CHI 2014
One of a CHInd

Conference Proceedings

Toronto, Canada | April 26 – May 1, 2014

Association for Computing Machinery

SIGCHI

The 32nd Annual ACM Conference on Human Factors in Computing Systems

Association for Computing Machinery

Advancing Computing as a Science & Profession

The Association for Computing Machinery
2 Penn Plaza, Suite 701
New York, New York 10121-0701

Notice to Past Authors of ACM-Published Articles
ACM intends to create a complete electronic archive of all articles and/or other material previously published by ACM. If you have written a work that has been previously published by ACM in any journal or conference proceedings prior to 1978, or any SIG Newsletter at any time, and you do NOT want this work to appear in the ACM Digital Library, please inform permissions@acm.org, stating the title of the work, the author(s), and where and when published.

ISBN: 978-1-4503-2473-1 (Digital)

ISBN: 978-1-4503-3288-0 (Print)

Additional copies may be ordered prepaid from:

ACM Order Department
PO Box 30777
New York, NY 10087-0777, USA

Phone: 1-800-342-6626 (USA and Canada)
+1-212-626-0500 (Global)
Fax: +1-212-944-1318
E-mail: acmhelp@acm.org
Hours of Operation: 8:30 am – 4:30 pm ET

Printed in the USA

Welcome to CHI 2014!

CHI is more than a conference, it is an international community of researchers and practitioners who want to make a difference. Everything we do is focused on uncovering, critiquing and celebrating radically new ways for people and technology to evolve together. People in their everyday contexts, in diverse regions of the world, from very different backgrounds, with alternative outlooks on life drive this innovation. As you take part in the conference sessions we really hope you will experience how powerful this people-centred approach to technological transformation can be. CHI as a conference is now in its 32nd year and has grown to become the premier international forum on human-computer interaction, gathering us all to share innovative interactive insights that shape people's lives. CHI draws together a multidisciplinary community from around the globe.

Our great strength is our ability to bring together students and experts, researchers and practitioners, scientists, designers and engineers, drawing from their rich perspectives to create new visions of humancomputer interaction. This year's conference theme is One of a CHInd. We chose this nearly two years ago as we began planning for this event. It has helped us focus our efforts and we hope you will use it to keep your eyes open to the bigger picture amongst all the excitement, range of presentations and activities at the conference.

CHI 2014 is One of CHInd because it is a celebration of the conference's one of a kind diversity; from the broad range of backgrounds of its attendees, to the diverse spectrum of communities and fields that the conference and its research have an impact on. CHI 2014 will take place at the Metro Toronto Convention Centre in Toronto, Canada, a city itself known for its one of a kind cultural diversity. But, CHI 2014 is more than a celebration of the diversity of our community and conference setting.

We hope that this year's event, more than anything, reminds you that the "people," "participants," "users" or "humans" that you hear described throughout this week are actually uniquely wonderful individuals full of hopes, concerns, joys and frustrations. CHI is here to serve all of these one of a kinds.

CHI 2014 features two outstanding keynote speakers: Booker prize winning author, Margaret Atwood and leading UX designer, Scott Jenson.

New for CHI 2014, we have Provoke! Wisdom! Impact! plenary talks first thing each morning on Tuesday, Wednesday and Thursday. Come along, join the crowd and be energised by our speakers who will each bring in their experience of the Big Picture to inspire us. The talks will be short - twenty minutes - and then the rest of the day's programme will begin.

We are also delighted to host a timely retrospective exhibition on wearable technology curated by Thad Starner and Clint Zeagler. CHI 2014 also includes two days of focused workshops and four days of technical content, including CHI's prestigious technical program, with 16 parallel sessions of rigorously reviewed research Papers, engaging Panels, Case Studies and Special Interest Groups (SIGs), an extensive Course program and invited talks from SIGCHI's award winners: Steve Whittaker, Gillian Grampton Smith and Richard Ladner.

We also host student research, design, and game competitions, provocative alt.chi presentations and last-minute SIGs for discussing current topics. Interactivity hands-on demonstrations showcase the best of interactive technology. We also highlight over 241 Work-In-Progress posters: this year we have added some features to these sessions to better help you get the most out of the exciting, early stage work on show; do go along and engage with the authors about their work. Evening events include the CHI 2014 conference reception, Sponsors and University events, local performances and the Job Fair.

We received over 3200 submissions and accepted nearly 1000 that will appear in the ACM Digital Library. To help you navigate through this immense program, there are a number of online and digital resources from the conference website to our mobile apps. You can also browse the videos, papers and extended abstracts on the CHI 2014 USB Key. But, CHI 2014 is about being in Toronto so perhaps the best way to select from and experience the event is by asking for pointers and chatting with your fellow attendees, our wonderful student volunteers, the information desk helpers or any of this year's committee.

We are all here to make your experience as useful and enjoyable as possible. We are deeply indebted to our vast number of volunteers, without whom CHI 2014 would not be possible, including over 3800 reviewers, over 180 senior members of the program committee, nearly 100 members of the CHI 2014 conference committee and, of course, the more than 180 student volunteers. We thank you all! We are honored and excited by the opportunity to host CHI 2014 and wish you a productive and enjoyable stay in Toronto!

Matt Jones,
Swansea University, Wales, UK
CHI 2014 General Conference Co-Chair

Albrecht Schmidt
University of Stuttgart, Germany
CHI 2014 Technical Program Co-Chair

Philippe Palanque
Université Paul Sabatier
CHI 2014 General Conference Co-Chair

Tovi Grossman
Autodesk Research, Canada
CHI 2014 Technical Program Co-Chair

From ACM SIGCHI's President and Vice President for Conferences

SIGCHI is proud to sponsor the premier annual conference in the field of human-computer interaction. We are extremely grateful to the CHI 2014 Conference Chairs Matt Jones and Philippe Palanque , to Technical Program Chairs Albrecht Schmidt and Tovi Grossman, and to their wonderful crew, who succeeded to build an impressive program and experience.

CHI 2014 is back in Toronto, Canada, returning to the same location of CHI 1987, 5 years after the first conference, on Human Factors in Computer Systems, in Gaithersburg, MD, March 1982. That first conference in Gaithersburg drew over 900 attendees, and since then CHI, with the official name: "ACM Conference on Human Factors in Computing Systems", has continued to grow and broaden its range of topics and contributing disciplines: the founding psychologists and software engineers began to meet new visions from ethnography, sociology, communication sciences and arts, among others. Relevant industries, as well as research institutes and academia, showed an increasing - and often long-lasting - interest and involvement (through volunteers and through sponsorship for conference expenses).

CHI is an ideal forum for people to meet formally as well as informally, to exchange knowledge and views, to share experiences, and to learn. The CHI conference brings together professionals from research and practice; people from industry, academia, and from government; long-term veterans of HCI, young professionals and students; all in an environment designed to encourage interaction. We invite you to actively participate in that interaction: introduce yourself to people, interact with presenters and speakers, renew old friendships and make new ones.

CHI is organized on behalf of ACM's Special Interest Group on Computer-Human Interaction (SIGCHI), an international community of professionals who share an interest in the many diverse facets of HCI. SIGCHI is committed both to advancing the field of HCI, to facilitate exchange of information within the SIGCHI community, and to support students to enter the domain.

The CHI conference is arguably the single most visible activity of SIGCHI, but we also sponsor and support a wide range of specialized conferences and workshops in areas ranging from interactive systems design to user interface technology to computer-supported cooperative work to "intelligent" user interfaces. Visit the SIGCHI website at **http://www.sigchi.org** to find our conference schedule, listing upcoming as well as past conferences.

SIGCHI and ACM produce some of the most respected publications in the field. All members receive interactions, a highly-acclaimed magazine covering the broad field of HCI and user interface design. ACM Transactions on Computer-Human Interactions (ToCHI), now in its 21st year, is our flagship journal - a quarterly publication with the top-quality archival research aimed at researchers and those translating research into practice.

SIGCHI is truly an international organization, with over 30 local chapters and 3 student chapters in 25 countries on 6 continents. We encourage all SIGCHI members to join their local chapter - or if there isn't one in your area, we would love to help you create one. And don't forget virtual communities! SIGCHI hosts dozens of electronic mailing lists on topics ranging from HCI and the Web, to HCI educations, to public policy and beyond. Those lists range from dozens of subscribers to thousands, and are an excellent way to keep up with the field and with friends and colleagues.

Finally, on behalf of ACM SGICHI, we again want to thank the conference committee and all of the hundreds of volunteers who make this conference possible. Their work makes this a rewarding experience for all of us.

Gerrit C. van der Veer
SIGCHI President

John "Scooter" Morris
SIGCHI Vice-President for Conferences

CHI 2014 Papers and Notes Chairs' Welcome

The CHI Papers and Notes programme is continuing to grow and this year we received more than 2000 submissions for the first time. We are pleased that CHI is still the leading conference for research in humancomputer interaction.

CHI 2014 continued the use of subcommittees to manage the review process. Authors selected the subcommittee they believed was best qualified to review their work: Due to the changing pattern of submissions we split some subcommittees into more manageable sizes and coalesced others. We are pleased with the subcommittee process: By dividing the work, each paper received much more careful discussion than would otherwise have been possible.

This year we considered 2036 submissions, including 1428 papers and 608 notes, representing a 4% growth over last year. We accepted 465 submissions (23%): 382 papers and 83 notes.

The CHI review process demands a tremendous amount of work from all areas of the human computer interaction community. As co-chairs of the process, we are amazed at the ability of the community to organize itself to accomplish this task. We would like to thank the 2866 individual reviewers for their careful consideration of these papers. We also deeply appreciate the huge amount of time donated to this process by the 205-member program committee, who paid their own way to attend the face-to-face program committee meeting, an event larger than the average ACM conference.

We are proud of the work of the CHI 2014 program committee and hope that you enjoy these papers and notes, which represent the best research in human-computer interaction.

Stephen Brewster,
Glasgow University
CHI 2014 Papers and Notes Chairs

Andy Cockburn,
University of Canterbury
CHI 2014 Papers and Notes Chairs

Table of Contents

Activity Recognition

Session Chair: Daniela Busse, *Samsung Research America (SRA)*

Managing Income

Session Chair: Sarita Yardi Schoenebeck, *University of Michigan*

Designing and Understanding Visualizations

Session Chair: Petra Isenberg, *INRIA*

Crowdfunding and Crowd Storage

Session Chair: Michael Muller, *IBM Research*

Novel Approaches to Navigation

Session Chair: Yuichiro Takeuchi , *Sony Computer Science Laboratories, Inc.*

Interfaces for Care and Support

Session Chair: Jesper Kjeldskov , *Aalborg University,*

April 29th, 2014 – Volume 2a

Interactive Visualization and Visual Elements

Session Chair: Eytan Adar , *University of Michigan*

Understanding and Designing Games

Session Chair: Lennart Nacke , *University of Ontario Institute of Technology*

Personal Values and Preferences

Session Chair: Katharina Reinecke , *University of Michigan*

April 29th, 2014 – Volume 2b

Learning and Education

Session Chair: Deborah Tatar , *Virginia Polytechnic Institute and State University*

April 30th, 2014 – Volume 3a

Telepresence and Connecting over Video

Session Chair: Kori Inkpen , *Microsoft Research*

Exergame Design

Session Chair: Sean Munson , *University of Washington*

Shape-Changing Interfaces

Session Chair: Abhijit Karnik , *Lancaster University*

Touch Input

Session Chair: Daniel Wigdor , *University of Toronto*

Risks and Security

Session Chair: Alexander De Luca , *University of Munich*

CHI for Social Development

Session Chair: Nithya Sambasivan , *University of California*

April 30th, 2014 – Volume 3b

Decisions, Recommendations, and Machine Learning

Session Chair: Jon Froehlich , *University of Washington*

Accessibility

Session Chair: Hironobu Takagi , *IBM Research*

Tangible Interactions and Technologies

Session Chair: Erin Solovey , *Drexel University*

Head-Worn Displays

Session Chair: Brian Bailey , *University of Illinois*

CHI 2014 Conference Organization

General Chair:	Matt Jones, *Swansea University, Wales, UK* Philippe Palanque, *Université Paul Sabatier, France*

Technical Program

Technical Program Co-Chairs:	Albrecht Schmidt, *University of Stuttgart , Germany* Tovi Grossman, *Autodesk Research, Canada*
Technical Program Chair Assistant:	Michael Glueck, *Autodesk Research, Canada*
Papers and Notes:	Stephen Brewster, *University of Glasgow, UK* Andy Cockburn, *University of Canterbrury, New Zealand*
Panels:	Gillian Hayes, *University of California, Irvine, USA* Khai Truong, *University of Toronto, Canada*
Case Studies:	Jonathan Arnowitz, *Google, USA* DJ Hoets, *SAP, USA* Michael Arent, *Rivendel Consulting, USA* *KAIST, Republic of Korea* in Henderson, *Flipside, The Netherlands*
Courses:	Regina Bernhaupt, *Ruwido, France* Elizabeth Churchill, *eBay Research Labs, USA*
Interactivity:	Steven Benford, *University of Nottingham, UK* Julie Rico Williamson, *University of Glasgow, Scotland, UK*
Video Showcase:	Jinwook Seo, *Seoul National University, Korea* Nicolas Roussel, *INRIA, France*
SIGs:	Enrico Rukzio, *Ulm University, Germany* Henry Duh, *University of Tasmania, Australia*
Doctoral Consortium:	Manfred Tscheligi, *University of Salzburg, Austria* Katherine Isbister, *New York University, USA*
Workshops:	Nadir Weibel, *University of California, San Diego, USA* Juergen Steimle, *Max Planck Institute, Germany*
Works in Progress:	Shelly Farnham, *Microsoft, USA* Shamsi Iqbal, *Microsoft, USA* Shaun Lawson, *University of Lincoln, USA*
Student Research Competition:	Celine Latulipe, *UNC Charlotte, USA* Floyd Muller, *University in Melbourne, Australia*
Student Design Competition:	Thecla Schiphorst, *Simon Fraser University, Canada* Youn-Kyung Lim, *KAIST, Korea*

Student Game Competition: Seth Cooper, *University of Washington, USA*
Alessandro Canossa, *Northeastern University, USA*

alt.chi: Daniela Rosner, *University of Washington, USA*
Lilly Irani, *UC San Diego, USA*

TOCHI Papers: Jeffrey Nichols, *IBM Research, USA*

Best of CHI Awards: Daniel Wigdor, *University of Toronto, Canada*
Karyn Moffatt, *McGill School of Information, Canada*

Spotlights

Spotlights Chairs: Kristina Höök, *Royal Institute of Technology, Sweden*
Ed Chi, *Google Research, USA*

Games & Entertainment: Magy Seif El-Nasr, *Northeastern University, USA*
Heather Desurvire, *Behavioristics, Inc, USA*
Lennart Nacke, *University of Ontario, Canada*

HCI For Development (HCI4D): Melissa Densmore, *Microsoft Research, USA*
Matthew Kam, *Carnegie Mellon University, USA*
Ban Al-Ani, *University of California, Irvine, USA*

Interaction Science: Andrew Howes, *University of Birmingham, UK*
Benjamin R. Cowan, *University of Birmingham, UK*
Stephen J. Payne, *University of Oxford, UK*
Paul Cairns, *University of York, UK*
Christian P. Janssen, *The Smith-Kettlewell Eye Research Institute, USA*
Anna L Cox, *University College London, UK*
Anthony J. Hornof, *University of Oregon, USA*
Peter Pirolli, *Palo Alto Research Center (PARC), USA*

Making Cultures: Jeffrey Bardzell, *University Bloomington, USA*
Shaowen Bardzell, *Shaowen Bardzell, USA*
Carl DiSalvo, *Georgia Institute of Technology, USA*
Ann Light, *Northumbria University, UK*
Daniela Rosner, *University of Washington, USA*

Art and Interaction: David England, *John Moores University, UK*
Joceyn Spence, *University of Surrey, UK*

Operations

Student Volunteer Coordinators: Lindsay Reynolds, *Cornell University, USA*
Jon Haber, *University of Calgary, Canada*

Technology Liaisons: Scooter Morris, *University of California, San Francisco, USA*
Sara Drenner, *University of Minnesota-Twin Cities, USA*

Webmaster: Liam Betsworth, *Swansea University, Wales, UK*

Social Media: Max Wilson, *Nottingham University, UK*
Katie Panciera, *University of Minnesota, USA*

Proceedings: Marco Winckler, *Université Paul Sabatier, France*
Yann Riche, *Microsoft, USA*
Stéphane Conversy, *ENAC, France*

Infrastructure Accessibility Chair: Jennifer Rode, *Drexel University, USA*

Digital Accessibility Chair: Jonathan Lazar, *Towson University, USA*

Community Sourcing & Scheduling: Paul André, *Facebook, USA*
Anant Bhardwaj, *MIT, USA*
Lydia Chilton, *University of Washington, USA*
Juho Kim, *MIT, USA*
Steven Dow, *Carnegie Mellon University, USA*
Rob Miller, *MIT, USA*
Haoqi Zhang, *Northwestern University, USA*

Mobile Apps: Stephen Oney, *Carnegie Mellon University, USA*
Eiji Hayashi, *Carnegie Mellon University, USA*
Jason Wiese, *Carnegie Mellon University, USA*
Célia Martinie, *Université Paul Sabatier, France*

Video Previews: Gene Golovchinsky *[in memory]*
Gonzalo Ramos, *University of Toronto, Canada*
Fanny Chevalier, *INRIA, France*

Conference Management: Janeé Pelletier, *Conference & Logistics Consultants, USA*
Allison Perrelli, *Conference & Logistics Consultants, USA*

Sponsors, Exhibits & Recruitment: Carol Klyver, *Foundations of Excellence, USA*

Registration: Yvonne Lopez, *Executive Events, Inc. USA*
Brooke Daley, *Executive Events, Inc. USA*

PCS Liaisons: Max van Kleek, *University of Southampton, UK*
Carol Klyver, *Foundations of Excellence, USA*
Scooter Morris, *University of California, San Francisco, USA*

Women's Breakfast Event: Allison Druin, *University of Maryland, USA*

CHI 2014 Papers and Notes Subcommittee & Associate Chairs

Subcommittee Chairs:

Mark Ackerman, *University of Michigan, USA*
Victoria Bellotti, *Xerox PARC, USA*
Laura Dabbish, *Carnegie Mellon University, USA*
Stephen Fairclough, *Liverpool John Moores University, UK*
Steven Feiner, *Columbia University, USA*
Jon Froelich, *University of Maryland, USA*
Vicki Hanson, *IBM Research, USA*
Jettie Hoonhout, *Philips Research, The Netherlands*
Hilary Hutchinson, *Google Research, USA*
Shahram Izadi, *Microsoft Research, UK*
David Kirk, *Newcastle University, UK*
Antonio Krueger, *DFKI, Germany*
Myriam Lewkowicz, *Université de Technologie de Troyes, France*
Youn-Kyung Lim, *KAIST, South Korea*
Joanna McGrenere, *University of British Columbia, Canada*
Bilge Mutlu, *University of Wisconsin-Madison, USA*
Fabio Paterno, *CNR ISTI, Italy*
Wanda Pratt, *University of Washington, USA*
mc schraefel, *University of Southampton, UK*
Sriram Subramanian, *University of Bristol, UK*
Bill Thies, *Microsoft Research, India*
Manfred Tscheligi, *CURE, Austria*
Ron Wakkary, *Simon Fraser University, Canada*
John Zimmerman, *Carnegie Mellon University, USA*

Associate Chairs:

Eytan Adar, *University of Michigan, USA*
Jason Alexander, *Lancaster University, UK*
Paul André, *Carnegie Mellon University, USA*
Judd Antin, *Yahoo! Research, USA*
Alissa Antle, *Simon Fraser University, Canada*
Paul Aoki, *Intel Labs, USA*
Daniel Ashbrook, *Nokia Research Center Hollywood, USA*
Gabriela Avram, *University of Limerick, Ireland*
Brian Bailey, *University of Illinois, USA*
Lynne Baillie, *Glasgow Caledonian University, UK*
Ravin Balakrishnan, *University of Toronto, Canada*
Jeffrey Bardzell, *Indiana University Bloomington, USA*
Richard Beckwith, *Intel Research, USA*
Hrvoje Benko, *Microsoft Research, USA*
Timothy Bickmore, *Northeastern University, USA*
Jeffrey Bigham, *Carnegie Mellon University, USA*
Mark Blythe, *Northumbria University, UK*
Alexander Boden, *University of Siegen, Germany*
Sebastian Boring, *University of Copenhagen, Denmark*
Duncan Brumby, *University College London, UK*
A.j. Brush, *Microsoft Research, USA*
Andreas Bulling, *Max-Planck Institut Für Informatik, Germany*
Daniela Busse, *Samsung Research America (SRA), USA*
Andreas Butz, *Ludwig-Maximilians-Universität München, Germany*
John Canny, *UC Berkley, USA*
Xiang Cao, *Lenovo Research & Technology, China*
Erin Carroll, *University of Rochester, USA*
Nicholas Chen, *University of Maryland, UK*
Yunan Chen, *University of California, USA*
Coye Cheshire, *UC Berkeley, USA*
Fanny Chevalier, *University of Toronto, Canada*
Keith Cheverst, *Lancaster University, England, UK*
Luigina Ciolfi, *Sheffield Hallam University, UK*
Rob Comber, *Newcastle University, UK*
Lorrie Cranor, *Carnegie Mellon University, USA*
Scott Davidoff, *Jet Propulsion Laboratory, USA*
Antonella de Angeli, *University of Trento, Italy*
Alexander de Luca, *University of Munich, Germany*
Rogerio de Paula, *IBM Research, Brazil*
Marco de Sá, *Facebook, USA*
Morgan Dixon, *University of Washington, USA*
Steven Dow, *Carnegie Mellon University, USA*
Pierre Dragicevic, *INRIA, France*
Mark Dunlop, *University of Strathclyde, Scotland, UK*
Darren Edge, *Microsoft Research Asia, China*
Serge Egelman, *University of California, USA*
Niklas Elmqvist, *Purdue University, USA*
Ylva Fernaeus, *KTH, Sweden*
Clifton Forlines, *Draper Laboratory, USA*
Jodi Forlizzi, *Carnegie Mellon University, USA*
Zhiyong Fu, *Information Art and Design Department, China*
Dominic Furniss, *University College London, UK*
Susan Fussell, *Cornell University, USA*

Associate Chairs: Natasa Milic-Frayling, *Microsoft Research Ltd, UK*
Robert Miller, *The Pennsylvania State University, USA*
Karyn Moffatt, *McGill University, Canada*
Tom Moher, *University of Illinois at Chicago, USA*
Wendy Moncur, *University of Dundee, Scotland,*
Dan Morris, *Microsoft Research, USA*
Tomer Moscovich, *INRIA, France*
Ingrid Mulder, *Delft University of Technology, The Netherlands*
Michael Muller, *Alexander Von Humboldt Institute for Internet and Society, USA*
Jörg Müller, *University of Arts, Berlin, Germany*
Sean Munson, *University of Washington, USA*
Lennart Nacke, *University of Ontario Institute of Technology, Canada*
Michael Nebeling, *ETH Zurich, Switzerland*
Carman Neustaedter, *Simon Fraser University, Canada*
Jeffrey Nichols, *IBM Research, USA*
Ian Oakley, *Ulsan National Institute of Science and Technology, South Korea*
Marianna Obrist, *Newcastle University, UK*
William Odom, *Carnegie Mellon University, USA*
Amy Ogan, *Carnegie Mellon University, USA*
Patrick Olivier, *Newcastle University, UK*
Alex Olwal, *Royal Institute of Technology (KTH), USA*
Claire O'malley, *University of Nottingham, UK*
Antti Oulasvirta, *Max-Planck Institut Für Informatik, Germany*
Andrea Parker, *Northeastern University, USA*
Sameer Patil, *Aalto University, Finland*
Mark Perry, *Brunel University, UK*
Christopher Power, *University of York, UK*
Aaron Quigley, *University of St. Andrews, UK*
Chris Quintana, *University of Michigan, USA*
Emilee Rader, *Michigan State University, USA*
David Randall, *University of Siegen, UK*
Pei-Luen Patrick Rau, *Tsinghua University, China*
Stuart Reeves, *University of Nottingham, England*
Katharina Reinecke, *Harvard University, USA*
Anne Roudaut, *University of Bristol, Germany*
Mark Rouncefield, *Lancaster University, UK*
Daniel Russell, *Google, USA*
Nithya Sambasivan, *University of California, USA*
Corina Sas, *Lancaster University, UK*
Martina Angela Sasse, *University College London (UCL), UK*
Christina Satchell, *The University of Melbourne, Australia*
James Scott, *Microsoft Research, UK*
Andrew Sears, *Rochester Institute of Technology, USA*
Abigail Sellen, *Microsoft Research, UK*
N. Sadat Shami, *IBM Research, USA*
Rajinder Sodhi, *University of Illinois at Urbana-Champaign, USA*
Erin Solovey, *Drexel University, USA*
Danae Stanton Fraser, *University of Bath, UK*
Jürgen Steimle, *Massachusetts Institute of Technology, USA*
Wolfgang Stuerzlinger, *York University, Canada*
Hironobu Takagi, *IBM Research, Japan*
Yuichiro Takeuchi, *Sony Computer Science Laboratories, Japan*
Deborah Tatar, *Virginia Tech,*

Associate Chairs: Jaime Teevan, *Microsoft Research, USA*
John Thomas, *IBM T.J. Watson Research Center, USA*
Melanie Tory, *University of Victoria, Canada*
Zachary Toups, *New Mexico State University, USA*Deborah Tatar, *Virginia Tech*
Elise Van Den Hoven, *University of Technology Sydney, Australia*
John Vines, *Newcastle University, UK*
Daniel Vogel, *University of Waterloo, Canada*
Amy Voida, *Indiana University, USA*
Annalu Waller, *University of Dundee, Scotland, UK*
Hao-Chuan Wang, *National Tsing Hua University, Taiwan*
Nadir Weibel, *University of California San Diego, USA*
Daniel Wigdor, *University of Toronto, Canada*
Lauren Wilcox, *Georgia Institute of Technology, USA*
Maria Wolters, *University of Edinburgh, UK*
Volker Wulf, *University of Siegen and Fraunhofer FIT, Germany*
Sarita Yardi Schoenebeck, *University of Michigan, USA*
Svetlana Yarosh, *AT&T Research Labs, USA*
Thorsten Zander, *TU Berlin, Germany*
Shengdong Zhao, *National University of Singapore, Singapore*
Michelle Zhou, *IBM Research - Almaden, USA*
Xiaomu Zhou, *Rutgers University, USA*

CHI 2014 Papers and Notes Reviewers

Konstantin Aal, *University of Siegen, Germany*
Parham Aarabi, *University of Toronto, Canada*
Francisco Abad, *Universitat Politècnica de València, Spain*
Julio Abascal, *University of the Basque Country, Spain*
Evgeniy Abdulin, *Texas State University, USA*
Saeed Abdullah, *Cornell University, USA*
Troy Abel, *Virginia Tech, USA*
Gregory Abowd, *Georgia Institute of Technology, USA*
Alessandro Acquisti, *Carnegie Mellon University, USA*
Lada Adamic, *University of Michigan, USA*
Anne Adams, *UCL Interaction Centre, USA*
Anne Adams, *Simplec, UK*
Dustin Adams, *University of California, USA*
Kim Adams, *University of Alberta, Canada*
Phil Adams, *Cornell University, USA*
Idris Adjerid, *Carnegie Mellon University, USA*
Rachel Adler, *Northeastern Illinois University, USA*
Tamara Adlin, *USA*
Daniel Afergan, *Tufts University, USA*
Ana Afonso, *Universidade de Lisboa, Portugal*
Stefan Agamanolis, *Akron Children's Hospital, USA*
Maneesh Agrawala, *University of California, USA*
David Ahlström, *Alpen-Adria Universität Klagenfurt, Austria*
Salman Ahmad, *Stanford University, USA*
Teemu Ahmaniemi, *Nokia Research Center, Finland*
June Ahn, *University of Maryland, USA*
Aino Ahtinen, *VTT Technical Research Centre, Finland*
David Akers, *Stanford University, USA*
Devdatta Akhawe, *UC Berkeley, USA*
Abdullah Al Mahmud, *Delft University of Technology, Netherlands*
Vicent Alabau, *Universidad Politécnica de Valencia (UPV), Spain*
Amro Al-Akkad, *Fraunhofer Institute for Applied Information Technology (FIT), Germany*
Gazihan Alankus, *Washington University In St. Louis, USA*
Turadg Aleahmad, *Coursera, USA*
Saleem Alhabash, *Michigan State University, USA*
Abir Al-Hajri, *UBC, Canada*
Dzmitry Aliakseyeu, *Philips Research, The Netherlands*
Doris Allhutter, *Institute of Technology Assessment, Austria*
Sonya Allin, *University of Toronto, Canada*
Norman Alm, *University of Dundee, UK*
Abdullah Al-Mahmud, *Delft University of Technology, The Netherlands*
Omar Alonso, *Microsoft, USA*
Basak Alper, *University of California Santa Barbara, USA*
Mohammad Al-Smadi, *Tallinn University, Estonia*
Florian Alt, *University of Munich, Germany*
Bashar Altakrouri, *University of Luebeck, Germany*
Reem Alzahabi, *Michigan State University, USA*
Saleema Amershi, *Microsoft Research, USA*

Morgan Ames, *Stanford University, USA*
Oliver Amft, *TU Eindhoven, Netherlands*
Farshid Amirabdollahian, *University of Hertfordshire, UK*
Swamy Ananthanarayan, *University of Colorado, USA*
Margarita Anastassova, *CEA, France*
Nazanin Andalibi, *Drexel University, USA*
Erik Andersen, *University of Washington, USA*
Fraser Anderson, *University of Alberta, Canada*
Ken Anderson, *Intel Corporation, USA*
Nazareno Andrade, *Universidade Federal de Campina Grande, Brazil*
Adrienne Andrew, *University of Washington, USA*
Christopher Andrews, *Virginia Polytechnic Institute and State University, USA*
Sean Andrist, *University of Wisconsin--Madison, USA*
Marvin Andujar, *Clemson University, USA*
Leonardo Angelini, *University of Applied Sciences Western Switzerland, Svizzera*
Michelle Annett, *University of Alberta, Canada*
Craig Anslow, *Victoria University of Wellington, New Zealand*
Lisa Anthony, *University of Florida, USA*
Thomas Apperley, *The University of New South Wales, Australia*
Caroline Appert, *Université Paris-Sud, France*
Bruno Araujo, *INESC-ID, Portugal*
Daniel Archambault, *Swansea University, UK*
Carmelo Ardito, *University of Bari, Italy*
Ahmed Arif, *Ryerson University, Canada*
John Arnott, *University of Dundee, UK*
Rosa Arriaga, *Georgia Institute of Technology, USA*
Kate Arrington, *Lehigh University, USA*
Thierry Artieres, *Université Pierre Et Marie Curie, France*
Mariam Asad, *Georgia Institute of Technology, USA*
Chieko Asakawa, *IBM Research - Tokyo, Japan*
Felix-Robinson Aschoff, *University of Zurich, Switzerland*
Debi Ashenden, *Cranfield University, UK*
Maryam Ashoori, *IBM, Canada*
Ilhan Aslan, *Universität Salzburg, Austria*
Zeina Atrash, *Northwestern University, USA*
Alan Au, *University of Washington, USA*
Anne Aula, *Google, USA*
Hane Aung, *University College London, UK*
Nikolaos Avouris, *University of Patras, Greece*
Daniel Avrahami, *Intel, USA*
Katerina Avramides, *London Knowledge Lab, UK*
Yuji Ayatsuka, *Koozyt, Japan*
Matthew Aylett, *Cereproc Ltd., UK*
Ruth Aylett, *Heriot-Watt University, UK*
Mobolaji Ayoade, *Glasgow Caledonian University, UK*
Phillip Ayoub, *Pennsylvania State University, USA*
Yadid Ayzenberg, *MIT, USA*
Shiri Azenkot, *University of Washington, USA*
Maryam Azh, *National University of Singapore, Singapore*
Tamara Babaian, *Bentley College, USA*
Chris Baber, *The University of Birmingham, UK*

Benjamin Bach, *INRIA, France*
Paula Bach, *The Pennsylvania State University, USA*
Myroslav Bachynskyi, *Max-Planck Institut Für Informatik, Germany*
Jonathan Back, *University College London, UK*
Maribeth Back, *FX Palo Alto Laboratory, USA*
Norm Badler, *University of Pennsylvania, USA*
Sangwon Bae, *Yonsei University, Seoul*
Seok-Hyung Bae, *KAIST, Republic of Korea*
Ronald Baecker, *University of Toronto, Canada*
Naveen Bagalkot, *IT University of Copenhagen, Denmark*
Zhen Bai, *University of Cambridge, UK*
Gilles Bailly, *CNRS, France*
Ryan Baker, *Teachers College, USA*
Suzanne Bakken, *Columbia University, USA*
Saskia Bakker, *Eindhoven University of Technology, The Netherlands*
Eytan Bakshy, *Facebook, USA*
Madeline Balaam, *Newcastle University, UK*
Aruna Balakrishnan, *Google, USA*
Guha Balakrishnan, *MIT, USA*
Matthias Baldauf, *FTW Telecommunications Research Center, Austria*
Rebecca Balebako, *Carnegie Mellon University, USA*
Elizabeth Bales, *University of Washington, USA*
Robert Ball, *Stephen F. KAIST, Republic of Korea in State University, USA*
Stinne Ballegaard, *KORA, Denmark*
Till Ballendat, *University of Munich, Germany*
Liam Bannon, *University of Limerick, Ireland*
Nikola Banovic, *Carnegie Mellon University, USA*
Francesco Banterle, *ISTI-CNR, Italy*
Xuan Bao, *Duke University, USA*
Evan Barba, *Georgetown University, USA*
Simone Barbosa, *Pontifical Catholic University of Rio de Janeiro (PUC-Rio), Brasil*
Jakob Bardram, *IT University of Copenhagen, Denmark*
Shaowen Bardzell, *Indiana University Bloomington, USA*
Javier Bargas-Avila, *Google, Switzerland*
Louise Barkhuus, *Stockholm University, Sweden*
Connelly Barnes, *Princeton University, USA*
Douglas Barnes
Pippin Barr, *University of Malta, Malta*
Barbara Barricelli, *University of West London, UK*
Barbara Barry, *MIT Media Lab, USA*
Tom Bartindale, *Newcastle University, UK*
Christoph Bartneck, *University of Canterbury, New Zealand*
Thomas Bartoschek, *University of Münster, Germany*
Lyn Bartram, *Simon Fraser University, Canada*
Santosh Basapur, *Illinois Institute of Technology, USA*
Rahul Basole, *Georgia Institute of Technology, USA*
Arianna Bassoli, *London School of Economics, UK*
Archer Batcheller, *University of Michigan, USA*
Scott Bateman, *University of Prince Edward Island, Canada*
Oliver Bates, *Lancaster University, UK*
Agathe Battestini, *Nokia, USA*
Olivier Bau, *Samsung Research America, USA*
Patrick Baudisch, *Hasso Plattner Institute, Germany*

Christine Bauer, *Vienna University of Economics and Business, Austria*
Jared Bauer, *University of Washington, USA*
Lujo Bauer, *Carnegie Mellon University, USA*
Eric Baumer, *Cornell University, USA*
Gordon Baxter, *University of St Andrews, UK*
Philip Beaman, *University of Reading, UK*
David Beattie, *Glasgow Caledonian University, Scotland, Uk*
Michel Beaudouin-Lafon, *Université Paris-Sud, France*
Elke Beck, *University of Salzburg, Austria*
S. Ann Becker, *Florida Tech, USA*
Benjamin Bederson, *University of Maryland, USA*
Roman Bednarik, *University of Eastern Finland, Finland*
Jenay Beer, *University of South Carolina, USA*
Andrew Begel, *Microsoft Research, USA*
Marios Belk, *University of Cyprus, Cyprus*
Rachel Bellamy, *IBM Research, USA*
Francesco Bellotti, *University of Genoa, Italy*
Raquel Benbunan-Fich, *Baruch College, USA*
Peter Benda, *The University of Melbourne, Australia*
Zinaida Benenson, *University of Erlangen-Nuremberg, Germany*
Steve Benford, *University of Nottingham, UK*
Mike Bennett, *Microsoft, USA*
Peter Bennett, *University of Bristol, UK*
Frank Bentley, *Motorola Mobility Inc., USA*
David Benyon, *Edinburgh Napier University, UK*
François Bérard, *CLIPS-IMAG, France*
Bettina Berendt, *KU Leuven, Belgium*
Alistair Beresford, *University of Cambridge, England*
Ofer Bergman, *Bar-Ilan University, Israel*
Kirsten Bergmann, *Bielefeld University, Germany*
Shane Bergsma, *Johns Hopkins University, USA*
Joanna Bergstrom-Lehtovirta, *Helsinki Institute for Information Technology HIIT, Finland*
Shlomo Berkovsky, *NICTA, Australia*
Gunilla Berndtsson, *Ericsson AB, Sweden*
Regina Bernhaupt, *IRIT, France*
Olav Bertelsen, *Aarhus University, Denmark*
Florent Berthaut, *INRIA, France*
Andrew Besmer, *UNC Charlotte, USA*
Michael Best, *Georgia Institute of Technology, USA*
Katrien Beuls, *Vrije Universiteit Brussel, Belgium*
Chris Bevan, *University of Bath, UK*
Nigel Bevan, *Professional Usability Services, UK*
Anastasia Bezerianos, *Université de Paris-Sud, France*
Konstantin Beznosov, *University of British Columbia, Canada*
Anant Bhardwaj, *Massachusetts Institute of Technology, USA*
Samit Bhattacharya, *IIT Guwahati, India*
Xiaojun Bi, *Google, USA*
Andrea Bianchi, *KAIST, Republic of Korea*
Nadia Bianchi-Berthouze, *University College London, UK*
Peter Bibby, *University of Nottingham, UK*
Nicola Bidwell, *CSIR-Meraka, South Africa*
Gerald Bieber, *Fraunhofer IGD, Germany*

Ralf Biedert, *German Research Center for Artificial Intelligence (DFKI), Germany*
Jacob Biehl, *FX Palo Alto Laboratory, USA*
Matthew Bietz, *University of California, USA*
Lukas Biewald, *CrowdFlower, USA*
Ali Bigdelou, *Technical University of Munich, Germany*
Dania Bilal, *University of Tennessee, USA*
Mark Billinghurst, *University of Canterbury, New Zealand*
Dorrit Billman, *NASA Ames, USA*
Jens Binder, *University of Manchester, UK*
Jon Bird, *City University London, UK*
Max Birk, *University of Saskatchewan, Canada*
Jeremy Birnholtz, *Northwestern University, USA*
Walter Bischof, *University of Alberta, Canada*
Pradipta Biswas, *University of Cambridge, England*
Staffan Björk, *University of Gothenburg, Sweden*
Pernille Bjorn, *IT University of Copenhagen, Denmark*
Alan Blackwell, *University of Cambridge, UK*
Rachel Blagojevic, *University of Auckland, New Zealand*
Renaud Blanch, *Université Grenoble I, France*
Ann Blandford, *University College London, UK*
Benjamin Blankertz, *Berlin Institute of Technology, Germany*
Eli Blevis, *The Hong Kong Polytechnic University, USA*
Brett Bligh, *Lancaster University, UK*
Jan Blom, *Nokia Research Center, Switzerland*
Katherine Blondon, *University of Washington, USA*
Marco Blumendorf, *Yetu AG, Germany*
Susanne Bødker, *Aarhus University, Denmark*
Mads Boedker, *Copenhagen Business School, Denmark*
Kirsten Boehner, *Cornell University, USA*
Cristian Bogdan, *KTH, Sweden*
Matthias Böhmer, *German Research Center for Artificial Intelligence (DFKI), Germany*
Susanne Boll, *University of Oldenburg, Germany*
Albertus Bongers, *University Technology Sydney, Australia*
Joe Bonneau, *USA*
Matthew Bonner, *Georgia Institute of Technology, USA*
David Bonnet, *Université Paris-Sud & CNRS, France*
Elizabeth Bonsignore, *University of Maryland, USA*
Kellogg Booth, *University of British Columbia, Canada*
Jan Borchers, *RWTH Aachen University, Germany*
Silvia Bordin, *TrentoRise, Italy*
Marcela Borge, *Penn State, USA*
Michelle Borkin, *Harvard University, USA*
Alan Borning, *University of Washington, USA*
Nis Bornoe, *Aalborg University, Denmark*
Gaetano Borriello, *University of Washington, USA*
Brennon Bortz, *Virginia Polytechnic Institute and State University, USA*
Nathan Bos, *University of Michigan, USA*
Claus Bossen, *University of Aarhus, Denmark*
Paolo Bottoni, *University of Rome - 'la Sapienza', Italy*
Matt-Mouley Bouamrane, *University of Glasgow, UK*
Stephane Bouchard, *Université Du Quebec En Outaouais, Canada*
Andy Boucher, *Goldsmiths College, UK*

Nadia Boukhelifa, *INRIA Saclay, France*
Anders Bouwer, *University of Amsterdam, Netherlands*
Judy Bowen, *The University of Waikato, New Zealand*
Chris Bowers, *University of Birmingham, UK*
John Bowers, *Newcastle University, UK*
Geoffrey Bowker, *UC Irvine, USA*
Doug Bowman, *Virginia Polytechnic Institute and State University, USA*
John Boyd, *Google, Na*
Erin Bradner, *Autodesk, USA*
Erin Brady, *University of Rochester, USA*
Andrew Bragdon, *Microsoft, USA*
Jonathan Bragg, *University of Washington, USA*
Giorgio Brajnik, *University of Udine, Italy*
Pedro Branco, *University of Minho, Portugal*
Joel Brandt, *Adobe Research, USA*
Stacy Branham, *Virginia Tech, USA*
Tone Bratteteig, *University of Oslo, Norway*
Cristian Bravo-Lillo, *Carnegie Mellon University, USA*
Matthew Brehmer, *University of British Columbia, Canada*
Margot Brereton, *Queensland University of Technology, Australia*
Robert Brewer, *University of Hawaii at Manoa, USA*
Jo Briggs, *Northumbria University, UK*
Pam Briggs, *Northumbria University, UK*
Willem-Paul Brinkman, *Delft University of Technology, The Netherlands*
Katie Brittain, *Newcastle University, UK*
Juliana Brixey, *UT Health Science Center at Houston, USA*
Anke Brock, *IRIT, France*
Eric Brockmeyer, *Disney Research, USA*
Gregor Broll, *DOCOMO Euro-Labs, Germany*
Geert Brone, *University of Leuven - Campus Antwerp, Belgium*
Jonas Brönstrup, *Technical University of Berlin, Germany*
Andy Brooks, *University of California, USA*
Mark Brosnan, *University of Bath, UK*
Ryan Brotman, *Intel Corporation, USA*
Anne-Marie Brouwer, *TNO Human Factors, Netherlands*
Barry Brown, *University of California San Diego, USA*
Deana Brown, *Georgia Institute of Technology, USA*
Michael Brown, *The University of Nottingham, UK*
Jed Brubaker, *University of California, USA*
Amy Bruckman, *Georgia Institute of Technology, USA*
Gerd Bruder, *University of Würzburg, Germany*
Pascal Bruegger, *University of Applied Sciences, Switzerland*
Clemens Brunner, *Graz University of Technology, Austria*
Miguel Bruns Alonso, *Eindhoven University of Technology, The Netherlands*
Anders Bruun, *Aalborg University, Denmark*
Nick Bryan-Kinns, *Queen Mary, UK*
Martin Brynskov, *Aarhus University, Denmark*
Michael Brzozowski, *Google, USA*
George Buchanan, *City University London, UK*
Sarah Buchanan, *University of Central Florida, USA*
Karolina Buchner, *Yahoo! Labs, USA*
Elizabeth Buie, *Northumbria University, UK*
Andrea Bunt, *University of Manitoba, Canada*

Cody Buntain, *University of Maryland, USA*
Judee Burgoon, *University of Arizona, USA*
Stefano Burigat, *University of Udine, Italy*
Moira Burke, *Facebook, USA*
Gary Burnett, *University of Nottingham, UK*
Margaret Burnett, *Oregon State University, USA*
Jesse Burstyn, *Queen's University, Canada*
Chris Burton, *University of Edinburgh, UK*
Jerry Busby, *Lancaster University, UK*
Marc Busch, *CURE - Center for Usability Research & Engineering, Austria*
Georg Buscher, *Microsoft, USA*
Monika Buscher, *Lancaster University, UK*
Stefano Bussolon, *Università di Trento, Italy*
Brian Butler, *UMD, USA*
D. Alex Butler, *Microsoft Research, UK*
Fabio Buttussi, *University of Udine, Italy*
Ayse Buyuktur, *University of Michigan, USA*
Daragh Byrne, *Arizona State University, USA*
Michael Byrne, *Rice University, USA*
Béatrice Cahour, *CNRS Télécom Paristech, France*
Kelly Caine, *Clemson University, USA*
Paul Cairns, *University of York, UK*
Maya Cakmak, *University of Washington, USA*
Jeffrey Calcaterra, *IBM Corporation, USA*
Roberto Calderon, *University of British Columbia, Canada*
André Calero Valdez, *RWTH Aachen University, Germany*
Janko Calic, *CVSS, UK*
Chris Callison-Burch, *Johns Hopkins University, USA*
Gaelle Calvary, *Grenoble Institute of Technology, France*
Licia Calvi, *NHTV Breda University of Applied Sciences, The Netherlands*
L Jean Camp, *Indiana University, USA*
Jose Campos, *Universidade do Minho, Portugal*
Heloisa Candello, *University of Brighton, UK*
Angelo Cangelosi, *Plymouth University, UK*
Cristina Cannone, *Università degli Studi di Milano, Italy*
Robert Capra, *University of North Carolina at Chapel Hill, USA*
Baptiste Caramiaux, *Goldsmiths College, London*
Giuseppe Carenini, *University of British Columbia, Canada*
Stefan Carmien, *University of Colorado, Spain*
Davide Carneiro, *University of Minho, Portugal*
Sheelagh Carpendale, *University of Calgary, Canada*
Luis Carriço, *University of Lisbon, Portugal*
John Carroll, *The Pennsylvania State University, USA*
Scott Carter, *FX Palo Alto Laboratory, USA*
Thomas Carter, *University of Bristol, UK*
Samuel Carton, *Northwestern University, USA*
Mark Cartwright, *Northwestern University, USA*
Géry Casiez, *University of Lille & INRIA Lille, France*
Alvaro Cassinelli, *University of Tokyo (todai), Japan*
Steven Castellucci, *York University, Canada*
Marcelo Cataldo, *Carnegie Mellon University, USA*
Grevet Catherine, *GVU Center, USA*
Abigail Cauchi, *Swansea University, UK*

Marc Cavazza, *University of Tesside, UK*
James Caverlee, *Texas A&M University, USA*
Melissa Cefkin, *IBM Research, USA*
Robert Cercos, *RMIT University, Australia*
Daniel Cernea, *University of Kaiserslautern, Germany*
Matteo Cesana, *Politecnico di Milano, Italy*
Pablo Cesar, *CWI, The Netherlands*
Ruy Cevantes, *UC Irvine, USA*
Elizabeth Cha, *Personal Robotics Lab, USA*
Samidh Chakrabarti, *Google, USA*
Matthew Chalmers, *University of Glasgow, UK*
Teresa Chambel, *University of Lisbon, Portugal*
Alan Chamberlain, *The University of Nottingham, UK*
Erik Champion, *Curtin University, Australia*
Deborah Chan, *University Health Network, Canada*
Joel Chan, *University of Pittsburgh, USA*
Liwei Chan, *Academia Sinica, Taiwan*
Angela Chang, *MIT Media Lab, USA*
Keng-Hao Chang, *University of California, Berkeley*
Remco Chang, *Tufts University, USA*
Peter Chapman, *University of Nottingham, UK*
Olivier Chapuis, *Université Paris-Sud, France*
Catherine Chase, *Carnegie Mellon University, USA*
Duen Horng (polo) Chau, *Georgia Institute of Technology, USA*
Beenish Chaudry, *Indiana University, USA*
Fang Chen, *Tsinghua University, Spain*
Gaowei Chen, *Pittsburg University,*
Hsiang-Ting Chen, *University of Tokyo, Taiwan*
Jay Chen, *New York University, USA*
Jilin Chen, *IBM Research, USA*
Judy Chen, *University of California, USA*
Liming Chen, *University of Ulster, UK*
Monchu Chen, *University of Madeira, Portugal*
Xiang 'Anthony' Chen, *Carnegie Mellon University, USA*
Yi-Shin Chen, *National Tsing Hua University, Taiwan*
Britte Cheng, *SRI International, USA*
Kai-Yin Cheng, *Microsoft Research Asia, Taiwan*
Lung-Pan Cheng, *National Taiwan University, Germany*
Shiwei Cheng, *Zhejiang University of Technology, China*
Mauro Cherubini, *Telefonica Research, Italy*
Marshini Chetty, *University of Maryland, USA*
Gifford Cheung, *University of Washington, USA*
Ed Chi, *Google, USA*
Pei-Yu Chi, *University of California, USA*
Sonia Chiasson, *Carleton University, Canada*
Mark Chignell, *University of Toronto, Canada*
Parmit Chilana, *University of Waterloo, USA*
Lydia Chilton, *MIT CSAIL, USA*
Alvin Chin, *Nokia Research Center, China*
George Chin, *Pacific Northwest National Laboratory, USA*
Clark Chinn, *Rutgers University,*
Winyu Chinthammit, *University of Tasmania, KAIST, Republic of Korea*
Eun Kyoung Choe, *University of Washington, USA*
Erik Choi, *Rutgers University, USA*

Ming Ki Chong, *Lancaster University, UK*
Wen Huei Chou, *Yunline University of Science and Technology, Taiwan*
Tanzeem Choudhury, *Dartmouth College, USA*
Ellen Christiansen, *Mads Clausen Institute, Denmark*
Georgios Christou, *Cyprus College, Cyprus*
Hao-Hua Chu, *National Taiwan University, Taiwan*
Jason Chuang, *University of Washington, USA*
Tyng-Ruey Chuang, *Academia Sinica, Taiwan*
Chia-Fang Chung, *University of Washington, USA*
Eunki Chung, *Carnegie Mellon University, USA*
Karen Church, *Telefonica Research, Spain*
Elizabeth Churchill, *eBay Research Lab, USA*
Marcelo Cicconet, *New York University, USA*
Jesse Cirimele, *Stanford University, USA*
Gabriel Cirio
Adrian Clark, *University of Canterbury, New Zealand*
Alan Clark, *Northwestern University, USA*
Lillian Clark, *University of Portsmouth, UK*
Rachel Clarke, *Newcastle University, UK*
James Clawson, *Georgia Institute of Technology, USA*
Adrian Clear, *Lancaster University, UK*
Tamara Clegg, *University of Maryland, USA*
Torkil Clemmensen, *Copenhagen Business School, Denmark*
Sue Cobb, *University of Nottingham, UK*
Michael Coburn, *RMIT University, Australia*
Gilbert Cockton, *Northumbria University, UK*
Gabe Cohn, *University of Washington, USA*
Marisa Cohn, *University of California Irvine, USA*
Michael Cohn, *Compukol Communications LLC, USA*
Jared Cole, *Carnegie Mellon University, USA*
Heather Cole-Lewis, *Columbia University, USA*
Lizzie Coles-Kemp, *Royal Holloway, UK*
Christopher Collins, *University of Ontario Institute of Technology, Canada*
Kevyn Collins-Thompson, *University of Michigan, USA*
Sébastien Combéfis, *Université Catholique de Louvain, Belgium*
Cristina Conati, *University of British Columbia, Canada*
Karin Coninx, *Hasselt University, Belgium*
Kay Connelly, *Indiana University Bloomington, USA*
Sunny Consolvo, *Google, USA*
Stéphane Conversy, *ENAC, France*
Gregorio Convertino, *Xerox Research Center Europe, Italy*
Perry Cook, *Princeton Computer Science, USA*
Michael Cooke, *Trinity College Dublin, Ireland*
Kovila Coopamootoo, *Newcastle University, UK*
Seth Cooper, *University of Washington, USA*
Andrew Cordar, *University of Florida, USA*
Raymundo Cornejo, *CICESE, Mexico*
Nicola Corradi, *Università di Padova, Italy*
Dan Cosley, *Cornell University, USA*
Joao Costa, *University of Ontario Institute of Technology, Canada*
Marc Cavazza, *University of Tesside, UK*
Gennaro Costagliola, *University of Salerno, Italy*
Enrico Costanza, *University of Southampton, UK*
James Coughlan, *Smith-Kettlewell Eye Research Institute, USA*

Tim Coughlan, *The University of Nottingham, UK*
Paul Coulton, *Lancaster University, UK*
Scott Counts, *Microsoft Research, USA*
Céline Coutrix, *Université Joseph Fourier, France*
Lynne Coventry, *University of Northumbria, UK*
Benjamin Cowan, *University of Birmingham, UK*
Anna Cox, *University College London, UK*
David Coyle, *University of Bristol, UK*
Michael Crabb, *University of Dundee, Scotland, UK*
Claire Craig, *Sheffield Hallam University, UK*
Scotty Craig, *Arizona State University,*
Henriette Cramer, *Yahoo! Labs, USA*
Meg Cramer, *UC Irvine, USA*
Angela Crandall, *iHub, Kenya*
Justin Cranshaw, *Carnegie Mellon University, USA*
Charles Crook, *University of Nottingham, UK*
Andrew Crossan, *University of Glasgow, UK*
R. Jordan Crouser, *Tufts University, USA*
Kevin Crowston, *Syracuse University, USA*
David Crundall, *University of Nottingham, UK*
Weiwei Cui, *Microsoft Research Asia, China*
Yanqing Cui, *Nokia Research Center, Finland*
Franco Curmi, *Lancaster University, UK*
Simone Cutini, *Università di Padova, Italy*
Edward Cutrell, *Microsoft Research India, India*
Chandrika Cycil, *Brunel University, UK*
Allen Cypher, *IBM Research - Almaden, USA*
Mary Czerwinski, *Microsoft Research, USA*
Alexei Czeskis, *Google, USA*
Raimund Dachselt, *Technische Universität Dresden, Germany*
Palle Dahlstedt, *Chalmers,*
Peng Dai, *Google, USA*
Florian Daiber, *DFKI German Research Center for AI, Germany*
Peter Dalsgaard, *Aarhus University, Denmark*
Ruth Dalton, *Northumbria University, UK*
Sashikanth Damaraju, *Texas A&M University, USA*
Chi Tai Dang, *University of Augsburg, Germany*
Andreea Danielescu, *Arizona State University, USA*
Darcy Dapra, *Google, USA*
Sauvik Das, *Carnegie Mellon University, USA*
Jennifer Davidson, *Oregon State University, USA*
Nigel Davies, *Lancaster University, UK*
James Davis, *UC Santa Cruz, USA*
Janet Davis, *Grinnell College, USA*
Katie Davis, *University of Washington,*
Richard Davis, *Singapore Management University, Singapore*
Rahmad Dawood, *Universitas Syiah Kuala, Indonesia*
Munmun de Choudhury, *Microsoft Research, USA*
Tjerk de Greef, *Delft University of Technology, The Netherlands*
Edward de Guzman, *Autodesk, USA*
Martin de Jode, *University College London, UK*
Daniele de Massari, *Fondazione Ospedale San Camillo, Italy*
Clarisse de Souza, *PUC-Rio, Brazil*

Cleidson de Souza, *Universidade Federal do Pará, Brazil*
David Dearman, *Twitter, USA*
Rob Deline, *Microsoft Research, USA*
Nicola Dell, *University of Washington, USA*
Robert Deloatch, *University of Illinois at Urbana-Champaign, USA*
Cagatay Demiralp, *Stanford University, USA*
Carrie Demmans Epp, *University of Toronto, Canada*
Nick Depalma, *Massachusetts Institute of Technology, USA*
Jan Derboven, *IBBT-KU Leuven, Belgium*
Katie Derthick, *University of Washington, USA*
Parag Deshpande, *Umeå Institute of Design, Sweden*
Audrey Desjardins, *Simon Fraser University, Canada*
Heather Desurvire, *Behavioristics, USA*
Sebastian Deterding, *Hans Bredow Institute for Media Research, Germany*
Laura Devendorf, *UC Berkeley, USA*
Guy Dewsbury, *Gdewsbury, UK*
Anind Dey, *Carnegie Mellon University, USA*
Barbara di Eugenio, *University of Illinois, USA*
Nicholas Diakopoulos, *Rutgers University, USA*
E.ilana Diamant, *University of Pittsburgh, USA*
Michael Dickard, *Ohio University, USA*
Margaret Dickey-Kurdziolek, *Virginia Tech, USA*
Sarah Diefenbach, *Folkwang University of the Arts, Germany*
Paul Dietz, *Microsoft, USA*
Tawanna Dillahunt, *Carnegie Mellon University, USA*
Jill Dimond, *Sassafras Tech Collective, USA*
Christian Dindler, *Aarhus University, Denmark*
Xianghua Ding, *Fudan University, China*
Abdigani Diriye, *Carnegie Mellon University, USA*
Betsy Disalvo, *Georgia Institute of Technology, USA*
Carl Disalvo, *Georgia Institute of Technology, USA*
Anke Dittmar, *University of Rostock, Germany*
Stephen Diverdi, *Adobe Systems Inc, USA*
Alan Dix, *Lancaster University, UK*
Sidney D'mello, *University of Notre Dame, USA*
Chuong do, *Coursera,*
Gavin Doherty, *Trinity College Dublin, Ireland*
Lynn Dombrowski, *University of California Irvine, USA*
Judith Donath, *MIT, USA*
Tao Dong, *University of Michigan, USA*
Birsen Donmez, *University of Toronto, Canada*
Marco Donnarumma, *Goldsmiths College, UK*
Jonathan Donner, *Microsoft Research India, USA*
Mira Dontcheva, *Adobe Research, USA*
James Doodson, *University of Leicester, England, UK*
Tanja Döring, *University of Bremen, Germany*
Marian Dörk, *Newcastle University, UK*
Brian Dorn, *University of Nebraska at Omaha, USA*
Michael Dorsch, *University of Michigan, USA*
Afsaneh Doryab, *Carnegie Mellon University, USA*
Jakub Dostal, *University of St Andrews, UK*
Wenwen Dou, *University of North Carolina at Charlotte, USA*
Andre Doucette, *University of Saskatchewan, Canada*

Audubon Dougherty, *MIT, USA*
Mark Doughty, *University of Lincoln, UK*
Paul Dourish, *University of California, USA*
John Downs, *The University of Melbourne, Australia*
Julie Downs, *Carnegie Mellon University, USA*
Toby Dragon, *Ithaca College, USA*
Christoph Draxler, *LMU München, Germany*
Martha Driessnack, *Oregon Health & Science University, USA*
Laurie Dringus, *Nova Southeastern University, USA*
Milena Droumeva, *Simon Fraser University, Canada*
Steven Drucker, *Microsoft Research, USA*
Allison Druin, *University of Maryland, USA*
Honglu Du, *Palo Alto Research Center, USA*
Ruofei Du, *Microsoft Research Asia, China*
Tina Du, *University of South KAIST, Republic of Korea ralia, Australia*
Carlos Duarte, *Universidade de Lisboa, Portugal*
Luís Duarte, *University of Lisbon, Portugal*
Emmanuel Dubois, *University of Toulouse, France*
Nicolas Ducheneaut, *Palo Alto Research Center, USA*
Andrew Duchowski, *Clemson University, USA*
Tobias Duckworth, *University of Salford, UK*
Casey Dugan, *IBM, USA*
Geoffrey Duggan, *University of Exeter, UK*
Susan Dumais, *Microsoft Research, USA*
Bruno Dumas, *Vrije Universiteit Brussel, Belgium*
Sean Duncan, *Indiana University, USA*
Lucy Dunne, *University College Dublin, Ireland*
Paul Dunphy, *Newcastle University, UK*
Andreas Dünser, *CSIRO - CCI, Australia*
Sophie Dupuy-Chessa, *University of Grenoble, France*
Shree Durga, *University of Wisconsin, USA*
Abigail Durrant, *Newcastle University, UK*
Erik Duval, *KU Leuven, Belgium*
Tim Dwyer, *Monash University, Australia*
Jason Dykes, *City University London, UK*
James Eagan, *Télécom-Paristech, France*
Sarah Eagle, *University of Bristol, UK*
David Ebert, *Purdue University, USA*
Florian Echtler, *Siemens Corporate Technology, Germany*
Dean Eckles, *Stanford University, USA*
Ernest Edmonds, *De Montfort University, UK*
Alistair Edwards, *University of York, UK*
Keith Edwards, *Georgia Institute of Technology, USA*
Kate Ehrlich, *IBM, USA*
Michael Eisenberg, *University of Colorado, USA*
Inger Ekman, *Aalto School of Economics, Finland*
Rana El Kaliouby, *University of Cambridge, UK*
Irene Eleta, *University of Maryland, USA*
Gunnar Ellingsen, *University of Tromsø, Norway*
Dan Ellis, *Columbia University, USA*
Geoff Ellis, *Lancaster University, UK*
Nicole Ellison, *University of Michigan, USA*
Lia Emanuel, *University of Bath,*
Bernadette Emsenhuber, *Johannes Kepler University of Linz, Austria*

Alex Endert, *Pacific Northwest National Laboratory, USA*
Klaus-Peter Engelbrecht, *Telekom Innovation Laboratories, Germany*
David England, *Liverpool John Moores University, UK*
Arvid Engström, *Mobile Life @ Stockholm University, Sweden*
Johan Engström, *Volvo Group Trucks Technology, Sweden*
Barrett Ens, *University of Manitoba, Canada*
Clayton Epp, *University of Saskatchewan, Canada*
Daniel Epstein, *University of Washington, USA*
Sheena Erete, *Northwestern University, USA*
Ingrid Erickson, *Rutgers University, USA*
Thomas Erickson, *IBM Research - T. J. Watson, USA*
Elina Eriksson, *KTH, Sweden*
Eva Eriksson, *Chalmers University of Technology, Sweden*
Lizbeth Escobedo, *Universidad Autonoma de Baja California, Mexico*
Parisa Eslambolchilar, *Future Interaction Technologies Lab, UK*
Sergio Espana, *Universitat Politecnica de Valencia, Spain*
Augusto Esteves, *University of Madeira, Portugal*
Michael Evans, *British Broadcasting Corporation, UK*
Vanessa Evers, *University of Twente, The Netherlands*
Marc Fabri, *Leeds Metropolitan University, UK*
Jerry Fails, *Montclair State University, USA*
Shamal Faily, *University of Oxford, UK*
Anthony Faiola, *Indiana University (IUPUI), USA*
Fiona Fairlie, *Glasgow Caledonian University, UK*
Majdi Faleh
Josef Faller, *Graz University of Technology, Austria*
Daniel Fallman, *Umeå University, Sweden*
Min Fan, *Simon Fraser University Surrey, Canada*
Xianyong Fang, *Anhui University, China*
Jill Fantauzza, *Georgia Institute of Technology, USA*
Jan Erik Farbrot, *Institute for Energy Technology / OECD Halden Reactor Project, Norway*
Elisabetta Farella, *DEIS - University of Bologna, Italy*
Shelly Farnham, *Microsoft Research, USA*
Umer Farooq, *The Pennsylvania State University, USA*
Karen Farris, *University of Michigan, USA*
Michael Farrugia, *UCD Dublin, Luxembourg*
Rosta Farzan, *University of Pittsburgh, USA*
Haakon Faste, *California College of the Arts, USA*
Andrew Faulring, *Carnegie Mellon University, USA*
Stu Favilla, *Swinburne University of Technology, Australia*
Melanie Feinberg, *University of Texas at KAIST, Republic of Korea in, USA*
Jean-Daniel Fekete, *INRIA, France*
Niels Feldmann, *Karlsruhe Institute of Technology (KIT), Germany*
Karla Felix Navarro, *University of Technology Sydney, Australia*
Deborah Fels, *Ryerson University, Canada*
Sidney Fels, *University of British Columbia, Canada*
Adrienne Felt, *Google, USA*
Jinjuan Feng, *University of Maryland, USA*
Robert Ferguson, *McGill University, Canada*
Jennifer Fernquist, *Google,*
Denzil Ferreira, *University of Oulu, Finland*
Pedro Ferreira, *Mobile Life @ KTH, Sweden*

Gabriele Ferri, *Indiana University, USA*
Brian Ferris, *University of Washington, USA*
Francesco Ferrise, *Politecnico di Milano, Italy*
Bruce Ferwerda, *Johannes Kepler University, Austria*
Mirko Fetter, *University of Bamberg, Germany*
Stephen Few, *Perceptual Edge, USA*
Christos Fidas, *University of Cyprus, Cyprus*
Rebecca Fiebrink, *Princeton University, UK*
Daniel Filonik, *Queensland University of Technology, Germany*
Leah Findlater, *University of Maryland, USA*
Thomas Finholt, *University of Michigan, USA*
Julia Fink, *Ecole Polytechnique Fédérale de Lausanne (EPFL), Switzerland*
Janet Finlay, *Leeds Metropolitan University, UK*
Andrew Fiore, *Facebook, USA*
Joel Fischer, *The University of Nottingham, UK*
Brian Fisher, *Simon Fraser University, Canada*
Danyel Fisher, *Microsoft Research, USA*
Stephen Fitchett, *University of Canterbury, New Zealand*
Daniel Fitton, *University of Central Lancashire, UK*
Elizabeth Fitzgerald, *The Open University, UK*
George Fitzmaurice, *Autodesk, Canada*
Geraldine Fitzpatrick, *Vienna University of Technology, Austria*
Zachary Fitz-Walter, *Queensland University of Technology, Australia*
Steve Flaherty, *Northeaster University, USA*
David Flatla, *University of Dundee, UK*
Ivan Flechais, *University of Oxford, England, UK*
Rowanne Fleck, *University College London, UK*
Scott Fleming, *University of Memphis, USA*
Martin Flintham, *The University of Nottingham, UK*
John Flowers, *University of Nebraska -- Lincoln, USA*
Allen Flynn, *University of Michigan, USA*
Brynn Flynn, *Carnegie Mellon University, USA*
James Fogarty, *University of Washington, USA*
Bj Fogg, *Stanford University, USA*
Sean Follmer, *MIT, USA*
Eelke Folmer, *University of Nevada, USA*
Peter Forbrig, *University of Rostock, Germany*
Alain Forget, *Carleton University, Canada*
Azadeh Forghani, *Simon Fraser University, Canada*
Laura Forlano, *Parsons The New School for Design, USA*
David Forsyth, *University of Illinois at Urbana-Champaign, USA*
Andrea Forte, *Drexel University, USA*
Jutta Fortmann, *University of Oldenburg, Germany*
Lesley Fosh, *The University of Nottingham, UK*
Elizabeth Foss, *University of Maryland, USA*
Derek Foster, *University of Lincoln, UK*
Stephen Foster, *UC San Diego, USA*
Marcus Foth, *Queensland University of Technology, Australia*
Brooke Foucault, *Northwestern University, USA*
Adam Fourney, *University of Waterloo, Canada*
Adam Fouse, *University of California, USA*
Allan Fowler, *Waiariki Institute of Technology, New Zealand*
Sarah Fox, *University of Washington, USA*

Suely Fragoso, *Federal University of Rio Grande do Sul (UFRGS), Brazil*
Anders Frank, *Swedish National Defence College, Sweden*
Mario Frank, *UC Berkeley, Germany*
Mike Fraser, *University of Bristol, UK*
Christopher Frauenberger, *University of Sussex, UK*
Dustin Freeman, *University of Toronto, Canada*
Euan Freeman, *University of Glasgow, Scotland, UK*
Andre Freire, *Universidade de Lisboa, Brazil*
Luanne Freund, *University of British Columbia, Canada*
Jill Freyne, *CSIRO, Australia*
Sarah-Christin Freytag, *Berlin Institute of Technology, Germany*
Enrique Frias-Martinez, *Telefonica Research, Spain*
Adrian Friday, *Lancaster University, UK*
Doron Friedman, *The Interdisciplinary Center, Israel*
Mathias Frisch, *MID Gmbh, Germany*
Chris Frisina, *Virginia Tech, USA*
Jonas Fritsch, *Aarhus University, Denmark*
Mario Fritz, *MPI Informatik, Germany*
Thomas Fritz, *University of Zurich, Switzerland*
Bernd Froehlich, *Bauhaus Universität Weimar, Germany*
Jon Froehlich, *University of Maryland, USA*
David Frohlich, *University of Surrey, UK*
Peter Fröhlich, *FTW Telecommunications Research Center, Austria*
Erik Frøkjær, *Københavns Universitet, Denmark*
Mads Frost, *IT University of Copenhagen, Denmark*
Wai-Tat Fu, *University of Illinois at Urbana-Champaign, USA*
Georg Fuchs, *Fraunhofer Institute Intelligent Analysis and Information Systems IAIS, Germany*
Johannes Fuchs, *University, Germany*
Verena Fuchsberger, *ICT&S Center, Austria*
Kaori Fujinami, *Tokyo University of Agriculture and Technology, Japan*
Kentarou Fukuda, *IBM Research - Tokyo, Japan*
Benjamin Fung, *McGill University, Canada*
Mathias Funk, *Eindhoven University of Technology, The Netherlands*
Silvia Gabrielli, *Create-Net, Italy*
Hind Gacem, *Télécom-Paristech, France*
Martin Gaedke, *Technische Universität Chemnitz, Germany*
Andrea Gaggioli, *Catholic University of Milan, Italy*
Sarah Gallacher, *UCL, UK*
Teresa Galvão, *Universidade do Porto, Portugal*
Maribeth Gandy, *Georgia Institute of Technology, USA*
Eva Ganglbauer, *Vienna University of Technology, Austria*
Ge Gao, *Cornell University, USA*
Ruth García-Gavilanes, *Universitat Pompeu Fabra, Spain*
Simson Garfinkel, *MIT, USA*
R. Kelly Garrett, *Ohio State University, USA*
Daniel Gartenberg, *George Mason University, USA*
Franca Garzotto, *HOC-Politecnico di Milano, Italy*
Nadia Gauducheau, *ICD-CNRS, France*
Steffen Gauglitz, *University of California, USA*
Paul Gault, *University of Dundee, UK*
William Gaver, *Goldsmiths College, UK*
Tom Gedeon, *KAIST, Republic of Korea ralian National University, Australia*

Nils Gehlenborg, *Harvard Medical School, USA*
Sven Gehring, *German Research Center for Artificial Intelligence (DFKI), Germany*
Johanna Gelderblom, *University of Pretoria, South Africa*
Hans Gellersen, *Lancaster University, UK*
Aaron Genest, *University of Saskatchewan, Canada*
Kallirroi Georgila, *University of Southern California, USA*
Elizabeth Gerber, *Northwestern University, USA*
Peter Gerjets, *Knowledge Media Research Center*
Jens Gerken, *ICT Innovative Communication Technologies AG, Germany*
Kathrin Gerling, *University of Lincoln, UK*
David Gerritsen, *Carnegie Mellon University, USA*
Paul Gestwicki, *Ball State University, USA*
Luc Geurts, *KU Leuven, Belgium*
Werner Geyer, *IBM Research - T. J. Watson, USA*
Giuseppe Ghiani, *ISTI-CNR, Italy*
George Ghinea, *Brunel University, UK*
Emilien Ghomi, *Université Paris-Sud, France*
Maysam Ghovanloo, *Georgia Institute of Technology, USA*
Alicia Gibb, *Nycresistor, USA*
Lorna Gibson, *University of Dundee, UK*
Eric Gilbert, *Georgia Institute of Technology, USA*
Kathleen Gilbert, *Indiana University, USA*
Alastair Gill, *University of Surrey, UK*
Kiel Gilleade, *Liverpool John Moores University, UK*
Nicholas Gillian, *MIT Media Lab, USA*
Stephen Gilroy, *Teesside University, UK*
Shuli Gilutz, *Interdisciplinary Center (IDC) Herzliya, Israel*
Shiry Ginosar, *University of California, USA*
Jeffrey Girard, *University of Pittsburgh, USA*
Audrey Girouard, *Carleton University, Canada*
Voula Gkatzidou, *Brunel University, UK*
Dylan Glas, *ATR, Japan*
Marie Glasemann, *Aalborg University, Denmark*
Michael Glueck, *University of Toronto, Canada*
Janet Go, *Autodesk, USA*
Kentaro Go, *University of Yamanashi, Japan*
Fernand Gobet, *University of Liverpool, UK*
Mayank Goel, *University of Washington, USA*
Anja Goeritz, *University of Freiburg, Germany*
Sean Goggins, *University of Missouri, USA*
Wooi Boon Goh, *Nanyang Technological University, Singapore*
Sergio Goldenberg, *Georgia Institute of Technology, USA*
Scott Golder, *Cornell University, USA*
Ilya Goldin, *Carnegie Mellon University, USA*
Dan Goldman, *Adobe, USA*
David Golightly, *Experian UK, UK*
Connie Golsteijn, *Eindhoven University of Technology, Netherlands*
Evan Golub, *University of Maryland, USA*
Richard Gomer, *University of Southampton, UK*
Antonio Gomes, *Queen's University, Canada*
Rafael Gomez, *Queensland University of Technology, Australia*
Steven Gomez, *Brown University, USA*

Jorge Goncalves, *Instituto Superior Técnico, Finland*
Daniel Gonçalves, *University of Oulu, Portugal*
Tiago Gonçalves, *FCUL, Portugal*
Nan-Wei Gong, *Massachusetts Institute of Technology, USA*
Amy Gonzales, *Indiana University, USA*
Berto Gonzalez, *University of North Carolina at Charlotte, USA*
Victor Gonzalez, *University of Manchester, UK*
Walkyria Goode, *SPARK Experience, USA*
Elizabeth Goodman, *UC Berkeley, USA*
Paul Gorman, *Oregon Health & Science University, USA*
Sandy Gould, *University College London, UK*
Rúben Gouveia, *University of Madeira, Portugal*
Nitesh Goyal, *Cornell University, USA*
Kazjon Grace, *UNC Charlotte, USA*
Michele Graffeo, *University of Trento, Italy*
Connor Graham, *National University of Singapore, Singapore*
Martin Graham, *Napier University, UK*
Nicholas Graham, *Queen's University, Canada*
Klaus Gramann, *Berlin Institute of Technology, Germany*
Dimitris Grammenos, *Foundation for Research and Technology - Hellas, Greece*
Sukeshini Grandhi, *Eastern Connecticut State University, USA*
Laura Granka, *Google, USA*
Raphael Grasset, *Graz University of Technology, Austria*
Colin Gray, *Indiana University, USA*
Rebecca Gray, *Michigan State University, USA*
David Green, *Newcastle University, UK*
Keith Green, *Clemson University, USA*
Michael Greenberg, *Northwestern University, USA*
Saul Greenberg, *University of Calgary, Canada*
Chris Greenhalgh, *The University of Nottingham, UK*
Peggy Gregory, *University of Central Lancashire, UK*
Catherine Grevet, *Georgia Institute of Technology, USA*
Harry Griffin, *University College London, UK*
Erin Griffiths, *University of Virginia, USA*
Thomas Grill, *University of Salzburg, Austria*
Rebecca Grinter, *Georgia Institute of Technology, USA*
Laurent Grisoni, *University Lille, France*
Alex Groce, *Oregon State University, USA*
Georg Groh, *TU Muenchen, Germany*
Diane Gromala, *Simon Fraser University, Canada*
Kaj Grønbæk, *University of Aarhus, Denmark*
Erik Grönvall, *IT University of Copenhagen, Denmark*
Mark Gross, *Carnegie Mellon University, USA*
Shad Gross, *Indiana University Bloomington, USA*
Tom Gross, *University of Bamberg, Germany*
Jens Grossklags, *The Pennsylvania State University, USA*
Jens Grubert, *University of Technology Graz, Austria*
Shion Guha, *Cornell University, USA*
Yves Guiard, *Télécom-Paristech CNRS, France*
François Guimbretière, *Cornell University, USA*
Rebecca Gulotta, *Carnegie Mellon University, USA*
Hatice Gunes, *University of Technology, Australia*
Philip Guo, *Stanford University, USA*

Ankit Gupta, *University of Washington, USA*
Sidhant Gupta, *University of Washington, USA*
David Gurzick, *Hood College, USA*
Sean Gustafson, *Hasso Plattner Institute, Germany*
Mattia Gustarini, *University of Geneva, Switzerland*
Francisco Luis Gutiérrez Vela, *University of Granada, España*
Ricardo Gutierrez-Osuna, *Texas A&M University, USA*
Mark Guzdial, *Georgia Institute of Technology, USA*
Tajin Ha, *KAIST, S. Korea*
Joerg Haake, *Fernuniversitaet Hagen, Germany*
Eija Haapalainen Ferreira, *University of Oulu, Finland*
Eben Haber, *IBM Research - Almaden, USA*
Jonathan Haber, *University of Calgary, Canada*
Martin Hachet, *Labri-INRIA University of Bordeaux, France*
Mieke Haesen, *Hasselt University - Tul - Iminds, Belgium*
Joshua Hailpern, *Hewlett Packard, USA*
Oliver Haimson, *University of California, USA*
Julia Haines, *University of California, USA*
Maria Håkansson, *Chalmers University of Technology, Sweden*
David Hakken, *Indiana University Bloomongton, USA*
Jonna Hakkila, *University of Oulu, Finland*
Jonna Häkkilä, *Soul4design, Finland*
Jukka Häkkinen, *Aalto University School of Science and Technology, Finland*
Timothy Hale, *Partners Healthcare Inc., USA*
Aaron Halfaker, *University of Minnesota, USA*
Joseph Hall, *The Center for Democracy & Technology, USA*
Michael Haller, *University of Applied Sciences Upper KAIST, Republic of Korea ria, Austria*
Lars Hallnäs, *Chalmers University of Technology, Sweden*
John Halloran, *Coventry University, UK*
Kim Halskov, *Aarhus University, Denmark*
Christine Halverson, *IBM Research - T. J. Watson, USA*
Tim Halverson, *Air Force Research Laboratory, USA*
Martin Halvey, *Glasgow Caledonian University, UK*
Perttu Hämäläinen, *Aalto University, Finland*
William Hamilton, *Texas A&M University, USA*
Jessica Hammer, *Carnegie Mellon University, USA*
Nils Hammerla, *Newcastle University, UK*
Tracy Hammond, *Texas A&M University, USA*
Jaehyun Han, *KAIST, Republic of Korea*
Jeonghye Han, *Computer Education, Republic of Korea*
Kyungsik (keith) Han, *The Pennsylvania State University, USA*
Teng Han, *University of Bristol, China*
Jeff Hancock, *Cornell University, USA*
Mark Handel, *The Boeing Company, USA*
Alina Hang, *University of Munich, Germany*
Benjamin Hanrahan, *Virginia Polytechnic Institute and State University, France*
Derek Hansen, *Brigham Young University, USA*
John Paulin Hansen, *IT University of Copenhagen, Denmark*
Kotaro Hara, *University of Maryland, USA*
Mona Haraty, *University of British Columbia, Canada*
Marian Harbach, *Leibniz University Hannover, Germany*

Gunnar Harboe, *University of Zurich, Switzerland*
Ellie Harmon, *UC Irvine, USA*
Morten Harning, *Dialogical ApS, Denmark*
Franklin Harper, *University of Minnesota, USA*
Richard Harper, *Microsoft Research, UK*
Simon Harper, *University of Manchester, UK*
Erik Harpstead, *Carnegie Mellon University, USA*
Rikard Harr, *Umeå University, Sweden*
Chris Harrison, *Carnegie Mellon University, USA*
Daniel Harrison, *University College London, UK*
Lane Harrison, *University of North Carolina at Charlotte, USA*
Jennefer Hart, *Lancaster University, UK*
Casper Harteveld, *Northeastern University, USA*
Björn Hartmann, *University of California, USA*
Mark Hartswood, *University of Edinburgh, UK*
Andrea Hartzler, *University of Washington, USA*
Catherine Harvey, *University of Nottingham, UK*
Khalad Hasan, *University of Manitoba, Canada*
Chelsea Hash, *Polytechnic Institute of NYU, USA*
Mitsuyo Hashida, *Soai Uiversity, Japan*
Marc Hassenzahl, *Folkwang University of the Arts, Germany*
Doris Hausen, *University of Munich, Germany*
Sabrina Hauser, *Simon Fraser University, Canada*
Kirstie Hawkey, *Dalhousie University, Canada*
Eiji Hayashi, *Carnegie Mellon University, USA*
Gillian Hayes, *University of California, USA*
Helen He, *University of Calgary, Canada*
Marti Hearst, *UC Berkeley, USA*
Brent Hecht, *University of Minnesota, USA*
Per-Olof Hedvall, *Lund University, Sweden*
Jaimee Heffner, *Fred Hutchinson Cancer Research Center, USA*
Tomi Heimonen, *University of Tampere, Finland*
Eric Hekler, *Arizona State University, USA*
Robert Held, *University of California, USA*
Bradley Hemminger, *University of North Carolina, USA*
Niels Hendriks, *University of Leuven, Belgium*
David Hendry, *University of Washington, USA*
Fabian Hennecke, *University of Munich, Germany*
Nathalie Henry Riche, *Microsoft Research, USA*
Niels Henze, *University of Stuttgart, Germany*
Cormac Herley, *Microsoft Research, Ghjhj*
Hamilton Hernandez, *Queen's University, Canada*
Davinia Hernandez-Leo, *Universitat Pompeu Fabra, Spain*
Marc Herrlich, *University of Bremen, Germany*
Morten Hertzum, *University of Copenhagen, Denmark*
Philipp Herzig, *SAP Research CEC Dresden, Germany*
Phil Heslop, *Newcastle University, UK*
Luke Hespanhol, *University of Sydney, Australia*
Jan Hess, *University of Siegen, Germany*
Susan Hessey, *Brithish Telecom, UK*
Wilko Heuten, *OFFIS - Institute for Information Technology, Germany*
Clint Heyer, *IT University of Copenhagen, Denmark*
Nadja Heym, *University of Nottingham, UK*

Jutta Hild, *Fraunhofer IOSB, Germany*
Benjamin Mako Hill, *University of Washington, USA*
Serena Hillman, *Simon Fraser University, Canada*
Juan David Hincapié-Ramos, *IT University of Copenhagen, Canada*
Ken Hinckley, *Microsoft Research, USA*
Jon Hindmarsh, *King's College London, UK*
Uta Hinrichs, *University of St Andrews, UK*
Sen Hirano, *University of California, USA*
Matthew Hirsch, *MIT Media Lab, USA*
Tad Hirsch, *University of Washington, USA*
Leanne Hirshfield, *Hamilton College, USA*
Chaya Hiruncharoenvate, *Georgia Institute of Technology, USA*
Christina Hochleitner, *CURE - Center for Usability Research & Engineering, Austria*
Nadia Hocine, *Montpellier 2 University, France*
Duncan Hodges, *University of Oxford, UK*
Gray Hodgkinson, *Massey University, New Zealand*
Orland Hoeber, *University of Regina, Canada*
Jesse Hoey, *University of Waterloo, Canada*
Guy Hoffman, *IDC Herzliya, Israel*
Bernie Hogan, *University of Toronto, Canada*
Trevor Hogan, *Cork Institute of Technology, Ireland*
Andrew Hogue, *University of Ontario Institute of Technology, Canada*
James Hollan, *UCSD, USA*
Simon Holland, *The Open University, UK*
Tobias Hollerer, *University of California, USA*
Nic Hollinworth, *University of Reading, UK*
Caitlin Holman, *University of Michigan, USA*
David Holman, *Queen's University, Canada*
Hrönn Holmer, *Cornell University, USA*
Stefan Holmlid, *Linköpings universitet, Sweden*
Lars Erik Holmquist, *Indep. Consultant, USA*
Kenneth Holmqvist, *Lund University, Sweden*
Bree Holtz, *Information Studies and Media, USA*
Christian Holz, *Yahoo! Labs, USA*
Andreas Holzinger, *Graz Medical University, Austria*
Hwajung Hong, *Georgia Institute of Technology, USA*
Jason Hong, *Carnegie Mellon University, USA*
Jin-Hyuk Hong, *Carnegie Mellon University, USA*
Lichan Hong, *Google, USA*
Kristina Höök, *KTH, Sweden*
Mohammed Hoque, *University of Rochester, USA*
Michael Horn, *Northwestern University, USA*
John Horton, *Harvard University, USA*
Matthew Horton, *Child Computer Interaction Group, UK*
Simo Hosio, *University of Oulu, Finland*
Steven Houben, *IT University of Copenhagen, Denmark*
Kirralie Houghton, *Queensland University of Technology, Australia*
Robert Houghton, *The University of Nottingham, UK*
Juan Pablo Hourcade, *University of Iowa, USA*
Rachid Hourizi, *University of Bath, UK*
Aaron Houssian, *Philips Research, The Netherlands*
Andrew Howes, *University of Manchester, UK*

James Howison, *Carnegie Mellon University, USA*
Kate Howland, *University of Sussex, UK*
Iris Howley, *Carnegie Mellon University, USA*
Idris Hsi, *Microsoft, USA*
Yi-Ta Hsieh, *University of Helsinki, Finland*
Chang Hu, *Microsoft, USA*
Jun Hu, *Eindhoven University of Technology, Netherlands*
Mengdie Hu, *Georgia Institute of Technology, USA*
Y. Charlie Hu, *Purdue University, USA*
Yuheng Hu, *Arizona State University, USA*
Chung-Ching Huang, *Indiana University, USA*
Haosheng Huang, *Research Group Cartography, Austria*
Jeff Huang, *University of Washington, USA*
Kevin Huang, *Georgia Institute of Technology, USA*
Shih-Wen Huang, *University of Washington, USA*
Jochen Huber, *MIT Media Lab, USA*
Bernardo Huberman, *HP Labs, USA*
Matthew Hudson, *The University of York, UK*
Scott Hudson, *Carnegie Mellon University, USA*
David Huffaker, *Google, USA*
Amanda Hughes, *Utah State University, USA*
Julie Hui, *Northwestern University, USA*
Alina Huldtgren, *Delft University of Technology, Germany*
Jessica Hullman, *University of Michigan, USA*
Shah Rukh Humayoun, *University of Kaiserslautern, Germany*
Seth Hunter, *MIT Media Lab, USA*
Stephane Huot, *Université Paris-Sud, France*
Annika Hupfeld, *University of Nottingham, UK*
Amy Hurst, *Carnegie Mellon University, USA*
Wolfgang Hürst, *Utrecht University, The Netherlands*
Christophe Hurter, *University of Toulouse, France*
Heinrich Hussmann, *Ludwig-Maximilians-Universität München, Germany*
Dugald Hutchings, *Elon University, USA*
John Hutchinson, *Lancaster University, UK*
C.j. Hutto, *Georgia Institute of Technology, USA*
Luke Hutton, *University of St Andrews, UK*
Ebba Thora Hvannberg, *University of Iceland, Iceland*
Inseok Hwang, *KAIST, South Korea*
Sungjae Hwang, *KAIST, South Korea*
Aulikki Hyrskykari, *University of Tampere, Finland*
Ioanna Iacovides, *UCL, UK*
Djilali Idoughi, *University A. Mira of Bejaia, Algeria*
Takeo Igarashi, *The University of Tokyo, Japan*
Klas Ihme, *University of Leipzig, Germany*
Masahiko Inami, *KMD, Japan*
Todd Ingalls, *Arizona State University, USA*
Stephen Intille, *Northeastern University, USA*
Alexandra Ion, *University of Applied Sciences Upper KAIST, Republic of Korea ria, Austria*
Iulia Ion, *Google, USA*
Panos Ipeirotis, *New York University, New York*
Shamsi Iqbal, *Microsoft Research, USA*
Ellen Isaacs, *PARC, USA*

Katherine Isbister, *Polytechnic Institute of New York University, USA*
Tobias Isenberg, *INRIA, France*
Kentaro Ishii, *The University of Tokyo, Japan*
Poika Isokoski, *University of Tampere, Finland*
Ali Israr, *Disney Research, USA*
Howell Istance, *De Montfort University, UK*
Yuichi Itoh, *Osaka University, Japan*
Bret Jackson, *University of New Mexico, USA*
Daniel Jackson, *Newcastle University, UK*
Steven Jackson, *Cornell University, USA*
Tanner Jackson, *Princeton, USA*
Robert Jacob, *Tufts University, USA*
Mattias Jacobsson, *Mobile Life @ SICS, Sweden*
Nassim Jafarinaimi, *Georgia Institute of Technology, USA*
Nils Jäger, *University of Nottingham, UK*
Mohit Jain, *University of Toronto, Canada*
Sharad Jaiswal, *Bell Labs India, India*
Timo Jakobi, *University of Siegen, Germany*
Mikkel Jakobsen, *University of Copenhagen, Denmark*
Hamid R. Jamali, *Kharazmi University, Iran*
Anthony Jameson, *German Research Center for Artificial Intelligence (DFKI), Germany*
Jacek Jankowski, *Digital Enterprise Research Institute, France*
Maddy Janse, *Philips Research, The Netherlands*
Bernard Jansen, *The Pennsylvania State University, USA*
Yvonne Jansen, *Université Paris-Sud, France*
Christian Janssen, *Smith-Kettlewell Eye Research Institute, USA*
Joris Janssen, *Eindhoven University of Technology, The Netherlands*
Ryan Janzen, *University of Toronto, Canada*
Tim Jay, *University of Bristol, UK*
K. Neil Jenkings, *Newcastle University, UK*
Tom Jenkins, *Georgia Institute of Technology, USA*
Carlos Jensen, *Oregon State University, USA*
Jennifer Jenson, *York University, Canada*
Seokhee Jeon, *ETH Zurich, Switzerland*
Jin-Woo Jeong, *Hanyang University, Republic of Korea*
Hans-Christian Jetter, *University of Konstanz, UK*
Jiepu Jiang, *University of Massachusetts Amherst, USA*
Nan Jiang, *Bournemouth University, UK*
Marina Jirotka, *University of Oxford, UK*
Kazuhiro Jo, *IAMAS, Japan*
Bonnie John, *IBM Research, USA*
Andrew Johnson, *University of Illinois at Chicago, USA*
Gabe Johnson, *Blank Slate Systems, USA*
Jeff Johnson, *UI Wizards, USA*
Kimberly Johnson, *Google, USA*
Maritza Johnson, *University of California, USA*
Mikael Johnson, *Helsinki University of Technology, Finland*
Steven Johnson, *Temple U., USA*
Aditya Johri, *Virginia Tech, USA*
Tero Jokela, *Nokia Research Center, Finland*
Brett Jones, *University of Illinois at Urbana-Champaign, USA*
J. Adam Jones, *University of Southern California, USA*

Malcolm Jones, *Northumbria University, UK*
Matt Jones, *Swansea University, Wales, UK*
Steve Jones, *University of Waikato, New Zealand*
William Jones, *University of Washington, USA*
Martin Jonsson, *Södertörn University, Sweden*
Sergi Jorda, *Universitat Pompeu Fabra, Spain*
Joaquim Jorge, *INESC-ID, Portugal*
Rui Jose, *Universidade do Minho, Portugal*
Anirudha Joshi, *Indian Institute of Technology, India*
Neel Joshi, *Microsoft, USA*
Ricardo Jota, *University of Toronto, Portugal*
M.-Carmen Juan, *UPV, Spain*
Oskar Juhlin, *Mobile Life @ Stockholm University, Sweden*
Satu Jumisko-Pyykkö, *Tampere University of Technology, Finland*
Heekyoung Jung, *University of Cincinnati, USA*
Malte Jung, *Cornell University, USA*
Tzyy-Ping Jung, *UCSD, USA*
Yumi Jung, *Michigan State University, USA*
Beyerer Jürgen, *Karlsruhe Institute of Technology (KIT), Germany*
Marko Jurmu, *University of Oulu, Finland*
Mike Just, *Glasgow Caledonian University, UK*
Antti Jylhä, *University of Helsinki, Finland*
Dennis Kafura, *Virginia Tech, USA*
Anne Kaikkonen, *Nokia Corporation, Finland*
Sanjay Kairam, *Stanford University, USA*
Yasuaki Kakehi, *Keio University, Japan*
Matthew Kam, *American Institutes for Research, USA*
Noreen Kamal, *University of British Columbia, Canada*
Alexander Kan, *The University of Melbourne, Australia*
Sean Kandel, *Stanford University, USA*
Eser Kandogan, *IBM, USA*
Bridget Kane, *Trinity College Dublin, Ireland*
Shaun Kane, *University of Maryland Baltimore County, USA*
Ruogu Kang, *Carnegie Mellon University, USA*
Marije Kanis, *Brunel University, UK*
Gopinaath Kannabiran, *Indiana University, USA*
Anne Marie Kanstrup, *Aalborg University, Denmark*
Ashish Kapoor, *Microsoft Research, USA*
Dennis Kappen, *University of Ontario Institute of Technology, Canada*
Evangelos Kapros, *Trinity College Dublin, Ireland*
Maurits Kaptein, *Eindhoven University of Technology, The Netherlands*
Victor Kaptelinin, *Umeå University, Sweden*
Mustafa Karagozler, *Disney Research, USA*
Karrie Karahalios, *University of Illinois, USA*
Amela Karahasanovic, *SINTEF ICT, Norway*
John Karat, *IBM Research - T. J. Watson, USA*
David Karger, *MIT, USA*
Thorsten Karrer, *RWTH Aachen University, Germany*
Christos Katsanos, *Hellenic Open University, Greece*
Brian Katz, *LIMSI-CNRS, France*
Larry Katz, *University of Calgary, Canada*
Andrea Kavanaugh, *Virginia Tech, USA*
Fahim Kawsar, *Phd Candidate, Japan*

Matthew Kay, *University of Waterloo, Canada*
Joseph 'jofish' Kaye, *Nokia, USA*
Gabriella Kazai, *Microsoft Research, UK*
Konstantinos Kazakos, *Newcastle University, UK*
Rubaiat Habib Kazi, *National University of Singapore, Canada*
Elizabeth Kaziunas, *University of Michigan, USA*
Wendy Keay-Bright, *University of Wales Institute, Wales, UK*
Daniel Keefe, *University of Minnesota, USA*
Brian Keegan, *Northeastern University, USA*
Flavius Kehr, *University of Koblenz-Landau, Germany*
Caitlin Kelleher, *Washington University, USA*
Wendy Kellogg, *IBM Research - T. J. Watson, USA*
Diane Kelly, *University of North Carolina, USA*
Ryan Kelly, *University of Bath, UK*
Logan Kendall, *University of Washington, USA*
Denisa Kera, *National University of Singapore, Singapore*
Dagmar Kern, *Bertrandt Ingenieurbüro Gmbh, Germany*
Andruid Kerne, *Texas A&M University, USA*
Andreas Kerren, *Linnaeus University, Sweden*
Karina Kervin, *University of Michigan, USA*
Cem Keskin, *Microsoft Research, UK*
Rilla Khaled, *University of Malta, Malta*
Mohammadreza Khalilbeigi, *Darmstadt University of Technology, Germany*
Vassilis-Javed Khan, *NHTV Breda University of Applied Sciences, The Netherlands*
Ahmed Kharrufa, *Newcastle University, UK*
Rohit Khot, *RMIT University, Australia*
Vera Khovanskaya, *Cornell University, USA*
Emre Kiciman, *Microsoft Research, USA*
Wolf Kienzle, *Microsoft Research, USA*
Johan Kildal, *Nokia, Finland*
Dongwhan Kim, *Seoul National University, Republic of Korea*
Hyang-Sook Kim, *St. Norbert's College, USA*
Hyung Nam Kim, *Northwestern University, USA*
Joy Kim, *Stanford University, USA*
Juho Kim, *Massachusetts Institute of Technology, USA*
Ju-Whan Kim, *KAIST, Republic of Korea*
Kibum Kim, *Kochi University of Technology, Japan*
Seung Wook Kim, *Samsung R&D Center Silicon Valley, USA*
Seungjun Kim, *Carnegie Mellon University, USA*
Si Jung Kim, *University of Central Florida, USA*
Sung-Hee Kim, *Purdue University, USA*
Sunyoung Kim, *Carnegie Mellon University, USA*
Taemie Kim, *Sociometric Solutions, USA*
Kenrick Kin, *University of California, USA*
Jennifer King, *University of California, USA*
Michael Kipp, *Augsburg University of Applied Sciences, Germany*
Reuben Kirkham, *Nottingham University, England*
Iacovos Kirlappos, *University College London, UK*
Alex Kirlik, *University of Illinois at Urbana, USA*
Ben Kirman, *University of Lincoln, UK*
Paul Kirschner, *Open Universiteit, Nederland*
David Kirsh, *University of California, USA*

Christopher Kirwan, *Parsons The New School for Design, USA*
Yoshifumi Kitamura, *Tohoku University, Japan*
Kris Kitani, *Carnegie Mellon University, USA*
Aniket Kittur, *Carnegie Mellon University, USA*
Funda Kivran-Swaine, *Rutgers University, USA*
René Kizilcec, *Stanford University, USA*
Scott Klemmer, *UC San Diego, USA*
Jayne Klenner, *King's College, USA*
Clemens Klokmose, *Aarhus University, Denmark*
Eric Klopfer, *MIT, USA*
Jarrod Knibbe, *University of Bristol, UK*
Bart Knijnenburg, *University of California, The Netherlands*
Cory Knobel, *University of California, USA*
Hendrik Knoche, *EPFL, Switzerland*
Bran Knowles, *Lancaster University, UK*
Masatomo Kobayashi, *IBM Research - Tokyo, Japan*
Michael Koch, *Bundeswehr University Munich, Germany*
Kenneth Koedinger, *Carnegie Mellon University, USA*
Lone Koefoed Hansen, *Aarhus University, Denmark*
Christian Koehler, *Carnegie Mellon University, USA*
Hyunseung Koh, *Indiana University, USA*
Kyle Koh, *Seoul National University, South Korea*
Hideki Koike, *University of Electro-Communications, Japan*
Mario Kolberg, *University of Stirling, UK*
Boriana Koleva, *The University of Nottingham, UK*
Beth Kolko, *University of Washington, USA*
Jon Kolko, *Frog Design, USA*
Thomas Költringer, *Ventum Consulting, Austria*
Steven Komarov, *Harvard University, USA*
Anita Komlodi, *University of Maryland, USA*
Andreas Komninos, *University of Strathclyde, UK*
Joseph Konstan, *University of Minnesota, USA*
Matthias Korn, *Aarhus University, Denmark*
Oliver Korn, *University of Applied Sciences Esslingen, Germany*
Gerd Kortuem, *The Open University, UK*
Robert Kosara, *Tableau Software, USA*
Timothy Koschmann, *Southern Illinois University, USA*
Ilpo Koskinen, *University of Art and Design Helsinki, Finland*
Vassilis Kostakos, *University of Oulu, Finland*
Ilkka Kosunen, *University of Helsinki, Finland*
Theodora Koulouri, *Brunel University,*
Matthias Kovatsch, *ETH Zurich, Switzerland*
Yong Ming Kow, *University of California Irvine, Hong Kong Sar*
Nicole Kraemer, *University of Duisburg-Essen,*
Adam Kramer, *Facebook, USA*
Jan-Peter Krämer, *RWTH Aachen University, Germany*
Matthias Kranz, *University of Passau, Germany*
Sven Kratz, *University of Munich, Germany*
Robert Kraut, *Carnegie Mellon University, USA*
Christian Kray, *University of Münster, Germany*
Shivsubramani Krishnamoorthy, *Amrita University, USA*
Ernst Kruijff, *Graz University of Technology, Austria*
John Krumm, *Microsoft Research, USA*
Erin Krupka, *University of Michigan, USA*

Ravi Kuber, *UMBC, USA*
Sebastien Kubicki, *CERV - Centre Européen de Réalité Virtuelle, France*
Alex Kuhn, *University of Michigan, USA*
Kai Kuikkaniemi, *Helsinki Institute for Information Technology HIIT, Finland*
Sari Kujala, *Aalto University, Finland*
Tuomo Kujala, *University of Jyväskylä, Finland*
Hannu Kukka, *University of Oulu, Finland*
Anand Kulkarni, *University of California, USA*
Chinmay Kulkarni, *Stanford University, USA*
Anuj Kumar, *Carnegie Mellon University, USA*
Arun Kumar, *IBM Research, India*
Neha Kumar, *University of California, USA*
Ranjitha Kumar, *Stanford University, USA*
Santosh Kumar, *University of Memphis, USA*
Ponnurangam Kumaraguru, *IIIT-Delhi, India*
Andrew Kun, *University of New Hampshire, USA*
Andreas Kunz, *Swiss Federal Institute of Technology Zurich, Switzerland*
Kai Kunze, *Osaka Prefecture University, Japan*
Liisa Kuparinen, *University of Jyväskylä, Finland*
Sri Kurniawan, *University of California, USA*
Gordon Kurtenbach, *Autodesk, Canada*
Arma an Kuru, *Middle East Technical University, Turkey*
Raja Kushalnagar, *Rochester Institute of Technology, USA*
Diana Kusunoki, *Drexel University, USA*
Kari Kuutti, *University of Oulu, Finland*
Stacey Kuznetsov, *Carnegie Mellon University, USA*
Youngshin Kwak, *Ulsan National Institute of Science and Technology, South Korea*
Bum Chul Kwon, *University of Konstanz, Germany*
Gyu Hyun Kwon, *Virginia Polytechnic Institute and State University, USA*
Jarmo Laaksolahti, *Swedish Institute of Computer Science, Sweden*
Richard Ladner, *University of Washington, USA*
Ben Lafreniere, *University of Waterloo, Canada*
Carl Lagoze, *University of Michigan, USA*
Susan Lai, *San Jose Gateway, Canada*
Denis Lalanne, *University of Fribourg, Switzerland*
Mary Lalomia, *Philips Medical, USA*
Shyong Lam, *Google, USA*
Anthony Lamarca, *Intel Research Seattle, USA*
Kristin Lamberty, *University of Minnesota, USA*
Cliff Lampe, *University of Michigan, USA*
Airi Lampinen, *Helsinki Institute for Information Technology HIIT, Finland*
James Landay, *University of Washington, USA*
Richard Landers, *Old Dominion University, USA*
Monica Landoni, *University of Lugano, Switzerland*
Pascal Landry, *Universitat Pompeu Fabra, Spain*
Steven Landry, *Purdue University, USA*
Peter Landwehr, *Carnegie Mellon University, USA*
Nicholas Lane, *Microsoft, China*
Patrick Langdon, *University of Cambridge, UK*
Marc Langheinrich, *Università Della Svizzera Italiana, Switzerland*
Joel Lanir, *University of Haifa, Israel*

Edward Lank, *University of Waterloo, Canada*
Rosa Lanzillotti, *Università di Bari, Italy*
Astrid Larssen, *Ashesi University College, Ghana*
Walter Lasecki, *University of Rochester Computer Science, USA*
Nancy Latham, *Boston University School of Public Health, USA*
Thomas Latoza, *UC Irvine, USA*
Celine Latulipe, *University of North Carolina at Charlotte, USA*
Manfred Lau, *Lancaster University, UK*
Felix Lauber, *University of Munich, Germany*
Carolyn Lauckner, *Michigan State University, USA*
Gael Laurans, *Delft University of Technology, The Netherlands*
Eric Laurier, *University of Edinburgh, UK*
Yann Laurillau, *University of Grenoble, France*
Debra Lauterbach, *Google, USA*
Joseph Laviola Jr., *University of Central Florida, USA*
Joseph Lawrance, *Oregon State University, USA*
Shaun Lawson, *University of Lincoln, UK*
Shawn Lawson, *Rensselaer Polytechnic Institute, USA*
Amanda Lazar, *University of Washington, USA*
Jonathan Lazar, *Towson University, USA*
Marco Lazzari, *University of Bergamo, Italy*
Lucian Leahu, *SICS, Sweden*
Alex Leavitt, *University of Southern California, USA*
Eric Lecolinet, *Télécom-Paristech, France*
Kerstin Leder Mackley, *Loughborough University, UK*
David Ledo, *University of Calgary, Canada*
Bongshin Lee, *Microsoft Research, USA*
Charlotte Lee, *University of Washington, USA*
Geehyuk Lee, *KAIST, Korea*
Joon Suk Lee, *Virginia Tech, USA*
Joyce Lee, *University of Michigan, USA*
Matthew Lee, *Philips Research, USA*
Michael Lee, *University of Washington, USA*
Min Kyung Lee, *Carnegie Mellon University, USA*
Stephanie Lee, *University of Washington, USA*
Uichin Lee, *KAIST, South Korea*
Young Lee, *Motorola Research, USA*
Colby Leider, *University of Miami, USA*
Darren Leigh, *USA*
Iolanda Leite, *Instituto Superior Técnico, Portugal*
Daniel Leithinger, *Massachusetts Institute of Technology, USA*
Luis A. Leiva, *Universitat Politècnica de València, Spain*
Eva Lenz, *Folkwang University of the Arts, Germany*
Pedro Leon, *Carnegie Mellon University, USA*
Chiara Leonardi, *Fondazione Bruno Kessler, Italy*
Stefania Leone, *University of South Carolina, USA*
Tuck Leong, *University of Technology, Australia*
George Lepouras, *University of Peloponnese, Greece*
Gilly Leshed, *Cornell University, USA*
Catherine Letondal, *ENAC, France*
Rock Leung, *University of British Columbia, Canada*
Vincent Levesque, *Immersion, Canada*
Peter Levin, *Intel Corporation, USA*

Vincent Lewandowski, *KTH, Sweden*
Clayton Lewis, *University of Colorado, USA*
Caroline Leygue, *University of Nottingham, UK*
Ian Li, *Carnegie Mellon University, USA*
Karen Li
Na Li, *Pennsylvania State University, USA*
Nan Li, *EPFL, Switzerland*
Wei Li, *Autodesk Research, Canada*
Hai-Ning Liang, *Xi'an Jiaotong-Liverpool University, China*
Rung-Huei Liang, *National Taiwan University of Science and Technology, Taiwan (r.o.c.)*
Fotis Liarokapis, *Coventry University, UK*
Ilaria Liccardi, *INRIA Paris, France*
Henry Lieberman, *Massachusetts Institute of Technology, USA*
Michael Liegl, *Lancaster University, UK*
Ann Light, *Northumbria University, UK*
Lassi Liikkanen, *Helsinki Institute for Information Technology HIIT, Finland*
Brian Lim, *Fraunhofer Center for Sustainable Energy Systems, USA*
Sohye Lim, *Ewha Womans University, Republic of Korea*
James Lin, *Google, USA*
Jialiu Lin, *Carnegie Mellon University, USA*
Min Lin, *Samsung Electronics, P. R. China*
Per Linde, *Malmö University,*
Robert Lindeman, *Worcester Polytechnic Institute, USA*
Rhema Linder, *Texas A&M University, USA*
Gitte Lindgaard, *Carleton University, Canada*
Siân Lindley, *Microsoft Research, UK*
Janne Lindqvist, *Rutgers University, USA*
Stephen Lindsay, *Swansea University, Wales, UK*
Conor Linehan, *University of Lincoln, UK*
Jessica Lingel, *Microsoft Research, USA*
Heather Lipford, *University of North Carolina at Charlotte, USA*
Roman Lissermann, *Technische Universität Darmstadt, Germany*
Eden Litt, *Northwestern University, USA*
Greg Little, *Massachusetts Institute of Technology, USA*
Linda Little, *Northumbria University, UK*
Jin Liu, *Cornell University, USA*
Leslie Liu, *University of Washington, USA*
Tracy Liu, *University of Michigan, USA*
Wei Liu, *Delft University of Technology, Netherlands*
Yefeng Liu, *Waseda University, Japan*
Ying Liu, *Charles Sturt University, Australia*
Ying Hsang Liu, *Intel, China*
Yun-En Liu, *University of Washington, USA*
Zhicheng Liu, *Georgia Institute of Technology, USA*
Zhicheng Liu, *Georgia Institute of Technology, USA*
Mark Livingston, *Naval Research Laboratory, USA*
Avishay Livne, *The University of Michigan, USA*
Sara Ljungblad, *LOTS Design AB, Sweden*
Markus Löchtefeld, *German Research Center for Artificial Intelligence (DFKI), Germany*
Dan Lockton, *University of Warwick, UK*

Thomas Lodato, *Georgia Institute of Technology, USA*
Courtney Loder, *UC Irvine, USA*
Sebastian Loehmann, *University of Munich, Germany*
Steffen Lohmann, *University of Stuttgart, Germany*
Benjamin Lok, *University of Florida, USA*
Lian Loke, *University of Sydney, Australia*
Derek Lomas, *Carnegie Mellon University, USA*
Benjamin Long, *Bristol University, UK*
Kiel Long, *Lancaster University, England, UK*
Chee Kit Looi, *NTU, Singapore*
Jack Loomis, *UCSB, USA*
Arminda Lopes, *Instituto Politecnico de Castelo Branco, Portugal*
Pedro Lopes, *Hasso Plattner Institute, Germany*
Fabien Lotte, *INRIA Bordeaux Sud-Ouest, France*
Danielle Lottridge, *San Francisco State University, USA*
Sandy Louchart, *Heriot-Watt University, Scotland, UK*
Oriana J Love, *Pacific Northwest National Laboratory, USA*
Hao Lu, *Intel, USA*
Hong Lu, *IBM Research, USA*
Jie Lu, *Samsung, USA*
Mei Lu, *CUNY Graduate Center, USA*
Pengfei Lu, *Fudan University, USA*
Tun Lu, *University of Washington, China*
Hao Lü, *Google, USA*
Andrés Lucero, *Nokia Research Center, Finland*
Bernd Ludwig, *University of Regensburg, Germany*
Patrick Lühne, *Hasso Plattner Institute, Germany*
Rowena Luk, *AMITA Telemedicine, Canada*
Kristian Lukander, *Finnish Institute of Occupational Health, Finland*
Jonathan Lukens, *University of Tennessee, USA*
Stephan Lukosch, *Delft University of Technology, The Netherlands*
Jay Lundell, *Intel Research, USA*
Kurt Luther, *Carnegie Mellon University, USA*
Wayne Lutters, *UMBC, USA*
Marianne Lykke, *Aalborg University, Denmark*
Peter Lyle, *Queensland University of Technology, Australia*
Leilah Lyons, *University of Illinois at Chicago, USA*
Michael Lyons, *Ritsumeikan University, Japan*
Heikki Lyytinen, *University of Jyväskylä, Finland*
Xiaojuan Ma, *Noah's Ark Lab, Hong Kong, China*
Catriona Macaulay, *University of Dundee, UK*
Craig Macdonald, *Pratt Institute, USA*
Carolyn Macgregor, *University of Waterloo, Canada*
Cristiano Maciel, *Universidade Federal de Mato Grosso, Brazil*
Giuliano Maciocci, *Qualcomm Research Cambridge, UK*
Wendy Mackay, *INRIA, France*
Scott Mackenzie, *York University, Canada*
Allan Maclean, *Image Semantics Ltd, UK*
Karon Maclean, *University of British Columbia, Canada*
Christopher Maclellan, *Carnegie Mellon University, USA*
Andrew Macvean, *Heriot-Watt University, Edinburgh*
Rui Madeira, *ESTSetúbal/IPS, Portugal*
Pattie Maes, *Massachusetts Institute of Technology, USA*

Rachel Magee, *Drexel University, USA*
Charlotte Magnusson, *Lund University, Sweden*
Mary Lou Maher, *University of Sydney, Australia*
Jalal Mahmud, *IBM Research - Almaden, USA*
Nasim Mahmud, *Hasselt University - Tul - IBBT, Belgium*
Angela Mahr, *German Research Center for Artificial Intelligence (DFKI), Germany*
Scott Mainwaring, *Intel Research, USA*
Julie Maitland, *Populus Global Solutions Inc., Canada*
Päivi Majaranta, *University of Tampere, Finland*
Yasutoshi Makino, *Keio University, Japan*
Sylvain Malacria, *University of Canterbury, France*
Miguel Malheiros, *University College London, UK*
Alessio Malizia, *University 'la Sapienza' of Rome, Italy*
Lone Malmborg, *IT University of Copenhagen, Denmark*
Lena Mamykina, *Columbia University, USA*
Hiroyuki Manabe, *NTT DOCOMO, Japan*
Clara Mancini, *The Open University, UK*
Regan Mandryk, *University of Saskatchewan, Canada*
Jennifer Mankoff, *Carnegie Mellon University, USA*
Daniela Mapelli, *Università di Padoa,*
Valérie Maquil, *Public Research Center Henri Tudor, Luxembourg*
Gabriela Marcu, *Carnegie Mellon University, USA*
Adam Marcus, *MIT CSAIL, USA*
Georgios Marentakis, *Institute for Electronic Music and Acoustics - Graz, Austria*
Gloria Mark, *University of California, USA*
Anders Markussen, *University of Copenhagen, Denmark*
Thomas Markussen, *Kolding School of Design, Denmark*
Jennifer Marlow, *Carnegie Mellon University, USA*
Elena Márquez Segura, *Uppsala University, Sweden*
Gary Marsden, *University of Cape Town, South Africa*
Andrea Marshall, *Drexel University Ischool, USA*
Catherine Marshall, *Microsoft, USA*
Joe Marshall, *University of Nottingham, UK*
Mark Marshall, *Sheffield Hallam University, UK*
Stuart Marshall, *Victoria University of Wellington, New Zealand*
Jean-Bernard Martens, *Eindhoven University of Technology, The Netherlands*
Stefan Marti, *Harman International, USA*
Anna Lisa Martin, *Zurich University of the Arts, Switzerland*
Aqueasha Martin, *Clemson University, USA*
Benoît Martin, *Université de Lorraine, France*
David Martin, *Xerox Research Center Europe, France*
Taylor Martin, *USU, USA*
Sarah Martindale, *The University of Nottingham, UK*
Diego Martinez Plasencia, *University of Bristol, UK*
Célia Martinie, *University Toulouse 3, France*
Misa Maruyama, *University of Hawaii at Manoa, USA*
Sergio Mascetti, *University of Milan, Italy*
Afra Mashhadi, *Alcatel-Lucent, Ireland*
Mikhil Masli, *Grouplens Research, USA*
Winter Mason, *Stevens Institute of Technology, USA*
Justin Matejka, *Autodesk, Canada*

Anijo Mathew, *Illinois Institute of Technology, USA*
Akhil Mathur, *University of Toronto, Canada*
Ben Matthews, *The University of Queensland, Australia*
Mark Matthews, *Cornell University, USA*
Tara Matthews, *IBM Research - Almaden, USA*
Denys Matthies, *University of Munich, Germany*
Frank Maurer, *University of Calgary, Canada*
Max-Emanuel Maurer, *University of Munich, Germany*
Deborah Maxwell, *University of Edinburgh, UK*
Aaron May, *Simon Fraser University, Canada*
Simon Mayer, *ETH Zurich, Switzerland*
Christopher Mayhorn, *North Carolina State University, USA*
Walterio Mayol-Cuevas, *University of Bristol, UK*
Oscar Mayora, *ITESM Cuernavaca, Mexico*
Rene Mayrhofer, *Lancaster University, UK*
Ali Mazalek, *Georgia Institute of Technology, USA*
Melissa Mazmanian, *University of California, USA*
Michelle Mazurek, *Carnegie Mellon University, USA*
Emanuela Mazzone, *University of Central Lancashire, Spain*
Victoria Mcarthur, *York University, Canada*
Simon Mccallum, *Gjøvik University College, Norway*
John Mccarthy, *University College Cork, Ireland*
Scott Mccrickard, *Virginia Tech, USA*
Sean Mcdirmid, *Microsoft Advanced Technology Center, Peoples Republic of China*
David Mcdonald, *University of Washington, USA*
Nora Mcdonald, *Drexel University, USA*
Mary F Mcdonough
Daniel Mcduff, *MIT Media Lab, USA*
Gregor Mcewan, *University of Saskatchewan, Canada*
Daniel Mcfarlane, *Lockheed Martin Advanced Technology Laboratories, USA*
Kevin Mcgee, *National University of Singapore, Singapore*
Mark Mcgill, *University of Glasgow, UK*
William Mcgrath, *Stanford University, USA*
Joanna Mcgrenere, *University of British Columbia, Canada*
Michael Mcguffin, *École de Technologie Supérieure, Canada*
Ross Mclachlan, *University of Glasgow, Scotland, UK*
Ryan Mcmahan, *University of Texas at Dallas, USA*
Donald Mcmillan, *SICS, Sweden*
Indrani Medhi-Thies, *Microsoft Research, India*
Richard Medland, *Queensland University of Technology, Australia*
Ben Medler, *EA, USA*
Elisa Mekler, *University of Basel, Switzerland*
Volkamer Melanie, *TU Darmstadt, Germany*
David Mellis, *Massachusetts Institute of Technology, USA*
Gustavo Mello Machado, *University of Stuttgart, Germany*
Nemanja Memarovic, *Universita Della Svizzera Italiana, Switzerland*
Maria Menendez, *University of Trento, Italy*
Sarah Mennicken, *University of Zurich, Switzerland*
Rachel Menzies, *University of Dundee, UK*
Emma Mercier, *University of Illinois at Urbana-Champaign, USA*
David Merrill, *Massachusetts Institute of Technology, USA*
Ronald Metoyer, *Oregon State University, USA*

Johanna Meurer, *University, Germany*
Jochen Meyer, *OFFIS - Institute for Information Technology, Germany*
Miriah Meyer, *University of Utah, USA*
Haipeng Mi, *Tsinghua University, China*
Nicholas Micallef, *Glasgow Caledonian University, UK*
Martin Mihajlov, *Ss. Cyril and Methodius University, Macedonia*
Silvia Miksch, *Vienna University of Technology, Austria*
David Millen, *IBM Research, USA*
Andrew Miller, *University of British Columbia, USA*
Gregor Miller, *Massachusetts Institute of Technology, Canada*
Scarlett Miller (herring), *Georgia Institute of Technology, USA*
Michael Minge, *Berlin University of Technology, Germany*
Aliaksei Miniukovich, *University of Trento, Italy*
Andrea Minuto, *University of Twente, The Netherlands*
Pejman Mirza-Babaei, *University of Ontario Institute of Technology, Canada*
Sonali Mishra, *University of Michigan, USA*
Taniya Mishra, *AT&T, USA*
Alex Mitchell, *National University of Singapore, Singapore*
Tanushree Mitra, *Georgia Institute of Technology, USA*
Tracy Mitzner, *Georgia Institute of Technology, USA*
Takahiro Miura, *The University of Tokyo, Japan*
Takashi Miyaki, *Inria, France*
Bart Moens, *Ghent University, Belgium*
Andrew Molineux, *Lancaster University, England*
Andreas Möller, *Technische Universität München, Germany*
Max Möllers, *RWTH Aachen University, Germany*
David Molyneaux, *Microsoft Research, England, UK*
Arthur Money, *Brunel University, UK*
Andrew Monk, *University of York, UK*
Andres Monroy-Hernandez, *Massachusetts Institute of Technology, USA*
Toni-Jan Keith Monserrat, *National University of Singapore, Philippines*
Kyle Montague, *University of Dundee, Scotland, UK*
Bob Moore, *PARC, USA*
Simone Mora, *Norwegian University of Science and Technology, Norway*
Stuart Moran, *University of Nottingham, UK*
Neema Moraveji, *Microsoft Research Asia, China*
Guillaume Moreau, *Ecole Centrale de Nantes, France*
Lourdes Moreno, *Universidad Carlos III de Madrid, Spain*
Jonathan Morgan, *University of Washington, USA*
Giulio Mori, *ISTI-CNR, Italy*
Joji Mori, *The University of Melbourne, Australia*
Carlos Morimoto, *University of Sao Paulo, Brazil*
Janine Morley, *Lancaster University, UK*
Fabio Morreale, *University of Trento, Italy*
Patricia Morreale, *Kean University, USA*
Margaret Morris, *Intel Corporation, USA*
Meredith Morris, *Microsoft Research, USA*
Ann Morrison, *Aalborg University, Denmark*
Cecily Morrison, *Microsoft Research, UK*
Richard Mortier, *The University of Nottingham, UK*
Lee Morton, *Glasgow Caledonian University, UK*
Christiane Moser, *ICT&S Center, Austria*
Vicki Moulder, *Simon Fraser University, Canada*

Christos Mousas, *University of Sussex, England, UK*
Mu Mu, *Lancaster University, UK*
Omar Mubin, *University of Western Sydney, Australia*
Christian Muehl, *Inria Bordeaux, France*
Florian "Floyd" Mueller, *Exertion Games Lab, Australia*
Stefanie Mueller, *Hasso Plattner Institute, Germany*
Christian Mueller-Tomfelde, *CSIRO ICT Centre, Australia*
Max Mühlhäuser, *TU Darmstadt, Germany*
Adiyan Mujibiya, *The University of Tokyo, Japan*
Heiko Müller, *IBM Research, Germany*
Gernot Müller-Putz, *Graz University of Technology, Austria*
Alessandro Mulloni, *Qualcomm Research KAIST, Republic of Korea ria, Austria*
Cosmin Munteanu, *National Research Council Canada, Canada*
Helmut Munz, *RMIT University, Austria*
Martin Murer, *University of Salzburg, Austria*
Dianne Murray, *Indep. Consultant, UK*
Ildar Muslukhov, *University of British Columbia, Canada*
Mirco Musolesi, *University of Birmingham, UK*
Brad Myers, *Carnegie Mellon University, USA*
Elizabeth Mynatt, *Georgia Institute of Technology, USA*
Mor Naaman, *Cornell University, USA*
Miguel Nacenta, *University of St Andrews, UK*
Frank Nack, *University of Amsterdam (uva), The Netherlands*
Till Nagel, *University of Applied Sciences Potsdam, Germany*
Tobias Nägeli, *ETH Zurich, Switzerland*
Hideyuki Nakanishi, *Osaka University, Japan*
Kevin Nam, *University of Michigan, USA*
Suranga Nanayakkara, *Singapore University of Technology and Design, USA*
Mathieu Nancel, *University of Canterbury, France*
Nitya Narasimhan, *edupreneur, USA*
Bonnie Nardi, *University of California, USA*
Amani Naseem, *RMIT University, Australia*
Chris Nash, *University of Cambridge, UK*
Meena Natarajan, *UC Berkeley, USA*
Lisa Nathan, *University of British Columbia, Canada*
David Navarre, *IRIT, France*
Elena Nazzi, *IT University of Copenhagen, Denmark*
Mark Neerincx, *TNO Human Factors, Netherlands*
Michael Neff, *UC Davis, USA*
Paolo Negri
Matei Negulescu, *University of Waterloo, Canada*
Matti Nelimarkka, *Helsinki Institute for Information Technology HIIT, Finland*
Les Nelson, *PARC, USA*
Cornelius Neufeldt, *University of Siegen, Germany*
Alena Neviarouskaya, *University of Tokyo, Japan*
Alan Newell, *Dundee University, Scotland, UK*
Mark Newman, *University of Michigan, USA*
Victor Ng-Thow-Hing, *Honda Research Institute USA, USA*
David Nguyen, *Nokia Research Center, USA*
Duyen Nguyen, *Cornell University, USA*
James Nicholson, *Northumbria University, England, UK*

Hugo Nicolau, *University of Dundee, UK*
Lene Nielsen, *IT University of Copenhagen, Denmark*
Gerrit Niezen, *Swansea University, UK*
Femke Nijboer, *University of Twente, The Netherlands*
Valentina Nisi, *University of Madeira, Portugal*
Xi Niu, *Indiana University, USA*
Sylvie Noël, *Universita di Trento, Italy*
Pedro Nogueira, *LIACC - Artificial Intelligence and Computer Science Laboratory, Portugal*
A. Imran Nordin, *University of York, UK*
Mie Nørgaard, *Aarhus School of Architecture, Denmark*
Francesco Nori
Maria Normark, *Södertörn University, Sweden*
Lauren Norrie, *University of Glasgow, Scotland, UK*
Chris North, *Virginia Polytechnic Institute and State University, USA*
Oded Nov, *Polytechnic Institute of New York University, USA*
Laurie Novak, *Vanderbilt University, USA*
Francisco Nunes, *Vienna University of Technology, Austria*
Petteri Nurmi, *Helsinki Institute for Information Technology HIIT, Finland*
Andreas Nürnberger, *Otto-Von-Guericke-University Magdeburg, Germany*
Stina Nylander, *Swedish Institute of Computer Science, Sweden*
Heather O'brien, *University of British Columbia, Canada*
Marita O'brien, *University of Alabama-Huntsville, USA*
Brendan O'connor, *Carnegie Mellon University, USA*
Lora Oehlberg, *INRIA, USA*
Anne Oeldorf-Hirsch, *University of Connecticut, USA*
Eyal Ofek, *Microsoft Research, USA*
Corinna Ogonowski, *University of Siegen, Germany*
Alice Oh, *KAIST, Republic of Korea*
Jonghwan Oh, *Seoul National University, Republic of Korea*
Kenton O'hara, *Microsoft Research, UK*
Harri Oinas-Kukkonen, *University of Oulu, Finland*
Aisling O'kane, *University College London, UK*
Bugra Oktay, *University of Nevada, USA*
Patrick Oladimeji, *Swansea University, UK*
Halla Olafsdottir, *Université Paris-Sud, France*
Erica Olmsted-Hawala, *U.S. Census Bureau, USA*
Dan Olsen, *Brigham Young University, USA*
Gary Olson, *University of California, USA*
Judith Olson, *U of Michigan, USA*
Katherine Olson, *Georgia Institute of Technology, USA*
Thomas Olsson, *Tampere University of Technology, Finland*
Sile O'modhrain, *University of Michigan, USA*
Jacki O'neill, *XRCE, France*
Stephen Oney, *Carnegie Mellon University, USA*
Wei Tsang Ooi, *National University of Singapore, Singapore*
Elisa Oreglia, *University of California Berkeley, USA*
Tihomir Orehovacki, *University of Zagreb, Croatia*
Eleanor O'rourke, *University of Washington, USA*
Valeria Orso, *University of Padova, Italy*
Martin Ortlieb, *Google, Switzerland*
Keith Ostfeld, *Children's Museum of Houston, USA*
Nuno Otero, *Linnæus University, Sweden*
Tom Ouyang, *MIT, USA*

Derya Özçelik, *Eindhoven University of Technology, The Netherlands*
Jeni Paay, *Aalborg University, Denmark*
Tyler Pace, *Indiana University Bloomington, USA*
Tim Paek, *Microsoft Research, USA*
Michel Pahud, *Microsoft Research, USA*
Helen Pain, *University of Edinburgh, UK*
Drew Paine, *University of Washington, USA*
Aditya Pal, *IBM Research - Almaden, USA*
Philippe Palanque, *ICS-IRIT, France*
Leysia Palen, *University of Colorado, USA*
Henri Palleis, *Ludwig-Maximilians-Universität München, Germany*
Susan Palmiter, *Design Technologies, USA*
Viktoria Pammer, *Know-Center, Austria*
Yingxin Pan, *IBM Research - China, China*
Yue Pan, *Indiana University Bloomington, USA*
Zhengzheng Pan, *Facebook, USA*
Katherine Panciera, *University of Minnesota, USA*
Sabrina Panëels, *McGill University, France*
Carolyn Pang, *Simon Fraser University, Canada*
Saurabh Panjwani, *Microsoft Research India, India*
Katrina Panovich, *MIT, USA*
Nadia Pantidi, *The University of Nottingham, UK*
Caroline Pantofaru, *Willow Garage, USA*
Eleftherios Papachristos, *University of Patras, Greece*
Savvas Papaioannou, *University of Oxford, UK*
Joseph Paradiso, *MIT Media Laboratory, USA*
Aditya Parameswaran, *Stanford University, USA*
Zachary Pardos, *UC Berkeley, USA*
Pablo Paredes, *University of Berkeley, USA*
Narcis Pares, *Universitat Pompeu Fabra, Spain*
Tapan Parikh, *UC Berkeley, USA*
Minsu Park, *KAIST, South Korea*
Souneil Park, *Univ. of Michigan, USA*
Sun Young Park, *University of California, USA*
Taiwoo Park, *KAIST, South Korea*
Young-Woo Park, *KAIST, South Korea*
Chris Parnin, *Georgia Institute of Technology, USA*
Kurt Partridge, *Google, USA*
Gaurav Paruthi, *University of Michigan, USA*
Marco Pasch, *University of Lugano, Switzerland*
Gert Pasman, *Delft University of Technology, The Netherlands*
Jerome Pasquero, *Research In Motion Limited, Canada*
Kayur Patel, *University of Washington, USA*
Nirmal Patel, *Georgia Institute of Technology, USA*
Rupa Patel, *University of Washington, USA*
Rupal Patel, *Northeastern University, USA*
Shwetak Patel, *University of Washington, USA*
Jessica Pater, *Georgia Institute of Technology, USA*
Andrew Patrick, *Carleton University, Canada*
Donald Patterson, *University of California Irvine, USA*
Sharoda Paul, *GE Global Research, USA*
Eric Paulos, *University of California, USA*
Dana Pavel, *University of Essex, UK*

Ioannis Pavlidis, *University of Houston, USA*
Andriy Pavlovych, *York University, Canada*
Stephen Payne, *University of Bath, UK*
Jennifer Pearson, *Swansea University, UK*
Fabrizio Pece, *University College London, UK*
Evan Peck, *Tufts University, USA*
Sonja Pedell, *Swinburne University of Technology, Australia*
Sonjs Pedell, *Swinburne University of Technology, Australia*
Esben Pedersen, *University of Copenhagen, Danmark*
Thomas Pederson, *IT University of Copenhagen, Denmark*
Peter Peltonen, *University of Helsinki, Finland*
Jorge Peña, *University of California, USA*
Wei Peng, *Information Studies, USA*
Gerald Penn, *University of Toronto, Canada*
Kylie Peppler, *Indiana University, USA*
Lucas Pereira, *Madeira Interactive Technologies Institute, Portugal*
Adam Perer, *IBM Research, USA*
Manuel Perez-Quinones, *Virginia Tech, USA*
Charles Perin, *INRIA Saclay, France*
Trevor Pering, *Intel Research, USA*
Ken Perlin, *New York University, USA*
Simon Perrault, *National University of Singapore, Singapore*
Daniel Perry, *University of Washington, USA*
Florian Perteneder, *University of Applied Sciences Upper KAIST, Republic of Korea ria, Austria*
Marianne Graves Petersen, *Aarhus University, Denmark*
Daniela Petrelli, *Sheffield Hallam University, UK*
Helen Petrie, *University of York, UK*
Tamara Peyton, *Penn State University, USA*
Laura Pfeifer Vardoulakis, *Google, USA*
Max Pfeiffer, *Leibniz Universität Hannover, Germany*
Thies Pfeiffer, *Bielefeld University, Germany*
Bastian Pfleging, *University of Stuttgart, Germany*
Martin Pielot, *Telefonica Research, Spain*
James Pierce, *Carnegie Mellon University, USA*
Jeffrey Pierce, *Samsung UX Innovations Lab, USA*
Emmanuel Pietriga, *INRIA, France*
Mary Pietrowicz, *National Center for Supercomputing Applications, USA*
Thomas Pietrzak, *University of Lille, France*
Hannah Pileggi, *Georgia Institute of Technology, USA*
Clément Pillias, *CNAM, France*
Laura Pina, *'UCSD' As In University of California at San Diego, USA*
Fabiano Pinatti, *Institute of Design and Assessment of Technology, Austria*
Kathleen Pine, *University of California, USA*
Claudio Pinhanez, *IBM Brazil, Brazil*
Volkmar Pipek, *University of Siegen, Germany*
Anne Marie Piper, *Northwestern University, USA*
Michael Pirker, *Ruwido KAIST, Republic of Korea ria Gmbh, Austria*
Peter Pirolli, *PARC, USA*
Catherine Plaisant, *University of Maryland, USA*
Andreas Pleuss, *University of Limerick, Ireland*
Bernd Ploderer, *The University of Melbourne, Australia*
Thomas Ploetz, *Newcastle University, UK*

Barry Po, *HSBC, Canada*
Henning Pohl, *University of Hannover, Germany*
Margit Pohl, *Vienna University of Technology, Austria*
Anna Pohlmeyer, *Delft University of Technology, Netherlands*
Ioannis Politis, *Eindhoven University of Technology, Netherlands*
John Pollak, *Cornell University, USA*
Marc Pomplun, *University of Massachusetts Boston, USA*
Heather Pon-Barry, *Informatics, USA*
Suporn Pongnumkul, *University of Washington, USA*
Erika Poole, *Penn State University, USA*
Alan Pope, *NASA Langley Research Center, USA*
Ana-Maria Popescu, *Pinterest, USA*
Leslie Poppe, *University of Washington, USA*
Kristi Potter, *University of Oregon, USA*
Tania Pouli, *Technicolor, France*
Ivan Poupyrev, *Disney Research, USA*
Sören Preibusch, *Microsoft Research, UK*
Chris Preist, *University of Bristol, UK*
Nora Presson, *University of Pittsburgh, USA*
Mike Preuss, *WWU Münster, Germany*
Blaine Price, *The Open University, UK*
Sara Price, *Institute of Education, UK*
Reid Priedhorsky, *Los Alamos National Laboratory, USA*
Rafael Prikladnicki, *Pucrs, Brazil*
Michael Prilla, *University of Bochum, Germany*
Suzanne Prior, *Media and Computer Games, UK*
Kathrin Probst, *University of Applied Sciences Upper KAIST, Republic of Korea ria, Austria*
Jason Procyk, *Simon Fraser University, Canada*
Halley Profita, *University of Colorado, USA*
Sebastian Prost, *CURE - Center for Usability Research & Engineering, Austria*
Janna Protzak, *Berlin Institute of Technology, Germany*
Emily Provost, *University of Michigan, USA*
John Pruitt, *Microsoft, USA*
Larissa Pschetz, *Microsoft Research Asia, Midlothian*
Deborah Ptak, *University of Toronto, Canada*
Pearl Pu, *EPFL, Switzerland*
Andreas Pusch, *Julius-Maximilians-Universität, Germany*
Cynthia Putnam, *Depaul University, USA*
Pardha Pyla, *Virginia Tech, India*
Huamin Qu, *HKUST, Hong Kong*
Novi Quadrianto, *University of Cambridge, UK*
Daniele Quercia, *Yahoo! Research, UK*
Whitney Quesenbery, *Whitney Interactcive Design, USA*
Alexander Quinn, *University of Maryland, USA*
Philip Quinn, *University of Canterbury, New Zealand*
Pablo-Alejandro Quinones, *University of Michigan, USA*
Andrew Quitmeyer, *Georgia Institute of Technology, USA*
Pernilla Qvarfordt, *FX Palo Alto Laboratory, USA*
Daphne Raban, *University of Haifa, Israel*
Mashfiqui Rabbi, *Cornell University, USA*
Robert Racadio, *University of Washington, USA*
Irene Rae, *University of Wisconsin, USA*

Matthew Rafalow, *University of California Irvine, USA*
Nikunj Raghuvanshi, *Microsoft Research, USA*
Tauhidur Rahman, *Cornell University, USA*
Kari-Jouko Räihä, *University of Tampere, Finland*
Andrew Raij, *University of South Florida, USA*
Roope Raisamo, *University of Tampere, Finland*
Eeva Raita, *Helsinki Institute for Information Technology HIIT, Finland*
Mikko Rajanen, *University of Oulu, Finland*
Thusha Rajendran, *UK*
Nitendra Rajput, *IBM Research, India*
Ismo Rakkolainen, *University of Tampere, Finland*
Raf Ramakers, *Hasselt University - Tul - Iminds, Belgium*
Ernesto Ramirez, *University of California, USA*
Gonzalo Ramos, *Microsoft, USA*
Adriane Randolph, *Kennesaw State University, USA*
Nimmi Rangaswamy, *Microsoft Research India, India*
Juhi Ranjan, *University of Virginia, USA*
Dimitrios Raptis, *Aalborg University, Denmark*
Umar Rashid, *University of Kent, UK*
Kirsten Rassmus-Gröhn, *Lund University, Sweden*
Rabindra Ratan, *Information Studies, USA*
Matt Ratto, *University of Toronto, Toronto*
Martina Rau, *University of Wisconsin, USA*
Janet Read, *University of Central Lancashire, England*
Kyle Rector, *University of Washington, USA*
Madhu Reddy, *Penn State University, USA*
Fiona Redhead, *Queensland University of Technology, Australia*
Johan Redström, *Umeå Institute of Design, Sweden*
Darren Reed, *University of York, UK*
Robert Reeder, *Google, USA*
Sarah Reeder, *Indiana University, USA*
Tim Regan, *Microsoft, UK*
Holger Regenbrecht, *University of Otago, New Zealand*
Derek Reilly, *Dalhousie University, Canada*
Peter Reimann, *University of Sydney, Australia*
Bryan Reimer, *MIT, USA*
Sofia Reis, *Universidade Nova de Lisboa, Portugal*
Wolfgang Reitberger, *Vienna University of Technology, Austria*
Harald Reiterer, *University, Germany*
Thomas Reitmaier, *UCT Centre In ICT4D, South Africa*
Jun Rekimoto, *University of Tokyo / Sony CSL, Japan*
Christian Remy, *University of Zurich, Switzerland*
Gang Ren, *University of Bath, UK*
Xiangshi Ren, *Kochi University of Technology, Japan*
Yuqing Ren, *Carnegie Mellon University, USA*
Karen Renaud, *University of Glasgow, UK*
Christian Rendl, *University of Applied Sciences Upper KAIST, Republic of Korea ria, Austria*
Stefan Rennick-Egglestone, *The University of Nottingham, UK*
Ronald Rensink, *University of British Columbia, Canada*
Paul Resnick, *University of Michigan, USA*
Glenda Revelle, *University of Arkansas, USA*
Gabriel Reyes, *Georgia Institute of Technology, USA*
Lindsay Reynolds, *Cornell University, USA*

Mark Rice, *Institute of Infocomm Research, Singapore*
Alex Richardson, *The KAIST, Republic of Korea ralian National University, Australia*
Alexander Richter, *Unibwm, Germany*
Jochen Rick, *Saarland University, Germany*
Angela Riechers, *School of Visual Arts, USA*
Jens Riegelsberger, *University College London, UK*
Soo Young Rieh, *University of Michigan, USA*
Andreas Riener, *Johannes Kepler University, Austria*
Alexander Rind, *Vienna University of Technology, Austria*
Lazlo Ring, *Northeastern University, USA*
Mikko Rissanen, *Move Correctly, Singapore*
Tobias Ritschel, *MPI Informatik, Germany*
Giuseppe Riva, *Università Cattolica Del Sacro Cuore, Italy*
Christopher Roast, *Sheffield Hallam University, UK*
Lionel Robert, *University of Michigan, USA*
Jonathan Roberts, *Bangor University, UK*
Judy Robertson, *Heriot-Watt University, UK*
Scott Robertson, *University of Hawaii at Manoa, USA*
Toni Robertson, *University of Technology, Australia*
Jeffrey Robins, *Google, USA*
Simon Robinson, *Swansea University, UK*
Carsten Röcker, *RWTH Aachen University, Germany*
Tom Rodden, *University of Nottingham, UK*
Edgar Rodriguez, *Wellington, New Zealand*
David Roedl, *Indiana University, USA*
Yvonne Rogers, *University College London, UK*
Daniel Roggen, *Newcastle University, UK*
Markus Rohde, *International Institute for Socio-Informatics, Germany*
Michael Rohs, *University of Hannover, Germany*
Daniel Romero, *Northwestern University, USA*
Mario Romero, *Delft University of Technology, Sweden*
Natalia Romero Herrera, *KTH, The Netherlands*
John Rooksby, *University of St Andrews, UK*
Chris Rooney, *Middlesex University, UK*
Carolyn Rose, *Carnegie Mellon University, USA*
Asta Roseway, *Microsoft Research, USA*
Joel Ross, *University of California, USA*
Chiara Rossitto, *Stockholm University, Sweden*
Mattias Rost, *Mobile Life @ SICS, Sweden*
Robert Roth, *University of Wisconsin-Madison, USA*
Virpi Roto, *University of Helsinki, Finland*
Nicolas Roussel, *Inria, France*
Maria Roussou, *Makebelieve Design & Consulting, Greece*
Debjani Roy, *IIT Bombay, India*
Quentin Roy, *CNRS LTCI UMR 5141, France*
Agata Rozga, *Georgia Institute of Technology, USA*
Elisa Rubegni, *Universita Della Svizzera Italiana, Switzerland*
Steve Rubin, *University of California, USA*
Michael Rubinstein, *MIT, USA*
Stefan Rüger, *The Open University, UK*
Jaime Ruiz, *Colorado State University, USA*
Enrico Rukzio, *Lancaster University, Germany*

Sonja Rümelin, *University of Munich, Germany*
Tuukka Ruotsalo, *Aalto University, Finland*
Derek Ruths, *McGill University, Canada*
Kimiko Ryokai, *MIT Media Laboratory, USA*
Jeffrey Rzeszotarski, *Carnegie Mellon University, USA*
Daniel Saakes, *Delft University of Technology, The Netherlands*
Selma Sabanovic, *Indiana University, USA*
Andreas Sackl, *FTW Telecommunications Research Center, Austria*
Ramik Sadana, *Georgia Institute of Technology, USA*
Alireza Sahami Shirazi, *University of Stuttgart, Germany*
Arnaud Sahuguet, *Google, USA*
Alan Said, *CWI, The Netherlands*
Daisuke Sakamoto, *The University of Tokyo, Japan*
Mona Sakr, *Institute of Education, UK*
Ben Salem, *Northumbria University, UK*
Pascal Salembier, *University of Technology of Troyes, France*
Mariana Salgado, *Laurea University of Applied Sciences, Finland*
Guarionex Salivia, *Minnesota State University, USA*
Eva Lotta Sallnäs Pysander, *Royal Institute of Technology, Sweden*
Katri Salminen, *University of Tampere, Finland*
Antti Salovaara, *Aalto University, Finland*
Anastasia Salter, *University of Baltimore, USA*
Frode Sandnes, *Oslo University College, Norway*
Aditya Sankar, *University of Washington, India*
Vagner Santana, *State University of Campinas, Brazil*
Pedro Santana-Mancilla, *University of Colima, Mexico*
Carmen Santoro, *ISTI-CNR, Italy*
T. Saponas, *Microsoft Research, USA*
Aleksandra Sarcevic, *Drexel University, USA*
Makoto Sasaki, *Iwate University, Japan*
Daisuke Sato, *IBM Research - Tokyo, Japan*
Munehiko Sato, *Disney Research, USA*
Yoichi Sato, *The University of Tokyo, Japan*
Debra Satterfield, *Iowa State University, USA*
Allison Sauppé, *University of Wisconsin-Madison, USA*
Valkyrie Savage, *University of California, USA*
Nadav Savio, *Google.org, USA*
Pete Sawyer, *Lancaster University, UK*
Walt Scacchi, *University of California, USA*
Christopher Scaffidi, *Carnegie Mellon University, USA*
Joey Scarr, *University of Canterbury, New Zealand*
Christopher Schaefbauer, *University of Colorado, USA*
Patricia Schank, *SRI International, USA*
Raimund Schatz, *Forschungszentrum Telekommunikation Wien (ftw.), Austria*
Florian Schaub, *Carnegie Mellon University, USA*
Benjamin Scheibehenne, *University of Basel, Switzerland*
Jesse Schell, *Carnegie Mellon University, USA*
Ansgar Scherp, *Business Informatics and Business Mathematics, Germany*
Gianluca Schiavo, *University of Trento & FBK, Italy*
Markus Schilling, *Simon Fraser University, Canada*
Thecla Schiphorst, *Simon Fraser University, Canada*
Steven Schirra, *Massachusetts Institute of Technology, USA*
Chris Schmandt, *Massachusetts Institute of Technology, USA*

Dominik Schmidt, *Hasso Plattner Institute, Germany*
Holger Schnädelbach, *University of Nottingham, UK*
Jodi Schneider, *National University of Ireland, Ireland*
Guy Schofield, *Newcastle University, UK*
Jean Scholtz, *Pacific Northwest Laboratory, USA*
Johannes Schöning, *Hasselt University - Tul - Iminds, Belgium*
Marén Schorch, *University of Siegen, Germany*
Falk Schreiber
Ronald Schroeter, *Queensland University of Technology, Australia*
Kai Schubert, *University of Siegen, Germany*
Daniel Schultheiss, *Ilmenau University of Technology, Germany*
Timothy Schultz, *Drexel University, USA*
Victoria Schwanda Sosik, *Cornell University, USA*
Tobias Schwartz, *Fraunhofer FIT, Germany*
Julia Schwarz, *University of Washington, USA*
Lauren Scissors, *Northwestern University, USA*
Stacey Scott, *University of Waterloo, Canada*
Peter Scupelli, *Carnegie Mellon University, USA*
Sue Ann Seah, *University of Bristol, UK*
A. Fleming Seay, *Carnegie Mellon University, USA*
Michael Sedlmair, *University of Vienna, Austria*
Magy Seif El-Nasr, *Northeastern University, USA*
Julian Seifert, *Ulm University, Germany*
Susanne Seitinger, *MIT Media Lab, USA*
James Self, *UNIST, South Korea*
Kate Sellen, *OCAD University, Canada*
Katherine Sellen, *University of Toronto, Canada*
Bryan Semaan, *University of Hawaii at Manoa, USA*
Shilad Sen, *University of Minnesota, USA*
Phoebe Sengers, *Cornell University, USA*
Sepandar Sepehr, *McMaster University, Canada*
Marcos Serrano, *IRIT, France*
Lauren Sessions Goulet, *Facebook, USA*
Leslie Setlock, *Cornell University, USA*
Burr Settles, *Carnegie Mellon University, USA*
Teddy Seyed, *University of Calgary, Canada*
Aviv Shachak, *University of Toronto, Canada*
Orit Shaer, *Tufts University, USA*
David Shaffer, *University of Wisconsin, USA*
Chirag Shah, *Rutgers University, USA*
Priti Shah, *University of Michigan, USA*
Qonita Shahab, *Eindhoven University of Technology, The Netherlands*
Noor Shaker, *IT University of Copenhagen, Denmark*
David Shamma, *Yahoo!, USA*
Ben Shapiro, *Tufts,*
Ehud Sharlin, *University of Calgary, Canada*
Moushumi Sharmin, *University of Memphis, USA*
Sarah Sharples, *University of Nottingham, UK*
Wes Sharrock, *Manchester University, UK*
Aaron Shaw, *Northwestern University, USA*
Richard Shay, *Carnegie Mellon University, USA*
John Shearer, *Newcastle University, UK*
Mohamed Sheik-Nainar, *Synaptics Inc, USA*
Chia Shen, *Harvard University, USA*

Dawei Shen, *Massachusetts Institute of Technology, USA*
S. Andrew Sheppard, *University of Minnesota, USA*
Yuanchun Shi, *Tsinghua University, China*
Patrick Shih, *The Pennsylvania State University, USA*
Choonsung Shin, *Carnegie Mellon University, USA*
Hiroyuki Shinoda, *The University of Tokyo, Japan*
Frank Shipman, *Texas A&M University, USA*
Sajad Shirali-Shahreza, *University of Toronto, Canada*
Mariya Shiyko, *Northeastern University, USA*
Buntarou Shizuki, *University of Tsukuba, Japan*
Irina Shklovski, *IT University of Copenhagen, Denmark*
Garth Shoemaker, *Google, USA*
Milad Shokouhi, *Microsoft Research, UK*
Jamie Shotton, *Microsoft Research Cambridge, UK*
Mark Shovman, *Yahoo! Inc., Israel*
George Siemens, *Athabasca University, Canada*
Beat Signer, *Vrije Universiteit Brussel, Belgium*
Six Silberman, *Bureau of Economic Interpretation, USA*
Elizabeth Sillence, *Northumbria University, UK*
Liz Sillence, *Northumbria University, UK*
Paula Alexandra Silva, *University of Hawaii at Manoa, Portugal*
Johanna Silvennoinen, *University of Jyväskylä, Finland*
Adalberto Simeone, *Lancaster University, UK*
David Simmons, *University of Glasgow, UK*
Ian Simon, *University of Washington, USA*
Judge Simon, *RAT Group, UK*
Laurent Simon, *University of Cambridge, UK*
Jolynna Sinanan, *The University of Melbourne, Australia*
Leif Singer, *University of Victoria, Canada*
Karan Singh, *University of Toronto, Canada*
Supriya Singh, *Royal Melbourne Institute of Technology, Australia*
Vikash Singh, *University of North Carolina at Charlotte, USA*
Valentina Sintsova, *EPFL, Switzerland*
Behzod Sirjani, *Northwestern University, USA*
David Sirkin, *Stanford University, USA*
Daniel Sjölie, *Umeå University, Sweden*
Mikael B. Skov, *Aalborg University, Denmark*
Marjorie Skubic, *University of Missouri, USA*
Roger Slack, *Bangor University, Wales, UK*
Bernhard Slawik, *University of Munich, Germany*
Manya Sleeper, *Carnegie Mellon University, USA*
Karin Slegers, *KU Leuven, Belgium*
James D. Slotta, *University of Toronto, Canada*
Petr Slovák, *Vienna University of Technology, Austria*
Jan Smeddinck, *University of Bremen, Germany*
Joshua Smith, *University of Washington, USA*
Madeline Smith, *Cornell University, USA*
Matthew Smith, *Leibniz Universität Hannover, Germany*
Ross Smith, *University of South KAIST, Republic of Korea ralia, Australia*
Thomas Smith, *Newcastle University, UK*
Michael Smyth, *Edinburgh Napier University, UK*
Jaime Snyder, *Syracuse University, USA*
Timothy Sohn, *Google, USA*
Tomas Sokoler, *IT University of Copenhagen, Denmark*

Jacob Solomon, *Michigan State University, USA*
Andreas Sonderegger, *University of Fribourg, Switzerland*
Hyunyoung Song, *University of Maryland, USA*
Junehwa Song, *KAIST, Korea*
Yale Song, *MIT CSAIL, USA*
Diane Sonnenwald, *UCD, Ireland*
Daniel Sonntag, *DFKI German Research Center for AI, Germany*
Vladimir Soroka, *IBM Haifa Research Lab, Israel*
Alexander Sorokin, *CrowdFlower, USA*
Iris Soute, *Eindhoven University of Technology, The Netherlands*
Caleb Southern, *Georgia Institute of Technology, USA*
Michiel Sovijärvi-Spape, *Aalto University, Finland*
Anna Spagnolli, *University of Padova, Italy*
Oleg Spakov, *University of Tampere, Finland*
Lucio Davide Spano, *University of Cagliari, Italy*
Mirjana Spasojevic, *Nokia, USA*
Chris Speed, *Edinburgh College of Art, UK*
Tess Speelpenning, *Philips Research, The Netherlands*
Wolfgang Spiessl, *BMW Research and Technology, Germany*
Tasos Spiliotopoulos, *Madeira Interactive Technologies Institute, Portugal*
Martin Spindler, *University of Magdeburg, Germany*
Adam Sporka, *Czech Technical University In Prague, Czech Republic*
Mary Ann Sprague, *Xerox, USA*
Srinath Sridhar, *Max-Planck Institut Für Informatik, Germany*
Saurabh Srivastava, *IBM India Research Laboratory, India*
Robert St. Amant, *North Carolina State University, USA*
Tad Stach, *Queen's University, Canada*
Frank Stajano, *University of Cambridge, UK*
Jeannie Stamberger, *Carnegie Mellon University, USA*
Brodie Stanfield, *University of Ontario Institute of Technology, Canada*
Kevin Stanley, *University of Saskatchewan, Canada*
Pieter Jan Stappers, *Delft University of Technology, The Netherlands*
Kate Starbird, *University of Washington, USA*
Thad Starner, *Georgia Institute of Technology, USA*
John Stasko, *Georgia Institute of Technology, USA*
Bogdan State, *Stanford University, USA*
Ian Stavness, *University of Saskatchewan, Canada*
Anthony Steed, *University College London, UK*
Ann Steele, *The University of Texas at KAIST, Republic of Korea in, USA*
Daniel Steffen, *German Research Center for Artificial Intelligence (DFKI), Germany*
Ben Steichen, *University of British Columbia, Canada*
Martin Stein, *University of Siegen, Germany*
Sebastian Stein, *University of Dundee, Scotland, UK*
Fabius Steinberger, *University of Technology, Australia*
Thomas Steiner, *Hamburg, Germany*
Aaron Steinfeld, *Carnegie Mellon University, USA*
Frank Steinicke, *University of Würzburg, Germany*
Sophie Stellmach, *Technische Universität Dresden, Germany*
Amanda Stent, *Yahoo! Labs, USA*
William Steptoe, *UCL, UK*
Sarah Stevenage
Gunnar Stevens, *University of Siegen, Germany*
Craig Stewart, *University of Glasgow, Scotland, UK*

Michael Stewart, *Virginia Polytechnic Institute and State University, USA*
Rainer Stiefelhagen, *Universität Karlsruhe (TH), Germany*
Jeremiah Still, *Missouri Western State University, USA*
David Stillwell, *University of Nottingham, UK*
Greg Stoddard, *Northwestern, USA*
Erik Stolterman, *Indiana University Bloomington, USA*
Margaret-Anne Storey, *University of Victoria,*
Cristiano Storni, *University of Limerick, Ireland*
Steven Strachan, *CEA, France*
Daniel Strazzulla, *INRIA, France*
Yolande Strengers, *AHURI-RMIT Research Centre, Australia*
Dagny Stuedahl, *University of Oslo, Norway*
Simone Stumpf, *City University London, UK*
Christian Sturm, *Hamm-Lippstadt University of Applied Sciences, Germany*
Norman Su, *University College Dublin, Ireland*
Ozge Subasi, *Vienna University of Technology, Austria*
Sriram Subramanian, *University of Bristol, UK*
Yusuke Sugano, *The University of Tokyo, Japan*
Masanori Sugimoto, *Hokkaido University, Japan*
Bongwon Suh, *Seoul National University, Republic of Korea*
Hyeon-Jeong Suk, *KAIST, South Korea*
Piyawadee Sukaviriya, *IBM Research - T. J. Watson, USA*
Gita Sukthankar, *University of Central Florida, USA*
Evan Suma, *University of Southern California, USA*
Chengzheng Sun, *Nanyang Technological University, Singapore*
David Sun, *UC Berkeley, USA*
Huatong Sun, *University of Washington Tacoma, USA*
Xiao Hua Sun, *IBM Research China, China*
Hari Sundaram, *Arizona State University, USA*
Petra Sundström, *Mobile Life @ SICS, Sweden*
Ja-Young Sung, *Georgia Institute of Technology, USA*
Siddharth Suri, *Microsoft Research, USA*
Alistair Sutcliffe, *The University of Manchester, UK*
Dag Svænes, *NTNU, Norway*
David Swallow, *University of York, UK*
Colin Swindells, *University of Victoria, Canada*
Cristina Sylla, *University of Minho, Portugal*
Anna-Liisa Syrjänen, *University of Oulu, Finland*
Daniel Szafir, *University of Wisconsin, USA*
Agnieszka (aga) Szostek, *Warsaw School of Social Psychology, Poland*
Gerd Szwillus, *Universität Paderborn, Germany*
Aurélien Tabard, *University of Munich, Germany*
Leila Takayama, *Willow Garage, USA*
Justin Talbot, *Stanford University, USA*
Chek Tien Tan, *University of Technology, Australia*
Hong Tan, *Microsoft Research Asia, China*
Kumiko Tanaka-Ishii, *University of Tokyo, Japan*
Joshua Tanenbaum, *Simon Fraser University, Canada*
Karen Tanenbaum, *Simon Fraser University, USA*
Anthony Tang, *University of Calgary, Canada*
Charlotte Tang, *University of British Columbia, Canada*
John Tang, *Microsoft Research, USA*
Stefano Targher, *University of Trento, Italy*
Andrea Tartaro, *Furman University, USA*

Craig Tashman, *Georgia Institute of Technology, USA*
Dan Tasse, *Carnegie Mellon University, USA*
Sarah Tausch, *University of Munich, Germany*
Alex Taylor, *Microsoft Research, UK*
Nick Taylor, *University of Dundee, UK*
Robyn Taylor, *Newcastle University, UK*
Stuart Taylor, *Microsoft Research, UK*
Robert Teather, *McMaster University, Canada*
Kimberly Tee, *SMART Technologies, USA*
Daniel Teibel, *Cassia, USA*
Paul Tennent, *The University of Nottingham, UK*
Monica Tentori, *UABC, Mexico*
Leong-Hwee Teo, *Carnegie Mellon University, Singapore*
Lucia Terrenghi, *Google, Switzerland*
Michael Terry, *University of Waterloo, Canada*
Loren Terveen, *University of Minnesota, USA*
Ambuj Tewari, *University of Michigan, USA*
Anuj Tewari, *UC Berkeley, USA*
Anja Thieme, *Newcastle University, UK*
Harold Thimbleby, *University of Swansea, Wales, UK*
Elizabeth Thiry, *Pennsylvania State University, USA*
Jennifer Thom, *Amazon, USA*
Katherine Thomas, *University of North Texas, USA*
Edison Thomaz, *Georgia Institute of Technology, USA*
Bart Thomee, *Yahoo Labs, Spain*
Robin Thompson, *Newcastle University, UK*
Feng Tian, *Chinese Academy of Sciences, P.r. China*
Lorenza Tiberio, *National Research Council of Italy (CNR), Italia*
Rob Tieben, *Eindhoven University of Technology, Netherlands*
Janko Timmermann, *OFFIS - Institute for Information Technology, Germany*
Nava Tintarev, *University of Aberdeen, Scotland, UK*
Mike Tissenbaum, *University of Toronto, Canada*
Hiroaki Tobita, *Sony CSL Paris, Tokyo*
Eran Toch, *Tel Aviv University, Israel*
Lisa Tolentino, *Arizona State University, USA*
Konrad Tollmar, *KTH, Sweden*
Peter Tolmie, *University of Nottingham, UK*
Catalina Toma, *University of Wisconsin-Madison, USA*
Christian Tominski, *University of Rostock, Germany*
Martin Tomitsch, *Vienna University of Technology, Australia*
Bill Tomlinson, *University of California, USA*
James Tompkin, *MPI Informatik, Germany*
KAIST, Republic of Korea in Toombs, *Indiana University Bloomington, USA*
Mercan Topkara, *IBM Research, USA*
Tammy Toscos, *Indiana University-Purdue University, USA*
Chad Tossell, *Rice University, USA*
W. Ben Towne, *Carnegie Mellon University, USA*
Cuong Tran, *University of California, USA*
Minh-Triet Tran, *University of Science, Vietnam*
Matthias Treder, *Technische Universität Berlin, Germany*
Jeffrey Treem, *Northwestern University, USA*
Shari Trewin, *IBM Research - T. J. Watson, USA*

Ha Trinh, *University of Dundee, UK*
Giovanni Maria Troiano, *Universitat Pompeu Fabra, Spain*
Khai Truong, *University of Toronto, Canada*
Janice Tsai, *Microsoft Research, USA*
Theophanis Tsandilas, *Inria, France*
Jason Tsay, *Carnegie Mellon University, USA*
Edward Tse, *SMART Technologies, Canada*
Nikolaos Tselios, *University of Patras, Greece*
Yuan-Chi Tseng, *National Cheng Kung University, Taiwan*
Jessica Tsimeris, *KAIST, Republic of Korea ralian National University, Australia*
Gill Tsouri, *Rochester Institute of Technology, USA*
Katherine Tsui, *University of Massachusetts Lowell, USA*
Oren Tsur, *Harvard University, USA*
Huawei Tu, *Swansea University, UK*
Alexandre Tuch, *University of Basel, Switzerland*
Zeynep Tufekci, *University of North Carolina, USA*
Kathleen Tuite, *University of Washington, USA*
Marcello Turconi, *University of Trieste, Italy*
Jayson Turner, *Lancaster University, UK*
Thea Turner, *USA*
Lisa Tweedie, *Tweedie Consulting, UK*
Michael Twidale, *University of Illinois at Urbana-Champaign, USA*
George Tzanetakis, *University of Victoria, Canada*
Brygg Ullmer, *Louisiana State University, USA*
Kent Unruh, *University of Washington, USA*
Connor Upton, *Intel Labs Europe, Ireland*
Blase Ur, *Carnegie Mellon University, USA*
Dina Utami
Stephen Uzor, *Glasgow Caledonian University, UK*
Kaisa Väänänen-Vainio-Mattila, *Tampere University of Technology, Finland*
Heli Väätäjä, *Tampere University of Technology, Finland*
Philip Vahey, *SRI International, USA*
Rajan Vaish, *University of California, USA*
Consuelo Valdes, *Wellesley College, USA*
Dimitar Valkov, *University of Muenster, Germany*
Anna Vallgårda, *IT University of Copenhagen, Denmark*
Philip Van Allen, *Art Center College of Design, USA*
Bram Van de Laar, *University of Twente,*
Robin Van Den Akker, *Belgium*
Jan Van Den Bergh, *Hasselt University - Tul - Iminds, Belgium*
Bart Van Den Hooff, *VU University Amsterdam, The Netherlands*
Janet Van Der Linden, *The Open University, UK*
Jelle Van Dijk, *Eindhoven University of Technology, Netherlands*
Aart Van Halteren, *Philips Research, Netherlands*
Frank Van Ham, *IBM Research, USA*
Nancy Van House, *University of California, USA*
Max Van Kleek, *MIT, UK*
Kristof Van Laerhoven, *TU Darmstadt, Germany*
Jos Van Leeuwen, *University of Madeira, Portugal*
Christof Van Nimwegen, *Utrecht University, The Netherlands*
Paul Van Schaik, *Teesside University, UK*

Peter Van Waart, *Rotterdam University of Applied Sciences, The Netherlands*
Davy Vanacken, *Hasselt University - Tul - Iminds, Belgium*
Jeroen Vanattenhoven, *KU Leuven, Belgium*
Andrew Vande Moere, *KU Leuven, Belgium*
Jean Vanderdonckt, *Université Catholique de Louvain (UCL), Belgium*
Kami Vaniea, *Carnegie Mellon University, USA*
Elina Vartiainen, *Nokia Research Center, Sweden*
Asimina Vasalou, *University of Birmingham, UK*
Radu-Daniel Vatavu, *University Stefan Cel Mare of Suceava, Romania*
Yolanda Vazquez-Alvarez, *University of Glasgow, UK*
Eduardo Veas, *Graz University of Technology, Austria*
Rajesh Veeraraghavan, *UC Berkeley, USA*
Laurian Vega, *Virginia Tech, USA*
Tiffany Veinot, *University of Michigan, USA*
Eduardo Velloso, *Lancaster University, UK*
Gina Venolia, *Microsoft Research, USA*
Colin Venters, *University of Huddersfield, UK*
Nervo Verdezoto, *Aarhus University, Denmark*
Arnold Vermeeren, *Delft University of Technology, The Netherlands*
Amber Vermeesch, *Michigan State University, USA*
Jo Vermeulen, *Hasselt University - Tul - Iminds, Belgium*
Frederic Vernier, *Université Paris XI, France*
Keith Vertanen, *Montana Tech, USA*
Roel Vertegaal, *Queen's University, Canada*
Janet Vertesi, *Princeton University, USA*
Carla Verwijs, *In Transition, Canada*
Chi Vi, *University of Bristol, UK*
Melodie Vidal, *Lancaster University, UK*
Timothy Vidas, *Carnegie Mellon University, USA*
Sarah Vieweg, *Qatar Computing Research Institute, Qatar*
Markel Vigo, *University of Manchester, UK*
Nicolas Villar, *Microsoft Research, UK*
Vinayak, *Purdue University, USA*
Jussi Virkkala
Jessica Vitak, *University of Maryland, USA*
Lisa Vizer, *University of Maryland, USA*
Vasillis Vlachokyriakos, *Newcastle University, UK*
Simon Voelker, *RWTH-Aachen University, Germany*
Christian Vogler, *Gallaudet University, USA*
Stephen Voida, *Indiana University, USA*
Martin Voigt, *TU Dresden, Germany*
Dirk Vom Lehn, *King's College London, Great Britain*
Ulrich Von Zadow, *Archimedes Exhibitions Gmbh, Germany*
Emanuel Von Zezschwitz, *University of Munich, Germany*
Mihaela Vorvoreanu, *Purdue University, USA*
Hana Vrzakova, *University of Eastern Finland, Finland*
Romain Vuillemot, *Harvard University, USA*
Dhaval Vyas, *University of Twente, The Netherlands*
Katarzyna Wac, *Carnegie Mellon University, USA*
Chat Wacharamanotham, *RWTH Aachen University, Germany*
Juan P. Wachs, *Purdue University, USA*
Greg Wadley, *The University of Melbourne, Australia*

Johanna Wagner, *Graz University of Technology, Austria*
Julie Wagner, *INRIA, Germany*
Patrick Wagstrom, *Carnegie Mellon University, USA*
Shahtab Wahid, *Virginia Tech, USA*
Brendan Walker, *The University of Nottingham, England, UK*
Bruce Walker, *Georgia Institute of Technology, USA*
Erin Walker, *Arizona State University, USA*
I Walker, *University of Bath, UK*
Lorna Wall, *UCL, UK*
Steven Wall, *System Concepts Ltd, UK*
James Wallace, *University of Waterloo, Canada*
Jayne Wallace, *University of Dundee, UK*
Guenter Wallner, *University of Applied Arts Vienna, Austria*
Jagoda Walny, *University of Calgary, Canada*
Greg Walsh, *University of Maryland, USA*
Tanja Walsh, *Tampere University of Technology, Finland*
Robert Walter, *Telekom Innovation Laboratories, Germany*
Lin Wan, *University of Siegen, Germany*
Chaoli Wang, *Michigan Technological University, USA*
Fei Wang, *IBM Research - Almaden, USA*
Jing Wang, *The Pennsylvania State University, USA*
Jingtao Wang, *University of Pittsburgh, USA*
Liang Wang, *Microsoft, USA*
Robert Wang, *Massachusetts Institute of Technology, USA*
Rongrong Wang, *Samsung Research America, USA*
Xiaoyu Wang, *University of North Carolina at Charlotte, USA*
Yang Wang, *Syracuse University, USA*
Yi-Chia Wang, *Carnegie Mellon University, USA*
Yuchen Wang, *University of Alberta, Canada*
Colin Ware, *University of New Hampshire, USA*
Andrew Warr, *Google, USA*
Rick Wash, *Michigan State University, USA*
Gloria Washington, *Clemson University, USA*
Takayuki Watanabe, *Tokyo Woman's Christian University, Japan*
Kari Watkins, *Georgia Institute of Technology, USA*
Diane Watson, *University of Waterloo, Canada*
Martin Wattenberg, *IBM Research, USA*
Leon Watts, *University of Bath, UK*
Jenny Waycott, *The University of Melbourne, Australia*
Kimberly Weaver, *Georgia Institute of Technology, USA*
Gerhard Weber, *Technische Universität Dresden, Germany*
Michael Weber, *University of Ulm, Germany*
Ina Wechsung, *TU Berlin, Germany*
Rina Wehbe, *University of Ontario Institute of Technology, Canada*
Xuetao Wei, *University of Cincinnati, USA*
Anne Weibert, *University of Siegen, Germany*
Christian Weichel, *Lancaster University, UK*
Karl-Heinz Weidmann, *Fachhochschule Vorarlberg, KAIST, Republic of Korea ria/Europe*
Alexandra Weilenmann, *IT-University of Göteborg, Sweden*
Tino Weinkauf, *Max-Planck Institut Für Informatik, Germany*
Astrid Weiss, *Vienna University of Technology, Austria*
Stephan Wensveen, *Eindhoven University of Technology, The Netherlands*

Elizabeth Wenzel, *NASA Ames Research Center, USA*
Wayne Westerman, *Apple, USA*
Adam Westerski, *Universidad Politecnica de Madrid, Spain*
Tara Whalen, *Dalhousie University, Canada*
Joseph Wherton, *Barts and The London School of Medicine and Dentistry, UK*
Brandyn White, *University of Maryland: College Park, USA*
Kevin White, *University of Maryland Baltimore County, USA*
Sean White, *Nokia, USA*
Anthony Whitehead, *Carleton University, Canada*
Michael Whitney, *University of North Carolina at Charlotte, USA*
Steve Whittaker, *University of California Santa Cruz, USA*
Jon Whittle, *Infolab21, UK*
Mikael Wiberg, *Umeå University, Sweden*
Hadley Wickham, *Rstudio, USA*
Josef Wiemeyer, *Sport Science, Germany*
Jason Wiese, *Carnegie Mellon University, USA*
Alexander Wiethoff, *University of Munich, Germany*
Andrea Wiggins, *University of New Mexico, USA*
Danielle Wilde, *Rmit University, Australia*
Erik Wilde, *UC Berkeley, USA*
Oliver Wilder-Smith, *Northeastern University, USA*
David Wilfinger, *University of Salzburg, Austria*
Wesley Willett, *INRIA, France*
Amanda Williams, *Wyld Collective Ltd., Canada*
Amanda Marisa Williams, *University of California, Canada*
Joseph Williams, *Stanford University, USA*
Kaiton Williams, *Cornell University, USA*
John Williamson, *University of Glasgow, UK*
Julie Williamson, *University of Glasgow, UK*
Andrew Wilson, *Microsoft Research, USA*
Graham Wilson, *University of Glasgow, Scotland, UK*
Mathew Wilson, *Swansea University, UK*
Max Wilson, *Swansea University, UK*
Raphael Wimmer, *University of Munich, Germany*
Marco Winckler, *ICS-IRIT, France*
Christian Winkler, *Ulm University, Germany*
Sarah Wiseman, *University College London, UK*
Pamela Wisniewski, *The Pennsylvania State University, USA*
Jason Wither, *Microsoft, USA*
Jens Witkowski, *Albert-Ludwigs-Universität Freiburg, Germany*
Dan Witzner Hansen, *IT University of Copenhagen, Denmark*
Jacob Wobbrock, *University of Washington, USA*
Jill Woelfer, *University of Washington, USA*
Donghee Yvette Wohn, *Northwestern University, USA*
Katrin Wolf, *Deutsche Telekom Laboratories, Germany*
Peter Wolkerstorfer, *CURE - Center for Usability Research & Engineering, Austria*
B.l. William Wong, *Middlesex University, UK*
Nelson Wong, *University of Saskatchewan, Canada*
Krist Wongsuphasawat, *University of Maryland, USA*
Gavin Wood, *Newcastle University, UK*
Simon Wood, *ABC, Australia*
Emma Woodberry, *Addenbrooke's Hospital, UK*

Rob Woodbury, *Simon Fraser University, Canada*
Allison Woodruff, *Intel Research, USA*
Kirk Woolford, *University of Surrey, UK*
Marcel Worring, *University of Amsterdam, The Netherlands*
Rita Wouhaybi, *Intel Corporation, USA*
Julie Wright, *Umass Boston, USA*
Michael Wright, *University of Bath, UK*
Peter Wright, *Newcastle University, UK*
Andy Wu, *Georgia Institute of Technology, USA*
Anna Wu, *Pennsylvania State University, USA*
Jiayu Wu, *Tsinghua University, China*
Mike Wu, *The University of Toronto, Canada*
Shaomei Wu, *Information Science, USA*
Yu Wu, *The Pennsylvania State University, USA*
Daniela Wurhofer, *University of Salzburg, Austria*
Susan Wyche, *Michigan State University, USA*
Peta Wyeth, *Queensland University of Technology, Australia*
Ruth Wylie, *Arizona State University, USA*
Lonce Wyse, *National University of Singapore, Singapore*
Robert Xiao, *Carnegie Mellon University, USA*
Xiao Xiao, *Massachusetts Institute of Technology, USA*
Xing Xie, *Microsoft Research Asia, China*
Anbang Xu, *University of Illinois at Urbana-Champaign, USA*
Heng Xu, *The Pennsylvania State University, USA*
Yan Xu, *Intel Labs, USA*
Kota Yamaguchi, *University of Tokyo, Japan*
Katsu Yamane, *Disney Research, USA*
Naomi Yamashita, *NTT Communication Science Laboratories, Japan*
Hirotake Yamazoe, *Osaka University, Japan*
de-Nian Yang, *Academia Sinica, Taipei*
Huahai Yang, *IBM Research - Almaden, USA*
Jiang Yang, *University of Michigan, USA*
Rayoung Yang, *University of Michigan, USA*
Rui Yang
Stephen Yang, *SUNY Cortland, USA*
Xing-Dong Yang, *University of Alberta, Canada*
Koji Yatani, *Microsoft Research Asia, China*
Yina Ye, *Helsinki Institute for Information Technology HIIT, Finland*
Nick Yee, *PARC, USA*
Tom Yeh, *University of Colorado, USA*
Yeliz Yesilada, *University of Manchester, UK*
Jude Yew, *National University of Singapore, Singapore*
Samantha Yglesias, *Virginia Tech, Montgomery*
Ji Soo Yi, *Purdue University, USA*
Emine Yilmaz, *University College London, UK*
Langxuan Yin, *Northeastern University, USA*
Ming Yin, *Harvard University, USA*
Jason Yip, *University of Maryland, USA*
Salu Ylirisku, *Aalto University, Finland*
Christian Yoder, *University of California, USA*
Daisy Yoo, *Carnegie Mellon University, USA*
Hyoseok Yoon, *KAIST, Korea*
Chuang-Wen You, *Academia Sinica, Taiwan*

Alyson Young, *UMBC, USA*
James Young, *University of Manitoba, Canada*
Chun Yu, *Tsinghua University, China*
Lixiu Yu, *Carnegie Mellon University, USA*
Michael Yu, *Carnegie Mellon University, USA*
Neng-Hao Yu, *National Taiwan University, Taiwan*
Zhiwen Yu, *School of Computer Science Xi'an, China*
Chien Wen Yuan, *Cornell University, USA*
Nicholas Yuan, *Microsoft Research Asia, China*
Beste Yuksel, *Tufts University, USA*
Stanislaw Zabramski, *Uppsala University, Sweden*
Lisl Zach, *Drexel University, USA*
Jose Zagal, *Georgia Institute of Technology, USA*
Panagiotis Zaharias, *Athens University of Economics and Business, Greece*
Bieke Zaman, *IBBT-KU Leuven, Belgium*
Massimo Zancanaro, *FBK-Irst, Italy*
Richard Zanibbi, *Rochester Institute of Technology, USA*
Michael Zarro, *Drexel University, USA*
Polle Zellweger, *Maczell Consulting, USA*
Shumin Zhai, *Research @ Google, USA*
Cheng Zhang, *Georgia Institute of Technology, USA*
Haimo Zhang, *National University of Singapore, Singapore*
Haoqi Zhang, *Harvard University, USA*
Pei Zhang, *Carnegie Mellon University, USA*
Tao Zhang, *North Carolina State University, USA*
Yan Zhang, *University of Texas at KAIST, Republic of Korea in, USA*
Yanxia Zhang, *Lancaster University, UK*
Chen Zhao, *Alibaba International UED, USA*
Dejin Zhao, *PSU, USA*
Jian Zhao, *University of Toronto, Canada*
Xuan Zhao, *University of Michigan, USA*
Bin Zheng, *University of Alberta, Canada*
Yangshuo Zheng, *Tsinghua University, China*
Jia Zhou, *Chongqing, China*
Lina Zhou, *University of Maryland, USA*
Yajin Zhou, *Raleigh, USA*
Bin Zhu, *Microsoft Research Asia, China*
Haiyi Zhu, *Carnegie Mellon University, USA*
Mengxiao Zhu, *Rutgers University, USA*
Zhigang Zhu, *The City College of New York, USA*
Martina Ziefle, *Rwth Aachen University, Germany*
Juergen Ziegler, *University of Duisburg-Essen, Germany*
Caroline Ziemkiewicz, *Brown University, USA*
Roshanak Zilouchian Moghaddam, *University of Illinois at Urbana-Champaign, USA*
Ryder Ziola, *University of Washington, USA*
Miriam Zisook, *Northeastern University, USA*
Hadar Ziv, *University of California, USA*
Goranka Zoric, *Stockholm University, Sweden*
Jo Zucco, *University of South KAIST, Republic of Korea ralia, Australia*
Sacha Zyto, *MIT, USA*

Special thanks for the financial support provided by the following sponsors:

CHI Champion Sponsors

AUTODESK.

Bloomberg

Google

Graphisme, animation et nouveaux médias
GRAND
Graphics, Animation and New Media

Microsoft

NAVER

Computer Science
UNIVERSITY OF TORONTO

CHI Contributing Sponsors

facebook.

NSF

YAHOO! LABS

Friends of CHI

Disney Research

Newcastle University

Printed on Rolland Enviro 100
100% post-consumer fiber
Certified EcoLogo
Processed chlorine free
Manufactured using biogas energy
Printed using soy-based inks

Odin: Contextual Document Opinions On The Go

Joshua Hailpern
HP Labs
1501 Pagemill Road
Palo Alto, CA 94304
joshua.hailpern@hp.com

Bernardo A. Huberman
HP Labs
1501 Pagemill Road
Palo Alto, CA 94304
bernardo.huberman@hp.com

ABSTRACT

Information overload is a systemic problem for knowledge workers in enterprise. For a long time, information was scarce and therefore valuable. While, the explosion of digital information has made information plentiful, time to read and process that content is now scarce. This problem is only exacerbated by our increased mobility, and the expectation to be "on top" of the continuous barrage of documents while on the go. Knowledge workers in enterprise need solutions that are designed with quick methods for finding *what* to read in a large collection of documents (e.g. financial reports, legal documents, news), and ways of *presenting* it within small visual real estate. Unlike reviews, document collections are long, more varied, and context is extremely important. In response, we present Odin, a mobile web-based window onto a user's document corpus. Rather than performing corpus summarization, Odin users can quickly find opinions and documents that are Aligned or Divergent from the corpus' consensus, or those that are the most Relevant given the overall corpus' of opinions. Odin presents this information through a simple and intuitive mobile interface. To the authors' knowledge, this is the first UI/system (and support algorithm) to allow mobile users to place documents and their opinions in context through alignment rather than raw word count or sentiment. Positive results from two evaluations are also presented.

Author Keywords

Consensus; Mobile; Interface; Interaction; Economics of Attention; Alignment; Divergence; Opinions

ACM Classification Keywords

H.5.m. Information Interfaces and Presentation (e.g. HCI): Miscellaneous

INTRODUCTION

While the web enables information access on a scale that would have been inconceivable a few years ago, it also creates the problem of information overload; access to a plethora of relevant content in a timely manner, without distractions from information which is marginal in value or relevance. The problem becomes even more acute when we acknowledge that knowledge workers (e.g. lawyers, financial investors, economists, CEOs) are increasingly accessing their large corpus on their mobile devices. Mobile enterprise workers must therefore be able to access large collections of documents on mobile devices' with small visual real estate and limited time/attention to process said content.

Consider: The executive that has a matter of minutes before a meeting, may have time to read only *one* document, and maybe not even its full length; The lawyer waiting fifteen or twenty minutes for his partners to arrive, can perhaps read two or three long documents; Meanwhile the financial analyst making an hour long train commute to work, may have more leisure to fully browse a corpus, though her time and UI must still be optimized as much as possible. Though each of these temporal and interaction constraints are different, the underlying goals of the user is constant: on a mobile device, quickly traverse a corpus of documents, find the best number documents that meet a time constraint, and naturally find key points in each document based upon a broader context.

This challenge is noticeably different from the solutions proposed by the existing literature. Real world knowledge workers must mitigate corpuses of documents that contain, on average, 1,262 documents [18]. Unlike reviews (e.g. product, restaurant, etc), documents are long, highly varied, many not be as focused, and context of a given opinion is extremely important. Further, mobile devices have extremely limited screen real-estate (which is not ideal for large document consumption) and mobile users have extremely limited time.

In response, we created a novel interaction model and system called **Odin**. By leveraging and exploiting our understanding of the economics of attention [38, 23, 1], we created the first system to allow mobile device users (tested within but applications beyond enterprise) to browse and find the most salient documents in a large corpus, by placing those documents and options in context of the full corpus using opinion alignment (rather than summarization, word count, or raw sentiment scores). Thus, users can find opinions and documents based on their relationship to the corpus' consensus on a given topic. In this way, Odin is like an implicit "wisdom of the crowd." The Odin UI and workflow is tailored for mobile devices and users that have limited time to consume documents. While there has been a large body of research on opinion mining, only one has investigated review mining on a smartphone (short Yelp reviews [22]) and none has examined document opinion mining on a mobile device nor using alignment of opinions (documents or reviews) to create mobile interfaces.

CHI 2014, April 26–May 1, 2014, Toronto, Ontario, Canada.

The foremost contribution of this work is a system and UI technique that allows the user to quickly find the document(s) needed given time and screen constraints, focus on the most important opinions in any document, while still being able to see how each article and opinion fits in its context (via a novel algorithm). Odin itself employes three key designs to provide this contribution and meet users' varying needs. First, to help users find a document that best meets their needs, Odin ranks each document on three different scales of importance: how **Relevant**, **Aligned** and **Divergent** it is from other documents in the corpus. Second, to help mitigate long document length, small screen sizes and limited time to consume each document, Odin provides an automatically generated **Executive Summary** of each document, highlighting key sentences and opinions for easy document digestion. Third, to address corpus size and complexity, the Odin UI has quick one-tap interactions to allow a user to find the most Relevant, Aligned or Divergent document without browsing, allowing users to get in-and-out of a corpus as quickly as possible.

In the remainder of this paper, we discuss how Odin builds on the existing literature and is situated within the broader set of solutions. We then present Odin's features and implementation, followed by positive results from two evaluations we conducted, and conclude with future and ongoing work.

RELATED WORK

Issues pertaining to information overload are not new, and were first codified in Simon's description of the relationship between attention and information [38]. More recently, information in the digital age has been shown to be a function of user access [1] and presentation [23]. Thus, we can look at these findings on economies of attention as a strong motivating and well grounded justification for new interfaces, especially those that focus on ease of information access to large document corpuses and presentation of content and opinions within a given document. Further, the need for document corpus management has been well established within the enterprise context [18], with corpuses averaging over 12,00 documents in size. This further motivates the need for solutions within a large, real-world context.

Likewise, there has been extensive work in automatic document summarization [3, 29, 40]. However, it is important to note that Odin is not a document summarization system or algorithm. Odin focuses on user interaction design, and systems to support the navigation of *key opinions* within a corpus on mobile devices by finding and placing opinions and documents in the context of a corpus.

Reading Documents

Research on document consumption/reading has identified four key activities: reading, annotating, collaborating, and authoring[9]. While all four are important, Odin focuses on the first activity *reading*, as it pertains to exploring the overwhelming collection of documents in a corpus on a mobile device. During this first activity, the reader enters a "planning phase" [31] when moving within and between documents. This is a critical step, in which, the readers focus on finding important facts so as to connect key "bits" of information. And as documents' length and complexity increase, difficulty increase as well (e.g. consuming a restaurant review is easier than consuming a 20 page financial report).

Yet on mobile devices, this initial "planning phase" is made harder by the limited screen size. Cui suggests that because mobile devices do not allow users to see multiple documents at the same time (or long documents where less is visible at one time), people must keep all salient information in working memory [12], which is quite finite. We therefore must conclude that there is a glaring need for solutions that directly support the planning phase, as well as minimizing cognitive overload in finding the "right" document and opinions because a user's working memory is in active use.

Technological solutions are well situated to help users wade through a large document, and find key sentences on which to focus. AKTiveMedia [11], Fishnet [6], and others [36, 39, 7]) use vibrant color highlighting within a document to draw users' attention to keywords based on queries issued. These techniques have proven successful in a desktop metaphor, and we build upon their success by using color to highlight sentences in a long document. In a similar vein, Ahmed's recent work on accessible skimming [2] attempts to merge document summarization and screen-readers to help visually impaired users find key points within a document. Given this success for interactive reading tools, we believe that there is much evidence for this need, and room for improvement.

Context, Visualization, and Opinions

Beyond supporting the process of reading itself, some research has examined document "context." Souneil Park [34] explored bias in news events by showing pairs of documents on contrasting ends of a political spectrum side-by-side. While this technique helps with directly comparing two *known* contrasting opinions (via two documents), it does so by showing contrasting documents physically side-by-side which, according to existing literature, does not port to a mobile context [12, 31]. Thus this approach lacks scalability and portability, which Odin directly addresses.

At a corpus level, tools can help users organize a document space. Popcorn [13] and many other tools [20] employ a wide range of visualizations to help users traverse a collection based on hierarchical semantic relationships (e.g. tree maps, network graphs). However, many of these visualization styles can be confusing [20, 10]. For example, while Tag Clouds (e.g. [26, 44, 16, 28, 27]), may be aesthetically pleasing from a content consumption perspective they are unusable, misrepresentative, and inferior to simple sorted lists [21, 26, 35, 19]. Further, while these and many other solutions [29, 25] help organize content by topic, they do not provide assistance to locate documents based on the relationship between a document's opinions and those in the corpus (are they aligned or divergent). It is in the space of unfulfilled needs that we situate our work on Odin.

Opinion Mining and Mobile Devices

Many research systems have focused on opinion mining [33]. However, the vast majority of the HCI approaches [44, 22] focus on reviews (e.g. Yelp). There is a large difference, computationally and from a user's perspective, between reviews and full length documents. As a result, many of the algorithmic and design considerations cannot be used directly. Within the document opinion mining literature, only one system, Echo, has investigated something akin to Alignment, Divergence or Relevance (as used in Odin) as a substrate for the UI design [18].

However unlike desktop interfaces, mobile device UI must be optimized both for the smaller screen-size and "on-the-go" use case of users. Thus systems like Echo [18] simply cannot function in a mobile environment (due to visual and interaction complexity and level of detail presented to the user). Until 2012, "none of that work has investigated opinion mining... for a smart phone" [22]. RevMiner[22] provided the first mobile UI system that helps users understand reviews on restaurants. Their UI is optimized for the small screens of mobile devices by utilizing a multi-facet view on the review data, and we can learn many lessons from their work. However, there are two distinct limitations of RevMiner. First, the opinions displayed to users are simply positive or negative. There is no sense of context for said opinions (are they aligned or divergent from the consensus of the corpus). Second, there is a substantial difference between reading short, to the point, reviews and reading long complex documents. Time required, content complexity, and document length greatly impact readability (especially on mobile devices) [12].

Other mobile UI research has focused on mapping multicolumn web content into mobile-friendly versions [43, 24, 45] or tree-like structures [32], or pagination. However, while these approaches do improve readability over the original text, empirical studies have shown that users greatly prefer scrolling text/lists[37, 17] and that users have the fastest information extraction when navigation is broad, with the fewest levels before reaching the desired content [17]. Based on this work, solutions must be created that get users to documents and content quickly, without pagination, while still providing context. The theory behind Odin is that these visual changes and text/document selection can be facilitated through opinion Alignment.

SCOPE & MOTIVATION

Odin is a *document* (not reviews) corpus reading solution for users on the go. Unlike previous approaches, Odin allows mobile users to have extremely easy access to the output of complex NLP and IR analysis on a corpus of documents. Within this scope, Odin is the first system that allows a mobile user to place and find documents and opinions via context within the corpus' distribution of opinions (unlike above solutions that rely upon only word count, topic modeling, or raw sentiment scores for reviews). The additional device constraints (e.g., small screen real-estate) the context of use (e.g. users with greatly decreased time availability to browse and consume) and type of input (documents vs. reviews) greatly change the functioning of our resulting solution, Odin.

In this paper, we will refer to sentences whose opinions are inline with those of the corpus as **Aligned**, and sentences with opinions that go against the grain of the corpus as **Divergent**. A weighting algorithm determines the rank, or presentation order, of each document and sentence based on how important its topics are, and how much the opinions are Aligned with or Divergent from the corpus. We also created a **Relevance** ranking which can be used to find the sentences or documents that are the most opinionated (regardless of if the opinions are Aligned or Divergent from the corpus). Relevant documents can therefore be thought of as documents that provide a broad perspective.

The authors wish to stress that this approach and it's underlying algorithm are *not* summarization tools. Odin focuses on using opinion alignment to improve document selection, and opinion highlighting, to make for a more meaningful and wide selection of crucial opinions. Odin automates this process by gathering the corpus' consensus (via a corpus of documents), distilling what is being talking about, and examining how the authors refers to those topics. In addition, the authors wish to stress that there is a large, substantive difference between reviews and mining full documents (which impact UI, interactions, and algorithms needed).

DESIGN REQUIREMENTS

Odin builds upon the existing literature above from the research community on reading, economics of attention, and opinion mining. From this background, Odin seeks to address five key design requirements:

R1 Support Planning Phase of Reading: Help readers quickly find important facts with little cognitive effort [31] from a range of opinions from the perspective most applicable to a given user's needs

R2 Support Finding Key Documents: Reduce cognitive load from managing multiple documents on mobile devices [12] from a range of opinions from the perspective most applicable to a given user's needs

R3 Mitigate Document Length: use visual techniques to help users find key sentences in documents regardless of document length [11, 6, 36, 39, 7]

R4 Document Selection by Alignment: allow users to find documents based on relation to corpus' opinion (unlike existing solutions which focus on summaries, word count, or raw sentiment scores only)

R5 Context Based Interaction: rather than a high-level abstract UI (unlike summarization or sentiment extraction tools), allow users to see all text within an individual document's context [32]

ODIN: DESIGN & INTERACTION

Odin is comprised of a web-based UI, that allows a user interact with documents and the broader corpus on *any* mobile device[1], and a back-end algorithm and system, that performs the data mining analysis of the document corpus. Any type of "document" corpus can be loaded, analyzed, and accessed: PDFs (e.g. legal documents or financial analysts reports),

[1]Screenshots that appear in this paper were taken from an iPhone5, though the system has been tested on Android as well.

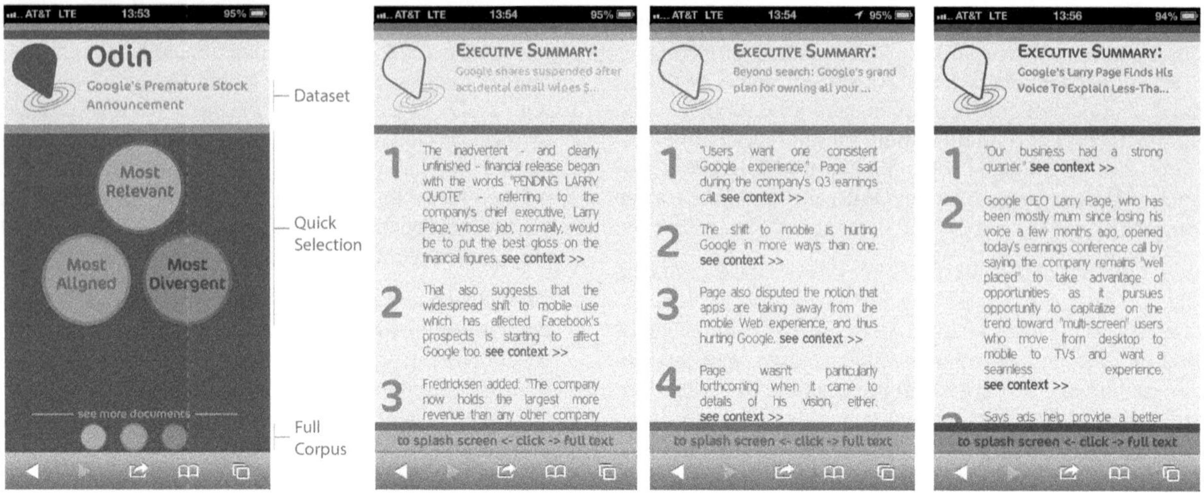

(a) Splash Screen of Odin (b) Most Relevant (c) Most Aligned (d) Most Divergent

Figure 1: Splash Screen & Executive Summary Screenshots

These screenshots also illustrate the three color schemes corresponding to the three ranking options available to the user: Relevant, Aligned, and Divergent

DOCX (e.g. student essays to be graded), HTML (e.g. product discussion blogs, online news, etc)[2] or streaming temporal documents (e.g. financial news on a company over time). Odin has been tested on a wide variety of data-sets from political articles to financial reports, to the more mundane domain of world/us news.

To illustrate the features and multiple uses of Odin, we present a series of three overly extensive scenarios. In practice, users may apply any subset of the following techniques at any time or in any order. Each scenario involve Anthony, a financial analyst, having progressively less time to react:

Anthony is a junior financial analyst for Kirby, Lee & Co. On October 19th, 2012 Anthony heard about Google's accidental earnings report release[3], and the negative Google's financial outlook. Anthony must quickly get a grasp on the flood of financial reports and get into a meeting with his boss to discuss how they should handle their company's investments. A corpus of financial reports was loaded into Odin.

Scenario 1: a Matter of Minutes

As news comes across Anthony's desk about Google's announcement, he gets a worried email from his boss requesting an immediate meeting. Antony grabs his mobile phone, and heads from his office to Boss' (a short distance away).

Anthony opens up Odin with a dataset of financial articles and is presented with the Odin splash screen (Figure 1a). While Odin has hundreds of documents, Anthony only has time to read one. Whichever document Anthony reads must provide him with the most information possible (R2). On the Odin splash screen, Anthony taps the large green button labeled "Most Relevant." This loads the Executive Summary (Figure 1b) for the most Relevant document (algorithm detailed later), which is entitled *Google shares suspended after accidental email wipes ....* We can conceptually think of the "Most Relevant" document, as the document with the broadest spectrum of opinions; those opinions that are on central topics, that are either very Aligned or Divergent with the corpus' conscious.

While the quick tap helped Anthony find a good document, it is still a very long piece of text – too long to read quickly, especially on a mobile device (even with pagination). Much like an executive assistant helps a CEO, Odin displays an Executive Summary with key sentences from that document, sorted in ranked order based on how Relevant they are (R1 & R4). Thus, Anthony can quickly and easily find the most interesting information in the document, covering a broad set of opinions regardless of the length of the original document or where the opinions occurred in the source text (R1 & R3).

Scenario 2: Meeting in a Few

We begin our scenario again, this time Anthony's boss asks for an all hands meeting in ten minutes. Anthony grabs his phone, and heads to the meeting room (he does not want to be late). While he waits for the meeting to begin, he brings up Odin to get up to speed. Given a slightly more relaxed time constraint, Anthony wants to explicitly see what the corpus' conscious is about the Google announcement. In addition, he wants to know what outlying opinions are being voiced so he can be prepared to discuss them.

Rather than click on Relevant, as in the above scenario, Anthony directs he attention to the two other large quick select buttons on the splash screen: "Most Aligned" in gold and "Most Divergent" in red (R4). Similar to the "Most Relevant" button, these other two quick select options will load the "most" Aligned or Divergent document into the Executive Summary view (Figure 1c and 1d respectively), showing the key sentences/opinions in ranked order. Within any of the three Executive Summary layouts, Antony can tap a given sentence and Odin loads the full document text, highlights

[2]These are not contributions of this work, and as a result, we do not include screen-shots or a description of the upload infrastructure.

[3]This scenario in no way reflects opinions on the value of Google stock. This is a test data-sets used to construct a narrative.

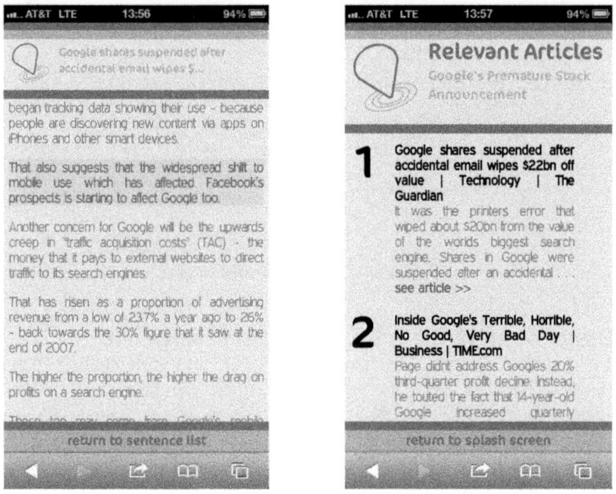

(a) Highlight Sentence in Context (b) Relevant Article List

Figure 2: Additional Odin UI Views

The above examples are from the Relevant sort view, and therefore are in green. Other sorts would use differing color schemes as seen in Figure 1d

the tapped sentence, and auto scrolls the full text to the location of the highlight (e.g. Figure 2a) showing that comment in context (R5).

The Aligned Executive Summary (Figure 1c) shows Anthony that the general consensus on Google is that the company has not monetized their mobile platform well. In the Divergent view Figure 1d, the power of Odin's algorithm truly shines; the most Divergent opinion in the most Divergent document is a quote, *"Our business had a strong quarter"*. This is a strikingly different point of view that goes against the grain. Anthony then can tap the sentence, and see the full full context of that sentence (R5), and can easily see that this is a quote from the chief business officer, who is attempting to spin lukewarm results in the best way possible. While this is so different from the consensus, Anthony now can see Google's perspective, why Google thinks they should be viewed positively, and Anthony also now realizes that these views are not shared by the financial analysts.

Scenario 3: On the Train-Ride to Work

The final scenario begins early in the morning (before work), when Anthony gets a message from his boss for a all hands meeting when everyone gets into the office. Anthony has roughly a thirty minute window of time, during his train commute, to get caught up with the financial reports to be discussed. Because the train is not the place to pull out a laptop, he turns on his phone and uses Odin.

While Anthony can use the quick tap buttons, as above, he can utilize his more flexible time to expand his understanding of the issues, and the opinions of the financial analysts[4]. Running along the bottom of the Odin splash screen are three smaller colored buttons (Figure 1a). Each button when clicked, loads the full corpus of documents (R2) sorted by how Relevant, Aligned, or Divergent the document is (Figure 2b) with the color corresponding to the sort order. Now Anthony can tap any document, and see the Executive Summary for *that* specific document. These Executive Summary screens function just as the ones in the above scenarios.

ALGORITHM & IMPLEMENTATION

The Odin interface is built in HTML, CSS and JavaScript allowing for corpus and document access on any mobile device (regardless of operating system). The server-side corpus analysis and upload system is constructed using Java. This section will discuss the seven-stage server-side algorithm that analyzes a corpus, and generates content for the Odin UI. This algorithm provides the analysis to directly support R4, which facilitates the UI components that satisfy R1 and R2. Odin can load documents in by hand, by being tied to a data base, streaming (e.g. RSS), or crawling the web (e.g. google news collections as corpuses).

Odin's algorithm has two key distinctions from existing research. First, Odin must calculate and situate the alignment of opinions (R4) within the implicit distribution of opinions within a corpus. Second, Odin provides users documents and opinions within a full context (R5) rather than simply displaying the output of a topic model or sentiment analysis. This requires a heuristic that can calculate the alignment at the document and sentence level, not just at the word (output of topic model) or modifier (sentiment analysis) level. This novel cross subject comparison/ranking with a scalar sentiment variation is a complex aspect of our algorithmic approach which builds upon [18].

Stage 1. Extract Content

Regardless of document format (e.g. PDF, HTML, DOCX, etc.), the raw paragraphs, sentences, and words must be extracted in order to perform any ML analysis. We borrow the term **Body Copy** from the layout and design community, to refer to the main text of a document, as compared to logos, images, title, advertisements, comments etc. Body Copy from text, PDF and DOCX files can be extracted with existing Java libraries (e.g. Apache PDFBox). However, HTML (uploaded by a user or crawled from a site like Google News) is more complex due to ads, navigation, comments, variation of page layout, etc. We therefore implemented the CETR algorithm [42] which extracts body-copy from webpages without use of a template through multidimensional clustering.

Stage 2. Identify Discussion Subjects

In order to determine *what* the corpus is talking about and what the most *important* subjects are, we leveraged LDA topic modeling[30] to extract topics and associated keywords across all documents. However, we first cleaned all body copy by filtering out all words that were not nouns using POS tagging[5]. Text was lemmatized using the Stanford NLP toolkit[41], and then fed into LDA.

To explain our use of LDA, we will define $\boldsymbol{A}$ to be the set of all topics ($a_0 \ldots a_v$), $\boldsymbol{B}$ to be the set of all documents in our

[4]By tapping the words *full text* along the bottom of the Executive Summary, will load the full text of the document, like Figure 2a, without the highlight.

[5]While an alternative could be Named Entity Recognition[15], entity disambiguation is an open challenge, and we opted to utilize a more conservative approach.

corpus ($b_0 \ldots b_m$), and C to be the set of all unique words ($c_0 \ldots c_n$) across all documents. Any given document (b_x) is made up of a subset of words from C. Likewise, each topic (a_w) is made up of a subset of words from C, each word having a probability $P(c_y|a_w)$ that if a word is randomly chosen from a_w, c_y is that particular word. Thus we can think of a_w and b_x as being probability distributions $\sum_{y=0}^{n} P(c_y|a_w) = 1$ and $\sum_{w=0}^{v} P(a_w|b_x) = 1$ respectively. In layman's terms, every word in a document is contributed by one of the topics.

Thus, LDA gives us the rank ($P(c_y|a_w)$) of each word (c_y) given a particular topic (a_w). However, these word probabilities cannot be compared across topics as they are conditional. We must therefor flip this conditional argument using Bayes' Rule, marginalizing out the topics for each word:

$$P(c_y) = \sum_{w=0}^{v} P(c_y|a_w)P(a_w) \tag{1}$$

This calculates a rank for each word that is topic independent, comparable across our document corpus, giving us a weight for how important or central each subject is in the corpus[6].

Stage 3. Detect Opinion Sentiment

Using the subjects identified, we attempt to find any opinions rendered on these important subjects. We consider all sentences that have one of the Stage 2 subjects in them[7]. Using a statistical parser [14] we can create a dependency tree (similar to sentence diagraming in grade school). From these parse trees we programmatically uncover the modifiers (e.g., adjectives) that were applied to any subject (and any negations).

For each modifier uncovered with the statistical parser, we lookup[8] a sentiment score with Senti-Wordnet[4], a hand-compiled list covering a large selection of common word modifiers. Senti-Wordnet thus associates each modifier on two 0.0-1.0 sentiment scales, Positive and Negative[9]. Thus, for each of the important subjects in Stage 2 (c_y), we uncover the set of opinions $\mathbf{D(c_y)} = d_1(c_y) \ldots d_u(c_y)]$ across every sentence of every document where the subject occurs: .

Stage 4. Calculate Corpus' Opinions

Unlike previous literature on opinion extraction, Odin presents opinions by alignment rather than simply positive or negative. Thus we must next place each unique opinion within the context of the "distribution" of per-subject opinions ($D(c_y)$). Stage 4 calculates that context. From $D(c_y)$, we can calculate a mean positive $\mu_{pos}(c_y)$ and negative sentiment $\mu_{neg}(c_y)$, which we can refer to as the corpus' opinion on a given subject. Given that each per-subject distribution is different, and we will need to compare opinions on different subjects against one another (e.g. *"which opinion is more Divergent"*), we must normalize. To this end, we calculate each per-subject standard deviation ($\sigma_{pos}(c_y)$ and $\sigma_{neg}(c_y)$) from the mean. As a result, all comparisons will be a measure of standard deviations away rather than absolute distance. We therefore can define opinion distance $\mathbf{E}(d_z(c_y)) = < E_{pos}(d_z(c_y)), E_{neg}(d_z(c_y)) >$:

$$E_{pos}(d_z(c_y)) = \frac{|d_{pos,z}(c_y) - \mu_{pos}(c_y)|}{\sigma_{pos}(c_y)}$$
$$E_{neg}(d_z(c_y)) = \frac{|d_{neg,z}(c_y) - \mu_{neg}(c_y)|}{\sigma_{neg}(c_y)} \tag{2}$$

Stage 5. Instance Alignment and Divergence

Given the above calculated context, we can now determine how Aligned or Divergent a given opinion is. Whereas $D(c_y)$ is the set of all opinions on a given word, we define the set of all opinions across all words in all documents as $\mathbf{F} = \bigcup_{q=0}^{p} (D(c_y))$. We therefore define an individual opinion on a specific instantiation of a word as $f_q = d_z(c_y)$. And therefore, f_q can be substituted for any $d_z(c_y)$ allowing us to easy calculate an Alignment (**G**) and Divergence (**H**) score:

$$E_S(f_q) = MAX(E_{pos}(f_q), E_{neg}(f_q))$$
$$G_{opinion}(f_q) = G_{opinion}(d_z(c_y)) \propto P(c_y) * E_S(f_q)$$
$$H_{opinion}(f_q) = H_{opinion}(d_z(c_y)) \propto \frac{P(c_y)}{E_S(f_q)} \tag{3}$$

These scoring functions were based on two principals: First, as Alignment should grows as distance from the corpus' opinion shrinks (hence in the denominator) while Divergence should shrink (hence as a multiplier); Second, both Alignment and Divergence grow as importance of the subject increases. In addition, we can consider an individual opinion of a specific instance of a word as being "Aligned" if $G > H$ (and "Divergent" if $H > G$).

Stage 6. Sentence Alignment, Divergence & Relevance

The inclusion of subject importance ($P(c_y)$) in our scoring functions in Stage 5 has an added benefit – both $G_{opinion}$ and $H_{opinion}$ become subject independent, and can be compared or combined at a sentence (or document) level with the $G_{opinion}$ and $H_{opinion}$ of another subject (which may have a different weight in the model from Stage 2). We can therefore define the set of all subject opinions ($\{f_q\}$) within a given sentence as $\mathbf{I} = \{f_q\}$. Subsequently, the Alignment or Divergence of the sentence is a sum over all opinions' Alignment or Divergence scores:

$$G_{sentence}(I) = \sum_{r=0}^{|I|} G_{opinion}(i_r)$$
$$H_{sentence}(I) = \sum_{r=0}^{|I|} H_{opinion}(i_r) \tag{4}$$

As described earlier, we defined Relevance as sentences or documents that have a broad set of opinions. To calculate a Relevance score (**J**), we combine both the Alignment and Divergence scores: $J_{sentence}(I) = G_{sentence}(I) + H_{sentence}(I)$. Thus, the more opinions rendered (Alignment, Divergence, or both) on the more important subjects, the higher the appropriate score will be, and are sorted accordingly based on their raw scores.

[6] To reduce complexity, and noise from topic modeling, we only consider the top 500 words.

[7] By filtering sentences, this improves run/computation time.

[8] Modifier lookup does not have word sense disambiguation (context). While their are many other sentiment calculation alternatives, Senti-Wordnet is a well regarded and robust system that provides fast and relatively accurate sentiment scoring.

[9] We maintain both positive and negative values because if combined on a single scale, most results trend towards neutral. Any negations detected will "swap" the positive and negative scores. Neutral opinions (both scores being 0) are dismissed.

Stage 7. Document Alignment, Divergence & Relevance

Calculating Alignment, Divergence or Relevance scores for documents follows a similar approach to that in Stage 6. We define the set of all opinions in a document as **K** = {I}, with scoring functions using sum, rather than mean, so as to give more weight to documents that have many opinions, rather than one strong opinion:

$$G_{doc}(I) = \sum_{o=0}^{|K|} G_{sentence}(k_o)$$
$$H_{doc}(I) = \sum_{o=0}^{|K|} H_{sentence}(k_o) \quad (5)$$
$$J_{doc}(I) = G_{doc}(K) + H_{doc}(K)$$

Documents, unlike sentences, have the potential to contain more opinions simply because they have more words (not because the document is more opinionated)[10]. Consider a corpus where all documents contain at least 1% Divergent comments. A longer document, which is largely Aligned, may appear to also be very Divergent, simply because of it's length (as compared to a short document which is 95% Divergent, but so short that the sum is smaller than the longer document). We therefore cannot rely upon the raw Alignment, Divergence scores. Rather we must look at documents that are highly Aligned or Divergent, which can be calculated as the delta between the two raw scores: $\delta_{Aligned}(K) = G_{doc}(K) - H_{doc}(K)$ and $\delta_{Divergent}(K) = H_{doc}(K) - G_{doc}(K)$. Thus, documents whose Alignment score is much larger than Divergent score will appear more Aligned, and documents whose Divergent score is much larger than Alignment score will appear more Divergent.

PILOT USER STUDY

An pilot study was conducted to understand how well our system, algorithm and UI could support corpus access for a mobile users and how Odin could be improved.

10 users participated (8 male, 2 female), and were shown a demonstration of Odin, its features and capabilities with multiple corpuses on finance, technology, and news[11]. Though a straw-man, we also showed users a page styled like Google News "more sources" (listing multiple documents on the same news story), and demonstrated how different news/article websites (e.g. CNN, ABC, etc.) rendered articles for mobile devices. Participants were given 5-10 minutes to explore Odin. During the informal 20-30 minute sessions, participants were encouraged to think aloud. At the end of the session, participants completed a brief questionnaire about their experience. Though our sample size is too small to conduct formal statistics (due to low confidence intervals) we do report quantitative responses to illustrate user reactions and comparisons to other approaches (Table 1).

[10]There are many IR techniques to normalize for a document's length itself. However, longer documents may simply have more sentences worth reading, and help a user quickly find key opinions, which is Odin's goal. We therefore did not account for document length itself.

[11]One of the corpuses users were shown, was the same document corpus as highlighted in the figures in this paper.

	Odin is...		Equal	Other is...	
Finding Documents	**Best (1)**	**Better (2)**	**(3)**	**Better (4)**	**Best (5)**
Google News	20%	60%	10%	10%	0%
Date Sorted List	40%	50%	10%	0%	0%
Popularity Sorted List	40%	50%	10%	0%	0%
Reading Documents					
Google News	20%	50%	20%	10%	0%
Date Sorted List	20%	40%	30%	10%	0%
Popularity Sorted List	30%	30%	20%	20%	0%

Table 1: Which Method Do You Prefer For ...
Participants were asked to respond on a 5 point scale

All were recruited from a large US corporation, had a mean age of 41.1. All of our participants reported using large collections of documents daily or a few times a week. Participants had varying educational backgrounds, both degree level (1 BS, 3 MS/MA, 6 Doctorate) and degree area (5 CS, 2 Statistics, 1 Math, 1 Business, 1 Engineering).

Results & Discussion

Participants were overwhelmingly positive in their feedback on Odin with respect to its ability to manage a large corpus:

It had a fluid look and feel that allowed for the rapid exposure to a number of articles with little thought about trying to "find" them. - P2

As a boss would say... 'give me the five minute rundown,' and you are asking for that, automatically. But now, you don't have to read everything to get that. You don't have to go 'not relevant, not relevant, not relevant'... if you don't have that hour, you can just go through it - which is great! - P7

and Odin's Executive Summary UI, that quickly brings key opinions within each document to the forefront:

[Executive summary] with aligned and divergent key sentences gives me a better overview than the standard abstract or summary - P10

Very useful, that it infers the main ideas and opinions, to give a higher-level understanding of the context of the corpus as a whole before I start to look at documents on a more detailed level. - P8

We asked participants *"If you could load any corpus into Odin or Google New's List View for mobile reading, which would you choose?"* 90% of participants chose Odin. Responses to other comparisons are included in Table 1.

Participants were also generally positive about the different features of Odin (Table 2). While the reaction was positive, we explicitly asked users what additional features could be useful to readers on the go. Surprisingly, each participant proposed a different idea:

- A quick tap button for documents that were read by many people viewing this corpus (social popularity)
- See articles that are aligned/divergent from the currently open document (relative alignment)
- Adapt the ranking based on individual user's viewing preferences or histories across multiple corpuses
- Summary statistics (e.g. number of Aligned opinions on topic A)

We asked participants what they thought of suggestions we heard from prior subjects. Unexpectedly, participants generally did not feel the others' suggestions would be valuable. Given that each participant justified their additional feature

	1	2	3	4	5
Different Executive Summaries (Relevance, Alignment, Divergence)	80%	10%	10%	0%	0%
Only Showing Key Sentences In Executive Summaries	50%	30%	10%	10%	0%
Seeing Each Sentence in Context	50%	40%	0%	10%	0%
Most Relevant Document	50%	40%	0%	10%	0%
Most Aligned Document	30%	40%	30%	0%	0%
Most Divergent Document	50%	20%	30%	0%	0%

Table 2: How Useful Is Each Feature of Odin
Participants were asked to respond on a 5 point scale, 1 was a "Key Feature" and 5 was "Provides no value"

within their own unique work or situation, we believe that this suggests that the features currently in Odin are universally critical, though additional features may be useful if turned on based on individual preference. This was echoed by P9:

> *In a world where you have inundation of information, and opinions you could spend 'how many?' hours a day trying to read much less put it together... I like it... and I think a lot of these [features] if you don't have them, you looses a lot. I would say most of [the features] are key features. Cause if you're not, then your missing too much. What you are looking for is a minimum ante to play the game... Odin solves that.* - P9

P1 discussed an interesting perspective of summarization UI (e.g. tag clouds, or summaries) versus Odin's approach of Alignment and Divergence (R4).

> *This is probably something generalizable, usually you get the official opinion... you see the same thing over and over again, but if someone says something different, now that is interesting so it is important that you find it quickly* - P1

He continued to articulate that traversing a corpus is more than just seeing key words, but seeing relative opinions.

All users also commented about the elegance and simplicity of the Odin UI. Often these comments were associated with praise that something could be so simple despite a powerful back-end and service (R1), especially for a mobile system:

> *It appears to allow for personalization of how the information is presented and allows it to meet the demands of the moment instead of dictating what you "should" be interested.* - P2

It is important to note that even while Odin was built using the most straightforward approaches used in the ML and NLP domains, participants explicitly stated that the key sentences were helpful and appeared to be picked out well by the system:

> *It behaves like a "smart" system. For what I've seen, results are always appropriate.* - P3

Many users even commented how strikingly different the documents were, and how they immediately saw the distinctions between the three ranking/categories. We strongly believe that this is due to the power of aggregating opinions based on the corpus' consensus, combining both subject importance in a topic model with sentiment detection and delta from the mean.

Overall, results from our study provide very promising. Encouraged by these results, a formal study was then conducted.

COMPARATIVE USER STUDY

Based on the feedback from our initial pilot user study, we conducted a second user evaluation of Odin[12] This study directly compared Odin to the only other research system that enables opinion mining on mobile devices, RevMiner[22]. We re-implemented the RevMiner system based on the description in the original paper[13]. We acknowledge that RevMiner was designed to synthesize Yelp Reviews, which are a extremely different type of data as compared to full length documents. While RevMiner *may* not be designed to function in the same use case as Odin, it is the only work that "has investigated opinion mining as a substrate for a smartphone interface,"[22]. In addition, by comparing Odin to RevMiner, users can contrast 'traditional' keyword-modifier pair/tag cloud style UI and the Executive Summary/Alignment in Odin. As in the first experiment, this study also presented users with a Google News style list UI as a straw man.

14 users participated (6 male, 8 female), and were able to experience each system (Odin, RevMiner, and the Google News styled UI) in turn[14]. For each system, users were given a demo, and then allowed to use it to explore a handful of corpuses. Users could select the corpuses they wished to read from a pre-loaded collection of 20 corpuses ranging from Financial Analysis, to Political Documents to more germane World and US news[15]. To motivate actual use of the three systems, we asked participants to try to summarize what the corpus was about after opening it (though this was not recorded).

At the conclusion of each session, participants were given a brief survey about the three systems, and specific aspects of their design. The survey contained a SUS usability metric[8], as well as more open-ended qualitative questions.

All were recruited from a large US corporation's Legal, Marketing a Consulting divisions (the target users of a system like Odin), had a mean age of 31.7. Participants reported suing large collections of documents daily, and had a variety of educational attainment: 6 had MS/MA, 6 BS/BA, 1 Doctorate or Equivalent Degree.

Results & Discussion

Participant responses were all strongly in favor of Odin over the other two solutions both in perceived value-add within their own work (Table 3b) and usability (Table 3a)[16], with almost all differences being statistically significant (Table 3c). Likewise, all participants selected Odin as the "best" system, the one they would chose to use in their day-to-day work. P4 described/justified her selection of Odin by stating:

> *RevMiner feels like a low-res version of Odin... It's like you pulled out all the useful features and obscured everything that matters.*

[12] Based on user feedback, one minor change was made to Odin; The letters R, A, D we added to the "see more document" circles. Each circle corresponds to the corpus list sort order (Relevance, Alignment and Divergence respectively) by color *and* typography.

[13] The 'Categories' tab was omitted as their is does not have a logical parallel in a document corpus.

[14] Presentation order was randomized to control for order effects

[15] Corpuses contained from 100 to 300 documents each

[16] It is worth noting that while both Google UI and Odin have similar SUS scutes (are equally usable), the benefits of Odin's additional synthesis improves its value add.

		Mean (SD)	Median [IQR]
Odin	Overall	86.79 (12.39)	87.5 [77.5, 97.5]
	Main Screen	89.64 (10.55)	90 [83.75, 98.75]
	Executive Summary	89.29 (12.14)	92.5 [82.5, 98.75]
RevMiner	Overall	63.93 (11.07)	62.5 [58.75, 66.25]
	Common	67.5 (13.54)	75 [61.25, 76.25]
	Special	55 (6.12)	52.5 [52.5, 60]
	Cloud	67.14 (12.11)	72.5 [55, 73.75]
Google	Overal	84.29 (9.43)	87.5 [76.25, 90]
	Article List	84.29 (19.19)	97.5 [67.5, 100]
	External Links	66.79 (14.41)	60 [58.75, 73.75]

(a) SUS Usability Scores

	Mean (SD)	Median [IQR]
Odin	4.71 (0.49)	5 [4.5, 5]
RevMiner	2.14 (0.9)	2 [2, 2]
Google	3.43 (0.98)	3 [3, 4]

(b) System Value-Add in Work Context

	Value Add	SUS Score
Odin vs.RevMiner	< 0.001	0.01
Odin vs.Google	0.01	0.26
RevMiner vs. Google	0.002	0.01

(c) T-Test Comparison P-Values

Table 3: Comparative User Study Results

SUS scores range from 0 to 100. 90-100 = A, 80-89 = B, etc.[5] — Value-Add Questions asked on 5 point scale (1=Low, 5= High) — T-Test Compared Overall SUS Scores

This view was echoed by P6 (R2, R3 R4):

> *when i am looking for something i need to read, i have 5 or 10 minutes. i want to get the most knowledge in that amount of time. So when i open the app, i want the relevance and alignment thing.*

These views and SUS scores overall, and for specific features, suggest that more abstract visual presentations (e.g. tag-clouds and word-modifier pairs) do not support the real-world tasks of knowledge workers who prefer the Executive Summary style of presentation based on Alignment. This is largely consistent with the literature discussed earlier. Within the extremely simple Google styled list UI (which had high SUS scores), participants preferred the Executive Summary and Alignment driven approach. P17 justified this by stating: *"I like the Executive Summary, not just [seeing] the first few lines [of the article shown in the Google UI]."* So while both are "usable" one has much more value (R3).

While there is a noticeable difference between Odin and RevMiner, we do not believe that these usability issues are generally true for the RevMiner system in its original use case. Rather, we believe that more traditional approaches to opinion mining (as used by RevMiner) do not map onto document corpuses on mobile devices. Along this line, P1 stated that *"Revminer just wasn't very useful, it's not that it wasn't hard to understand."* This difference, highlights the need for new algorithmic and UI approaches when handling different types of textual data (e.g. reviews vs. documents).

LIMITATIONS & FUTURE WORK

Given the informal nature of the first study, and the unstructured exploration (rather than explicit task) in the second, the findings should not be interpreted as a final validation of Odin. However, these results do provide an insight into feature utility, and the potential use of Odin in the real world. Presently, we are undertaking a long-term ecological deployment of Odin, integrating it within a corporate environment. This will allow us to better understand how Odin quantitatively impacts job performance.

While Odin leverages standard Machine Learning algorithms to perform its analysis, there are many additional topic and sentiments analysis libraries on the "bleeding edge." As Odin development continues and expands, we aim to continue to integrate more advanced APIs and techniques or sentiment analysis (taking sentence context into account), keyword extraction (with n-gram phrases and Named Entity Recognition) and topic modeling (combining supervised and unsupervised techniques). As stated above, however, participants' initial reaction to Odin's performance was quite good.

Lastly, another direction of future work would be the inclusion of social aspects of corpus reading as suggested by many of our participants. While Odin focuses on the written corpus itself to weight rankings, we wish to explore how we can integrate user's view habits into the algorithm to "bubble up" popular articles and opinions. Further, we wish to explore taking source "credibility" into the algorithm's weight. Whether the source is the enterprise hierarchy of the author, or the veracity of the journal/author from more public domains, we believe source can play a powerful role.

CONCLUSION

The digital age has resulted in increased informational awareness, which has caused a growing scarcity of human time and attention. This problem is exacerbated by the growing ubiquity of mobile devices as a major information consumption platform, in that they have smaller screen real-estate and mobile device users have far less time to consume content. In this paper we presented Odin, a fundamentally new approach to mitigating information overflow by creating an algorithm and mobile UI that allows a user to view a corpus from three distinct perspectives; Relevance, Alignment and Divergence. Thus, rather than simply seeing a summary of a corpus keywords, Odin lets a user quickly access key opinions and documents by their relation to the corpus' conscious. Odin is fundamentally a different approach from the standard summarization, topic modeling, or sentiment analysis, and is deeply grounded in a breadth of literature from many disciplines. Two user studies provide strong support for the quality and utility of a system like Odin within real-world scenarios. Thus, the foremost contribution of this work is an interaction model and algorithmic approach that allows users to place each document and opinion within the larger corpus of opinions while "on the go."

REFERENCES

1. E. Adar and B. A. Huberman. The economics of surfing. *Quarterly Journal of Electronic Commerce*, 2000.
2. F. Ahmed, Y. Borodin, A. Soviak, M. Islam, I. V. Ramakrishnan, and T. Hedgpeth. Accessible skimming: faster screen reading of web pages. In *UIST '12*. ACM Request Permissions, Oct. 2012.

3. N. Archak, A. Ghose, and P. G. Ipeirotis. Show me the money!: deriving the pricing power of product features by mining consumer reviews. In *KDD '07*. ACM Request Permissions, Aug. 2007.
4. S. Baccianella, A. Esuli, and F. Sebastiani. Sentiwordnet 3.0: An enhanced lexical resource for sentiment analysis and opinion mining. In *Proceedings of the 7th Conference on Language Resources and Evaluation*, 2010.
5. A. Bangor, P. Kortum, and J. Miller. Determining what individual SUS scores mean: Adding an adjective rating scale. *Journal of usability studies*, 2009.
6. P. Baudisch, B. Lee, and L. Hanna. Fishnet, a fisheye web browser with search term popouts: a comparative evaluation with overview and linear view. In *AVI '04: Proceedings of the working conference on Advanced visual interfaces*. ACM, May 2004.
7. D. Billsus, D. M. Hilbert, and D. Maynes-Aminzade. Improving proactive information systems. In *the 10th international conference*, pages 159–166, New York, New York, USA, 2005. ACM Press.
8. J. Brooke. SUS-A quick and dirty usability scale. *Usability evaluation in industry*, 1996.
9. A. J. B. Brush, D. Bargeron, A. Gupta, and J. J. Cadiz. Robust Annotation Positioning in Digital Documents . In *the SIGCHI conference*, pages 285–292, New York, New York, USA, 2001. ACM Press.
10. G. Carenini, R. T. Ng, and A. Pauls. Interactive Multimedia Summaries of Evaluative Text . In *the 11th International Conference*, page 124, New York, New York, USA, 2006. ACM Press.
11. M. Chakravarthy and P. Ciravegna. Cross-media document annotation and enrichment. 2006.
12. Y. Cui and V. Roto. How people use the web on mobile devices. In *WWW '08*. ACM, Apr. 2008.
13. S. Davies, S. Allen, J. Raphaelson, E. Meng, J. Engleman, R. King, and C. Lewis. Popcorn: the personal knowledge base. In *the 6th ACM conference*, pages 150–159, New York, New York, USA, 2006. ACM Press.
14. M. C. De Marneffe and B. MacCartney. Generating typed dependency parses from phrase structure parses. In *Proceedings of LREC '06*, 2006.
15. J. R. Finkel, T. Grenager, and C. Manning. Incorporating non-local information into information extraction systems by gibbs sampling. *ACL'05*, 2005.
16. K. A. Ganesan, N. Sundaresan, and H. Deo. Mining tag clouds and emoticons behind community feedback. In *WWW '08*. ACM, Apr. 2008.
17. V. Giller, R. Melcher, J. Schrammel, R. Sefelin, and M. Tscheligi. *Usability Evaluations for Multi-device Application Development Three Example Studies*, volume 2795 of *Verena Giller, Rudolf Melcher, Johann Schrammel, Reinhard Sefelin and Manfred Tscheligi*. Lecture Notes in Computer Science, Berlin, Heidelberg, 2003.
18. J. Hailpern and B. A. Huberman. Echo: the editor's wisdom with the elegance of a magazine. In *EICS '13: Proceedings of the 5th ACM SIGCHI symposium on Engineering interactive computing systems*. ACM Request Permissions, June 2013.
19. M. J. Halvey and M. T. Keane. An Assessment of Tag Presentation Techniques . In *the 16th international conference*, page 1313, New York, New York, USA, 2007. ACM Press.
20. M. A. Hearst. User interfaces and visualization. *Modern information retrieval*, 1999.
21. M. A. Hearst and D. Rosner. Tag clouds: Data analysis tool or social signaller? *... on System Sciences*, 2008.
22. J. Huang, O. Etzioni, L. Zettlemoyer, K. Clark, and C. Lee. RevMiner: an extractive interface for navigating reviews on a smartphone. In *UIST '12*. ACM Request Permissions, Oct. 2012.
23. B. A. Huberman and F. Wu. The economics of attention: Maximizing user value in information-rich environments. *Advances in Complex Systems*, 2008.
24. B. Kim and B. Aeschliman. Experimental assessment of a visual interface designed for web documents on mobile devices. *ICCIT 2011*, pages 231–236, 2011.
25. T. Kriplean, J. Morgan, D. Freelon, A. Borning, and L. Bennett. Supporting reflective public thought with considerit. In *CSCW '12*. ACM Request Permissions, Feb. 2012.
26. B. Y.-L. Kuo, T. Hentrich, B. M. Good, and M. D. Wilkinson. Tag clouds for summarizing web search results. In *the 16th international conference*. ACM, May 2007.
27. S. E. Lee, T. Chun, and S. S. Han. Using Qtag to Extract Dominant Public Opinion in Very Large-Scale Conversation. In *2009 International Conference on Computational Science and Engineering*, pages 753–758. IEEE, 2009.
28. S. E. Lee, D. K. Son, and S. S. Han. Qtag: tagging as a means of rating, opinion-expressing, sharing and visualizing. In *SIGDOC '07*. ACM Request Permissions, Oct. 2007.
29. B. Liu, M. Hu, and J. Cheng. Opinion observer: analyzing and comparing opinions on the Web. In *the 14th international conference*, page 342, New York, New York, USA, 2005. ACM Press.
30. A. K. McCallum. Mallet: A machine learning for language toolkit. 2002.
31. K. O'Hara and A. Sellen. A Comparison of Reading Paper and On-Line Documents. In *the SIGCHI conference*, pages 335–342, New York, New York, USA, 1997. ACM Press.
32. J. Otterbacher, D. Radev, and O. Kareem. News to go: hierarchical text summarization for mobile devices. In *SIGIR '06*, 2006.
33. B. Pang and L. Lee. Opinion Mining and Sentiment Analysis. *Foundations and Trends in Information Retrieval*, 2(1-2), Jan. 2008.
34. S. Park, M. Ko, J. Kim, and H. Choi. NewsCube2. 0: An Exploratory Design of a Social News Website for Media Bias Mitigation. In *Workshop on Social Recommender Systems*, Mar. 2011.
35. A. W. Rivadeneira, D. M. Gruen, M. J. Muller, and D. R. Millen. Getting our head in the clouds: toward evaluation studies of tagclouds. In *CHI '07: Proceedings of the SIGCHI conference on Human factors in computing systems*. ACM Request Permissions, Apr. 2007.
36. B. Sereno, S. B. Shum, and E. Motta. ClaimSpotter: an environment to support sensemaking with knowledge triples. In *the 10th international conference*. ACM Request Permissions, Jan. 2005.
37. S. Shrestha. Mobile Web Browsing: Usability Study. In *the 4th international conference on mobile technology, applications, and systems and the 1st international symposium*, page 187, New York, New York, USA, 2007. ACM Press.
38. H. A. Simon. Designing organizations for an information-rich world. *Computers, Communication, and the Public Interest*, (The Johns Hopkins Press), 1969.
39. B. Suh, A. Woodruff, R. Rosenholtz, and A. Glass. Popout prism: adding perceptual principles to overview+detail document interfaces. In *CHI '02: Proceedings of the SIGCHI conference on Human factors in computing systems: Changing our world, changing ourselves*. ACM Request Permissions, Apr. 2002.
40. J.-T. Sun, X. Wang, D. Shen, H.-J. Zeng, and Z. Chen. CWS: a comparative web search system. In *WWW '06*. ACM, May 2006.
41. The Stanford Natural Language Processing Group. Stanford CoreNLP.
42. T. Weninger, W. H. Hsu, and J. Han. CETR: content extraction via tag ratios. *WWW 2010*, 2010.
43. X. Xie, G. Miao, R. Song, J.-R. Wen, and W.-Y. Ma. Efficient Browsing of Web Search Results on Mobile Devices Based on Block Importance Model. In *PERCOM '05*. IEEE Computer Society, Mar. 2005.
44. K. Yatani, M. Novati, A. Trusty, and K. N. Truong. Review Spotlight: A User Interface for Summarizing User-generated Reviews Using Adjective-Noun Word Pairs . In *the 2011 annual conference*, page 1541, New York, New York, USA, 2011. ACM Press.
45. X. Yin and W. S. Lee. Using link analysis to improve layout on mobile devices. In *WWW '04*. ACM, May 2004.

Monadic Exploration: Seeing the Whole Through Its Parts

Marian Dörk
Potsdam University of
Applied Sciences, Germany
doerk@fh-potsdam.de

Rob Comber
Culture Lab, School of
Computing Science,
Newcastle University, UK
robert.comber@ncl.ac.uk

Martyn Dade-Robertson
School of Architecture
Planning & Landscape,
Newcastle University, UK
martyn.dade-robertson@ncl.ac.uk

ABSTRACT
Monadic exploration is a new approach to interacting with relational information spaces that challenges the distinction between the whole and its parts. Building on the work of sociologists Gabriel Tarde and Bruno Latour we turn to the concept of the monad as a useful lens on online communities and collections that expands the possibility for creating meaning in their navigation. While existing interfaces tend to emphasize either the structure of the whole or details of a part, monadic exploration brings these opposing perspectives closer together in continuous movements between partially overlapping points of view. We present a visualization that reflects a given node's relative position within a network using radial displacements and visual folding. To investigate the potential of monadic exploration we report on an iterative design process of a web-based visualization of a highly cross-referenced book and its six-month deployment.

Author Keywords
Information seeking; exploratory search; philosophy; theory; information visualization; network visualization.

ACM Classification Keywords
H.5 Information Interfaces & Presentation

INTRODUCTION

> *"A monad is not a part of a whole, but a point of view on all the entities taken severally and not as a totality."*
> – Bruno Latour et al. [14]

There is increasing prevalence of large, relational data sets in the everyday practices of individuals. Most prominently, people are interacting with large-scale social data in the form of social network sites, and vast media collections such as photo archives, library catalogs, and blogs. With such data sets people are often interested in the content of particular elements as well as the entirety of elements as a whole. For instance, one might want to look at both a specific friend's profile page, while also gaining some idea of who their friends are. Or one might read an individual post and then wish to see how it relates and resonates within a community.

CHI 2014, April 26–May 1, 2014, Toronto, Ontario, Canada.

http://dx.doi.org/10.1145/2556288.2557083

As digitisation proceeds further we witness the popularisation of interconnected data sets and the desire to afford new modes of navigation to make sense of them. In this paper we explore a type of interaction with relational information spaces, which incorporates both the individual and the whole. We aim to harness the rich connections embedded in collections to devise new methods for moving along linked elements.

Some recent efforts in graph visualization defy the long-standing overview-first dogma in favor of filtered and local perspectives [10, 20]. These developments correspond to recent sociology theory promoting the part over the whole, as a richer and more nuanced view on social networks [14]. Our work here follows these lines of research in visualization and sociology and explores how information spaces can be navigated along individual entities in the context of their collection. We are inspired by the concept of the *monad*, which offers a relational perspective on the world by shifting emphasis from aggregation of the whole to movement among particular points of view [14, 17]. In fact, Bruno Latour explicitly challenged the CHI community to develop interfaces that support the visualization and navigation of monads [13].

This paper introduces *monadic exploration* as a new way of navigating relational information spaces. We propose three basic principles of the monadic perspective—having, difference, and movement—to inspire a new class of visual interfaces for exploring collections. The monadic perspective brings the contradictory representations of individual elements and entire collections closer together and suggests continuous movements between partially overlapping vantage points. Based on these ideas, we present a visualization that uses search queries or element selections to provide unique perspectives on the network through radial displacements and visual folding. We applied this visualization technique to a highly cross-referenced book and deployed it for a six-months period on the Web. We report on the largely positive feedback and discuss future directions for research and design.

VISUALIZING NETWORKS AND COLLECTIONS

Visualizations have played a significant role in the analysis of social networks. Starting from manual drawings of 'sociograms', there has been a gradual movement towards computer-supported methods for graph layouts [7]. The main aim of such visualizations has been to analyse the structure of networks, and secondarily to communicate derived understandings. Some efforts focused on graph visualization for more casual audiences, for example, by encouraging the playful exploration of one's own friend networks [10].

A range of alternative visualizations have been developed that provide different perspectives on networks and support various types of analyses. For example, node properties can be aggregated into higher-level representations thus allowing for a meta analysis of connection patterns [22]. Graphs can also be summarized by histograms representing facet distributions across neighborhoods and graph-theoretical qualities such as node and edge specific metrics to characterize and compare large networks [12]. A hybrid representation between node-link diagrams and matrices has been shown to support the analysis of local communities as well as global structure [11]. However, most network visualizations tend to provide a global perspective on a graph by attempting to represent it in its entirety or aggregating its nodes and edges based on their properties. Such global approaches can make it difficult to discern relations among particular nodes and neighborhoods.

In contrast to the emphasis on high-level views on networks, there has been some work favoring more local perspectives. Without requiring a global view, egocentric networks around particular nodes can support the analysis of, for example, group communication patterns and people's social roles [6]. In the context of online communities, it has been shown that 'starting with what you know' can serve as a more useful approach [10] than the established principle of 'overview first' [16]. When dealing with particularly large networks, search relevance can be used to initially establish a partial context and then expand the visualization from there [20]. While emphasizing individual nodes and their neighbors, local views lack the wider context of the network and thus can make it difficult to connect the part back to the whole.

The tension between global and local views relates to a long-standing research effort on focus+context visualization [2]. For example, radial graph layouts arrange a focus node at the center and connected nodes as context into concentric circles, e.g. [26]. The visualization we will introduce also features a circular layout, but integrates keyword search with the exploration of collection elements. Our work extends prior work on focus+context techniques to exploratory information seeking involving both search and navigation in rich collections.

Information visualizations are increasingly used to support the visual exploration of rich collections. This development coincides with a growing interest in more exploratory forms of information seeking without specific information needs, but rather a more open-ended desire to learn, play, and discover [15, 25]. Such positive and exploratory information practices have been conceptualized using the analogy of the flaneur curiously strolling through streets and experientially making sense of a city [4]. To foster such forms of serendipitous information seeking and spawn interest in collections, visualizations can offer unconventional and inviting views [18]. Presenting faceted relations as visual paths and connecting interface states through transitions can support lateral movements through interconnected collections [5]. Continuing these efforts in visualization and building on the concept of the monad, we will develop an approach to information exploration that takes search queries and particular elements as vantage points onto a collection.

TARDE'S MONADOLOGY

> *"Each monad draws the world to itself,*
> *and thus has a better grasp of itself."*
> – Gabriel Tarde [17]

The people and artifacts in our lives define us, just as our relationships to them alter the meanings we ascribe to them. Friendships, interests, and professions are rich sources for understanding ourselves as well as our social and material environment. Such a relational perspective on the world coincides with a growing prevalence of richly interconnected information spaces on the Web such as social networks and media-sharing communities. However, this growing relational embeddedness of digital resources is still neglected by the interfaces used to navigate such collections. While each entity in these informations spaces, e.g., a person or a photo, is connected with many other entities, the existing interfaces downplay the rich interconnectedness that is becoming increasingly prevalent. To conceptualize the relational aspects of data sets and conceive new methods for interacting with them we draw from work in sociology.

Resembling the tension between global and local views on networks, there has been a struggle between the macro and micro scale in social science since its earliest days [14]. The social network model has grown as an analytic lens among social scientists as a means to study the structure of society [21], due in part to the widespread public use of social network sites. While social network sites are used in diverse ways, the underlying social network model and its representation as web-based interface provide only limited mechanisms for individual meaning making in navigation. The social network model tends to flatten relations, assuming them to be univariate and mutual [3]. Although social networks describe complex relations among individuals, they do not represent the richness of those ties. Moreover, as these social ties are decontextualized from the relational world in which they exist, they potentially further reduce the meaningful history of a relationship. Such reductions result in a top-down model of society, in the form of a highly abstract network—resembling the reductions that most visualization techniques rely on to provide overviews of large data sets.

While ostensibly operating at the global level, in-grained in this perspective is an assumption that the individual, as a fundamental social unit, has also changed [23]. Such 'networked individualism' asks the individual to become devolved from their context to preserve the value of a dispersed network (for instance in the actualization of social capital). It is thus argued that the social network profile, together with its many counterpart fragments across various social media channels, gives rise to the isolation of the individual from its context. In the case of the individual human actor, it is argued that online social networks change who we are as individuals because they allow us to deliberately write ourselves into being across distributed spaces [19], configuring local networks in global contexts. In contrast, we do not argue that individuals are isolated from each other, in fact, the opposite effect is often possible, but rather that the network model reinforces a dichotomy of the local and global, the part and the whole.

Among those scholars who resist this dichotomization, such as Tarde, Bahktin, Simmel, Elias, and Latour, a relational worldview is espoused. In this text, we follow this argument as forwarded by Tarde [17] and, later, Latour et al. [14], to rethink the exploration of information spaces. We agree that the dichotomy of element and aggregate is unnecessary and unfounded, and that alternative theoretical accounts of the social world might be better founded on the relationships between those elements. This is the perspective put forward by Gabriel Tarde in his text 'Monadology and Sociology' [17]. Drawing on Lorenc's reading of Tarde [17], we identify three principles of monadology, which can positively contribute to the study and design of novel exploration interfaces.

On Having, Not Being

Tarde sees a monad as an element's own relational perspective onto the world—whether social or physical. The notion of the element and the characterization of the world as fundamentally relational can be seen in Tarde's appeal to the Newtonian principle of reciprocal action: as each monad exerts its influence upon another, it is equally influenced by that other. Thus any attribute (reiterating the Newtonian link, we could consider weight) is defined by the relation (i.e., gravity) between elements, and not by the a priori being of the entity. He posits that the essential qualities of an entity is not that of 'being', but of 'having'. Specific attributes then are those belonging to an entity, but to which, conversely, the entity also belongs. For instance, the monad of 'me' has the attribute 'academic', while the monad 'academic' has 'me'.

Having suggests the primacy of relational aspects embedded in collections. Therefore each element should be understood as an entity mainly in so much as it has relations to other entities. For example, a photo meaningfully exists insofar as it relates to people, places, and events. Furthermore, we might also suggest that all elements have relations to all other elements, even when a relation is of total difference. In this way, a monadic interface represents the social world of an information space by visualizing the varying relations among the elements of a collection. While, this principle prioritizes the relations among elements, it does not preclude the use of individual properties of elements such as color or size.

The Essential Difference

Central to Tarde's monadology is the argument that the element takes precedence over the aggregate. There is a critical point in this assertion, namely that difference is pivotal in the construction of monads. The monad is defined by its particular perspective on its world, which is defined by the unique relations to others. The monadic perspective then is dependent on the extent to which each monad is expended in the constituting monads of the others. Thus each monad is defined by the overlapping spheres of monadic influence of others. Given that monads are not mutually exclusive (elements can contain shared characteristics), we can assume that two monads that occupy fully identical spaces are, in fact, the same monad. By extension, the way in which we understand a monad is not in its similarity, but difference to others. Therefore, while a monad may exert influence over other monads, it must do so without itself becoming extinguished in the other—it must retain difference.

Difference as the second defining feature of an element should be recognized within the information space. In contrast to a focus on similarity among elements (e.g., products in online shops), a monadic perspective emphasizes an element's distinguishing qualities. In line with 'having', difference is not an a priori property of the element but its unique position in the world. We propose therefore that each element must stamp its particular identity on the relational world, which is its own monad. That is, the difference of the element must be conveyed by taking the monad's perspective on the world.

Meaning in Movement

The principles of having and difference construe the monad as a unique perspective onto the world achieved through the relations with other entities. However, the monad's perspective on the world is not simply inscribed by mechanistic laws. Tarde stresses that a monad is not a configuration of static relations, but rather a highly dynamic and contingent arrangement. This is a fundamental break away from the structuralist perspective of many of Tarde's contemporaries (and those who followed them). For him, this is a significant consideration for sociology, as it is equally for us with regard to information exploration: in what way can we understand the whole through the dynamic relations among the parts? Tarde is joined in this concern by many others, most notably Simmel. As Frisby reiterates Simmel, the question of understanding the whole (famously 'What is Society?') is reliant on exploring "all those modes and forces of association which unites its elements" [8]. How can we make these forces of association in collections visible? This question corresponds to Latour et al.'s challenge "to account for longer lasting features of social order by learning to navigate through overlapping 'monads'" [14]. This emphasis on navigation ascribes a unique role to movement as a way to experience the relations and differences among elements.

Movement suggests a way of making sense of an information space by navigating along elements as overlapping monads. While the principles of having and difference highlight the relational quality of an element's unique position in an information space, the principle of movement relates to the dynamic quality of an element and the potential of exploration as a form of interpretative sense-making. The movement between monads should serve as a meaningful proxy for the viewer's movement through an information space. The principle of movement is an invitation to explicitly consider the purpose of animation to support exploration.

Taking the principles of having, difference, and movement together, we propose *monadic exploration* as a way to make sense of the relationships among entities exerting their influences throughout an information space. Monadic exploration is, therefore, the meaning-making movement between overlapping vantage points in a relational world.

DESIGNING FOR MONADIC EXPLORATION

A monadic perspective suggests an approach to relational information spaces that promises new types of explorations. To substantiate this approach, we have undertaken an iterative design process that started with above elaborations about monads, continued with more practical considerations about design goals for an interface, and finally led to a prototype. In parallel, we engaged with a community behind a particular information space that provided us with the opportunity to get feedback and a sense for the potential for monadic exploration. While we envision a wide range of interfaces to be based on the idea of monadic exploration, we present here one initial design that serves as a concrete example. This design is not the only or necessary one, but it is explicitly intended for monadic exploration of a densely interconnected information space. In this section we focus on the decisions behind the design of the visual interface. In the subsequent section, we describe the findings from the case study of a highly cross-referenced book and its six-month deployment.

From Profiles and Graphs to Monads

The dichotomy between micro and macro in the social sciences finds resemblance in the contrast between profile pages and graph visualizations of social networks. The typical structure of a profile page can be found on almost any web-based information space far beyond social network sites. While a few related entities are displayed on a given page, revealing the relationships among other entities and the rest of the information space requires conventional navigation from one page to the next. In contrast to profiles, a graph visualization represents the whole network typically using a globally optimized graph-drawing algorithm. To convey higher-level structures in a network, graph visualizations tend to diminish the individual differences between nodes and their particular relations among each other.

Considering the monadic principles developed in the previous section, it becomes apparent how neither profiles nor graphs facilitate the movement between elements to discern their differences and explore their influence on the collection. The profile focuses on the individual details of one node without much consideration of the larger context and a graph portrays the abstract structure of an entire network neglecting the richness of individual elements at the node level.

We seek to find a way to retain the individual and relational aspects of elements when representing an interconnected information space. To support monadic exploration, we aim to design a visualization of elements as both vantage and navigation points providing both nuanced perspectives on and inviting gateways through relational information spaces. Based on this general aim and the principles of having, difference, and movement, we posit these design goals:

Offer elastic layout. Visual arrangements of a collection should portray both subtle and marked differences in relations among elements. Based on the explorer's steps, the layout should fold and stretch as elements shrink, expand, and move.

Reveal differences. During the exploration of the collection the variation of attraction among elements should be represented as animated transition of positions, opacities, and labels. The resulting movements should convey difference.

Integrate navigation and search. The explorer should be able to shift between different forms of information seeking. Both open-ended navigation and more targeted keyword search should be supported within the same visual arrangement.

Representation: Taking a Monadic View

We first discuss the representational considerations for a monadic visualization of a relational information space. The premise is that elements have some relationships among each other, feature textual and/or visual attributes, and can have a type to distinguish, for example, between people and artifacts.

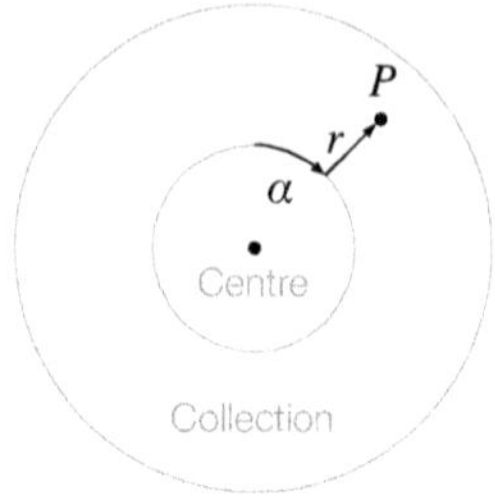

Figure 1. A monad has a search query or an element selection at its center and a circular arrangement of a collection's elements around it.

A Monad As a Circular Layout

We define a *monad* as the visual arrangement of a collection around the explorer's interest that is manifested at the center of the monad and expressed either as a search query or an element selection. We adopt a polar coordinate system to negotiate the overall structure of a whole with the differences among the parts. As shown in Figure 1, an element is positioned at point P with angular coordinate α encoding any collection-wide ordering (e.g., by type or name) and radial coordinate r being inversely proportional to the search relevance or the attraction strength to the selected element.

By using a combination of node specific and collection wide encodings for position, the monad has both dynamic as well as stable qualities. In this sense, the monad offers an elastic lens, which dynamically draws the elements to the center or pushes them towards the periphery within a stable structure of a global ordering around the circle. The radial movements of elements only represent changes in attraction, making the movement a meaningful visual variable to discern difference.

Subtle Attractions

The radial coordinate is intended to convey likely interestingness of a given element based on its relationship to an explorer's search query or element selection. The effect is that the more relevant an element is, the closer it gets positioned towards the center than those that are less relevant. Search relevance can be computed, for example, by counting the occurrences of the query across each element's text fields (e.g., title, teaser, and text). A more robust technique is tf–idf, a common measure used in information retrieval to determine how relevant a result is for a given set of search terms; if one of the terms is more common in the collection than the others it will contribute less in the overall ranking.

Besides a search query, an element itself can be the basis for determining the possible interestingness of each element in a collection. For this we assume that a direct connection between the selected element and another element in the collection is an indicator for attraction. However, a connection between nodes is binary and does not account for the dense pathways contained in interconnected information spaces.

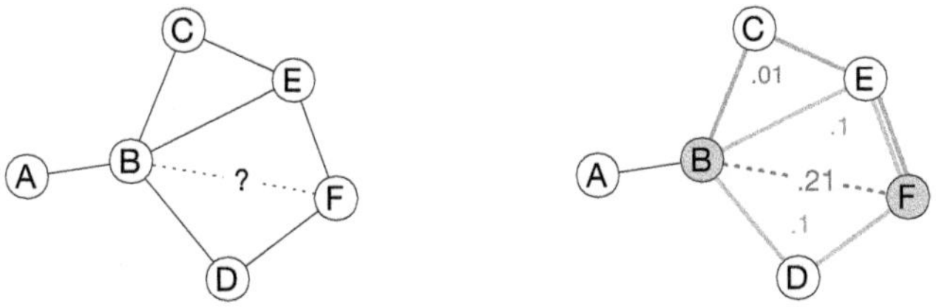

	A	B	C	D	E	F
A		1	0	0	0	0
B	1		1	1	1	0
C	0	1		0	1	0
D	0	1	0		0	1
E	0	1	1	0		1
F	0	0	0	1	1	

Adjacency matrix

→

	A	B	C	D	E	F
A		1	.11	.1	.11	.02
B	1		1.1	1.01	1.11	.21
C	.11	1.1		.11	1	.11
D	.1	1.01	.11		.21	1.01
E	.11	1.11	1	.21		1.01
F	.02	.21	.11	1.01	1.01	

Attraction matrix

Figure 2. Both direct and indirect connections contribute to the relationship between nodes. Based on the information from the adjacency matrix, the attraction matrix captures more nuanced relationships.

To get a more nuanced sense of relationship between two nodes we can additionally consider the indirect connections between them. Consider the graph depicted in the top left of Figure 2. There may be no direct link between B and F, however, there are three paths via C, D and E that suggest an implicit attraction nevertheless (top right). To consider a more nuanced indication of attraction between elements, we include indirect paths between elements in addition to direct links. The attraction score $A_{I,J}$ between two nodes I and J then corresponds to the weighted sum of paths p_i:

$$A_{I,J} = p_1 + w_2 \cdot p_2 + w_3 \cdot p_3$$

with p_1 equal 1 if directly linked, otherwise 0, p_2 and p_3 as the number of two-hop and three-hop paths, and w_2 and w_3 as weights (through iterative refinement we settled with 0.1 and 0.01). Given a binary adjacency matrix we can calculate an attraction matrix containing the strength of attraction for each pair of nodes (see Figure 2, bottom). We assume that edge weights equal 1; this can be adapted to account for weighted edges by introducing additional weights for each summand.

When there is neither an active search query nor element selection, the displacement of elements is based on a node's degree, i.e., number of direct connections, as a straightforward measure of centrality. Node degree serves as a proxy for potential interest inviting the explorer to select an element without having to enter a search query to see some elements.

Dots and Labels

Labeling is a computationally complex challenge in visualization, especially when displaying many elements. We address this problem in two ways: 1) only elements with relatively high attraction scores are labeled, and 2) labels are displayed in radial arrangements around the circular layout around which each element has a dedicated segment. The only time label overlaps occur is when two similarly relevant elements are neighbors in the circular ordering. Using the mouse pointer one can clarify and read them individually.

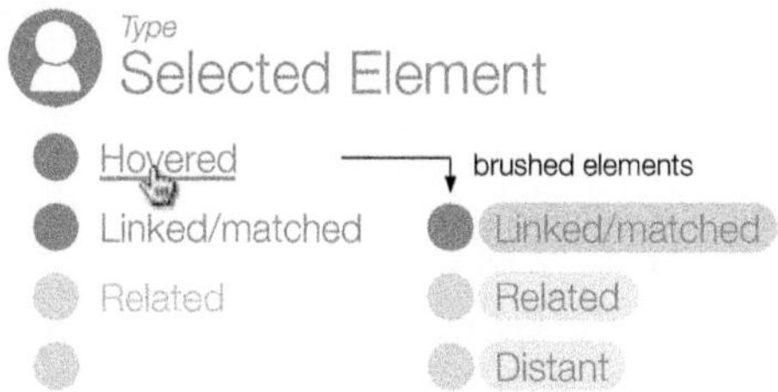

Figure 3. An illustration of the varying visual appearances of elements according to their attraction value as well as interaction state. If an element is directly connected with the hovered element, a brighter tone of the element's dot color is added as a background behind its label.

Elements are displayed as a dot and optional label. As illustrated in Figure 3, the visual appearance of dots and labels is varied to reflect different relationships and interaction states. There are two types of relationships to convey: adjacency as the binary relationship of having a direct connection, and attraction as the more nuanced relationship based on direct and indirect paths or search relevance. The attraction values are already encoded by an element's position using the circular layout discussed above. Position allows for the discernment of smaller differences that is adequate to represent more nuanced differences in attraction. The binary connectivity is conveyed by the opacity and therefore darkness of the dot and label: linked elements are displayed significantly darker. Similarly for search, if an element has at least one occurrence, the element is drawn darker. There are only two levels of opacity used for the dots, making the visual discrimination between these two effortless.

An element's label is simply the title of the represented entity, e.g., the name of a person or the title of an article. Labels are placed facing towards the outside of the display, and rotated according to the angular coordinate used for element placement. Similar to how the dot's opacity varies, the label is shown only in full opacity for elements that have either a direct connection with the activated element or are matched against the search query. If the attraction value is weaker the label is shown either with reduced opacity or not at all—depending on the number of displayed elements.

The color used for the dot and label denotes the type of that element. While distinguishing elements by color is optional, it can help to discern the distribution of element types in a heterogenous information space. However, considering the perceptually limited discriminatory power of color, we suggest to use it when the number of types is lower than ten. The size of the dot represents the element's degree, that is the number of connections to other elements in the collection.

When an element is selected as the center of the monad, its dot and label move into the middle of the visualization and are increased in the respective sizes. Within the dot a symbol is embedded indicating the element's type. Below symbol and title, a brief description and an optional figure is displayed providing more detail for that element. Displaying elements as circles of varying sizes allows for non-disruptive transitions between these different states. Together with the selection of colors and fonts, the symbols can be used to reflect the aesthetic identity of a given collection.

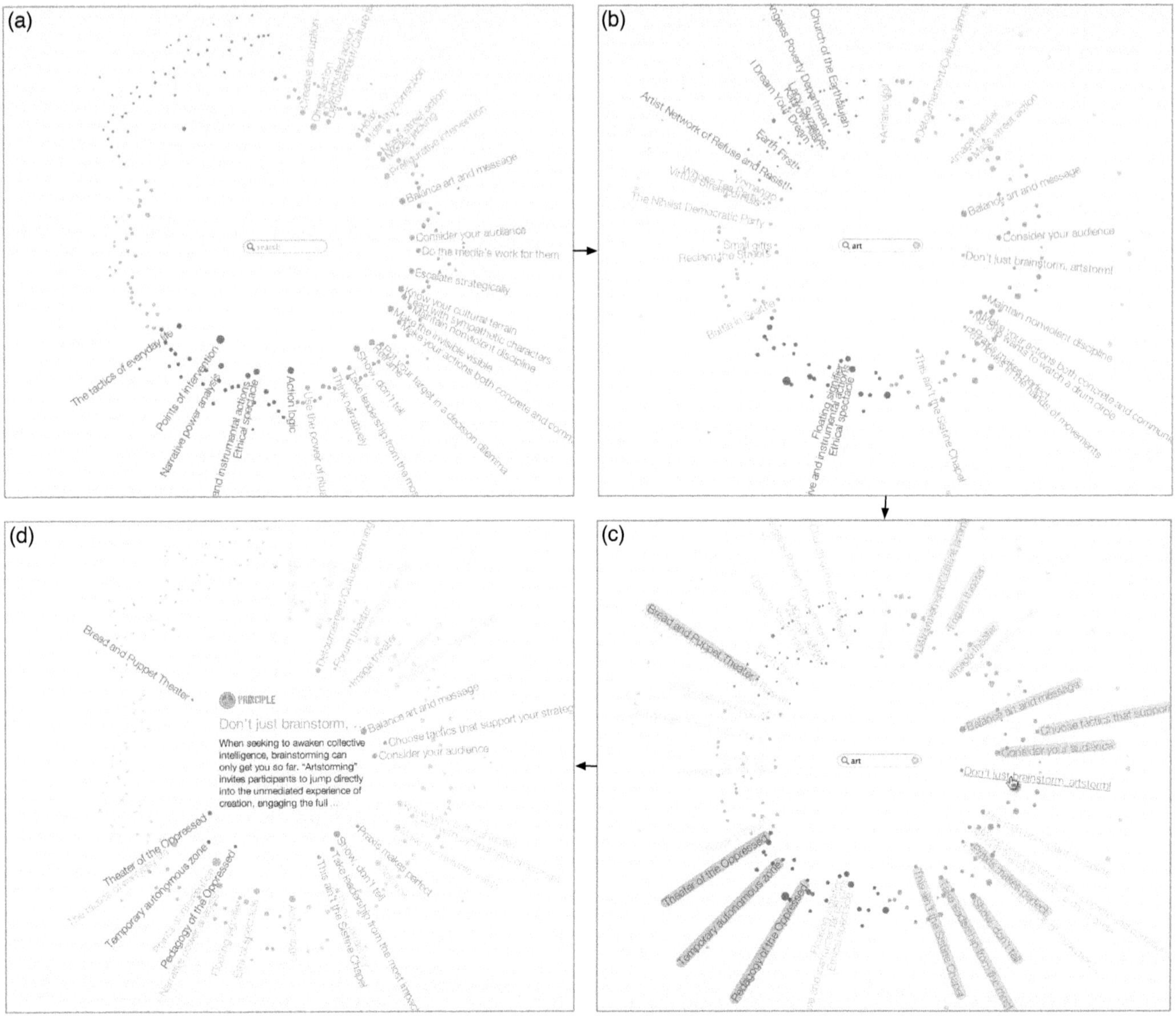

Figure 4. From views based on (a) node degree and (b) search relevance to (c) hover highlights and (d) selection of a specific node as the monad.

Interaction: Moving Between Monads

The visualization supports three basic types of interaction: search, hover, and select. The intention behind offering these three interaction methods is to allow for targeted, provisional, and exploratory movements through a collection. The search allows the formulation of a query based on an existing interest, while the hover function lets one peek around without changing the layout; by selecting an element one can navigate through a collection along its elements. When a person opens the visualization with no active element, the elements are placed around the circular layout based on their node degrees (see Figure 4, top left). Highly connected elements are positioned closer to the center and are displayed with a label in contrast to less connected elements that are arranged towards the outside with no label shown. At this point the viewer can decide to either enter a search query or hover over any of the displayed nodes.

Search

When no element is selected, the search box is placed into the center. Once a few letters are entered, elements are moved according to their relevance scores (see Figure 4, top right). As the query changes, elements move in or outward and reveal or hide labels to reflect the changing relevance scores. The effect is that the person entering a query can get a general sense of the impact that query changes have by seeing the movements toward and away from the center in the immediate visual periphery of the search box. While many search interfaces already offer query suggestions or display results while a query is being entered, query changes lead to abrupt display changes. In contrast, changing the query in the monad does not disrupt the overall organization of the visualization. Instead, elements either get gradually expanded and pulled in when they become more relevant, or if not, they are gradually folded and pushed towards the outside.

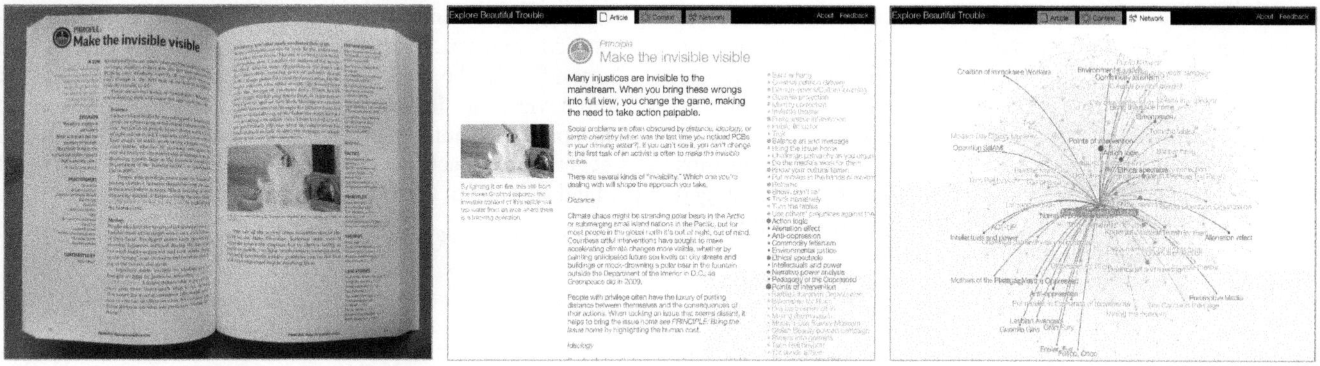

Figure 5. A book on creative activism (left) is used as a case study for monadic visualization. The interface represents the book's contents using a monadic Context view (see Figures 4) and additionally as Article (middle) and Network (right) views.

Hover

Moving the mouse pointer over any element shows how it relates to other elements (see Figure 4, bottom right). Regardless whether a search query is active or an element has been selected, hovering over dot or label of an element highlights connected elements of that hovered element (foreshadowing which elements move closer when clicked). The hovering function allows the viewer to inspect whether two elements share an element as a neighbor. On the flip-side, it is possible to discern which elements are neighbors of the hovered element, but not of the centered element by looking for those highlighted elements with brighter dots. Furthermore, if an element's label is not shown (due to a low attraction value), hovering over its dot reveals the label. Thus one can deviate from the emphasized elements in the center and investigate peripheral elements that differ from a search or selection.

Select

Clicking on any element turns it into the current selection of the monad (see Figure 4, bottom left). If there is an active search or a selected element, it is replaced by the element. The dot and label increase in size and move into the center. Below the label is a description of the active element. As a new active element changes the relative attraction values of the other elements they will gradually move and adjust their opacity. During this transition the hover highlights remain visible allowing the viewer to follow elements that are linked with the newly selected element. After the moving transition is over, the hover highlights eventually fade out.

CASE STUDY: BEAUTIFUL TROUBLE

To better understand the potential of monadic exploration we used the book 'Beautiful Trouble: A Toolbox For Revolution' [1] as a case study. Being highly cross-referenced, the book serves as an intriguing example of a relational information space. This book is also a particularly interesting dataset for our purpose here, because of the interest and passion that the editors and readers have for the subject matter. To contrast the use of the monadic perspective with established representations, we created an interface that also offered profile and graph views on the book's contents. In collaboration with the team behind the book, we deployed the interface for six months on the book's official website and invited readers to explore the book's contents with it.

Setup and Interface Design

The book contains 194 modules about creative forms of protest and civic engagement. The modules are categorized into five types: tactics, principles, theories, case studies, and practitioners. In total, there are 1938 references linking related modules; in the book these references are shown on the margins of the pages (see Figure 5, left). The references turn the book into a densely interlinked information space. To integrate the visual design of the interface with the book, we adopted the same color scheme from the website and used the same symbols representing the module types.

The interface used for the deployment had three views: Context, Article, and Network. The *Context* view is the visualization discussed in the previous section. The *Article* view approximately resembles the display of many information spaces on the Web, such as posts on blogs or profile pages in online communities (see Figure 5, middle). The purpose of the Article view is to show great detail about an entity, allow for its close examination, and provide links to related pages. While there are many ways of visualizing networks, most network visualizations use force-directed algorithms and display all edges among nodes. The aim with the *Network* view was to provide one such perspective on the interconnections among modules (see Figure 5, right). The Network view uses the Fruchterman-Reingold layout [9] as is provided by the network visualization environment Gephi. Curved edges among nodes are shown in faint shades of grey, except for the selected element whose edges are displayed in dark tones of the element's color. Node labels are only shown for the selected element and directly connected neighbors.

Each of these three views provides a different perspective on the book's contents emphasizing different aspects and granularities. We integrated these three views into the same interface to allow for a close consideration of these distinct, yet related perspectives. The rationale behind this was not to illustrate the superiority of one of these views over another (admittedly we focused our design on the Context view), but rather to contrast typical ways of displaying relational information spaces with a view designed towards monadic exploration. By juxtaposing these views in one interface we can compare how they are used and received, and think how the experience differs between the three approaches.

The visual design and interactivity is integrated across the different views. The interface has a tab for each view on the top indicating which is active and allowing the viewer to switch modes, which results in an animated transition moving elements to their new positions in the respective layout. The intention behind this integration is to see the relationships between these views and notice how elements are arranged differently. For example, when switching from Context to Article view, the circular arrangement of elements gradually morphs into the linear list on the side of the Article view.

To integrate the interface with the book's website we worked closely with the technical lead of the team behind it. We had access to the book's modules via their content management system, and deployed the interface on a subdomain of the book's website.[1] Both website and visual interface were integrated with links between module pages and the respective states in the views. The team announced the visualization on their blog, mailing lists, and social media accounts as an experimental interface for exploring the book. Visitors were encouraged to give feedback in the interface. During the six months of the deployment, we received 124 feedback submissions and the visualization attracted 4890 visitors.

Editors: "Feels Like Home"

Following the initial deployment, we asked the editors to give their perspective on the final prototype. Having discussed the concept of the monad with them, we wanted to know how they felt the interface lived up to their expectations. Feedback was provided via e-mail responses. In what it contributes to their website, the editors felt that the visualizations *"highlight the web of relationships among the content elements"* [Andrew] and provide a *"variety of ways to interact with the content"* [Phillip]. Further comments from Andrew and Phillip reveal a difference in how they value the various views within the interface. For Andrew the Context view "feels like home". He draws on this sense of familiarity, and compares those ways the overview of the book has been presented in print format with how the Context view extends upon them:

> *"It's like a dynamic table of contents – a very organic and responsive and navigable 'map' of the book's content and relationships – with an ability to glance at or skim the surface of the actual content."*

The Context view is, in this sense, an overview that captures the monadic perspective of the whole. Although this appears to stand aside from the content, Andrew insists that there is an organic connection between the Article and Context views:

> *"The Article View offers a focus or spotlight on a particular piece of content, one that you can organically 'drop into' from the Context View."*

For Phillip, it is the Article view that holds the most value as:

> *"The Article view is a nice compromise: showing both the module content and the relations in a way that makes it visually apparent that certain other modules are more or less related to the one in focus."*

[1] `http://explore.beautifultrouble.org`

One possible solution is proposed as Andrew asks for a unified monadic interface, where the Article view is fully embodied in the Context view. Although we envisaged the three views as interwoven, this was not incorporated into the prototype interface. Both Andrew and Phillip provide negative feedback on the Network view, which they felt to stand apart from the symbiosis between the other views:

> *"The Network View feels disconnected from the other two views, more like a side-show novelty. It's also a map, but not one that feels particularly welcoming or navigable or responsive or useful, compared to the Context View."*

Asked to speculate about future directions of using visualization to explore the content, Andrew is considering the *"possibility of making a combined Context-Article View THE interface for the site"*—not as an alternative, but a replacement of the existing website. Phillip mentioned that the interface does not support mobile devices, something which would need to be taken care of in the long term.

Participants: "Learning While Walking Around"

Feedback from visitors was collected through an online feedback tool built into the deployed interface. Visitors were asked to share "thoughts, impressions, and suggestions about the interface and the different views." This feedback points, in the main, to positive and enjoyable experiences. More interesting for us are both the ways in which the constructed monadic perspective serves navigation and the limitations of the views achieving this. Much like the book editors, users also felt that the interface generally accomplished that which the monadic perspective requires. All feedback submissions that explicitly compared the different views favored the Context and Article views over the Network; for example:

> *"I liked the article and context pages and found it easy to use them–the visualization of relationships on the context page was exciting. Not so the Network page."*

Several comments suggest immersive qualities of the interface, such as: *"It feels like I could spend hours..."* and *"Makes you want to read another article."* This suggests a complex relationship between aesthetics and substance, where the visuals seem to encourage a close engagement with the content, one where exploration supports meaning making. One user calls to mind the metaphor of the flaneur, reconstructing the flow of meaning making in transition: *"It's nice and funny! :-) learning while walking around."* Another user reiterates this sentiment, but draws attention to the potential for overload:

> *"When I first looked at it, I was a bit fazed by how it was organised... but it is remarkably intuitive and after the first few minutes, exploration became really enjoyable. There's so much visually present that the occasional overlapping titles create a sense of information overload, but the system encourages its own familiarisation."*

This is an intrinsic familiarization, where the interaction techniques produce an evolving knowledge. Users drew specific concerns with the Network view—as *"messy," "over-*

whelming, and therefore, counterproductive." For some this is a fundamental difficulty with the system. In viewing the prototype system, users were concerned with the lack of directed navigation and information seeking:

> *"Not sure how useful this interface would be if I were looking for guidance in a particular area..."*

Some users see the interface to be prohibitive for information seeking: *"The cross-indexing is very complex; I'm not sure it serves to quickly zero in on particular content..."* (The search function was not introduced until after the first four weeks of deployment.) However, the same visitor follows on to see this limitation as a potential:

> *"...it's a treasure hunt for discovering. Be prepared to wade in and be immersed in the collective [...] wisdom of the best social change agents active now."*

DISCUSSION

The shared feedback largely resonates with Tarde's characterization of monads in constant movement with a drive to grasp the world and shape it to their desires [17], which raises some interesting questions about monadic exploration.

For the purpose of exploration, we defined the monad as a visual arrangement of elements communicating relationships and allowing for gradual movements through a collection. While these movements are triggered by human explorers, we have not considered their role in the visualization itself. As a person navigates using the monad, could the monad itself be seen as their avatar in an information space? With the desire of the monad to exert influence on the world we recognize the poetic, aesthetic, and imaginary interest of the information flaneur [4] as a central driver in making meaning of information spaces. However, can we position the flaneur as a monad into the world in which they navigate? We refer to Latour's expression that "another experience of 'being in a whole' should be explored that has little to do with 'being a part' of a 'structure'..." [14]. The information flaneur relates to the collection, as the urban flaneur to the city, as not 'part' of the city, but nonetheless in it. In this sense, the flaneur reveals the space as a continuation of being therein, where "the added value is no longer the power of prediction, but the progressive shift from confusing overlaps to successive clarifications of provisional wholes" [14]. This is also crucial for the realization of the monadic perspective, as the interests of the flaneur might transcend the collection in question.

While the monadic view responds to the explorer's transient interest, their ongoing meaning making could form a more gradually evolving basis for attraction forces. Furthermore, the interaction histories of many explorers could inform collective attraction forces [24]. As Tarde explicitly rejects the monad as a machine with a static "distribution and direction of pre-existing forces" [17], people's changing inclinations and contingent movements through an information space can give rise to unexpected discoveries and changes to a collection. Considering attraction forces among elements and explorers to evolve over time, a monad becomes a temporally specific perspective on an information space. The visualization we introduced is atemporal, however, a simple addition would be the introduction of temporal elements representing time spans meaningful for a given collection. However, besides treating time as metadata fields, the challenge is to meaningfully represent temporal dynamics in relational information spaces. Could time-sensitive monads help us recognize stories in evolving information spaces?

During the creation of a particular monadic interface, we found it useful to translate the conceptual principles of the monadic perspective (having, difference, and movement) into three concrete design goals (offer elastic layout, reveal differences, and integrate navigation and search). Due to the engagement with a community of book editors and their readers, we observed two additional design principles that appeared to be beneficial for monadic exploration: 1) provide stable, yet dynamic arrangements, and 2) consider the visual style of a given collection. First, by devising a layout that (paradoxically) integrated a reliable order with dynamic displacements, it was possible to negotiate the influence of the collection and the explorer; it seemed that this negotiation was crucial to provide a sense of orientation and facilitate meaning making. Second, the visualization design was meant to be sensitive to the aesthetics of the represented collection (especially via colors and symbols), which seemed to help the explorers to trust the interface to be truthful to the content.

CONCLUSION

We adopted the perspective of the monad, as advanced by Tarde and Latour, to problematize the dichotomy between aggregate and element. Based on the idea of a monad as an element's relational perspective onto the world, we introduced *monadic exploration* as a method to navigate relational information spaces along overlapping vantage points. We have presented one particular visualization that is based on this approach that merges the macro and the micro in a circular arrangement of elements. We applied this visualization to a cross-referenced book and deployed it as part of an experimental interface for six months. The feedback about the potential of monadic exploration was very promising; participants felt that the monadic view provided an inviting way to explore the book's contents and appreciated the visualization's immersive qualities.

In summary, we have made the following main contributions:

- A theoretical treatise about the concept of monads that identifies key principles to inform new types of interfaces.
- A visualization technique that represents a collection as a circular arrangement of elements designed to support both exploratory and targeted forms of information seeking.
- A case study of a highly cross-referenced book contrasting a monadic visualization with conventional representations.

During this work, interesting questions came up about the role of the explorer in a monadic interface and the treatment of temporal dynamics. How can a monad support explorers in following their changing interests? In what ways can the temporal dynamics be exposed that are latent in an information space? These are some of the questions we wish to pursue further in future work on monadic exploration.

The distinction between the whole and its parts has been a useful one for information visualization to cope with the scale differences at these two granularities, however, it also introduced an artificial boundary between high-level structure and low-level detail. While we do not claim that the presented interface resolves this dichotomy once and for all, we hope that the monadic perspective can bring fruitful considerations for interaction and visualization design to make the relational qualities of collections visible and navigable. To quote Bruno Latour from his CHI 2013 keynote: "the future belongs to those who are able to navigate through overlapping monads" [13]. In particular in the context of cultural archives, digital humanities, and the arts, we see great potential for monadic interfaces to support new types of engagements with relational information spaces.

ACKNOWLEDGMENTS

We are indebted to the Beautiful Trouble team, especially Andrew Boyd and Phillip Smith, for their willingness to collaborate with us. Thanks also to Tom Schofield, Mitchell Whitelaw, Tim Dwyer, and Annika Haas for their insightful feedback and to our colleagues at Culture Lab for stimulating discussions related to monads. We are also very grateful for the constructive feedback from the reviewers. This research was funded by the RCUK PATINA Project (EP/H042806/1) and the EPSRC SIDE Project (EP/G066019/1).

REFERENCES

1. Boyd, A., and Mitchell, D. O., Eds. *Beautiful Trouble: A Toolbox For Revolution*. OR Books, 2012.
2. Cockburn, A., Karlson, A., and Bederson, B. A review of overview+detail, zooming, and focus+context interfaces. *ACM Computing Surveys 41*, 1 (2008), 1–31.
3. Donath, J., and boyd, d. Public displays of connection. *BT Technology Journal 24* (2004), 71–82.
4. Dörk, M., Carpendale, S., and Williamson, C. The information flaneur: A fresh look at information seeking. In *CHI '11: Proceedings of the SIGCHI Conference on Human Factors in Computing Systems*, ACM (2011), 1215–1224.
5. Dörk, M., Riche, N. H., Ramos, G., and Dumais, S. PivotPaths: Strolling through faceted information spaces. *TVCG: Transactions on Visualization and Computer Graphics 18*, 12 (2012), 2710–2719.
6. Fisher, D. Using egocentric networks to understand communication. *Internet Computing 9*, 5 (2005), 20–28.
7. Freeman, L. Visualizing social networks. *Journal of Social Structure 1* (2000).
8. Frisby, D. *Simmel and Since: Essays on Georg Simmel's Social Theory*. Sociology: Cultural studies. Routledge, 1992.
9. Fruchterman, T. M., and Reingold, E. M. Graph drawing by force-directed placement. *Software: Practice and experience 21*, 11 (1991), 1129–1164.
10. Heer, J., and boyd, d. Vizster: Visualizing online social networks. In *InfoVis 2005: Symposium on Information Visualization*, IEEE (2005), 32–39.
11. Henry, N., Fekete, J., and McGuffin, M. NodeTrix: A hybrid visualization of social networks. *TVCG: Transactions on Visualization and Computer Graphics* (2007), 1302–1309.
12. Kairam, S., MacLean, D., Savva, M., and Heer, J. GraphPrism: Compact visualization of network structure. In *AVI 2012: Advanced Visual Interfaces*, ACM (2012), 498–505.
13. Latour, B. From aggregation to navigation: A few challenges for social theory. Closing plenary keynote at CHI '13, Paris, May 2, 2013.
14. Latour, B., Jensen, P., Venturini, T., Grauwin, S., and Boullier, D. The whole is always smaller than its parts – a digital test of Gabriel Tardes' monads. *British Journal of Sociology 63*, 4 (Dec 2012), 590–615.
15. Marchionini, G. Exploratory search: From finding to understanding. *Comm. of the ACM 49*, 4 (2006), 41–46.
16. Shneiderman, B. The eyes have it: A task by data type taxonomy for information visualizations. In *Proc. of the IEEE Symposium on Visual Languages* (1996), 336–343.
17. Tarde, G. *Monadology and Sociology*. re.press, January 2012. Originally published 1893. Edited and translated by Theo Lorenc.
18. Thudt, A., Hinrichs, U., and Carpendale, S. The bohemian bookshelf: Supporting serendipitous book discoveries through information visualization. In *CHI '12: Proceedings of the SIGCHI Conference on Human Factors in Computing Systems*, ACM (2012), 1461–1470.
19. Turkle, S. *Life on the Screen*. Simon & Schuster, 2011.
20. van Ham, F., and Perer, A. "Search, show context, expand on demand": Supporting large graph exploration with degree-of-interest. *TVCG: Transactions on Visualization and Computer Graphics 15*, 6 (2009), 953–960.
21. Wasserman, S., and Faust, K. *Social network analysis: methods and applications*. Cambridge University Press, 1994.
22. Wattenberg, M. Visual exploration of multivariate graphs. In *CHI '06: Proceedings of the SIGCHI Conference on Human Factors in Computing Systems*, ACM (2006), 811–819.
23. Wellman, B. Little boxes, glocalization, and networked individualism. In *Digital cities II: Computational and sociological approaches*. Springer, 2002, 10–25.
24. Wexelblat, A., and Maes, P. Footprints: history-rich tools for information foraging. In *CHI '99: Proceedings of the SIGCHI Conference on Human Factors in Computing Systems*, ACM (1999), 270–277.
25. White, R. W., Kules, B., Drucker, S. M., and m.c. schraefel. Supporting exploratory search: Introduction. *Comm. of the ACM 49*, 4 (2006), 36–39.
26. Yee, K.-P., Fisher, D., Dhamija, R., and Hearst, M. Animated exploration of dynamic graphs with radial layout. In *InfoVis 2001: Symposium on Information Visualization* (2001).

Photographing Information Needs: The Role of Photos in Experience Sampling Method-Style Research

Zhen Yue
University of Pittsburgh
135 North Bellefield Ave.
Pittsburgh, PA 15213, USA
zhy18@pitt.edu

Eden Litt
Northwestern University
2240 Campus Drive Evanston
Chicago, IL 60208, USA
eden.litt@u.northwestern.edu

Carrie J. Cai
MIT CSAIL
32 Vassar Street
Cambridge, MA 02139, USA
cjcai@mit.edu

Jeff Stern
Elon University
100 Campus Drive
Elon, NC 27244, USA
jstern@elon.edu

Kathy Baxter, Zhiwei Guan, Nikhil Sharma, George Zhang
Google Inc.
1600 Amphitheatre Pkwy, Mountain view, CA 94043, USA
{kathyb*, zguan, nikhilsh, georgez}@google.com
*corresponding author

ABSTRACT
The Experience Sampling Method (ESM) enables researchers to capture information about participants' experiences in the moment. Adding an end-of-day retrospective survey also allows participants to elaborate on those experiences. Although the use of photos in retrospective interviews and surveys for memory elicitation is well known, little research has investigated the use of photos in ESM studies. As smartphone adoption increases facilitating ESM studies and making photo sharing easier, researchers need to continuously evaluate the method and investigate the role of photos in such studies. We conducted a large-scale ESM and retrospective survey study via Android smartphones with more than 1,000 US participants, and analyzed participants' photo submissions, including how photo use correlated with participants' data quality and what, if any, value photos added for researchers. Our study sheds light on the role of photos in ESM and retrospective studies that researchers can reference when constructing future study designs.

AUTHOR KEYWORDS
Experience sampling method; photo-elicitation; information need; retrospective study method.

ACM CLASSIFICATION KEYWORDS
H.5.2. Information interfaces and presentation (e.g., HCI): User Interfaces (Evaluation/Methodology).

CHI 2014, Apr 26 - May 01 2014, Toronto, ON, Canada
ACM 978-1-4503-2473-1/14/04.
http://dx.doi.org/10.1145/2556288.2557192

INTRODUCTION
The Experience Sampling Method (ESM) [1] refers to a method for collecting data from a participant in the natural context of everyday life. In an ESM study, participants are reminded randomly during fixed windows of time and asked what they are doing in that moment. It is based on the work of Edmund Husserl's "pure phenomenology," which says that the only things we can really know are the events represented in our individual streams of consciousness [13]. The ESM was also influenced by William James who stated that a person's life can be seen as the sum of all of his or her experiences accumulated over a lifetime [16]. The ESM is designed to be a reliable measure of events over time. Compared to a survey, diary and other self-reported study methods, the ESM is less susceptible to subjective recall errors because the focus is on the participant's immediate experience [14]; however, it can be disruptive to participants' current activities. One way of reducing disruption is to ask participants to enter briefly what they are doing when alerted and then later on have them fill out a more extensive survey. To aid in participant recall, participants are sometimes encouraged to take photos or videos for later review in retrospective interviews or surveys [2]. Russell and Oren [27] found in a study on search behavior that cuing participants with their screen captures aided in their recall accuracy. With smartphone use increasing in popularity, researchers are also turning to the technology for ESM studies making photo submissions for retrospective purposes a viable study design option. Despite the proven value of photos in other types of studies, there has been minimal work evaluating the role of photos in ESM studies. In particular, most studies focus on how photos help participants recall events, while the value of photos to researchers is neglected.

[1] The method is sometimes referred to as Ecological Momentary Assessment (EMA) when used in the medicine domain [29].

In this paper, we discuss a large scale ESM study with retrospective surveys conducted to explore people's daily information needs with the goal of identifying innovation opportunities for a search engine. Previous studies using search logs analysis [17] provide us with a landscape for what people use a search engine; however, people do not solve all information needs online. Logged search queries may be just a small fraction of people's daily information needs. Diary studies [30] are often the alternative to log analysis for understanding information needs.

We used the ESM combined with a retrospective survey because we wanted a more reliable way of capturing people's information needs in a natural context. In this study, participants provided text descriptions of their information needs throughout the day for five days and were encouraged to submit photos if it would help better describe their needs. We recognize that taking a photo for every information need could be burdensome or socially inappropriate at times, so we made it an optional activity [4]. In addition, participants were asked to complete a retrospective survey at the end of the day to describe more about their information needs. While the original purpose of this study was to collect peoples' information needs, the focus of this paper is on the evaluation of the methodology and the role that photos played in the study design more generally. Who submits photos? Do participants stay on task and submit relevant photos for the primary goals of the study? Do photos help participants provide higher quality responses during the retrospective parts of the study [27], or do they interfere with the participants' goals and the study's goals? Do researchers understand the photo submissions and find them useful or might they only be useful to participants? In this paper we address the aforementioned challenges through the following research questions:

RQ1. Who submits photos and when?

RQ2. Do photos help participants provide higher quality data without interfering with the participants'/study's primary goals (e.g., their information seeking)?

RQ3. Do photos help researchers understand participants' responses (e.g., their information needs) better?

RELATED WORK

The ESM has grown in popularity since Csikszentmihalyi, Larson and Prescott published a report on one of the first and most well-known ESM studies in 1977 [5]. The method is revered for its ecological validity and reduction in memory bias as well as its ability to capture contingent observations and within-person processes [28]. The ESM is commonly used in psychology to study concepts surrounding experiences of the self like mind-wandering [31], work stress and satisfaction, and relationship satisfaction. Researchers have also used the ESM to study experiences with games [7], ubiquitous computing systems [4], and programming software [15]. All of these studies are able to collect data from people in their natural environment over an extended period of time. Most ESM studies last one to two weeks [28] during which participants are 'pinged' (alerted) 2-12 times throughout the day at random times and asked to report their behavior or mood. Early studies were limited by technology, requiring participants to either set an alarm or receive a phone call at home. In these studies, participants would either anticipate the ping, or researchers were limited to only studying participants in their homes. Advances in technology have eliminated these early methodological problems and, now, researchers are using smartphone technology to help facilitate ESM studies. Smartphone applications such as Maestro [22] and the Personal Analytics Companion (PACO) [2] alert the participant, present them with a set of questions, and automatically log the data. These applications eliminate the need for participants' access to pen and paper or additional devices, potentially making the methodology less intrusive to participants' daily routines.

However, the ESM has some drawbacks. The act of being pinged frequently throughout the day may be intrusive and the people that agree to participate in such studies may lead to a self-selection bias [28]. Some studies have suffered from low completion rates; studies that sample 8 or more times per day over one to two weeks get a 50-80% completion rate [7]. These drawbacks aside, research has shown that the ESM is a viable method for collecting behavioral or emotional activity directly from people in their natural context over time [28]. However, questions still exist about what collected information is most useful for researchers and participants. In particular, the value of photo submissions in ESM studies, including how to collect and utilize photos is unclear.

Photos may be particularly relevant to ESM studies because of *elicitation*, or their ability to aid participants in providing retrospective interview and survey responses [12]. For example, Collier [3] observed that when a researcher used photos during an interview, participants' responses tended to be longer and more pointed than those in the control group. Others have used photo elicitation to enhance memory and learning. For example, Lee and Dey [19] designed a life-logging system with automatic photo and audio-capture to assist people with memory impairments by cuing them to remember details from their daily experiences [19]. Photo elicitation may also be a positive anchoring tool in educational contexts [6]. Not only can photos stimulate discussion and learning via vivid and lucid imagery [9], but they may also serve as effective verbal prompts, potentially increasing recall rates [6].

Photos have been used in some diary studies [2,8] and ESM studies [4,14] to help participants capture their experiences and recall memories. For example in a study evaluating ubicomp applications, researchers found photo submissions

[2] https://quantifiedself.appspot.com/main.jsp

helpful in highlighting what was important to participants however, the researchers did not further analyze the photo's role or usefulness. Similarly, Intille and colleagues [14] prototyped a non-intrusive image-based ESM that automatically took photos of participants' contexts, but no formal study was conducted to evaluate the method. Gabridge and colleagues [8] evaluated users' information-seeking behaviors in a photo diary study on library systems, but focused on the information needs found rather than the role of photos in eliciting those needs. Despite the usage of photos in research studies, little research has systematically investigated the extent to which photo taking is related to eliciting responses from participants or helping researchers understand participant responses better.

As smartphone use popularizes, and photo sharing online also continues to gain popularity [25], increasing the likelihood of photo-sharing uptake in studies, more researchers are considering incorporating photos in their ESM-style research designs. However, more inquiry is needed to see if there may be biases in who actually participates and submits photos. For example, background factors like age and gender tend to relate to who shares photos online more generally; women are more likely to engage with photo-sharing services online than men, and tend to upload more images [e.g., 21,32]. Young adults are also more likely to post their own photos online than older adults [26]. Additional factors related to one's technological experience are also associated with who shares online [10], including if and how people share their photos [23]. In this paper, we examine whether photo submissions in ESM studies are randomly distributed throughout the sample, or whether there are also similar systematic patterns among photo-sharers online and photo-sharers in research studies online, and the implications behind such potential patterns.

The lack of a systematic evaluation of participants' photo use and focus on the value they have for researchers, combined with the relatively small number (<50) of participants in prior photo-related studies, leaves many questions unanswered. Some researchers have debated the potential shortcomings of the use of auto-photography and elicitation in research [33]. Allowing participants to determine what to photograph also limits the researcher's control over what information can be elicited [24]. A study comparing three media (photos, audio, and tangible artifacts) in diary studies [2] found that photos lead to more specific recall than the other two, but only 11 participants were included. Our study incorporates data from a large-scale ESM study of more than 1000 people, systematically investigates photo submission as it relates to the quality of responses, and probes the extent to which such responses are in practice useful to researchers.

Based on prior research, it is clear that the use of photos in ESM and retrospective studies is an important topic, but many questions remain. The goal of this article is to address this gap in the literature.

METHODOLOGY

The ESM and end-of-day study design

We recruited more than 1,000 Android phone users across the US through a vendor as well as through our own participant database. The study ran between March and May 2013, and was conducted in five waves that each lasted five days, with 200-250 participants per wave. Fifty-two percent of the participants were male and participants ranged in age from 18 to over 60. Participants represented 46 out of 50 states in the country as well as Washington, D.C.

Participants were asked to install the Android app "PACO" from the Google Play Store [3] on their smartphone. Participants that successfully installed the app were sent notifications randomly 8 times a day (between 9am and 7pm in the participants' local time) and asked to complete a form about their information needs. The form asked basics about the information need including what it was ("What"), how important it was ("Importance") and how urgent it was ("Urgency"). For the "What" survey item, we instructed participants to describe their most recent information need using a sentence and provided an open text field. The "Importance" question was a single-selection question with a 5-point Likert scale and the "Urgency" question was a single-selection question with a 7-point Likert scale.

During each notification (beneath the "What" question), participants also had the opportunity to submit a photo with their entry. This was optional. The instructions stated, "When to include a photo? - Whenever it gives us insight about the information you needed and why." Participants had one hour to submit information before the notification timed out and was marked as "missed." Participants also had the option of manually submitting information without having received a notification, whenever they had a need they wanted to share.

At the end of the day, participants were sent a final notification to complete a survey on their desktop or laptop. The retrospective survey showed participants their text and photo submissions (if applicable) from that day and asked more information about their needs including why they needed the information ("Why"), how much of the information they were able to find that day ("Success") and how easy or difficult it was to find the information ("Ease"). The participants were required to answer all of the questions for each of their submitted information needs. For the "Why" survey item, we instructed participants to describe why they wanted to know the information using a whole sentence and left an open text field. The "Success" question was a single-selection question with a 5-point Likert scale, and the "Ease" item was a single-selection question with a 7-point Likert scale. The survey asked additional questions related to information seeking such as

[3] https://play.google.com/store/apps/details?id=com.pacoapp.paco

sources participants used to look for the information, but we do not analyze these in the current paper.

Participants were asked to respond to at least 5 of the notifications per day and complete each end-of-day survey for 5 days. The amount of compensation was based on industry standards for a 5-day rigorous engagement. If they completed 3 responses and the end-of-day survey for 3 days, they received $150 in incentives. If they responded to 5 or more notifications plus the end-of-day survey for 5 days, they received $200 in incentives.

Quantitative analysis method

The analysis unit in this study is a response from a participant that describes one information need. In the following part of this paper, we refer to this as a "DIN" (Daily Information Need). Excluding notifications that did not get responses, we have 33,180 DINs in the original dataset. If a participant responded to a notification but did not complete the end-of-day survey, the DIN was marked as incomplete. If the participant responded "nothing," "no need," etc., or if the response was about the study itself, the DIN was marked invalid. After removing the incomplete and invalid responses, there were 25,368 DINs from 1,013 participants.

Because photo submissions were optional, not all DINs were associated with a photo. Among all the DINs in the cleaned dataset, 889 (3.5%) DINs were associated with a photo. Therefore, two types of participants were identified for our analysis: 1) Photo-sharers, or participants who submitted at least one DIN with a photo; 2) Non-photo-sharers, or participants who did not submit any DINs with a photo. However, photo-sharers did not always submit photos with their DINs, so we categorized the whole dataset into three groups (shown in Table 1). The first group (G1) includes DINs from non-photo-sharers. The second group (G2) includes DINs from photo-sharers that did not have a photo submission associated with it. The third group (G3) includes DINs from photo-sharers that have associated photos. Comparing G1 and (G2+G3) allows us to analyze any differences between photo-sharers and non-photo-sharers, whereas comparing G2 and G3 enables us to examine any differences between DINs without photos and DINs with photos.

	From non-photo sharers (G1)	From photo sharers but without photos (G2)	From photo sharers and with photos (G3)
# DINs	17,182	7,297	889

Table 1: Three groups of DINs.

In order to answer RQ2 (Do photos help participants provide higher quality data without interfering with the participants'/study's primary goals (e.g., their information seeking)?), we measured both data quality and the "Ease" and "Success" of participants' original primary goal, information seeking. One set of measurements used for evaluating the data quality is the rate of incomplete and invalid DINs. From the original dataset of 33,180 DINs, we removed about 7,000 incomplete and 1,000 invalid DINs. We compared the incomplete and invalid rates among the three groups with the assumption that higher incomplete and invalid rates indicate lower data quality.

To further evaluate data quality, we also measured the length of participant responses to the "What" and "Why" questions. We chose to focus on response length because previous research has shown word count to be an effective quality measure [1], typically allowing for more opportunity to understand participant responses. We thus used the number of words as one measurement. Because many responses were submitted through mobile interfaces, we note that each additional character adds extra effort for the participants. Therefore, we also used the number of characters as another measurement of data quality. In the analysis, we assumed that the higher the word or character count, the higher the quality.

Participants' responses to the "Success" and "Ease" questions were used to measure the success and ease of their information seeking for each DIN. For the analysis, we assume that the higher the ratings, the more successful participants were at solving their information need and the easier it was for them to find the information.

Qualitative analysis method

To determine the extent to which photos can provide additional information to researchers, we recruited 12 researchers to manually code all 889 photos in the dataset. The photographs were divided into four subsets of 222 or 223 photos, which were randomly assigned to the researchers such that each photo was ultimately coded by three researchers. The coding process was conducted using a Web interface. To help researchers isolate the content they could surmise from text alone, the webpage first presented the "What" and "Why" responses without the photo. Once the coder clicked "Show image," the photograph appeared along with two questions for the coder. The first question captured whether the photo was relevant or not and asked "Is this photo RELEVANT to the information need that he/she wrote above?" The second question measured the photo's usefulness to researchers and asked, "Does this photo help you understand more about the information need BEYOND what he/she wrote above?" Each question had only "Yes" or "No" as answer options, but researchers were allowed to skip a maximum of 5% of trials in rare cases when they were unable to make a decision. If researchers mistakenly answered "No" to relevance but "Yes" to usefulness, they were given a pop-up warning that prevented them from advancing to the next trial until they reevaluated their choices.

Prior to coding, researchers were trained on standards of relevance and usefulness, and arrived at a consensus regarding the usefulness of a photograph. A photo was deemed useful if the researchers thought the photo helped them understand the participants' information beyond what was written in the text alone. To determine overall relevance and usefulness, answers for each photo were aggregated via a majority vote among the three coders. If a photo was deemed relevant in the first question by at least two raters, we then determined its usefulness using a majority vote on the second question. We treated a skipped photo as a vote for "Skip," so if more than one rater skipped the photo, we removed it from the qualitative analysis.

RESULTS

In this section, we report results for each of the three research questions.

Who submitted photos and when?

Photo-sharer versus Non-photo-sharer

While participants were not required to submit photos during the study, almost a third (30.80%), or 312 participants submitted at least one photo. Participants submitted 889 photos during the study, accounting for roughly 3.50% of DINs. On average, photo-sharers uploaded approximately three photos during the study (M=2.84). Table 2 showcases information on photo-sharers in comparison to non-photo-sharers.

		Photo-sharer	Non-photo-sharer	Statistic test
Gender	Female	170	316	$\chi2$=7.28 p =0.007
	Male	142	385	
Age	18-23	39	128	$\chi2$=11.65 p =0.02
	24-30	83	222	
	31-40	109	214	
	41+	80	135	
Mobile phone usage	Low	80	199	$\chi2$=0.91 p =0.634
	Medium	146	310	
	High	86	192	
Phone Search frequency	Low	106	274	$\chi2$=4.55 p =0.103
	High	205	427	

Table 2: Photo-sharer vs non-photo-sharer (some participants did not provide responses to some of these questions).

Upon examining photo-sharers in comparison to non-photo-sharers, we find photo submissions are not randomly distributed among participants, but rather certain people are more likely to submit photos than others. Similar to photo sharing online, females were more likely to submit photos in this ESM study than males. More than a third of females (34.97%) submitted photos in comparison to just over a quarter of males (26.94%). However, in contrast to photo sharing online, younger adults (18-23) were less likely to submit photos with their DINs than those over 40 years of age. Less than a quarter (23.35%) of the participants aged 18-23 submitted photos compared to over a third (37.2%) of participants aged 41 and older. This result holds true even when controlling for gender effects.

In addition, we do not see any correlation between who submitted photos and self-reported technology use, such as how often participants use their mobile phone and how often they generally search for information. For example, we see no significant difference of photo sharing between people who use their mobile phones frequently in comparison to those who use their phones less often.

When photos were submitted

To get a better sense of the photo submission timeline, we analyzed when participants submitted photos. In general, participants seemed to be more participatory in the beginning of the study as they were more likely to respond to notifications sent to them and more likely to include a photo on the first day of the study in comparison to the other days. However the decay rate was starker for the percent of DINs with photos. When we compare photo-containing DINs with the total number of DINs submitted per day, we still observe that participants were more likely to submit photos on the first day. A total of 272 photos were submitted on the first day, accounting for 5% of the DINs submitted on the first day, compared with only 2.9% on the final day of participation (χ^2 = 50.219, df = 4, p < 0.01). Post-hoc analyses suggest that the participants submitted a higher rate of DINs with photos on the first day. While participants still submitted photos on all five days, there may have been a novelty effect with photo submissions that diminished after the first day.

	Day1	Day2	Day3	Day4	Day5
DINs w/ photos	272	178	146	144	145
Total DINs	5,410	5,130	4,959	4,820	5,027

Table 3: DINs for each day.

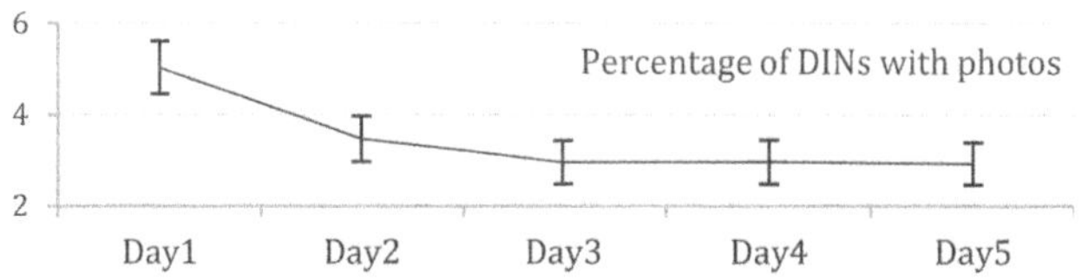

Figure 1: Percentage of DINs with photos for each day.

We did not find any significant differences using chi-square tests in reported "Urgency" or "Importance" of the information needs between DINs with photos and DINs without photos. Hence, our findings did not suggest a correlation between photo submission and urgency or importance of the information needs.

DIN quality and photo interference

A goal of any study is to obtain high quality data without placing undue burden on participants. The purpose of RQ2 was to discover whether photo submissions were associated with higher quality data, (e.g., DINs) and, if so, whether submitting a photo could interfere with the participant's primary goals, in this case, the information seeking process.

DIN quality

Based on prior research on photo elicitation, we hypothesized that DINs with photos were less likely to be incomplete DINs because photos might trigger the participant's memory while taking the end-of-day survey. Our results (as shown in Table 4) indeed show that DINs with photos have the lowest rate of missing an end-of-day survey (17.1%) and the lowest rate of invalid DINs (1.8%). Compared to the DINs from non-photo-sharers, DINs from photo-sharers but without photos actually had the highest incompletion rate (22%). Chi-square analyses highlighted that the overall differences on both incomplete and invalid rates were significant among the three groups. Post-hoc analyses further indicated the differences on incomplete rates between any two groups were significant, and the invalid rate for DINs with photos was significantly lower than the other two groups. Overall, these results indicated DINs with photos were more likely to be higher quality in comparison to DINs without photos, while DINs from photo-sharers without photos were less likely to be higher quality than DINs from non-photo-sharers.

	From non-photo-sharers	From photo-sharers (no photos)	From photo-sharers (with photos)	Statistic test
Incomplete DINs (%)	20.5	22	17.1	$\chi2=19.58$ $p<.001$
Invalid DINs (%)	2.9	2.5	1.8	$\chi2=19.04$ $p<.001$

Table 4: Percentage of incomplete and invalid DINs.

Furthermore, we found significant differences among the three groups in terms of the length of "What" and "Why" responses. We predicted that DINs with photos would have shorter "What" responses because participants may have used photos as partial replacement for text, and we hypothesized that "Why" responses in the EOD survey would be longer because photos would help them recall and describe their information needs more comprehensively.

	From non-photo-sharers	From photo-sharers (no photos)	From photo-sharers (with photos)	Statistic test
# word in "What"	8.00	8.23	9.13	F=32.53 $p<.001$
# char in "What"	42.17	43.10	47.16	F=24.48 $p<.001$
# word in "Why"	13.54	14.88	16.27	F=90.55 $p<.001$
# char in "Why"	67.89	74.77	81.66	F=87.79 $p<.001$

Table 5: Length of "What" and "Why".

Our results (as shown in Table 5) show that DINs with photos had both the longest "What" (9.13 words or 47.16 characters) and "Why" (16.27 words or 81.66 characters) among the three groups. DINs from non-photo-sharers had the shortest length of "What" (8 words and 42.17 characters) and also the shortest length of "Why" (13.54 words and 67.89 characters). One-way ANOVA tests show that the overall differences among the three groups were significant for each of the four measurements on length. Post-hoc analyses with Bonferroni correction also indicate the differences between any two groups were significant for each of the four measurements on length. Hence, DINs from non-photo-sharers tended to have shorter responses than DINs from photo-sharers. More importantly, among all the DINs submitted by photo-sharers, those with photos were associated with longer responses than those without photos.

The above analysis shows that submitting a photo correlated with higher data quality, operationalized in terms of response length and valid DINs.

Photo interference

Because photo submission required extra effort from the participant, an important question to address is whether submitting photos could affect the participant's original primary goal at hand, finding information. We analyzed two self-reported questions about participants' "Ease" and "Success" regarding finding information for DINs from photo-sharers, including those without photos (G2) and those with photos (G3). We excluded DINs from non-photo-sharers (G1) to control for the possibility that "Ease" and "Success" of finding information could be highly related to the search expertise of participants. Because G2 and G3 were DINs from the same set of photo-sharing participants, we can mitigate the possible effect of search expertise. Because the responses for these two questions were ordinal and the distributions were skewed, we use Wilcoxon Signed Rank Test. The results (as shown in Table 6) indicate that there was no significant difference on either "Ease" or "Success" between G2 and G3. Hence, we find no evidence that submitting photos had a negative (or positive) impact on the participants' ability to fulfill their primary goal.

	From photo-sharers (no photos)	From photo-sharers (with photos)	Statistic test
Median "Ease"	3	3	W=2445314 p = 0.49
Median "Success"	2	2	W=2460039 p = 0.10

Table 6: "Ease" and "Success" of finding information

Relevance and usefulness of photos

Our third research question investigated whether the photos are helpful to researchers. Researchers coded 882 photos (skipping seven photos) into one of three categories: irrelevant, relevant but not useful, and relevant and useful (For confidentiality and privacy, we provide simulated but representative photo examples for each category as shown in Figures 1, 2 and 3). The Fleiss' Kappa inter-rater reliability (IRR) for the relevance question was 0.53 and the IRR for the usefulness question was 0.35, which indicated that researchers had moderate agreement on the relevance and usefulness of photos. The final category of each photo was determined by majority voting. While these are acceptable IRRs [18], we see that even with training, researchers still had some difficulty in agreeing upon the usefulness of the photos for data analysis.

Irrelevant photos

Researchers rated 8.9% of the photos as irrelevant, indicating the researchers did not think that particular photo aligned with the participant's DIN text. A closer look at the photos revealed that many were unrelated images of the individuals, images that contained shots of their immediate context, and photos that were undecipherable. For example, one need was "[Wanted] to know if there was an evening Zumba class at any Mountainside Fitness location" and was accompanied by a picture of the participant holding a pen. While these irrelevant photos may have been useful to the participants in triggering their memories later on, the researchers found them irrelevant, and sometimes even distracting, when understanding the information need.

Figure 2: Left: An example of an irrelevant photo of the participant (What: How many days until my trip? / Why: I'm going on a vacation soon and was thinking about when it started); Right: An undecipherable photo coded as irrelevant.

Relevant but not useful photos

Researchers marked the majority of photos as relevant, but not providing any new information (*56% of total*), indicating that while oftentimes the photo was related to the need, it did not provide a deeper understanding. One common theme among this group of photos was a capturing of the information-seeking *tool* itself. For example, a DIN was, "why do my hands burn after putting on lotion?" The accompanying photo was of a search engine results page with the stated need as a search term. It merely signaled how the participant sought to fulfill the need, but it did not clarify or elaborate on the need itself. This was not useful because participants already reported the source they used for each DIN in the end-of-day survey. Furthermore, some photos contained a relevant context, but they were often too general to be useful. For example, one information need stated, "Is the horse hostile to humans?" and the photo was of a horse very far away making it impossible to recognize the horse's breed. A frequent need participants had was about weather conditions ("Is it going to be sunny tomorrow?") and the accompanying photos were often of the current weather itself. Other photos were too blurry or low quality to be useful for the researcher.

Figure 3: Left: An example of a relevant but not useful photo of an information-seeking medium (What: Where is the best pizza in New York? / Why: I wanted to get pizza for lunch and was trying to decide where to go); Right: A relevant but not useful photo about weather conditions (What: Is it going to be sunny tomorrow? / Why: I wanted to plan for a picnic tomorrow).

Relevant and useful photos

The final category, which comprised 35.1% of the dataset, are photos that were relevant to the DIN text *and* provided the researcher with additional information about the participant's need. This type of photo was most helpful to the researcher. Common themes emerging from this group were photos that clarified non-specific nouns (e.g., text said "this fish"; photo showed the type of fish in question), disambiguating nouns (e.g., text said "keyboard"; photo showed a computer keyboard rather than a musical keyboard). While it is possible that participants would not have used ambiguous or non-specific nouns had they not included the photo, results from the quantitative analysis indicate that the "What" and "Why" text is longer (and possibly more specific) among DINs with photographs.

Figure 4: Left: An example of a relevant photo that disambiguates the type of 'pet' referenced (What: What does this animal eat? / Why: My friend showed me his pet and I was curious what it ate.); Right: A relevant photo that provides more information about the style of keyboard and disambiguates it from a musical keyboard (What: Where can I buy a new keyboard? / Why: My old keyboard broke).

Lastly, some photos in this category provided new information to the text by giving more nuance to the information need. For example, a need stated, "My granddaughters are staying with me this summer. I am looking for crafts to keep them busy." The photograph showed two young girls, identifying the approximate age and number of granddaughters.

Overall we found that while participants submitted relevant photos in the study, for the purposes of our study, the majority of photos did not help researchers understand the participants' needs beyond what they had already included in text responses.

DISCUSSION

Although the ESM has been used as a research method for decades, as smartphone adoption rises and access to potential participants becomes easier through apps like PACO and Maestro, ESM-related studies are also becoming more prevalent. As researchers increasingly use this method for data collection, it is important to evaluate its effectiveness on various levels. Using results from an ESM study of more than 1,000 participants, we investigated whether any systematic biases exist between photo-sharers and non-photo-sharers, how photos relate to participants' data quality, and whether or not photo submissions are helpful for researchers.

In our study design in which photo submissions were optional, we found that photo submission was not common. Even within the third of participants who shared at least one photo during the study, photo submissions only accounted for a small percentage of their responses. Furthermore, we found that some people were more likely to submit photos than others. Females were more likely to share photos with the researchers than males. This finding echoes similar past research, which suggests that because of differing communication patterns and desires, women may be more likely to participate online and share their photos [34]. Surprisingly, in contrast to photo-sharing trends online, we found that those aged 41 and older in our study were more likely to submit photos than those 18-23 years old, even when controlling for gender. Although research on online photo sharing more generally has found a negative relationship with age [26], such findings may be attributable to people's Internet skills [11], which have been linked negatively with age (see [20] for a review). This trend might not hold among participants in our study, who were Android smartphone users and may thus be more technologically savvy than the average adult. The age patterns may also be linked with a social or psychological variable not explicitly measured in this study, such as time availability, privacy concerns, financial motivations, and conscientiousness. Regardless of the specific explanatory variable, the main conclusion here is that photo-sharers tended to be different from non-photo sharers. This is important for researchers who are designing similar studies involving photo submissions. For example, if researchers only focus on submissions containing photos, they may unintentionally bias the overall findings by systematically leaving out certain people.

Researchers considering incorporating photos into their ESM studies should also keep in mind that photo submissions dropped substantially throughout the study. While this may be a limitation of this particular study, which did not provide explicit feedback to participants regarding how their photo submissions were being used, it is also possible that this novelty/drop-off effect may persist in other multi-day studies, in which participants are eager and compliant in the beginning of the study, but by the end they may drop off due to repetition and fatigue.

Beyond photo submissions being related to participants' background characteristics, we also witnessed greater quality of responses when photos were involved. Participants were more likely to complete the end-of-day survey and more likely to share longer responses about their information needs. Although we did not conduct a systematic text analysis to discover whether longer responses were in fact more articulate, our findings are consistent with prior research suggesting the role of photos in memory elicitation [3,6]. Photos may have helped some participants articulate more details about why they needed the associated information, carrying memory triggers beyond what had been written in the text responses alone.

Although our results provide some evidence that photos may be helpful for participants, we also found that photos may not be as helpful or relevant to researchers and data analysis. In accordance with the instruction on submitting a relevant photo, the overwhelming majority of participants submitted relevant photos. While researchers had more difficulty in objectively determining the usefulness of the photos, they found just over a third of photos helped them understand participants' information needs beyond what they had written. This tended to be particularly true when the photos helped disambiguate participants' nouns, clarified their non-specific nouns, or added more nuance to their information needs. Although researchers found the "selfies" (i.e. photos of the participants) and blurry photos irrelevant, it is possible that these photos may have still helped the participant in responding to the end-of-day survey. In the future, researchers may choose to include the photo-sharing option in their study if they desire longer responses from participants, but whether it is worthwhile for researchers to analyze the entire photo dataset remains an open question. Additionally, researchers may find photos useful for other objectives beyond data analysis such as communicating findings in presentations, or creating personas and use cases for design/product development.

CONCLUSION

Overall, our findings suggest both advantages and drawbacks to photo submissions in ESM- and retrospective survey-related studies. Researchers can take these into account for future work and adjust their study designs based on their own primary goals. For example, on the one hand, requiring or encouraging photo submissions may lead to more biased samples. On the other hand, photo submissions may be linked with signals of higher quality data like longer and more valid responses. Furthermore, as our study demonstrated, researchers may find at least a subset of photos critical to understanding participants' responses.

While our study raises important insights for researchers incorporating ESM techniques and photos into their studies, it is important to keep in mind this study's limitations. For example, although our research allowed for large-scale data collection in participants' everyday environments, our primary study had a specific set of goals, instructions, compensation, and quality indicators. Future research can explore the applicability of these results and issues in more depth by investigating topics such as how variations in instructions may affect photo submission compliance or how participant interviews may impact photo elicitation.

Researchers and developers creating ESM-style technology can also work to optimize (a) when to encourage photo submissions, and (b) when researchers should access the photo data for analysis. For example, the research technology (e.g., PACO) could alert a user to include a photo after automatically detecting an issue such as after the use of a non-specific noun or ambiguous keyword. During analysis, researchers can in turn use some of the themes identified in this paper to pinpoint text responses that may need to be analyzed in conjunction with photo data. Participants could also aid in the process by manually flagging when their photo is vital to understanding the response. Moreover, since many irrelevant photos captured the individuals' immediate context rather than relating to their information need, researchers may consider providing more feedback on how the photos will be used or allow greater flexibility in when participants can submit photos. These may be particularly necessary if the researcher's priority is for the photos to provide additional information.

Future research should investigate the specific factors that influence whether and when participants choose to include photos from the participants' perspective, such as through in-depth interviews. Furthermore, future work can examine if there are any patterns in the types of responses that are more likely to receive photos. Likewise, a more structural analysis of text responses (e.g., using part of speech tagging) may help shed light on precisely what additional verbal content is being included in longer text submissions. Lastly, while our qualitative study provided insight into researchers' perspective on the usefulness of photos, we recognize that other studies and research opportunities may find the photos more or less useful depending on their specific objectives. While it is clear there are both benefits and drawbacks of incorporating photo submissions in ESM- and retrospective survey-style studies, researchers can utilize these findings when constructing future studies.

ACKNOWLEDGEMENTS

We would like to express our gratefulness to Aaron Sedley, Ann Hsieh, Bob Evans, Kerwell Liao, LaDawn Jentzsch, and Marianne Berkovich for their help in this study. We would also like to thank Dan Russell, Ed Chi, John Boyd and the anonymous reviewers for their valuable feedback and suggestions.

REFERENCES

1. Blumenstock, J.E. Size matters: word count as a measure of quality on wikipedia. *Proceeding of the 17th international conference on World Wide Web - WWW '08*, ACM Press (2008), 1095–1096.

2. Carter, S. and Mankoff, J. When participants do the capturing: The Role of Media in Diary Studies. *Proceedings of the SIGCHI conference on Human factors in computing systems - CHI '05*, ACM Press (2005), 899–908.

3. Collier, J. Photography in anthropology: a report on two experiments. *American Anthropologist 59*, 5 (1957), 843–859.

4. Consolvo, S. and Walker, M. Using the experience sampling method to evaluate ubicomp applications. *IEEE Pervasive Computing 2*, 2 (2003), 24–31.

5. Csikszentmihalyi, M., Larson, R., and Prescott, S. The ecology of adolescent activity and experience. *Journal of Youth and Adolescence 6*, 3 (1977), 281–294.

6. Fanning, S. Visual Methodologies: Photo-Elicitation in the University Classroom. *The Proceedings of the 10th European Conference on Research Methodology for Business and Management Studies*, (2011).

7. Fischer, J.E. and Benford, S. Inferring player engagement in a pervasive experience. *Proceedings of the 27th international conference on Human factors in computing systems - CHI 09*, ACM Press (2009), 1903–1906.

8. Gabridge, T., Gaskell, M., and Stout, A. Information seeking through students' eyes : The MIT photo diary study. *College & Research Libraries 69*, 6 (2006), 510–523.

9. Grady, J. Working with visual evidence: an invitation and some practical advice. In *Picturing the social landscape: visual methods and the sociological imagination.* Routledge, London, 2004, 18–32.

10. Hargittai, E. and Walejko, G. The Participation Divide: Content creation and sharing in the digital age. *Information, Communication & Society 11*, 2 (2008), 239–256.

11. Hargittai, E. Beyond logs and surveys: In-depth measures of people's web use skills. *Journal of the American Society for Information Science and Technology 53*, 14 (2002), 1239–1244.

12. Harper, D. Meaning and work: A study in photo elicitation. *Current Sociology 34*, 3 (1986), 24–46.

13. Husserl, E. *Logical Investigations, volume 1*. Routledge, New York, 2001.

14. Intille, S., Kukla, C., and Ma, X. Eliciting user preferences using image-based experience sampling and reflection. *CHI '02 extended abstracts on Human factors in computing systems - CHI '02*, ACM Press (2002), 738–739.

15. Jakobsen, M.R. and Hornbæk, K. Fisheyes in the field: Using Method Triangulation to Study the Adoption and Use of Souce Code Visulization. *Proceedings of the 27th international conference on Human factors in computing systems - CHI 09*, ACM Press (2009), 1579–1588.

16. James, W. *The Principles of Psychology, 2 vols*. Henry, New York, 1890.

17. Jansen, B.J. and Spink, A. How are we searching the World Wide Web? A comparison of nine search engine transaction logs. *Information Processing & Management 42*, 1 (2006), 248–263.

18. Landis, J.R. and Koch, G.G. The measurement of observer agreement for categorical data. *biometrics*, (1977), 159–174.

19. Lee, M.L. and Dey, A.K. Using lifelogging to support recollection for people with episodic memory impairment and their caregivers. *Proceedings of the 2nd International Workshop on Systems and Networking Support for Health Care and Assisted Living Environments*, (2008), 1–3.

20. Litt, E. Measuring users' internet skills: A review of past assessments and a look toward the future. *New Media & Society 15*, 4 (2013), 612–630.

21. Madden, M. Online photo services. 2005. http://www.pewinternet.org/Commentary/2005/December/Online-Photo-Services.aspx.

22. Meschtscherjakov, A., Reitberger, W., and Tscheligi, M. MAESTRO: Orchestrating User Behavior Driven and Context Triggered Experience Sampling. *Proceedings of the 7th International Conference on Methods and Techniques in Behavioral Research*, ACM Press (2010), 1–4.

23. Miller, A.D. and Edwards, W.K. Give and take: A study of consumer photo-sharing culture and practice. *CHI '07*, ACM Press (2007), 347–356.

24. Noland, C.M. Auto-Photography as Research Practice : Identity and Self-Esteem Research. *Jounal of Research Practice 2*, 1 (2006), 1–19.

25. Pew Research Center's Internet & American Life Project. *SNS and Facebook survey 2010*. Washington D.C., 2010.

26. Rainie, L., Brenner, J., and Purcell, K. *Photos and videos as social currency online*. 2013.

27. Russell, D.M. and Oren, M. Retrospective Cued Recall : A method for accurately recalling previous user behaviors. (2009), 1–9.

28. Scollon, C.N. and Kim-Prieto, C. Experience Sampling: Promises and Pitfalls, Strengths and Weaknesses. *Journal of Happiness Studies 4*, 1 (2003), 5–34.

29. Shiffman, S., Stone, A.A., and Hufford, M.R. Ecological Momentary Assessment. *Annual Review of Clinical Psychology 4*, 1 (2008), 1–32.

30. Sohn, T., Li, K.A., Griswold, W.G., and Hollan, J.D. A diary study of mobile information needs. *Proceeding of the twenty-sixth annual CHI conference on Human factors in computing systems - CHI '08*, ACM Press (2008), 433–442.

31. Stawarczyk, D., Majerus, S., Michalina Maj, M.V. der L., and D'Argembeau, A. Mind-wandering: phenomenology and function as assessed with a novel experience sampling method. *Acta Psychologica*, (2011), 370–381.

32. Stefanone, M.A. and Lackaff, D. Reality television as a model for online behavior: Blogging, photo, and video sharing. *Journal of Computer-Mediated Communication 14*, 4 (2009), 964–987.

33. Tagg, J. *The Burden of Representation: Essays on Photographies and Histories*. The University of Massachusetts Press, Boston, MA, 1988.

34. Thelwall, M. Privacy and gender in the social web. In S. Trepte and L. Reinecke, eds., *Privacy Online*. Springer, Berlin, Heidelberg, 2011, 251–265.

Design Insights for the Next Wave Ontology Authoring Tools

Markel Vigo
University of Manchester
School of Computer Science
markel.vigo@manchester.ac.uk

Caroline Jay
University of Manchester
School of Computer Science
caroline.jay@manchester.ac.uk

Robert Stevens
University of Manchester
School of Computer Science
robert.stevens@manchester.ac.uk

ABSTRACT
Ontologies have been employed across scientific and business domains for some time, and the proliferation of linked data means the number and range of potential authors is set to increase significantly. Ontologies using the Web Ontology Language (OWL) are complex artefacts, however: the authoring process requires not only knowledge of the application domain, but also skills in programming and logics. To date, there has been no systematic attempt to understand the effectiveness of existing tools, or explore what users really require to build successful ontologies. Here we address this shortfall, presenting insights from an interview study with 15 ontology authors. We identify the problems reported by authors, and the strategies they employ to solve them. We map the data to a set of design recommendations, which describe how tools of the future can support ontology authoring. A key challenge is dealing with information overload: improving the user's ability to navigate, populate and debug large ontologies will revolutionise the engineering process, and open ontology authoring up to a new generation of users.

Author Keywords
Ontologies; semantic web; authoring tools;

ACM Classification Keywords
H.5.m. Information Interfaces and Presentation (e.g. HCI): Miscellaneous; I.2.4 Knowledge Representation Formalisms and Methods: Semantic networks

INTRODUCTION
The use of ontologies to capture the knowledge or semantics of a field of interest has grown over the past two decades as a consequence of the needs of applications to query, integrate and analyse data on the basis of the nature of the entities being described in those data. Ontologies have been widely used in the biomedical and healthcare domains, as well as many other areas of science, and commerce. The production of linked data has also led to a widespread use of ontologies to describe its entities and their relationships.

An ontology attempts to represent knowledge of the entities in a field of interest. Entities are typically described as classes of individuals, and the relationships between those individuals. For example, we may describe the class of all Person as a set of objects all of which has a Sex, a Father and a Mother, with the latter two entities also being classes of individuals of class Person that have a specified Sex and are parents of a Person. These classes of objects may be related via relationships such as hasSex, hasFather and hasMother.

Many ontologies are represented using the Web Ontology Language (OWL) [4]. OWL has its roots in description logics, a decidable fragment of first order logic. An ontology written in OWL is a collection of axioms describing the classes, individuals and the relationships between them. A consequence of OWL's strict semantics is that an OWL ontology can be subjected to automated reasoning. Thus an OWL ontology can be a complex artefact, with thousands of axioms from which implications can be deduced. The strict semantics, potentially numerous axioms – sometimes in complex patterns – from which deductions can be drawn means that an OWL ontology is difficult both to build and understand.

There are a range of tools that support the ontology authoring lifecycle. Typically, these tools assist authors in carrying out particular tasks including ontology building, reasoning or debugging. In such a fragmented landscape, the few tools that aim to support the chore processes of ontology authoring are consequently extremely popular, Protégé being a notable example [2]. Considering the potential complexity of ontologies, little is known about how well the mentioned tools help ontology authors to accomplish their tasks.

Previous work on ontology authoring dynamics addresses the socio-technical issues of distributed collaborative authoring, highlighting that reaching consensus on the use, purpose and scope of a given ontology may generate tensions among the authors [3]. In contrast to collaborative ontology building, axiom addition is carried out individually. To gain a better understanding of the individual ontology authoring process and how tools support it, we interviewed 15 ontology authors about the problems they encounter and the strategies they employ. Our results suggest that the next generation of ontology authoring tools should provide support to navigate and populate large ontologies, be able to reason on-the-fly and aid the debugging process by identifying the most relevant problems.

STUDY

Method
Ontology authors were recruited through convenience/snowball sampling. Participants worked in a wide variety of disciplines: genetics, anatomy, archaeology,

CHI 2014, Apr 26–May 1, Toronto, ON, Canada
ACM 978-1-4503-2473-1/14/04.
http://dx.doi.org/10.1145/2556288.2557284

amino acids and the food industry. The semi-structured interviews, which were conducted either face-to-face or via video-conferencing, followed this script:

- Can you describe the authoring tasks you perform?
- How do you use tools to support you in these tasks?
- What sort of problems do you encounter?

The mean interview time was 41 minutes and 31 seconds (sd = 15 minutes, 20 seconds). The interviews were recorded and transcribed.

Participants

We interviewed 15 ontology authors (11 female participants) with an mean age of 37 years (sd = 7). Thirteen of these were based in the UK and 2 were based in the US. Nine were computer scientists, 4 were biologists and the remaining 2 had a background in science. All of them had more than 4 years of experience working with ontologies. Participants were awarded with a £10 book store gift certificate.

The participants' interaction with ontologies can be classified into 3 different groups (5 participants in each): ontology researchers (R), curators (C) and ontology developers (D). Ontology researchers are typically computer scientists investigating the properties of ontologies, building test ontologies or building reasoning engines. Curators are individuals with a deep knowledge about a domain and maintain large ontologies (a magnitude of 100,000 axioms). They receive requests from ticketing systems or a consortia to add terms, update entities or add branches into existing ontologies. Ontology developers are computer scientists that work very closely with domain experts in order to model and validate a specific domain. The ontologies they build are normally used by applications such as search engines or web applications.

The tools participants use are: Protégé (14 users), OWL API (6), OBO-Edit (4), Bioportal (3), AmiGO (1), ArrayExpress (1), Corona (1), Ontodog (1), Ontofox (1), Ontogene (1), OLS (1), QuickGO (1), Topbraid (1) and Zooma (1).

Analysis

The transcriptions of the interviews were uploaded to the qualitative data analysis software, Dedoose 4.5. Transcripts were thematically analysed in an open coding fashion following established analysis methods [1]: (1) familiarising with data, (2) generating the initial codes, (3) searching for themes and (4) iteratively reviewing themes. The generated codebook was agreed between the authors. Then, an independent coder was given the codebook and transcripts in order to establish coding reliability.

RESULTS

The principal emerging themes that were identified are the tasks ontology authors typically tackle, the problems they encounter and the strategies they employ to overcome such difficulties. The inter-coder reliability analysis yielded a Cohen's $\kappa = 0.61$, which is considered a substantial agreement.

Sensemaking, exploration and searching

Sensemaking problems relate to the loss of contextual awareness and to the difficulties grasping the current state of the tool and the ontology: "*You just lose the overview. If you have a small ontology I know every single axiom I put in there, I can remember it, whereas with big ontologies I wouldn't be able to remember every single existential restriction.*" (P4, R).

Exploration problems describe the difficulties encountered when navigating and traversing the ontology: "*We have classes and instances about clinical statements; moving from instances to classes is not so good because instances appear as a plain list [...] As the number increases it is more difficult to track back which instance belongs to which class.*" (P7, D).

Search problems are about unsatisfactory searching capabilities of tools or because tools cannot search in multiple ontologies. The latter is crucial because before adding new terms to ontologies, authors check the existence of similar terms in other ontologies in order to reuse them. "*I forgot what the primary label was; then it is very difficult because you cannot search on synonyms or other metadata.*" (P14, C).

Strategies (15 instances)

Authors get an overview from looking at the top element of the hierarchy, especially if authors are not familiar with the domain: "*The first thing would be to start from the top level of genes and just investigate the hierarchy and try to learn about it.*" (P1, R).

If the author is familiar with the domain and the ontology, finding one's way through the ontology is done by navigating the class hierarchy, which is shaped as an expandable tree: "*If you edit an ontology full-time you get very familiar with it [...] all of us can drill-down the ontology and find it quite easily.*" (P12, C).

Resorting to domain specific information retrieval engines allows authors to obtain information about terms and finding whether a given term exists in another ontology. "*I would look at the ontology directly in Bioportal to see whether a term is in the hierarchy and also to figure out what it means.*" (P10, C).

Ontology building

One of the foremost problems encountered by authors is efficiently building and populating an ontology with many entities "*If you want an ontology with 100-1000 nodes Protégé is useful for the higher levels and abstract classes.*" (P7, D).

Ontologies do not necessarily have to be shaped as trees. In theory, ontologies are a set of axioms, which is a view mostly supported by computer scientists and logicians: "*An ontology is a set of axioms, end of story.*" (P2, R). We call the particular style of building ontologies as a set of axioms and letting the reasoner build the relationships between nodes definition-oriented ontology development. However, existing tools do not support definition-oriented ontologies well because the interfaces drive authors to build hierarchies by hand. "*I would say that this interface makes us make use of the hierarchy feature the main structuring block for classes.*" (P5, R). This has a number of inconveniences including maintenance problems. "*Definition-oriented development is better for main-*

tenance because the hierarchies are not anymore subject to human decision [...] you don't have to decide upfront where you want to locate your thing." (P5, R).

Strategies (17 instances)

Reusing existing ontologies is embedded into the ethos of the semantic web community. Consequently and in theory, only a few ontologies have to be built from scratch. "*We only add new content to the ontology if no other ontology contains that.*" (P6, C). To reuse and import existing terms, authors try to match or map their terms with those described in other ontologies (which may use a different term to refer to the same concept). Some authors resort to Bioportal, which can be used as an information retrieval system that searches over the annotations and metadata of some ontologies on the life sciences domain. "*There is so far no available tool but we do use some ontology mapping tool which is Bioportal.*" (P11, D). Those who are computer scientists use programming libraries such as the OWL API to efficiently populate ontologies. "*If it is 2 classes I do it manually, if it is 10 classes in Protégé and if it is 100 I do it programmatically.*" (P7, D). On the other hand, curators and those who work closely with domain experts have template based tools that are given to domain experts to fill out. These templates are then automatically processed and their content is placed into ontologies. "*We had biologists filling out the templates, then we instantiate lots of axioms with these templates.*" (P6, C).

Reasoning

The size of the ontology and the complexity of the axioms cause problems when running the reasoner. "*I don't like to work with ontologies that are so big or complicated that I can't reason reasonably quickly.*" (P15, C).

Strategies

The following strategies are often used to speed-up the otherwise lengthy reasoning process.

- Externalising reasoning by employing continuous integration (3 instances). "*Reasoning is so memory intensive we have to do all the reasoning separately.*" (P12, C).
- Complex entities are taken out of the ontology and reasoning is done separately (3 instances). "*The disjoints are kept in a separate file and they are all combined in this set of checks that run every time*" (P12, C).
- Using low expressivity languages has some positive consequences (2 instances): these tend to be more human readable, seen as less error prone and faster to reason.

Debugging

Debugging is one of the most challenging tasks due to the lack of relevant information and appropriate instructions to fix problems. "*If the ontology is big enough, it is very difficult to work out why particular axioms are not working.*" (P8, D).

Strategies

In a debugging scenario, ontology authors exhibit particularly elaborate strategies.

- Injecting test axioms or using description logic (DL) queries (3 instances). "*You build the test classes so you can break down a class, you use a DL query to check which one stops working.*" (P6, C).
- Frequent reasoning not to accumulate problems over time (8 instances). "*Every axiom change, every class addition, every refactor I always run the reasoner.*" (P8, D).
- Fixing first those entities which are more prone to propagate problems (2 instances). If these are removed high number of problems disappear. "*Go to most general inconsistent concept and try to figure out most common concepts of inconsistencies.*" (P9, D).
- Users try to fix the ontology by making changes in a trial and error fashion, almost randomly (3 instances). "*It's a little bit trial and error, we don't really have a methodology.*" (P9, D).

Evaluation

In the context of ontology authoring, evaluation entails checking if the ontology does what is expected. This quality assurance stage is poorly supported either by tools or processes "*We don't have a formal mechanism for checking. We rely on the fact that the ontology is being used.*" (P14, C). Only those who work in larger teams where the ontology authoring process is carried out in a more systematic way employ evaluation procedures.

Strategies (7 instances)

Sitting next to experts and using domain specific databases are the main strategies employed for evaluation purposes. "*It's reasonable to have experts to confirm what is correct or what is wrong.*" (P1, R). Natural language statements about what is expected from an ontology are also formalised as competency questions.

Resorting to Protégé

Protégé is intended to be a tool that gives support at every step of the ontology authoring process. Conversely, we found that a number of users employ Protégé only in particular situations and for very specific tasks:

- To convert and classify non-OWL ontologies (5 instances). "*I transform my document into OWL and then I will load it with Protégé and classify it.*" (P6, C).
- To have an overview and visualise the effect of actions (7 instances). "*If I need to check a small piece of code that I have in mind I just pull up Protégé and I quickly do it.*" (P13, D).
- To show ontologies to domain experts (2 instances). "*We show the ontology to the clinicians. If you give them the whole ontology that's not really useful for them.*" (P11, D).

DISCUSSION

Results indicate that tools aiming to support the chore processes of ontology building (e.g. Protégé) fail to do so. These tools are primarily used to build small ontologies and to visualise medium-sized ontologies that have been built using other means. Assistance for populating, reasoning, debugging and evaluation is limited and not sufficiently supported by tools.

From the strategies users employ when carrying out the authoring tasks we derive a number of design insights. Following these will enable tools to better support the ontology authoring process.

Sensemaking, exploration and search

Provide situational awareness
Existing tools do not clearly show the consequences of the actions taken (i.e. the *undo* command). When the modification of a single axiom can affect the underlying logic and structure of an entire ontology that contains hundreds of thousands of classes, support for situational awareness is crucial. This may be obtained through textual and visual feedback: the former would inform about the problems that may have arisen (background reasoning would be necessary for this), while the latter can highlight the updated elements.

Overview, filtering and linking features
Navigating ontologies is prone to information overload and disorientation. This is especially true of the larger and the heavier axiomatised ontologies. Implementing fundamental principles of information visualisation by providing overviews and filters can alleviate this problem. Overviews may help those who are not familiar with the domain, whereas filters will speed up the navigation of domain experts. Considering how intertwined the elements of an ontology are, hyperlinking the class hierarchy, entities and axioms may help authors to use the information scent in links to traverse the ontology.

Ontology building

Support for ontology retrieval and reuse
Extending the search capabilities of tools to well known ontology search engines (e.g. Bioportal), established terminologies (e.g. the Gene Ontology) or manually aggregated sources would allow authors not only to retrieve those resources that match a query, but also to select and incorporate these into the working ontology. Support for dealing with discrepancies between the working ontology and existing ones should provide mechanisms for mapping, aligning and merging ontologies.

Efficient ontology population methods
Current GUI tools fail to support the massive number of additions and modifications that need to be done in large ontologies, which calls for efficient population methods. Templates, which are mostly used by curators, are especially relevant if domain experts are involved in the building process.

Support for definition driven ontologies
Whilst definition-driven ontologies have several advantages over hand-crafted deep trees, current tools drive authors to build the latter type of ontologies and do not support the former. Tools should cater for different building styles without imposing one in particular: for those who are not familiar with description logics, tree structured ontologies may be easier to understand.

Debugging and evaluation

On-the-fly reasoning
The complexity of ontologies leads some authors to invoke the reasoner at every modification they make or when complex axioms are added. Some adopt this strategy in order to avoid the propagation of problems. Considering how demanding reasoning is, tools and reasoners should allow authors to reason over subsets of ontologies and axioms to speed up the process. Ideally, authoring tools should provide background reasoning capabilities, as do the compilers of software development IDEs.

Error filtering
Debugging is often dealt with by identifying first the most relevant problems among highly overloaded explanations. It should be relatively straightforward for tools to identify these problems, and removing these initially will minimise the number of explanations.

Incorporating unit tests
Having pre-built axioms to test the ontology helps to unearth problems. When these axioms are shaped as competency questions the authors can evaluate whether the ontology meets the initial requirements in terms of coverage and capabilities.

CONCLUSION

We provide design recommendations to ease the authoring process of large logical artefacts that are potentially complex and are becoming more pervasive, i.e. ontologies. The possibilities of ontology use are opening up to a wide range of people, including those who may never have encountered this form of knowledge representation before. A consequence of this is that ontology authoring will move from being a specialist enterprise that is the preserve of experts, to being a tackled by mainstream – even amateur – developers. Adopting these design insights will help to ensure this evolution in ontology development realises its full potential.

ACKNOWLEDGMENTS

Research funded by the EPSRC project: *WhatIf: Answering "What if... " Questions for Ontology Authoring*. EPSRC reference EP/J014176/1.
The authors would like to thank Samantha Bail for her help in analysing the data.

REFERENCES

1. Braun, V., and Clarke, V. Using thematic analysis in psychology. *Qualitative Research in Psychology 3*, 2 (2006), 77–101.
2. Cardoso, J. The semantic web vision: Where are we? *IEEE Intelligent Systems 22*, 5 (2007), 84–88.
3. Randall, D., Procter, R., Lin, Y., Poschen, M., Sharrock, W., and Stevens, R. Distributed ontology building as practical work. *International Journal of Human-Computer Studies 69*, 4 (2011), 220 – 233.
4. W3C OWL Working Group. OWL 2 Web Ontology Language Document Overview, 2012. `http://www.w3.org/TR/owl2-overview/`.

The Role of Interactive Biclusters in Sensemaking

Maoyuan Sun
Virginia Tech
Blacksburg, VA USA
smaoyuan@vt.edu

Lauren Bradel
Virginia Tech
Blacksburg, VA USA
lbradel1@vt.edu

Chris North
Virginia Tech
Blacksburg, VA USA
north@vt.edu

Naren Ramakrishnan
Virginia Tech
Blacksburg, VA USA
naren@vt.edu

ABSTRACT
Visual exploration of relationships within large, textual datasets is an important aid for human sensemaking. By understanding computed, structural relationships between entities of different types (e.g., people and locations), users can leverage domain expertise and intuition to determine the importance and relevance of these relationships for tasks, such as intelligence analysis. Biclusters are a potentially desirable method to facilitate this, because they reveal coordinated relationships that can represent meaningful relations. Bixplorer, a visual analytics prototype, supports interactive exploration of textual datasets in a spatial workspace with biclusters. In this paper, we present results of a study that analyzes how users interact with biclusters to solve an intelligence analysis problem using Bixplorer. We found that biclusters played four principal roles in the analytical process: an effective starting point for analysis, a revealer of two levels of connections, an indicator of potentially important entities, and a useful label for clusters of organized information.

Author Keywords
Biclustering; Visual Interaction; Intelligence Analysis.

ACM Classification Keywords
H.5.m. Information Interfaces and Presentation (e.g. HCI): Miscellaneous

INTRODUCTION
Intelligence analysts face complex and difficult challenges in analyzing large, unstructured, text datasets. They often seek the help of visual analytic technology, combining the computational benefits of statistical models and knowledge discovery algorithms with the cognitive abilities of humans, to support sensemaking [7]. The challenge is to design a system that integrates these areas, creating efficient visualizations to present computed, structural relationships, and a usable workspace for analysts to perform sensemaking.

Identifying coordinated relationships from text (e.g., find three people who have all visited the same four cities on the same set of days) is a common problem in intelligence analysis. We posit that integrating biclusters into a spatial sensemaking workspace provides a potential solution to identify these connections. A bicluster is a complete bipartite graph where every vertex of one set is connected to all vertices of another set [6], which can be viewed as a bundling of individual relationships into a pair of sets. There are three steps to compute biclusters from the text dataset. First, extract useful entities (e.g., people, location, date) from the text, and then establish relationships between individual entities based on co-occurrence (e.g., a person at a location). Finally, biclusters are formed by grouping entities that share the same relationships (e.g., three people at the same four locations) with algorithms such as CHARM [10]. Spatial workspaces provide a flexible and expressive visual medium to support sensemaking [1]. For example, analysts can organize documents in spatial structures to help synthesize hypotheses. Integrating biclusters into the spatial workspace can enable users to interact with them in a facile way within their analytic process.

Bixplorer
Bixplorer is a visual analytics prototype that combines biclustering algorithms with visual representations (linked matrices) within the spatial workspace [3]. Two considerations of the sensemaking workspace motivate the design of Bixplorer. First, the system must provide a sufficiently rich abstraction of information (e.g., biclusters) that can serve as the basis of more detailed navigation and perusal. Second, sensemaking by users' manual exploration must be seamlessly integrated with the results of knowledge discovery algorithms.

Bixplorer has three major views: a data browser, a preview panel and a spatial workspace, shown in Figure 1. The data browser allows users to search and browse lists of documents, biclusters and entities. The preview panel previews the browsable content, and the workspace enables the visual organization of information. In total, 18 interactions in 6 categories are provided in Bixplorer: 1) ***Open*** documents and biclusters of interest in the data browser and move them to the workspace. 2) ***Remove*** unwanted documents and biclusters from the workspace. 3) ***Show*** related biclusters or documents from a selected document or bicluster. 4) Create user defined ***Links*** between biclusters and documents. 5) ***Extract*** a row or a column of interest from a bicluster. 6) ***Save*** the workspace.

The workspace shown in Figure 1 presents a typical usage scenario in Bixplorer, in which there are 2 biclusters and 5 documents. Bic 40 shows coordinated relationships between 3 dates and 3 people. Based on fbi19, "25 April, 2003"was the date of this FBI report, "23 April, 2003"was the date that person2 bought the train ticket, and "29 April, 2003"was the day that these 3 people planned to meet on the train. Bic 105 shows coordinated relationships between people and organizations, in which AMTRAK was the train that the 3 people

CHI'14, April 26–May 1, 2014, Toronto, Canada.

http://dx.doi.org/10.1145/2556288.2557337

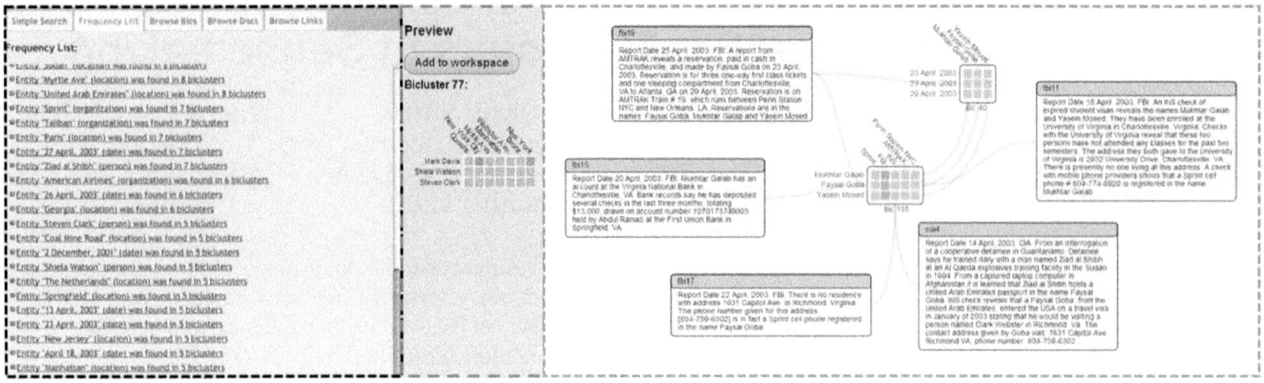

Figure 1. Three views in Bixplorer: the data browser (left), the preview panel (middle) and the spatial workspace (right).

would meet, Penn Station NYC was a train station, and all others were organizations in US. Based on the important plots reported in cia4 (person4 received explosive training before, and entered USA with a United Arab passport in the name of person1), and fib11 (person1 and person3 were registered as students in UVA, but they never came to any classes), analysts may make a hypothesis that a planned explosive attack would be performed by the three people on 29 April, 2003 at the AMTRAK train #19.

Previously we discussed some preliminary results of features usage in Bixplorer (e.g., number of used biclusters and user-generated links) [3]. However, the following questions still remain unanswered: How are biclusters integrated into the sensemaking process and used within the sensemaking loop? Do biclusters serve as a helpful guidance for foraging related information or a meaningful summary for synthesized information? To answer these questions and to inform the design of future visual analytics tools, we conducted a user study.

RELATED WORK

Many visual analytic tools allow users to explore individual relationships, based on text co-occurrence, between entities extracted from raw text documents. For example, Jigsaw's List View [9] visually represents relationships similarly to parallel coordinates, whereas Analyst Notebook and Entity Workspace [2] use entity-relationship network diagrams. Although they provide solutions to visually represent individual relationships, these tools have limited capability for coordinated relationships discovery. Too many edges between entities visually obscure coordinated relationships. Besides, filtering edges by interactively selecting entities requires users to manually search all possible combinations of entities to find the combinations that share common relationships.

Biclusters, incorporated in visual analytics tools, provide a potential solution, which has been explored in the realm of bioinformatics and social network analysis. BicOverlapper [8] uses a bubble map to infer similarities between biclustering results for microarray analysis. BiCluster Viewer [4] applies biclusters in the form of matrix diagrams to assist gene expression data analysis. NodeTrix [5] facilitates exploration of social networks (e.g., co-authorship) through a hybrid visualization that combines adjacency matrices for dense subgraphs, similar to biclusters, with node-link diagrams for sparse connections between subgraphs. Although biclusters appear to be useful for sensemaking tasks, there are few studies on how people use biclusters in human analytic process.

METHODOLOGY

The user's task in this study was to analyze a set of fictitious intelligence reports, identify any planned attacks, and hypothesize about the terrorist plot. The dataset used in this study (called Sign of the Crescent) contains 41 documents regarding a coordinated terrorist plot in three US cities. 24 reports are relevant to the plot and 17 reports are irrelevant. We used CHARM [10] to generate biclusters from the dataset with the "support"parameter set to 3, which assured that each bicluster has at least 3 rows and 3 columns. This resulted in 284 unique entities, 495 relationships, and 109 biclusters. These settings were selected to match the needs of typical text analysis scenarios.

This study included 15 participants between the age of 20 and 27, and each was compensated for participation. 4 participants were graduate students, and 11 participants were undergraduate students. 6 participants had prior experience with visual analytics tools, but none had prior experience with biclusters. The study procedure consisted of three parts. First we explained the nature of the dataset to users, and used a separate dataset to demonstrate all features in Bixplorer without instructions on any particular analytical approach. Second, users were asked to assume the role of an analyst and investigate the dataset for 1.5 hours to identify any threats of attacks. Finally, we asked users to explain their findings, and interviewed them on their use of Bixplorer to find how biclusters impacted their analysis. Data were collected from log files, workspace screenshots, observations and interviews. Three components of each interaction were logged: the time stamp, interaction type and the target object (e.g., a bicluster or a document that is interacted with by users).

RESULTS

We found that biclusters in Bixplorer played four principal roles in intelligence analysis: 1) an effective starting point for analysis, 2) directing attention toward connections at both the micro and macro level, 3) an indicator of potentially important entities, and 4) a useful label for clusters of organized

User	Number of docs opened by users before opening their 1st bic	Timestamp users opened the 1st bic (min:sec)	Relevance of the 1st doc opened before / after users opening their 1st bic	Percent of bic based interactions used to find relevant docs	Percent of bics with non-uniform color in the workspace	Identified attack number
U1	6	41 : 52	irrelevant / relevant	51%	68%	1
U2	1	52 : 31	irrelevant / irrelevant	34%	73%	1
U3	0	01 : 19	none / relevant	79%	78%	2
U4	3	04 : 11	relevant / relevant	55%	76%	1
U5	NA	NA	NA	NA	100%	2
U6	0	01 : 09	none / relevant	64%	NA	1
U7	0	04 : 10	none / relevant	100%	93%	2
U8	0	01 : 08	none / relevant	89%	NA	2
U9	NA	NA	NA	NA	80%	1
U10	1	01 : 22	relevant / irrelevant	86%	85%	1
U11	0	00 : 52	none / relevant	78%	62%	2
U12	0	01 : 15	none / relevant	75%	92%	1
U13	0	00 : 50	none / relevant	35%	82%	1
U14	6	29 : 31	irrelevant / relevant	10%	0%	1
U15	0	02 : 45	none / relevant	48%	100%	2

Table 1. Summary of user data in the study. Denote: bic(s) for bicluster(s) and doc(s) for document(s).

information. Table 1 summarizes the data in this study. Unfortunately, log files for users 5 and 9 (henceforth, U5 and U9) and workspace screenshots for users 6 and 8 (henceforth, U6 and U8) were corrupted, so we excluded U5 and U9 for log analysis, and excluded U6 and U8 for workspace analysis. Overall, using Bixplorer, all users were able to identify at least one of the 3 hidden attacks and the coordinator of the 3 attacks, although none found all 3 attacks.

An Effective Starting Point for Analysis

Biclusters quickly direct users to important relevant documents as a starting point for analysis. In this study, we did not provide any instructions about how to start analysis, so all users started their analysis based on their preference. Based on the second column in Table 1, 5 of 13 users began by reading documents; The other 8 users began by examining biclusters. Based on the third column, 2 (U4 and U10) of the 5 who began with documents quickly abandoned this approach within 5 minutes and switched to using biclusters. This indicates that there was some preference for starting with biclusters.

For 7 of the 8 users (except U2) who began with biclusters, the documents that they opened based on their first bicluster were relevant to the solution. We observed that 5 of these users used their first bicluster to identify important entities that they then used to search for relevant documents. The other 2 used the bicluster to directly show relevant documents. Of the 5 users who did not begin with biclusters, 3 began with irrelevant documents because they began reading documents in an arbitrary order. These 3 users persisted reading documents for about 30 minutes or more before opening biclusters. This trend indicates that biclusters provided an efficient way to find relevant documents at the beginning of analysis.

Directing Attention Toward Connections

On the micro level, each bicluster revealed a set of relationships between entities of two groups. For example, U13 mentioned that he used biclusters "*to see the relationships between items within*". On the macro level, a bicluster could indicate semantic connections among shared lexical items in multiple documents. Micro level connections led users to explore macro level connections, thus enabling them to connect more detailed information from the documents and synthesize semantic hypotheses. For example, U2 mentioned using biclusters "*to find connections between news [documents] and people, places and news [documents]*". In Bixplorer, users can perform eight different interactions with a bicluster (e.g., extract a row), only one of which is used to show documents related to the bicluster. Based on the fifth column in Table1, most of the users' interactions with biclusters were to find documents and therefore better understand the detailed connections between them. Also, through biclusters, users connected documents together frequently by placing them near each other in the spatial layout and occasionally with user-defined links. Taken together, biclusters helped users perceive connections at both levels: co-occurrence of entities at the micro level, and relevance for documents at the macro level.

An Indicator of Potentially Important Entities

Biclusters enhance the capability of users to recognize potentially important entities. Each bicluster in Bixplorer is represented as a grid of cells, and each cell presents a relationship between two entities. The cell color indicates the frequency of co-occurrence for the two related entities. Thus, uniform coloring of cells within a bicluster means that all relationships within this bicluster have the same frequency, and non-uniform coloring means that at least one relationship has different frequency. An example of uniform and non-uniform biclusters in Bixplorer is shown in Figure 2.

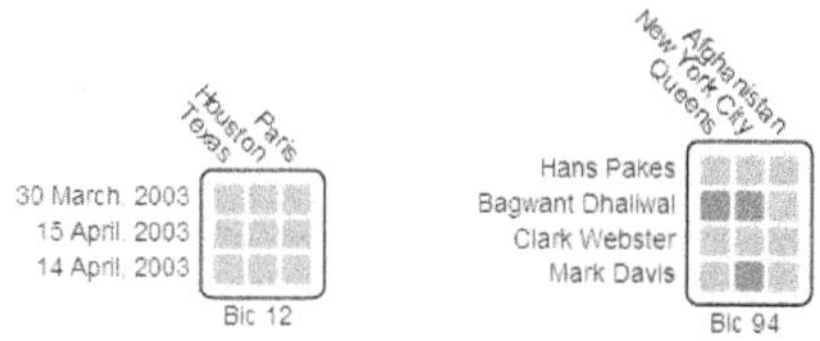

Figure 2. A uniform bicluster (left) and a non-uniform bicluster (right).

For the Crescent dataset, the number of non-uniform biclusters found by Bixplorer happens to be 72% of the total number of biclusters found. From the sixth column in Table 1, the non-uniform biclusters rate in 10 users' workspace is higher than 72%. Thus, the ratio of non-uniform to uniform biclusters found on these users' workspaces is greater than the ratio of non-uniform to uniform biclusters found in the dataset. This indicates that users preferred non-uniform over uniform biclusters in their analysis. Some users interpreted that high frequency relationships in non-uniform biclusters indicate important entities. U10 mentioned that "*I mostly focused on biclusters with a large variation in color, since those biclusters usually yielded the strongest correlations*". Although the rate of non-uniform biclusters in U11's workspace is lower than 72%, U11 still admitted that "*The ability to see how many documents connect each two pieces of information just by looking at the shade of the color was a useful thing for quick glances*". U14 removed almost all biclusters (except one) from the workspace at the end of the study, so the rate of non-uniform biclusters in U14's workspace is 0%. In fact, in this dataset, the high frequency cells typically represented the important persons who organized the correlated activity.

A Useful Label for Clusters of Organized Information

According to the screenshots of their final spatial workspaces, users frequently used biclusters as a label for the surrounding spatially organized information. A typical example of such spatial layout from U13's workspace is shown in Figure 3. A bicluster with one column and one row is placed in the center as a semantic label for the cluster of eight biclusters. This special bicluster was created by U13 using the *extract* interaction. In this bicluster, the row name is "Mark Davis", and the column name is "Queens". All surrounding biclusters list more detailed relevant relationships associated with "Mark Davis"and/or "Queens".

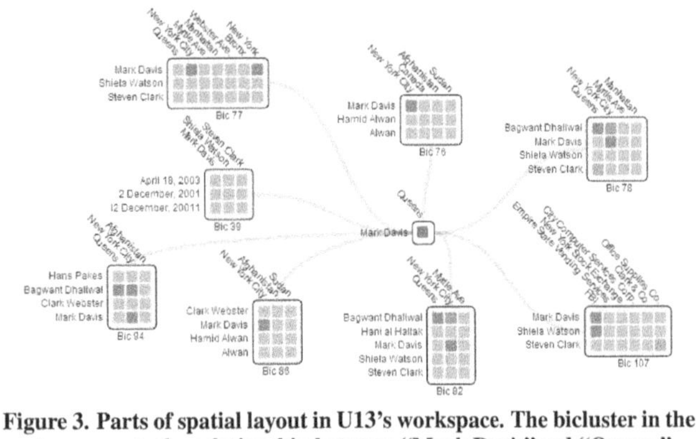

Figure 3. Parts of spatial layout in U13's workspace. The bicluster in the center presents the relationship between "Mark Davis"and "Queens".

In fact, 7 of 13 users' final workspaces had spatial layouts similar to that shown in Figure 3, and 6 of these 7 users mentioned that biclusters provided the labeling capability to assist their analysis. For example, U3 mentioned that "*[I] chose one [bicluster] that had..., something that sounded terrorist-like*"and U7 said that, "*[I] used them [biclusters] to title clusters of documents*". By referring to a bicluster as a label, users can quickly retrieve useful information from the spatial layout. For example, when reporting his findings, U12 looked at a specific bicluster in his workspace and then mentioned that "*[personA] has connections to [personB] who allegedly visited [personC] at a non-existent address...*" From U12's workspace screenshot, we found that this bicluster presents a collection of information related to *personA*.

CONCLUSION

A bicluster in Bixplorer is a highly abstracted set of relationships. Considering the sensemaking loop, biclusters are useful for foraging information in three ways: directing users to relevant documents as a starting point, discovering potential connections of both the micro level and the macro level, and indicating potentially important entities. Biclusters are also helpful for synthesis by labeling organized information.

ACKNOWLEDGMENTS

This research was partially supported by NSF grant #CCF-0937133.

REFERENCES

1. Andrews, C., Endert, A., and North, C. Space to think: large high-resolution displays for sensemaking. In *Proceedings of the SIGCHI Conference on Human Factors in Computing Systems*, ACM (2010), 55–64.
2. Bier, E. A., Ishak, E. W., and Chi, E. Entity workspace: an evidence file that aids memory, inference, and reading. In *Intelligence and Security Informatics*. Springer, 2006, 466–472.
3. Fiaux, P., Sun, M., Bradel, L., North, C., Ramakrishnan, N., and Endert, A. Bixplorer: Visual analytics with biclusters. *Computer 46*, 8 (2013), 90–94.
4. Heinrich, J., Seifert, R., Burch, M., and Weiskopf, D. Bicluster viewer: a visualization tool for analyzing gene expression data. In *Advances in Visual Computing*. Springer, 2011, 641–652.
5. Henry, N., Fekete, J.-D., and McGuffin, M. J. Nodetrix: a hybrid visualization of social networks. *Visualization and Computer Graphics, IEEE Transactions on 13*, 6 (2007), 1302–1309.
6. Jin, Y., Murali, T., and Ramakrishnan, N. Compositional mining of multirelational biological datasets. *ACM Transactions on Knowledge Discovery from Data (TKDD) 2*, 1 (2008), 2.
7. Pirolli, P., and Card, S. The sensemaking process and leverage points for analyst technology as identified through cognitive task analysis. In *Proceedings of International Conference on Intelligence Analysis*, vol. 5 (2005), 2–4.
8. Santamaría, R., Therón, R., and Quintales, L. Bicoverlapper: a tool for bicluster visualization. *Bioinformatics 24*, 9 (2008), 1212–1213.
9. Stasko, J., Görg, C., and Liu, Z. Jigsaw: supporting investigative analysis through interactive visualization. *Information visualization 7*, 2 (2008), 118–132.
10. Zaki, M. J., and Hsiao, C.-J. Charm: An efficient algorithm for closed itemset mining. In *SDM*, vol. 2 (2002), 457–473.

SmartVoice: A Presentation Support System for Overcoming the Language Barrier

Xiang Li
Interfaculty Initiative in Information Studies,
The University of Tokyo
7-3-1 Hongo, Bunkyo-ku,
Tokyo 113-033, Japan
kular.me@me.com

Jun Rekimoto
Interfaculty Initiative in Information Studies,
The University of Tokyo
7-3-1 Hongo, Bunkyo-ku, Tokyo 113-033, Japan
Sony Computer Laboratories, Inc
3-14-13 Higashigotanda, Shinagawa-ku,
Tokyo 141-0022, Japan
rekimoto@acm.org

ABSTRACT
In most cases, speeches or presentations at an international event are required to be given in a common language (e.g. English). However, for people who are not proficient in that common language, delivering presentations fluently is very difficult. Simultaneous translation seems to be a solution, but besides its high cost, simultaneous translation undermines the nature of the presentation by substituting the real voice of the lecturer as well as his/her emotions. In this paper, we propose "SmartVoice", a presentation support system, which aims to overcome language barriers. By tracking the lip motion of the lecturer, SmartVoice controls the playback of the narration, which is a sound data prepared in advance or created automatically using a voice synthesizer. SmartVoice also controls the intonation of the sound based on the position and shape of the lecturer's mouth. As the lecturer can talk at his/her own pace with the voice automatically following, it appears as if he/she talks in his/her own voice. In our user evaluation, we confirmed that audiences find it difficult to distinguish between the narration generated by SmartVoice and that by a real voice. We also discuss the possibility of applying SmartVoice to fields other than multi-language presentation support, such as Automated Dialogue Replacement and language study.

Author Keywords
User Interface; Lip Sync; Presentation Support; Face Tracking; Facial Actions; Language Barrier.

ACM Classification Keywords
H.5.m. Information interfaces and presentation: [HCI]

INTRODUCTION
In events such as international conferences, lecturers are usually asked to use a common language (e.g., English). However, this is difficult for a person who has a different native language. Even though reading a manuscript is permitted in some cases, significant effort is still needed to pronounce words correctly and speak fluently. There is also the need to deliver the presentation in other languages when the majority of the audience does not understand the common language. For example, a presentation given in English in Asian countries may not be well understood by the audience with no translation. In both cases, the language barrier is a serious problem for presentations.

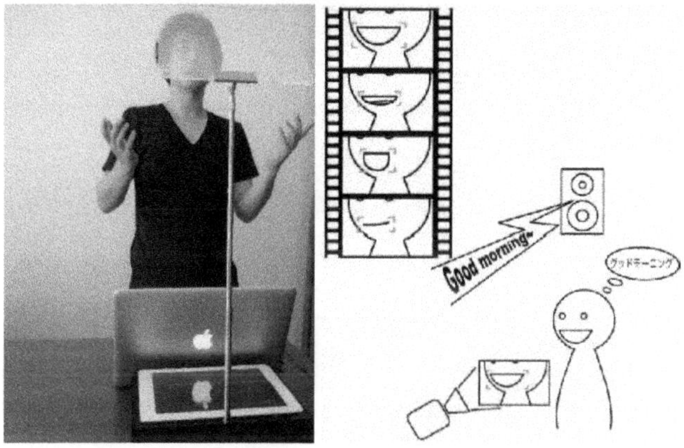

Figure 1. Presentation using SmartVoice

Simultaneous translation is one possible solution for such situations in which a lecturer and audience do not share the same native language. However, in addition to the considerable cost of hiring interpreters, there will be a delay between the voice of the lecturer and that of the simultaneous translation, which not only sounds unnatural but also fails to convey non-linguistic information such as the tempo, pauses, stresses, and intonation of the speech.

It might also be possible for the lecturer to perform a lip sync presentation if he/she records the narration of the manuscript in advance. However, this means that the lecturer will have to practice in order to be familiar with the speed of playback, and when the presentation begins, the lecturer could easily lose control of it.

CHI 2014, April 26–May 1, 2014, Toronto, Ontario, Canada.

http://dx.doi.org/10.1145/2556288.2557161

With the help of a voice synthesizer, text in any language can be converted to sound data. Although a voice synthesizer can pronounce each word correctly, the narration of long sentences sounds artificial and robotic. A human lecturer will make a pause or speak louder to emphasize that something important is about to be mentioned, but a voice synthesizer speaks with the same tone consistently all the time. Due to the lack of intonation and emotional expression, voice synthesizers are still not a suitable substitute for a human narrator.

As a solution to the problems above, this paper proposes a support system based on a method with the name "smart lip-syncing." A smart lip-syncing system automatically controls the playback of sound data based on the motions of the lecturer's lip. The sound data can be either a narrated recording or created by a voice synthesizer. With this method, the lecturer can take full control of the presentation; he/she can pause or change the speech speed during the presentation to emphasize important points or gain the attention of the audience. In addition to the playback control, the change in volume as well as intonation can also be controlled in realtime by natural facial gestures. As a result, the audience recognizes that the lecturer standing right before them is delivering a talk with his/her own voice. We call the system based on this smart lip-syncing method "SmartVoice."

To give a better explanation of SmartVoice, we compare it with three known concepts, which is looping, pre-scoring and lip sync (see Figure 2).

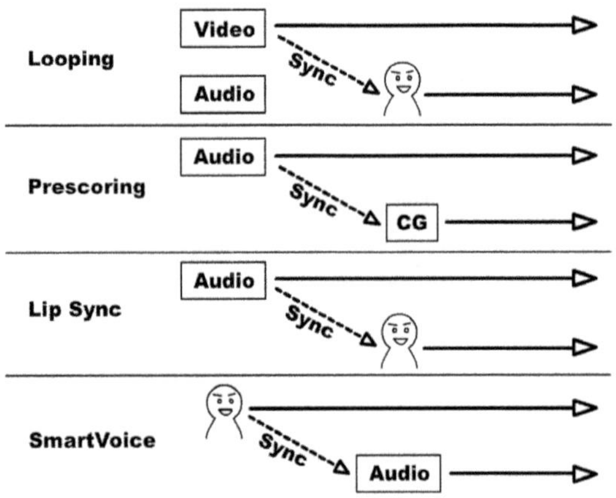

Figure 2. Comparison among Looping, Pre-scoring, Lip sync and SmartVoice

In the case of looping, video is recorded previously with no sound. Then, dubbing artists will narrate the script while watching the video in order to match their voice to the lip motion of the characters in the video.

Contrary to looping, in pre-scoring, which is widely used in American cartoon production, sounds are recorded in advance. Then, graphics are created according to the timing of the sound. Lip sync can be considered as a variety of pre-scoring if the graphics are substituted with a real person.

In all the cases discussed above, humans try to adjust themselves to either un-editable video or un-editable audio. However, in SmartVoice, although the audio file is created beforehand, its playback fits the pace of the lecturer giving the presentation, so that it is the human being that takes all the control in SmartVoice.

PRESENTATION USING SMARTVOICE

To give a presentation with SmartVoice, a user needs to prepare a text file with the presentation's manuscript and then create the sound data of the same manuscript. As mentioned above, the sound data can be a recording of the narration by the user himself or another narrator, or be generated by a voice synthesizer.

After the user feeds both the manuscript text file (.txt) and the sound file into the system, SmartVoice semi-automatically matches the text and the sound on a phrase-to-phrase basis. Phrases in the manuscript that are correctly matched to the sound will then be displayed on the screen of a half-mirror prompter.

Ensuring that SmartVoice is successfully tracking the user's face, he/she can control the sound playback of each phrase shown on the prompter by lip sync. If the user closes his/her mouth after reading one phrase, the playback will pause and that phrase will slide up on the prompter while the next phrase is emphasized. By opening his/her mouth again, the user can resume playback with the corresponding sound. Between every phrase, a user can pause as long as he/she likes. In addition, playback speed and intonation can be controlled in realtime based on the user's lip sync speed and the position of his/her mouth and eyebrows, respectively.

SMART LIP-SYNCING IN SMART VOICE

By mapping the playback control, pitch, speed and volume to the lecturer's lip motions and other facial actions in realtime, SmartVoice sends out the sound correctly and properly at the lecturer's pace of lip sync. Figure 1 shows a scene of giving a presentation with SmartVoice.

Playback Control

We introduce a prompter to our system to act as a SmartVoice interface for the user. With the prompter showing the phrase to read, the user can always confirm the progress of the presentation. To achieve this, we need to correctly match the manuscript with the sound. In SmartVoice, this matching is semi-automatic.

Generally, a lecturer will pause during a presentation to maintain the correct tempo. In order to ensure that the audience will not feel confused with incongruous pauses during the presentation, our system first extracts phrases from both the manuscript text and the sound data and then matches them. For the manuscript text, we extract phrases that are separated by commas and periods. For the sound data, we extract phrases separated by silent sections, which are characterized by low volume levels (see Figure 3).

To be specific, the silent section is determined as the region whose audio levels is less than 10% of the average audio level on the entire sound data and last at least 100 milliseconds. The results will be cached in an array of raw silent sections. Noise or breath sound, usually consisting of very short bursts of high volume, may exist in the sound data. In order not to regard noises as silent sections, we add an algorithm, which loops the array of the raw silent sections to find pairs of raw silent sections whose distance is less than 200 milliseconds, and then appends them to a single silent section, to identify and ignore noise or breath sound to guarantee that there are no silent sections separated by noises.

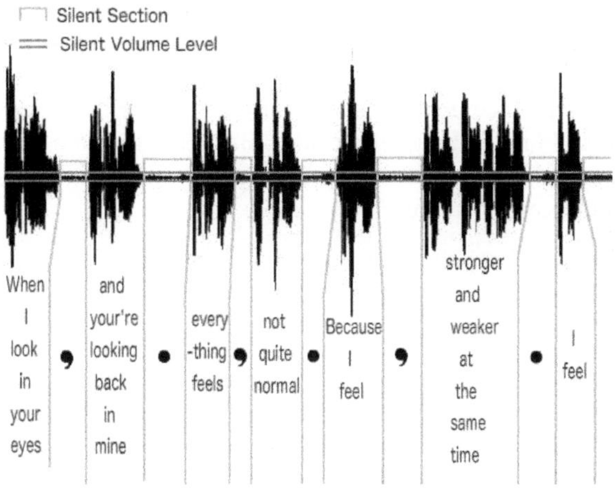

Figure 3. Phrase extraction from sound and text

With the phrases extracted from both the manuscript text and the sound data, our system semi-automatically matches them using a process we explain in detail below. Since the phrases extracted from both sides are matched on a phrase-to-phrase basis, SmartVoice guarantees that each phrase shown on the prompter is correctly matched to its sound and that after one phrase is read, the next phrase slides up and is ready with its corresponding sound so that the correct phrases in the sound data will be played in time with the user's lip sync.

We intend not to match the lip motion to exactly at each syllable, because not all syllables or words can be detected from the lip motion. Instead, the user can merely start a phrase by opening his/her mouth to indicate the system to start or resume. As long as the playback does not encounter a silent section with the user's mouth closed, SmartVoice will not take into account whether the lip motion/shape matches the syllable or word being played within a phrase.

Pitch, Speed & Volume Control

With SmartVoice, not only the playback but also the pitch, speed, and volume can be controlled by the user's facial gestures in realtime. This results in a more natural presentation experience, although the manuscript text is narrated by a voice synthesizer.

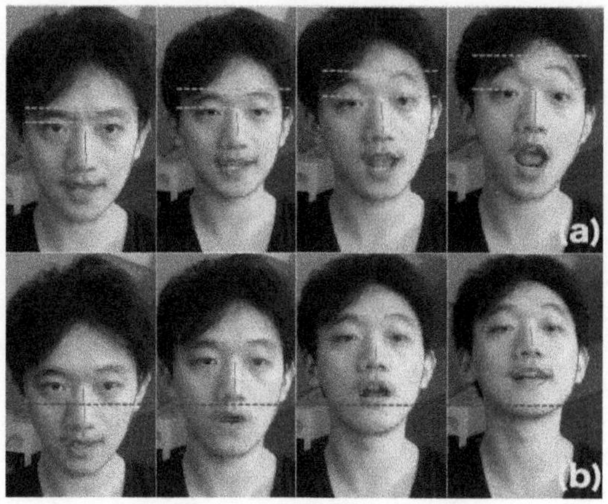

Figure 4. (a) Volume control (b) Pitch shifting control

We take into consideration the physical constitution of human beings when speaking and developed a method for controlling pitch, speed, and volume. Pitch is shifted up or down with the position of the user's head (see Figure 4(b)). If the user performs a rapid lip sync, the playback speed will be accelerated and vice versa. We attempted to control the volume by the openness of the eyes, but we eventually changed the controller to follow the height of the eyebrows (see Figure 4(a)). We return to this issue later.

SYSTEM ARCHITECTURE

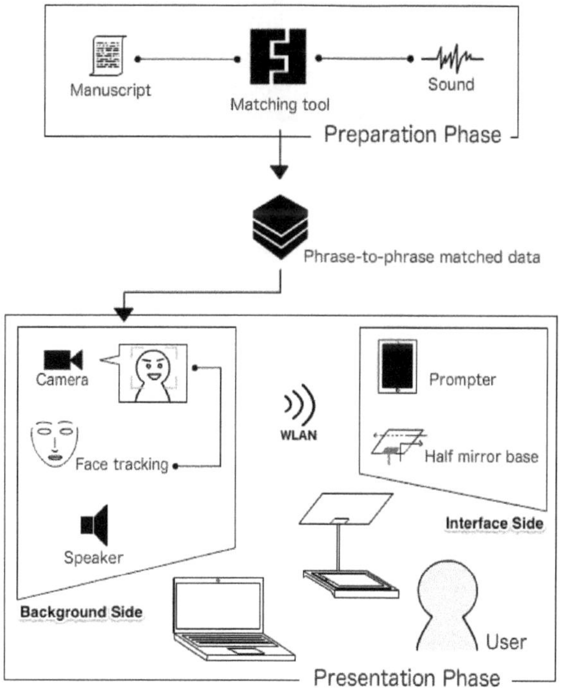

Figure 5. System architecture

In this section, we present details of the prototype of our presentation support system.

There are two main parts to our system. One is on the background side and the other is on the interface side. The background side consists of a camera, which is used for detecting and tracking the user's face, a speaker, and a computer used for processing. The interface side basically consists of a prompter containing a tablet PC and a prompter base. The two sides are connected via wireless LAN (see Figure 5).

Background side

Since we want to achieve a natural presentation experience and at the same time free the user from complicated operations, everything is completely controlled only by the user's lip motions and facial actions. Not only can the user determine the pauses and resumption of the playback, but also can make the sound generated by a voice synthesizer more vivid by altering the volume, pitch and speed in realtime.

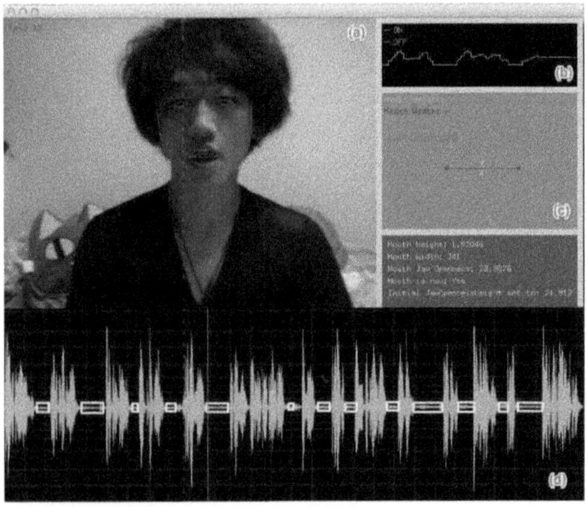

Figure 6. Background side program. (a) Real-time frame captured with camera with ofxFaceTracker markers as annotation, (b) mouth openness pattern, (c) indicator of the mouth height and width, and (d) sound waveform with silent sections shown as white rectangles

Face Detecting & Tracking

When in use, SmartVoice tracks the user's face position and lip motions. This is achieved by adopting the openframeworks add-on "ofxFaceTracker" for our system. Openframeworks is a C++ based multi-platform open source tool kit [1]. OfxFaceTracker is one of the many add-ons of openframeworks and has features to detect the position, inclination, and shape of a human face as well as all the parts on the face, such as mouth, eyes, nose, and eyebrows [2]. C++ ensures the high performance of our system because any delay will sound unnatural and may confuse the audiences during a presentation. Compared to other computer vision implementation for face tracking, ofxFaceTracker is easy to attach to our system because it is well moduled as an add-on with outstanding performance on tracking the human face as well as facial parts (The empty sample of ofxFaceTracker runs at over 100fps on a laptop). In our prototype, we track the position and shape of the user's face and other facial parts in the video captured by a laptop with a built-in web camera and display this information as annotations or charts in realtime (see Figure 6).

Phrase-to-phrase Matching

A pause within a single word may confuse the audience; this should be avoided. As we mentioned in the previous chapter, our system conforms to a phrase-to-phrase matching principle. In order to guarantee that the text in the manuscript correctly matches the sound at the phrase level, we introduce a semi-automatic matching tool.

First, the matching tool analyzes the sound data to find all silent sections. To be specific, the background side program will search all frames in the sound data (a wav file) for areas that both are significantly low in volume and last for over 100 milliseconds. We call these areas silent sections, which are assumed to be the intervals between adjacent phrases. However, since noise exists, usually consisting of very short bursts of high volume, especially when recording, our system can identify and ignore it to ensure that there are no silent sections separated only by noise.

Second, the matching tool generates temporary sound data with a voice synthesizer for each text phrase separated by punctuation in the manuscript file and caches the duration of each phrase.

Since the duration of each phrase generated by a voice synthesizer may be quite different from the length of each phrase in the sound file, especially when the sound is a recording of a human narrator, we choose not to match the two targets directly. We find that the ratio of the phrase duration to the full presentation length is a stable value in both cases; hence, the matching tool is based on this ratio.

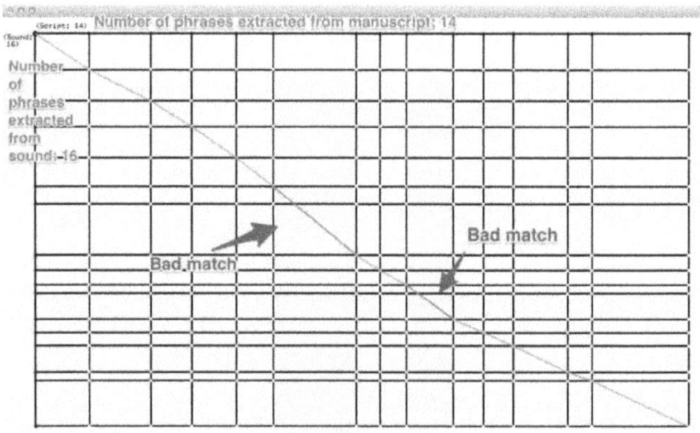

Figure 7. Matching tool conducts DP matching with the ratio of the phrase duration to the full presentation length respectively.

We refer to the DP Matching algorithm to match the two patterns and Figure 7 shows the results. The dots connected with green line segments are good matches that indicate that the phrase-to-phrase matching is successful, while red line segments indicate bad matches that will need to be fixed manually by the user.

There are two main kinds of bad matches. One occurs when the sound pauses where there is no punctuation in the manuscript text (see Figure 8). In this case, the user can choose to either add punctuation to the text or tell SmartVoice to ignore the silent sections within that particular "long" phrase. The other one occurs when the narrator ignores punctuation such as a comma or period so that the number of phrases in the manuscript is different from that in the sound data (see Figure 9). In this case, the user will have to delete the punctuation ignored by the narrator. For both cases, our matching tool provides the user an interface showing the target phrase(s) and waveforms to easily fix any mismatches manually.

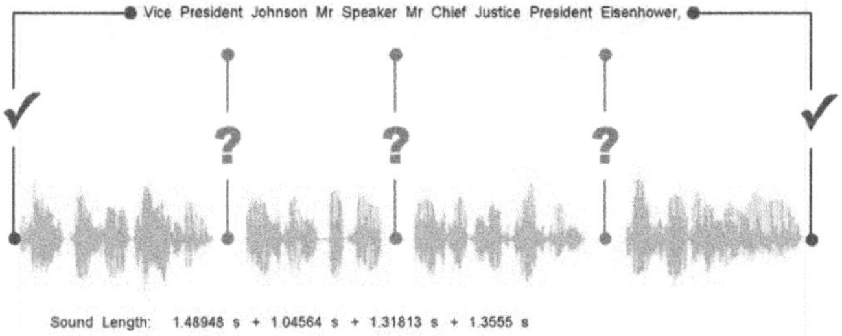

Figure 8. Bad match in which number of phrases in the text is less than that of phrases in the sound (blue line segments are automatic matching results; red line segments require manual fixing)

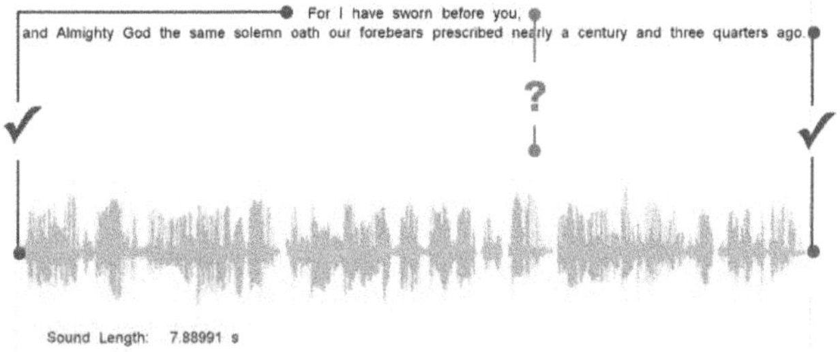

Figure 9. Bad match in which number of phrases in the text is more than that of phrases in the sound (blue line segments are automatic matching results; red line segments require manual fixing)

Playback Control, Intonation & Expression

In SmartVoice, we assign the authority to determine the duration of each pause to the user. Every time the playback pauses at a silent section, the duration of the silent section will be skipped so that when the user opens his/her mouth, the playback continues immediately with no lag.

As we discussed above, due to lack in intonation, the narration generated by a voice synthesizer may sound artificial even if the pronunciation of each word is perfect.

SmartVoice makes it possible to make the narration generated by a voice synthesizer sound vivid and natural by altering the volume, changing the playback speed, and shifting the pitch in realtime. This feature is implemented with the help of Dirac3, an open source C/C++ based multi-platform time and pitch manipulation library. [3] Based on the experimental results and the nature of human beings when speaking, we set the fluctuation band for pitch shifting to +/- one semitone in increments of 0.2 semitones and we constrained the speed variation to a range of 0.7–1.6 times normal. Volume was set to 70% of full loudness initially and could be altered between 50–100%.

Mapping

To allow the user to concentrate on the presentation, all operations are mapped to the user's face and facial parts that are detected and tracked with our system.

Pause and resume are mapped to a user's mouth openness. If the user closes his/her mouth when the current playback position is within any one of the silent sections, the playback will pause. Since the playback position will then be set to the start of the next phrase, when the user opens his/her mouth again, the playback continues with the phrase immediately. One thing to note is that when the playback position is within a phrase, the playback will not be paused until the next silent section even if the user closes his mouth. With the basic functions of SmartVoice detailed here, the audience is made to believe that a real presentation in another language has been given.

SmartVoice can also change the volume, pitch, and playback speed in realtime. As mentioned in Section 2, the pitch shifting is mapped to the position of the user's face. By calculating the *y*-direction difference between the current frame and the initial frame captured with the camera, SmartVoice shifts the pitch up when the user looks slightly up and vice versa. We initially mapped the volume to the openness of the user's eyes, but the rate of change of eye openness is so small that we finally chose to map the volume to the average height of both eyebrows, which moves in conjunction with the openness of eyes, but have a bigger rate of change. Like the mapping principle for pitch shifting, the difference between the current status and initial status determines the current volume. As for playback speed modification, we map it to the speed of lip sync. By comparing the difference in the mouth's area between the current and previous frame and calculating the rate of change, we can quickly grasp whether the user is speaking rapidly or not, so that our system will adjust the playback speed to the speed of lip sync.

Interface

Prompter

In our system, we introduce a prompter to provide an interface that interacts with the user during a presentation. In our prototype, we use a tablet PC (iPad) as the prompter screen, which shows the manuscript, and a half-mirror prompter base. With this prompter, it is possible for the user to read the manuscript while facing the audience naturally.

Co-operate with Background side

The main run environment on the interface side is an iPad that communicates with the background side program over WLAN. The reason for this is that we want to keep the prompter as simple as possible and keep all preparations completely on the background side computer. For instance, the manuscript shown on the prompter display is actually a text file loaded on the background side program sent to the iPad via WLAN before the presentation begins.

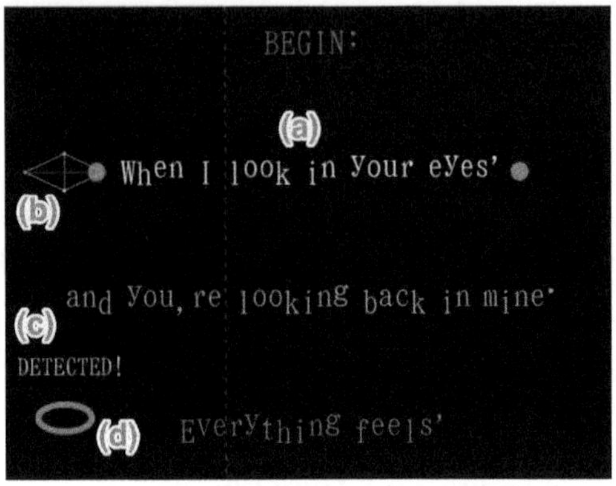

Figure 10-1. Prompter Screen

Because the user actually only interacts with the prompter during the presentation, we make it possible for the user to confirm all system behaviors from the prompter display. As shown in Figure 10-1(c), there is a label saying "DETECTED!" to notify the user that SmartVoice is successfully tracking his/her face. (The label changes to "???" if the user's face is not being tracked.)

As mentioned above, the manuscript and sound data have been correctly matched by the matching tool on a phrase-to-phrase base; hence we also break the manuscript into phrases to display them on the prompter. As Figure 5 shows, either the phrase currently being read or to be read after the current pause is emphasized and the phrase slides up after being read. (see Figure 10-1(a)).

Compared to the effects of changing the volume or pitch, the change in playback speed is difficult to immediately notice. To inform the user of the current playback speed, we add to the prompter screen an animation of a mouth whose frame rates alter with current playback speed. The mouth will be closed if the playback pauses (see Figure 10-1(d)). In addition, mouth height and width, the two parameters that determine playback speed, are represented as two orthogonal bars that change their length dynamically as the user lip syncs (see Figure 10-1(b)).

We realize that knowing the manuscript is insufficient for the user to lip sync if the manuscript is in a language that is totally strange to him/her, so we also designed another version of prompter screen, which is shown in Figure 10-2. In this version of the prompter screen, we add the translation to each phrase of the manuscript in the native language of the user (see Figure 10-2(a)) and suggest the sound level by displaying the waveform (see Figure 10-2(d)), and a pink bar is displayed as an indicator to let the user know the progress of the playback (see Figure 10-2(e)).

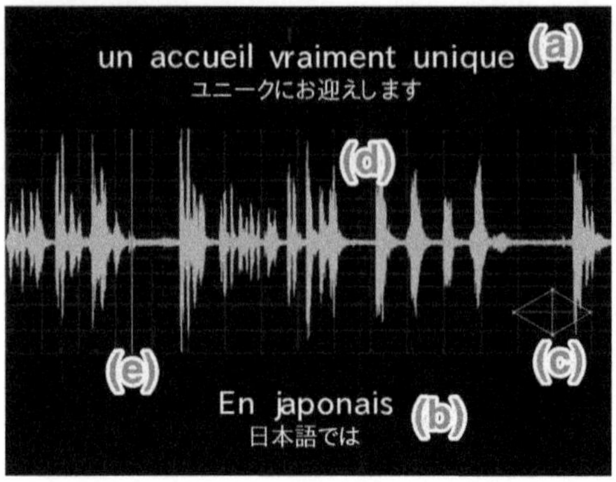

Figure 10-2. Prompter Screen ver. 2

(a) Current phase of the manuscript and its translation in native language of the user (b) next to read phrase (c) orthogonal bars showing the height and width of mouth dynamically (d) waveform (e) playback progress indicator

Performance

The phrase-to-phrase matching between manuscript text and sound data is conducted semi-automatically by the matching tool. In the case where the narration is generated by a voice synthesizer, the correct rate is 100% because the voice synthesizer always obeys the punctuation in the text file. However, if the punctuation is ignored or inserted when a human narrator reads the manuscript, there will be mismatching results that need to be fixed manually.

The background side laptop is a MacBook Pro running OSX 10.8.4 with a 2.4GHz Intel Core i5 CPU and 4GB DDR3 RAM. The tablet PC running the prompter program is a 4th generation iPad. The built-in FaceTime HD camera on the background side laptop can capture up to 720p videos at 30fps at maximum, and we set the resolution to 640x480 manually.

The background side program maintains a minimum of 55fps; hence no noticeable delay occurs with any user operations in a presentation.

EVALUATION

We conducted a user evaluation experiment to confirm the effectiveness of SmartVoice. In the user test, we showed volunteers a video that was edited with clips of real speech and speech moderated by SmartVoice. During the video playback, volunteers were asked to click and hold their mouse button whenever they thought the speech was lip synced. In order to avoid the effect of different vocal effects, the sound data used for SmartVoice was the same voice as that used for the real speech. Eight volunteers participated, all with a background in computer science.

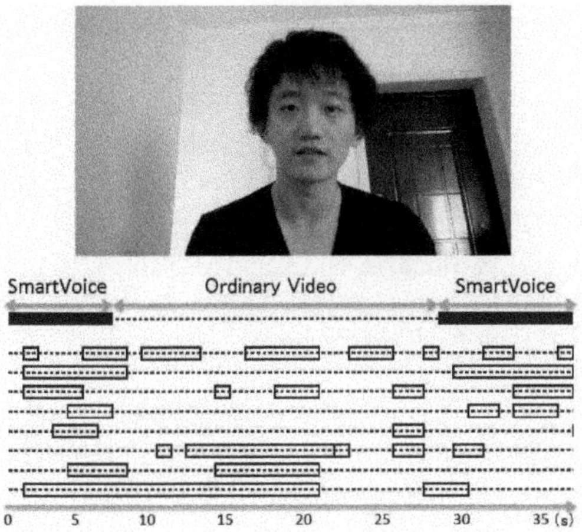

Figure 11. Results of the evaluation experiment (white rectangles in each of the eight lines indicate the sections of speech that each tester thought were generated by SmartVoice.)

Figure 11 illustrates the results. The white rectangles in each of the eight lines indicate the sections of speech that each tester thought were generated by SmartVoice. There were instances that were real speech but thought to be SmartVoice and instances that were SmartVoice speech but considered to be real. Hence, we conclude that there is no significant noticeable difference, even when we compare SmartVoice with a real presentation.

DISCUSSION

Related Work

Using facial actions as a controller is not novel. The Mouthesizer is a system that uses a mini head-mount CCD camera to track the shadow area inside the mouth using color and intensity thresholding to map it to MIDI control and instrument playing [4]. The researchers showed that although there is no difference between the Mouthesizer and the piano pedal with respect to a non-hand controller, the Mouthesizer is more intuitive and easier to learn, also suggesting the possibility of machine interfaces driven by facial actions. [5]

Facial actions are not only used for making sounds. There is also research involving a user's facial actions to control the facial expressions of CG avatars in realtime. [6]

Future Work

Integrate Voice to Video

Sometimes when we have to add narration to a demo video, especially when the narration is in a foreign language, a voice synthesizer seems to be the best choice. However, the narration generated by a voice synthesizer is too artificial to be satisfactory. By adding intonation to the synthesized voice in realtime, SmartVoice may be practical for integrating voice data generated by a voice synthesizer to videos and animations.

Ad lib

As we discussed above, the sound data used by SmartVoice needs to be prepared in advance, but it is common for a lecturer to talk about something not in the manuscript. If we are able to hide the incongruity when switching between SmartVoice and a real voice, ad-libs during a presentation may be possible.

Looping

In video production and filmmaking, video and dialogues are usually recorded separately and the dialogue is added during the automated dialogue replacement process by voice casters. The video input source is not limited to the realtime frames captured with the camera; SmartVoice is able to track the face of characters in a video as well. As a result, we may be able to use SmartVoice to do automatic looping.

Singing and Foreign Language Learning

Speeches and presentations should not be the only targets that SmartVoice aims to support. For example, SmartVoice has a prompter that is similar to that of a Karaoke system. Since both pitch and speed can be controlled in realtime with SmartVoice, our system may be able to help people who have a bad sense of pitch and rhythm to sing in the right key and tempo with practice.

For people who have to give a presentation in a foreign language, SmartVoice works as tool for practicing with a native voice. As they practice, they can memorize the pronunciation and intonation and finally get ready for the presentation with their own voice. Foreign language learners who wish to speak a language like a native may find it difficult to habitually speak with correct pronunciation and intonation, even though they often mimic native speakers. By adding a feature to compare the voice of the user to the native one for practice, we believe it may be possible for foreign language learners to develop native-like intonation with the help of SmartVoice. If the precision of detecting facial muscles is precise enough, a pronunciation correction feature is also feasible.

CONCLUSION

We proposed a presentation support system, SmartVoice, with the aim of overcoming language barriers. By matching the manuscript and sound data on a phrase-to-phrase basis, we guarantee that the sound of each phrase is correctly played according to the corresponding lip sync speed. We also attempted to solve the artificial intonation of narration generated from a voice synthesizer by changing it dynamically according to the user's facial actions. To evaluate the effectiveness of our system, we conducted a user experiment and concluded from the results that there is no significant difference between SmartVoice and real presentations. We believe that our system will enable a variety of new applications and may be the basis for substantial follow-up research.

ACKNOWLEDGMENTS
We thank all the volunteers who participated in our evaluation experiment for their help and precious advice.

REFERENCES

1. openframeworks. http://www.openframeworks.cc/.
2. ofxFaceTracker. http://github.com/kylemcdonald/ofxFaceTracker/
3. Dirac3L. http://dirac.dspdimension.com/
4. Lyons. M. J., Haehnel. M, and Tetsutani. N. The Mouthesizer: A Facial Gesture Musical Interface. In *Conference Abstracts, SIGGRAPH 2001*, ACM (LA, 2001), 230.
5. Lyons. M. J., Tetsutani. N. Facing the Music: A Facial Action Controlled Musical Interface. In *Proc, CHI 2001, Conference on Human Factors in Computing Systems 2001*, ACM (Seattle, 2001), 309-310.
6. T. Weise, S. Bouaziz, H. Li, and M. Pauly (2011). Realtime Performance-Based Facial Animation. *ACM Trans. Graph.*, *30*(4), 77.

PitchPerfect: Integrated Rehearsal Environment for Structured Presentation Preparation

Ha Trinh[1,2] **Koji Yatani**[1] **Darren Edge**[1]
[1] Microsoft Research
Beijing, China
[2] University of Dundee
Dundee, UK
hatrinh@computing.dundee.ac.uk, koji@microsoft.com, darren.edge@microsoft.com

ABSTRACT
Rehearsal is a critical component of preparing to give an oral presentation, yet it is frequently abbreviated, performed in ways that are inefficient or ineffective, or simply omitted. We conducted an exploratory study to understand the relationship between the theory and practice of presentation rehearsal, classifying our qualitative results into five themes to motivate more structured rehearsal support deeply integrated in slide presentation software. In a within-subject study (N=12) comparing against participants' existing rehearsal practices, we found that our resulting PitchPerfect system significantly improved overall presentation quality and content coverage as well as provided greater support for content mastery, time management, and confidence building.

Author Keywords
Presentation rehearsal; Slideware; PowerPoint

ACM Classification Keywords
H.5.2. Information interfaces and presentation: User Interfaces.

INTRODUCTION
Oral presentations are an integral part of academic and professional life, with virtually all related literature advocating proper rehearsal as a cornerstone of success. Appropriate rehearsal strategies potentially enable presenters to increase content familiarity, identify verbal transition issues, improve time management, and practice vocal delivery and stage presence [11, 33, 34]. Research in public speaking pedagogy has also highlighted practice time as a significant predictor of presentation quality [27].

Despite the importance of rehearsal, survey studies show it is often neglected [15, 9]. An extensive survey of 2,501 professionals [15] revealed that 35% of respondents rarely or never rehearse for their presentations. Factors contributing to rehearsal avoidance include insufficient preparation time, limited tool support, inadequate presentation training, and unawareness of expert recommendations. The intrinsic factor of communication apprehension can also lead to rehearsal avoidance, often resulting in degraded performance [3].

CHI 2014, April 26 - May 01 2014, Toronto, ON, Canada

ACM 978-1-4503-2473-1/14/04...$15.00.
http://dx.doi.org/10.1145/2556288.2557286

Our research explores how technology could facilitate a more manageable and efficient approach to presentation rehearsal than is supported in existing presentation software. We began with an interview study of 16 presenters, eliciting the problems, practices, and concerns that shape their rehearsal experiences. Five themes emerged to describe fundamental processes that structure the activity of rehearsal. Inspired by these findings and our literature survey, we developed PitchPerfect – a system offering a structured approach to presentation rehearsal. Our system integrates a range of targeted rehearsal tools to progressively develop the presenter's confidence to speak spontaneously and fluently within a prepared structure. Implemented as an add-in for Microsoft PowerPoint 2013 [22], PitchPerfect comprises:

1. *Extended authoring*. Planning of verbal content, flow, and timing in parallel with visual slide design, through use of element notes, flow paths, and slide time targets.
2. *Cued-recall testing*. Rapid recall practice to master the flow of visual content and its associated verbal notes.
3. *Scaffolded speech rehearsal*. Realistic spoken rehearsal supported by visual time guides and structured notes, with the ability to progressively withdraw scaffolding support using an automatic note compression technique.

In a two-session study with 12 participants, we compared structured rehearsal with PitchPerfect against existing practices with PowerPoint. We measured the overall experiences of both presenters and audience through subjective ratings of participants' presentation videos and qualitative analysis of semi-structured interviews. Results showed that PitchPerfect led to small but significant differences in overall presentation quality and content coverage. Qualitative findings indicated a strong user preference toward PitchPerfect, confirming its benefits in terms of content mastery, time management, confidence building, and preparation time efficiency. We show that PitchPerfect can encourage many practices recommended in the literature while providing greater support than conventional presentation tools. Our contributions include:

1. Derivation of five grounded themes that characterize rehearsal practices and motivate integrated tool support;
2. Development of the PitchPerfect system to support structured rehearsal in an integrated environment;
3. Validation of PitchPerfect in a comparative study that demonstrates its potential to improve the overall experiences of both presenters and audiences.

RELATED WORK

We divide the related work into three sections. We discuss recommendations on how to learn presentations, and explain the relationship between rehearsal and presentation quality, before concluding with a review of rehearsal tool support.

Learning and presentations

The needs of audiences learning from presentations are tightly intertwined with the needs of presenters preparing to deliver such presentations. Nancy Duarte [10] suggests that the fear of failing to remember what to say in the moment discourages presenters from giving up text-heavy slides, which then fail to result in audience connection. Her "3 Rs of Letting Go" is a systematic way to help presenters speak naturally to slides that visually complement their narration:

1. *Reduce* reliance on slide text by rehearsing with a single highlighted word per bullet until only the highlighted words are needed as prompts (or better, use images);
2. *Record* spoken rehearsals, using a script or notes if required, listening back in idle moments to absorb content auditorily and further reduce text reliance;
3. *Repeat* the presentation by speaking to it, writing it down, and reciting it mentally many times, and continue until the key points and flow are committed to memory.

When presenters are no longer dependent on their slides, they become free to leave the lectern and engage directly with the audience [28]. Reduced slide text also avoids the involuntary audience reflex of reading the slide, allowing presenters to draw attention with interpretations, examples, and other details that justify their presence and enhance their credibility [33]. A special case of adding value to slides is through closure – saying something conclusive before moving to the next slide rather than "rebooting" with an empty transition such as, "Now I'd like to talk about…" [34]. Repeated mental review in a slideshow mode can help reveal problems with such transitions, as well as overall flow [11].

While mentally reviewing slides is helpful, "a truly effective presentation is impossible" without verbalization: speaking aloud, accompanied by slides, just as intended when in front of the audience [33]. Reluctance to verbalize can stem from feelings of self-consciousness, anxiety, and foolishness, leading to the suboptimal, disembodied practice of speaking *about* slides rather than speaking *to* slides [33].

Advice for spoken rehearsals is to practice first with the clock counting up, trimming content until the talk fits within the desired timeframe, then practicing with a timer counting down until the talk fits the timeframe consistently [11]. An advantage of recording such rehearsals is to identify unconscious use of filler words [2]. These can be remediated through the strategy of "phrase and pause" [34], which adds animation to the presenter's voice and reduces the audience's sensory overload [34]. Video-taping rehearsals provides an additional opportunity to check stage presence, eye contact, facial expressions, gestures, and ease of movement [11], but risks making the presenter self-conscious and nervous [34].

Learning through multimedia

Many of these recommendations on how and why to avoid text-heavy slides is further supported by cognitive science. Replacing text with images is motivated by the Picture Superiority Effect – concepts are remembered for longer when presented as images rather than words [24]. Slides designed in a minimalist manner can thus serve as instant visual mnemonics [33]. Reviewing materials both visually and auditorily is also supported by the Dual Coding theory of memory [26], in which visual and verbal information are encoded in separate mental representations that act as cues for the recall of one another. A benefit of this practice is that the same effects apply to the audience during delivery, summarized by the principles of Multimedia Learning [19]:

1. *Multiple Representation*: use both pictures and words;
2. *Continuity*: use pictures and words at the same time;
3. *Coherence*: use fewer words and pictures at a time;
4. *Split Attention*: augment pictures with speech not text;
5. *Individual Differences*: applies more to visual learners.

The "Beyond Bullet Points" method [2] is explicitly based on these principles, encouraging presenters to communicate one idea per slide and to clearly differentiate the roles of slide visuals and speaker notes by first building their slides in the Notes Page (handout) view, rather than in the Normal view.

Learning through cued-recall

Once visuals have been added to slides, the challenge is then to mentally associate these visuals with the script or notes. One approach is cued-recall learning [6], in which the learner attempts to recall a target item (e.g., speaker notes) given a cue (e.g., slide visuals). Such learning leverages two effects:

1. *Testing effect*: tests strengthen memory more than extra study, even without spoken or written responses;
2. *Spacing effect*: for a given time of exposure, multiple short exposures are better than one long exposure.

Typical cued-recall systems progressively increase test intervals to optimize for long-term learning efficiency. However, for specific short-term needs, it is often effective to test the same items multiple times in the same session [29]. This is called *overlearning*, and can have confidence-boosting effects when preparing to speak under stressful circumstances (e.g., second language conversations [12]). Another common strategy is to rehearse in the slideshow mode without notes to encourage higher levels of content mastery than is required in practice [11].

Rehearsal and Presentation Quality

Previous research has reported consistent findings on the impact of rehearsal on presentation performance [3, 21, 27]. In a study with 119 students, positive correlations were found between presentation quality and rehearsal time (both silent and spoken), number of verbal rehearsals (alone and to an audience), and preparation of speaking notes [21]. Similarly, after an analysis of speech preparation journal entries from 95 students, rehearsal time was suggested as a significant predictor of presentation quality [27].

Related research has examined the relationship among communication apprehension (CA), speech preparation practices, and public speaking competency [3, 4]. Affecting at least 20% of the population, CA can be defined as fear or anxiety in either real or anticipated communication with others [20]. Students with high CA have also been found to spend more preparation time on non-communicative tasks (e.g., writing notes) in avoidance of rehearsal [3]. As a result, they required substantially greater preparation time but received lower speech grades than their low apprehensive peers, who focused their time on rehearsals. These findings indicate that presentation success is determined more by preparation strategy than duration. To complicate the issue, a significant, positive correlation has been found between CA and public speaking procrastination [4]. Consequently, presenters with high CA tend to reserve inadequate time for preparation, leading to poor delivery quality. Appropriate "anti-procrastination" strategies, such as dividing a rehearsal into an incremental series of small and targeted components, could be beneficial for such apprehensive presenters [4].

Presentation Rehearsal Systems

Commercial slideware packages, including Microsoft PowerPoint [22] and Apple Keynote [1], provide timing, audio recording, and presenter view features to aid rehearsal. However, very little work has been published on the usability of these facilities or their use in practice.

Several projects have addressed the need for effective feedback mechanisms in presentation rehearsal. In the Presentation Sensei system [18], speech and image processing are used to provide automatic feedback on the presenter's speaking rate, eye contact, frequency of verbal fillers and timing. Hypervideo techniques have also been used to create a peer-review support framework for the collection and organization of audience comments during and after rehearsal [25]. While appropriate feedback strategies are undoubtedly useful, they implicitly assume that the presenter is sufficiently prepared to perform a full timed and recorded spoken rehearsal of their intended final delivery. The question remains as to how technology can help presenters move beyond the completion of slide authoring to reach such an advanced stage of readiness.

Several presentation tools, such as NextSlidePlease [30] and HyperSlides [13], also incorporate facilities for rehearsal. NextSlidePlease allows the presenter to specify individual slide time budgets in the authoring environment. During rehearsal and delivery, the system displays visual feedback on time expenditure at both slide and overall presentation levels, thereby facilitating time management. HyperSlides enables the creation of hierarchically structured scenes and expandable points in a presentation where each point can be dynamically revealed on demand. In rehearsal, this flexible structure opens up opportunities for cued-recall testing [6] of points to be communicated. However, no existing system gives explicit and systematic support that progressively guides presenters through the different stages of rehearsal.

REHEARSAL IN PRACTICE: AN EXPLORATORY STUDY

To gain an insight into the problem of presentation rehearsal, we conducted an interview study exploring the practices of presentation preparation. Our aim was to identify fundamental concerns that shape the activity of rehearsing, as well as discrepancies between everyday practices with presentation systems and best practices from the literature.

Participants

We recruited 16 students and professionals (4 female, 12 male, ages 21–40+, PA1–16). Our participants comprised 7 native English speakers and 9 non-native English speakers from 4 nationalities, with backgrounds in computer science, physics, life science, and finance. They had diverse linguistic, cultural, and educational backgrounds as well as presentation experience levels, in ways that might influence presentation preparation strategies and desired tool support.

Procedure and Findings

We conducted semi-structured interviews with open-ended questions about the participants' presentation experiences, focusing on post-authoring preparation strategies and related supporting tools. The interviews were recorded, transcribed and coded using thematic analysis techniques [5]. Our initial open coding resulted in 113 process codes capturing actions in data. We categorized these codes into five overarching themes that help to structure the activity of rehearsing.

1. Appropriating notes with personal notations

As a common tactic in presentation planning, writing and styling speaking notes assists presenters in verbally expanding on visual elements (e.g., bullet points and images on a presentation slide), both during rehearsal and delivery:

> *"I wrote down just short explanations next to each bullet point … what for each one I was trying to say but in my words, not in formal words like you put on the slide."* [PA6]

Presenters utilize various means of note taking, from paper notebooks, physical cue cards, and annotated slide printouts, to digital documents and slide note sections in slideware. While some presenters prepare verbose notes or scripts, others prefer just *"slightly more expanded bullet points"* [PA5] or even more condensed notes containing only keywords and referable values. Specific wordings are sometimes scripted and memorized for a strong introduction and conclusion, or for a verbal transition that *"leads from one slide to the other"* [PA2]. Creative use of notes includes cumulative timing targets that prompt and remind the presenters of a specific point in the presentation time by which they should have arrived at a particular slide.

During rehearsal and especially during delivery, the ability to quickly refer to notes corresponding to the point being communicated is of critical importance. Although existing slideware allows presenters to view on-screen notes during a presentation, these notes are often *"hidden away"* [PA6]. Various ad-hoc strategies are used to overcome this issue, such as segmenting notes with colors, highlighting keywords or styling slide content notes and transition notes differently.

2. Tuning cued-recall through rapid practice
Presenters often treat visual elements, e.g., bullet points or images on a slide, as prompts for retrieval of verbal content. Rapid, mental rehearsal enables presenters to review and refine the intended visual-verbal associations, *"making sure what I want to say is reflected on the slides"* [PA4], as well as practice recalling verbal points from visual cues:

"I just have a quick scan on my slides to remind me in each slide what I should do. So actually I've already got a structure, so I review stuff just to make sure that I don't forget the points." [PA9]

Mentally rehearsing visual elements also allows presenters to check and absorb the presentation flow, ensuring they *"know the ordering of the slides, which is important"* [PA1]. Anxious or unprepared presenters may have to *"look often at the slides to make me remember what I want to say"* [PA11], causing unpleasantness for both presenter and audience.

3. Scaffolding realistic delivery in rehearsal
As a step closer to realistic delivery, presenters often perform end-to-end rehearsals, speaking full sentences verbally or mentally, with support from private notes and time guides:

"I'll have slides on my TV and the notes in front of me. I'll time myself and I'll start working my way through the presentation. And at the end of it, I'll check my time. I'll check if there's anything I need to change, then go back and do it again." [PA2]

Prior to full rehearsal, presenters may derive an initial timing plan based on their knowledge of slide and note content as well as previous presentation experiences. During and after rehearsal, these timing targets provide presenters with guidance on *"roughly how long I should spend on a particular area"* [PA1], assisting them in adjusting the amount of presentation content in accordance with time constraints. Developing realistic time estimates is a time-consuming process, *"because you need to go through the presentation yourself 2 or 3 times to understand how long you are going to spend on each slide"* [PA7]. Existing tools for time tracking range from a watch to timing features in slideware, which allow presenters to check individual slide timings in addition to overall presentation duration.

Detailed speaking notes, e.g., complete scripts, may be used in initial rehearsals, while repeated rehearsals with more condensed notes help to reduce the presenter's note reliance. These notes can also be specially structured to aid presenters in controlling speaking rate: *"the way I've done it, it's 3 or 4 words, so you can take a little break after every one"* [PA7].

Besides timing control, end-to-end rehearsal helps presenters refine the presentation flow and practice verbal transitions between slides. These can be scripted beforehand in notes or improvised from the next slide preview in slideware.

4. Committing provisional speech for judgment
Performing full verbal rehearsal allows presenters to obtain feedback on various aspects of their presentation, from slide content, flow, and pacing to vocal delivery, wording, and pronunciation issues. Such feedback may come from an audience or from self-judgment on recorded speech:

"So I'll hit the record on the presenter mode…So what it does is it records the audio along with the timing of the slides as well. So I will go and I'll get the presentation to my laptop screen, talking at the screen as if I'm giving a presentation. And then I'll play back and listen and I'll look at these areas where I delayed or skipped over things too quickly." [PA1]

While a few presenters who have recorded rehearsal praise its benefits, this practice is often neglected. Common reasons include lack of suitable environments and equipment for recording, *"feeling stupid speaking to a recorder"* [PA4], *"sounded awful"* [PA3], and presenters who *"never saw the point of doing that"* [PA2]. As a tedious and time-consuming task, recording and reviewing spoken rehearsal is often skipped under time pressure. Second language presenters tend to be even more reluctant to record rehearsals due to language barriers. Instead, silent rehearsal, described as *"just look at my slides and think about what I want to say"* [PA12], is a less overwhelming and hence a more common practice.

Although errors detected through recorded rehearsal can help presenters highlight areas for improvement, they can also lower their self-confidence, because *"if I don't think about having made mistakes during rehearsal, I won't be dwelling about whether I will make mistakes in the real thing"* [PA5].

5. Reducing notes, times, and errors until ready
Presenters often aim to reduce rehearsal times, errors, and note details through iterative rehearsals. Manually condensing notes in each iteration is a frequently described strategy to help decrease presenters' note reliance:

"I generally write out cue cards… I then use them when I'm rehearsing it. And then I sort of reduce them to just very small pointers that remind me of what was in the original cue cards. Then eventually I'll use something on the slides as a reminder of what the pointers were. So it is a very convoluted kind of method, starting with putting a lot of notes in, then moving down to having none but cues on the slides." [PA5]

By improving timing accuracy, by aiming for successive error-free rehearsals, and by practicing with increasingly compressed notes, presenters can decrease their speech anxiety and progressively build up their confidence to deliver a timely and fluent speech in a natural and spontaneous manner. Producing artefacts that embody different levels of readiness (e.g., notes at different levels of detail) also supports all future deliveries (e.g., falling back to appropriately reduced notes rather than the complete script).

DESIGN OF PITCHPERFECT

Informed by the findings of our interview study and literature review, we designed PitchPerfect as rehearsal environment embedded within Microsoft PowerPoint. We now present an overview of the supported activities and interaction design.

Structured Presentation Preparation

PitchPerfect incorporates three-level support for presentation preparation: planning verbal delivery with three forms of *extended authoring*, forming mental associations with two forms of *cued-recall testing*, and verbalizing within a *scaffolded speech rehearsal* environment.

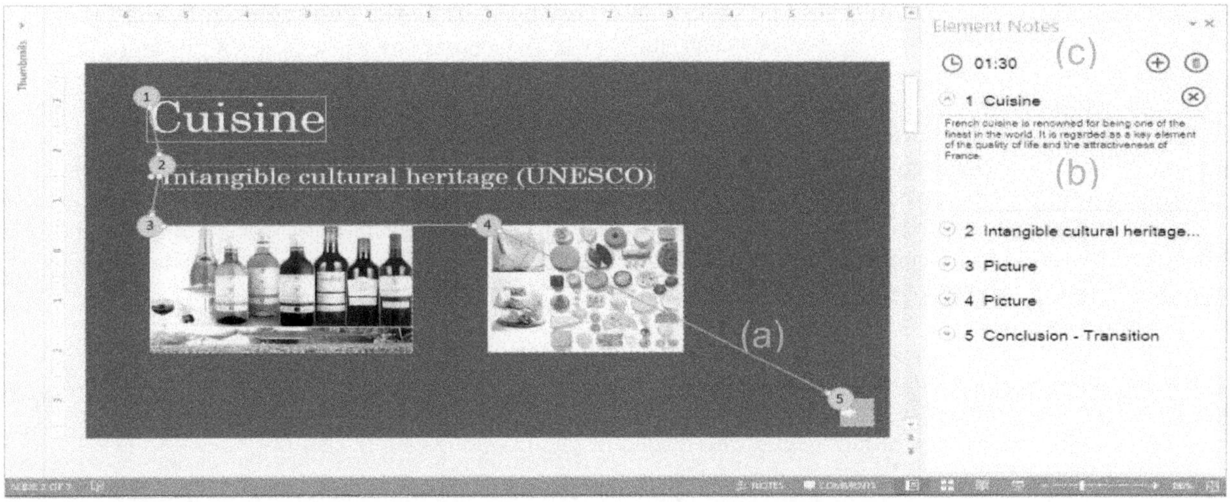

Figure 1. Extended authoring mode with (a) visualized flow path; (b) element notes; and (c) time target.

At the bottom level of planning, extended authoring enables the presenter to prepare to verbally expand on slide visuals with element notes, arrange the speaking order of slide visuals with flow paths, and specify a timing plan with time targets for both individual slides and the overall presentation. Compared to existing slide notes, our element notes provide enhanced support for creating visual-verbal associations by allowing for attachment of speaking notes to specific slide visuals (e.g., titles, bullet points, images, shapes, or groups).

At the middle level of memory-building, PitchPerfect uses a flashcard-like approach for cued-recall testing of element notes and flow paths. Element note rehearsal allows presenters to practice recalling their intended speaking points for each visual element. Flow path rehearsal trains the presenter's ability to recall the content of visual elements and the verbal path through them. Together, they help presenters to drill both visual and verbal points into their memory, refining if necessary, before progressing to verbalization.

At the top level of speech rehearsal, PitchPerfect allows presenters to verbalize with scaffolding support from element notes and time guides specified and refined at lower levels. Our system visualizes actual slide timings versus time targets, aiding time management. In addition, PitchPerfect accounts for trial and error during speaking by supporting record-review-revise cycles for speech at various levels. To help presenters reduce their note reliance, we also incorporate note compression capabilities, which applies NLP techniques to trim note text while retaining key words.

Together, these support mechanisms form a structured approach to presentation rehearsal that guides presenters through the processes of preparation in ways that conform to recommendations from the literature while offering greater support than conventional presentation tools. Although we target formal, time-controlled presentations, we anticipate that the mental associations formed during rehearsal would also provide a platform for more improvisational delivery of the same content. We now describe the three core features.

Extended Authoring

The presenter begins by authoring PowerPoint slides as usual, then proceeds to extended authoring by clicking the corresponding control on the PowerPoint ribbon. As the presenter selects a slide, a visualized flow path through all visual elements of the slide is automatically generated and overlaid on the slide, representing a default speaking order of the slide visuals (Figure 1a). An element note placeholder is automatically created for each node of the flow path and displayed on the side panel (Figure 1b). The presenter can edit these notes to specify how they intend to elaborate upon each visual element with speech. These element notes are initially arranged according to the chronological creation order of their associated visual elements. They can be manually rearranged through drag-and-drop operations on the element note list to reflect the intended speaking order, or deleted if desired. The flow path automatically updates.

In addition to element notes for slide visuals, we also attach a special "transition note" to the end of the note list (shown as an icon in the bottom-right slide corner, Figure 1). This encourages the presenter to prepare a verbal linkage to the next slide – a key way to create a smoothly flowing delivery.

In parallel to creating, editing, and authoring element notes, the presenter can also set time targets for the overall presentation and individual slides. The overall presentation time target can be entered into a designated control on the PowerPoint ribbon while slide time targets can be automatically calculated by evenly distributing the overall time across slides. The presenter can manually adjust time targets of specific slides on the element notes side panel (Figure 1c). As the presenter modifies a slide time target, all other device-generated slide time targets will be updated accordingly. In addition to helping the presenter stay or get back on track during delivery, such time targets can also assist the presenter in preparing an appropriate amount of content for the slide. These time targets can also be adjusted in the three rehearsal modes described next.

Cued-recall Testing

PitchPerfect has two targeted cued-recall rehearsal modes. In the element note rehearsal mode, presenters train themselves to recall the contents of element notes (i.e., their intended speaking points) for each visual element. Interaction proceeds with the system highlighting a visual element and prompting the presenter to anticipate the associated element note (Figure 2a). The presenter then presses the right arrow key to reveal the associated element notes and mentally compare them to what they had anticipated. If the presenter correctly anticipated the actual element notes, they can proceed to the next visual element specified in the flow path. Otherwise, they can press the left arrow key to navigate back, and repeat the process. Training to a level of reliable error-free completion can increase the presenter's confidence that they will be able to recall their verbal points even when under real delivery pressure. This process also helps to identify visuals that did not support recall. In this and all other targeted rehearsal modes, it is always possible to rapidly exit the rehearsal environment, make refinements to slide visuals and notes, then rehearse again in an iterative cycle.

In the flow path rehearsal mode, presenters train themselves to recall the visual elements on a slide and their intended speaking order. Interaction proceeds in a similar fashion to the element note rehearsal, with the system hiding visual elements further along the flow path and prompting the presenter to anticipate what is coming next (see Figure 2b). A press of the right arrow key then reveals the target visual element along with its associated note. This process enables the presenter to check and commit the presentation flow and visual contents into memory. This in turns helps delivery of the presentation without constant reference to the slides.

Scaffolded Speech Rehearsal

This rehearsal mode encourages the presenter to practice timed and recorded verbalization. The element notes and time targets specified in the extended authoring stage are shown to guide the exploration of how to speak about each visual element and for how long (Figure 2c). We arrange all the element notes of a slide onto a single note page, segmenting them by colored headings to facilitate note retrieval. These combined notes provide a big picture of all speaking points for the slide, helping the presenter smoothly connect points with speech. While the presenter is speaking, we continuously update time information on two time bars: a *slide time bar* displaying the speaking time of the current slide relative to its time target (Figure 2i), and a *presentation time bar* showing the cumulative timed recordings of all slides relative to the presentation time budget (Figure 2ii). We also display a *presentation target bar* of all time targets, allowing the presenter to compare planned versus actual timings (Figure 2iii).

We capture the presenter's speech through auto-recording with silence detection. As the presenter starts speaking, their speech is detected using the Microsoft Speech Recognition API [23]. A new recording segment is immediately added to the existing recording of the slide, as shown on the slide time bar. As soon as any pause exceeds two seconds, recording and timing stop. A pause marker is added to the slide time bar to indicate the end of the current recording segment, as shown in Figure 2iv. All non-speech durations are therefore not included in cumulative time totals. The purpose of this feature is to reduce the pressure on the presenter, helping them review notes and slides or think about what they want to say without the constant feeling of time ticking by.

At any time, the presenter can click on a recording segment for playback or deletion, with the most recent one selected by default. This allows the presenters to review and revise parts that they did not say well enough without having to re-record the entire slide or presentation. Double-clicking on a slide on the presentation time bar enables the presenter to select the entire slide recording for playback or deletion. Manual recording controls can also be used at any time.

The accumulated speech intervals recorded in this manner comprise an "ideal delivery" containing little or no disruptive pauses, performed in an ideal environment with support from both time guides and speaking notes. In each successive rehearsal, the presenter can aim to approach this ideal delivery while reducing rehearsal times, errors, and note reliance. To help the presenter gradually lessen their note reliance, we developed an automatic compression method.

Note Compression

With note compression, we aim to progressively reduce the text of the notes across successive rehearsals, while preserving essential information. We view this as a simplified problem of automatic sentence compression addressed in previous research [7]. Our purpose is to retain words that can act as appropriate cues for recall of original notes (i.e., the intended speaking points) rather than to ensure the grammatical correctness of the compressed notes. Thus, we adopted a basic telegraphic text reduction approach [16].

Unlike statistical methods using word frequencies [7, 14], in this approach the judgment of importance of information is based upon linguistic criteria drawn from cognitive and information retrieval research [17, 32]. Our compression algorithm is guided as follows:

1. Words are filtered based on their ability to act as retrieval cues for target text (e.g., nouns generally contribute most, adjectives and adverbs less, and verbs the least [17]; subject nouns are better cues than object nouns [32]).
2. Number, comparative and superlative phrases should be retained as they tend to convey important information.
3. The number of compression levels and the compression rates should be carefully considered to avoid dramatic note reduction between two consecutive levels, thereby allowing a gradual process of withdrawing note support.

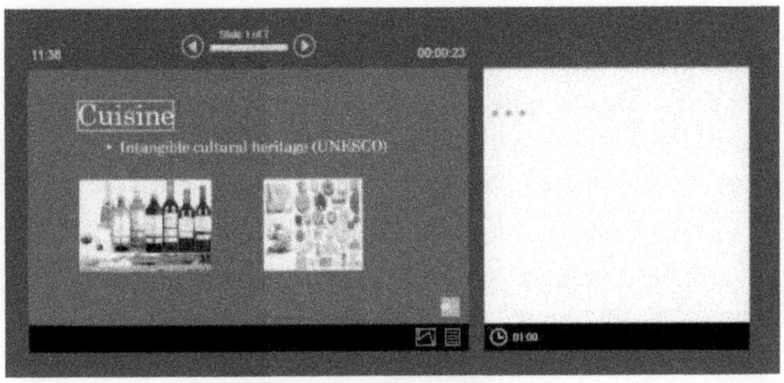

(a) Element Note Rehearsal

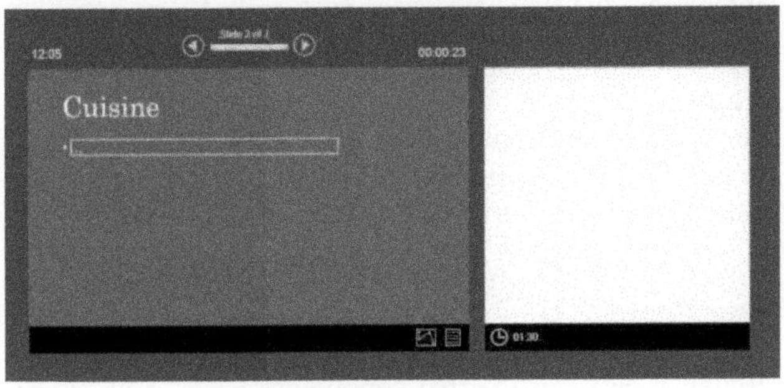

(b) Flow Path Rehearsal

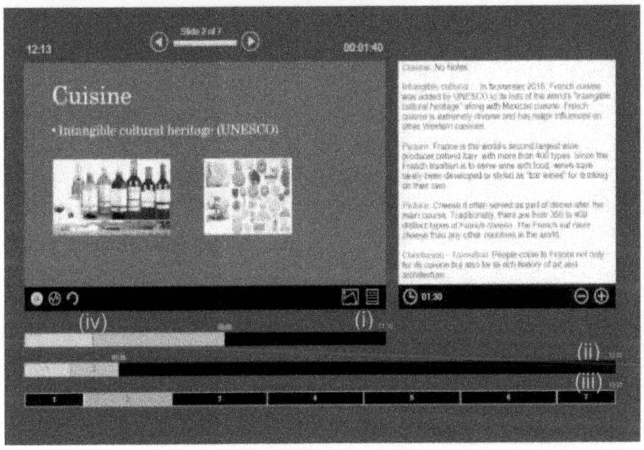

(c) Timed Speech Rehearsal

Figure 2. Three targeted modes in PitchPerfect supporting cued-recall testing and recorded spoken rehearsal.

Level 1: Original notes
"French cuisine is renowned for being one of the finest in the world."

Level 2: Nouns - proper nouns - verbs - adjectives - adverbs - numbers
"French cuisine is renowned ... being one ... finest ... world."

Level 3: Nouns - proper nouns - adjectives - comparative, superlative and number phrases
"French cuisine ... renowned ... one ... finest ... world."

Level 4: Subject nouns - proper nouns - comparative, superlative and number phrases
"... cuisine ... one ... finest ..."

Level 5: No notes

Figure 3. Five levels of notes in PitchPerfect: An example showing how a sentence is compressed at each level.

To compress a sentence in the notes, our system analyzes the grammatical structure of the sentence using the Stanford Part-of-Speech (POS) tagger [33] and typed dependency parser [8]. At each compression level, the system removes a new set of words according to a pre-defined set of rules.

To tune the compression levels, we collected over 8000 PowerPoint presentations using Microsoft Bing web search and extracted all slide note text. 21% of the presentations contained notes, resulting in a notes corpus of 1.1M words in total. We analyzed the grammatical structure of these notes and computed the POS tag frequencies on the corpus. We experimented with removing different POS tags from the corpus following our first principle while calculating the resulting compression rates based on the POS tag frequencies. Through this process, we derived five levels of compression rates (0%, 33%, 54%, 82%, and 100%).

In PitchPerfect, the presenters can set a global level for all slide notes using controls in the PowerPoint ribbon. In the speech rehearsal mode, they can move between different note levels for a specific slide by pressing the associated buttons on the slide note pane. Figure 3 shows an example.

EVALUATION OF PITCHPERFECT

We conducted a user study comparing the structured approach of PitchPerfect against participants' existing practices with PowerPoint. Our focus was to examine whether structured rehearsal with PitchPerfect can improve both the presenter experience of presentation preparation and presentation quality perceived by an audience.

Procedure

From our interviews, we learned that delivering a presentation created by somebody else is a common scenario. We therefore focused our evaluation purely on rehearsal and delivery of prefabricated presentation material, which would also support controlled comparisons with existing approaches to rehearsal. We therefore asked each participant to rehearse and deliver two 10-minute presentations on similar topics (French and Italian culture) in English. Each slide deck contained 7 slides with 27 visual elements in total, including headings, bullet points and images. Supporting notes formed approximately 900 words, containing 27 key points for all the visual elements.

The study was a within-subject, baseline-intervention design across two sessions. Each session lasted between 90-120 minutes, with 1–6 days between sessions. The ordering of slide decks was counterbalanced across participants. We adopted the baseline-intervention design because counter-balancing the conditions could risk the transfer of rehearsal approaches from the PitchPerfect to the PowerPoint condition, which would not provide an accurate picture of existing practices. We also expected the learning effect from the PowerPoint condition to be minimal with experienced presenters, controlling any potential threat to validity.

Session 1: In this baseline session, we asked participants to rehearse and deliver the presentation using their own preparation strategies with PowerPoint. Notes had been added to the corresponding slide note sections in PowerPoint in advance. All points in the notes were arranged in the intended speaking order and clearly separated by blank lines.

At the beginning of the session, we gave participants the scenario of preparing to present a pre-made slide deck. We instructed them to cover the key points in the notes to the best of their ability given the preparation time available. We also introduced participants to the three rehearsal support features of PowerPoint 2013: timing, recording, and presenter view. The session was set up with two screens, allowing the participants to rehearse with the presenter view should they wish. We explained that they could use any subset of these features or other approaches according to their preferences. Following this introduction, we allowed participants one hour to rehearse before giving a final, video-recorded presentation. We concluded with a semi-structured interview probing their preparation strategies and task experiences.

Session 2: In this intervention session, we asked participants to rehearse and deliver the presentation in a structured way using PitchPerfect. All key points in the notes were attached to the corresponding visual elements beforehand.

We gave participants the same scenario as in Session 1, followed by an introduction to the element notes and the three rehearsal modes of PitchPerfect, which lasted approximately 10 minutes. Following this introduction, we allowed participants one hour to rehearse before giving a final, video-recorded presentation. We divided this 1 hour into three ordered sections: 10 minutes using the element notes, 20 minutes using the cued-recall testing modes, and 30 minutes using the speech rehearsal mode. In the cued-recall testing modes, we instructed participants to use either or both the element note rehearsal and the flow path rehearsal, in any order they liked. We asked participants at the end of the time allocated to each section to move on to the next. The interview protocol followed that of Session 1 and prompted critical reflection on the use of PitchPerfect.

In both sessions, participants used the same tool to deliver their presentations (i.e., the presenter view of PowerPoint with the presence of notes, timer, and next slide preview).

Participants

We recruited 12 students and researchers with technical backgrounds and varying levels of presentation experience (3 female, 9 male, ages 22-32, mean 24, PB1–12). All spoke English in their work environment, 7 as a second language. All were frequent users of PowerPoint or Keynote or both.

Presentation Ratings

We recruited three raters (2 female, 1 male, R1–3) to independently evaluate the relative quality of the 12 pairs of video-recorded presentations. The raters were research students working in our lab and blind to the study protocol. Raters compared each presentation pair (PowerPoint vs. PitchPerfect) on six criteria: organization, content coverage, note reliance, speech, timing and pacing, and overall quality. Each criterion was judged on a 4-point ordinal scale of "no difference", "slight difference", "moderate difference", and "substantial difference", with the superior presentation indicated in the case of perceived differences. We later converted results into a 7-point numeric scale ranging -3 to 3 (negative values favor PowerPoint, positive PitchPerfect).

For content coverage, we gave raters a checklist of the 27 key points in the notes that should be covered in each presentation. We asked raters to award one point for each piece of content presented in its entirety (but not necessarily word-for-word). We calculated the average content coverage score across the three raters for each recorded presentation and used them for comparison.

Results

We performed Shapiro-Wilk tests to check the normality of our data. Parametric tests were used for normally distributed data and non-parametric tests were used otherwise.

Average content coverage was 19.36 (*SD* 5.17) with PowerPoint and 21.83 (*SD* 3.68) with PitchPerfect. Analysis using repeated measures ANOVA showed a significant difference between the two conditions ($F_{1,11}$= 9.57, p<.01, partial η^2=0.47).

For overall quality, a t-test on the average ratings of the three raters showed a significant difference between the two conditions in favor of PitchPerfect (p<.05). Wilcoxon signed-rank tests on the ratings of each rater indicated that R1 and R2 had significant preferences for the PitchPerfect presentations (p=.04 for both), but not in R3's ratings (p=.5). The inter-rater reliability of the three raters was moderate (Cronbach's alpha=0.482), but explained by the inherent difficulty of the rating task, the subjective rating criteria, and the limited training given to raters. Despite this, PitchPerfect achieved significantly higher average ratings and was preferred by the majority of the raters, showing potential to improve overall talk quality. No significant differences were found in the other four quality criteria.

Qualitative Findings

We performed high-level coding on the transcribed interviews, and found that all participants reported strong preference toward PitchPerfect and their reasons.

Planning Visual-Verbal Associations with Element Notes

Participants appreciated the ability to connect slide visuals and intended speaking points using element notes. With conventional slide notes, *"sometimes you don't remember what note is assigned to what element"* [PB5]. Participants had to manually organize and style slide notes into element-based subsections, often discouraging them *"from taking notes in the first place"* [PB9]. In contrast, our element notes provided a *"nice, clean and simple"* [PB8] way of structuring notes, making *"the idea more clear"* [PB5]. Participants could quickly refer to specific segments, making it *"easier to find"* what they want [PB2], and allowing them to *"focus on just one particular part of the slide"* [PB12].

The clear ordering of the notes and the visual flow paths also helped participants to learn and absorb the presentation flow: *"every time I see a slide, there was a map hidden in my mind"* [PB1]. One participant suggested that these features would be most useful when learning slides made by others.

A recommended improvement for the element notes was to allow adding and ordering of note sections without attaching them to a visual element. This feature could be particularly beneficial for presenters with minimal slide visuals.

Mastering Content with Cued-recall Testing

By allowing presenters to quickly step through each slide visual and element note in the intended speaking order, our cued-recall testing enabled them to *"get the structure of the PPT faster"* [PB3]. Moreover, by hiding slide visuals and element notes, this process encouraged participants to actively recall what to say for each element – *"because if I can see all of them, I will be lazy, I will just read it and won't think about it"* [PB6]. As a result, they developed *"a deeper understanding or feeling of what I should say"* [PB3]. Through cued-recall practices, participants could also highlight *"which part I didn't remember well"*, allowing them to *"strengthen the memory of that part"* [PB2] and subsequently increase their confidence in content mastery.

Reducing Note Reliance with Note Compression

Practicing with note compression was reported to be helpful, mainly by native English speaking participants. It provided useful cues for recall of verbal notes – *"it's amazing that the shown words are very important words"* [PB6]. It also helped with *"memorizing key points"* [PB9] as opposed to relying on the notes during delivery. Participants often described the process of manually condensing notes for their own presentations as *"really tedious and time consuming"* [PB10], and felt that our note compression would greatly reduce this effort. Repeated practices with compressed notes was another effective method PitchPerfect offered to build confidence – *"when I look at the few keywords of a sentence and I can say the whole sentence, I think it makes me feel very confident"* [PB6]. An area for improvements pointed out by participants was that note compression operated on individual sentences rather than the whole note, sometimes making note recall *"a little bit difficult"* [PB10] when the logical connections between sentences became unclear.

Encouraging Recorded Spoken Rehearsal

Participants commented that recording their rehearsal with PowerPoint was generally unnecessary unless they wanted to elicit feedback from others, because *"I don't have time to re-watch my recording"* [PB1]. Many of them reported to often rehearse mentally, or just *"normally whisper"* [PB10].

In contrast, the recording environment in PitchPerfect encouraged participants to perform recorded verbalization, thanks to the multiple benefits it offered. The auto-recording with silence detection provided a more accurate estimate of presentation length compared to conventional recording facilities, *"because when you do rehearsal, you have a lot of empty voice time, and you have pauses"* [PB1]. The ability to account for trial and error during speaking was also well received, because *"every time I was thinking about how to change or edit my voice, it provides me with a function that I can delete some period of my voice or I can add something"* [PB1]. Cycles of record-review-revise for speech at both segment and slide levels helped participants to quickly check their speaking rate and identify wording issues, highlighting *"which word and which sentence I want to adjust"* [PB2].

Several participants noticed that they had to speak louder because otherwise, PitchPerfect did not record their speech. But, they enjoyed the experience because *"it encouraged me to properly practice it instead of just whispering"* [PB9]. Visualization of pauses during recording also helped participants identify problem areas because *"you can see the points when I was obviously hesitating"* [PB8].

Many participants reported an increase in confidence arising specifically from the spoken rehearsal mode. One of our participants, who was originally very reluctant to rehearse aloud, expressed how PitchPerfect would influence his future behavior: *"I used not to speak aloud...If I have this tool, it would be very helpful because I can edit my voice. But if I don't have this tool, I will find a way to edit my voice"* [PB1].

Improving Time Management

Time keeping was a major concern for participants. In PitchPerfect, breaking down the presentation time budget into slide time targets helped participants to *"control the time for each slide better"* [PB4]. Visualizations of time expenditure relative to the time targets also enhanced participants' time awareness: *"the bar is growing and growing, it can push you"* [PB7]. Visual time guides also helped participants to dynamically adjust speech, whether they should be *"more detailed or less detailed"* [PB7]. Time information also helped with speaking rate and pace control – *"I was a bit more paced and taking time before moving on to the next point, whereas normally I'd just ramble and get it out as quickly as possible"* [PB11].

Breaking Down Rehearsal into Achievable Milestones

Participants appreciated the structured rehearsal approach in PitchPerfect and reported that the explicit and achievable goals set by each stage would encourage them to rehearse: *"each step we have a very clear destination or target...I think if we finish these targets it will be truly helpful"* [PB3]. Clear indications of readiness also helped participants to *"estimate what score I can get"* [PB7], whereas *"[with PowerPoint] you are not sure after 1 hour how well you are prepared"* [PB2]. Rehearsing with PitchPerfect also improved preparation time efficiency, allowing them to *"make full use of the time – every minute I do things"* [PB7]. Participants, as a result, described their experiences with PitchPerfect as *"happier"* [PB7] since it *"focused my mind"* [PB10], let them feel *"more relaxed,"* and *"not so worried"* [PB2]. PitchPerfect thus progressively guided participants through the set of efficient training for confident delivery.

CONCLUSIONS AND FUTURE WORK

This work uncovers mismatches between best rehearsal practices as recommended in the presentation literature, the actual rehearsal practices, and support for rehearsal in conventional slideware. The result of this exploration is PitchPerfect: an integrated rehearsal environment with three targeted rehearsal modes for structured presentation preparation in PowerPoint. Our user study with 12 participants demonstrated that PitchPerfect led to small but significant improvements in perceived presentation quality and coverage of prepared content after a single hour of use, arising from more effective support for the presenter's content mastery, time management, and confidence building.

We aim to integrate our system into a persuasive rehearsal framework, employing personalization techniques to tailor our support for each individual presenter and providing appropriate feedback and reminder mechanisms at all stages of the preparation process. We also plan to examine the effectiveness of a structured rehearsal approach in more naturalistic settings through a longitudinal deployment.

REFERENCES

1. Apple Keynote. http://www.apple.com/iwork/keynote.
2. Atkinson, C. (2005). Beyond bullet points: Using Microsoft PowerPoint to create presentations that inform, motivate, and inspire. Microsoft Press.
3. Ayres, J. (1996). Speech preparation processes and speech apprehension. Communication Education, 45, 228-235.
4. Behnke, R. R., Sawyer, C. R. (1999). Public speaking procrastination as a correlate of public speaking communication apprehension and self-perceived public speaking competency. Communication Research Reports, 16(1), 40-47.
5. Braun, V., Clarke, V. (2006). Using thematic analysis in psychology. Qualitative Research in Psychology, 3(2), 77-101.
6. Carpenter, S. K., Pashler, H., Wixted, J. T., Vul. E. (1998). The effect of tests on learning and forgetting. Memory & Cognition, 36(2), 438-448.
7. Clarke, J., Lapata, M. (2006). Models for sentence compression: A comparison across domains, training requirements and evaluation measures. ACL'06.
8. De Marneffe, M.C., Manning, C. (2008). The Stanford typed dependency representation. Coling'08.
9. Distinction Communication, Inc. (2009). Executive survey. http://www.distinction-services.com.
10. Duarte, N. (2008). Slide:ology: The art and science of creating great presentations. O'Reilly Media.
11. Duarte, N. (2012). HBR guides to persuasive presentation. HBR Press.
12. Edge, D., Fitchett, S., Whitney, M., Landay, J. (2012). MemReflex: Adaptive flashcard for mobile microlearning. MobileHCI'12, 431-440.
13. Edge, D., Savage, J., Yatani, K. (2013). HyperSlides: dynamic presentation prototyping. CHI'13, 671-680.
14. Filippova, K., Strube, M (2008). Dependency tree based sentence compression. INLG'08.
15. Goodman, A. (2006). Why bad presentations happen to good causes. Andy Goodman & Cause Communication.
16. Grefenstette, G. (1998). Producing intelligent telegraphic text reduction to provide an audio scanning service for the blind. AAAI'98, 111-118.
17. Jing, Y., Croft, B. (1994). An association thesaurus for information retrieval. RIAO'94.
18. Kurihara, K., Goto, M., Ogata, J., Matsusaka, Y., Igarashi, T. (2007). Presentation sensei: A presentation training system using speech and image processing. ICMI'07.
19. Mayer, R. E. (2001). Multimedia learning. New York: Cambridge University Press.
20. McCroskey, J. C. (1978). Validity of the PCRA as an index of oral communication apprehension. Communication Monographs, 45, 192-203.
21. Menzel, K. E., Correll, L. J. (1994). The relationship between preparation and performance in public speaking. Communication Education, 43, 17-26.
22. Microsoft PowerPoint. http://office.microsoft.com/en-us/powerpoint.
23. Microsoft Speech Platform SDK. http://msdn.microsoft.com/en-us/library/hh361572(v=office.14).aspx.
24. Nelson, D.L., Reed, U.S., Walling, J.R. (1976). Pictorial superiority effect. Journal of Experimental Psychology: Human Learning & Memory, 2, 523-528.
25. Okamoto, R., Kashihara, A. (2011). Back-review support method for presentation rehearsal support system. KES'11. Springer Berlin Heidelberg, 165-175.
26. Paivio, A. (1990). Mental representation: A dual coding approach. Oxford University Press.
27. Pearson, J.C., Child, J.T., Kahl, D.H. (2006). Preparation meeting opportunity: How do college students prepare for public speeches?. Communication Quarterly, 54(3), 351-366.
28. Reynolds, G. (2012). Presentation Zen: Simple ideas on presentation design and delivery. New Riders.
29. Rohrer, D., Taylor, K., Pashler, H., Wixted, J. T., Cepeda, N. J. (2005). The effect of overlearning on long-term retention. Applied Cognitive Psychology, 19, 361-374.
30. Spicer, R., Lin, Y. R., Kelliher, A., Sundaram, H. (2012). NextSlidePlease: Authoring and delivering agile multimedia presentations. TOMCCAP, 8(4).
31. Thios, S. J. (1975). Memory for general and specific sentences. Memory & Cognition, 3(1), 175-177.
32. Toutanova, K., Klein, D., Manning, C., Singer, Y. (2003). Feature-rich part-of-speech tagging with a cyclic dependency network. HLT-NAACL'03, 252-259.
33. Weissman, J. (2009). Presenting to win: the art of telling your story. FT Press.
34. Weissman, J. (2009). The power presenter: techniques, styles, and strategies from America's top speaking coach. Wiley.

DemoWiz: Re-Performing Software Demonstrations for a Live Presentation

Pei-Yu (Peggy) Chi[1,2], Bongshin Lee[1], Steven M. Drucker[1]
[1]Microsoft Research
{bongshin, sdrucker}@microsoft.com
[2]University of California, Berkeley
peggychi@cs.berkeley.edu

ABSTRACT

Showing a live software demonstration during a talk can be engaging, but it is often not easy: presenters may struggle with (or worry about) unexpected software crashes and encounter issues such as mismatched screen resolutions or faulty network connectivity. Furthermore, it can be difficult to recall the steps to show while talking and operating the system all at the same time. An alternative is to present with pre-recorded screencast videos. It is, however, challenging to precisely match the narration to the video when using existing video players. We introduce DemoWiz, a video presentation system that provides an increased awareness of upcoming actions through glanceable visualizations. DemoWiz supports better control of timing by overlaying visual cues and enabling lightweight editing. A user study shows that our design significantly improves the presenters' perceived ease of narration and timing compared to a system without visualizations that was similar to a standard playback control. Furthermore, nine (out of ten) participants preferred DemoWiz over the standard playback control with the last expressing no preference.

Author Keywords

Demonstration; demo; software demo; presentation; video

ACM Classification Keywords

H.5.m. Information interfaces and presentation (e.g., HCI): Miscellaneous.

INTRODUCTION

Performing a software demonstration can be an effective way to communicate with the audience during a live presentation. By illustrating actions within a working system, presenters can guide the audience through an interaction flow and show results in real time. However, it is not always easy to perform an effective live demo. Problems such as software crashes, network connectivity issues, and configuration changes (e.g., screen resolution) may break a demonstration. Furthermore, talking while interacting with the system creates a high cognitive load on presenters. In addition, the stress of public speaking, especially during a high-stakes presentation, makes it difficult for presenters to deliver effective messages in a timely manner without forgetting to cover a set of core values of the system. An alternative is to present with pre-recorded screencast videos that capture the correct flow and information. Even though technical problems are less likely to occur with a video, it is challenging for presenters to talk over a video with appropriate timing because they have to mainly rely on their memories for the sequence and timing of interactions. Such a "canned" demo can often result in a less understandable or engaging presentation when a video is not tightly prepared to attract the audience's attention to anticipate the results [6].

The presenter view in PowerPoint or Keynote attempts to help presenters during slide show presentations by showing notes along with an upcoming slide. A teleprompter, commonly used for news programs or political speeches, prompts presenters with an electronic visual text of a speech or script. With this, speakers can appear to be speaking spontaneously as they look at the audience while reading the script. Inspired by these tools, we built DemoWiz (Figure 1), a system that assists presenters in giving software demonstrations with a screencast demo video during a live presentation. DemoWiz augments a screencast video with visualizations, enabling presenters to *anticipate* the video content rather than react to it; overlaying glyphs to guide presenters to the next action along with the time remaining before the action occurs.

DemoWiz supports the entire authoring process from capturing a screencast video; to rehearsing it and adjusting timings; to performing live presentation of the demo. During the recording phase, DemoWiz captures the screen pixels and logs input events, including event types and locations with timestamps. This event information is then processed and provided to presenters in the form of an adjustable timeline of events. During the rehearsal phase, presenters can speed up or slow down specific segments while navigating through the video recording using the timeline. In addition, they can add *pause markers* and short *text notes*. During the presentation, similar to current presentation tools like PowerPoint and Keynote, DemoWiz shows two views–one for the presenter and the other for the audience. The *Presenter View* is augmented with timed notes and a visualization of the captured events to help presenters synchronize their narration with the video.

CHI 2014, April 26 - May 01 2014, Toronto, ON, Canada
Copyright 2014 ACM 978-1-4503-2473-1/14/04$15.00.
http://dx.doi.org/10.1145/2556288.2557254

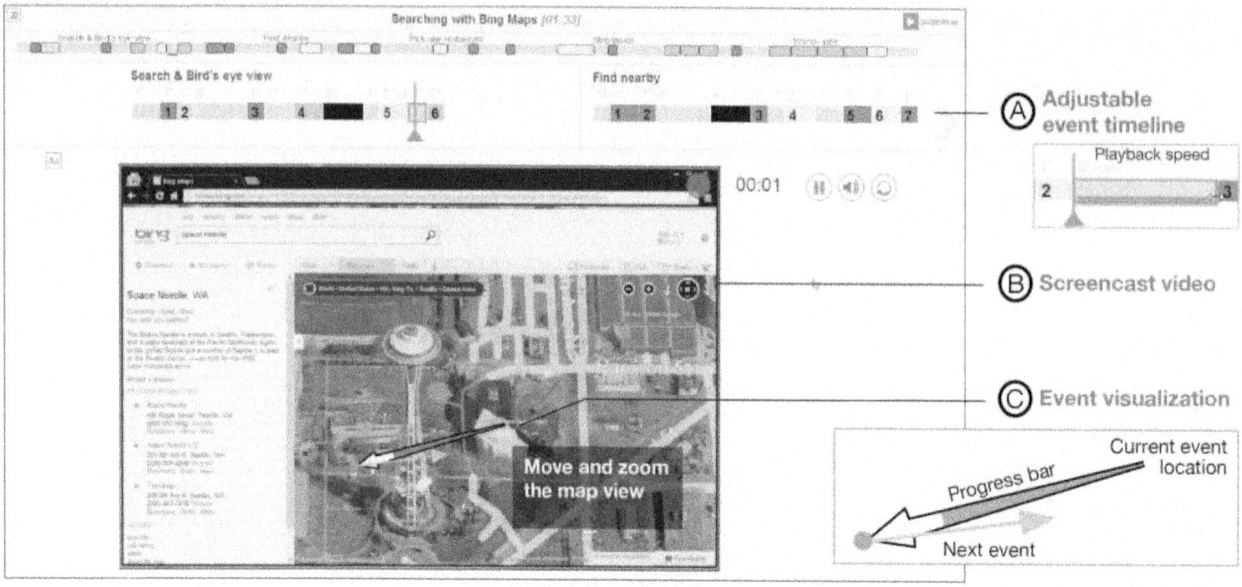

Figure 1. DemoWiz visualizes input events in a screencast video to help presenters anticipate the upcoming event for narrating a software demonstration in a live presentation.

To explore the effectiveness of the DemoWiz system, we performed a user study, comparing it with a version similar to a conventional video player. Our results show that, with DemoWiz, participants anticipated upcoming actions better and rated themselves as having narrated the video better. Moreover, 9 out of 10 participants preferred DemoWiz to a system without visualizations.

The contributions of this work are:

- An interactive video playback interface to help presenters control demo videos during a live presentation. It is combined with visual augmentation of screencast videos to enable presenters to anticipate upcoming actions and to be better aware of timing for narration.
- A lightweight workflow for presenters to record, rehearse and edit, and present demo videos. To support automatic video segmentation, we employ a hybrid approach to combine screencast videos and input event logs.
- Evaluation of the overall effectiveness of DemoWiz, incorporating visualizations into the presenter view of a video, across the workflow.

RELATED WORK

Workflow Capturing and Tutorials

There has been a considerable amount of research and many commercial tools devoted to revealing input events and operation sequences for software applications. Researchers have shown that visualizing input events in real-time during operations can provide better learnability of applications [8]. Tools such as Mouseposé[1] and ScreenFlow[2] capture mouse and keyboard events and apply special effects, such as drawing a circle around a mouse cursor. Workflows can also be captured from existing screencast videos [1] and screenshots [34]. In addition to visually enhancing events, presenting operation history helps users review the workflow. Approaches include annotating screenshot images with markers and arrows [15, 29], showing a list of before and after thumbnails and video clips [17], and creating a union graph of operations for workflow comparison [21]. These projects demonstrate the benefits of recognizing and visualizing events. Our work is related in that we use the stream of input events, but is focused on enhancing *a speaker's* experience in a live presentation by visualizing events *in advance* of the happening moments.

Another closely related area is the design of various tutorial formats that help viewers operate an interactive system. Work includes embedding video snippets in application tooltips [16], mixed-media tutorials that combine operation-based video segments with text descriptions and screenshots [5], and application-in-tutorial design enhanced by community-shared workflows [22]. These designs show possible ways for viewers to explore application features interactively, but again, differ from our goal of real-time assistance for presenters.

Visualizing and Navigating Video Content

Videos can be navigated at the content level beyond log events, such as visualizing subject movements in a storyboard design [12] and enabling direct manipulation of a target in 2D [9, 13, 20] or 3D [30]. These techniques help viewers understand content flow and playback videos, and have been applied to screencast videos [7]. It is also possible to automate video control based on user actions for scenarios such as operating software applications [31] and block assembling tasks [18]. Such novel forms of video navigation

[1] Mouseposé http://www.boinx.com/mousepose

[2] ScreenFlow http://www.telestream.net/screenflow

inspired us to explore new visual designs for revealing the video content that support live presentations.

Presentation Tools

Modern presentation tools have supported embedding video recordings and animation. Recent research has proposed advanced designs for content creation and navigation beyond simple slideshow composition, including: tools that help presenters compose content in a large canvas [14] as a path [26] or a directed graph [33] derived from zoomable graphical interfaces [3]; structure slides using markup languages [11] or sketching [25]; and define animation programmatically [35]. There has also been work on analyzing slide content for search and reuse [4, 32] and comparing revisions in a design process [10]. Our work shares similar goals of structuring a presentation based on event inputs that can be navigated and edited. However, we focus more on presentation enhancements of video content specifically for software demonstrations rather than on the authoring experience of the presentation itself.

Research on presenting information that can be perceived at a glance [28] helps presenters recall the content during a presentation, such as a callout to show finer resolution of an overall view [2]. Closely related, Time Aura provides ambient cues of a pile of slides using colors and a timeline for pacing [27]. Recent research shows that people like to have better control of the presentation even though it requires more effort [23], and earlier studies suggest that designing an integrated presentation tool for complicated tasks could be challenging [19]. These findings inspired our design on revealing content of a demo video with information that can be perceived with minimum attention.

DEMOWIZ DESIGN

To motivate and inform the design of a tool to support live presentations, we collected preferences for software demonstrations using an online survey. We describe the three design goals derived from the survey results.

Understanding Demo Preferences

To understand both presenters' and audiences' preferences for performing and viewing system demonstrations, we conducted an online survey in a software company and a university research lab. Our goal was to collect people's feedback on giving and seeing software demonstrations during live presentations. We received 73 responses from researchers, graduate students, software engineers, and designers. Their main research areas include human-computer interaction (64.4%), software engineering (21.9%), and machine learning (20.6%); 66.7% were male. Among all the respondents, 35.6% indicated that they were very experienced at giving software demos to the audience during a live presentation; 46.6% had demoed at least once; 13.7% had not demoed but attended talks that showed a software demonstration.

We asked respondents who had demo experience ($N = 60$) how they preferred to perform a demo. Their answers were: a live demo (25 out of 60), pre-recorded videos (15), a mixed format of a live demo and videos (12), static screenshots (4), and other (4). In Table 1, we list the top 2-3 reasons for their preferences. Giving a *live demo* can be more engaging with a working system and match the audience's interests, but presenters can encounter unexpected problems and forget to show important features within a given time constraint. On the other hand, presenting with *a demo video* avoids such problems by extracting the most important parts, and can allow visual highlighting (labelling or zooming), but can be less engaging. In addition, it is hard to narrate.

We were also interested in reactions as an audience member. For respondents who had seen software demos ($N = 70$), we asked how they preferred to see the demonstration performed. We found a slightly different preference: a live demo (36 out of 70), a mixed format of a live demo and videos (24), pre-recorded videos (7), and other (3). However, the reasons were well aligned with presenters' concerns. A *live demo* shows a working system and can be more engaging, but the audience might need to wait for system problems to be resolved or sometimes see presenters rambling. A *demo video* can show the most important parts, sometimes assisted by visual highlighting, but it can be hard to tell which parts of a demo are real, and can be less engaging to the audience.

Design Goals

From the survey results, we understand that giving a live demo is often more preferable than showing demo videos. However, we cannot, in general, address some of the main concerns with giving a live demo – that is, stability of the software system and variations in the presentation environment which can cause the demo to fail. Therefore, we

	Presenters		Audience	
	Advantages	**Disadvantages**	**Advantages**	**Disadvantages**
Live Demo	• More engaging (88.3%) • Show a working system (86.7%) • Easy to adjust a demo based on audience's interests (45%)	• May encounter unexpected system problems (86.4%) • May forget to show important features (33.9%) • Hard to control time (35.6%)	• Show that it's a working system (97.1%) • More engaging (72.9%)	• May need to wait for problems to be solved (78.6%) • Presenters may end up rambling (37.1%)
Demo Video	• Avoid system problems (95%) • Work with a partially working system or a mockup (51.7%) • Can edit to remove mistakes or add highlights (51.7%)	• Less engaging (57.6%) • Hard to match their narration to the video content (30.5%)	• Avoid problems (81.4%) • Show the most important parts with visual highlights (60%) • Work with a partially working system or a mockup (45.7%)	• Hard to tell which parts are real (62.9%) • Want to see how the actual system works (44.3%) • Less engaging (37.1%)

Table 1: Survey of software demonstration preferences from presenters' (N=60) and audience's (N=70) point of views.

instead aim to address some of the drawbacks with demo videos while preserving their advantages. More specifically, our goal is to make demo videos *more engaging* by assisting presenters in adjusting their narration to guide the audience through the material. In this section, we describe our design goals to support more effective demo video presentations.

G1. Show what's coming next, where and when it will occur.
To engage the audience with the demonstration, it is important for presenters to guide the audience's attention to the right place at the right time. To do so, presenters should be fully aware of upcoming actions – specifically *what* actions will happen, *where* they will occur on the screen, and *when* they will happen.

G2. Minimize required attention or interpretation.
While it is our desire to help presenters understand and anticipate impending events, we should not overburden a presenter who is already narrating a specific set of talking points. As a tradeoff between providing more information and minimizing cognitive load, any augmentation of the video needs to be offered in a glanceable fashion, i.e., information can be interpreted quickly and without the presenter's full attention.

G3. Support light-weight editing during rehearsal.
Different presentations may require more or less extensive explanations, and when first recording a demo video, it may not be possible to perform the demo at the same rate necessary for a live presentation (e.g., typing can be difficult or system response times may be variable). In addition, it should be easy to review, practice, and modify the pace for a particular presentation. For all these reasons, lightweight editing and rehearsal are necessary.

Using these principles as a guiding rubric for our design, we iterated on several versions of the DemoWiz system.

DEMOWIZ

Augmented Workflow

For presenters to narrate "live" over a video recording, we propose augmenting a typical workflow from capturing a screencast video; to rehearsing it and adjusting timings; and finally to live presentation of the demo video (Figure 2).

DemoWiz first captures a screencast video and input events during a software demonstration from a user-defined rectangular region. Once the recording is done, DemoWiz analyzes the low-level event stream and transforms it into higher-level events such as mouse clicks, double-clicks, and drags. DemoWiz then allows presenters to edit the timing and notes while practicing their presentations with the presenter view equipped with an adjustable event timeline (Figure 1a). Finally, presenters can give a live presentation using the same UI (i.e., presenter view) and show the audience view without visualization to the viewers.

Figure 2. DemoWiz workflow: Presenters captures a software demonstration, edit the recording while rehearsing with our playback UI, and present the edited video to the audience using a presenter view.

Visualizations

To enable presenters to focus on their narration and the original video contents, DemoWiz augments the screencast recording by automatically overlaying simple glyphs.

Input Event Glyphs

DemoWiz overlays visual annotations of events on the screencast recording in a graphical way where the events happen. For example, in Figure 1, the presenter clicks and drags the map view to the right. DemoWiz uses the following simple, distinctive glyphs to differentiate event types as Figure 3 shows:

- Mouse click: a red circle with a radius of 20-pixels,
- Double-click: a green circle with a radius of 20-pixels,
- Mouse drag: a thin, orange line with a dot at the start point and an arrowhead at the end point,
- Mouse scroll: a thin, yellow line, 80 pixels long, with an arrowhead, and
- Keystrokes: text in blue.

At any given time during the video playback, DemoWiz shows the current event and the upcoming event on the video. We tried to show more than two events within a fixed time period in our initial prototypes. However, we noticed several issues. First, the view becomes too cluttered to understand at a glance, especially when the original video is visually complex. Second, it is not easy to convey the order of the events. Third, it is difficult to observe when multiple events are spatially close. Therefore, we provide minimum but essential events for recall.

Visual Guides to the Next Events

In order to help guide the presenter's attention, DemoWiz overlays a motion arrow between the current and upcoming events on the demo video (Figure 1c). This is inspired by storyboard design used in filming where an arrow effectively shows the movement of a camera or an actor in a single shot [12]. We expand the idea of guiding attention for a specific purpose: the arrow in DemoWiz shows the movement from one action (e.g., click a checkbox) to another action (e.g., click a button). By overlaying this motion arrow, the visualization matches the flow of a presenter's attention when they observe the video content.

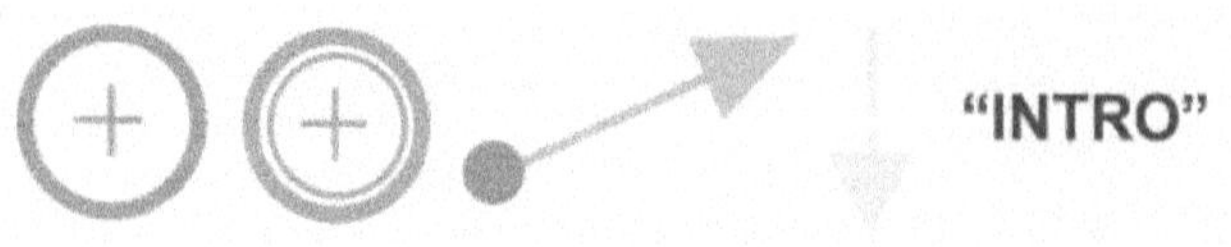

Figure 3. DemoWiz visualizes input events in a graphical way. From the left to right we show a mouse click, double-click, a drag, a mouse scroll, and keystroke events. These glyphs are overlaid on the video recordings.

Since the distance between two consecutive event segments vary, we created three visual designs to make sure the arrows are visible to lead a presenter's attention:

- For two events that are located far away (e.g., clicking an "OK" button after selecting a checkbox on a page), apply a *straight* arrow (Figure 4a).
- For events that are nearly at the same location (e.g., click the "Next" button twice to navigate a list of selections), apply a *round* arrow that points to the current location (Figure 4b).
- Otherwise, apply a *curved* arrow (Figure 4c).

Sense of Timing

DemoWiz provides a sense of timing for an upcoming action so that presenters can adjust their narration. First, DemoWiz embeds *a progress bar* in the motion arrow to show relative time (Figure 1c). The green bar shows the proportional time that has been passed before reaching the next event (Figure 5 top). When a motion arrow is filled up with green, it fades away and guides the presenter to the next action. We were concerned that people may associate the length of an arrow to the length of time. Therefore, we also incorporated a *countdown* visualization where circles will fade out in the last three seconds before the next action starts (Figure 5 bottom) to convey absolute timing.

Visualization Examples

Figure 6 presents examples of DemoWiz visualizations with four different systems. The glyphs effectively show the start and end points of mouse drags and the locations of mouse clicks. Motion arrows help direct the presenter's attention between events, such as start the end of the drag event to clicking a button (Figure 6a, 6b), clicking between several options (Figure 6c), or selecting a specific slide after scrolling down (Figure 6d).

Lightweight Editing During Rehearsal

During rehearsal for their demonstration, presenters can modify the video timing and add reminder notes for their narration. DemoWiz shows the type and length of each event in a sequence in a timeline (Figure 1a). Each segment is shown as a block whose width indicates its length in time. To simplify the timeline and avoid fine-grained adjustment, lengths of event blocks are rounded to the second. Presenters can modify the playback speed of a segment by dragging the boundaries of a segment on the timeline. For example, presenters can speed up to shorten long text inputs, and slow down for fast mouse drag inputs that select multiple objects.

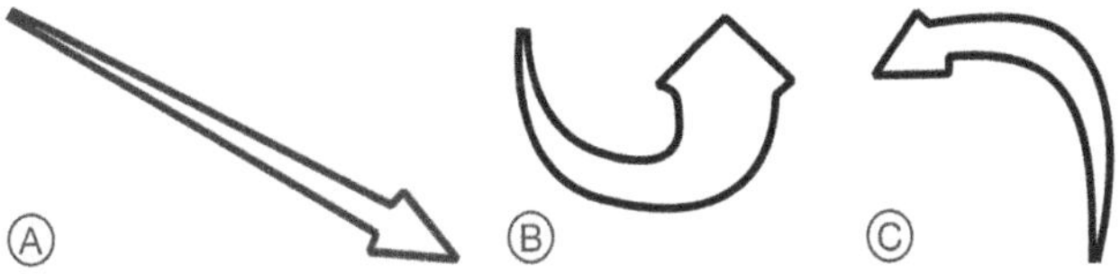

Figure 4. Three types of motion arrows in DemoWiz that guide presenters to the next event of different distances at a (A) far, (B) nearly the same, and (C) near location.

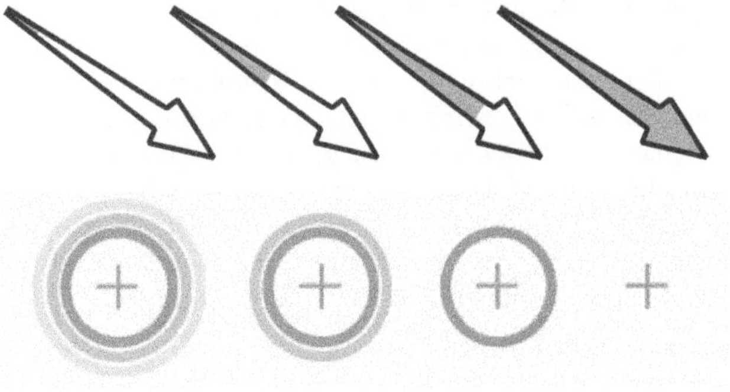

Figure 5. A progress in time guides the presenter from the current event (left) gradually to the upcoming action (right) using relative timing with a progress bar (top) and absolute timing (bottom).

Figure 6. Examples of DemoWiz visualizations with four different systems and input event sequences.

Sometimes a change in the playback speed may result in an awkward effect that is noticeable to the audience, especially when showing a UI transition. Therefore, DemoWiz supports two special time control markers to enable breaks in the narration. Presenters can add an adjustable *pause* segment, at which the system will pause at the last frame of the previous segment for the specified length of time. If presenters prefer full control on pause length, a *stop* marker ensures the video stays paused at the last frame of the previous segment and will not proceed until presenters manually resume the playback of the video.

DemoWiz enables presenters to add a short text note (such as the reminder "*Move and zoom…*" in Figure 1) so that they could remind themselves of upcoming actions at a higher level. The note can be positioned manually at any location on a video so that it does not block important video content, and will be shown for 3 seconds before the associated event.

For every edit that is associated with time changes (including playback speed and pauses), DemoWiz computes and updates the total presentation time as well as updating the progress bar and countdown to provide accurate timing.

Presenter View

During presentation, DemoWiz shows two views in separate windows. Presenters can observe visualizations using the presenter view, while the audience will see the audience view with a full-screen video that has no enhanced information. DemoWiz synchronizes the videos in both views based on presenters' editing decisions to ensure the same playback speed and time. As with a conventional video player, presenters can control the video, to pause and play at any time. In addition, when a video is paused (or stopped), presenters can hover the mouse over the demo video in the presenter view to point out an important area, as many presenters currently do in a live demo. DemoWiz then simulates and synchronizes a mouse cursor in the audience view to help the audience follow the demonstration.

Implementation Details

During recording, DemoWiz captures the screen within a specified region and logs low-level system input data with *timestamps* (with an accuracy of 0.1 seconds) from the operating system, including:

- *Mouse events* (mouse downs, mouse ups, and mouse wheel movements) and their *positions* (in x-y coordinates relative to the screen-captured region).
- *Key-press events* (keyboard input).

Once presenters finish their demonstrations, DemoWiz analyzes the low-level event stream and transforms it into high-level event metadata. For mouse events, we pair each mouse down and up into mouse *clicks*, *double-clicks*, or *drags*. We group any consecutive mouse wheel events within a time threshold of 2 seconds to one *scroll* event and any key-press events within the same threshold to one *keystroke* event (e.g., combine keys d-o-w-n-t-o-w-n to "downtown"). For each high-level event, we log the *start* and *end time* (timestamps of the first and the last low-level event).

Based on the start and end times of these high-level events, DemoWiz segments the screencast video recording into *event segments*. Any gap between two consecutive input events is marked as an *inactive segment*, which may include mouse hovering, UI transitions of the demo system, or static frames with no visual changes. DemoWiz adjusts the boundaries of these event segments to avoid any short visual effect that cannot be observed. DemoWiz examines segments in a linear order to ensure each segment lasts at least t_{min} seconds long, which is set as one second based on our early testing. For an event segment S_i of time (t_{start}, t_{end}) that $t_{end} - t_{start} < t_{min}$, DemoWiz expands 0.5 second forward and backward if S_{i-1} and S_{i+1} are inactive. If the adjusted S'_{i-1} and S'_{i+1} are shorter than t_{min}, DemoWiz merges it to the shorter neighbor segment. Currently, DemoWiz does not analyze these inactive segments, but techniques including computer vision and video analysis [1, 5] can be applied for finer segmentation.

The capturing program is implemented in C#. Two APIs were used: 1) the Windows Event Log API for mouse and keyboard hooks and 2) the Expression Encoder 4 API for screen recording running on Microsoft Windows 7. The recorded metadata (stored in a JSON object) and screencast video (in MP4) are read by the Presenter UI, which is implemented using standard Web technologies, including HTML5, CSS3, JavaScript, and jQuery. In particular, the visualization is rendered on the canvas element on top of the video object on the fly based on the video playback time. The audience view is generated by the main browser window of presenter view for video control.

EVALUATION

To evaluate the DemoWiz design, we conducted a controlled experiment in which participants recorded and edited a demo video, and gave a presentation with the edited video. Specifically, we wanted to see if presenters would evaluate their own performances higher with the support of our augmented visualizations and control of timing.

Baseline Condition: DemoWiz without Visualization

Since DemoWiz allows for rapid editing of the video, it would have been unfair to compare it with a conventional video player without supporting any editing during the rehearsal phase. We therefore modified our system to serve as the baseline condition, providing participants with the same lightweight editing of the video in each condition. However, during presentation, the baseline condition was similar to a conventional video player that shows only the video without event timeline and augmented visualizations. It also did not support the *stop* markers and *text notes*, i.e., participants could only adjust playback speed of each segment and add variable length *pauses*. During presentation, participants only saw the video with a traditional timeline. They could, however, pause (or stop) and resume the video manually at any time during playback.

Study Design

We conducted the study as a within-subjects design in a usability room. After recording and editing a video using the same system, each presenter gave a presentation with both systems to an experimenter. To control the effect of order and learning, we prepared two tasks that included similar interaction flows and counterbalanced the order of the two systems—DemoWiz and Baseline—but we fixed the order of tasks. Even though presenting to a single audience member in a usability room is not the same as using the system with a large conference audience, it is important to control the tasks and presentation as closely as possible to understand the relative benefits of the system in comparison with a baseline condition.

For each condition, we observed and coded the *timing* of narration that matched the video content and noted the time in seconds when an event was described *before*, *at*, or *after* the action happened in the demo video. We also marked obvious *breaks* between narrations, *errors* when the narration was not about the current or following events (e.g., discussing actions in a different order than they actually occurred), and *misses* when an important action was not mentioned. To avoid unconscious bias that might influence the coding of the videos, we neutrally named the recordings and coded them all in a batch. We focused on objective timing measurements as much as possible, measuring deviation from specific video events and their corresponding narrations down to a second. Finally, we gathered qualitative feedback through satisfaction and preference questionnaires.

Participants

We recruited 12 participants (10 males and 2 females) from a software company. However, we excluded the data from two participants (1 male and 1 female); one was due to a software bug during one condition and another was because the participant requested to restart a presentation in one condition. The average age of the effective 10 participants was 37.3 ranging from 24 to 64 years of age. We recruited participants who had experience at showing a software demonstration to an audience such as giving a presentation at a conference. Four participants were native English speakers and the rest were fluent in English. The expertise of participants included audio processing, computer graphics, human-computer interactions, machine learning, networking, and software engineering. Each participant was compensated with lunch coupons worth $20.

Procedure and Tasks

Each session consisted of one training task and two experimental tasks. For the training task, to introduce the common features for recording and editing the video, we designed a simple workflow of five steps to demonstrate editing of a slide using PowerPoint. The experimenter briefly demonstrated an example and then introduced the recording program that captured the screen. Participants were then asked to practice and record using the recording program.

The two tasks consisted of a similar sequence and interactions: 1) searching with Bing Maps to show the 2D map view and the Bird's Eye view, looking for a restaurant, and navigating to the interior view of a specific restaurant; and 2) searching with Google Shopping to show the search results with the Grid view, filtering and voting for reviews, and navigating the 3D product view of an espresso machine. For each task, we provided a specific scenario along with a list of subtasks. The experimenter walked through this list with participants to ensure that they could easily find the features that needed to be demonstrated. Participants were then asked to practice (3-5 minutes), record (about 2 minutes), and rehearse and edit (5-10 minutes).

To help simulate a conference setting where participants would not be able to present immediately after having recorded a demonstration, we inserted an intentional 1-minute gap between rehearsal and presentation. During this gap before giving the presentation, we asked participants to watch a conference showcase video. Participants were then asked to stand up and gave a 2-3 minute presentation to the experimenter in a usability room.

After each task, participants filled out a questionnaire of 8-10 questions asking about their experience (8 for the Baseline condition, and 10 for the DemoWiz condition). At the end of the session, an online questionnaire was provided for them to present overall preferences and leave comments. Each session lasted about 1.5 hours.

Experiment Setup

Each participant used a desktop computer running Windows 7, Expression Encoder 4 for screen recording, and a web browser for the DemoWiz user interface. A regular mouse and keyboard were provided, along with two 27-inch displays, one for editing (during rehearsal) and showing the audience view (during presentation), and the other for the presenter view on a stand-up table. The resolution of both displays was 1920×1200 pixels. The average captured screen area was 1311×857 pixels. In the presenter view, the video resolution was within 1000×600 pixels; in the audience view, the screencast videos were resized to fill the entire display with at least 100-pixel wide border in black. During the study, the experimenter stayed in the room, providing instructions and sitting behind the participants during the recording and editing phases.

Results

Ten participants successfully recorded, rehearsed, and gave a demo with both systems.

Subjective Preference

Figure 7 shows the average subject responses (on the 7-point Likert scale) from presenters for both systems. We analyzed these subjective responses using a Wilcoxon signed-rank test. We found significant differences in responses for ease of narration (DemoWiz $\mu = 6.2$ over Baseline $\mu = 4.5$, $p = .018$) and ease of presentation (6.4 over 5.2, $p = .048$). We also found marginally significant differences in participants' overall satisfaction with their presentations (5.5 over 4.7, $p = .062$). Participants also tend to agree that DemoWiz helped them interpret timing (6.1 over 4.4, $p = .067$).

In addition, 9 out of the 10 participants preferred DemoWiz to the system without visualization and would choose to present with DemoWiz if they were asked to give a public software demo; the remaining participant indicated no preference for both questions. The general feedback was also encouraging. For example, P1 commented "*Awesome system. I'd use it today.*" and P5 "*felt more confident in being able to present what I wanted to.*"

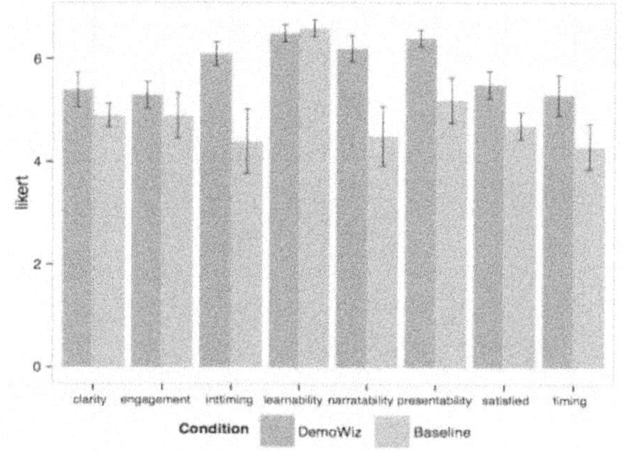

Figure 7. User feedback from questionnaire on the 7-point Likert scale.

Visualization as a Supportive Cue

Participants answered that they were able to understand DemoWiz visualization of input events (μ = 6.0) and found it supportive for their presentations (μ = 6.3). They also commented that the DemoWiz visualization supported the presentation in various aspects: "*the visualization reminds of the order of the content*" (P1), "*Really liked the ability to know what was coming up*" (P2), "*It provides better insight of the progress of the video*" (P6), and "*viz gave me an idea about timing or something I was going to forget to say*" (P9).

Narration Timing

We coded the 20 recordings of participants' final presentations to observe the timing of narration of each action in correspondence with the video content (11 key events for both tasks). With DemoWiz, participants tended to *anticipate* the upcoming events rather than talk afterwards, where the average timing was -0.1 seconds with DemoWiz (i.e., narrated the action before it happened) and 0.4 seconds with the Baseline condition (i.e., explained the action after it was shown). We found a significant difference in the number of times that events were anticipated by the narration, co-occurred, or occurred after the fact ($\chi^2(2,220) = 8.6, p = .01$, see Figure 8).

In general, this supports our suspicion that DemoWiz would help in anticipating an event as opposed to talking about it after it occurred. More important though, was how often a narrator spoke about an event within several seconds of when the event actually occurred. By defining *better* timing as when a presenter's explanation came within 2 seconds of a shown event (either prior, exact, or after), there was marginal significance by condition (p = .089 with DemoWiz performing better). In addition, with the Baseline condition, the timing of narration was less consistent and off more, varying from 6 seconds early or 10 seconds late with a variance of 3.9 seconds, in comparison to the DemoWiz condition with at most 3 seconds early to 3 seconds late and a variance of 1.9 seconds.

Five participants had an obvious *error* (forgot the next action or incorrectly narrated another action), had a long *break* (waiting for more than 2 seconds until the action was made),

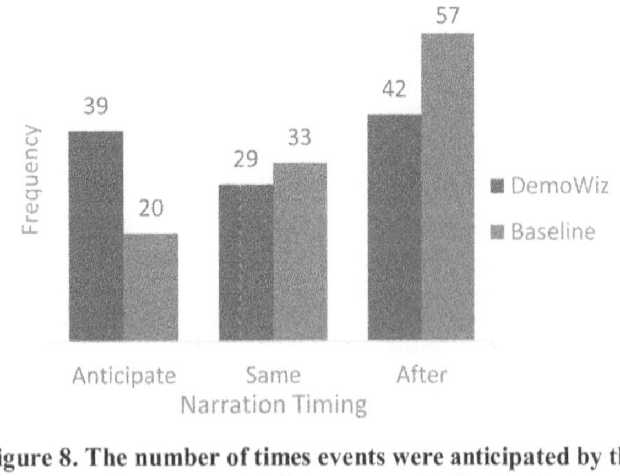

Figure 8. The number of times events were anticipated by the narration, co-occurred, or occurred after the fact.

or *missed* an action (did not explain an important feature) when presenting with the Baseline condition. On the other hand, in the DemoWiz condition no errors were made, and there were only one long break and one miss from two different participants, respectively.

Participants' comments also support the fact that DemoWiz helped presenters anticipate the upcoming events. P7 explained, "(I) *felt better able to time my speech to coincide with visual events, rather than trailing after them. Without the event visualizations, I felt like I was talking about what the audience had just seen, rather than having my words and visuals combine to a single message.*"

Editing Experience

We collected comments on the workflow. Participants found it easy to record (μ = 6.4) their demonstrations with DemoWiz. For editing features, they found it easy to edit in general (6.6), including controlling the playback speed (6.5) and adding pauses and stops (6.5), but it was less easy to add text notes (4.8); only two participants used this as reminders.

Although using different strategies, all of the participants adjusted the playback speed for matching their narration. Some sped up whenever possible and added stop markers for transitions; some slowed down the repetitive actions (such as drags) to demonstrate effects. P6 said, "*I really liked being able to add 'stop' events so I could 'fake' my demo better.*" DemoWiz made it easy for participants to separate the capturing and presentation preparation as P5 explained, "*Overall, recording was very easy. In fact, as I got to the second task, I realized that I really don't need to think about the words as I record because later on I will be able to slow down and speed up time ...*"

On average, the length of demo videos was 2'09" before editing and 2'05" after editing, and the presentation was 2'38" long. Each participant spent 7.5 minutes on average to edit. For each demo of 44 segments on average, participants adjusted 3.15 segments for speedup and 4.25 segments for slowdown, and added 0.55 pause markers. In the DemoWiz condition, 1.2 stop markers and 0.2 text notes were added.

DISCUSSION AND FUTURE WORK

New Tool to Present Video in Real-Time

DemoWiz is an attempt to make demo videos more engaging by helping presenters anticipate the upcoming events rather than reacting to them, leveraging a refined workflow with augmented visualizations. Overall, participants liked the DemoWiz visualization, finding it supportive rather than distracting. For examples, P4 said, "*Event visualization was very powerful – definitely the way to go.*" and P2 (who first experienced Baseline) was originally skeptical when he first saw the visualization but immediately found it helpful and not distracting. This corresponds with our goal of designing the visualization with a minimal cognitive load.

Editing Capabilities

Lightweight editing during rehearsal not only makes it easy to edit the recorded video but also lowers the burden of the initial recording. Presenters do not have to prepare a complete script for exact timing. They also do not have to repeat recording many times to grab the best recording.

Some participants appreciated our design choice of providing only minimum but essential editing capabilities to make the process as light as possible. P2 mentioned that "*Ironically, I think it's better to have limited editing feature set -- this system was very easy to learn/use.*" A few participants expressed the need for more editing features: P1 explained, "*(I wish the system could be) cutting events in parts so that I can slow down/speed up/remove portions of, e.g., a mouse trajectory*"; P3 wanted to "*flip segments around*" and P8 thought "*break up or merge blocks*" would be helpful. We found these interesting as the system enabled more possibilities, but there is a tradeoff between providing a powerful tool and lowering the burden in editing. We believe that this is a design choice that needs to be balanced.

Our system does not support combining two or more video clips for a presentation. Sometimes, presenters may also want to update part of the existing material to show new features of their developing systems. For example, P4 explained that he would like to see "*the ability to record multiple clips and insert them in a timeline.*" This would be straightforward future work because the current DemoWiz framework is designed to be able to implement this.

Editing can still be limited to support fine timing control of narration. P10 explained, "*The length of narration changes each time I present, and it is difficult to perfectly align the timing.*" Automatically navigating a video based on presenters' performances could be an interesting avenue of exploration, similar to scenarios of following a tutorial [31] or performing music [24]. However, we decided not to pursue this approach because it would present its own form of risk relying on unreliable speech recognition during a live presentation. Also, considering the time constraints presenters usually have, we chose to provide full control for presenters rather than trying to intelligently update a video.

Study Audience Engagement

In our user study, we gathered presenters' opinions as to how engaging their presentation was, and we explored the relative timing of the narration to events in the video. Ultimately, however, our goal is to help increase audience engagement. Measuring audience engagement is an ongoing topic of research, and we would like to explore ways of quantifying the relative impact of the DemoWiz system, but that work was out of scope for this project.

Enhance the Audience View

Some participants commented that it would be helpful to highlight certain input events for the viewers to observe subtle changes. For example, P10 wanted to enable, "*visualize mouse events such as clicks and scrolls for the audience so they know what is going on.*" The current DemoWiz framework makes it easy to achieve this goal by highlighting the audience view *only* when the event happens. In other words, presenters and audience will see different visual effects, where the former observe events in advance and the latter see a visualization synchronized with the demo video content.

Beyond Software Demonstrations

Although our current implementation is focused on software demonstrations, we argue that it is possible to expand our system design to more advanced inputs. By defining event types that a system recognizes (e.g., a pinch gesture on a multitouch device or a specific pose detected by a 3D sensor), it is possible to log the events and align them with the captured video for later use. In addition, the enhanced presentation mode can be potentially applied to other domains where knowing the timing and the sequence of events is crucial, such as narrating over animated presentation slides with dynamic graphical objects. DemoWiz is an important first step towards validating this general approach and we believe our work could inspire future research in these directions.

CONCLUSION

This paper introduces DemoWiz, a system with a refined workflow that helps presenters capture software demonstrations, edit and rehearse them, and re-perform them for an engaging live presentation. DemoWiz visualizes input events and guides presenters to see what's coming up by overlaying visual annotations of events on the screencast recording where the events happen in a screencast video. It also provides lightweight editing for presenters to adjust video playback speed, pause frames, and add text notes. A user study showed that DemoWiz was effective in helping presenters capture timing and narrate over a demo video.

REFERENCES

1. Banovic, N., Grossman, T., Matejka, J., and Fitzmaurice, G. Waken: reverse engineering usage information and interface structure from software videos. *UIST '12*, ACM Press (2012), 83–92.
2. Baudisch, P., Good, N., and Bellotti, V. Keeping things in context: a comparative evaluation of focus plus context screens, overviews, and zooming. *CHI '02*, ACM Press (2002), 259–266.
3. Bederson, B.B. and Hollan, J.D. Pad++: a zooming graphical interface for exploring alternate interface physics. *UIST '94*, ACM Press (1994), 17–26.
4. Bergman, L., Lu, J., Konuru, R., MacNaught, J., and Yeh, D. Outline wizard: presentation composition and search. *IUI '10*, ACM Press (2010), 209–218.
5. Chi, P.-Y., Ahn, S., Ren, A., Dontcheva, M., Li, W., and Hartmann, B. MixT: automatic generation of step-by-step mixed media tutorials. *UIST '12*, ACM Press (2012), 93–102.
6. Cohen, P. Great Demo! How to Create and Execute Stunning Software Demonstrations. iUniverse, Bloomington, IN, USA, 2005.

7. Denoue, L., Carter, S., Cooper, M., and Adcock, J. Real-time direct manipulation of screen-based videos. *IUI '13 Companion* (2013).

8. Dixon, M. and Fogarty, J. Prefab: implementing advanced behaviors using pixel-based reverse engineering of interface structure. *CHI '10*, ACM Press (2010), 1525–1534.

9. Dragicevic, P., Ramos, G., Bibliowitcz, J., Nowrouzezahrai, D., Balakrishnan, R., and Singh, K. Video browsing by direct manipulation. *CHI '08*, ACM Press (2008), 237–246.

10. Drucker, S.M., Petschnigg, G., and Agrawala, M. Comparing and managing multiple versions of slide presentations. *UIST '06*, ACM Press (2006), 47–56.

11. Edge, D., Savage, J., and Yatani, K. HyperSlides: dynamic presentation prototyping. *CHI '13*, ACM Press (2013), 671–680.

12. Goldman, D.B., Curless, B., Salesin, D., and Seitz, S.M. Schematic storyboarding for video visualization and editing. *ACM Trans. Graphics (SIGGRAPH '06) 25*, 13 (2006), 862–871.

13. Goldman, D., Gonterman, C., and Curless, B. Video object annotation, navigation, and composition. UIST *'08*, ACM Press (2008), 3–12.

14. Good, L. and Bederson, B.B. Zoomable User Interfaces as a Medium for Slide Show Presentations. *Information Visualization* 1, 1 (2002), 35–49.

15. Grabler, F., Agrawala, M., Li, W., Dontcheva, M., and Igarashi, T. Generating photo manipulation tutorials by demonstration. *ACM Trans. Graphics (SIGGRAPH '09) 28*, 3 (2009).

16. Grossman, T. and Fitzmaurice, G. ToolClips: an investigation of contextual video assistance for functionality understanding. *CHI '10*, ACM Press (2010), 1515–1524.

17. Grossman, T., Matejka, J., and Fitzmaurice, G. Chronicle: capture, exploration, and playback of document workflow histories. *UIST '10*, ACM Press (2010), 143–152.

18. Gupta, A., Fox, D., Curless, B., and Cohen, M. DuploTrack: a real-time system for authoring and guiding duplo block assembly. *UIST '12*, ACM Press (2012), 389–402.

19. Johnson, J.A. and Nardi, B.A. Creating presentation slides: a study of user preferences for task-specific versus generic application software. *ACM Trans. Computer-Human Interaction 3*, 1 (1996), 38–65.

20. Karrer, T., Weiss, M., Lee, E., and Borchers, J. DRAGON: a direct manipulation interface for frame-accurate in-scene video navigation. *CHI '08*, ACM Press (2008), 247–250.

21. Kong, N., Grossman, T., Hartmann, B., Agrawala, M., and Fitzmaurice, G. Delta: a tool for representing and comparing workflows. *CHI '12*, ACM Press (2012), 1027–1036.

22. Lafreniere, B., Grossman, T., and Fitzmaurice, G. Community enhanced tutorials: improving tutorials with multiple demonstrations. *CHI '13*, ACM Press (2013), 1779–1788.

23. Lee, B., Kazi R. H., and Smith, G. SketchStory: Telling more engaging stories with data through freeform sketching. *IEEE TVCG (InfoVis '13) 19*, 12 (2013), 2416–2425.

24. Lee, E., Wolf, M., and Borchers, J. Improving orchestral conducting systems in public spaces: examining the temporal characteristics and conceptual models of conducting gestures. *CHI '05*, ACM Press (2005), 731–740.

25. Li, Y., Landay, J.A., Guan, Z., Ren, X., and Dai, G. Sketching informal presentations. *ICMI '03*, ACM Press (2003), 234–241.

26. Lichtschlag, L., Karrer, T., and Borchers, J. Fly: a tool to author planar presentations. *CHI '09*, ACM Press (2009), 547–556.

27. Mamykina, L, Mynatt, E., and Terry, M.A. TimeAura: Interfaces for Pacing, *CHI '01*, ACM Press (2001), 144–151.

28. Matthews, T.L. Designing and Evaluating Glanceable Peripheral Displays. PhD thesis, EECS Department, University of California, Berkeley (2007).

29. Nakamura, T. and Igarashi, T. An application-independent system for visualizing user operation history. *UIST '08*, ACM Press (2008), 23.

30. Nguyen, C., Niu, Y., and Liu, F. Direct manipulation video navigation in 3D. *CHI '13*, ACM Press (2013), 1169–1172.

31. Pongnumkul, S., Dontcheva, M., Li, W., Wang, J, and Bourdev, L. Pause-and-play: automatically linking screencast video tutorials with applications. *UIST '11*, ACM Press (2011), 135–144.

32. Sharmin, M., Bergman, L., Lu, J., and Konuru, R. On slide-based contextual cues for presentation reuse. *IUI '12*, ACM Press (2012), 129–138.

33. Spicer, R., Lin, Y.-R., Kelliher, A., and Sundaram, H. NextSlidePlease: Authoring and delivering agile multimedia presentations. *TOMCCAP 8*, 4 (2012), 1–20.

34. Yeh, T., Chang, T.-H., and Miller, R.C. Sikuli: using GUI screenshots for search and automation. *UIST '09*, ACM Press (2009), 183–192.

35. Zongker, D.E. and Salesin, D.H. On creating animated presentations. *SCA '03*: 2003 ACM SIGGRAPH/Eurographics symposium on Computer animation, 2003.

TurningPoint: Narrative-Driven Presentation Planning

Larissa Pschetz[1,2,3]
[1] Microsoft Research
Beijing, China

Koji Yatani[1]
[2] University of Edinburgh
Edinburgh, UK

Darren Edge[1]
[3] University of Dundee
Dundee, UK

lpschetz@ed.ac.uk, koji@microsoft.com, darren.edge@microsoft.com

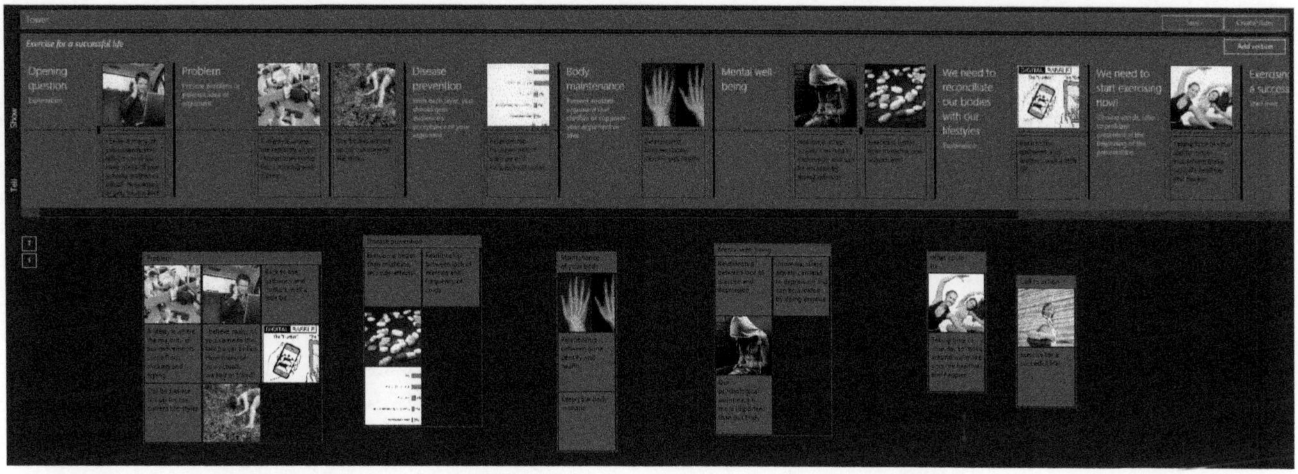

Figure 1. TurningPoint probe for presentation planning, showing narrative strip (top) and content canvas (bottom)

ABSTRACT

Once upon a time, people told stories unencumbered by slides. What modern presentations gain through visual slide support, however, is often at the expense of storytelling. We present TurningPoint, a probe to investigate the potential use of narrative-driven talk planning in slideware. Our study of TurningPoint reveals a delicate balance between narrative templates focusing author attention in ways that save time, and fixating attention in ways that limit experimentation.

Author Keywords

Slide presentations; narrative templates; storytelling

ACM Classification Keywords

H.5.2. Information interfaces and presentation: User Interfaces

INTRODUCTION & RELATED WORK

It is easy to identify what makes a talk good or bad, but much more difficult to explain what makes a talk great. The "TED Commandments" sent to upcoming speakers at TED [14] offer an insight into the ingredients of a great talk, but the most apparently obvious, "Thou Shalt Tell a Story", is strangely absent from the majority of slide presentations we see today. In contrast, the presentation literature is full of advice to engage in storytelling, since *"it is the story, not the slides that will capture your audience's attention"* [6].

ACM 978-1-4503-2473-1/14/04...$15.00.
http://dx.doi.org/10.1145/2556288.2557389

We reviewed ten such books and identified a shift away from slides, software, and visual design to messages, narrative structures, and storytelling (e.g., from [2] to [3] and [11] to [12] respectively). The majority [2, 3, 6, 11, 12, 13, 16] recommend a bottom-up, brainstorming approach to presentation planning, generating as many ideas as possible through divergent thinking. This is followed by the convergent process of filtering and clustering ideas into key messages. The final step before slide creation is to fit this material into one of several *narrative structures* that shape the overall flow of the presentation (e.g., contrasting how things are and how they could be [3]). The converse, top-down approach of generating content to fit a predetermined narrative structure is recommended in two books [1, 9], but the difference is primarily in the ordering of preparation processes rather than the nature of the processes themselves.

Although modern presentation software has evolved in many ways, e.g. by providing new visual paradigms such as 3D environments [5] and zoomable canvases [8, 10], it still fails to differentiate provisional plans and polished presentations. Recent HCI work has identified *telling stories with slides* as a core concern of presenters wanting to "hit the right tones, inspiring, motivational" [4]. The related HyperSlides system generates hyperlinked presentation slides from a structured hierarchy of narrative points, but neither HyperSlides nor any other system offers guidance on how to sequence such points for maximum effect. Within HCI research on narrative and storytelling in general (e.g. [7, 15]), there is also no prior work specifically targeting oral presentations. Based on our analysis of existing literature, systems, and interview transcripts, we therefore developed a probe, TurningPoint, to explore the potential for narrative-driven design in slideware.

PRESENTATION PLANNING IN PRACTICE

To understand presentation planning by real presenters, we reanalyzed 36 transcripts of interviews from prior studies exploring presentation practices in general. Informants (I1-36) had diverse expertise, age, gender, nationality, and background. We discovered three main ways in which actual practices contradicted best practices advised in the literature.

Planning on slides saves time but limits creativity

Many informants open slideware as their first planning step. Some create a text outline first, some create a style first, and several combine the two to create a "prototype" (I5), e.g.:

"I start with the slides that I want to produce – the style, the structure, the title of the slides – then I just start filling it in" (I3)

Others appropriate slides as space in which to draft an overall plan before moving to the prototyping process. Relatively few informants follow advice to "resist the temptation during the initial phase to sit down with presentation software" [3], but there were some mentions of recommend extra-slideware practices such as mindmapping (I1), sketching (I2), and long-term idea collection with paper and digital notes (I6, 7). However, the use of multiple tools incurs transcription costs:

"With my EverNote I start labeling each section [...] then I label each section in PowerPoint, then every time I make changes in EverNote I also make changes in PowerPoint" (I7)

Continuous iteration between collecting, planning, and styling (I4) further encourages the low-cost solution of planning on slides.

Reusing slides saves time but dilutes the message

Informants reported a great reluctance to delete slides, even draft slides representing earlier thoughts and dead ends (I6), because of their potential reuse value. Multiple participants also go to the extreme of creating "megadeck" archives of hundreds of slides that can be hidden or revealed in place or sampled for inclusion in more targeted presentation files (I9). Informants also reported bootstrapping from the last deck:

"I reuse, I take the last one that has everything on it" (I6)

This is justified not only as a way of saving time and being more efficient by "not reinventing the wheel" (I10), but also avoiding the feeling of starting "from a blank sheet" (I11). While convenient, "regurgitating" existing slides in this way weakens the presenter's message whenever the slides do not suit the audience [3] or result in a weak, disconnected flow.

Lack of knowledge limits continual skill development

Various informants were motivated to improve their presentation skills, e.g., by thinking "not about the words but the flow" (I13) and by trying "to do storytelling" (I14). Some informants also identified their own weaknesses, e.g.:

"I see amazing presentations and I'm not there" (I11)

However, knowing how to make such improvements is difficult. While some informants reported judicious use of online videos and articles, very few read presentation books and one believed that only a coach could really help (I3).

Implications for Design Part I

Following our analysis we derived the following guidelines:

1. Support the collection, organization, and reuse of content in slideware, but in a manner independent of slides;
2. Support learning of storytelling forms by providing narrative templates with which to structure content;
3. Support timesaving by quickly generating prototype slides from narrative templates populated with content.

Based on these guidelines, we developed an open-ended technology probe that uses narrative templates to either inspire content generation or fit content already generated.

TURNINGPOINT

TurningPoint, is an add-in for Microsoft PowerPoint that provides a planning environment from which slides can be automatically generated. It comprises two distinct areas.

The content canvas (Figure 1, bottom) is an area in which the user creates sticky-like notes as either images or text. These modular notes can be freely repositioned and dragged into clusters that snap automatically and can be given a label.

The narrative strip (Figure 1, top) supports the sequencing of notes into a narrative structure drawn from the literature and chosen from a menu of templates. The strip is vertically divided into two horizontal streams: show (top) and tell (bottom). In the "show" stream, the user adds notes representing visual content (slide text, images, or descriptions thereof). In the "tell" stream, they add notes representing what they will say verbally to describe and elaborate on that visual content. Dragging a note or cluster to a show or tell placeholder in the narrative strip adds it to the current narrative but preserves the original on the canvas for later editing and reuse. Element text edits are synchronized across canvas and narrative strip, but deletions are localized.

Above the narrative strip is space for the core message of the presentation that should be kept in mind (if known). Each template is also divided horizontally into sections representing the structure of its high-level narrative. Each section includes a description of the target content and guides the user to sequence content accordingly.

We included 6 narrative templates in our TurningPoint probe, adapted from structures proposed in the books of our initial literature review [1, 3, 6, 9, 16]. These templates were:

a) **Ping-Pong**. A repeated *opposition* of two aspects or ideas, e.g., two sides of an argument;
b) **Mystery**. Sets up a *question* or problem that is only resolved towards the end of the presentation;
c) **Melodrama**. A *chronological* account of complications that grow, climax, and resolve among a cast of characters;
d) **Tower**. A logical *progression* that builds up multiple layers of information to support a final conclusion;
e) **Vision**. A repeated *contrast* between how things are and how things could be to share a vision of the future;
f) **Beyond Bullet Points**. An *elaboration* of a set first act through a structured second act to a synthesizing third act.

Once a narrative is created, the user can add markers to define slide boundaries. They can then click a button to generate slides accordingly: within each slide boundary, content from "show" and "tell" streams is added to the slide and note areas of a new PowerPoint slide respectively. This is a one-way process and requires subsequent slide styling. Users can return to the planning environment at any point to regenerate slides or experiment with different templates. Both canvas and strip content persist across sessions (in the XML of the .pptx file) as well as saved versions of the deck.

USER STUDY

We conducted a formative user study with TurningPoint to investigate how people might come to understand, use, and appropriate narrative templates if they were incorporated into slideware such as PowerPoint.

Data was gathered in single sessions of 4 stages: a semi-structured interview about participants' general presentation practices (10 min); an introduction to TurningPoint (20 min); free use of TurningPoint to create a narrative-driven presentation on "the importance of exercise" (guide time 40 min, actual time 36-82 min, mean time 53 min); and a final semi-structured interview on their experiences of using TurningPoint as well as their thoughts on narrative-driven presentation design in general (20 min).

We recruited 15 participants (6 male and 9 female, ages 18-45, mean 27) of 7 different nationalities, from four organizations working in research and development, sales, marketing, and public relations. All participants give presentations at least once a month and considered them important for their career advancement (half considered presentations to be of critical importance). Self-reported expertise varied from below intermediate (4), via intermediate (2), to above or well above intermediate (9).

Prior Practices

Unlike the informants whose interview transcripts we reviewed in our preliminary analysis of presentation building practices, most participants in this study reported typically starting their planning process outside of slideware. Example tool use included paper (P2, P4, P8, P9, P11), whiteboard (P6, P7), note-taking software (P5), and general text editors (P2, P6, P11, P12, P14, P15). Some still reported going to PowerPoint first to organize their ideas (P1, P3, P10, P13). Three participants (P7, P11, P12) further explained they would go to PowerPoint first if the outcome of the presentation was not especially important.

Findings

We now organize our discussion by the main study findings relating to the order of ideation and template selection, the saving or spending of time with respect to brainstorming, and the focusing but sometimes fixating narrative structures.

Choosing a template before brainstorming saves time by constraining current options for content filling or fitting

Most participants (11 in total) started by choosing a template. One group (P3, P4, P6, P10) had no initial idea of what to include in the presentation and picked the template that seemed the easiest to fill: *"I chose this template because it seemed very easy, I thought if I tried to fill the blanks, very likely I would think about a topic I wanted to talk about"* (P6). Others chose a template because they perceived a match between the structure of the problem and the structure of the template (P1, P2). These participants (P1, P2, P3, P4, P6, P10) felt that templates reduced the amount of effort necessary to plan a presentation *"it kind of does the work for you"* (P10), *"it's easier than if I try to build the logic myself"* (P4). Another reported reason for choosing a template first was the desire to simply *"try something new"* (P8).

Another group (P5, P11, P13, P14) started the process based on a preconceived idea. They looked for the template that formed the best fit with this idea, then started thinking about the content: *"it's like having a kind of negotiation with the template. I have something in my mind [...] and the template gives me some choices. I will see which one best matches"* (P13). These participants reported that their content would likely be the same regardless of the template chosen, but that the organization would vary: *"at first my thoughts were not 100% logical or not 100% consistent but with the help of the template I kind of rearranged the order of my thoughts so it looks more logical"* (P11). Overall, template-first participants appreciated the ability of templates to guide them through an unfamiliar process and instruct them in the art of crafting a narrative: *"this is educative, this is already a crash course for how to make a presentation better"* (P11).

Participants did not try to modify the structure of the chosen template. When asked about the reasons, most argued that they did not feel like changing it: *"I feel that I'm not really the type of person that really changes templates a lot, like this is the structure and it works and if it is not broke, don't break it"* (P13). Others (P6, P9, P11) said they would change it if necessary, but in this case they preferred to use it as a guide: *"if I have something like a very static story I would change the structure of the section, but in this case it is very comfortable to fill the blanks"* (P6).

The content canvas was still used in the template-first case, but as an area for low-level ideation: "*So this system helps me to not forget the fragmented single ideas, I can just note the single ideas somewhere in here [content canvas]"* (P1). The combination of content canvas and narrative strip also supported fluid reordering of narrative content: *"I like to move things around... It was nice because I didn't have to waste time copying and pasting and retyping and adjusting it again, because it was all in the same area"* (P13). However, two participants totally shunned any use of the content canvas beyond the essential because of the perceived time cost of more divergent thinking and the belief that brainstorming is best conducted as a group activity (P4, P11).

Brainstorming first is a time investment that reduces fixation on the first template tried and increases future options

A much smaller group of participants started by individually 'brainstorming' on the content canvas before selecting a template that best matched their emerging structure (P7, P9, P12, P15). Examples include, *"I was actually surprised that the tower fit what I was thinking, the ideas I was throwing around"(P7)*, and *"I started with the brainstorming, I started like writing random texts and as I was writing the texts I realized what I wanted to do, and what I wanted to do was the Ping-Pong" (P9).* Only in this brainstorming case did participants change templates during the process (P7, P9, P12): *"I put some things in the brainstorming part and then thought a little bit more... then I fixed the template"* (P12).

The ability to save random thoughts on the content canvas was mentioned by three participants (P7, P9, P12) as an important characteristic of the system: *"the main difference is that this brainstorming area gives more freedom than just PowerPoint which only allows you to put something in front of something else"* (P7). The non-linearity was also seen to be valuable to participants who had adopted a template-first approach to the task: *"when we are writing the script of the presentation in a doc or when we are making the slides of a presentation, we usually start from the introduction and then reason, reason, reason and conclusion. But here is like you can do it in whatever sequence you want"* (P14).

Support for presentation design should carefully integrate narrative templates that elaborate with evolving content

The primary feedback we received regarding the overall system was that it helped participants to keep on track. In some cases "on track" concerned keeping focused on content that really matters for the specific narrative (P7, P8, P9, P11, P12, P14, P15), e.g., *"I think this focuses on the topic... If I weren't using this I would put so many things"* (P12), while in other cases it referred to keeping focused within the given timeframe (P3, P4, P10, P12, P13, P15): *"if I didn't have the tool [...] it definitely would take much longer to already have the idea of the structure here"* (P4). In other cases it referred to keeping focused on the content instead of other features of presentation software (P10, P13), e.g., *"I like it because I'm always messing around... and then I'm just like what have I done, spent like three hours doing that"* (P13).

There are two main ways in which templates kept presenters on track. The first was by providing a high-level overview, e.g., *"I think it is very important to get a big picture... I think in PowerPoint, especially if you have many slides, it is very easy to get lost"* (P14). The second was by providing narrative structures that closely fit the problem or idea.

Among all templates the least popular was the melodrama –it was not chosen by any of the participants for the reason that is was unclear how to tell a character-driven story for the theme of "the importance of exercise". Beyond Bullet Points was chosen only once (P15) and mentioned in several interviews, for being either too long (P7, P14, P15), too typical (P8, P7, P6), or too complex (P13). The Vision template turned out to be the most popular, chosen by five participants, followed by Tower, Ping-Pong and Mystery. Although the templates were explained in the same way to all participants and each one was accompanied by a set of instructions, participants had different interpretations for all of them. Sometimes, when they explained how the narrative related to the template, little of the original logic remained.

IMPLICATIONS FOR DESIGN PART II & CONCLUSION

We have reported on a literature review, interview analysis, probe design, and user study investigating the potential for the narrative-driven design of slide presentations. The main design implication is to be cautious in exposing the full details of a narrative structure at the outset. Templates should be able to elaborate their structure as appropriate for the evolving content matter, in ways that provide initial guidance without being overly prescriptive. With reduced feelings of premature commitment to fine-grained narrative structures, authors may also feel freer to explore alternative templates, without incurring heavy transaction costs that deter the valuable and creative process of narrative experimentation.

Our revised, post-study design implications are therefore:

1. Support the collection, organization, and reuse of content in slideware, but in a manner independent of slides *and only reveal possible narrative structures when there is enough raw material to begin supporting them*;
2. Support learning of storytelling forms by providing narrative templates with which to structure content *and only reveal the next level of narrative structure when it gives an achievable target for the next round of ideation*;
3. Support timesaving by quickly generating prototype slides from narrative templates populated with content *and encourage more time to be spent on experimentation.*

Future work in the form of more naturalistic studies will further develop our understanding of how narrative-driven presentation planning can facilitate content reuse. Controlled comparisons of preparing presentations with and without narrative support will also help us to understand the extent to which such support impacts the final audience experience.

REFERENCES

1. Atkinson, C. (2005) Beyond Bullet Points. Microsoft
2. Duarte, N. (2008). Slideology. O'Reilly Media
3. Duarte, N. (2010). Resonate. Wiley.
4. Edge D., Savage, J. & Yatani, K. (2013). Hyperslides: Dynamic Presentation Prototyping. CHI'13, 671-680
5. Emaze. http://www.emaze.com
6. Gallo, C. (2009). The Presentation Secrets of Steve Jobs. McGraw Hill
7. Landry, B.M. & Guzdial, M. (2006). iTell: supporting retrospective storytelling with digital photos. DIS'06, 160-168.
8. Lichtschlag, L., Karrer, T. & Borchers, J. (2012). Fly: A Tool to Author Planar Presentations. CHI'12, 547-556
9. Lloyd-Hughes, S. (2011). How to be Brilliant at Public Speaking. Pearson
10. Prezi. http://www.prezi.com
11. Reynolds, G. (2008). Presentation Zen. New Riders
12. Reynolds, G. (2010). The Naked Presenter. New Riders
13. Sykes, M., Malik, N. & West, M.D. (2012). Stories That Move Mountains. Wiley
14. TED talks. http://www.ted.com
15. Thiry, E., Lindley, S., Banks, R. & Regan, T. (2013). Authoring personal histories: exploring the timeline as a framework for meaning making. CHI'13, 1619-1628
16. Weissman, J. (2009). Presenting to Win. FT Press

Supporting Treatment of People Living with HIV / AIDS in Resource Limited Settings with IVRs

Anirudha Joshi[1] (anirudha@iitb.ac.in), **Mandar Rane**[1] (mrane@iitb.ac.in),
Debjani Roy[1] (debjani.r@gmail.com), **Nagraj Emmadi**[1] (nagrajmumba@gmail.com),
Padma Srinivasan[1] (padma.srinivasan90@gmail.com), **N Kumarasamy**[2] (kumarasamy@yrgcare.org),
Sanjay Pujari[3] (sanjaypujari@gmail.com), **Davidson Solomon**[4] (Shadows_Org@rediffmail.com),
Rashmi Rodrigues[5] (rashmijr@gmail.com), **DG Saple**[6] (clinicaltrial@drsaple.com),
Kamalika Sen[7] (ksen@grameenfoundation.in), **Els Veldeman**[8] (EVELDEMA@its.jnj.com),
Romain Rutten[8] (RRUTTEN@its.jnj.com)

[1] Indian Institute of Technology, Bombay; [2] YRG CARE, Chennai; [3] Institute of Immunological Diseases, Pune;
[4] SHADOWS, Chirala; [5] St. John's Hospital, Bangalore; [6] HHRF, Mumbai; [7] Grameen Foundation, New Delhi;
[8] Janssen Pharmaceutica, Brussels.

ABSTRACT
We developed an interactive voice response (IVR) system called TAMA (Treatment Advice by Mobile Alerts) that provides treatment support to people living with HIV / AIDS (PLHA) in developing countries, who are on antiretroviral therapy (ART). We deployed TAMA with 54 PLHA in 5 HIV clinics in India for a period of 12 weeks. During the study, we gathered feedback about TAMA's design and usage. Additionally, we conducted detailed qualitative interviews and analysed usage logs. We found that TAMA was usable and viable in the real life settings of PLHA and it had many desirable effects on their treatment adherence. We developed insights that inform the design of TAMA and some of these can be generalised to design of other long-term, frequent-use IVR applications for users in developing countries in the healthcare domain and beyond.

Author Keywords
IVR; HIV; AIDS; healthcare; developing countries; treatment support; frequent-use applications; TAMA

ACM Classification Keywords
H.5.m. Information interfaces and presentation (e.g., HCI): Miscellaneous.

INTRODUCTION
Human Immunodeficiency Virus (HIV) affects 35 million people worldwide and is a cause of about 2 million deaths annually. A large majority of these people live in developing countries. In India there are about 2.4 million people living with HIV / AIDS (PLHA), and about 170,000 people die each year due to HIV [16, 35].

HIV is not curable yet, however it is manageable. The treatment of HIV is called ART. ART drugs suppress the replication process of HIV. Once a PLHA gets stabilised on ART, viral load reduces and gets suppressed, her immunity increases (which is tracked by CD4 counts) and can lead a productive life [11, 34]. However, the PLHA needs to be adherent to ART and needs to continue taking the medication for life. It is also important to take the medication on time. ART drugs stay in the blood for a limited amount of time. A drop in the drug level gives HIV opportunities to replicate and to develop resistance to the drug. If and when the virus develops resistance, the PLHA needs to take the next "line" of ART drugs, which suppress another part of the process of HIV replication. Though several lines of ART medication have been developed, the first line is the cheapest, the most widely available, and gives the PLHA the best chance for a simple regimen with a long term treatment success [34]. With high adherence, a large majority of PLHA can stay on the first line of ART for several years.

Over the last two decades, ART drugs have become available all over the world. Costs too have come down significantly, and in several countries, including developing countries, the first two lines of ART medication are available for free. It is therefore a surprise that though the treatment is available and affordable, many PLHA die each year. Could information and tools help in this situation?

The last decade has seen a rise in the use of mobile phones in developing countries. In this paper, we investigate whether it is possible to support the treatment of the PLHA with the help of mobile phones that they already own. A technology commonly available on all mobile phones is IVR. However, IVRs are not normally associated with personal, frequent-use applications. We designed an IVR ap-

CHI 2014, April 26 - May 01 2014, Toronto, ON, Canada

ACM 978-1-4503-2473-1/14/04□$15.00.
http://dx.doi.org/10.1145/2556288.2557236

plication called TAMA for the PLHA, and a web-interface for the clinician. As a pilot study, we deployed TAMA for 12 weeks with 54 PLHA in 5 clinics across India and collected feedback about its design and usage.

The next section reviews the related work. After that we describe the design of TAMA and our study. The fourth section describes our findings, followed by discussions and conclusions.

RELATED WORK

There have been several studies that describe why PLHA from developing countries have poor adherence to ART. Costs of ART and financial status of the patient are important reasons for discontinuing medication and poor adherence [5]. However, giving away free medication does not work either. A study reports that respondents receiving free drugs had lower adherence [28]. Severe depression, less education, being unemployed, high CD4 count, hospitalisation, side effects, and pill burden were the other factors associated with lower adherence. Reasons for missed doses were ran out of pills, travelling away from home, simply forgot, busy with work, or intolerable side effects [37].

There is some literature about ways of supporting treatment. Klein et al. describe an "adherence loop" wherein a patient needs to believe that she has a disease, to develop a mental model of the condition and the therapy, to know what she needs to do, and to act and to have the ability to do so [10]. While their work was not specific to HIV and was done in developed countries, other studies corroborate the importance of patient education, and social and emotional factors. Patient's knowledge about side effects, belief towards ART, having developed reminder tools for taking medication, and patient's trust and confidence in the doctor improves adherence [37]. Studies have shown a positive correlation between family support and adherence [3], though family support is usually less in case of PLHA because of the stigma.

There has been work related to using technology for treatment support. Computer-based and mobile-based interventions were found to be effective in developed countries because of lower cost and higher flexibility than human-delivered interventions [17, 20, 31, 33, 36]. SMS-based HIV preventions strategies were found to be particularly useful in developing countries, including Uganda [4], Kenya [12] and South Africa [6, 25]. SMS-based systems have also been used for daily or weekly adherence reminders and for collecting adherence feedback in Africa [22].

However, SMS content is not secure and hence not suitable in case of PLHA who have not yet disclosed their HIV status to their family members, which limits the use of SMS. Further, SMS-based systems cannot reach everyone in developing countries because of low literacy. A specific problem in the context of India is that even literate people are unable to input text, and hence do not use SMS.

Intuitively, IVR systems seem to have several advantages over SMS. IVRs are suitable in oral cultures, can be richer in communication than text, and because the content is stored at the server end, IVRs can be potentially made more secure. IVRs have been traditionally used for customer service. More recently, applications based on IVRs have been used as a mechanism to enable citizen journalism in rural areas [15], for broadcasting audio messages to commercial sex workers [27] and as an agricultural information service [19]. The IVR platform has been extended as a "Spoken Web" with many applications [1].

IVRs have also been used in the healthcare domain. DocTalk attempts to extend doctors' visits by allowing them to share pre-recorded messages on IVRs [23]. In a recent study, IVR was used to provide thrice a week adherence reminder for a daily pill, and report a small improvement in Hb levels of intervention group over control group [18]. Authors speculate that the findings were not significant due to small sample size. But another possible reason could be that the calls were "about the adherence" and not actual daily pill-time reminder calls. They also provide a systematic review of healthcare studies using technology.

In recent times, IVRs have been used to support HIV treatment, mainly for adherence reminders. IVR has been used to collect adherence data [7]. IVR was found to be better than SMS for weekly adherence calls [26]. Tucker et al used IVRs to provide self-monitoring of adherence for up to 10 weeks to PLHA who were substance users in rural USA [31]. They found that daily reports were correlated positively with 4-day and 7-day recall reports, though 7-day recall yielded higher adherence claims.

In our prior study with 65 PLHA in 5 clinics across locations in India, we found that while adherence is important, there is a need and an opportunity to do more [9]. While most PLHA are counselled on initiation of ART, these efforts are not sufficient. We suggest a more holistic intervention that repeats, localises and personalises information, provides conceptual clarity in addition to factual and procedural knowledge, complements current efforts in clinics, leverages the social position of treating doctors, and discreetly supports PLHA who have not disclosed their HIV status to family members.

However, increasing the features of an IVR system carries the risk of making it complex and unusable. In a follow-up experimental study, we reported that the IVR systems with these levels of complexity could be made usable even by low-literate users [24]. However, a product that works in a lab with healthy users need not be as effective in real-life settings with PLHA. The objective of the current study is to evaluate the design in a real-life setting with PLHA.

TAMA (TREATMENT ADVICE BY MOBILE ALERTS)

We designed a system called TAMA to complement and extend the care provided by the HIV clinics. TAMA consists of an IVR for the PLHA and a web-interface for the clinics. It provides pill-time reminder calls to PLHA, allows them to look up recommendations for common symptoms, plays short informational messages called "health tips" and reminds about appointments (figure 1).

Pill-time Reminders

It is important that a PLHA is adherent to her ART regimen and takes her doses on time. TAMA calls the PLHA to remind her to take her pills. The PLHA can choose to get daily or weekly reminder calls. If the PLHA chooses daily calls, TAMA calls her just after the pill time and asks if she has already taken her dose, if she plans to take it later, or if she will not be taking the dose (figure 1A). If the PLHA indicates that she has taken the dose, TAMA gives feedback about her adherence over the last 28 days.

At times the PLHA may be busy or away from her pills at pill-time, and may report that she will take the pill later. At other times, the pill-time call may not go through because of range or battery issues. In such cases, TAMA calls back after 30 minutes. TAMA repeats such calls for up to 2 hours after the first scheduled pill-time call. The PLHA is free to proactively call TAMA at any time (either before or after the pill-time) to report her dose. This is useful if the PLHA does not want to be disturbed at pill-time.

If the PLHA reports that she will not be taking the current dose, the doctor's voice comes on the line and gives feedback about the importance of adherence. When the PLHA misses her dose for the first time, (or if her adherence level has been generally high), the feedback is a gentle reminder. For frequent *pill-missers* (and for those with low / falling adherence), the feedback gradually gets sterner and reminds about several negative consequences, including possible viral resistance, and the risk of needing more expensive medication in future.

Those who feel that daily pill-time calls may intrude their lives too much can opt for a weekly call. The PLHA indicates a "best call time" (e.g. Sundays at 5 pm) for an unhurried call once a week. In that case, TAMA calls the PLHA once a week, reminds about adherence, and collects self-reported adherence feedback based on a 4-day recall.

Symptoms and Recommendations

ART drugs are known to cause side-effects. However, not every symptom is a side effect of ART. A symptom may also be caused by an opportunistic infection, by a condition called immune reconstitution syndrome, or due to treatment failure of the ART drugs. Currently, the PLHA needs to visit the clinic to manage a symptom. Symptoms require varied interventions. Some symptoms require no action as they disappear within a few weeks as the body gets used to ART. Others require minor lifestyle adjustments (e.g. taking

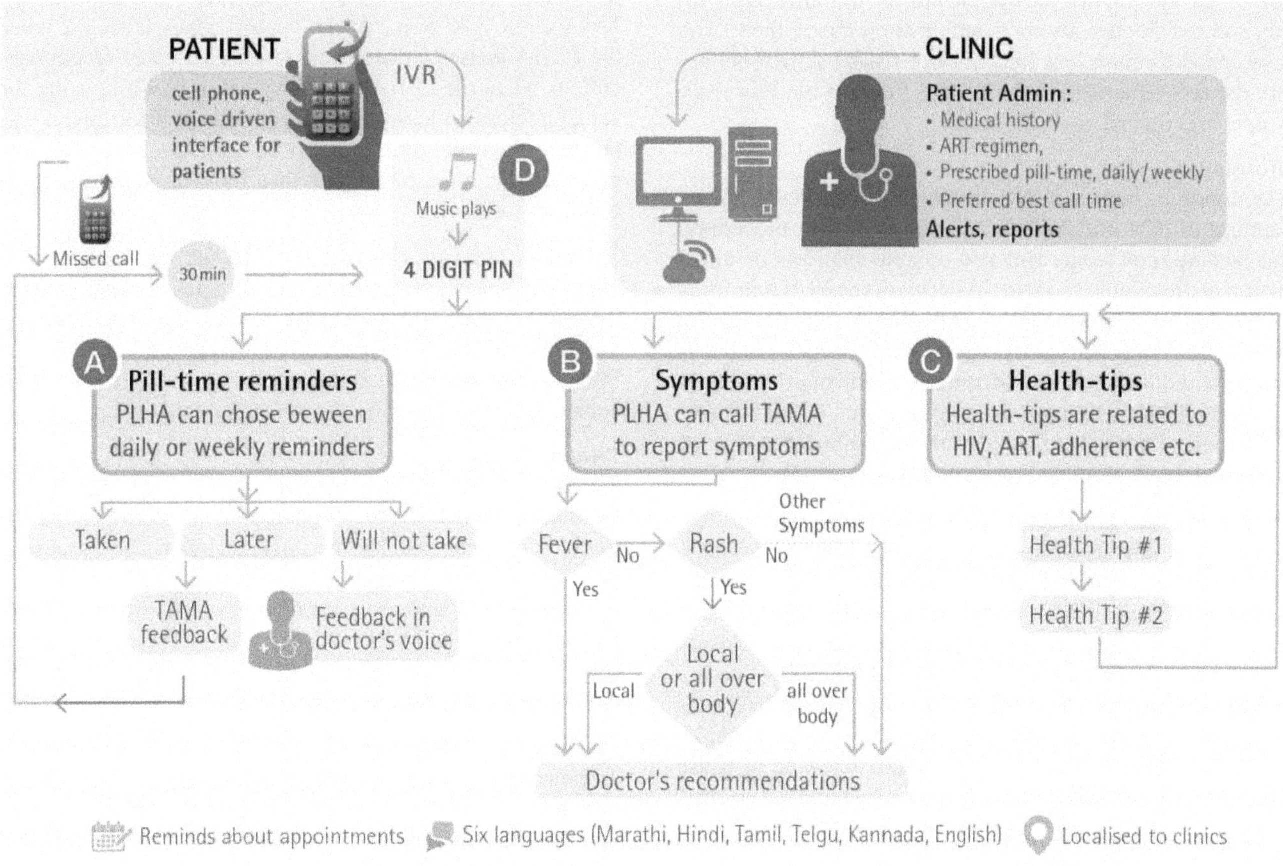

Figure 1. TAMA patient services daily (A) pill-time reminder, (B) symptoms look-up, (C) health tips, and (D) PIN.

medication half an hour before dinner). Others require symptomatic medication for a short duration that is available over the counter without a prescription in most drug stores (e.g. paracetamol). Some symptoms may require the PLHA to stop or change her ART regimen. Some symptoms require urgent medical attention.

If the PLHA is not feeling well, she can call TAMA (figure 1B). TAMA asks her about a probable symptom (e.g. "fever"). If the PLHA answers "no", TAMA asks about the next probable symptom (e.g. "rash"). If the PLHA answers "yes", TAMA may ask the PLHA for further details (e.g. "is the rash all over the body, or is it localised"). Depending on the PLHA's answers, TAMA makes one of four possible recommendations: ignore the symptom for now but discuss it with the doctor on the next visit, take *x* over-the-counter medication for *y* days, a lifestyle change, or meet the doctor immediately. In each case, TAMA also advises on whether or not to continue ART. In critical cases, TAMA connects the PLHA directly to a doctor for further management. The symptoms, their sequence, and the recommendations are based on an algorithm that is personalised depending on factors such as regimen of ART, age, gender, BMI, baseline CD4, hypertension, diabetes etc. This algorithm was created by a panel of practicing HIV specialists.

TAMA dialogues and algorithms are designed to err on the side of safety, and at times at the cost of usability. As a result, some dialogues are long, and in some cases, the PLHA is screened through less frequent but riskier symptoms before the recommendation for a more frequent but less risky symptom is played.

Information

It is important that a PLHA develops a conceptual understanding of HIV and ART in addition to having procedural and factual knowledge. But few reliable channels of information are available to them. Majority of the PLHA in India do not have access to the internet. Those who do, do not always find localised and personalised information that is relevant, and do not always trust the information they find. Currently, PLHA are counselled on initiation of ART. However, counselling is hard as a lot of information needs to be given and the PLHA is not in a condition to absorb it.

TAMA provides information in a question and answer format in short chunks of about 30 seconds each on demand. We call these "health tips". In the version used in the study, TAMA had 32 such health tips related to HIV, ART, adherence, tracking CD4, nutrition, family, children, disclosure etc. When a PLHA selects the option, two health tips are played back to her (figure 1C). The sequence is based on when she is likely to need that information. For example, the initial health tips have information relevant to those who are new to ART (e.g. adherence, tracking CD4 etc.), while the later ones are related to nutrition or family.

Security

PLHA are not likely to trust a system that has the slightest risk of an accidental disclosure. An accidental disclosure could lead to strain in the family, a loss of job, and / or public disgrace. TAMA is protected by a 4-digit personal identification number (PIN) (figure 1D). The PLHA chooses her PIN when she registers into TAMA. When TAMA calls a PLHA, or when the PLHA calls TAMA, a piece of music is played without any instruction. To access TAMA, the PLHA inputs her PIN. If the PIN is incorrect, the music is played again, and the PLHA tries again. If the PIN is correct, the relevant menu of TAMA begins.

Other Design and Technology Aspects

PLHA are often lost to follow up by clinics. Based on the last clinic visit date, TAMA reminds the PLHA to fix up an appointment for the next clinic visit. Once an appointment is fixed, TAMA reminds about the appointment itself.

In this study, TAMA was made available in 6 languages (Marathi, Hindi, Tamil, Telugu, Kannada and English). The scripts of TAMA were written in a conversational style. Translations (especially symptoms) were carefully localised and reviewed. Apart from languages, TAMA was also localised to clinics. This was done to leverage the trust that the doctors enjoy with patients. The opening greeting mentions the name of the clinic and / or the name of the treating doctor. E.g. "Welcome to PQR clinic", or "Welcome to Dr. Xyz's clinic". A "voice of the doctor" gives feedback when the PLHA misses a dose. This voice also gives recommendations when the PLHA reports symptoms. While using the actual doctors' voices would have been ideal for this, it was not feasible as the doctors are not fluent speakers in all languages. (We must remember that India is a multi-lingual country).

As Indian languages do not have robust text-to-speech or automatic speech recognition technologies, all dialogues in TAMA are recorded in human voices. Input is received through touchtone navigation. For outgoing calls, TAMA IVR is accessed by dialling a toll-free number. Incoming calls in India are free.

Clinical Tools

TAMA provides a web interface for clinics to register and maintain patients. During registration, the clinic enters the PLHA's medical history, the ART regimen, the prescribed pill-time (e.g. 10 pm daily), the preference to receive daily or weekly calls, and the preferred best call time (e.g. Sundays at 5 pm). As the PLHA uses TAMA, the web interface raises alerts about symptoms or falling adherence so that clinics can track patient progress and follow up in critical cases.

To help the clinics train the PLHA for using TAMA, an 18-minute long video was produced. With the help of scenarios, the video demonstrates the use of TAMA, including the use of the PIN, adherence reporting, symptoms look-up, and health tips. The video also shows some best practices such as taking one's pills on time and proactively calling TAMA rather than waiting for TAMA's call. Like TAMA, the videos too are localised in languages and to the clinics and include photographs of local doctors. (As a clinical trial is currently underway, and it uses the same videos, these have not been referenced here.)

THE STUDY

IVRs work on all mobile phones, and hence have a wide reach. However, IVRs are not easy to use and are not typically used as a personal, frequent-use application for providing holistic treatment support. The key question that we wanted to answer was, "*Can TAMA IVR with as many features be safely used for supporting treatment of HIV in a real-life setting in a developing country?*" Further, we wanted to investigate which design decisions worked, why, and what can be learnt beyond the immediate context of supporting HIV treatment?

We deployed TAMA in five well-known HIV clinics in four large cities and one small town in India (Mumbai, Pune, Bangalore, Chennai, and Chirala). The locations were selected in high HIV prevalence states and to represent the diversity in languages and the types of clinics. Clinics often got patients who spoke different languages. Hence localised versions of TAMA IVR and the training videos were developed for each location for each language spoken there. In all, 16 localisations of TAMA IVR and training videos were created. Since all clinicians could speak, read, and write English fluently, only the English version of the web interface was developed. At least two doctors and / or clinic staff in each clinic were trained to use the web interface and to administer the protocol for the study.

During the study, TAMA IVR was provided for use at home for a period of 12 weeks to PLHA who had been on ART for 0-6 months, and who volunteered participation. On recruitment, participants were trained by the clinic with the help of the video and demonstrations. While recruitment was open to all eligible PLHA, we requested the clinics to ensure variability in terms of gender, languages, income groups, education, and age. In the first four weeks, all participants were required to be on a daily pill-time calls option. After that if the clinician found that the participant has been adherent, he could move her to a weekly call on request. The participants were followed up after weeks 2, 4, 8 and 12. A buffer of ± 2 days was allowed to account for convenience. If a follow-up happened beyond this window, the data from that participant for that follow-up was not considered for the purposes of the study (though the medical treatment continued as usual). The study took 9 months.

Our objective was to evaluate TAMA in a real-life setting. Apart from training the doctors and clinic staff on TAMA, we did not provide any additional administrative assistance. Apart from TAMA and TAMA training, the participants received the "standard of care" (i.e. the same treatment at the same cost as they would have otherwise got). Specifically, we did not provide any medication or cost of medication

Qualitative Interviews

Authors conducted semi-structured qualitative interviews with a subset of the participants. Before each interview, the interviewers reviewed TAMA logs. The interviewers asked the participants several open-ended questions to identify design problems or difficulties faced while using TAMA. Participants were encouraged to share experiences, opinions, and feedback about TAMA's design and usage and were asked for suggestions about how TAMA could be improved. Interviewers followed up on specific incidents noticed in usage logs. Interviewers probed about perceptions of effects on adherence and accuracy of information provided by TAMA. Interviews typically lasted 40 minutes. After a gap of a few weeks, interviews were repeated with some of the participants to explore if perceptions changed over time.

Quantitative Questionnaires

During each follow-up, the participants answered a questionnaire. The first 10 questions were the same as the System Usability Scale (SUS) questionnaire [2], which were modified only to replace the words "the system" with the word "TAMA", and translated. An additional set of 12 questions were asked to elicit feedback about TAMA's design and the participant's usage. The questionnaire was orally administered by a trained clinic staff or a treating doctor in the language of the participant's choice. The administrator read out the questions to the participant. In case the participant did not understand a question the administrator repeated the question, but did not give additional explanation.

The study was done ethically. It was done only in clinics specialising in treating HIV patients. Apart from the phone number and the medical history, no other personal data was collected from the PLHA. Patient data of a particular clinic was only handled within that clinic. PLHA interviews were scheduled by clinic staff and were conducted by researchers within the clinic premises. The design of TAMA and the study were approved by ethics committees of all participating organisations.

PARTICIPANTS

Initially doctors found it difficult to recruit women, rural participants, and those with less education. However, in due course doctors managed to recruit participants with reasonable variability. A total of 54 PLHA (35 male, 19 female) were recruited. Each clinic recruited between 5 to 15 PLHA. There were 28 urban, 10 small town, and 11 rural participants. 15 participants chose TAMA IVR in Telugu, 14 in Marathi, 8 in Tamil, 8 in Hindi, 6 in Kannada, and 3 in English. 9 participants had less than 4 years of school education, 10 from 4 to 7 years, 15 from 8 to 10 years, and 20 had more than 10 years of education. Their mobile phone experience ranged from 6 months to 17 years (mean 6.6 years, SD 4.5 years).

A total of 50 qualitative interviews (including 15 repeat interviews) were conducted with 35 participants. 12 of these were conducted after 2 weeks of TAMA usage, 12 after 4 weeks, 11 after 8 weeks, and 14 after 12 weeks. 10 participants interviewed were of the age 23 to 30, 16 of age from 31 to 40, and 9 of age 40 to 64.

FINDINGS

The overall qualitative feedback on TAMA was very positive. TAMA was found to be usable even by people with few technology skills. A participant could not unlock her own phone, but could answer TAMA calls by herself.

Many participants, and particularly those who had no other support system, liked TAMA. They felt that through TAMA someone was keeping track of their treatment like a family member, taking care of them, and giving them knowledge, advice and counselling. Participants consistently agreed with the statement "When I use TAMA, it feels like I am in touch with my HIV clinic" (4.30/5 to 4.44/5 across weeks 2-12). A large majority of participants said they were willing to pay for such a service. The minority who said they wouldn't, said so either because they could not afford to pay or because they were financially dependent on someone else. When asked what might be the effect once TAMA was shut down after the study, some said they would miss TAMA, and it might make them miss their pills. Others said they will have to manage without TAMA by making alternative arrangements such as mobile alarms.

The qualitative interviews produced detailed feedback about specific features and design aspects of TAMA.

Pill-time Reminders

Many participants said that their adherence to ART regimens had improved because of TAMA. Some participants said they now were more "serious" about adherence than earlier. Four participants believed that they had been adherent earlier, but even they thought that TAMA served as a backup "in case I forget – which is bound to happen at times". Three participants who had used mobile alarms for pill times said that TAMA was better "because it calls several times". The 30 minute gap between calls was considered to be ideal. Many thought that a larger gap would make them late, and a shorter gap too much of a nag. Logs indicate that for 6,904 pills scheduled to be taken by participants, they received 5,787 incoming pill-time reminder calls (84%). It is interesting to note that 8,203 pill-time calls attempted by TAMA were either not completed (possibly due to range or battery issues), or missed, declined, snoozed, or left incomplete by participants. Thus, the remind-me-in-30-minutes feature got used extensively.

TAMA helped people develop good adherence habits. Participants strongly agreed with the statement "TAMA helps me take my medicines on time" (4.47/5 to 4.74/5 across weeks 2-12). Distractions (festivals, work etc.) still affected some people's pill-times, but TAMA's calls prod them to be punctual. Some started associating their pills with routine activities like dinner. In the questionnaire, participants were asked whether their adherence would have been less or more than current had they not been using TAMA. Their opinion changed marginally over the 12 weeks. After the first 2 weeks of TAMA usage, the participants' opinions tended towards somewhat less than current adherence (2.26/5). By the 12th week, the opinions had drifted towards somewhat more than current adherence (2.53 in week 4, 2.67 in week 8, 2.77 in week 12). Though the differences are not statistically significant, the drift is consistent

The adherence percentage feedback seems to have worked. Several participants could recall their current adherence percentage. Some participants could explain correctly what the numbers meant, though a majority was confused. One participant asked, "Does it mean that I am late?" Some participants felt that TAMA underestimated their adherence. And yet, in all cases, their "daily scores" seemed to prod them on towards better adherence. They were keen to find out their adherence levels and waited to hear their current percentage before hanging up the call.

We were interested to find out if people "cheated" TAMA (i.e. answered that they had taken the pill, but actually took it later). A majority of participants said they did not do so. One remarked, "Why should I do that? It is about my life after all". Six participants admitted to have cheated TAMA, and at least one of these admitted that once he had forgotten to take his pill after he reported it as taken.

We were interested to find out if participants called TAMA proactively to report doses. If a user calls proactively, it could mean that she is not overly dependent on TAMA's reminder calls. Surprisingly, as per the logs, as many as 52/54 participants made at least one outgoing call to record adherence. For 6,904 scheduled pills, 1,095 (16%) such outgoing calls were made. But many participants did not want to call TAMA proactively every time and said it was "too tedious". Some asked why they should bother, as "TAMA calls for the purpose of reminding". One said, "I will call TAMA only if I have a problem". Even the participants claiming that that they took their pills before TAMA calls them said they waited for TAMA to call. Twelve participants said that they "called back" after TAMA had called them once at their pill-time. Three said that they called TAMA if a later call from TAMA was likely to disturb their work or sleep, or if they were likely to be in company. Only one participant called TAMA routinely, and he too missed on occasions.

A related issue was the toll-free number. Though many users did have TAMA's toll-free number "written down somewhere", only one tech-savvy participant had saved it in his phone. Most preferred to call back the same number that TAMA called from (a toll number).

Opinions were mixed about whether TAMA calls were intrusive. When TAMA's call came in front of others, some thought that was intrusive but most participants managed to answer TAMA calls in public or in company. To the statement "I often get disturbed in my work when TAMA calls" participants disagreed consistently (1.62/5 to 2.17/5). In contrast, participants reported that weekly calls by TAMA (the "best call time" calls) were not useful and were intrusive. The few participants who were set to receive weekly calls opted out when they found out they could. Only one participant asked to be switched from daily pill-time reminders to a weekly call.

Symptoms and Recommendations

Some participants reported that they did not have any symptoms, and naturally many of these did not access the symptoms menu. Among those who had symptoms, six preferred to call or visit the doctor first, either in cases where the doctor was easily accessible, or because the participants were not sufficiently trained to use the symptom menu in TAMA. (This happened in case of some early participants in the study.)

But a majority of participants called TAMA first. Logs show that 42/54 participants accessed the symptoms menu in a total of 216 calls. Among these 75 were outgoing calls made by 31/54 participants (presumably calls because of a symptom or out of curiosity). 33/47 participants reported one or more symptoms in TAMA through 100 calls. (*Due to a technical difficulty, this part of the data is available for 47/54 participants.*)

Of the 100 reported symptom calls, in 40 calls TAMA diagnosed the case as critical and attempted to connect to a doctor after giving the recommendation. In 29 of these 40 calls, TAMA could connect the 14 participants to a doctor successfully. In many of the clinics, more than one doctor was set up to receive such escalated calls in a sequence. In spite of this, TAMA could not complete calls to doctors in 11/40 cases for 10 participants. This data reflects the real life. Doctors typically get hundreds of calls from patients every day, and they do miss many calls. In the study, TAMA was deployed to a small fraction of the patients in each clinic, thus it did not have any 'triaging' effect on the number of calls that doctors receive. Hopefully when TAMA is deployed to all patients in the clinic, some of the problems will be resolved by the system, thereby allowing doctors to handle more calls that are critical.

During the interviews, many of those who accessed the symptoms menu said they trusted in TAMA's recommendations, but some still needed a reconfirmation from the doctors. Eight participants reported that they had "explored" the symptoms menu out of curiosity even when they did not have any symptoms. Two participants admitted that they had reported a "fake" symptom, and were surprised to find that it was taken seriously. TAMA gave them a recommendation and even connected them to a doctor. While it is not desirable to have fake symptoms reported, exploration helped three participants report a real symptom. They explored all the available symptoms in one pass, and reported a true symptom in a second pass soon after.

Information

Logs indicate that 42/54 participants accessed health tips in 718 calls. Among these, 158 calls (22%) were proactive outgoing calls made by 32/54 participants, the rest being incoming calls. Information was perceived to be useful and believable. Over the 12 weeks, participants consistently agreed with "TAMA is helping me to know more about ART and HIV" (4.15/5 to 4.51/5) and disagreed with statements "TAMA does not give useful information" (1.31/5 to 2.00/5) and "I find the information given by TAMA hard to believe" (1.77/5 to 2.44/5).

A majority of those who had heard health tips remembered them. The health tips that could be readily recalled were actionable. They were regarding nutrition, about not sharing ART pills, that there are multiple lines of ART, about how HIV can and cannot spread, and why one should track CD4 regularly. However, six participants could not recall any health tip, though logs indicate that they had heard some of them. The participants who heard health tips demanded more of actionable health tips. They wanted to know about the "latest research", more about children and family issues, sexual behaviour, nutrition, about the "real" differences between ART medications available at various prices and in different clinics, about alcohol, smoking, becoming "negative", life expectancy, and prognosis. Those who had reported symptoms wanted personalised health tips related to those symptoms. Several participants report a change of behaviour after hearing health tips. Participants said they often had questions after hearing a health tip. Perhaps there could be a "discussion board" around each health tip.

24 participants accessed 10 or more health tips in a single call at least once (looping through the menu 5 or more times). This behaviour was not anticipated. Some participants said that they had heard "all" the health tips available. A particular rule in TAMA is that once a health tip is played, it is not repeated within 15 days. So those who heard many health tips "ran out". Perhaps this rule is not needed, as repetition is useful.

Five participants who never heard health tips said they did not know that TAMA had this feature. Eight participants had heard health tips only once or twice. Surprisingly, when we asked these participants what could be added to TAMA, they often asked for "more information" (often of the type that was already present in TAMA).

Other Issues

While participants were concerned about accidental disclosure, almost all felt that the PIN was secure enough. Over the 12 weeks they consistently disagreed with the statement "TAMA will cause un-wanted disclosure – people who don't know about TAMA suspect something" (1.62/5 to 2.00/5). Participants reported surprisingly few PIN malfunctions. One user pressed the "green button" after entering the PIN once. Another user "backspaced" a wrong PIN to correct it (like one can do on a handset). But users learnt to get over these problems quickly.

While most participants said that TAMA calls reminded them of their pills, one participant said it reminded her of her disease. We found that while some people learned to "barge in" the IVR menus, many continued to wait till the menu was completed.

We discovered some operational issues related to the study during the interviews. In some cases, participants' data was not completely entered in TAMA, which prevented TAMA from playing health tips. We found that participant training was inconsistent across clinics particularly for early participants. When the training was improved, later participants faced fewer issues. Some problems were related to the mismatch between the doctor's advice during consultation and the settings in TAMA.

Quantitative Feedback

The mean SUS score across all participants across 12 weeks is 83.73 (SD 13.8, 95% CI 81.7 to 85.8). SUS scores above 81 convert to a percentile rank of above 90% of reported studies [29, 32]. We present the detailed SUS scores grouped by weeks, languages and clinics in an appendix online [30]. The quantitative questions were analysed by comparing the responses of participants against a uniform distribution using the Kolmogorov Smirnov goodness of fit test for ordinal variables with a D statistic. All questions returned significant results at $p < 0.05$. We present the details of these quantitative findings also in the appendix [30].

DISCUSSIONS

It is known that low literate users lack several abstraction skills and find it difficult to navigate hierarchies [14]. While it is true that many of our users needed to be trained to use IVRs, we found that a small amount of training helped the participants overcome the initial barriers and use TAMA effectively over the longer term. Though such training may not be feasible for one-time use applications, it makes sense for long-term, frequent-use applications. Future research could focus on evaluating the costs and benefits of training low-literate users for such applications.

While providing technology support for a routine task such as pill-taking, we must remember that it should mainly serve as a backup. There is always the risk that people may get too dependent on technology. A study showed that adherence could drop due to over-dependence on technology or due to device failure [13]. The participants' opinion about what their adherence would have been without TAMA drifted from "somewhat less than their current levels" after 2 weeks of usage to "same as current levels" after 12 weeks. Though the differences are not statistically significant, the drift is consistent. A possible reason could be that TAMA's pill-time reminders were useful to the beginners, but as the participants got used to ART they became less dependent on them (at least in their perception). A design feature that possibly contributed to this trend was that TAMA calls the participant 5 minutes *after* the scheduled pill-time. A focussed study is required to confirm this trend empirically.

To further wean people away from over-dependence on TAMA, we originally considered that it might be better if PLHA were to proactively call TAMA to report adherence instead of waiting for TAMA's call. While that may still be the better option, after the study we are convinced that TAMA is usable and viable in real life settings, and it could be reliably used by PLHA for pill-time reminders. Though many participants occasionally called TAMA, routine proactive calling for reporting pill-time adherence does not seem feasible to most users.

Surprisingly, participants found the *weekly* "best call time" calls more intruding than the *daily* pill-time reminders. By hindsight the reason is clear. The daily pill-time calls are actionable ("take your pill now") and fit into a routine, and hence do not intrude. While the weekly calls remind about the importance of adherence, they are pedantic. They do not actually help adherence, and hence are found intrusive.

Trust is an important factor to consider while disseminating information on sensitive topics. Literature in agricultural domain suggests that though users say they prefer to get information from an expert, they tend to act more often on an IVR message from a peer rather than an expert [19]. Our experiment with PLHA peer group discussions also indicates that peers are trusted [8]. However, PLHA also have tremendous trust in the local doctors. We tried to leverage that trust in the doctors by localising TAMA and the training videos to clinics, and by using "the voice of the doctor" to give critical advice. We found that the recommendations were usable, useful and trusted. After the study, our sense is that the participants trusted TAMA recommendations only because these came from the doctors. Perhaps trust is a function of the domain (agriculture vs. healthcare) and type of task (practical agriculture vs. treatment).

The proportion of participants who reported symptoms in TAMA seems to be somewhat larger than in the clinical practice. Though we did not investigate this systematically (and two participants did admit to reporting fake symptoms), the difference indicates that the participants may be reporting minor symptoms that they may have otherwise ignored, perhaps because TAMA makes reporting symptoms easy. This calls for more investigation in future.

Dialog design in IVRs should be related to frequency of use. In TAMA the symptoms menu is meant to be used rarely. The symptoms menu was accessed in only 216 calls, and a symptom was reported in only 100 calls. This suggests that such menus should allow for exploration at the same time they should not lead to wrong entries of medical data. Balancing these requirements and yet keeping such dialogs usable by less educated users has been a challenge. On the other hand, for frequently used IVR menus (e.g. pill-time reminder menus), length of dialogs is an important design consideration. Our prior work suggests that longer, expansive menus help novices understand prompts better [24]. However, not many of our participants had learnt to barge in after 12 weeks. For long-term, frequent-use IVR applications, menus could be progressively shortened to improve speeds of experienced users, with longer menus could act as backup.

Some of the participating doctors were surprised to see the popularity of health tips and the demand for even more despite the extensive counselling that they provide. However, we believe that more could be done to help PLHA understand their disease and its treatment, and to give them emotional and social support. The participants who did not access health tips too were keen for more information. A reason they did not access the existing information could be the health tips had to be "pulled". In contrast, the adherence feedback (which was "pushed") was always heard. People with less exposure to digital technologies are not used to active "information foraging" as is understood traditionally [21]. For them, perhaps the cost of interaction is too high compared to the utility of information gained. They prefer to stumble upon information by serendipity (e.g. friends, TV etc.) and would readily hear pushed information.

For the clinics, TAMA is an enabling tool rather than an automated system. When it is scaled up TAMA needs to be better integrated with the operations of the clinic. This may include activities such as more extensive patient training, saving TAMA numbers in their phones, tracking their usage routinely, follow-up in cases of poor adherence or symptoms etc. In a way, it may increase the clinic's work, though it also allows them to extend their care beyond the clinic.

CONCLUSIONS

IVRs can reach a large majority of human population today and are particularly suitable for countries like India with many languages and several low-literate users. IVRs are known for poor user experience and are usually associated with pesky customer service calls. However, in a study in five HIV clinics with 54 PLHA for 12 weeks we found that it is possible to improve adherence and build a deeper relationship between PLHA and the clinic using a holistic, well-designed, localised, personalised IVR application. Our study shows that TAMA was usable and works in real-life settings. The quantitative feedback reassured us about the appropriateness of our broader design approach to TAMA. The qualitative interviews unearthed the insights of why things work, what can be improved, what failed, and why.

While some of these lessons are specific to TAMA, we find that many of these can be generalised to other frequent-use IVR applications in the healthcare domain. We found that a 4-digit PIN on IVRs is usable and provides sufficient perception of security to HIV patients. It should be sufficient for most other ailments. We found that a daily pill-time reminder call is not considered intrusive as it is actionable, while even a weekly call may be intruding if it is pedantic. Our 30-minute duration between follow-up calls turned out to be just right for the users. Patients suffering from serious health conditions are hungry for authenticated, personalised, and localised information beyond what they receive from clinicians and caregivers. The delivery of such information needs to fit their information seeking behaviour. Pushing information to them may be better than asking them to pull it.

Our immediate next step in this project is a randomised clinical trial, wherein biological outcomes of a cohort of HIV patients using TAMA will be compared with a control group. Looking beyond, several such long-term, frequent-use applications based on IVR technologies seem feasible for a wide range of users in developing countries, though many unanswered questions call for more research.

ACKNOWLEDGEMENTS

This project was funded through a grant from Johnson & Johnson Limited. We thank the doctors, counsellors, moderators, and the people living with HIV / AIDS for participating in this project and sharing their insights.

REFERENCES

1. Agarwal, S., Jain, A., Kumar, A., Nanavati, A., Rajput, N. The Spoken Web: A Web for the Underprivileged. *ACM SIGWEB* (2010).
2. Brooke, J. SUS: A "Quick and Dirty" Usability Scale. In Jordan, P. et al. Usability Evaluation in Industry. *Taylor and Francis* (1996).
3. Cauldbeck, M., O'Connor, C., O'Connor, M., Saunders, J., Rao, B., Mallesh, V., Laing, R., Satish, K. Adherence to anti-retroviral therapy among HIV patients in Bangalore, India. *AIDS Research and Therapy* (2009).
4. Chang, L., Kagaayi, J., Nakigozi, G., Packer, A., Serwadda, D., Quinn, T., Gray, R., Bollinger, R., Reynolds, S. Responding to the Human Resource Crisis: Peer Health Workers, Mobile Phones, and HIV Care in Rakai, Uganda. *AIDS patient care and STDs* (2008).
5. Duraisamy, P., Ganesh, A., Homan, R., Kumarasamy, N., Castle, C., Sripriya, P., Mahendra,V., Solomon, S. Costs and financial burden of care and support services to PLHA and households in South India. *AIDS care* (2006).
6. Fabricant, R. Project Masiluleke. *Interactions* (2009).
7. Haberer J., Kiwanuka J., Nansera D., Wilson I., Bangsberg D. Challenges in using mobile phones for collection of antiretroviral therapy adherence data in a resource-limited setting. *AIDS and behavior* (2010).
8. Iyengar, A., Joshi, A. Evaluating anonymous social networking for PLHA with social prototypes. *ACM Dev* (2013).
9. Joshi, A., Rane, M., Roy, D., Sali, S., Bharshankar, N. Kumarasamy, N., Pujari, S., Solomon, D., Sharma, D., Saple, D., Rutten, R., Ganju, A., Van Dam, J. Design opportunities for supporting treatment of PLHA in India, *INTERACT*, Springer (2011).
10. Klein, D., Wustrack, G, Schwartz, A. Medication adherence: Many conditions, a common problem. *HFES Annual Meeting*, SAGE (2006).
11. Kumarasamy, N., Solomon, S., Chaguturu, S., Cecelia, A., Vallabhaneni, S., Flanigan, T. The changing natural history

of HIV disease: Before and after the introduction of generic antiretroviral therapy in southern India. *CID* (2005).

12. Lester, R., Karanja, S. Mobile phones: exceptional tools for HIV / AIDS, health, and crisis management. *Lancet Infectious Diseases* (2008).

13. Mannheimer, S., Morse, E., Matts, J., Andrews, L., Child, C., Schmetter, B., Friedland, G. Sustained benefit from a long-term antiretroviral adherence intervention. *JAIDS* (2006).

14. Medhi, I., Toyama, K., Joshi, A., Athavankar, U., Cutrell, E. A comparison of list vs. hierarchical UIs on mobile phones for non-literate users. *INTERACT* (2013).

15. Mudliar, P., Donner, J., Thies, W. Emergent practices around CGNet Swara, voice forum for citizen journalism in rural India. *ICT4D* (2012).

16. National AIDS Control Organisation Facts and Figures. http://www.naco.gov.in/NACO/Quick_Links/Publication/State_Fact_Sheets/Fact_Sheets/ (2012).

17. Noar, S., Black, H., Pierce, L. Efficacy of computer technology-based HIV prevention interventions: a meta-analysis. *Aids* 23.1 (2009).

18. Pai, N., Supe, P., Kore, S., Nandanwar, Y., Hegde, A., Cutrell, E., Thies, W. Using automated voice calls to improve adherence to iron supplements during pregnancy: A pilot study. *ICTD* (2013).

19. Patel, N., Savani, K., Dave, P., Shah, K., Klemmer, S., Parikh, T. Power to the Peers: Authority of Source Effects for a Voice-based Agricultural Information Service in Rural India. *ITID* (2013).

20. Patrick, K., Griswold, W., Raab, F., Intille, S. Health and the mobile phone. *AJPM* (2008).

21. Pirolli, P., Information foraging theory: Adaptive interaction with information. Oxford Univ. Press (2007).

22. Pop-Eleches, C. Thirumurthy, H., Habyarimana, J., Zivin, J., Goldstein, M., Walque, D., MacKeen, L., Haberer, J., Kimaiyo, S., Sidle, J., Ngare, D., Bangsberg, D. Mobile phone technologies improve adherence to antiretroviral treatment in a resource-limited setting: a randomized controlled trial of text message reminders. *Aids* 25 (2011).

23. Ramkrishnan, P., Vashistha, A., Cutrell, E., Thies, W. DocTalk: Extending doctors' visits with personalized voice messages. *ACM Dev* (2013).

24. Rashinkar, P., Joshi, A., Rane, M., Sali, S., Badodekar, S., Emmadi, N., Roy, D., Sheikh, R., Shrivastav, A. Healthcare IVR system for non-tech savvy users. *USAB: Information Quality in e-Health. Springer* (2011).

25. Rivett, U., Tapson, J. The Cell-Life project: converging technologies in the context of HIV/AIDS. *IJCRE* (2009).

26. Rodrigues, R., Shet, A., Antony, J., Sidney, K., Arumugam, K., Krishnamurthy, S., D'Souza, G., DeCosta, A. Supporting adherence to antiretroviral therapy with mobile phone reminders: results from a cohort in South India. *PloS one* (2012).

27. Sambasivan, N., Weber, J., Cutrell, E. Designing a phone broadcasting system for urban sex workers in India. *ACM SIGCHI* (2011).

28. Sarna, A., Pujari, S., Sengar, A., Garg, R., Gupta, I., Dam, J. Adherence to Antiretroviral Therapy & its Determinants Amongst HIV Patients in India. *IJMR* (2008).

29. Sauro, J. Measuring Usability With the System Usability Scale. http://www.measuringusability.com/sus.php.

30. Supporting Treatment of People Living with HIV / AIDS in Resource Limited Settings with IVRs, Appendix (Quantitative Data) http://www.idc.iitb.ac.in/~anirudha/TAMApilotsAppendix.html (2014).

31. Tucker J., Simpson, C., Huang, J., Roth, D., Stewart, K. Utility of an interactive voice response system to assess antiretroviral pharmacotherapy adherence among substance users living with HIV/AIDS in the rural South. *AIDS Patient Care STDS* (2013).

32. Tulis, T. and Albert, B. Measuring User Experience, *Morgan Kaufmann* (2008).

33. Vidrine, D., Arduino, R., Lazev, A., Gritz, E. A randomized trial of a proactive cellular telephone intervention for smokers living with HIV/AIDS. *Aids* (2006).

34. WHO: Consolidated guidelines on the use of antiretroviral drugs for treating and preventing HIV infection. http://www.who.int/hiv/pub/guidelines/arv2013/ (2013).

35. Wikipedia, List of countries by HIV/AIDS adult prevalence rate. http://en.wikipedia.org/wiki/List_of_countries_by_HIV/AIDS_adult_prevalence_rate.

36. Winchester, W. Catalyzing a perfect storm: Mobile phone-based HIV-prevention behavioral interventions. *Interactions* (2009).

37. Wu, X. Factors associated with adherence to antiretroviral therapy among HIV/AIDS patients in rural China. *Aids* (2007).

Reflection through Design: Immigrant Women's Self-Reflection on Managing Health and Wellness

Deana Brown, Victoria Ayo, Rebecca E. Grinter
School of Interactive Computing and GVU Center
Georgia Institute of Technology
85 5th Street, Atlanta, GA 30308
{deana.brown, vayo3, beki} @gatech.edu

ABSTRACT
Women comprise nearly half of the immigrant population worldwide and are susceptible to a wider range of health challenges compared to immigrant men. We present the findings of four participatory design sessions with immigrant women from the Caribbean to identify health and wellness challenges they faced and to conceptualize technologies to help them manage these issues. Stress, dietary challenges (specifically obesity), mental health, and domestic abuse, as identified by the women, form the focal themes for the design sessions. Their design approaches emphasized *rebuilding the support structure*, *reducing stressors through entertainment and relaxation* and *encouraging positive gradational lifestyle changes*. In conceiving health and wellness technologies for immigrant women, our work highlights opportunities for HCI to consider *the role of others* (and who benefits) and to *reflect on the role of design* and the underlying values and themes designs encompass. Finally, we emphasize how the technologies conceived by these women support rather than replace social solutions to the health and wellness challenges faced by these and other immigrant women.

Author Keywords
Participatory design, health and wellness, immigrant women, Caribbean, culture

ACM Classification Keywords
H.5.m. Information interfaces and presentation (e.g., HCI): Miscellaneous.

INTRODUCTION
African and Caribbean immigrants make up a large percentage of the immigrant population in the United States [10]. Minority immigrants, such as Africans, face health challenges that make them more prone to health disparities even compared to African Americans [29]. In our research we sought to gain a deeper understanding of the health-related challenges and barriers faced by immigrant women from the English-speaking Caribbean, and found many of those—stress, dietary challenges, mental wellness, and domestic abuse—lent themselves to technological interventions. The participatory design that followed, yielded solutions that stemmed from the women's own reflection on how they manage their health and wellness which revealed three key strategies: rebuilding social and organizational support structures to connect immigrant women with people and resources ii) reducing stressors through entertainment, relaxation and spirituality and iii) encouraging positive gradational lifestyle changes (such as to one's diet).

Our research contributes to HCI by highlighting the needs that particular groups face when it comes to health and wellness. It also highlights the role immigrant women themselves can play in shaping these designs through participatory approaches and reflection through design. We present considerations for individuals designing health and wellness technologies for immigrants or displaced people outside their countries of origin, though these could also apply more broadly to the design of general health technologies: i) consider the role of others (whether the health challenge lends itself to private, personal interventions, or if intervention by others is a more appropriate solution, whether it should benefit the individual or instead provide collective benefit within groups undergoing similar health challenges), ii) when utilizing participatory approaches, reflection on the resulting designs can be even more informative than the designs itself, as in our case it highlighted needs and gaps not yet fulfilled by the field, and iii) consider how technologies can help to support social solutions rather than replacing them, and when not designing is best.

CHI 2014, April 26 - May 01 2014, Toronto, ON, Canada
Copyright 2014 ACM 978-1-4503-2473-1/14/04...$15.00.
http://dx.doi.org/10.1145/2556288.2557119

RELATED WORK
Immigrant Women, Health and Wellness
Immigrants make up about 12% of the US population [27] and of that, the number of females comprise about half [17]. New immigrants may be uncertain of the benefits of preventative care and lack information about medical opportunities available to them in the new host country [4]. They also face issues with accessing healthcare that stem from the limitations of health insurance or the perceived cultural insensitivity of doctors who often lack knowledge about their countries of origin [15]. There are also cultural

barriers which may prevent them from seeking assistance, like African immigrants who hold deeply rooted stigmas towards HIV/AIDS and mental health [29].

Immigrant women in particular face physical, physiological, and psychological [23] challenges stemming from a traumatic separation from family and their support group [4], changes in lifestyle and diet [17], family tension and new domestic roles [11], mental distress [11,23] and the general struggles of starting over in a new country and accessing proper health care [4,6]. These altogether induce stress and affect their health and wellness [1,4,6,7]. Receiving countries are often not prepared to appropriately cater to the cultural footprints they bring that have implications for health [4]. Moreover, health services may not accommodate the distinctive needs of these newcomers or integrate with settlement services, making them unnecessarily difficult to navigate [6]. As such, it is unsurprising that immigrants in the US have been found to have better access to health care in their home countries than in the new host country [1]. For example, 58% of recent asylum seekers/grantees in New York had access to health services and 14% had insurance in their home country but only 43% had access to services and none had insurance after coming to the United States largely due to unemployment and fragile legal status [1]. Additionally, providers lack understanding of culture on health and help seeking. For instance, the cultural legacy of 'being strong' has been shown to influence African Caribbean women in that they are more likely to hide distress and unlikely to seek help services due to cultural legacies of 'being strong' [23]. Another omission concerns the role of religion and spirituality, which are considered to be an integral part of health and wellness in many sending counties [7].

Cultural Technologies for Health and Wellness

There is a growing body of HCI research that acknowledges the role culture plays in health, and seeks to incorporate this in technology design [3,12,22]. For example, given dietary habits are culturally-situated, Grimes et al sought to incorporate the socio-cultural practices of low-income African-American in the design of tools to promote eating healthfully for this demographic. Their design EatWell, allows communities to share with each other via voice messages, their experiences eating healthfully [12]. This collectivist approach accounted for the cultural dimensions particular to this community including *environmental effects on eating practices*, *common health attitudes and behaviors within cultures* and support *culturally-relevant behavioral modification suggestions*, leading to a welcomed and potentially more effective intervention [12].

Siek et al also sought to uncover culturally appropriate solutions to preventing chronic diseases that threaten children from at-risk low-income populations [22]. By conducting participatory-based design workshops with children and caregivers from these communities, they discovered socio-economic barriers that called for a more holistic approach to assistive systems that helped not just with encouraging healthier habits (e.g. with reminder systems), but with activities such as budgeting time and resources and parenting [22].

And as a final example, Sakpal has created virtual patients to teach cultural competency to health care providers given the link between cultural sensitivity and eradicating health disparities [20]. Our work contributes by further emphasizing the need to consider culture in health technology designs particularly for immigrants.

Recognition for the unique health needs of immigrants and implications for technology design still remains sparse in HCI literature. There has been research that seek to help immigrants foster community and get access to resources which may help to mitigate some stress-related challenges [15]. And seeing that immigrant women are especially vulnerable to poor mental health due to the migration, researchers have introduced ways for them to portray and share their stories and struggles with each other to promote mental wellness [5]. Given only a few health and wellness tools are designed with immigrant women specifically in mind, our work addressed this gap.

METHODS

In this study we conducted four focus group sessions followed by participatory design activities. We enrolled a total of 20 Afro-Caribbean women, 25–70yrs old, who emigrated from the English-speaking Caribbean and are currently living in South Florida. Most were middle-aged, middle-income, retired or employed in a range of jobs from domestic help to teaching among other professions. All were fully literate and had moderate technology use. Some were recent migrants while others had immigrated more than 10 years to the US. Though the reasons for migration varied, the majority came as young adults to reunite with families or to seek economic opportunities as part of work abroad programs which allowed them to transition to permanent residents. Participants were recruited by word of mouth from local churches and schools. Each of the four groups included members already familiar with each other whether employed or worshipping at the same place.

The session was divided into two parts: a) a focus group and b) a design session with group presentation at the end. The combined focus group and participatory session lasted about 2 hours. All 20 participants took part in both sections of one session held at the usual meeting location for the group. In the focus group, participants were asked to discuss challenges they had faced as new female immigrants to the United States that had an impact on their health and wellness. They were also asked to reflect on their experiences transitioning to the United States and gaining access to health services and resources. Participants themselves led the discussion and the researcher's role was to document the themes that arose organically from the discussion on a flip chart. The researcher also chimed in to keep the conversation on track if it steered away for more than a brief period of time from a discussion of health and wellness related topics. For instance, because of familiarity with each other, participants at times transitioned into stories unrelated to health and wellness. In the design session, participants were asked to select one of the themes that came up during the focus discussion and to storyboard ideas for how technology could help new immigrant women manage that particular health and wellness challenge. To promote participation by all, the researcher split the groups into smaller teams and demonstrated the storyboard process of an 'out of the box' idea with very rudimentary sketches. This helped to set the expectations at a level that encouraged contribution by those less confident in their skills. All but the first group (since no other group preceded them), upon completing their designs, were asked to 'remix' i.e. critique and expand on the storyboard designs created by previous groups (similar to a process used with kids [14]). Finally, a presentation and larger group discussion took place. Given the first author knew individuals who were affiliated with some of these organizations, several participants had prior familiarity with or knowledge of the researcher. The researcher also engaged with key leaders of the groups beforehand who then introduced her with a tone of familiarity to the participants. This improved trust, openness and engagement between participants and the researcher, and the relationship has continued in a non-research capacity following the study.

Inductive coding helps to condense raw research data which is huge and varied into a summarized version which highlights the links between the study's objectives and the findings which emerge from the data itself rather than purported beforehand [21]. Two researchers carried out inductive coding of the transcripts of the focus groups and design sessions as well as the final design artifacts that emerged. The researchers first coded one session separately using qualitative coding software and assigning short codes to describe snippets of the transcript, then compared and discussed the codes that emerged to gain similarity in coding style. Both researchers then individually recoded that session as well as the remaining sessions. Low-level codes were then merged and sorted into broader themes. For instance, the low-level codes such as *family separation/tension*, *new lifestyle challenges to health/wellness*, *low finance/resources*, *existing health issues exacerbate post-migration* were collectively grouped into the higher theme of *migration-induced challenges*.

MIGRATION'S IMPACT ON HEALTH AND WELLNESS

Our discussion of the challenges identified by the women as disrupting their health and wellness post-migration (many of which are identified in health literature [1,4,6,7,17,23]), situates the challenges within the experiences of the women. This helps to set the context for the resulting designs which highlight how reflective the women were on their health and wellness challenges.

Migration-Related Stressors

Participants reported several stressors that they faced upon migrating that either triggered new or exacerbated existing health conditions. In this section we describe challenges associated with readjustment and accessing health services.

Readjustment to a new country proved challenging for many of the women especially in the absence of family or a support network to ease the burden. Conflict with a new host family who did not meet expectations or the culture shock experienced in a new country generated stress. Starting over with limited resources and unemployment also generated stress as women had to quickly seek employment to get settled, cover new expenses, and meet family needs. Finding day care for young children and meeting the cost of education for older children were some examples of this. At times this meant getting multiple jobs or working longer hours than they did in their home country. Older children were sometimes obligated to work creating guilt for mothers. Such changes in lifestyle and responsibilities only introduced more stress for these women: *"I don't want to blame that, but everything together created high blood pressure for me. As I say it's a combination. Coming to this country is stressful, you know you have to start dealing with so many issues (Pam)."*

Access to healthcare costs and insurance was a barrier to appropriate healthcare, whether due to lack of it, or the limitations it imposed. For those who had insurance, it narrowed the pool of doctors they could choose from, which at times meant not covering the doctor of their choice. One woman had to pay out of pocket to visit her preferred doctor despite having insurance: "*My problem was finding a doctor that I'm comfortable with. And when you have found a doctor that you're comfortable with, the insurance you have they do not use it. So each time I went…I had to pay a lot of money (Paulina).*"

The patient-doctor relationship was another challenge. Differences in expectations about the relationship led some of the women to generalize American doctors as having poor 'bedside manners' and consequently experiencing dissatisfaction with the health care experience. For example, Paulina said "*Some of them they just see you and it's like they are not in tune with you, they don't have the time to sit and talk with you about anything…so you don't even feel satisfied with whatever they do with you.*" A finding consistent with the experiences of immigrant women from other countries [11]. We confirmed the presence of different visit expectations through interviewing a doctor licensed to work in the English-speaking Caribbean. He explained that laboratory tests were much more abundant in countries like America, while in many of the Caribbean countries from which the women originated, doctors spend more time with patients to elicit their information.

The difference in treatment routines frustrated some of the women. They perceived American doctors as being quick to prescribe medications and overlook basic procedures such as checking the eyes and nose. Additionally, they were used to having a primary doctor who they consulted for everything. The abundance of specialized doctors in the United States however, meant the women were referred to multiple doctors for diagnosis and/or treatment of illnesses. This posed an additional barrier to their building a relationship with the doctor: "*Back home to you went to one doctor and they see you for everything. Here you have, doctor for everything and if you say that this is happening to you, they're gonna send you wherever. You will end up going to one doctor and they [send] you to six other doctors and you have to go through the process again of adjusting to whomever they send you to (Paulina).*"

Migration and Stress-induced Health Challenges

In this section we describe three groups of stress-induced health challenges: diet, mental health and the physical and psychological issues associated with domestic abuse.

First, after migrating, many participants reported adopting a busier lifestyle leading to poor dietary choices. Unhealthy 'fast food' was usually the most convenient given it was easily obtained: *"The fast food places and the different restaurants, is just at your fingertips. You are so busy that [you buy it] instead of getting a chance to go home and cook (Paulina)."* Additionally, the women adopted a more sedentary lifestyle. For instance, they found they relied on taking transportation more instead of walking, as some often did in their home country. This led to weight gain and obesity which for some triggered other health issues, such as diabetes, hypertension and high cholesterol: *"You just grab something to go and 99% of the time it's not the healthiest thing you're grabbing. You're just getting the one that's close to you. You supersize, and then build up your cholesterol and all those things (Olivia)."*

Also, the women had to deal with the expectations of others. For instance, people in their home country often expected them to gain weight when they migrated as this was seen as a sign of health and prosperity: *"I go back home and people marvel because the tendency is once you come here [to the United States], when you go back [to your home country] you're going to be fat. So when they see you and you still look so slender, don't have on a lot of weight they wonder if it's because you are ill (Olivia)."* On the other side, stress-induced or poor nutrition that resulted in weight loss was another problem they reported.

Second, our participants reported mental health issues. Some triggered by the stress (e.g. stress disorder), others by the traumatic separation from family, abandonment or neglect and readjustment challenges (e.g. depression), and for others from the domestic abuse they endured (e.g. Post Traumatic Stress Disorder): *"I had one year of counseling for Post Traumatic Stress-PSTD. The same thing that soldiers go though. Then I had to get medical intervention (Millie)."* These symptoms of mental health challenges manifested in different ways for some of the women including mood swings and suicidal thoughts.

Third and finally, the women reported family tension and abuse resulting from stress as well as role changes brought about by migration. *"When they come some men change because the adjustment is rough on them. So it comes back on the women (Dawn).";* Women may assume new roles as breadwinners which may trigger power issues: *"They want you to go and work and they have a ball (Millie)."*

Family members who encountered difficulty adjusting created problems for others: *"When my husband joined me here [in the US], he was more of a problem than the babies...I insisted, if he's going to be here he has to go to school (Jennifer)."*

Prolonged, the adjustment challenges of others (often spouses), in addition to other factors, fed into domestic abuse of a verbal, emotional, and/or physical nature. At times, women had no support group to get through that, leading to a feeling of being trapped and isolated. Some resorted to the legal system while others to their faith: *"I didn't have anyone to help me with that [spousal abuse]. I had to tell myself 'pray', my mom keep saying 'I don't like divorce'. I pray, I keep saying that it can work, it can work. I stayed in that for four years until I let it go (Louise)."*

The post-migration experience however, at times brought about positive health outcomes. For some, like Paulina, having access to better health facilities meant improved detection and treatment of existing health issues that previously went undetected: *"I had cholesterol problems. I didn't know [until I migrated] I had that problem. When I found out they were able to treat me, so that was not a negative for me, that's more like a positive"*. Hence despite the stress, the migration played a positive role at times.

DESIGN INTERVENTIONS

Following the focus group discussions, we asked the women to generate design ideas for technologies that would help them tackle their health and wellness challenges. The designs they produced spoke to health issues that they thought lent themselves to design (rather than those that did not) and experiences they had had using technologies to manage their own wellness. For instance, women spoke about using existing tools to tackle dietary and mental health challenges, and high-threat situations that could lead to abuse. They also discussed technology limitations (some of which we describe below) given that the tools they had were not specifically designed to tackle their challenges. Hence, some themes were chosen as a means of improving on the limitations of existing non-suitable tech solutions. On the other hand, for challenges such as severe mental illness (manifesting in suicidal thoughts) and physical abuse, technologies were seen as working alongside, rather than competing with non-tech solutions such as counseling or escaping the home, which were seen as more effective.

Our goals in having the women design technologies were two fold. First, we wanted to see what they produced as designs, particularly in terms of the values reflected. Second, we wanted to understand what role technologies might already play, and what more could be done (e.g., reducing the limitations of current systems by improving the relevance of the application). In the discussion, we will take up a third question: when should we not design.

Rebuilding Social and Organizational Support

A number of the designs reflected the importance of social and organizational support in dealing with migration induced or exacerbated health conditions. In this we join others who encourage the development of pro-social health systems [24].

Social Support

Social support is the notion that one is loved, 'belongs' and has help available at hand [25]. Immigrants especially those who did not endure challenging or prolonged readjustment periods, explained the important role people—whether family, colleagues or people in groups they joined—played in orienting them to the new country and culture. Support in the form of accommodation, transportation, childcare or guidance (key needs of immigrants [6]) by individuals during the initial transition period helped to alleviate some of their worries: *"Family support [helped to ease the transition]. And when I got on campus I got connected to the Baptist student fellowship and from I got there I was picked up Sunday morning and Wednesday night for church. I had no problems. So that kind of community, that fellowship, that Christian love is very important when you leave your country to get acclimated into another country (Jennifer).*" One design solution that involved a strong theme of rebuilding social support was what the women who designed it called the Mood Plant (Fig 1).

(a) (b)

Figure 1: (a) Mood Plant & (b) Remixed Version (right)

It is an ambient device that shares an awareness of other people's moods. Each person in the group would talk to their plant and given mood is transient, the plant would only store the mood for up to an hour until it fades away. The design started out as a one-way support i.e. one person's mood being tracked by a friend (Fig 1a) but was remixed by another group to provide two-way support i.e. a group of friends tracking each other's moods (Fig 1b). The design is similar to ambient technologies such as Buddy Wall, which allows users to make emotional connections with others remotely, through the use of ambient lights and voice communication [19].

This design, echoes their need to build and maintain new social networks in the country that they have migrated to. Ambient technologies may be particularly interesting to explore since they create lower barriers to creating a connection while simultaneously preserving privacy. The Mood Plant does not require sustained conversation with others (only with your plant), it does not present information about what goes on inside the home, potentially making it easier for people to use who are in the process of forming relationships rather than being old friends, or whose relationship is a bond of expatriate status rather than a close friendship.

Additionally, the women mentioned that social support was important for helping with the recovery process from traumatic situations such as spousal abuse and for staying motivated and keeping one's health goals. For this, they also turned to technology, social media and cellphones, to maintain relationships with people in their home country.

Organizational Support

The women spoke about support they received from organizations they worked for or those they joined upon arrival (such as religious or ethno-racial community groups). For instance, those who arrived as part of a work abroad or recruitment program mentioned how seamless the transition was in terms of getting a job, accommodation, access to health care and for some even access to scholarships to further their education and childcare for young children that accompanied them. Grace, who migrated to work as a university auxiliary staff reported, *"When I came here, [the university] took care of me. I worked on campus and also in the dorms and they provided healthcare. I had two jobs on campus, life was good."* The importance of these organizations in the lives of migrants cannot be underestimated—nor can technologies replace the role that these institutions serve. However, given this was not the experience for most, some of their designs did reflect the need to connect new immigrant women to organizations that could provide resources to aid in their transition, readjustment and any difficulties faced along the way.

One such design incorporating a strong organizational support theme was the Safety Alert Necklace (Fig 2). This design was conceived from the limitations—the high visibility—of a pager issued by the court to a victim of spousal abuse. The pager allowed the woman to alert the court if her husband violated his restraining order and she was potentially in danger. A problem with this was that ex-spouses knew that pagers were used for this purpose and tried to take them away from the wearer, violently. The new design was meant to be inconspicuous so the assailant would not have any knowledge that the jewelry was an alert

(a)

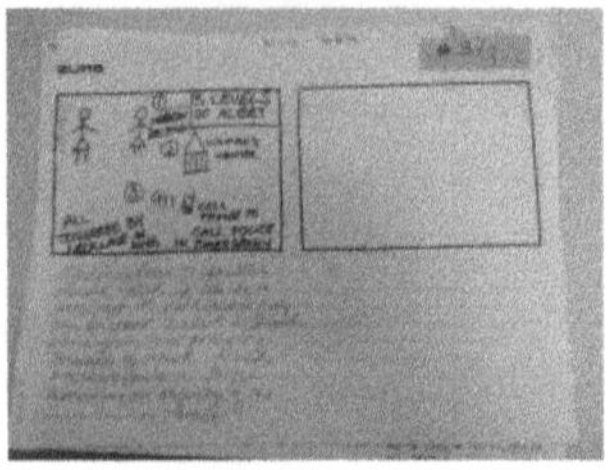

(b)

Figure 2: (a) Safety Alert Necklace & (b) Remixed Version

system or whether it was being used. An abused woman would wear the necklace or other jewelry triggering it when in danger by pressing the pendant. The pendant, based on the severity and number of presses would alert a friend (level 1), a friend and the women's shelter (level 2) or in high alert situations the police and both the previous options (level 3). Individuals would call to ease the tension (level 1), support her 'escape' from the home and/or provide her with shelter, as well as arrange for counseling and legal support to help her through the difficult transition (level 2 and 3).

The safety necklace speaks to an important limitation of technology in this situation, that phones and pagers are the obvious mode of contact for a victim of spousal abuse. Thus these technologies, whose uses are meant to protect, become a potential source of danger. Second, the design itself illustrates how the women saw social and organizational networks as the key factors to help victims escape. The technology was not a replacement for those networks but rather a means to bring them together. "*What I know is, it wasn't technology per se, but what the judge did, the different places that I used to visit with [my husband], he was forbidden, even the very place we worshipped (Millie).*"

Jennifer, spoke about the importance of religion in migration. Indeed, she attributed her ability to survive to the spiritual *"[The transition] should have stressed any normal person out…I got through that with just the Lord."* Religion, for Jennifer and others, was a source of more than spiritual support however, proving social and organizational help too. Indeed, participants offered recommendations for religious new immigrants to connect with places of worship as a means of relieving stress and promoting wellness "*especially since most of us who come from the Caribbean we are church people (Paulina).*"

For example, one remixed design produced was an e-journal (Fig 3) that included writing letters to God as part of journaling the experiences of migration. The technology behind the e-journal included the ability to process the words and from that infer the mood of the writer. The e-journal was also collaborative, the entries of different women would be accessible to the computer and on detecting that someone was feeling low it would encourage someone else who seemed happy to send the depressed person a message. Another component of the system

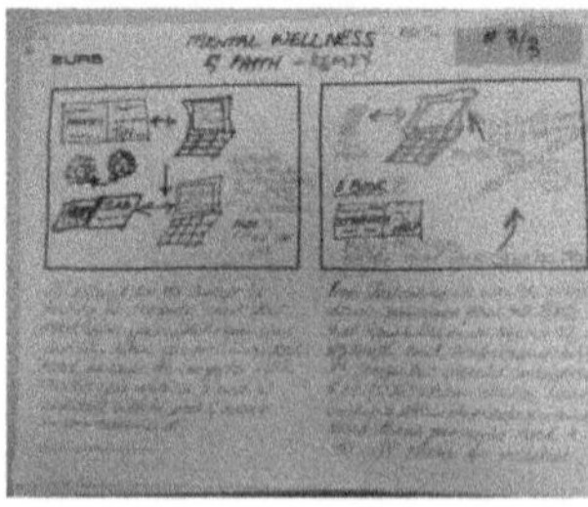

Figure 3: Letters to God (Let Go) - Remixed

encouraged writers to share Bible passages that had helped them, with other journalers using the system.

Existing research acknowledges the role religion and spirituality can play in mental health care for women post-migration. Researchers have seen some immigrant Caribbean women adopt a process called 'being strong' and a reliance on spirituality which provided strength in the absence of others and an effective framework for combating depression [7]. Within HCI, there is a body of work on religion and technology which collectively argues the centrality of the former and its influence on when and how technology is used [26]. Much of it has focused on the infusion of technology into religious practices. Our focus on migration illustrates how religion also provides divine, social and organizational support during times of considerable flux.

Reducing Stressors: Entertainment and Relaxation

Designs also emphasized the importance of entertainment and relaxation for reducing stress. Some provided activity recommendations that promote relaxation. For instance, the Mood Plant above (Fig 1) included a screen embedded in the plant's pot which provided activity recommendations such as '*go walk in the park*' or *'go to the beach'* 'when it detects a negative mood. And another design, the Stress Free Headphones (Fig 4), played music when it detected that an individual's stress level was high from a 'futuristic watch' worn by the user.

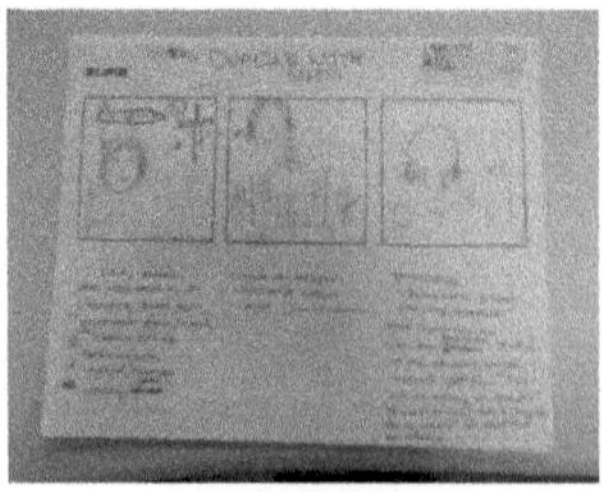

(a)

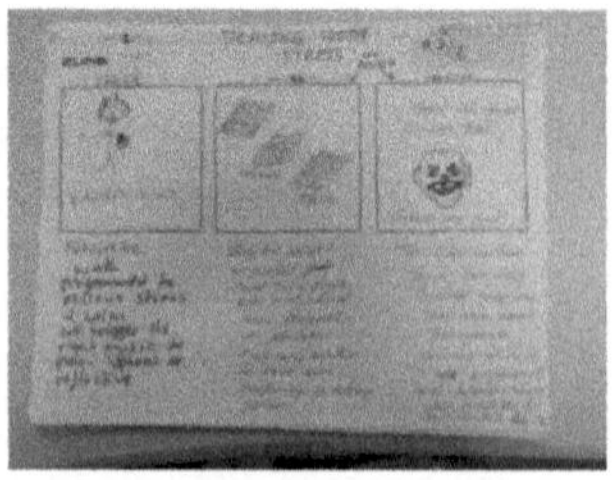

(b)

Figure 4: (a) Stress Free Headphones & (b) Futuristic Watch & Pocket Pals

The device also included a support component, displaying to others the kind of music being listened to and facilitating connections if desired by the wearer, reflecting the value of social support again. Realizing the limitations however, of wearing headphones all the time in public, a participant in another session conceived the 'Make-me-laugh pocket pals' (Fig 4b) as an alternate solution to relieving stress through entertainment. The key-chain-sized device stimulates laughter by providing a joke or through simulating laughter: *"When you're really stressed you can tickle the nose and it will just tell you something, its pre-programmed, it goes 'hahahaha!' The minute you hear that you start laughing (Sonia)."*

The women valued relaxation, laughter and entertainment as part of their health and wellness and imagined solutions that would help them overcome negative moods and stress. These designs reflect their thinking of being healthy in terms that are broader than the health HCI literature has tended to emphasize. It is interesting to consider entertainment-oriented work as part of a health agenda. What should HCI's agenda be around promoting laughter? Perhaps none, but what these women suggest is that entertainment matters for health and wellness.

Encouraging Positive Gradational Lifestyle Changes

The decision to migrate is a significant and rapid lifestyle change. So perhaps its not surprising that the women saw value in encouraging positive and progressive (as opposed to drastic) lifestyle changes. For instance, the Belt and Ring Alert devices (Fig 5) were conceived to promote healthier eating.

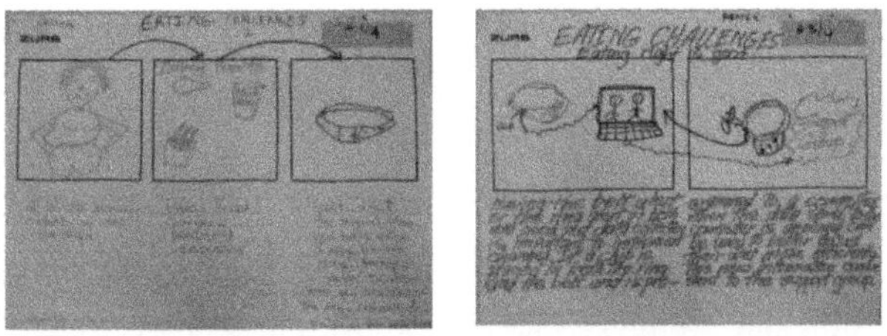

(a) (b)

Figure 5: (a) Belt Alert & (b) Ring Alert

These wearable devices would help support reflection on one's dietary habits through the tracking of the properties of food consumed (e.g. calories, sodium content) and portion size. Belt Alert helps with portion control while Ring Alert displays the nutritional intake of foods so women can make more informed decisions about their diet while still enjoying cultural foods. *"When you are used to something, you don't change immediately. You can't its like your body goes into a shock. You have to gradually change the amount you eat and the type of things you eat. So you'd say instead of not eating chicken, you're gonna eat less fried chicken, and instead of frying it in the deep oil fryer, you'll say, why not try it oven fried, why not bake it (Paulina)."*

The devices also provided *just-in-time feedback*, which has been shown to promote a gradual adoption of wellness practices leading to long-term positive behavioral changes and healthier practices [16]. The women hope that in seeing the benefits of the small changes one is making, a new immigrant woman will be inclined to make long-term adjustments such as exploring new foods, controlling her portions, adjusting cooking methods to be healthier or exercising to maintain health results. The women didn't incorporate a fitness aspect with their diet monitoring solution, but indicated this as something the woman would initiate once she begins to see positive results such as weight loss.

It was in these designs (and as reported in other research) we saw the value of paying attention to the cultural significance of food [3,12,22]. Hence, what was important for the women was that the devices help to support their existing reflection practices rather than, as many existing tools do, i.e. impose with assumptions about food and what the user should eat without accounting for culture. For migrants the desire to eat familiar foods may be especially strong when so much of the new country is unfamiliar.

DISCUSSION

Stemming from the focus group and workshops, we see that immigrant women face many challenges that pose a threat to their health and wellness. Stress, often related to the many difficulties of readjusting to a new country, makes up a large part of the problems and feeds into other issues such as dietary and mental health challenges. We have heard how it has at times triggered family tension that may manifest in abuse. The issues are vast and multi-dimensional and so are the solutions. The field of HCI has seen a vast number of health technologies designed to address dietary [12] and mental health challenges for instance [8,9]. However, designs that focus on the needs of immigrant women who are essentially experiencing displacement until they have fully settled into the country and new lifestyle are not as present. Based on the designs the women conceived, we set forth a few considerations for individuals who may be designing health and wellness technologies for immigrants though this could extend to individuals living outside of their place of origin.

Consider the Role of Others

The technologies the women conceived outlined three roles that other individuals could play in a proposed intervention and the extent to which they would benefit: *no role*, a *one-way role* (either as a supporter or as a beneficiary) and a *reciprocal role* (both as a supporter and a beneficiary).

Technologies where others played *no role* tended to be discrete wearables, personal in nature. These designs facilitated self-support or the provision of support through the capabilities of the technology itself. Consider for instance the wearable *Belt and Ring alert* solution in Fig 5. This involved persuasive strategies such as *self-monitoring* (of one's activities) and *suggesting at the right time* i.e. alerting the user at the point of need [18]. This allowed for the individual to reflect on their choices and make decisions to adjust their habits accordingly. And in other instances, the technology itself provided the support; a pair of glasses that monitored an individual's blood glucose level, would administer insulin when critical and the Stress Free Headphones in Fig 4 monitored stress levels and automatically played soothing music when necessary. As such, health issues which seemed to lend themselves well to this type of approach were those that were measurable and so able to be triaged accurately by the technology as well as those which required highly individual solutions (for instance what constitutes as stress for one person may not be for another). Thus devices designed solely with the purpose of promoting self-support or built-in support through the technology, do not prompt other individuals to get involved. The benefit is geared towards the individual, and is addressed by focusing privately on the person.

In the case of a *one-way role*, a design intervention was introduced as a means of obtaining support for a beneficiary from one (one-to-one) or more (one-to-many) people. Designs of this kind alerted others to play a part in the intervention of the individual where self-support is not sufficient but the issue at hand still unique. For instance, the *Safety Necklace* (Fig 2) included tiered support based on the severity of the domestic abuse situation. Health issues which can be detected but the severity not easy to triage (e.g. mood or danger), may lend itself to a one-way intervention by others since the technology can do the initial detection and facilitate an alert, though not a solution (left up to those being alerted).

In the case of a *reciprocal role* a design intervention was introduced as a means of obtaining support from and for all people involved in the intervention. In this type of many-to-many support, reciprocity is key and everyone included is ideally both a beneficiary and a recipient. Design interventions of this nature facilitated the connection of groups of individuals. For immigrant women, this facilitated the rebuilding of mutual support groups. For instance, the *Mood Plant* and e-journal solutions included a group-monitoring component. Originally, both were created for one-way monitoring of one person by another. Two other groups however, given combating isolation is about rebuilding the support system (one has been uprooted from), modified the original designs to include two-way group monitoring in which a group of friends would monitor and be monitored by each other. One participant summed this up perfectly: *"Life is a circle. We're all going through so many things and maybe we were where you are, so I've been where you are and you have probably been where I am and so you can share with me how you dealt with it. How you got to be in your happy place (Pam)."*

Health issues then, which are common in nature with common solutions may lend itself to this type of design which provides dual benefit i.e. to one self as well as others. We see the benefit of this approach outlined in research which seeks to promote collectivism in eating healthfully through cultural technologies [13].

We pose then, questions individuals can ask to determine the potential role of others when designing health and wellness technologies—Does the health challenge lend itself to being measured by the technology or self-monitored, or is intervention by others a more appropriate solution? Is it a challenge that requires a highly individualized solution and conversely a design that benefits just the individual or is it a commonplace issue with a solution that could provide collective benefit within a group of individuals undergoing similar challenges?

Reflecting on the Role of Design

In addition to highlighting the many different ways that the immigrant women wanted to interact with and through technology, the designs also yielded some other points to reflect upon. In this section we review each in turn.

One significant challenge that disproportionally affects minorities (racial, cultural, ethnic) in the U.S. is the challenge associated with mapping medical information about health and wellness into actual practice. For example, nutritional advice is often not sensitive to the types of foods eaten by low-income African Americans [12]. The first value of the designs is as a means to understand what people know, how they translate and interpret ideas about their health in their lives, with respect to foods they eat, the income they earn, the place they live, their cultural traditions, their religious practices. The designs are not right or wrong per se, but serve as opportunities for people to come to a shared understanding of what might most help people in the community and how to effectively communicate it.

A second value of the designs was that they encouraged the women to reflect on their own health and share with each other. Most of the designs stemmed from the women's reflection on their personal practices in managing their health and wellness challenges. At times, based on the common tales they told, such practices stemmed from observation of others or indigenous knowledge passed on to them. Millie, one of our over 65 participants, believed that *"If anything is going wrong with me, my plants tell you. If I feel down, they look sick like I do."* This inspired the design of the Mood Plant and triggered similar stories from others. *Ring Alert* was borne out of Olivia's reflection on her approach to monitoring her sodium level. If the ring on her finger grew tight, this was an indication that she had had food with a high sodium level and she would thus adjust her portions or avoid that particular food next time. *"I want to tell you something. I wear this ring all the time. And I realize that every time I eat too much salt, my fingers get swollen, and the ring cannot go on"*. And Dawn conceived the futuristic watch to detect stress level because she maintains *"my pulse always [damages] the watches, beat it out of sync,"* when her blood pressure level is too high.

Additionally they reflected on this together. For instance, in one group, those who in the past experienced domestic abuse had no idea others in their familiar circle had also endured the same challenge. They later informed the researcher how the project had allowed them to make a connection that persisted beyond the session. They now had someone to speak openly with. This type of sharing, community building, has been shown to matter, particularly for those who feel marginalized and excluded by the medical establishment [12]. Given the migrant women's reports of frustration with a health system that they are unfamiliar with, we see potential opportunities to create conversations within these groups that support communities sharing advice with each other.

Finally, some although not all of the designs revealed a desire to manage the challenges of migration discretely. The conversations around mood plants and jewelry for example highlighted not just safety concerns but also a desire for whatever they had to blend in as Olivia explained "*Its that you don't want something that everyone is gonna know. You want something that looks normal.*" Not only does this suggest that the material form matters, it also encourages reflection on what it means to design health technologies that promote wellness discretely (in contrast to those that publish step counts on Facebook) or tweet a user's weight [28].

Consider the Limits of HCI and Design

In recent years HCI has given more thought to questions of when technology is not appropriate, when the implication should be not to design [2]. For migrant women technology design is not a replacement for the social and organizational support that we found to be at the core of how the women wanted to manage and get help with health issues stemming from migration. And in our design exercise we uncovered instances of when technology was in fact doing more harm than good. Consider the beeper issued through the court system to women in domestic abuse situation. It was visible and making trouble for migrant women. Thus it is always a good idea to ask whether technology will potentially cause harm, but for migrants who are vulnerable through the stress of the experience, it seems essential to examine the risks of technologies. Moreover, many migrants migrate for economic opportunities and it should be assumed that they do not have significant resources for expensive technologies, especially when they first arrive (and when they might most need support). Considering alternatives to technology or building on existing low cost technologies already accessible to this demographic is a valuable reflection for any community.

We engaged in participatory design as a means of highlighting the women's voices. One tension that arises however is that the solutions, though originating from the women themselves, still need to be critically unpacked in alignment with HCI practices. Baumer and Silberman encourage HCI researchers to ask questions about the feasibility of design proposals for instance [2]. As we encountered, some of the designs produced by the women are likely not feasible. For example, it is unclear whether Natural Language Processing (particularly of small data sets) is intelligent enough to predict mood. And given the topic of health, the question arises of the relationship between participatory design and medical expertise. So as not to overlook critical reflection, while at the same time balancing the value of the women's own designs, we consulted with a doctor (as mentioned earlier) as part of the research. In addition to contextualizing some of the differences in health practices (such as the nature of doctor visits), he also offered his medical insights into the designs that the women produced. For example, he suggested that the Ring Alert device (Fig 5b) had some medical validity because "*Salt causes water retention so that could lead to swelling.*" He also saw problems with other concepts, such as the glasses that monitored one's blood glucose levels as there were medical limitations to vision-based blood glucose monitoring as envisioned by the women.

CONCLUSION

The migration process is one wrought with stress and consequently implications for health and wellness for immigrants especially women [4]. Rebuilding the social and organizational support structure, reducing stressors through rest and relaxation and encouraging positive gradational lifestyle changes were three approaches conceived by immigrant women to tackle some of the major challenges they endured. The women's conception and 'remixing' of designs brought out consideration for the role of others (and the direction of benefit the technology provides), called for reflection on the role of design and consideration for the limits of HCI and design to tackle the challenges these women faced. Consider for instance, how, beyond providing technologies to help immigrant women monitor their health and wellness, opening up access to healthcare itself or aiding healthcare providers in becoming more sensitive to the cultural background, traditions and expectations of these immigrant women can help to improve the doctor-patient relationship and promote health and wellness for new immigrants.

ACKNOWLEDGMENTS

We thank the women who provided insights into the challenges they face and conceived these designs. We also thank Andrew Miller, Andrea Parker, Lana Yarosh, the doctor with whom we consulted as well as the anonymous reviewers for their valuable input in the writing of this paper. This work was supported by the Cultural Technology and Wellness NSF Grant (#1016394).

REFERENCES

1. Asgary, R., Charpentier, B., and Burnett, D.C. Socio-Medical Challenges of Asylum Seekers Prior and After Coming to the US. *Journal of immigrant and minority health/Center for Minority Public Health 15*, 5 (2013), 961–8.

2. Baumer, E.P.S. and Silberman, M.S. When the Implication is Not to Design (Technology). *CHI '11 - Proceedings of the 2011 annual conference on Human*

factors in computing systems, ACM Press (2011), 2271–2274.

3. Boujarwah, F.A., Nazneen, Hong, H., Abowd, G.D., and Arriaga, R. Towards a framework to situate assistive technology design in the context of culture. *Assets*, ACM Press (2011).
4. Carballo, M. and Mboup, M. International Migration and Health. Global Commission on International Migration (2005).
5. Clarke, R., Wright, P., and McCarthy, J. Sharing narrative and experience. *Proceedings of the 2012 ACM conference on Human Factors in Computing Systems, Extended Abstracts*, ACM Press (2012), 1505.
6. Collins, E., Shakya, Y.B., Guruge, S., and Santos, E.J. Services for Women: Access, Equity and Quality. In *Working with Women: Issues and Strategies for Mental Health*. 2008, 119–133.
7. Collins, E. Recognizing Spirituality as a Vital Component in Mental Health Care. In *Working with Women: Issues and Strategies for Mental Health*. 2008, 89–102.
8. Coyle, D., Doherty, G., Matthews, M., and Sharry, J. Computers in talk-based mental health interventions. *Interacting with Computers 19*, 4 (2007), 545–562.
9. Doherty, G., Coyle, D., and Matthews, M. Design and evaluation guidelines for mental health technologies. *Interacting with Computers 22*, 4 (2010), 243–252.
10. Dumont, J.-C., Spielvogel, G., and Widmaier, S. International Migrants in Developed, Emerging and Developing Countries: An extended Profile. 2010.
11. Elliott, S.J. and Gillie, J. Moving Experiences: A Qualitative Analysis of Health and Migration. *Health & Place 4*, 4 (1998), 327–39.
12. Grimes, A., Bednar, M., Bolter, J.D., and Grinter, R.E. EatWell: sharing nutrition-related memories in a low-income community. *Cell*, ACM (2008), 87–96.
13. Grimes, A. and Harper, R. Celebratory Technology: New Directions for Food Research in HCI. *Proceedings of the SIGCHI Conference on Human Factors in Computing Systems*, ACM (2008).
14. Guha, M.L., Druin, A., Chipman, G., Fails, J.A., Simms, S., and Farber, A. Mixing Ideas: A New Technique for Working with Young Children as Design Partners. *Interaction Design and Children*, (2004), 35–42.
15. Hirsch, T. and Liu, J. Speakeasy. *Proceedings of the 2004 conference on Designing interactive systems processes, practices, methods, and techniques - DIS '04*, ACM Press (2004), 345.
16. Meyer, J., Boll, S., Lee, Y., Mayora, O., Siek, K.A., and Röcker, C. Wellness interventions and HCI: theory, practice, and technology. *ACM SIGHIT ... 2*, 2 (2012), 2–4.
17. Popovic-Lipovac, A. and Strasser, B. A Review on Changes in Food Habits Among Immigrant Women and Implications for Health. *Journal of immigrant and minority health* (2013).
18. Prochaska, J.O., Redding, C.A., and Evers, K.E. The Transtheoretical model and stages of change. *Health Behavior and Health Education*, (2008), 97–121.
19. Quintanilha, M.S. and Design, V.C. BuddyWall : A Tangible User Interface for Wireless Remote Communication. (2008), 3711–3716.
20. Sakpal, R. Virtual patients to teach cultural competency. *Proceedings of ICMI '12*, (2012), 349.
21. Seidman, I. *Interviewing as Qualitative Research*. Teachers College Press, 2005.
22. Siek, K.A., LaMarche, J.S., and Maitland, J. Bridging the information gap: Collaborative Technology Design with Low-income At-risk Families to Engender Healthy Behaviors. *Proceedings of the 21st Australia conference on Computer-Human Interaction*, (2009).
23. Sisley, E.J., Hutton, J.M., Louise Goodbody, C., and Brown, J.S.L. An interpretative phenomenological analysis of African Caribbean women's experiences and management of emotional distress. *Health & social care in the community 19*, 4 (2011), 392–402.
24. Skeels, M.M., Unruh, K.T., Powell, C., and Pratt, W. Catalyzing Social Support for Breast Cancer Patients. *Proceedings of the SIGCHI Conference on Human Factors in Computing Systems*, ACM (2010), 173–182.
25. Turner, R.J. Social Support and Coping. In A. V Horwitz and T.L. Scheid, eds., *Handbook of coping Theory research applications*. Cambridge University Press, 1999, 198–210.
26. Wyche, S.P., Hayes, G.R., Harvel, L.D., and Grinter, R.E. Technology in Spiritual Formation: An Exploratory Study of Computer Mediated Religious Communications. *CSCW '06 Proceedings of the 2006 Conference on Computer Supported Cooperative Work*, (2006), 199–208.
27. Zallman, L., Himmelstein, D.H., Woolhandler, S., et al. Undiagnosed and Uncontrolled Hypertension and Hyperlipidemia among Immigrants in the US. *Journal of immigrant and minority health / Center for Minority Public Health 15*, 5 (2013), 858–65.
28. Withings Scale. http://www.withings.com/.
29. *National African HIV/AIDS Initiative NAHI - Summit Reports*. Atlanta, GA, 2007.

DDF Seeks Same: Sexual Health-Related Language in Online Personal Ads For Men Who Have Sex With Men

Oliver L. Haimson
University of California, Irvine
Department of Informatics
Irvine, CA, USA
ohaimson@uci.edu

Jed R. Brubaker
University of California, Irvine
Department of Informatics
Irvine, CA, USA
jed.brubaker@uci.edu

Gillian R. Hayes
University of California, Irvine
Department of Informatics
Irvine, CA, USA
gillianrh@ics.uci.edu

ABSTRACT
The HIV/AIDS crisis of the 1980s fundamentally changed sexual practices of men who have sex with men (MSM) in the U.S., including increased usage of sexual health-related (SHR) language in personal advertisements. Analyzing online personal ads from Craigslist, we found a substantial increase in SHR language, from ~23% in 1988 to over 53% today, echoing continuing concern about rising HIV rates. We argue that SHR language in Craigslist ads can be used as a sensor to provide insight into HIV epidemiology as well as discourse among particular communities. We show a positive significant relationship between prevalence rate of HIV in an ad's location and use of SHR language in that location. Analysis highlights the opportunity for SHR information found in Craigslist personal ads to serve as a data source for HIV prevention research. More broadly, we argue for mining large-scale user-generated content to inform HCI design of health and other systems, and explore use of such data to examine temporal changes in language to facilitate improved user-interface design.

Author Keywords
Health informatics; HIV/AIDS; personal ads; LGBT; online dating; digital identity; Craigslist; computational linguistics.

ACM Classification Keywords
H.4.3 Communication Applications; J.3 Life and Medical Sciences: Health; K.4.1 [Computers and Society]: Public Policy Issues: Computer-related health issues.

INTRODUCTION
When designing large-scale health systems, data giving insight into user practices and language choices can help HCI designers to inform choices in data structure and system features. Traditional data collection methods can be slow, expensive, and inaccurate, particularly when focusing on sensitive communities and practices. By exploring relationships between user-generated content and established data collection methods, we seek to augment existing practices and make data collection faster, cheaper, and possibly more accurate.

"Public health surveillance is the continuous, systematic collection, analysis and interpretation of health-related data needed for the planning, implementation, and evaluation of public health practice" [40]. Surveillance is frequently employed to provide early warning for public health emergencies, monitor health progress at the population level, and inform public health policy. However, public health professionals, in attempts to curtail HIV infection rates, have noted "an urgent need to address gaps in our ability to monitor changes in HIV, STDs, and sexual practices among MSM" [39:884] (MSM is short for men who have sex with men, an inclusive term used in public health literature). Conducting frequent population-based surveys along with facility-based surveillance, while effective [2,39], requires considerable time and resources, and often only reaches more visible segments of the MSM community [2].

In this paper, we explore the potential of using publicly available personal ads as a proxy for HIV and STI (sexually transmitted infection) statistics to augment current collection methods and provide more comprehensive data. Since the advent of online personal ads in the 1990s, MSM have willingly shared SHR information on sites such as Craigslist to facilitate sexual contact. Such data is free, plentiful, and readily accessible to researchers. The accessibility, affordability, and anonymity of Internet personal ads [11] make the Internet an "ideal medium for sexual pursuits" [9:74], but also an ideal environment for mining user-generated content.

As compared to survey-based research, online personal ads give researchers quick access to millions of anonymous ads, which contain information analogous to data found through surveys and surveillance [16,17]. Ads can be continuously and systematically collected, with only minimal costs such as computational time spent gathering data. Thus, online personal ads have the potential to make a substantial difference in HIV research and prevention efforts.

We analyzed online personal ad content and explored its relationship to HIV prevalence to demonstrate an

CHI 2014, April 26–May 1, 2014, Toronto, Ontario, Canada.

ACM 978-1-4503-2473-1/14/04...$15.00.
http://dx.doi.org/10.1145/2556288.2557077

application of mining online, publicly available data for use in real-world contexts. First, through our analysis of 252,786 MSM Craigslist ads, we identified SHR language currently used online. Second, through a comparison with print personal ads from the 1980s, we demonstrate an increase in the use of SHR language, signifying that even 30 years after the beginning of the HIV/AIDS crisis, health concerns among MSM persist and can be measured empirically online. Finally, by comparing use of SHR language in 95 locations, we find that HIV prevalence rates and SHR language in Craigslist ads have a significant positive relationship. Taken together, these contributions demonstrate the potential for publically available online data to be used as a surveillance tool and provide description of one method to create such tools.

We present this work as an example of mining user-generated online media content and using it as a sensor for secondary purposes. Large, publicly available online datasets are important sources of information for HCI researchers. To properly design large-scale health data systems, HCI research must be conducted on the information architecture of such data and its potential use as a sensor. Similar methods and techniques could be used in other domains (*e.g.*, urban or civic informatics). Additionally, our work highlights issues around the timescale of codifying large-scale data from online media, particularly given evolving language.

Our research also addresses gaps in the study of sexuality within HCI, particularly the shortage of research dealing with sexual orientation and homosexuality [24]. Research on the intersections of technology and sexuality contributes to the development and growth of the field of HCI [1]. By studying the online dating practices of MSM, we address the dearth of sexuality research within HCI.

The remainder of this paper is structured as follows: We first provide some background on HIV/AIDS and the use of personal ads by MSM, followed by a discussion of related research. We then describe the methods and results of our empirical work as conducted in three phases: developing a sexual health dictionary; determining presence of SHR language in Craigslist ads and comparing current metrics with those from the 1980s; and building and analyzing statistical models to explore the relationship between SHR language and HIV prevalence. We close with a discussion of HCI design implications and a summary of our findings.

BACKGROUND

HIV/AIDS

In the early 1980s, many gay men contracted and died from a mysterious disease initially known as "gay cancer." The disease was eventually identified as AIDS, caused by the virus HIV and commonly spread through sexual contact. The HIV/AIDS crisis in the United States has been a considerable public health problem that has historically and continues to disproportionately affect MSM [5]. As a result, HIV/AIDS has fundamentally changed sexual practices in the U.S., particularly among MSM [39].

Highly Active Antiretroviral Therapy (HAART), a treatment first distributed in the United States in 1996, has succeeded in controlling HIV infections and decreasing AIDS deaths [28]. However, research has shown that some MSM conflate HAART's benefits with a reduction in the risk of unsafe sex with HIV-positive partners, which has been shown to lead to a higher tendency to engage in unprotected sex [13]. Thus, HIV infection rates, especially those of MSM, have continued to increase.

MSM accounted for 63% of all new HIV cases in 2010, and make up 52% of all HIV cases in the United States [5]. Taking into account the fact that MSM only make up 2% of the U.S. population [5], these statistics are especially alarming. Particular MSM subgroups, such as those under the age of 24 and young African-Americans, experience even higher rates of HIV infection [5]. Considering these statistics, it is unsurprising that disclosure of HIV status and use of SHR language is part of courtship for MSM.

Personal Advertisements and MSM

Personal ads have historically been useful in facilitating exchange between interested people when dating preferences lie outside of traditional markets, such as MSM [10]. Multiple studies have found that MSM meet sexual partners online significantly more often than others [19,30,31]. Given the relative frequency with which MSM use the Internet for sexual communication and their disproportionate risk of contracting HIV, how can the online content generated by MSM be used as a sensor for public health efforts to reduce the spread of HIV?

Contradictory research has argued that online personal ads can either help or hinder HIV prevention efforts. An increase in MSM sexual contact brought about by online personal ads may have had negative effects on disease control [7,18,27]. For example, those who met sex partners online were more at risk to contract HIV and other STIs than those who did not [27]. Likewise, the launching of Craigslist for a particular city was found to predict an increase in contraction of both AIDS and syphilis in that city, and the number of MSM personal ads linked to a particular city was found to be a significant predictor for AIDS cases [7]. Additionally, Craigslist's search function may enable risky behavior by allowing users to search for behaviors that they desire, such as "bareback" (sex without a condom), a functionality that would not be possible offline or in print personal ads [18].

On the other hand, online dating could support HIV prevention by allowing sexual partners to discuss HIV status and protection preferences prior to meeting [31,38]. Just as Craigslist allows for searching for risky behaviors [18], it could also facilitate searching for safe behaviors. However, relying solely on information that sexual partners provide online can increase risk if it eliminates further discussion of safe sex practices, particularly if sexual partners are unsure or incorrect about their HIV status [37].

While this debate is ongoing, in this paper, we adopt a new approach. We focus on the information that can be gleaned through an analysis of personal ads rather than on the practices that surround them. We demonstrate that computational analysis of language in MSM Craigslist personal ads can provide one source of public health surveillance for MSM. The information found in these ads has potential to aid in HIV prevention strategies that, if successful, could mitigate the negative effects that Craigslist has arguably had on the spread of HIV and STIs.

RELATED WORK

This paper draws from and contributes to several bodies of literature that have explored health implications of personal ads by MSM. Although previous studies have examined the use of SHR language in MSM personal ads [14,18,22] and others have argued that Craigslist ads can be used for public health surveillance and HIV/STI epidemiology research [16,17], we posited that further insight could be gained by joining these two research methods. We thus build on previous research by combining linguistic analysis of personal ads with epidemiological analysis to understand how online MSM personal ads can be used as a sensor for public health surveillance.

Several studies have examined the content of personal ads on Craigslist and how it relates to sexual health and risk of HIV and other STIs in MSM [8,18,22,29,32]. Health-related language has been found to be more prevalent in ads posted by HIV-positive MSM [22], giving evidence of serosorting ("preferentially selecting sex partners with concordant HIV status and … using condoms with partners of discordant status" [4:2497]), a method shown to reduce risk of HIV transmission [4]. One risk indicator is the volume of ads posted by any individual MSM, which predicted more likeliness to engage in unsafe sexual practices [29], while the marital status of MSM can also correlate with perceived safety [8,32]. These studies show how content of personal ads correlates with the sexual risk behaviors of those posting and replying to these ads.

One notable focus relevant here can be seen in epidemiological work on HIV and Craigslist. Several studies have found relationships between the content or volume of Craigslist ads and real world prevalence of HIV and other STIs, showing that online personal ads and Craigslist in particular are effective tools for HIV epidemiology research [7,16,17]. For example, Fries *et al.* computationally extracted HIV status information from millions of Craigslist ads and found a positive predictive relationship with HIV rates by location, demonstrating that HIV status information disclosed in Craigslist ads can be used as a proxy for HIV rates among MSM [17]. These rates can in turn be used in "understanding or anticipating STI outbreaks" [17:13]. In addition to HIV rates, Craigslist posters include information about many risk behaviors that allow for public health surveillance [16]. Similarly, Chiasson *et al.* argue that the Internet is an ideal place to conduct research on the sexual health of MSM [9].

Personal ads have been used to study changes over time in the use of health-related language long before the advent of the Internet. Sociologist Alan G. Davidson analyzed the percentage of personal advertisements that included health-related language in each of four years: 1978, 1982, 1985, and 1988 [14]. He found a "significant increase in personal advertisements suggesting a concern with health" from 1982 – 1985 [14:125], the time during which many gay men first learned about AIDS [26], and again from 1985 – 1988, showing that the effects from the first time period persisted [14]. Davidson's work highlights how the gay community responded to the outbreak of HIV/AIDS by changing the language that they used to describe themselves and their sexual and dating preferences [14].

Personal ads can be "useful data sources for assessing the meanings people attach to their sexuality, as well as for assessing changes in these meanings over time" [14:136]. Although the format and medium for personal ads has shifted from newspapers to websites, the implications of their power to convey sexual representations and practices has persisted and grown along with their volume. Thus, Davidson's work led us to address the research question of how sexual health discourse among MSM has changed over time and across mediums, both in content and volume

The literature on Craigslist and HIV/STIs has shown that Craigslist ads can be used as a kind of sensor. We demonstrate that when used to collect and analyze health data, this sensor can provide information about disease rates, risk of spreading disease, and particular communities who may be at risk of contracting disease. When used in a public health context, this information could have powerful effects on HIV prevention and provides a real world example of the kind of outcomes promised by publicly available "big data". Our work leverages linguistic analysis of personal ads as a potential way to harness such data.

DATA

Our initial goal was to replicate Davidson's 1991 study, to determine how time and platform affected use of SHR language in MSM personal ads. Davidson compared the use of SHR language in gay male personal ads published during 1978, 1982, 1985, and 1988 in the *Village Voice*, a weekly New York City (NYC)-based newspaper [14]. Our goal framed choices in data analysis, which began with NYC for the sake of comparison with Davidson.

Although methods of posting personal ads have changed in the last 25 years, we turned to Craigslist, a popular online classifieds website, as a modern equivalent of print personal ads. Like print personal ads, Craigslist posts are anonymous and stand-alone (as contrasted with profile-based online dating sites) and allow disclosure of sexual practices and health-related language. Differences between *Village Voice*

Population Range	Locations	Mean Population Density (SD) [33]	Mean HIV Estimated Diagnosis Rate (SD) [6]	Ads (% of Total)
> 5 Million	8	1897.6 (2231.7)	26.4 (7.2)	91,110 (36.04%)
2M – 5M	23	668.9 (444.3)	17.6 (10.0)	105,874 (41.88%)
1M – 2M	21	486.0 (317.4)	20.3 (11.6)	35,345 (13.98%)
< 1M	43	364.4 (252.8)	12.2 (8.7)	20,457 (8.09%)
TOTAL	95	594.1 (808.3)	16.5 (10.3)	252,786 (100%)
New York City		7231.6	36.5	10,737 (4.25%)

Table 1. Locations and Sample Sizes.

and Craigslist personal ads include message length, cost, and possibility of censorship. *Village Voice* personal ads had no word limit per se, but authors were charged on a per-line basis, while Craigslist ads are free with no word limit. Although the *Village Voice*'s censorship policies were not stated in the four 1978-1988 issues we accessed, the paper "reserves the right to reject or edit any advertisement" [35]. In comparison, Craigslist does not reject, remove, or edit ads unless other users flag ads for removal, and does not restrict adult content [12].

Our dataset comprises 252,786 personal ads posted to the "men seeking men" (m4m) subsection of Craigslist. Craigslist maintains a separate website for each of many cities and towns in the United States. Using a custom-built RSS scraper, we collected all m4m ads within a two-week period in August and September 2013 in 95 metropolitan statistical areas (MSAs) (see Table 1). Locations were selected to correspond with location-specific statistics on HIV prevalence rates as reported by the U.S. Centers for Disease Control and Prevention (CDC) in a 2011 report [6]. We excluded seven locations on the CDC's list of MSAs because a corresponding Craigslist site did not exist. Craigslist sites were selected to best approximate the geographic area of each MSA.

Our data collection methods captured each ad as it was first posted, meaning that our dataset includes ads that may have later been flagged by users and/or subsequently removed. In practice, ads are often removed when the poster wants no more responses; such ads are still relevant for analysis. Meanwhile, duplicate ads within a location were removed from our dataset prior to analysis. During manual coding of 500 ads, we identified a 0.2% rate of irrelevant ads.

There is a risk that people misrepresent their HIV status on Craigslist or may not be aware of it. However, at a population level, we are interested in capturing use of SHR language of any kind, not the specifics of any individual's personal status and claims. While there are almost certainly inconsistencies in individual ads, in aggregate, the data are relatively accurate [17].

Though we cannot claim that our sample is representative of all MSM in the U.S., research has shown that more than 85% of MSM find sexual partners online [3,20]. Additionally, the existence of a relationship between HIV prevalence rates in CDC data and the use of SHR language in our data, along with previous literature that has found similar positive correlation [17], signals the appropriateness of using Craigslist as a source to study MSM sexual health.

On average, large cities included more ads than small cities: the eight cities with populations over five million comprised 36.04% of total ads, and the 31 cities with populations over two million comprised 77.92% of total ads. A majority of ads (88.77%) included the poster's age. Of those ads with age included, excluding ads with reported age 99 or <10, the mean age in NYC was 34.59 (SD = 9.40; range 18-80), while the mean in the overall dataset was slightly older: 34.81 (SD = 10.24; range 10-98).

SEXUAL HEALTH DICTIONARY

Methods

To analyze the use of sexual-health related (SHR) content in personal ads, we first created a dictionary of SHR language. Davidson provided a dictionary of health-related language based on ads from 1978-1988 [14], but instead of adopting Davidson's dictionary or analyzing the data using a pre-supposed list of words and terms, we used open-coding techniques to find the SHR language that MSM used in our dataset [14]. This method allowed the discourse used by the MSM community in their personal ads to shape the dictionary [14]. Four coders, including two gay-identified men, were given a sample of Craigslist ads from the dataset, and were asked to independently determine SHR words or terms in each ad. 500 ads in total were coded, 125 by all four coders for inter-rate reliability. Use of multiple coders allowed us to detect SHR language that may not be familiar to or identified by one coder alone. Agreement levels were acceptable at 72% with a Fleiss' Kappa of .708. Words or terms were added to the dictionary if one or more of the coders identified the term as SHR. Two additional terms were added to our dictionary even though our coders did not identify them. These terms, "seeding" (and its shorter form, "seed") and "uninhibited", were mentioned in previous similar studies [18,32] and occurred in our full dataset, but not in the subset used for open-coding.

Next, to facilitate more detailed analysis, we divided our dictionary into 6 categories: disease, HIV (a sub-category of disease), protection, risk (a sub-category of protection), safety, and health. Table 2 shows our full dictionary as compared with Davidson's dictionary [14].

We intentionally excluded drug related terms to focus the scope of our paper on sexual health, replicate Davidson's methods, and compare current levels of SHR language to the 1980s. Terms that referenced drugs without explicitly

Sexual health-related language, Craigslist 2013	
Category	**Words and terms**
Disease	bug free, clean, ddf [drug and disease free], disease free, std free, tested
HIV (sub-category of Disease)	AIDS, HIV+, HIV-, neg, negative, pos, positive, poz, undetectable
Safety	safe, safely, safe sex
Protection	condom, protection
Risk (sub-category of Protection)	bareback, bb [bareback], bred, breed, breeding, raw, seed, seeding, uninhibited
Health	health, healthy
Davidson's health-related language, *Village Voice* 1978-1988 [14]	
Category	**Words and terms**
Health-Related	health, healthy, health conscious, clean, unaffected, unused, taking the current situation very seriously, interested in safe dating, safe for us both, HIV negative, safe-sex romance, safe, tested disease-free, AIDS-free relationship
Sexual Exclusivity Subcode	monogamous, monogamy, exclusive, 1-to-1, one to one, non-promiscuous, dislike promiscuity

Table 2. Sexual Health-Related Dictionaries, Craigslist 2013 and *Village Voice* 1978-1988.

mentioning sex were not included in Davidson's study and were subsequently omitted here. However, drug use and sexual health are often bound up with each other, and future research should examine drug use and its relationship to sexual health and HIV/AIDS among MSM.

Results

There are four important differences between our 2013 SHR language dictionary and Davidson's 1978-1988 dictionary (Table 2) [14]. First, Davidson's dictionary included a subset of terms related to monogamy and relationship exclusivity, while our dictionary does not [14]. In the 1980s, exclusivity was often motivated by HIV/STI prevention, which is no longer the case [23]. Davidson analyzed monogamy-related terms separately [14], allowing us to compare our findings to only his health-related terms.

Second, in the disease category and HIV sub-category, the 1978-1988 dictionary includes relatively few terms: "tested disease-free", "HIV negative", and "AIDS-free relationship." In 2013 the corpus of disease language has both increased (now including words such as "bug", "clean", and "std") and settled on shorter phrases and/or abbreviations to describe one's own STI status and to convey a preference for a partner's STI status: "ddf", "HIV+" or "poz", "HIV-" or "neg".

Third, in our 2013 Craigslist dictionary, we found the word "safe" primarily used in a list of words describing the poster or his desired partner (*e.g.* "very discreet, safe, sane, clean, d&d free, you also"). While Davidson's dictionary includes "safe", it also appears as part of several longer phrases that use "safe" in a dating context: "interested in safe dating", "safe-sex romance" [14]. Again, we see 2013 Craigslist ads using shorter phrases than the 1978-1988 dictionary.

Finally, words describing protection or lack of protection occur regularly in our 2013 data, but not at all in the 1978-1988 data [14]. This suggests that contemporary MSM are more likely to communicate about protection techniques and preferences in personal ads than 1980s MSM.

In the 25 years since Davidson's 1988 dataset was collected, MSM have standardized and abbreviated their SHR language, allowing for rapid and efficient communication. Surprisingly, even though physical and financial word count barriers have been eliminated in the Craigslist personal ad medium, our Craigslist SHR language dictionary includes shorter and more to-the-point terms than the print ad dictionary. This is likely a result of the fact that SHR information is now routinely communicated, demonstrated by the use of abbreviations. The differences between our dictionary and Davidson's show how SHR language has evolved beyond a topic of discussion or an ideal, and into the world of personal stats – akin to height, age, and weight.

Additionally, our analysis shows how personal ad text evolves over time, leaving open questions about adoption of language as indicated by the changes between Davidson's dictionary and ours. Differences in SHR language between 1980s personal ads and current Craigslist ads highlight the constant evolution of SHR language.

SHR LANGUAGE IN PERSONAL ADS OVER TIME

Methods

The next step in our comparison to Davidson's work was to detect the presence of SHR language across our larger dataset. We started our analysis with ads posted to NYC-area Craigslist. The text of each ad was compared to the terms included in our dictionary, and each ad was assigned a single binary indicator for the presence of SHR language.

In addition to the dictionary entries listed in Table 2, we also searched for variations in phrasing, punctuation, and spacing. For example, in addition to "disease free", we also searched for "disease-free", "no diseases", "diseased free", and "diseased-free", all of which appeared in the data. A term such as "ddf" (an abbreviation for "drug and disease free") likewise was expanded to include "dd free", "d&d free", "d&df", "d/df", "dd/f", etc. Other terms in our dictionary (*e.g.* "clean") had to be distinguished from longer terms (*e.g.* "clean cut") that were not part of our dictionary and would not result in an indication of SHR language. To reduce false positives in our risk category, negations of the SHR term were detected and ignored or reassigned as necessary. For example, an ad including the phrase "no bareback" would be put in the protection category, but not the risk category.

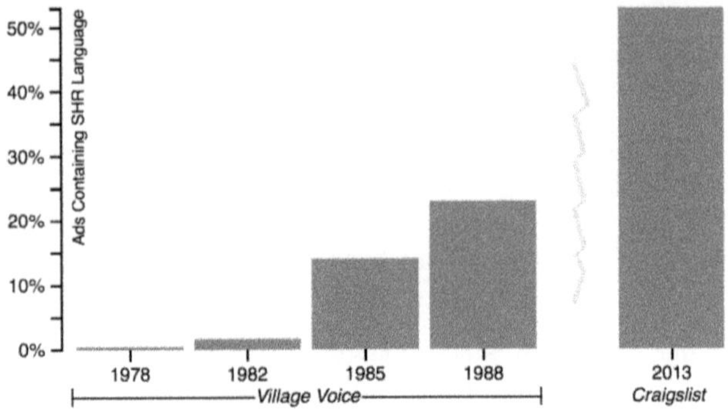

Figure 1. Sexual Health-Related Language in MSM Personal Ads Over Time, New York City Area.

Results

We began by comparing data from the NYC metro area with historical data. Use of SHR language increased substantially, from 22.99% to 53.50% from 1988 to 2013 (see Table 3 and Figure 1). In our full dataset, we see an even greater percentage of SHR language: 53.96%.

The increase in usage of health-related language that Davidson observed in the 1980s and attributed to concern with and response to HIV/AIDS [14] has not only persisted but has continued to grow throughout the last 25 years. Use of SHR language, including disclosing HIV status and safe sex preferences, has become a standard in MSM personal ads, occurring in over half of the ads in our sample.

Across our categories of SHR language, disease-related is the most common (48.34%). Within that category, 30.53% of ads with disease-related content include mention of HIV. This provides evidence to support our argument that the increase in health-concern in MSM personal ads over the past 25 years is greatly motivated by disease prevention, HIV prevention in particular.

Following disease, safety is the next most common category (12.85% of ads). Protection-related terms, including many connoting risky sexual practices, were less common (4.78%), however, ads that used language specifically associated with a preference for unsafe sexual activity occurred in 3.38% of ads. This is comparable to Grov's finding that 3% of Craigslist MSM ads in 2009 sought unprotected sex [18]. Although a relatively small percentage compared to our other categories, 3.38% corresponds to approximately 8,544 ads seeking risky sex encounters in only two weeks. In NYC alone, a smaller percentage of ads included risky SHR language (2.35%), but this still corresponds to 252 ads in two weeks.

SHR LANGUAGE AND HIV PREVALENCE

Methods

To explore relationships between characteristics of MSM and their locations and use of SHR language in personal ads, we constructed seven multivariate logistic regression models (see Table 5). Dependent variables were binary indicators of the presence of SHR language overall in each

Category	*Village Voice* (1988)	Craigslist, NYC only (2013)	Craigslist, 95 locations (2013)
Overall SHR	22.99%	53.50%	53.96%
Disease	NA	46.30%	48.34%
HIV (sub-category of Disease)	NA	17.03%	14.76%
Safety	NA	17.87%	12.85%
Protection	NA	3.56%	4.78%
Risk (sub-category of Protection)	NA	2.35%	3.38%
Health	NA	2.12%	1.23%
Davidson's health-related dictionary [14]	22.99%	34.35%	32.73%
Davidson's sexual exclusivity subcode [14]	13.41%	0.07%	0.15%

Table 3. Presence and Types of Health-Related Language in Craigslist 2013 and *Village Voice* 1988.

of our six SHR language categories: disease, HIV, safety, protection, risk, and health. We used the author's age, the ad's word count, and the ad location's HIV prevalence (rate per 10,000 population) [6], population [34], and population density [33] as regressors. Ads in which authors did not indicate an age, as well as those with a reported age of 99 or <10 were excluded from analysis (11.33% in total).

Ads were placed into one of six age groups based on the poster's age, as reported in Table 4. Because use of SHR language varies significantly among age groups, age is used as a categorical rather than a continuous variable. Great care was taken to construct age groups based on HIV/AIDS history. Those in the youngest two age groups (born after 1986) represent those "too young to remember life before HAART" [21:176]. Further divisions were made based on stage of life during the 1980s, when most people learned of HIV/AIDS. Those 45 and over compose one group, as these men were likely sexually active during the 1980s. Another group includes men 21 and younger, who may exhibit higher risk behaviors than older men [25]. Each age group has a similar sample size, with the exception of the youngest age group, which includes substantially fewer people, but is still important to keep separate due to the potential differences in risk preference between this group and the others [36]. Age groups were used as dummy variables, with the oldest age group as reference value.

Age in 2013	Sample size	During AIDS outbreak (~1983-1988)	Remember life before HAART?
10 - 21	15,832	not born	no
22 - 26	41,557	not born	no
27 - 31	40,800	born	yes
32 - 37	39,315	child	yes
38 - 44	41,029	teenager	yes
45 - 98	45,619	adult – likely sexually active	yes

Table 4. Age Groups.

	Sexual Health-Related (1)	Disease (2)	HIV (3)	Safety (4)	Protection (5)	Risk (6)	Health (7)
Predictor	Odds ratio (95% confidence interval)						
Word count	1.0089**** (1.0086, 1.0091)	1.0074**** (1.0072, 1.0076)	1.0044**** (1.0041, 1.0046)	1.0052**** (1.0049, 1.0054)	1.0053**** (1.0050, 1.0056)	1.0037**** (1.0033, 1.0040)	1.0062**** (1.0058, 1.0066)
HIV prevalence rate	**1.0004**** (1.0003, 1.0004)**	**1.0003**** (0.0002, 0.0003)**	**1.0010**** (1.0009, 1.0011)**	**1.0005**** (1.0005, 1.0006)**	**1.0003**** (1.0001, 1.0004)**	**1.0003*** (1.0001, 1.0004)**	**1.0005**** (1.0002, 1.0007)**
Population	1.0000**** (1.0000, 1.0000)	1.0000**** (1.0000, 1.0000)	1.0000**** (1.0000, 1.0000)	1.0000**** (1.0000, 1.0000)	1.0000**** (1.0000, 1.0000)	1.0000**** (1.0000, 1.0000)	1.0000** (1.0000, 1.0000)
Population density	0.9999**** (0.9999, 0.9999)	0.9999**** (0.9999, 0.9999)	0.9997**** (0.9997, 0.9997)	0.9999**** (0.9999, 1.0000)	0.9998**** (0.9998, 0.9999)	0.9998**** (0.9998, 0.9999)	1.0000 (1.0000, 1.0001)
(Ages 45 - 98)	1.0000	1.0000	1.0000	1.0000	1.0000	1.0000	1.0000
Ages 38 - 44	1.0625**** (1.0337, 1.0922)	1.0513**** (1.0232, 1.0802)	1.1363**** (1.0943, 1.1801)	1.0356* (0.9968, 1.0762)	1.2033**** (1.1319, 1.2792)	1.2693**** (1.1825, 1.3625)	0.5887**** (0.5317, 0.6513)
Ages 32 - 37	0.9996 (0.9722, 1.0278)	0.9797 (0.9544, 1.0070)	1.1834**** (1.1398, 1.2294)	1.0495** (1.0096, 1.0908)	1.2361**** (1.1622, 1.3146)	1.2570**** (1.1698, 1.3506)	0.3554**** (0.3142, 0.4010)
Ages 27 - 31	0.8251**** (0.8029, 0.8481)	0.8347**** (0.8123, 0.8576)	1.1035* (0.9955, 1.0751)	0.9394*** (0.9033, 0.9770)	1.0009 (0.9385, 1.0673)	0.9746 (0.9033, 1.0514)	0.2995**** (0.2628, 0.3403)
Ages 22 - 26	0.7319**** (0.7122, 0.7520)	0.7748**** (0.7541, 0.7960)	1.0165 (0.9781, 1.0565)	0.7121**** (0.6831, 0.7422)	0.8249**** (0.7712, 0.8821)	0.7742**** (0.7145, 0.8386)	0.2108**** (0.1813, 0.2439)
Ages 10 - 21	0.5947**** (0.5731, 0.6172)	0.6544**** (0.6306, 0.6791)	0.8586**** (0.8125, 0.9069)	0.5357**** (0.5024, 0.5707)	0.8662*** (0.7901, 0.9483)	0.6596**** (0.5851, 0.7415)	0.0861**** (0.0596, 0.1198)

* $p < .10$; ** $p < .05$; *** $p < .01$; **** $p < .001$

Table 5. Results of Logistic Regression Models.

Results

Across all regression models (1-7), the prevalence rate of HIV in the ad's location was a significant positive predictor of use of SHR language, even after controlling for population, population density, word count, and age. Although the effect size is relatively small and the high significance level may be due to the very large sample size, our results show a meaningful effect. In model 1, for instance, an increase in HIV prevalence rate of 100 people per 100,000 population (*i.e.* an increase of 0.1%) predicts an increase of 4% in SHR language.

Though our results are correlational, the positive relationship between HIV prevalence and use of SHR language supports an extension of Davidson's findings that the HIV/AIDS crisis may have triggered increased health-concern in MSM personal ads [14]. In the previous section we showed that overall use of SHR language has increased substantially in the past 25 years. Here we see that the magnitude of this trend varies geographically, and may be motivated in part by HIV prevalence.

Cities with larger populations are more likely to have higher incidence of SHR language in MSM Craigslist ads (see Table 5 and Figure 2). In the regression models (1-7), population is a significant positive predictor of SHR language in all six categories and overall. The scatterplot (Figure 2) demonstrates this relationship and also allows us to see several outliers, such as the San Francisco Bay Area, which has the highest use of SHR language but only an average HIV prevalence rate. Boise, Idaho, similarly, has a very low prevalence of HIV but a high use of SHR language. Outliers in the opposite direction include Jackson, Mississippi and Wichita, Kansas, both of which have a relatively high prevalence of HIV and low use of SHR language. Outliers may signify the effectiveness of HIV prevention strategies in these locations. Identifying HIV/STI outreach and education approaches in locations such as Boise and the San Francisco Bay Area may be of use to outliers in the opposite direction (Jackson, Wichita), where similar approaches may help with HIV prevention.

Use of SHR language differs significantly across age groups, with men 21 and under using significantly less SHR

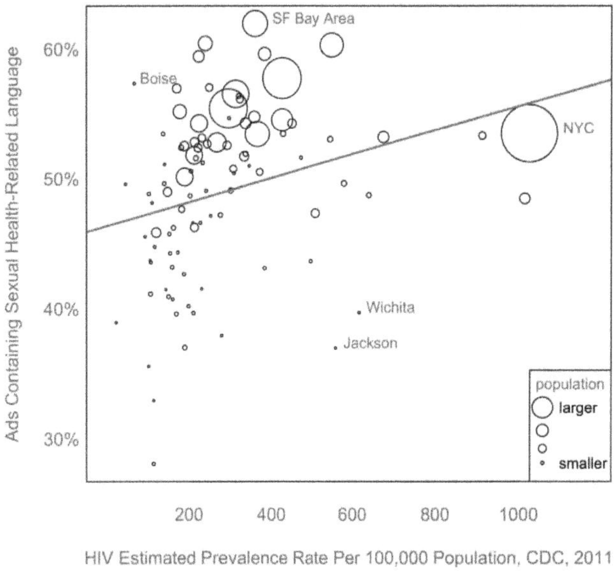

SHR language = 46.360 + 0.009 * prevalence rate, p=0.009

Figure 2. Relationship Between HIV Estimated Prevalence Rate and Use of SHR Language in 95 Locations.

language in all categories (models 1-7) than men in the reference group. This may be a result of the fact that young MSM exhibit higher risk preferences, or do not remember life before HAART [25]. However, MSM under 21 also use significantly less SHR language demonstrating a preference for unsafe sexual behavior than other age groups (model 6).

Overall (model 1), men aged 38 – 44 are the most likely to use SHR language, even more so than men who were adults during the beginning of the HIV/AIDS crisis. Perhaps these men, who were teenagers during the 1980s HIV/AIDS outbreak, came of age during a time when the importance of safe sex was especially emphasized.

Models 3 and 5 show that men aged 32 – 37 are relatively highly likely to use terms in our HIV and Protection categories. This may be a result of the multitude and prevalence of HIV/AIDS outreach and awareness campaigns in the 1990s [15], when these men were teenagers, which may have instituted a higher awareness of HIV/AIDS and sexual safety.

Interestingly, in our health category (model 7), age and use of SHR language have a positive relationship, meaning that as age increases, use of terms in this category ("health" or "healthy") increases. "Health" is a term that was featured prominently in Davidson's dictionary and in his paper, implying that use of the words "health" and "healthy" were important ways for MSM of the time to convey their HIV/STI status and preferences for safe sex [14]. Use of these words in this context has since tapered off in favor of standardized and abbreviated terms such as "ddf". However, the results of the regression model (7) indicate that those MSM who were using the words "health" and "healthy" to convey HIV/STI status in the 1980s may still be using these terms, while younger MSM are not.

Our analysis showing that an ad location's HIV prevalence rate is a significant predictor for use of SHR language in that ad (models 1-7) led us to further question whether the relationship holds in the other direction, *i.e.* whether the use of SHR language in a location predicts HIV prevalence rate in that location. Table 6 shows the results of a linear regression model testing this hypothesis (model 8). Though this relationship is not as strongly significant as the former (models 1-7), it is significant at the 10% level, even after adding control variables. The sample size is limited to the 95 locations from the CDC's dataset [6]. A similar model might show the same effect at a higher significance level if data were available from more locations, showing potential for the use of Craigslist ads for public health surveillance.

	HIV Prevalence Rate (8)	
Variable	Coefficient	Standard error
Intercept	537.30*	(315.18)
Mean SHR language	613.02*	(311.24)
Population	-0.00	(0.00)
Population density	0.16****	(0.03)
Count of ads	0.01	(0.01)
Mean word count	-3.62	(3.03)
State's Internet penetration	-605.46*	(348.14)
Adjusted R^2	*0.32*	

* $p < .10$; ** $p < .05$; *** $p < .01$; **** $p < .001$

Table 6. Results of Linear Regression Model, Dependent Variable = HIV Prevalence Rate Per 10,000 Population.

LIMITATIONS

There are several limitations to our analysis. First, the full dataset may include SHR terms that were not identified by our coders. Next, the circulation area of the *Village Voice* and the readership area of NYC Craigslist ads do not match exactly. Another limitation of comparing our dataset with Davidson's is that while his includes only single gay men, excluding bisexual or heterosexual MSM and couples [14], ours includes all MSM. Further research could examine the differences in SHR language between gay-identified and non-gay-identified MSM.

Although we removed duplicate identical ads, our dataset does include some similar or nearly-duplicate ads, presumably posted by the same user during our data collection period. Were a single user to generate a substantial portion of the ads in a particular location, this may compromise our analysis. Other limitations include the possibility of foreign language or spam ads, which were minimal but were not excluded from our dataset.

With large-scale computational linguistics techniques, some margin of error is to be expected. Comparing our computational coding to a human-coded random sample of 100, we identified two non-SHR ads that the computer coded as false positives, and zero false negatives. Thus, we can assume a margin of error of approximately 2%.

One important limitation is the inability of our search algorithm to evaluate the context of a term. For example, the word "clean" is often used in a SHR context. However, it can also be used to discuss hygiene, drug use, etc. While a human can usually identify whether "clean" is being used in a SHR context or not, this is not an easy task for a computer. In fact, the two false positives that were found when calculating our computational margin of error both were instances of "clean" being used in a non-SHR context. The margin of error helps to mitigate this limitation.

DESIGN IMPLICATIONS

This study argues for computational analysis of online media content as a research method to discover insights about user populations, which is useful for HCI designers in a variety of contexts. First, when designing large-scale health data systems, designers must be cognizant of the ways in which users represent their health conditions, preferences, and activities. Computational linguistic analysis of data sources such as Craigslist ads can inform the information architecture of such systems. Next, many HCI domains would benefit from mining user-generated content to answer questions about how users communicate and represent themselves. In this paper we present an example of this in a health context, but similar methods could be used in the areas of urban informatics (to inform the design of city-wide technologies), user experience (to inform the design of user interfaces), and many more.

This work also highlights temporal issues surrounding the use of language in user interfaces. We have explored how SHR language used by MSM has evolved in the last quarter century. While dropdown menus for HIV status and safe sex preferences on online dating sites would make computational analysis easier, as well as supporting serosorting and negotiation of sexual safety before meeting [37,38], such solutions are perhaps too simple if they do not take into account the evolution of language. Analysis of the constantly changing nature of language over time opens up opportunities for natural language processing and machine learning techniques to identify new SHR terms as they emerge, an area for future research. We encourage HCI research to develop tools to detect evolving language for use in user-interface design.

CONCLUSION

In this work, we examined the potential for online personal ad content to serve as a sensor for real world health behavior. This kind of low-cost, efficient sensing can augment existing data collection methods. Additionally, data collected through these mechanisms can inform systems designers about the necessary information architecture for large-scale health systems as well as the potential for online health interventions. Concretely, we analyzed sexual health-related language in a large sample of MSM Craigslist personal ads. We first built a dictionary of SHR terms, then calculated the proportion of ads with SHR content and demonstrated a rising use of SHR compared to print personal ads in the 1980s. We then built regression models to determine demographic and location-based characteristics that predict use of SHR language.

Our SHR language dictionary allowed us to examine the differences between ways that MSM currently communicate health-concerns to practices directly following the HIV/AIDS epidemic. Despite the longer length of online personal ads, SHR language is more standardized and abbreviated when compared to language documented in the 1980s. At the same time, we found a substantial increase in the percentage of ads using SHR language, from 22.99% in 1988 to 53.50% in 2013. This suggests that health-concerned language has become a core attribute of MSM personal ad content. The largest category of SHR language was disease-related, including much HIV-related language, and 3.38% of ads indicated preferences for unsafe sexual practices.

Our statistical models (1-7) identified that the prevalence rate of HIV in an ad's location was a significant predictor for use of SHR language. This suggests that the substantial increase in SHR language that occurred over the past 25 years may have been motivated by concern with HIV. These results highlight the potential for Craigslist ads to be used as a way to quickly gather information about MSM sexual health and practices for public health surveillance purposes to assist in HIV prevention. Additionally, we found that young MSM, a group with higher preference for risky behavior [25], were less likely to use SHR language in their ads, and we identified several outlying locations with high HIV prevalence but low use of SHR language. A SHR language sensor could potentially help to identify communities such as these who may benefit from HIV education and outreach.

By employing data science techniques to analyze SHR language in a large, publicly available dataset, this research demonstrates that SHR language on Craigslist can serve as a sort of sensor. This sensor provides insight not only into epidemiological public health data and sexual practices and discourse among particular communities, but into the potential for similar sensors to transform publicly available, online data into design implications. Future research could consider ways to improve such a sensor, such as by computationally identifying more information about an ad's author's demographics and sexual practices, or could ascertain new applications for the sensor. Another future research direction could contrast use of SHR language among different communities on Craigslist, to identify differences in sexual practices, discourse, and representation of online identity. Finally, research could examine the use of SHR discourse, or lack thereof, in profile-based online dating sites and mobile apps such as Match.com and Grindr, and the implications of censorship of SHR language on disease control.

ACKNOWLEDGMENTS

Thank you to Karen Cheng, Kate Ringland, Steven Frost, and members of STAR and LUCI for their generous help and support with this paper. This work was conducted as part of the UC Irvine Competitive Edge program and funded in part by a Eugene Cota-Robles Fellowship.

REFERENCES

1. Brewer, J., Kaye, J., Williams, A., and Wyche, S. Sexual interactions: why we should talk about sex in HCI. *Proc. CHI 2006*, ACM (2006), 1695–1698.
2. Brown, T. Behavioral surveillance: Current perspectives, and its role in catalyzing action. *J. of Acquired Immune Deficiency Syndromes International Perspectives on HIV 32*, (2003), S12–S17.
3. Bull, S.S., McFarlane, M., Lloyd, L., and Rietmeijer, C. The process of seeking sex partners online and implications for STD/HIV prevention. *AIDS Care 16*, 8 (2004), 1012–1020.
4. Cassels, S., Menza, T.W., Goodreau, S.M., and Golden, M.R. HIV serosorting as a harm reduction strategy: Evidence from Seattle, Washington. *AIDS 23*, 18 (2009), 2497–2506.
5. Centers for Disease Control and Prevention. *HIV in the United States: At A Glance*. 2013.

6. Centers for Disease Control and Prevention. *HIV Surveillance Report, 2011*. 2013.
7. Chan, J. and Ghose, A. Internet's dirty secret: Assessing the impact of online intermediaries on HIV transmission. Soc. Sci. Research Network, 2013.
8. Cheeseman, K., Goodlin-Fahncke, W., and Tewksbury, R. "Looking for a married hookup": An examination of personal ads posted by men seeking sex with married men. *J. of Men's Studies 20*, 2 (2012), 144–157.
9. Chiasson, M.A., Parsons, J.T., Tesoriero, J.M., *et al.* HIV behavioral research online. *Journal of Urban Health 83*, 1 (2006), 73–85.
10. Cocks, H.G. *Classified: The Secret History of the Personal Column*. Random House, 2009.
11. Cooper, A. Sexuality and the Internet: Surfing into the new millennium. *CyberPsy&Beh 1*, 2 (1998), 187–193.
12. Craigslist Terms of Use. *Craigslist.org*, 2012.
13. Crepaz N, Hart TA, and Marks G. Highly active antiretroviral therapy and sexual risk behavior: A meta-analytic review. *JAMA 292*, 2 (2004), 224–236.
14. Davidson, A.G. Looking for love in the age of AIDS: The language of gay personals, 1978-1988. *The Journal of Sex Research 28*, 1 (1991), 125–137.
15. Davis, J. Evolution of an Epidemic: 25 Years of HIV/AIDS Media Campaigns in the U.S. Henry J. Kaiser Family Foundation, 2006.
16. Fries, J.A., Ho, T.Y., Polgreen, P.M., and Segre, A.M. Using Craigslist messages for syphilis surveillance. *Int. Meeting on Emerg. Diseases and Surveil.* (2011).
17. Fries, J.A., Segre, A., Polgreen, L., and Polgreen, P. The use of Craigslist posts for risk behavior and STI surveillance. *Int. Society for Disease Surv.* (2011), 13.
18. Grov, C. Risky sex- and drug-seeking in a probability sample of men-for-men online bulletin board Postings. *AIDS and Behavior 14*, 6 (2010), 1387–1392.
19. Gudelunas, D. Online personal ads. *Journal of Homosexuality*, 49, 1 (2005), 1–33.
20. Gudelunas, D. There's an app for that: The uses and gratifications of online social networks for gay men. *Sexuality & Culture*, 16, 4 (2012), 347–365.
21. Handel, M.J. and Shklovski, I. Disclosure, ambiguity and risk reduction in real-time dating sites. *Proc. GROUP 2012*, 175–178.
22. Hatala, M.N., Baack, D.W., and Parmenter, R. Dating with HIV: A content analysis of gay male HIV-positive and HIV-negative personal advertisements. *J. of Social and Personal Relationships 15*, 2 (1998), 268–276.
23. Hoff, C.C. and Beougher, S.C. Sexual agreements among gay male couples. *Archives of Sexual Behavior 39*, 3 (2010), 774–787.
24. Kannabiran, G., Bardzell, J., and Bardzell, S. How HCI talks about sexuality: discursive strategies, blind spots, and opportunities for future research. *Proc. CHI 2011*.
25. Mansergh, G. and Marks, G. Age and risk of HIV infection in men who have sex with men. *AIDS 12*, 10 (1998), 1119–1128.
26. Martin, J.L. The impact of AIDS on gay male sexual behavior patterns in New York City. *American Journal of Public Health 77*, 5 (1987), 578–581.
27. McFarlane, M., Bull, S.S., and Rietmeijer, C.A. The Internet as a newly emerging risk environment for sexually transmitted diseases. *Journal of the American Medical Association 284*, 4 (2000), 443–446.
28. Mocroft, A., Brettle, R., Kirk, O., *et al.* Changes in the cause of death among HIV positive subjects across Europe: results from the EuroSIDA study. *AIDS 16*, 12 (2002), 1663–1671.
29. Moskowitz, D.A. and Seal, D.W. "GWM looking for sex—SERIOUS ONLY": The interplay of sexual ad placement frequency and success on the sexual health of "men seeking men" on Craigslist. *Journal of Gay & Lesbian Social Services 22*, 4 (2010), 399–412.
30. Mowlabocus, S. *Gaydar Culture: Gay Men, Technology and Embodiment in the Digital Age.* Ashgate Publishing, 2010.
31. Mustanski, B., Lyons, T., and Garcia, S.C. Internet use and sexual health of young men who have sex with men: A mixed-methods study. *Archives of Sexual Behavior*, 40, 2 (2011), 289–300.
32. Rosenbaum, M.S., Daunt, K.L., and Jiang, A. Craigslist exposed: The Internet-mediated hookup. *J of Homosexuality 60*, 4 (2013), 505–531.
33. U. S. Census Bureau. Population, housing units, area, and density: 2010 - United States -- metropolitan and micropolitan statistical areas. 2010. http://factfinder2.census.gov/faces/tableservices/jsf/pages/productview.xhtml.
34. U. S. Census Bureau. Annual estimates of the population: April 1, 2010 to July 1, 2012. 2012. http://www.census.gov/popest/data/metro/totals/2012/.
35. Village Voice. Classifieds. *Village Voice*, 1978-1988.
36. Wickman, M.E., Anderson, N.L.R., and Smith Greenberg, C. The adolescent perception of invincibility and its influence on teen acceptance of health promotion strategies. *J of Pediatric Nursing 23*, 6 (2008), 460–468.
37. Winchester III, W.W., Abel, T.D., and Bauermeister, J. The use of partner-seeking computer-mediated communication applications by young men that have sex with men (YMSM): Uncovering human-computer interaction (HCI) design opportunities in HIV prevention. *Health Systems 1*, 1 (2012), 26–35.
38. Wohlfeiler, D., Hecht, J., Volk, J, *et al.* How can we improve online HIV and STD prevention for men who have sex with men? Perspectives of hook-up website owners, website users, and HIV/STD directors. *AIDS and Behavior*, 17, 9 (2013), 3024–3033.
39. Wolitski, R.J., Valdiserri, R.O., Denning, P.H., and Levine, W.C. Are we headed for a resurgence of the HIV epidemic among men who have sex with men? *Amer. J. of Public Health 91*, 6 (2001), 883–888.
40. World Health Organization. WHO | Public health surveillance. *World Health Organization*, 2013. http://www.who.int/topics/public_health_surveillance/.

Support Matching and Satisfaction in an Online Breast Cancer Support Community

Tatiana A. Vlahovic[1*], Yi-Chia Wang[2*], Robert E. Kraut[1], John M. Levine[3]

Human-Computer Interaction Institute[1]
Language Technologies Institute[2]
Carnegie Mellon University
{tvlahovic, yichiaw, robert.kraut}@cmu.edu
*These authors contributed equally to this work.

Department of Psychology[3]
University of Pittsburgh
jml@pitt.edu

ABSTRACT
Research suggests that online health support benefits chronically ill users. Their satisfaction might be an indicator that they perceive group interactions as beneficial and a precursor to group commitment. We examined whether receiving emotional and informational support is satisfying in its own right, or whether satisfaction depends on matches between what users sought and what they received. Two studies collected judgments in a breast cancer support community of support users sought, support they received, and their expressed satisfaction. While receiving emotional or informational support in general positively predicted satisfaction, users expressed less satisfaction when they sought informational support but received emotional support. There was also a tendency for users to express more satisfaction when they sought and received informational support. On the other hand, users were equally satisfied with emotional and informational support after seeking emotional support. Implications for membership commitment and interventions in online support groups are discussed.

Author Keywords
Social support; support groups; computer-mediated communication; health informatics; breast cancer

ACM Classification Keywords
H.5.3. Information Interfaces and Presentation: Group and Organization Interfaces: Asynchronous interaction, Computer-supported cooperative work, Evaluation/methodology, Web-based interaction.

INTRODUCTION
Research across decades shows that social support can improve psychological functioning, mental and physical health, and longevity [14, 24]. Many people with chronic or life-threatening illnesses, especially cancer patients and survivors, participate in online health support groups [5]. A recent meta-analysis demonstrates that online support groups are often effective in reducing depression and increasing self-efficacy and quality of life [15].

The straightforward prediction from many theories of social support, such as the classic stress-buffering theory of support [6], is that people will both receive more benefit and perceive they are receiving more when they receive more support. However, the empirical evidence is not so simple [21, 25]. Previous studies suggest that whether the support people receive matches or mismatches the support they need or seek is important in determining their benefits and satisfaction [e.g., 8, 9, 16, 28]. However, it is difficult to draw firm conclusions about the importance of matching from prior research due to the variations in the way matching is defined, populations and support types studied, and the outcome measures used.

The current research focuses on recipients' expressed satisfaction with support and the group that provided it in an online breast cancer support community. Satisfaction can be an immediate outcome linked to a specific episode of support, unlike longer-term outcomes like depression or quality of life. As Hecht observed, "Satisfaction is commonly conceived of as the affect experienced when expectation-type standards are fulfilled" (p. 357) [10]. Therefore, satisfaction is a proxy for benefits because satisfied individuals perceive they are getting benefit from an exchange. Satisfaction is also an important determinant of people's commitment to a group, which determines whether they will stick around to receive benefits from it. For example, Anderson et al. found that satisfaction has positive associations with cohesion and consensus [1].

Receiving emotional and informational support
Because exchanges of informational and emotional support dominate conversation in health support groups [e.g., 19, 18], most research has focused on them. Ridings and Gefen reported that 76% of people who join online health groups do so to exchange emotional and informational support [17].

Our first research question is whether receiving emotional or informational support by itself is sufficient for increasing

CHI 2014, April 26 - May 01 2014, Toronto, ON, Canada
Copyright 2014 ACM 978-1-4503-2473-1/14/04···$15.00.
http://dx.doi.org/10.1145/2556288.2557108

expressed user satisfaction in an online breast cancer support community.

Emotional support refers to the provision of caring, sympathy, or encouragement. An example in our breast cancer support community is: [...] *I do understand the frustration and anger and sadness of when medicines fail you and then returning to unknown territory once more* [...] *I wish you the best on the Ixempra* [...]. [1] Previous work has shown that peer discussion that centers on emotional support bolsters the psychological outcomes of individuals with cancer [13].

Informational support refers to the provision of information or advice. An example in our support community is: [...] *It was explained to me that microcalcifications look like as if one were to throw rock salt on a blacktop driveway and they would "cluster and fall" in many locations* [...]. Individuals in cancer support groups share experiences regarding their illness, medical care, side effects, physician interactions, financial difficulties, etc. Previous work has found that sharing information in cancer support groups is a key component in improving psychological health [12].

Matching support seeking and support provision

Our second research question is whether users express more satisfaction when the emotional and informational support they receive matches the support they sought. While Uses and Gratifications Theory offers a broad framework to examine matching between user needs and various types of media use [e.g., 20], we focus here on the social support literature because our research questions address support received and support matching in an online cancer support group.

The support people receive is not necessarily the support they seek. In a survey study of women with breast cancer, Reynolds and Perrin found that matching between desired and received support had a greater impact on psychosocial functioning than did the amount of support received [16]. In particular, getting support that one did not want (i.e., mismatched support) was negatively related to psychosocial functioning.

Cutrona proposed that support is successful when support matches needs arising from causes of stress [7]. In a lab-based test of this claim, Curtona and Suhr had married participants talk about stressors with their partners [9]. Although the authors treated controllability as a proxy for support seekers' needs, they did not directly measure the support sought. In general, participants were more satisfied with the more informational and emotional support they received from their spouses. While emotional support was satisfying irrespective of controllability of stressors, satisfaction with informational support varied with controllability of stressors for support givers and receivers.

Cutrona et al. examined support matching (specified as emotional disclosure leading to emotional support and advice/information requests leading to informational support) on perceptions of partner sensitivity and marital satisfaction [8]. Partner sensitivity was rated higher when participants expressed their emotions and got emotional support in return. However, when participants made information requests, support matching or mismatching did not significantly influence partner sensitivity ratings. In addition, a mismatch in which one partner expressed emotions and received informational support in return reduced martial satisfaction. However, Cutrona et al. acknowledged that their coding system did not adequately capture support seekers' intent [8]. Thus, it is impossible to understand from this study what support seekers were actually looking for.

Wolff et al. examined the relationship between needed and gotten emotional support on complaints about health and experience of negative affect among older and younger people [28]. This research used a daily survey and did not assess support sources. Degree of matching was equated to a "balance score" computed by subtracting daily ratings of emotional support needed from daily ratings of emotional support received (p. 70) [28]. Younger participants had more complaints about health and more negative affect when they received too little or too much emotional support relative to their needs (i.e., a matching effect). In contrast, the more emotional support older participants got, the less negative affect they reported. However, this research is limited in that it only explored emotional support.

Support matching has also been examined in online health support groups. In an Internet-based support community for self-harm called "SharpTalk," Smithson et al. examined the type of support "opening posters" seemed to be seeking and their reactions to the support they received from group members who replied to their posts [22]. Using conversation analysis, they found "[...] posters often prioritized the telling of their problems, while respondents often oriented to possible advice [...] [P]osters did appear to respond to requests to elaborate, and to statements of 'being here' [...] better than they did to offers of advice, which they often rejected or ignored" (p. 498) [22]. Even when opening posters requested advice, these users appeared to be searching for empathy or "[...] a way into a supportive conversation" (p. 498) [22]. Thus, there was no evidence that support matching was beneficial in the case of asking for and receiving advice. What appeared to be beneficial for these users was receiving emotional support in general. However, given the qualitative nature of this study, what users wanted from the group could only be inferred from their reactions.

Thus, prior research suggests that support matching may be important, but due to variations in populations,

[1] All quoted posts from the examined online community are lightly disguised in this paper to preserve user anonymity.

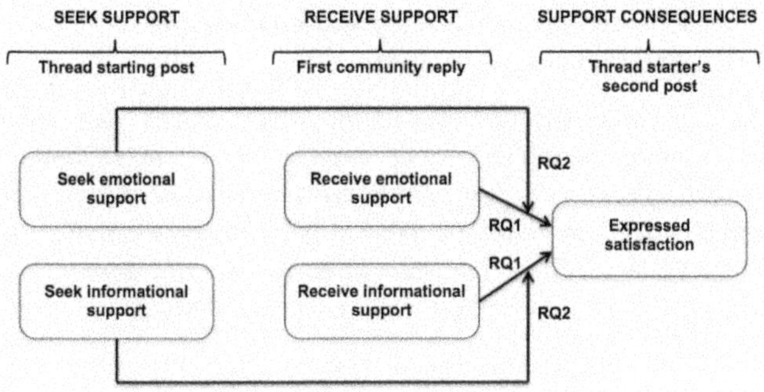

Figure 1. Conceptual model of relationships between seeking support, receiving support, and satisfaction

operationalization of matching, support types, and outcomes measured, previous work shows mixed findings. We systematically investigated the benefits of receiving support in general and receiving support matched to support sought within an online breast cancer support community.

STUDY 1: MATCHING BETWEEN SEEKING AND RECEIVING SUPPORT

To address gaps in prior work, we gathered observers' judgments of support seeking (message intent) in the thread starting post, support received in the first reply from the community, and satisfaction the thread starter expressed in her first follow-up post in the same thread. Figure 1 shows our conceptual model of examined relationships between support sought, support received, and user satisfaction.

Research Site

This study investigated threads from the discussion boards of a large online breast cancer support community. In these discussion boards, breast cancer patients, survivors, and caregivers post questions, self-disclose personal stories and health information, and learn about others' experiences. These discussion boards are organized by forums, containing topic threads.

One thousand threads were randomly selected from this online community's discussion boards (containing 66 forums at the time of data collection), and these threads served as the units of analysis (thread length: M = 20.97 posts; Mdn = 9 posts; min = 1 post; max = 2327 posts). For each thread, we analyzed support processes occurring at three times (Figure 1): (1) the thread starting post, which we sometimes refer to as simply the initial post; (2) the first reply to that post, which we sometimes refer to as the first reply; and (3) the thread starter's second or follow-up post in the same thread. Following Barak and Gluck-Ofri's methods [3], we chose the first reply for analysis because reply structure (i.e., who is replying to whom) can become complex as threads get longer. In contrast, the first reply is most likely a response to the thread starting post. Furthermore, Wang et al. found similar results when examining the relationships between thread starting posts and the support they received in analyses based on the first reply or the first five replies [27]. Six hundred thirty-eight threads in our sample contained a follow-up post by the thread starter. The number of community replies between thread starter users' first and second posts was M = 4.04; Mdn = 2; SD = 5.86; min = 0; max = 75.

Measuring support sought, support received, and expressed satisfaction

We posted tasks as Human Intelligence Tasks (HITs) on the crowdsourcing online marketplace Amazon Mechanical Turk (MTurk) and had workers from this community (Turkers) read portions of the cancer support threads and make judgments of support sought, support received, and satisfaction in posts from the breast cancer support community threads. Buhrmester et al. reported that MTurk data quality matched or surpassed psychometric standards of traditional studies [4]. Furthermore, Snow et al. demonstrated that the combined ratings of between five to seven Turkers yielded judgments of textual content comparable to judgments made by experts, including expressions of emotion, event timing, similarity of words, disambiguation of word meaning, and language-based entailment/implication [23].

To qualify for our HITs, Turkers had to have a United States location and a 98% approval rate for their previous work on MTurk. Turkers received \$0.05 per HIT when they judged the amount people were seeking and receiving support (seeking support task and receiving support task) and \$0.12 per HIT when they judged satisfaction (satisfaction task). To increase their attention while doing HITs, Turkers also highlighted portions of the post text that supported their numerical judgments. Ten Turkers completed each HIT (a Turker could complete multiple HITs in the same task if he chose to, but he could not complete the same HIT twice), and tasks were completed by different sets of Turkers. The judgments Turkers made in seeking support, receiving support, and expressed satisfaction tasks are described below.

Seeking support in thread starting posts

Turkers were provided with brief definitions of emotional support elicitation ("When seeking emotional support, the writer is trying to get understanding, encouragement, affirmation, sympathy, or caring.") and informational support elicitation ("When seeking informational support, the writer is trying to get advice, referrals or knowledge."), taken from Bambina [2]. They then read a thread starting post and rated how much the post was seeking emotional support and seeking informational support on Likert scales with end-points "1 (not at all)" and "7 (strongly)".

Social support received from community replies

Turkers were provided with brief definitions of emotional support ("Emotional support messages provide understanding, encouragement, affirmation, sympathy, or caring.") and informational support ("Informational support messages provide advice, referrals or knowledge."). They read a thread starting post for context and the first reply it

Variable	*M*	*SD*	Min	Max	ICC
Seek emo support	2.75	1.66	1	7	0.91
Seek info support	4.21	2.01	1	7	0.95
Receive emo support	2.68	1.43	1	6.5	0.92
Receive info support	2.93	1.47	1	7	0.92
Composite satisfaction	4.80	0.71	1.93	6.58	0.92

Table 1: Descriptive statistics and intra-class correlations for seeking emotional and informational support in thread starting posts (*N*=1000); receiving emotional and informational support in first replies (*N*=974); and satisfaction in thread starters' second posts (*N*=638).

received and rated the amount of emotional support and informational support provided by the reply on Likert scales with end-points "1 (none)" and "7 (a great deal)".

Satisfaction in thread starters' second posts

To assess expressed satisfaction, Turkers were shown a pair of posts – a thread starter's initial post and her second post in the same thread, but none of the intervening replies – and then answered four questions about the exchange. (1) "Overall, how satisfied was this person in her second message with the conversation that she participated in?" (2) "How satisfied was this person in her second message with the health information that she received from the other members of this online community?" (3) "How much did this person's level of distress change from her first message to her second message?" and (4) "How much did this person's closeness to the other members of this online community change from her first message to her second message?" Questions 1 and 2 were assessed on Likert scales with end-points "1 (Completely dissatisfied)" and "7 (Completely satisfied)", and Questions 3 and 4 were assessed on Likert scales with end-points "1 (Decreased very much)" and "7 (Increased very much)".

Analytic Methods

To assess agreement among judges, we computed the intra-class correlations (ICC) for each task. The ICC can be interpreted as the proportion of variance in judgments that is attributable to the stimuli that were judged (rather than error or biases among different judges). Table 1 shows the ICCs for Study 1 variables.

We aggregated Turkers' judgments by calculating the mean Turker rating for each question. The four questions form a highly reliable composite satisfaction scale (Cronbach's alpha = 0.89). We combined ratings from the four question measures into a composite satisfaction measure by first reversing the distress question and then averaging across questions. Table 1 provides unstandardized descriptive statistics for Study 1 variables.

Below we provide an example of a thread starting post, the first community reply, and the thread starter user's follow-up post. (The initial post also had two additional replies, which are not shown.) The thread starter expressed an above average amount of satisfaction in her follow-up post.

Thread starting post (seek emotional support = 1, seek informational support = 6.1):

Can someone explain this to me. What does it mean for them to be clustered? I have many flecks, according to mammo results, within of this pacman shaped thing. The lump is deep and can't be felt, but is visible on mammo...but nothing was shown on US. They looked like three little circles that, if connnected, would create a triangle.

First community reply post (receive emotional support = 2.2; receive informational support = 4.6):

[User name omitted for privacy],

It was explained to me that microcalcifications look like as if one were to throw rock salt on a blacktop driveway and they would "cluster and fall" in many locations. They usually don't appear on a sonogram but as I've read do line the ducts of the breast so they seem to be scattered but they can be running through one duct that may extend throughout several places in the breast. Dr. Susan Love's book is very detailed in explaining this and I'd much rather you get a hold of that book and read her expert description than mine.

Good luck with your research. Hope I could be of some assistance.

Thread starter's second post to the thread (composite satisfaction = 5.4):

Thank you all so much for your thoughts. This web site is fantastic and everyone here is delightful. My doctor has requested a biopsy, it will be conducted on the 30th. Like many here until then I am waiting on pins and needles. Since the biopsy is a synthesis of my biggest fears, needles, heights and cancer...I'm feeling VERY nervous, but hopefully that the results will be OK. Again, thanks for everyone's support.

Results

Six hundred thirty-eight threads in our sample had a follow-up post from the thread starter, introducing potential selection bias because over one third of the thread starters did not have a follow-up post. This is of concern because the act of posting a second time might be influenced by the replies the initial post received and may itself reflect satisfaction. To control for selection bias, we employed Heckman selection models [11], which control for a thread starter's propensity to write a follow-up post when analyzing the effects of support receiving and matching on user expressed satisfaction.

Table 2 presents Heckman models predicting expressed satisfaction from the extent to which initial posts sought support and replies provided it. The number of replies between thread starters' first and follow-up posts is included as a control variable. Model 1 presents main effects of the predictors, and Model 2 presents main and interaction effects. The dependent variable in both

		Model 1 Satisfaction main effects (RQ1)			Model 2 Satisfaction main effects (RQ1) and interaction effects (RQ2)		
	Variables	**Coef.**	**SE**	***p***	**Coef**	**SE**	***p***
Predictor variables (Outcome: Composite satisfaction)	Seek emotional support	-.080	.052	.118	-.088	.053	.096
	Seek informational support	.122	.052	.020	.159	.054	.003
	Receive emotional support	**.154**	**.050**	**.002**	**.136**	**.051**	**.008**
	Receive informational support	**.179**	**.047**	**.000**	**.164**	**.048**	**.001**
	Posts between thread starter posts 1 and 2	.248	.038	.000	.227	.039	.000
	Seek emo support X Receive emo support				**.012**	**.038**	**.752**
	Seek emo support X Receive info support				**-.006**	**.037**	**.866**
	Seek info support X Receive emo support				**-.090**	**.040**	**.025**
	Seek info support X Receive info support				**.079**	**.041**	**.052**
	Constant	.543	.072	.000	.493	.075	.000
Selection variables (Selection: Having a second post in the thread)	Has profile	.265	.075	.000	.242	.075	.001
	Post count before thread	-.003	.040	.934	-.001	.038	.969
	Seek emotional support	.230	.050	.000	.236	.050	.000
	Seek informational support	.134	.052	.010	.140	.051	.006
	Receive emotional support	-.051	.050	.304	-.058	.049	.242
	Receive informational support	.042	.048	.375	.038	.047	.420
	Constant	.259	.056	.000	.272	.056	.000

Table 2: Heckman selection models predicting composite satisfaction in a follow-up post (*N* = 638) from seeking emotional and informational support in the thread starting post, and receiving emotional and informational support in the first reply post. Model 1 includes only main effects, while Model 2 includes main effects and interactions. Effects in bold pertain to RQ1 and RQ2. Models 1 and 2 include selection models that predict whether a thread starter would have a follow-up post. The Likelihood Ratio test shows the selection and prediction equations were not independent. Model 1 LR test of indep. eqns. $x^2 = 14.92$ ($p = 0.0001$). Model 2 LR test of indep. eqns. $x^2 = 15.96$ ($p = 0.0001$).

Heckman models was composite satisfaction. To control for selection biases, Models 1 and 2 in Table 2 also contain selection models which predict if a thread starter would have a follow-up post based on whether the thread starter created a profile on the site (*Has profile*), the number of posts the thread starter created before initiating the thread (*Post count before thread*), seeking emotional and informational support in thread starting posts, and receiving emotional and informational support in first replies. The *Has profile* and *Post count before thread* variables were included to identify active users, who might be more likely to return and have a follow-up post. Variables included in the Heckman models in Table 2 (except *Has profile*) were centered and standardized (*Posts between thread starter posts 1 and 2*, and *Post count before thread* were log transformed).

Predicting second thread posts of thread starters

Selection models demonstrate that a thread starter creating a profile and seeking emotional and informational support in her initial post were significant positive predictors of having a follow-up post (Models 1 and 2, Table 2). The number of posts by a thread starter before she posted her thread starting post and receiving emotional and informational support in the first community reply were not significant predictors of having a follow-up post (Models 1 and 2, Table 2).

Predicting expressed satisfaction

Regarding RQ1, people expressed more satisfaction in their follow-up posts when they received emotional and informational support in the first reply to their initial post. These main effects were qualitatively similar in both Heckman models (see the bolded lines in Models 1 and 2 in Table 2). In addition, and unrelated to our research questions, people expressed more satisfaction when they sought informational support in their initial posts, independent of the support they received. Seeking emotional support did not predict expressed satisfaction. The number of community replies between thread starters' first and follow-up posts was a significant positive predictor of satisfaction, suggesting the more replies a thread starter received, the more satisfied she was.

The interaction effects in Model 2 of Table 2 addressed RQ2, that matching between sought and received support would influence satisfaction. The data do not support a matching hypothesis when women sought emotional support, with no interaction on satisfaction between seeking emotional support and receiving either emotional support ($b = .012$, $p > .75$) or informational support ($b = -.006$, $p > .86$). That is, women were equally satisfied with receiving emotional or informational support after seeking emotional support.

There was, however, support for a matching hypothesis when women sought informational support. The significant

Variable	*M*	*SD*	Min	Max	ICC
Positive emo disclosure	1.55	0.96	1	6.7	0.90
Negative emo disclosure	2.39	1.52	1	6.7	0.94
Positive info disclosure	1.89	1.09	1	6.6	0.85
Negative info disclosure	3.58	1.72	1	7	0.91
Question asking	4.94	2.17	1	7	0.91

Table 3: Descriptive statistics and intra-class correlations for self-disclosure and question asking in thread starting posts (N=1000).

negative interaction between seeking informational support and receiving emotional support (b = -.090, p < .05) suggests dissatisfaction when women sought informational support and received emotional support. Moreover, the positive interaction between seeking informational support and receiving informational support (b = .079, p = .052) suggests that women were more satisfied with informational support when they actually sought it.

STUDY 2: MATCHING BETWEEN BEHAVIORAL SPEECH ACTS AND RECEIVING SUPPORT

We conducted a second analysis to predict satisfaction from speech acts that might elicit social support rather than from observers' judgments of support elicitation. Previous research indicates that people explicitly ask questions when seeking informational support, but use self-disclosure as an implicit way of eliciting emotional support [2, 27]. It is possible that Study 1 found no support for a matching hypothesis when women sought emotional support because Turkers had more difficulty recognizing implicit elicitation of emotional support than informational support.

Given that users employ different linguistic strategies to elicit emotional and informational support, we examined RQ1 and RQ2 using judgments of thread starting post behavioral speech acts (self-disclosure and question asking) in place of judgments of thread starting post intent (seeking emotional and informational support). Study 2 methods were similar to Study 1 and used the same thread sample and data for support received and expressed satisfaction in Study 1. However, Study 2 examined Turker judgments of question asking and four kinds of self-disclosure collected for the same thread starting posts as Study 1.

An example of negative emotional and informational self-disclosure from our data is: [...] *I had been so depressed this entire weekend my results showed progression and so met with doctor today and hes taking me off gemzar and going to begin ixempra* [...]. An example of positive emotional and informational self-disclosure from our data is: [...] *Today is my three year cancerversary!!* [...] *In some sense it is difficult to believe it has been three years and in other ways it seems like it has been way longer. Either way, I feel very blessed to be here and living a wonderful life (even through constant therapy)* [...]. Wang et al. found that emotional and informational self-disclosure (both positive and negative kinds) were effective ways to evoke emotional support from the community; these relationships were mediated by the extent to which a user was perceived to be seeking emotional support [27].

An example of question asking from our data is: *Can someone explain this to me. What does it mean for them to be clustered?* [...]. Wang et al. also found that question asking was an effective way to evoke informational support from the community, and this relationship was mediated by the extent to which a user was perceived to be seeking informational support [27].

Measuring self-disclosure and question asking

Separate judgment tasks were presented for emotional self-disclosure, informational self-disclosure, and question asking, and tasks were completed by different sets of Turkers. Ten Turkers completed each emotional self-disclosure HIT and each informational self-disclosure HIT. Six Turkers completed each question asking HIT. Turkers received $0.05 per HIT for emotional self-disclosure and informational self-disclosure tasks and $0.03 per HIT for question asking tasks.

Self-disclosure in thread starting posts

Turkers rated the amount of self-disclosure in thread starting posts. All self-disclosure tasks specified, "Self-disclosure is defined as the process by which one person reveals something about oneself to others."

Emotional self-disclosure tasks specified, "Emotional self-disclosure is concerned with the extent to which the writer has discussed her feelings and emotions with others, such as happiness, fears, sadness, and anger." Turkers read the thread starting post and rated the amount of positive emotional self-disclosure and the amount of negative emotional self-disclosure on Likert scales with end-points "1 (Not at all)" and "7 (Very much)".

Informational self-disclosure tasks specified, "Informational self-disclosure is concerned with the extent to which the writer has discussed her personal information with others, such as health conditions, diagnosis results, and family status." Turkers read the thread starting post and rated the amount of positive informational self-disclosure and the amount of negative informational self-disclosure on Likert scales with end-points "1 (Not at all)" and "7 (Very much)".

Question asking in thread starting posts

Question tasks specified, "When asking a question, the writer is requesting a response from the group. Questions can be asked directly and indirectly." Turkers read the thread starting post and rated how much the post was asking a question on a Likert scale with end-points "1 (Definitely does not contain a question)" and "7 (Definitely contains one or more questions)".

Analytic Methods

Analytic methods were the same as those used in Study 1. Table 3 shows unstandardized descriptive statistics and

		Model 1 Satisfaction main effects (RQ1)			Model 2 Satisfaction main effects (RQ1) and interaction effects (RQ2)		
	Variables	**Coef.**	**SE**	***p***	**Coef.**	**SE**	***p***
Predictor variables (Outcome: composite satisfaction)	Positive emotional disclosure	-.026	.063	.684	-.041	.065	.534
	Negative emotional disclosure	-.055	.057	.338	-.050	.059	.397
	Positive informational disclosure	.080	.064	.209	.080	.065	.218
	Negative informational disclosure	-.017	.064	.794	-.033	.067	.622
	Question asking	.176	.052	.001	.231	.055	.000
	Receive emotional support	**.149**	**.048**	**.002**	**.119**	**.051**	**.020**
	Receive informational support	**.193**	**.044**	**.000**	**.186**	**.045**	**.000**
	Posts between thread starter posts 1 and 2	.227	.038	.000	.205	.039	.000
	Positive emo disclosure X Receive emo support				**.043**	**.056**	**.447**
	Negative emo disclosure X Receive emo support				**.003**	**.047**	**.949**
	Positive info disclosure X Receive emo support				**-.009**	**.059**	**.881**
	Negative info disclosure X Receive emo support				**.056**	**.055**	**.307**
	Positive emo disclosure X Receive info support				**.008**	**.058**	**.894**
	Negative emo disclosure X Receive info support				**-.022**	**.048**	**.644**
	Positive info disclosure X Receive info support				**-.012**	**.054**	**.826**
	Negative info disclosure X Receive info support				**-.034**	**.054**	**.533**
	Question asking X Receive emo support				**-.097**	**.041**	**.019**
	Question asking X Receive info support				**.073**	**.046**	**.107**
	Constant	.476	.072	.000	.432	.076	.000
Selection variables (Selection: Having a second post in the thread)	Has profile	.244	.078	.002	.221	.077	.004
	Post count before thread	.005	.042	.899	.002	.040	.965
	Positive emotional disclosure	.131	.067	.050	.123	.066	.061
	Negative emotional disclosure	.098	.059	.098	.098	.059	.095
	Positive informational disclosure	.073	.066	.265	.081	.065	.213
	Negative informational disclosure	.132	.064	.039	.131	.064	.039
	Question asking	.130	.052	.013	.131	.052	.011
	Receive emotional support	-.059	.050	.232	-.065	.049	.189
	Receive informational support	.049	.047	.296	.046	.046	.323
	Constant	.269	.056	.000	.282	.056	.000

Table 4: Heckman selection models predicting composite satisfaction in a follow-up post ($N = 638$) from self-disclosure and question asking in the thread starting post, and receiving emotional and informational support in the first reply post. Model 1 includes only main effects, while Model 2 includes main effects and interactions. Effects in bold pertain to RQ1 and RQ2. Models 1 and 2 include selection models that predict whether a thread starter would have a follow-up post. The Likelihood Ratio test shows the selection and prediction equations were not independent. Model 1 LR test of indep. eqns. $x^2 = 10.51$ ($p = 0.0012$). Model 2 LR test of indep. eqns. $x^2 = 12.17$ ($p = 0.0005$).

ICCs for self-disclosure and question asking. Units of analysis were the same as Study 1, except that Turker ratings for seeking emotional and informational support in thread starting posts were replaced with Turker ratings for self-disclosure and question asking. For example, the thread starting post in the example provided in Study 1 methods has the following Turker ratings: positive emotional self-disclosure = 1, negative emotional self-disclosure = 1, positive informational self-disclosure = 1.2, negative informational self-disclosure = 2.3, asking question = 6.17.

Results

Heckman models were also employed for analysis. Table 4 presents Heckman models that predict expressed satisfaction from speech act variables in thread starting posts and support received in community replies. The number of community reply posts between thread starters' first and second posts was again included as a control predictor. Model 1 presents main effects of predictors, and Model 2 presents main and interaction effects. The dependent variable in both models is the composite satisfaction in thread starters' follow-up post in a thread. Models 1 and 2 in Table 4 also contain selection models which predict if a thread starter would have a second post to a thread from the selection variables of whether the thread starter created a profile on the site (*Has profile*), the number of posts by the thread starter before she posted her thread starting post (*Post count before thread*), question asking and four kinds of self-disclosure in thread starting posts, and receiving emotional and informational support in first replies. Variables included in the Heckman models in Table

4 (except *Has profile*) were centered and standardized (*Posts between thread starter posts 1 and 2*, and *Post count before thread* were log transformed). Refer to Table 4 selection models for significant and not significant predictors of a thread starter having a follow-up post in a thread.

Predicting expressed satisfaction

Heckman analyses with behavioral speech acts (Models 1 and 2, Table 4) were very similar to Study 1 findings. Regarding main effects, users expressed more satisfaction when they received either emotional or informational support (RQ1). They also expressed more satisfaction when they asked questions in their thread starting posts and when they received more replies. There was no support for a matching hypothesis when thread starters expressed speech acts that elicit emotional support (i.e., no interactions between any type of self-disclosure type in thread starting posts and getting either emotional or informational support in first replies (RQ2)). There was support for the matching hypothesis when users asked questions. They were less satisfied with the emotional support they received after asking questions than the emotional support they received without asking questions ($b = -.097$, $p < .02$). However, they were not more satisfied with informational support following questions than not following questions ($b = .073$, $p < .11$).

DISCUSSION

This research sheds light on what makes social support effective and how these processes unfold in a large online breast cancer support community. We addressed gaps in previous work by collecting quantitative, independent measures of seeking support, receiving support, and reactions to support. Our findings were very similar for two ways of operationalizing support elicitation: direct judgments of seeking social support (Study 1) and judgments of behavioral speech acts that typically elicit support (Study 2).

Regarding RQ1, users expressed more satisfaction the more they received either emotional or informational support. This suggests that judges perceive that receiving emotional and informational support is beneficial for online breast cancer support users, at least for brief exchanges. However, the results also suggest that in some situations, women's satisfaction depended on what they were seeking in the first place. Specifically, matching was associated with more satisfaction when women were seeking informational support but not emotional support.

When users sought emotional support, they were equally satisfied when they received either emotional or informational support in return. Our findings diverge from Cutrona et al. who found that the match between emotional disclosure and emotional support positively influenced reactions toward partners' sensitivity [8].

However, receiving emotional support was not always satisfying in this online cancer support community. Both studies demonstrate a mismatch effect: when women sought informational support or asked questions and received emotional support in return, they were less satisfied with the support than under other conditions in which they received emotional support. This result is analogous to Reynolds and Perrin's findings that mismatched support had a negative relationship to psychosocial functioning in women with breast cancer [16]. However, this finding is inconsistent with arguments in the couples support literature that providing emotional support is a good support strategy in general, regardless of what someone sought [e.g., 9].

Moreover, Study 1 is consistent with a matching hypothesis when people were seeking informational support: when women in this community sought informational support and then received it, they were more satisfied with the support than when they got informational support under other circumstances. These findings consistent with matching for informational support diverge from the findings of Smithson et al., where requesting advice on SharpTalk (i.e., seeking informational support) appeared to be a strategy to elicit empathy from the community and a springboard for the thread starters to talk more about their issues [22]. Our results also suggest that just as matching needed and gotten emotional support is beneficial in everyday life of younger people [28], matching sought and received informational support might be beneficial in exchanges among users in online breast cancer support.

Thus, our findings contribute a piece to the puzzle about when support matching is beneficial, but differ from previous work where different populations, definitions of matching, and outcome measures were used. One of the most interesting results of our research is that seeking emotional support did not moderate the effects of receiving social support, particularly the lack of a matching effect between seeking and getting emotional support on satisfaction. One explanation could be that seeking emotional support might be based on longer-term needs than seeking answers to questions [26], requiring more time for support matching to occur. Another explanation is that when seeking emotional support, it might be that just being responded to (receiving either emotional or informational support) is sufficient to feel recognized and supported in online breast cancer support communities. That is, it might be the act, rather than the content, that signals support.

For instance, in the following example with Turker ratings, the user is seeking more emotional support than informational support in her thread starting post, receives more informational support than emotional support in the first reply (the two community replies after the first reply are not shown), and has a composite satisfaction score that is above the mean composite satisfaction score.

Thread starting post (seek emotional support = 5.6; seek informational support = 3.2; positive emotional self-disclosure = 1.3; negative emotional self-disclosure = 4.5; positive informational self-disclosure = 2.6; negative informational self-disclosure = 5.2; asking question = 4.83):

This is more a question for my psychological health than for any other thing. My five years on tamoxifen will be finished in April and i will place myself into menopause so I can switch to an AI (haven't decided whether to begin with lupron or go immediately for the ooph). I am experiencing a lot of anxiety about the double issue of both menopause and beginning an AI. I am not scared of menopause -- I experienced it with chemopause for a bit and it wasn't that bad for me, also its inevitable, I'm 47 years of age. But I am scared of the side effects of sopping up all the remaining estrogen in addition to sudden menopause. My gynecologist, who is also a surgeon and takes out many ovaries, claims that there won't be many extra SEs from the AI. My onc is less optimistic. Anything someone could say to make me feel better about this, I would welcome. I am especially nervous about the sexual side effects and also, since I am a runner, the outcome on my joints.

First community reply post (receive emotional support = 1.2; receive informational support = 4.4):

I've had many joint problems from AIs that I haven't had from only menopause. The AIs tend to cause many tendon problems, and that's what's been aggravating my hip and wrists. From the literature, it's not certain if these tendon problems are reversible or not...great.

Menopause hasn't been my favorite experience. But it's doable. I haven't been plagued by hot flashes, but certainly less libido, belly fat, and vaginal atrophy.

Some individuals have more issues with one brand of AI than a different one. Arimidex crippled me, Femara seemed not problematic, and Aromasin has hurt my hip and wrists, but not as intensely as Arimidex did...

[User name omitted for privacy]

Thread starter's second post to the thread (composite satisfaction = 5.43):

Thanks ladies. Very reassuring.

Future work should therefore examine whether the quantity of feedback matters more when seeking emotional or informational support.

Limitations

The main limitation of this work is that all measures of support sought, support received, and expressed satisfaction were made by judges who were not participants in the cancer support community. Future work would benefit from acquiring measures from support group participants. Other limitations include that only first replies to thread starting posts were coded, and not all posts in a given thread were included in analyses, which may not have fully captured thread complexity. We did, however, control for an important aspect of thread structure that positively influenced satisfaction in both studies: the number of community reply posts between thread starters' first and second posts. Our studies also only examined the satisfaction of users who started threads. However, given that no posts come before a thread starting post in a thread, this is the best place to measure support initially sought, and our Heckman models controlled for whether users came back to post a second time. Lastly, we only studied one disease (breast cancer) that impacts mostly older women, and therefore support group dynamics might differ for different diseases, ages, and gender.

Design implications and future work

Using machine learning and survival analysis, Wang et al. discovered that linguistic emotional support encountered by users was linked with elevated commitment to an online breast cancer support community, but linguistic informational support did not greatly impact user commitment [26]. Since users express satisfaction in their language, a machine learning model could also be built to measure the level of satisfaction in all posts in an online support community. Thus, expressed user satisfaction could be monitored by a machine learning model in real time and across time as users post, and facilitators and/or relevant community members could be alerted to provide feedback to users flagged as dissatisfied. Future work on satisfaction in online health support would also profit from an analysis of whether linguistically expressed satisfaction predicts membership commitment.

ACKNOWLEDGMENTS

This research was supported by NSF grant IIS-0968485 and the CUPS Doctoral Training Program Fellowship. We thank Carolyn Rosé, Miaomiao Wen, Dan Tasse, Jeffrey Rzeszotarski, and our reviewers for helpful comments.

REFERENCES

1. Anderson, C.M., Martin, M.M., and Riddle, B.L. Small group relational satisfaction scale: development, reliability and validity. *Communication Studies 52*, 3 (2001), 220-233.
2. Bambina, A. *Online social support: the interplay of social networks and computer-mediated communication.* Cambria Press, NY, 2007.
3. Barak, A., and Gluck-Ofri, O. Degree and Reciprocity of Self-Disclosure in Online Forums. *CyberPsychology & Behavior 10*, 3 (2007), 407-417.
4. Buhrmester, M., Kwang, T., and Gosling, S.D. Amazon's Mechanical Turk: A New Source of Inexpensive, Yet High-Quality, Data? *Perspectives on Psychological Science 6*, 1 (2011), 3-5.
5. Chou, W.S., Liu, B., Post, S. and Hesse, B. Health-related Internet use among cancer survivors: data from

the Health Information National Trends Survey, 2003–2008. *Journal of Cancer Survivorship*, (2011), 1-8.

6. Cohen, S., and Wills, T.A. Stress, social support, and the buffering hypothesis. *Psychological Bulletin 98*, 2 (1985), 310-357.
7. Cutrona, C.E. Stress and social support – in search of optimal matching. *Journal of Social and Clinical Psychology 9*, (1990), 3-14.
8. Cutrona, C.E., Shaffer, P.A., Wesner, K.A., and Gardner, K.A. Optimally Matching Support and Perceived Spousal Sensitivity. *Journal of Family Psychology 21*, (2007), 754-758.
9. Cutrona, C.E., and Suhr, J.A. Controllability of Stressful Events and Satisfaction With Spouse Support Behaviors. *Communication Research 19*, (1992), 154-174.
10. Hecht, M.L. Measures of communication satisfaction. *Human Communication Research 4*, 4 (1978), 350-368.
11. Heckman, J. Sample selection bias as a specification error. *Econometirica 47*, 1 (1979), 153-162.
12. Helgeson, V.S., and Cohen, S. Long-term effects of educational and peer discussion group interventions on adjustment to breast cancer. *Health Psychology 20*, 5 (2001), 387-392.
13. Helgeson, V.S., Cohen, S., Schultz, R., and Yasko, J. Group support interventions for women with breast cancer: Who benefits from what? *Health Psychology 19*, 2 (2000), 107-114.
14. Holt-Lunstad, J., Smith, T.B., and Layton, J.B. Social relationships and mortality risk: a meta-analytic review. *PLoS Medicine 7*, 7 (2010), e1000316.
15. Rains, S.A., and Young, V.A. Meta-Analysis of Research on Formal Computer-Mediated Support Groups: Examining Group Characteristics and Health Outcomes. *Human Communication Research 35*, 3 (2009), 309-336.
16. Reynolds, J.S., and Perrin, N.A. Mismatches in Social Support and Psychosocial Adjustment to Breast Cancer. *Health Psychology 23*, (2004), 425-430.
17. Ridings, C.M., and Gefen, D. Virtual Community Attraction: Why People Hang Out Online. *Journal of Computer-Mediated Communication 10*, 1 (2004).
18. Rimer, B.K., Lyons, E.J., Ribisl, K.M., Bowling, J.M., Golin, C.E., Forlenza, M.J., and Meier, A. How new subscribers use cancer-related online mailing lists. *J Med Internet Res 7*, 3 (2005), e32.
19. Rodgers, S., and Chen, Q. Internet Community Group Participation: Psychosocial Benefits for Women with Breast Cancer. *Journal of Computer-Mediated Communication 10*, 4 (2005).
20. Ruggiero, T.E. Uses and Gratifications Theory in the 21st Century. *Mass Communication & Society 3*, 1 (2000), 3-37.
21. Shrout, P.E., Bolger, N., Iida, M., Burke, C., Gleason, M.E.J., and Lane, S.P. The Effects of Daily Support Transactions During Acute Stress: Results from a Diary Study of Bar Exam Preparation. In K. Sullivan and J. Davila (Eds.), *Support Processes in Intimate Relationships* (175-199). Oxford University Press, New York, NY, 2010.
22. Smithson, J., Sharkey, S., Hewis, E., Jones, R., Emmens, T., Ford, T., and Owens, C. Problem presentation and responses on an online forum for young people who self-harm. *Discourse Studies 13*, 4 (2011), 487-501.
23. Snow, R., O'Connor, B., Jurafsky, D., and Ng, A.Y. Cheap and Fast---But is it Good? Evaluating Non-Expert Annotations for Natural Language Tasks. In *Proc. EMNLP 2008*, Association for Computational Linguistics (2008), 254-263.
24. Taylor, S.E. Social Support: A Review. In H.S. Friedman (Ed.), *The Oxford Handbook of Health Psychology* (189-214). Oxford University Press, New York, NY, 2011.
25. Uchino, B. Understanding the links between social support and physical health: A life-span perspective with emphasis on the separability of perceived and received support. *Perspectives on Psychological Science 4*, 3 (2009), 236-255.
26. Wang, Y.-C., Kraut, R., and Levine, J.M. To Stay or Leave? The Relationship of Emotional and Informational Support to Commitment in Online Health Support Groups. In *Proc. CSCW 2012*, ACM Press (2012), 833-842.
27. Wang, Y.-C., Kraut, R., and Levine, J.M. How to Get Support? A Computer-Aided Content Analysis Approach to Examine Online Social Support Dynamics. (in preparation).
28. Wolff, J.K., Schmiedek, F., Brose, A., and Lindenberger, U. Physical and emotional well-being and the balance of needed and received emotional support: Age differences in a daily diary study. *Social Science & Medicine 91*, (2013), 67-75.

Between Theory and Practice: Bridging Concepts in HCI Research

Peter Dalsgaard, Christian Dindler
Center for Participatory IT
Department of Aesthetics and Communication
Aarhus University
{dalsgaard, dindler}@cavi.au.dk

ABSTRACT

We present the notion of 'bridging concepts' as a particular form of intermediary knowledge in HCI research, residing between theory and practice. We argue that bridging concepts address the challenge of facilitating exchange between theory and practice in HCI, and we compare it to other intermediary forms of knowledge such as strong concepts and conceptual constructs. We propose that bridging concepts have three defining constituents: a theoretical foundation, a set of design articulations and a range of exemplars that demonstrate the scope and potential of their application. These constituents specify how bridging concepts, as a form of knowledge, are accountable to both theory and practice. We present an analysis of the concept of 'peepholes' as an example of a bridging concept aimed at spurring user curiosity and engagement.

Author Keywords

Experience-oriented design; Interaction design theory; Engagement; Analytical frameworks.

ACM Classification Keywords

H.5.2 [Information Interfaces and Presentation]: User Interfaces – Theory and Methods, User-Centered Design.

INTRODUCTION

The notion of design thinking - i.e. the modes of understanding and acting upon design challenges that characterize designers - has become a topic of much discussion in the CHI community in recent years. While a number of contributions and discussions have developed our understanding of design thinking, there is also a consensus that there is still a need to clarify and articulate (e.g. [28]) what constitutes design thinking, and indeed to discuss how we may arrive at such articulations (e.g. [40]). There are different ways of adding to the discourse of design thinking. Among these, one can draw more or less directly upon existing theoretical positions (e.g. cognitive psychology), 'import', in the terminology of Rogers [39], and develop existing positions and theories within the frame of HCI (e.g. activity theory [22]) or one can develop theoretical constructs from design practice and examples of interactive systems (e.g. design patterns [42]). One of the persistent challenges for interaction design researchers and practitioners is that there often seems to be a gap between theory and the specific design instance; by nature, theories are abstract, since they must account for a variety of instances, and thus they can be difficult to translate and operationalize in relation to the particular design situation. In this article, we are interested in exploring knowledge constructs that exist in the middle ground between theory and practice. Some of the wider known concepts and forms of knowledge in HCI such as patterns and heuristics occupy this space, arguably because they draw upon a wider set of input than the specific design situation, yet are operational and aimed at helping designers address the specific situation.

CHI 2014, April 26 - May 01 2014, Toronto, ON, Canada

ACM 978-1-4503-2473-1/14/04…$15.00.
http://dx.doi.org/10.1145/2556288.2557342

In this paper, we introduce the notion of 'bridging concepts' as an intermediary form of knowledge residing between abstract theory and design practice and we argue that bridging concepts are distinguished by their ability to facilitate exchange between theory and practice. Articulating knowledge in the form of bridging concepts, prompts us to formulate knowledge in a way that specifies the accountability to both theory and practice. While continuous exchange between theory and practice is important in academia in general, it is arguably even more so for HCI. Within HCI, much theory has been imported from other more established disciplines such as psychology and sociology [39]. For interaction design researchers and practitioners, this prompts constant articulations of how and to what extent newly imported theories are useful. To complicate matters, the subject matter of research in HCI – ever-evolving interactive interfaces and reconfigurations of human-computer relations - is under constant development. This accentuates the need for continuous reflection on how new materials, interaction styles and products challenge our theories, and in turn how theories can be employed to understand these new developments. Bridging concepts provide one way of facilitating this exchange by articulating the knowledge construct both in terms of its ties to theory and particular design exemplars. Specifically, we propose that bridging concepts are composed of three constituents: a theoretical grounding, a series of design articulations and a set of exemplars that embody the properties of the concept, reflecting the span from theory and practice.

In the following sections we begin by positioning and developing bridging concepts in relation to existing intermediary forms of knowledge that have been discussed in the CHI community. We then present the concept of 'peepholes' as an example of a bridging concept and analyse it in terms of theoretical grounding, design articulations and a selection of exemplars. We conclude the paper by providing two additional brief examples of established concepts that may be considered as bridging concepts, and then discuss more broadly the potentials and applications of bridging concepts.

We consider the main contributions of the paper to the CHI community to be 1) the presentation and discussion of bridging concepts, and 2) the development of peepholes as a particular instance of bridging concepts, including theoretical foundations, design articulations and exemplars from design practice. The intended audience for the paper is therefore researchers focusing on the development of the discourse on interaction design and HCI research and articulation of new forms of knowledge within this domain, as well as practitioners and researchers within the field of experience-oriented design.

INTERMEDIARY FORMS OF KNOWLEDGE IN HCI

Recently, Höök and Löwgren [21] introduced the notion of 'strong concepts' as an intermediate-level knowledge construct in the space between theory and design particulars; the notion of strong concept was also the subject of a debate at CHI 2013. In their words, "Strong concepts are design elements abstracted beyond particular instances which have the potential to be appropriated by designers and researchers to extend their repertoires and enable new particular instantiations" [21 p. 5]. Strong concepts are thus specifically developed to occupy the middle ground by accounting for recurring phenomena in interaction design, and to offer a richer understanding of said phenomena by looking at their commonalities. As an example, the authors employ this approach to discuss 'social navigation' as a strong concept - a concept which can be found in a variety of different forms in existing systems and services, and which is now articulated on the basis of recurring aspects and qualities. This approach, which bears family resemblance to other knowledge constructs such as design patterns, can be said to be inductive, in that it draws from particulars to form a more generalizable concept. Höök and Löwgren consider their work on strong concepts to be an extension of Stolterman and Wiberg's [41] 'conceptual constructs', a wider definition of forms of knowledge that occupy this middle ground between theory and practice. In our view, Stolterman and Wiberg's conceptual constructs differ markedly from Höök and Löwgren's strong concepts in that "the point of departure is conceptual/theoretical rather than empirical" [41 p. 98] and in that Stolterman & Wiberg's objective is theoretical advancement, or in their words developing "innovative concepts that lead to intellectual development through definitions, conceptual constructs, and theories." [41 p. 112]. One example of such an innovative concept is the Dynabook [25], which was never developed as a final product, but has inspired a wide array of subsequent research.

Stolterman and Wiberg thus differ radically from Höök and Löwgren both in terms of the approach to developing intermediary forms of knowledge and the objectives for doing so: strong concepts are primarily developed bottom-up or inductively with the main purpose of generating knowledge that can be employed in design practice, whereas conceptual constructs are primarily developed top-down with the main purpose of enriching the theoretical foundations of HCI. In light of our argument for the need for concepts that can mediate between theory and practice, the two forms of knowledge represent opposite positions, which we seek to connect: The two sets of concepts serve different purposes for different audiences, in that strong concepts primarily support design practitioners in developing products, whereas conceptual constructs serve to help design researchers make theoretical advancements. This is an important distinction to make, both in regards to understanding where the concepts emerge from, how they can meaningfully be employed, and on which grounds they should be evaluated.

In a wider perspective, intermediary forms of knowledge can emerge from design research in several ways. In some instances, they emerge from examination of concepts informed and inspired by theory; in other cases, they emerge through developing specific cases and abstracting knowledge from them; and finally, they may emerge through both these processes concurrently. Koskinen et al. [26] conceive of 'Labs' as constructive design research approach in which theoretical concepts serves to inform and inspire the design of novel artefacts, which in turn come to embody the concept. Often several artefacts are created to examine the potential of the concept. Alexander's 'patterns' [1] also occupy a middle ground between practice and theory, but stand out from Labs since they are developed from recurring, successful examples in practice with the intent of supporting design practitioners in finding and combining well functioning patterns, which can be assembled and developed to form a new artefact. Zimmerman's 'framing constructs' [44] are similarly developed from recurring design patterns, but seek a stronger link to theory by examining how theory can be operationalized as part of the product, which in turn can also lead to new understandings about applying theory in design processes. Bowers' 'annotated portfolios' [2] present design cases and seek to abstract knowledge from them in order to create intermediary level knowledge, as design practitioners simultaneously document and reflect upon connections between different examples of their work.

We do not consider one way of generating intermediary knowledge as being inherently better than the other ones - e.g. operationalizing theory through concepts [26] versus abstracting concepts from practice [1, 19, 44]; indeed, we consider both forms crucial to the development of the discourse on design research. It is in this light that we present and discuss bridging concepts as a particular form of intermediary knowledge.

BRIDGING CONCEPTS AS A PARTICULAR FORM OF INTERMEDIARY KNOWLEDGE

Bridging concepts are a form of intermediary knowledge distinguished by their ability to facilitate exchange both ways between overarching theory and practice, rather than by being developed from theory or practice or with the specific aim of informing either theory or practice. As a knowledge construct, a bridging concept can be developed in any of the ways discussed above, and can support movement from theory to design and vice versa. Our motivation for introducing the notion of bridging concepts is primarily that it can shed light on how exchanges back and forth between overarching theory and practice can be facilitated.

In relation to the accounts of intermediary forms of knowledge outlined above, the concept thus stands out in that it can be developed from both theory and practice – often in a continuous process of theoretical and practice-based explorations, which is characteristic of many experimental design projects – and that it can subsequently be employed to both inform specific interaction design projects and to further develop theoretical understandings of the field of HCI. As such, bridging concepts are akin to Höök and Löwgren's strong concepts, in that they can be inspired by significant examples of existing installations, 'exemplars' in the terminology of Krippendorff [27], but stand out from strong concepts since they can simultaneously be developed from theory, rather than being predominantly abstracted from design practice. As such, the theoretically grounded development of a bridging concept is more in line with Stolterman and Wiberg's [41] conceptual constructs. However, it departs from the definition of the conceptual construct in that it is a generative concept also intended to inspire, inform and guide design practice, rather than one primarily focused on theoretical advancement. We have chosen to label this form of knowledge a bridging concept, since it is developed to bridge the gap from theory to interaction design practice. This does not mean that a bridging concept is detached from practice. Indeed, in our view it must be directed towards concrete issues in interaction design practice and should be evaluated on how well it ultimately helps us understand and act on these issues. A bridging concept can thus draw upon both existing exemplars from interaction design practice, as well as upon one or more strands of theory.

	Conceptual constructs	Strong concepts	Bridging concepts
Primary origins	Theory	Design cases	Inspired by exemplars as well as theory
Primary intent	Theoretical advancements	Informing design practice	Facilitating exchange between theory and practice

Table 1: Comparison of the roots and objectives of conceptual constructs [41], strong concepts [21] and bridging concepts.

Table 1 offers a rough overview of the departure points and objectives of conceptual constructs, strong concepts, and bridging concepts, respectively. There are nuances that escape this rough categorization. As an example, conceptual constructs may well contribute to design practice, even if that is not the primary intent; and strong concepts can be theoretically substantiated, even if developed from design cases. As such, both conceptual constructs and strong concepts can potentially be developed to serve as bridging concepts. We must stress that we do not consider bridging concepts to be a critique of conceptual constructs, strong concepts, or the other intermediary forms of knowledge outlined above. Rather, we consider it a complimentary form of knowledge residing in the space between theories and specific design instances; in the same vein, Höök and Löwgren [21] point out that other concepts such as design patterns and heuristics can also be considered part of this middle ground between theory and practice (Figure 1).

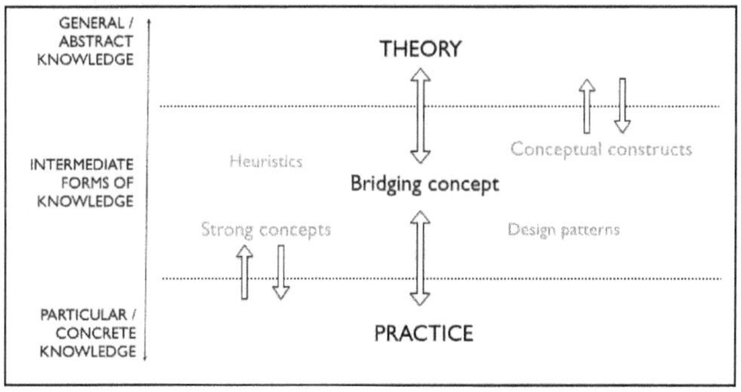

Figure 1: Bridging concepts as one form of intermediary knowledge bridging between theory and practice.

Summing up, a bridging concept has the following features:

- It inhabits the middle ground between theory and practice

- It is accountable to both practical exemplars, the parameters that shape the concept (articulations) and theoretical grounding.

- Its purpose is to bridge and span the gap between theory and practice and thereby unveiling and articulating untried design opportunities and potential theoretical advancements.

We propose that bridging concepts, in order to serve as bridges, are composed by three constituents which can help interaction design practitioners and researchers understand their grounding and potential and offer advise on how to employ them in practice. First, bridging concepts have a theoretical grounding. In the case of the peepholes bridging concept, we draw primarily on pragmatism and philosophy of technology. Second, drawing on exemplars as well as theoretical insights, bridging concepts can be illuminated through the formulation of design articulations. Inspired by Krogh and Petersen [29], we use the term 'design articulations' to refer to the parameters that are important in expressing the qualities of a concept. Third, bridging concepts may be explored through exemplars that clearly illustrate critical aspects of the concept. Exemplars may illustrate similar salient aspects of a particular concept or may be critical in the sense that they delineate the boundaries of the concept.

PEEPHOLES: A BRIDGING CONCEPT FOR UNDERSTANDING AND DEVELOPING ENGAGING INTERACTIONS

Having outlined the anatomy of bridging concepts in general, we will now present and discuss the notion of peepholes as a particular example of a bridging concept. In keeping with the properties of bridging concepts outlined above, we first explore a theoretical grounding of peepholes, which builds upon pragmatist philosophy. This constituent ties the intermediary concept to theory. Second, we explore design articulations for the concept of peepholes. By design articulations we refer to the salient parameters that designers can manipulate to change the interaction and experience of an artefact. We couple these articulations to the theoretical grounding. And third, using the design articulations, we analyse design exemplars that are critical in terms of showing the potential and scope of the concept of peepholes in terms of practice and theory. We have previously addressed the notion of peepholes in a design case study [11] and a preliminary discussion of the design of peephole installations [6]. Here we focus on peepholes as an example of a bridging concept.

By peepholes we refer to interactive artefacts that provide a limited view into a larges space. Peepholes play on the tension between what is hidden and what is revealed to spark engagement. In the physical world, keyholes or cracks in a fence provide the viewer with a limited view to a larger space and appeal to our inquisitive nature providing us with views into hidden, secret or even forbidden spaces. Within architecture and art, peepholes are well known as a means for enticing the curious viewer. Architects use light, acoustics and physical structures to suggest that the space holds places that are not immediately visible but can be found if people actively explore. From art and architecture to interaction design, the qualities of peepholes are no less attainable, as the malleable qualities emerging from the fusion between physical and digital materials provide designers with a broad palette of opportunities. Peepholes may be moveable, change size, provide clues of orientation and the universe to which they provide a glimpse may be changed and subject to interaction.

Within the CHI community, the notion of peepholes has been explored to some extent. Most often, peephole interaction is used as a means for providing views into large information spaces. As early as the 1990's, scholars at PARC explored the concept of portholes as means of supporting awareness in distributed work. Early efforts also explored portholes in the form of palmtop computer used to access information in ubiquitous computing environments [17]. More recently, several authors have used the similar concepts of peephole displays, peephole interaction or peephole pointing where studies have explored visualization and interaction techniques for providing users views of large information spaces (e.g. [24, 33, 38, 43]). In these studies, the peephole displays are most often realized using various handheld devices that are mapped onto larger surfaces or information spaces. Common to these contributions is a focus on providing users with an effective and manageable way of accessing large information spaces of various kinds. A notable exception is provided by Gaver et al. [19], who discuss the design and rationale behind the Drift Table – a coffee table with a small screen in the middle providing a moveable birds eye view of a map. The authors use the installation as a means for exploring how technology can support ludic engagement. This work most clearly resonates with our idea of the peepholes concept in this paper, in that it examines a particular form of interaction, which inspires the user to explore and discover the content of the installation. The concept of peepholes presented here is thus situated within the HCI discourse on user experience that reaches beyond usability and effectiveness exploring aesthetic, playful and engaging qualities of interaction (e.g. [31, 32, 37]). At a glance, the concept of peepholes appears similar to well-established HCI notions such as affordances in the sense of providing an invitation for people to interact. However, where affordances typically refer to qualities that clearly indicate to the user what she or he should do and what results will be achieved, peepholes have a more voyeuristic character. They provide enticements and play on the tension between what is hidden and what is revealed. Their virtue is the way they spark imagination about what is hidden beyond the immediate scope of our senses. This difference in perspective resonates with Overbeeke and Wensveen [36], who distinguish between affordances and 'irresistibles', stressing the qualities of attraction and temptation rather than functional perception.

Theoretical grounding of peepholes

Our conception of peepholes builds on pragmatist philosophy, specifically the works of John Dewey. Dewey is considered one of the founding fathers of pragmatism and developed his position in an extensive range of books and papers from the 1880es to the 1950es. We primarily refer to his later work on art, experience, inquiry, and technology [12, 13, 14, 15].

Pragmatist aesthetics have been a source of inspiration for several contributions to HCI, especially in the domain of experience-oriented aspects of interaction design. Among others, Forlizzi and Battarbee [18] developed their work on understanding experience in interactive systems on Dewey's conception of experience, Petersen et al. [37] drew on Dewey and contemporary pragmatist Richard Shusterman in their exploration of aesthetic interaction, and McCarthy and Wright's [32] work on technology as experience is developed from Dewey and Bakhtin. Our conception of peepholes is inspired by these works, as well as Dalsgaard's [5, 8, 9] notion of inquisitive use, which explores the Deweyan notion of conflict as a starting point for engaging experiences, a proposition that resonates with key characteristics of peepholes.

We draw upon five concepts from Deweyan pragmatism in our development of the peepholes concept, namely situatedness, conflict, inquiry, technology, and the intertwined nature of thinking and doing. Due to space constraints, we will only offer a rough outline of these concepts, focusing on the implications it has for the design, use and experience of interactive systems.

Situatedness

All human experience and action is inherently dependent on, and must be understood in relation to, the situations in which we find ourselves. According to Dewey, "we never experience nor form judgments about objects and events in isolation, but only in connection with a contextual whole." [16 p. 66-67]. If we wish to understand how a user will perceive of, and potentially interact with, an interactive system, we must consider not just the relation between user and system, but also the factors of the situation, including the physical space, socio-cultural aspects, other people, and other forms of physical objects and technologies, all of which may influence the user-system relation.

Conflict

Dewey proposes that conflict "stirs us to observation and memory. It instigates to invention. It shocks us out of sheep-like passivity, and sets us at noting and contriving. Not that it always effects this result; but that conflict is a sine qua non of reflection and ingenuity." [12 p. 207]. In other words, the perception of conflict or tension in a situation is what prompts us to investigate, seek new understandings, and potentially try to overcome the conflict. For designers of interactive systems, this presents conflict and tension as elements that may be employed to prompt action and reflection with users.

Inquiry

While many aspects of our lives are guided by routine, inquiry is the process by which we seek to alter a situation when a form of conflict arises. Inquiry is aimed a transforming or rearranging one or more elements of a situation so that it makes sense and/or resolves tensions. A person facing a conflict will often draw upon a range of resources at hand, including a variety of technologies and work with other people to change the situation so that the conflict is resolved. For the design of interactive systems, this prompts designers to consider both how the process of inquiry can be supported and which elements may be included in guided inquiries.

Technology

Most human activity is mediated by some form of technology. In a pragmatist perspective, technology has a dual nature in that it is both frames how our perception of the world and augments our potential for changing the world. For good or bad, technologies influences the way we make sense of our surroundings. Some technologies do this quite directly, e.g. sensors that make things visible to us. Others technologies do so less directly by inviting us to focus on the aspects in our surroundings that we can act on, hence the phrase "if all you have is a hammer, everything looks like a nail." This conception of technology invites designers of interactive systems to consider not only how a system may support specific actions, but also how it may frame the users sense making and perception of options.

The intertwined nature of thinking and doing

Deweyan pragmatism proposes that thinking and doing are tightly interwoven, to the extent that distinguishing between the two is at times untenable. We form thoughts and hypotheses in response to events in the world, and often with an intended action in mind; and we often start acting in the world because it helps us think and examine potential futures. Sketching is a well-known example of the intertwined nature of thinking and doing in interaction design. This conception prompts designers of interactive systems to consider how the interplay between action and reflection may be scaffolded in a system.

Taken together, these pragmatist concepts has informed our definition of peepholes as a bridging concept: Peepholes are interfaces that seek to engage users and invite them to explore the content of a system by creating a tension between what is hidden and what is revealed. They frame users' perception of the content by providing initially limited access to it, while also hinting at the potential for access by offering means for exploring that which is hidden from plain sight. Peepholes thus rely on elements of conflict to spur engagement and inquisitive use.

Design articulations for peepholes

Building upon the theoretical foundations of peepholes, we propose that there are a series of issues that are of particular salience to designers of peephole installations.

The design articulations presented here are all concerned with the interaction gestalt [30], i.e. the way in which the interaction unfolds between user and system. The articulations serve to give an understanding of the parameters that give peepholes their particular qualities, and to prompt designers to put a particular effort into considering these aspects. It is for this reason that we address the dimensions as articulations, rather than e.g. heuristics or guidelines. In addition to being informed by theory, the articulations are also substantiated by our analysis of a range of peephole installations, three of which are outlined in the following section on peephole exemplars.

Manoeuvring between hidden and revealed

The central tension afforded by peepholes is the relationship between what is hidden and what is revealed. In the physical world, keyholes are fixed in their position and the scenery that they unveil is also typically stable. Interactive peephole installations must strike a balance between obscurity and revelation, and unlike static physical peepholes, this balance must be maintained throughout the user's interaction if the tension is to be intact. Thoughtful design of peephole interactions can both draw upon and support reciprocal processes of thinking and doing with users by striking the right balance. In some installations, a peephole strategy may be employed to attract people and subsequently be replaced by other means of engagement once users are drawn in, whereas other installations may maintain the peephole format throughout. Some peepholes have a fixed position and always provide a limited view into a particular world. Other peepholes however can be moved at the discretion of the user or may move automatically. Special consideration must be given to the potential for both framing the user's perception of the installation and offering means of altering it: How much is visible? How can the user manoeuvre and manipulate the viewpoint? How will further content be revealed through user input? An interactive system may provide a moveable peephole, whereas the scenery remains the same; or it present a fixed peephole while the scenery changes; or it may present dynamics in both peepholes and content. The manoeuvrability, then, can both be a quality of the peephole itself and of the scenery to which it provides a view.

Navigational clues

When there is a potential for interacting with a peephole, be it via dynamics in the peephole, the content, or both, designers must consider how they can provide navigational clues. The choice of navigational clues is an important one since is plays a major part in maintaining the tension between what is hidden and what is revealed. This can be a tricky affair and if navigational clues become extensive and the user consequently gains too much of an overview, the peephole looses its intrigue. On the other hand, too few navigational clues may leave the user frustrated to the extent that installation becomes unattractive.

Sensory qualities and modalities

In the physical world, peepholes are by definition visual. Interactive installations traditionally often rely on visual components as well, but they need not be limited to one sensory modality. They may involve more senses and/or forego the visual side entirely. To the extent that e.g. audio-based installations may draw upon the same tensions and strategies for intrigue and engagement as visually oriented installations, they may also be considered instances of peepholes. In many cases, designers may choose to combine different sensory modalities to promote user engagement. E.g. an installation may combine tangible and visual components (as is the case with *Tangible 3D Tabletop* which we shall return to). A combination of different sensory modalities can be used to reinforce a particular experience, and may also be employed to increase the tension by delivering intentionally contradictory messages, e.g. an audio track may invite the user to carry out certain actions, but the tangible and visual components can resist or delay user input so as to further up the stakes.

Metaphors for prompting inquisitive use

Analogue, physical peepholes embody a series of familiar affordances and constraints – we know what to expect from the peepholes themselves and to some extent we also know what to expect when we look through them. The same does not go for interactive peepholes, unless they quite directly mirror their analogue counterparts. Two important design decisions are therefore to determine how to present the peephole itself, and how to build up expectations about what can be experienced through it. One way of doing this is to create a metaphor that is familiar to users. This can establish an understanding of what to expect of the peephole as well as the content. However, as has been seen through the history of visual interfaces, users do not always correctly decipher metaphors, and incongruences between analogue and digital properties may cause metaphors to break down, potentially ruining the user experience. As is the case with combinations of different sensory modalities, designers can also intentionally use metaphors to build up expectations and then surprise users by breaking those expectations. The Out of Bounds installation [35] uses the metaphor of a flashlight, but when users shine the flashlight on a wall, they see through the wall into the next room.

Peephole exemplars

In order to demonstrate how the design articulations above may shape the qualities of peepholes, this section provides an analysis of five peephole installations. During our work on developing the concept of peepholes, we have identified a range of peephole installations, as well as taken part in the design of several. We have selected these five peephole installations because they illustrate how the concept may be employed across a range of use cases, and how different forms of interaction may support peephole interfaces.

Hydroscopes and Drift Table

The *Hydroscopes* installation, co-developed by the authors, was designed for a marine centre as part of an installation where visitors could construct their own fish using physical building blocks. The first part of the video accompanying this paper shows the Hydroscopes in use at the marine centre. Visitors could mix qualities from various species putting together different fins, bodies and heads to explore how various fish have different characteristics. Having constructed their fish, visitors could release them into a virtual ocean that was only visible in glimpse by pushing the Hydroscopes around the floor surface (figure 2). As visitors moved the hydroscopes, they could explore the fish created by other visitors.

Figure 2: Children push a Hydroscope to explore a virtual ocean. See also the accompanying video for demonstration.

The Hydroscopes employ a very direct metaphor, providing users the idea of life in the ocean being partially hidden beneath the surface, only visible through the Hydroscopes. The movement of the Hydroscopes is mapped directly onto the virtual ocean, so as to offer a clear navigational mapping between the peephole and the content. In terms of interaction, the Hydroscopes thus exemplify a peephole that is mobile in two dimensions. While the Hydroscopes are primarily visually oriented, small loudspeakers were imbedded in the casing providing an ocean soundscape.

The Hydroscopes resemble the aforementioned Drift Table (figure 3) in the sense of providing a limited visual view from above. In terms of interaction and metaphor they are however quite different. The Drift Table elegantly uses the weigh of everyday objects to steer the view. The metaphor is, by conscious choice, more ambiguous. While the view and the pace of the moving view may resemble a hot air balloon, the metaphor breaks down when using weights to change direction. Moreover, the view is scaled down in order to make the table more akin to a normal coffee table than a screen and also making navigation challenging. In terms of the attention to detail, the design of Drift Table reflects great care for supporting the experience of looking down at a landscape far below, using Fresnel lens to support the illusion of depth. Our point here is not to say that designers should opt for the most consistent metaphor, but to show how two relatively similar installations can be shaped very differently in terms of interaction qualities.

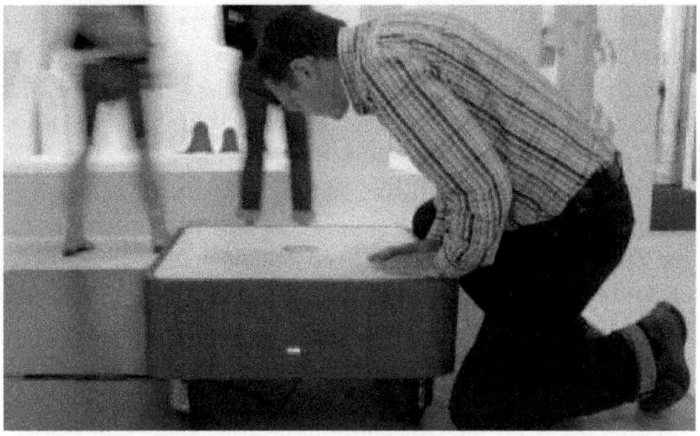

Figure 3: The Drift Table offering a small peephole view.

Tangible 3D Blueprints and Jurascopes

Tangible 3D Blueprints, an installation co-developed by the authors, combines tangible tabletop interaction with 3D projection in such a way that the tangible objects may be augmented with visual material corresponding to their physical shapes, positions, and orientation [7]. The second part of the video accompanying this paper shows the Tangible 3D Blueprints in use. A static two-dimensional floor plan is shown on the tabletop, and when a tangible is placed on the tabletop, it provides a three-dimensional view into a building (figure 4). This enables the user to examine aspects of the building that are not represented in the blueprint (e.g. height of walls), as well as enhancing some of those that are (e.g. textures and lighting).

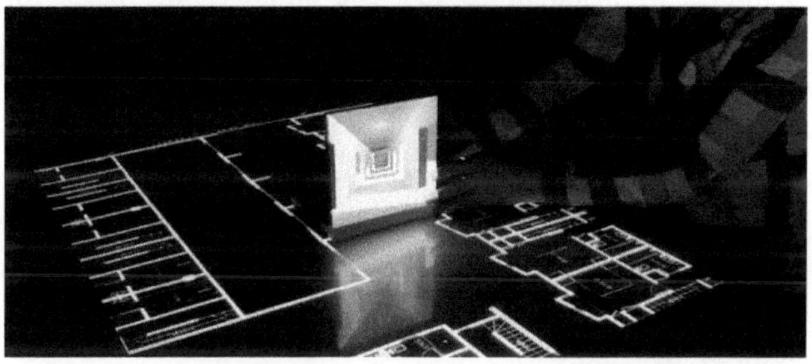

Figure 4: Tangible 3D Blueprints use tangible interaction and visual feedback to offer a peephole into a building blueprint. See also the accompanying video for a demonstration.

The Tangible 3D Blueprints installation is designed with the intent of offering users who are unfamiliar with engineering blueprints an alternative way of experiencing building plans so that they may contribute to co-design of future buildings. Contrary to the Hydroscopes, it provides very clear navigational clues in terms of the floor plan that provides clear bounds and orientation in the virtual building. While the tangible in itself does not build on a specific form of metaphor, the physical, spatial form in combination with the 2D blueprint provides an intuitive form of interaction and navigation.

The draw of the 3D tabletop is not so much that people wonder which room they are 'walking' into. Rather, the installation invites exploration by changing the sensory qualities from two- to three-dimensional visuals and providing an alternative point of view, which contains enough novel information to prompt users to explore the different parts of the building. As such, it builds up tension with the intent of making users understand and interact with the proposed building plans. For the purpose of this paper, the installation serves the purpose of showing the scope of the peephole concept since it can be considered a means to an end, i.e. informed participation in a co-design event. In this respect it differs from most of the other peephole installations we discuss, which can be considered discrete and self-contained. An example of such an installation is *Jurascopes* from the Museum of Natural History in Berlin. The two installations are similar in the sense that navigation is straightforward. The Jurascopes, however, provide peepholes in time as the skeletons come to life and materialize in their natural surrounding (figure 5).

Figur 5: Jurascopes use a binocular metaphor and offer a glimpse into the Jurassic era.

Listen Here!

Moving on from two exemplars that primarily employ tangible and visual sensory modalities, there are also examples of installations that use audio as the basis for peepholes. Similar to the keyhole as an archetypical peephole, the practice of eavesdropping shares many of these qualities. The eavesdropper is provided an auditory glimpse of private conversation, and just as the keyhole, the access is restricted. An example of an auditory peephole is the Listen Here! concept by Nicola Hume [20]. Here, a map is synchronized to microphones placed around the city and people can explore sounds from around the city using a stethoscope (figure 6).

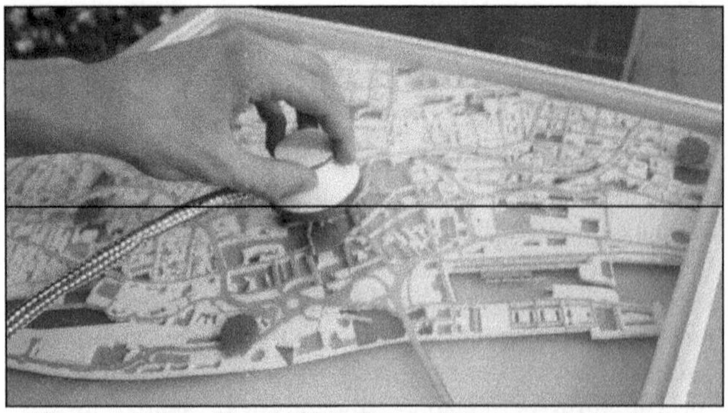

Figure 6: Listen Here! [20] offers auditory peepholes to live audio streams from urban locations.

Similar to the 3D tabletop, the Listen Here! concept is very clear in terms of navigational clues as red markers clearly indicate where microphones are placed. The combination of the stethoscope and the map is interesting as there are two layers to the installation. The stethoscope is a strong metaphor for listening to the sounds of a particular place, and at the same time, the map clearly indicates where to microphones are located. In a way, the red markers work as peepholes and the stethoscope is the device with which to access these. Contrary to the 3D tabletop and the Hydroscopes, the peepholes in the Listen Here! concept are not mobile. The user can move the stethoscope around the map but the peepholes remain in the same position. Rather the soundscape into which the user is provided a view is likely subject to change as people pass the microphones in the city.

OTHER EXAMPLES OF BRIDGING CONCEPTS: PERCEPTUAL CROSSING AND AFFORDANCES

We have presented and discussed peepholes at some length in order to give a detailed example of a bridging concept. However, there is a range of other existing concepts, which we consider to embody the characteristics of bridging concepts. We will briefly mention two such concepts: 'perceptual crossing' from the work of Deckers [10] and 'affordances'.

Perceptual crossing refers to the phenomenon that one person's perception influences a co-present person's perception and vice versa. It is "the interplay of perceiving while being perceived (...) We share a common space in which we can build a history in the course of our interaction." [10 p. 7] We will classify this as a bridging concept, since a) it is rooted in theory, specifically phenomenology of perception and ecological psychology; b) it is illustrated by a range of exemplars and analyses of interactions; c) it is developed as a model, which in turn results in d) a series of design considerations that can guide design practice. While still a new concept, it is one that, in our view, holds the potential to both strengthen the theoretical understanding in HCI of an important aspect of how and why interactive systems are perceived and used, and offer guidance for designing systems in practice. It thus lives up to the bridging concept principle of accountability to both theory and practice.

Looking at a much more well-established concept, 'affordances' is arguable one of the best known terms in HCI. The debates and developments surrounding affordances in HCI illustrate the strength of concepts that facilitate exchanges between practice and theory. The concept is specific enough to have inspired designers in their work yet also has a strong theoretical basis. The theoretical aspects have been the subject of some debate since Norman [34] introduced the concept in HCI. Debates arose about the extent to which affordances as they were used in HCI did justice to their theoretical origins in ecological psychology, and later contributions have tried to further develop the concept with both strong ties in theory and potential for concrete application [3, 23]. The discourse on affordances in HCI have spanned almost three decades and provides a good example of how a bridging concept can promote continuous exchange and prompt accountability both in terms of practical applicability and theoretical grounding.

CONCLUSIONS AND FUTURE WORK

When Rogers [39] in 2004 took stock of the achievements in HCI research she stated that the field appeared to be in a state of flux; new theories where imported and developed and design practices and technologies where changing at an apparently ever increasing rate. While much has since been achieved within HCI, we appear to be facing roughly the same situation ten years on. While a highly dynamic field is arguably a desirable quality of HCI, it also challenges us to continuously explore the coherence and interplay between theory and practice. If connections between theory and practice are not maintained and re-articulated, the risk is a drift, where theoretical developments are made but these are out of sync with the object of study. Bridging concepts insist on articulating the connections between theory and practice through theoretical grounding, design articulations, and exemplars and thus promote accountability to both theory and practice. We find similar calls for alignment between theory and practice in the work of Stolterman [40].

Bridging concepts are inherently unstable constructs – perhaps best illustrated by the history of affordances in HCI. Obviously a bridging concept such as peepholes could be grounded in several theoretical positions apart from pragmatism; similarly, it can be informed through an evolving range of exemplars. Our point is thus not to seek a stable grounding of bridging concepts, but rather to show that they call for exploring different forms of grounding and articulation. This in turn can alter the exemplars and vice versa. It is exactly this process of grounding, re-grounding, articulation and re-articulation that facilitates exchanges and thus reflections on the ties between theory and practice. A bridging concepts, then, can have value beyond being a finalised form of knowledge, since the very process of creating and criticising bridging concepts within a research community is essential to its on-going development.

Looking more specifically at peepholes as a bridging concept this work has, for us, indicated untried design opportunities. As regards the sensory qualities and modalities of peepholes, our research indicates that most interactive peepholes rely primarily on visual modalities. In our survey we have not been able to find examples of installations that, for example, create taste or touch peepholes. This is arguably unsurprising, given the historical predominance of visual interfaces in HCI. However, we have strived to offer examples of how other modalities can supplement and/or replace visuals, such as embodied interaction with the Hydroscopes, the tangible interaction of Tangible 3D Blueprints and the auditory components of Listen Here! Explicating the concept of peepholes may motivate the exploration of examples of how different sense modalities can be employed to create peepholes.

Moving the other way across the bridge, the development of bridging concepts can also point towards inadequate theoretical foundations and potentials for 'importing', appropriating or developing new theoretical positions in HCI. In terms of importing or appropriating theoretical frameworks, our work on peepholes shows how pragmatist philosophy may be relevant for addressing specific aspects of engagement and inquiry in interaction. In terms of identifying underdeveloped theoretical positions, a concept such as 'touchpoints' in service design has enjoyed a large uptake in service design discourse, yet seems underdeveloped in terms of theoretical grounding. Developing the theoretical grounding could potentially make this concept a useful conceptual bridge between the theory and practice of service design.

ACKNOWLEDGMENTS

We thank our anonymous CHI shepherd for encouragement and insightful support of our work. This work has been funded by Center for Interactive Spaces, Center for Digital Urban Living (Danish council for Strategic research grant 2128-07-0011) and Center for Participatory IT.

REFERENCES

1. Alexander, C. *A Pattern Language: Towns, Buildings, Construction*. USA: Oxford University Press (1977).
2. Bowers, J. The logic of annotated portfolios: communicating the value of 'research through design'. In *Proc. DIS 2012*. ACM Press (2012), 68-77.
3. Bærentsen, C., Trettvik, J. An activity theory approach to affordace. *Proc. NordiCHI 2002*, ACM Press (2002).
4. Cao, X., Li, J.J., Balakrishnan, R. Peephole pointing: modeling acquisition of dynamically revealed targets. *Proc. CHI 2008*, ACM Press (2008), 1699-1708.
5. Dalsgaard, P. 2009. Designing Engaging Interactive Environments: A Pragmatist Perspective. Aarhus University, Denmark.
6. Dalsgaard, P., Dindler, C. 2009. Peepholes as means of engagement in interaction design, Proc. of Nordes 2009, Oslo, Norway.
7. Dalsgaard, P., Halskov, K. 2012. Tangible 3D Tabletops: Combining Tangible Tabletop Interaction and 3D Projection, Proc. of NordiCHI 2012, ACM, New York, NY, USA, 109-118.
8. Dalsgaard, P. Designing for Inquisitive Use. Proc. DIS 2008, ACM Press (2008), 21-30.
9. Dalsgaard, P. Pragmatism and Design Thinking. International Journal of Design 8,1 (2014).
10. Deckers, E. Perceptive Qualities in Systems of Interactive Products. Eindhoven University of Technology (2013).
11. Dindler, C., Krogh, P.G., Beck, S., Stenfeldt, L., Nielsen, K.R., Grønbæk, K. 2007. Peephole Experiences

- Field Experiments with Mixed Reality Hydroscopes in a Marine Center, in Proc. of DUX 2007, ACM, New York, NY.

12. Dewey, J. *The middle works*. 15 volumes, 1976-83 Edition (Boydston, J.A. eds.) Southern Illinois University Press, Carbondale, 1899-1924.

13. Dewey, J. *The later works.* 16 volumes. 1981-1990 Edition (Boydston, J.A. eds.), Southern Illinois University Press, Carbondale, 1925-1953.

14. Dewey, J. *Art as Experience*. 2005 edition, Perigree, New York, 1934.

15. Dewey, J. *Logic: the theory of inquiry*. Holt, Rinehart and Winston, New York, 1938.

16. Dewey, J. *The Essential Dewey: Ethics, logic, psychology*. (Hickman, L., Alexander, T. eds.). Indiana University Press, Bloomington, 1998.

17. Fitzmaurice, G. Situated information spaces and spatially aware palmtop computers. *Communications of the ACM 36*, 7 (1993), 39-49.

18. Forlizzi, J., Battarbee, K. Understanding experience in interactive systems. *Proc. DIS 2004*, ACM Press (2004), 261-268.

19. Gaver, W.W., Bowers, J., Boucher, A., Gellerson, H., Pennington, S., Schmidt, A., Steed, A., Villars, N., Walker, B. The Drift Table: Designing for Ludic Engagement. *Proc. CHI 2004*, ACM Press (2004), 885-900.

20. Hume, N. *Listen Here!*, http://www.nicolahume.co.uk/listen-here/, accessed on September 17th 2013.

21. Höök, K., Löwgren, J. Strong concepts: Intermediate-level knowledge in interaction design research, *ACM TOCHI 19*, 3 (2012).

22. Kaptelinin, V., Nardi, B.A. Activity theory: basic concepts and applications. *Proc. CHI 1997*, ACM Press (1997).

23. Kaptelinin, V., Nardi, B. Affordances in HCI: toward a mediated action perspective. *Proc. CHI 2013*, ACM Press (2013), 967-976.

24. Kaufmann, B. Ahlström, D. Studying spatial memory and map navigation performance on projector phones with peephole interaction. *Proc. CHI* 2013, ACM Press (2013), 211-220.

25. Kay, A. A personal computer for children of all ages. Palo Alto, CA: Xerox Palo Alto Research Center, 1972.

26. Koskinen, I., Zimmerman, J., Binder, T., Redstrom, J., & Wensveen, S. *Design Research Through Practice: From the Lab, Field, and Showroom.* Morgan Kaufmann (2011).

27. Krippendorff, K. On the Essential Contexts of Artifacts or on the Proposition That "Design Is Making Sense (Of Things)". *Design Issues 5*, 2 (1989), 9-39.

28. Krippendorff, K. *The Semantic Turn: A New Foundation for Design*. Taylor and Francis, Boca Raton, 2006.

29. Krogh, P. G., Petersen, M.G. Design Articulations for Aesthetics of Interaction. *Proc. DPPI 2009*, ACM Press (2009).

30. Lim, Y.K., Stolterman, E., Jung, H., Donalson, J. Interaction gestalt and the design of aesthetic interactions. *Proc. DPPI 2007*, ACM Press (2007), 239-254.

31. Locher, P., Overbeeke, K., Wensveen, S. Aesthetic Interaction: A Framework, *Design Issues 26*, 2 (2010), 70-79.

32. McCarthy, J, Wright, P. *Technology as Experience*, MIT Press, Cambridge, 2004.

33. Mehra, S., Werkhoven, P., Worring, M. Navigating on handheld displays: Dynamic versus static peephole navigation, *TOCHI 13*, 4 (2006), 448-457.

34. Norman, D. *The Psychology of Everyday Things*, Basic Books, NY, USA, 1988.

35. O'Shea, C. *Out of Bounds*. 2007, http://www.chrisoshea.org/projects/out-of-bounds/, accessed on September 17th 2013.

36. Overbeeke, K., Wensveen, S. From Perception to Experience, from Affordances to Irresistible. *Proc. DPPI 2003*, ACM Press (2003), 92-97.

37. Petersen, M.G., Iversen, O.S., Krogh, P.G., Ludvigsen, M. Aesthetic interaction: a pragmatist's aesthetics of interactive systems. *Proc. DIS 2004*, ACM Press (2004), 269-276.

38. Rohs, M., Essl, G., Schöning, J. Naumann, A., Schleicher, R., Krüger, A. 2009. Impact of item density on magic lens interactions. *Proc. MobileCHI 2009*, ACM Press (2009).

39. Rogers, Y. New Theoretical Approaches for HCI, *Annual Review of Information Science and Technology* 38, 1 (2004), 87-143.

40. Stolerman, E. The Nature of Design Practice and Implications for Interaction Design Research. *International Journal of Design 2*, 1 (2008).

41. Stolterman, E., Wiberg, M. Concept-Driven Interaction Design Research. *Human-Computer Interaction 25,* 2 (2010), 95-118.

42. Tidwell, J. *Designing Interfaces: Patterns for Effective Interaction Design.* O'Reilly and Associates, 2005.

43. Yee, K.P. Peephole displays: pen interaction on spatially aware handheld computers. *Proc. CHI 2003*, ACM Press (2003), 1-8.

44. Zimmerman, J. "Designing for the self: making products that help people become the person they desire to be." In *Proc. CHI 2009*, ACM, (2009), 395-404.

Evolution of Design Competence in UX Practice

Colin M. Gray
Indiana University Bloomington
201 N. Rose Avenue, #2276
Bloomington, IN 47405 USA
comgray@indiana.edu

ABSTRACT
There has been increasing interest in the adoption of UX within corporate environments, and what competencies translate into effective UX design. This paper addresses the space between pedagogy and UX practice through the lens of competence, with the goal of understanding how students are initiated into the practice community, how their perception of competence shifts over time, and what factors influence this shift. A 12-week longitudinal data collection, including surveys and interviews, documents this shift, with participants beginning internships and full-time positions in UX. Students and early professionals were asked to assess their level of competence and factors that influenced competence. A co-construction of identity between the designer and their environment is proposed, with a variety of factors relating to tool and representational knowledge, complexity, and corporate culture influencing perceptions of competence in UX over time. Opportunities for future research, particularly in building an understanding of competency in UX based on this preliminary framing of early UX practice are addressed.

Author Keywords
Competence; UX practice; design capability; expertise; identity.

ACM Classification Keywords
H.5.m. Information interfaces and presentation (e.g., HCI): Miscellaneous.

INTRODUCTION
In the past decade, there has been a dramatic shift in the adoption of UX practices in a variety of industries, an increasing need for qualified job candidates, and an expansion of programs to train interaction designers and user researchers. In parallel, curricula in interaction design has changed to a studio model of education in a number of institutions in order to accurately reflect the workplace where students will practice. This study presents the complexity of this expanding space as UX students are initiated into the professional design community as a rich area for future HCI research. The contributions of this work address how interaction design students translate their educational experience into the workplace; and more broadly, how the competencies of a UX designer change or adapt over time in relation to a specific design environment.

CHI 2014, April 26 - May 01 2014, Toronto, ON, Canada

ACM 978-1-4503-2473-1/14/04...$15.00.
http://dx.doi.org/10.1145/2556288.2557264

While there has been some attempt to document competencies of usability engineers and other practitioners within the HCI domain over the past two decades, these have been limited to documentations of specific practices, and have often been constrained to one or two companies [e.g., 2, 4, 7, 14, 22]. In this exploratory work, a broader range of companies are included in a 12-week longitudinal study, with the goal of understanding the critical first three months of practice as interaction design students transition into jobs or internships in the UX field. Over these three months, we asked interns and early practitioners (EPs) to document perceptions of their competence, both individually and in relation to their work environment. Through this study, we begin to address the issue of competence in UX, both as a concept that spans the discipline and is related to professional practice and preparatory pedagogy, and as a personally situated construct that is co-constructed over time through the relationship of a UX designer to their organization.

Within this framing, the contribution of this work includes three primary elements: 1) Documenting the shifts in competence as interaction design students take their first jobs or internships in a variety of corporate settings; 2) Understanding more fully how a beginning designer co-constructs their identity in reaction to the organization they work for, especially in regard to their competence; and 3) Beginning an exploration into the factors that affect the development of competence for UX practitioners, which may eventually lead to a fuller understanding of what UX competence should include in a more general sense.

REVIEW OF LITERATURE
To address the issue of competence, both in the framing of UX and as it exists as a concept within the broader design literature, several main issues will be introduced in this review of literature. These include nascent definitions of competence that already exist in the HCI literature linked to

broader constructions of competence in the workplace; a linkage of competence with an overall development of design capability or ability to engage in design thinking; and how a deeper look at practical knowledge helps us understand how academic notions of competence might be translated into the everyday work of a UX practitioner. While significant research has occurred in this area, there are fragments of knowledge across a wide range of fields, complicating the process of synthesis and extension into UX; this review of literature seeks to address the range of research being carried out in this area, with implications for how we view competence in an emergent sense in HCI.

What is competence?

There are a wide range of views on what competence is or should be, and how this concept might apply to educational and professional settings. In this review, literature is synthesized across multiple domains of research and theory, including practical knowledge, expertise, learning and increase in ability, and as a complex system of ability or skills enacted in a performative sense.

As a System of Abilities Applied in Context

In a general sense, competence is defined as "a roughly specialized system of abilities, proficiencies, or skills that are necessary or sufficient to reach a specific goal [that] can be applied to individual dispositions or to the distribution of such dispositions within a social group or an institution" [33]. Expanding on the role of place and context, Rychen and Salganik [25] define competence as "the ability to successfully meet complex demands in a particular context through the mobilization of psychosocial prerequisites [... where the] primary focus is on the results the individual achieves through an action, choice, or way of behaving, with respect to the demands [... of] a particular professional position, social role, or personal project." In these broad definitions we see the relationship of an individual to a specific context in which the individual *performs* using cognitive and non-cognitive skills, abilities, or judgments.

As a Designer

When viewing competence in this systemic way, there are important linkages between a holistic sense of competence, a cataloguing of *key competence* that might be desirable in a given discipline, and an overarching *metacompetence* that allows for awareness of one's own actions and the ability to introspect. *Metacompetence* appears to link most strongly with literature on design competence, including a focus on reflection [26] and active internalized and externalized communication. Donald Schön's [26] seminal work on reflective practice has been adopted widely in design education and practice, with an emphasis on reflecting in a dialogic way with specific design situations ("reflection-in-action") as well as reflecting in an intentional, metacognitive way after designing ("reflection-on-action").

In engineering design, a number of taxonomies of competence have been proposed, including: broad multidisciplinary frameworks comprised of skills, abilities, and metacognitive dimensions of behavior (visions and concepts, design methods, tools and materials, user and actor perspectives, versatility, design theory and research, and continuous competence development) [13], holistic competencies around generic capacities (capabilities, attitude, knowledge, skills, and experiences) [14], and systemic views of design (analysis and interpretation of context, development of the system, representation and communication of the system) [19]. Arvola and Artman [1] have also taken preliminary steps to explore competencies of interaction designers in the context of an educational environment, concluding that communication is as important as technical skill in the development and expression of professional competence. This *digital design competence* moves beyond technical skill or use of specific methods or tools to "learning the communicative practices of design work by mastering the articulation of envisioned future use" [1].

As Expertise

In design, most attention is paid to the study of expertise either as conflated with competence in a theoretical sense [20], or as the development of design ability through increasing levels of expertise [8]. Cross [7] considers the application of expertise in the domain of design, noting several key elements of "expert" practitioners: 1) the use of problem decomposing strategies, 2) exposure to large numbers of exemplars in a particular domain (e.g., Schön's [26] repertoire, Lawson's [18] schemata, gambits, and precedent), and 3) a solution-focused rather than problem-focused orientation. Dorst [8] has also addressed the issue of competence in design through the lens of expertise, utilizing and extending the Dreyfus model of expertise [9] into a set of seven stages of expertise, moving from naïve to visionary.

As Learnable and Teachable

While some competencies, particularly those bound to intelligence or cognitive ability, are inborn, most competencies are "learnable and teachable" [25]. Trier [31] points out the importance of both formal education and the growth of the knowledge economy as factors in understanding the development of competence over time. This underscores the need for formal educational systems to build baseline competencies, often independent of a specific career path or domain of use [3,16,31], but also the need for "professional training and education [...] as a process that continues throughout life" [31]. This process is generally self-led within a domain of individual interest, and results in what we readily recognize as an experienced practitioner; these practitioners often seem to automatically draw on tacit knowledge to make quick, yet reasoned, judgments [7,18,20,23,32].

Competence in HCI

While competence has been addressed to some degree in the HCI literature, research has generally focused on highly situated elements of UX practice in particular organizations, or through the lens of particular practices (e.g., participatory design). The CHI community has shown interest in this area through panels and workshops [e.g., 10,11,21,30], but relatively little formalized literature addressing design competence in UX exists. Most examples draw on competencies from an organizational lens, such as: Buur and Bødker [6] in a reframing of usability work, evaluation of design processes at B&O [3], cooperative design in a Scandinavian company [4], or management practices around UX adoption at Microsoft [29]. Despite this range of work, no definitive set of UX competencies has been proposed.

HCI Pedagogy

In positioning this paper, it is crucial to note the impact of the formal pedagogical process in preparing students for work in HCI-related disciplines, UX in particular. In the past two decades, changes to pedagogy have addressed the rigor and applicability of education in HCI to practice, most notably including use of the studio model of education [1,15,17,24]. The goal of these environments is to encourage the development of design thinking, introducing students to the reality of the discipline through active project work, collaboration, and use of HCI methods and technology. As Brandt, et al. [5] have theorized, the studio can be seen as a "bridge" that links the professional and academic communities of practice, and in this way, students are able to work in an environment that links them to their academic context, while also projecting their developing identities toward their eventual professional role. Additional work in this framing has addressed how students develop in a studio-based HCI program, including the kinds of barriers they have to address to reach competence [27], connections between technical skill and communication of concepts [1], and additional factors that affect their individual development of a designerly identity [12].

PURPOSE OF RESEARCH

The intent of this paper is to explore how students become UX practitioners, and the competencies that surround the success of this evolution in the identity of an individual designer. While students and practitioners have been studied in isolation, the transition between these two roles and the process of *becoming* that the student goes through in this transition have not been adequately discussed. While many studies have chosen to address competence from the lens of the workplace or through the perspective of a particular desirable method, this study focuses on assessments of competence by an individual designer. To target this perspective more powerfully, the participants for this study are recruited to represent the liminal space between formal educational preparation and UX practice, documenting the initiation of these participants into the UX community.

This process of *becoming* through the lens of competence is an especially important question to answer as we consider how we are currently preparing students for practice in UX settings. It is important to validate the education students are being provided, ensuring that it aligns with the realities of practice as UX adoption continues to spread. It is important to understand how designers are initiated into their work, and to assess whether the pedagogy is preparing them adequately to succeed.

RESEARCH APPROACH

This study relies on a longitudinal survey instrument with follow-up interviews for triangulation of data and increased thickness of detail. This method allowed the researchers to capture changes in the perceptions of competence over time in a relatively granular way, using the interviews to gain a greater understanding of the overall experience of the designer in relation to their perceptions of competence. This data collection was situated in a larger ethnographic study, which drew on a superset of this study population.

The 11 participants for this study were first (6) and second (5) year HCI students in a residential Master's program in a large Midwestern university. These students were recruited through an email solicitation, and both graduating students taking their first UX job and first year students completing an internship over the summer were solicited and recruited into the study. 10 of the 11 participants completed the data collection period.

Data Collection

Two primary methods of data collection were used in this study: weekly surveys and monthly interviews. All participants were requested to complete an online survey for 12 weeks, starting after the first week of their new job or internship. For internships, the data collection period covered the entire internship. The survey instrument included quantitative questions tracking their perceived level of competence, and asked the participants how that competence was applied in terms of design activity, critique, sharing of knowledge, and learning skills on the job through open ended questions. The following two ordinal questions were asked of the participants each week, with a 1 to 10 rating scale: 1) How competent do you feel as a UX designer? and 2) How competent do you feel as a UX designer as compared to your work colleagues?

In addition to the weekly surveys, an interview was requested at one-month intervals. This allowed the researchers to triangulate this thicker record with the survey results, resulting in a more complete picture of each student/practitioner's experience. These interviews also allowed for the researcher to identify potential causative agents in the overall rankings of competence, and check them with the student/practitioner for relevance. During the final interview, students were shown their survey results as a trend line and asked whether this agreed with their job or internship experience during the collection period.

Theme	Description
tool / representational knowledge	Use or description of tools that allow a designer to share their work with others. These could be digital or analog, created as deliverables or as representations of a design to generate a response.
dealing with complexity	Externalization of the amount of work expected in the designer's work environment—either in quantity or scope. Issues surrounding time management or processes relating to work practices.
vocabulary / language / communication	Reference to contextually-relevant vocabulary (e.g., jargon), talking to non-UX designers, developers, or managers, or facilitating the communication process about a design or project.
design leadership	Showing initiative and leadership in relation to design or design thinking. This includes broader views of problem scoping/framing, drawing on the [20] conception of being a design leader.
internal / external up-skilling	Learning new skills inside or outside of the organization, or the sharing of attained skills or knowledge with coworkers.
reconciling corporate reality/culture	Perception of the culture of the designer's work environment, and how that constrains or shapes their work practices, expectations of quality, or scope of projects.
designerly identity	The development and evolution of a personal identity in relation to design practice, including change/adaptation to a work environment, or a push/pull of identity from the corporate culture.

Table 1: Emergent themes used to analyze survey data.

ANALYSIS

Quantitative analysis of the measures of competence was performed to document shifts in competence over time, and then expanded through thematic analysis to explain the quantitative results more fully. A total of 111 survey responses were collected from 11 participants, and 23 interviews were conducted with 10 participants. Five participants completed all 12 surveys in a timely manner, while the remaining participants completed 7 to 11 surveys during the 12-week data collection period. Out of the 10 participants that completed the data collection period, six completed all three interviews, one participants participated in a two interview, and three participated in two interviews.

All ordinal data were plotted on a scatterplot to analyze how the trend for each individual changed over time. Because a clear definition of competence was not provided to the participants, analysis of an individual's trend line over time was the focus, rather than a comparison of quantitative rankings between participants.

Once the initial trend lines of competence rankings were completed, an analysis of the remaining open-ended survey results began. This process included a close reading of all survey data by two researchers. A set of emergent themes were identified, drawing from emergent themes in the close reading and elements of competence indicated by the literature. This emergent set of themes (Table 1) was then comprehensively applied to the entire corpus of survey data in a non-exclusive manner, yielding 628 excerpts with an average of 1.66 codes applied per excerpt.

After this analysis, a second researcher validated the theme application, reviewing all excerpts and code application. Any discrepancies were resolved through discussion with the primary researcher. Interview data was used to triangulate responses and resolve any issues in ascertaining meaning or relevance.

RESULTS

We first overview the kinds of companies the participants work in, as either full time employees or interns, and the array of UX contexts these companies represent. We then discuss participant perceptions of competence over time, and the shifts that resulted.

Types of Participants/Companies

Participants represented a range of company size, from small to multinational, and with the exception of one company in Scandinavia, all jobs and internships were located in the United States. Sectors included technology, energy, travel services, healthcare, digital agency, and management consulting. All positions were the equivalent of an entry-level position, but there were a broad range of job expectations: from a UX leadership role in several internships and jobs to a more supportive relationship in existing departments. Two of the participants worked on NSF funded research with a UX component, spanning both product development and writing. A range of UX adoption existed in the 10 represented companies, with some hiring UX talent as interns in groups that did not have a history of UX presence—what we refer to as "low UX" environments. Most internships and jobs were in this context, with little mentoring or senior UX professionals available. There were also two positions where the existing management framework included individuals with significant UX competence.

Perceptions of Competence

The participant's perception of competence was not static over the reporting period. In contrast, the weekly surveys revealed a turbulent change over time with large dips and increases in ranking over a single week. This rapid change in self-assessed competence was shared by both interns and EPs, although there was some difference in the kinds of shifts that took place and at what point in the reporting period. It is important to note that no definition of competence was provided to the participants to aid their self-assessment on a 1-10 scale. Therefore, no comparisons can directly be made between them, but because each trend line is completed by the same participant these trend lines can be compared as a whole, including analysis of shifts and the relative location of these shifts.

Interns

Many of the five participants interning at various organizations in a UX capacity shared a similar cycle of self-assessed competence: they began a moderate level of competence at the outset which grew over time as their comfort with the position and their responsibilities increased (Figure 1). While their assessment of individual competence leveled off near the end of the three-month reporting period, almost every intern experienced some "drop" or crisis between weeks five and nine. Compared to individual assessments of competence, the participants assessment of competence as compared to their colleagues and their assessment of the helpfulness of their education to everyday tasks were more stable overall, with steady gains over time in most cases. In almost every case, the participants ended with approximately the level of self-reported competence with which they began, although as revealed in the open-ended responses, this does not indicate that little or no growth in competence took place. This merely represented a "raising of the bar," where the participants gained a better sense of what competence in professional practice included.

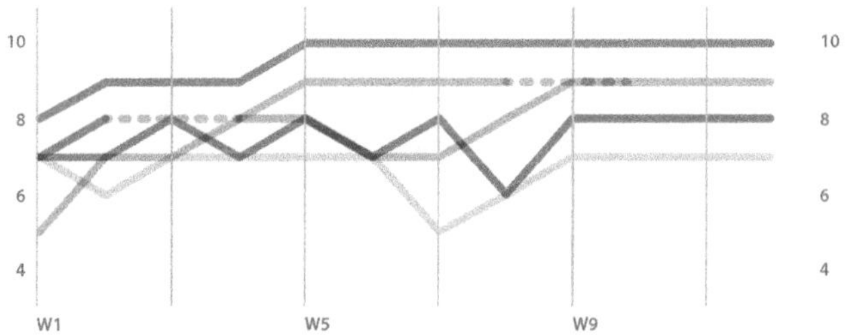

Figure 1: Individual competence of interns over time.

Early Practitioners

The five participants entering a full-time UX position generally shared a more chaotic path in their perception of individual competence, especially in the middle to end of the reporting period. Many of these participants ended the reporting period with roughly the same reported level of individual competence (Figure 2) and competence in relation to their colleagues, but the more chaotic transition period in the second month represents a promising area for further study. As with the interns, EPs had to rapidly adjust their expectations of what competence included in their position, even though all of these participants had taken part in internships similar to the other participants in this study.

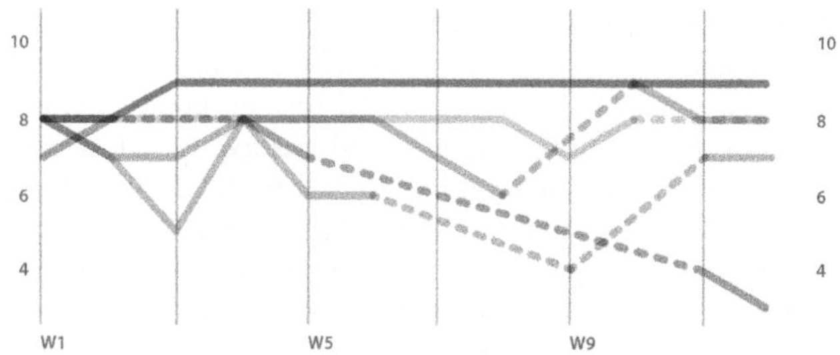

Figure 2: Individual competence of professionals over time.

Issues with Self-Reporting

Perceptions of competence are always grounded in a personal understanding of what competence includes. This perception was strongly influenced by the kind of UX environment the interns or EPs worked in, and reflected the relative amount of mentorship available in many cases. Interns were more likely to work in a "low UX" environment where they had little mentorship in matters relating to UX, and some of these participants consistently ranked themselves highly in terms of competence, while their peers in environments with higher UX competence seemed to rank themselves lower. Additional research is needed to ascertain whether the UX competence of an organization is a causal agent in personal assessment of competence.

Another issue in the reporting of competence is the directionality or object of comparison. Most participants ranked themselves against their immediate colleagues, interns or junior level UX designers, with only a minority mentioning higher management. This difference in level of comparison also affected the overall results. When asked in the exit interview to rank their competence against an experienced UX professional, most participants who had ranked themselves at the level of an 8-10 altered their assessment of individual competence to a 4 or 5. This indicates a more inclusive and consistent measurement of competence in relationship to others, which may be dependent on environmental, management, or educational factors.

Emergent Elements of Competence

Based on the thematic analysis of open-ended survey responses, guided by elements discussed in the literature, initial elements of competence addressed by participants in the context of UX practice can be constructed. Most of these themes are not unique to UX, but emerged in a categorical way as primary considerations for early career designers. Much of these themes revolve around the specificity of the individual corporate environment in which design is carried out. This environment serves as a demarcator of experience, so while some practices are common or valued in one organization (e.g., tool use, design processes, types of deliverables, scope of work), they are not universal to UX practice. These broad themes are helpful to begin to address the diversity of practice, and understand how students from a single HCI design program co-constructed their identity within their work environment.

Tool/Representational Knowledge

Interns and EPs each began their positions with the expectation that most of their work would rely on good software skills in prevailing wireframing and creative products; one EP noted "I think that getting a good proficiency in Photoshop, Balsamiq, and Axure will be necessary" (Week 1), while an intern expressed a need to gain skills wireframing, explaining "I have experience doing this, but I'd like to gain a lot more" (W1). These expectations of tool use grew in the early weeks of the job, and competence developed in a more integrative way, focusing more on depth than breadth. One EP reflected on the learning of tool skills on an as-needed basis, explaining: "we weren't ever really taught how to use 'this feature' or 'that feature' in the products that we used. This is something you just have to learn from day to day" (W3).

As interns and EPs were enculturated by their workplaces and their competence stabilized, an increasing focus was placed on analog skills for representation, rather than just software tools. One intern related her experience learning about "internal sketch style and research sharing formats" including "a technique for idea/sketch generation from the Basel School for Design [...] which involves creating many iterations of a highly constrained thing in order to come up with surprising stuff" (W6). Comparisons in tool and representational skill also developed over time, especially around representations by visual designers; one EP related: "I found that even though I have had adequate sketching skill, my visual design peers are really good at articulating ideas rapidly and with extreme depth" (W6).

Ultimately, these participants grew to think about tools and representational systems in a different way, not constrained by prevailing notions of "correct use." This included a much more substantial component of individual design judgment and pragmatism: "I've learned to stop worrying about what software I'm using and leverage what I know" (Intern, W7).

Dealing with Complexity

Virtually all participants reported a need to intellectually and experientially deal with the demands of their work environment, either in the scope of work expected, the deadlines or time pressures of design, or the problem space and requirements of projects. Early on, the common refrain from many participants was similar to this EP: "I felt a little more overwhelmed with the scope of this project" (W2). While some participants had to deal with complexity in relation to scope, others dealt with complexity in a more collaborative sense; another EP relates their first experience working with new designers: "It. Was. Utter. Chaos. Here I'm talking about collaborative design. I stupidly didn't step forward to be a lead, so these incredibly green designers did, and it was a huge waste of time. Next time, I will volunteer myself. Most of the problems stem from poor project/time management." (W4).

For others, managing the multiple projects and responsibilities was a bigger issue, with one intern reflecting that "time management is a big skill I have yet to master. I think the small deadlines will help me balance my tasks out more." (W4). For EPs, while time management was still reported, the balancing of complexity dealt more with the shaping and scope of the overall projects or tasks. For one EP, "[t]he main difference I encounter in my job is that the goal and problem is not clearly identified. In school, projects had a clear problem space defined in the form of a brief. Although school projects still required reframing and narrowing of the space, work projects aren't even at that point." (W5). For another EP, the need for domain-specific knowledge was challenging: "The domain expertise I need for each project, at least this first one and I assume every subsequent one, is slow to acquire." (W8). Finally, many EPs were dealing with the realities of complex systems for the first time, "solving for some of the cases that are not so 'happy path' [...] They sort of test the limit of what our 'nice' designs do once they get thrown into a more complex and outlier situation. It's a lot about making a judgment call and keeping up with consistency." (W8).

Vocabulary/Language/Communication

Communication with others in the organization was one of the big challenges facing many of these participants, with industry-specific jargon or unfamiliar work processes often standing in the way. Early on, this could be almost crippling, with one intern noting their need "to continue to find the proper vocabulary to express my ideas" (W2), and another intern admitting their unfamiliarity with "polished, corporate speak" (W2). An EP dealt with this lack of vocabulary in a more blunt manner: "I ask a lot of questions and won't let a question go until it is explained in a cut-the-crap-and-big-words-say-what-you-really-mean manner. If I don't understand, I keep asking questions until someone can give examples or paint a picture." (W1).

Over time, participants found strategies to increase communication with others, including honing presentation skills and building arguments that are convincing for developers or stakeholders. One EP explained: "I've learned and am learning how to present to a massive corporation in a way that resonates with them." (W6); while another intern used "sketches and mockups [to] drive the discussion" (W8) with their team. Communicating with developers was a common struggle, with one EP noting the barrier of "learning how to 'talk to developers'" (W9) and another intern describing their strategy of "draw[ing] insights quickly from research [to] build a convincing argument for developers to get onboard" (W5).

Design Leadership

A common theme among almost all of the participants was the lack of understanding about what UX could "do" for an organization. Many interns were placed in positions without substantial UX talent or mentoring, and several EPs were similarly serving in roles where they had minimal control over applying UX on a broad scale. An intern explains this frustration early in their experience, reflecting: "I am not sure my team knows what to do with me. I feel they recognize the need for UX, but in a way I have to tell them where I can help." (W2). Another intern struggled with "justifying the value of HCI and design" in a more general sense (W4).

Despite the organizational pushback that many participants experienced, they attempted to implement design processes in their respective organizations. An EP was able to lead in this area, demonstrating his "ability to think about systems, articulate rationale, and lead project teams to success" with "numerous people com[ing] up to [him] asking for advice about leading teams, from interns to professionals" (W6). Although there were some stories of leadership around design processes, another EP was more constrained, "find[ing] himself making things and not knowing why other than 'he/she/it told me to do it'" (W9). Ultimately, leadership in design and UX on an organizational level was highly situated and politically charged, and participants had differing levels of success in producing change.

Internal/External Upskilling

Participants readily assumed roles of self-learning, drawing on the experiences of others in their team, while sharing their own skills. While these skills were often situated in UX, including sharing expertise around wireframing, presentation skills, or "func-specs," this also included knowledge specific to an individual, such as one intern's "engineering and knowledge of physical materials [in] a certain robotics-y project" (W2). There was also a nuance to how individual skills came to bear on a particular situation, with one EP evaluating their own presentation skills in relation to their colleagues: "It's not actually delivery that's their problem, it's that their contributions could be more insightful. I haven't actually said, 'hey, asshat, stop and think for a moment,' but I think people can learn by example, so I try to be thoughtful in my comments." (W2).

The participants appeared to be actively focused on acquiring skills they perceived would be of use, ranging from competitive analysis research to "soft skills" development to learning how to create an empathy map. One EP noted this acquisition process, explaining their need "to work toward absorbing more information from other teams as well as people on my team" (W9). Another EP projected their need for acquisition of skills in a more pragmatic sense, situated in their project development: "I need to NOT start from scratch as often [...] inventing only when absolutely necessary." (W11).

Reconciling Corporate Reality/Culture

This theme framed many of the participants' reflections on their development in competence and early experiences in a UX position. Their educational experience, in many cases, had not prepared them for the level of bureaucracy, limited control, and tight deadlines of practice, and participants had to reconcile this with their personal approach to design. Two primary aspects of this reconciliation with corporate culture appeared to be evident: 1) learning about the corporate culture in order to engage it more effectively, and 2) adjusting their expectations to match reality.

Learning about the culture was an inevitable part of the transition process, and began in the first weeks, with one intern "starting to see the focus on the revenue" (W3) and an EP "adjusting to corporate hierarchy and learning the ladder of communication" (W4). Another intern dealt with specific issues in getting her user study approved: "I need to get acquainted with protocols and bureaucracy" (W3).

While most participants adapted to their new environment more willingly, others were more frustrated, like this intern: "The more I learn about the consulting business the less I like. My co-workers, namely those above me, guard their clients like bulldogs. I had to listen in on a client conversation and as a designer I felt I was coming into the project way too late. This seems to be typical." (W4). Others had to adjust to more menial parts of the process, such as the generally slower pace of work, or the movement from more "blue sky" to "laser focused" tasks. One EP explains this movement: "on a professional project, you get a list of requirements, try to follow *all* of them. In school, if you get a list of requirements, you can usually get away with following 1-2 of them really well. At work, you can attempt to do the same thing, but you have to show how the rest of the requirements fall into line. Also, if you pick the WRONG 1-2 requirements to follow, [...] it isn't a great move. The problem space isn't as wide open as it is at school." (W1).

Designerly Identity

As with the constant presence of the corporate culture, there was a constant sense in which the participants had to engage with their identity as a designer in a co-constructive manner with their environment. This played out in both positive and negative respects, with some participants struggling to adapt to their environments, and others deciding whether to or how to determine their value as a person through their work performance.

Some participants wrestled with basic work/life balance, such as: "will the bulk of my professional satisfaction [be located] in the workplace?" (EP, W2) or "want[ing] time to myself" (Intern, W6). Others noted the more positive aspects of their work: "It simply felt good to contribute to something." (EP, W2). One intern celebrated his individual skills in comparison to colleagues: "Some people are taken aback by my willingness to scrap and idea" (W11).

It seemed as if participants all had their own way of coping with their new work environment, with some worried about how others would see them—"I don't want to appear to not be a self-starter, and I don't want to eventually get overwhelmed if I take on too many projects." (EP, W2)—and others fighting for their approach: "We had a phone call with a client today. We were briefed before to only speak if "teed" up to speak. That is such an abrasive thought for a HUMAN computer interaction designer. Where, the [Master's] program tells me to talk to all stakeholders." (Intern, W3).

DISCUSSION

The development and expression of competence by these participants over a relatively short period of time brings several issues relating to the development of competence to the foreground. Rather than being a static entity or documentable system, I propose that competence is more fluid and personally and organizationally situated, drawing on elements unique to the context of use [25,33], while also drawing equally on the unique contributions and life experiences of the individual designer. This fluidity appears to be especially relevant in a nascent discipline like UX.

Corporate Culture as the Center of Experience

[20] concludes that being a design leader involves being "in service"—exceeding the original expectations of the client or stakeholder. In these initiatory moves into UX practice, both interns and EPs were met with the realities of their own designerly identity and the culture of the organization in which they worked. In many cases, they were confronted with the question: Does being a good designer mean being or becoming a good design leader?

This leads us to a fuller discussion of identity development within an organization, and the role of the organization and underlying corporate culture—both as a push and pull—in shaping an individual's designerly identity. In this relatively brief reporting period, these participants—interns and EPs alike—demonstrated their ability to affect their organizational culture by introducing new UX practices, designerly ways of thinking, and design leadership. But at the same time, the organization and corporate culture also affected these designers in a deep way. They were forced to assess how their "blue sky" visions of design fit into complex, integrated systems, and how their effectiveness as a designer is situated within the larger bureaucracy. To succeed as a designer, most participants ended with the self-realization that they must understand the culture in which they work in order to produce lasting change.

Mentoring and upskilling as a UX designer is another dimension in which the corporate culture has a significant role. Based on the level of UX adoption and underlying mentoring resources, the culture can allow an individual designer to either expand their projected worth, or diminish their sense of designerly identity. The level of UX adoption is not deterministically bound to either condition, but is highly dependent on the co-construction of identity between the organization and the individual designer. For instance, a designer in an organization with high UX competence might feel diminished in their personal competence due to aspirational role models, while they might have an inflated sense of competence if they are the sole UX or designer force in the organization or working group. In contrast, when a designer is out on their own, they must justify their existence in many cases, working to translate their work into empiricist or positivist arguments that can be accepted by developers or engineers. This requires great personal strength, and may result in greater competence than merely being mentored.

Descending Reliance on Tool Knowledge

As others have documented [28], tool knowledge is not bound to specific software, but rather to the judgment of the designer. While some participants innately knew this, they came into their work environments with the expectation that they would need specific software competencies in order to produce adequate representations for their projects. Many participants seemed surprised, however, by their ability to learn something new on the fly, often "picking up" a new skill in the course of a week. And as the weeks progressed, there was less stated reliance on knowing tools—especially software—and more focus on the ability to lead others in a communicative sense through representations to and understand the core of their design practice.

Many participants came into their organizations with the perception that they would need to know specific software, especially to produce digital wireframes or high fidelity prototypes. While some organizations relied on these representations, many UX positions relied more on analog or low fidelity methods of representation for buy-in, and in some instances, the creation of higher fidelity mockups using software diminished effectiveness and wasted time.

In a somewhat unusual turn, especially as dozens or hundreds of wireframing and visualization tools are available to designers, some organizations seemed more concerned with reinforcing the need for strong analog skills, particularly in sketching and rapid forms of representation. This competence was taught at a baseline level in the formal education of participants, but not to the level of proficiency some jobs required. These visual competencies, along with the related manual skills, were the most referenced skills needed on the job, yet the least addressed in formal curricula.

Self-Learning

The ability to direct self-learning appears to be a primary indicator for future growth in competence, yet it is only addressed by a few models of competence [13,31]. Participants addressed this need for increase in competence in a variety of ways—directed both on a holistic level (e.g., how UX should be addressed in this environment) and a highly tactical level (e.g., specific software tools, methods, or techniques). The literature does not substantially address how these individual acts of competence development fuel future growth, or the potential role of project work and practice experience.

Participants had to quickly make a transition from being "fed" content in a classroom setting to leading their own efforts to be a better or more competent UX practitioner.

While most participants came into their job with strong self-learning skills, others felt less confident and were surprised at how quickly they could "pick up" a new skill and execute with a relatively high degree of competence (e.g., patent drawings, marker sketches).

There is also a strong orientation among these participants towards taking on a variety of work, and learning along multiple dimensions at once. While some of this may be directed by the overarching corporate culture, some participants also took steps to increase the variety of their work on their own, pushing themselves to learn or execute in different ways (e.g., creation of podcasts, execution of a user study). There does seem to be some value in viewing proactive/reactive orientations in this regard, and additional work around the co-construction of competence is needed.

Implications for Pedagogy

The variety of experiences of these participants underscores the question for pedagogy: How do we prepare students for such a diversity of jobs? The role that the studio model of learning might play in developing this "studio bridge" between academic and practice communities has not been substantively explored, but must be addressed to understand not only what skills UX practitioners need, but also what types of identity formation *should* happen in education.

In particular, participants pointed out what an educational program "could not do." These included organizational skills, such as working with developers to execute on a design, types of professional communication around presenting and working with constraints, and the realities of both "blue sky" and more "laser focused" projects. Some participants seem to have been lured into thinking of their role in a strategic sense much too broadly and optimistically, and then were frustrated when they couldn't have as much impact as they desired. Thus, there seems to be an importance in building both optimism and pragmatism into a design curriculum: preparing students to be exceptional and aspirational, but also to embrace the culture and constraints of a particular organization. This also indicates the importance on the part of the pedagogy in directing students towards the kinds of UX jobs that match their personality and skillset—especially in a field as broad and diverse as HCI. This cannot be accomplished as only a technical match of competencies; an identity "fit" with an organization is equally important to the overall success of a new UX practitioner.

OPPORTUNITIES FOR FUTURE RESEARCH

This paper offers substantial contributions towards our understanding of competence in UX practice, but there are also limitations on generalizability relating to the population of students and EPs recruited as participants. Limitations include a relatively small sample size, somewhat mitigated through depth of data collection methods. There were also multiple instances of missing survey/interview data from some participants, which constrains our overall understanding of changes in competence over time for some individuals. Finally, there is a selection bias from students within this HCI Master's program—these 11 participants represent less than 15% of the student population, and are not necessarily fully representative of the entire student population. Additionally, these experiences are constrained to participants originating from a single HCI Master's program, which limits the generalizability of these findings to less design-focused HCI programs.

Despite these limitations, this study captured the responses of a wide range of individual experiences mediated by a substantial number of UX environments. Future work in this framing could increase our awareness of this diversity further, and as our expectations of what competence in UX includes solidifies, more consistent rankings could allow for a finer grained analysis of shifts in competence over time. There is a need for in-depth research on UX practice, which has not traditionally been a strong focus in the HCI community. This work allows us to address the diversity of UX practice through the framing of a developing UX designer's experience, allowing for additional understanding not only of work environments in which UX practice takes place, but also how individual competencies influence this role.

CONCLUSION

This exploratory research on the development and perception of competence by interns and EPs in UX underscores the importance of research on UX practice. The literature does not adequately address the competencies that result in successful UX practice, and the linkages between the academic and professional communities are not well explored.

This paper takes some first steps towards documenting how shifts in perception of competence take place as students are initiated into UX practice, including ways that these participants co-construct their identity in relation to the organization and corporate culture in which they work. A preliminary thematic analysis reveals some factors that might affect or contribute to this development and perception of competence over time, and points to promising areas for future research in the areas of tool development, the effect of corporate culture in shaping UX practice, the types of self-learning necessary for success, and the role of the pedagogy in developing students ideally suited for the diversity of UX practice. More research is needed in each of these areas to further frame activities in the practice community that lead to increasing levels of competence.

ACKNOWLEDGMENTS

This work is supported in part by the National Science Foundation (NSF) Grant Award no. 1115532. Opinions expressed are those of the author and do not necessarily reflect the views of the entire research team or the NSF. Additional thanks to Omar Sosa Tzec for his thoughtful contributions and support.

REFERENCES

1. Arvola, M. and Artman, H. Studio life: The construction of digital design competence. *Digital Kompetanse 3,* 2 (2008), 78-96.
2. Bærentsen, K.B. and Slavensky, H. A contribution to the Design Process. *Comm. of the ACM 42,* 5 (1999), 72-77.
3. Blokhuis, F.T.L. *Evidence-based design of workplace learning*. University of Twente, 2006.
4. Bødker, S., Ehn, P., Sjögren, D. and Sundblad, Y. Co-operative design —perspectives on 20 years with 'the Scandinavian IT Design Model'. *Proc. NordiCHI,* (2000), 22-24.
5. Brandt, C.B., Cennamo, K., Douglas, S., Vernon, M., McGrath, M. and Reimer, Y. A theoretical framework for the studio as a learning environment. *International Journal of Technology and Design Education,* (2011).
6. Buur, J. and Bødker, S. From usability lab to "design collaboratorium": reframing usability practice. *Proc. DIS*, ACM (2000), 297-307.
7. Cross, N. Expertise in design: an overview. *Design Studies 25,* 5 (2004), 427-441.
8. Dorst, K. Design research: a revolution-waiting-to-happen. *Design Studies 29,* 1 (2008), 4-11.
9. Dreyfus, S.E. Formal models vs. human situational understanding: Inherent limitations on the modeling of business expertise (ORC 81-3). Berkeley: Operations Research Center, University of California, (1981).
10. Friedland, L., Innes, J., Longoria, R., Hom, W., Henry, P. and Anderson, R. Outsourcing & offshoring: impact on the user experience. *Proc. CHI,* ACM (2005), 1170-1171.
11. Gobert, D., Howlett, V., Snyder, C., Tamler, H., Tullis, T.S. and Wilson, C. What the best usability specialists are made of. *Proc. CHI,* ACM (2002), 706-707.
12. Gray, C.M. Informal peer critique and the negotiation of habitus in a design studio. *DRS // CUMULUS,* (2013), 702-714.
13. Holmlid, S. and Arvola, M. 2007. Developing a thematic design curriculum as a Bologna master. *International Conference on Engineering and Product Design Education* (2007), 13-14.
14. Horváth, I. Design competence development in an academic virtual enterprise. *Proc. IDETC/CIE*, (2006), 10-13.
15. Hundhausen, C. D., Narayanan, N. H., and Crosby, M. E. Exploring studio-based instructional models for computing education. *Proc. SIGCSE*, 2008, 392-396
16. Knight, P. and Page, A. The assessment of wicked competences: Report to the Practice-based Professional Learning Centre. 2007.
17. Koutsabasis, P. and Vosinakis, S. Rethinking HCI Education for Design: Problem-Based Learning and Virtual Worlds at an HCI Design Studio. *International Journal of Human-Computer Interaction 28,* 8 (2012), 485-499.
18. Lawson, B. Schemata, gambits and precedent: some factors in design expertise. *Design Studies 25,* 5 (2004), 443-457.
19. Morelli, N. Globalised Markets and Localised Needs. *Educating Designers for a Global Context,* (2006).
20. Nelson, H.G. and Stolterman, E. *The design way: Intentional change in an unpredictable world.* MIT Press, Cambridge, 2012.
21. Nieminen, M.P., Runonen, M., Nieminen, M. and Tyllinen, M. Designer experience: exploring ways to design in experience. *Proc. CHI,* ACM (2011), 2449-2452.
22. Olsson, E. What active users and designers contribute in the design process. *Interacting with computers 16,* 2 (2004), 377-401.
23. Polanyi, M. *The tacit dimension*. Anchor Books, Garden City, New York, 1966.
24. Reimer, Y.J. and Douglas, S.A. Teaching HCI design with the studio approach. *Computer Science Education 13,* 3 (2003), 191-205.
25. Rychen, D.S. and Salganik, L.H. A holistic model of competence. In *Key competencies for a successful life and a well-functioning society*. Hogrefe & Huber, Göttingen, Germany, 2003, 41-62.
26. Schön, D.A. *The reflective practitioner: How professionals think in action*. Basic Books, New York, 1983.
27. Siegel, M.A. and Stolterman, E. Metamorphosis: Transforming Non-designers into Designers. In *Proc. DRS*. Sheffield, UK, 2008, 378:1-13.
28. Stolterman, E. and Pierce, J. Design tools in practice: studying the designer-tool relationship in interaction design. *Proc. DIS*, (2012), 25-28.
29. Szóstek, A. A look into some practices behind Microsoft UX management. *Proc. CHI,* ACM (2012), 605-618.
30. Thompson, C.F., Anderson, R.I., Au, I., Ratzlaff, C. and Zada, N. Managing user experience: managing change. *Proc. CHI,* ACM (2010), 3143-3146.
31. Trier, U.P. Defining educational goals: A window to the future. In D.S. Rychen and L.H. Salganik, editor., *Defining and selecting key competencies*. Hogrefe & Huber, Seattle, WA, 2001, 241-246.
32. Vickers, S.G. Judgment. In *The Vickers Papers*. Harper & Row, London, 1984, 230-245.
33. Weinert, F.E. Concept of competence: A conceptual clarification. In D.S. Rychen and L.A. Salganik, editor, *Defining and selecting key competencies*. Hogrefe & Huber, Seattle, WA, 2001, 45-66

Causal Interactions

Adam Darlow, Gideon Goldin, Steven Sloman
Department of Cognitive, Linguistic & Psychological Sciences, Brown University
Box 1821, 190 Thayer St., Providence, RI 02912, USA
{adam_darlow, gideon_goldin, steven_sloman}@brown.edu

ABSTRACT
In this paper we present two design guidelines, causal order and continuity, to be used as rules of thumb for designing intuitive interactions based on principles of causal reasoning. We propose that designing interactions to behave like real-world systems of cause and effect makes them more intuitive. Using these basic principles avoids the limitations inherent to specific metaphors. In three experiments, participants solved puzzles using variations of a novel graphical interface. Participants using interfaces that were consistent with the causal guidelines consistently solved the puzzle faster than participants using inconsistent interfaces. We also discuss common interactions already consistent with the causal guidelines as well as areas where the guidelines are likely to apply successfully. The causal order guidelines provide specific utility while also demonstrating how principles of causal psychology can be applied to help interface designers better convey the functionality of their interfaces.

Author Keywords
Causal reasoning; Psychology; Graphical interfaces; GUI; Design guidelines; Interaction design

ACM Classification Keywords
H.1.2 User/Machine Systems: Software Psychology; H.5.2 User Interfaces: Graphical User Interfaces (GUI)

INTRODUCTION
The interface design philosophy of Direct Manipulation [11,17] states that interfaces should behave like environments where users can directly manipulate the objects of interest for their task, as opposed to behaving like intermediaries between users and their tasks. To this end, an interface benefits from behaving like a predictable environment containing task-relevant objects that interact in predictable ways.

Often an interface achieves directness by mimicking a specific real-world environment, called a metaphor [5]. Common metaphors include the desktop and folders metaphor for organizing files and the tools and canvas metaphor for creating and manipulating images. However, metaphors are not without their problems. They can be too limiting when they introduce artificial constraints merely because those constraints exist in the real-world environment. They can also be confusing when users make assumptions based on the metaphor that aren't maintained in the interface. For example, users can estimate the length of a book based on its visual size in the real world, but not on a computer desktop.

CHI 2014, April 26–May 1, 2014, Toronto, Ontario, Canada.
Copyright ©ACM 978-1-4503-2473-1/14/04...$15.00.
http://dx.doi.org/10.1145/2556288.2557216

Our approach attempts to capitalize on users' real-world experience without committing to a specific metaphor by supporting the reification of interface elements. The reification principle states that both control and data elements should be conceptualized as objects and not mere abstract representations of actions or properties [3,13]. We apply basic principles of causal psychology, how people think about interactions between objects and events, and translate them into interaction design guidelines. The goal of these guidelines is to make an interface feel like it functions via realistic causal mechanisms, making the parts of the interface behave more like objects and making their functionality easier to learn.

Causal Reasoning in Graphical Interfaces
Two typical questions for a user learning a novel interface are "What does this [button] DO?" and "What CAN BE DONE to this [text]?" These questions ask about the *causal roles* of objects in the interface. Whenever objects interact and one object causes a change in another, e.g. a baseball breaking a window, the causal roles of the source object (baseball) and destination object (window) determine what will happen. An object's causal source roles refer to what it is capable of doing to other objects and its causal destination roles refer to what other objects are capable of doing to it [9,19]. The combination of the baseball's source roles of being hard and reasonably heavy and the window's destination role of being fragile leads to the window breaking when they interact.

The same causal analysis applies even more concisely to GUIs because GUI objects have fewer causal roles than real-world objects do. Most objects in an interface have either source roles, e.g. buttons, or destination roles, e.g. text in a word processor, but not both. Once a user has learned those roles, they have learned how to use the interface. Therefore, the important question is how we can make learning causal roles easier. To this end, we explore the psychological principles of causal reasoning and attempt to translate them into design guidelines for making causal roles and relations easier to learn. In this paper, we present two principles and their respective guidelines, causal order and continuity.

Causal Order

Not only do causes necessarily precede their effects, but people find it easier to think about causal systems when they observe and attend to causes prior to their effects. For example, prediction is easier than diagnosis [7,18]. It's easier to infer that a person was late for work if you know their train was delayed and harder to infer that their train was delayed if you know they were late to work. People are also better at learning the structure of a causal system when they observe a cause before observing its effects, even when they know the order of observations is irrelevant [14]. Students also prefer to write mathematical equations according to their causal order [16]. For equations representing multiple causes of a single effect, students choose to structure the equation such that all of the causes lie on one side of the equation and the sole effect on the other. They also find the equations easiest to understand in this form.

When extended to objects and their causal roles, the causal order principle suggests that it is easier to think about an interaction between objects when attending to the object with the causal source role before the object with the causal destination role. This leads to the causal order design guideline:

In any interaction that changes an element of the interface, the element that changes should be the last element the user interacts with.

In other words, the causal order guideline suggests having users click (or touch, gesture at, or otherwise stimulate) buttons, menus, and other controls before clicking on the objects that they influence. The brush tool in painting programs is causally ordered because the user first selects the brush then applies it to the canvas. The bold and other style buttons in word processors are not causally ordered because the user first selects the text to be changed. The highlighting tool in Microsoft Word is mixed because it can be used in either order.

We assert that causally ordered interactions are easier to learn than inconsistent interactions. Experiments 1 and 2 test this assertion with novel interfaces that differ only in the order of interactions, but first we describe the second causal guideline.

Continuity

Another fundamental property of a causal relation is that it's built upon a continuous process leading from cause to effect, called a mechanism. Mechanisms are how causes bring about their effects and are central to people's concept of causality [1]. The plausibility of mechanisms helps distinguish rational causal beliefs from mere superstition, e.g. attributing a broken window to the kids playing outside or to a black cat encountered earlier. When the mechanism is visible, such causal attribution becomes obvious. If you see the path of a baseball from the hand of a pitcher to a window as it breaks, you don't pause to consider why the window broke or who is responsible. Cases like this involve causal *perception* in that the causal relation is directly perceived, not inferred [15]. Therefore, the continuity guideline suggests making mechanisms visible in interactions in order to make the causal interactions obvious.

Any change to an object should follow a continuous visible path from the interaction with the object that controls the change, to the changed object when it changes.

In other words, when a user interacts with a button or other control object to make another object change, the change should flow visibly from the control object to the changing object. Note that there are multiple ways to implement continuity; it is not necessary to add superfluous animations to an interface. The brush tool in painting programs is continuous because the cursor changes to represent the brush and follows a continuous path to wherever the brush is applied on the canvas. The bold button in text editors is not continuous because the text becomes bold when the button is pressed without any visible process connecting the two. The highlight tool in Microsoft Word is again mixed because it can behave like either of the above, depending on the order of interactions. In the discussion section we address why causal order and continuity tend to be correlated, but first we present experiments testing the usefulness of the guidelines. We assert that continuous interactions are easier to learn. Experiment 3 tests the assertion by comparing novel interfaces that differ only in whether the animations triggered by their interactions make the interactions continuous.

EXPERIMENTS

The following three experiments test the efficacy of the causal guidelines in making interactions easier to learn by presenting participants with a novel interface which they need to use in order to solve a puzzle. Minimal variations on the interfaces manipulate whether they are consistent with the guidelines. Experiment 1 tests the causal order guideline. Experiment 2 separates the measures of learning and efficiency by examining learning curves. Finally, Experiment 3 tests the continuity guideline.

Experiment 1 – Causal Order

This experiment tests the causal order guideline by asking participants to solve a puzzle with a novel interface. In this puzzle, properties are transferred from one object to another either by selecting the source first and then the destination (causal order condition), or by selecting the destination then the source (non-causal order condition; see Figure 1).

Interfaces

As seen in Figure 1, each interface consisted of eight objects (circles with 62 pixel diameters and 48 pixel margins) arranged in a three-by-three grid. Participants interacted with the objects by clicking on pairs of objects to use one to modify the other, but the order differed between interfaces as shown in Figure 2. In the causal order interface, participants first clicked on the object to use and then on the object to modify and in the non-causal order interface the order was reversed.

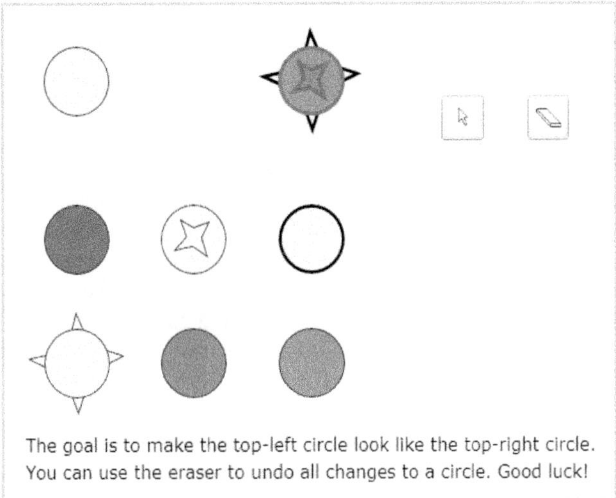

Figure 1: The puzzle interface from Experiments 1 and 2. The instructions read "The goal is to make the top left circle look like the circle on the right. You can use the eraser to undo all changes to a circle. Good luck!"

The effect of modifying an object depended on both objects. The blank circle in the top-left was passive. It could be modified, but couldn't modify other objects. Each of the bottom six objects had a central property that defined both how it modified other objects and how it was modified by other objects. In order from top-left, the objects' properties were blue, inner star, thick border, outer star, green, and red. For example, applying the blue object to the thick border object made its thick border blue but didn't change its fill color. Modifying a star object modified the star instead of modifying the circle. This enabled participants to chain modifications, which was required to solve the puzzle. For example, in order to give the blank object a blue border, a participant first had to modify the border object as described above and then use it to modify the blank object.

The other parts of the interface included the goal object in the top-right of the grid and the cursor and eraser buttons. The goal object didn't respond to interactions and was displayed for comparison to the blank object. The eraser button changed the cursor to an eraser that would return any object to its initial state. The cursor button returned the cursor to its normal function.

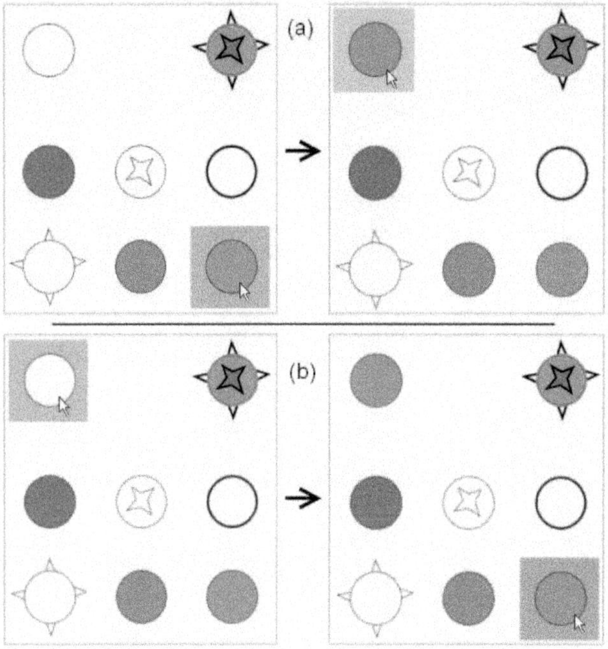

Figure 2: In order to make the blank object red in the *causal order* interface (a), the user first selects the red object then the blank object. To do the same in the *non-causal order* interface, the user first selects the blank object then the red object.

The puzzle was implemented using Microsoft Silverlight and ran in the participant's browser of choice.

Procedure

Participants received only minimal instruction, as seen in Figure 1. To solve the puzzle, they had to make the blank object match the goal object. The interface recorded each click on an object, but analyses focused on the overall time and number of clicks taken to solve the puzzle. The fastest solvers in each condition received a bonus. Participants could take as much time as needed, but after 10 minutes were offered (without forewarning) the opportunity to quit without penalty.

Participants

Participants did the study online and were recruited through Amazon Mechanical Turk (AMT). Of 33 participants, 17 were randomly assigned to the causal order condition, and 16 to the non-causal order condition. All participants reported normal color vision.

Results

All participants in the causal order condition solved the puzzle, compared to only 63% of participants in the non-causal order condition (p<.006, binomial test) as seen in Figure 3. We included participants' quitting time as a lower bound on how long it would have taken them to solve the puzzle.

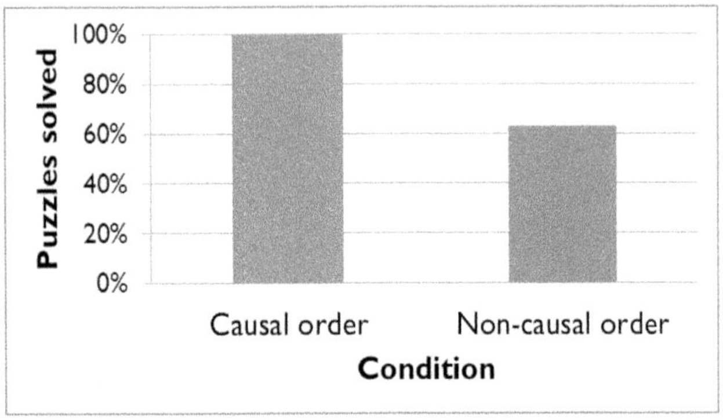

Figure 3: In Experiment 1, all participants using the *causal-order* interface solved the puzzle as opposed to two-thirds of participants using the *non-causal order* interface.

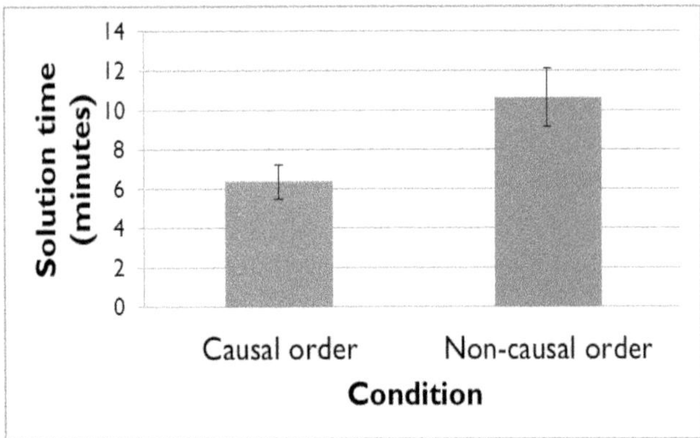

Figure 4: Participants using the *causal order* interface solved the puzzle faster than those using the *non-causal order* interface.

Participants in the causal order condition completed the puzzle in less time (t=2.46, p<0.03, M=6.35 min., SD=3.68) and fewer clicks (t=3, p<0.01, M=151 clicks, SD=96.84) than participants in the non-causal order condition (M=10.63 min., SD=5.97; M=282 clicks, SD=140.60).

These results support our hypothesis that an interface is easier to use when it is consistent with causal order. Participants took longer to complete a task with a novel interface when the interface dynamics were inconsistent with natural causal order.

Discussion

Participants were more effective in the causal order condition, demonstrating the effectiveness of the causal order guideline. The guideline was designed to aid users in forming a causal model of the interface and we propose that this explains the advantage. However, there is an alternative explanation. The causal order guideline prescribes that the user should interact last with the element that changes, making it easier to notice and remember which actions generated which outcomes. This means that the user is attending to where the change occurs when it occurs. It is possible that regardless of users' causal understanding of an interface, simply making sure that changes occur where they are attending is what makes the interface easier to learn. Although this does not undermine the value of the causal order guideline, it does raise the question of why the guideline is effective. We control for a similar explanation in Experiment 3 and discuss the attentional account further in the general discussion.

Experiment 2 - Learning Curves

Participants solved the puzzle faster when the interface was consistent with the causal order guideline. Our hypothesis is that the guideline made the interface easier to learn, but a possible alternative is that it made the interface more efficient to use. Experiment 2 presented participants with a series of puzzles, each with a different goal object, to distinguish learning from efficiency. We predict that the causal order interface is easier to learn, not necessarily more efficient to use, and so participants' performance in this condition should improve faster *over time*, i.e. a higher learning rate, than in the non-causal order condition.

To better understand any effects of learning, we also investigated the effect of explicit, verbal instruction. Some participants were told how the puzzle works before attempting to solve it.

Interfaces

Both the causal order and non-causal order interfaces were identical to those used in Experiment 1.

Procedure

The procedure for solving each puzzle was the same as in Experiment 1, except that participants didn't receive a bonus for faster solutions and didn't get the option to quit. Unlike Experiment 1, participants solved eight consecutive puzzles. All of the puzzles used the same interface, but each iteration involved a new randomly generated goal. All of the puzzles were equally difficult as measured by the number of moves in the optimal solution.

In addition, some of the participants using each interface received extra instructions before the first puzzle, including a description of how the interface works, similar to the description above, and accompanied by the appropriate half of Figure 2.

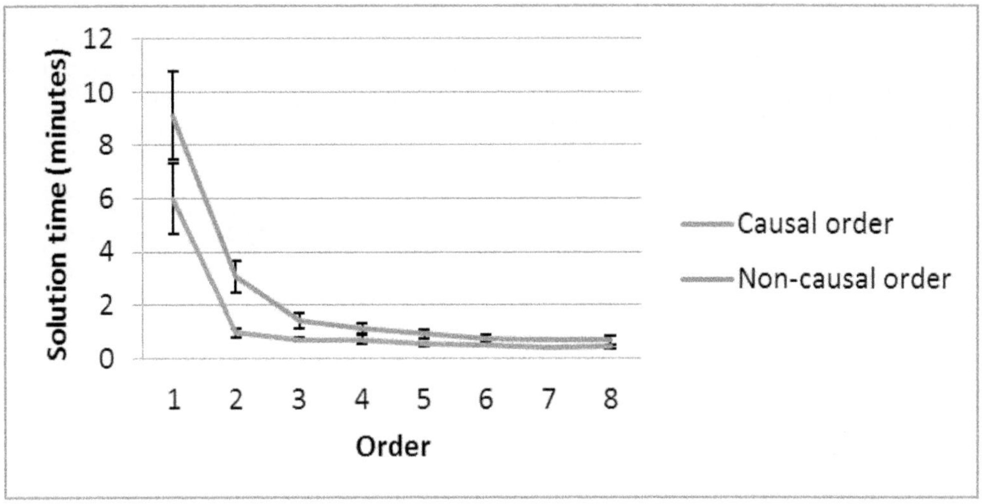

Figure 5: Average learning curves with the causal order and non-causal order interfaces.

Participants
34 undergraduates with normal color vision participated in exchange for course credit. 15 took part in the *non-causal order* condition, of which 8 received explicit instructions. The remaining 19 participated in the *causal order* condition, and 11 of them received explicit instructions.

Results
Figure 5**Error! Reference source not found.** shows the average learning curve for each interaction order. We analyzed the solutions with split-plot ANOVAs of solution time and number of clicks as functions of interaction order, iteration, and instructions. Participants solved the puzzles faster with practice ($F(1,30)=365.83$, $p<.001$). Participants using causal interactions were faster than those using non-causal interactions ($F(1,29)=22.27$, $p<.001$), although the difference decreased with practice as performance approached asymptote ($F(1,30)=5.28$, $p=.029$). Instructions had no significant effect on solution times and had no interactions with other variables. Therefore, further analyses ignored whether participants received instructions. The analysis of number of clicks showed a similar pattern.

In order to distinguish whether the causal order was improving learning or efficiency, we fit an exponential model to each participant's learning curve [10] using an MCMC (Markov Chain Monte Carlo) model fitting procedure. The model is expressed in the equation $f(t)=A+Be^{-\alpha t}$ which has separate parameters for learning rate (α), efficiency (B), and asymptotic performance (A). Figure 6 compares the distribution of participants' model

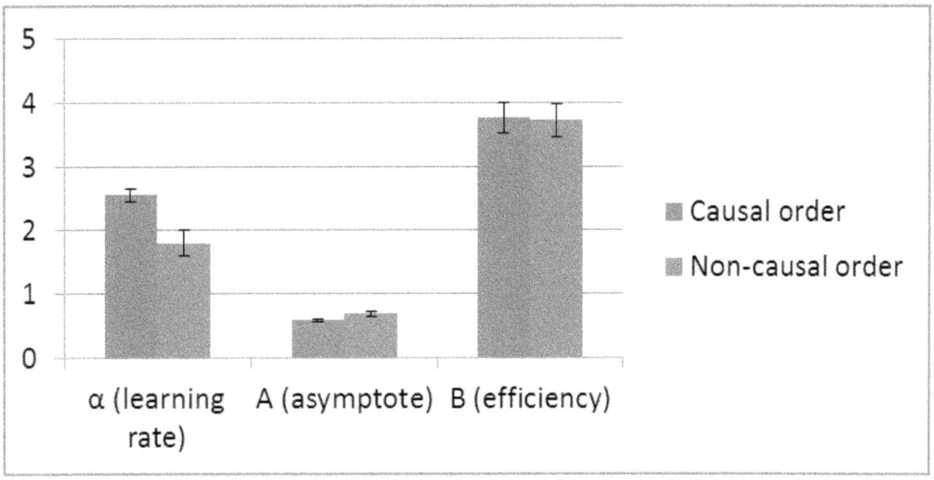

Figure 6: Comparison of learning curve model parameters shows a higher learning rate with the causal order interface.

parameters across interaction orders. Participants using causal order had a higher learning rate than those using non-causal order (t(32)=3.48, p=.001). In contrast, there was no difference in the effectiveness parameter. Participants using causal order also had slightly better asymptotic performance (t(32)=2.06, p=.047). A similar analysis using a power law model instead of the exponential model yielded similar results.

Discussion

The results of Experiment 2 show that it is learning and not efficiency that is supported by the causal order guideline, as predicted. The finding supports the claim that causal order makes interactions more intuitive and easier to learn.

Experiment 3 - Continuity

Experiments 1 and 2 explored the causal order guideline and found that it helps users learn a novel puzzle interface faster. Experiment 3 investigates the continuity guideline using the same puzzle but a slightly different interface. The continuity guideline states that when interacting with one object in an interface that affects another object, the effect should flow along a continuous path from the source to the destination.

Our first attempt at exploring continuity tested whether changing the cursor to represent the effect, as per the tool metaphor, is more effective than displaying the effect in a static location. Participants were faster with the continuous interface, but there were too many differences between the interfaces to pinpoint what made the continuous condition more effective. We designed Experiment 3 to control for those differences.

First, in Experiment 3, all conditions were animated and the animations took the same time in all conditions. The only difference between the continuous and discontinuous interfaces was whether the animations created paths from source objects to destination objects.

Second, Experiment 3 included two different continuous interfaces to compare with the discontinuous interface and with each other. One continuous interface included a simple animation from source to destination and the other included an animation that followed the cursor's path. One reason for the different continuous interfaces was to test whether some implementations of the continuity guideline, as described earlier, are more effective than others. The second reason was to test whether learning depends on keeping the transferred property close to the focus of attention, in this case the cursor.

Finally, Experiment 3 was designed to distinguish between continuity of the representation of a change, as stated in the guideline, and continuity of visual attention. Similar to the attentional explanation in Experiment 1, the continuity guideline could be effective either by aiding causal learning or by guiding attention. In addition to comparing the two continuous conditions, we aimed to distinguish the two possibilities artificially by adding distractors that capture visual attention automatically. Distractors were added to the interface as described below in order to disrupt continuity of visual attention in all conditions.

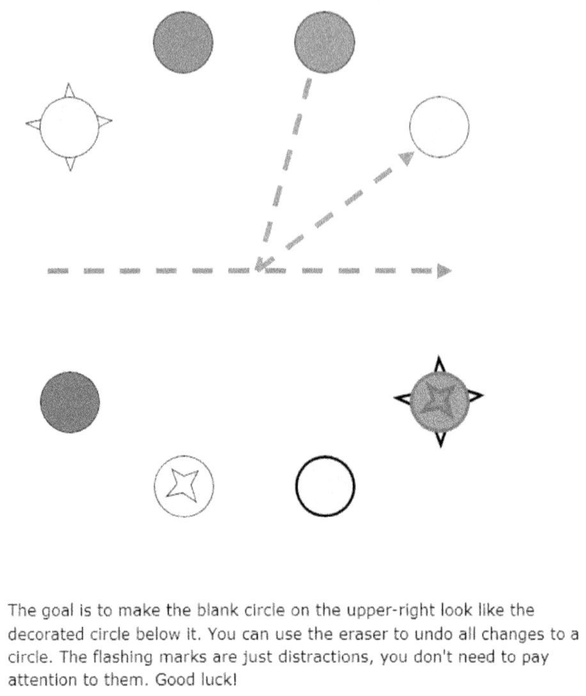

Figure 7: In Experiment 3, the objects were arranged in a circle and the effect of the current interaction was presented in the center (except in the *follow* interface). The blue and red arrows show the paths of the effect animation in the *continuous* and *discontinuous* interfaces when applying the red object to the blank one.

Interfaces

The interface in Experiment 3 included the same objects as the interface from previous experiments, but all interactions were in causal order and the objects were arranged in a circle to support displaying property animations during the interactions (see Figure 7). Each animation presented the effect being applied in that interaction, began when the source was selected and ended when the destination changed. For example, if a participant made the blank object red, a red circle appeared when they clicked on the red object, was animated along its path, and disappeared when the blank object turned red. Visual aspects of the animations, such as size, speed, and duration, were also matched across all variations of the interface.

The distinction among the three variations of the interface was the path that the animated property followed and whether it connected the interaction's source to its destination, as seen in Figure 7. In the *discontinuous* interface animations began at the leftmost point on the circle, paused in the center of the circle and finally ended at the rightmost point on the circle after a destination was selected. The leftmost and rightmost points of the circle were left empty so that regardless of which objects were chosen as the source and the destination, the animation did not create a continuous path between them. In the *follow* interface animations began at the source object, followed the path of the cursor and ended at the destination object after it was selected. Finally, the *continuous* interface animations began at the source object, paused in the center, and finally ended at the destination object. The animations in the *follow* and *continuous* interfaces satisfied the continuity guideline by creating continuous paths from sources to destinations. The *follow* interface linked the property to the cursor and the *continuous* interface kept them independent, representing implementations that change the cursor and add simple animations respectively. For the sake of brevity, we don't report another experiment that changed the appearance of the cursor instead of adding a follow animation and found an advantage for the continuous interface. Experiment 3 included the follow interface because it is more comparable to the other interfaces.

In order to distinguish between continuity of the representation of the effect and continuity of visual attention, the interfaces also included visual distractors designed to automatically capture visual attention. Each distractor was a crosshair 25 pixels across that randomly appeared in one of four locations inside the circle every 1.5-2.5 seconds. In addition to the random distractors, one of the left distractors flashed each time a source was chosen. This was meant to draw attention towards the beginning of the animation in the discontinuous condition and away from the animation in the continuous conditions. Similarly, one of the right distractors flashed just before each destination changed. Participants were instructed to ignore the distractors. As evidence that the distractors were effective, participants took longer to solve the puzzle than in a pilot study that was identical except that it did not have distractors.

Procedure
The procedure was the same as in Experiment 1, where participants solved a single puzzle. The fastest solvers received a bonus and participants had the option to quit after 10 minutes.

Participants
137 participants were recruited through AMT and were assigned randomly to the three interfaces. Each participant was paid for their participation, and the fastest 10% of participants in each condition received an additional bonus. We used TurkGate [8] to exclude participants that already participated in any of the previous experiments.

Results
87% of participants solved the puzzle and there was no difference between interfaces (S_c=87%, S_f=89%, S_d=85% ; $\chi^2(2)=0.34$, $p=0.85$). The remaining analyses only include participants who solved the puzzle. Figure 8 shows how long it took participants to solve the puzzle with each interface, as measured by number of clicks. We focus on number of clicks because of uncertainty in whether participants were slowed down by waiting for animations to complete. We also analyzed the solution times in minutes, and the results were analogous except where noted below.

Planned comparisons tested whether participants solved the puzzle faster with the continuous interfaces, *continuous* and *follow*, relative to the *discontinuous* interface and whether they solved it faster in the *follow* condition than in the *continuous* condition. ANOVA contrasts yielded a significant difference between the continuous interfaces and the *discontinuous* interface (M=113.87 clicks, SD = 70.87; $t(116)=2.06$, $p=.04$) but no difference between the two continuous interfaces ($t(116)=0.5$, $p=.61$), *follow* (M=88.88, SD=54.72) and *continuous* (M=98.72 , SD=56.86).

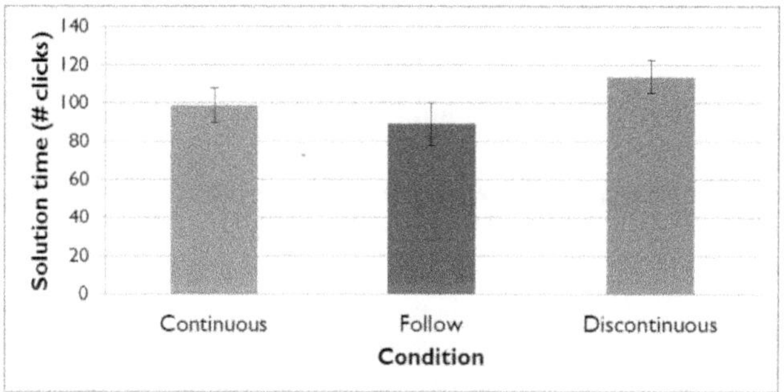

Figure 8: Comparison of solution times in Experiment 3 measured in number of clicks. Solution times were faster with the continuous interfaces (*continuous* and *follow*) when combined than with the *discontinuous* interface. There was no significant difference between the continuous interfaces.

Analyzing the solution times in minutes gave the same results, except that the non-significant difference between the continuous interfaces was in the opposite direction, the continuous condition was faster than the follow condition. This further supports the conclusion that there was no real difference between the different continuous interfaces.

Discussion
Participants using the interfaces consistent with the continuity guideline solved the puzzle faster than those that solved the puzzle using the inconsistent interface regardless

of the implementation. The solutions in all conditions were slower than in previous experiments and slower than in a similar study with no distractors. We attribute this to the distractors successfully grabbing participants' attention and to participants waiting for animations between clicks. In this way we controlled for the attentional explanation that was not addressed in Experiments 1 and 2. Together with the lack of difference between the continuous conditions, this reinforces our proposal that the causal guidelines are effective because they support causal learning.

DISCUSSION

Our experiments found that each of the causal guidelines helped design novel interfaces that were easier to learn. In this section, we discuss what interfaces are most likely to benefit from causal interactions as well as which common interactions are causal and which are not. The following discussion assumes that the causal guidelines are effective because they support causal learning although most of our claims hold even if our effects have a different source, such as locus of attention. Because causal relations are often perceived directly rather than reasoned about, causality and attention can be very difficult to separate. In addition to people's expectations about causal relations guiding their attention, where a person's attention is focused in a visual display influences what causal relations they perceive [6]. Although further studies are needed to determine the exact role of attention in the effectiveness of the guidelines, we believe the causal framing of the guidelines is the most appropriate because it highlights where they are effective.

Where do causal interactions make sense?

The causal guidelines are guidelines about how graphical objects in an interface should interact. Therefore, they only apply to graphical interfaces. Some variation of them may apply to command line interfaces, e.g. preferring verb-noun order over noun-verb order, but this issue is outside the current scope. The more interesting question is what constitutes an *object* in a graphical interface. In our view, any relatively stable graphical representation in the interface is an object. This includes both data objects, e.g. text or a canvas, and controls, e.g. buttons or menus. A context menu that appears next to an object when you right-click it, for example, is transient and therefore doesn't count as an object in itself. Therefore, it isn't clear that the causal guidelines apply to it.

Furthermore, the guidelines only apply to interactions that generate changes in the interface. If the results of an interaction aren't represented in the interface, e.g. changing the type of connection to a server, then the guidelines don't apply. Ideally, though, an interface should represent any part of a system that the user can interact with. Not doing so interferes with the sense that the interface *is* the system, which is a central principle of direct manipulation.

Even given these limitations, the causal guidelines apply to a surprisingly broad range of interfaces. For example, in the TurkGate application [8] the continuity guideline inspired a novel interaction design for what was originally a standard web form. This web page is used to generate a script for embedding in an AMT recruitment page to add extra security and experimental control. In order to support easy and intuitive revision of the form data after generating a script, the form and results are presented side-by-side as seen in Figure 9. The results panel slides out from under the form only when the form is submitted, thus maintaining continuity between the form and the generated script. The form remains visible and the user can edit their input at any time. If they submit again, the results panel slides back under the form, changes while hidden to reflect the updated input, and slides back out. User feedback has indicated that this design makes the form easier and quicker to revise than typical web forms.

Similar to other methods related to reification of interface elements, causal guidelines are likely to become even more relevant as we move beyond WIMP interfaces. The interfaces that should benefit the most are those that intertwine the physical world and the digital one, such as augmented reality and tangible interfaces [12]. When both physical objects and digital ones are part of the interface, the causal principles become a matter of the internal consistency of the interface instead of the consistency between the interface and a separate real world.

Which existing interaction patterns are causal?

When reviewing existing interactions under the lens of the causal guidelines, we found that many interactions fall into one of two categories, selection-based or tool-based. Selection-based interactions involve selecting the object that the user wants to change and then interacting with other objects that determine how it will change. When making text bold in a text editor, the user first selects the text and then presses the bold button to make it bold. Selection-based interactions are very common, but aren't causal. In tool-based interactions, users first select an action to apply to other objects in the interface and the cursor changes to represent the chosen action. The user can then apply the action to objects to change them. Tool-based interactions are less common than selection-based interactions, but they are causal. Our assertion is that all else being equal, tool-based interactions are more intuitive than selection-based interactions, and are therefore preferable.

The experiments here were designed so that the information conveyed in the causal and non-causal conditions were closely matched. Experiment 3 was also designed to control for the attentional explanation. Tool-based interfaces need not administer these controls and thus benefit from both supporting causal learning and guiding users' attention without the delays introduced by animations. Therefore, the results of these studies likely underestimate the advantage of tool-based interfaces over selection-based interfaces.

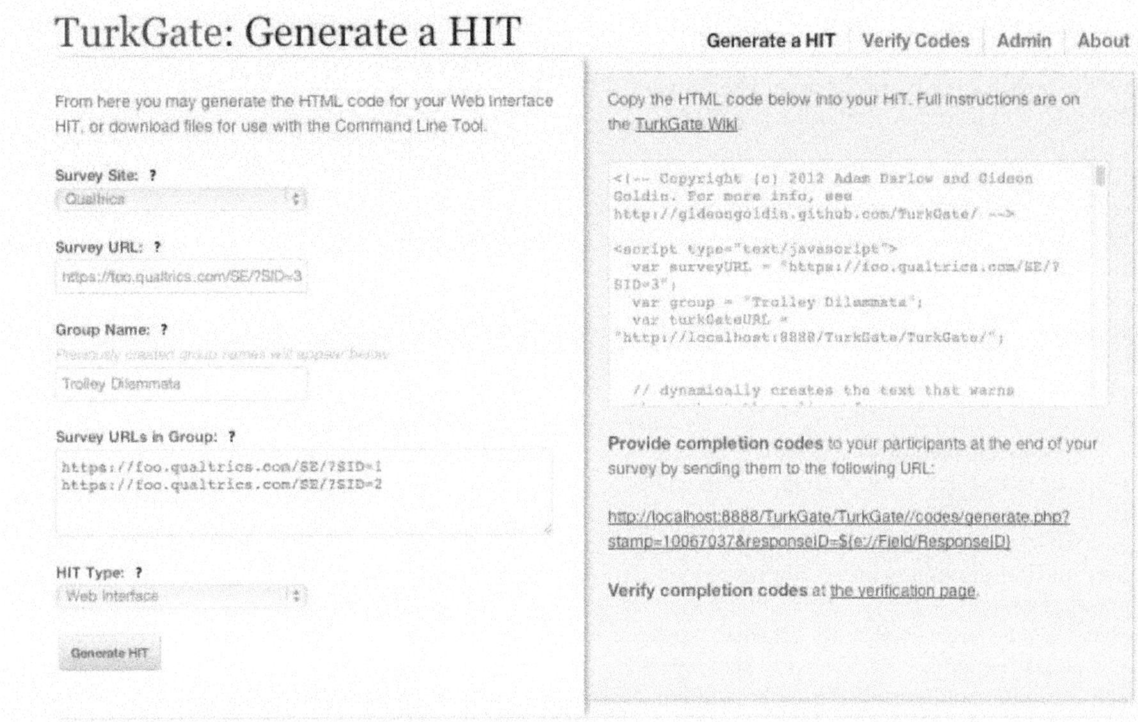

Figure 9: The TurkGate web form implements the continuity guideline by obscuring the results section behind the input section when generating its content and only then sliding it out to make the content visible.

If tool-based interactions are more intuitive, that raises the question of why selection-based interactions are more common. One possibility is that interface designers don't conceive of controls in the interface as objects [4]. Certainly in text editors, style controls like the bold button behave like properties of the selected text, not like independent objects. For example, the state of the bold button changes when text is selected to reflect the current style of the text. Selection-based interactions make sense given the conceptualization of controls representing properties and not objects. However, that raises the question of why the properties have their own stable graphical representations, independent of what text they are properties of. Recent versions of Microsoft Word, for example, have added a floating toolbar of styles that appears when text is selected. This is a better way to represent properties of text because it is transient and closely linked to text selection, and therefore doesn't suggest that the properties are objects in their own right. With the causal guidelines, we hope to help interface designers distinguish between objects and non-objects in their interface and make their behavior more consistent.

The other possible reason that selection-based interactions are more common is that all else is not equal and selection-based interactions have advantages that are not directly related to causality. Two possible advantages relate to persistence and the finality of selection. In selection-based interactions, the object selection is persistent and the user can easily make multiple changes to the object by interacting with multiple controls, e.g. making text bold and italic. In tool-based interactions, it is the chosen action that is persistent and it can be applied to multiple objects, e.g. painting on multiple areas in a canvas. Selection persistence isn't always more efficient, but it is more efficient in tasks with a few complex objects where you make many different changes to each object. In contrast, action persistence is more efficient when you make the same simple changes to many objects. However, action persistence is frowned upon in modern design guidelines [2] because it's considered modal: The behavior of the program is dependent on the action selected. Modal interfaces are used only when absolutely necessary, e.g. when there are no individual objects to select. Our research suggests that tool-based interactions should be considered more often as long as the interface can overcome the problems with modality by making the mode salient and easy to change.

Another concern regards how interfaces freely mix causal and non-causal interactions. For example, again in Microsoft Word, the highlighting tool can be used in either a selection-based manner or a tool-based manner, presumably because of the familiar metaphor of real-world highlighters as well as the efficiency of action persistence in the workflow of marking up a document. The highlighter coexists with strictly selection-based interactions, e.g. the style buttons, and a few strictly tool-based interactions, e.g. the format painter. The inconsistency only becomes apparent with the causal analysis and future research should explore whether this inconsistency confuses users.

CONCLUSION

In this paper we presented two design guidelines based on principles of human causal reasoning. The guidelines enable interaction designers to create interactions that are consistent with causal temporal order and the continuity of mechanisms, so that their interfaces are perceived as a causal system. We demonstrated how following these guidelines makes novel interfaces easier to learn using several different implementations of the guidelines. We also used the guidelines to distinguish two common classes of interactions, selection-based and tool-based, and discussed the trade-offs involved in choosing between them. Finally, we presented a novel design pattern for forms inspired by the continuity guideline. We hope that this research will encourage researchers to explore other psychological principles that can be translated into effective design guidelines and encourage interaction designers to adopt the guidelines and to think about the interfaces they design as causal systems.

ACKNOWLEDGMENTS

This research was conducted as part of the first author's dissertation research. We wish to thank David Laidlaw and David Badre as well as fellow members of the Sloman Lab who provided helpful feedback during the research and on previous versions of the written work.

REFERENCES

1. Ahn, W. and Kalish, C.W. The role of mechanism beliefs in causal reasoning. *Explanation and cognition*, (2000), 199–225.
2. Apple Computer Inc. *Macintosh human interface guidelines*. Addison-Wesley, Reading, MA, 1992.
3. Beaudouin-Lafon, M. and Mackay, W.E. Reification, polymorphism and reuse. *Proceedings of the working conference on Advanced visual interfaces - AVI '00*, ACM Press (2000), 102–109.
4. Beaudouin-Lafon, M. Designing interaction, not interfaces. *conference on Advanced visual interfaces*, (2004), 15–22.
5. Blackwell, A.F. The reification of metaphor as a design tool. *ACM Transactions on Computer-Human Interaction 13*, 4 (2006), 490–530.
6. Choi, H. and Scholl, B.J. Effects of grouping and attention on the perception of causality. *Perception & psychophysics 66*, 6 (2004), 926–42.
7. Fernbach, P.M. and Darlow, A. Causal Conditional Reasoning and Conditional Likelihood. *Proceedings of the 32nd annual meeting of the Cognitive Science Society*, (2009), 1088–1093.
8. Goldin, G. and Darlow, A. TurkGate. *[Software]*, 2013. http://gideongoldin.github.com/TurkGate/.
9. Harré, R. and Madden, E.H. *Causal powers: A theory of natural necessity*. Rowman and Littlefield, 1975.
10. Heathcote, A., Brown, S., and Mewhort, D.J.K. The power law repealed: The case for an exponential law of practice. *Psychonomic Bulletin & Review 7*, 2 (2000), 185–207.
11. Hutchins, E., Hollan, J., and Norman, D.A. Direct manipulation interfaces. *Human-computer interaction 1*, 4 (1985), 311–338.
12. Ishii, H. Tangible bits: beyond pixels. *Proceedings of the Second International Conference on Tangible and Embedded Interaction*, (2008).
13. Jacob, R.R.J.K., Girouard, A., Horn, M.S., and Zigelbaum, J. Reality-based interaction: a framework for post-WIMP interfaces. *Proceedings of the ...*, ACM (2008), 201–210.
14. Lagnado, D.A. and Sloman, S.A. Time as a guide to cause. *Journal of Experimental Psychology: ... 32*, 3 (2006), 451.
15. Michotte, A. and Miles, T.R. *The perception of causality*. Methuen London, Oxford, England, 1963.
16. MOCHON, D. and SLOMAN, S.A. Causal models frame interpretation of mathematical equations. *Psychon Bull Rev 11*, 6 (2004), 1099–1104.
17. Shneiderman, B. Direct manipulation: a step beyond programming languages. *Sparks of Innovation in Human-Computer Interaction 08*, (1993), 57.
18. Tversky, A. and Kahneman, D. Judgment under uncertainty: Heuristics and biases. *Science 185*, 4157 (1974), 1124.
19. White, P.A. A theory of casual processing. *British Journal of Psychology*, 4 (1989), 431.

Personas is Applicable – A Study on the Use of Personas In Denmark

Lene Nielsen
Center for Personas Research & - Application, IT University, Copenhagen
Rued Langgaardsvej 7, 2300 Copenhagen, Denmark
lene@itu.dk

Kira Storgaard Hansen
Center for Personas Research & - Application, IT University, Copenhagen
Rued Langgaardsvej 7, 2300 Copenhagen, Denmark
kist@itu.dk

ABSTRACT

The persona method is gaining widespread use and support. Many researchers have reported from single cases and novel domains how they have used the method. Few have conducted literature studies in order to identify and discuss the different understandings of the method. Fewer still have reported on ethnographic studies of practice. This paper falls within the last category, reporting on a study on how practitioners in Denmark use the method, and their perceptions of benefits and challenges when using the method. Finally, different casts of personas obtained from the involved companies are analysed. The findings are compared to reported studies of practice. Contrary to the existing findings the study reports that the method is well integrated into existing practices.

Author Keywords
Personas; scenarios; application; practice-study

ACM Classification Keywords
H.5.m.

INTRODUCTION

The persona method has developed from being a method for IT system development to being applied in many other contexts, including development of products, marketing, communication strategy, and service design [29]. So far most research focus either on single cases of application or on the introduction of the method in novel domains. Only a few include experienced designers in their studies and fewer still have studied more than one organization. There is therefor a need to understand how designers apply the method, how it is used in organisations, when in the design process it is used, and for what. Furthermore, there is a need for a deeper understanding of the pros and cons of the method.

CHI 2014, April 26–May 1, 2014, Toronto, Ontario, Canada.

ACM 978-1-4503-2473-1/14/04..$15.00.
http://dx.doi.org/10.1145/2556288.2557080

To bridge the gap of understanding of how personas are used in practice we conducted 28 interviews in 13 Danish companies, within both the private and the public sector. We furthermore got access to 47 confidential persona descriptions. The study examines the practitioners' perceived benefits, experienced challenges when using the method, and at how they have improved and adapted the method. Finally, different casts of personas are analysed. This provides insight not only in regard to how and for what the method is used, but also in how the companies develop the method adopting it to new areas and creating novel ways of using the method.

In this paper we compare the findings from the study to existing literature on personas use in practice. Contrary to the findings in the literature we found that personas are perceived as a success and used for design decisions throughout the design process. The method co-exists with other User Experience (UX) methods and is most often not used for all projects, but only when it is deemed as the best method for the project. There are a number of challenges most notably that the method does not provide instructions of use and that it becomes difficult to create personas when the audience is international.

This study contributes with a much-needed generalizability to current understandings of personas, and it provides valuable insights across different lines of businesses into how a large group of practitioners use and perceive the method. This enables both a deeper understanding of the method and provides practitioners with applied experiences to learn from.

PERSONAS

In the literature there is a common understanding that personas should be based on field data such as surveys, user interviews, observations, and a combination hereof, that they are created in the beginning of the design process, and should be used for different design activities [7, 28, 32].

Furthermore a set layout for the persona descriptions can be observed in the literature. The persona has a name, the description is most often 1-2 pages long, and has several subsections that describe the persona's characteristics, life, behaviours, goals, and preferences. Often a photo accompanies the description [19].

These are theoretical understandings and recommendations, but studies of the method in use paint a somewhat different picture.

Studies of personas use

Most research on personas in use is based on single case studies that report and/or evaluate the method, how it was used, and the benefits and pitfalls of the method, [e.g. 9, 21, 34]. Based on the case, the method is criticized, and/or refinements to the method are suggested [e.g. 15], or the inclution of new user groups is suggested e.g. system attackers [2]. This line of research is similar to multi-case studies that evaluate use across cases [e.g. 4].

Others have reported on use in novel domains such as creating child-personas [1], using personas within e-health [e.g. 20, 36], for service design [14], or using dramaturgical methods together with personas [e.g. 16, 31].

Some have developed the method using quantitative data for personas elicitation [e.g. 24], the design of a conceptual model for automatically creating and validating personas [26], also reports on creating personas based on assumptions have been made [10]. Furthermore, some have developed and evaluated the method by looking at single aspects of it e.g. segmentation [18], attributes [6], or the effect of using photos versus drawings or action figures [19, 27]. The last mentioned are classical comparison studies where groups of designers or students try out different versions of the same material. The results are then compared.

Literature studies are rare in the field of personas. The authors have been able to find two studies that look at the literature on personas: a discursive study on texts that describe the persona technique [22], and an overview of persona kinds, attributes and characteristics based on literature studies that divides personas into three categories: 1) personas founded on data 2) personas founded on data with fictitious elements and 3) fictitious personas. Each category holds a unique level of detail for the persona description [11].

Studies of practice

This paper reports on a study that falls within a rare group, as there exist very few larger studies of the personas method in practice. The small number is insufficient in order to make meaningful conclusions on the pros and cons of, and usage practices for personas. Moreover, it makes results difficult to compare, as the prerequisits are different. Furthermore, only 3 prior studies have included experienced designers and of these, only 2 have studied more than one organization.

The role of the researcher in the literature on personas in practice can be divided into three different categories: 1) researchers have been part of the design process either as facilitators or researchers. This category of studies, report from both single and multi-case studies. 2) Researchers were not part of the studied cases, but initiated the research and observed the use of the method in practice. 3) Researchers captured and analysed practitioners' perceived understandings of the method and reported use.

The first category holds numerous studies while observations and studies of perceived understandings are few. This current study falls into the third category and we will in the following treat literature from both category 2 and 3 as they can be compared to our study.

In the following we introduce six studies that fall within the second and third category: A discourse analysis of decision-making in a design company [12], an ethnographic study on a project where the material and data covers several sites [13], an ethnographic study of personas in use in an interaction design team [3], a study of experts' view on the benefits of personas in the design process, the experts were asked to prioritize and create consensus on the benefits [25], a study of 14 experienced UCD practitioners' perception and use of personas, all from the same company [23], and finally [5] the results from an online survey among IXDA members on how personas are created.

An overview of the findings in the literature reveals that:

Personas are not used for design: Two studies on application of personas report that personas are used not for design, but solely for communication purposes [13, 23]. The reasons stated for not using them in design are: lacks of relevance [13], designers prefer scenarios to personas [3], misleading descriptions [5], and finally poor introduction and incorporation of the method into the design process [3].

Moreover, designers find that personas are not relevant for fundamental technical solutions only for interface decisions [13]. Scenarios written out of scope can make programmers reject all scenarios [13], and a study revealed that scenarios play a greater role than personas [3]. Finally, poor introduction of the method and unclear separation between the process of creating personas and the use of personas in the design process are potential reasons for personas not being used in design [3].

Designers do not refer to personas in their discussion, but to their own opinions and impressions: A discourse analysis revealed that designers did not use personas in their discussions; instead they used their own opinions and impressions in appeals. The designers who had developed the personas, referred to them slightly more. These designers were perceived as persona custodians and used the personas in critical instances [12].

The persona descriptions can be problematic: The content of the persona descriptions might also create resistance to the method. Designers found that personas are abstract and impersonal, and that personifying information misleads and distracts [23] and programmers became critical because of certain details in the descriptions [13].

Personas are not created entirely from data: Designers use input from different users to create the description, the content comes from user studies, but also from the designers' own assumptions [5].

Personas are not created at the beginning of a design process: Contrary to the recommendations personas are created throughout the design process and not only at the beginning [5].

Benefits of the method: Other research points to the benefits described and advocates for the use of personas and describes the method in detail, such as [7, 8, 32, 33]. The reported benefits include: Personas help prioritize audiences and bring about a focus on the most important audience(s) [25]. In line with this personas bring assumptions to the surface and challenge long-standing (and often incorrect) organizational assumptions about the customers [25]. Personas focus product development on users/customers and their goals [25] including that the method support advocating for user needs with the development team [23]. Personas also help individuals realize how the users/customers are different from themselves [25]. Furthermore, personas help prioritize product requirements and help determine if the right problems are being solved [25] enabling practitioners to advocate their designs and prevent stakeholders from making design decisions for themselves [23].

A STUDY OF THE USE OF PERSONAS IN DENMARK

This paper reports on a qualitative study among Danish companies who has experience in creating and using personas. All participants have been involved in creating and, in most cases, using personas within their current employment. The study took place from October 2012 to January 2013.

To find and recruit companies that have experience in using personas online channels, such as LinkedIn groups, were used. Additionally advertisements in two expert fora newsletters and word of mouth were used. Finally, to broaden the perspective and get companies outside our existing network, Google searches were performed using keywords such as: personas and usability, and the companies found were contacted. We succeded in approaching 13 large, medium-sized and small companies from both the public and private sector, of these 6 have worked with international personas [30]. We are aware of that the self-selected recruiting method creates a bias as it makes it more likely that participants with a positive experience with personas will participate. Despite this we managed to find one company and do interviews with two participants with a negative experience.

Interviews

We set up interviews with 28 participants. The interviews were performed as single interviews, interviews with 2-3 participants present from the same company, and several interview sessions within the same company. The decision on how to conduct the interviews depended on company size as small companies often have only one employee working with personas while large coorporations have many working in different positions, departments, and contexts.

All participants had experience with personas and most of them had been working within project development and management. Most were domain experts with no formal design education.

The interviews were conducted as qualitative, semi-structured research interviews. In the interviews participants were asked to describe: their process of working with personas, who initiated the use of personas, how they collect and use data, the design process, how personas are communicated and shared, and how they use the personas. Furthermore, they were asked to reflect upon benefits and challenges inherent to the method. During the process of interviewing two subjects occurred that we followed up on in later interviews: new approaches to the method where role-play is applied and the extended benefits and challenges of the method when companies have an international perspective on personas.

METHOD OF ANALYSIS

The goal of the study has been to gain knowledge about how personas are created and used in Danish companies. The interviews were analysed for statements on creation and use. Furthermore, the aim of the analysis has been to provide insights into the general tendencies for persona use generated from statements shared by many participants and insights into novel initiatives generated from statements shared by few participants. Moreover, to find the causal relations that can describe why companies act as they do in regard to persona creation and use.

In line with Kvale's [17] advice to start the analysis already when interviewing, we began identifying the recurring issues of working with personas already in the interview situations. Furthermore, while listening to the recorded interviews, different sound bites were identified through the method of condensation [17]. The condensed transcripts were analysed for statements on use and use situations.

In order to identify which general benefits, challenges, and problems the companies face when using personas and which strategies they use to overcome the challenges the statements were mapped into categories.

Moreover, the companies gave access to 47 persona descriptions. These were analysed for coherence, methods of communication, visual expression, and content.

FINDINGS FROM THE INTERVIEWS

As it can be seen in Table 1 most companies started using personas around 2008-9 and have by now approximately four years of experience with the method. Two companies are "novices" and started introducing the method as late as a year ago (2012) while four companies have more than 8 years of experience.

Most describe their work with personas as satisfactory or very satisfactory. Only one of the companies interviewed had an altogether failed attempt to use personas and had, as a consequence of the failure, abandoned the method. In the interviews it is a recurring theme that the current successful use is based on several failed attempts. Reasons for former failures vary and among the reasons mentioned are material created by foreign departments, lack of management support, lack of organizational maturity, and lack of considerations on how personas can be useful. An example of failed attempt is expressed in the following quote:

C5: "The people who were part of the project were critical towards the method. It was not the best choice to say: "we have these results" and then get somebody who opposes the method to implement it. That was a wrong decision. [...] At least one person should have been passionate about it [the method]."

The current successes are based upon support from management and employees, understanding of the usefulness of the method and, not least, integration of the method into the design process.

Persona development

We identified three different approaches to personas development; either entirely in-house, or development is outsourced to consultants, or a mix hereof where the project team cooperates with a consultancy to create the personas (see Table 2).

From the analysis we found a connection between company size, experience, and resources spent on personas. Companies tend to spend more resources on personas the larger they are and the more experienced they are.

Company size and type	Type of product	Years of personas use	Interviewee role	Personas examples provided
Large, Private	Product	1-4	1: Innovation specialist. 2: Business Excellence Developer. 3: International Product Manager	8 personas
Large, Private	Software	8+	1+2: UX designers. 3: PM lead. 4: UX research lead	An overview of the persona cast, but not the actual descriptions
Large, Private	Software	-1	1: Project Manager. 2: Online training specialist. 3: Technical Writer	3 persona examples + additional material (postcard sent from the personas)
Large, Private	Service	-1	1+2: IT developers. 3: Project manager.	None
Large, Public	Services	1-4	1: Chief consultant. 2: Principal	6 personas
Large, Public	Service	1-4	1: Area manager. 2: Librarian Researcher	4 personas
Medium, Private	Consul-tancy	8+	1: Senior UX Manager. 2: UX consultant	None
Medium, Private	Consul-tancy	8+	1: Chief Advisor. 2: UX developer	None
Medium, Public	Service	1-4	1: Consultant in digital communication	7 personas
Medium, Public	Service	4-8	1: IT Consultant	6 personas
Small, Private	Consul-tancy	1-4	1: Project manager. 2: Head of secretariat. 3: Student assistant	10 personas + 34 persona sketches
Small, Private	Consul-tancy	1-4	1: Project manager	An overview of a persona cast, but no actual descriptions
Small, Private	Service	8+	1: Trainee	2 personas

Table 1: Overview of companies and interviewees

Persona creation

There is great variety in the amount of data that is the foundation of the persona descriptions. Most participants refer to projects with extensive ethnographic studies others to small-scale research, and a few projects have no data but have built the personas entirely on own existing assumptions.

There is a correlation between large amounts of data and high satisfaction with the persona method. Surprisingly, there is also a correlation between no data and high satisfaction. The participants who expressed less satisfaction with the method were found in the companies that had some data, but where the data sample was not experienced as being rich. An explanation of this apparent paradox could be that those with no data do not know that they lack data, but experience the positive effects of the method such as alignment of communication and having a steering tool for development. While those that lack rich data, understand that the data sample could be better.

Personas in use

All interviewed from companies with successful or very successful persona experience - all companies except two - perceive the method as well embedded in their organisation. This was observed in the interviews when the respondents from the companies, where the method was described as thoroughly embedded in the organization, referred to the personas by name as if they are persons they know and described the personas as something that resides in the back of their minds constantly.

However, there is a great difference in how the method is in fact used within the companies and we can distinguish between two approaches to the use of personas: personas as an integrated part of the development process or an ad hoc approach where the method is used less systematically. Most of the companies have an ad hoc approach, where use of personas varies from project to project both in relation to where in the process they are used and how they are described. The rationale behind the different approaches to the persona method seems to lie in the communication challenges that correspond to company size. In small companies there is no need for a formalized approach to gather and communicate user knowledge. For large companies it is a challenge to disseminate knowledge. The strategies are either to have a formalized development process that includes personas (reported from one company) or to tie user knowledge together with the specific project (reported in most companies). This latter approach makes it more random for participants in other projects to encounter the persona descriptions. This is not a problem in small companies where the information typically is tied to the individual and stays with the one who works on the project.

Most companies have a specific group that develops the personas - in rare occasions together with external partners or consultants. Other project teams have inherited persona descriptions from previous internal projects and the descriptions have been redesigned to fit the present projects. Finally, some companies have a cast of personas that is in constant development, and it is an on-going process to keep them updated and suitable for current projects.

The lifespan for a cast of personas depends on the project horizon. Some projects run for several years, while others lasts only a couple of months. Within a company there might exist both short and long project horizons. More than half of the companies have the same cast of personas that is used for more projects. In four companies the project team developed new casts of personas for each projects, whereof three are forced to do so as they have different clients.

What are personas used for?

As can be seen in Table 2 personas are used in all phases of project development. The companies use personas in multiple design situations: they are used for website-, app-, and product development, for planning of physical environments, and for service design. The method is used for alignment of communication, definition of target groups, and for design of interaction. Most projects involve some sort of interaction with a screen, but many report that they have used personas for product development of physical objects and for communication purposes. Around half of the participants report that they use personas to solve specific design tasks such as web design, IT development,

Development	Creation	UX methods	Use	Purpose	Satisfaction
• Developed in-house. • Developed by consultants. • Developed both by consultants and in-house.	• Large amount of data (7 companies) • Medium amount of data (2 companies) • No data (4 companies)	• Always use of UX methods these include personas. • Always use of UX methods sometimes personas. • Sometimes use of UX methods sometimes personas.	• Integrated in the development process. • Ad hoc use.	• Ideation and design (10 companies). • Cooperation and communication (10 companies). • Management (7 companies). • Sales and marketing (7 companies).	• Very Satisfied with personas (5 companies). • Satisfied with personas (7 companies). • Not satisfied with personas (1 company).

Table 2: Overview of categories identified in the interviews

interior design, sales strategies, and marketing material. The method is also used for development of strategies.

There is a common tendency that personas are used more in the initial than in the later phases of a project. In the initial stages personas are mainly used for ideation and tests of prototypes. As expressed by this participant it makes the designer think of the users right from the start:

"C4: We use them for example when we write use cases, when we design user interfaces, and the navigation, [...]. I use a lot of other methods besides personas when I develop, but I find personas a useful tool as foundation - and it gets the human into the early, more technical, phases."

In the later stages they are used for recruiting users to usability tests.

It is noteworthy that the company that discarded the persona method reported that they had no understanding of when in the process personas should be applied and how it could provide value.

In the analysis of the interviews we found that for personas to be successful, the method needs to provide for more than an understanding of who the users are. Additionally, the tasks that can be solved by using personas need to be considered from the beginning of the project. Finally, the method is a success when: it is used to develop scenarios of use, personas are directly involved in the development process, whether it is design or sales, and when it is a design tool.

Role-play as a new approach

In parallel with the more traditional representation of personas as posters and hand-outs interviewees from five companies reported that the project participants have created different forms of persona performance. Additionally, interviewees from three companies report that they have cooperated with companies that have used role-play, but that they did not actively participate in the performances [31].

The role-play is mainly used to act out scenarios for user journeys and to explore the information flow and characteristics of the persona's search behaviour. It is performed both with hired actors and with internal personnel that act as the personas, and both with and without props such as; masks, figures, and dollhouses. Most describe that the acting occurs as a spontaneous design activity. By acting out the personas the designers get an understanding of the persona as a character and of the flow of use. The performance occurs as a natural extension of the persona method, but not as something explicitly inherent in the method. Even though role-playing is mentioned in several interviews, the interviewees perceive themselves as the first to try out the different ways of role-play.

The value of persona in an international perspective

In the companies with a global audience and globally distributed project teams the benefits and challenges of using personas are perceived as even bigger than within a national setting. The benefits are twofold: a shared language to discuss and talk about users that are nationally and culturally diverse, and a shared understanding across departments and national borders [30]. The challenges are mostly connected to data collection, as it is described as especially challenging to get enough data and to know when there is enough data. The project participants try to solve this by collecting data from different parts of the world, but none of the participants have data from all the markets they address.

The companies either develop persona descriptions that represent users from different countries (e.g. one Finnish, one Polish, etc.), or descriptions that are so general that they can fit a wide variety of countries. Some companies combine the two strategies, by dividing the persona descriptions into an overall part and a part that singles out national differences. The global perspective can be observed in both naming and the connected images.

C8: "One is from Frankfurt, one from Poland, and one from Norway. [...] In order to create a broad representation of users and contacts we must have some personas from around the world. We asked our reference group: "Do we need personas from around the world?" [...] They said it makes good sense as we sell worldwide. [...] It is not randomly selected countries, each are chosen to represent several countries."

Opposition to the persona method

Even though the method is perceived as successful several incidents of opposition are mentioned in the interviews. Opposition against the method comes both from clients, in-house project participants, and management. Clients, project participants, and management question whether you can earn money on using the method. Management expresses opposition due to lack of strategy for what the method is to be used for and how it can provide value. Additionally, as the personas method is perceived as a fun, its' ability to add value is questioned. Furthermore, if personas are entirely based on qualitative data, there is opposition against the research approach, as quantitative data is perceived as more credible than qualitative data. Finally, it can be difficult to identify with a user who is far away from, especially, the developers' world and skills.

Benefits

The successful implementation rests on a row of benefits. Shared by all is that personas provide a common language, this covers both the method's ability to provide internal and external project participants with a common language and a common understanding of the users. For the large companies it is a common language between departments and across national borders. The following quote is from a participant that works in a large international company:

C12: "One thing is for sure it has provided a common language [...] I become quite warm [at heart] when at meetings where you hardly know anyone and then somebody says: "then Alex would think like this". Then we all know whom we are talking about. [...] – And this is internally in our department and right out to our subsidiary companies."

In line with this, personas give deeper insights into the users including insight into what value the product will create for the users. Personas provide insights into user needs and focuses the decision processes on both user needs and company goals. Including that the process of developing personas has in itself the benefit of gaining deeper insight into the users and to mainting focus on the users. In line with this the process enables discussions of the project participants' implicit assumptions, thus making them explicit. In the following quote a participant expresses how personas have changed the company's design process:

C11: "We are still quite technically oriented and nerdy when we develop. Now we describe the customers' needs first [...]. This is completely different from what we did before. And personas have helped us understand what needs you are to cover."

Another benefit is that personas becomes a management tool in the development process that guides development towards what the users want instead of what is novel. In line with this personas reduce time and money spent as the right products and solutions are developed. For the tasks personas help define their nature including creation of use cases and scenarios. Furthermore, personas used in present day scenarios create clarity in the decision processes as it provides precision in users needs and company goals.

Challenges

Personas include a row of challenges that can be hard to overcome. One such is that it takes time and money to create personas, this is perceived as the only actual downside of the method.

C12: If you want to have valid [personas] then it easily costs between 250.000 and 500.000 Danish Kroner. That is quite a lot to put into a method. For a large organization and to be done well it also demands a proper validation and large sets of data. I find it an expensive tool.

Some mention that it is challenging to keep the descriptions updated so they reflect reality. And it can be hard to keep in mind that the personas are not real users and cannot replace meetings with real users. If you have a large cast of personas – more than 10 - it becomes difficult to encompass all in the design process.

A challenge that regards the use of personas is that the method in itself does not provide instructions on how to use the personas, as the focus is on descriptions of people. In line with this it can be a challenge to create useful descriptions with enough or proper information for design decisions. This is expressed in the following quote:

C2: "These persons they can't feel because they are fictitious. That I find is the biggest downside. And you can't ask them."

In an organisational perspective it can be difficult to get the personas anchored in and communicated to both the organization and clients. Furthermore, it can be difficult to get management support. This includes that some organizations/project participants do not understand the qualitative nature of the method and questions the validity of a small number of interviewed and thus finds that the method cannot cover all users.

FINDINGS FROM THE PERSONA DESCRIPTIONS

In most literature the persona descriptions relate to Cooper's method where goals are a central part of the persona description [7, 8]. This seems not to be the case in Denmark, but there is a common understanding of what a persona description should contain and a standard for length, visual, and textual layout has been developed.

All descriptions have a length of approximately one page, there is a photo depicting the persona, and the text is divided into small sections with headings. The format makes it easy to get an overview of how many personas there is in a cast and how they differ. The differences are further supported by color-coding and for some descriptions by different tag lines or sentences.

Persona naming

All persona descriptions have a name, but some have in addition a tagline that characterizes the persona, it can be a role, quote, motto, demographics or marketing characteristics e.g. 'Baby-boomer'. Some have personality types added to the name e.g. 'optimistic'. A few persona casts had several taglines. Both name and taglines enables the reader to identify differences between the personas.

Consistency

There is a relation between how long the personas exist and how thorough the descriptions are. In the companies that create new personas for each project the descriptions are less thorough and have less consistency between the different personas in a cast.

There is furthermore a tendency towards that the persona casts from companies that are new to the method are less coherent. This is especially observed in the companies where the persona method is not a core method, but a minor and more ad hoc practice. Furthermore, companies that have not had external consultants to help them with the persona descriptions have less coherence in their persona cast, with incoherence in wording and layout.

The photo

All the persona descriptions we have had access to, have worked with visual strategies to get the descriptions to foster empathy. However, the visual strategies differ in connection to how the company/project group perceives the concept of personas. Is the persona a representation of an average user based on quantitative and/or qualitative data? Is it rather a management tool aimed at embracing variety of user behaviour? Or is it an extreme user created for design purposes? The differences in perception of the persona concept is expressed in the following two quotes from different companies

C1: "What it [personas] really is, are patterns in data."

C12: "To us the advantage of a persona is that it is an extreme user. If you for example design an elevator, then there is a need that a wheel chair can enter – that is an extreme user. [...] And this is important to explain; a persona is a representative for a user group, it is not the average of a user group.

The strategies differ in the following ways: some create mood-boards that show pictures from the personas everyday life, in line with this the illustrations can be true to real life situations and leave an impression of the persona being an actual person. Other descriptions are created to look artificial e.g. one description is illustrated by the same persona at different ages and different representations wearing clothes in the same shades of colour, which points to the persona not being a real person.

Texts

All persona descriptions have text divided into subsections that portray personality features and characteristics and subsections that include information relevant for the specific project. It is different how much weight is put on the two parts. Some descriptions have a clear division between the sections that creates empathy and the sections that inform on use- or work related issues. Other descriptions integrate the two kinds of information.

In one persona cast the descriptions of present time scenarios were intertwined with the persona description. This made the persona description hard to use, as the whole concept behind personas is to use them in the design of future products. This might explain why this company cancelled using the method.

Extra material

Several projects had developed extra material such as post cards and life-size personas in order to enable empathy and to sustain the use of personas. The companies, where the persona method is well integrated, have considered how to promote the persona descriptions in the workspace, e.g. by hanging persona posters at central places in the company or placing posters on the floor.

DISCUSSION

We will in the discussion compare our analysis with the previous mentioned findings from the literature.

Personas are not used for design

In the literature it is reported that personas are used only for communication purposes and not for design. In design the method of building scenarios play a greater role than personas. In the rare occasions where personas are used for design it is only for interface decisions and not for fundamental technical solutions.

It is noted that designers who develop the personas refer to them more and that the designers who develop the personas become persona custodians.

The analysis of the presented study shows a somewhat different picture than in the existing literature. First and foremost, personas are used for design decisions, this was found across disciplines from IT development to architecture. The participants report that the personas only become valuable when they are used directly in the design process. Moreover, several participants report that personas are used in discussions and that designers refer to them and argue from their needs in order to take the right design decisions.

We did not experience a distinction between technical solutions and interface design. Furthermore, we did not see scenarios without personas all participants refer to personas and scenarios as a combined method. What we did see in the analysis is that there are designers who unknowingly become a sort of ambassador and drives the introduction of the method and the following use of personas. But there is more to the picture, it is not always the designers who use the personas that have developed them and most often many designers are involved in the use of a cast.

Designers do not refer to personas in their discussion

In the literature it is found that designers refer to their own opinions and impressions in discussions instead of to the personas.

As we did not take part in any discussions we have not been able to verify or falsify this. But in the interviews we did hear a lot of actual references to the personas and references to how including personas in discussions had helped in the design process.

Problems with persona descriptions

For the persona descriptions it is found in the literature that personas are perceived as abstract and impersonal, and that personifying information misleads and distracts. Additionally, some programmers can be critical because of specific details in the descriptions.

The first issue is not recognised in the Danish study, whereas the programmers' critical stance can be found in the oppositions towards the method where some mention that it can be difficult to identify with personas that are very different from one self.

Personas are not created entirely from data

In the literature it is presented that personas can be based entirely on data, they can be based on data and fictitious elements, or they can be based solely on fiction and the foundation range from based on ethnographic immersions to produced on the fly.

As reported in the analysis the personas in the Danish companies are created on very different material, from huge user studies to designers' own assumptions. Different from the literature is that the participants are aware of when they use their own assumptions.

It is difficult to tell the level of fictional components from the descriptions we have had access to. There seems to be fictional components in all the descriptions when it comes to the more personal parts.

In our research we never encountered any projects where the creations were produced on the fly. The descriptions were produced on very different sets of data, but even the companies that had no data had created a very thorough process to obtain as much internal knowledge as possible.

Personas are not created at the beginning of a design process

A common finding in the literature is that, contrary to recommendations personas are created throughout the design process and not only at the beginning.

This does not correlate with our findings. Companies where personas are created from project to project create the personas mainly in the beginning of the design process and use them at different stages in the process. Other companies have a set cast of personas that are used for multiple projects, thus they are not created in the beginning of the project, but they are used from the start to the end of the project.

Benefits

The literature mentions several benefits of using the method: Personas help individuals realize how the users/customers are different from themselves. They help prioritize audiences and bring about a focus on the most important audience(s). For product development they help focus on users/customers and their goals. In line with this personas help prioritize product requirements and help to determine if the right problems are being solved. Finally, personas are useful when communicating with non-designers and non-UX practitioners.

The reported benefits from the literature are seen in this study as well. The benefits are perceived as understanding users and their needs, but also providing a common language that enables discussions on users. Furthermore, the method is perceived as a management tool that reduces wrong decision-making. The process of developing personas enhance the insights into the users and in line with this the project participants' implicit assumptions are discussed and thus becomes explicit. We have no explicit reports on the benefits when discussing with non-designers and non-UX practitioners, but what we can see is that it is used in many different phases of the design process involving many different work roles.

CONCLUSION

In the study of use of personas in Danish companies we found both similarities and differences in comparison with the existing literature. Most significant is that personas are created in the beginning of the design process and that they seem to be well integrated into the existing design practices and used for design. This may also explain why some companies have used the method for more than eight years and why most companies are satisfied or very satisfied with the method. But despite the current achievement, in many companies the success rests upon several failed attempts to use the method.

Concerning data, descriptions purely made on own assumptions, were observed, but contrary to the literature there is an awareness of the difference between data and own assumptions.

There is accordance between the perceived benefits in the literature and our study.

This study broadens the understanding of the application of personas in that it has found that companies develop the method e.g. when introducing role-play together with personas. Furthermore, it reports on the extended challenges and benefits that arise when companies have a transnational market and creates an international cast of personas.

Finally, we found a challenge inherit in the method as the lack of guidance of use in the persona descriptions. This needs to be looked upon in future studies.

ACKNOWLEDGMENTS

This research is supported by InfinIT- Danish network for innovative utilization of IT. We thank Line Mulvad and Sabine Madsen for support.

REFERENCES

1. Antle N.A. Child-Personas: Fact or Fiction? *Proc. DIS 2006,* (2006).
2. Atzeni, A., Cameroni C., Faily S., Lyle J., and Flechais I. Here's Johnny: A Methodology for Developing Attacker Personas. *Proc. ARES '11*, IEEE, (2011) 722–727.
3. Blomquist, Å. And Arvola M. Personas in Action: Ethnography in an Interaction Design Team. *Proc. NordiChi 2002*, ACM, (2002) 195–198.
4. Bødker, S., Christiansen, E., Nyvang, T, and Zander, P-A. Personas, People and Participation: Challenges from the Trenches of Local Government." *Proc. PDC 2012.* ACM Press, (2012) 91–100.

5. Chang, Y. Lim, Y. and Stolterman, E. Personas: From Theory to Practices. *Proc. Building Bridges*, ACM, (2008) 439–442.
6. Chapman, C.N., Love, E., Milham, R.P., ElRif, P., and Alford, J.L. Quantitative Evaluation of Personas as Information." *Proc. HFES 52nd Annual Meeting,* (2008) 1107–1111.
7. Cooper, A., Reimann, R., Cronin, D. *About Face 3.0: The Essentials of Interaction Design*. Wiley, (2007).
8. Cooper, A.: *The Inmates Are Running the Asylum*. Indianapolis. SAMS, (1999).
9. Dotan, A., Maiden, N. Lichtner, V. and Germanovich. L. Designing with Only Four People in Mind? – A Case Study of Using Personas to Redesign a Work-Integrated Learning Support System. *Proc. HCI '09* Springer, (2009) 497–509.
10. Faily, S. and Flechais I. Persona Cases: a Technique for Grounding Personas." *Proc. CHI '11*, ACM (2011) 2267–2270.
11. Floyd, I. R., Jones, C. M., and Twidale, M. B. Resolving Incommensurable Debates: A Preliminary Identification of Persona Kinds, Attributes, and Characteristics. *Artifact 2, 1,* (2008) 12–26.
12. Friess, E. The Sword of Data: Does Human-Centered Design Fulfill Its Rhetorical Responsibility?" *Design Issues 26, 3,* (2010) 40–50.
13. Gudjónsdóttir, R. and Lindquist, S. Personas and Scenarios: Design Tool or a Communication Device? *Proc. COOP'08*, (2008) 165-176.
14. Hosono, S. Hasegawa, M. Hara, T. Shimomura, Y. and Arai T. A Methodology of Persona-centric Service Design. *Proc. 19th CIRP*, (2009) 541-547.
15. Junior, P. T. A., and Filgueiras, L. V. L. User Modeling with Personas. *Proc. CLIHC '05*, ACM Press, (2005) 277–282.
16. Kantola, V., Tiitta, S. K. Mehto, K. and Kankainen, T. Using Dramaturgical Methods to Gain More Dynamic User Understanding in User-centered Design. *Proc, C&C 07*, ACM Press. (2007) 173–18.
17. Kvale, S. I*nterView*. Hans Reitzel. (1997).
18. Laporte, L., Slegers, K. and De Grooff, D. Using Correspondence Analysis to Monitor the Persona Segmentation Process. *Proc. NordiChi 2012,* ACM, (2012) 265–274.
19. Long, F. Real or Imaginary - the Effect of Using Personas in Product Design. *Proc. IES Conference, 2009*. Irish Ergonomics Review, (2009).
20. Ma, J. and LeRouge, C. Introducing User Profiles and Personas into Information Systems Development. *Proc. AMCIS 2007*, (2007) paper 237.
21. Markensten, E. and Artman, H. Procuring a Usable System Using Unemployed Personas." *Proc. NordiCHI 2004*, ACM Press, (2004) 13–22.
22. Massanari, A. L. Designing for Imaginary Friends: Information Architecture, Personas and the Politics of User-centered Design. *New Media & Society, 12, 3,* (2010) 401–416.
23. Matthews, T., Judge, T. and Whittaker, S. How Do Designers and User Experience Professionals Actually Perceive and Use Personas?" *Proc. CHI ' 12*, ACM, (2012) 1219–1228.
24. McGinn, J. and Kotamraju, N. Data-driven Persona Development." *Proc. CHI '08* ACM Press. (2008) 1521–1524.
25. Miaskiewicza, T., Kozarb, K. A.: Personas and User-centered Design: How Can Personas Benefit Product Design Processes? *Design Studies 32, 5,* (2011) 417–430.
26. Negru, S. and Buraga S. Towards a Conceptual Model for Describing the Personas Methodology. *Proc ICCP '12* IEEE (2012).
27. Nieters, J. E., Ivaturi, S. and Ahmed, I. Making Personas Memorable. *Proc. CHI '07*, ACM Press, (2007) 1817–1824.
28. Nielsen, L. *Engaging Personas and Narrative Scenarios*. Vol. 17, PhD Series. Samfundslitteratur (2004).
29. Nielsen, L. *Personas - User Focused Design*. Human-Computer Interaction. Springer (2012).
30. Nielsen, L., Nielsen, K. S., Stage, J. and Billestrup, J. Going Global with Personas. *Proc. INTERACT 2013*. Springer, (2013).
31. Nielsen, L. and Nielsen, K. S. Personas - from Poster to Performance. *Proc. PIN-C*. 1, Chap. 273, (2013) 270–273.
32. Pruitt, J., Adlin, T. *The Persona Lifecycle*. Morgan Kaufmann (2006)
33. Pruitt, J., Grudin, J. Personas: Practice and Theory. http://research.microsoft.com/en-us/um/people/jgrudin/publications/personas/pruitt-grudin.pdf (2003)
34. Rönkkö, K. Hellman, M. Kilander, B. and Dittrich, Y. Personas Is Not Applicable: Local Remedies Interpreted in a Wider Context." *Proc. PDC 2004*, ACM, (2004) 112–120.
35. Sinha, R. Persona Development for Information-rich Domains. *Proc. CHI2003*. ACM, (2003).
36. van Velsen, L. van Gemert-Pijnen, L., Nijland, N. Beaujean, D. and van Steenbergen, J. Personas: The Linking Pin in Holistic Design for eHealth. In *proc. eTELEMED 2012* (2012).

GestKeyboard: Enabling Gesture-Based Interaction on Ordinary Physical Keyboard

Haimo Zhang*
National University of Singapore
13 Computing Drive, Singapore
z-haimo@comp.nus.edu.sg

Yang Li
Google Research
Mountain View, CA 94043, USA
yangli@acm.org

Figure 1: Gesturing on a physical keyboard. The green overlays show the keys that have been pressed and the red ones show the currently pressed keys. The red line running across keys illustrates the captured gesture stroke.

ABSTRACT

Stroke gestures are intuitive and efficient but often require gesture-capable input hardware such as a touchscreen. In this paper, we present GestKeyboard, a novel technique for gesturing over an ordinary, unmodified physical keyboard—that remains the major input modality for existing desktop and laptop computers. We discuss an exploratory study for understanding the design space of gesturing on a physical keyboard and our algorithms for detecting gestures in a modeless way, without interfering with the keyboard's major functionality such as text entry and shortcuts activation. We explored various features for detecting gestures from a keyboard event stream. Our experiment based on the data collected from 10 participants indicated it is feasible to reliably detect gestures from normal keyboard use, 95% detection accuracy within a maximum latency of 200ms.

Author Keywords

Physical keyboard; gesture detection; modeless interaction.

ACM Classification Keywords

H.5.2 [User Interfaces]: Input devices and strategies. I.5.2 [Design Methodology]: Classifier design and evaluation.

CHI 2014, April 26 - May 01 2014, Toronto, ON, Canada
Copyright is held by the owner/author(s). Publication rights licensed to ACM.
ACM 978-1-4503-2473-1/14/04…$15.00.
http://dx.doi.org/10.1145/2556288.2557362

INTRODUCTION

Gesture-based interaction is intuitive and efficient for many interaction tasks, and has become a promising interaction modality on various new-generation devices such as smartphones, tablets and tabletops. However, gesture-based interaction has not seen significant adoption in traditional computing environments and devices such as desktop computers or laptops. One important reason is that either traditional devices lack appropriate gesturing input mediums or existing input devices have been occupied for other purposes.

Existing work that enables gesture-based interaction on a traditional computing device usually introduces additional hardware [6][8][11]. Although it is possible to use existing path-making devices such as a mouse or a trackpad for gestural input, an explicit mode switch is often required to disambiguate the gestural input from other uses of these devices such as target acquisition.

In this paper, we present GestKeyboard, a technique that allows a user to perform gestures on an ordinary, physical keyboard. It requires no additional hardware, allows modeless switching between gesturing and the designed use of a keyboard—text entry and shortcut activation, and reduces homing effort—users can complete many tasks without having their hands to leave the keyboard switching to other input devices.

Previously, physical keyboards have been augmented with additional sensors for various purposes such as pressure-sensing [3] or touch display keyboards [2], and gesture support on keyboards has not been the focus of prior work. In contrast, we intend to enhance a regular keyboard for

* This work was done during an internship with Google Research.

gesture input with no physical modification or additional hardware. Our basic idea is straightforward. We view each key on the keyboard as a binary sensor that tells if a key is pressed, and the entire keyboard as an array of such sensors. By tracking when each key is pressed and released, we can recover a low-resolution trajectory of finger movement on the keyboard that can be fed to a gesture recognizer for interpretation.

However, enabling such a gesturing capability is not without challenges. The keyboard provides a limited spatial resolution and when sliding the finger on the keyboard, key events are often noisy. For example, not every key on the finger travel path is registered and a key press might generate multiple events. In addition, we need to quickly differentiate gesturing from regular keyboard uses especially text entry. In this paper, we contribute the following:

- A user study for understanding gesturing and regular keyboard behaviors and soliciting subjective feedback on gesturing on the keyboard;
- A method for detecting gesturing from typing on the keyboard that achieves high accuracy (95%) within reasonable latency (maximally 200ms);
- A process for transforming a keyboard event sequence into a spatial trajectory for gesture recognition and an adaptation of a template-based recognizer;
- Two examples of GestKeyboard that demonstrate its use at both the platform system and the application level.

In the rest of this paper, we first discuss the characteristic of physical keyboards and clarify our research problems. Two challenges in realizing GestKeyboard: gesture occurrence detection and gesture recognition. We then describe our user study, by which we collected user data for investigating these problems as well as acquiring user feedback on the usefulness of keyboard gestures. Next, we discuss our solutions and report their performance. We present two applications of GestKeyboard and discuss its limitation and future work. Finally, we discuss related work and conclude the paper.

TECHNICAL PREAMBLE

We started our investigation by understanding our target gesture sensing device—existing physical keyboards, including its hardware characteristics, its event representation and geometry that transforms an array of binary events into a spatial trajectory.

Keyboard Hardware

Most keyboards detect key presses and releases via a matrix of circuits [4][7], consisting of columns and rows of wires that are not in contact with each other. Keycaps are located at the intersections between column and row wires. When pressed, the keycap would bring the respective column and row wires into contact. The location of the key press is therefore detected by successively setting a high voltage on each column wire, and detecting the high voltage signal on each row wire. This scheme creates two issues, "ghosting" and "masking", when multiple pairs of column and row wires are connected at the same time, which creates ambiguous key presses. "Ghosting" refers to a key press being incorrectly reported even when it is not pressed, due to multiple other keys being pressed simultaneously (usually more than three keys) that short circuit the column and row wires underneath the "ghosting" keycap; and "masking" refers to the pressing and releasing of the "ghosting" key not seen by the keyboard controller, which considers the "ghosting" key to be always pressed.

The "ghosting" and "masking" phenomena can be avoided by using diodes, which prevents the wires from being shorted via other pressed keys. However, this mechanism is still absent in most keyboards. For GestKeyboard to be usable for as large an audience as possible, we decide to focus on single-finger gestures to avoid the ghosting and masking effect, since a single finger is less likely to press more than three keys simultaneously.

Keyboard Events

In most operating systems, a keyboard event encapsulates information about one single change of the keyboard state, which includes the timestamp that change occurs, the keycap that change involves, and the type of that change. The time is often in milliseconds or microseconds, the keycap is often uniquely identified with a scancode, and the type can be press, release, or repeat of that keycap. Although much of the details are system and hardware dependent, this generic model of keyboard event suffices for our discussion of GestKeyboard.

Keyboard Geometry

To capture spatial movement on a keyboard for gesture detection, we model two aspects of a specific keyboard: the bounding box of each keycap relative to the top-left corner of the keyboard and the binary adjacency between keycaps. By modeling the keyboard geometry, we are able to calculate various features that are useful for gesture detection and recognition. For example, we can calculate the shortest distance between two consecutive key press events. Due to the existence of large keycaps such as the space bar or the "+" key on the numeric pad, the shortest distance between two keycaps cannot be simply calculated as the distance between their centers. Instead, we first "thin" each keycap as a line segment and then calculate the shortest distance between segments (see Figure 2).

Figure 2: Centroid distances (red line) versus segment-segment shortest distance (blue line) for non-square keys such as the space bar ("thinned" as the black line).

RESEARCH PROBLEMS

There are two important aspects of the problem. First, we need to understand how users would perceive gesturing on a physical keyboard regarding its usefulness and usability including the ergonomic issues. Second, we need to address the technical challenges regarding gesture detection and classification to yield a usable system.

User Perception on Keyboard Gestures

As we introduce gesturing as a new behavior to the keyboard, it is important to understand how users perceive its usefulness and what potential applications or interaction scenarios are for keyboard gestures. We hope to understand if it is feasible to use a physical keyboard as a gesture articulation device ergonomically. A keyboard does not offer a smooth surface and is not as easy or comfortable as a touchscreen or touchpad for sliding fingers above it. If a user presses her finger heavily, it is difficult to slide it across keys but if a user does so lightly, keys might not be registered and a trajectory will not be captured completely.

Gesture Detection & Classification

Due to limited spatial resolution of keys on a keyboard and possible sensor failures such as ghosting and masking of keys, we focus our research on single-finger unistroke gestures and assume that typing and gesturing occur in an interleaved way but not in parallel.

Both regular keyboard uses such as typing and keyboard shortcuts and gesturing produce keyboard events, with unobvious differences, and they can be highly interleaved. To allow a user to freely transition between these two types of behaviors without explicit mode switching, we need to determine if the user is gesturing from a stream of keyboard events—the gesture detection issue. Our solution needs to meet two criteria.

To not interfere with the major function of the keyboard--text entry and shortcut activation, our detection algorithm needs to be *highly accurate*. Missing a gesture—false negatives—would result in unintended operations such as gibberish characters entered as text and unintended hotkey combinations invoked that changes the system behavior. Capturing a gesture mistakenly—false positives—would lead to unresponsive interfaces, e.g., typed characters do not appear in a text editor, or unintended gesture execution.

In addition to accuracy, a related issue is the *decision latency*, i.e., the time needed for reliably detecting a gesture occurrence. For example, the user expects to see typed text to appear in a text editor with as little latency as possible. As a result, the detection algorithm should try to reject gesturing as early as possible, to allow for normal dispatching of keyboard events as for typing, of course, without missing intended gestures.

Once a gesture occurrence is detected, we need to recognize the gesture for invoking corresponding actions, given a sequence of keyboard events that are identified by the gesture detection phase. We currently focus on a template-based recognition approach that matches an unknown gesture against a predefined gesture set, because the approach is easy to implement and highly customizable.

We intend to find out if the low resolution of spatial trajectories captured by the key events would hamper the recognition accuracy. Because we aim at supporting both directional (e.g., sliding downwards for scrolling down) and symbolic gestures (e.g., "?" for help), which are useful for assisting common interaction tasks, we need to enhance existing template-based recognizers to support both types of gestures.

USER STUDY

We started our exploration by conducting a user study, to understand user behaviors and perception on keyboard gestures and to collect training data for gesture detection and classification. To facilitate our investigation, we selected a set of 16 target gestures by adapting a previous gesture set [13] (see Figure 3). In particular, we try not to include gestures with complex trajectories that can be inappropriate for a low-resolution gesture-sensing device—the physical keyboard.

Note that both directional and symbolic gestures are included in the gesture set. In particular, the four straight gestures are sequence-sensitive, e.g., if the articulation direction of the two horizontal gestures is reversible, they would become indistinguishable. The remaining (symbolic) gestures in the set are sequence-invariant. For example, a circle gesture should allow for both clock-wise and counter clock-wise articulation sequences.

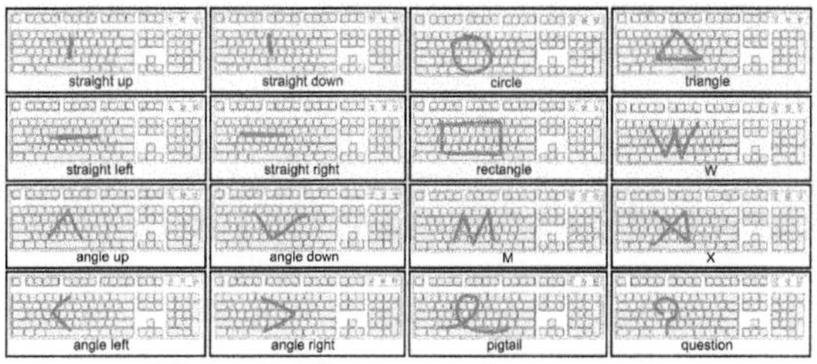

Figure 3: The proposed gesture set.

Keyboard Conditions

We expect the physical form of different keyboards to be an important factor for the applicability of GestKeyboard. On keyboards with a large vertical travel distance (the height of a key) and rugged keycap profile, such as the HP SK-2880 keyboard (Figure 4-a), sliding the finger on the keyboard would require the finger to laterally squeeze against the sharp edge of the keycap, in order to activate the keys along the path of the gesture. Performing a gesture on this kind of keyboard might induce uncomfortable physical experience and hinder speed and accuracy. In contrast, gesturing might be easier and more comfortable on keyboards with a small travel distance and smooth keycap profile, such as the Apple MB110LL/B Keyboard (Figure 4-b).

To observe the effect of different keyboards on gesturing experiences, we used two types of keyboard in our study, the HP SK-2880, representing the mainstream PC keyboards (thereafter referred as *full-size* keyboards), and the Apple MB110LL/B, representing the keyboards commonly found in laptops and Mac computers (thereafter referred as *compact* keyboards).

a) HP SK-2880 keyboard ("full-size" keyboard)

b) Apple MB110LL/B keyboard ("compact" keyboard)

Figure 4: The two types of keyboards used in our study.

Experimental Tasks & Procedures

We recruited 10 participants (2 females and 8 males, all right-handed, aged between 19 and 40, M=27). The participants had a various background including software engineers, project managers and attorneys. Half of the participants used full-size keyboards primarily, while the other half used compact keyboards more often.

To understand how the key events generated by gesturing on the keyboard are different from those by regular usage, our experiment involves two tasks: *gesturing* and *typing*. For brevity, we use typing to refer to regular uses of keyboard such as text entry using alphanumeric, punctuation, and the space keys and key combinations served as shortcuts, such as Ctrl+C/Ctrl+V for copy/paste, and meta characters, such as delete, home/end keys, and platform-dependent meta keys such as Macintosh's Command key. Each participant was asked to use both types of keyboard for typing and gesturing. The order of the keyboard use is counterbalanced. In each keyboard condition, a participant first completed a typing task and then a gesturing task.

Our typing task captures a typical text entry scenario. Participants were asked to type a plain-text document in English, and then follow the instructions to stylize the document using various keyboard shortcuts (see Figure 5). Participants were instructed to complete the typing task as naturally as possible, with their natural typing speed and shortcut habit, e.g., the preferred modifier location such as left versus right "Shift" key and the landing order in a key combination such as Ctrl+Alt+Del versus Alt+Ctrl+Del.

The typing task used a different document (with a similar complexity) in each keyboard condition such that participants do not enter the same document twice. Each document had about 1000 characters that involved about 50 unique characters and 4 different formatting styles from a set of bold, italic, hyperlink, center-aligned, underline and right-aligned. We provide a cheat sheet of 14 shortcuts for text editing and formatting to the participants.

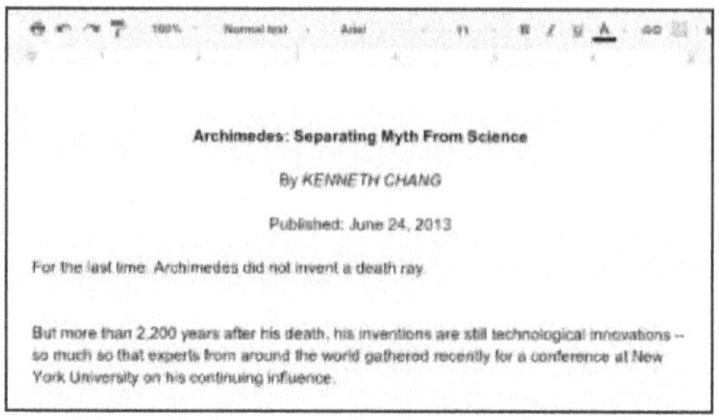

Figure 5: An example of our typing task.

In the gesturing task, participants were asked to perform keyboard gestures, by following an on-screen stimulus that shows one of the 16 gesture in Figure 3. Participants were informed that the presentation of the gesture in the stimuli is for the illustration purpose only, and they should perform the gesture in the way they are most comfortable with, regarding the size, speed, and location of the articulation on the keyboard. The visual presentation of the gesture is hidden once participants start gesturing to refrain them from precisely replicating the gesture. Participants were allowed to redo a trial if a mistake happens. The occurrence of the 16 target gestures is randomized with five repetitions for each gesture in total.

Experimental Apparatus

A desktop computer with Intel i7 processor and 16G RAM running Ubuntu 12.04 LTS operating system was used in the study. A low-level key logger recorded all the keyboard events throughout the study by reading from the /dev/input/event* file, which Linux uses to expose input events. The timestamps for the beginning of each trial and gesture stimuli were recorded, which allow us to segment and label the continuous keyboard event stream as chunks of typing and gesturing data as well as corresponding gesture categories in post processing.

Results

In total, we collected 1600 gesture samples (10 participants x 16 gestures x 5 repetitions x 2 keyboards), from which we excluded 6 samples that participants mistakenly entered (clearly belong to other categories).

We conducted a paired two-sample T test on the task completion time. On average, a typing task took 4162 seconds (SD=142 seconds) on the full-size keyboard, and 4607 seconds (SD=162 seconds) on the compact keyboard. $t(9)=3.0$, $p=0.015$. In contrast, for gesturing, the compact keyboard allowed a significantly faster gesture articulation speed (M=768ms, SD=385ms) than the full-size keyboard

(M=979ms, SD=604ms), $t(9)=2.941$, $p=0.016$, after log-transformation. The effect of keyboard conditions on the number of key presses generated from each gesture is not significant ($p>0.05$), with a mean of 10.2 keys, SD=4.2 (see Figure 6), which roughly reflects the resolution of these keyboards on sensing gestures.

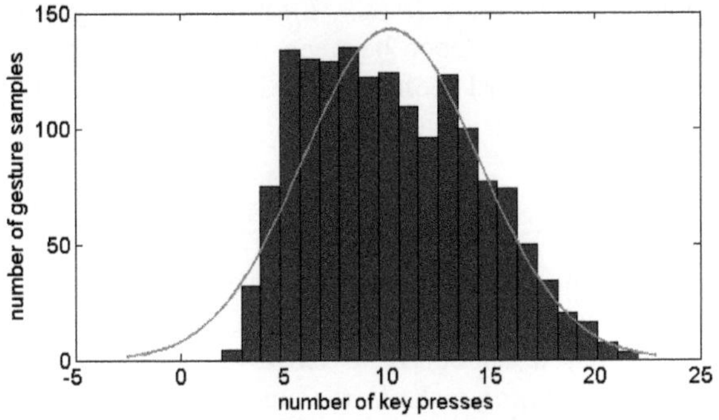

Figure 6: The distribution of the number of key press events generated from each gesture.

Gesture Articulation Characteristics. To understand how participants perform these gestures on the keyboard, we analyzed the articulation characteristics of the gesture samples. Although the four straight-line gestures have a designated direction, we deliberately left the articulation direction of the rest gestures undefined. For example, a circle can be drawn in either a clockwise or a counter clockwise fashion. This gives us an opportunity to observe users' preferences in performing these gestures on a physical keyboard.

We model the profile of gesture articulation direction by projecting each gesture stroke segment (a primitive finger motion as sensed by the keyboard) of collected samples onto three separate dimensions: horizontal, vertical and angular. For example, in the horizontal dimension, a movement can be left to right, right to left or no movement.

We found that gesturing tended to involve more left-to-right (59.4%) than right-to-left motion (40.2%), more downward (31.9%) than upward motion (21.3%) and more clockwise (58.9%) than counter clockwise motion (34.3%). Because all the participants in the study were right-handed, this observation implied that the participants preferred to contact the keycaps using the soft finger pad, instead using the tip or back of the finger.

We observed that the participants adopted various alternative articulation strategies in performing the gestures, such as using the soft pad on the tip of the index finger for a downward gesture, and using the back of the nail for an upward gesture. Several participants used the non-gesturing hand to hold the keyboard for stabilization while gesturing, while others completed the gestures single-handedly.

These observations have several implications for designing a keyboard gesture set. First, since participants tend to use their finger pad in most cases, it is important to have handedness in mind. For example, a left-to-right straight gesture might be easy for right-handed users, but uncomfortable for left-handed users. Second, it is advisable to design for gestures without much curvature in the path, since curvature would require the use of different parts of the finger to perform the gesture, which could be less comfortable. Third, some gestures might be easier to perform with alternative articulation strategies, such as using the thumb. It is useful to make users aware of these alternative strategies for increased performance and comfort.

Subjective Feedback. We solicit the feedback from participants to understand their perspective on the potential use of gesturing on the keyboard. Overall, the participants were excited about being able to issue gestures on a regular keyboard. In particular, the participants suggested several scenarios where GestKeyboard can be useful, such as shortcuts for editing a document while in a rush, web navigation using directional gestures (e.g., backward or forward) and shortcuts for launching specific applications. This feedback inspired us to develop two applications to showcase GestKeyboard that we will discuss later.

All the participants preferred using the compact keyboard over full-size keyboard. They felt that they were more accurate, more comfortable, and less frustrated when performing gestures on the compact keyboard, which is consistent with the gesture completion time we discussed earlier. Two participants felt that these keyboard gestures will shoulder part of functionality of existing keyboard shortcuts. In particular, keyboard gestures can be performed in an eye-free fashion.

DETECTING GESTURE OCCURRENCES

Because we intend to allow users to switch between gesturing and typing without explicit mode switching, we need to detect the occurrence of a gesture from a continuous stream of keyboard events. A naïve strategy is to assume every key event to be a potential start of a gesture. However, this will require us to run gesture detection on every key event that induces a constant overhead for event processing. Instead, we view the event stream as a sequence of typing and gesturing segments and between two consecutive segments, the keyboard is idle, i.e., no key is pressed for a certain interval. Ideally, the "heavy-lifting" of executing the detection algorithm should only happen at the start of each segment. Once the segment type is determined to be typing or gesturing, the subsequent keyboard events can simply carry the same segment type and be dispatched immediately until another idle stage occurs. Therefore, our first task in gesture occurrence detection is to segment the event stream.

Segmenting the Keyboard Event Stream

We segment a keyboard event stream based on if the idle stage before a new event (signals the start of a segment) or after the previous event (signals the end) is larger than a certain interval. Based on the gesturing data collected from our user study, on average, a gesture contains 3.7 idle stages for the full-size keyboard, and 2.5 for the compact keyboard. Based on the cumulative distribution of all idle durations (see Figure 7), we use the duration value at the 99% cut-off point on the empirical CDF as the timeout interval, which turns out to be 420ms for the full-size keyboard and 120ms for the compact keyboard—only 1% of the idle stages would lead to incorrect segmentation.

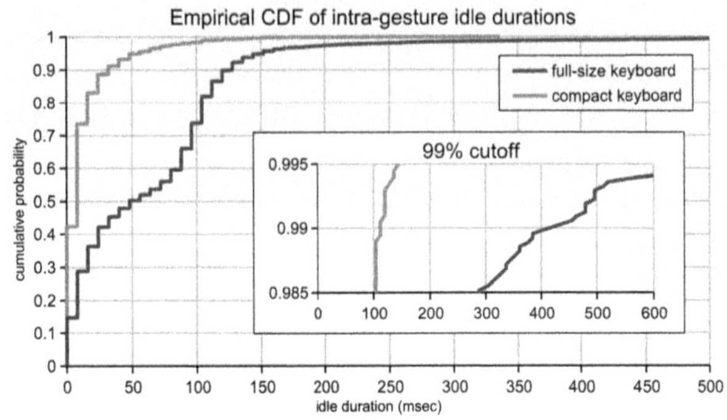

Figure 7: The empirical Cumulative Density Functions of intra-gesture idle durations. Inset shows the 99% cutoff.

These acquired timeout intervals will be applied to a continuous event stream at runtime for identifying the starting point of a segment and invoking gesture occurrence detection algorithms. For our offline analysis, we use these timeout intervals to segment the typing data into chunks, which are served as negative samples for training a gesture occurrence detector. Applying the timeout intervals on typing data results in 1,493 typing samples for the full-size keyboard, and 2,327 samples for the compact keyboard.

Creating a Gesture Occurrence Classifier

With the typing and gesturing samples generated in the previous steps, our gesture detection task reduces to a binary classification problem. To create an efficient classifier, we first look into various features that characterize gesturing versus typing behaviors, including both spatial and temporal aspects.

Keystroke Transition Distances

One obvious observation about gesturing on a keyboard is that consecutive keystrokes (key presses) in the stream tend to be close in distance, as the fingers slide across keys. In contrast, two consecutive keystrokes in typing can be quite distant on the keyboard depending on the target word or shortcut being entered.

To capture this difference, we look at both the mean distance M_K between consecutive keystrokes and its variance for the K keystrokes that have been observed so far in an unknown segment:

$$M_K = \frac{\sum_{i=2}^{K} D(E_{i-1}, E_i)}{K-1}, \quad K \geq 2 \qquad (1)$$

where E_i is the keycap name of the ith keystroke on the keyboard, and function $D(E_{i-1}, E_i)$ returns the segment-to-segment shortest distance between two keycaps, based on the specific keyboard geometry (see Figure 2). The variance, V_K, is in turn calculated as:

$$V_K = \frac{\sum_{i=2}^{K} \left| D(E_{i-1}, E_i) - M_K \right|^2}{K-1}, \quad K \geq 2 \qquad (2)$$

At this point, we can directly use these features to participate in the process for training a gesturing-typing classifier, based on our data. However, our typing data, from the two typing tasks in the study, is hardly inclusive for describing all possible keystroke transitions in day-to-day typing behaviors. To address this issue, we used an English language model (http://invokeit.wordpress.com/) to synthesize the typing data that can better reflect keystroke transitions in typing based on the follow procedure.

We start with the N-gram-frequency pairs from the language model, where the value of N ranges from 2 up to 5. Then for each N-gram, we generated the corresponding keystroke sequences. It is possible that an N-gram could be entered in multiple ways, due to alternative modifier key locations. For instance, either of the two "Shift" keys might be used to enter uppercase letters such as "A" or "?" character. Lacking empirical data on the probability of such alternative keystroke sequences, we simply generated all possible keystroke combinations for each N-gram with an equal frequency, summing up to the N-gram frequency. Finally, for each such synthesized keystroke sequence, we computed the mean distance and variance for the first K keys—K ranges from 2 to 5.

Note that the synthesized dataset is only useful for capturing keystroke transitions and it lacks other properties of the behavior that can only be observed in actual typing, such as temporal aspects. As a result, we only use the synthesized dataset to determine an optimal threshold for M_K and V_K, to discretize these features. We also computed M_K and V_K for K from 2 to 5 for each gesture sample from a dataset that we collected for the 16 gestures in a pilot study—that is separate from the user study reported earlier.

For each K, we want to determine an optimal threshold that can best separate gesturing from typing based on M_K or V_K. We achieve so through an ROC (Receiver Operating Characteristic) analysis on M_K and V_K for gesturing and synthesized typing (see Figure 8 for M_K for the compact keyboard). Note that each typing M_K and V_K is weighted based on the frequency of their originating N-gram in the ROC analysis. Based on these thresholds, we discretize M_K and V_K as M'_k and V'_k by assigning 1 if they are above their threshold and 0 otherwise.

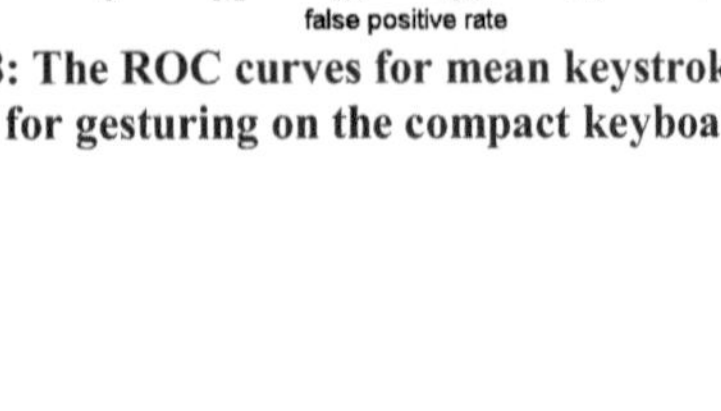

Figure 8: The ROC curves for mean keystroke distances for gesturing on the compact keyboard.

Adjacency Rates

Following on the keystroke transition distance feature family, we look into a similar but different aspect—the adjacency of two consecutive key presses. Note that two keystrokes that are spatially close are not necessarily adjacent. It is noticed that for gesturing, consecutive key press events often happen for adjacent keys on the keyboard, whereas it is not the case for typing. This spatial characteristic is captured as the adjacency rate, A_K, for the first K key press events in a sequence:

$$A_K = \frac{\left|\{E_i | E_i \in Adj_{i-1}, i \in [2, K]\}\right|}{K-1}, \quad K \geq 2 \qquad (3)$$

where E_i is the same as Equation 1, and Adj_{i-1} is the set of keycaps adjacent to the keycap of the i-1th key press event, which is acquired from the keyboard geometry. The numerator therefore denotes the number of pairs of consecutive key press events that are also spatially adjacent in the first K key presses. Note that a keycap should not be considered adjacent to itself: we expect gesturing to have a high adjacency rate and repeatedly pressing the same keycap, which is rare in gesturing but common in typing, should not increase the adjacency rate.

Revisitation Rates

Typing frequently involves the repetition of the same key, such as the space bar, or highly recurrent letters such as letter "e" in "succeeded". Gesturing, in contrast, rarely involves revisiting previously pressed keys—only when a gesture stroke intersects itself, e.g., the pigtail gesture. The keycap revisitation rate, R_K, is defined as the number of unique keycaps in the first K keystrokes of an unknown segment over the total number of keystrokes, i.e., K.

Idle Rates

Lastly, we observed that the keyboard is hardly ever at an idle state while gesturing, since the fingers would remain pressed on some keys. However, the dominant pattern for finger motion while typing is discrete striking of keycaps that presses and releases a keycap in a short time interval. This temporal characteristic is captured as the percentage of time that the keyboard is idle—the idle rate, I_K—during the first K key presses.

Combining Individual Features

Consider features generated from the same featurization process but for different K values a feature family. With the five feature families, M'_k, V'_k, A_K, R_K, and I_K, with K ranging from 2 to 5, a total of 20 features (4 lengths x 5 feature families) are computed for each sequence segment. If a segment contains fewer than K key press events, the feature F_k, $F \in \{M', V', A, R, I\}$, is assigned a default value -1, to indicate a missing value.

Based on these features, we used the C4.5 decision tree of WEKA to predict if an unknown segment is gesturing or typing from the 2nd to the 5th key press event since the start of a sequence, a separate binary decision tree model is trained for each, using all available features up to that event.

Because segmented typing samples are significantly more than the gesture samples for each keyboard condition from our user study, we balance the dataset by duplicating gesture samples to roughly have the same size as the typing samples. Based on this dataset, we tested each model with a 10-fold cross-validation. Figure 9 shows the mean accuracy for each individual feature family and for the decision tree combination of them.

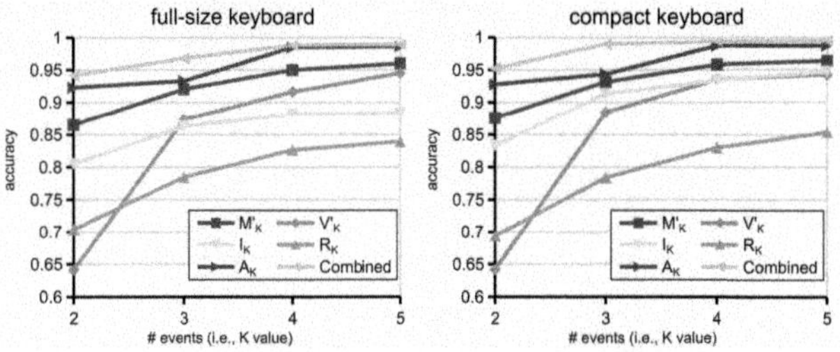

Figure 9: The detection accuracy for the full-size and the compact keyboard for the number of key press events used.

The results clearly show that adjacency rates (A_K) and mean keystroke distances (M'_k) are the more discriminative than other feature families. They require as few as two key press events to achieve over 85% accuracy. Idle rates (I_K) also consistently performed well. Combining all the five feature families with the decision tree outperformed each individual feature family with 94% accuracy based on only 2 key press events. By using 5 key press events and combining all the feature families, the decision tree reaches 99.5% and 98.9% accuracy on the compact and full-sized keyboard, respectively.

In terms of overall accuracy, using the full-size keyboard is almost as accurate as using the compact keyboard, which suggests the generalizability of the proposed features for different types of keyboard. One interesting observation is that, the type of keyboard has a more significant effect on the accuracy of the idle rate feature family than on other feature families. This phenomenon may be due to the large spacing and vertical travel distance for the full-size keyboards, which results in more idle stages even when gesturing, making it less distinguishable from typing.

Making Time-Sensitive Decisions

In the online situation, as keyboard events come in, our gesture detector should make a decision about if the user is gesturing or typing as soon as possible and at the same time minimize decision mistakes. The gesture detector is capable of making a decision once it sees two key press events, however, it needs to balance if it should make the decision now or wait until more events are observed.

A decision tree can give a confidence value for its classification result, and we need to determine an appropriate confidence threshold for accepting or ignoring a classification result. Although more events will lead to better accuracy (see Figure 9), it is important for the detector to resolve within a certain time limit. In addition, since keyboard events come in at an unexpected interval, which is not time-bounded, we need to impose a resolution timeout in our decision process, i.e., if a resolution timeout is reached, the sequence is force-resolved to typing. For a given confidence threshold and resolution timeout, it is necessary to understand the performance of the gesture detector, with respect to elapsed time since the start of the sequence (see Figure 10).

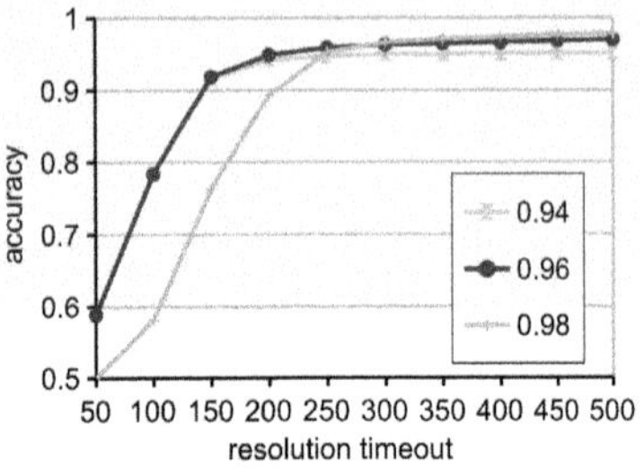

Figure 10: The detection accuracy for different resolution timeouts and confidence thresholds on the compact keyboard.

Each resolution timeout bounds the worst-case latency from the user starting to type to seeing the actions permanently committed to the system. We select 200ms resolution timeout and the 0.96 confidence threshold for our online detection process. This setting achieves 95% detection accuracy on both types of keyboard—on average 1 in every 20 detections is wrong, either a gesture sequence is detected as typing, or vice versa. Note that the 200ms latency only occurs when detection is triggered—a timeout followed by a keystroke, and could be reduced to tradeoff accuracy for responsiveness of the system.

RECOGNIZING GESTURES

Upon identifying a gesturing segment from the keyboard event stream, we need to recognize the gesture. We first transform the keyboard events of the segment to a sequence of timed 2D coordinates and then classify the sequence with a template-based recognizer adapted from previous work.

If we consider each keycap as a binary sensor with two possible states: pressed or released, a keyboard event essentially describes a state change of one of these binary sensors. A key press or release event triggers the transition from one state to another, and a key repeat event has no change in the pressed state. In turn, the entire keyboard can be viewed as a low-resolution sensor array. Each individual sensor could be of large and irregular shapes. We use the keyboard geometry—the bounds of each keycap relative to the top-left corner of the keyboard—to transform a

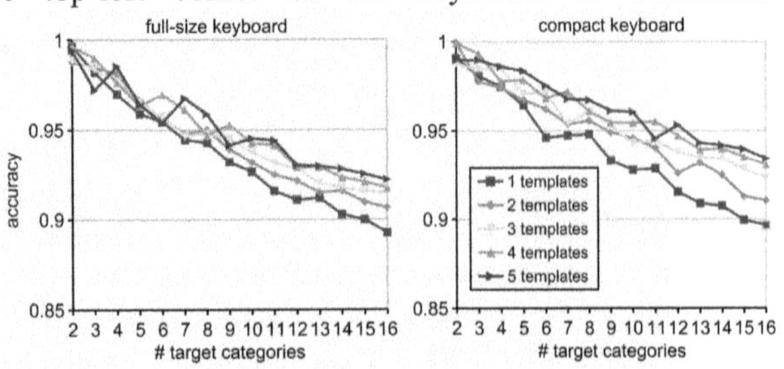

Figure 11: The recognition accuracy for each keyboard.

keyboard event stream into a timed 2D trajectory, i.e., an approximation of the finger's trajectory.

We maintain a set of currently pressed keys to reflect the current "footprint" of the user fingers, which is initially empty as we always start from an idle stage. Whenever a press or release event occurs, we add the key to the set or remove it from the set. For each update, we calculate the centroid of the footprint, C, as the following:

$$C = \frac{\sum \vec{p}_i a_i}{\sum a_i} \quad (4)$$

where p_i is the bounding box center of the ith keycap in the footprint key set, and a_i is its bounding box size. The centroid along the timestamp of the key event is appended to a 2D trajectory (see Figure 1).

We employ Protractor, a template-based gesture recognizer [9] for recognizing an acquired 2D trajectory, which matches a 2D trajectory against a set of templates. Protractor allows a developer to configure how sensitive the recognizer should be to orientation variation of a gesture. Because our gesture set involves gestures that would be indistinguishable from each other without considering orientation, e.g., four straight lines or gesture "M" versus "W", we set Protractor to be orientation sensitive.

Although several gestures in our target set are irreversible such as straight lines, many of our gestures are reversible, e.g., gesture "M" can be drawn from left to right or right to left. We could ask participants to perform additional gestures to capture both articulation directions. However, this would lengthen the study time and increase user fatigue and frustration. Instead, for each sample of a reversible gesture, we synthetically add its reverted trajectory to the template set. This allows the recognizer to support both types of gestures simultaneously without needing additional data. To find out the recognition accuracy of these keyboard gestures, we conducted a cross-validation splitting on participants—picking one participant's data for training and the rest 9's for testing and repeating the process for each participant. For each round, we varied the number of templates (training samples) from 1 to 5 and the number of target gesture categories (classes) from 2 to 16 (see Figure 11). Gesturing on the compact keyboard seems to be more accurate (M=95.3%, SD=2.5%) than on the full-size keyboard (M=94.5%, SD=2.6%), $t(df=74)=9.260$, $p<0.005$. For the most difficult classification condition (16 target gestures and 1 template gesture), the accuracy is 89.3%. When 5 templates per class is used to classify the 16 gestures, the accuracy is significantly increased to 92.2%. These results indicated that it is feasible to sense gestures on a physical keyboard.

EXAMPLE APPLICATIONS

We developed two applications using GestKeyboard: one allows a user to invoke applications anytime and the other allows a user to edit text, using GestKeyboard gestures.

System-Wide Deployment: GestRun

We developed an application launcher, named "GestRun" (see Figure 12), as a system-level service. Without going to a specific application (or the Desktop screen), a user can launch an application anytime, by performing a keyboard gesture. We leveraged shape mnemonics to ease learning of the gestures, such as the "circle" gesture for the Chrome browser, the "rectangle" gesture for terminal and gesture "V" for the Vim editor. GestRun provides a system-wide access to common applications, without consuming screen estate or requiring long click-throughs or search to find a specific application.

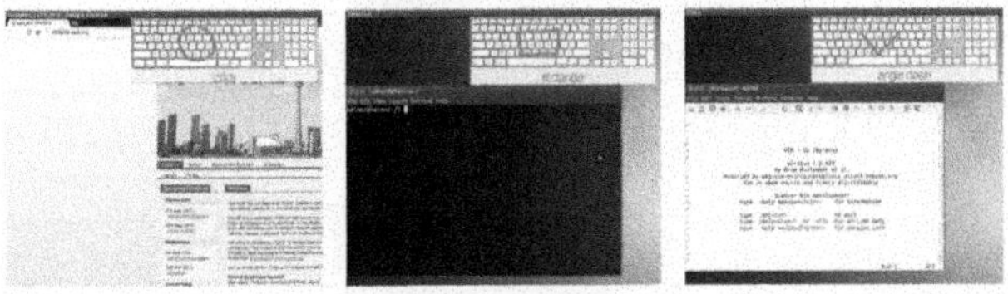

Figure 12: The GestRun application launcher. The recognized gesture is shown above the corresponding application for the illustration purpose.

Application Specific Deployment: GestEdit

We also used GestKeyboard to enhance text editing. We developed GestEdit that allows a user to use keyboard gestures for common styling tasks (see Figure 13), such as vertical swipes for super or subscripting, and angle gestures for font style manipulation. Many of these styling operations have no shortcuts defined in existing text editors.

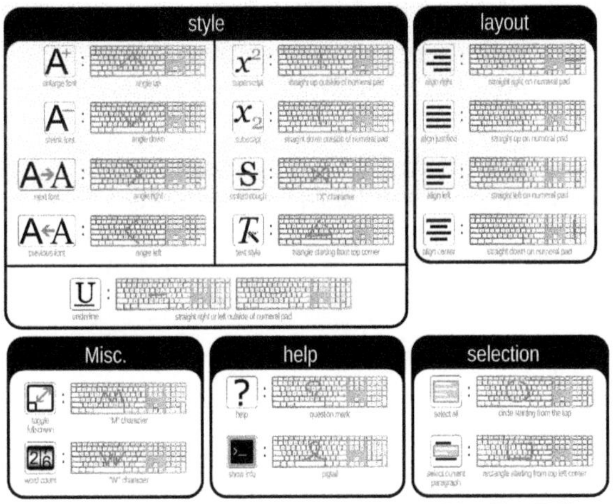

Figure 13: The gesture commands used in GestEdit.

In case a user is unsure which gesture to use, the user can pause the articulation by holding down the current keys. After a short dwell time (e.g., 500ms), an in-place popup menu is shown to present the gesture set and associated functions. At this point, the user can continue sliding her fingers to finish the target gesture. Alternatively, the user can cancel the ongoing gesture by pressing a key that is not adjacent to the current footprint,

GestEdit also leverages in which area of the keyboard a gesture is performed and invokes different functions for each area, e.g., the straight-line gestures map to alignment functions if they are performed on the numeric keypad.

LIMITATIONS AND FUTURE WORK

GestKeyboard allows a user to perform a set of useful gestures on a regular physical keyboard that is equipped on every desktop and laptop computer. However, the ghosting and masking effect with most existing keyboard hardware prevents us from exploring gestures that require multiple simultaneous touch points, such as multi-touch or shape gestures [10]. In particular, shape gestures such as rolling the palm or fist across the keyboard can be easier to perform than stroke gestures that involve lateral friction.

Before gesture detection is resolved, there are two options to process the key events that have occurred for an unknown segment. GestKeyboard can hold on these events until the decision is made, and then dispatch them as well as the following events to either typing or gesturing, which continues until another segmentation timeout occurs and gesture detection is invoked again. This would incur a maximum of 200ms latency in interaction. Alternatively, GestKeyboard can dispatch each event right away but at the same time inform the application GestKeyboard has not yet made a decision. This removes the latency but shoulder the effort for handling uncertainty to application developers.

GestKeyboard itself is currently implemented as an application based on Linux. It is more appropriate for it to run at the core of keyboard event processing in the operating system, to take full control of the keyboard status. It is also worthwhile to implement GestKeyboard in a web environment, e.g., as a browser plugin so that it becomes instantaneously available to user on various computing devices that have a physical keyboard.

One important component in GestKeyboard is the keyboard geometry about the bounds of each key on the keyboard, which is often keyboard-specific. To automatically extract the geometry from a keyboard, we can potentially use computer vision and OCR to recognize each keycap from a photo of the keyboard.

Aside from the technical aspect, GestKeyboard's practicality should be further examined in the context of existing shortcut mechanisms, particularly in comparison with hotkeys. Keyboard gestures that are enabled by GestKeyboard have several potential advantages, including eye-free interactions, easy to learn and flexible to perform. Performing these gestures does not require the user to adapt for the specific keyboard layout or semantic designations of the modifier keys, which tend to significantly impact how a user performs hotkeys. Future research on these characteristics of keyboard gesture would provide direct implications on the usage scenario for GestKeyboard and further reveal the advantage and shortcomings of keyboard gestures.

RELATED WORK

Using physical key presses to sense trajectories has briefly been demonstrated previously. Jannotti [5] presented a scheme to simulate the shape of characters on the numeric keypad for text entry on a reduced keypad such as a TV remote. EdgeWrite uses four keys (arranged as a square) to capture spatial sequences for text entry [12]. All this prior work inspired us to explore gesturing on a physical keyboard in depth.

Extensive work has been conducted on gesturing on a soft keyboard for text entry based on a touchscreen or a stylus-enabled surface [14]. Although relevant, our work is vastly different because we focus on a different sensing device—an ordinary physical keyboard, which raises different challenges. For example, separating gesturing and typing on a touchscreen keyboard would be trivial because a touchscreen provides a much higher resolution than a physical keyboard does.

Traditional computing devices, such as a desktop or laptop computer, enabled limited gesture behaviors. For example, Apple MacBook allows a user to bring up Expose (windows overview) through a three-finger swipe gesture on the trackpad. However, stroke gestures are generally not supported on traditional computing devices that lack a dedicated gesturing device.

Previously, various efforts have been devoted to augmenting a keyboard with additional hardware [1][2][3]. In particular, the Pressure-Sensing Keyboard [3] is manufactured with additional press sensors in imprinting but its spatial resolution is unchanged. Touch Display Keyboard [2] enable flexible ways of using the keyboard, such as reassigning the keyboard functions or changing keyboard layout, by augmenting the keyboard with capacitive touch sensors and a projector instrumented in the environment. Actuated Keys [1] augments existing hotkey behaviors by mechanically raising keycaps when a modifier key is pressed. All this work did not focus on gesture articulation on the keyboard. In contrast, we aimed at enabling stroke gestures on existing unmodified keyboards.

CONCLUSION

We present GestKeyboard, a novel technique for gesture-based interaction on an existing physical keyboard, without any additional hardware or modification. It does not interfere with existing keyboard usage and allows a user to switch between the regular usage—typing or performing hotkeys—and gesturing in a modeless way. Based on a user study with 10 participants, we explored various characteristics about gesture articulation on a physical keyboard. We contributed a set of algorithms for detecting gesture occurrences. In particular, we designed features that can effectively separate gesturing from typing by using typing behaviors synthesized from a language model. GestKeyboard is able to detect gesturing from regular typing, with 95% accuracy with a maximum latency of 200ms. Based on the experiment as well as two applications using GestKeyboard, we found gesturing on a regular physical keyboard is useful and feasible.

REFERENCES

1. Bailly, G., Pietrzak, T., Deber, J., and Wigdor, D. Métamorphe: augmenting hotkey usage with actuated keys. In *Proc. CHI 2013*, ACM Press (2013), 563-572.
2. Block, F., Gellersen, H., and Villar, N. Touch-Display Keyboards: Transforming Keyboards into Interactive Surfaces. In *Proc. CHI 2010*, ACM Press (2010), 1145-1154.
3. Dietz, P., Eidelson, B., Westhues, J., and Bathiche, S. A Practical Pressure Sensitive Computer Keyboard. In *Proc. UIST 2009*, ACM Press (2009), 55-58.
4. Dribin, D. Keyboard Matrix Help. http://www.dribin.org/dave/keyboard/one_html/.
5. Jannotti, J. Iconic Text Entry Using a Numeric Keypad. Unpublished, 2002. http://pdos.csail.mit.edu/~jj/jannotti.com/papers/iconic-uist02.pdf.
6. Kane, S., Avrahami, D., Wobbrock, J., Harrison, B., Rea, A., Philipose, M., and LaMarca, A. Bonfire: A Nomadic System for Hybrid Laptop-Tabletop Interaction. In *Proc. UIST 2009*, ACM Press (2009), 129-138.
7. Keyboard Ghosting Explained. http://www.microsoft.com/appliedsciences/antighosting explained.mspx. Retrieved September 15, 2013.
8. Leap Motion. https://www.leapmotion.com/. Retrieved September 15, 2013.
9. Li, Y., Protractor: A Fast and Accurate Gesture Recognizer. In *Proc. CHI 2010*, ACM Press (2010), 2169-2172.
10. Wigdor, D., Benko, H., Pella, J., Lombardo, J., and Williams, S. Rock & Rails: Extending Multi-Touch Interaction with Shape Gestures to Enable Precise Spatial Manipulations. In *Proc. CHI 2011*, ACM Press (2011), 1581-1590.
11. Wilson, A. Robust Computer Vision-Based Detection of Pinching for One and Two-Handed Gesture Input, In *Proc. UIST 2006*, ACM Press (2006), 255-258.
12. Wobbrock, J., Myers, B., and Rothrock, B. Few-Key Text Entry Revisited: Mnemonic Gestures on Four Keys. In *Proc. CHI 2006*, ACM Press (2006), 489-492.
13. Wobbrock, J., Wilson, A., and Li., Y. Gestures without libraries, toolkits or Training: a $1.00 Recognizer for User Interface Prototypes. In *Proc. UIST 2007*, ACM Press (2007), 159-168.
14. Zhai, S., Kristensson, P.O., Gong, P., Greiner, M., Peng, S.A., Liu, L.M., and Dunnigan, A. ShapeWriter on the iPhone – From the Laboratory to the Real World. In *Proc. CHI EA 2009*, ACM Press (2009), 2667-2670.

Gesture Script: Recognizing Gestures and their Structure using Rendering Scripts and Interactively Trained Parts

Hao Lü[1,2], James Fogarty[1], Yang Li[2]

[1]Computer Science & Engineering
DUB Group, University of Washington
Seattle, WA 98195
{hlv, jfogarty}@cs.washington.edu

[2]Google Research
1600 Amphitheatre Parkway
Mountain View, CA 94043
hlv@google.com, yangli@acm.org

ABSTRACT
Gesture-based interactions have become an essential part of the modern user interface. However, it remains challenging for developers to create gestures for their applications. This paper studies unistroke gestures, an important category of gestures defined by their single-stroke trajectories. We present Gesture Script, a tool for creating unistroke gesture recognizers. Gesture Script enhances example-based learning with interactive declarative guidance through rendering scripts and interactively trained parts. The structural information from the rendering scripts allows Gesture Script to synthesize gesture variations and generate a more accurate recognizer that also automatically extracts gesture attributes needed by applications. The results of our study with developers show that Gesture Script preserves the threshold of familiar example-based gesture tools, while raising the ceiling of the recognizers created in such tools.

Author Keywords
Gesture recognition; interactive machine learning.

ACM Classification Keywords
H.5.2. [User Interfaces]: Input devices and strategies, Prototyping.
I.5.2. [Pattern Recognition]: Classifier design and evaluation.

INTRODUCTION
The continuing rise of ubiquitous touchscreen devices highlights both needs and opportunities for gesture-based interaction. Symbolic gestures are an important category of gestures, defined by their trajectories (e.g., a circle, an arrow, a spring, each character in an alphabet). Symbolic gestures have been extensively studied [3,17,27,32,34], and are increasingly common in everyday interaction. However, implementation of gesture recognition remains difficult. Because of this difficulty, many developers either decide against adopting gesture recognition or instead limit themselves to simple gestures to make recognition easier.

Extensive research examines tools to support developers creating gestures for their applications [14,15,18,19,27].

CHI 2014, April 26–May 1, 2014, Toronto, Ontario, Canada.

ACM 978-1-4503-2473-1/14/04...$15.00.
http://dx.doi.org/10.1145/2556288.2557263

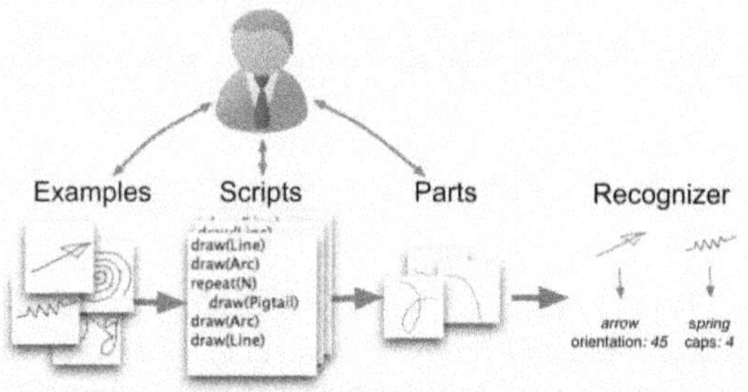

Figure 1: Developers use Gesture Script to incorporate gesture recognizers in their applications. They provide example gestures, create scripts, and define parts to build recognizers capable of both classifying gestures and recovering important attributes from the gestures.

This paper addresses symbolic, unistroke gestures. Current approaches to tool support focus on *example-based* training. One well-known exemplar of such tool support is the $1 Recognizer [34]. The $1 Recognizer allows developers to create a gesture recognizer by providing examples of each class of gesture. It then recognizes gestures using a nearest-neighbor classifier based on a distance metric that is scale and rotation invariant. At runtime, the recognizer compares new gestures to the provided examples and outputs a recognized class. Such an example-only approach hides recognizer complexity, but has key limitations.

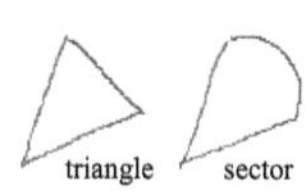

First, example-only approaches provide little control to developers creating a recognizer. Consider a scenario where a recognizer is having trouble reliably distinguishing between a triangle and a sector. In a strictly example-only system, a developer's only recourse is to provide more examples and hope the system eventually learns to differentiate the gestures. A better approach would allow developers to provide more information about the gestures. For example, a developer might indicate that a triangle is made of three lines, while a sector is made of two lines and an arc.

Second, example-only approaches limit the complexity of gestures developers can create for applications. Without any other knowledge, it is hard to efficiently learn gestures from only examples. For example, consider a spring gesture that can contain a varying number of zigzags. Such a gesture does not have a fixed shape, so it will be difficult for the $1 Recognizer to learn. With current example-only tools, a developer is left to provide many examples that attempt to cover the range of variation (e.g., illustrating examples of

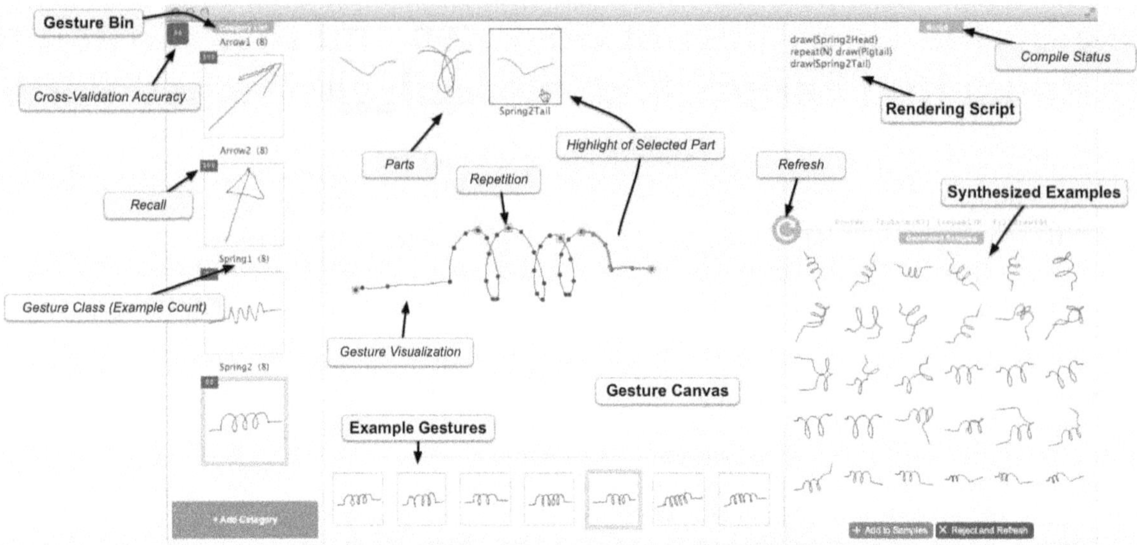

Figure 2: The main Gesture Script interface. Developers use the gesture bin on the left to define gesture classes and understand recognition accuracy for each class. They also work with example gestures and the gesture canvas in the center to define and inspect gestures and parts. On the right they author rendering scripts and incorporate examples synthesized from these scripts.

springs containing all possible numbers of zigzags). This can be tedious and inefficient, and it often still does not yield an acceptable recognizer.

Third, many applications require *attributes* of gestures beyond just their recognized class. For example, an application that recognizes an arrow gesture may also need to know its orientation and length. Prior work has focused on recognizing the correct class [3,17,27,32,34], so a developer is generally left to recover such attributes on their own. In our example, a developer might write custom code to infer an arrow's orientation and length by analyzing the gesture's two most distant points. Although straightforward for an arrow, some attributes can require analyses that are as complicated as the recognizer (e.g., recovering the number of zigzags in a spring). A better approach would allow developers to leverage the primary recognizer to recover attributes of a gesture needed by an application.

This paper presents Gesture Script, a new tool for developers incorporating gesture recognizers in their applications. As in previous example-based tools, Gesture Script allows developers to create a recognizer by simply providing examples of desired gestures. But we also enhance this core capability with several novel and powerful techniques as shown in Figure 1. Gesture Script allows developers to describe the structure of a gesture using a *rendering script*. A rendering script describes the process of performing a gesture as drawing a sequence of user-defined parts. The parts of a gesture can be learned from provided examples, and they can also be interactively specified. Scripts and their parts allow synthesis of new examples, helping developers quickly add greater variation to their training examples. Taken together, these capabilities allow developers to create more powerful gesture recognizers than prior example-based gesture tools. At runtime, the resulting recognizers are also able to recover specified attributes of the structure of gestures, extracting them and providing them to applications together with the gesture's recognized class.

The contributions of this work include:

- Introduction of rendering scripts as a technique to allow developers to combine example-based training with more explicit communication of gesture structure.
- A novel developer tool that uses rendering scripts to learn more accurate gesture recognizers, gives developers additional control over learning, and supports automatic recovery of gesture attributes.
- A set of interactive techniques for specifying the primitive parts of gestures and for adding greater variation to an example gesture set.
- A set of algorithms for learning the primitive parts of gestures from example gestures, rendering scripts, and interactive feedback on primitive parts, as well as algorithms for learning a gesture recognizer.
- Validation of Gesture Script in both initial experiments with developers and in detailed analyses of recognition reliability for multiple gesture datasets.

The next section discusses how a developer uses Gesture Script to interactively create a recognizer for a set of unistroke gestures and how they extract important attributes from those gestures. We then more formally introduce our rendering scripts and discuss what gesture structures can be described. Next, we discuss our algorithms for learning user-defined parts, synthesizing gesture examples, and learning the final gesture recognizer. We then evaluate Gesture Script through an initial study with developers and examination of recognition rates on multiple gesture datasets. Finally, we survey related work, discuss limitations and opportunities for future work, and conclude.

INTERACTING WITH GESTURE SCRIPT

We introduce Gesture Script by following a developer as she implements a recognizer for a small set of unistroke gestures. Ann needs to recognize four gestures in her application, as shown in Figure 2: *Arrow1* will create a solid arrow of the same orientation and length as the gesture, *Arrow2* will create a hollow arrow in the same orientation and length as the gesture, *Spring1* will add a resistor with the same number of zigzags as the gesture, and *Spring2* will add an inductor with the same number of coils as the gesture. Note that Ann's application needs to know the orientation and length of arrows as well as the number of zigzags and coils in springs in order to support simulations informed by the gestures.

Example-Based Demonstration of Gestures

Like prior example-only systems, Gesture Script allows developers to quickly create a recognizer simply by demonstrating examples of each gesture class within the Gesture Script interface. Ann first creates four gesture categories in the gesture bin and names them accordingly (i.e., *Arrow1*, *Arrow2*, *Spring1*, and *Spring2*). For each gesture category, Ann records a few examples by drawing on the gesture canvas in the center column of Figure 2's view of the interface. After the examples are recorded, Ann immediately has a gesture recognizer. Although Ann will extend the capabilities of her recognizer beyond what is possible with prior example-only systems, Gesture Script preserves the core interaction of quickly training a recognizer by example (i.e., Gesture Script raises the ceiling for gesture recognizer tools but preserves the same low threshold as prior example-only systems [17,27,34]).

Experimental Cross-Validation

To experimentally test her recognizer, Ann clicks the blue button in the upper-left corner of Figure 2's gesture bin. Gesture Script performs a random 10-fold cross validation on the recorded gesture set and updates the blue button to show result of the cross-validation as an estimate of the accuracy of the current recognizer. Gesture Script also displays the recall value for each gesture class next to its thumbnail to inform the developer how many of the provided examples are correctly recognized.

The cross-validation can only be interpreted as recognition performance over the recorded gestures. When the recorded gesture set fails to capture the qualities of real-world gestures, the cross-validation can report high accuracy for a recognizer that will actually perform poorly in practice. This can occur if the gesture set is too small to illustrate a space of gestures, or if the example gestures are too similar and fail to demonstrate real-world variation within a class. To produce a high-quality recognizer, Ann therefore needs a good cross-validation result on a realistic set of example gestures demonstrating real-world variation.

Describing Gestures with Rendering Scripts

When Ann sees that her cross-validation reports a low accuracy, she seeks ways to improve her recognizer. She could provide additional examples, or she can write rendering scripts that describe the structure of her gestures.

Gesture	One option	Alternative
Arrow1 	**draw**(Line) **draw**(Head1) 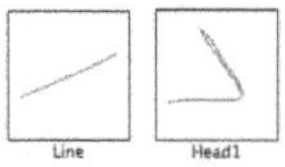	**draw**(Line) **draw**(ThickLine) **draw**(Line) 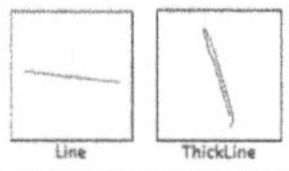
Arrow2 	**draw**(Line) **draw**(Head2) 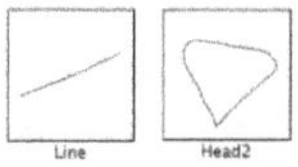	**draw**(Line) **draw**(Line) **draw**(Line) **draw**(Line) 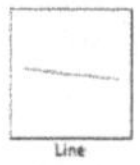
Spring1 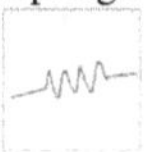	**draw**(String1Head) **repeat** draw(Cap) **draw**(String1Tail) 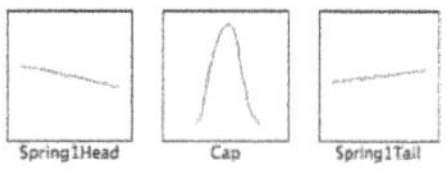 or 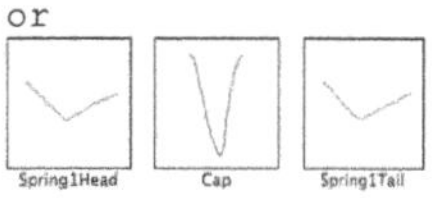	**draw**(Line) **draw**(Line) **repeat** **draw**(V) **draw**(Line) **draw**(Line) 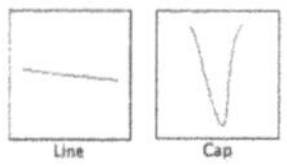
Spring2 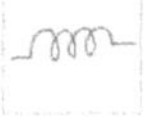	**draw**(String2Head) **repeat** draw(Coil) **draw**(String2Tail) 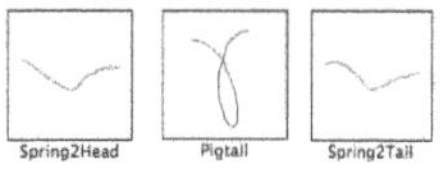	**draw**(Line) **draw**(Arc) **repeat** **draw**(Coil) **draw**(Arc) **draw**(Line) 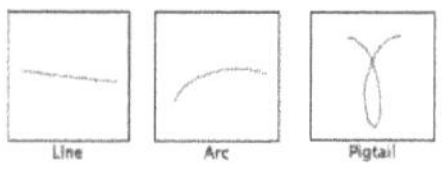

Figure 3: Scripts provide multiple ways to define a gesture. For instance, this table presents two different scripts for each gesture. There can also be alternative interpretations of a part for the same script, as shown in gesture *Spring1*.

Ann creates a simple rendering script that uses a sequence of *draw* commands to describe *Arrow1* as drawing a part called *Line* followed by a part called *Head1*, as in Figure 3. Similarly, Ann defines the slightly different *Arrow2* as first drawing a *Line* and then a *Head2*. Importantly, parts are all user-defined. Gesture Script does not have any pre-existing notion of a line or an arrowhead, but will learn these parts from Ann's examples and interactive guidance. Part names are globally scoped, so the *Line* part in *Arrow1*'s script is the same as the *Line* part in *Arrow2*'s script.

Spring1 and *Spring2* are a bit more complicated, as the bodies of the gestures contain repetitive patterns. Gesture Script supports such gestures with a *repeat* command. Ann describes *Spring1* as first drawing a *Spring1Head*, then a series of one or more *Cap* parts, and finally a *Spring1Tail*. She similarly defines *Spring2* to include a *Spring2Head*, one or more *Coil*, and a *Spring2Tail*.

There are multiple scripts that can describe the same gesture, including multiple potential alternatives for each of

Ann's scripts. Even for the same script, multiple interpretations of the named parts might be consistent with provided examples. Figure 3 shows example alternative scripts for each of Ann's gestures as well as two different interpretations of the parts in her *Spring1* script. Some scripts are more effective in improving recognition. In our experience, a good strategy is to reuse parts among scripts when possible, as this helps the recognizer isolate and focus on the other more discriminative parts of gestures.

Interactively Training User-Defined Parts

Scripts define a global set of user-defined parts. However, the shapes of those parts are unknown (i.e., Gesture Script does not have any pre-conceived notion of a line as the shortest path between two points, nor of the two different styles of arrowhead in Ann's scripts). When a gesture class is selected, Gesture Script shows its current understanding of the appearance of each part defined in the gesture's rendering script (see the top center of Figure 2). An empty box is shown if Gesture Script has not yet learned a shape.

After defining her scripts, Ann clicks on the refresh button in the center of the Gesture Script interface. Gesture Script then tries to learn all of the parts defined in Ann's scripts. It tries to learn the appearance of each part from the example gestures (i.e., searching among potential shapes of parts to find those that best fit the gesture examples). The learned parts are then visualized.

Unfortunately, the space of possible shapes for parts is very large. Given computational constraints, Gesture Script is only able to find a set of local minima and pick the best. When gestures are simple, Gesture Script is generally able to find parts that match the developer's intent. However, it does not always find the best shapes for parts. Figure 4 shows an example where Gesture Script has not identified the intended distinction between *Line* and *Head2* in Ann's *Arrow2* gesture. Gesture Script provides developers with two methods for interactively guiding part learning.

Interactively Labeling Part Segmentation

A developer can interactively specify one or more segmentation points in any of their example gestures by clicking that point in the gesture visualization. For example, Ann can label the end of the *Line* in any of her examples of *Arrow2*. Interactively provided segmentations thus guide search to the intended part shapes (e.g., see Figure 4a).

Providing Examples of User-Defined Parts

With a large number of examples, labeling segmentations can be laborious. Gesture Script also allows providing a rough part shape by directly drawing the part within the box intended to visualize that part (i.e., within the boxes at the top center of Figure 2). The demonstration is then used as a rough indication of the desired shape of that part and guides search to the intended part shapes (e.g., see Figure 4b).

Synthesizing Additional Examples

As we previously discussed, training a high-quality recognizer requires that a developer obtain examples that

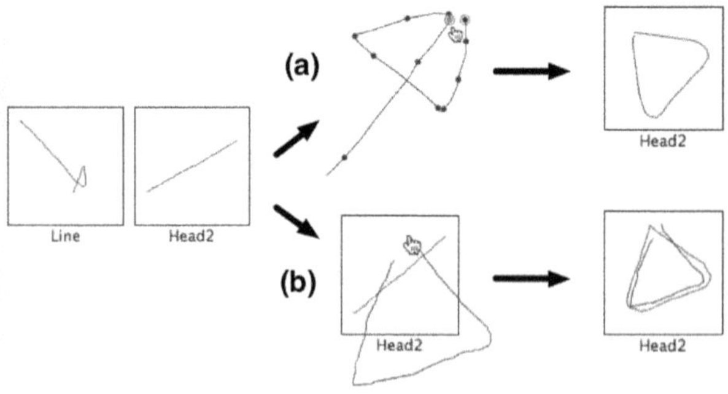

Figure 4: Gesture Script presents feedback in red when developers interactively define parts. When an undesired shape is learned for a part, developers have two options: they can manually label a segmentation point, or they can draw over the visualized part to define its appearance.

```
draw(Line)    ➜  +rotate(dir)
draw(Head1)      draw(Line)
                 draw(Head1)
```

Recovering the Direction of *Arrow 1*

```
draw(S1Head)       ➜  draw(S1Head)
repeat                repeat(n)
  draw(Cap)             draw(Cap)
draw(S1Tail)          draw(S1Tail)
```

Recovering the Repetitions of *Spring 1*

Figure 5: Script variables are used to define the attributes that will be extracted from a gesture. Here the developer specifies *dir* to extract a gesture's initial rotation, and *n* to extract the number of repetitions in a gesture.

illustrate sufficient variation to enable good performance on future real-world data. To help developers include greater variation in their example gestures, Gesture Script uses rendering scripts and learned parts to generate new potential examples of gestures, as displayed in the bottom right of Figure 2. Gesture Script introduces variation by changing the relative scale of each part and the angles of rotation between parts. Ann can quickly scan the synthesized examples, select interesting cases, and add them to her training set. When she finds examples that demonstrate so much variation that she no longer considers them an example of the gesture, she selects them and clicks the "Reject and Refresh" button. Gesture Script uses this feedback to guide its generation of additional examples.

Recovering Attributes of Gesture

Gesture Script allows developers to include *variables* in scripts that specify attributes that should be recovered from a recognized gesture. Specifically, we currently support recovering the number of times a part is repeated within a given gesture as well as the angles between parts in a particular gesture. For example, in Figure 5 Ann recovers the orientation of the *Line* in *Arrow1* gesture by adding a *rotate* command using the *dir* variable. Similarly, she recovers the number of repeated *Cap* parts in a *Spring1* gesture by adding the variable *n* to her *repeat* command. When using the recognizer in her application, Ann can access these attributes by simply accessing the variables *dir* and *n* on recognized instances of these gestures.

Iterative Improvement and Evaluation

The overall process of training an effective recognizer is highly iterative and exploratory. Ann adds more examples, modifies her rendering scripts, interactively defines parts, and examines the cross-validation performance of her recognizer as she works. Gesture Script also allows Ann to interactively test her current recognizer. When Ann gestures in the test window, Gesture Script presents the current recognizer's predicted class and any extracted gesture attributes. If Ann creates an example that is misrecognized or otherwise interesting, she can directly add it to her example gestures. When complete, Ann has a reliable recognizer that automatically extracts gesture attributes.

Incorporating the Recognizer

This paper focuses on creating the recognizer. After a recognizer is created, incorporating it in the developer's application is analogous to prior work [34]. Ann will add two things: (1) the recognition module containing the algorithms and (2) the model files for her gestures as created, trained, and exported from Gesture Script.

DESCRIBING GESTURES USING RENDERING SCRIPTS

Prior to discussing our implementation, we first detail our rendering script language, as it defines how developers can communicate the intended structure of gestures and is important to the effectiveness of Gesture Script.

Unistroke gestures have been extensively studied, and we surveyed gestures found in the research literature and commercial applications [1,5,16,21,23,28,33,35]. Unistroke gestures can be arbitrarily complex in theory, but in practice are much simpler. One reason is that people must be capable of remembering and reliably producing the gesture. We have found most unistroke gestures can be broken into a fixed number of parts, while others contain repetition. Our script language supports this, describing gestures as a sequence of structures. Each structure can be either a user-defined part or a repetition of a user-defined part.

Under such a description, possible gesture attributes include the angles between structures, the number of repetitions of a part, and the angle between repetitions. The size and location of a particular part can also be useful and is easily retrieved from the bounding box of a part.

The syntax of our script language is defined as:

```
Script :- Structure*;
Structure :-
  [rotate(X)]?
    [repeat[(N[, Y)]?]?]?
      draw(P);
```

P is gesture part. *X*, *N*, and *Y* are script variables. They do not describe gestures, but rather allow developers to indicate what gesture attributes are of interest.

ALGORITHMS

We now present the algorithms Gesture Script uses to learn parts, synthesize gesture examples, and learn a recognizer.

Learning Gesture Parts

The provided rendering scripts introduce a set of global parts. This section first addresses the unsupervised learning problem, where we learn parts from only gesture examples.

As a high-level overview, we first heuristically generate a shape for each part. We then use these initial part shapes to segment each example in the way that best matches the corresponding parts in its script. We score the match that results from segmentation of each example and then compute a total score over all examples. After segmenting all the examples, we have a set of gesture segments corresponding to each part, which we then use to update our estimate of the shape of the part. We iteratively improve our estimate of the shapes of parts until there is no improvement in the total score. We repeat this process several times (20 in our current implementation), each time with different initial random part shapes. This subsection details each step and how we incorporate interactive feedback (i.e., part segmentation and provided part shapes).

Preprocessing and Initial Shapes

Gestures typically contain hundreds of points, and considering every point as a segmentation boundary becomes computationally prohibitive. We therefore first approximate the gesture as a sequence of line segments using the bottom-up segmentation algorithm described by Keogh et al. [13]. We then only consider endpoints of these line segments as candidates for boundaries between parts.

As in prior instance-based gesture recognition [17,34], we represent a part by sampling a set of equidistant points along its trajectory, normalized by its vector magnitude: $(x_1, y_1, x_2, y_2, \ldots, x_n, y_n)$, with $n = 32$ in our implementation.

To generate initial part shapes, we find the simplest example corresponding to a script that contains the part (i.e., the example with the fewest segmentation candidates). We then randomly pick a segment as the initial part shape.

Matching a Gesture to a Script

To segment an example gesture to match a script, we first define our similarity metric. Our similarity metric is based on Protractor [17]. When a gesture segment is matched to a simple part, their distance is the cosine distance defined as:

$$d(G^{seg}, V^{part}) = \arccos(V^{seg} \bullet V^{part}) \quad (1)$$

where V^{seg} is a resampling of G^{seg} rotated to an aligned angle. We assume vectors are normalized by magnitude.

When a gesture segment is matched to a repetition, we find the best way to break it into subsegments that each matches the part shape, then use the average distance of the subsegments to the part shape as a distance measure:

$$d(G^{seg}, R(V^{part})) = \min_{n,\theta;\Delta;\Gamma}\{\sum_i \frac{1}{n} d(G^{seg}_{\Gamma_i}(\theta + i \times \Delta), V^{part})\} \quad (2)$$

where n is the number of repetitions, θ is the initial angle, Δ is the change in angle between each repetition, and Γ is the segmentation.

Given these metrics for the distance between a gesture segment and an individual part or a repetition, the overall distance between an example gesture and a script can then be defined as the average distance of its segments to the corresponding structures:

$$d(G,S_{0:K-1}) = \min_{\Gamma}\{\sum_{0\le i<K}\frac{1}{K}d(G^{\Gamma_i},S_i)\} \quad (3)$$

where S_i is a structure (i.e., either a repetition or a part) and Γ is the segmentation.

We segment an example gesture to best match a script by solving equation (3). We use dynamic programming:

$$d(G_{a:b},S_{j:K-1}) = \min_{a<i\le b, j<K}\{\frac{1}{K}d(G^{a:i},S_j)+d(G_{i:b},S_{j+1:K-1})\} \quad (4)$$

where a, b and i are end points in the gesture, and $a{:}b$ means a gesture segment between point a and point b.

For equation (2), we use a greedy algorithm. Although dynamic programming can be used, it has many states (n, θ, Δ) and it is nested within the dynamic programming for equation (4). Solving equation (2) using dynamic programming is therefore costly. We instead scan the end points in G^{seg} and find the segment with the lowest distance to equation (1)'s part V^{part}. We use this as the first segment. We then repeat and update θ and Δ along the way until we reach the end point. To compensate for a lack of lookahead in the greedy approach, we then perform a back scan to merge segments that further reduce the distance.

Updating Part Shapes and Iteration

We can now match gesture examples to scripts and thus obtain a set of gesture segments for each part. To update the current estimate of the shape of a part, we compute the average of segments after normalization and alignment:

$$V^{part} = Normalize(\frac{1}{T}\sum_{0\le i<T}V^{seg_i}) \quad (5)$$

We then iterate between segmenting gesture examples and updating parts until the total distance between gestures and scripts can no longer be improved.

Incorporating Interactive Feedback

As previously discussed, developers can improve learning of parts by manually labeling the part segmentation points and by drawing examples of individual part shapes. We can integrate this interactive guidance into our unsupervised learning. For interactively labeled part segmentation points, we modify our matching algorithm in equation (2) and (4) to require selection of interactively labeled segmentation points. In the case of interactively provided examples of part shapes, we use them as the initial shapes in the search. This explicit developer guidance is more effective than random selection of an initial part shape.

Gesture Synthesis

After part shapes are learned, we can synthesize gesture examples by following the procedural steps specified in a rendering script. The goal is to help developers introduce variation into their examples. Synthesized examples can vary in their parameters (i.e., the angles between parts, the relative scale of parts, and the number of repetitions). However, we cannot simply use random values for these parameters. If the number of parameters is n and the number of values for each parameter is about m, the total number of different examples will be m^n, most of which will not be meaningful. Randomly generated parameters are unlikely to generate helpful suggested examples.

We therefore choose to vary one parameter at a time. We first use our part matching algorithm to find the values of one parameter in the existing examples, then map them in one dimension. We identify the largest gaps in this space (i.e., where no values have been previously selected), as these are promising regions for exploring variation. We then vary the parameter using values from these gaps.

When developers reject generated examples, those parameter values are marked in their value space. We then prioritize the gaps between positive and negative example values, which may contain the most information.

Gesture Recognition

We now discuss creating the recognizer from examples, scripts, and parts. We compute features for each example, and then we train a linear SVM multi-class classifier.

If there are N gesture classes, the features for a gesture consist of N+1 groups of features. The first group of features can be represented as $\{f_0, f_1, ..., f_{N-1}\}$, where f_i is the minimum cosine distance of the gesture to example gestures in the i-th class. These features are the same distances used in Protractor [17], and including them preserves Protactor's strong example-only performance.

The remaining N feature groups are generated from the script of the i-th gesture class, giving the recognizer access to additional information the script provides about gesture structure. For the i-th group, with a script containing K structures, an example gesture's features are represented as $\{d_0, d_1, ..., d_{K-1}, r_{0,1}, r_{1,2}, ..., r_{K-2,K-1}, s_1, s_2, ..., s_{K-1}\}$. The example gesture is first matched to the script using our matching algorithm. We then compute features as follows: d_i is the distance between the i-th structure to the corresponding gesture segment per equation (1) or (2); $r_{i,i+1}$ is the angle between the aligned angle of the i-th structure and that of the (i+1)-th structure; and s_i is the scale ratio of the i-th matched gesture segment to the first matched gesture segment. In essence, these features encode how well an example matches the parts in a script and how an example's parts are arranged in terms of their relative angles and relative scales.

We scale each feature to the range of -1 to 1, then train a multi-class SVM classifier with a linear kernel. At runtime, the SVM predicts gesture category and we use the results of our matching to extract gesture parts and attributes.

The computational cost of our recognizers is comparable to Protractor. In the simplest case with no scripts, the cost is that of Protractor plus a smaller cost from a linear SVM. When scripts are specified, the additional cost for each script over Protractor is $O(k^2 + k*m^2*c + k'*m^4)$, where k is the number of parts, m is the number of segmentation candidates, c is the number of sampling points, and k' is the number of parts with repetition. Assuming $k = 4$, $m = 10$, $k' = 1$, and $c = 32$, this is about the cost of an additional 1000 examples in a Protractor recognizer. This is practical and has not been an issue in our experiments.

VALIDATION

To validate and gain insight into Gesture Script, we now present a series of experiments. First is an initial laboratory study with four developers, observing their use of and reactions to Gesture Script. Second is our collection of data to evaluate the performance of Gesture Script's recognition. Finally, we analyze recognition performance from several perspectives: (1) we test recognizers that developers created in our study, (2) we examine recognition with a larger set of gesture classes, and (3) we examine recognition of simple, compound, and high-variation gesture datasets.

Study with Developers

To obtain initial feedback on the usability of Gesture Script and the usefulness of its features, we conducted a laboratory study with 4 programmers recruited from our organization (2 male and 2 female). None had previously programmed gesture recognition, but all had used machine learning.

Study Setup

We asked each participant to train a gesture recognizer for the seven gestures in Figure 6 and to extract gesture attributes including the direction of each arrow and number of repetitions in each spring. The size of the gesture set was chosen to be appropriate for a laboratory study. The specific gestures were chosen so they are not easily distinguishable to a simple instance-based recognizer. They require non-trivial effort to add examples, iterate on scripts, and train parts to achieve a good recognition performance.

We first gave participants a tutorial on Gesture Script. We then walked through the process of creating a recognizer for two simple gestures, a triangle and a rectangle. Next, participants completed a warm-up task to train a recognizer for Figure 8's "v" and "delete".

We then asked participants to work on the main task, creating a recognizer for the seven gestures from scratch. We asked participants to think as developers looking to create the recognizer for their software. The goal was to train a quality recognizer and to improve its recognition until satisfied. We limited the task time to one hour. Finally, participants completed a post-study questionnaire.

The study was conducted on a ThinkPad X220 Tablet PC with stylus support. Participants had a keyboard and mouse, and all used the stylus for gesture input.

Results

All 4 participants completed the study with satisfactory recognition performance. Participants added a total of 341 gesture examples (i.e., 12.2 examples per class per participant) and wrote a total of 26 scripts (with 82 non-empty lines and 36 parts). Popular features included gesture synthesis (participants used 106 synthesized gestures) and providing examples for parts (participants

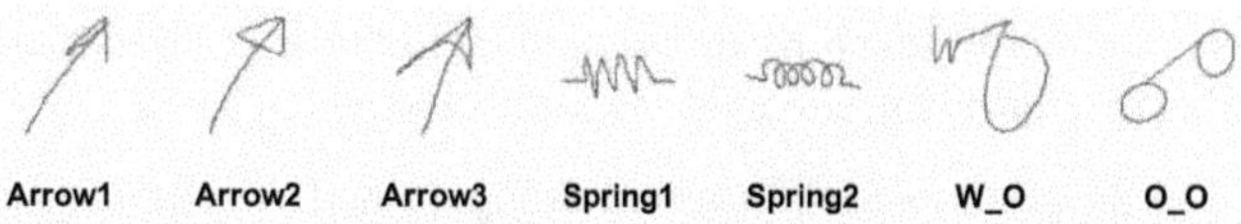

Figure 6: Our study includes seven gestures. The arrows can point any direction, springs can have arbitrary number of repetitions, and the W_O and O_O gestures can place the circle part at arbitrary locations indicating region for action.

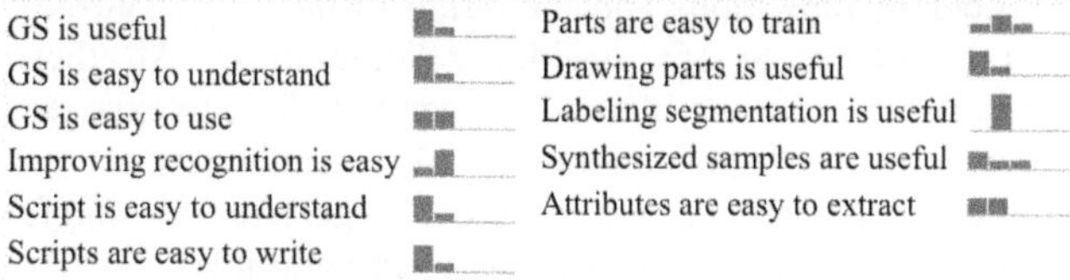

Figure 7: The Likert scales from our post-study survey, presented from strongly agree to strongly disagree.

provided 20 examples for individual parts). In the post-study questionnaire, all participants agreed Gesture Script is useful, easy to understand, and that it was easy to improve recognition. Figure 7 presents all Likert scales.

When asked what they liked best, all participants mentioned Gesture Script's ease of use. One commented "*it provides a very high-level API for developers to construct a recognizer.*" Another participant liked that they could "*write scripts to break down a complicated gesture into parts.*"

When asked what had been most confusing, participants expressed the frustration of understanding why a recognizer was failing: "*[what is] the reason behind why one gesture is confused with another gesture.*" Consistent with prior machine learning tools [10,24,25], participants adopted iterative and exploratory strategies to improve their recognizers. Participants wanted an ability to see misclassified gestures, as they found accuracy and recall helpful to understand overall performance but also wanted to see how specific instances failed.

We also added two features based on feedback from the participants. First, we added support for adding misclassified gestures directly to the training set from the testing window. Second, we added the ability to clear all user-labeled segmentations. As the participants iterated on scripts and parts, previously labeled segmentations could become incorrect and a hassle to remove or correct.

3 participants suggested in the post-study questionnaire that they wanted the script language to be more powerful. They suggested being able to specify constraints on aspects of a script, such as referencing variables from multiple locations in a script. This aligns with our vision for future work.

Data Collection

To obtain additional data for further evaluating Gesture Script, we collected 24 gesture classes from 10 participants. Each participant was asked to perform 10 gestures for each class, yielding a total of 2400 gestures. Data collection was done on a ThinkPad X220 Tablet PC, and all gestures were input with the stylus. All participants were right handed.

We explicitly asked participants to include variation in how they performed gestures of the same class.

The 24 gestures are illustrated in Figure 8. The leftmost 16 are from the website for the $1 Recognizer (except for "zigzag", these are identical to the gestures in [34]). The rightmost 8 are new gestures with more flexible structures. For instance, the springs can have an arbitrary number of repetitions and the *circle* in the "w_o" gesture can be placed at any position relative to *w*. All these gestures are from the literature or commercial contexts, and have practical applications. In the remainder of our analyses, we refer to the leftmost 16 gestures as *simple*. We refer to the rightmost 8 as *compound* gestures.

Recognition Evaluation

We first tested the four recognizers created in our study against the newly collected data. We tested only the 7 gesture classes the developers had trained, a total of 700 gestures. We compare the results against recognizers trained using the $1 Recognizer, Protractor, and Gesture Script without scripts. Results are presented in Figure 9. With an average accuracy of 89.6%, these results show that the recognizers from the study have much better accuracy than existing example-only methods. The best recognizer is from P4, whose accuracy is 94.7%. When scripts are not used, as in the other three conditions, accuracies drop to an average of 68.7%. Enabling a developer who has never programmed gestures to build an accurate recognizer for a non-trivial set of gestures in less than an hour is promising.

To further examine Gesture Script recognition, we next conducted cross-validation experiments with our full dataset. We expected recognition of *compound* gestures to be more difficult, so we considered them separately from *simple* gestures. To examine the impact of the number and diversity of training examples, we conducted two cross-validations. *Train-on-1* considered limited training data, training on examples from 1 person and testing on examples from the other 9. *Train-on-9* considered greater training data availability, training on examples from 9 people and testing on examples from the other 1. We again compare Gesture Script with the $1 Recognizer, Protractor, and Gesture Script without scripts. In the Gesture Script condition, the authors created a script for each gesture.

Results are presented in Figure 10. For *compound* gestures, Gesture Script obtains the best results in both the *train-on-1* and *train-on-9* conditions. Gesture Script obtains 89.6% accuracy in the *compound train-on-1* data, compared to an average of 68.0% for example-only conditions. Gesture Script obtains 99.5% accuracy in the *compound train-on-9* data, compared to an average of 92.1% for example-only conditions. On *simple* gestures, all recognizers have similar performance. These results are consistent with our goal of raising the ceiling for gesture creation tools while preserving the low threshold of existing example-only tools.

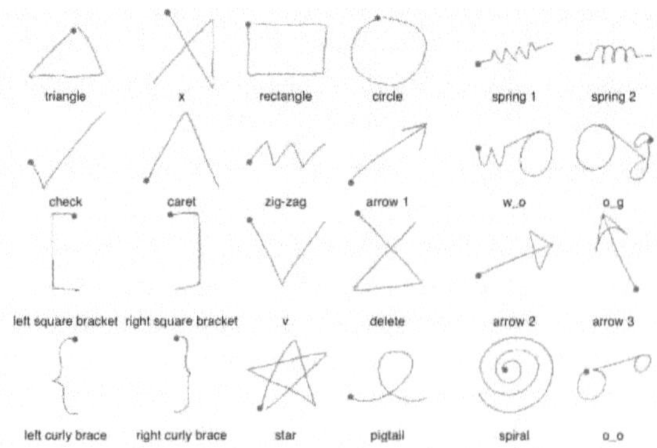

Figure 8: The 24 types of gestures in our data collection, with 16 *simple* on the left and 8 *compound* on the right.

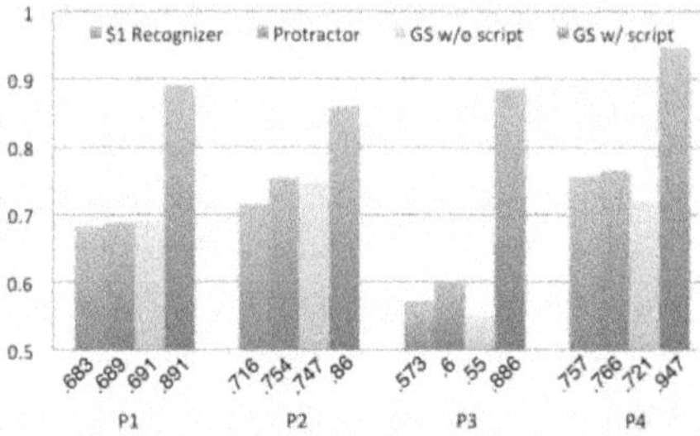

Figure 9: Gesture Script recognizers created by the developers in our study obtain better recognition results than example-only methods.

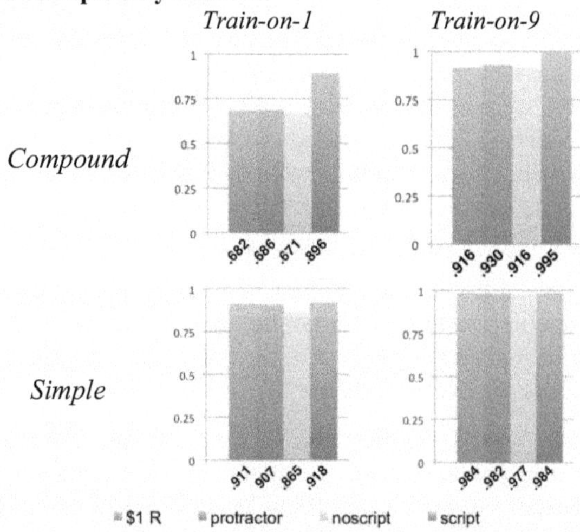

Figure 10: Gesture Script obtains better results on *compound* gestures, while being no worse on *simple* gestures. This is consistent with raising the ceiling for gesture creation tools while preserving the low threshold of example-based tools.

Given the extreme accuracy of all *train-on-9* recognizers for simple *gestures*, we suspected a ceiling effect (i.e., the experiment was too easy to differentiate the recognizers). We suspected this is because of the high consistency in *simple* gestures (i.e., low variation in how they were performed). As an early investigation, we created a new *high-variation* dataset. This consists of 10 examples of each *simple* gesture, created by the authors to exhibit high variation in form. We then tested the recognizers from our previous *train-on-1* and *train-on-9* cross-validations against the *high-variation* data. Recall these were trained on data containing little variation, so our goal was to test how methods perform on examples containing previously unseen variation. Results are shown in Figure 11. This provides an early indication that Gesture Script is overall more accurate and robust to variation, even in simple gestures.

We also examined performance of our parts matching by randomly verifying 5 example gestures per script from the 26 scripts collected from the 4 developers in our study (i.e., 130 total gestures). We marked a match as correct if we would have matched the parts in exactly the same way; partially correct if one or two segmentation points were slightly off; and otherwise incorrect. Figure 12 illustrates a correct match and two examples of erroneous matches. In the 130 gestures we examined, 98 (75.4%) are correct, 29 (22.3%) are partially correct, and 3 extractions (2.3%) are incorrect. This indicates the matching is largely effective.

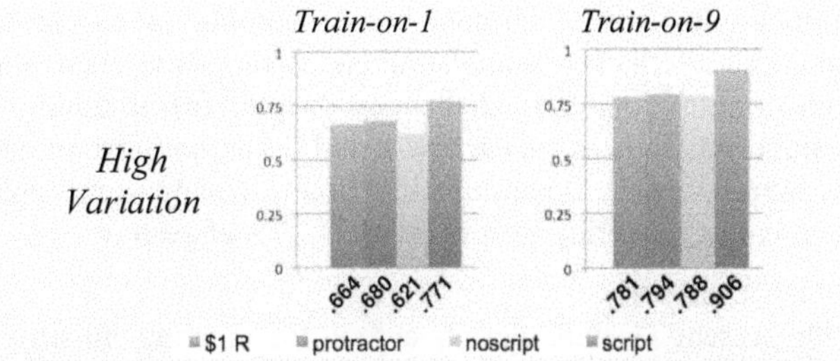

Figure 11: Gesture Script obtains better results when tested against *high-variation* data. This provides an early indication Gesture Script is more accurate in the presence of variation.

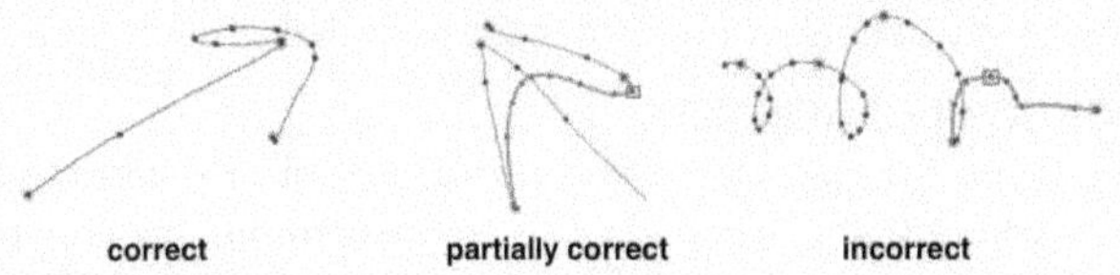

Figure 12: We manually inspected gesture segmentations to gauge how well they matched expectations. Here we show three cases highlighting the segmentation that was found (in red) versus that our annotator preferred (in green).

RELATED WORK

Many symbolic gesture recognition algorithms have been developed, with learning-based approaches gaining significant popularity. Various models have been studied, including neural networks [26], decision trees [27,28], Hidden Markov Models [2,6,30], and instance-based learning [3,17,32,34]. Instance-based approaches have recently received extensive attention, due to their ease of implementation and good performance. $1 and $N recognizer use the Euclidean distance of two aligned gestures [3,34]. Protractor instead uses cosine distance [17]. Although Gesture Script learns its gesture recognizer from examples using a SVM, Gesture Script enhances example-based learning with declarative guidance through explicit structures in rendering scripts. Moreover, existing tools only recognize gesture class. Gesture Script is able to extract gesture attributes to support application needs.

From an algorithmic point of view, a symbolic gesture is largely the same as a sketched symbol. Extensive work has examined recognizing and understanding sketches [12,29]. While enhancing example-based learning with rendering scripts is a novel approach, our work relates to this rich body of work in several ways. First, declarative scripts are used to define gestures in systems such as LADDER [8]. While Gesture Script also includes scripts, our rendering scripts are not gesture definitions but serve as optional information in addition to the example gestures. As a result, our scripts are much simpler and developers can be less precise. Second, many sketch recognition systems use parts in recognition [29], most based on identifying predefined primitive shapes using perceptual attributes such as curvature. In contrast, our parts are user-defined and can be of arbitrary shape, and we currently do not rely on perceptual attributes. While other systems have looked at arbitrary part shapes [31] and features [22], no prior work has the problem of learning user-defined part shapes across classes in an unsupervised setting. Third, Hammond and Davis [9] also study generating examples from scripts. While their purpose is to debug scripts, ours is to directly incorporate generated examples in learning. Moreover, in addition to having a different script language, our method considers both scripts and developer-provided examples.

Gesture tools are also well studied [14,15,18,19,20,27]. The example-based approaches [18,19,27] allow developers to create and test gestures by recording examples. Gesture Script preserves this core interaction, but enables much more. We support interactive user guidance about the structure of a gesture, and believe this general strategy can be extended to recognition tools for other types of data.

DISCUSSION AND FUTURE WORK

Implementation

Gesture Script is implemented using Java. The parser for rendering scripts is implemented using ANTLR [4]. The SVM within the gesture recognizer is provided by LIBSVM [7]. Our code and data are available under open license at *https://code.google.com/p/gesture-script/.*

Variation in Gestures

As in Figure 11, and as discussed by Kane et al. [11], recognizer performance can be dramatically impacted by variations. Because gesture tools capture gestures outside any application context, it is important for developers to include gesture examples that exhibit the gesture variation expected in real use. In our data collection, although we explicitly asked the participants to vary their performance of gestures, the amount of variation was still limited. One hypothesis is people tend to perform gestures consistently and it is hard to manually introduce variation. Gesture Script synthesizes gestures to introduce additional variation. The initial feedback from developers was positive. One opportunity for future work is to investigate the impact of synthesized gestures on the recognizer performance.

Alternative Ways to Perform a Gesture

The gestures discussed in this paper each have a unique way they are performed (e.g., a circle must be counter-clockwise). Instance-based learning is robust to multiple alternative demonstrations of the same class, but rendering scripts face challenges due to: (a) assuming a unique way to perform each part, and (b) assuming a unique ordering of parts. One future direction is to support multiple alternative rendering scripts for each class of gesture.

CONCLUSION

We present Gesture Script, a tool for creating unistroke gestures. It enhances example-based learning with declarative guidance through rendering scripts, preserving the low threshold of example-based gesture tools while raising the ceiling of the recognizers created in such tools.

ACKNOWLEDGEMENTS

We thank Morgan Dixon and Daniel Epstein for comments on earlier drafts. This work is sponsored in part by the National Science Foundation under award OAI-1028195, the Intel Science and Technology Center for Pervasive Computing, and by a Google Faculty Research Award.

REFERENCES

1. Alvarado, C. and Davis, R. SketchREAD: A Multi-Domain Sketch Recognition Engine. *UIST 2004*, 23-32.
2. Anderson, D., Bailey, C., and Skubic, M. Hidden Markov Model Symbol Recognition for Sketch-Based Interfaces. *AAAI Fall Symposium*, (2004), 15-21.
3. Anthony, L. and Wobbrock, J.O. A Lightweight Multistroke Recognizer for User Interface Prototypes. *GI 2010*, 245-252.
4. ANTLR 4. http://www.antlr.org/.
5. Appert, C. and Zhai, S. Using Strokes as Command Shortcuts. *CHI 2009*, 2289-2298.
6. Cao, X. and Balakrishnan, R. Evaluation of an On-Line Adaptive Gesture Interface with Command Prediction. *GI 2005*, 187-194.
7. Chang, C.-C. and Lin, C.-J. LIBSVM: A Library for Support Vector Machines. *ACM TIST,* 2 (3), 2011, 1-27.
8. Hammond, T. and Davis, R. LADDER, A Sketching Language for User Interface Developers. *Computers & Graphics*, 29 (4), 2005, 518-532.
9. Hammond, T. and Davis, R. Interactive Learning of Structural Shape Descriptions From Automatically Generated Near-Miss Examples. *IUI 2006*, 210-217.
10. Hartmann, B., Abdulla, L., Mittal, M., and Klemmer, S.R. Authoring Sensor-Based Interactions by Demonstration with Direct Manipulation and Pattern Recognition. *CHI 2007*, 145-154.
11. Kane, S.K., Wobbrock, J.O., and Ladner, R.E. Usable Gestures for Blind People : Understanding Preference and Performance. *CHI 2011*, 413-422.
12. Kara, L.B. and Stahovich, T.F. Hierarchical Parsing and Recognition of Hand-Sketched Diagrams. *UIST 2004*, 13-22.
13. Keogh, E., Chu, S., Hart, D., and Pazzani, M. Segmenting Time Series: A Survey and Novel Approach. *Data Mining in Time Series Databases*, 57, 2004, 1-22.
14. Kin, K., Hartmann, B., DeRose, T., and Agrawala, M. Proton: Multitouch Gestures as Regular Expressions. *CHI 2012*, 2885-2894.
15. Kin, K., Hartmann, B., DeRose, T., and Agrawala, M. Proton++: A Customizable Declarative Multitouch Framework. *UIST 2012*, 477-486.
16. Kurtenbach, G. and Buxton, B. GEdit: A Test Bed for Editing by Contiguous Gestures. *ACM SIGCHI Bulletin,* 23 (2), 1991, 22-26.
17. Li, Y. Protractor : A Fast and Accurate Gesture Recognizer. *CHI 2010*, 2169-2172.
18. Long, A.C., Landay, J.A., and Rowe, L.A. Implications for a Gesture Design Tool. *CHI 1999*, 40-47.
19. Lü, H. and Li, Y. Gesture Coder: A Tool for Programming Multi-Touch Gestures by Demonstration. *CHI 2012*, 2875-2884.
20. Lü, H. and Li, Y. Gesture Studio: Authoring Multi-Touch Interactions through Demonstration and Composition. *CHI 2013*, 257-266.
21. Morris, M.R., Wobbrock, J.O., and Wilson, A.D. Understanding Users' Preferences for Surface Gestures. *GI 2010*, 261-268.
22. Oltmans, M. Envisioning Sketch Recognition: A Local Feature Based Approach to Recognizing Informal Sketches. Doctoral Dissertation. 2007.
23. Ouyang, T.Y. and Davis, R. A Visual Approach to Sketched Symbol Recognition. *IJCAI 2009*, 1463-1468.
24. Patel, K., Bancroft, N., Drucker, S.M., Fogarty, J., Ko, A.J., and Landay, J. Gestalt: Integrated Support for Implementation and Analysis in Machine Learning. *UIST 2010*, 37-46.
25. Patel, K., Fogarty, J., Landay, J.A., and Harrison, B. Investigating Statistical Machine Learning as a Tool for Software Development. *CHI 2008*, 667-676.
26. Pittman, J.A. Recognizing Handwritten Text. *CHI 1991*, 271-275.
27. Rubine, D. Specifying Gestures by Example. *SIGGRAPH 1991*, 329-337.
28. Rubine, D. Combining Gestures and Direct Manipulation. *CHI 1992*, 659-660.
29. Saund, E., Fleet, D., Larner, D., and Mahoney, J. Perceptually-Supported Image Editing of Text and Graphics. *UIST 2003*, 183-192.
30. Sezgin, T.M. and Davis, R. HMM-Based Efficient Sketch Recognition. *IUI 2005*, 281-283.
31. Sharon, D. and Van De Panne, M. Constellation Models for Sketch Recognition. *SBIM 2006*, 19-26.
32. Vatavu, R.-D., Anthony, L., and Wobbrock, J.O. Gestures as Point Clouds: A $P Recognizer for User Interface Prototypes. *ICMI 2012*, 273-280.
33. Wobbrock, J.O., Morris, M.R., and Wilson, A.D. User-Defined Gestures for Surface Computing. *CHI 2009*, 1083-1092.
34. Wobbrock, J.O., Wilson, A.D., and Li, Y. Gestures without Libraries, Toolkits or Training: A $1 Recognizer for User Interface Prototypes. *UIST 2007*, 159-168.
35. Zhai, S. and Kristensson, P.-O. Shorthand Writing on Stylus Keyboard. *CHI 2003*, 97-104.

Type–Hover–Swipe in 96 Bytes: A Motion Sensing Mechanical Keyboard

Stuart Taylor[1], Cem Keskin[1], Otmar Hilliges[2], Shahram Izadi[1], John Helmes[1]
[1]Microsoft Research, [2]ETH Zurich
{stuart|cemke|shahrami|v-johelm}@microsoft.com, otmarh@ethz.ch

Figure 1. We present a novel mechanical keyboard combining motion gestures on and directly above the keys with regular tactile typing. A low-resolution but high-speed sensor (A) is embedded into an off-the-shelf keyboard (B). IR proximity sensors are interspersed between the keycaps (C). This results in a low-resolution raw intensity image when hands are interacting above (D). A sequence of these images are accumulated into proximity (E) and motion (F) history images. Together these form a *motion signature* (E+F) which can be used to robustly recognize a number of dynamic on-keyboard (G) and hover gestures (H) using a machine learning-based classifier.

ABSTRACT
We present a new type of augmented mechanical keyboard, sensing rich and expressive *motion gestures* performed both *on* and directly *above* the device. A low-resolution matrix of infrared (IR) proximity sensors is interspersed with the keys of a regular mechanical keyboard. This results in coarse but high frame-rate motion data. We extend a machine learning algorithm, traditionally used for static classification only, to robustly support dynamic, temporal gestures. We propose the use of *motion signatures* a technique that utilizes pairs of motion history images and a random forest classifier to robustly recognize a large set of motion gestures. Our technique achieves a mean per-frame classification accuracy of 75.6% in leave–one–subject–out and 89.9% in half-test/half-training cross-validation. We detail hardware and gesture recognition algorithm, provide accuracy results, and demonstrate a large set of gestures designed to be performed with the device. We conclude with qualitative feedback from users, discussion of limitations and areas for future work.

Author Keywords
Input devices; Keyboard; Gesture recognition;

ACM Classification Keywords
H.5.2 User Interfaces: Input devices and strategies

INTRODUCTION
Since the invention of the typewriter in the 1860s, mechanical keyboards have remained the preferred method for text entry. Their haptic nature ensures they are still central to much of today's desktop productivity and gaming scenarios, despite the recent popularity of alternative natural user interfaces (NUIs) such as touch, speech and 3D input.

Given their widespread adoption, research has explored how to *augment* keyboards with additional sensing capabilities. In particular, previous work has demonstrated multi-touch capabilities combined with soft (i.e. non-moving) [36] and mechanical keyboards [3, 10, 11, 12]. The aim of such systems is to *co-locate* gestural interaction with regular typing so that the user can quickly move between a resting 'home-position' and either typing or touch-based interactions. Previously studies have shown advantages of combining keyboard use with touch-based 2D pointing[11, 12]. We build on this related work by presenting a new type of augmented mechanical keyboard, capable of sensing *motion gestures*. These are rich, expressive interactions which are performed both *on* and *directly above* the device.

Our hardware design comprises of a low-resolution matrix of infrared (IR) proximity sensors interspersed between the keys of a mechanical keyboard. This low spatial resolution is intentional, allowing the mechanical qualities of the keyboard to be preserved, and providing the ability to support frame-rates of up to an order of magnitude more than previous touch and in-air sensing systems ($325Hz$). We demonstrate that this trade-off between temporal and spatial resolution allows for a rich set of motion gestures.

The coarse but high-speed motion data generated by our prototype requires a new approach to gesture recognition. We demonstrate a novel machine learning algorithm based on randomized decision forests (RDF) [5]. RDFs have been shown to be effective for classification of static hand gestures

CHI'14, April 26–May 01 2014, Toronto, ON, Canada

http://dx.doi.org/10.1145/2556288.2557030

[19], hand pose [18], body pose [30] and objects [13], and generally provide high classification accuracy, are robust to noise and are relatively fast to train [5, 9]. However, one limitation of standard RDFs is that they operate on single images and therefore are not well suited for temporal data.

Given the sensor speed, the temporal domain becomes a rich source of information. We present an extension to standard RDFs which natively supports temporal gestures. We propose the use of *motion signatures* a technique that utilizes pairs of motion history images and an RDF based classifier to robustly recognize a large set of motion gestures on and above the keyboard. The technique automatically performs temporal segmentation, is invariant to linear changes in speed and runs in real-time on commodity hardware.

The structure of the rest of this paper is as follows: We review the relevant literature in the domain of augmented keyboards, touch and in-air motion sensing. After highlighting compelling motion gestures and interactions, we detail the sensing hardware (Fig. 1, A-C), followed by a more in-depth exploration of the gesture design space (Fig. 1, G+H). One of the key contributions of our work is the concept of *motion signatures*, we explain the working principle and detail how they can be used to robustly recognize dynamic gestures (Fig. 1, D-F). We present our initial results in terms of recognition accuracy. Finally, we discuss advantages and limitations and conclude with directions for future work.

RELATED WORK

There has been extensive work on the augmentation of standard input devices such as mice, styluses, touch pads and keyboards, highlighting that this is indeed a rich design space for novel interaction. Systems have added multi-touch [33], pressure [6], and display capabilities to mice [38], as well as touch [31] and proximity sensing [23] to styluses.

Augmented Touchpads

Touch pads have for some time supported multi-touch capabilities [1, 29]. Choi et al. [7, 8] extend prior work [16, 17, 24] that uses discrete proximity sensors for multi-touch displays to create a touch and hover pad. A later variant [14] uses a flexible compliant surface with proximity sensors around the edge to support both touch, pressure and hover in a single sensor. The system is intended to replace the standard touch pad on laptops with a wider sensor, occupying a laptops entire width underneath the keyboard, and support both simultaneous or sequential keyboard and touch input.

Whilst the combination of separate touch pad and keyboard is interesting, the sensors must still reside in two physical locations. Systems therefore enforce highly sequential use and require the user to reposition their hands, acquiring the touch pad much the same way as a mouse. This may increase interaction time and interrupt flow especially for quick, modal gestures that do not require the same precision as targeting.

Multi-touch & keyboards

The limitation of using a dedicated gesture device alongside the keyboard has led researchers to explore other configurations where the two are more tightly coupled. The pressure sensitive keyboard [10] allows simple gestures based on sensing the force applied to each key. Fingerworks produced a flat keyboard (without moving keys) with support for multi-touch gestures [36]. The recently announced Microsoft TouchCover 2* uses a resistive force sensing scheme to detect a small number of gestures, performed by exerting small amounts of force while gesturing directly on top of the keys but does not allow for gestures above the keyboard or gesturing without pressing down. PreSense [27] and SmartPad [28] demonstrate single finger capacitive sensing above a mobile phone keypad and number pad, using a single capacitive matrix behind the keypad.

Touch-based pointing on keyboards

Fallot-Burghardt first describe the concept of touch sensing above a full mechanical keyboard to support regular typing and single finger pointer control [12]. A study of the system shows improved time-to-completion over a standard mouse and keyboard configuration [11]. Due to inadvertent triggering of pointing whilst typing, the system required an explicit mode switch (via a mechanical button) to transition between gesturing or typing. Later variants of this system [15] were also capable of sensing multi-touch on top of the physical keys, but did not solve the problem of false triggering when hands are resting or typing on the keyboard. Block et al. [3] combined the concept of coarse, per-key capacitive sensing with projection capabilities, to display a variety of content such as dynamic keyboard legends.

Above keyboard gestures

Other researchers have placed an RGB camera above a mechanical keyboard [37] or two depth cameras above a desk [34] to detect pinch gestures in mid-air for a variety of tasks such as map navigation and CAD. More recently, commercial products such as LEAPMotion† and 3Gear Systems‡, have added in-air gesturing capability either above or in-front of a keyboard using consumer or custom depth sensors. These systems focus on in-air gestures and do not support transitions between on surface to above surface input.

Whilst capacitive systems have some inherent hover capabilities, to our knowledge we are the first mechanical keyboard to support rich motion gestures on and above the keyboard with a single integrated hardware unit and no use of external cameras. Our system does not require an explicit mode switch to transition between gesturing and typing. We achieve a wide range of motion gestures using a robust gesture recognition technique described in detail later.

INTERACTING WITH THE MOTION KEYBOARD

Our system couples coarse motion and hover gestures with a mechanical keyboard, whilst preserving its core function. Fig. 2 illustrates a number of interesting motion keyboard interactions. For example, a user pans and zooms a map using multi-touch style bi-manual gestures directly on the key caps (A). Slightly lifting the splayed left hand off the keyboard and quick subsequent taps invoke the visual task switcher to quickly jump between applications (B). In a graphics application pressing the 'C' key brings up a color wheel and a motion gesture performed with the other hand changes the selected

*http://www.microsoft.com/surface/

†https://www.leapmotion.com/

‡http://www.threegear.com

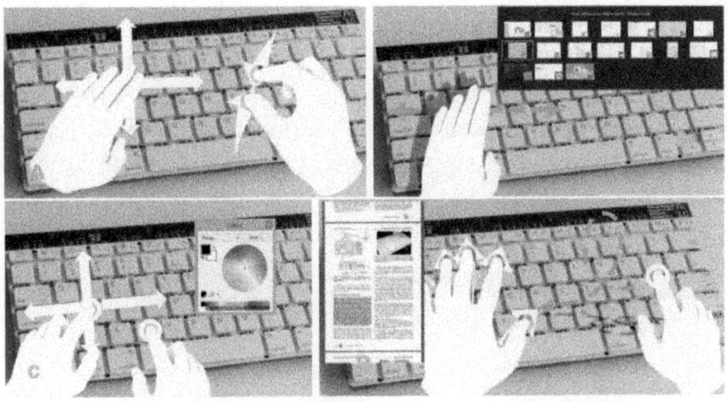

Figure 2. Usage scenarios. (A) Panning and Zooming a document. (B) Open hand hovering above keyboard invokes task switcher. (C) Pressing 'C' brings up color wheel and non-dominant hand selects color. (D) Coarse flicks scroll whole page; index finger performs a touch and hover 'loop' gesture to next/previous paragraph.

color (C). In a document, swiping above the keyboard with the whole hand advances an entire page while a single finger in-air 'loop' advances by a single paragraph (D).

In summary a key goal of enhancing a keyboard in this manner is to enable fast, easy, low-effort gestures and smooth transitions back to typing, where the user's hands always remain in the 'home position'. The motion keyboard enables this in a single, self-contained mechanical package, as opposed to having an external sensor such as a 2D or depth-sensing camera. Our solution coarsely approximates depth, but does allow for rich gestural interaction directly on the keycaps and in a narrow band above.

HARDWARE

Physically the motion keyboard prototype does not differ much from commercially available keyboards. Large parts of the sensor electronics have been integrated into the electro-mechanical 'sandwich' of an off-the-shelf keyboard, which we dismantled, modified and then reassembled with additional custom sensing electronics embedded within it.

The sensor comprises of a two-dimensional array of 64 IR proximity sensors (Avago HSDL-9100-021, Fig. 3), arranged as four rows of 16, where each row lies between two rows of keys. Sensor nodes are surface-mounted on a PCB which is inserted between the array of keycaps and silicone rubber membrane which sits underneath.

Sensor electronics

The sensor LEDs are wired in a matrix fashion, with row and column lines driven by FET switches (Fig. 4). Using this addressing scheme allows individual LEDs to be illuminated by activating just a single row and column. Alternatively, blocks of multiple LEDs can be illuminated by driving several rows

Figure 3. Motion keyboard prototype hardware components. Left: individual IR proximity sensor in metal housing. Middle: Bare PCB with board-mounted 16x4 array of IR proximity transceivers. Note holes cut into the PCB, through which the membrane key switches protrude. Right: IR transceivers interspersed with regular keycaps.

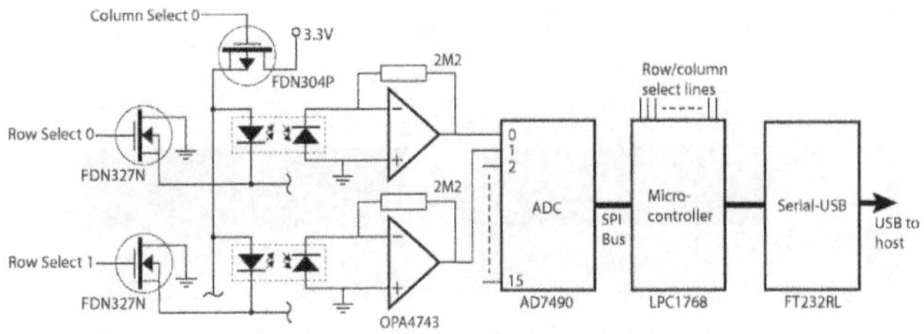

Figure 4. Sensor circuit diagram.

and/or columns simultaneously. One advantage of illuminating multiple LEDs per read is that the hover range above the keyboard can be increased programmatically.

Previously, similar sensor designs [16] have measured a capacitor's discharge time, regulated by the photo-diode, for analog-to-digital conversion. This readout scheme introduces an inherent latency as the charge level must drop to logic state zero. In contrast we use a design where the output from the photodiodes is fed to 16 OPA4743UA quad op-amps in a high-gain configuration, before being passed to four 16-channel, 12-bit analog-to-digital converters (ADCs). The conversion timing and data transfer from the ADCs is performed over an SPI bus (see Fig. 4). This more direct readout scheme allows us to run the circuitry at more than 20× the frame rate of the original Thinsight system [16]. We use an NXP LPC1768 ARM Cortex M3 microcontroller for LED control, co-ordinating ADC readings and transferring data frames to the host PC via USB.

Sensor Data

Capturing one complete frame of proximity data is achieved with a raster scanning process. In sequence, the firmware activates the first row/column line driver (turning on the IR emitter for $24\mu s$), and then instructs the appropriate ADC to perform a conversion of the corresponding amplified photodiode reading. This sequence repeats for each of the sensors, in column order, collecting a complete frame of 64×12-bit ADC readings (i.e. 96 bytes per full frame). The frame is then sent over USB to the host computer for post processing and gesture recognition.

Fig. 5 illustrates typical sensor data from hands moving above the keyboard. Despite the low resolution of only 64 pixels, there is clear signal as the user is swiping or hovering. However, this resolution is not intended for accurate localization of a fingertip. Although fingertip contact is sensed reliably, there are often scenarios where only a single sensor will detect signal, making up-sampling or interpolation of an accurate touch location difficult.

Additionally, the sensor output can be read at high frame rates ($325Hz$), this can benefit in discriminating between intentional gesturing, and regular typing – a much cited issue in previous touch sensing keyboards [11]. Another big advantage of using proximity sensors is that the signal contains data about fingers and hands hovering over the key caps, illustrated through false-color rendering in Fig. 5, (C).

Sensor characteristics and calibration

Each individual sensor node returns raw intensity values that map roughly to proximity. In a first step we establish the

Figure 5. Sensor data. (A) Hand moving across the keyboard, including brief hover period (middle). (B) Sensor data is low-res but can be read at high frame rate (intensity encodes proximity). (C) False-color rendering, scale from blue (0mm) to red (400mm).

noise floor for each cell by capturing a series of empty frames which are accumulated into a background model that can later be used for foreground subtraction.

We conducted experiments to find a model that best linearizes the raw intensity values and maps them to proximity estimates. Fig. 6 (left) shows the response curve for a single sensor. Measurements where made of a 100mm square of gray cardboard mounted on a motorized stage, and human finger stabilized on the same stage. Both targets were measured at fixed intervals from the sensor, parallel to the keycaps. Fig. 6 (right) plots sensor readings against the reciprocal of squared distance, showing that, for both targets, the sensor response tracks the inverse square law reasonably well. These experimental results show that the sensor readings are meaningful in a range from 6mm-33mm (as indicated by the dotted green line). We use these curves to linearize the data and define coarse depth estimates $D = \frac{1}{\sqrt{I}}$ from raw intensity values I.

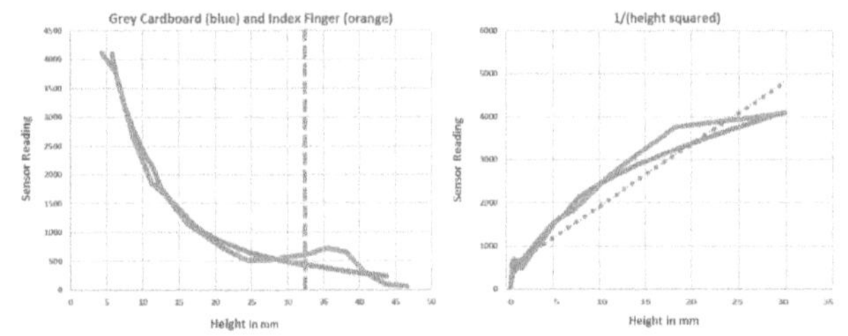

Figure 6. Left: Response curves for a single sensor where gray cardboard (blue) and human finger (orange) are positioned at varying distances from the sensor. Right: Raw intensity values approximate inverse square law (dotted line).

GESTURE RECOGNITION

Now that the reader has a feeling for the hardware configuration and the sensor data, we want to shift the focus towards sensing and gesture recognition. In this section we first introduce a number of gestures that we seek to enable, followed by an in-depth description of our recognition engine.

The gestures discussed here are not necessarily an attempt to design a final end-user experience but serve the dual purpose of exploring the sensor characteristics, illustrating the flexibility and power of the gesture recognition engine, and further highlight the interactive capabilities of our system.

On-Keyboard swipes

The most basic class of gestures we support are on-keyboard swipes, shown in Fig. 7. These directional swipes may be used to scroll and pan large documents, to trigger scrolling or to flick through a collection of images. Swipes may be performed with either hand, single or multiple fingers and anywhere on the keyboard. Our recognition engine can discriminate gestures performed by left and right hand (assuming hands are never crossed) and between large swipes across the central areas of the keyboard (see Fig. 7, left) and shorter swipes crossing the edges of the physical keyboard (see Fig. 7, right). We can separately create compound gestures such as swiping in an out across an edge of the keyboard.

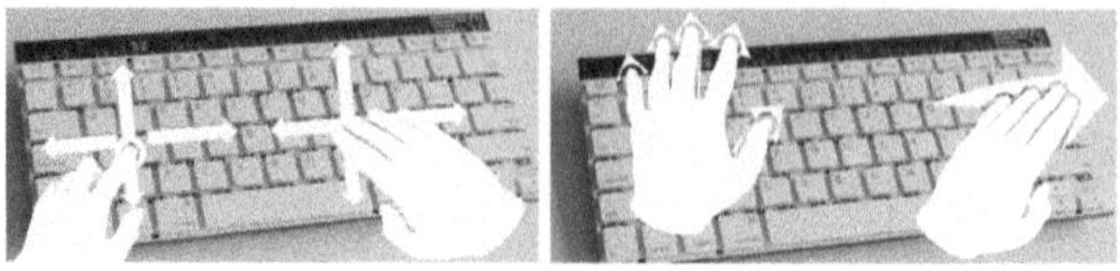

Figure 7. On-Keyboard swipe gestures. Gestures can be performed by either hand with single finger or whole hand.

On-Keyboard shapes

A variant of the coarse swipes for navigational purposes, are shape or stroke based gestures which could be used to trigger discrete commands. These gestures make use of the physical keyboard as visual landmark to aide recall. For example, one gesture is performed by 'drawing' an up arrow onto the keyboard, which causes a window to maximize (Fig. 8, left). The stroke starts with "Left-Alt" moving to "Y" and ending on the "Right-Alt" key. Similarly, a user can use strokes to perform complex keyboard shortcuts and leverage muscle memory to better memorize them, for example a "Ctrl-Shift-D" stroke inverts a selection in Photoshop (Fig. 8, right).

Figure 8. On-Keyboard shapes. Shape drawing to perform discrete commands. Physical keyboard as landmark may help as mnemonic aide in gesture memorization.

Multi-touch gestures

We also recognize a number of multi-touch inspired gestures. For example, a static pinch gesture where the index finger touches the thumb may invoke an OS wide search functionality. Furthermore, dynamic variants of these gestures can be recognized as well where a user may pinch to zoom in and out of a map or photo.

Micro-hover gestures

These are a class of gestures where both hands remain in home position, ready to type or are already typing when the user quickly lifts one or several fingers to issue commands. For example, quickly lifting the open left hand of the keyboard and lowering it back to resting may invoke a marking menu on screen (Fig. 9, left). Coarse swipes can then be used to navigate the menu and selection could happen by quickly lifting and lowering the outstretched index finger of the right hand (Fig. 9, right).

Our system also recognizes static variants of these gestures such as a single finger held for a short duration hovering above the keyboard, or a victory sign also held hovering above the keyboard. These could be used to switch between two modes in an application.

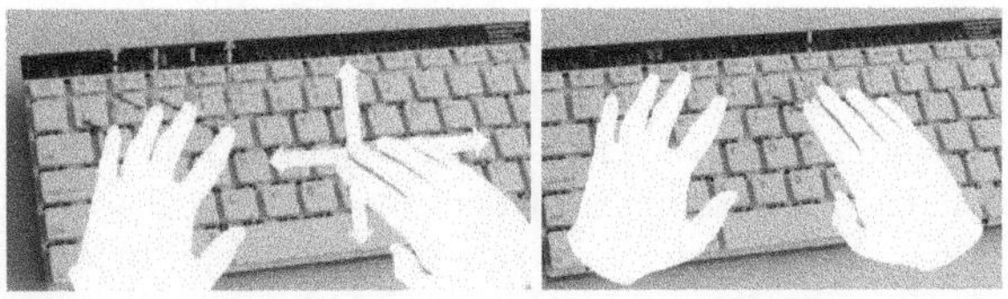

Figure 9. Micro-hover gestures. Hands remain in home position while typing or resting. Quick lifts off fingers triggers different commands.

Dynamic hover gestures

We exploit the proximity sensing capability to add further commands to the gesture set by discriminating stroke-based gestures that are performed entirely on the keyboard from those that contain an in-air portion. One example of this class is a horizontal stroke starting roughly on "LKJ" keys after which the finger lifts off the keyboard performs a tight loop and ends the stroke by touching roughly on "GFD" keys (Fig. 10, left). This gesture may perform an undo while the opposite direction may perform a redo. Another hover gesture could forgo the in-air loop and simply include a hover segment in an otherwise straight stroke (Fig. 10, right), for example invoking a task switcher with a preview function such as Window's Aero Peek.

Figure 10. Dynamic hover gestures. Part of the gesture trajectory is performed in narrow band above the keyboard.

This gives a flavor for the types of gestures we wish to implement. There are two aspects that are important to highlight.

First, whilst our sensor is coarse, the gesture set described here is already reasonably *large*. To perform all the motion and static gestures described earlier in this section, in all the different directions across the keyboard would result in needing to discriminate between a total of 28 gestures, from only 96 bytes of raw proximity data.

Second, many of the gestures share similarities in their trajectories. Our approach is capable of distinguishing gestures that follow the exact same path but with one performed entirely on the keyboard and the other containing a hover section.

These two aspects suggest that heuristic-based recognition approaches would struggle to robustly discriminate between gestures (this is an intuition actually born out of our own experiences during the development of this system). We therefore have explored a novel machine learning based technique for gesture recognition.

METHOD

Our approach leverages randomized decision forests (RDFs) for frame-by-frame gesture classification. RDFs have been shown to be effective for a number of high-level computer vision problems such as object recognition [13], body part [30] and hand shape classification [18] and generally provide high classification accuracy at low computational cost.

However, RDFs are a per-frame technique that is they do not inherently lend themselves to the classification of temporal activities such as human gestures. One of our contributions in this context is a simple but powerful way to represent temporal (and associated proximity) data so that it can be used in one-shot, direct motion classification using RDFs.

The basic idea is that of training a classifier to recognize a *motion signature* rather than a single image of an object. This motion signature encodes the accumulation of motion information over a number of frames (a temporal signature) into a single image. A second image encodes a running average of the proximity information over the same duration.

At training time we annotate a series of these motion signatures with ground truth gesture labels (data capture and labeling is described later), and train a RDF with three trees. At test time, we classify each pixel in the motion signature image into one of the gestures. Note that this approach does not introduce latency, each accumulated image contains a motion signature that allows the RDF to recognize the gesture even before it is completed. The technique can also cope with different gesture execution speeds and variations in motion trajectory (within limits of the training data).

Our approach has some similarities to the method of [25]. However, this previous approach requires the extraction of a large number of features and relies on already available per-pixel body part classification from depth images. We extend the capability to directly classify temporal actions in a way that operates on essentially unprocessed data and does not require computationally expensive feature extraction.

Building motion signatures

Figure 11. Generating a motion history images. Each MHI contains 160 frames of history. All frames t_1 to t_2 are labeled as a specific gesture in the training data. At test time each pixel in the MHI is classified. All MHIs within $t_1 - t_2$ range will be labeled as the corresponding class.

To represent important temporal information necessary to robustly recognize gestures from a single image we build upon and extend the concept of motion history images (MHI)[4]. MHIs are formed by accumulating binary foreground masks, weighted according to their age in a fixed size temporal window. More weight is assigned to recent frames, producing visually recognizable motion trajectories, shown in Fig. 11.

Note that MHIs can be used to recognize both dynamic and static gestures, without motion the MHI is identical to a single foreground mask. However, the binary foreground mask alone does not contain depth information and is thus not suitable to represent the type of hover gestures we seek to recognize. To retain the proximity information in the signal, we accumulate a second image representing motion from weighted intensity images instead of binarized foreground masks.

During training and classification time, we use *both* the binary-MHI (bMHI) and intensity-MHI (iMHI). The bMHI do not contain hover information, and the iMHIs are ambiguous to whether changes correspond to motion over time or changes in depth. Hence, neither bMHI nor iMHI alone are sufficient to robustly detect all types of gestures. However, by using the pair of images together as *motion signature*, we can distinguish between static, dynamic, and hover gestures.

At each time-frame t, the sensor data consists of low resolution 16x4 IR intensity image I_t (12-bit intensity values). We threshold I_t to discard sensor noise to form I_t^s, and binarize it producing the foreground mask I_t^m. These masks are summed $\sum_{i=0}^{k-1} w_{k-1-i} I_{t-i}^m$, where $w_i = \frac{2i}{k(k-1)}$, and k is the number of frames used in the history and i is the current frame index. To form the iMHI, we first normalize the data and produce an approximated depth image I_t^d by applying the reciprocal of the inverse-square law. The iMHI is then the weighted sum of the last k depth images as before.

Training data

In order to train a classifier to robustly recognize a large gesture set with significant variation in terms of execution speed and motion trajectory, we need a database which reflects as much of this natural variation as possible.

We asked 11 subjects recruited from the lab to perform many examples of the 28 gestures outlined previously. Instances of each gesture were semi-automatically delimited and annotated with a class label according to the current gesture. To avoid biases introduced by learning and fatigue effects, gestures were performed in a random order, and counterbalanced appropriately. To capture a wide variation of gesture styles, subjects received minimal instruction on how to perform gestures. Only clear outliers were removed from the database.

We recorded raw frames at $325Hz$ and captured a total of 28 gestures $\times 10$ repetitions $\times 11$ subjects resulting in 3080 sequences. We additionally recorded large amounts of data containing many different types of miscellaneous non-gestural interactions, including typing but also hands moving to and away from the keyboard. This data adds roughly 30% to the entire database and is collectively labeled as 'Typing'. This catch all class for *non-gestures* greatly increases overall robustness as it allows the classifier to learn tighter decision boundaries around the actual gesture classes.

A key contribution is our motion signature representation. Instead of using the entire sequence as an example gesture, we use clusters of (iMHI, bMHI) pairs. At training time we compute these pairs for every tenth frame in all sequences, since consecutive images are very similar due to high frame-rate. The sequences are split into a gesture onset period t_0 to t_1 and a gesture completion period t_1 to t_2 (see Fig. 11). Assuming that the (iMHI, bMHI) pairs from t_1 onward carry a unique signature of the gesture to reliably classify it at test time. We have experimented with different sequence split ratios and have found $t_1 = 0.2 \times t_2$ to be a good compromise between recognition latency and accuracy. MHI pairs extracted from the onset periods are included in the non-gesture class to prevent early false triggering of the recognizer.

Classification

We use a standard RDF classifier similar to previous body [30] and hand pose [19] estimation methods. These approaches use ensembles of decision trees to classify depth images. Decision trees consist of internal split nodes, used to analyze the data, and leaf nodes, used to infer the posterior probability of the class label. At test time, each split node sends the incoming input to one of its children according to the test result. For the final decision, the posterior probabilities estimated by all the trees in the ensemble are averaged.

Tests typically are of the form: $f_n(F_n) < T_n$, where f_n is a function on features F_n and T_n is a threshold, for the split node n. The training of a decision tree involves determining the tests and collecting statistics from a training set in a supervised manner. In the case of RDFs, f_n operates on a subset of the features selected during training. This is done by randomly selecting multiple function candidates and choosing the one that best splits the data. For more details see [9].

Here, we follow the same methodology, but instead of depth features (correlating to the shape of the object) we use MHI pixel intensity differences, which correlate to the dynamic signature of the gesture for bMHI, and to the proximity of the hand for iMHI. Furthermore, during training time the technique selects features from both the bMHI and iMHI, as both can contain information crucial for gesture discrimination. Given an MHI $I(\boldsymbol{x})$, where $\boldsymbol{x}$ denotes location, we define a feature $F_{\boldsymbol{u},\boldsymbol{v}}(I, \boldsymbol{x})$ as follows:

$$F_{\boldsymbol{u},\boldsymbol{v}}(I, \boldsymbol{x}) = I(\boldsymbol{x} + \boldsymbol{u}) - I(\boldsymbol{x} + \boldsymbol{v}) \quad (1)$$

The offsets $\boldsymbol{u}$ and $\boldsymbol{v}$ are vectors relative to the pixel in question. At training time, each split node is assigned a pair of offsets and a threshold that best separates the labeled training data. The leaf nodes are assigned the histograms of class labels of the pixels that end up in those nodes.

At run-time, every pixel is evaluated independently with each tree in the forest. The histograms at the leaf nodes are then normalized and averaged to obtain the posterior likelihood of each pixel. These posteriors are pooled across the image to form a final likelihood for the entire frame. The sequence of posteriors is then smoothed with a running mean filter, and the class label of the mode is assigned to the current frame.

Discussion of Method

Our gesture set includes the static, dynamic and hover gestures illustrated earlier. We picked an RDF classifier over other methods, mainly because they are accurate and robust to noise and can classify each gesture type without modifying the model. Furthermore, RDFs are fast enough to enable classification in real-time, can skip high level feature extraction and work directly on images, and local feature tests can be very simple pixel operations. RDFs are also highly parallelizable (every tree and every pixel is independent).

Whilst in principle it is feasible to use other classifiers in combination with *motion signatures*, we briefly want to highlight potential issues with other classification approaches. Hidden Markov Models (HMMs) [26] or Support Vector Machines (SVMs) [2] are not easily applicable to classification of such motion signals. HMMs typically model feature sequences rather than image sequences. It is an open research question which features would work for our low-res IR images. Designing HMMs that can model both dynamic and static signals is also difficult and uncommon. More importantly, continuous recognition is not straight-forward and usually requires mechanisms for gesture spotting [22]. SVMs on the other hand, lend themselves primarily to the classification of static gestures. A common approach is to extract a single feature vector from a fixed number of images to train the SVM. This again brings up the non-trivial feature selection problem, and other pre-processing steps such as noise reduction may prove necessary. Note that using an MHI as a 64 dimensional feature vector would lead to gestures being conditioned on their locations, which is undesirable. RDFs do not suffer from this issue by using relative features only.

SYSTEM EVALUATION

We have introduced a novel scheme to directly and per-frame recognize dynamic or motion gestures using RDF classifiers. Our approach is centered around the idea of *motion signatures* capturing the essence of both static and motion gestures. In this section we detail experiments we have conducted to evaluate the performance of our classification scheme.

Test Data and Forest Parameters

The forest size (number of trees) and the depth of the trees are the two main parameters affecting classifier performance. Increasing the forest size enhances the accuracy at a linear computational cost. To ensure that recognition is fast enough for real-time interaction at $325Hz$, we set the number of trees to 3. Table 1 summarizes performance at different tree depths.

To evaluate the accuracy of our gesture recognition technique we collected an additional data set of 28 gestures in total collected from 11 users. 6 of these gestures are essentially the same motion, performed by left or right hand on different locations of the keyboard (e.g. swipe-right with left or right hand). We merged these gestures such that there is no distinction between left and right hands at the RDF level. The hand type is determined at a higher level based on where the gesture is performed. After these modifications we have 21 gesture classes and one non-gesture class. We report results using both leave–one–subject–out cross–validation and by using half of the gesture samples in the set for training and the remaining half for validation.

	15	16	17	18	19	20
Tr PPCR	0.69	0.74	0.79	0.83	0.86	0.89
Tr SCR	0.80	0.82	0.85	0.89	0.92	0.95
Ts PPCR	0.57	0.58	0.59	0.6	0.60	0.59
Ts SCR	0.74	0.73	0.75	0.76	0.75	0.75

Table 1. Classification accuracy for half training / half test (Tr) and leave–one–subject–out (Ts) cross validation. PPCR stands for per-pixel classification rate and SCR for state classification rate. Columns report accuracy for different tree depths. Over-fitting starts at depth 19.

Table 1 summarizes overall classification accuracy, averaged over all recognized gestures. Increasing tree depth improves classification accuracy but also increases training time and memory footprint. Over-training starts at depth 19, so we set the tree depths to 18.

The accuracy of the leave–one–subject–out technique directly depends on the inter-personal variation in the dataset. Users have their own preferences for natural gestures, and the variation is quite high. As the number of subjects increases, so does the variation covered in the training set, and the model generalizes better to previously unseen subjects. At depth 18 the accuracy of leave–one–subject–out technique converges in our case and over-training starts when depth is increased more. This accuracy can be viewed as a lower bound. Half training–half test scheme is provided to give a better estimate of the power of the proposed method. Overall, recognition performance is very good even with very shallow trees for this technique (cf. Table 1).

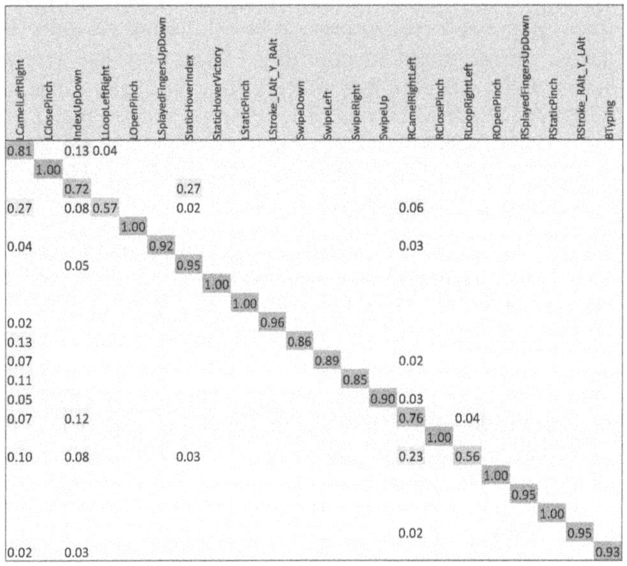

Figure 12. Confusion matrix for all 22 recognized gestures, test data recorded from 11 participants. Results from our forest-based classifier; mean success rate 88.9%.

Fig. 12 summarizes classification accuracy as a confusion matrix for the entire gesture set that an RDF has been trained on. Our technique achieves generally very good classification accuracies with a mean per-class accuracy (mean of the confusion matrix's diagonal) of 88.9%. Furthermore, many gestures achieve close to 100% accuracy per frame. Please keep in mind that these are raw, per frame classification rates. Simple temporal low-pass filtering will further improve these and for most gestures real-world accuracy should be higher. It is worth noting very successful, per-frame classification approaches such as the Xbox Kinect body-tracker, which is based on [30], 'only' reports 60% per-frame mean accuracy yet provides good enough performance when combined with temporal tracking for a mass market product.

The results show excellent classification performance for dynamic and static gestures on the keyboard, and some confusion between the dynamic hover gestures 'Wave' and 'Loop'. The primary reason for the reduced accuracy for the hover gestures is the loss of signal when the hand is out of range of the sensor. The remainder of the motion signature is very similar for both gestures, making it hard to distinguish between the signals.

Also important to highlight is the 'non-gesture' classification rates of 93%, as indicated previously this is the state in which users were typing, resting their hands, and not performing a gesture. This accuracy level is compelling and adds more substance to the machine learning based approach outlined.

PRELIMINARY USAGE OBSERVATIONS

So far we have concentrated on evaluating the gesture recognition accuracy and specifically the impact of *motion signatures*, which we deem one of our main contributions. We also ran some very informal 30 min sessions with 8 users (6 male, 2 female) recruited from our lab, just to gather initial feedback and observations regarding the prototype.

Uniformly all participants instantaneously 'stress-tested' the system to see if it still worked for real text input. All participants expressed real surprise at how little the gestures impacted the keyboard functionality. Once they had learned some of the gestures they quickly tried to explore and understand the whole corpus. The left-right swipes Fig. 7 and the hover gestures that do not require much lateral motion, were well received (Index Up/Down, SplayedHand Up/Down (Fig. 9), Index Loop (Fig. 10, left)).

While other gestures received some criticism for being cumbersome to perform (Swipe Up/Down) or difficult to remember (Hover Stroke) (Fig. 10, right). The former might be due to the keyboard's form-factor which has only limited depth and hence larger hands have very little room to travel in the up/down direction. Finally, one idea that was seen as something with a lot of potential was that of combining the benefits of the keyboard (visual landmarks, haptic feedback) with that of stroke based character recognition or 'shape writing' [20] (e.g., Maximize/Minimize (Fig. 8)) to augment or replace keyboard short cuts – similarly too prior work on touch keyboards [21]. Compound gestures comprising of key presses and swipes such as the color picker example Fig. 2 (C) were also received favorably. Some users even generated several new ideas based on these examples. For example, controlling volume, screen brightness and other continuous OS settings in such a manner.

Of course these observations are only preliminary. Our gesture set was in part designed to evaluate the range of variation our recognizer can cope with. Nonetheless, the current gestures illustrate the utility of enriching mechanical keyboards with gesture sensing capabilities, especially those that go beyond simple 2D pointing. A key benefit seems to be the fact that the system can robustly detect very quick and subtle gestures such as the rapid 'SwipeLeft', 'SwipeRight' gestures and the 'IndexFingerLoop' gesture. Furthermore, users commented that the absence of an explicit mode switch is very compelling. This can be seen as partial confirmation of our initial design goal of low-effort gestures, allowing user's hands to always remain in the 'home position' and of smooth transitions between typing and gesturing.

A final important observation was that of user's initial concerns and reservations with the concept of a sensor embedded in a keyboard, which is perhaps understandable given the importance of the keyboard for their day-to-day work life. However, all of the participants expressed their surprise in how robust the system is in delineating resting and typing motion from intentional gesturing. Hence, many participants indicated that they would use such a system in earnest if, and only if, it provided close to zero false gesture activation. We feel this backed up by our initial accuracy rates, and highlights the importance of a sophisticated and robust gesture recognition engines such as the one outlined here.

DISCUSSION

The initial quantitative and qualitative results of the motion keyboard in use are compelling. Classification results based on motion gestures performed by a variety of users on the keyboard illustrates that even our initial prototype can be used for a diverse set of gestures, even with the low resolution and noise characteristics of our sensor. To our knowledge this is the first time that a touch and hover based keyboard has been demonstrated, especially with this level of robustness for gesture recognition. One important aspect to note is that given our recognition engine is machine learning based, new gestures can be added simply by providing new examples, and retraining our system.

There are also clearly many areas of improvement, which we discuss in this section, outlining limitations and future work. As with all vision systems, ambient light is an issue. We have experimented with IR cut-off filters to alleviate common ambient IR sources (e.g. natural lighting, and room and desk lights), but strong direct light sources are still an issue.

More resolution

In this paper we have intentionally designed a keyboard with low spatial resolution sensing. First, we have wanted to use this device for coarse and lightweight (i.e. low precision but also low effort) gestures that are easy to perform. This takes an opposite approach to systems such as [11], which have looked at replacing the mouse. We on the other hand wish to complement mouse interactions with motion gestures mapped to other UI actions. There have also been mechanical and electronic constraints and cost and power considerations which have also pushed us to choose our current sensing resolution. Clearly, there are ways to improve the spatial resolution in the future. One interesting possibility is to use a denser [23] arrangement of IR proximity sensors. Reverse-biased IR LEDs could also give more flexibility removing the need for an emitter/receiver pair, and instead integrating both sensing or illumination into a single unit (which could be driven using interesting sampling strategies as described below). Higher resolution sensing could allow for fine grained gestures to be coupled with coarser gestures using different readout schemes. For example, the sensor could operate by default in a "coarse" mode of operation allowing regular motion gestures to be sensed, but once detected, could switch to finer scale sensing, allowing fingertip interactions.

How unique are motion signatures?

One interesting finding from experiments is that even with the coarseness of the current sensor configuration we are able to use RDFs to distinguish between diverse *static* gestures robustly (as well as dynamic). There is clearly signal present even at this coarse resolution, which is being learned by our RDF. So clearly our input has some unique signature even for a single frame of data (rather than multiple frames in a motion signature). The question then becomes whether this per-frame signature is unique enough to identify coarsely the overall hand pose, potentially super-resolving the shape of the hand, from the low resolution signal. Inspired by recent work on image retrieval from tiny images [32, 35], we think it may be possible to apply a database look-up scheme to retrieve high-res images of the user's hand, whereby the 96-byte raw sensor data is used as hashing index. To this end we have recorded sequences of 2D images from a top down camera pointing at our sensor, and captured interactions with the sensor using a single finger sliding across the surface.

At test-time we estimate the hand configuration (and in this case the fingertip location) by performing a nearest neighbor lookup into the database (Fig. 13). Initial experiments are promising and seem to indicate some uniqueness per frame even for subtle hand pose differences.

Figure 13. Fingertip localization. Left: Ground truth data. Middle: best candidate from kNN search. Right: Hand contour is traced and fingertip extracted and tracked over time.

Intelligent sampling

Relating to the issue of teasing out more data from the signal we have, is the ability to use more sophisticated sampling mechanisms. Currently, we use a simple scan-line based sampling scheme where each emitter is turned on for a small fraction of time ($24\mu s$) sequentially. However, there might be other ways of sampling. For example, rather than turning a single emitter on in sequence, we could turn a neighborhood of 3×3 around the current sensor on (i.e. 8 other emitters, with the one in the middle sensing). Given the speed of the sensor, we could do this type of sampling every other frame. This could become a separate iMHI and bMHI, which could improve the "uniqueness" of motion signatures, potentially improving our kNN approach outlined earlier.

Per-pixel calibration

Whilst we have started to characterize the response of the proximity sensors within our keyboard, we have yet to exploit this knowledge fully during calibration. Fig. 4 plots the response curve of a single pixel, and as noted, the readings become non-linear the further we move away from the sensor (essentially following the inverse square law). One can accommodate for some of these non-linearities by correcting all pixels (based on the simple inverse square law approximation), as currently implemented. However, we have empirically noted that each sensor has a different response curve, so instead it might be possible to correct each sensor independently. This is akin to radiometric calibration of cameras.Here operating the sensors occasionally in "shadow mode" where no active illumination is used for a single frame, could also allow subtraction of ambient light to help reduce external IR interference.

Interestingly despite our current naive calibration process, our classifier is robust to these differences in per pixel responses. Clearly with radiometric aligned responses from the sensors, our classification could potentially be improved further. However, the RDF is also encoding and learning this mapping in an implicit way. Another avenue of future work therefore could be to have the RDF more explicitly learn the individual response curves of each pixel.

Other hardware/software configurations

Another interesting area of research is to think about both our sensor and gesture recognition in new contexts. Whilst we have demonstrated the advantages of our sensor in a mechanical keyboard, in the future it might be interesting to consider new form-factors such as a stand-alone touch and hover pad. One of the limitations of our current device is extended depth. One interesting possibility is to combine our bottom-up sensing approach with top-down depth cameras to capture interactions in this extended space, using both sensor modalities depending on the proximity to the keyboard. We also feel that our motion signature classification algorithm is general and can be applied to other sensor modalities beyond the motion keyboard, such as depth cameras. Obviously, another big area of future experience is in investigating more specific application scenarios for the motion keyboard, especially ones such as gaming or CAD, where the proximity could be directly mapped to 3D interaction.

CONCLUSIONS

We have presented a new input device, a motion sensing mechanical keyboard. Our sensor allows a variety of gestures on and directly above the keyboard. The device allows very lightweight gestures to be performed without moving your hands away from the keyboard. Our main contributions can be summarized as follows: 1) a new motion sensing keyboard prototype which for the first time demonstrates both touch and hover gestures; 2) a new gesture recognition engine for robustly identifying both static and temporal gestures using a single *motion signature* and RDF framework; 3) a large example gesture set realized using our novel hardware prototype and classification algorithm.

ACKNOWLEDGMENTS

We thank Christoph Rhemann, Alex Butler and Christopher Zach for insightful discussions and Emily Whiting for providing the video voiceover.

REFERENCES

1. Apple Inc. Magic TrackPad, 2010.
2. Bahlmann, C., Haasdonk, B., and Burkhardt, H. Online handwriting recognition with support vector machines - a kernel approach. In *Proc. Frontiers in Handwriting Recognition, 2002.* (2002), 49–54.
3. Block, F., Gellersen, H., and Villar, N. Touch-display keyboards: transforming keyboards into interactive surfaces. In *Proceedings of ACM CHI* (Apr. 2010), 1145–1154.
4. Bobick, A., and Davis, J. The recognition of human movement using temporal templates. *IEEE PAMI 23*, 3 (Mar. 2001), 257–267.
5. Breiman, L. Random Forests. *Machine Learning 45*, 1 (Oct. 2001), 5–32.
6. Cechanowicz, J., Irani, P., and Subramanian, S. Augmenting the mouse with pressure sensitive input. In *Proceedings of ACM SIGCHI* (Apr. 2007), 1385–1394.
7. Choi, S., Gu, J., Han, J., and Lee, G. Area gestures for a laptop computer enabled by a hover-tracking touchpad.

In *Proceedings APCHI*, ACM Press (New York, New York, USA, Aug. 2012), 119–124.
8. Choi, S., Han, J., Kim, S., Heo, S., and Lee, G. ThickPad: a hover-tracking touchpad for a laptop. In *Adjunct Proceedings of ACM UIST* (Oct. 2011), 15–16.
9. Criminisi, A., and Shotton, J., Eds. *Decision Forests for Computer Vision and Medical Image Analysis*. Springer London, London, 2013.
10. Dietz, P. H., Eidelson, B., Westhues, J., and Bathiche, S. A practical pressure sensitive computer keyboard. In *Proceedings of ACM UIST* (Oct. 2009), 55–58.
11. Fallot-Burghardt, W., Fjeld, M., Speirs, C., Ziegenspeck, S., Krueger, H., and Läubli, T. Touch&Type. In *Proc. NordiCHI '06* (Oct. 2006), 465–468.
12. Fallot-Burghardt, W., Speirs, C., Ziegenspeck, C., Krueger, H., and Läubli, T. Touch&TypeTM: a Novel Input Method for Portable Computers. In *Proc. INTERACT* (2003), 954–957.
13. Gall, J., Yao, A., Razavi, N., Van Gool, L., and Lempitsky, V. Hough forests for object detection, tracking, and action recognition. *IEEE PAMI 33*, 11 (Nov. 2011), 2188–202.
14. Gu, J., Heo, S., Han, J., Kim, S., and Lee, G. LongPad: A TouchPad Using the Entire Area below the Keyboard on a Laptop Computer. In *ACM CHI'13*, ACM Press (Paris, France, 2013).
15. Habib, I., Berggren, N., Rehn, E., Josefsson, G., Kunz, A., and Fjeld, M. DGTS: Integrated Typing and Pointing. In *Proc. INTERACT*, vol. 5727 of *Lecture Notes in Computer Science*, Springer Verlag (Berlin, Heidelberg, 2009), 232–235.
16. Hodges, S., Izadi, S., Butler, A., Rrustemi, A., and Buxton, B. ThinSight: versatile multi-touch sensing for thin form-factor displays. In *Proceedings of ACM UIST* (Oct. 2007), 259–268.
17. Hofer, R., Naeff, D., and Kunz, A. FLATIR: FTIR multi-touch detection on a discrete distributed sensor array. In *Proceedings of TEI '09*, ACM Press (New York, New York, USA, Feb. 2009), 317.
18. Keskin, C., Kiraç, F., Kara, Y. E., and Akarun, L. Hand Pose Estimation and Hand Shape Classification Using Multi-layered Randomized Decision Forests. In *ECCV 2012*, Lecture Notes in Computer Science, Springer Verlag (Berlin, Heidelberg, Oct. 2012), 852–863.
19. Keskin, C., Kiraç, F., Kara, Y. E., and Akarun, L. Randomized decision forests for static and dynamic hand shape classification. In *2012 IEEE CVPR Workshops*, IEEE (June 2012), 31–36.
20. Kristensson, P.-O., and Zhai, S. SHARK 2. In *Proceedings of ACM UIST* (Oct. 2004), 43.
21. Kristensson, P. O., and Zhai, S. Command strokes with and without preview. In *Proc. ACM CHI* (Apr. 2007), 1137.
22. Lee, H.-K., and Kim, J. H. An HMM-based threshold model approach for gesture recognition. *IEEE PAMI 21*, 10 (1999), 961–973.
23. Liu, S., and Guimbretière, F. FlexAura: a flexible near-surface range sensor. In *Proceedings of ACM UIST* (Oct. 2012), 327–330.
24. Moeller, J., and Kerne, A. ZeroTouch: an optical multi-touch and free-air interaction architecture. In *Proceedings of ACM CHI* (May 2012), 2165.
25. Nowozin, S., and Shotton, J. Action Points: A Representation for Low-latency Online Human Action Recognition. Tech. rep., Microsoft Research Cambridge, 2012.
26. Rabiner, L., and Juang, B. An Introduction to Hidden Markov Models. In *IEEE Acoustic Speech Signal Processing Magazine* (1986), 3–4.
27. Rekimoto, J., Ishizawa, T., Schwesig, C., and Oba, H. PreSense: interaction techniques for finger sensing input devices. In *Proceedings of ACM UIST* (Nov. 2003), 203–212.
28. Rekimoto, J., Oba, H., and Ishizawa, T. SmartPad: a finger-sensing keypad for mobile interaction. In *CHI '03 extended abstracts*, ACM Press (New York, New York, USA, Apr. 2003), 850–851.
29. Rosenberg, I., and Perlin, K. The UnMousePad: an interpolating multi-touch force-sensing input pad. *ACM Transactions on Graphics 28*, 3 (July 2009), 1.
30. Shotton, J., Fitzgibbon, A., Cook, M., Sharp, T., Finocchio, M., Moore, R., Kipman, A., and Blake, A. Real-time human pose recognition in parts from single depth images. In *CVPR 2011*, IEEE (2011), 1297–1304.
31. Song, H., Benko, H., Guimbretiere, F., Izadi, S., Cao, X., and Hinckley, K. Grips and gestures on a multi-touch pen. In *Proceedings of ACM CHI* (May 2011).
32. Torralba, A., Fergus, R., and Freeman, W. T. 80 million tiny images: a large data set for nonparametric object and scene recognition. *IEEE PAMI 30*, 11 (Nov. 2008), 1958–70.
33. Villar, N., Cao, X., Chen, B., Izadi, S., Rosenfeld, D., Benko, H., Helmes, J., Westhues, J., Hodges, S., Ofek, E., and Butler, A. Mouse 2.0: multi-touch meets the mouse. In *Proceedings of ACM UIST* (Oct. 2009).
34. Wang, R., Paris, S., and Popović, J. 6D hands: markerless hand-tracking for computer aided design. In *Proceedings of ACM UIST* (Oct. 2011), 549–558.
35. Wang, R. Y., and Popović, J. Real-time hand-tracking with a color glove. In *ACM Transactions on Graphics*, vol. 28 (July 2009).
36. Westerman, W., Elias, J. G., and Hedge, A. Multi-Touch: A New Tactile 2-D Gesture Interface for Human-Computer Interaction. *Proceedings of the Human Factors and Ergonomics Society Annual Meeting 45*, 6 (Oct. 2001), 632–636.
37. Wilson, A. D. Robust computer vision-based detection of pinching for one and two-handed gesture input. In *Proceedings of ACM UIST* (Oct. 2006), 255–258.
38. Yang, X.-D., Mak, E., McCallum, D., Irani, P., Cao, X., and Izadi, S. LensMouse: augmenting the mouse with an interactive touch display. In *Proceedings of ACM SIGCHI* (Apr. 2010), 2431–2440.

B#: Chord-based Correction for Multitouch Braille Input

Hugo Nicolau[1], Kyle Montague[1], Tiago Guerreiro[2], João Guerreiro[2], Vicki L. Hanson[3, 1]
[1]University of Dundee, Dundee, Scotland
[2]University of Lisbon, Lisbon, Portugal
[3]Rochester Institute of Technology, NY, USA
{hnicolau, kmontague}@dundee.ac.uk, tjvg@di.fc.ul.pt, joao.p.guerreiro@ist.utl.pt, vlh@rit.edu

ABSTRACT
Braille has paved its way into mobile touchscreen devices, providing faster text input for blind people. This advantage comes at the cost of accuracy, as chord typing over a flat surface has proven to be highly error prone. A misplaced finger on the screen translates into a different or unrecognized character. However, the chord itself gathers information that can be leveraged to improve input performance. We present B#, a novel correction system for multitouch Braille input that uses chords as the atomic unit of information rather than characters. Experimental results on data collected from 11 blind people revealed that B# is effective in correcting errors at character-level, thus providing opportunities for instant corrections of unrecognized chords; and at word-level, where it outperforms a popular spellchecker by providing correct suggestions for 72% of incorrect words (against 38%). We finish with implications for designing chord-based correction system and avenues for future work.

Author Keywords
Chord; Braille; Error Correction; Touchscreen; Mobile

ACM Classification Keywords
H.5.2. Information interfaces and presentation

INTRODUCTION
Since the advent of Apple's iPhone and its built-in accessibility features, blind people have increased access to mainstream mobile applications. However, the flat surface poses challenges that are only partially solved. Particularly, typing is still slow compared to what sighted people experience [4]. To address this issue, multitouch Braille chording approaches have been presented and are very effective in improving input speed [1,6]; however, they are characterized by a decrease in typing accuracy [6].

One common approach to improve typing accuracy is the usage of spellcheckers. Indeed, there have been efforts in developing spellcheckers for disabled people, taking into consideration common typing errors and keyboard layout [3]. Further, Sandnes and Wang [5] presented a texting alternative for desktop computers, which relied on chording with spatial mnemonics and automatic word correction. However, to our knowledge, there are no reports of correction approaches that leverage Braille chording information. As a result, when decoding multitouch actions to characters, useful knowledge about the users' intent is lost. The sequence of chords provides more information about the desired word than do the characters, as each chord becomes the atomic unit of information. Distances are computed considering that a chord may be partially correct enriching the selection of the most probable suggestions.

In this paper we present B#, a correction system for multitouch Braille input that resorts to the chord itself as the basis for similarity analysis between words. At character-level, an unrecognized chord is used along with n-gram features to decide the closest character. At word-level, we extended the *Damerau-Levenshtein* distance to assess proximity between chords, and thus use this information to search for the most probable corrections. The contributions of this paper are: first, an analysis of chording errors on multitouch Braille input; second, a correction system that leverages chord-level information; and finally, an analysis on the effectiveness of character- and word-level correction.

COLLECTING TYPING DATA
We conducted a user study with 11 Braille-knowledgeable blind participants (light perception at most, ages between 22-62, 3 females) aimed at understanding the most common errors in multitouch Braille input (Grade 1). None of the participants owned a touchscreen phone. The prototype draws inspiration from BrailleTouch's [6] usage setup (Figure 1-a), combined with finger tracking techniques [1].

Procedure
Participants were given warm-up trials (10 minutes) starting from writing individual characters, words, and finally sentences. They were then instructed to write a set of 22 sentences (completion dependent of participant's availability), whereas the first two were practice trials. Error correction (delete) was not available in order to capture errors and uninterrupted typing behaviours. An auditory signal was used to indicate that a letter had been entered. Participants were instructed to continue to the next character even if they recognized they had made an error. Each sentence comprised five words, with an average size

CHI 2014, April 26–May 1, 2014, Toronto, Ontario, Canada.

http://dx.doi.org/10.1145/2556288.2557269

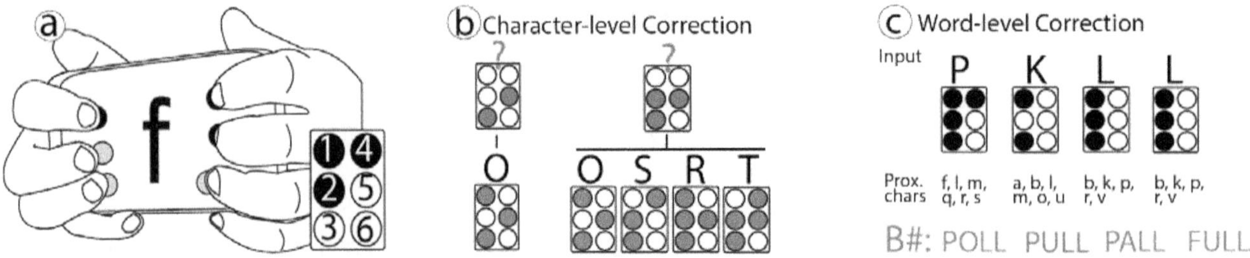

Figure 1. B# is a novel correction system for multitouch Braille input. (a) The user types the letter 'f'. (b) Character-level correction; the closest characters in terms of Braille distance for 2 unidentified chords. (c) Word-level correction; top suggestions return by B# considering the letters that are at a Braille distance of one from the entered chord.

of 4.48 characters. These sentences were extracted from a Portuguese written language corpus, each one having a minimum correlation with language of 0.97.

Major Results

Participants wrote a total of 168 sentences and 5972 characters. Data analysis revealed insights on the most prominent Braille touch typing behaviors, which were the basis for B#'s error correction algorithm principles.

High error rate. Multitouch Braille typing solutions are known to be fast and error prone [6]. Similarly, in this study, participants obtained an average typing speed of 14 words per minute and error rate of 17.7%, of which 72.4% was due to character substitutions errors.

Single dot errors. Chord-level analysis revealed that 35.2% of substitutions were due to a single dot error within the braille cell. This difference occurred either due to a single omitted or extra dot. If we include a single adjacent finger transposition, this accounts for 42.5% of substitution errors.

Unrecognized Characters. Participants entered a total of 263 Braille chords that were not recognized as a valid letter (4.4% of all chords). In these cases, the characters are automatically classified as errors, and this information is usually discarded from traditional correction systems.

B#: LEVERAGING CHORD INFORMATION

B# deals with mistyped words that result from entering incorrect chords on a touchscreen device. In the remainder of this section, we propose: first, a distance function that enables us to compare Braille chords, and therefore predict misspells; second, a character-level disambiguation mechanism; and finally, a word-level correction algorithm that leverages chord information.

Braille Distance

Our approach to word correction is based on similarity between Braille chords. The proposed distance function aims to model users' behaviours while chording on a touchscreen. The 3x2 Braille matrix is viewed as a vector of 6 bits and thus, the difference between two vectors can be computed as a binary distance. Four types of chording errors can occur whilst chording: omissions (finger was not on the screen), insertions (additional finger on the screen), transpositions (finger was on an adjacent position), and substitutions (wrong finger on the screen).

Our distance function draws inspiration from the *Damerau-Levenshtein* distance with a slight variation. The distance between chords is the sum of the differences between hands; that is, the first and last three bits that correspond to each hand are treated independently. This approach prevents transposition errors from occurring between hands. Overall, omission, insertion, and transposition errors are considered as a one-bit error (distance of one), because these are the most common misspellings, and substitution errors (i.e. wrong fingers), are treated as a 2-bit error.

Character-Level Correction

Character-level correction is achieved by exploiting redundancy in the alphabet. The Braille cell allows the representation of 64 different patterns. However, standard text entry applications do not use its maximum capacity. If we only consider the letters of the English alphabet (26), and the blank space, then this yields 58% redundancy. In cases where the user enters an invalid chord, the closest valid character in terms of Braille distance can be selected (Figure 1-b). There are several situations where this approach retrieves more than one valid character, introducing ambiguities in the correction process. In these cases, we leverage basic linguistic features, such as letter and n-gram frequencies to select the most probable character. Our algorithm uses the maximum of previous available letters to disambiguate invalid chords. Although this approach may not deal with all spelling errors, we are interested in analyzing its effect as a stand-alone solution, as well as in combination with word-level correction.

Word-Level Correction

B# word-level correction algorithm uses a similar approach to traditional spellcheckers by matching the transcribed word against a wordlist. A key difference is that it operates at chord-level. This means that even partially correct or invalid chords can be used to retrieve better matches. Even non-alphabetic characters, which are usually ignored by traditional spellcheckers, can provide useful information.

For each transcribed word, B# creates a list of likely suggestions and ranks them using a word distance score. If the word exists in the wordlist, then it is automatically the first suggestion. Our algorithm deals with three types of typing errors: insertions (unintentionally added chords), substitutions (incorrect chords), and omission (omitted

chords). Transposition errors were not considered since Braille input is a sequential task with no overlap between chord entries. A *minimum string distance* (MSD) score is used to calculate the distance between users' input and suggestion candidates. We systematically check chord permutations in the transcribed word against the wordlist.

Since computing all permutations of chords is computationally inefficient, we reduce our search space by only checking against letters that are at a Braille distance of one from the transcribed chord. This distance accounts for 1-bit errors, responsible for most character substitutions. A Trie tree structure is used for checking the existence of the word in the wordlist, while employing character insertion, omission, and substitution rules during the spelling correction stage. A blank space filter is used to separate two words that were transcribed without a space between them. Finally, a word frequency score is computed and subtracted from the MSD score.

B# EVALUATION

In order to evaluate B#, we ran the correction algorithms on the set of sentences previously collected. Analysis was performed using an Android Virtual Device (Galaxy Nexus). From the 751 words, we identified and tagged 364 (48.5%) incorrect entries that could be corrected by B#. We applied Shapiro-Wilk normality tests to observed values in all dependent variables. Parametric tests were applied for normally-distributed variables and non-parametric tests otherwise. Greenhouse-Geisser's sphericity corrections were applied whenever Mauchly's test showed a significant effect. Bonferroni corrections were used for post-hoc tests.

Character-Level Results

Character-level correction was applied to unrecognized characters, i.e. inexistent chords in the native alphabet. To evaluate character correction, we compared B# disambiguation with the baseline substitution errors. Additionally, we included a version of B# without the linguistic features in order to assess its effect on correction accuracy. The letters' relative frequencies, bigrams, and trigrams were extracted from a corpus with more than 11 million letters and 2 million words.

Chord and Linguistic features enable Disambiguation. We obtained an average of 12.8% (sd=8.6%) substitution errors. By only exploiting the redundancy of the Braille alphabet, substitution errors slightly decreased to 12.2% (sd=7.3%). On the other hand, B# character-level disambiguation successfully corrected 2.4% of substitution errors, reaching an average of 10.4% (sd=5.9%). A Friedman test revealed a significant effect on methods [$\chi^2_{(2)}$=18.474, p<.001]. Wilcoxon pairwise comparisons showed significant differences between B# disambiguation and both baseline [p<.005, r=.2] and redundancy-only [p<.01, r=.1] results. As 33.6% of substitution errors were due to unrecognized characters, it means that 18.8% of all chord ambiguity errors were automatically corrected combining redundancy and simple language features. Overall, B# disambiguation corrected 29 words (8% of all incorrect words).

Word-Level Results

In order to evaluate B# word-level correction, we compare our solution with a popular spellchecker for mobile devices: Android (AOSP) spellchecker, which for brevity purposes will herein be referred to as AOSP. This solution makes no use of contextual information, similarly to B#. Additionally, to conduct a fair comparison between correction methods, we used the same wordlist (213,133 words) and word frequencies. All required words used in the data collection stage existed in the wordlist. To assess the effect of each correction component, the results presented here were obtained without character-level disambiguation. We also analyze a variant of B# that uses the Hamming distance (XOR between binary vectors) to compute similarity between chords enabling us to assess our effectiveness against a commonly used metric to compare vectors.

Method	Top 1	Top 2	Top 3	Top 4	Top 5
AOSP	28 (12)	34 (12)	36 (13)	37 (13)	38 (13)
Hamming	53 (19)	63 (19)	66 (21)	62 (22)	69 (22)
B#	56 (17)	65 (18)	69 (20)	70 (21)	72 (20)

Table 1. Mean percentage (standard deviation) of correct words returned for the top n suggestions (1≤n≤5).

B# is consistently more accurate. Table 1 shows the results for the top n suggestions ($1 \leq n \leq 5$), while Figure 2 illustrates the results. The percentage of accurate words returned by the AOSP spellchecker is rather small and never exceeds 38%. On the other hand, chord-based solutions outperform the AOSP spellchecker, with mean accuracy rates between 53% and 72%. Indeed, when analyzing the first suggestion, there is a significant effect [$F_{(1.102,11.021)}$=19.279, p<.001, partial η^2=.66], with both B# [p<.005] and Hamming [p<.01] methods being more accurate than AOSP spellchecker. This result suggests that leveraging chord information plays a major effect on correction accuracy. No significant effect between B# and Hamming variant was found for the first suggestion. Overall, B# would be able to correct 204 of 364 incorrect words automatically, i.e. without user intervention. The Hamming variant and AOSP would correct 193 and 100 words, respectively.

B# is more accurate for the top three suggestions. While we agree that the most important result is to propose the correct word as the first suggestion, we also acknowledge that providing the highest possible fraction of accurate suggestions at the top of the list is critical, especially, when user intervention is needed. Therefore, although B# and Hamming variant methods are equally accurate for $n=1$ and $n=2$, B# significantly outperforms its counterpart for $n=3$ [Z=-2.023, p<.05, r=0.08], $n=4$ [Z=-2.023, p<.05, r=0.11], and $n=5$ [$t_{(10)}$=-2.25, p<.05, Cohen's d=.17].

No gain beyond top five suggestions. We can observe in Figure 2 that the highest gain is achieved from $n=1$ to $n=2$

with an increase of 6.6%, 9.5%, and 9.5% for AOSP spellchecker, Hamming variant, and B#, respectively. For *n>2* improvements are smaller and then start to fade at *n=5*. B# and Hamming curves are very similar, which can be explained by the similar correction paradigm; however, Hamming is consistently outperformed by B#. This result suggests that indeed the proposed extension to the *Damerau-Levenshtein* distance is effective in dealing with Braille chording misspellings. B# continues to provide useful suggestions for $n \leq 5$, with significant differences for $1 \leq n \leq 2$ [Z=-2.803, $p<.005$, r= 0.26], and $2 \leq n \leq 3$ [Z=-2.201, $p<.05$, r= 0.09], $4 \leq n \leq 5$ [Z=-2.023, $p<.05$, r= 0.05].

B# provides a low number of incorrectly corrected words. All methods obtained low false positives (top suggestion incorrect): 1.4% (sd=1.9%), 1.7% (sd=2.2), and 1.7% (sd=2.2). In fact, a Friedman test revealed no significant effect on method [$\chi^2_{(2)}=2$, $p=.368$]. B# high accuracy comes at no cost regarding incorrectly corrected words.

Chord information matters. In order to measure how important chord-level information is on providing accurate suggestions, the word frequency factor was removed from our spellchecker. This means that the scoring solely depended of Braille chord similarity. Results showed an accuracy rate of 44.8% (sd=15%) for the top suggestion, which is a significant decrease of accuracy (*n=1*) from the B# condition. This result shows that word frequency features are important to obtain the best possible suggestion. Despite the decrease in performance, this condition still outperforms AOSP's spellchecker [$t_{(10)}=3.182$, $p<.01$, Cohen's d=1.3], suggesting that taking advantage of the chord similarity is crucial correct errors.

Combined character-word-level correction is ineffective. We also assess the effect of feeding disambiguation results into the word-level component. Overall, the combined solution presents a similar accuracy curve to word-level correction; however, it is outperformed for all $1 \leq n \leq 10$. A paired t-test showed a significant effect for methods [$t_{(10)}=3.080$, $p<.05$] with the word-level correction outperforming the combined solution for *n=1* (m=50.1%). This suggests that erroneous corrections at character-level affect word-level accuracy. The spelling component loses important chord information that would otherwise be used.

IMPLICATIONS FOR DESIGN

Leverage input method information. Results showed that leveraging chord distances significantly improves word correction accuracy. Even simple distance functions allow improvement over traditional spellcheckers. As previously suggested [2], one should take advantage of common misspellings, tightly related to each method, and use that knowledge to improve spelling accuracy.

Do not discard chord information. Data showed that combining character- and word-level is an ineffective solution, mostly because information is lost in the first correction stage. Therefore, if using character-level correction to provide instant feedback to users, allow the word-level component to receive the original chords.

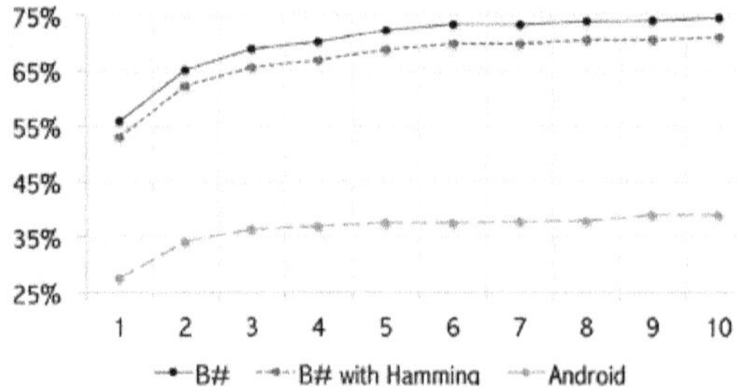

Figure 2. Mean percentage of correct words returned for the top n suggestions (1≤n≤10)

Focus on top 5 suggestions. Most spellcheckers provide a list of most probable suggestions enabling users to intervene when corrections are inaccurate. Results showed that B#'s top two suggestions yield most corrections; however, if possible, the top five should be considered.

CONCLUSION AND FUTURE WORK

We presented B#, a chord-based spellchecker for multitouch Braille input. Results show that B# is more effective than other spellcheckers by leveraging a distance of similarity between chords. These results should encourage researchers to develop more accurate correction algorithms tailored to novel text-input techniques. Future work will explore the design of non-visual interfaces to leverage chord-based suggestions.

ACKNOWLEDGMENTS

This work was supported by RCUK Digital Economy Programme grant EP/G066019/1 – SIDE; FCT Multiannual Funding Programme, and grant SFRH/BD/66550/2009

REFERENCES

1. Azenkot, S., Wobbrock, J., Prasain, S., Ladner, R. Input finger detection for nonvisual touch screen text entry in Perkinput. In *Proc. GI* (2012).
2. Deorowicz, S., & Ciura, M. G. Correcting spelling errors by modelling their causes. *Int. journal of applied mathematics and computer science* (2005), *15*(2), 275.
3. Kane, S., Wobbrock, J., Harniss, M., & Johnson, K. TrueKeys: identifying and correcting typing errors for people with motor impairments. In *Proc IUI* (2008).
4. Oliveira, J., Guerreiro, T., Nicolau, H., Jorge, J., Gonçalves, D. Blind people and mobile touch-based text-entry: acknowledging the need for different flavors. In *Proc. ASSETS* (2011).
5. Sandnes, F. E., Huang, Y. P. Chording with spatial mnemonics: automatic error correction for eyes-free text entry. In *Journal of information science and engineering*, 22, 5 (2006).
6. Southern, C., Clawson, J., Frey, B., Abowd, G., Romero, M. An evaluation of BrailleTouch: mobile touchscreen text entry for the visually impaired. In *Proc. Mobile HCI* (2012).

Representatively Memorable: Sampling the Right Phrase Set to Get the Text Entry Experiment Right

Luis A. Leiva and Germán Sanchis-Trilles
PRHLT Research Center, Universitat Politècnica de València
{luileito,gsanchis}@dsic.upv.es

ABSTRACT

In text entry experiments, memorability is a desired property of the phrases used as stimuli. Unfortunately, to date there is no automated method to achieve this effect. As a result, researchers have to use either manually curated English-only phrase sets or sampling procedures that do not guarantee phrases being memorable. In response to this need, we present a novel sampling method based on two core ideas: a multiple regression model over language-independent features, and the statistical analysis of the corpus from which phrases will be drawn. Our results show that researchers can finally use a method to successfully curate their own stimuli targeting potentially any language or domain. The source code as well as our phrase sets are publicly available.

Author Keywords

Text Entry; Sampling; Memorability; Representativeness

ACM Classification Keywords

H.5.2 Information interfaces and presentation: User interfaces—*Input devices and strategies, Evaluation/Methodology*

INTRODUCTION

In text entry experiments, participants are prompted with phrases (short sentences) that must be entered as quickly and accurately as possible. Although it may seem more natural to have users enter free text and increase thus the external validity[1] of the experiment, it is critical to make the text entry method the only independent variable in the experiment, and increase thus its internal validity.[2] Indeed, if users were asked to type "as fast as possible" they would introduce rather biased text. Hence, researchers typically use pre-selected phrases, measuring the dependent variables (e.g., input speed or error rates) in a text-copy task. This eliminates noise and facilitates the comparison of text input techniques.

In general, copy-tasks should prefer memorable stimuli [7, 8, 13]. Unfortunately, to date there is no automated method to achieve this effect. Researchers resort to using manually curated English-only phrase sets, which are typically small according to modern standards, or rely on sampling procedures that cannot guarantee memorability. In contrast, today text is entered into mobile devices in many different languages, where text entry methods might perform very differently (c.f., English vs. Arabic). This fact evidences the necessity of an adequate sampling method, aimed at exploiting the huge amount of text corpora available in many languages.

We present a method for sampling memorable *and* representative phrase sets, based on a multiple regression model over language-independent features, so that it can generalize to other languages, and the statistical analysis of the (large) corpus from which phrases will be drawn. An interesting property of our method is that, being data-driven, phrases may contain unusual vocabulary as long as it is representative of the task or domain. Our method is validated in two user studies, showing that researchers can now gather their own stimuli for a given language or domain. It is available at `http://personales.upv.es/luileito/memrep/`.

RELATED RESEARCH

For the past decade, text entry researchers have predominately used the MacKenzie and Soukoreff phrase set [8], which contains 500 phrases that were manually selected according to three criteria: moderate in length, easy to remember, and representative of general English. More recently, Vertanen and Kristensson [13] released a phrase set based on genuine mobile emails. Unfortunately, both phrase sets are *1)* manually curated, *2)* only available in English, and *3)* relatively small according to today's standards. In contrast, repositories like the Linguistic Data Consortium, Data Wrangling LLC, or the ELRA catalog provide a plethora of large multilingual corpora that could be curated to automatically build phrase sets tailored to specific tasks or languages.

Paek and Hsu [10] devised a procedure for creating representative phrase sets by randomly sampling sets of n-grams and choosing the set with less entropy with regard to the original dataset. Although mathematically sound, this procedure does not guarantee that sampled phrases are memorable. Moreover, the phrase set generated in this way (the NGRAM dataset) contains incomplete sentences and near two thirds of the words are out of vocabulary,[3] sometimes with extremely unusual punctuation symbols. This might pose a threat to the internal validity of text entry experiments.

In a text-copy task, phrases can be briefly shown at the start or left visible throughout. Kristensson and Vertanen [6] observed that in the latter case entry rates are consistently higher

[1] The extent to which the observed effect is generalizable.

[2] The extent to which the observed effect is due to the test conditions.

[3] Most words are not regular English, according the NEWS dataset.

CHI 2014, April 26–May 1, 2014, Toronto, Ontario, Canada.

ACM 978-1-4503-2473-1/14/04..$15.00.
http://dx.doi.org/10.1145/2556288.2557024

at the cost of higher error rates and longer task times. They reported that the NGRAM phrase set is memorable, but we suspect it is because all sentences are exactly 4 tokens long.

On Entropy and Memorability

Genzel and Charniak [3] postulated in their "entropy rate" principle that speakers tend to produce sentences with similar entropy, so that they can be easily understood. Therefore, too informative sentences (high entropy) should be harder to process and, in consequence, less memorable. However, entropy has been shown to be a weak predictor of processing effort, being the latter better correlated with word length and word frequency [5]. Danescu-Niculescu-Mizil *et al.* [2] analyzed the memorability of movie quotes, concluding that "stand-alone" sentences built on common syntactic scaffolding are likely to be memorable. In general, shorter and frequent words take less time to read and therefore are easily understandable [4]. These observations are key to our work.

METHOD

We are interested in a sampling method to select, from a fairly large text corpus $\mathcal{C}$, those sentences that are good candidates for conducting text entry experiments. Such a method should select phrases that are:

1. **representative** of the task, domain, or language, for ensuring the external validity of the experiment;
2. **memorable**, for ensuring internal validity;
3. **complete**, since fragmented phrases are often confusing.

We assume that the corpus $\mathcal{C}$ contains text that users are likely to write in a real-world context. So, a statistical analysis should uncover commonalities of $\mathcal{C}$, such as phrase length or word frequencies, and the sampled subset should present similar characteristics. In contrast, memorable phrases should be easy to process and write out, which implies that *1)* phrases must be moderate in length, and *2)* words should not be infrequent overall. Then, representativeness and memorability can be pictured as antagonist forces, since e.g. phrases that are very short and contain short and common words will be very memorable, but will rarely be representative either of general language or the task. For instance, a dataset containing only phrases like "this is it" or "and so on" would not be very appropriate for conducting a text entry experiment. We therefore devise a single-pass procedure where each phrase is assigned an expected memorability value that is compensated with a representativeness score.

Modeling Memorability

We first looked at readability tests such as the Coleman-Liau index [1] or ARI [12]. However, they were designed to gauge the understandability of whole documents and are overly simplistic; i.e., they only contemplate sentence and word lengths, and systematically retrieve extremely short phrases. Fortunately, the accuracy (or quality) of a transcribed sentence, measured as the character error rate (CER), is widely accepted to be a good proxy of memorability [6, 7, 13]. Therefore, we focus on modeling CER to predict memorability.

Together with the previously discussed observations, we will attempt to express CER as a function of language-independent features, among which we chose the following:

- `Nw`: Number of words in the phrase. Longer phrases are generally harder to process.
- `OOV`: Number of infrequent words, relative to `Nw`. The higher this ratio, the harder the phrase is to process.
- `Mchr`: Average number of characters per word. Shorter words are easier to process.
- `SDchr`: Standard deviation of the number of characters per word. Higher variability leads to higher processing effort.
- `Ppl2` and `Ppl3`: Perplexity (or cross-entropy) of the phrase using word bigrams and trigrams, respectively. Lower perplexities may indicate that the phrase is easier to process.
- `LProb`: Natural logarithm of the probability of the phrase. Phrases with high probability are likely to be more usual expressions and so they should be easier to memorize.

Ideally, to compute `OOV`, `Ppl2`, `Ppl3` and `LProb` as accurately as possible we would need full knowledge of the "universe" of the target language or domain. Being this impossible, we resort to using a sufficiently large corpus $\mathcal{U}$ and consider that such corpus is descriptive of the desired language, task, or domain. In our experiments, $\mathcal{U}$ is the NEWS corpus[4] (Table 1). Then, *1)* infrequent words are those that do not appear in $\mathcal{U}$; *2)* perplexities are measured with respect to a language model built on $\mathcal{U}$; and *3)* word frequency counts within `LProb` are estimated on $\mathcal{U}$. Note that $\mathcal{C} \not\subseteq \mathcal{U}$, otherwise it would lead to over-trained estimations for the phrases in $\mathcal{C}$ (e.g., no word would be considered infrequent).

Language	Sentences	Running words	Vocabulay size	Singletons
English	68.5M	1.6G	3.4M	1.8M
Spanish	13.4M	0.4G	1.2M	0.6M

Table 1: Statistics of the NEWS corpus.

Model Estimation

The CER model was fitted according to generalized linear regression [9], since it allows for any distribution of the model features. We suspected that not all of the features described above, besides being intuitively useful, would be strong CER predictors. For instance, linear models assume that factors are independent of each other. So, in order to decide the best features for the model, we used the Bayesian Information Criterion (BIC) approach [11]. BIC was chosen over other criteria in the literature because it tends to build a simple model and converges as the number of observations increases.

We trained the model with the data released by Vertanen and Kristensson [13], which was drawn from the ENRONMOBILE dataset and provides 22,390 CER-labeled sentence memorization tasks completed by 386 MTurk workers. All workers were from the United States and India, either native speakers or having a competent English level. Workers had to memorize a sentence and then type it after pressing a continue button. Having 10 observations per phrase, intra-phrase observations that exceeded 1.5 times the interquantile CER range were considered outliers (e.g., a worker being distracted or

[4] `http://statmt.org/wmt13/translation-task.html`

writing a completely different sentence), and the remaining observations were averaged on a phrase basis. Eventually 2,390 "data points" were considered.

BIC revealed that the significant features to predict CER were only **Nw**, **OOV**, **SDchr**, and **LProb**. The model yielded a good fit (adj. $R^2 = 0.63$), with the following combination of features:

$$\texttt{CER} \approx -11.65 + 0.83 \cdot \texttt{Nw} + 0.48 \cdot \texttt{SDchr} + 6.94 \cdot \texttt{OOV} - 1.00 \cdot \texttt{LProb} \quad (1)$$

As observed, **Nw**, **SDchr**, and **OOV** have positive weights, implying that CER increases when sentences get longer, words are more infrequent, and words have a highly variable amount of characters. Conversely, **LProb** having a negative weight implies that the more likely the sentence, the less prone users are to make mistakes. In addition, **OOV** receives a much higher weight than the rest of the features, indicating that infrequent words are specially correlated with high CER values.

Ensuring Representativeness

Presumably, selecting sentences with the lowest CER estimates would yield the most memorable ones, although such sentences would end up being those with few and short words. To compensate this effect, we also need to ensure that sentences are representative either of general language, the sentence corpus, or the desired task for the text entry experiment. To achieve this, we estimate the empirical probability of the features present in Eq. (1), and reward those phrases that have a higher probability according to such prior distribution. Assuming Gaussian distributions, we can estimate the mean μ_i and standard deviation σ_i of each feature h_i on the target corpus $\mathcal{C}$. Then, the representativeness of a sentence is given by:

$$\texttt{Repr} = \prod_i P_{\mathcal{C}}(h_i; \mu_i, \sigma_i) \quad (2)$$

where $P_{\mathcal{C}}(h_i; \mu_i, \sigma_i)$ is the probability distribution of each feature h_i according to $\mathcal{C}$. Moreover, adjusting the meta-parameters μ_i and σ_i allows text entry researchers to fine-tune the kind of phrases that will be eventually used in the text entry experiment.

Finally, since we want to retrieve phrases with high memorability (low **CER**) and high representativeness (high **Repr**), we define the final score assigned to a phrase by the following expression:

$$\texttt{sc}(\text{phrase}) = \frac{\texttt{CER}}{\texttt{Repr}} \quad (3)$$

so the lower the score, the better. This way, our sampling method provides a closed-form solution to sample the (hopefully) right phrases to get the text entry experiment right.

EVALUATION

We tapped into the MACKENZIE dataset (500 sentences) and the NGRAM dataset (500 4-gram sentences). Both datasets have been reported to be memorable by native English speakers [6], so we replicated the analysis with non-natives. We also sampled 500 sentences at random from the public EUROPARL dataset (1.8M sentences from the proceedings of the European parliament), and 500 more following our method. Because EUROPARL contains overly long sentences (28 words per sentence on average) we restricted both samplings to lowercased phrases of 3–10 words, otherwise the random condition would be placed at a disadvantage; and punctuation symbols were removed (as in MACKENZIE). Moreover, $P_{\mathcal{C}}(\texttt{Nw})$ was set to that of MACKENZIE, resulting in phrases of 5–6 words, since estimating μ_i for **Nw** according to EUROPARL would be heavily skewed and therefore would tend to retrieve the longest sentences. Even though such sentences would be representative of this specific topic (parliamentary proceedings), they may not be reflective of everyday language and thus would not be very appropriate for conducting text entry experiments, where memorability is important.

We recruited 20 native Spanish speakers aged 28–38 using the available University's mailing lists. All participants had a qualified intermediate or advanced English degree according to CEFR.[5] Each participant was shown a phrase for 5 seconds or until the first keystroke, whatever happened first. Next, the phrase disappeared and users had to write it (as much as they could remember) with a physical QWERTY keyboard. Participants entered 20 phrases in a randomized order from each dataset, resulting in 1,600 annotated phrases in total. The results are show in Table 2. Together with CER (in %), we report the words per minute (WPM) to give an overview of the participants performance in terms of input speed. We also report the time since the phrase was loaded until the first keypress (T_k, in seconds), which provides an estimate of the time spent memorizing each phrase.

Dataset	WPM	CER	T_k
MACKENZIE	67.90 (12.23)	2.04 (2.58)	2.62 (0.74)
NGRAM	65.70 (11.34)	3.07 (2.45)	2.64 (0.74)
EUROPARL random	64.80 (13.63)	6.63 (4.68)	3.47 (0.80)
EUROPARL ours	65.49 (11.47)	1.40 (1.48)	3.27 (0.90)

Table 2: Evaluation results for English. SDs in parentheses.

An ANOVA test revealed that differences between datasets were statistically significant for CER [$F_{3,72} = 10.75, p < .0001, \eta_p^2 = 0.31$] and memorization time [$F_{3,72} = 5.89, p = .0012, \eta_p^2 = 0.20$]. Post-hoc pairwise t-tests (Bonferroni-Holm corrected) revealed that the phrase set derived by our method compares favorably to state-of-the-art phrase sets (no differences were found), and that participants performed significantly worse in the random sampling condition, both in terms of CER and memorization time. Overall, we observed more variability in our data in comparison to previous literature [6], which motivates the need to provide participants with sentences in their native language.

In light of the previous study, we generated 3 phrase sets of 500 sentences each by tapping into the Spanish version of EUROPARL. We used random sampling, the n-gram sampling procedure (with $n = 6$), and our method. In all cases, we used lowercased phrases of 3–10 words with punctuation symbols removed. We then repeated the same experiment with the same participants. The results are show in Table 3. Again, differences between datasets were found to be statistically

[5] http://www.coe.int/lang-CEFR

significant for CER [$F_{2,54} = 5.90, p = .0048, \eta_p^2 = 0.18$] and memorization time [$F_{2,54} = 20.94, p < .0001, \eta_p^2 = 0.44$]. Post-hoc pairwise t-tests (Bonferroni-Holm corrected) revealed that the random and n-gram conditions performed equally similar, and that our method performed significantly better than the other sampling procedures. This study shows that our method generalizes well to Spanish, which is a language quite different from English.

Dataset	WPM	CER	T_k
EUROPARL random	70.21 (13.70)	2.33 (1.96)	3.32 (0.60)
EUROPARL ngram	72.04 (15.71)	3.10 (2.53)	3.20 (0.66)
EUROPARL ours	74.51 (14.19)	0.85 (1.55)	2.24 (0.37)

Table 3: Evaluation results for Spanish. SDs in parentheses.

In both studies, a common complaint from participants was that "some phrases are incomplete [...] they are distracting and difficult to memorize." This observation backed up our intuitions regarding the desired properties of a phrase set for text entry experiments (see Method section).

DISCUSSION AND CONCLUSION

Many text entry methods require constant visual attention, such as eye typing or dialing a contact while driving. For experiments trying to emulate these or similar situations, memorability is critical since it can be difficult for participants to consult often the reference text. Memorability is also desirable to unburden the participants and let them exclusively focus on the text entry method. Until now, sampling methods aimed to select "representative" phrases, but memorability was largely ignored. This work therefore significantly contributes to HCI by making it possible to curate large text corpora in potentially any language and any task or domain.

Our findings are of special relevance to text entry researchers interested in conducting experiments tailored to the linguistic capabilities of their participants. Memorability was found to be correlated with sentence length, word variability, word frequency, and ratio of infrequent words. In sum, shorter phrases with frequent vocabulary are easier to remember. These findings were consistent in all of our experiments, and ultimately are aligned to previous key findings in the literature. Table 4 provides an overview of the type of phrases that can be deemed as being either of good or bad quality, as scored by our method. This illustrates a means to filter (un)desired phrases from the phrase set used as stimuli, in order to ensure the validity of the text entry experiment.

We have shown that our method can generalize to different domains and languages different from English. This provides text entry researchers with a scalable and unprecedented capability. However, it must be noted that our features may not be applicable to every possible language. For instance, Chinese words are not even formed by individual letters. Therefore, there is still an opportunity for future work. Thus one possibility would be experimenting with other memorability predictors, which could lead to better models that would in turn improve our sampling method. We hope that this work will be suitable for use in a variety of text entry evaluations.

Phrase set	Quality	Sample phrases
MACKENZIE	+	mary had a little lamb
	+	february has an extra day
	-	if you come home late the doors are locked
	-	rent is paid at the beginning of the month
NGRAM	+	will receive a unit
	+	is likely to propose
	-	& cyndi clark [mailto:bcclarks.att.net
	-	and skills–attend critical information-packed=20
EUROPARL	+	i forgot to mention it
	+	all human life is valuable
	-	two questions still remain however
	-	secondly the economic and financial crisis

Table 4: Good (+) and bad (-) phrase examples to conduct text entry experiments, according to Eq. (3). Good examples were scored the lowest.

ACKNOWLEDGMENTS

This work is supported by the 7th Framework Program of the European Commision (FP7/2007-13) under grant agreements 287576 (CASMACAT) and 600707 (tranScriptorium).

REFERENCES

1. Coleman, M., and Liau, T. L. A computer readability formula designed for machine scoring. *Journal of Applied Psychology 60*, 1 (1975).
2. Danescu-Niculescu-Mizil, C., Cheng, J., Kleinberg, J., and Lee, L. You had me at hello: How phrasing affects memorability. In *Proc. ACL* (2012).
3. Genzel, D., and Charniak, E. Entropy rate constancy in text. In *Proc. ACL* (2002).
4. Just, M. A., and Carpenter, P. A. A theory of reading: From eye fixations to comprehension. *Psychological Review 87*, 1 (1980).
5. Keller, F. The entropy rate principle as a predictor of processing effort: An evaluation against eye-tracking data. In *Proc. EMNLP* (2004).
6. Kristensson, P. O., and Vertanen, K. Performance comparisons of phrase sets and presentation styles for text entry evaluations. In *Proc. IUI* (2012).
7. MacKenzie, I. S., and Soukoreff, R. W. Text entry for mobile computing: Models and methods, theory and practice. *Human-Computer Interaction 17*, 2 (2002).
8. MacKenzie, I. S., and Soukoreff, R. W. Phrase sets for evaluating text entry techniques. In *Proc. CHI EA* (2003).
9. Nelder, J. A., and Weddrburn, R. W. M. Generalized linear models. *J. R. Statist. Soc. 135*, 3 (1972).
10. Paek, T., and Hsu, B.-J. P. Sampling representative phrase sets for text entry experiments: a procedure and public resource. In *Proc. CHI* (2011).
11. Schwarz, G. E. Estimating the dimension of a model. *Annals of Statistics 6*, 2 (1978).
12. Senter, R. J., and Smith, E. A. Automated readability index. Tech. Rep. AMRL-TR-6620, Wright-Patterson Air Force Base, 1967.
13. Vertanen, K., and Kristensson, P. O. A versatile dataset for text entry evaluations based on genuine mobile emails. In *Proc. MobileHCI* (2011).

Sketching in Circuits: Designing and Building Electronics on Paper

Jie Qi
MIT Media Lab
75 Amherst St, E14 548
Cambridge, MA 02142
jieqi@media.mit.edu

Leah Buechley
MIT Media Lab
75 Amherst St, E14 548
Cambridge, MA 02142
buechley@mit.edu

ABSTRACT

The field of new methods and techniques for building electronics is quickly growing—from research in new materials for circuit building, to modular toolkits, and more recently to untoolkits, which aim to incorporate more off-the-shelf parts. However, the standard mediums for circuit design and construction remain the breadboard, protoboard, and printed circuit board (PCB). As an alternative, we introduce a method in which circuits are hand-made on ordinary paper substrates, connected with conductive foil tape and off-the-shelf circuit components with the aim of supporting the durability, scalability, and accessibility needs of novice and expert circuit builders alike. We also used electrified notebooks to investigate how the circuit design and build process are affected by the constraints and affordances of the bound book. Our ideas and techniques were evaluated through a series of workshops, through which we found our methods supported a wide variety of approaches and results—both technical and expressive— to electronics design and construction.

Author Keywords

Paper computing; toolkits; sketchbooks; circuit prototyping.

ACM Classification Keywords

J.5 Arts and Humanities

INTRODUCTION

More and more communities are becoming interested in creating their own hardware, as the tools of design and application space of electronics become more diverse and accessible. Despite advances in the technology itself, the standard mediums people use to design and build electronics remains largely the same: the breadboard, the protoboard, and the printed circuit board (PCB).

The breadboard provides a press-fit grid for quick connections and disconnections for testing circuits and modification. Since these circuits are built using only press-fit connections, breadboards are great for fast prototyping but quite fragile as final products. Protoboards are a more permanent solution in which components are soldered down to a board that is precut with a grid of holes. The PCB is the most permanent solution, in which components are soldered onto a pre-designed circuit board. Unlike breadboards and protoboards, PCBs also give users the freedom to arrange components spatially on the board with the help of CAD software. Their digital nature also allows PCB designs to be easily checked by CAD, shared and replicated. However, the PCB design process requires users to wait for the board to be fabricated—which can take a few hours to a few days—before designs can be tested. Once produced, PCBs are difficult to modify, making this process ideal for amplification but slow and inconvenient for prototyping purposes.

CHI 2014, April 26–May 1, 2014, Toronto, Ontario, Canada.

ACM 978-1-4503-2473-1/14/04...$15.00.
http://dx.doi.org/10.1145/2556288.2557391

An interesting alternative approach to prototyping and building circuits is *ugly construction*, in which circuit components are soldered directly to each other in mid-air over a rigid ground board [22]. This method allows creators to spatially arrange their components, create permanent circuits, and test their creations immediately. However, the circuit connections are often unclear because these three-dimensional circuits are difficult to plan and tend to be constructed organically. In addition, the exposed component leads make short circuits very common.

In this paper, we introduce an alternative method in which circuits are hand-made on paper substrates with conductive foil tape and off-the-shelf circuit components. This process incorporates the tinkerability and immediate feedback of breadboards, protoboards and ugly construction. It also allows users to visually and spatially lay out their circuit as with PCBs. Paper as a circuit substrate also affords all the qualities of any other paper-based craft. For example, users can sketch and annotate, cut and fold, digitally scan, or even bind their circuits into books for archival. In addition to exploring the techniques on paper, we also investigate how building circuits in book form through electrified sketchbooks—recalling the process of traditional sketching—affects the circuit design process and resulting artifacts.

RELATED WORK

This work builds upon a body of research most notably centered around the concept of untoolkits [13], materials approaches to building circuits on paper, and electronically augmented books.

Untoolkits

Given the growing research in non-traditional approaches to building electronics, many researchers are now looking at incorporating more off-the-shelf and existing components and materials, the untoolkit approach, to make these techniques more accessible and reach more diverse audiences. From a craft perspective, squishy circuits [9] is a circuitry sculpting technique using conductive modeling clay and Perner-Wilson [15] systematically studied a variety of traditional craft practices, to see how existing materials and techniques could be applied to circuit building. Mellis et. al. [13] used off-the-shelf microcontrollers, traditional craft materials, conductive ink and open hardware and software tools to create an approach to circuit building that is friendly to new circuit builders by relying on familiar craft techniques. In Invent-Abling [8], soft circuit kits were designed to be as simple and bare as possible, to encourage users to incorporate other local materials. Finally, the MakeyMakey kit [12] is a board that specifically requires users to find common materials to complete the circuit-building activity. Inspired by these approaches, we designed our method to incorporate materials that are familiar and easy to use and off-the shelf for accessibility.

Building circuits on paper

There have also been many explorations of how to incorporate circuits with paper from a materials perspective. Some approach this challenge through materials science investigations on new conductive inks for drawn [18], printed [10] and painted [2] circuits. Others, in addition to the examples mentioned above, have looked at repurposing existing materials for circuit building. [3] is a toolkit of magnetic circuit boards that cling to conductive painted traces, [17] looks at a variety of industrial shielding materials for electronically interactive pop-up scenes on paper, and [4] even embeds circuit elements within the pulp during the paper making process. While these were techniques for handmade circuits, [14] presents a method for CNC vinyl-cutting copper foil tape to create circuit boards and [20] presents digital design tools for making electronically interactive paper-based artifacts. These techniques and explorations show the wide variety of existing and emerging material and techniques that integrate circuits with paper.

Electrified Books

Finally, despite the growing trend in digitization, researchers have become increasingly interested in researching methods for preserving the physical book form while augmenting them with electronic qualities. In addition to [17], many have integrated digital features to the traditional book format, allowing users to remotely communicate through book interfaces [5], interact with sound while reading a story [1], and connect a physical book to a web interface [21]. Others have looked specifically at how digital features can help note-taking through augmented notebooks [10] and [11]. Workshops [18] and [6] have also emerged to both preserve and guide the evolution of physical books in this increasingly electronic and digital age. In our work, we are similarly inspired to analyze the affordances of the physical book, especially in the note-taking and design aspect, and transfer this to the process of circuit building.

METHOD FOR MAKING PAPER CIRCUITS

The following process summarizes a flexible and hand-made approach to building circuits on paper using off-the-shelf electronic components and common household supplies (Figure 1).

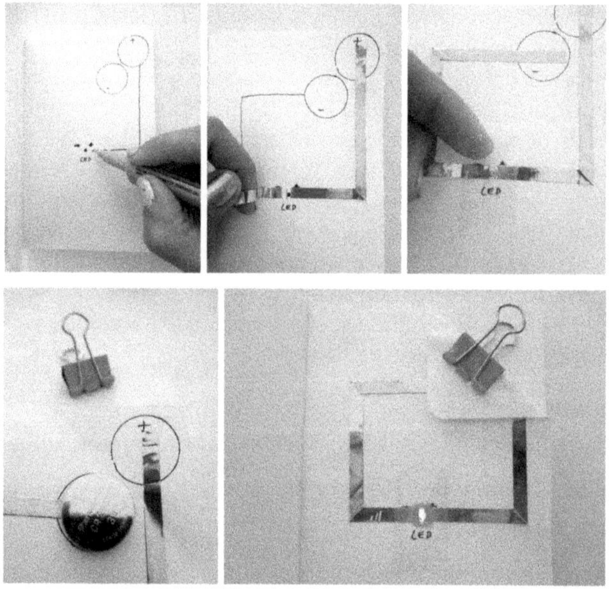

Figure 1. Method for making basic paper circuit: Plan the circuit, place conductive traces, connect components, and add power.

Plan the Circuit (optional)

Decide where components will be organized on the page, and trace the component footprints. It is helpful to label these footprints with their functionality and pinouts. Then draw lines to indicate the necessary electronic connections. Using multiple colors helps keep traces organized. To connect external components to the page, draw traces to the page edge for alligator clips to attach.

Add foil traces

Cover the drawn traces with conductive foil tape. Make alligator clip pads for external components by folding conductive foil over the edge of the page. Connect multiple foil pieces by soldering or folding over the end of the foil and taping metal surface to metal surface. Connections made by simply sticking two foil tapes together, even those with conductive adhesive, tend to degrade quickly over time. To jump across a trace without connecting, make a bridge by sandwiching paper or high-temperature resistant tape between the two traces. Finally, to make sharp turns, use the folding turn gadget in Figure 2.

Figure 2. Making sharp turns: (a) Fold the foil tape back on itself, (b) so the sticky side faces up. (c) flip it over while simultaneously folding the corner and flatten.

Do-it-yourself circuit components
Create quick paper switches by folding over the end of a foil tape, so that the adhesive is no longer exposed, and placing this over another trace (the other half of the switch). Stick a paper spacer underneath the tab to prevent accidental connections. This is a momentary switch. To create a permanent slide switch, slide a pair of magnets over the foil to clip the switch closed down.

Connect standard components
Populate the circuit by soldering surface mount components on as with a standard printed circuit board. For circuits using only smaller, simpler (two or three-pin) surface mount components like LEDs, elements can be secured in place by taping over with clear tape.

Add power
For connection with coin cell batteries, fold down a corner of the paper, place the positive and negative leads on either side of the fold and use a binder clip or disc magnets to hold the battery in place (Figure 1). This technique was designed in collaboration with Hannah Perner-Wilson for the electronic postcard project [16]. External power supplies can also be clipped on with alligator clips.

Programming
Microcontrollers in the circuit can be connected to standard programmers through foil pads for alligator clips to the programmer, or a foil footprint to press on a standard programming headers.

Repeat and iterate
Once the circuit is built, it is still open for revision. Foil trace connections can be cut with a knife or untaped. It is even possible to lift entire sections of circuitry intact and tape them elsewhere for rearranging the circuit. Additional circuitry can be added to the circuit by creating more paper bridges, or even covering entire networks of traces with a sheet of paper to create a new layer of blank space.

PAPER CIRCUITS WORKSHOPS
To share, evaluate and evolve our techniques, we ran a series of workshops with a diverse community of users. We started by investigating paper electronics techniques, introducing them first through templates and then moving on to guided activities with free time for open exploration.

Starting with templates
Our goal for the preliminary workshop was to see if participants could successfully apply these new techniques to reproduce given circuits on paper templates, with the hope of ultimately experimenting with circuits for expressive applications.

This workshop had 11 total participants, 8 female and 2 male between the ages of 19 and 21. All participants were undergraduates majoring in graphic design with experience in arts and crafts. Regarding their technical backgrounds, 60% reported having little to no experience in programming and 67% reported having little to no experience making electronics.

Participants were given three different printed circuit templates with directions on where to place metal foil tape and electronic elements (Figure 3). The templates showed how to turn on one LED, turn on multiple LEDs in parallel and create paper switches with pop-up mechanisms. We led students through constructing the first template and introduced the electrical concepts along with techniques like soldering on foil over paper. Students completed the two remaining templates with little guidance.

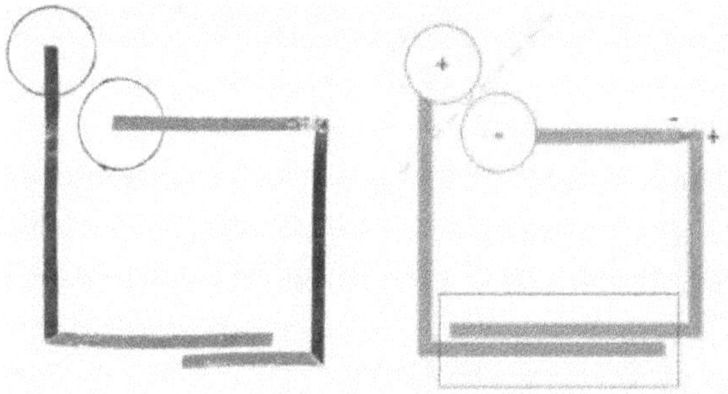

Figure 3. Original scanned circuit (left) and digitized template (right) for flickering slide switch circuit.

After the session, students had the option to complete a personal interactive book project with these techniques. Three books were made; two incorporating circuits and techniques covered during the workshop and one used a commercial sound-recording module.

Our workshop results confirm that such techniques are indeed accessible and engaging for novice circuit builders. The templates successfully communicated how to create circuits on paper.

Circuits on paper
Next we taught a series of four workshops in parallel, one to a group of art and design students and the other to a group of

science and engineering students, for a total of eight workshop sessions. These sessions met once a week and took place over a period of five weeks—the fifth session was a final project presentation. The goal of these workshops was to test out the full suite of paper electronics with "experts," those who are used to working with technology and those who are experienced in crafting creative and expressive work.

Of the art and design students, there were a total of 19 unique participants, eight of whom were women, ranging in age from 18 to 26 years old. They were mostly undergraduate students who majored in graphic design, industrial design, furniture, architecture or apparel. Of the science and engineering students, there were 16 total unique participants, thirteen women and three men, age 18 to 37 years old. Participants were generally split between undergraduate students who majored in mathematics, mechanical engineering or computer science and graduate students studying electrical engineering, computer science, microbiology and physics, with the exception of one medical student. 9 of the art and design participants and 7 of the science and engineering participants were able to make it to at least three of the four workshops.

Each workshop began with technical instruction, followed by free time to experiment, design and create a personalized project. The workshops covered four main topics: basic paper electronics techniques with LEDs, copper tape and soldering, preprogrammed ATTINY85 microcontrollers with switches as inputs; preprogrammed ATTINY85 microcontrollers with pressure sensors, light sensors, microphones and piezoelectric elements as inputs; and actuating thermochromic ink and shape memory alloys. In this paper, we will focus on results from the first three sessions, since the fourth session covered uncommonly used electronic materials.

Participants produced a wide variety of projects and explorations, a few of which are shown in Figure 4. There were technical explorations involving the circuitry as well as physical mechanisms. Others focused on more aesthetic properties—looking at how light could be diffused with different materials. Yet others looked at interaction and application to finished projects. The diversity of these results show that the paper electronics techniques do support an experimental, sketch and design approach to building circuits. This enables participants to explore and bring in their own personal interests into the circuit building process, even those interests that have nothing to do with electronics.

ANALYSIS:

One goal for this work was to present electronics in a way that is accessible to grasp conceptually and feels intuitive to work with physically. The focus was on exploring and expressively applying the electronics concept, guided by the participants' own interests. Ultimately, we hoped participants would feel empowered and inspired by the magical interactive qualities of electronics to apply it in their own works. These goals were reached to various extents within the workshop.

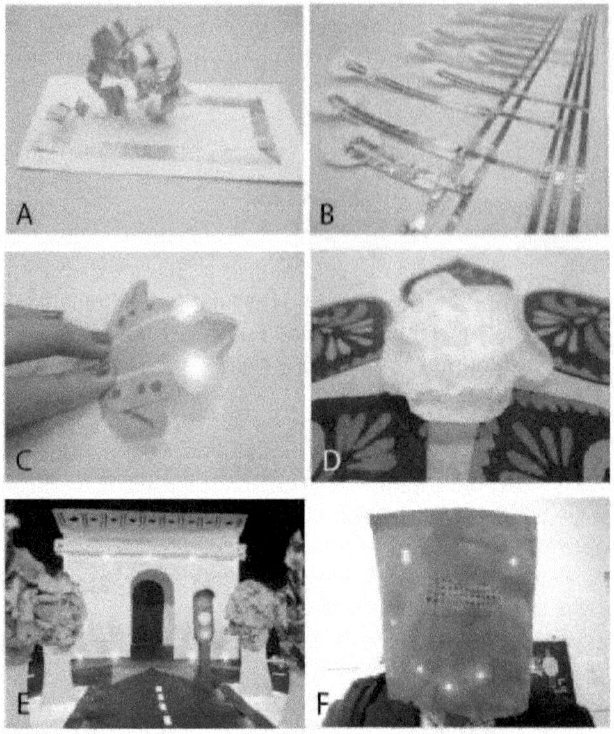

Figure 4. Example paper electronics projects: copper foil sculpture (A), bracelet with decorative foil traces (B), origami frog that glows right before jumping (C), LED diffusion through paper flower (D), Arc du Triomphe diorama (E), Mask that smiles when you speak (F).

Participant reactions

Regarding the templates used during the preliminary workshop, students responded positively. One student reported, "*the cards she made us were VERY helpful and easy to comprehend, I feel I could go back in 2 years and still understand what I learned.*" However, we have learned that while the circuit templates made it very easy for students to construct working circuits, their specificity limited students' exploration. Since most participants made the exact circuit printed on the templates, most did not try incorporating the circuit physically nor conceptually into their artworks. In the personalized book project, two of the participants embedded a circuit made during the workshop directly into their final projects rather than creating a new circuit.

As a result, in subsequent workshops we used the templates only as supplemental materials and found that participants were just as capable of making functioning circuitry without them. Free of template guidelines, people's works also became far more diverse and this format allowed each person to focus on the techniques they were most interested in and through their own learning styles.

Even without templates, one of the most frequently observed results from the workshops was that participants found electronics surprisingly easy to build. After the first workshop session, one science and engineering participate responded wrote, "*I really enjoyed how easy it was to incorporate lights into almost any static or dynamic paper craft, using only simple components and without even needing soldering!*"

Asked about paper electronics as a whole, an art and design participant wrote, "*the workshop made me realize that electronics were in my reach.*" Another participant from the science and engineering group, an astronomy PhD student, found the paper electronics approach especially illuminating for learning electronics. At the end of all four sessions, he wrote the following about his experience:

"Step-by-step you had us work our way up to more and more complicated projects, and now I really feel empowered to explore electronics (paper, or otherwise!) on my own. Doing everything with the attitude that things could always be peeled up and retaped or unsoldered and resoldered or programmed and reprogrammed made it a really fun environment to learn."

This simplicity also gave some participants enough freedom and fluency to use these techniques in an expressive fashion. One science and engineering participant wrote "*Good to think I can focus on the concept, making use of the techniques rather than the other way around.*"

Diversity in artifacts produced

The resulting projects show the wide range of physical projects people could create—from glowing dioramas (Figure 4.E), to personalized interactive greeting cards, to science fictional plants that respond to light. Projects could be technically simple but expressively complex, such as an origami frog that glowed right before jumping (Figure 4.C) made with a simple switch and two LEDs. They could also be more complex, such as the mask that smiled when the wearer spoke (Figure 4.F). Here, the mask listened to the wearer through a microphone and microcontroller, while the expressions were drawn with LEDs embedded in the mask.

Others focused on the technical aspects of paper electronics and used the workshops as opportunities to learn electronics and add this powerful tool to their creative toolboxes for later applications. Some decided to explore the material affordances, such as the copper tape sculpture circuit (Figure 4.A). Others experimented with materials and effects, such as light diffusion (Figure 4.D).These projects demonstrate that experts and beginners alike—in making technology, art and craft—are all able to tinker with paper electronics and invent new techniques, mechanisms and approaches for making technology in creative ways.

Diversity in participation

The workshops engaged a diverse audience of participants, from college and graduate students to working adults. In fact, contrary to general trends in technical fields, the majority of people who attended were women. We recruited with posters that emphasized the materials and electronics covered using crafted example circuits and posted these on workshop websites and in university hallways. Our goal was to spread the idea of expressive electronics and inspire more diverse participation in terms of technical and expressive background, rather than particular demographics.

Interestingly, at the art and design school 8 out of 19 participants were female, though in general the school itself is 70% female and 30% male. While at the technical school 14 out of 17 participants were female while the general school is 54% male and 46% female. One explanation for this reversal is that the mixed approach of technical as well as expressive instruction allowed those who were trained technically to explore the expressive side of their medium, while those trained in arts and design were able to try out new tools to express their visions. At the same time, the materials of paper electronics were designed specifically to support as wide a range of approaches and thinking styles—from non-directed and experiential to problem-driven and analytical—so that everyone could learn and create in a style they were comfortable with.

Because these techniques incorporate paper craft, which is widely accessible and familiar, people were able to bring in their prior experiences, knowledge and skills in exploring electronics without being overwhelmed by completely new information. This made the material easier to grasp and thus conceptually accessible. Those who were technically advanced were given the freedom to explore their craft from a new perspective. Introducing electronics through craft helped participants enter a mindset of creative exploration.

Design implications

Looking at creating technology with these expressive materials also brought up many unanswered questions. One main question that persisted was how to gracefully use technology and interactivity to enhance the art and expression. Although electronics and craft were successfully integrated physically, many participants observed the dominance of technology over the rest of the project. Others worked only with the technology and did not attempt to make expressive statements, perhaps because doing so requires more than just knowing how to physically implement. In this case, building the circuit is the easy part; the real challenge comes in developing a concept. This can be read as a success of paper electronics—that expression is not hindered by the medium, but by the idea behind it.

WHY PAPER ELECTRONICS?

We curated these paper electronics materials and techniques for ease of use, accessibility and scalability. The goal was to make the medium successful as a tool for learning, making and expressing with circuits for both novice and expert circuit builders.

First, the materials are comfortable to work with. They are soft, flexible, light and can be easily manipulated by hand with only few special tools. A pair of scissors and a soldering iron are enough to construct most projects presented. By being very tangible and non-discrete—that is, people can cut and glue materials rather than relying on modular units—the materials give more creative freedom and intuitive control over the construction and its results.

Next, the paper materials are familiar, plentiful and relatively cheap, so users do not need to worry about breaking or wasting precious materials. This takes the pressure off of experimentation and making mistakes while encouraging iteration, which are vital to both learning and invention.

For making electrical connections, we chose to focus on metal foil tapes for their low resistance and solderability— so that users can create circuit that are as complex and technically advanced as with traditional means like breadboards and PCBs. Finally, they are friendly for handcraft-- requiring no additional wait to be ready as in the case of conductive paints or clays; adhering to a variety of surfaces; and by nature staying neatly in place but can be untaped and reworked. Allowing for easy undo and redo enables experimentation both while learning and during the creative process. The foil tape can be easily cut if a connection is incorrect, or untaped if placed in the wrong location. Even entire circuits can be peeled off of the page and taped down in new locations or cut and collaged. This is useful, for example, to make room for additional circuitry or to recycle pre-made circuits.

These techniques also allow for a range of permanence—from fast prototypes to final products. Since the circuitry can be quickly taped down on a piece of paper and reworked, it is great for prototyping. However, since components are soldered down, it is also more permanent than a circuit on a breadboard. Unlike traditional PCBs, modified paper-electronics circuits generally appear as clean and intentional as the original circuit. This is because the materials used to make the modifications are the same as those used to make the original circuit, while in a PCB, jumper wires are used to replace the traces printed on the board. This is important because it encourages users to make modifications, when necessary or beneficial, without worrying that it will ruin the aesthetics of their piece.

For the electronic components, we rely on surface-mount package components because their small size and flat base make them sit comfortably on flat but flexible paper substrates. In fact they are small enough to fit onto the pages of a normal sketchbook, with room for the book to close. Since these parts are off the shelf, users can take full advantage of the variety, accessibility and affordability of commercially available components. This helps scale the complexity of circuits, since novices and experts alike can use the techniques to create circuits relevant to them. The same component also may come in various-sized surface mount packages, allowing for different degrees of accessibility, bigger components for ease of use and smaller components for more control over aesthetic integration.

Next, paper circuits give full control over spatial and geometric organizations of traces and components—in other words, components and traces can be stuck anywhere. This also applies to layering, where non-connected traces can overlap and require only a simple piece of tape between them for insulation. For those learning electronics, it allows students to organize their circuit for visual and conceptual clarity. For example, components can be arranged by function—such as placing the ground trace at the bottom of the page and power trace at the top. They can also be spaced far apart to leave room for notes, or to make components and traces more accessible for modification and debugging.

As an expressive medium, this means that makers can design the circuit to visually and stylistically fit their creative visions. The circuit can be cut down to fit small or uniquely shaped spaces, or even taped over three-dimensional surfaces. Being able to easily layer traces gives the creator more freedom to build up their circuit in an improvisational way, without needing to fully plan out all the connections beforehand.

In paper electronics all of the circuitry lays flat against a surface, all the connections are out in the open and accessible for changing. This is unlike in traditional breadboards where the actual connections are hidden away inside the board and in PCBs where traces are often masked and components are rigidly stuck in place once soldered down. Such openness supports readability of the circuit, which is especially useful for learning and debugging. From a creative perspective, having the circuit in the open also means it is accessible for future modifications and additions, opening the space for creators to revisit and tinker with their ideas.

Placing circuitry on paper surfaces also means that marks can be made around the electronics. This allows for note taking right on and around circuit, which is extremely useful when learning how the circuitry works as well as for aesthetic decoration of the circuit. Having the circuitry on thin flexible paper is useful for documentation and archiving, since it takes up little room and can even be assembled into books.

Finally, the nature of the materials—mostly borrowed from traditional crafts—is expressive and creative. This created a bridge for audiences to use existing knowledge and skills to understand and learn new electronic concepts. It also helps peoples think of electronics as a powerful expressive tool, enabling new ways to look at circuit building and design.

After building circuits on sheets, we moved on to the bound book, specifically looking at sketchbooks for circuits.

POWERED SKETCHBOOKS

Building circuits on paper also comes with the affordances of documentation and archival—the individual electrified pages could all be bound into books. Would the circuit building experience be improved if circuits were made in books to begin with? Exploring this idea, the following are three approaches to creating a sketchbook for circuits. Every functioning circuit needs a power source, so we began by adding these to the bound book form.

Custom bound sketchbook and power clip

One option is to create a custom bound book that interfaces with a removable power clip (Figure 5).

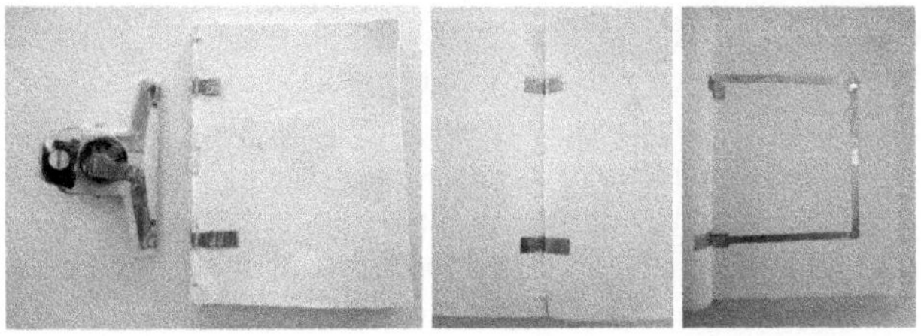

Figure 5. Custom bound book with battery clip, interior with power tabs, example circuit.

The sketchbook is composed of pages folded in half—called folios—stacked together and stab bound into a book. All folios have two conductive foil stripes taped across the spine in the same place, so that when stacked corresponding conductive foils touch. When bound together, these patches create a conductive track along the spine of the book and are accessible on alternating spreads inside the book.

The power clip is composed of a standard wide document clip, insulated to prevent short-circuiting to the clip's metal body. A coin cell battery is taped in place with two foil traces leading to the mouth of the clip. These leads are designed to match the conductive foil track on the spine of the sketchbook. When the power clip is attached to the book, every page is connected to the power supply. This allows users to power multiple pages simultaneously, or if desired, use switches for powering individual pages.

This approach was designed to allow a single removable power supply to power multiple circuit sketchbooks. A future revision may include a power clip that also functions as a cover, so that the pages within function like inserts in a binder.

Hacked rechargeable sketchbook

Yet another approach was to permanently embed a rechargeable power supply inside a standard sketchbook (Figure 6).

Here, we deconstructed an off-the-shelf USB phone charger and embedded the circuit with rechargeable battery into the back cover of a standard sketchbook. Our goal was to make the sketchbook look and feel as much as possible like a traditional book.

The USB connector and on/off switch are on the top and bottom spine extremes of the book, respectively, and LED indicators for power status and battery life are on the outside spine. An additional power indicator light is on the inside back cover, for use when the book is open.

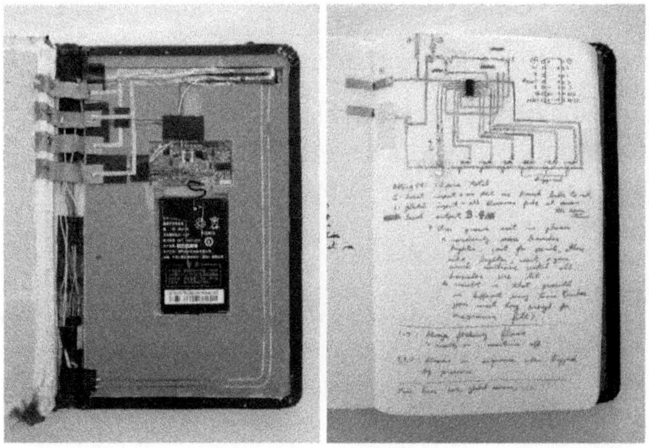

Figure 6. Rechargeable sketchbook with charging circuit in back cover and interior with power tabs and example circuit with notes.

To connect the power output of the circuit to the pages of the sketchbook, first we unbound the sketchbook and added two conductive foil tapes to both sides of every folio along the centerfold. We then sewed these folios back together into signatures with standard nonconductive thread. Next, we connected conductive fabric tapes to the positive and negative leads of the power output. Finally, we sewed the signatures to the conductive fabric tapes using a separate piece of conductive for each tape, to prevent shorting the power leads. The result inside the book is two conductive foil tabs—positive and negative leads to the power supply—in the center of each spread. All tabs are powered when the book is turned on.

Circuits page by page

The last and most accessible approach to creating a circuit sketchbook is simply building circuits sequentially on the pages of standard a book, using a movable power supply for each page. For this third model, we used the coin cell battery and binder clip to create a collection of circuits in an off-the-shelf mini-sketchbook (Figure 7).

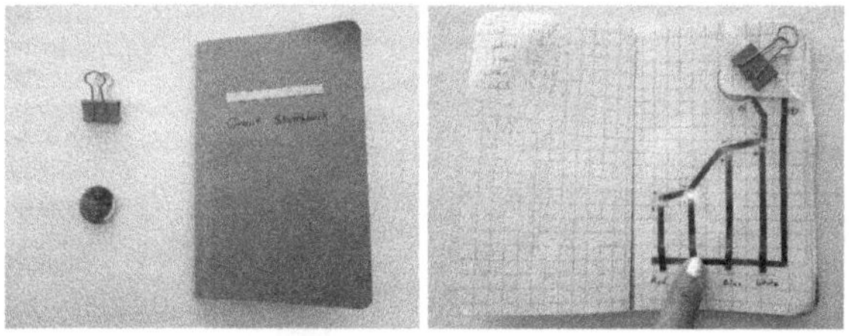

Figure 7. Standard sketchbook with coin cell and binder clip power supply. Example page.

In this setup, the battery can be stored with the notebook by simply clipping it in place with the binder clip. This method is most accessible since it only uses off the shelf parts but preserves the sequential, and archival qualities of building circuitry in a sketchbook format. Also, by using a normal sketchbook, there is less worry about preciousness—in the other circuit sketchbooks there was a sense that powered the pages shouldn't be wasted. Even though the tool was design for experimentation, its limited pages encouraged more careful making and they were used more for display and archival rather than sketching and testing.

As a first look into using sketchbooks for circuit building, we did preliminary workshops with standard sketchbooks and removable batteries to test how novice users responded.

Circuits in sketchbooks

To see what effects crafting in actual sketchbooks would have for users, we ran a two-day workshop on circuit building in sketchbooks for a group of high school art students and two educators, who already used sketchbooks in their everyday work.

In this workshop we had 19 total participants, 12 of whom were female, with an age range of 15 to 50 years old. 78% percent of participants reported having little to no experience in building electronics, but 90% reported a lot to expert levels of experience in making crafts.

On the first day of the workshop, we introduced five circuits along with paper electronics techniques like soldering and building paper switches. Students learned to turn on a single LED, multiple LEDs in parallel, create two types of paper switches and make a paper pressure sensor. We gave participants off-the-shelf sketchbooks and a coin cell battery with binder clip to power their books. Participants were instructed to create one circuit per page and to leave a blank page between circuits. The second day was open for creating a final project outside of their sketchbooks.

All participants successfully created the booklet of functioning circuit examples. Some wrote down notes on how the circuit worked, and others decorated around the circuits in their sketchbooks or illustrated the blank illuminated pages between circuit pages (Figure 8). During the final project-building phase, many participants flipped through the sketchbooks to look at the various circuit options and study how they were built. Some also used the sketchbook circuits to test lighting effects.

Figure 8. Sample participant circuit sketchbooks. Decorating around the circuit (left), illustrating a light (center), planning a circuit (right).

While some final projects were inspired by drawings and circuits previously made in their sketchbooks, and some groups sketched out circuits for their final projects in the books, no groups constructed any new circuits in their sketchbooks towards their final projects. Instead, most decided to build and prototype directly onto the final project materials.

Analysis

Our goal for the sketchbooks was to make them useful for circuit prototyping. However, our results seem to show participants prefer using these for documentation, archival and sharing.

While the participants did not use the sketchbooks as a place for prototyping circuits, they did flip through their examples many times in the process of brainstorming ideas and ways to implement their final projects. As such, the book of functional circuits worked as an encyclopedia—filled with inspiration—as well as a notebook, reminding participants how a particular circuit is constructed.

The sequential nature of the pages showed a learning process and strand of thoughts that went into producing the circuits. Participants often decorated their circuits with a particular theme or even narrative thread. The sketchbooks also provided a protective cover—the pages and the cover of the book itself—for circuits created, allowing students to toss them into their bags without worrying about damaging the circuit. Finally, the sketchbooks allowed many circuits to be compiled and organized into one portable object, making them handy as participants were able to carry their entire collection of circuits in a compact form.

Finally, because they were so portable and personalized, many participants enjoyed sharing and trading their circuit sketchbooks with each other to show off both the different circuits they created as well as the personalized illustrations that accompanied the light effects.

As we further develop the circuit sketchbook idea, beyond serving as a portable power supply, we hope to make the sketchbooks more supportive of the electronics design and prototyping process. We imagine embedding a programmable microcontroller in addition to the power supply to enable greater functionality and encourage users to use the sketchbook for prototyping software as well as hardware. Beyond adding physical features, our priority now is to do more extensive user studies with more diverse audiences, to see how experts might respond to such tools.

FUTURE RESEARCH

There are many avenues in which we would like to further explore paper electronics and the idea of circuit sketching. A few of these include accessibility and convenience, digitization and sharing, creativity and expression.

From an accessibility point of view, how can we make these techniques further simple enough to use so that students and engineers alike might decide to sketch circuits on paper, in addition to prototyping on breadboards and drawing PCBs?

As flat circuits, these can all be scanned to serve as visual schematics. How can we take advantage of this to be able to digitize these handmade circuits, so that they can be shared as digital files and read by CAD programs? Conversely, how can we create CAD programs to help generate templates and learning materials to be used for sharing and teaching electronics?

Finally, from the expressive perspective: now that these techniques enable more diverse communities of people to engage in creating interactive electronics, how do we support personal expression that integrates the technology and interaction without overly focusing on the electronics themselves? How do we inspire creators to think about not only how to make a circuit work, but why we want to build them in the first place?

CONCLUSION

In this paper we present a method for creating circuits on paper with off-the-shelf components and everyday household items in hopes it can provide an alternative to traditional methods of designing, prototyping and building electronics. We hope that these friendly but scalable techniques will lead to new explorations in circuit making as well as new types of artifacts, by being accessible to more diverse communities. We also present concepts for circuit sketchbooks, to enable users to further take advantage of the properties of paper for documentation, archival and convenience. We aim to continue this line of research, creating tools and resources to spread these techniques as well as share what others create as more creators adopt paper electronics as a method for making and expressing with technology.

REFERENCES

1. M. Back, et al. Listen reader: an electronically augmented paper-based book. in Proceedings of the SIGCHI Conference on Human Factors in Computing Systems 2001. Seattle, Washington, USA: ACM.
2. Bare Conductive. http://www.bareconductive.com.
3. L. Buechley, S. Hendrix, and M. Eisenberg. Paints, paper, and programs: first steps toward the computational sketchbook. In *TEI '09*, pages 9–12. ACM, 2009.
4. M. Coelho, L. Hall, J. Berzowska, and P. Maes. Pulp-based computing: a framework for building computers out of paper. In *CHI '09*, pages 3527-3528. ACM, 2009.
5. N. Freed, J. Qi, A. Setapen. Sticking together: handcrafting personalized communication interfaces. In *IDC '11*. ACM, 2011.
6. N. Freed, J. Qi, C. Sylla, and P. Branco. Beyond the binding: exploring the future book. In *Proc. C&C '11*, pages 445-446. ACM, 2011.
7. F. Guimbretière. Paper Augmented Digital Documents. In *Proc. UIST '03*, pages 51-60. ACM, 2003.
8. S. D. Guler, M. E. Rule. Invent-abling: Enabling Inventiveness through Craft. In *IDC '13,* pages 368-371.
9. Johnson, S. and Thomas, A. P. Squishy Circuits: a tangible medium for electronics education. In *Proc. CHI EA '10*, pages 4099-4104. ACM 2013.
10. Y. Kawahara, S. Hodges, B. S. Cook, C. Zhang, and G. D. Abowd. Instant inkjet circuits: lab-based inkjet printing to support rapid prototyping of UbiComp devices. In *Proc. UbiComp '13*, pages 363-372. ACM, 2013.
11. W. E. Mackay, G. Pthier, C. Letonda, K. Boegh. The Missing Link: Augmenting Biology Laboratory Notebooks. In *UIST '02,* pages 41-50. ACM 2002.
12. MakeyMakey http://makeymakey.com/.
13. D. A. Mellis, S. Jacoby, L. Buechley, H. Perner-Wilson, and J. Qi. Microcontrollers as material: crafting circuits with paper, conductive ink, electronic components, and an "untoolkit". In *Proc. TEI '13*, pages 83-90. ACM, 2013.
14. N. Peek. How to make flexible vinyl cut circuits. http://fab.cba.mit.edu/content/processes/PCB/vinylcut.html
15. H. Perner-Wilson. A kit-of-no-parts. Master's thesis, MIT, 2011.
16. H. Perner-Wilson. Light up postcard tutorial. http://highlowtech.org/?p=1149
17. J. Qi and L. Buechley. Electronic popables: exploring paper-based computing through an interactive pop-up book. In *TEI '10*, pages 121–128. ACM, 2010.
18. D. K. Rosner, H. Perner-Wilson, J. Qi, and L. Buechley. Fine bookbinding meets electronics. In *Proc. TEI '11*, pages 345-348. ACM, 2010.
19. A. Russo, B. Y. Ahn, J. J. Adams, E. B. Duoss,J. T. Bernhard, and J. A. Lewis. Pen-on-paper flexible electronics. *Advanced Materials*, pages 3426-3430. 2011.
20. G. Saul, C. Xu, and M. D. Gross. Interactive paper devices: end-user design and fabrication. In *TEI '10*, pages 205–212. ACM, 2010.
21. W. Węgrzyn. *Elektrobiblioteka.* 2012. http://www.info.elektrobiblioteka.net/.
22. Ugly Construction. http://www.qrp.pops.net/ugly.asp.

Do-It-Yourself Cellphones: An Investigation into the Possibilities and Limits of High-Tech DIY

David A. Mellis
MIT Media Lab
75 Amherst St., Cambridge, MA 02142, USA
mellis@media.mit.edu

Leah Buechley
MIT Media Lab
75 Amherst St., Cambridge, MA 02142, USA
leah@media.mit.edu

ABSTRACT
This paper describes our do-it-yourself cellphone and our use of it to investigate the possibilities and limits of high-tech DIY practice. We describe our autobiographical approach – making the phone and using it in our daily lives – and our work disseminating the cellphone in workshops and online. This informs a discussion of the implications of technology for DIY practice. We suggest an understanding of DIY as an individual's ability to combine existing technologies into a desired product, enabled and limited by ecosystems of industrial actors and individuals. We distinguish different pathways into high-tech DIY practice, consider the relationship between prototyping and production, and discuss the effect of technology on DIY's relevance and tools, and on notions of transparency. We conclude by reflecting on the relationship between DIY and empowerment: the extent to which making devices gives people control over the technology in their lives.

Author Keywords
Digital Fabrication; Electronics; DIY; Cellphone; Microcontrollers; Toolkits; Prototyping

ACM Classification Keywords
J.6 Computer-Aided Engineering

INTRODUCTION
Neil Gershenfeld, a leading visionary of the personal fabrication movement, tells us that it's now possible for an individual to "make almost anything" [6]. In many respects, this is true. Digital fabrication machines enable precise, one-off production of a diversity of forms in a variety of materials. Combined with the increasing power and accessibility of embedded computation, individuals can create complex electronic devices in small quantities or as one-off pieces. The design files for these objects can be shared online, enabling their reproduction and adaption to others' needs. Locations like FabLabs and maker spaces provide access to machines and like-minded individuals. Online services provide access to more sophisticated machines and processes. All of this is a huge change from the capital investments, big companies, and mass markets of traditional manufacturing.

CHI 2014, April 26 - May 01 2014, Toronto, ON, Canada

ACM 978-1-4503-2473-1/14/04..$15.00.
http://dx.doi.org/10.1145/2556288.2557309

Still, there's a big gap between having access to the technology and actually building devices for use in one's daily life. Our research seeks to investigate this gap, exploring both "the myth and the mess" of personal fabrication (to borrow a phrase from Dourish and Bell's book on ubiquitous computing [3]). We're interested in individual's use of digital fabrication and embedded computation to make electronic devices, a practice we refer to as *high-tech DIY*. For example, how does this practice relate to and differ from other forms of DIY? What determines the extent to which people are able to make sophisticated devices for use in their daily lives? How can we introduce people to these practices and to what difficulties and limitations will they encounter? What tools or technologies would allow them to go further? To what extent and in what ways does making a DIY device empower people in their lives and in their relationships with technology?

This paper explores these questions through our experience in using digital fabrication to produce what is perhaps the quintessential device of our day: the cellphone. This is a deliberate attempt to push the limits of DIY practice in order to better understand its possibilities and limitations. The requirements and constraints of mobile phones – in terms of functionality, size, battery life, usability, and more – make them a particularly enlightening case study. A cellphone is something that most of us carry with us every day, rely on for many purposes, and have a complex relationship with. And yet, cellphones (at least in a Western context) lack the rich DIY heritage of, say, early radios or personal computers. As such, it seems important to ask what will happen when we try to make cellphones for ourselves. To what extent can we even build a phone that will function well enough for us to use it in our daily life? What parts of the design space will we and others be able to explore – and what will prevent us from going further? How much will people be able to understand of a device that's composed of sophisticated and often opaque components and designed using complex tools?

We've taken multiple approaches to this investigation. The first is an autobiographical method, in which the first author designed, made, and used multiple iterations of a DIY cellphone. This process, including more than nine months in which these phones have served as the author's primary phone, has addressed two main research themes: (1) approaches to and constraints on developing a complex DIY device and (2) the experience of using a DIY device in daily life. Second, the author conducted two workshops in which others made the phones: one focused on designers, the other including members of the general public. These workshops explored the extent to which participants were able to meaningfully engage with the process of building a device for themselves and the value they were able to derive from it. Finally, the cellphone has attracted interest from others, both friends of the authors and strangers who saw the project online. We draw on their experiences to discuss some lessons for the dissemination of DIY devices.

These activities have yielded insights about technology, design, and people, revealing both opportunities and challenges. They show how new technology requires more nuanced notions of DIY – notions that acknowledge the complex networks of actors and layers of technology that go into making a modern device. In such ecosystems, DIY is about the ability to put together available parts and processes into a desired product – rather than the knowledge of how to make everything for oneself. High-tech devices can provide new relevance and motivation for DIY practice but only if DIY tools and toolkits can keep pace with technological development. Further, the complexity of these devices reveals DIY as a deep and multi-faceted process, only some parts of which may be possible to explore in a given activity or with a particular audience. Digital fabrication and embedded computation turn DIY into an ever more digital activity, increasing the importance of software and interfaces as an enabling and limiting factor in DIY practice. The ease-of-use and functionality of a CAD tool, for example, may impose more constraints than the fabrication process itself. Access to source code for communicating with an electronic component may be as important as access to the component itself. In short, the cellphone starts to reveal the ways in which technology transforms DIY practice.

In the next section, we discuss related work; then, we present a short overview of the DIY cellphone. This is followed by a discussion of our personal experience making and using the phone. Then we describe the two workshops and other dissemination. These experiences inform the discussion, which explores in-depth the implications of new technology for DIY practice. Finally, we conclude with a more general discussion about the relationship between technology, DIY, and empowerment.

RELATED WORK

Here, we discuss related work on electronics prototyping platforms, digital fabrication, and DIY.

DIY electronics and prototyping platforms.

Electronics prototyping and toolkits have a long history, both within and outside of the HCI community. Mitchel Resnick and collaborators have developed a series of projects to introduce programming and engineering to children ([21], [22]). These research projects helped to inspire the Lego Mindstorms products and PicoCrickets. Other toolkits have focused more specifically on designers, like Phidgets [8]. Popular commercial products include Basic Stamp, Arduino, and the Raspberry Pi. Some platforms, like d.tools [9], combine electronics modules with tools to help in the creation of onscreen interfaces. More recently, some projects – like .NET Gadgeteer [28] – have started to look at the combination of an electronics toolkit with digital fabrication. Other researchers have taken a more general look at the role of prototyping in the design process [14]. In this work, we're interested in going beyond prototypes to looking at ways to help people assemble finished devices for use in their daily lives. In this way, we're inspired by tools like Fritzing [11], that help people translate electronic prototypes into fabricated circuit boards.

Figure 1. The DIY cellphone.

Digital fabrication and human-computer interaction.

In recent years, a variety of research projects have looked at the intersection of digital fabrication and human-computer interaction, a topic summarized in a workshop at last year's CHI [16]. Some have focused on creating new interfaces for computer-aided design or fabrication. These include a number of systems for real-time, interactive control of fabrication machines ([4], [19]). Others provide tangible or software interfaces for computer modeling for fabrication ([5], [10], [24]). Other projects look at ways to use digital fabrication to create interfaces that integrate with various forms of sensing or actuation ([25], [29]). Still others have created new fabrication machines with interactive capabilities ([29], [30]). We're interested in combining digital fabrication with electronics to create final products, an approach similar to that explored in our previous work ([17], [18]).

DIY and Technology Practice

Another strand of HCI research has looked at the effect of technology on DIY and craft practices, both traditional and technological ([2]). For example, [13] surveyed contributors to online DIY communities, while [27] examines maker culture more broadly. Other work has focused specifically on repair as a form of DIY and creativity ([15]). Other researchers have looked at technology and DIY practice within specific domains, such as craft [1], environmental sensing [12], furniture hacking [23], or knitting and gardening [7].

Figure 2. The circuit board (top and bottom).

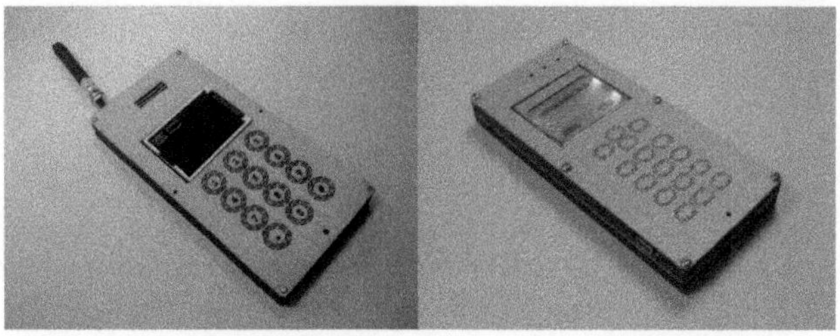

Figure 3. First generation prototype and second generation w/ LCD.

THE DIY CELLPHONE

The DIY cellphone is an attempt to satisfy two somewhat contradictory objectives: it should be as easy as possible to individually assemble by hand; and it should be functional enough to serve as one's primary phone. The phone's electronics and enclosure have been iteratively designed to satisfy these objectives. For the electronics, this requires balancing the overall size and functionality of the device against the difficulty of soldering the components. For the enclosure, the challenge has been to create a robust, attractive form that can be produced using digital fabrication, minimizing the time, cost, and number of processes required.

In its current form, the DIY cellphone makes and receives phone calls and text messages, stores up to 250 phone numbers and names, shows the time, and serves as an alarm clock. It connects to GSM networks (like AT&T and T-Mobile in the United States) and includes a socket for a standard, full-size SIM card. The phone is powered by a 3.7 volt, 1000 milli-amp hour rechargeable lithium polymer (LiPo) battery and rechargeable via a mini-USB port. In total, there are a little over 60 individual components on the board, including 16 buttons, a microphone and speaker, a magnetic buzzer for generating ring tones and the alarm, and either a black and white LCD display (84x48 pixels) or an 8-character LED matrix (where each character is a 5x7 grid of LEDs). The phone uses the same GSM module (the Quectel M10) and antenna as those found on the Arduino GSM Shield; these components handle the major functionality of connecting to the cellular network and processing audio input and output. The phone's firmware is a ~1000 line Arduino program running on an ATmega1284P micrcontroller; it controls the user interface and communicates with the GSM modules, using the Arduino GSM library, custom extensions to it, and other Arduino libraries. All the components can be individually ordered from three suppliers (Digi-Key, SparkFun, or the Arduino store). The total cost of the components (in the quantities required to make a single phone) is around $105 for the LCD version, $135 for the LED matrix version. The cost of the circuit board varies from around $10 to $60 each, depending on the desired quantity and turn-around time.

A variety of enclosures have been designed for the phone, both by the author and others. The standard one consists of two halves sandwiching the PCB, which is visible from the side. Each half is made from laser-cut 0.25" plywood covered with laser-cut veneer. The halves are held together with small bolts.

The phone is open-source, with design files for both the electronic circuit and enclosure available online,[1] along with the source code for the Arduino-based firmware and libraries.[2] The circuit was designed in Eagle, the enclosure in Inkscape.

DESIGN FOR PERSONAL MANUFACTURING AND USE

Through the process of designing, making, and using DIY cellphones, we hoped to derive more general lessons about the possibilities and limits of do-it-yourself technology. In this, we were inspired by autobiographical approaches (e.g. [20]). In particular we were interested in the opportunities and constraints of available technology and in the experience and meaning of using devices that we'd designed ourselves.

I went through a number of iterations in making the DIY cellphone. (Note: in this section, "I" refers to the first author.) These started with a breadboard prototype, then a first-generation proof-of-concept (which could make and receive calls but not much else), then multiple iterations of the second generation (described in the previous section). These second generation prototypes have served as my main phone for the past nine months. To facilitate learning from the process, I kept a rough diary of my experiences with the phone, both making and use. Reviewing these notes and reflecting on my experiences yields some practical insights.

Component Availability Enables and Limits DIY

Picking the right electronic components was the core of the technical design work and highlights some of the main opportunities and challenges of making DIY devices. (Laying out the circuit boards, assembling the prototypes, and writing the software took time, but was fairly deterministic.) On the one hand, it is only the availability of increasingly sophisticated components that made it possible for me to build a phone at all. On the other hand, my choice of components was surprisingly limited, given that I want to hand-solder the boards, limit the overall size, cost, and complexity of the resulting circuit, and only use components that other people will be able to get.

The GSM module was perhaps the most complicated component. There are not many modules available for individual purchase (at least in the U.S., where the authors are based), and those that are often have a connector that it is difficult or impossible to solder by hand. Luckily, the module on the Arduino GSM shield (the Quectel M10) is easier to solder and I was able to work with Arduino both to receive samples and to

[1] `https://github.com/damellis/cellphone2hw`

[2] `https://github.com/damellis/cellphone2`

make the module publicly available for individual purchase. The only other source I've found for the module is the Chinese e-commerce site AliExpress. This module may not be a long-term solution, however, as the GSM networks it relies on are slowly being phased out, at least by AT&T and T-Mobile in the U.S. It's not clear if a suitable replacement exists for use with newer 3G or LTE networks, without which it may be impossible to create a DIY cellphone.

The display and speakers were two other components with limited options. While there are many displays available to hobbyists, the LCD I used initially seemed to break after about a month of use. Other LCDs seemed even less robust, leading me to switch to an LED matrix, for which I could find only a single satisfactory option. Similarly, given my constraints on size, electrical resistance, and solder-ability, I could only locate a single viable speaker.

These examples (the GSM module, display, and speaker) highlight the extent to component availability constrains high-tech DIY. Despite the large number of electronic parts available to hobbyists, there may be few options satisfying specific functional requirements. On the other hand, only the sophistication of these parts enables the creation of high-tech DIY devices.

Open Ecosystems Enable Bricolage

The process of designing and building the various versions of the phone hasn't necessarily required specific deep technical expertise. Instead, it's been more of a process of bricolage: assembling the device from existing resources and information. For example, the antenna design was borrowed from the Arduino GSM shield (by literally copying the original Eagle file) but didn't require me to learn anything about radio frequency (RF) circuit design. Surprisingly for me, every version of the phone has connected to the cellular network and seemed to get reasonable reception, despite a lack of any specific RF testing or expertise on my part.

Other parts of the circuit's design have been borrowed from various other sources. The GSM module's datasheet described the requirements for its connection to the SIM socket, microphone, and speaker. The LiPo charging chip was selected because it's the one that SparkFun uses on their boards (and has performed reasonably in practice). Its datasheet suggests the PCB footprint I've adopted to enable adequate heat dissipation.

It's not just the hardware that draws on existing resources. The phone's software uses a variety of open-source libraries, enabled by its use of an Arduino-compatible microcontroller. For example, in various prototypes I've tried out a total of four different displays and was able to find an existing library (or more than one) for each. In many cases, I needed to understand or modify the source code to the libraries I used, though, which wouldn't have been possible with proprietary code.

Both the hardware and software, then, have been pieced together from various sources. This can be a slow and difficult process, of course, but it doesn't require the expertise or low-level knowledge that would be needed to design the phone from scratch. It does rely, however, on access to a variety of information and open-source designs, both hardware and software.

The Joys and Frustrations of Using a DIY Phone

In retrospect, the version of the phone that I first start using was very rough. It had sharp corners, large bolts extending out the back, a hole in the back for a programming header, and many missing features in the software. While it had a phone book, it wouldn't show people's names when they called. There was no way to generate the DTMF tones needed to interact with automated menus and, consequently, no way to enter the password to check my voicemail. There was no way to change the volume or check the battery life.

In large part, my willingness to tolerate all these shortcomings was the result of the excitement I felt at being able to start using the phone in my daily life. The initial prototype of the second generation phone went into my pocket immediately after I screwed it together, a process that was repeated with every subsequent iteration. Typically, I'd intend these as prototypes to be refined before I started using them – but, inevitably, as soon as they were finished, they became my primary phone. This was true even in one case when I had finished the circuit board but not the case, so I carried the bare PCB for a couple of days before finishing the enclosure.

This excitement was sometimes shared by others seeing me use the phone. Even people that knew I was working on DIY cellphones were often surprised to see me actually pull one out of my pocket. They would express astonishment that was this was the phone I had been previously talking to or texting them with. I was actually conscious to keep the phone in my pocket most of the time to avoid conversations with strangers about it, but was pleasantly surprised by the attention it received from the waiters in a variety of restaurants. Friends who had seen the phone would often encourage me to show it to others.

At other times, the phone led to friendly teasing from friends, for example, about the fact that I couldn't use it to look up something on the web. One friend joked "what, do I have to call you now?" when I went a weekend without receiving an email he had sent me, and knowing that the phone doesn't sound an alert when I get a text message. On another occasion, my aunt called to wish me a happy birthday, and the call dropped a couple of times. She gave me a hard time about it, although it wasn't clear if the problem was my phone, the connectivity in the spot I was standing, or on her end. Friends would chide me for reading about new iPhones, as if I were cheating on my phone.

Any problems with the phone were a source of intense stress. The frustration with a non-working device seemed increased because I knew that I had no one else blame: I designed it, built it, and was the one using it. For example, the LCD on early iterations of the phone would became unreliable, I would compulsively check to see if it would turn on, and developed elaborate tricks involving pressing on various spots of the display as I turned it on. Once, my phone was continuously crashing, even when I removed and reinserted the battery; I was pre-occupied until I could get to my computer and figure out the cause (an overly-long text message).

In short, the current state (working or not) of the latest prototype could become a proxy for my feelings towards the whole endeavor: excitement and satisfaction when everything worked, stress and frustration when anything was wrong. I have to remind myself that certain problems (like not having a friend's number in my phone book or forgetting my charger) have nothing to do with the DIY cellphone per se but could happen with any device. Now that the device is relatively stable, it's become less of an emotional experience – but the process of getting it to that point has been intense and personal.

DISSEMINATION

In order to help other build the DIY cellphone, we've conducted two workshops, helped friends to make the device, and published detailed instructions on our website.

Workshop 1: Designers

As an initial effort to understand how others might respond to the process of making or modifying the cellphone, we invited colleagues and friends with experience in design and technology to attend a workshop. Nine people participated, three female and six male. Their ages ranges from 21 to 36; six were white, two black, and one Asian. On a pre-workshop survey, many of the participants self-reported an expertise in design but only some experience with electronics and programming. Participants had some experience with soldering, less with microcontroller programming, and even less with circuit board design. All reported regular smartphone use and liking their phones.

The workshop started with an opening discussion. Then participants brainstormed and sketched a concept for a phone that would be ideal for either themselves or someone they knew. Most of the rest of the first day was spent soldering the phones together. In theory, the second day was meant to be used for modifying the circuit or designing and making an enclosure. In practice, we had to finish programming and debugging that day. Some people had other obligations as well, and could only attend for part of the time. Still, everyone was able to successfully assemble the electronics and program the firmware. After completing the assembly and debugging, some participants used their cellphone circuit boards (without enclosures) to call friends or experimented with calling each other from various locations in the building. The workshop ended with a closing discussion, including thoughts from participants on the directions they would take the DIY cellphones if they continued to work on them.

Two participants did create custom enclosures for the phone, although both did so in advance of the workshop itself. One enclosure was modeled in SolidWorks and 3d-printed on a MakerBot Replicator. It consisted of seven parts (top, bottom, keypad, and plugs to cover the screws) and required about five hours in total to print, including two iterations of the bottom and keypad. The other enclosure had a bottom half of wood, which was also modeled in SolidWorks and CNC milled on the ShopBot. The fabrication took about five hours (including two iterations), after approximately the same amount of time for modeling. The top half of the enclosure was created by placing silkworms on top of the circuit board and allowing them to spin a silk covering, a process which was only somewhat successful.

Figure 4. Variants created by workshop partipants.

Figure 5. Workshop participants assembling their phones.

Workshop 2: With the Public

For this workshop, we wanted to work with a more general audience to see how they would respond to the process of making a cellphone for themselves. We recruited using fliers in local coffee-shops and other locations. Five participants found out about the workshop in this way, six others joined through word-of-mouth from the authors. Participants were charged a $150 materials fee. Three of the participants were female, eight male. Their ages ranged from 24 to 45. Professions varied, although many participants had experience in an area involving engineering or technology but not specifically electronics, like mechanical engineering, computer science, or graphic design. Participants reported less extensive use of cellphones and expressed less positive feelings towards them than the participants in the previous workshop.

This workshop was two days long (1 to 6 pm on a Saturday and Sunday) and deliberately focused on assembling the DIY cellphone in its existing form. The only customization was selecting a graphic to be laser-etched into the veneer on the back of the phone. After an opening discussion, each participant received a PCB and the necessary electronic components, and most of the first day was spent soldering the boards together. The second day consisted of programming the boards and, mostly, debugging various problems. These issues took a variety of forms, including one unexpected problem: the buzzers of nine of the eleven phones failed to ring when an incoming call was received. This was eventually identified (after the workshop) as a result of a difference

Figure 6. Phones made by friends.

in the firmware between two batches of GSM modules. Many participants (six of the eleven) returned after the workshop to continue to troubleshoot or to implement a workaround to get their buzzers to work. Some returned multiple times to continue to debug and would coordinate their visits to work on their phones together. Eventually, all but one participant was able to complete a functional phone.

While many participants reported a desire to use their DIY cellphones in their daily lives, a variety of practical obstacles have interfered. At least two participants are still lacking a SIM card from a GSM carrier. Another reported that the phone doesn't get good reception in their apartment. Two mentioned that the lack of a silent mode would be an obstacle to adoption.

Other Dissemination

In addition to the workshops, we've begun to disseminate the DIY cellphone in other ways. We've documented the phone online so that others can make it and worked with friends to build their own. This has yielded additional insights about the possibilities for and obstacles to getting the phone out into the world.

Some people have built their own phones with little or no help from us beyond the information posted on our website. Others have asked questions over email and then made the phone on their own. We find these examples meaningful as an indication that the components and processes required to create the phone are, at least for some, independently accessible. This suggests that there is in fact value in designing and sharing the hardware and software for these DIY devices.

In other cases, people have encountered various obstacles to making the phone, pointing out some of the limitations of this sort of distributed production. Some have reported difficulty getting some of the necessary parts in Europe, including the small (M0) screws used to hold the enclosure together. (In response, the design has since been updated to allow for the use of slightly larger M2 screws as well.) Others reported high costs to order a single PCB, or were uncertain about how to do so. (In response, we've improved the directions on our site for ordering a circuit board from an online manufacturer.) These examples highlight the importance of having others (in different places with different resources) try to replicate a device as part of the process of refining its design.

I've also worked with friends to make their own DIY cellphones. This has included several custom enclosures, including one CNC-milled from solid, purple-heart wood, another hand-cut from cardboard, and a third assembled from multiple 3d-printed pieces. Two friends have used the phones in their daily lives, at least temporarily. One seemed undaunted by usability issues, commenting, for example, that the lack of labels on the buttons isn't a problem. Another made requests for new features, like battery-life and signal strength indicators that were later implemented. Both have encountered practical obstacles that have prevented more in-depth use: one doesn't get good reception at home, the other hasn't found the time to make a necessary repair. With friends, as with participants in the workshop, organizing a dedicated time to get together and work on the phone has helped them fit the activity into their lives.

DISCUSSION

Reflecting on the experiences and comments of the people involved in these dissemination activities, we discuss some of the broader implications of the DIY cellphone.

High-Tech DIY Exists in an Ecosystem

With modern industrial supply chains, companies depend on complex systems of third-party parts and knowledge to produce devices. Our experience with the cellphone shows that similar ecosystems exist in DIY practice. The phone builds on components, materials, and processes that are produced at an industrial scale and embody deep, domain-specific expertise. Intermediate actors (like Arduino, SparkFun, or BatchPCB) make these high-tech parts and processes available to individuals. The DIY cellphone, in turn, draws on – and is limited by – the elements that these actors make available. This ecosystem suggests a nuanced notion of DIY, one that consists of the ability of individuals to create devices from the parts, resources, and processes available – rather than their ability to do everything themselves, from scratch.

Participants in the workshops seemed to share this perspective, commenting on their new-found understanding of the way in which devices are assembled from existing parts:

"When I'm choosing a phone, I'm choosing the phone based on what I see, how it looks, I never thought about where the speaker might be, what's the speaker like underneath it, a speaker to me is this set of holes, but then there's this speaker component inside that. I don't know what it looks like in my phone but I know what it looks like in this other phone [the DIY cellphone]. All the different elements, I know what they look like and what they are." (Workshop 1, Participant 1)

"It's cool that you can treat this all as a black box. You can pull out components and you can make a phone that works with stuff you can buy at home, off-the-shelf. You don't have to know how the part works to know the part is working. You don't have to know how the GSM works but how to connect it." (W2-P3)

This perspective (of DIY within an ecosystem) highlights the extent to which DIY practice depends on the decisions of actors, like industrial manufacturers or hobbyist services, that may or may not have an interest in supporting it. For example, while we were able to find the components necessary to build a functional phone, we had few choices available. Furthermore, we're not able to access many of the technologies in modern smartphones – and probably couldn't work with them even if we could get them. The decisions of industrial and commercial actors has significant potential to change the possibilities for DIY practice. The availability of new hand-solderable components could dramatically expand the possibilities for DIY devices, as could easier access to automated assembly processes. Conversely, the discontinuation of essential components or changes to required infrastructure (like the cellular network) could prevent continued making or use of DIY devices.

Consequently, effecting changes in these supply chains can expand the possibilities for DIY practice as much as the creation of new tools or toolkits or the production of new educational resources. Our experiences with the phone suggests some ways that individuals can effect changes in these ecosystems. By working with Arduino to make the GSM module available, for example, we greatly expanded the number of people that could build the phone. By making the phone's hardware and software available online as open-source, we enabled others to build a phone without designing it themselves. Similarly, we were enabled by the decisions of others to open-source libraries for talking to various electronic components. These examples show that while industrial and commercial entities may shape much of the ecosystem surrounding high-tech DIY, it's still possible for individuals to make meaningful changes in the technologies available for DIY practice.

DIY Technology Supports Multiple Forms of Engagement

A single device, especially one as complex as a cellphone, provides for many different kinds and levels of engagement with DIY practice. For example, some workshop participants were most interested in building a device they could use in their daily life; others wanted to understand how a modern device works. Some wanted to experiment with new interaction design possibilities, like alternative form factors and interfaces, or simply ways to re-engage people with actually talking on the phone. Others were seeking an alternative to buying a phone from a big company. In these different perspectives, we see some of the diversity of activities and interests that can fit within an undertaking like making DIY cellphones.

Our efforts at dissemination have shown some different aspects of the process that people have or haven't engaged with. Specifically, while people have explored different possibilities for the DIY cellphone's enclosure, including a variety of materials and fabrication processes, almost none have modified the circuit itself. In part, this seems to reflect people's previous skills, which have tended to be stronger in design than electronics. Still, many of the workshop participants and others who have made the phone have significant experience with electronics prototyping. Other factors discouraging the experimentation with the electronics may be the seemingly complete nature of the existing cellphone design, the lack of available expansion points on the circuit, the time required to design and fabricate a new circuit board, or simply the greater appeal of creating an enclosure, with its opportunity for aesthetic exploration and personalization.

This emphasizes the importance of being deliberate about the intended audience or outcomes of a DIY process. Even within a specific set of tools and products – like assembling electronic components into a cellphone – there are opportunities for many different workshop structures and emphases. For example, in holding another workshop for designers, we would emphasize the exploration of different form factors and interfaces, a prototyping process that suggests a very different structure from a workshop targeted at individuals interested in producing a device for daily use. (We discuss this tension more in the following section.) Both of these would be very different from a workshop aimed at teaching people about electronics or cellular communication technology.

Across all of these different entry points, it's important to consider social factors. Hosting workshops provides an opportunity for people to come together, learn from the instructor and each other, observe each other's work, etc. Some workshop participants attended with people they knew, suggesting that perhaps they wouldn't have come without the social connection. Our friends, too, seemed to prefer to make the phone together with others, making it a social occasion as well as a DIY activity – a connection seem in some, but not all, forms of non-technical DIY [7].

In addition to different types of engagement, the complexity of the cellphone as a device highlights the importance of providing for different levels and durations of involvement. Assembling the device can provide motivation for further exploration. In the words of participants:

"I think the workshop's definitely long enough to assemble the stuff that you've designed, but I think then, once you've done that, it takes time for that to sink into people's brains and then be able to think about not just how they would want to customize it but the ways in which they would be able to. Cause at the beginning of yesterday morning, you can have ideas about the kind of phone that you want, but now I have a better idea of how that might be manifested: what things might be easier to include or not include." (W1-P2)

"I think that definitely I don't want to stop at the cellphone, now I want to make more things. This has definitely motivated me to try making other stuff and not just stop here." (W2-P5)

These quotes highlight the importance of not just finding ways to engage people initially but also helping them to progress to more in-depth and meaningful forms of high-tech DIY practice.

Bridging the Gap Between Prototyping and Production

The cellphone's constraints on form and function highlight some of the tensions between prototyping (rapid exploration of the design space) and production (robust, reproducible devices). In optimizing the circuit, we've limited its flexibility as a prototyping platform. The use of a single, unified circuit board soldered directly to off-the-shelf electronic components helps to contain the phone's size and increase its robustness, but a modular toolkit would allow for more variation in form-factor and interface. The latter was much requested by the designers in the first workshop. On the other hand, prototyping tools may not always be appropriate for production use; as a participant in the first workshop pointed out, an Arduino board plus the Arduino GSM shield is even larger and less flexible than the DIY cellphone's PCB.

Our experience with the phone suggests some approaches that could enable an easier transition between prototype electronics and production devices. The regular pin spacing of the LED matrix, for example, enabled it to be tested in a breadboard and then soldered directly into the final PCB. Regular pin spacing on other components would make it easier for them to function in both prototypes and final products. Another option is illustrated by the Quectel module on the Arduino GSM shield. The existence of the shield enables prototyping, but the module itself can be hand-soldered, allowing the same component (and associated software) to be used in both prototype and product. Furthermore, the module itself a high-level encapsulation of functionality like that found in many toolkits, but it's in a form that's robust and optimized enough to permit its use in production devices.

Open-source also facilitates the transition between prototype and production. Open-sourcing a toolkit's hardware allows the design of a prototyping module to serve as the basis for part of a production circuit (as with the cellphone's borrowing of the antenna design from the GSM shield). Better hobbyist software for routing circuit boards could facilitate mashups of existing open designs or adapting of circuits to new components or designs. Open-source software also helps, allowing for the adaptation of prototyping libraries or examples to production use, as, for example, in our changes to the LED matrix library and additions to the GSM library. If we had used proprietary libraries for prototyping and encountered similar bugs or missing features, we would have to had to re-implement the libraries for production use. Furthermore, it might not be feasible to purchase proprietary software for each production device, even if the cost were acceptable as part of the prototyping process.

Digital fabrication helps close the gap between prototyping and production, by minimizing the time and effort required to go from a reproducible digital design to a physical object that can be experimented with. With direct access to fabrication machines, it may be possible to try multiple iterations of a design in a day – and then immediately put those prototypes into use. Of course, different processes have different speeds but, in general, digital fabrication allows for faster iteration than production processes which are completely separate from the relevant prototyping techniques.

The experience of the few people who have used the DIY cellphone in their daily lives suggests some interesting lessons for the requirements of a production DIY device. In general, these people (including the first author) seemed willing to accept tradeoffs in functionality (e.g. versus a smartphone) and ease-of-use (like the the lack of labels on the buttons) but not in robustness or reliability. For example, the limited lifespan of the initial LCD was problematic but the limited resolution of the LED matrix, while limiting, is acceptable. Similarly, while the failure to store text messages after they're read reduces ease-of-use, it's less of a problem than the failure to get reception in someone's home (a reliability issue).

Modern Technology Gives Relevance to DIY Practice

Talking with the participants in the workshops made it clear that building cellphones appeals to people and motivations not present for simpler devices or more general-purpose toolkits. As one person put it in an email after building the cellphone independently:

"I have had an Arduino Uno board for months, and I've fiddled around with it a little. However, until this cellphone project, I have not felt inspired to really dig in and test the limits of this platform. Now, I am completely captivated... I anticipate a long and very enjoyable journey down the perverbial rabbit hole."

The relevance was also reflected in the excitement of workshop participants at successfully completing their phones, an excitement far beyond what we've encountered in previous workshops on other DIY devices (e.g. radios or speakers). This makes sense when we consider how ubiquitous cellphones are in our daily lives and how little understanding most people (at least in our Western society) have of how they work or what they're made of. As one participant said:

"I like that you grabbed our attention and forced us to slow down and say this is how you build a thing you use every single day. It's just, I guess you know the DIY movement is saying don't take everything for granted, see how it actually works." (W2-P3)

For a DIY experience to affect someone in this way, it seems important for it to engage with the things that people encounter in their daily lives. In the realm of technology, the rapid change in consumer devices means that the devices people want to make are likely to change rapidly as well. The DIY cellphone, for example, may be more advanced than a DIY radio but it's a lot simpler than today's smartphones. For those of us interested in supporting or researching DIY practice, new technology is thus both an opportunity and a challenge. If we can create tools and experiences for creating modern devices, we can provide DIY with increased appeal and value – but, unless we keep up, DIY will offer fewer and fewer possibilities for the devices that people use in their daily lives.

If we can help DIY practice keep pace with technological development, however, our experience suggests that it will continue to have meaningful parts of the design space to explore – spaces left largely unexploited by industry but still of interest to designers and members of the general public. In the cellphone industry in the developed world, the tremendous efforts of many huge companies has been largely focused on a narrow segment of devices: powerful, general-purpose smartphones. Going into the workshop, we expected that participants would be interested in pushing the DIY cellphone in that direction. Instead, multiple participants in both workshops expressed interest in simpler, special purpose devices, whether for use in their own lives, for someone else they knew, or as a design exploration. In addition, the enclosures we and others have designed for the phone showcase very different materials and aesthetics from those found in most commercial devices – whether wood, cardboard, or even silk. This suggests that regardless of the resources an industry invests, there are factors that may make certain kinds of functionality or aesthetics better suited for DIY production.

High-Tech DIY Practice Relies on Software

Just as the products of DIY practice need to keep up with modern technology to stay relevant, the tools for DIY practice need to keep up in order to make modern technology accessible. The cellphone workshops shows that even when a technology is accessible, the tools for working with it may not be. A circuit board, for example, can be ordered by anyone with an internet connection and a credit card – but the tools for modifying them were not suited to the skills of the workshop participants or the level of abstraction at which they were interested in working. In many kinds of physical making, there is a long heritage of tools that have evolved to support the construction of specific types of functionality or aesthetics. As DIY moves into high-tech realms like CAD and embedded software, it becomes an increasingly digital practice. This requires increasing attention to the nature of these digital tools and their adaptation to the various domains and audiences of DIY. There is an opportunity for HCI research and practice to develop new software tools and interfaces that increase the accessibility of design tools for sophisticated circuits and digitally-fabricated forms.

Technology Requires New Conceptions of Transparency

The workshop participants' understanding of the cellphone demonstrates the changing nature of transparency as it relates to modern electronics. By opening up a cellphone and allowing participants to assemble one for themselves, the workshops gave them an understanding of its overall composition and components. This traditional approach to transparency, however, breaks down when it comes to the microcontroller and GSM module, both of which are complex assemblages that can't be deconstructed physically. Instead, transparency of these components depends on access to information, like datasheets and source code. This suggests that notions of openness and transparency from the software world will be increasingly relevant for DIY devices. It also means that transparency is increasingly dependent on decisions made by manufacturers that may not be interested in or supportive of DIY practice.

CONCLUSION: TECHNOLOGY, DIY, EMPOWERMENT

After all this, some fundamental questions remain: So what? Does this actually give anyone control over the technology in their lives? Even if someone invests the time to design and build their own device, aren't they still dependent on technology from big companies? Is there any chance for DIY to replace mass production in even a small fraction of high-tech devices?

At the core of these questions is the relationship between DIY and empowerment, as applied to technology – specifically, the extent to which making something for oneself (DIY) gives someone the ability and confidence to control the technology in their life (empowerment). This relates to broader conversations about the rhetoric and reality of DIY and maker activities (e.g. [26]). There are clearly limits: even of the small group that have assembled a phone, few have used it in their daily life. For those few, this is just one of many devices they interact with. For all the workshop participants, having assembled a phone doesn't mean that they have the knowledge or motivation to design one themselves. Even if they did, the functionality of the cellphone is, to a large extent, limited by the decisions of entities that individuals have little control over. All in all, despite our extensive efforts, we've made little obvious impact on people's use of technology.

Still, building the cellphone has helped people make steps towards taking control over the technology in their lives in at least three important ways:

1. *Having a Choice to Produce Technology.* Through the workshops and other dissemination, we've shown people that it is possible to make a cellphone for oneself instead of buying one. Even if someone doesn't end up doing so, there's power in just knowing that such a thing is possible. Here, we see parallels to craft and DIY in other domains, like knitting or woodworking, in which, even if someone still buys most of the products (like clothing or furniture) that they use, DIY gives them control in the form of a choice about whether to make or buy any particular artifact.

2. *Understanding How Devices are Put Together.* In making the cellphone, people opened up what is, to most, a black box – something taken for granted. Understanding the way a cellphone is assembled from existing parts, and the ecosystem that those parts exist within, provides a valuable perspective on the technology in people's lives. It's also an important first step towards re-thinking those devices and the ways they're put together.

3. *Questioning the Control of Technology.* Perhaps most importantly, we hope that by giving people a perspective on the possibilities and limits of DIY technology, we can encourage them to reflect on the questions we're considering here: to what extent do they have control of the technology in their daily lives? Do they want to live in a world in which only big companies have access to the technology needed to make a modern device? Understanding the limits of the available DIY possibilities may spur people to pursuing other (e.g. political or economic) approaches to technological empowerment.

So, when we ask whether DIY leads to empowerment in the form of control over the technology in our lives, the immediate answer may be no, not directly. However, in helping people to understand how their devices come to be and the ways that process might be different, we offer them new choices in their relationship with technology and an understanding of the limits on those choices – both important steps towards empowerment.

ACKNOWLEDGEMENTS

Thanks to the workshop participants and others who have built their own phones!

REFERENCES

1. Buechley, L., and Perner-Wilson, H. Crafting technology: Reimagining the processes, materials, and cultures of electronics. *ACM Trans. Comput.-Hum. Interact. 19*, 3 (Oct. 2012), 21:1–21:21.
2. Buechley, L., Rosner, D. K., Paulos, E., and Williams, A. Diy for chi: methods, communities, and values of reuse and customization. In *CHI EA '09*, ACM (2009), 4823–4826.
3. Dourish, P., and Bell, G. *Divining a Digital Future: Mess and Mythology in Ubiquitous Computing*. The MIT Press, 2011.
4. Follmer, S., Carr, D., Lovell, E., and Ishii, H. Copycad: remixing physical objects with copy and paste from the real world. In *UIST '10*, ACM (2010), 381–382.
5. Follmer, S., and Ishii, H. Kidcad: digitally remixing toys through tangible tools. In *CHI '12*, ACM (2012), 2401–2410.
6. Gershenfeld, N. *Fab: The Coming Revolution on Your Desktop–from Personal Computers to Personal Fabrication*. Basic Books, Inc., 2007.
7. Goodman, E., and Rosner, D. From garments to gardens: negotiating material relationships online and 'by hand'. In *CHI '11*, ACM (2011), 2257–2266.
8. Greenberg, S., and Fitchett, C. Phidgets: easy development of physical interfaces through physical widgets. In *UIST '01*, ACM (2001), 209–218.
9. Hartmann, B., Klemmer, S. R., Bernstein, M., Abdulla, L., Burr, B., Robinson-Mosher, A., and Gee, J. Reflective physical prototyping through integrated design, test, and analysis. In *UIST '06*, ACM (2006), 299–308.
10. Jacobs, J., and Buechley, L. Codeable objects: computational design and digital fabrication for novice programmers. In *CHI '13*, ACM (2013), 1589–1598.
11. Knörig, A., Wettach, R., and Cohen, J. Fritzing: a tool for advancing electronic prototyping for designers. In *TEI '09*, ACM (2009), 351–358.
12. Kuznetsov, S., Davis, G. N., Paulos, E., Gross, M. D., and Cheung, J. C. Red balloon, green balloon, sensors in the sky. In *UbiComp '11*, ACM (2011), 237–246.
13. Kuznetsov, S., and Paulos, E. Rise of the expert amateur: Diy projects, communities, and cultures. In *NordiCHI '10*, ACM (2010), 295–304.
14. Lim, Y.-K., Stolterman, E., and Tenenberg, J. The anatomy of prototypes: Prototypes as filters, prototypes as manifestations of design ideas. *ACM Trans. Comput.-Hum. Interact. 15*, 2 (July 2008), 7:1–7:27.
15. Maestri, L., and Wakkary, R. Understanding repair as a creative process of everyday design. In *C&C '11*, ACM (2011), 81–90.
16. Mellis, D., Follmer, S., Hartmann, B., Buechley, L., and Gross, M. D. Fab at chi: digital fabrication tools, design, and community. In *CHI EA '13*, ACM (2013), 3307–3310.
17. Mellis, D. A., and Buechley, L. Case studies in the personal fabrication of electronic products. In *DIS '12*, ACM (2012), 268–277.
18. Mellis, D. A., Gordon, D., and Buechley, L. Fab fm: the design, making, and modification of an open-source electronic product. In *TEI '11*, ACM (2011), 81–84.
19. Mueller, S., Lopes, P., and Baudisch, P. Interactive construction: interactive fabrication of functional mechanical devices. In *UIST '12*, ACM (2012), 599–606.
20. Neustaedter, C., and Sengers, P. Autobiographical design in hci research: Designing and learning through use-it-yourself. In *DIS '12*, ACM (2012), 514–523.
21. Resnick, M. Behavior construction kits. *Commun. ACM 36*, 7 (July 1993), 64–71.
22. Resnick, M., Martin, F., Berg, R., Borovoy, R., Colella, V., Kramer, K., and Silverman, B. Digital manipulatives: new toys to think with. In *CHI '98*, ACM (1998), 281–287.
23. Rosner, D., and Bean, J. Learning from ikea hacking: i'm not one to decoupage a tabletop and call it a day. In *CHI '09*, ACM (2009), 419–422.
24. Saul, G., Lau, M., Mitani, J., and Igarashi, T. Sketchchair: an all-in-one chair design system for end users. In *TEI '11*, ACM (2011), 73–80.
25. Savage, V., Zhang, X., and Hartmann, B. Midas: fabricating custom capacitive touch sensors to prototype interactive objects. In *UIST '12*, ACM (2012), 579–588.
26. Sivek, S. C. "we need a showing of all hands" technological utopianism in make magazine. *Journal of Communication Inquiry 35*, 3 (2011), 187–209.
27. Tanenbaum, J. G., Williams, A. M., Desjardins, A., and Tanenbaum, K. Democratizing technology: pleasure, utility and expressiveness in diy and maker practice. In *CHI '13*, ACM (2013), 2603–2612.
28. Villar, N., Scott, J., Hodges, S., Hammil, K., and Miller, C. .net gadgeteer: a platform for custom devices. In *Pervasive '12*, Springer-Verlag (2012), 216–233.
29. Willis, K., Brockmeyer, E., Hudson, S., and Poupyrev, I. Printed optics: 3d printing of embedded optical elements for interactive devices. In *UIST '12*, ACM (2012), 589–598.
30. Zoran, A., and Paradiso, J. A. Freed: a freehand digital sculpting tool. In *CHI '13*, ACM (2013), 2613–2616.

3D Printed Interactive Speakers

Yoshio Ishiguro
Disney Research Pittsburgh,
4720 Forbes Avenue,
Pittsburgh, PA 15213 USA
yoshio.ishiguro@disneyresearch.com

Ivan Poupyrev *
Disney Research Pittsburgh,
4720 Forbes Avenue,
Pittsburgh, PA 15213 USA
ivan.poupyrev@disneyresearch.com

Figure 1. 3D printed speakers: (a) Speaker is embedded into toy (b) The entire 3D printed object is a speaker, (c) Printed speakers can have arbitrary geometries

ABSTRACT
We propose technology for designing and manufacturing interactive 3D printed speakers. With the proposed technology, sound reproduction can easily be integrated into various objects at the design stage and little assembly is required. The speaker can take the shape of anything from an abstract spiral to a rubber duck, opening new opportunities in product design. Furthermore, both audible sound and inaudible ultrasound can be produced with the same design, allowing for identifying and tracking 3D printed objects in space using common integrated microphones. The design of 3D printed speakers is based on electrostatic loudspeaker technology first explored in the early 1930s but not broadly applied until now. These speakers are simpler than common electromagnetic speakers, while allowing for sound reproduction at 60 dB levels with arbitrary directivity ranging from focused to omnidirectional. Our research of 3D printed speakers contributes to the growing body of work exploring functional 3D printing in interactive applications.

Author Keywords
3D printing; speakers; audio; ultrasonic; tracking; rapid prototyping; tangible; additive manufacturing

ACM Classification
H.5.2. [Information Interfaces and Presentation]: User Interfaces---Auditory feedback, Haptic I/O.

* Currently at Google's Motorola ATAP division

CHI 2014, April 26 - May 01 2014, Toronto, ON, Canada

ACM 978-1-4503-2473-1/14/04···$15.00.
http://dx.doi.org/10.1145/2556288.2557046

INTRODUCTION
3D printing technology has expanded from being a tool for rapid prototyping of shapes to printing *functional objects*, including everything from providing a simple enclosure for a printed circuit board to replacing a broken airplane part [4]. Furthermore, with the development of sophisticated multi-material 3D printers [18,27] it is becoming possible to take the next step and fabricate not only passive mechanical components, but functional electromechanical devices as well. Here the shape and functionality are designed simultaneously and then fabricated in one step [18]. Although still in the early stages, recent research has demonstrated how functional Zn-air batteries, organic-polymer transistors and electromechanical relays can be fabricated using additive 3D fabrication techniques [17]. With the continued development of novel materials and 3D printing technologies [26], we believe that the capability to 3D print functional electrical circuits and conductive electrode surfaces as an integral part of a 3D printed object is within reach.

The importance of 3D printing techniques has been recognized in the human-computer interaction (HCI) community. There is a rapidly growing body of work that explores applications of this emerging fabrication technology, including the possibility of creating novel 3D printed interface controllers [9,23,28], of developing interactive tools for the design and rapid fabrication of interactive systems [13,20,22] and many others [2,5,14,28].

We, in particular, are inspired by the vision of a future where interactive devices are not assembled from mass-produced components, but rather designed and 3D printed on-demand locally as individual objects. The establishment of such a manufacturing technology would have a profound and lasting impact on the way future interfaces and interactive devices are designed and developed. It would introduce an unprecedented degree of personalization and customization and a much higher degree of interface components integration, which would allow for nearly arbitrary product geometries. Furthermore, the physical interfaces can be designed and re-designed in an ad-hoc manner by the end user in a way that may terrify professional product and interaction designers, but that could unleash unprecedented freedom and creativity within the broader user community. As noted in [28] the ability to "... *digitally fabricate high fidelity, highly customized, 'ready-to-go' devices will be a powerful enabling technology for HCI research.*"

In this paper we contribute to this vision by presenting the design, fabrication principles, experimental evaluation and some potential applications of an *interactive 3D printed loudspeaker.* The production of the 3D printed speaker is based on principles of *electrostatic sound reproduction* (ESR) which were investigated in depth as early as the 1930s [8] but have not been broadly used before today except in high performance audio systems [e.g. 29]. However, in the course of our research we discovered that there is a natural fit between 3D printing technology and ESR speaker design. Because of the simplicity of ESR, it allows us to design and fabricate speakers that are seamlessly integrated into physical objects of arbitrary geometries, including spherical and omnidirectional shapes. Furthermore, 3D printed speakers can produce both audible and ultrasound frequencies and, therefore, can provide tracking and object identification in addition to sound reproduction. Experimental evaluation demonstrates that our technology produces high quality sound at 60 dB levels. Figure 1 presents 3D speakers that we have designed and manufactured.

The current design and implementation of 3D printed speakers still requires manual steps because we are unable to access multi-material printers that are capable of printing with 3D print conductive polymers and inks [26]. Therefore, all conductive layers in our prototypes were painted using commodity conductive spray paints. However, the fundamental principles of the design and application of 3D printed speakers outlined in this paper are general and are not contingent on the limitations of technology available today. In the near future 3D printers capable of printing with conductive materials will become commonplace, and the vision of printing functional speakers embedded into objects with no human involvement will become the reality.

This paper's contributions are as follows:

1) We introduce the concept and implementation of 3D printed speakers, including the principles of their operation, as well as details of their design and fabrication;

2) We report their properties as well as results of our experimental evaluation of 3D printed speakers; and

3) We describe applications, advantages and limitations of 3D printed speaker technology, including their interactive applications, e.g., ultrasound tracking and identification.

RELATED WORK

In the last two decades there has been rapid growth in the application of print-based techniques in device manufacturing, including printing circuits using electro-conductive inks, printing transistors, microprocessors and even displays [3,6,10,16]. At the same time, free-form 3D printing technology based on additive fabrication techniques has been used to create both passive objects as well as integrated functional devices, such as actuators, relays, batteries and other items [17].

Recently, growing efforts have been focused on developing new materials and processes to 3D print integrated objects where enclosures, shapes, and functional elements (such as electronics, power, storage and optics) are all printed in one step. An example of such an effort is Printed Optics [28] that uses the Objet Eden260V multi-material printer to integrate custom optical elements, such as light pipe bundles, into passive 3D printed shapes. When combined with some minimal electrical components, it allows for the design of novel interactive display and input devices that are not feasible using any other current fabrication technology.

We are not aware of any previous attempt to investigate the fabrication of 3D printed speakers. *A loudspeaker* is one of the most fundamental output devices in interactive systems. It is a transducer that converts an input electrical signal into an audible acoustic signal. The most common speakers are based on electromagnetic and piezoelectric operational principles that have important limitations.

Electromagnetic speakers include a voice coil and a magnet, and the sound is generated by the vibration of a paper cone induced by moving the magnet. Electromagnetic speakers are relatively large and consist of multiple materials and moving parts. The shape of the electromagnetic speaker is usually limited to a classic cone or one of its variations. Although mass-produced speakers are relatively cheap, designing and producing custom speakers is expensive and requires a significant engineering effort. It would be difficult, if not impossible, to 3D print a functional electromagnetic speaker of an arbitrary shape.

Piezoelectric speakers consist of two electrodes with a thin piezoelectric element, e.g., lead zirconate titanate (PZT), sandwiched in between. As a signal is applied to the electrodes the piezoelectric element bends, producing an audible vibration. Although piezoelectric speakers are simple and inexpensive, they are produced by baking ceramic paste at very high temperatures. Therefore, it is difficult and expensive to produce them in anything other than a flat shape, particularly in small quantities. Increasing the size of the piezoelectric elements is particularly challenging because their audio response rapidly decreases with increased size and thickness. Piezoelectric speakers are also capable of creating *ultrasonic* sound sources and they are commonly used in designing various sensors.

Classic speaker technologies, by the very nature of sound production, place significant constraints on their form factors, thus limiting their application. It is relatively difficult and expensive, for example, to create *omnidirectional* speakers that produce sound equally in all directions. There have been many efforts to overcome the form factor limitations and produce alternative speaker designs. *Film speak-*

ers, for example, can be very thin, flexible and transparent. They are usually based on vibrating thin sheets of film with PZT or electroactive polymer actuators [25]. *Stretchable speakers* use silicon substrates and ionic conductors to produce audible sound [11]. *Cylindrical speakers* create omnidirectional sound by using PZT tubes [12] or arrays of transducers placed on cylindrical surfaces [1,24].

Currently one of the least commonly used techniques for sound production is *electrostatic loudspeaker* (ESL) technology which was intensively investigated in the early 1930s through 1950s [8,15,19]. ESL technology had certain limitations that inhibited its wider adoption, and we discuss them in the next section. Nevertheless, ESL technology has very attractive properties for 3D printing: it is very simple, it has almost no moving parts, and it can be made out of inexpensive common materials. ESL does not require complex assembly or involved production processes; in fact, speakers can easily be made at home by hand and can take various geometrical shapes. Electrostatic sound production forms the basic foundation of the 3D printed speaker technology we propose in this paper.

3D PRINTED SPEAKERS

This section presents the design of 3D printed free-form speakers based on *electrostatic sound reproduction principles* (ESR). It discusses the principles of their *operation and design* and then outlines the basic *categories of 3D printed speakers* investigated in this paper. We discuss the details of speaker fabrication techniques, their properties, and report on their experimental evaluation.

Electrostatic Sound Reproduction

The basic principles of electrostatic sound reproduction are simple and were explored in depth in the 1930s. A thin conductive diaphragm and an electrode plate are separated by insulating material, e.g., air, with the dielectric permittivity ε (Figure 2a). The audio signal is amplified to ~1000 V and applied to the electrode, charging it relative to the ground level that is connected to the diaphragm. As the electrode is charging, an electrostatic attraction force is developed between the electrode and diaphragm. According to Columb's Law this attractive force can be calculated as follows:

$$\vec{F} = \frac{q_1 q_2}{2\varepsilon S} = \frac{\varepsilon S V^2}{2d^2}, \qquad (1)$$

where ε is permittivity, S is electrode surface size, d is distance and V is a potential difference between the electrode

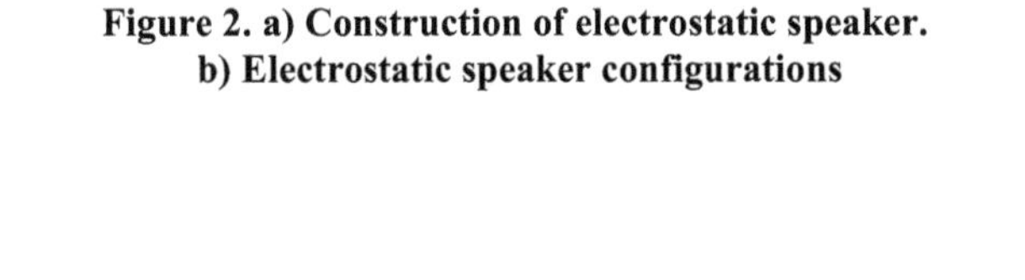

Figure 2. a) Construction of electrostatic speaker. b) Electrostatic speaker configurations

and the diaphragm [8,15]. This electrostatic force would deform or displace the diaphragm by Δx (Figure 2a) and, as an alternating audio signal is provided, the displaced air would create an audible signal. Thus, the diaphragm actuated with electrostatic force would create a speaker.

The sound quality of an ESR speaker depends on several factors. According to Equation 1, a larger surface, a higher insulator permittivity and a smaller distance between plates creates a stronger force, increasing both Δx and sound pressure levels. We cannot increase the size of the electrode and diaphragm indefinitely: a lighter diaphragm produces better speaker response. Therefore, a lighter speaker would by louder then a larger ESR device with a heavy diaphragm.

The ESR speaker forms a capacitor and, therefore, another key property is the electrical time constant τ, which defines how fast the induced charge builds on the capacitor plates:

$$\tau = C \cdot R = \frac{\varepsilon S R}{d}, \qquad (2)$$

where R is the input impedance of the speaker. A larger τ would degrade speaker response at higher frequencies. The design of the speaker, therefore, is a question of tradeoffs between loudness and the frequency response.

It has been demonstrated that ESR speakers allow for high quality sound reproduction, outperforming traditional electromagnetic speakers in both high and medium sound frequency ranges [15]. Nevertheless, they have a number of limitations that inhibite their broad application. The sound reproduction industry was established in the 1930s, and high voltage amplification was difficult before the invention of the transistor. Even today, the selection of high-voltage audio drivers is very limited. Furthermore, achieving high sound volume in a living room, for example, depends on large diaphragms (~0.5m^2) with a uniform surface tension. This requires relatively high precision manufacturing, limiting ESL applications to the HiFi audio niche. These limitations, however, become significantly less crucial when ESR technology is used for low cost, low sound volume speakers embedded in toys and embodied interaction devices.

In the ESR speakers reported here we connect the ground to the diaphragm and the audio signal to the electrode (Figure 2b right). This is contrary to the ESR speaker design proposed previously [8,15], where the signal was connected to the diaphragm or a two-electrode configuration was used (Figure 2b left and middle). In designing home audio speakers the choice is irrelevant. However, it becomes important in 3D printed speakers embedded in toys and objects that can be touched by the user. The grounded diaphragm protects the user touching the speaker from the high-voltage audio source, making it safe to handle and manipulate the object with embedded speakers. This becomes particularly important in the interactive applications that we describe later in the paper.

Designing 3D Printed Speakers

The overall design of 3D printed speakers is presented in Figure 3 using the example of a toy character with an inte-

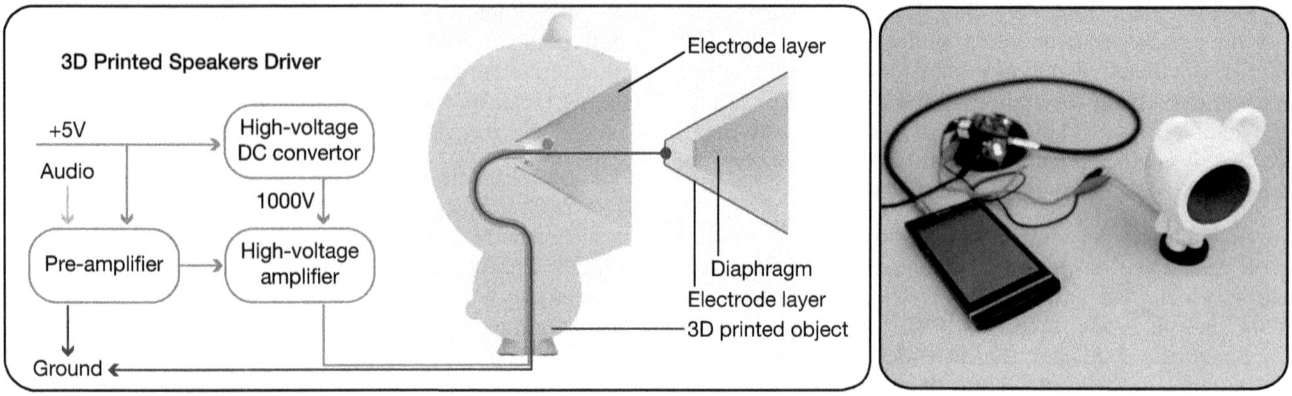

Figure 3. 3D printed speaker system diagram, here the speaker is integrated into the toy character

grated speaker. The body of the toy is 3D printed using currently available 3D printing technology. In our case, we used an Objet Eden260V 3D printer with triple material printing head. However, it is not capable of printing conductive materials, and thus was supplemented with a nickel-based conductive spray paint (MG Chemicals Super Shield™ Nickel conductive coating). Painting conductive layers is a simple procedure; it will become unnecessary when printing heads capable of printing conductive materials become available. In the future the painting process will be eliminated altogether.

The conductive layer painted on the body of the toy becomes an inner electrode layer where the audio signal in injected (Figure 3). The sound-producing diaphragm is then 3D printed and painted with conductive paint as well. In addition, it is also coated with a silicone-based coating spray (TechSpray® 2102-12S) that insulates the electrode and sound-making diaphragm. The diaphragm is next inserted into the toy and held in place using the 3D-printed connector ring. The diaphragm and painted electrode are finally connected to both the ground and audio outputs of the custom-designed high-voltage audio driver.

The *audio driver* for printed speakers amplifies the input audio signal from nominal amplitude (~1.0 V peak-to-peak) to 1000 V peak-to-peak signal by using a high-voltage transistor amplification circuit. A miniature step-up converter (EMCO QH10-5) boosts voltage from 5 V DC to 1000 V DC, which is used as a voltage source for the transistor amplifier. The output current of the voltage converter and, therefore, the audio driver is ~1.25 mA. The entire driver runs at 5 V DC and consumes 250 mA maximum current.

Air electrical breakdown can occur between high-voltage traces [21]. Therefore, it is important that an appropriate distance (> 1 mm) is maintained between all high-voltage traces and connectors on the controller board. In addition, silicone-based insulator spray can be used to improve the insulation between the contacts.

The implemented printed speaker system is presented in Figure 3 on the right. It can operate using either a standard Li-Ion battery or a USB connection. It accepts any standard audio source, such as a mobile phone.

3D Printed Speakers Design Space

3D printed speakers can take a variety of forms and shapes leading to many unique applications. Figure 4 explores some of the forms that become possible with printed speaker technology. It is obvious that we can create traditional flat planer speakers (Figure 4, top) that are common today and that have been explored before. Therefore, we do not explore this category of speaker in this paper.

At the next level of complexity speakers can take a variety of basic 3D geometrical shapes including traditional cone-shaped speakers, cylindrical, spherical and others (Figure 4, middle). All these shapes produce sound in all directions around the speaker, i.e., omnidirectional sound production. Note that designing 3D geometrical speakers using traditional speaker technologies is challenging. Using our 3D printed speaker approach, however, designing various geometrical speakers is a relatively trivial problem. We will discuss it later in the paper.

The most challenging and important aspect of 3D printed speakers is that they can be integrated into objects of arbitrary shapes, becoming an unobtrusive and invisible part of their design (Figure 4, bottom). 3D printed speaker technology provides an alternative to traditional techniques of integrating loudspeaker functionality into objects and devices.

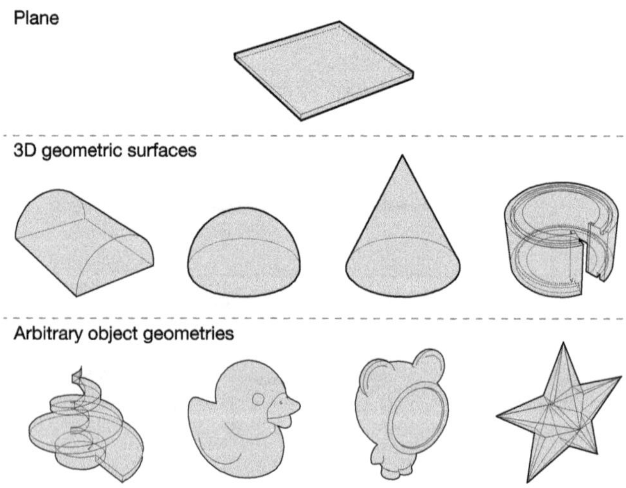

Figure 4. 3D printed speakers design space

Here speakers take arbitrary shapes making them an integral part of the object. In some cases only parts of an object may have speaker functionality and in other cases the entire body of the object generates sound.

Diaphragm Design for 3D Printed Speakers

The key factor influencing the sound quality of printed speakers is *the design of the diaphragm*. Figure 5 presents the results of the displacement measurements for two 3D printed diaphragms with the thicknesses of 1.0 mm and 0.5 mm and weighing 5.94 g and 3.65 g, respectively, driven by a 100 Hz sinusoid signal. The Keyence® LK-H057 laser displacement sensor is used to measure the movement of the diaphragm at a 20 kHz sampling rate with 0.025 μm accuracy. In addition to displacement, an Extech® 407730 Sound Level Meter (SLM) is used to measure sound pressure levels (SPL) 30 cm away from the speaker.

The experiments demonstrate that a) printed speakers work as designed, and b) lighter and thinner diaphragms produce significantly larger displacement and therefore louder sound. In fact, the displacement nearly doubles when we decrease the thickness of the diaphragm by half. The emitted speaker energy increases with the increase of the displacement, which is supported by the measurements that resulted in 54.8 dB_{SPL} and 53.2 dB_{SPL} for 0.5 mm and 1.0 mm diaphragms using 2 kHz input signal.

The latter observation, while seeming straightforward, is not obvious. As diaphragms become thinner, they also become much more flexible. Initially it was not clear to us that thinner, yet more flexible, diaphragms would outperform slightly thicker and stiffer ones. The experiments demonstrate that the stiffness of a diaphragm is not as important as its thickness and weight. This finding allows us to significantly expand the range of materials and processes that may be used to create effective diaphragms for 3D printed speakers.

Directionality and Geometry of 3D Printed Speakers

Printed speakers allow for transforming the surface of an object into a sound producing device. Among other things, this allows us to design speakers that have either highly directive or, adversely, omnidirectional sound. This is a unique and exciting property of ESR speaker technology.

Indeed, designing speakers that are either highly directive or omnidirectional is a challenging problem. It usually requires designing speaker arrays where each speaker has to be individually controlled and calibrated, both of which are expensive and labor intensive. In the case of 3D printed speakers, the entire surface of an object contributes to sound production. The sound direction is normal to the diaphragm geometry [25]. Therefore, the directionality of sound can be partially controlled by the object's surface geometry.

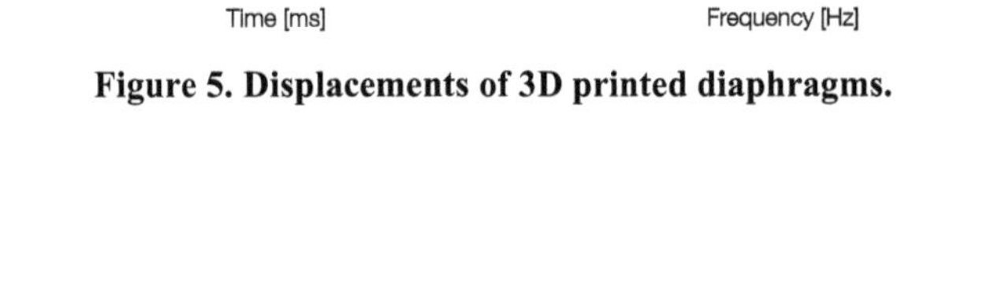

Figure 5. Displacements of 3D printed diaphragms.

To investigate this observation, four speaker shapes are designed, including a classic speaker *cone*, a *half cylinder*, a *full cylinder* and a *slit* speaker where the vibrating diaphragm is inside (Figure 6). The diaphragm area for all speakers is kept constant at 5625 mm^2. Common aluminum metallized polyester film is used for diaphragms. Metalized polyester offers an inexpensive and easy to use alternative to 3D printed diaphragms for simple geometrical shapes: it is light, durable, thin (~0.127 mm) and easily accessible.

We evaluated the directionality of each printed speaker using input signal frequencies at 2 kHz and 10 kHz. A printed speaker is placed on a laser-cut experimental base plate with engraved registration marks for sound level meter (SLM) locations. We move the SLM by hand between measurements. The duration of measurements are 5 sec for each SLM location. Because the sound pressure produced by small printed speakers is relatively low, the measurement volume is small (~$1m^3$). Therefore, we are able to isolate the experimental setup from the environment noise by carefully shielding the measurement apparatus with accessible soundproof materials.

Figure 6 shows the results of the SPL measurements at different angles for each of the 3D printed speakers. The graph is normalized in relation to the sound pressure levels at 0 degrees and plotted with a 22.5 degree interval. The results of the measurement demonstrate that sound directionality is indeed defined by the surface geometry of the printed speaker. Each point of the diaphragm emits sound in an approximately normal direction, as is expected. The directionality is stronger at higher frequencies, which is also expected. We are particularly impressed with 3D printed cylindrical speakers: the sound distribution is nearly perfectly uniform (Figure 6d), making a relatively high quality yet very inexpensive omnidirectional speaker.

The *slit speaker* allows for the production of directional sound and is presented on Figure 7. Note that we were not able to measure sound pressure levels in $90^\circ - 270^\circ$ diapason at 10 kHz because the sound pressure levels were below the SPL sensitivity thresholds. A 3D printed slit speaker provides a very useful configuration where the speaker has to be placed inside of the object, e.g., inside of a toy character with a mouth opening. This creates the impression of sound coming directly from the character's mouth – increasing both realism and engagement. Furthermore, the slit design protects the user from the electrical circuitry.

Electrode Arrays in Printed Speakers

3D printed speakers can be designed with any electrode configuration and number of electrodes. In the case of electrode arrays, each electrode acts as an *independent 3D printed speaker*, even though all of them share a single diaphragm.

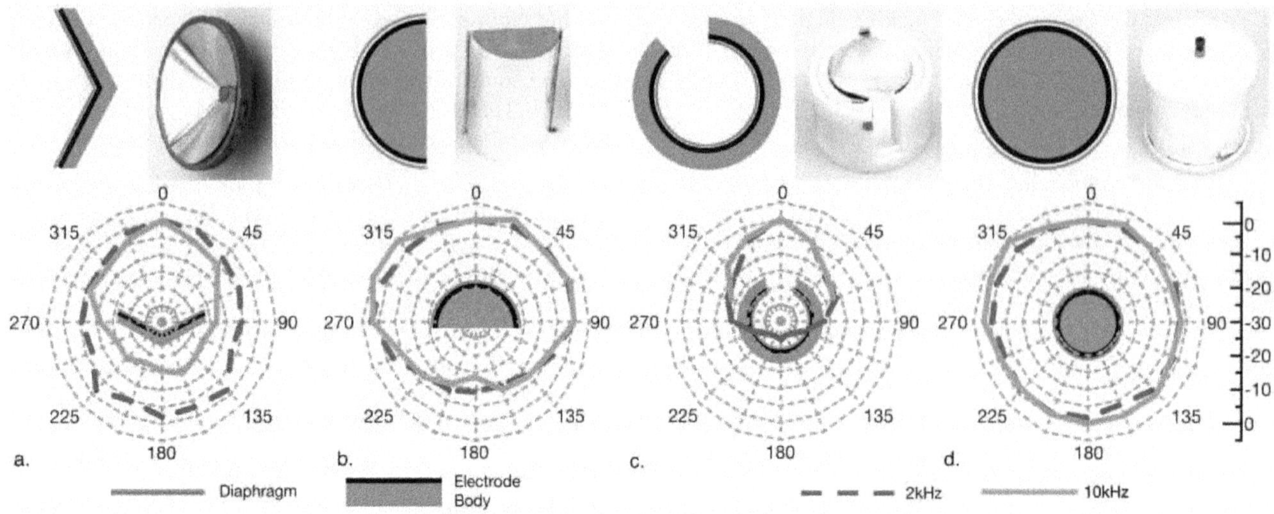

Figure 6. Directionality and geometry of 3D printed speakers.

To test 3D printed electrode arrays we measured sound pressure level distributions for a half cylindrical speaker with painted electrodes at 20° – 90°, 30° – 330° and 340° – 270° degrees (Figure 8). A single metalized polyester diaphragm is used as in previous experiments (Figure 6b). The same measurement setup is used in the directionality measurements reported above.

Figure 8 shows the measurement results using a 2 kHz input signal for each electrode. We can clearly observe that each painted electrode produces directive sound output in its respective direction. This demonstrates the versatility of printed speaker technology: A single object can have multiple electrodes sharing the same diaphragm and yet acting as individual speakers, with individual and directive sound output. Location-based audio displays, both on a small-object scale and on the scale of entire environments, can be easily created using 3D printed speakers.

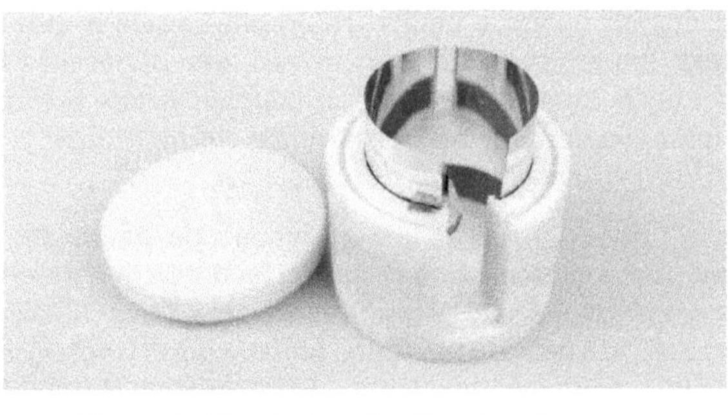

Figure 7. The design of a slit printed speaker

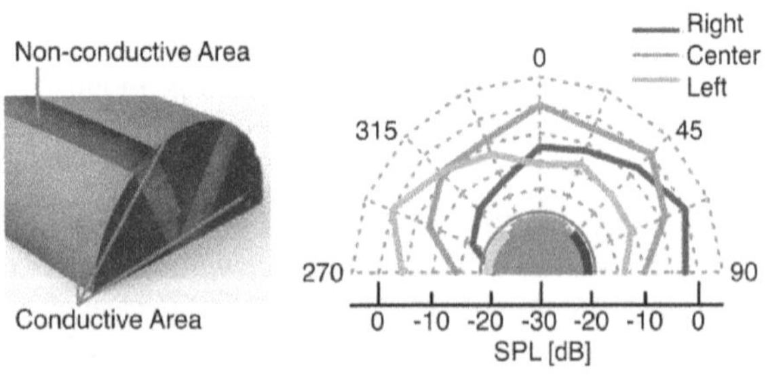

Figure 8. Multi-electrode 3D printed speakers

Integrating 3D Printed Speakers into Objects

The vision behind 3D printed speakers is the integration of loudspeaker functionality into objects at the design stage. Although our current prototypes presently require a certain amount of hand assembly, in the future we envision designers picking and dropping speakers into objects and devices as one of the elements of their CAD programs [28]. In this section we investigate possible means for integrating loudspeaker functionality into objects.

The most straightforward way to integrate speaker functionality into an object is to simply place one of the basic geometrical speakers (Figure 4) into the appropriate place in the object. As an example of this approach we created a toy bear with a speaker embedded within the head (Figure 1, 3). Such integration is trivial and any of the geometric speaker shapes can be used. The disadvantage of this approach is that the speaker is visible and, although the design process is simplified, from the user's perspective there is no difference between the printed speaker and a traditional speaker.

An alternative approach to embedding the speaker is to enhance the actual body of the object with loudspeaker functionality: the entire object's surface or any part of it would become the speaker, seamless and invisible to the user. In the simplest approach, only the *parts of the object surface* that can be augmented with 3D printed diaphragms would be, turning the object into the speaker. Figure 9 demonstrates a *Spiral Speaker*. The 3D printed diaphragm is shown on the left and an assembled speaker is shown on the right. The diaphragm is attached on the speaker body using a soft silicon compound. Similarly, any other object that has any number of flat faces can be easily turned into a speaker. Thus, we can imagine toys, decorations, household items and other objects augmented with loudspeaker functionality.

Another approach to augment objects with loudspeaker functionality is to turn the entire body of the object into a

Figure 9. 3D printed Spiral Speaker.

Figure 10. 3D printed Duck Speaker.

Figure 11. Thin film diaphragm fabrication.

speaker by covering the object with the diaphragm. Figure 10 demonstrates a *Duck Speaker* where the entire 3D printed duck toy is wrapped in a compliant diaphragm, creating one *single* sound-emitting surface.

The challenge in designing full body object speakers is creating a diaphragm that is thin, robust and covers the entire body of the object. The experimental evaluation reported earlier in the paper has demonstrated that a thinner and softer diaphragm produces louder sound pressure levels. However, the minimum thickness of a 3D printed diaphragm using our Objet printer is limited to ~0.3 mm, resulting in a relatively heavy diaphragm, reducing sound levels.

In order to create thin, reliable, full-body object compliant diaphragms we developed a new fabrication procedure that uses film coatings and molds to create diaphragms that are ~0.14 mm thin and weigh 1.1 g. Figure 12 demonstrates the process. First, negative molds are 3D printed using the same CAD model as for the object (Figure 11). Then both the mold and the object are sprayed with nickel-based conductive paint. The mold is then coated with polyethylene coating spray (3M Paint Defender™ Spray Film), forming a thin soft film bonded to the conductive paint (Figure 12c).

The polyethylene coating spray is a poor insulator inappropriate for high-voltage applications. Therefore, the object body is then coated with a silicone-based insulation spray over the nickel-based paint layer. We fast dry the molds in an oven and carefully remove the formed film from the mold (Figure 12d). The resulting diaphragm is strong, conductive, thin, and mirrors the object shape. It is used to cover the entire body of the object, turning it into a speaker.

INTERACTIVE USES OF 3D PRINTED SPEAKERS

The basic purpose of 3D printed speakers is to produce an effective sound display. In addition, however, 3D printed speakers also allow for additional interactive functionality that we discuss in this section.

Ultrasonic Tracking and Identification

Figure 13 demonstrates the frequency response of cone-shaped 3D printed speakers. It shows that they can effectively reproduce sound over 20 kHz, i.e., in ultrasonic frequencies. Thus, objects enhanced with 3D printed speakers can both output audible sound and produce signals at ultrasonic frequencies that can be used for lightweight *data transmission* and *object tracking*.

To make a compact audio driver we use a small high-voltage regulator with current-limited output. Therefore, there is an amplitude drop at ultrasonic frequencies (Figure 13). This is because, with the increase of signal frequency, the impedance drops and the regulator cannot support the subsequent current increase. A larger 3W high-voltage power supply allows for a nearly flat response. However, we have found that for short-range tracking and data transmission the ultrasound signal produced with printed speakers is efficient even with lower signal amplitude.

We explored two interactive applications of printed speakers that are enabled by their ultrasonic capabilities. These consist of lightweight *character identification* in a storytelling application and *distance tracking* between a computer and a 3D printed character. In both applications no additional equipment has to be provided: we use a standard microphone embedded in the laptop computer.

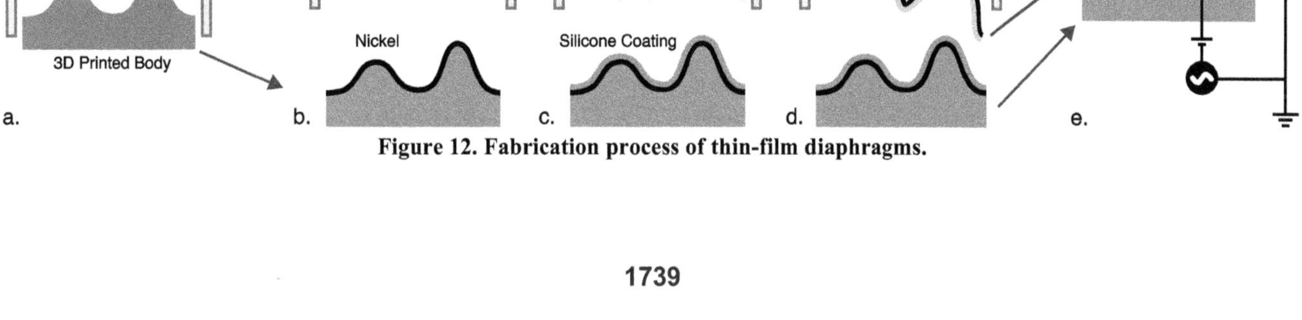

Figure 12. Fabrication process of thin-film diaphragms.

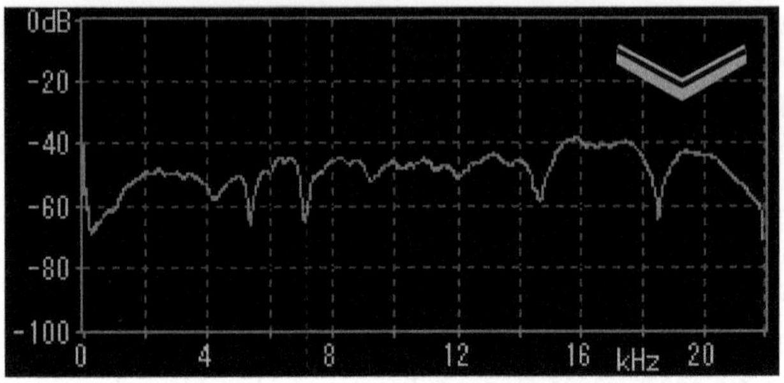

Figure 13. The frequency response of printed speakers.

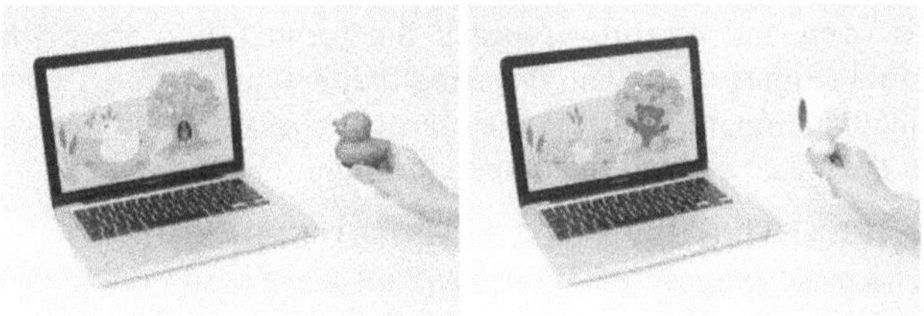

Figure 14. Character identification.

Figure 15. Distance tracking.

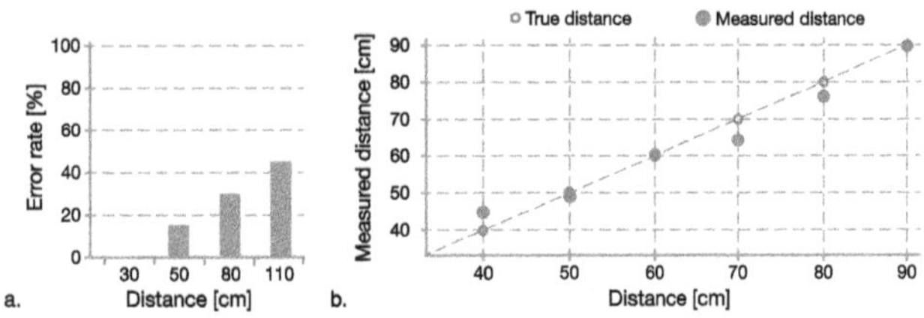

Figure 16. a) Identification error b) Distance measurement error

Character identification

The ultrasound Frequency Shift Keying (FSK) modulation is used to create unique object IDs for two 3D printed characters: a duck and a bear. The FSK ID is an 8-bit long ASCII code and has no parity bits. When the user brings characters within ~1m of the computer microphone, the application software detects a modulated ultrasound signal, decodes the character ID and presents feedback by animating the appropriate cartoon character on the screen (Figure 14). Note that no physical connection between the computer and character is required, i.e., character identification can be completely ad hoc.

Figure 16a presents the results of identification error measurements for the bear-shaped speaker at 30, 50, 80 and 110 cm distance of the computer microphone. The character ID is sent 20 times with a 500ms interval for each test distance. The measured error rate is approximately 0, 15, 30, and 45 percent at each distance, respectively. It also means that we can achieve 100 percent accuracy when all 20 measurements are used for object identification. The experiments demonstrate that at close distances (~1m) the object identification is effective and can be significantly improved by introducing data redundancy and error correction codes. The error rate is also affected by the speaker orientation and can be minimized by using an omnidirectional design.

Distance tracking

The 3D printed bear toy is used to implement and evaluate ultrasonic distance tracking (Figure 15). The bear is connected to the computer, which outputs a 20KHz ultrasonic impulse on the embedded 3D printed speaker. The application software detects the impulse by using a built-in microphone and Discrete Fourier Transform (DFT), then measures the time difference between the initial and returned impulses and calculates the distance. The resulting distance can then be used for 3D interaction and gesture recognition, games and storytelling applications.

Figure 16b presents the results of preliminary distance error measurements for the bear-shaped speaker at various distances from the computer microphone. The tracking impulse signal is outputted 30 times at each position. The root mean square error of tracking is 3.83 cm and standard deviation is 4.04. The tracking accuracy is sufficient for most of the envisioned interactive applications. We believe that, with better data processing and low-level optimization of the internal audio processing, the tracking error can be reduced to a minimum. Furthermore, with the improved performance more detailed and rich gesture interaction can potentially be implemented, for example, by using the Doppler effect [7]. A stereo microphone or a microphone array would allow for the tracking of the 3D position of the character with the embedded 3D printed speaker. We are electing to leave this research for future work.

Touchable and Tactile Feedback

A 3D printed speaker can be touched and held by the users and still function effectively as a speaker. In ESR speakers the entire thin, elastic diaphragm participates in creating sound and, therefore, even when users touch and hold some part of the diaphragm, the rest of it still functions as a speaker (see Figure 17).

We measure the effect of touching and holding a 3D printed cone speaker on sound output levels at different frequencies. Figure 18 presents the measurement for no touch, pinching with three fingers and full hand contact conditions. The data show that the effect of a single digit touching the speaker is negligible, and, indeed, during the experiments we were unable to hear any discernable difference. When a whole hand is placed on the speaker the sound pressure level drops ~10dB on average, which is expected. Indeed, any sound source is muffled when covered with a human hand.

This property of ESR printed speakers is quite unique, as the same does not hold true for traditional electromagnetic loudspeakers. In electromagnetic speakers only the voice coil vibrates, other speaker parts are passive, solely transfer-

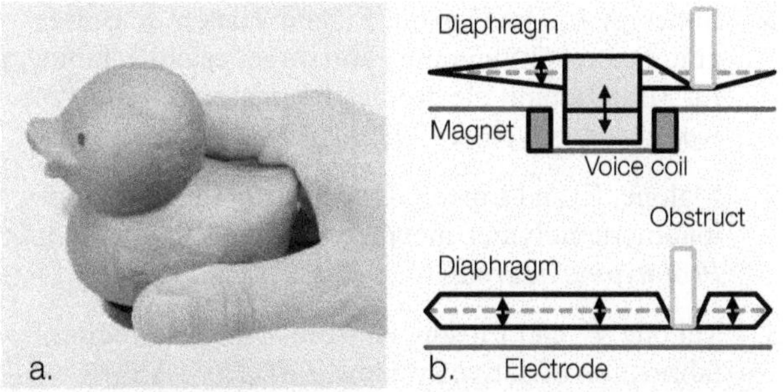

Figure 17. The diaphragm can vibrate when user holds an object creating effective tactile feedback.

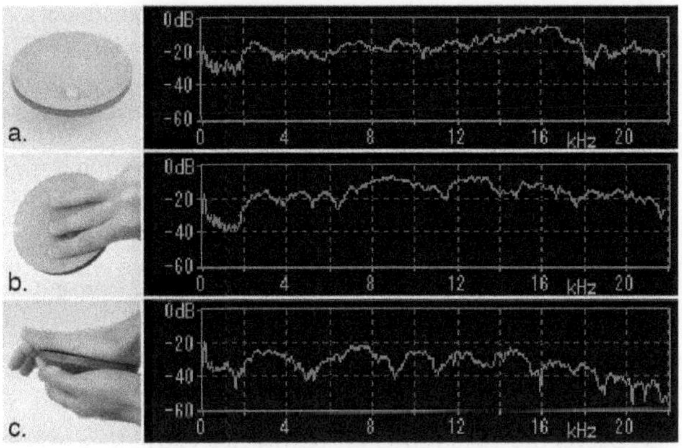

Figure 18. Printed speaker performance when touched by the user: a) no touch, b) three finger pinch and c) holding with both hands.

ring and amplifying these vibration forces. Therefore, touching the diaphragm of an electromagnetic speaker *anywhere* significantly impedes its operation (Figure 17).

The fact that printed speakers can be touched and held in the hand means that we can use them to communicate simple tactile feedback to the user. In our early tests we discovered that the user can clearly feel bursts of signals at the 20 ~ 120 Hz frequency range. We will investigate this exciting and unique property of printed speakers in future work.

DISCUSSION AND CONCLUSIONS

This paper reports on the design and investigation of 3D printed speaker technology based on electrostatic sound reproduction principles. Experimental evaluation of 3D printed speakers demonstrates that, among other things:

1. It is possible to produce audible sound with a broad range of speaker geometries at about 60 dB_{SPL};
2. We can effectively control the directivity of sound by changing the shape of the speakers and using various electrode arrays;
3. Multiple speaker shapes can be designed and embedded into objects and devices;
4. 3D printed speakers provide unique interaction properties, such as tracking and identification using ultrasonic frequencies;
5. Speakers can be touched and manipulated by the user's hand without a noticeable decrease in speaker sound quality, providing the possibility for simple tactile feedback; and
6. The resulting speakers are simple, inexpensive, low powered and can be run from a battery.

There are also a number of *limitations* of 3D printed speaker technology that warrant further research efforts:

First, the current implementation of 3D printed speakers requires manual assembly. 3D printers that are capable of printing with conductive materials are not accessible at this moment. However, the principles of the design and application of 3D printed speakers are general and scalable. They do not depend on the limitations of current technology. We believe that in the near future 3D printers capable of printing with conductive materials will become commonplace, and the vision of 3D printed speakers will become a reality.

Second, although a large variety of shapes can be used to make effective 3D printed speakers, there are also limitations. The most critical limitation is avoiding shapes that result in a charge concentration along sharp edges. Such a charge concentration would result in isolation breakdown and a short circuit between the body and diaphragm, with adverse effect on sound reproduction.

Third, the direction of sound strongly depends on object shape. Therefore, special care should be taken in using object shapes that allow for the sound directions that are appropriate for the applications where the object is used.

Fourth, the sound level produced by 3D printed speakers is appropriate for small hand-held objects and devices but may not be effective in large scale or outdoor applications unless the size of the diaphragm is significantly increased.

Fifth, the ESR technology and 3D printed speakers are less effective for low frequency sound playback than for medium and high frequency sounds. The human voice, birds, animals, nature sounds, stringed instruments and computer-generated blips are some of the examples of the content that can be effectively reproduced on 3D printed speakers.

In the future we plan on exploring the interactive applications of 3D printed speakers, especially focusing on ultrasonic tracking, tactile feedback and enhancing both of these applications with touch sensitivity. Additional planned research will focus on exploring printed speaker arrays and developing techniques for printing very large printed speakers.

REFERENCES

1. Brown, J.A., Dunphy, K., Leadbetter, J.R., Adamson, R.B.A., and Beslin, O. Fabrication and performance of a single-crystal lead magnesium niobate-lead titanate cylindrical hydrophone. *The Journal of the Acoustical Society of America 134*, 2 (2013), 1031–1038.

2. Calì, J., Calian, D.A., Amati, C., et al. 3D-printing of non-assembly, articulated models. *ACM Trans. on Graphics 31*, 6 (2012), 1–8.

3. Clemens, W., Fix, W., Ficker, J., Knobloch, A., and Ullmann, A. From polymer transistors toward printed electronics. *Journal of Materials Research 19*, 07 (2011), 1963–1973.

4. Economist. *Print me a Stradivarius*. Economist, 2011. http://www.economist.com/.

5. Follmer, S., Carr, D., Lovell, E., and Ishii, H. CopyCAD: remixing physical objects with copy and paste from the real world. In *Adjunct proc. UIST '10*, ACM Press (2010), 381–382.

6. Gong, N.W., Hodges, S., and Paradiso, J.A. Leveraging conductive inkjet technology to build a scalable and versatile surface for ubiquitous sensing. In *Proc. UbiComp '11*, ACM Press (2011), 45–54.

7. Gupta, S., Morris, D., Patel, S., Tan, D. SoundWave: using the doppler effect to sense gestures. In *Proc. CHI '12*, ACM Press (2012), 1911–1914.

8. Hanna, C.R. Theory of the electrostatic loud speaker. *The Journal of the Acoustical Society of America 2*, 2 (1930), 143–149.

9. Hodges, S., Taylor, S., Villar, N., Scott, J., and Helmes, J. Exploring physical prototyping techniques for functional devices using .NET gadgeteer. In *Proc. TEI '13*, ACM Press (2013), 271–274.

10. Kawahara, Y., Hodges, S., Cook, B.S., Zhang, C., and Abowd, G.D. Instant inkjet circuits. In *Proc. UbiComp '13*, ACM Press (2013), 363–372.

11. Keplinger, C., Sun, J.Y., Foo, C.C., Rothemund, P., Whitesides, G.M., Suo, Z. Stretchable, Transparent, Ionic Conductors. *Science 341*, 6149 (2013), 984–987.

12. Langevin, R.A. The Electro-Acoustic Sensitivity of Cylindrical Ceramic Tubes. *The Journal of the Acoustical Society of America 26*, 3 (1954), 421–427.

13. Lau, M., Mitani, J., and Igarashi, T. Digital Fabrication. *Computer 45*, 12 (2012), 76–79.

14. Leigh, S.J., Bradley, R.J., Purssell, C.P., Billson, D.R., and Hutchins, D.A. A simple, low-cost conductive composite material for 3D printing of electronic sensors. *PloS one 7*, 11 (2012), e49365: 1–6.

15. LLoyd, B., Goldman, R.B., and Roop, R.W. Design and Performance of a High-Frequency Electrostatic Speaker. *The Journal of the Acoustical Society of America 27*, 6 (1955), 1128–1133.

16. Lopes, A.J., MacDonald, E., and Wicker, R.B. Integrating stereolithography and direct print technologies for 3D structural electronics fabrication. *Rapid Prototyping Journal 18*, 2 (2012), 129–143.

17. Malone, E. and Lipson, H. Freeform fabrication of ionomeric polymer-metal composite actuators. *Rapid Prototyping Journal 12*, 5 (2006), 244–253.

18. Malone, E. and Lipson, H. Multi-material freeform fabrication of active systems. *ESDA '08*, ASME (2008), 1–9.

19. Medley, A.P., Billson, D.R., Hutchins, D.A., and Davis, L.A.J. Properties of an electrostatic transducer. *The Journal of the Acoustical Society of America 120*, 5 (2006), 2658–2667.

20. Mueller, S., Lopes, P., and Baudisch, P. Interactive construction: interactive fabrication of functional mechanical devices. In *Proc. UIST '12*, ACM Press (2012), 599–606.

21. Peek, F.W. *Dielectric Phenomena in High Voltage Engineering*. McGraw-Hill, 1929.

22. Saul, G., Lau, M., Mitani, J., and Igarashi, T. SketchChair: An All-in-one Chair Design System for End Users. In *Proc. TEI '11*, ACM Press (2011), 73–80.

23. Savage, V., Chang, C., and Hartmann, B. *Sauron: Embedded Single-Camera Sensing of Printed Physical User Interfaces* | EECS at UC Berkeley. .

24. Sayin, U., Artís, P., and Guasch, O. Realization of an omnidirectional source of sound using parametric loudspeakers. *The Journal of the Acoustical Society of America 134*, 3 (2013), 1899–1907.

25. Sugimoto, T., Ono, K., Ando, A., Morita, Y., Hosoda, K., and Ishii, D. Semicylindrical acoustic transducer from a dielectric elastomer film with compliant electrodes. *The Journal of the Acoustical Society of America 130*, 2 (2011), 744–752.

26. TTPgroup. Chemical, ceramic and even biological 3D printing is now a reality as TTP unveils new multi-material breakthrough. http://www.ttpgroup.com/news/press/.

27. Vidimče, K., Wang, S.P., Ragan-Kelley, J., and Matusik, W. OpenFab: A programmable pipeline for multi-material fabrication. *SIGGRAPH 2013*, ACM Press (2013), Article 136.

28. Willis, K., Brockmeyer, E., Hudson, S., and Poupyrev, I. Printed optics. In *Proc. UIST '12*, ACM Press (2012), 589–598.

29. STAX Ltd., http://www.stax.co.jp/.

Circuit Stickers: Peel-and-Stick Construction of Interactive Electronic Prototypes

Steve Hodges[1,2], Nicolas Villar[1], Nicholas Chen[1], Tushar Chugh[1], Jie Qi[3], Diana Nowacka[2,1] and Yoshihiro Kawahara[4,3]

[1]Microsoft Research [2]Culture Lab, Newcastle University [3]MIT Media Lab [4]University of Tokyo

{shodges,nvillar,nchen,tchugh}@microsoft.com, jieqi@media.mit.edu, d.nowacka@newcastle.ac.uk,kawahara@akg.t.u-tokyo.ac.jp

ABSTRACT

We present a novel approach to the construction of electronic prototypes which can support a variety of interactive devices. Our technique, which we call *circuit stickers*, involves adhering physical interface elements such as LEDs, sounders, buttons and sensors onto a cheap and easy-to-make substrate which provides electrical connectivity. This assembly may include control electronics and a battery for standalone operation, or it can be interfaced to a microcontroller or PC. In this paper we illustrate different points in the design space and demonstrate the technical feasibility of our approach. We have found circuit stickers to be versatile and low-cost, supporting quick and easy construction of physically flexible interactive prototypes. Building extra copies of a device is straightforward. We believe this technology has potential for design exploration, research prototyping, education and for hobbyist projects.

Author Keywords

Conductive inkjet; silver ink; rapid prototyping; physical computing; solderless electronics; tangible interfaces.

ACM Classification Keywords

H.5.m. Information interfaces and presentation (e.g., HCI): Miscellaneous.

INTRODUCTION

In recent years there has been an explosion in the availability and use of electronic prototyping platforms in a range of disciplines such as design exploration, technology education, research prototyping and within the hobbyist communities [1,2,10,13]. These tools typically comprise electronic hardware modules which are readily connected together to produce compact and robust assemblies. However, traditional techniques like hand soldering and the use of solderless breadboards still have the edge for many applications and are therefore frequently used too.

In this paper we present a new approach to prototyping with electronics which we call *circuit stickers*, see Figure 1. In our scheme, the hardware building blocks for constructing a device are simple elements in the form of small printed circuit board (PCBs). These are connected together physically and electrically to form a working prototype by sticking them onto a cheap and easy-to-make substrate. A battery can be included for standalone operation, or the resulting assembly can be interfaced to a microcontroller or a PC.

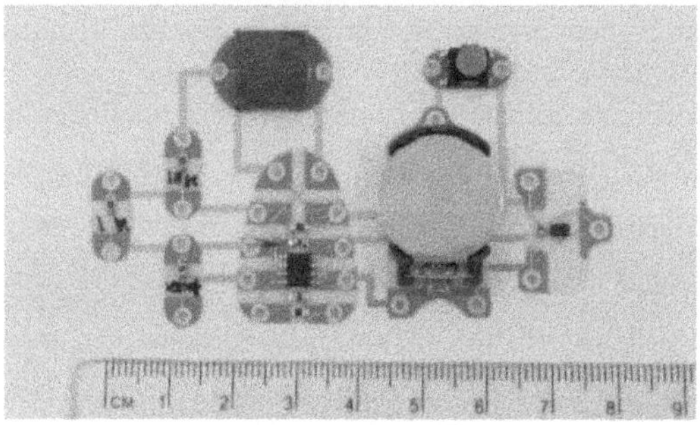

Figure 1: An example circuit sticker design. The stickers needed for a coin-cell powered musical toy are stuck to a sheet of paper which has been inkjet printed with silver conductors.

Whilst our technique is not a panacea, it provides a useful alternative to established approaches. We believe it is particularly well-suited to building reasonably compact and robust interactive devices. It is simple to use, versatile, easy to replicate and results in physically flexible prototypes.

In the remainder of this paper we describe the design and use of circuit stickers. Following a discussion of related work, we describe the concept in more detail and outline some of the sticker elements we have built so far. The conductive substrate which the circuits are attached to may be hand-crafted or designed digitally; we describe the processes we have used in our research to date. We then present different prototypes built using circuit stickers to validate the potential of our approach. We imagine applications in several domains such as design exploration, research prototyping, education and home use. We do not provide a formal evaluation but rather aim to establish the concept, explore the possibilities it affords and demonstrate its potential. We conclude with a number of areas of future work.

RELATED WORKS

Electronics Prototyping

Users who are prototyping electronic circuits have several construction options. A common approach is the use of

CHI 2014, April 26–May 1, 2014, Toronto, Ontario, Canada.

ACM 978-1-4503-2473-1/14/04...$15.00.

processor boards like Arduino [1] in conjunction with discrete wires, components and breadboards. The use of wires allows flexibility when positioning interface elements like LEDs and switches and the resulting circuits can readily be modified to explore different designs or debug problems. However, they can be relatively cumbersome and fragile, and the wiring process can be tedious and error-prone.

More modular platforms address some of the issues associated with using discrete wires and components. LittleBits [2], VooDooIO [12], Phidgets [6] and .NET Gadgeteer [13] use higher level abstractions and custom hardware to simplify assembly and reduce the iteration cycle. This added convenience comes at a tradeoff, however – the size and layout of the resulting circuit is constrained, and the range of components and possible configurations may be limited.

Quick-turnaround, low-volume PCB manufacturing is another option for constructing prototypes. PCBs support fine-grained positioning of components and bypass the need to manually wire them up, enabling complex yet compact designs which are physically robust. However, assembling and modifying a PCB-based prototype can be difficult.

Circuit stickers combine positive elements from the above techniques, offering a prototyping "sweet spot" for some applications. Circuit stickers are faster and cheaper to use than PCBs, more reliable and compact than breadboards, and more versatile than higher-level modular systems. They can also make it easier to replicate, evaluate and ultimately extend prior work in this area including the above systems. The aim of this paper is to illustrate what is possible with this easy-to-use technique and to facilitate further research.

Producing and Attaching to Conductive Substrates

Circuit stickers rely on a conductive substrate to provide electrical interconnection. This substrate can be created by hand using conductive ink and paint (e.g. http://electroninks.com and http://bareconductive.com), or can be designed on a computer and then printed. We have explored both, but in this paper we primarily focus on the latter. In particular, we build on our previously published technique of Instant Inkjet printing [9] which produces conductive silver traces with a domestic inkjet printer. The high spatial resolution and low resistance of inkjet-printed traces enables end-users to easily and rapidly output complex patterns on a thin paper or plastic substrate, which is ideal for connecting and powering circuit sticker elements.

Conductive epoxy has previously been used to attach components to a flexible substrate [6], and in [9] we suggested the use of anisotropic electrically conductive adhesive transfer tape (ECATT) [4]. ECATT is essentially double-sided conductive tape that only conducts from one side to the other and not across either surface, and it is much easier to use than epoxy. Unfortunately it results in electrically and mechanically fragile bonds when the contact area is small, which is the case for most electronic components. Circuit stickers work around these problems by mounting electronic components onto intermediate PCB carriers. This simple step is a key contribution of this work because it increases the substrate contact area and therefore makes the use of ECATT practical for a wide range of applications.

Flexible Circuits

Physically flexible circuits have been explored by many researchers. Buechley [3] developed several solder-less techniques for constructing working electronic circuits on paper – enabling games, interactive paintings and sculptures. Similarly, Freed et al. [5] used conductive tapes to build a kit of flexible sticky circuit pieces. Mellis et al. [10] presented ways to construct interactive artifacts using conductive ink, paper, off-the-shelf electronic components, and hardware and software tools. Savage et al. [11] demonstrated a new way to design and fabricate flexible touch sensors.

Circuit stickers, by virtue of their flexible substrate and conductive adhesive offer another point in the design space. They can be combined with all of these existing systems to improve ease of use or extend the design possibilities.

CIRCUIT STICKER IMPLEMENTATION DETAILS

Our initial approach was to create stickers encapsulating very basic circuit elements, such as individual components and simple sub-circuits. We designed a number of these to illustrate the concept and gain experience with simple interactive designs. Our *generic stickers* include a single electronic component footprint such as an 0805 passive or SOT-23 transistor. These are ideal for trying out new ideas because a wide range of electronic components can be soldered directly to them. More specific *sub-circuit stickers* which house a small group of components can be designed when a particular electronic device needs to be adopted, e.g. an analog accelerometer with decoupling and filtering or a simple microcontroller with support circuitry. Some of our initial circuit stickers are shown in Figure 2.

Figure 2: Circuit stickers. From left: generic 0805, piezo sounder, LED, coin-cell battery holder, 555 timer, hall-effect sensor, accelerometer, push button.

Figure 3: One-wire and I2C bus-based circuit stickers. The touch sensor (right) has extra connections for touch electrodes.

Circuit stickers are not a panacea. A knowledge of electronics is required and there is scope for human error when using them. Circuits with more than 10-15 stickers can become cumbersome. To mitigate these shortcomings we have also developed some *bus-based sticker* designs. In this case the stickers are used primarily for input and output, with computation, storage and communications offloaded to a conventional microcontroller or a PC. To explore this pattern of use, we created a bus-based sticker design, where several parallel traces are inkjet printed on the substrate to form a 1-wire or I2C bus between multiple stickers. The bus needs to carry power as well as data and the stickers have corresponding interfaces. See Figure 3.

All of our sticker prototypes adhere to some basic design rules determined through experimentation. The contact pads on the bottom of a sticker are typically 10-20mm^2 with a minimum dimension of 1.5mm and at least 1mm between adjacent pads. This ensures good electrical connection to the substrate but avoids short-circuits. We also ensured a total sticker size of at least 50mm^2 for mechanical stability. We have used two different PCB materials, FR4 and the more flexible Kapton, both ~0.15mm thick. To assemble, we either apply ECATT to the underside of the PCB and then trim off the excess material, or we apply a piece of ECATT to the substrate and then affix a bare sticker.

DIGITAL DESIGN TOOLS FOR CIRCUIT STICKERS

Instant inkjet circuit designs can be created using any software with a 'printable' output, e.g. Adobe Illustrator or Microsoft PowerPoint. However, manually creating a design which is compatible with the underside of each sticker and which also provides the necessary interconnections from scratch can be time consuming and error prone. To give a flavor of what is required, Figure 4 shows an example audio-frequency oscillator connected to a piezo sounder.

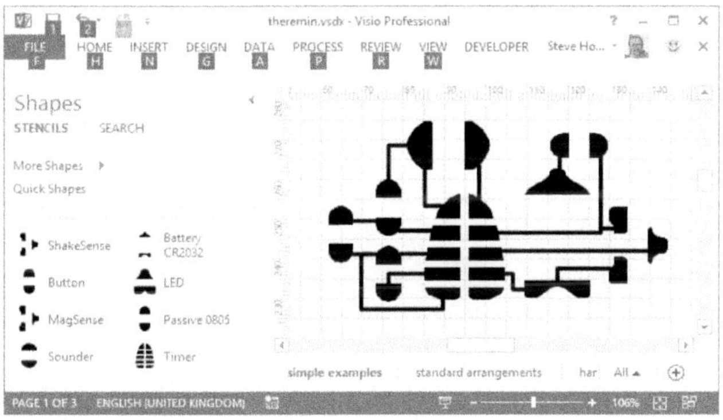

Figure 4: Using Visio to lay out a sticker circuit design.

To support the design process we built custom extensions to Microsoft Visio. We used the 'stencil' feature of Visio to define shapes which match the underside of each sticker circuit. The pads which make up these stencils are easily interconnected using the standard Visio 'connector' object.

A library of "pre-wired" common circuit sticker configurations was created to support re-use of previously developed and tested circuitry. This simplifies the creation of new designs. In addition, we used custom automation in Visio to allow it to automatically wire-up bus-based stencils. We use a simple algorithm which snakes the bus across the page, passing through each sticker on the bus (see Figure 7).

It is also possible to use standard PCB design tools like Eagle and Altium to design circuit sticker substrates. These have the necessary design rules built in and are much more powerful than our Visio extension, with interactive routing capabilities, trace impedance analysis etc. However, they also have a much higher learning curve.

CONSTRUCTING INTERACTIVE PROTOTYPES

To gauge the validity of our design decisions, we evaluated four different sticker circuit applications, each illustrating a different point in the design space. We hope that these will further explain our technique and how it can be used.

Simple lighting effects

Our earliest experiences with circuit stickers involved simple LED-based circuits built from substrates hand-crafted using conductive ink, self-adhesive copper tape, conductive threads and fabrics. These largely aesthetic designs (see Figure 5) were useful for validating the circuit sticker concept and refining our design rules.

A self-contained, creative musical toy

As a next step, we constructed a simple circuit using 8 different stickers. The center of the design was a 555 timer IC driving a piezo to create a noise-making toy. We incorporated a Hall effect sensor so that a magnet could be used to change the frequency of the 'note' being played. A coin cell powered the device via a push-button. See Figure 1.

Experimenting with gestural input

Our third example illustrates how circuit stickers can be combined with traditional electronics prototyping, by instrumenting a glove to sense the relative movement of the wearer's fingers. For this, we designed and printed a flexible circuit and trimmed it to match the shape of the glove. We placed accelerometer stickers at the fingertips and applied a 'connector sticker' to allow the circuit to be hooked up to an external microcontroller. A .NET Gadgeteer [4] system was used to create a microcontroller-based display and logger for the accelerometer values. See Figure 6.

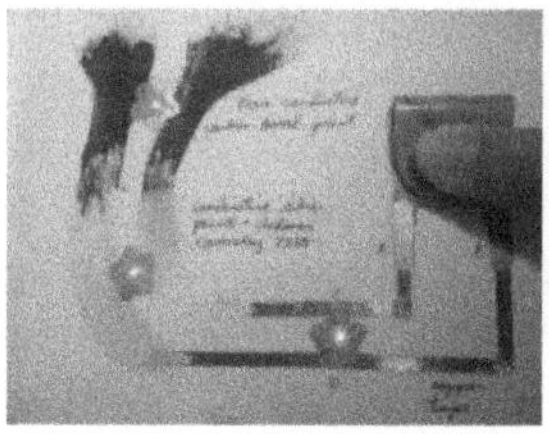

Figure 5: Mixed media.

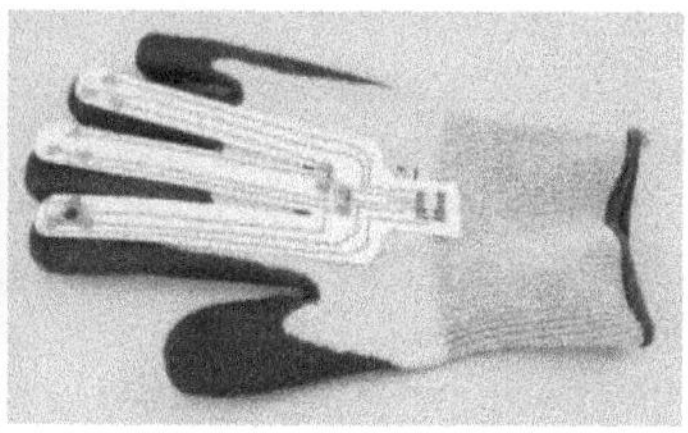

Figure 6: Glove sensor.

Prototyping touch-based interfaces using an I2C bus

Instant inkjet printing is a natural fit for experimenting with touch sensing electrodes. To facilitate this, we built a 'touch sensor sticker' which connects a Freescale MRP121 I2C touch sensor IC to 8 printed electrodes in addition to the I2C bus (see Figure 3). The sticker also has a multi-color LED. We connected four of these across a sheet of A4 paper to wire the bus to a Gadgeteer I2C bus master programmed to light LEDs based on touch interactions. This prototype is shown in Figure 7.

DISCUSSION AND FUTURE WORK

Performance

In our experience circuit stickers are pretty easy to work with. As long as care is taken to ensure correct alignment, applying them is quick, easy and natural. They show good mechanical and electrical robustness; we have circuits that work well several months after being built. Stickers may be re-used by removing them carefully and cleaning the underside (we use "Sticky stuff remover" by "De-Solv-it".)

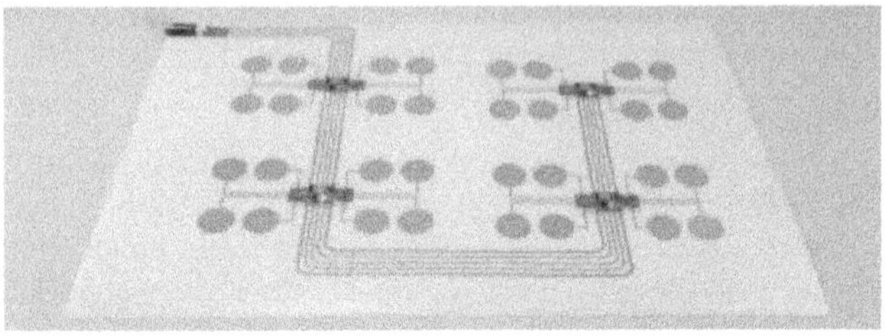

Figure 7: I2C bus-based design with distributed touch sensors and color LEDs. An I2C bus master connected by the yellow wires (top left) polls the touch sensors and controls the LEDs.

The sheet resistance of the Instant Inkjet traces introduces a measurable voltage drop, but for the circuits we constructed running an I2C bus at 100kbps was not an issue. However, it could be problematic for long traces or high currents. A solution for reducing resistive losses that we have successfully prototyped is to use a higher bus voltage in conjunction with a DC-DC converter on each sticker.

Further Aspects of Design

We would like to combine graphical elements using inkjet over-printing, and use laser cutting to support visually and functionally richer designs. We would also like to see how the stickers interface with other substrates, especially when cut, bent and folded into different configurations.

Other Application Areas

We have started exploring the use of circuit stickers in applications beyond creative design exploration and functional prototyping. For example, our approach could be a useful tool in education, encouraging a computational thinking mindset and helping students develop a better intuition of how electronic devices work. We imagine conductive worksheets which are used in conjunction with a class kit of circuit stickers. Basic stickers could be cheap enough for students to permanently keep working circuits.

Encouraging adoption

We would like others to build on our work. We have put design resources relating to our work online at http://research.microsoft.com/circuitstickers. In addition, at the time of writing, a basic range of open-source stickers including LEDs of different colours, specific controllers for these and a simple microcontroller are available to purchase at http://chibitronics.com. A new manufacturing technique developed by Andrew "bunnie" Huang allows kapton-based stickers to be supplied with ECATT pre-applied, making them easier to use. In addition to hobbyists and educators, we also imagine applications in design studio and research lab settings and are excited to explore these in future work.

CONCLUSION

By building and evaluating a number of different prototypes, we have demonstrated that circuit stickers can provide a practical alternative to traditional breadboarding and custom PCBs. When used in conjunction with the growing number of conductive printing technologies, circuit stickers support quick, versatile and easy electronics prototyping like breadboards, but they result in more compact and robust prototypes. Like PCBs, they are relatively easy to clone should more be needed, but they are much cheaper and quicker to make and naturally provide physical flexibility. Although PCBs can support more dense, sophisticated and durable prototypes, we believe that circuit stickers may have a useful role when these are not key considerations.

Our ultimate goal is to extend the tools and processes available for designing interactive prototypes. As we do this we hope to inform other practitioners working in this area by sharing our ideas and experiences in enough detail to enable them to adopt and adapt our work in new ways.

REFERENCES

1. Arduino. http://www.arduino.cc.
2. Ayah Bdeir. Electronics as material: littleBits. In *Proc of TEI '09*, pp. 397-400.
3. Buechley, L. et al. "Paints, Paper, and Programs: First Steps Toward the Computational Sketchbook" In *Proc. of TEI '09*, pp. 9-12.
4. 3M Electrically conductive adhesive transfer tape.
5. Freed, N. et al. Sticking together: handcrafting personalized communication interfaces. In *Proc IDC '11*.
6. Gong, N.-W.et al. Leveraging conductive inkjet technology to build a scalable and versatile surface for ubiquitous sensing. In *Proc of UbiComp '11*, pp. 45-54.
7. Greenberg, S., & Fitchett, C. Phidgets: Easy development of physical interfaces through physical widgets. In *Proc. of UIST '01*, ACM, 209-218.
8. Hartmann, B., Reflective physical prototyping through integrated design, test and analysis. In *Proc. UIST '06*.
9. Kawahara, Y et al., Instant Inkjet Circuits: Lab-based Inkjet Printing to Support Rapid Prototyping of UbiComp Devices. In *Proc of UbiComp '13*.
10. Mellis, D. A. et al. Microcontrollers as material: crafting circuits with paper, conductive ink, electronic components, and an "untoolkit". In *Proc of TEI '13*, pp. 83-90.
11. Savage, V. et al. Midas: fabricating custom capacitive touch sensors to prototype interactive objects. *Proc. of UIST '12*, 579–588.
12. Villar, N. & Gellersen, H. A malleable control structure for softwired user interfaces. In *Proc. of TEI '07*.
13. Villar, N. et al. .NET Gadgeteer: A Platform for Custom Devices. In *Proc. of Pervasive '12*, pp. 216-233.

Modeling the Perception of User Performance

Max Nicosia
School of Computer Science
University of St Andrews
St Andrews, Fife, UK
ln73@st-andrews.ac.uk

Antti Oulasvirta
Max Planck Institute for
Informatics and Saarland
University, Germany
oantti@mpi-inf.mpg.de

Per Ola Kristensson
School of Computer Science
University of St Andrews
St Andrews, Fife, UK
pok@st-andrews.ac.uk

ABSTRACT
This paper studies how users perceive their own performance in two alternative user interfaces. We extend methodology from psychophysics to the study of interactive performance and conduct two experiments in order to create a model of users' perception of their own performance. In our studies, two interfaces are sequentially used in a pointing task, and users are asked to rate in which interface their performance was higher. We first differentiate the effects of objective performance (speed and accuracy) versus interface qualities (distance between elements and width of elements) on perceived performance. We then derive a model that predicts the amount of change required in an interface for users to reliably detect a difference. The model is useful as a heuristic for predicting if a new interface design is better enough for users to reliably appreciate the obtained gain in user performance. We validate the model via a separate user study, and conclude by discussing how to apply our findings to design problems.

Author Keywords
Perception of user performance; psychophysics

ACM Classification Keywords
H.5.2 Information Interfaces and Presentation: User Interfaces—*Theory and methods*

INTRODUCTION
Present-day computer users are bombarded with possibilities to upgrade, modify, and switch software and hardware. Such changes trigger them to exercise judgment on the interface being presented to them. This could encompass the study of their perceived utility, perceived usability, or perceived user performance. This paper focuses on the perception of performance.

Despite the obvious importance of this topic to human-computer interaction (HCI), the question of how users perceive changes in interactive performance has not received serious attention. Knowledge on this topic would help designers with many tasks where they usually have to run empirical studies. For example, interface designers could focus on usability features where noticeable differences can be gained and marketers could focus advertisements of a new interface on aspects of an interface that users will most likely recognize as improvements. Theories and designers' conceptions of user experience [11, 12] make the point that it is not objective performance that matters but the user's experience and perception of it. However, the link between the perception of user performance and user interface design is not well understood.

CHI'14, April 26–May 1, 2014, Toronto, ON, Canada

http://dx.doi.org/10.1145/2556288.2557355

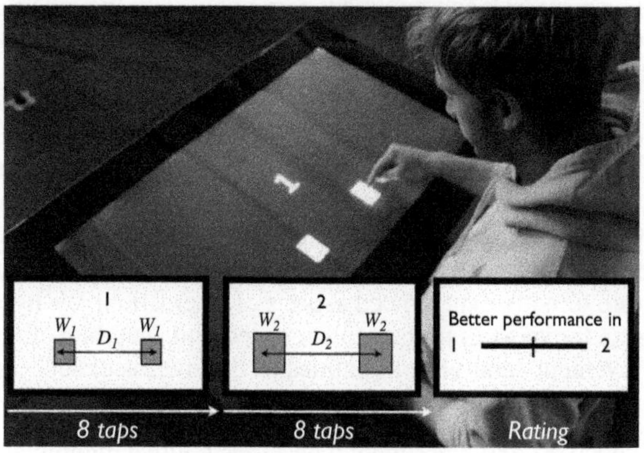

Figure 1. The experimental method in this paper is based on retrospective subjective comparison of two interfaces. Trial 1 and Trial 2 are followed by a rating screen.

This paper builds on *psychophysics methods* to study users' perception of which of two interfaces yields better performance for the same HCI task. In computer science, psychophysical models are used to optimize computer graphics [19], image processing [17], haptics [2], audio [27], and video [13]. In HCI, some psychophysics laws have gained recognition as design guidelines [14]. However, research has been limited to *time perception*, with applications to system response times and progress bars [10, 21].

Our goal is to extend psychophysical methodology to *interactive* tasks. One challenge is that user performance is not passive perception—it involves active engagement of the user over a longer period of time. Another challenge is that the standard psychophysics experiments typically consider relationships between two variables [5, 24]. However, user performance cannot be reduced to a single quality: users can base their judgment on two main categories of cues: *perceived qualities of the interface* and *perceived qualities of the user's own sensorimotor performance*. Important instances of the former in HCI are the size, distance, and density of interface elements. Examples of the latter are the speed and number of errors when performing a task, which constitute human performance more generally [20]. Complicating this further is the fact that such variables are necessarily interrelated. For example, a new design that enlarges the sizes of the targets, also affects the time and accuracy of users' target selections. For these reasons, the standard psychophysical methodology has not been readily applicable to interactive tasks.

The method we introduce in this paper includes an *aimed movement* task consecutively carried out with two alternative designs: the standard (the "old" interface), and the alternative (the "new" interface). A participant completes a tapping task with one design (Trial 1), then completes the same task with another design (Trial 2), and is finally asked to rate in which his or her performance was better (Figure 1). This emulates the use of two interfaces that are compared retrospectively. We regard perception of user performance as a second-order representation that is most likely constructed based on other, more directly experienced aspects of interaction. We hypothesize the most important to be: speed and accuracy of aimed movements and visual qualities of the interface, such as the distance to and the width of the target.

The key to our experimental design is that we manipulate *index of difficulty* (*ID*) (see for example [15, 20]) to exert a predictable effect on user performance. *ID* is the difficulty of movement required to select an interface element with a distance *D* and a width *W*; $ID = \log_2\left(\frac{D}{W}+1\right)$. By manipulating *ID*, and thus the difficulty of sensorimotor responses, we emulate the fact that the alternative design changes the user performance only indirectly: by affecting the demands placed on sensorimotor control and by changing the perception of the layout.

ID is controlled in two ways in the two experiments reported here. In Experiment 1, we keep the *ID* of the standard and the alternative design constant, but we change *D* (distance) and W (width). In Experiment 2, we use a *staircasing method*: the ΔID between the standard and the alternative interface is gradually increased until the user can reliably notice the difference in performance. These two manipulations allow us to address two central research questions:

Experiment 1: What are the criteria users use to judge that performance in one design is better than an alternative design?

Experiment 2: How large does a difference in user performance have to be for users to reliably notice it?

The two experiments map to two common decision contexts in interface design. Experiment 1 addresses what we call a *within-ID design*. In this case, the qualities of interface elements cannot be changed independently of each other. Limited display space would pose such a scenario: the size of the elements cannot be changed independent of inter-element distance. The second experiment addresses the *between-ID* case where the qualities of the new design *can* be changed independently. For example, smartphones with two different screen sizes would have different average *ID*s.

The results from our experiments expose several previously unreported phenomena on the contribution of different factors and biases. Based on the experimental data we develop a predictive model in the form of a mathematical function that can be used to estimate the percentage of users that will be able to identify a performance change between two interfaces with different *ID*s. Our model characterizes the probability of a user being able to reliably judge that there is a difference between two designs with different *ID*s. This model is validated via a separate task, a *Whac-A-Mole* type of game.

In summary, we contribute to the HCI literature by presenting a novel variation of a psychophysical method that we have adapted to interactive tasks. This methodology can be generalized to other studies of user performance in other interactive tasks. The presented model and obtained results are limited to *target acquisition* tasks. While this is a common sub-task in HCI, for example in command selection and typing [15], it leaves room for future work on other task domains. We conclude this paper with a discussion on how to use of this model and deploy the method to other task domains.

RELATED WORK

Psychophysics is the study of a human's perceived ability to distinguish a difference in physical stimuli and events. The classic psychophysics model, the *Weber–Fechner law*, states that equal stimulus ratios produce equal subjective ratios [24]. The *Just Noticeable Difference* (JND) is proportional to the size of the standard stimulus: JND = kS, where S is the size of the standard stimulus and k is a constant (a so-called Weber fraction). k is the proportionate increase the standard stimulus needs to change before it can be reliably discriminated. JND thresholds using the Weber–Fechner law and other models have been charted for perceptual events and for user interface qualities one can expect to be relevant: visual length and area, visual distance, visual velocity, visual flash rate, and duration [24].

Psychophysics research in HCI has focused on time perception, with applications to system response time and progress bars (e.g,. [10, 21]). Recently, cognitive load was found to affect time perception in an HCI task [3]. We are unaware of work in HCI addressing aspects of interactive tasks more broadly.

Evidence from psychology suggests that *interactive performance* can turn out to be special. Studies in psychology have found time perception to be affected by the allocation of attention during the task and the structuring of the stimulus environment [8]. Both attention and the stimulus environment are affected by the interface. More generally, it has been found that judgment tasks that involve *action* by the perceiver at times differ from passive tasks. In such cases, JND functions are not always Weberian and complex interactions emerge. Such tasks include the perception of motion as opposed to stationary stimuli [26] and visually-guided grasping [6]. Moreover, JND thresholds can change during an action. For instance, a moving hand is less sensitive to external stimuli than a static hand [18, 25]. Another complication is posed by multimodal perception. Visual and haptic information can produce superior discrimination when used jointly, compared to using either modality alone [7]. Similar multimodal-unimodal differences have been reported elsewhere (e.g. [4, 22]).

Given this brief overview, we deduce two requirements for our experimental method. First, the Weber–Fechner law, or any other known JND function, cannot be expected to apply. Thus the experimental method should allow a function of any shape to emerge. Second, the experimental method must be able to link perception to both 1) the observable qualities of the interface and 2) the observable qualities of performance.

GENERAL APPROACH

Our research interest is exploratory and encompasses two goals: The first is to understand the factors that affect the perception of user performance and the second is to chart JND thresholds for user performance.

Within a range of commonly studied HCI tasks—such as navigation, command selection and search—we chose *target acquisition* [15] for two reasons. First, visually controlled discrete aimed movements executed with the hand are prevalent in present-day HCI, and thus studies of target acquisition are relevant to a wide range of user interfaces. Second, there exists a well-established predictive model that links interface characteristics with user performance for target acquisition. Fitts' law [15, 23] predicts the movement time (MT) required for a user to hit a target with width W at distance D as:

$$MT = a + bID = a + b\log_2\left(\frac{D}{W} + 1\right), \qquad (1)$$

where a and b are empirically determined parameters[1]. Fitts' law implies that a user's information capacity, as measured by throughput (TP) in bits/s, stays relatively constant as a function of ID [23][2]:

$$TP = \frac{ID}{MT}. \qquad (2)$$

The two experiments in this paper exploit this tendency.

In Experiment 1, we hold ID constant and change D and W within an ID condition. This means that MT should stay at the same level for the the two to-be-compared interfaces, although the interface qualities D and W change. If judgments are based on TP, they should not favor either interface. If this is not the case, we will be able to assess the individual contributions of speed, accuracy, D, and W.

In Experiment 2, we manipulate ID with a so-called staircasing method [5]. We start from a minimum difference between two interfaces and subsequently increase the difference between the IDs (ΔID) with a constant step size until participants are able to reliably tell that their performance has changed. This exploits the prediction of Fitts' law that increasing ΔID increases the difference in MT as well (and possibly inaccuracy). The staircasing method thus allows charting judgment reliability as a function of ΔID.

[1] We use the Shannon variant of ID since the values are positive [15].

[2] For a critical view of this standard approach, see Guiard and Olafsdottir [9].

Knowing that aimed movements at different scales can be associated with different sensorimotor requirements[3], we sample the whole permissible range of IDs afforded by a large interactive surface (a Microsoft PixelSense, model Samsung SUR40). In the two experiments, we study four base-ID conditions ranging from very small (ID = 1.2, or "tray icon-sized") to large but still comfortable targets (ID = 2.4, similar to the Windows Start Menu). This allows us to examine if the size of the standard ID affects JND thresholds similar to the Weber-Fechner law.

To measure perception we use a rating scale where two sequentially used interfaces are directly compared on a slider ranging from −100 to 0 to +100. Participants are instructed to use the slider to express in which interface he or she experienced a "better performance". Performance is explained as the combination of how *quickly* and how *accurately* they were able to do the task [20]. Although rating is a motor task, we do not expect this to affect the reported differences. A measurement via a rating allows participants to use whatever criteria they deem reasonable to make the judgment. Moreover, the scalar value allows them to express their level of certainty. The known drawbacks of the rating scale are non-linearity of responses, order effects, and scale non-uniformity [5]. We address these in our analysis by making no assumptions of linearity or uniformity, and in the experimental design by randomizing the order of interfaces.

EXPERIMENT 1: CONSTANT INDEX OF DIFFICULTY

Our first experiment investigated if perception of performance is affected by four variables that characterize user performance—perceivable interface qualities: the width W and the distance D between targets; and objective performance qualities: speed and accuracy.

The ID of the two to-be-compared interfaces was kept constant, but W and D were manipulated. In order to examine if sensorimotor demands affect users' perception of performance, we investigated four different IDs.

Method

Participants and Experimental Design

We recruited 18 participants from a university campus. The mean age was 24 years, ranging from 19 to 31 years (sd = 3.2). Eight were female, ten were male. Their sight was normal or corrected-to-normal, and they reported no motor or neural disorders.

The experiment was a within-subjects design with one independent variable, ID, with four levels: 1.2, 1.6, 2.0 and 2.4. Sixty trials were carried out in each ID condition by each participant, each trial consisting of two interface designs. Participants performed eight target acquisition tasks in each interface design per trial. A *trial* consisted of two successive sub-trials followed by a rating task in which the participant rated which interface design (the former or the latter, or Trial 1 or Trial 2) resulted in a better perceived performance.

[3] For example, the wrist and the fingers may be used more for targets with small D and W.

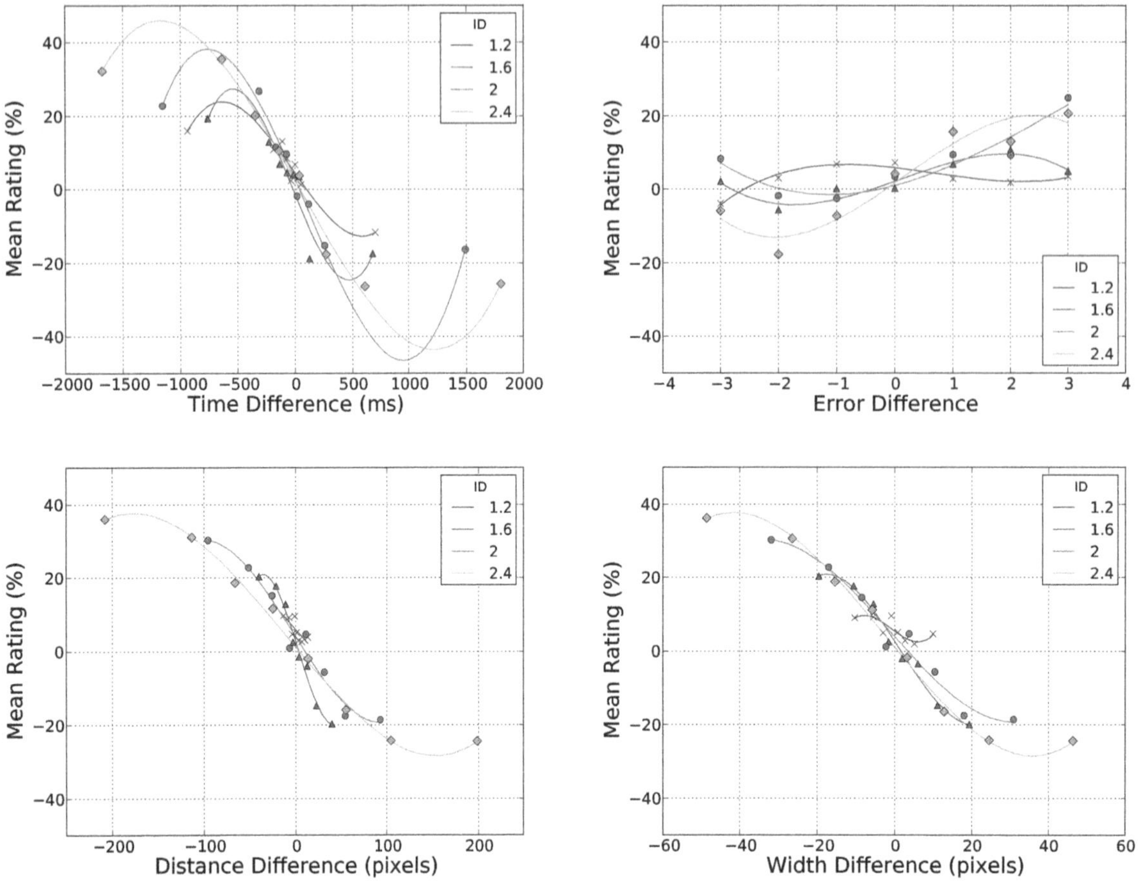

Figure 2. Contributions of *Time*, *Error*, *Distance*, and *Width* on the perception of performance in Experiment 1. Markers denote observed means for each bin, lines are regression models described in Table 1. The x-axes show the differences between interfaces in Trial 1 and Trial 2, the y-axes show the ratings: positive values refer to a preference for Trial 2 (the latter interface), while negative values refer to a preference for Trial 1.

For each trial, D and W were randomly sampled from a uniform distribution covering all permissible combinations within the ID condition. W was restricted to an interval ranging from 30 pixels (13.84 mm) to 173 pixels (79.80 mm) and D to an interval ranging from 39 pixels (17.99 mm) to 740 pixels (341.33 mm). The minimum D was limited by the feasibility of the minimum width for the smallest ID, while the maximum D was based on the screen resolution. ID conditions were balanced using a Latin square design.

Apparatus

The experiment was carried out on a Microsoft PixelSense, model Samsung SUR40. It had a resolution of 1920 × 1080 pixels (885.6 x 498.15 mm). The experimental software was developed in C# and used the Microsoft XNA framework and the Surface SDK. The software was designed to register touches through the surface API. A tolerance threshold was used in order to mitigate tracking errors that may occur on the apparatus for very fast movements. The precision of the timing data was in the order of microseconds.

Task and Procedure

Before starting the experiment, participants were instructed to familiarize themselves with the interface. The experimental task consisted of tapping two targets presented on the surface, sequentially, and as fast as possible without missing the target (see Figure 1). The current target was highlighted with a green color. The target areas were shaped as vertical columns, as in the original Fitts' unidimensional tapping task. Participants were instructed to aim for the middle part of the column that contained the target. However, the whole column was considered the target from the system's point of view. If the participant missed the target but was still within the tolerance range defined by the column, the system accepted the touch.

Each task had two interfaces (Trial 1 and Trial 2) followed by a judging task. Each trial consisted of eight reciprocal target acquisition tasks for a particular interface. Afterwards, the participant made a judgment on the performance of the interfaces by providing a rating on a continuous rating scale shown as a slider on the display (see Figure 1). The numbers "1" and "2" referred to the first and second interface with the corresponding label. Participants were instructed to treat the slider as a continuous rating scale, where the mid point was 0% difference in the interfaces, and each extreme meant a 100% difference in favor of either interface 1 or 2. We instructed participants to think of "performance" as the combination of how quickly and how accurately they were able to do the task.

In total, each participants performed 240 judging tasks (60 trials × 4 *IDs*), with two types of breaks interleaved to prevent fatigue. A 20-second break was scheduled for every 10 pairs of trials and a 1.5 minute break was scheduled for every 50 pairs of trials.

Results

The dependent variable *Rating* was calculated from the position of the slider as positioned by the participant. The left end of the slider was mapped to -100%, i.e. completely better performance in Trial 1 and the right end of the slider was mapped to +100%, i.e. completely better performance in Trial 2.

The predictive variables were calculated as the difference between Trial 1 and 2. *Time* was calculated as the difference in time taken to complete the tapping task in milliseconds, *Error* was calculated as the difference between the number of taps outside the target, *Distance* was calculated as the difference in the distance between the targets, and *Width* was calculated as the difference in the widths of the targets.

We here report general observations from the data and provide models for the effect of *Time*, *Error*, *Distance*, and *Width*. Observations outside three standard deviations were removed. Remaining ratings were grouped into bins per dependent variable, each bin containing roughly the same amount of observations. Binning for *Distance*, *Width* and *Time* was done by allocating 8 bins covering the entire range for each *ID* condition. The sizes of the bins increases with each *ID* as higher *IDs* span over greater ranges. Within each *ID*, bins also increase in width for larger values. For *Error* however, only the bins at either extreme contain more than one error value, all others contain a single error value.

Recency Bias

Overall, the average rating is close to zero, which is expected, because the *ID* was held constant and the order was randomized in both interfaces. However, participants demonstrated a slight *recency bias*—a bias towards the second and more recent interface they used (the second sub-trial) under all *ID* conditions. The bias was particularly pronounced in the lowest-*ID* condition. Calculated biases for *IDs* 1.2, 1.6, 2.0 and 2.4 were 5.80%, 1.35%, 3.94% and 3.82%.

Effects of Time, Error, Distance and Width

Figure 2 shows the effects of *Time*, *Error*, *Distance*, and *Width*, respectively. The markers represent the averaged observations per bin and the curves the fitted models listed in Table 1. Ratings range from -100.00% to 100.00%, where negative values correspond to a perception of better performance in the first interface (Trial 1), and positive values to better performance in the second interface (Trial 2). A rating of 0% expresses no noticeable difference. The following observations were made on the effects of the variables on the perception of user performance:

1. **Time**: *Time* had the strongest effect. Figure 2 shows a strong correlation between the rating and *Time*. The plot also reveals that the $\Delta Time$ required for participants to adjust the rating was affected by the *ID* condition. For $ID = 1.2$ the time difference was 500 ms, for 1.6 it was 700 ms and for *IDs* 2.0 and 2.4 they were 1000 ms and 1500 ms respectively. In the case of $ID = 1.2$, participants exhibited a clear recency bias. This may be due to the fact that perceiving a difference in D or W is relatively more difficult with larger and closer targets.

2. **Error**: Errors were not always taken into account when judging performance. $ID = 2.4$ showed a strong correlation between *Error* and rating ($r = 0.90$), while *ID*s 1.6 and 2.0 had a lower correlation ($r = 0.69$). For *IDs* 1.6 and 2.0, participants tended to be biased towards the second interface regardless of the number of errors in each trial. Again, $ID = 1.2$ is an outlier: participants tended to rate the first interface as providing higher performance even if they made more mistakes with it. However, as Figure 2 shows, this effect was negligible.

3. **Distance and width**: Figure 2 shows that *Distance* and *Width* affected judging performance for *ID*s 1.6, 2.0 and 2.4 but, again, *ID* 1.2 did not provide reliable grounds for performance judgments. In this case, the ratings were dominated by the recency bias. This is because the ratings tended to be positive if *any* difference in D or W was present.

Regression Models

Table 1 lists the regression models that best explained the data. Line plots for the models are shown in Figure 2, together with the observed points. The regression models for D and W can explain 94–95% of the variance for *ID*s 1.6–2.4. Interestingly, these models for *ID* 1.2 can only explain 51% and 42% of the variance respectively. For $ID = 1.2$, the strongest predictor appears to be *Error* ($R^2 = 0.91$) and *Time* ($R^2 = 0.88$). To conclude, except for $ID = 1.2$, the observations reported in the previous subsection could be captured by psychometric functions.

Regression Model		
Time	*ID*	R^2
$4.04 \times 10^{-8}x^3 + 2.99 \times 10^{-6}x^2 - 4.50 \times 10^{-2}x + 4.50$	1.2	0.88
$1.00 \times 10^{-7}x^3 + 1.05 \times 10^{-5}x^2 - 7.67 \times 10^{-2}x - 1.34$	1.6	0.79
$3.36 \times 10^{-8}x^3 - 9.63 \times 10^{-6}x^2 - 7.32 \times 10^{-2}x + 2.88$	2	0.96
$1.30 \times 10^{-8}x^3 - 9.28 \times 10^{-7}x^2 - 5.60 \times 10^{-2}x + 2.50$	2.4	0.98
Error		
$3.47 \times 10^{-1}x^3 - 7.13 \times 10^{-1}x^2 - 1.88x + 5.87$	1.2	0.91
$-5.64 \times 10^{-1}x^3 + 1.55 \times 10^{-1}x^2 + 5.64x + 2.12$	1.6	0.80
$-1.73 \times 10^{-1}x^3 + 1.57x^2 + 4.20x + 9.67 \times 10^{-1}$	2	0.81
$-7.56 \times 10^{-1}x^3 + 3.81 \times 10^{-1}x^2 + 1.11 \times 10^{1}x + 1.68$	2.4	0.85
Distance		
$-2.78 \times 10^{-1}x + 5.94$	1.2	0.51
$1.83 \times 10^{-4}x^3 - 1.50 \times 10^{-3}x^2 - 7.96 \times 10^{-1}x + 2.73$	1.6	0.97
$1.46 \times 10^{-5}x^3 + 1.68 \times 10^{-4}x^2 - 3.92 \times 10^{-1}x + 4.04$	2	0.94
$3.65 \times 10^{-6}x^3 + 1.24 \times 10^{-4}x^2 - 2.98 \times 10^{-1}x + 1.25$	2.4	0.99
Width		
$5.39 \times 10^{-3}x^3 + 1.40 \times 10^{-2}x^2 - 7.65 \times 10^{-1}x + 5.42$	1.2	0.42
$1.47 \times 10^{-3}x^3 - 6.11 \times 10^{-3}x^2 - 1.60x + 2.64$	1.6	0.97
$3.84 \times 10^{-4}x^3 + 1.57 \times 10^{-3}x^2 - 1.17x + 3.96$	2	0.95
$2.85 \times 10^{-4}x^3 + 2.39 \times 10^{-3}x^2 - 1.28x + 1.07$	2.4	0.99

Table 1. Regression models for the judgment of performance separately for the independent variables *Time*, *Error Distance* and *Width* for each of the four base-*ID* conditions in Experiment 1.

EXPERIMENT 2: STAIRCASING

In Experiment 2, the difference between the two interfaces, or ΔID, was manipulated using the *staircasing* method with

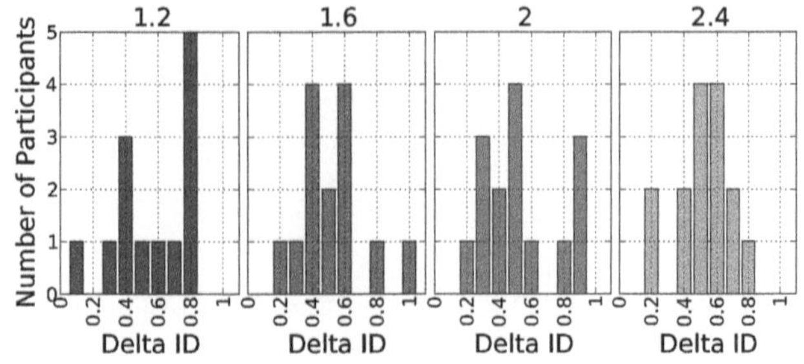

Figure 3. The number of participants that correctly judged 91% (or more) of the trials in Experiment 2 as the ΔID was increased.

a constant increase (0.1) between the steps. We started comparisons from four base-*ID* conditions (1.2, 1.6, 2.0, 2.4), increasing ΔID of the two to-be-compared interfaces gradually until the user could notice a difference with >90% reliability. The term *sub-stair* refers to a trial with a particular ΔID.

Method

We here only report the differences in method compared to Experiment 1.

Participants, Apparatus and Materials

We recruited 16 participants from a university campus. The mean age was 30.5 years, ranging from 22 to 55 years (*sd* = 8.4). Five were female, 11 were male. There sight was normal or corrected-to-normal, and they reported no motor or neural disorders. None of the participants had participated in Experiment 1.

Task and Procedure

Unlike Experiment 1, in Experiment 2 participants were explicitly told that the *ID* of the two interfaces (Trial 1 and 2) were different. This was necessary because the difference would become salient as the ΔID increased. They were told that there were four different difficulty levels (base-*IDs*) and that promotion to the next level only occurred when they identified the interface that yielded the highest performance in more than 90% of the trials (10 out of 11 judgments). They were instructed to judge their performance using the same definition of performance provided in Experiment 1. In the case they could not notice any difference, participants were instructed to provide their best guess and to avoid a 0% rating. If a participant was *unable* to judge a difference correctly by the 10th attempt, he or she was promoted to the next base-*ID*. In the case of the last stair, a *limit* was set by the maximum *ID* allowed. This *limit* was set because randomly sampling combinations of *D* and *W* for *ID*s higher than 3.2 provided too many distances that are far beyond the physical limits imposed by the resolution of the multitouch display used in the experiment. If participants made too many target selection errors the system beeped and forced the same sub-stair to be repeated.

Results

Our main dependent variable for Experiment 2, *Judgment-Reliability*, was the probability of perceiving an interface with a lower *ID* to yield a better user performance. It was calculated as the proportion of trials correctly judged out of the

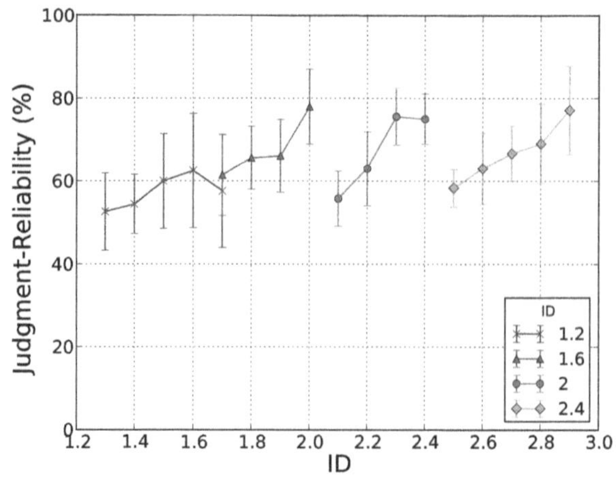

Figure 4. Mean judgment as a function of sub-stair in Experiment 2. Each base-ID is plotted as a separate line. The plot shows only sub-stairs that have at least 2/3 of participants remaining. Error bars show 95% confidence intervals.

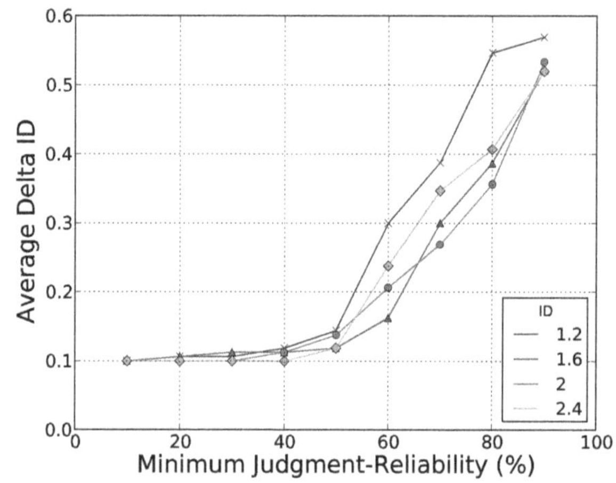

Figure 5. Average ΔID for each minimum Judgment-Reliability level by stair in Experiment 2.

total trials for a sub-stair. A participant was considered to judge correctly when he or she rated the sub-trial with the lower *ID* as providing higher performance, ultimately reducing judgment to a binary decision.

Figure 3 shows a histogram of the number of participants that correctly identified a performance difference on each sub-stair for each stair-*ID*. There are two key observations. First, no stair showed a 100% completion rate; that is, not all participants were able to achieve a correct judgment above 90% before being pushed onto the next stair. Second, completion rate increased through the stairs. The number of participants that successfully detected a difference was 13, 14, 15 and 15 for *IDs* 1.2, 1.6, 2 and 2.4 respectively.

Figure 4 shows mean Judgment-Reliability per sub-stair for each of the base-*IDs*. Only sub-stairs including at least 2/3 of the participants are included in the figure, to ensure representativeness of the whole user group. Figure 4 reveals the

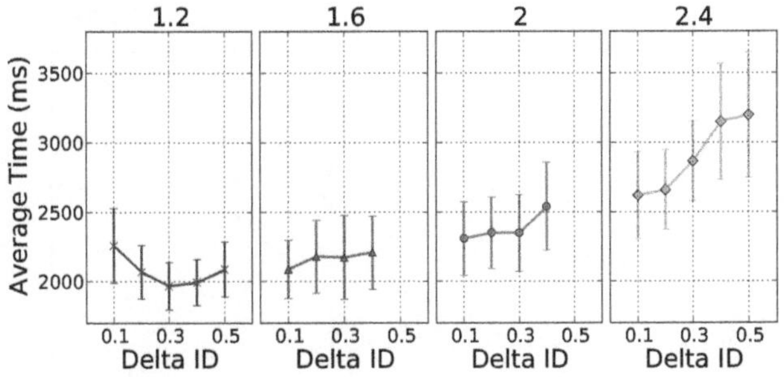

Figure 6. Average time in milliseconds per sub-stair for each stair in Experiment 2. Only sub-stairs containing at least 2/3 of participants are shown.

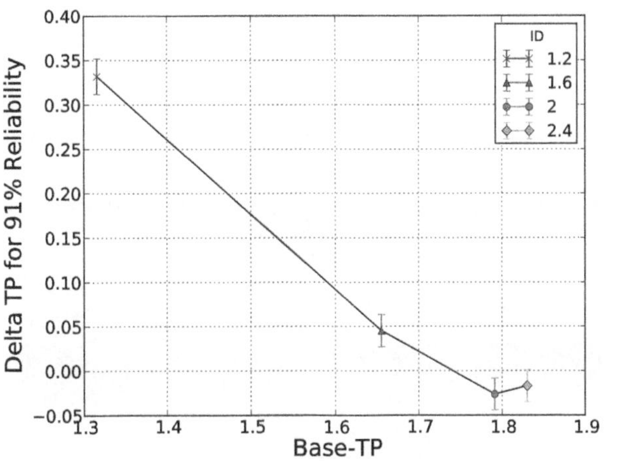

Figure 7. Average ΔTP required for a 91% reliable judgment in performance in Experiment 2, where $TP = ID/MT$. Error bars show 95% confidence intervals.

expected trend that the reliability of perceiving a performance difference increased as participants progressed "up" the sub-stairs, coinciding with increases in completion rates.

Figure 5 shows the average ΔID by minimum Judgment-Reliability. Figure 5 confirms the already mentioned trend that the reliability increased as participants progressed "up" the sub-stairs. Moreover, it also shows that the intuition that can be gained from the histogram in Figure 3 of approximately six sub-stairs being necessary for most participants ($\sim$70%) to reliably notice a difference holds. Base-*ID* $= 1.2$ is the exception, for reasons observed in Experiment 1: for this base-*ID*, participants struggled to reliably judge differences due to the small changes in *Distance* and *Width*.

Relationship between ID and Time

Participants tended to take longer to complete the pointing task on later stairs. Figure 6 shows the average *Time* in milliseconds for each sub-stair that still contains at least 2/3 of the participants. The plot shows that *Time* remains fairly constant for the first two stairs, but it increases steadily on the last two stairs, revealing the increased difficulty in tapping the targets. In other words, there is a linear component as presumed by Fitts' law, and some curvature at the extremes due to changes in sensorimotor demands.

Effect of Throughput (TP)

An outstanding question is to what extent it is (TP) that is predictive of Judgment-Reliability, rather than ID.

Figure 7 shows the difference in TP required for a 91% reliable judgment, shown as a function of base-TP. TP was calculated as $TP = ID_e/MT$, where $ID_e = \log_2((D/W_e) + 1)$. W_e was calculated as 4.133 multiplied by the standard deviation of all total widths for the condition [15], where a total width was defined as the distance from the center of the target to the x-coordinate where the user touched.

If Interface A is able to provide TP_a bits/s and Interface B TP_b bits/s, how likely is that difference noticeable? We chose the 91 percent cut-off as it corresponds to the stair advance rule used by our method. However, because we did not manipulate throughput (TP) but ID in our experiment, we have a narrower range of TP-differences in the data. This analysis should therefore be regarded as tentative.

The main observation is that *smaller* TP differences are required for larger base-TPs. In other words, when user performance is high, only a small difference is required. However, when it is very high (here, above 1.7 bits/s), TP does not predict the reliability of judgments. Instead, users use some other criteria. In contrast, for low-TP conditions, users require a relatively large (0.35 bits/s) difference. Comparing the curve to our analysis of ID, we conclude that ID is a more powerful predictor for this task.

Individual Differences

To learn about individual differences, we split participants into two groups according to the median of *Judgment-Reliability*. "Better judgers" showed a tendency to stick to two particular strategies when rating their performance: differences in *Width* and *Distance*, or differences in *Time*. For stair-*ID*s 1.2 and 1.6 these participants judged correctly when the *Time* difference was above 500 ms. This practice decreased in the higher stairs as the increase in distance reduced the capacity to estimate *Time*. Participants instead chose shorter *Distances* and smaller *Widths* (depending on the interface quality they looked at) when being unable to estimate *Time*. In contrast, the worse judgers do not reveal an obvious behavioral pattern.

Modeling

Table 2 presents regression models fitted on the data that predict the probability that a participant detected a performance difference for a given ΔID.

To make the models presented in Table 2 more generalizable and reduce the proneness to overfitting we set out to identify a

Regression Model	ID	R^2
$1.38/\left(1+e^{(-0.23-\log x)/0.46}\right)$	1.2	0.96
$0.88/\left(1+e^{(-0.81-\log x)/0.24}\right)$	1.6	0.99
$1.05/\left(1+e^{(-0.73-\log x)/0.39}\right)$	2.0	0.98
$1.08/\left(1+e^{(-0.70-\log x)/0.30}\right)$	2.4	0.97

Table 2. Regression models predicting the probability a participant reliably detected a performance difference as a function of ΔID in Experiment 2.

simplified general predictive model. We found such a model in the form of a variant of the logistic function. This model, referred to as the *generalized model* from now on, predicts the probability $p(x)$ that a user will judge his or her performance as different between two alternative interfaces separated by an ID step-size of x is:

$$p(x) = \frac{1}{1 + e^{-(ax-b)}}, \quad (3)$$

where a and b are model parameters. Based on our data we estimate $a = 8$, $b = 4$. The generalized model is shown with a dashed line in Figure 8 (*GenMod*). We evaluated this model against the actual judging data we collected in Experiment 2 and found that it had good fit for the actual observed frequencies of users being able to reliably judge their performance as being noticeably better for a given ID step-size. The R^2 goodness of fits were 0.71 for $ID = 1.2$, 0.94 for $ID = 1.6$, 0.92 for $ID = 2.0$, 0.98 for $ID = 2.4$, and 0.94 for all IDs.

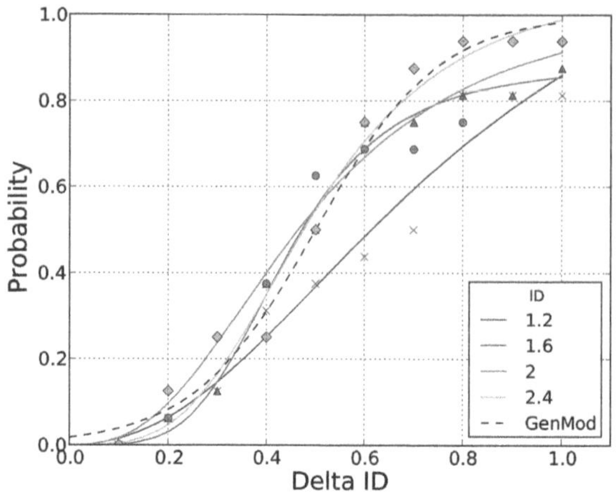

Figure 8. Cumulative probability of reliable judgment in Experiment 2. The models are rendered for base-*ID*s, and the generalized model (see the text) is shown with a dashed line. The plotted points are the cumulative number of participants that had detected the *ID* change by that sub-stair.

Figure 9. An illustration of the *Whac-a-Mole* game.

MODEL VALIDATION STUDY

Having identified the generalized model from data collected in Experiment 2, we validated its predictive power on an alternative task outside of the experimental framework that shaped its functional form. For this purpose we created a variant of the *Whac-A-Mole* game for the Microsoft PixelSense, model Samsung SUR40. In the game, the user has to hit two sets of five circular targets (see Figure 9) in a predetermined order as quickly as possible. Thereafter the user chooses which of the trials resulted in a higher performance.

Method

Each of the circular targets were set with a constant ID. The width of the target was sampled uniformly from an interval between 30 pixels (13.84 mm) and 199 pixels (91.79 mm). The distance to the target was then fully determined by the fixed ID and the width of the target. The configuration of the five targets was randomly generated within the constraints given above. In the game, when the user hit the "Start" button a pre-determined circular target was highlighted. The user was instructed to hit this target as quickly as possible. Thereafter another circular target was highlighted. When the user had hit all the highlighted targets the game was over. The highlighted sequence guided the user through a series of target acquisitions that all had the same ID for an individual game, but all the targets had randomly generated widths and heights within the constraints given above.

We recruited 11 participants from a university campus. The average age was 26.3 years, ranging from 20 to 55 years (*sd* = 11.2). Five were female, six were male. None of the participants had participated in Experiment 1 or 2.

Using the same definition of performance as in Experiment 1 and 2, participants were asked after every two games to choose the game in which they perceived they experienced a better performance. Each pair of games compared a particular base-ID against an alternative ID. To make the results of our validation exercise stronger we took two measures to reduce the possibility of false-positives. First, we took three out of three correct judgments as proof of a participant recognizing a change in performance, thus the probability of choosing the correct ID by chance was only $\frac{1}{8}$. Second, we selected a single base-ID of 0.9. This choice was made based on the observations from Experiment 2, where we noticed that participants had greater difficulty in recognizing differences in low-ID conditions. Coincidentally, this makes the prediction task of our generalized model more challenging as the chosen base-ID for the game is lower than the lowest base-ID of 1.2, which had the worst R^2 fit in Experiment 2.

In the game we compared nine ΔIDs: $0.1, 0.2, \ldots, 0.9$ for a single base-ID of 0.9. Thus, the ID comparisons ranged from 0.9–1.8. In total, each user played 1 base-ID $\times$ 9 ΔIDs $\times$ 3 pairs of games per ID comparison = 54 games (27 pairs of games). It took a user circa 7–8 minutes to play all 54 games, which mimics a typical walk-up use-scenario for a tabletop interface.

Results

We calculated the probabilities of a user detecting a change in the base-ID in the data. The procedure was identical to Experiment 2. We then compared the generalized model of perceivable performance gain using the same parameters $a = 8$, $b = 4$ we found in Experiment 2.

We found that the judgments about the *ID* differences in the game had an R^2 goodness of fit of 0.72. This should be compared against the closest comparable base-*ID* we used in Experiment 2 (*ID* = 1.2) and its R^2 model fit of 0.71, which was obtained in a much more controlled setup with less noisy data and more participants. Our good model fit for the game data indicates that our generalized model of perceivable performance gain does generalize beyond the experimental task that shaped its functional form and model parameters.

SUMMARY AND DISCUSSION

Psychophysics models are of paramount importance in graphics, audio, and multimedia, thanks to their ability to directly inform design and engineering. Psychophysics could be a useful asset in the HCI toolbox, too, if it allows us to make reliable quantitative predictions about the effect of a change in an interface on users' perception of interaction. This paper has extended the application of psychophysics in HCI from passive perception to interaction.

To this end, we have presented a method for operationalizing another important psychophysical dependent variable in HCI: a user's *perception* of his or her own performance in a user interface. By definition, user performance is the efficiency of a user carrying out a task [20], which in HCI is measured in terms of speed and accuracy aggregated over acts exhibited in the course of a task. We have presented an adaptation of psychophysics methodology into an interactive task. A central insight is that a change in interface design assumes its potential effect via two interconnected routes: via overt perceivable changes and via changes in a user's objective performance. Changing something in a layout may be noticeable via perception of the elements and/or via how it changes the speed and accuracy of a user's performance. This was operationalized by manipulating the *difficulty* of sensorimotor movement via *ID*. We registered both interface qualities and objective user performance to predict the user's judgment. A drawback in comparison to more realistic tasks is that the two interfaces in our experiments are used immediately after one another, whereas in actual use they are probably separated more in time.

The results in this paper provide insights into users' perception of interaction. In Experiment 1, we found that:

- Users can indeed reliably judge their performance, but they also exhibit slight biases. Low-*ID* conditions were markedly different from others: interfaces consisting of large targets close to each other provide no reliable ground for judging one's performance.
- *Width* and *Distance* are not as important cues as *Time*: when interfaces look similar, the differences in the user's own performance dominate the judgment.

In Experiment 2, a staircasing design enabled us to learn what happens when *ID* changes between two to-be-compared interfaces. We learned that, depending on the base-*ID*, users' judgment capabilities change. In particular:

- For small base-*ID*s, users struggle to consistently identify differences.
- Higher base-*ID*s perform better because participants can obtain more information to make their judgment, such as greater changes in *Distance*, *Width* and *Time*. These differences are needed to improve the reliability of users' judgments.
- Throughput (*TP*) is not as strong a predictor as *ID* is. Judgment reliability seems to only be predictable for low-*TP*s.
- In no case was the user's perception of performance reducible to *ID* alone, which confirms that the perception of performance is disjoint from actual performance as measured by *TP*.
- There are inter-subject differences in judgment ability.

Further, we have discovered a mathematical model that predicts the probability that a user will notice a performance difference, as defined by a change in *ID*. The model was validated in a *Whac-A-Mole* game, which demonstrated that the model's predictions generalized to at least one other HCI task involving discrete aimed movement.

However, we acknowledge that there could be other effects influencing the user, which he or she could not perceive, especially over a prolonged period of time. For example, when the visual layout is more complex, users will have more cues than distance and width of targets that they can use to assess the user interface. Moreover, when the interaction task is a compound task (i.e. it consists of many subtasks), users might base their performance judgments with respect to any of the subtasks. However, we believe that the results in this paper are promising enough to motivate further research in this direction.

Application to Design Problems

Currently, the models derived in this paper can be considered heuristics for interfaces where pointing is important. Such activities involve command selection (menus, hotkeys, etc.), text entry and gaming.

The regression models in Table 1 require knowing the *ID* of the two user interfaces to be compared, and the difference that is most pronounced between them: this can be the user's speed, accuracy, target distances, or target widths. A model should be selected based on this information.

The regressions models in Table 2 require knowing the *ID*s of the two user interfaces that are being compared. The lower of these should match or must be matched to the closest base-*ID* in the table. The output of the model is an estimation of the probability that a user will be able to *reliably* notice the difference in user performance.

It is important to note that the regression models in Table 2 are likely to suffer from overfitting. For general design problems we recommend using the generalized model in Equation 3.

CONCLUSIONS

Psychophysics modeling could have numerous applications in HCI beyond its current limited use. We envision that the ability to better anticipate the subjective perception of interaction might save substantial money in interface development.

The methodology presented in this paper is a starting point for understanding the perception of user performance more fully. With little effort, the paradigm could be extended to continuous aimed movements [1], allowing the study of steering and pursuit tasks common in for example gaming and driving. The methodology can also be extended to tasks involving timing and rhythm, such as music [16]. To extend it beyond aimed movements, the challenge is to find models that allow manipulating user performance with predictable effects.

ACKNOWLEDGEMENTS

This research was supported by the Scottish Informatics and Computer Science Alliance, the Max Planck Centre for Visual Computing and Communication and the Cluster of Excellence for Multimodal Computing and Interaction at Saarland University. Max Nicosia's undergraduate internship in St Andrews was supported by a donation from Nokia.

REFERENCES

1. Accot, J., and Zhai, S. Beyond Fitts' law: models for trajectory-based HCI tasks. In *Proc. CHI 1997*, ACM Press (1997), 295–302.
2. Biggs, S. J., and Srinivasan, M. A. Haptic interfaces. In *Handbook of Virtual Environments*, K. M. Stanney, Ed. Lawrence Earlbaum, 2002, 93–116.
3. Block, F., and Gellersen, H. The impact of cognitive load on the perception of time. In *Proc. NordiCHI 2010*, ACM Press (2010), 607–610.
4. Brewer, B. R., Fagan, M., Klatzky, R. L., and Matsuoka, Y. Perceptual limits for a robotic rehabilitation environment using visual feedback distortion. *IEEE Transactions on Neural Systems and Rehabilitation Engineering 13*, 1 (2005), 1–11.
5. Cunningham, D., and Wallraven, C. *Experimental Design: From User Studies to Psychophysics*. AK Peters, Ltd., 2011.
6. Ganel, T., Chajut, E., and Algom, D. Visual coding for action violates fundamental psychophysical principles. *Current Biology 18*, 14 (2008), R599–R601.
7. Gephstein, S., and Banks, M. S. Viewing geometry determines how vision and haptics combine in size perception. *Current Biology 13*, 6 (2003), 483–488.
8. Grondin, S. Timing and time perception: a review of recent behavioral and neuroscience findings and theoretical directions. *Attention, Perception, & Psychophysics 72*, 3 (2010), 561–582.
9. Guiard, Y., and Olafsdottir, H. B. On the measurement of movement difficulty in the standard approach to Fitts' law. *PloS ONE 6*, 10 (2011), e24389.
10. Hamada, K., Yoshida, K., Ohnishi, K., and Koppen, M. Color effect on subjective perception of progress bar speed. In *Proc. INCoS 2011*, IEEE Press (2011), 863–866.
11. Hassenzahl, M. The thing and I: understanding the relationship between user and product. *Funology* (2005), 31–42.
12. Law, E. L.-C., Roto, V., Hassenzahl, M., Vermeeren, A. P. O. S., and Kort, J. Understanding, scoping and defining user experience: A survey approach. In *Proc. CHI 2009*, ACM Press (2009), 719–728.
13. Le Gall, D. MPEG: A video compression standard for multimedia applications. *Communications of the ACM 34*, 4 (1991), 46–58.
14. Lidwell, W., Holden, K., and Butler, J. *Universal Principles of Design*. Rockport Publishers, 2010.
15. MacKenzie, I. S. Fitts' law as a research and design tool in human-computer interaction. *Human-Computer Interaction 7*, 1 (1992), 91–139.
16. Maury, S., Athénes, S., and Chatty, S. Rhythmic menus: toward interaction based on rhythm. In *Ext. Abstr. CHI 1999*, ACM Press (1999), 254–255.
17. Nadenau, M. J., Winkler, S., Alleysson, D., and Kunt, M. Human vision models for perceptually optimized image processing—a review, 2000. Unpublished manuscript.
18. Rank, M., Shi, Z., J. Müller, H., and Hirche, S. Perception of delay in haptic telepresence systems. *Presence: Teleoperators and Virtual Environments 19*, 5 (2010), 389–399.
19. Reddy, M. Perceptually optimized 3D graphics. *IEEE Computer Graphics and Applications 21*, 5 (2001), 68–75.
20. Sanders, A. F. *Elements of Human Performance: Reaction Processes and Attention in Human Skill*. Lawrence Erlbaum, 1998.
21. Seow, S. C. *Designing and Engineering Time: The Psychology of Time Perception in Software*. Addison-Wesley, 2008.
22. Shi, Z., Hirche, S., Schneider, W. X., and Muller, H. Influence of visuomotor action on visual-haptic simultaneous perception: A psychophysical study. In *Proc. Haptics 2008*, IEEE Press (2008), 65–70.
23. Soukoreff, R. W., and MacKenzie, I. S. Towards a standard for pointing device evaluation, perspectives on 27 years of Fitts' law research in HCI. *International Journal of Human-Computer Studies 61*, 6 (2004), 751–789.
24. Stevens, S. S. On the psychophysical law. *Psychological Review 64*, 3 (1957), 153–181.
25. Yang, X. D., Bischof, W. F., and Boulanger, P. Perception of haptic force magnitude during hand movements. In *Proc. ICRA 2008*, IEEE Press (2008), 2061–2066.
26. Zanker, J. M. Does motion perception follow Weber's law? *Perception 24* (1995), 363–372.
27. Zwicker, E., and Zwicker, U. T. Audio engineering and psychoacoustics: Matching signals to the final receiver, the human auditory system. *Journal of the Audio Engineering Society 39*, 3 (1991), 115–126.

Edit Distance Modulo Bisimulation: A Quantitative Measure to Study Evolution of User Models

Himanshu Zade[1,2], S. A. Adimoolam[1], Sai Gollapudi[1], Anind K. Dey[2], and Venkatesh Choppella[1]

[1]Pascal Lab, SERC, IIIT-Hyderabad, India — [2]Ubicomp Lab, HCII, CMU, Pittsburgh, USA

ABSTRACT
When a user learns to use a new device, her understanding of it evolves. A progressive comparison of the evolving *user models* towards the device *target model*, for analysing learning, involves determining the behavioral proximity between them. To quantify the gap between a user model and a target model, we introduce an *edit distance* metric for measuring their behavioral proximity using a bisimulation-based equivalence relation. We define edit distance to be the minimum number of edges and states with incident edges required to be deleted from *and/or* added to a user model to make it bisimilar to the target model. We propose an algorithm to compute edit distance between two models and employ the heuristic procedure on experimental data for computing edit distance between target and user models. The data is organised into two experiments depending on the device the user interacted with: (a) a simple device resembling a vending machine and (b) a close to real-world vehicle transmission model. The results validate our proposed metric as edit distance converges with progressive user learning, increases for erroneous learning, and remains unchanged indicating no learning.

Author Keywords
Learning; finite state machines; behavioral proximity.

ACM Classification Keywords
H.1.2 User/Machine Systems: Human Factors; F.1.1 Models of Computation: Relation between models; D.2.2 Design Tools and Techniques: State diagrams

INTRODUCTION
The rapid proliferation of technology challenges users to quickly become familiar with any new device that they may encounter. User interface (UI) designers, on the other hand, are challenged to provide UIs that are easy to learn and use. In order to do so, they need to understand how a user gets acquainted with a new device. Insight about how a user learns to use a device helps in designing better UIs, creating new interventions to assist learning, quantifying the speed of learning, all of which improve both the efficiency and effectiveness of the user's interaction and experience with the device.

CHI 2014, April 26–May 1, 2014, Toronto, Ontario, Canada.

http://dx.doi.org/10.1145/2556288.2557191

Mental models (*i.e.* mental representations of a user's understanding) are important in learning how to operate a device [24]. We use the term *user model* to refer to a finite state machine (FSM) representing the user's understanding of a device [20, 33]. In contrast to the user model, we use the term *target model* to refer to the FSM representing the behavior of the device, which the end user is trying to learn [37]. For a user to understand the complete behavior of a device, it is essential that her final user model is bisimilar to (*i.e.* its behavior is indistinguishable from) the target model [26]. The user may attain such a model if her multiple user models progressively approach the target model, while interacting with the device to learn it. Relatively little attention has been paid to how user models evolve as a part of a user's learning process.

FSMs have long been used to represent mental models [20]. In this paper, we build on the past work in FSMs, contribute an edit distance metric for comparing the differences between FSMs, and apply this to represent the process of how a user learns to use a new device, by tracing the evolution of user models towards a target model. We study user learning through a progressive comparison of the user model and target model over time. (Bi)simulation relations allow behavioral comparisons between two models [26]; they hold true for a user model indicating complete understanding of a device, false otherwise. However during learning, user models may be incomplete, erroneous and contradictory [14]. It is therefore important to quantify the amount of learning. This translates to the problem of determining the proximity between the two models. (Bi)simulation relations by themselves do not provide such a metric to measure proximity; they capture the notion of order, and not measure. To quantify the gap between a user model and a target model, we introduce *edit distance* for measuring behavioral proximity between them.

The edit distance metric is based on two propositions: (a) A target model can simulate a user model by deleting some edges from the user model. (b) The *edited* user model can now be made bisimilar to the target model by adding some edges and states with incident edges. We define edit distance as the sum of the minimum number of such deletions and additions, as proposed above. We use a heuristic procedure for manually calculating edit distance between FSMs and employ this procedure on our experimental data.

Our proposed representational technique provides an intensional description of the process involved in learning a new device. As the two experiments discussed later in the paper show, it allows us to examine several questions of interest to the HCI community about the learning process: When are two user models close? Do successive user models converge for all users? *etc.* The key here is not to show a mere convergence of the user models, but to capture and represent the process of their evolution to show that the convergence (or divergence) follows a user's ability to learn the system. Such a representation allows designers to identify the problem areas in a UI by differentiating instances when a user model is improving from instances where it is not.

The paper is laid out as follows. First we provide the conceptual foundations for our edit distance approach. We then describe related literature that highlights the need for a novel approach. Then we report on the exploratory study that helped us formulate our solution. Next, we describe the *edit distance* approach in detail and demonstrate the computation of edit distance between two models. We then present our first experimental study that heuristically validates our approach using a simple machine. Later, we strengthen our findings through another study conducted using a close to real-world vehicle transmission system. Using our algorithm, we calculate the heuristic edit distances of successive user models, and demonstrate that they converge or diverge for progressive or regressive user learning respectively, validating our metric.

CONCEPTUAL FOUNDATIONS

This section describes in brief the concepts that are instrumental for understanding the work presented in the paper.

What is an interactive machine?

Most of the devices that people use are interactive in nature. An interactive machine can be succinctly described as a control system whose user inputs can (at least in part) be administered by a user through a UI. Apart from the UI, an interactive machine also has a set of capabilities that a machine offers to the user. It is essential for a user to get acquainted with the UI in order to learn its functional behavior and use it effectively [40]. In our paper, we represent an interactive machine as an FSM, and refer to it as a *target model.*

Finite state machines

An FSM has internal states, transitions between these states and observable outputs associated with each state.

DEFINITION 0.0.1. *An FSM with outputs is a tuple* $\langle X, q, \delta, I, Y, H\rangle$ *where*

- X *is a set of* states, $q \in X$ *is the* start *state,* I *is the set of* user inputs *and* Y *is the set of* outputs.
- $\delta : X \times I \rightarrow 2^X$ *is a* transition *function. We write* $s \xrightarrow{a} s'$ *if* $s' \in \delta(s, a)$.
- $H : X \rightarrow Y$ *maps each state in* X *to an output in* Y.

An FSM is *deterministic* if $|\delta(s, a)| \leq 1$ for all $s \in X$ and $a \in I$, else *nondeterministic*. In this paper, we restrict ourselves to deterministic FSMs since we model deterministic devices.

Simulation and bisimulation

A simulation relation is a relation between the states of two different FSMs such that whenever there is a transition in one FSM, there is a corresponding transition in another FSM with respect to the relation. A bisimulation relation is a simulation relation whose inverse is also a simulation. Formally, we define the simulation and bisimulation relation as follows.

DEFINITION 0.0.2 (SIMULATION RELATION). *Let* $L_1 = \langle X_1, q_1, \delta_1, I, Y, H_1\rangle$ *and* $L_2 = \langle X_2, q_2, \delta_1, I, Y, H_2\rangle$ *be two finite state machines. A relation* $R \subseteq X_1 \times X_2$ *is called a simulation* of L_1 by L_2 *if, for each pair* $(s_1, s_2) \in R$,

1. $H_1(s_1) = H_2(s_2)$, *i.e., the output of both states is same.*
2. *Whenever* s_1 *makes a transition, then* s_2 *makes a transition such that the corresponding pair of next states are also in the relation* R, i.e., *if* $s_1 \xrightarrow{a} s_1'$, *then there exists a state* $s_2' \in X_2$ *such that* $s_2 \xrightarrow{a} s_2'$ *and* $(s_1', s_2') \in R$.

DEFINITION 0.0.3 (BISIMULATION). *A simulation relation* R *of* L_1 *by* L_2 *is also a bisimulation relation between* L_1 *and* L_2 *if* R^{-1} *is a simulation relation of* L_2 *by* L_1.

Simulation establishes that all behaviors in the simulated machine are reflected in the other (simulating) machine. Bisimulation is a two-way simulation that establishes behavioral equivalence between two machines. The concept of simulation and bisimulation thus allows for behavioral comparison and equivalence respectively [26]. Successful simulation of the user model by the target model implies that the user's learning is coherent with the behavior of the machine. However, this does not indicate whether the user has learnt the behavior of the machine entirely. To ascertain that the user's understanding is complete and coherent, we require a bisimulation relation between the user model and the target model encompassing all the states of both the models. We now discuss past research that we build upon, and use it to motivate our FSM and bisimulation approach.

RELATED WORK

Here, we discuss earlier efforts by others related to the topics of quantitative analysis of UIs, formal methods in HCI, model representation and simulation. Various approaches have aimed to improve user productivity through quantitative analysis of UIs [19]. Typical examples include *KLM* [5], *GOMS* [23] and *TAG* [28]. Such approaches require task analysis at a low level and hence are suitable when a user's behavior is either well understood [21] or error-free [7]. The inability of these approaches to deal with incomplete and imperfect user behavior [13] limits their utility for analysing user learning. We therefore propose a new approach to trace and measure user learning when defined as the progressive convergence of the gap between the target and the user model.

Mental models have long been in use in Learning and Cognitive Sciences [22]. Moreover, there is considerable debate on whether a mental model in general [27], or its FSM representation in particular, is in itself a sufficient description of what the user has in her mind. In our work, the novelty is not in using FSMs to represent mental models, but in representing the evolution of an individual's mental model during a guided learning process. Most works on guided learning are domain specific. *E.g.* Cognitive tutors [2] use separation of memory types into declarative and procedural to provide individualized support. However, learning an interactive system mostly involves procedural knowledge unlike learning algebraic concepts. We, therefore, focus on measuring a user's knowledge specific to learning an interactive system.

Formal methods have been widely used to specify, model and verify user interactions [16, 25, 32]. Several investigations have reported different methods for identifying and bridging the gap between what users know and what they need to know [4]. Systems engineering principles have helped to hide the irrelevant complexity of a machine from the UI [36]. Heymann *et al.* [18] used formal methods in proposing a systematic procedure for automatic generation of correct and succinct UIs. Several of the limitations of automatic UI generation have been described in detail [12, 29, 35]. Moreover, most of these techniques assume every user behaves in a similar and ideal manner, and therefore do not apply to novice users. This encourages us to propose a new technique to understand, evaluate and analyse individual user interactions with machines without the assumption of a generic user model.

The representation of a model is a key aspect that determines the effectiveness of any analysis technique. Different notations like maps, graphs and mathematical specifications have been used to represent user models [10, 15, 17, 30]. Some of these representations offer poor support for scalability and hinder a detailed analysis of the user models. Traces of user interactions with a machine form the primary source of data for user modeling and should ideally be analyzed as a time series. However, Dix *et al.* [1] have demonstrated how statistical and machine learning techniques fail to analyse such user traces but they can easily be applied if the representation of the behavior focuses on the state transitions. The formal language of automata has been used by others like [33] to represent both the target and the user model. This facilitates the use of mechanized techniques like model checking to automatically discover any scenarios that cause any divergence in the behaviors of the two models [34]. It also allows us to contribute towards safety and due diligence in safety critical interactive systems by identifying any instances in the machine that may lead to incorrect user understanding [38].

In our paper, we capture and compare the user models of an individual to understand the process of user learning. Milner used bisimulation to demonstrate behavioral comparison of two FSM models [26]. In [8], Combefis and Pecheur used a bisimulation-based equivalence relation to address the mode confusion problem. They demonstrate the possibility of generating user models for an imperfect user and take into account the deviations in her behavior. This motivates us to extend the idea of bisimulation-based equivalence to study how users learn a new machine by extracting, not one but multiple user models in sequence as the user interacts with the machine. To investigate the potential of our proposed idea, we conducted an exploratory study as described below.

EXPLORATORY STUDY

In order to investigate the process of how a user learns to use a machine, we conducted an exploratory study with 27 participants (17 males, 10 females) with an engineering background and captured the process of formulating user models for a machine which is unfamiliar to the user.

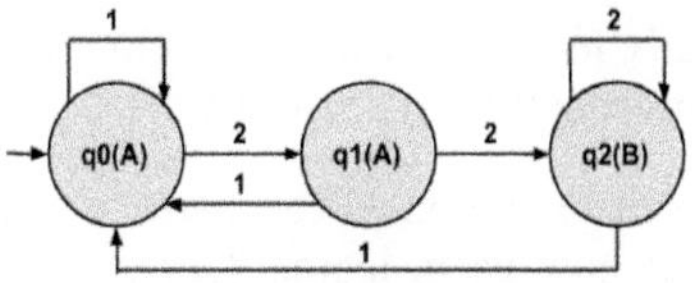

(a) Target model

(b) User Interface

Figure 1. The target model and UI of the unfamiliar machine presented to participants during exploratory study and experimental study I.

Not surprisingly, users trust an unfamiliar machine quickly if it is simpler, due to their ability to predict the machine's behavior [39]. This trust in the machine's behavior assists users in breaking out of any incorrect user understanding and further learn the machine correctly. Therefore, we chose a simple machine (Figure 1) for our study. We labelled the states as q_0, q_1 and q_2 with observable outputs, *A* or *B*, alongside. The UI consisted of one output text box and two input buttons labelled *1* and *2*. The output display language consisted of letters *A* and *B*. As a subject pressed either of the two buttons, the output would display the previous history of outputs appended by either letter *A* or *B* following its deterministic machine behavior. These strings of letters *A* and *B* would remain in the text box over time.

Our chosen machine closely resembles a simple tea/coffee vending machine [26] that starts at state q_0, accepts a coin and makes a transition to state q_1, outputs tea, and returns to the initial state q_0. By accepting another similar coin in state q_1, it goes to state q_2 and outputs coffee before returning to state q_0. The machine does not change its state when a user inserts coins in state q_2. Also, it does not output tea or coffee without accepting any coins. In Figure 1, the transitions labelled *2* correspond to coin transactions, while the transitions labelled *1* correspond to a user accepting tea or coffee. Thus, we present an unfamiliar machine to the participants by introducing small changes into a familiar machine.

A confirmatory approach to extract, represent and analyze a user's understanding of a concept allows researchers to validate only a subset of a user's understanding [6]. We therefore chose the exploratory approach for this study. The unfamiliarity with the machine compelled the user to construct a model of her understanding in order to be able to successfully predict and use the machine. The users predicted the next character in sequence after each click of the buttons labelled *1* and *2* and thought aloud what they believed to be the behavior of the machine at regular intervals. Later, we attempted to represent the user knowledge gathered through verbal responses as FSMs. From our experiences in this exploratory study, we drew the following conclusions:

1. The users were able to perform similar tasks better when they interacted more with the machine. Therefore, we hypothesize that user learning can be represented as a series of user mental constructs.

2. The uncertainty within user responses to reason about a change in the machine made it difficult to translate well the user narratives of machine's behavior into an FSM. Therefore, we decided to recruit computer science literate partic-

ipants who could directly report their understanding as an FSM, rather than we infering it from a narrative.

3. Investigating evolution of user models can be of tremendous help for reasoning how users learn. Our proposed measure of user understanding should therefore allow for a rigorous analysis of the evolving user models, which may be incomplete *and/or* incorrect by nature.

These realizations helped us formulate our edit distance solution approach, as explained in the following section.

SOLUTION APPROACH: EDIT DISTANCE

Once the user model and the target model are formally captured and rendered, then learning can be operationally treated as the process of evolution of the user model towards the target model. In most cases, a user model deviates from the target model because of incomplete, as well as, incorrect learning. For a fine grained analysis of user learning, we need to quantify the gap between these two models. To measure the behavioral closeness of these models, we rely on the graph-theory technique of *edit distance*, a quantitative value which represents the gap. In our work, the user learning process is then hypothesized as a reduction in the edit distance: the progressive convergence of the gap between what the user believes to be the system's behavior (user model) and what truly is the system's behavior (target model). To address the concerns raised in our exploratory study, we used a bisimulation-based technique to calculate edit distance ensuring that our metric allows analysis of incomplete and incorrect user models. Next, we discuss the process of making a model bisimilar to another model by performing some edit operations.

Restricting edit operations to generate a bisimilar model

In general, an edit operation on an FSM can be any change in terms of deletion or addition of an edge or a node. But it is easy to observe that the presence or absence of an isolated node (without any incident edges) would not affect bisimilarity. Thus, deletion of a node simply corresponds to deletion of multiple edges modulo bisimilarity. Therefore, we do not consider removing a node as an edit operation. We define an edit operation on an FSM as deletion of an edge, addition of an edge or addition of a node with only one incident edge.

It is also easy to see that any two FSMs can be made bisimilar to each other by deleting all edges of one FSM and adding nodes and edges corresponding to the other FSM. This is a naive way of making two FSMs bisimilar. Furthermore, this would ensure structural (graph based) proximity and not behavioral proximity. We have had examples of user models from our experiments that were very structurally different from the target model but were behaviorally close to it. Therefore, we ensure that our chosen algorithm for edit distance modulo bisimilarity not only captures behavioral proximity as opposed to structural proximity, but also restricts the required edit operations using the following propositions.

PROPOSITION 0.0.4. *Let* $L_u = \langle X_u, q_{0u}, \delta_u, I, Y, H_u \rangle$ *and* $L_t = \langle X_t, q_{0t}, \delta_t, I, Y, H_t \rangle$ *be two FSMs. Let* $R : X_u \times X_t$ *be a relation such that if* $(q_{0u}, q_{0t}) \in R$ *and* $(s, q) \in R$, *then* $H_t(q) = H_u(s)\ \forall s \in X_u$. *Then there exists an FSM* L'_u *obtained by deleting only those edges of* L_u *that are not simulated by* L_t *via R, such that R becomes a simulation of updated FSM* L'_u *by* L_t.

PROPOSITION 0.0.5. *Let* $L_u = \langle X_u, q_u, \delta_u, I, Y, H_u \rangle$ *and* $L_t = \langle X_t, q_t, \delta_t, I, Y, H_t \rangle$ *such that* L_u *is simulated by* L_t *through a relation* $R \subset X_u \times X_t$. *Then there exists an FSM* L'_u *obtained by addition operations on* L_u *such that* L'_u *is bisimilar to* L_t *by the relation defined by R extended to the added states. Furthermore, the additions can be restricted to correspondence with only those transitions in target FSM not simulated by user FSM.*

We have described the formal proofs for both the propositions in detail in [3]. Proposition 0.0.4 says that a user model can be simulated by the target model by deleting a limited number (may be less than the total number) of edges from the user model. Further, Proposition 0.0.5 says that if a user model is simulated by the deterministic target model, then addition of a limited number (may be less than the total number) of nodes and edges to the user model would make the two models bisimilar. Based on this, we define the edit distance and hypothesize that it captures behavioral proximity. This hypothesis is validated through the experiments in the paper.

Calculating edit distance between 2 FSM models

Given a user model L_u and a target model L_t, and an arbitrary relation $R \subseteq X_u \rightarrow X_t$, there exists a model L'_u obtained by making the minimum possible number of edit operations on L_u such that R becomes a simulation of L'_u by L_t. Through the proof of Proposition 0.0.4 [3], it is easy to see that the model is unique to a relation defined. We can define multiple relations and for each relation there is a model. Let $S(L_u, L_t)$ denote the set of all such models. The minimum number of delete operations required to generate L'_u from L_u such that L'_u is simulated by L_t is denoted as $M_d(L_u, L_t, L'_u)$.

Now, there exists an L''_u, the FSM obtained by making addition operations on L'_u so that L''_u is bisimilar to L_t by an extension of the relation R to added nodes. This follows from Proposition 0.0.5. Denote $M_a(L'_u, L_t)$ as the minimum number of additions required to obtain one such model among all possible bisimilar models. Then, we define the edit distance between L_u and L_t as

$$e(L_u, L_t) = \min_{L'_u \in S(L_u, L_t)} [M_d(L_u, L_t, L'_u) + M_a(L'_u, L_t)] \quad (1)$$

Although it is computationally difficult to find the edit distance between two arbitrary FSMs due to the number of possible relations from states of one automaton to other, it may be found easily for small FSMs by associating the start states of the target and user FSM by the simulation relation and applying heuristic calculations. The catch here is the start states of the two FSMs normally correspond to each other. So, we take them as related states of the desired bisimulation relation. We illustrate the heuristic calculations with an example case taken from our experimental study I. Our example is described by the series of Figures 2, 3 and 4. We denote the user and target model in consideration as L_u and L_t in Figure 2 and find the edit distance between them. The model on

Start	Button	End	o/p
u0	1	u0	A
u0	2	u1	B
u1	2	u1	B

Table 1. State transitions of the target machine in Figure 2 as perceived by the user.

Start	Button	End	o/p
t0	1	t0	A
t0	2	t1	A
t1	1	t0	A
t1	2	t2	B
t2	1	t0	A
t2	2	t2	B

Table 2. Actual state transitions of the target machine.

the left is the user model and on the right is the target model. Each row of Table 1 and Table 2 respectively decribe the state transitions of the user model and the target model in Figure 2.

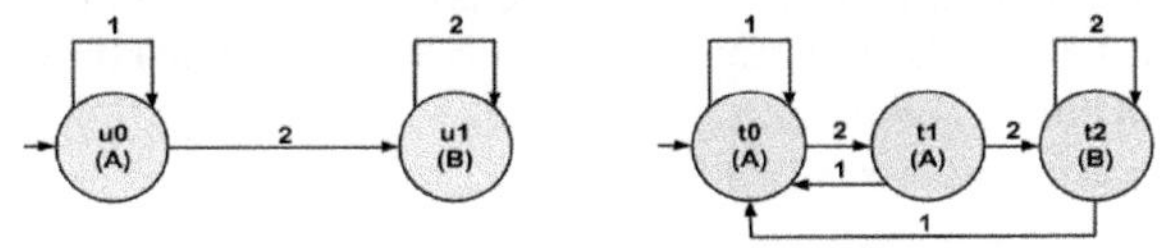

Figure 2. An example of a user model (left) and target model (right) taken from experimental study I.

The first step (Figure 3) in the process of calculating edit distance is to heuristically find a model L'_u by making a minimum number of edge deletions from L_u such that L_t simulates L_u. This is done by recursively associating states of L_u to those of L_t and deleting edges from L_u as necessary. The explanation follows. Initialize $L'_u = L_u$. The start state u_0 of L'_u should unequivocally be associated to the start state of L_t *i.e.*, $(u_0, t_0) \in R$. This association is correct with respect to the transitions $u_0 \xrightarrow{1} u_0$ and $t_0 \xrightarrow{1} t_0$ and hence we keep these transitions intact. Although $u_0 \xrightarrow{2} u_1$ and $t_0 \xrightarrow{2} t_1$, the output of u_1 (*i.e.*, B) and t_1(*i.e.*, A) are not the same (see Table 1 and Table 2). Hence, we do not map u_1 to t_1. Instead, we map u_1 to t_2 because $u_1 \xrightarrow{2} u_1$ and $t_2 \xrightarrow{2} t_2$ allowing the state t_2 to simulate u_1. This also mandates the deletion of the transition edge $u_0 \xrightarrow{2} u_1$ for preserving simulation of L'_u by L_t. This can be clearly seen in Table 1 that the user model is missing a state equivalent to state t_1 of the target model. The updated user model L'_u is now simulated by L_t and is obtained by a minimum possible number of edge deletions from L_u.

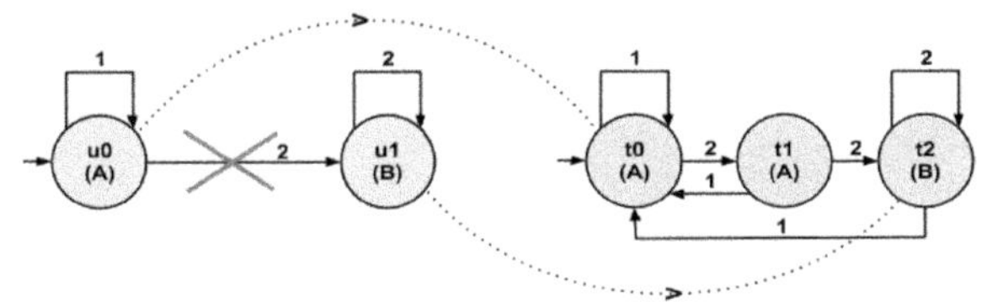

Figure 3. The simulation mapping of states of user model to those of target model and the requisite deletion operations from the user model such that the mapping enables the target model to simulate the user model.

In the next step as illustrated in Figure 4, because L'_u is simulated by L_t, we can get a L''_u bisimilar to L_t by adding edges or states with incident edges to L'_u. In the present case, a state u_2 is added to L'_u and also edges $u_0 \xrightarrow{2} u_2$, $u_2 \xrightarrow{2} u_1$, $u_2 \xrightarrow{1} u_1$ and $u_1 \xrightarrow{1} u_0$. Now after making L''_u and L_t bisimilar, we calculate the edit distance as the sum of the total number of deletions and the total number of additions $= 1+4 = 5$, as stated by equation 1. In the following sections, we describe two experimental studies we conducted to validate our proposed edit distance metric for user learning.

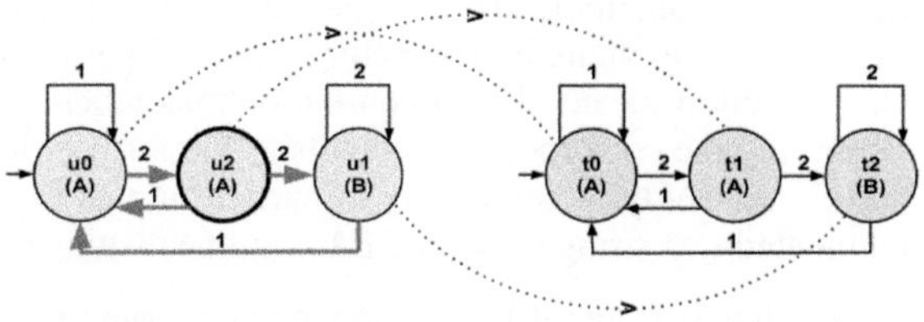

Figure 4. The required addition operations and the extension of the mapping to new states such that the new mapping is a bisimulation between the user model and the target model.

VALIDATION OF THE EDIT DISTANCE METRIC

Experimental Study 1

We setup a simple within-subjects experimental study to validate our proposed measure of user learning. We presented participants with a newly created unfamiliar machine and tasked them with learning its functionality by interacting with it. Each participant was routinely asked to self-report her impression of the functionality as an FSM, which represented her user model for that round. Over the course of an entire interaction, several rounds of user models and one final user model were captured. We compared this series of user models to the target model. Finally, we derived a trend by comparing each subject's stream of user models against the singular target model. The reliability of the proposed measure is confirmed by observing that the user models converge towards the target model with progressive learning of the user.

Participants

20 undergraduate/graduate students (16 males, 4 females), participated in the experiment. Their ages ranged from 21 to 43 years (average was 23). All participants were computer science literate comfirming their prior knowledge of FSMs.

Stimuli

The functional behavior of the machine, that was presented to the participants as a novel machine for learning, was modeled after the FSM described in Figure 1. The software also captured experiment duration, inputs provided, outputs generated, and the timing of such events. We used this information along with the self-reported user models for data analysis.

Procedure

We captured the demographic information of each participant and provided them with an overview of the experiment. A set of two questions were then asked: (1) Have you studied FSMs before? and (2) Do you feel comfortable to represent the behavior of a simple machine as an FSM? After obtaining her consent, the subject was lead into the experiment.

For the experiment, we initially trained the participant using a counter that allowed her to increase or decrease the displayed number by one ranging from *0* to *4* with the help of two buttons. The UI of the training machine was similar to the one described in Figure 1. The researchers helped the participant in representing her understanding of this training machine as an FSM to get the participant acquainted with (1) the UI of the machine, (2) the task that she was expected to perform and (3) how to represent an interactive behavior as an FSM.

After the training period, all participants were instructed to learn the functionality of the new machine, which was about to be displayed to them, by interacting with it. Operationally, each interaction meant clicking on the buttons labelled *1* or *2*, observing the corresponding outputs in the form of letters *A* and *B*, and studying the history of earlier outputs (*e.g.*, an accumulated text string of *AABABBA* ... in the display box).

The participants were informed that while they were interacting with the machine, they would be interrupted after every 3 interactions, each interaction being one click, and asked to draw an FSM that represented their understanding of the machine. This drawing served as their user model for that round. The subjects would also have to answer the question: "How well does your user model represent what is in your mind?" The possible answers were: (a) this is a very good representation of what I have in my mind, (b) this is a partial but a fair representation of what I have in my mind, and (c) this is an incomplete representation of what I have in my mind.

We allowed the participants to interact with the machine for any number of rounds. When the participant felt that she had a complete understanding of the machine, she could stop interacting and draw a final FSM, which was labelled as final user model (Uf) for that subject. To conclude the experiment, participants answered 3 final questions: (1) was this machine new to you? (2) when encountering a new machine, what do they think is more important: the number of interactions, *and/or* amount of time spent with the machine? (3) what is your preferred way of interacting with a new machine?

Results

All 20 participants had previously studied FSMs in their university curricula. In addition, 18 of them felt comfortable in using an FSM to represent their mental understanding of the machine. Most of the participants (18) felt that the machine was sufficiently new to them. Although the remaining 2 participants suspected a partial exposure to a similar device in their past, neither of them guessed the FSM correctly.

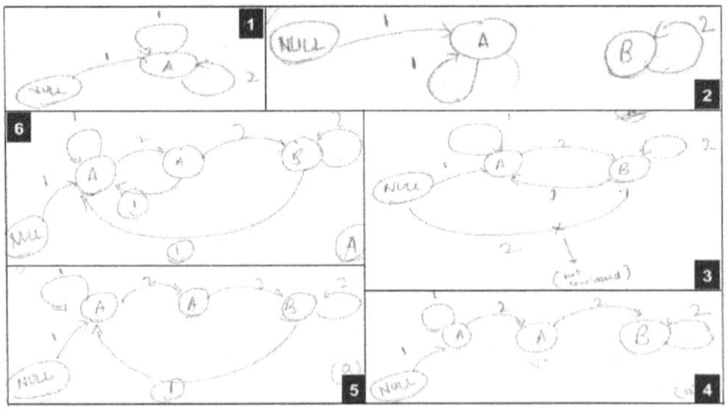

Figure 5. A sequence of user models self-reported by a participant during study I. Each model represents her understanding of the machine represented in Figure 1 at different rounds of interaction.

18 participants reported that their self-reported user model in the various rounds of the experiment was at least a good to fair representation of what was in their mind, with 10 even claiming it to be a very good representation. 13 of the 20 (65%) felt that when learning a new machine, it is the interactions with the machine (and not necessarily time spent with it) that is important for better understanding the machine. The remaining 7 felt that interactions *and* the time spent on the machine contribute to learning. However, when asked about how they have learnt about the functionality of a new machine in the past, 6 of these 7 said that they would consult a manual, and 1 said that he would look for a pattern. All agreed that they would indeed interact and explore the machine to learn it.

Our data revealed that every participant spent an average of 9:31 minutes in learning this new machine (maximum: 19:54, and minimum: 4:08). All interacted with the machine for at least 3 rounds; 15 completed 5 rounds, 7 completed 6 rounds, and only 1 person went up to round 8. The average time spent in each round was typically around 1:56 minutes.

The participants self-reported their user models as hand-drawn FSMs (Figure 5). The average number of user models per participant was 4.89 (SD=1.12). Almost all (19 out of 20) had the output symbols (letters *A* and *B*) as states, and input buttons *1* and *2* as the transition arcs. One participant chose to represent the state machine with multiple letters (as in A, AA, AB, *etc.*). Structurally, there were dissimilarities between the hand-drawn models across different users, but common features included A as the start state, at least 2 states, 4 transitions, *etc.* We computed the edit distance for each user model using our algorithm and plotted the trend against the multiple rounds of interaction for each participant in Figure 6. The overall convergence in the trend of edit distances validated our metric. A detailed comparison of the self reported user models and the resultant trend of edit distance can be found in the Discussion Section of this paper.

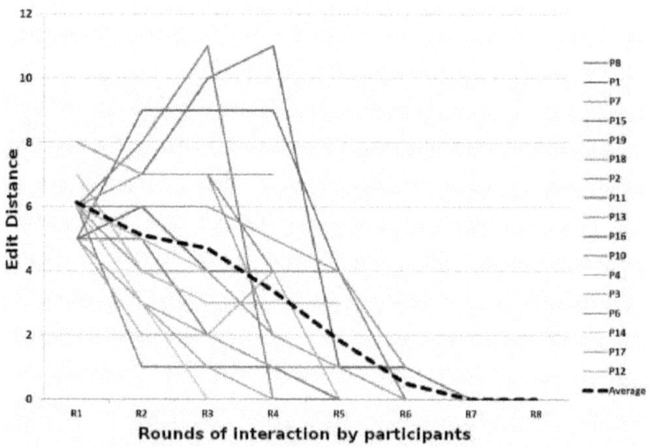

Figure 6. The trend of edit distance as it converges for different users across several rounds of user interaction. The dotted line indicates that the average of edit distances calculated for models of all users during the corresponding rounds of interaction shows a monotonic convergence.

Experimental Study 2

We conducted the previous study using a simple machine with low functional complexity. In order to further confirm the validity of our approach, we conducted another study involving a variation of a digital vehicle transmission system (VTS),

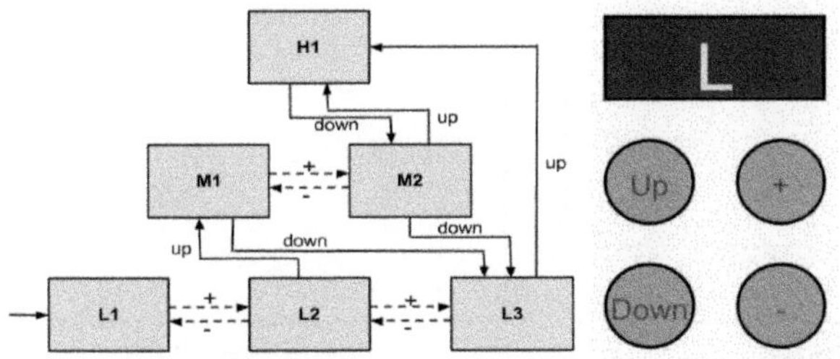

(a) Target model (b) User Interface

Figure 7. The target model and the UI of the digital vehicle transmission system (VTS) with variations to make it simpler. This machine was presented to participants of the experimental study II.

taken from [8]. VTS is a classic example of an interactive system that resembles a sufficiently complex system with limited transparency and issues of mode confusion.

Participants

The experiment involved twelve participants, 9 males and 3 females, with ages ranging from 18 to 62; average age was 27.25 with a standard deviation of 11.69.

Stimuli

We presented the participants with a variation of a VTS model, taken from [8], as an unfamiliar machine. The participants interacted with this machine described in Figure 7, that represents the target model and the new UI for this study.

Procedure

The protocol for this study remained largely similar to the previous study, except for our approach for extracting the user models. From the different techniques available for extracting user models, such as structured interview, questionnaire and talk back, an open method is less useful than a more structured approach when the complexity of a machine increases [31]. The digital VTS model presented to the participants, even with the variations meant to simplify it, was sufficiently complex for an unfamiliar user and necessitated a structured approach to extract user models. Therefore, we provided partial guidance to the study participants in identifying the states of the target model. The participants received this guidance in the form of sheets of paper having a minimum of all the states, which were necessary to represent the target model, printed upon them. They were expected to use these sheets to self-report their understanding of the machine, thus reducing the task of drawing FSMs to identifying the valid states and mapping the transitions between them. This helped the researchers to minimize the noise captured within a user model due to a participant's inefficacy, while reproducing her understanding as an FSM. We provided a few superfluous states on the sheets to (1) ensure that particpant were not influnced by the number of states marked on the sheets and (2) allow them to express their understanding as an FSM that may be structurally different, but bisimilar to the VTS target model.

While conducting the study, we started by collecting the demographics of the participant and her prior knowledge about FSMs and her ability to draw one. Since the target model was a variation of a VTS, we also enquired if the participant had any experience with using a car gear box. The participant was shown a simple FSM with 2 states and 1 transition, and was asked to think aloud to explain it. After ensuring a correct understanding of the concept of an FSM, the participant received training on how to represent an interactive behavior as an FSM. We used the same training example of a number counter, taken from the first study.

The participants were provided with a brief explanantion of a VTS model having a few main gear levels and a few sub-levels within each of the main gear levels. We informed them that we would be using a variation of a VTS with 3 main gear levels: low, medium and high, and each level would have a minimum of 1 and a maximum of 4 sub-levels. However, the software would only display a character corresponding to the main gear level (*i.e.* L, M or H), irrespective of the sub-level. It was possible to separately identify all the sub-levels within a main gear level through sufficient interaction.

The participants were tasked to learn the behavior of the machine (Figure 7) by interacting with it for an unlimited number of rounds, where each round consisted of four clicks. They were free to distribute the 4 clicks in each round amongst the 4 buttons on the UI (*i.e.*, Up, Down, + and -) as they saw fit. Then, they were asked to self-report their understanding of the machine as an FSM, one on each sheet of the paper with the possible states indicated on them. We notified the participants that the most succint representation of the VTS would not take more than 9 states; but they were free to utilise all 16 states shown on the provided sheets.

A round of interaction was complete when a participant answered the following questions about her user model for that round: (1) What fraction of the machine's behavior did she understand till then?- *(a)* 0-25% *(b)* 25-50% *(c)* 50-75% *or (d)* 75-100% and (2) How well did the FSM represent her understanding of the machine?- *(a)* poor *(b)* fair but partial *or (c)* fair and complete. The response of the former question reflected the gain, if any, in participant's understanding of the machine; while the latter reflected the efficiency and completeness of her representation, similar to the first study.

At the end of the second and the final round of interaction, we tested the participants' understanding. We asked them to indicate, using the smallest number of clicks, how to transition between two states of the model, *e.g.*, start state of the machine to any of the medium sub-levels. These responses reflect if the participant learnt anything during the several rounds of interaction or not. Each participant answered the same set of 3 final questions, taken from the previous study, after her interaction session with the machine was complete.

Results

9 (out of 12) participants had studied FSMs and thought they would be able to plot an interactive behavior as an FSM. Except one, all participants had an average of 6.1 years driving experience (SD=12.6). The brief explanation of a VTS model (prior to the study) ensured that each participant had at least some knowledge of how a car gear box works. Despite this, 11 participants confessed that the VTS model was unfamiliar to them; this included a participant who had a thorough

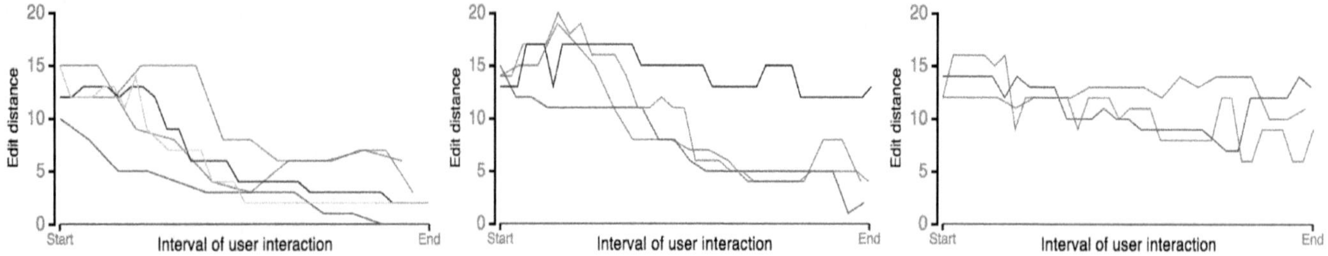

(a) Group 1: 3/3 sequences correct (b) Group 2: 2/3 sequences correct (c) Group 3: None or 1/3 sequence correct

Figure 8. The edit distances for all user models, computed using our algorithm, collected in the experimental study II performed using the vehicle transmission model. We have grouped the users as per their final understanding of the machine, reflected by the number of correct user responses. X axis denotes the normalised duration of time that each participant spent trying to learn the machine and actually made any changes to her user model.

knowledge of the internal strucure and working of a car gear box. One of the participants, with prior driving experience, reported the behavior to remotely resemble a game to launch a rocket at different speeds depending on the player interaction with the knob to release the rocket. She also tried to relate it to a new type of clutch that decides how to shift gears, depending on how hard it is pressed.

5 participants reported the number of interactions allowed with the machine to be the primary reason for them to understand the behavior of the VTS model, while 6 participants gave an equal priority to number of interactions and the time to think between them. One participant found her knowledge of the previous state where he left the machine to be more important. When questioned about the preferred way to understand the working of an unfamiliar machine, 9 preferred to interact with it; 2 preferred using a manual, while one said that she would interact with a simple machine but refer to a manual if the machine were sufficiently complex.

The participants interacted with the machine for an average of 28.5 rounds each (minimum 10 and maximum 43), with a standard deviation of 11.04. In the end, all the participants reported having understood most of the machine (reported as 75-100%) and were confident about their representation to be fair and complete, 5 participants stopped interacting once their model was complete, while 7 continued to interact further and used their final few rounds to confirm their previous understanding as represented by their last FSM. The participants took an average of 55:30 minutes (SD=21:30 minutes) to interact with the machine before they thought they understood it completely; the minimum was 27:37 minutes while the longest was 108:57 minutes.

We classified the users depending on the correctness of their responses (required sequence of clicks) to perform certain state transitions as requested by the researchers into 3 groups. We plotted the edit distances for user models, as computed by our algorithm, across the normalised duration of time that each participant spent trying to learn the machine, separately for each group in Figure 8. The normalised duration excludes the time spent by participants in past few rounds for verifying their previous knowledge of the machine during which they neither changed their user model, nor their confidence about their understanding of the machine or their representation of it. A detailed discussion of these follows in the next section.

DISCUSSION FOR BOTH EXPERIMENTS

By using the self-reported user models in both studies as our primary source of data, we trace user learning and measure the gaps between the user models and the target model in progressive rounds of interaction. We quantify this gap using our proposed measure edit distance. We then compute the edit distances for each of the user models per participant, and plot them against their corresponding rounds of interaction as observed during study I in Figure 6. The simplicity of the machine used in study I ensured that all the participants learnt some fraction of the machine's behavior through user interaction. Considering the complexity of the VTS model, we classified the participants of study II into 3 separate groups to facilitate a better analysis of the results as shown in Figure 8: participants who answered all 3 understanding questions correctly, answered 2 correctly, and 1 or none correctly.

The graph in Figure 6 clearly indicates that the overall trend of edit distances converges with every passing round as a user interacts more with the machine. A similar trend of convergence can be seen in Figure 8a. This graph reflects how edit distance converges for a user who learns the VTS model correctly (*i.e.*, answers all understanding questions correctly). 5 participants from experimental study I learned the machine partially. This is captured as a converging but non-zero edit distance. A similar convergence can be seen in Figure 8b (except for one user) despite their inability to perform all the given tasks correctly. Our measure successfully illustrates their process of acquiring this partial understanding.

As Figure 6 indicates, a few participants in study I have their trend of edit distances higher than the average. On examining their user models, we realised that initially the users who contributed to the 2 highest peaks, struggled with the concept of FSMs since they could not distinguish between the outputs and the states of the machine and resorted to plotting their user models as a sequence of outputs as opposed to an FSM. We also notice an outlier in Figure 8b showing no significant convergence in edit distance despite providing correct user responses to our state transition questions. A further probe into her user models indicated that the she identified behaviorally similar states as separate without mapping all the necessary transitions between them to ensure bisimilarity. The replication of behaviorally similar states in a user model, in turn replicates the number of missing transitions, if any. Our edit distance algorithm includes each missing transition and outputs a higher edit distance indicating user confusion. We consider that a user with a partial understanding and a larger number of states in her model is more likely to be confused than a user with similar understanding but fewer states. We suspect this to indicate higher cognitive load. Our metric thus identifies these cases as partially incorrect user learning.

The next peak in Figure 6 comes from a participant who demonstrated an erroneous learning of the machine thus justifying an increase in the edit distance towards round 2. This participant's user models indicate that she recreated her user model following round 4 when she realised her error, as is evident from the steep decline in her edit distance plot indicating a positive knowledge gain. Similar instances of erroneous learning can be seen in trends of several users during study II. The rise in edit distance for one participant in Figure 8a resulted from an erroneous learning which was reflected in her correct, but not the shortest, sequence of clicks for the third task. Figure 8c especially highlights cases where users either could not rectify their erroneous learning or were unable to learn constructively about the VTS model. The absence of any convergence in this graph implies no user learning, thus further indicating the reliability of our proposed edit distance.

Thus, our proposed measure edit distance successfully traces cases of complete, partial, erroneous and no user learning. These trends will allow us to identify users that need some help in learning an interface or UIs that need to be redesigned. In the future, this approach can be used to investigate the rate at which a user attains her understanding of an unfamiliar device by investigating how fast do the user models converge towards the target model. Our proposed technique of edit distance is useful for allowing a behavioral comparison between any two models that can be represented as FSMs. *E.g.* comparing different UIs for the same system, comparing business process models as they evolve with time, *etc.*

Ideally, edit distance would be the minimum number of edges and states with incident edges required to be added and deleted from the user model such that it bisimulates the target model. However, it would be computationally very expensive to compute the edit distance by an automated algorithm due to a large number of possible relations between the states of the user model and the target model. The heuristic edit distance that we computed manually using our algorithm, therefore, may vary from the ideal edit distance and compromise its minimality; however it is logically and scientifically consistent, as shown in Proposition 0.0.4 and Proposition 0.0.5.

A non-deterministic user model can certainly be made bisimilar to the target model by using a naive $O(|G1| + |G2|)$ algorithm, which essentially deletes G1 edges and reconstructs G2 edges. However, such an edit distance is not minimal. The problem of computing the minimum edit distance is NP-Hard. On the other hand, efficiently finding the minimum edit distance between two non-deterministic FSMs modulo bisimilarity is an open problem. While not optimal, our present algorithm performs better than the naive $O(|G1| + |G2|)$ algorithm and measures the edit distance between two deterministic models. This restriction to deterministic user models is not a theoretical limitation of our work; instead it prevents the user from expressing ambiguity by reporting only deterministic approximations of the machine, which the user was informed to be deterministic.

Although we have defined (bi)simulation in the context of FSMs, bisimulation is a general concept used to capture the notion of behavioral equivalence and extends across different domains *e.g.* [11]. Thus, the idea presented in the paper can be applied even when user interactions are represented in different notations and is not restricted to FSMs.

CONCLUSION

The paper focuses on a behavioral comparison of user and target models when represented as finite state machines. We propose the *edit distance* metric for mathematically capturing the gap between evolving user models and a target model using bisimulation equivalence. In our experiments, we observed that the edit distance between the user and target model converges with progressive user learning, increases for erroneous learning and remains unchanged indicating no learning. Thus, the paper demonstrates that user learning can be witnessed, captured, and measured formally, allowing for a better understanding of how users learn to use a new device.

Our proposed edit distance metric is of significant importance to UI designers to identify instances when user understanding is not improving and to develop dynamic adaptive interventions to address them [9]. A quantified measure of user learning will help researchers to develop techniques that expedite the process of training a user for successfully operating a new device. In the future, we plan to use our proposed framework for segmentation of the feature space of a device depending on which features a user could understand completely or partially, and those, which he could not use at all. Ensuring complete knowledge of some features will be crucial to safety critical systems for meeting minimum standards of safety. Such an effort will also help in identifying new design principles leading to better user interaction.

REFERENCES

1. A. Dix, J. F., and Beale, R. Analysis of user behaviour as time series. In *HCI'92: People and Computers VII*, Cambridge University Press (1992), 429–444.
2. Anderson, J. R., Corbett, A. T., Koedinger, K. R., and Pelletier, R. Cognitive tutors: Lessons learned. *The Journal of the Learning Sciences 4*, 2 (1995), 167–207.
3. Arvind, S., and Choppella, V. A definition of edit-distance modulo bisimulation. Tech. Rep. IIIT/TR/2014/1, IIIT-Hyderabad, January 2014.
4. Baecker, R., Booth, K., Jovicic, S., McGrenere, J., and Moore, G. Reducing the gap between what users know and what they need to know. In *CUU '00*, 17–23.
5. Card, S. K., Moran, T. P., and Newell, A. The keystroke level model for user performance time with interactive systems. *Commun. ACM 23*, 7 (1980), 396–410.
6. Carley, K., and Palmquist, M. Extracting, representing, and analyzing mental models. *Social Forces 70*, 3 (1992), 601–636.

7. Carroll, J. M., and Olson, J. R., Eds. *Mental models in human-computer interaction: research issues about what the user of software knows*. National Academy Press, Washington, DC, USA, 1987.
8. Combéfis, S., and Pecheur, C. A bisimulation-based approach to the analysis of human-computer interaction. In *EICS '09*, ACM (2009), 101–110.
9. Dhawan, R., M. O., and Borman, M. Mental models and dynamic decision making: an experimental approach for testing system methodologies. In *24th International Conference of the System Dynamics Society* (2006).
10. Doherty, G., Campos, J. C., and Harrison, M. D. Representational reasoning and verification. *Formal Aspects of Computing 12* (1998), 260–277.
11. Dong, Q. A bisimulation approach to verification of molecular implementations of formal chemical reaction networks, 2012.
12. Falb, J., Popp, R., Rock, T., Jelinek, H., Arnautovic, E., and Kaindl, H. Fully-automatic generation of user interfaces for multiple devices from a high-level model based on communicative acts. In *HICSS* (2007), 26–26.
13. Fischer, G. User modeling in humancomputer interaction. *User Modeling and User-Adapted Interaction 11*, 1-2 (2001), 65–86.
14. Gentner, D., and Stevens, A. *Mental models*. Cognitive Science - Lawrence Erlbaum Associates. Lawrence Erlbaum Associates, Incorporated, 1983.
15. Harrison, M. Modelling user structures within system specifications. In *Formal Methods in HCI: III, IEE Colloquium on* (1989), 1/1–1/4.
16. Harrison, M., and Thimbleby, H. *Formal Methods in Human Computer Interactions*. Cambridge Middle East Library. Cambridge University Press, 1990.
17. Hermann, M., and Weber, M. When three worlds collide: a model of the tangible interaction process. In *OZCHI '09*, ACM (2009), 341–344.
18. Heymann, M., and Degani, A. Formal analysis and automatic generation of user interfaces: approach, methodology, and an algorithm. *Human Factors 49*, 2 (Apr. 2007), 311–30.
19. Hinckley, K., Cutrell, E., Bathiche, S., and Muss, T. Quantitative analysis of scrolling techniques. In *CHI '02*, ACM (2002), 65–72.
20. Ippel, M. J., and Beem, A. L. Mental models as finite-state machines: Examples and computational methods. Tech. Rep. 9911, United State Air Force Armstrong Laboratory, October 1998.
21. John, B. E., and Kieras, D. E. The goms family of analysis techniques: Tools for design and evaluation. Tech. rep., Carnegie Mellon University, 1994.
22. Johnson-Laird, P. N. *Mental models: Towards a cognitive science of language, inference, and consciousness*, vol. 6. 1983.
23. Kieras, D. E. Towards a practical goms model methodology for user interface design. *Handbook of human-computer interaction* (1988), 135–158.
24. Kieras, D. E., and Bovair, S. The role of a mental model in learning to operate a device. *Cognitive Science 8*, 3 (1984), 255 – 273.
25. Long, J., and Dowell, J. Formal methods: the broad and the narrow view. In *Formal Methods and HCI: II, IEE Colloquium on* (1988), 5/1–5/8.
26. Milner, R. *A Calculus of Communicating Systems*. Springer-Verlag New York, Inc., 1982.
27. Norman, D. Some observations on mental models. *Mental models 7* (1983).
28. Payne, S. J., and Green, T. R. G. Task-action grammars: a model of the mental representation of task languages. *Human-Computer Interaction 2*, 2 (June 1986), 93–133.
29. Popp, R., Falb, J., Raneburger, D., and Kaindl, H. A transformation engine for model-driven ui generation. In *EICS '12*, ACM (2012), 281–286.
30. Qian, X., Yang, Y., and Gong, Y. The art of metaphor: a method for interface design based on mental models. In *VRCAI '11*, ACM (2011), 171–178.
31. Read, J. C., MacFarlane, S., and Casey, C. What's going on?: discovering what children understand about hand-writing recognition interfaces. In *IDC '03*, 135–140.
32. Reeves, S. Principled formal methods in hci research. In *Formal Methods in HCI: III, IEE Colloquium on* (1989), 2/1–2/3.
33. Romera, M. E. Using finite automata to represent mental models. Master's thesis, San Jose State University, 2000.
34. Rushby, J. Using model checking to help discover mode confusions and other automation surprises. In *Reliability Engineering and System Safety*, vol. 75 (2002), 167–177.
35. Schneider, K., and Cordy, J. Abstract user interfaces: A model and notation to support plasticity in interactive systems. In *Interactive Systems: Design, Specification, and Verification*, vol. 2220. Springer, 2001, 28–48.
36. Thimbleby, B., Blandford, A., Cairns, P., Curzon, P., and Jones, M. User interface design as systems design. In *People and Computers XVI - Memorable yet Invisible*, Springer (2002), 281–301.
37. Thimbleby, H. *Press On — Principles of Interaction Programming*. MIT Press, 2007.
38. Thimbleby, H. Contributing to safety and due diligence in safety-critical interactive systems development by generating and analyzing finite state models. In *EICS '09*, ACM (2009), 221–230.
39. Tullio, J., Dey, A. K., Chalecki, J., and Fogarty, J. How it works: a field study of non-technical users interacting with an intelligent system. In *CHI '07*, 31–40.
40. Zade, H., and Choppella, V. Functionality or user interface: Which is easier to learn when changed? In *IHCI '12* (2012), 1–6.

The Law of Unintended Consequences: The Case of External Subgoal Support

J. Gregory Trafton
Naval Research Laboratory
Washington, DC
greg.trafton@nrl.navy.mil

Raj M. Ratwani
MedStar Institute for Innovation
Washington, DC
raj.ratwani@medicalhfe.org

ABSTRACT

Many interfaces have been designed to prevent or reduce errors. These interfaces may, in fact, reduce the error rate of specific error classes, but may also have unintended consequences. In this paper, we show a series of studies where a better interface did not reduce the number of errors but instead shifted errors from one error class (omissions) to another error class (perseverations). We also show that having access to progress tracking (a progress bar) does not reduce the number of errors. We propose and demonstrate a solution – a predictive error system – that reduces errors based on the error class, not on the type of interface.

Author Keywords

Error Prediction; Progress Tracking; Interface subgoal support; Computer Human Interaction

ACM Classification Keywords

H.5.2. User Interfaces

H.1.2. User/Machine Systems

INTRODUCTION

When performing a routine procedural task, people occasionally make errors despite having the correct knowledge of how to perform the task and despite being well practiced on the task. These procedural errors, also called skill-based errors [1], generally have a low base rate, and occur less than five percent of the time [2; 3]. However, in high risk domains like aviation, medicine, nuclear energy, or military systems, procedural errors can have disastrous consequences [4; 5].

An interesting finding from researchers who have studied routine procedural tasks is that the very last step of a procedure is especially error-prone [2; 6-10]. Forgetting to include an attachment to an email or leaving the original on the glass after making copies or clicking twice on a credit card button after ordering something from an online store are all relatively common errors that occur at the end of a procedure [10-12].

CHI 2014, April 26 - May 01 2014, Toronto, ON, Canada
Copyright 2014 ACM 978-1-4503-2473-1/14/04…$15.00.
http://dx.doi.org/10.1145/2556288.2557422

Interface designers have spent a fair amount of energy attempting to minimize the probability of errors on these types of routine tasks. The typical goal is to not only prevent errors, but to also be unobtrusive about it and to provide a good user experience as well. The most popular method for preventing procedural errors is to provide interface support for what the user has accomplished; this is goal-state information.

Interface support comes in multiple methods, but we will focus on two ways that modern interfaces support goal-state tracking for the user. Gray [13] refers to the process of goal state tracking as global placekeeping and Maxion and Reeder [14] refer to this as external subgoal support. When users have to keep track of which subgoals have been accomplished, a cognitive burden is introduced by way of an increased memory load. If the interface provides explicit information about which goals have been accomplished overall, user workload can be reduced since the goal state information no longer needs to be maintained in memory.

The need for interface cues as an indicator of what the user has accomplished so far has been well documented [15] and is a general guideline that is part of most design criteria. These indicators are particularly important for well-structured, procedural tasks. For example, most interface or web guidelines have wording similar to that given by the International Organization for Standardization's Guidance on World Wide Web, "For well-defined user tasks such as purchasing a product, the navigation structure guides users through that task and gives users a clear indication of their current position within the task." We will focus on two common methods for providing subgoal support in interfaces.

As users complete work on a procedural task, simply leaving that information on the interface provides a method for users to know which components of the task have been completed. Take, for example, the task of placing an order on Amazon.com. As the user completes the various data fields, such as entering the name, address and credit card information, that information remains on the screen even as the user progresses through the task of entering additional order information. This trail of information on the interface serves as a place keeper to cue the user as to which fields have been completed and which are yet to be completed. Most procedural task interfaces display information that has been entered in the data fields to prevent the user from having to remember what data fields have been completed. We call this presentation method "information trails."

A more explicit method of providing external subgoal support is to use a checklist or progress tracker. The progress tracker provides an explicit representation of the subgoals in the procedural task and indicates which subgoals have been completed, which are to be completed, and the order of subgoals in the task. Generally, the progress tracker is displayed at the top of the interface so that the user can clearly understand where they are in the task hierarchy.

Error Types

Our primary focus in this paper is on errors that occur on the last step. Errors in procedural tasks consist of perseverations, omissions/anticipations, and intrusions [16]. Perseveration errors are repeats of a previous action [17]. For example, putting cream in a cup of coffee multiple times is a perseveration error. Omissions are skipped steps, while anticipation errors are skipped steps that are quickly rectified. For example, an omission error would be completely forgetting to put cream in a cup of coffee, while an anticipation error would be attempting to pour from an unopened container. It can be quite difficult to differentiate omission and anticipation errors [18]. Intrusion errors (sometimes called capture errors) occur when an action comes from a different, usually related, task. For example, a capture error would occur when attempting to make coffee a person gets distracted by a tea bag and instead makes tea. In this paper, we will focus on omission errors and perseveration errors that occur at the last step of a well-learned procedure. We chose to focus on the last step of the procedure in this paper because, while errors are quite rare on well-learned tasks, they are more common on the last step [2; 6-10], and it is easier to see patterns and generate statistics.

Unintended Consequences

One possible concern about "improving" the interface is that those improvements can have unintended consequences. For example, in recent years the medical field has added computerized patient order entry forms and these systems and interfaces have saved hospitals money and patient's lives [19]. However, dosage errors [19] and patient identification errors have increased [20; 21].

Many times these unintended consequences are difficult to spot empirically because researchers focus on specific variables and sometimes do not look at how an interface may shift errors from one class to another or decrease performance in an "unrelated" area. In this paper we show how improving or changing the interface not only can have unintended consequences (in our case, shifting errors from one class to another), but also propose and demonstrate a solution that reduces errors based on the type of error, not on the type of interface.

EXPERIMENT 1

When tasks are routine, people make very few errors on them because those tasks have been performed hundreds or thousands of times. To allow meaningful analysis of the data, different researchers have examined errors by making the task difficult to remember [22; 23], added a secondary working memory task [7; 8] or interrupted participants during the routine task [24]. We used an interruption paradigm because interruptions have high ecological validity and have been shown to increase error rates even on well-learned tasks [2; 9; 25].

Experiment 1 focused on information trails. In the "No Information Trails" condition, no external subgoal support was available to participants. As participants entered order information into the data fields of the interface, the information was removed from the data fields upon completion of the subgoal. Thus, participants in this condition were forced to remember which subgoals had been completed. In the "Information Trails" condition, external subgoal support was provided by displaying the information that was entered into the data fields of each subgoal allowing participants to use this information to track their progress in the task. We should note that no designer would use the "No Information Trails" interface and that it was used here as an experimental control.

Method

Participants

63 undergraduate students participated in the experiment for course credit.

Materials

The primary task was a complex financial management task. The goal of the task was to successfully fill clients' orders for different types of stocks. The orders were to either buy or sell a stock and were presented four at a time at the top of the screen (see Figure 1). The current prices of the stocks associated with the orders were presented in the center of the screen in the Stock Information column. The actual stock price fluctuated every 45 s.

To complete an order, participants first had to determine which of the client orders was valid by comparing the client's requested price with the actual market price of the stock from the Stock Information column. Once an order was determined to be valid, the participant clicked the Start Order button for the respective stock. To actually fill the order, the participant had to enter details from the order itself and the Stock Information column into eight different modules on the screen. Participants had to follow a specific procedure to complete the order; the specific sequence was as follows: Quantity, Cost, Order Info, Margin, Stock Exchanges, Transaction, Stock Info, and Review. The spatial layout of the interface is intuitive (working down the left column and then the right column of Figure 1) and made sense to participants when asked during post-experiment interviews.

After entering information in each module, the participant clicked the Confirm button and could then move on to the next module. The Confirm button used the standard interface button practice of "blinking" after it was pushed to let the user know that their mouse click had been recorded by the interface. As part of training, participants were shown that the button blink occurred any time the button was clicked. After clicking Confirm on the final module (the Review module), a pop-up window appeared confirming the details of the order. The participant then had to acknowledge the window by clicking Ok. Finally, to complete the order the participant clicked the Complete Order button (upper right corner).[1]

All of the information required to complete the task was directly available on the task interface. If a participant attempted to work on a module or clicked a button that deviated from the strict procedure, the computer emitted a beep signaling that an error was made. The participant then continued working on the task until the correct action was completed.

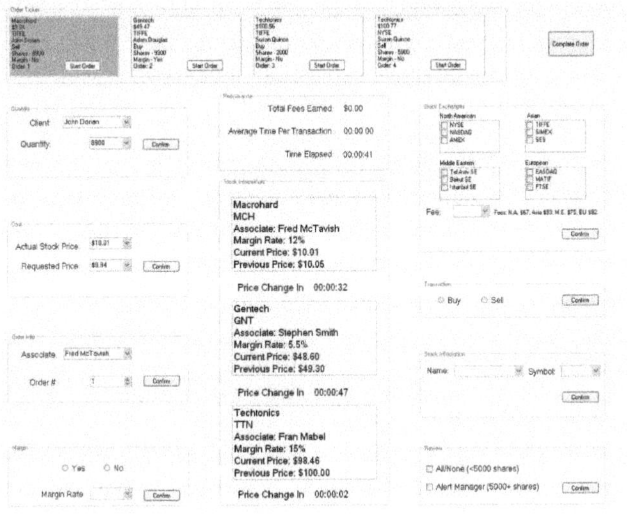

Figure 1. Screenshot of the financial management task with information trails.

The interrupting task consisted of multiple choice addition problems. Each problem contained five single-digit addends and five possible solutions (4 incorrect, 1 correct). A single addition problem and solution set was presented at one time; participants completed as many problems as possible during the interruption.

[1] Previous work has shown that the location of the complete order button does not impact error rates (Trafton, in preparation).

Design

Participants were randomly assigned to one of two conditions in a between-participants design. In the No Information Trails condition (N = 33), there were no explicit methods for external subgoal support provided. When information was entered into each module it disappeared after the confirm button was pressed. In the Information Trails condition (N = 30) information that was entered in each module remained after the confirm button was pressed.

In each condition, non-interruption and interruption trials were manipulated in a within-participants design. The completion of one order on the financial management task constituted a trial. Participants completed 12 trials; six were non-interruption and six were interruption trials. The order of non-interruption and interruption trials was randomized. Each interruption trial contained two interruptions. There were eight possible interruption points. These points occurred after clicking the Confirm button following the first seven modules and after acknowledging the order, just prior to the last action. The location of the interruptions was randomized with the constraint that exactly two interruptions occurred just prior to the last step and at least one interruption occurred at each of the other seven possible locations. The interruption itself lasted for 15 s.

Procedure

Participants were seated approximately 47 cm from the computer monitor. After the experimenter explained the financial management and interrupting tasks to the participant, the participant completed two training trials (one with and one without interruptions). To begin the experiment, participants had to complete two consecutive error-free trials to ensure the task was well learned.

Each participant was instructed to work at his / her own pace. When performing the interrupting task, participants were instructed to answer the addition problems as soon as the solution was known.

Error Categorization

Mouse-click data were recorded to determine the types of errors that were made on the last step (clicking the "Complete Contract" button). Error actions at the last step were categorized as either omissions or perseveration errors. An omission error was defined as skipping the step of clicking the Complete Contract button and making an action that is related to a new order on the financial management task (e.g., erroneously attempting to click the Start Order button or attempting to work on the first module). A perseveration error was defined as repeating an action on an already completed subgoal (e.g. clicking on the confirm button in the review module).

For each participant in all conditions, the percent of omission and preservation errors on the last step was calculated as a ratio of the actual number of each error type to the opportunities to make an error.

Results

We only analyzed the error rate at the last step of the procedure – the complete contract button. This was done because errors at the last step are more common than mid-trial errors and it is easier to see patterns and generate informative statistics.[2] In addition to the traditional ANOVA results below, we also performed analyses using count data and poisson distributions; the results were quite similar, so we present the ANOVA results that are more familiar to most readers.

Interruptions

Our first analysis examined the effect of interruptions. Consistent with other research [26-31], participants made more errors on the last step when it was preceded by an interruption (M = .31) than when it was not preceded by an interruption (M = .008), $F(1, 59) = 67.8$, $MSE = 0.04$, $p < 0.05$. However, interruption did not interact with any other variable (all $p > 0.05$), so it will be collapsed for the remainder of the analyses.

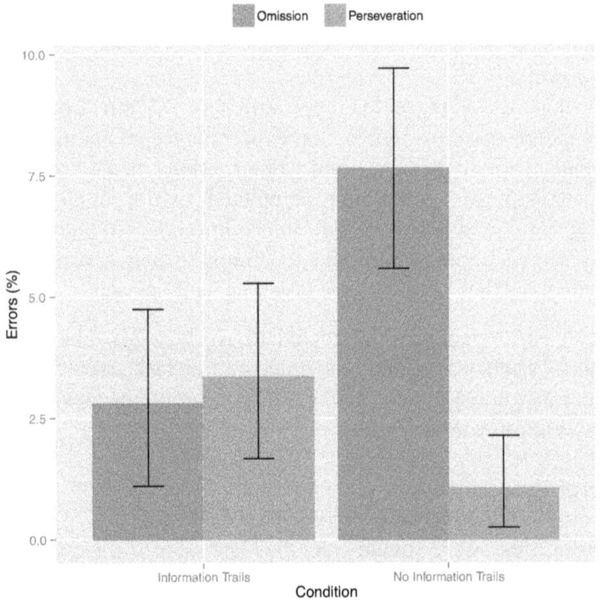

Figure 2. The error % in Experiment 1 for both omission errors and perseveration errors. Error bars are 95% CI.

Overall Error Rates

Somewhat surprisingly, there was not a difference between conditions in terms of overall error rate, $F(1, 61) = 2.5$, $MSE = 0.002$, $p > 0.10$. However, as Figure 2 suggests, there were overall more omission errors than perseveration errors, $F(1, 61) = 10.5$, $MSE = 0.003$, $p < 0.05$. More importantly, error type interacted with condition: the error rate for both omissions and perseverations was about the same for information trails, but when there was no information trail, omissions were much higher than perseveration errors, interaction $F(1, 61) = 13.2$, $MSE = 0.003$, $p < 0.05$; see Figure 2.

[2] Many results were similar when mid-trial errors were examined, but space precludes a detailed discussion.

Discussion

If we were to look only at one specific type of errors – omissions – we would conclude that information trails greatly reduced errors. Indeed, as Figure 2 shows, information trails reduced omission errors approximately three fold. However, a more detailed analysis shows that this is an incomplete story. An interface with information trails does not actually reduce the number of errors.[3] Rather, information trails change the class of errors at the last step. Without information trails, most of the errors are omission errors. However, with information trails, both omission and perseveration errors occur with approximately equal frequency.

Why would having information trails shift the class of errors from omission errors to perseveration errors? Previous researchers have suggested that the last step of the procedure may be skipped because people think they have already completed the last step [2;7;10]; this will obviously occur when there are fewer environmental cues. When there are environmental cues (e.g., information trails), people do seem to fall into a pattern of making perseveration errors [32; 33]. Thus, information trails shift the class of errors from omission errors to perseveration errors, perhaps because information cues make it easier to remember that the last step has not yet been completed, but decay and interference still cause some perseveration errors.

Note that overall error rates were quite low: less than 10%. This is confirmatory evidence that users knew and understood the task. Also, our view is that it is almost impossible to completely eliminate errors from any given task that a person is performing; our goal is to keep overall error rates < 1%. This study suggests that information trails shift errors from omission to perseveration but do not reduce the number of errors.

EXPERIMENT 2

Experiment 1 showed that information trails did not reduce the number of errors, but merely shifted the class of errors from omission errors to perseveration errors. There are, of

[3] Note that there were no differences between conditions in terms of the error rate. We interpret this result cautiously, but believe it should be taken seriously because (1) the standard deviation (3.5%) is larger than the difference between conditions (1.3%) and (2) the interaction was statistically significant, suggesting that it was not a power issue. Experiment 2 also helps address this concern by replicating the finding.

course, other ways of providing external subgoal support; a common method is to provide a progress checker, typically in the form of a progress bar at the top of the interface. Experiment 2 explored whether having a progress bar and information trails could reduce the number of errors or, as in Experiment 1, merely shift errors from one class to another. Experiment 2 also provides the opportunity to replicate the somewhat surprising findings of Experiment 1 that providing information trails did not reduce the number of errors.

There were two types of subgoal support in this experiment: information trails and progress trackers. The information trails conditions were identical to that used in experiment 1. The progress tracker condition used a progress bar that was modeled on popular retail web sites (e.g., Amazon, Toys R Us) and was displayed at the top of the interface so that the user could clearly understand where they are in the task hierarchy.

Method

Participants

64 undergraduate students participated in the experiment for course credit. No one in experiment 2 participated in experiment 1.

Materials

The primary task was the financial management task used in experiment 1; the interrupting task was the same as experiment as well.

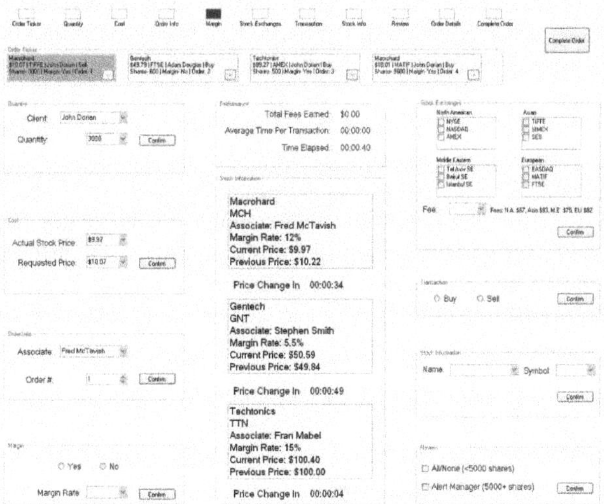

Figure 3. Screenshot of the financial management task with information trails and progress tracker.

Design

The Information Trail conditions were the same as that used in Experiment 1. The Progress Tracker conditions contained a progress bar at the top of the screen that showed the user exactly where they were in the task and what subgoal they were currently working on. The progress tracker changed states as a step was correctly completed (the confirm button was pushed). It did not change if the user made an error. The progress tracker was always perfect information and always available to the user.

Participants were randomly assigned to one of four conditions in a between-participants design. The No Information Trails/No Progress Tracker condition (N = 18) contained no explicit methods for external subgoal support. The No Information Trails/Progress Tracker condition (N = 16) contained no information trails but did provide a progress bar. The Information Trails/No Progress Tracker condition (N = 14) provided information trails but no progress bar. The Information Trails/Progress Tracker condition (N = 16) provided full external subgoal support by providing both information trails and a progress bar.

The No Information Trail/No Progress Tracker condition was the same as the No Information Trail condition from Experiment 1. The Information Trail/No Progress Tracker condition was the same as the Information Trail condition from Experiment 1.

Procedure

The procedure for experiment 2 was the same as that for experiment 1. If a participant was in a Progress Tracker condition, the experimenter clearly explained how the progress bar worked and exactly what it showed.

To begin the experiment, participants again had to complete two consecutive error-free trials to ensure the task was well learned.

Error Categorization

Errors were categorized into omissions and perseverations in the same manner as experiment 1. Percent errors were calculated the same way as in experiment 1.

Results

Interruptions

We again examined the effect of interruptions. Consistent with experiment 1, participants made more errors on the last step when it was preceded by an interruption (M = .18) than when it was not preceded by an interruption (M = .009), $F(1, 56) = 57.9$, $MSE = 0.02$, $p < 0.05$. Interruptions did not interact with any other variable (all $p > 0.05$) and will therefore be collapsed for the remainder of the analyses.

Overall Error Rates

We analyzed the error rate for both Information Trails and the Progress Tracker. Surprisingly, but consistent with experiment 1, participants who did not have access to Information Trails did not make more errors than participants who did have access to Information Trails, $F(1, 60) < 1$, $MSE = 0.003$, NS. Also surprisingly, having access to a progress tracker did not reduce the number of errors compared to participants not having access to a progress tracker, $F(1, 60) < 1$, $MSE = 0.003$, NS.

Information Trails and Progress Tracking did not interact, $F(1, 60) < 1$, $MSE = 0.003$, NS.

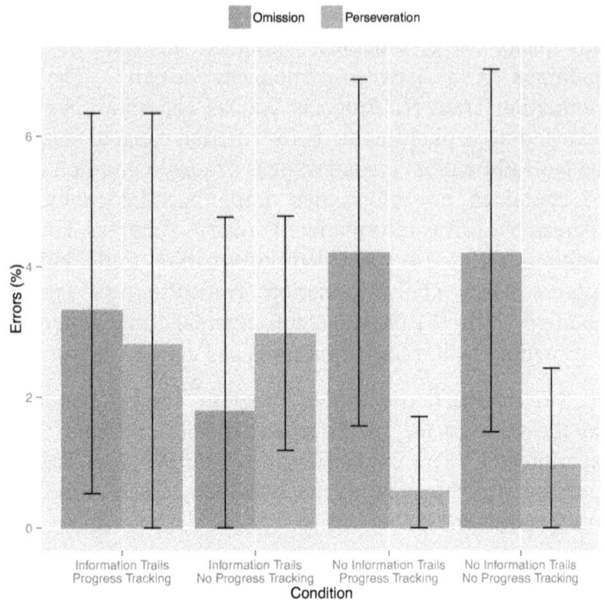

Figure 4. The error % in Experiment 2 for both omission errors and perseveration errors. Error bars are 95% CI.

As suggested by Figures 4 and 5 and consistent with experiment 1, there were more omission errors than perseveration errors, $F(1, 60) = 4.3$, $MSE = 0.002$, $p < 0.05$. Also consistent with experiment 1 and as shown in figure 5 which collapses across the Progress Tracker conditions, error type interacted with Information Trail: the error rate for omission errors were higher than perseveration errors when there was no information trail, but was about the same when there was an information trail, $F(1, 60) = 5.3$, $MSE = 0.002$, $p < 0.05$. Having access to a progress tracker did not, however, interact with the type of error, $F(1, 60) < 1$, $MSE = 0.002$, NS. Finally, there was not a three-way interaction between Information Trail, Progress Tracker, and error type, $F(1, 60) < 1$, $MSE = .002$, NS.

Discussion

This experiment examined two different types of subgoal support: information trails and progress tracking, both singly and in combination. The results were rather surprising. First, the pattern of results for information trails replicated the results of experiment 1: having information trails does not reduce the total number of errors. Experiment 2 also showed that when there was no information trail, there were more omission errors than perseveration errors on the last step of a procedure, but that when users did have access to information trails the error rate for omission errors and perseveration errors were about the same. This again shows that improving the interface may have unintended consequences: in our case it shifted the class of errors from one type to another but did not decrease the overall rate of errors.

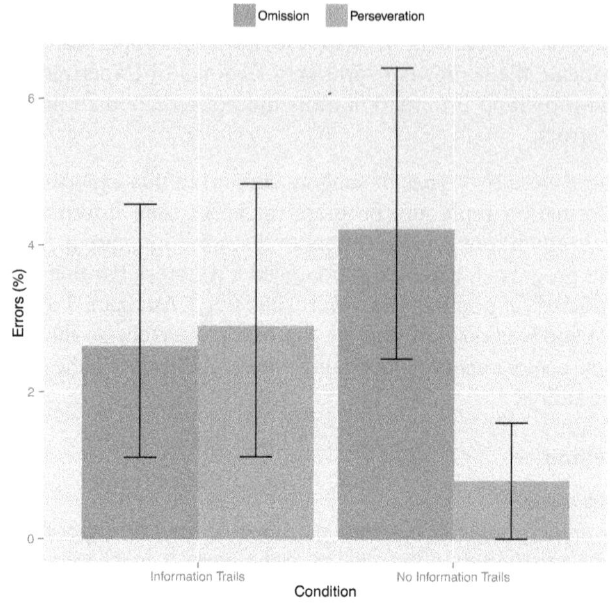

Figure 5. The error % in Experiment 2 for both omission errors and perseveration errors, collapsed across progress tracking. Error bars are 95% CI.

Another surprising result is that having a progress tracker did not reduce the number of errors at all. This is surprising because not only is a progress bar a very well known part of modern interfaces, but it showed with perfect accuracy the step that the user should have been working on. In fact, all the user had to do in order to completely eliminate errors was to look at the progress bar and execute the appropriate subgoal. The fact that the progress bar did not impact overall error rates suggests that people are not using the progress bar or perhaps not looking at it when they need it. It follows that people may not think they need it or because it required an additional gaze and was an additional level of (albeit small) work [34; 35].

One of the main aspects of experiments 1 and 2 is that people still make errors on the last step of a task, even though they know the task well. Critically, improving the interface by providing explicit subgoal support does not seem to reduce the number of errors that users make, at least on the last step of the task.

There are, however, several ways to reduce errors that could be tried. One possibility is to display only a single widget at a time and force users to fill in that information before continuing. This "single entry option" would almost assuredly reduce errors, but the user would likely be unimpressed with the interface. First, it is not uncommon to need information that has already been filled in (e.g., details of the task). Second, adding that additional step (similar to our "Confirm" button) increases time and work for the user. Third, making changes becomes much more difficult because the user must navigate backwards.

A second way to reduce errors would be to provide explicit subgoal support by way of an explicit cue on every single step. For example, the interface could point an arrow at the step that the user was working on. Again, this approach would likely reduce errors, at least for new users. However, users are likely to become frustrated and annoyed with a cue that is always present [36]. Second, on interfaces that contain a large amount of information, a cue that is always present can contribute to visual clutter on the interface [37]. Finally, users often become accustomed to information that is always present on an interface, and users can begin to ignore this information [38]. For these reasons, a constant cue may become ineffective over a long period.

A third approach is to attempt to predict when a user is going to make an error and present a just-in-time cue only when it is likely to be needed [2]. This is the approach we will use here.

In previous work, we developed a theoretical model that predicted when a user would make an error before the error actually occurred. The model itself was based on the Memory for Goals theory [32; 39; 40] and was quite successful when converted to a real-time system. Details are available elsewhere [2], but the system was able to track a user's eye-movements and predict the likelihood that the user would make an error. When the probability reached a sufficiently high level (75% for this model), the system provided a just-in-time, blatant cue that guided the user to the next correct step. We chose this approach because it has support from different researchers [8; 41], it is not annoying because the cue is only presented when it is needed and it does not constantly increase visual clutter.

There are two important caveats to this model. First, the model was developed with interfaces that had no explicit subgoal support (neither information trails nor progress tracking), so it is unclear whether it would reduce errors on interfaces that do provide subgoal support. Second, the model was developed to work only for the last step of a procedure; it does not work for other steps in a procedure because the reason that people make errors differs according to the type of step the user is executing. However, this last caveat is actually a strength for this project: it can be used to reduce end-of-procedure errors on the current task, which is the focus of this paper.

EXPERIMENT 3

Experiments 1 and 2 showed that providing explicit subgoal support did not reduce the number of errors that users made. The goal of this paper is not only to understand how the interface impacts errors, but also to determine a method of reducing error rates on the last step of a routine procedural task.

To accomplish this, we used a real-time system that predicts when users will make an error on the last step of a procedure [2].

Method

Participants

54 undergraduate students participated in the experiment for course credit. No one in experiment 3 participated in experiment 1 or 2.

Materials

The primary task was the financial management task used in experiments 1 and 2; the interrupting task was the same as experiments 1 and 2 as well.

Design

The control condition in this experiment was the same as the Information Trails/Progress Tracker condition of experiment 2. This condition provided both Information trails and a progress bar that showed the user exactly where they were in the task and what subgoal they were currently working on. The Cue condition was exactly the same as the Information Trails/Progress Tracker, but also ran the predictive model [2].

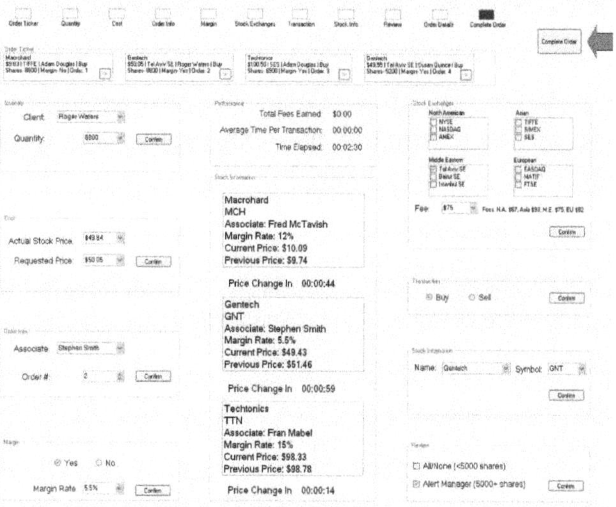

Figure 6. Screenshot of the financial management task running the predictive cue. The arrow shows that the model predicted the current user would make an error, so presented a real-time cue to the participant.

The model has three components (described more fully in [2; 10; 25]: time, the total number of fixations, and whether or not the last step was fixated. The motivation for these three variables followed directly from cognitive theory. The time predictor represents goal decay. The total number of fixations also represents decay, but it may also capture individual differences in decay rates and differences in visual and cognitive processing demands [42; 43]. Finally, the fixation on the last step represents (in)attention to the last step and associative priming provided by the last action button on the task interface.

As the user starts working on the last step of the procedure, the predictive system calculates the probability that the user would make an error based on the aforementioned components. If the probability reached or exceeded 75% (determined through ROC analyses; see [2]), a cue would fire, alerting the user to the correct action that should be taken. The alert is shown in figure 6.

Participants were randomly assigned to one of two conditions in a between-participants design. The control condition (N = 29) presented full external subgoal support by providing both information trails and a progress bar. The cue condition (N = 25) looked and behaved identically, except that the predictive cue was shown when the probability threshold reached or exceeded 75%.

Hypotheses
Our hypothesis was that the Cue condition would reduce the overall number of errors compared to the control condition.

Procedure
The procedure for experiment 3 was the same as that for experiments 1 and 2. Participants in both conditions were calibrated on the eyetracker as well. For both conditions, the experimenter clearly explained how the progress bar worked and exactly what it showed.

To begin the experiment, participants again had to complete two consecutive error-free trials to ensure the task was well learned.

Error Categorization
Errors were categorized into omissions and perseverations in the same manner as experiment 1. Percent errors were calculated the same way as in experiment 1.

Collecting Eye Movements
Eye track data were collected using an SMI RED 250 operating at 250 Hz. A fixation was defined as a minimum of five eye samples within 30 pixels (approximately 2° of visual angle) of each other, calculated in Euclidian distance. The eyetracker was used as an input to the model to predict when a user had a high probability of making an error.

Results

Interruptions
We began by examining the effect of interruptions. Consistent with the previous two experiments, participants made more errors on the last step when it was preceded by an interruption (M = .15) than when it was not preceded by an interruption (M = 0.0), $F(1, 51) = 12.6$, MSE = 0.03, $p < 0.05$. As in experiments 1 and 2, interruptions will be collapsed for the remainder of the analyses.

Overall Error Rates
We first examined how well the model was able to predict when a user made an error in the control condition. Consistent with previous results, it accurately predicted 85% of the errors made.

We next analyzed the overall error rate for both the Control and Cue conditions. Consistent with our hypothesis and as suggested by Figure 7, we found that users who received the predictive cue made fewer errors than uses who did not receive the predictive cue, $F(1, 52) = 12.1$, MSE = 0.001, $p < 0.05$.

This study also showed a larger number of perseveration errors than omission errors, $F(1, 52) = 14.43$, MSE = 0.06, $p < 0.05$. We also found a significant interaction between error type and condition, $F(1, 52) = 6.6$, MSE = 0.001, $p < 0.05$, suggesting that the Cue condition helped perseveration errors more than omission errors.

Discussion
This experiment was extremely successful: it showed that errors can be greatly reduced by running a predictive model. The predictive model successfully reduced both omission errors and perseveration errors. Critically, the model brought error rates to under 1% (see figure 7).

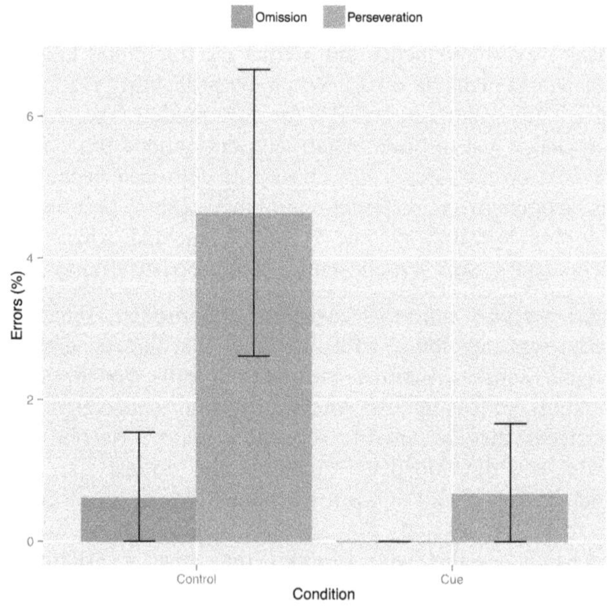

Figure 7. The error % in Experiment 3 for both omission and perseveration errors. Error bars are 95% CI.

CONCLUSION

Imagine a professional in the medical domain who has noticed that when emergency room doctors are especially busy, they sometimes forget to log off one patient and switch to a current patient, entering orders for the wrong patient [20]. This professional then requests a re-design of the interface to provide subgoal support so this omission error (forgetting to logoff one patient) is reduced. A later study does, in fact, show that by adding subgoal support, the number of omission errors are reduced. However, an unintended consequence of this interface change was that it increased the number of times some orders got entered, so some patients had duplicate procedures performed and medications doubled (a perseveration error).

The last step of a routine procedural task frequently has one of the highest error rates [6; 9] and this paper has presented three experiments that have focused on methods for reducing the number of errors on the last step of a procedural task.

Experiment one showed that providing information trails to users did not, in fact, reduce the number of errors. Information trails did, however, have an impact on the class of errors: users who did not have information trails made more omission errors while users who did have access to information trails made approximately the same number of omission and perseveration errors. This shifting of errors from one class to another was an unintended consequence of improving the interface.

Experiment two presented two different types of external subgoal support – information trails and progress tracking. Experiment two showed that providing strong subgoal support did not decrease the number of errors. Specifically, having access to a progress bar did not reduce the number of errors, nor did having access to information trails. However, adding information trails again shifted the class of errors from omission errors to perseveration errors.

Experiments 1 and 2 suggested that, short of removing the step entirely, these end-of-procedure errors are quite resistant to interface methods of error reduction. In order to reduce the number of errors at the last step, we described a theoretical error model that predicted when people made errors on the last step of a procedure and used that model to provide a cue when the probability of making an error reached a predetermined threshold. Experiment three compared an interface with both information trails and progress tracker support to an interface with external subgoal support and the predictive cue system. Our predictive error system was able to reduce the number of errors made on the last step of the procedure to < 1%.

We believe that, as long as a person is involved, errors will occur. There are many ways to reduce or mitigate the number or type of errors that occur, including providing additional training, an excellent interface, double-checking information, etc. However all of these methods have costs in one form or another. Additional training can only reduce errors so much; double checking information (like airline pilots do) requires additional people, training, money, and errors still occur. Improving the interface can reduce the number of errors (not shown in this paper, but shown by others), but may have unintended consequences like shifting errors from one class to another.

It should be noted that in all of the current studies, the overall error rate was quite low (less than 10%). This low error rate is actually an important aspect of procedural tasks: they are well learned and thus the error rates should be low. For some tasks (e.g., making tea or making copies), making an error is either easily fixed or the consequences are not severe. However, for safety-critical tasks like nuclear power plant operations, medical procedures, airplane piloting, long-haul trucker driving, etc., errors can be disastrous. The low error rate of these types of tasks makes studying errors more challenging, but because most actions that people do are routine [3], it is critical that we understand not only why people make errors, but also how to prevent them.

The approach presented in this paper is tied to cognitive science theory and our goal is to understand why people make errors [7; 32; 39; 40; 44]. This understanding can then allow theoretically based predictive models to be built that should work across a variety of interfaces but that are focused on specific error classes (e.g., anticipation errors) or steps (e.g., the last step of a procedure). The model can then be used to predict and hopefully prevent errors as we did here. One of the advantages of class- or step- predictive models is that the interface itself may not matter as much. Thus, the interface designer can focus on creating an excellent user experience and worry less about preventing errors.

ACKNOWLEDGMENTS

This work was supported in part by the Office of Naval Research to JGT. The views and conclusions contained in this document are those of the authors and should not be interpreted as necessarily representing the official policies, either expressed or implied, of the U.S. Navy.

REFERENCES

[1] Rasmussen, J. 1982. Human errors. A taxonomy for describing human malfunction in industrial installations. Journal of occupational accidents.

[2] Ratwani, R. M. and Trafton, J. G. 2011. A real-time eye tracking system for predicting and preventing postcompletion errors. Human–Computer Interaction. 26, 3, 205-245.

[3] Reason, J. 1990. Human Error. Cambridge University Press.

[4] Perrow, C. 1981. Normal accident at three mile island. Society. 18, 5, 17-26.

[5] Perrow, C. 2011 Normal accidents: Living with high risk technologies. Princeton University Press.

[6] Brumby, D. P., Cox, A. L., and Back…, J. 2013. Recovering from an interruption: Investigating speed− accuracy trade-offs in task resumption behavior. Journal of Experimental Psychology: Applied

[7] Byrne, M. D. and Bovair, S. 1997. A working memory model of a common procedural error. Cognitive science. 21, 1, 31-61.

[8] Chung, P. H. and Byrne, M. D. 2008. Cue effectiveness in mitigating postcompletion errors in a routine procedural task. International Journal of Human Computer Studies. 66, 217-232.

[9] Li, S. Y. W., Blandford, A., Cairns, P., and Young, R. M. 2008. The effect of interruptions on postcompletion and other procedural errors: An account based on the activation-based goal memory model. Journal of Experimental Psychology: Applied. 14, 4, 314-328.

[10] Ratwani, R. M., McCurry, J. M., and Trafton, J. G. 2008. Predicting postcompletion errors using eye movements. CHI.

[11] Botvinick, M. M. and Plaut, D. C. 2006. Such stuff as habits are made on: A reply to Cooper and Shallice (2006). Psychological Review.

[12] Cooper, R. P. and Shallice, T. 2006. Hierarchical schemas and goals in the control of sequential behavior. Psychological review.

[13] Gray, W. D. 2000. The nature and processing of errors in interactive behavior. Cognitive Science. 24, 2, 205-248.

[14] Maxion, R. A. and Reeder, R. W. 2005. Improving user-interface dependability through mitigation of human error. International Journal of Human-Computer Studies. 63, 1, 25-50.

[15] Hix, D. and Hartson, H. R. 1993 Developing user interfaces: ensuring usability through product & process. John Wiley & Sons, Inc.

[16] Reason, J. 2000. Human error: models and management. British Medical Journal.

[17] Sandson, J. and Albert, M. L. 1984. Varieties of perseveration. Neuropsychologia.

[18] Cooper, R. and Shallice, T. 2000. Contention scheduling and the control of routine activities. Cognitive Neuropsychology.

[19] Campbell, E. M., Sittig, D. F., Ash, J. S., Guappone, K. P., and Dykstra, R. H. 2006. Types of unintended consequences related to computerized provider order entry. Journal of the American Medical Informatics Association. 13, 5, 547-556.

[20] Koppel, R., Metlay, J. P., Cohen, A., Abaluck, B., Localio, A. R., Kimmel, S. E., and Strom, B. L. 2005. Role of computerized physician order entry systems in facilitating medication errors. JAMA: the journal of the American Medical Association. 293, 10, 1197-1203.

[21] Koppel, R., Wetterneck, T., Telles, J. L., and Karsh, B.-T. 2008. Workarounds to barcode medication administration systems: their occurrences, causes, and threats to patient safety. Journal of the American Medical Informatics Association. 15, 4, 408-423.

[22] Giovannetti, T., Schwartz, M., and Buxbaum, L. 2007. The Coffee Challenge: A new method for the study of everyday action errors. Journal of Clinical and Experimental Neuropsychology. 29, 7.

[23] Ruh, N., Cooper, R. P., and Mareschal, D. 2008. The Hierarchies and Systems that Underlie Routine Behavior: Evidence from an Experiment in Virtual Gardening. Cognitive Science 2008.

[24] Botvinick, M. M. and Bylsma, L. M. 2005. Distraction and action slips in an everyday task: Evidence for a dynamic representation of task. Psychonomic Bulletin and Review.

[25] Ratwani, R. M. and Gregory Trafton, J. 2010. A generalized model for predicting postcompletion errors. Topics in Cognitive Science. 2, 1, 154-167.

[26] Hodgetts, H. M. and Jones, D. M. 2006. Interruption of the tower of london task: Support for a goal activation approach. Journal of Experimental Psychology: General. 135, 103-115.

[27] Hodgetts, H. M. and Jones, D. M. 2006. Contextual cues aid recovery from interruption: The role of associative activation. Journal of Experimental Psychology: Learning, Memory & Cognition. 32, 1120-1132.

[28] McFarlane, D. C. 2002. Comparison of four primary methods for coordinating the interruption of people in human-computer interaction. Human Computer Interaction. 17, 1, 63-139.

[29] Monk, C., Boehm-Davis, D., and Trafton, J. G. 2002 The attentional costs of interrupting task performance at various stages. In Human Factors Annual conference of 2002,

[30] Monk, C., Boehm-Davis, D., and Trafton, J. G. 2004. Recovering from Interruptions: Implications for Driver Distraction Research. Human Factors. 46, 4, 650-663.

[31] Monk, C., Trafton, J. G., and Boehm-Davis, D. 2008. Goal decay and the resumption of suspended goals; Evidence for an activation-based theory of interruption recovery. Journal of Experimental Psychology: Applied. 14, 4, 299-313.

[32] Trafton, J. G., Altmann, E. M., and Ratwani, R. M. 2011. A memory for goals model of sequence errors. Cognitive Systems Research. 12, 2, 134-143.

[33] Trafton, J. G., Jacobs, A., and Harrison, A. M. 2012. Building and verifying a predictive model of interruption resumption. Proceedings of the IEEE. 100, 3, 648-659.

[34] Ballard, D. H., Hayhoe, M. M., Li, F., Whitehead, S. D., Frisby, J. P., Taylor, J. G., and Fisher, R. B. 1992. Hand-eye coordination during sequential tasks [and discussion]. Philosophical Transactions of the Royal Society of London. Series B: Biological Sciences. 337, 1281, 331-339.

[35] Gray, W. D., Sims, C. R., Fu, W. T., and Schoelles, M. J. 2006. The soft constraints hypothesis: A rational analysis approach to resource allocation for interactive behavior. Psychological Review. 113, 3, 461-482.

[36] Ceaparu, I., Lazar, J., Bessiere, K., Robinson, J., and Shneiderman, B. 2004. Determining causes and severity of end-user frustration. International journal of human-computer interaction. 17, 3, 333-356.

[37] Heiner, A. P. and Asokan, N. 2008. Using Salience Differentials to Making Visual Cues Noticeable. UPSEC.

[38] Burke, M., Hornof, A., Nilsen, E., and Gorman, N. 2005. High-cost banner blindness: Ads increase perceived workload, hinder visual search, and are forgotten. ACM Transactions on Computer-Human Interaction (TOCHI). 12, 4, 423-445.

[39] Altmann, E. M. and Trafton, J. G. 2002. Memory for goals: An activation-based model. Cognitive Science. 26, 1, 39-83.

[40] Altmann, E. M. and Trafton, J. G. 2007. Timecourse of Recovery from Task Interruption: Data and a Model. Psychonomic Bulletin & Review. 14, 6, 1079-1084.

[41] Byrne, M. D. and Davis, E. M. 2006. Task structure and postcompletion error in the execution of a routine procedure. Human Factors: The Journal of the Human Factors and Ergonomics Society. 48, 4, 627-638.

[42] Just, M. A. and Carpenter, P. A. 1976. Eye fixations and cognitive processes. Cognitive Psychology. 8, 4, 441-480.

[43] Rayner, K. 1998. Eye movements in reading and information processing: 20 years of research. Psychological Bulletin. 124, 372-422.

[44] Gray, W. D. 2000. The nature and processing of errors in interactive behavior. Cognitive Science. 24, 2, 205-248.

CAUSALITY – A Conceptual Model of Interaction History

Mathieu Nancel
University of Canterbury
Christchurch 8140, New Zealand
mathieu@nancel.net

Andy Cockburn
University of Canterbury
Christchurch 8140, New Zealand
andy@cosc.canterbury.ac.nz

ABSTRACT
Simple history systems such as Undo and Redo permit retrieval of earlier or later interaction states, but advanced systems allow powerful capabilities to reuse or reapply combinations of commands, states, or data across interaction contexts. Whether simple or powerful, designing interaction history mechanisms is challenging. We begin by reviewing existing history systems and models, observing a lack of tools to assist designers and researchers in specifying, contemplating, combining, and communicating the behaviour of history systems. To resolve this problem, we present CAUSALITY, a conceptual model of interaction history that clarifies the possibilities for temporal interactions. The model includes components for the work *artifact* (such as the text and formatting of a Word document), the system *context* (such as the settings and parameters of the user interface), the *linear timeline* (the commands executed in real time), and the *branching chronology* (a structure of executed commands and their impact on the artifact and/or context, which may be navigable by the user). We then describe and exemplify how this model can be used to encapsulate existing user interfaces and reveal limitations in their behaviour, and we also show in a conceptual evaluation how the model stimulates the design of new and innovative opportunities for interacting in time.

ACM Classification Keywords
H.5.2 [Information interfaces and presentation]: User Interfaces. - Graphical user interfaces.

Author Keywords
History Systems; Undo; Conceptual Model; Paradoxes

INTRODUCTION
Supporting the ability for users to Undo and Redo commands has been an expected part of interactive computing systems since the first graphical user interfaces [26]. The simple metaphor of allowing users to step back and forward through time enables users to revert to previous states and encourages exploratory learning because erroneous actions can be easily reversed or redone. Other forms of history systems can make interaction more efficient by providing rapid access to recently used tools or data (e.g., [11]). Yet more advanced history systems allow sophisticated manipulations of temporal aspects of interaction, such as parallel editing of alternative versions of a document [27], recycling past sequences of commands or command parameters [12, 15], undoing commands within a portion of the document [8, 9, 25], and concurrent collaborative work [23]. In short, previous research on interactive history systems is extremely rich.

CHI 2014, April 26 - May 01 2014, Toronto, ON, Canada

ACM 978-1-4503-2473-1/14/04...$15.00.
http://dx.doi.org/10.1145/2556288.2556990

A number of these works address technical aspects of interacting with command histories, including how to visualize them [8, 12, 14] and navigate through them [22, 24]. However items of prior work generally address separated problems or functionalities. Combining these systems or their features in a real-world application remains challenging as they often rely on different and sometimes incompatible paradigms and models, or generate different effects for the same operation. Many also exhibit conceptual problems caused by their underlying model. As a simple example, most interactive systems 'forget' undone commands or previous document states when the user triggers an editing command after having performed undo. Consequently, pressing 'undo' then accidentally triggering an action will, in many systems, eliminate the possibility of returning to the pre-undo state. Therefore, although built primarily for error recovery, such systems can be surprisingly error intolerant. Yet this need not be the case – an interface may maintain the undone command, or the data state, or both. Through this paper we demonstrate a variety of counter-intuitive, illogical or restrictive effects that can arise with history systems, and we attribute them to the lack of an underlying model with sufficient expressiveness to adequately contemplate temporal interactions.

The key problem that we address is that designers and researchers currently lack the conceptual tools for supporting, combining and generating temporal behaviours. To solve this problem, we introduce CAUSALITY, a conceptual model of interaction history in which commands, application parameters and document states are described as a *causal* and *unforgetting* system that is both linear and branching.

CAUSALITY, as illustrated in Fig. 1, consists of five main components that model different elements necessary for complete coverage of temporal interactions. 1) *Artifact* stores the state of the work object at discrete points, and is represented by the green bar in Fig. 1. The middle images of the figure show how the artifact develops through time, although the images are not part of the model. 2) *Context* stores the application state at discrete points, including parameter settings and the state of user interface controls. It is represented by the grey bar. For example, in a drawing application, *context* might store the current colour and line-width, etc. 3) *Com-*

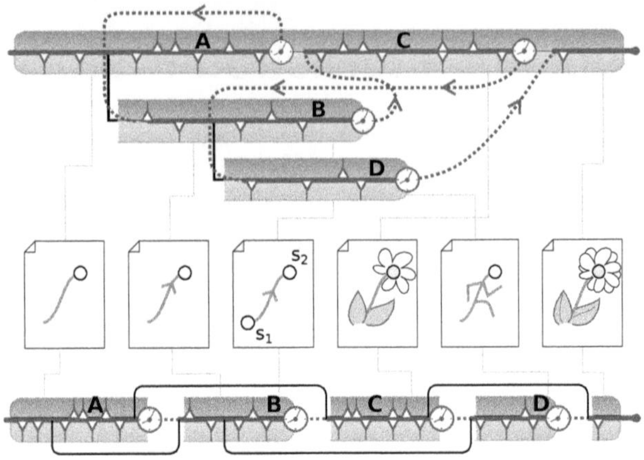

Figure 1. CAUSALITY overview: branching chronology (top 3 rows); linear timeline (bottom, and blue line in top 3 rows); lettered and illustrated states match in both visualizations. Application context is the grey bar; Artifact state is the green bar. Commands shown as blue triangles; time-travel as clocks and dotted lines within the linear timeline. Black strokes between states represent branching in both visualizations.

mands (blue triangles in the figure) cause state changes in the artifact (downward pointing) or context (upwards). For example, a drawing action constitutes a command affecting the artifact. In CAUSALITY, each command references all the elements of the artifact and context that it uses and affects. 4) *Linear timeline* stores the commands as a linear sequence of events (bottom of Fig. 1 and blue line in top 3 rows). 5) *Branching chronology* stores a tree-like virtual chronology of artifact and context, with each branch constructed by first using the interface to traverse through time (represented by the clock icons on the linear timeline) and then using a command to modify the artifact, context or chronology at that point.

The model's separation of *artifact* from *context* is particularly important. This is because some commands affect only the artifact (e.g., drawing), some only the context (e.g., changing line colour), and some both (e.g., cutting a drawn object). In general, the model (which includes other components described later in the paper) can encapsulate and describe existing interactive behaviours, and it also facilitates identifying and describing new possibilities for history interactions.

After reviewing previous research on temporal interaction from the HCI and general computing literature, we detail and exemplify the technical and conceptual issues that arise when interacting with time. We then fully describe the CAUSALITY model and explain how it solves these issues and how it can be used to implement the techniques and systems in the literature. Finally, we use a painting application scenario as a conceptual evaluation to show how CAUSALITY inspires powerful and exciting new interface behaviors. The contributions of the paper are (i) a comprehensive review of history in computing systems, (ii) an analysis of the limitations of prior models for history systems, and (iii) the provision of an exact set of 'thinking tools', instantiated in CAUSALITY, for designers and researchers to explore powerful and novel interactions with history. This paper presents the conceptual foundations of a larger project; specific implementations of CAUSALITY and their evaluation are left to future work.

HISTORY IN COMPUTING SYSTEMS

The following subsections briefly review key items from the extensive history systems literature, categorised by the main objective of each study: error recovery, command reuse, version management, and history models. In addition, many papers have examined interactive visualisations of past events for a variety of application domains (see [13] for a review). Although visualisations might be used to help the user navigate branching chronologies generated by CAUSALITY (described later), this review focuses on conceptual foundations, rather than their visual representation.

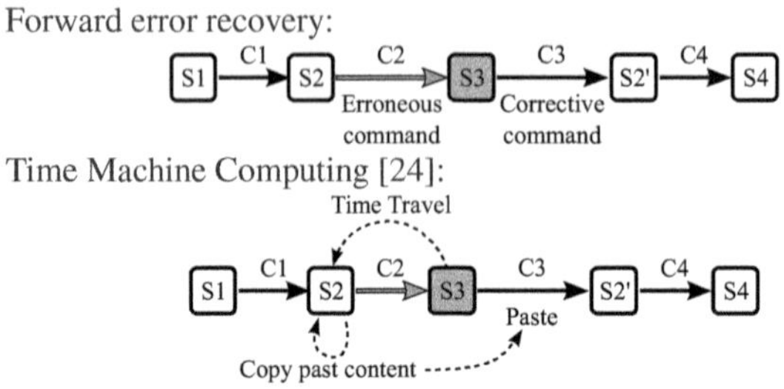

Figure 2. History of an artifact, with its different states (S) and commands (C). Forward error recovery (top) consists in applying corrective commands to recover from an erroneous action. TMC [24] helps this process by providing access to past versions of the artifact (bottom).

Error recovery

The primary goal of many history systems is to allow the user to recover from erroneous or mistaken actions. Abowd and Dix [1] distinguish backward and forward error recovery. *Forward* error recovery consists of performing additional editing actions to either cancel or correct the erroneous action(s) (Fig. 2). For example, using an eraser tool to cancel the effects of a drawing action, rather than undoing its creation. Rekimoto's Time Machine Computing [24] supports a variant of forward error recovery that allows users to reuse past data in modifying the current state (Fig. 2-bottom).

Figure 3. Undo (left) temporarily restores previous states of the artifact; undone commands are discarded if the user resumes editing (right).

Backward error recovery alters the command history of the artifact to restore past versions or cancel unwanted operations. The most common backward error recovery facility is linear undo/redo, often implemented with the 'Command' design pattern [10]. 'Undo' takes the work artifact back to its state before the last command (Fig. 3-left) and can be repeated to visit earlier artifact states. 'Redo' moves through time in the opposite direction, reapplying the commands, until the latter-most artifact state is reached. While undo is normally available in desktop applications for discrete commands influencing the data state, it has not generally been applied to mobile interactions, continuous interactions, nor for commands that affect view state (e.g., zooming). Recent research, however, has addressed these limitations: Dwell-and-Spring supports undo for direct manipulation; [2] and Loregian [16] examines undo on mobile devices.

The linear model of undo/redo systems has also been augmented in a number of ways to improve error recovery. *Selective Undo* [23] allows the user to cancel distinct commands without deleting all later history. The user is thus able to interfere with the history of the document instead of simply restoring previous versions chronologically. Chimera [14] and '3Rs' [4] allow the user to go back in time within a document or the whole system, applying changes to past data and/or commands, and then replay every later actions on the newly defined past. Chen *et al.* propose a subset of these functionalities in [8]: users can select past editing commands that required dialog windows and alter the parameters of these commands, then replay every later command.

However, modifying only parts of the history of a document can generate temporal paradoxes [19], which are conflicts in the course of actions that chronologically follow the undone or modified command(s). For example, if changing a past command results in a data object no longer existing, then every later command applied to that object is meaningless. Advanced history manipulations therefore require recovery mechanisms to detect and cope with paradoxes. Systems like Joyce [22] and Script [3] reject commands that generate paradoxes. *Cascading undo* [6] takes a different approach, tracking forward through every conflicting command, and triggering undo mechanisms to remove the conflict(s).

Command reuse

Accessing and reusing past commands can improve user performance, e.g. by repeating a command or by generating macros that apply complex operations in a single step. Kurlander and Feiner [15] described a system for selecting past sequences of commands and re-applying them to the current version of the document with different parameters. Their system identifies the required parameters of the macro, requesting input from the user; and it permits macro debugging. Bueno *et al.* [5] proposed a tool for collaborative editing of vector graphics, allowing users to merge work across different timelines. Chronicle [12] allows users to invoke dialogs from past commands with the same parameters.

Version management

Some history systems maintain alternative versions of a document, allowing users to explore different designs at the same time without needing to undo their previous edits. Subjunctive interfaces [18] allow the user to view and control alternative scenarios for a variety of uses including simulations and document editing. Terry *et al.*'s system [27] supports alternative document designs and provides interface mechanisms for quick editing and visual comparison. Chen *et al.* apply revision control mechanisms to binary files [8], enabling branching and merging similar to SVN.

History structure

Depending on their purpose, history systems record commands and states as either a list, tree or graph. *List* structures are the most widespread, recording artifact states and/or commands in a linear fashion, often chronologically [5, 21, 28]. This structure enables a variety of single-history operations, from Linear [10] to Selective [23] and Regional Undo [25]. *Tree* structures allow histories to diverge from a common past state, usually at the user's explicit command, so that several versions of a document can coexist in parallel. They enable exploration of alternative modifications of a single document [27] or the whole file system [22]. Finally, directed *graph* structures enable merging of parallel branches of history, such as those produced by multiple users [19] or from a single user's alternative designs [8].

ISSUES WITH HISTORY SYSTEMS

Although there is a wealth of prior research on history systems, most of this research has focused on meeting the requirements of a specific target domain. A smaller proportion of prior work has carefully specified the temporal model that underlies the behaviour of the systems disclosed, but again, when described, these models have generally been directed to the requirements of their intended domain or of specific functionalities. This specificity of application creates problems for designers who wish to apply features in new domains.

In this section we describe three main limitations of existing models of history: 1) they lack structural and functional *inter-compatibility*, which makes it challenging to combine their functionalities in actual applications; 2) they can cause *conceptually inadequate* effects, i.e. command results that go against the goals of the very system they support; and 3) their structure may *limit the vocabulary* of the possible history operations, and thus fail to support the user's intentions.

Inter-compatibility between history systems

As described above, the literature on history systems features a variety of functionalities including advanced error recovery, command reuse, history visualisation, version management, and underlying models. Although the total set of interactive behaviours described are tremendously diverse, there are substantial limitations in facilitating the reuse and combination of the methods disclosed. In particular, there are no tools to assist determining whether the techniques described in article A comply with the assumptions or methods proposed in article B. Example problems are described in this section.

Structural incompatibility occurs when two models cannot be merged. This can occur when the model's structure is incompatible (e.g., linear- vs. graph-based structures) or when the methods for linking commands within the structure are incompatible. An example of incompatible linking methods is given by the combination of Cass *et al.*'s [6] model, which links user commands along predefined process dependencies, with Parallel Paths [27], which logs alternative courses of events. While undoubtedly useful, neither of these systems maintain strict chronological order of commands, meaning that past commands (including operations on history) cannot be accessed or undone chronologically: they cannot trivially be combined with classic undo/redo. Critically, though, the ways that they deviate from chronological behaviour are fundamentally different, and therefore there are also complexities in their combination (resolved by CAUSALITY).

Functional incompatibility occurs when two systems react differently to seemingly identical commands. For example, when undoing a past command C: Linear Undo undoes all commands more recent than C; Script [3] and 3Rs [4], in contrast, attempt to re-run the command sequence that follows C and will cancel the undo if it generates paradoxes; Cascading Undo [6] also undoes the commands that share dependencies with C. These effects are all reasonable consequences of an Undo command, so there are design complexities in modelling and combining these behviors in a single system.

Conceptual inadequacies

Conceptual inadequacies are system behaviours that oppose its own primary goals. We identify two main conceptual inadequacies in existing history systems, and they stem from limitations of the underlying data model: their unforgiving nature [22]; and illogical undo.

Unforgiving Undo

Many history systems were designed primarily for error recovery, yet they can be surprisingly error-intolerant. With linear undo histories, undone commands and the resulting history states are typically deleted when new commands are triggered (Fig. 3). The replacing commands can be undone afterwards, but the discarded piece of history cannot be retrieved, and therefore mistaken manipulations during use of these systems can lead to non-recoverable loss of work. For example, if the user realizes that she shouldn't have undone some commands or if she inadvertently triggered an editing command in the middle of an undo navigation. This problem also occurs with advanced history systems, like Cascading Undo [6]. The inadequacy is a consequence of the traditional linear modeling of history[1]: old commands and document versions must be deleted to make space for new ones.

By modeling history as a tree or a graph, some systems [19, 22, 27] can prevent parts of history from being mistakingly forgotten by saving them in a parallel subtree. However, the creation of a branch has to be triggered by the user and thus can only partially help with error recovery: undos can still delete commands or states that were not explicitly saved.

Illogical Undo

History models also cause illogical behaviors when dealing with non-linear undo of past commands. For example, the seminal Amulet system [20] enables Selective Undo by storing the previous value of a modified property in the Command object itself (the `OLD_VALUE` slot) and uses it in the `undo()` method of this Command object. As illustrated by the authors, "[if] a command turns an object from blue to yellow, selectively undoing the command will make it blue, no matter what its current color is" [20].

This is an example where a data model only supports the simplest cases of a technique's principle. For example, as illustrated in Fig. 4, say that a vector object has undergone three `setColor` commands A (from black to red), B (red → green) and C (green → blue); say also that the user selectively undoes B then C (not shown in Fig. 4). The last two color changes have been undone: one could expect that the object turns back to the result of A, i.e. red. However,

[1] Cass *et al.*'s system [6] models *processes* as a tree, but modifications of this tree are applied linearly.

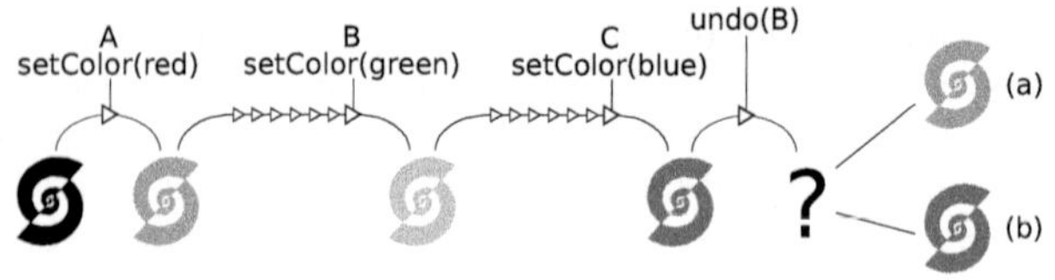

Figure 4. Possible effects of a Selective Undo: either restore a previous parameter value (a) or remove a command from history (b).

following Amulet, the last undo command (on C) triggered `setColor(OLD_VALUE)`, causing the object to turn green, i.e. the effect of B, which was undone first.

Limited vocabulary

History systems are usually designed to deliver the 'best' response to specific problems or functionalities. Consequently, their models often allow only one outcome to a user command even when other reasonable responses could be considered. Indeed, studies showed that the users' expectations to non-trivial modifications on history are not always fully consensual [7] and can depend on the platform [16, 17]. We illustrate this with two examples.

Case 1: Possible outcomes of Selective Undo

Using the previous `setColor()` example, say that the user selectively undoes only B, not C. Following Amulet, the system calls B's `undo()` method that is `object.setColor(OLD_VALUE)`, so the object turns red despite the later command C (Fig. 4-a). This outcome makes sense if the user's intention was to restore the object's color to before B was applied. However B could also have been selected and undone as part of a batch of commands corresponding to a higher-level editing process, in which case she would probably prefer this object to remain blue as the later (and not undone) command C set it (Fig. 4-b).

Case 2: Paradox resolution with Cascading Undo

In [6], Cass and Fernandes describe a scenario where selectively undoing the creation of a virtual section in a structured document results in automatically undoing the (later) generation of a table of contents, because their model logged a functional dependency between the table of contents and the section. Again this could be the user's intent, but she could also completely change the structure of her document yet still want a table of contents at its beginning. In this case, the proper outcome would be to update the table of contents to the 'new' structure. Both outcomes are valid depending on whether the user considers the generation of the table of contents to be a consequence of the creation of the section or not, and possibly more outcomes could be imagined, but the history model only enables one of them.

THE CAUSALITY MODEL

CAUSALITY is a new model of interaction history that reflects the causal system of a process along with its virtual chronology and real-time ordering. It provides persistent, transitive relationships between the user actions, their parameters and their consequences on the edited artifact throughout its history. We designed it in order to solve the problems described in the previous section while enabling most existing history techniques and systems of the literature. Its structure also enables whole new paradigms of interaction histories, that we will illustrate in the next section.

The upcoming description of CAUSALITY is intended to be exact and precise, as is necessary for designers and researchers to be able to make use of it. Core concepts are described earlier, with details deferred to later subsections. A reader initially uninterested in the details required for replication might consider skim-reading once past the core concepts. However, we hope that such as reader will return to the details once inspired by the example applications of CAUSALITY presented in the following section.

Artifact and Context

CAUSALITY considers both the *artifact* (e.g. the edited document and its composing elements) and the editing *context* (i.e. the different states and values of the application's or system's parameters). The context is composed of elements that are used in editing operations but do not affect the artifact directly. For example, changing the foreground and background colors in Adobe Photoshop has no effect on the image but can affect the result of later actions such as painting. A command that influences the context may also concurrently influence the artifact – for example, when a text region is selected, clicking the bold button affects both the text in the artifact and the parameters in the context (toggling the bold state). In most cases the artifact will be a single-file document, and the context will relate to its editing software, but these notions can be extended: a Java project can be considered an artifact composed of its packages, files and binaries. Further, the entire file system can be considered an artifact [2, 4, 24], in which case the context parameters could be those of the operating system or of the file browser.

History is thus separated into the artifact history and the context history, which are composed of the various versions of the artifact and context linked by the user commands. The artifact and context histories describe the evolution of different datasets but are temporally connected: changing a parameter of the application generates a new state in the context history but not in the artifact history, and vice-versa. Some commands generate new states in both histories; for example, the 'Cut' command pushes new content to the clipboard (context) and deletes part of the file content (artifact).

Linear Time and Branching Chronology

CAUSALITY models history as a tree and uses *systematic branching*. When a command is applied to a history state S a new 'child' of S is generated, regardless of the number of children that S already has (Fig. 5-left). Similarly, every change to an existing portion of history (e.g. modifying, deleting or inserting a command C) generates a new subtree that replicates the original history but includes the changes; this new subtree thus starts with C and branches from the last state of history before C (Fig. 5-right). This way, the original sequence of commands is preserved. This duplication can happen any number of times from any state.

One consequence of using a tree-like branching chronology is that states that belong to parallel branches cannot be formally ordered, e.g. context states A and B in Fig. 1. However commands themselves can be ordered since they take place in real time. CAUSALITY thus defines a *linear timeline* that is the unalterable set of commands issued by the user as they occurred in real time. Linear time disconnects from the branching chronology when the user 'travels' in time, as illustrated in Fig. 5. The linear timeline thus contains every command performed by the user, including operations that modify history that we describe later in the paper.

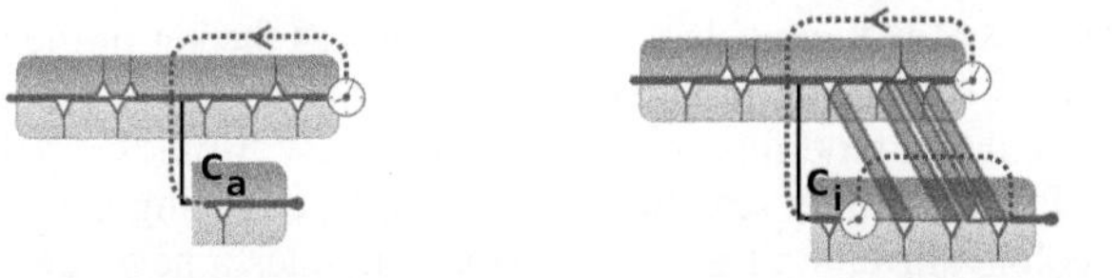

Figure 5. Left: *applying* a command C_a to a past state always generates a new state of history regardless of its existing 'children'. Right: *inserting* a command C_i in an existing sequence of commands generates a new subtree, with replicated commands from the original branch (blue halo). The user travels to the end of the branch to see the effect of the insertion.

This allows commands or states to be retrieved based on either *real time*, e.g. "what I did before lunch", or virtual *chronology*, e.g. "before this paragraph was edited". Chronology-based navigation follows the order of states in the tree structure, regardless of when these commands were invoked in real time; time-based navigation, in contrast, follows the order of commands as they were invoked by the user regardless of the branching chronology tree structure. For example, in Fig. 1, the lettered context states happened in alphabetical order in real time; but in the branching chronology, it can only be said that A preceded C and that B preceded D. Any visualizations based on the linear time, e.g. Fig. 1-bottom, can be used to easily spot clusters of commands that correspond to specific editing processes, as with the Chronicle timeline [12]. In contrast, any visualization based on the branching chronology enables a rich view of actions upon different versions of the interaction context or artifact.

References as Versions or Subscriptions

The artifact and context are composed of elements that are modeled as encapsulated data structures composed of other elements and/or data fields, similar to member variables in Object-Oriented programming. Fig. 6 illustrates how a particular vector drawing artifact state might be composed of several elements, each of which having its own history.

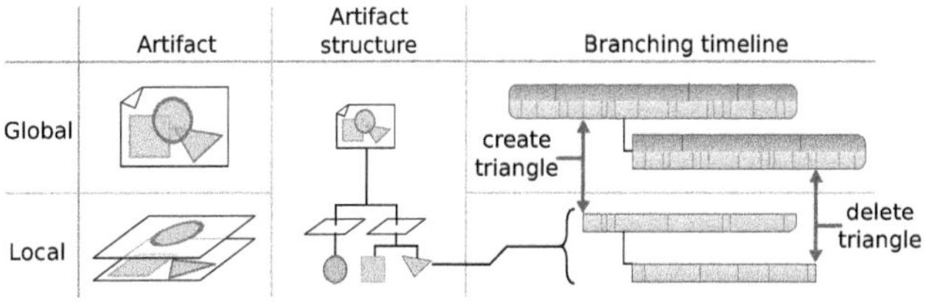

Figure 6. A vector document (left) and its structure (center), and their corresponding history (right). The local history of an element of the artifact (bottom right) is composed of the subset of the commands that affected it (from creation to deletion, branch-wise) and of its own versions along history. Command (triangles) are not represented for readability.

CAUSALITY considers these elements as the set of their versions within the timeline, as shown in Fig. 7. A user command that modifies an element effectively 'ripples' up the artifact or context structure. For example, changing the 'border color' attribute of a vector shape generates a new version of that attribute, as well as a new version of the shape, then recursively of everything that contains it, e.g. groups and layers, up to the artifact itself.

The Command objects in CAUSALITY use *References* to these data objects rather than copies of the objects themselves, as in previous approaches [20]. Importantly, *References* can be one of two types, either *Versions* or *Subscriptions*, as illustrated in Fig. 7.

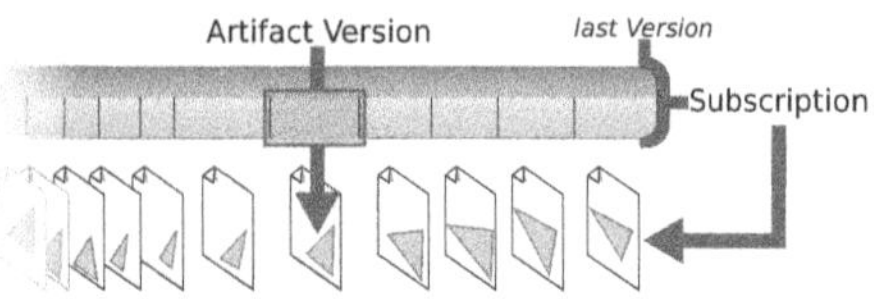

Figure 7. Local history of a triangle shape in a vector document. Versions are fixed in history while Subscriptions 'follow' the corresponding element to the last state of a branch.

A *Version* is a fixed reference in history: it represents a snapshot E_S of an element E at a given state S of history. Later modifications of E generate new Versions $\{E_{i,i \neq S}\}$ but do not alter the commands referencing E_S. However, going back in time to change E_S may affect the commands' outcome.

A *Subscription*, in contrast, is a dynamic link to the last Version of an element in a given branch, regardless of when it was referenced in real time or history. For example, the 'clone' function in Inkscape creates a duplicate T' of a shape T that will mirror every change applied to T: T' is a Subscription to T. Formally, a Subscription E^B echoes every modification of an element E within the branch B. If E is deleted at some state D in this branch, E^B references the last Version E_D of E in that branch. If branching occurs in a branch containing Subscriptions, the user needs to specify which of the original or the replicated branch the Subscription should follow, or duplicate the Subscription.

Since the branching chronology is modeled as a tree, the full sequence of commands and intermediate states that led to a given version of the artifact (or of one of its elements) can be retrieved (Fig. 6), enabling local histories to be exported [15], or represented, as in Chronicle [12] or Chimera [14]. Representations of the artifact can be attached to Versions and Subscriptions as well. Classic editor views typically *subscribe* to the whole artifact: they update their content to its last version within a given branch. Attaching several Subscriptions to a single view enables quick comparison of design alternatives, as in Parallel Paths [27]. Versions provide persistent views of specific artifact states that can be used as visual references, or to observe the effects of a set of modifications on the artifact through probes [12] or with flickering [8].

Commands

CAUSALITY links data describing commands to References of the elements that they influence or use. Every element in the context or artifact is thus linked to its 'causes', i.e. the commands that affected it and the parameters of these commands. CAUSALITY defines commands as septuples:

LABEL$_{\text{String}}$ identifies the command, similarly to Amulet's `LABEL` slot. It can be format-specific, e.g. 'Create ellipse' in any vector graphics, or application-specific, e.g. a Photoshop filter. The Label is meant to be interpreted by applications or systems, e.g. to re-run past histories or export histories across applications; it cannot be null.

USER$_{\text{String}}$ identifies the user that triggered the command.
DATE$_{\text{long}}$ is the time(-stamp) of the command in real time.

TARGETS$_{\{\text{String, Type, Version+}\}*}$ contains the elements to which the command is applied or that will be modified by it. This is similar to Amulet's `OBJECT_MODIFIED` slot except (a) these elements are referenced as Versions rather than as elements, so their previous values can be accessed through history and do not need to be stored in the command, and (b) elements of the context can be referenced as Targets as well. For example, commands that change the application's primary and secondary colors can be accessed, as in Chronicle [12]; however, these commands are linked to the elements they modify through the their Target's set, while in [12] the user has to find a color change in the Color track and find the corresponding event in the Tools track. Targets cannot be Subscriptions since commands are applied to definite history states. Targets can be empty if no element is altered nor created by the command, e.g. 'Save'.

INPUTS$_{\{\text{String, Type, Reference}\}*}$ records the user input(s) that were used to compute the effect of the command, e.g. a drawing stroke or a set of values entered through a dialog window. Temporal inputs such as strokes can be used to replay commands in real time, as with [8, 12]. The Inputs set only contains the user inputs that were used for computing the command's effects: CAUSALITY filters out less relevant user actions and periods of time, e.g. random cursor movements or pointing to a button before clicking it. Storing these input movements is also much lighter than whole video streams. Inputs are References, and they can be empty.

PARAMETERS$_{\{\text{String, Type, Reference+}\}*}$ contain every Reference (Versions or Subscriptions) to artifact and context elements that were used to compute the effect of the command, e.g. the last Version of the clipboard for a 'paste' command or the current brush attribute for a 'paint' command. Parameters, in combination with Inputs, should enable the command to be re-run exactly as originally performed. Using Subscriptions as parameters enables higher-level interactions such as Inkscape's cloning. Parameters can be empty as well.

RESULTS$_{\{\text{String, Type, Version+}\}*}$ references every new Version that the command generated, including new state(s) of history and the new Versions of elements that have been created or altered by the command. For example, the Results set of text entry includes the modified range of caret locations, and the Results set of a paint stroke includes the pixel region that was modified by it. Similarly to Targets, the Results set is bound to the newly generated state(s) of history and thus cannot contain Subscriptions; it can also be empty if no element was modified nor created by the command, e.g. deleting elements in the artifact. The Results and Targets sets need not be equal; e.g., inserting text Targets a caret *location* and Results in a new character *range*.

Targets, Inputs, Parameters and Results are named and typed (respectively 'String' and 'Type' components). *Names* identify command attributes for later access, modification or reuse. For example, a 3D scaling operation can require three different scaling factors (x, y and z) as parameters. Modifying one of these parameters requires knowing which value corresponds to which factor. *Types* enable coherent reuse of existing command parameters. They can be structured, similarly to Object-Oriented programming; for example, a 'pen stroke' in Photoshop consists of the shape, velocity- and pressure profiles of the actual stroke; themselves are composed of temporal data points. CAUSALITY is 'weakly typed': elements of compatible Types can be swapped, e.g. Integer to Float or ARGB color to HSV color.

Each element of Targets, Parameters and Results may consist of more than one Reference (hence the '+'). For example, one could imagine a vector graphics function that subtracts a set of shapes S from a single shape s and then deletes the shapes in S. Being all modified by the command, s and all the shapes in S are Targets, however they have different roles: the elements of S are considered indistinctly as a group.

Note that this septuple contains the minimal requirements of CAUSALITY and can be augmented for the needs of specific functionalities or applications, e.g. for command filtering based on application-dependent command types [9, 12, 24] or hierarchies of commands [9, 20, 28].

Interferences and Paradoxes

CAUSALITY's branching chronology permits the creation of parallel histories that differ from the linear timeline experienced by the user. Modifications of history generate new branches by *replicating* sets of commands (Fig. 5-right), which causes the generation of a new set of artifact and context Versions. The linear timeline, however, will not contain the replicated commands; only the triggering action executed by the user. Any explicit user command that causes a branch to be created (thus replicating commands) is call an *interference*. Although replicated commands are not included in the linear timeline (Fig. 5), they do appear in the Results set of the interference that generated them, with an updated Date attribute.

By changing courses of actions in the replicated branch, interferences can generate *paradoxes*, i.e. causal conflicts that prevent deterministic computation of further history states. A command is deemed "paradoxical" if at least one of the references necessary to the computation of its effects has been altered or deleted in its (chronological) past; its resulting state(s) cannot be rendered until the paradox is resolved. CAUSALITY defines two types of paradoxes:

Inconsistencies are paradoxes that prevent commands from being run. They occur when at least one element of a command's Parameters or Targets sets no longer exists in the history state from which it is referenced, e.g. changing the font size of a paragraph whose creation has been undone.

Ambiguities are paradoxes that result in multiple possible outcomes. They occur when at least one element of a command's Parameters or Targets sets has changed in the history state from which it was originally referenced. For example, if a shape with a color C1 is copy-pasted at some point in history, and if the user goes back in time to alter the original shape's color ($\rightarrow$ C2) before the copy-paste operation, then there is an uncertainty about whether the pasted shape's color should be the 'original' one from before the interference (C1), or the 'chronological' one that it would have had if the copy-paste command had been triggered in this new branch (C2).

Paradoxes are transitive: every command that targets or uses parts of the Results set of a paradoxical command is also paradoxical. The earlier a paradox is resolved chronologically, the fewer paradoxical commands and states have to be resolved by the user. Paradox resolution can also be deferred. For example, if a user goes back in time to insert several commands one after the other, she should not need to decide what resolution method to use until the whole process is complete, i.e. after the last command is inserted.

As discussed earlier, there can be several sensible ways to resolve a given paradox. CAUSALITY's structure of commands enables a variety of resolution methods adapted from the literature without deleting history:
- *Remove* the command from the replicated subtree, similar to Cascading Undo [6]. The new subtree is created as if the paradoxical command never occurred. Every further command of that subtree that references elements from the Results set of the removed command will be marked paradoxical.
- *Recompute* the outcome of the modified portion of history regardless of its original branch, similar to the Replay operation in [4]; this is only possible with Ambiguities, for Inconsistencies cannot be run by definition.
- *Ignore* the paradox by reusing the Results of the original command in the replicated branch. This can be compared to the default behavior of Amulet [20], except these elements are referenced, not copied: if an interference modifies these Results later in real time, the user will have the possibility to reflect these changes in the Ignored command as well.
- *Substitute* the altered or missing Targets or Parameters with compatible replacements chosen by the user, as suggested in [15, 17], in the form of References from other history states.

Resolution methods do not generate new subtrees, as opposed to interferences: their goal is to 'fix' newly replicated subtrees. They only appear in the user timeline and, as for other commands, they can be accessed and modified later.

EXAMPLES OF USE IN IMAGE EDITING

In this section we use a painting scenario to illustrate several novel, powerful and exciting interaction possibilities that are made available by modeling history with CAUSALITY. As the focus of this paper is on the underlying model, we describe functionalities without considering how that functionality might be accessed and controlled through interactive components or visualizations. Thus, the interfaces in the figures are only illustrative and should not be considered for their usability or visual design.

The basic scenario concerns a user editing a scene image with digital painting software that models history using CAUSALITY. The scenario starts with the painting in the state shown Fig. 8-left, with everything painted on a single layer. The river on the right was painted most recently. The user wants to change the painting as follows: the house should be bigger (but not the boat next to it), and another similar house should be shown partially occluded by the original one (Fig. 8-right).

Figure 8. Original image and target image after modifications.

One forward method to perform these changes is to (a) select the pixels of the house and copy them, (b) scale these pixels to make the house bigger, (c) create a new layer with that bigger selection as a negative mask, so that the first house remains in the foreground, (d) paste the copied pixels in the new layer, (e) scale them down to make the second house look smaller, then (f) flatten the image. However this method raises a number of issues: first, it only works with applications that support layers (c, d); second, it requires a non-novice knowledge of selection tools (a) and of the way layers and masks work (c, d, f); third, scaling pixels up or down (b, e) results in regions of the image with visibly different resolutions; fourth, if the user wants to change the size of the foreground house again, he will have to repeat the whole process.

CAUSALITY allows the user to alter his own past actions: he can change the *history* of the painting as if these changes had been made from the start and without needing layers or complex selections. We will illustrate the following process: (a) select the *commands* that correspond to painting the house, (b) scale up the corresponding *strokes*, i.e. the user's input when he painted the house and the paint brush sizes, (c) copy these commands and apply them again in their own past so that the original house is drawn on top of them, then (d) scale their stroke inputs and brush sizes down as in step (b).

(a) Selecting commands

We need to select the commands that were used to paint the house in order to modify them. To do so, we will use the various components of a CAUSALITY command: we will filter them by their name, the location of their effect, the time they occurred and their color parameter.

First, we are only interested in painting commands, so we can use this Label as a first filter. Second, the Results set of a 'paint' command references the pixel region that it affected; conversely, any pixel region of the document is linked to the commands that affected it. The commands that were used in the global vicinity of the house can thus be accessed from a simple selection operation (Fig. 9-left). The selected commands can be displayed on a timeline[2] thanks to their Date attribute (bottom panels in Fig. 9).

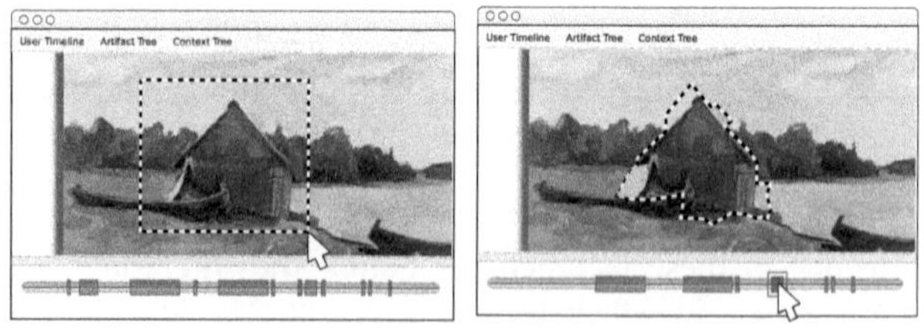

Figure 9. Left: selecting pixels on the image highlights the commands that affected them and the time these command occurred (bottom panel, blue). Right: hovering the timeline with the cursor highlights the pixels resulting from the corresponding command (top panel, green) and has been used to unselect commands.

Third, the selected commands form clusters on the timeline: most of the house-painting commands were performed at approximately the same time, while the ones corresponding to the sky, the grass, the trees, the boat and the river inside the selection rectangle were performed at different times. Similar to pixels, periods of time are linked to the commands that were invoked within them: one can thus unselect commands by toggling their corresponding time region on the timeline. To facilitate this process, the interface could highlight the pixel region affected by the currently hovered command (green in Fig. 9-right).

Filtering commands by name, location and time provides fast and coarse selection, however some unwanted commands may remain selected if they occurred close to the house and approximately at the same time of the house-painting commands, e.g. sky-colored paint strokes added near the top of the roof for edge adjustment. The Parameters set of a 'paint' command references the application's 'primary color' attribute at the time of the command, the user can thus recover the list of colors that were used by the selected painting commands (Fig. 10-left) and use it to unselect the remaining non-house-painting commands (Fig. 10-right).

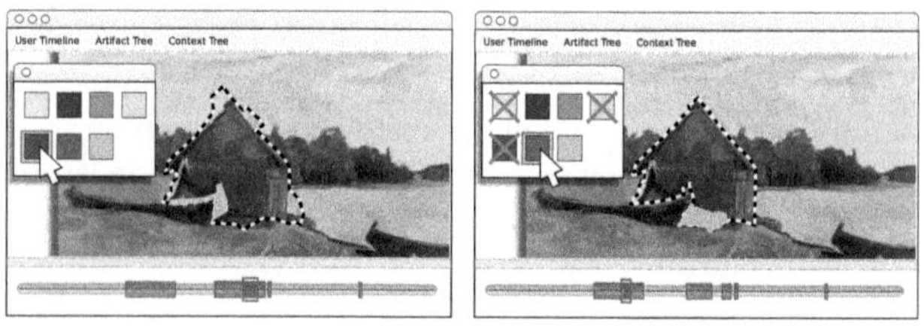

Figure 10. Left: the colors used in the selected set of commands can be displayed (foreground window); hovering them highlights the corresponding pixels and commands in the top and bottom panels. Right: removing colors from this set unselects the corresponding commands.

(b) Scaling paint strokes

The Inputs set of a 'paint' command contains the user's stroke in the form of a set of cursor locations, and possibly a velocity and pressure profile. Its Parameters set also refers to the brush that it used to compute its effect. The user can apply any transformation on this data; in this case, he will scale both the

[2] In this section we will only show periods of time (rather than actual commands) for the sake of readability.

strokes and the brush widths (Fig. 11, right) and recompute the artifact's history to observe its effects.

This is a modification of history: a parallel branch is generated (bottom panel in Fig. 11-right), branching from the last Version of the artifact that is common to both branches. These modifications cause Ambiguity paradoxes to be raised: later 'paint' commands have their resulting pixel regions intersecting the ones of the modified commands (yellow in Fig. 11-right). Some of these Ambiguous commands must be deleted from the new branch, e.g. overlapping landscape-painting commands that were performed after the house was painted (chronologically). As a result, the modified house looks as if it was drawn this big from the start, without any loss of resolution. This is an interesting application of history: modifying inputs provides vector-like functionalities to tools intended to manipulate raw data (e.g. pixels).

Figure 11. Left: displaying the stroke shapes corresponding to the selected 'paint' commands (right panel). Right: scaling these strokes generates a parallel branch (bottom panel) and raises paradoxes (in yellow) with later, intersecting 'paint' commands.

(c, d) Reusing commands in the 'past'

CAUSALITY considers commands as Versions, similarly to artifact and context elements, that can thus be referenced and reused as well. The commands used to draw the house can be copied as a group, even if they weren't all contiguous in time, and reapplied anywhere in history (Fig. 12-top).

Remember however that the color and brush Parameters of a 'paint' command are References: duplicating a paint command somewhere in time means to either perform a similar painting *stroke* with the brush and primary color of the history state at which they are replicated, or to reproduce the actual paint operation including color and brush. In the former case, the brush and color Parameters reference the Version of the application's brush and primary color attributes where the commands were applied. In the latter, they reference the same Version of these attributes as the original commands.

In our case, the user duplicates these commands using the original parameters and *before* the ones corresponding to the original, now bigger house (Fig. 12-bottom); these new commands thus happen earlier in chronology, so their result will be partly hidden by the bigger house. This will again generate a new subtree with some Ambiguous commands (Fig. 12-bottom). Finally, the stroke Inputs of these commands can be scaled down using the same process than in the previous step.

Discussion

This scenario illustrates how CAUSALITY enables safe, flexible and understandable modifications of history that are substantially more powerful than existing history mechanisms.

Figure 12. Top: re-applying all the selected commands in their own past generates a new parallel branch; the replicated commands are linked to the original ones. Bottom: after relocation and scaling, these commands generate new paradoxes.

Commands can be modified, duplicated and reordered: the user can recover from earlier errors or rethink the document without losing any previous work. Further, it reduces the need for users to form a strategy for completing their work before beginning to work with the interface.

The functionalities described in this scenario are but a glimpse of the possibilities that CAUSALITY can offer. Our goal is not to replace advanced editing but to increase the vocabulary of corrective and editing operations available to interaction designers, and ultimately to the user. In our example, modifying the construction of the scene by classic means requires some training in layers, masks and selection techniques. It also implies local changes of resolution and erasing existing parts of the landscape. CAUSALITY enables a process-oriented approach where users can simply re-access, manipulate and alter the operations they know they did without erasing any previous actions or result.

Our scenario used a graphical application because it is easy to describe and illustrate. As a conceptual model, CAUSALITY can be applied to any kind of editing software, from basic text editors to video and audio editing software or multi-file project managers. It is however challenging to define a universal implementation framework from it, for different application domains will likely have very different performance and data requirements. For example, systematically storing all the states of a multi-layer graphic document might become very voluminous, while some of them could be made *accessible* through recomputation without being *stored*. Additionally, fully integrating CAUSALITY into pre-existing software systems would require information that is seldom available from software APIs, necessitating access to source code.

CONCLUSION AND FUTURE WORKS

This paper introduced CAUSALITY, a new conceptual model of interaction history that keeps track of past commands and states of the edited artifact in the form of a causal system. CAUSALITY can model most of the existing systems and techniques of the literature and it enables more flexible opportunities for temporal interactions. It can also provide a richer vocabulary of effects and consequences. As well as exactly stipulating components of CAUSALITY, as necessary for its deployment, we also provided examples of its use in an advanced painting application scenario.

Our next step will be to implement and evaluate CAUSALITY in usable applications, focusing on the following two points. First, we will implement CAUSALITY both as the core of a specific application for evaluation, and as a plugin of a scriptable application such as Adobe Photoshop or Eclipse; the latter will help us evaluate how far we can go with CAUSALITY's functionalities when using APIs. Second, we will design and evaluate user interfaces that provide access to the power of the novel interactions inspired by CAUSALITY. Visualizations, such as those suggested in our painting scenario, are likely to have a major impact on the effectiveness of the user's interaction. As illustrated by the scenario, CAUSALITY permits the invention of new interactive techniques for manipulating the history of a document based on reuse and modification of the links between interaction causes and effects. Ultimately, we hope that CAUSALITY will inspire others to invent, implement and evaluate new, learnable and powerful tools for interacting with time.

REFERENCES

1. Abowd, G. D., and Dix, A. J. Giving undo attention. *Interact. Comput. 4*, 3 (Dec. 1992), 317–342.
2. Appert, C., Chapuis, O., and Pietriga, E. Dwell-and-spring: undo for direct manipulation. CHI '12 (2012), 1957–1966.
3. Archer, Jr., J. E., Conway, R., and Schneider, F. B. User recovery and reversal in interactive systems. *ACM Trans. Program. Lang. Syst. 6*, 1 (Jan. 1984), 1–19.
4. Brown, A. B., and Patterson, D. A. Rewind, repair, replay: three r's to dependability. SIGOPS European Workshop 10 (2002), 70–77.
5. Bueno, C., Crossland, S., Lutteroth, C., and Weber, G. Rewriting history: more power to creative people. OzCHI '11 (2011), 62–71.
6. Cass, A. G., and Fernandes, C. S. T. Using task models for cascading selective undo. TAMODIA'06 (2007), 186–201.
7. Cass, A. G., Fernandes, C. S. T., and Polidore, A. An empirical evaluation of undo mechanisms. NordiCHI '06 (2006), 19–27.
8. Chen, H.-T., Wei, L.-Y., and Chang, C.-F. Nonlinear revision control for images. SIGGRAPH '11 (2011), 105:1–105:10.
9. Edwards, W. K., Igarashi, T., LaMarca, A., and Mynatt, E. D. A temporal model for multi-level undo and redo. UIST '00 (2000), 31–40.
10. Gamma, E., Helm, R., Johnson, R., and Vlissides, J. *Design Patterns: Elements of Reusable Object-Oriented Software*. 1995.
11. Greenberg, S., and Witten, I. H. Supporting command reuse: empirical foundations and principles. *Int. J. Man-Mach. Stud. 39*, 3 (Sept. 1993), 353–390.
12. Grossman, T., Matejka, J., and Fitzmaurice, G. Chronicle: capture, exploration, and playback of document workflow histories. UIST '10 (2010), 143–152.
13. Heer, J., Mackinlay, J., Stolte, C., and Agrawala, M. Graphical histories for visualization: Supporting analysis, communication, and evaluation. *IEEE TVCG 14*, 6 (Nov. 2008), 1189–1196.
14. Kurlander, D., and Feiner, S. A visual language for browsing, undoing, and redoing graphical interface commands. In *Visual Languages and Visual Programming* (1990), 257–275.
15. Kurlander, D., and Feiner, S. A history-based macro by example system. UIST '92 (1992), 99–106.
16. Loregian, M. Undo for mobile phones: does your mobile phone need an undo key? do you? NordiCHI '08 (2008), 274–282.
17. Loregian, M., and Locatelli, M. P. An experimental analysis of undo in ubiquitous computing environments. UIC '08 (2008), 505–519.
18. Lunzer, A., and Hornbæk, K. Subjunctive interfaces: Extending applications to support parallel setup, viewing and control of alternative scenarios. *ACM Trans. Comput.-Hum. Interact. 14*, 4 (Jan. 2008), 17:1–17:44.
19. Martin, R., Demme, J., and Sethumadhavan, S. Timewarp: rethinking timekeeping and performance monitoring mechanisms to mitigate side-channel attacks. *SIGARCH Comput. Archit. News 40*, 3 (June 2012), 118–129.
20. Myers, B. A., and Kosbie, D. S. Reusable hierarchical command objects. CHI '96 (1996), 260–267.
21. Naderlinger, A., and Templ, J. A framework for command processing in java/swing programs based on the mvc pattern. PPPJ '08 (2008), 35–42.
22. O'Brien, J., and Shapiro, M. Undo for anyone, anywhere, anytime. SIGOPS European Workshop 11 (2004).
23. Prakash, A., and Knister, M. J. A framework for undoing actions in collaborative systems. *ACM Trans. Comput.-Hum. Interact. 1*, 4 (Dec. 1994), 295–330.
24. Rekimoto, J. Time-machine computing: a time-centric approach for the information environment. UIST '99 (1999), 45–54.
25. Seifried, T., Rendl, C., Haller, M., and Scott, S. Regional undo/redo techniques for large interactive surfaces. CHI '12 (2012), 2855–2864.
26. Shneiderman, B. Direct manipulation: A step beyond programming languages (abstract only). CHI '81 (1981), 143.
27. Terry, M., Mynatt, E. D., Nakakoji, K., and Yamamoto, Y. Variation in element and action: supporting simultaneous development of alternative solutions. CHI '04 (2004), 711–718.
28. Washizaki, H., and Fukazawa, Y. Dynamic hierarchical undo facility in a fine-grained component environment. CRPIT '02 (2002), 191–199.

Conversing with Children: Cartoon and Video People Elicit Similar Conversational Behaviors

Jennifer Hyde[1], Sara Kiesler[2], Jessica K. Hodgins[1,3,4], and Elizabeth J. Carter[3]

[1]Computer Science Department,
[2]HCI Institute, [3]Robotics Institute
Carnegie Mellon University
Pittsburgh, PA 15213
{jdtam, kiesler, ejcarter}@cs.cmu.edu

[4]Disney Research, Pittsburgh
4720 Forbes Avenue
Lower Level, Suite 110
Pittsburgh, PA 15213
jkh@disneyresearch.com

ABSTRACT

Interactive animated characters have the potential to engage and educate children, but there is little research on children's interactions with animated characters and real people. We conducted an experiment with 69 children between the ages of 4 and 10 years to investigate how they might engage in conversation differently if their interactive partner appeared as a cartoon character or as a person. A subset of the participants interacted with characters that displayed exaggerated and damped facial motion. The children completed two conversations with an adult confederate who appeared once as herself through video and once as a cartoon character. We measured how much the children spoke and compared their gaze and gesture patterns. We asked them to rate their conversations and indicate their preferred partner. There was no difference in children's conversation behavior with the cartoon character and the person on video, even among those who preferred the person and when the cartoon exhibited altered motion. These results suggest that children will interact with animated characters as they would another person.

Author Keywords

Children; conversation; behavior; avatar; agent; animated character; facial motion

ACM Classification Keywords

H.4.3. Communications Applications: Computer conferencing, teleconferencing, and videoconferencing; H.5.1. Multimedia Information Systems: Evaluation/methodology

INTRODUCTION

Over the past decade, the use of animated human characters has increased dramatically in education, entertainment, and therapy. They assist customers on shopping websites, occupy virtual worlds on behalf of users in games such as *The Sims* and *World of Warcraft*, serve as teachers or virtual peers in educational software, and act as mock job interviewers who provide feedback to users. Animated characters can provide corporeal representations when none are available, impart anonymity, and add entertainment value. People's interactions are complex, with verbal and nonverbal cues that can often be very subtle and meaningful. The benchmark of a successful conversational agent, as proposed by Cassell and Tartaro [12], is if an agent can interact with a people similarly to how people interact with one another.

Extensive research has focused on how additions of human-like behaviors to agents create more successful human-agent interactions. These studies have incrementally tested how adding various behaviors, such as smiles, emotional facial expressions, gaze, and mirroring, can influence human behavior [1, 8, 18, 20]. Although researchers have shown that these behaviors improve human-agent interaction, they have not shown that these interactions are similar to human-human interaction. These studies also focused on how to improve adult human interactions with agents; however, many animated characters are created for children.

Much of children's entertainment and educational programming features interactive or pseudo-interactive animated characters. As of 2003, approximately 70% of children under two had watched television, and over 90% of childrn have done so by age six [31]. The characters often wear bright colors and have simple, exaggerated features. The bright colors are supposed to grab children's attention, and the simple, exaggerated features (e.g., large eyes) are supposed to help children focus on particular parts of the screen [21]. These characters have also been given human-like behaviors (e.g., blinking) to make them seem more "alive" and interactive. It is unclear whether these characters are actually more appealing or engaging than real people. Is Steve from *Blue's Clues* a better host than Dora from *Dora the Explorer*? What about Fred Rogers and Daniel Tiger from *Mr. Rogers'/Daniel Tiger's Neighborhood*?

Some previous research has compared how children speak differently to real and animated people. The researchers identified possible differences in children's language patterns, but the researchers could not explain whether the differences were due to different language patterns in the real and animated partners or appearance differences [4, 29]. We ran an experiment to examine children's preferences, attention, and language when conversing with an adult partner who appeared via videoconference as herself and as a cartoon character. The cartoon characters' facial motion was driven by

CHI 2014, April 26–May 1, 2014, Toronto, Ontario, Canada.

ACM 978-1-4503-2473-1/14/04..$15.00.
http://dx.doi.org/10.1145/2556288.2557280

our adult confederates in realtime; thus, we removed the issue of natural language generation, allowing us to focus on the appearance of the characters and their motion to better understand their effects on children's interactions. In our experiment, character appearance was a within-subjects variable and motion was a between-subjects variable. The characters displayed human behaviors, including facial expressions and mirroring. We also manipulated facial motion magnitude by exaggerating and damping the characters' spatial motion. Exaggerated facial motion magnitude has been associated with easier emotion recognition and perceptions of increased emotional intensity [3, 9, 22]. By exaggerating our characters' faces, we hoped to make them more expressive.

In contrast to previous research, we found that despite having strong preferences about confederate appearance, the children behaved similarly across conditions. Our participants behaved and conversed with animated and real people in similar ways, suggesting that appearance does not affect children's speech and that animated characters could be suitable substitutes for real people in conversational applications. Moreover, this research highlights the importance of using both self-report and behavioral measures when conducting experiments about design.

RELATED WORK

Children interact with animated characters on a frequent basis. Often, these characters are on television shows or in educational games, in which case the interactions are staged and the characters cannot respond to unexpected behaviors. Simulated interactions on television are important because they help engage children and improve learning [24, 26]. Since the successful launch of *Blue's Clues*, children's educational television programs have followed a similar format of characters looking directly at the viewers, asking questions, pausing, and then "acknowledging" viewers' responses (for a review, see [21]).

Although children will interact with animated characters, they do not always treat these characters as they would other people [4, 29]. For example, a prior study found that children used more gestures and words when conversing with adults than with computer characters [4]. As intelligent agents become more human-like, the hope is that children will interact with the agents as they do real people.

Children learn from a young age to pay attention to socially relevant information, including eye gaze, gestures, and emotional displays (for a review, see [2]). Children's comprehension of facial expressions develops over time (for a review, see [37]). When children are between two and three years old, facial expressions are categorized as positive or negative. The number of categories grows and the criteria for each category narrow as the children develop. Most 4- and 5-year-olds can recognize basic emotions on the face although their accuracy may not be very high. By the time children are 9 and 10 years old, they are almost as accurate as adults [25, 37]. Because exaggeration can make facial expressions easier to recognize [10, 22], we hypothesized that exaggerating the facial motion of animated characters may improve child-character interactions.

Although young children pay attention to people who are physically present, there has been a question as to how children view people who appear on screens. As adults, we understand that people who are not physically present may still provide useful information to us. For example, we listen and learn from newscasters about what traffic to avoid or how to prepare for the weather. Children, on the other hand, do not necessarily listen and learn from people on television, especially if there is no interaction. Troseth and colleagues [36] conducted several studies in which two-year-old children watched people on monitors or in the same room give useful hints for a game. Only the physically present people and the people on monitors who interacted with the children were able to get the children to use the hints. These results emphasize the importance of interaction if young children are to pay attention to animated characters.

Very little research has compared how children interact with animated characters and other people. Oviatt [29] conducted a study with ten 6- to 10-year-old participants. The researcher compared how children spoke with an animated character to an adult experimenter, and she found that children had fewer disfluencies in their speech with the characters than with the adult. Although participants were encouraged to ask questions in both interactions, the tasks were not identical. In the character condition, participants spoke with multiple animated animals to learn more about the different species. When participants spoke to the experimenter, they played a game of Twenty Questions where the children asked the questions.

In another experiment comparing child-computer interaction to child-human interaction, Black and colleagues [4] compared nine 4- to 7-year-olds' interactions with an animated human agent on a computer to those with an adult experimenter in person. The comparison tasks were more similar: there was a single animated human character who asked questions that were similar to the questions that the adult experimenter asked. The researchers found that children were less verbose and spoke slower when speaking with the agent rather than the adult; however, the researchers also noted that their agent used fewer words and spoke slower than the adult partner. This work supports the idea that children will emulate the speaking style of their conversational partners, as suggested by other researchers [16, 17]. Additionally, they reported that the children looked away from the adult more than from the animated human character. To build upon these two previous studies, we wanted to examine more precisely how children's patterns of engagement would differ between a human and an animated character by having the children take part in two nearly identical interactions using the same apparatus. We hypothesized that they would attend more to the character.

CONTRIBUTION

We designed our experiment to limit confounds and inconsistencies. We used two different confederates and corresponding animated characters to ensure that effects were not a result of a specific character's design. Additionally, comparison tasks were very similar, semi-structured conversations

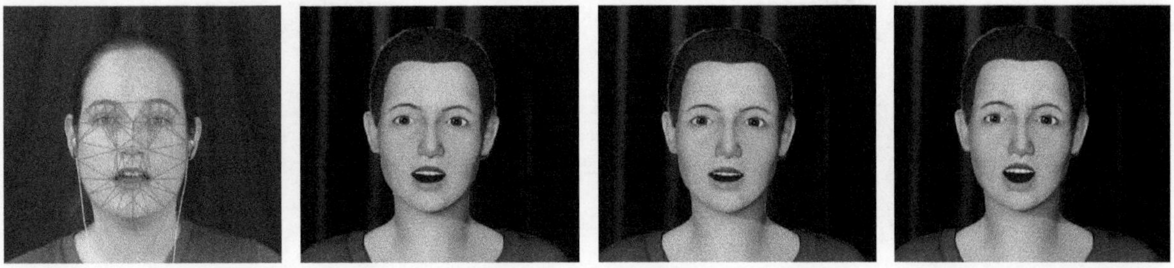

(a) Video with AAM tracking (b) Normal cartoon (c) Damped cartoon (d) Exaggerated cartoon

Figure 1. Example frames of confederate video tracking and corresponding character being animated with different levels of facial motion. In this frame, the exaggeration/damping is most clearly shown in the mouth.

that were counterbalanced so that conversation topics were not confounded with participants' interaction partner. For both tasks, the interactive partner was an adult confederate who appeared on-screen. In one task, she was shown through video; in the other task, she was shown as a cartoon character. The confederate's cartoon character was human and was customized to her appearance. The confederate was blind to her appearance on the participant's screen. Also, we created questionnaires to determine the correspondence between subjective measures and participant behavior. Through this combination of control measures, we examined the precise effects of character appearance and motion on children's experiences. Our results indicate that children are resilient to the appearance and motion of their conversation partners, regardless of their personal preferences. Therefore, it should be possible to design conversational agents that elicit natural behavior from children.

METHOD

In this section, we explain the technique we used to animate a character with our confederate's facial motion in realtime. We also describe our equipment, study materials, participants, procedure, and measures.

Apparatus

Our goal is to create believable interactive animated characters, with motion that mimics the pacing, style, and facial gestures of humans; to that end, we opted to have two confederates "puppet" the characters. To ensure that the confederates were blind to the study condition, they were animated using a markerless, computer vision method for face tracking: active appearance models (AAMs) [13, 14, 27]. This method tracks a person's face in realtime, permitting it to be mapped onto a character's face without noticeable delay. We designed a desktop-like audiovisual telecommunications system so that research participants could interact with confederates who both appeared as themselves through video and as animated characters while using natural eye contact and speech.

Active Appearance Models

AAMs mathematically model the face shape and appearance of people and characters. To animate a character using human motion, an AAM can be customized to an individual, and a corresponding AAM can be created for the character. To create a custom AAM, images of an individual's face in different poses are manually labeled so that a mesh of 79 vertices fit to the individual's face. Once the face and appearance space have been learned from the training images, the individual's face can be tracked from new video in realtime. Animating a character requires a mapping from the individual's AAM to the character's AAM. When the individual moves his/her face, the 79 mesh vertices change position. The change in position is mapped to the character's mesh, and then the character's appearance is warped to illustrate movement (see Figure 1). We purposefully created characters that resembled the confederates so that the remapped motion would be as accurate as possible. For further information on the creation and use of AAMs, please see [13, 14, 27].

Given that each vertex changes position during movement, we followed previous procedures [5, 35] to multiply those changes in position by specific scale factors, thus exaggerating or damping the spatial movements across all features of the face. We selected damped and exaggerated scale factors based on a previous perceptual study in which the adult threshold of facial motion level sensitivity was determined [23]. We selected equally perceptible levels of damping (-20%) and exaggeration ($+25\%$). For example images of exaggerated and damped character motion, see Figure 1.

We used 2D AAMs for this research. Therefore, our characters always faced forward. We added rigid points around the tops of the characters' heads and damped the face border and nose points by 50% to ensure that the character would not warp excessively if the confederate turned her head. Body motion was not tracked, so the torsos of the characters moved rigidly with respect to a pivot located at their mouths. The confederates practiced extensively with the characters prior to the experiment to ensure that they did not generate movements that appeared unnatural or otherwise distracting when presented on the characters.

Telecommunications System

Our audiovisual telecommunications system is diagrammed in Figure 2. It was designed to maximize natural interactions: both people appear life size and can make eye contact as they would in person. Two setups were positioned in separate rooms with a control room in between. All video and audio data from each setup was relayed through the control room for video and audio processing before being presented to the other setup. Each setup consisted of a black box hous-

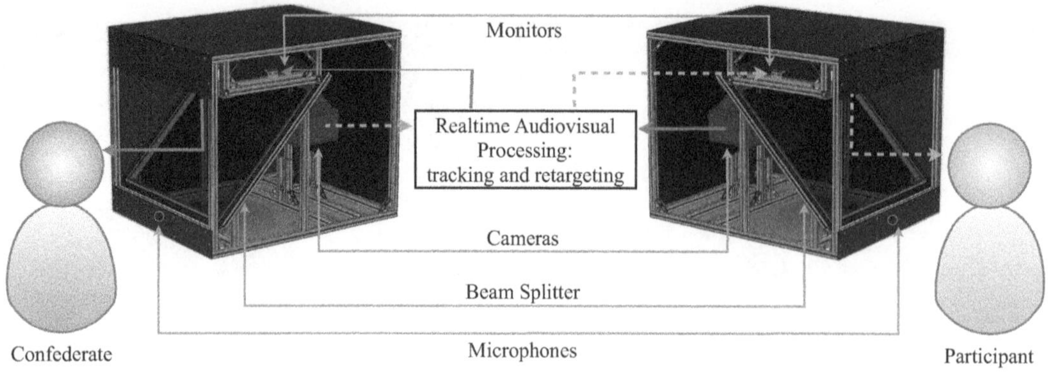

Figure 2. Diagram of the telecommunications system.

ing a monitor, camera, microphone, and beam splitter, and the box was positioned on a height-adjustable table to ensure that the camera was at eye level for the user. A speaker was also placed within the participant's setup, but headphones were used on the confederate's setup to avoid auditory feedback. We used a beam splitter made of reflective material between the user and the camera so that the camera was hidden directly in front of the user, allowing for eye contact between users, often an impossibility in audiovisual telecommunications. The monitor was placed above the beam splitter in order to project visual information directly in front of the user. A shotgun microphone was mounted below the beam splitter to capture audio.

A computer attached to each setup controlled the presentation of visual information. When animating a character, the participant's computer tracked the confederate, retargeted the motion to the animated character, and displayed the character on the participant's monitor. If the system was displaying a video feed, the computer was used to add a small amount of delay to the presentation of the video in order to replicate the delay induced by tracking and animating the confederate character. A sound mixer in the control room was used to add delay to the audio and ensure that the audio and video/animation remained in sync. Our measurements indicated that the delay inherent in our system is 100 ms for video and 166 ms for animation. Because the confederate always saw video of the participant, the delay for the confederate was 100 ms; however, because the participant saw both video and animated conditions we kept the participant's delay at 166 ms. Previous research with a similar system validated that these delays have a negligible effect on conversation between adults [34].

Storybook

In order to introduce the children to the task, we created storybooks for each of the confederates and possible task orders. Each storybook starred one of two confederates and described how she enjoyed playing pretend, sometimes as a cartoon character. She particularly enjoyed pretending to own a bakery. Depending on the order of tasks assigned to a particular participant, the storybook then described one of two tasks: designing a cake or an ice cream sundae. For the cake task, the children were told that the confederate had already created three cakes and needed the child's help to make a fourth, selecting the flavor of cake, the frosting, and a topping from a list. In the ice cream task, the children were asked to help design a fourth sundae by selecting the ice cream flavor, a sauce, and a topping from a list. After the child completed the first task, the experimenter read the second part of the story that described the other task. Participants were randomly assigned a task order and confederate.

Visual Aids

We used felt fabric to create facsimiles of all of the food components described in tasks so that the participants could see their creations at the end of each task and have a more concrete representation of the items for imagination and recall.

Questionnaires

To obtain participant feedback, we used a modified smileyometer with written labels. Smileyometers have been used frequently with children as they are understandable and reliable; however, we included written labels because they are better for older children [6, 30]. The traditional smileyometer includes a neutral midpoint; however we removed the midpoint as prior work [7] found that four response options and no neutral midpoint obtained the most reliable responses from children. Our participants were all familiar with the various types of smileys as they were used in the other experiments that participants completed on the same day. Unfortunately, eliciting truthful responses from 4- to 5-year-olds can be very difficult as they are susceptible to satisficing, and they will often select the most positive response [38]. When presenting the rating scale, the experimenter verbally stated each option while pointing to the corresponding smiley. The experimenter also verbally confirmed each of the participants' responses. After each task, the experimenter verbally asked the children four questions and offered possible answers while showing the questions and a rating scale:

1. How much did you like talking to [name] just now? (Really liked, kind of liked, didn't really like, did not like)
2. How much fun did you have talking to [name] just now? (Lots of fun, kind of fun, kind of bored, bored)
3. How nice was [name] to you just now? (Very nice, kind of nice, kind of mean, mean)
4. How much did you like talking to [name] about [topic]? (Really liked, kind of liked, didn't really like, did not like)

After both tasks, the children answered an additional three questions. Again, participants were verbally read the questions and possible responses as well as shown images of the responses. Participants were given response options in a random order:

1. Did you like talking to [name] more when she looked like a real person or when she looked like a cartoon character? (photo of confederate and cartoon character)
2. If you could speak to [name] again, would you want to see her as a real person or as a cartoon character? (photo of confederate and cartoon character)
3. Did you like talking about ice cream or cake more? (image of ice cream sundae visual aid and cake visual aid)

To measure participants' extroversion, we asked parents to answer a short, six-question survey. The six items were selected to represent the six facets of extroversion, as defined in the NEO-PI-R [15], a well-known and validated personality measure for adults. The items were selected from the M5-PS-35 [19, 32], a measure created and validated to assess preschool children's personality.

Participants

Children between the ages of four and ten years were recruited to take part in a series of short, unrelated experiments, including this study, that lasted a total of approximately 90 minutes. In total, 69 children (mean age = 7.17 years, standard deviation = 2.02 years, 36 boys and 33 girls) participated successfully in this paradigm. Five additional children were excluded from analyses due to technical or behavioral issues. See Figure 3 for participant breakdown. Participants were recruited using email lists and advertisements in local gathering places, and they were compensated for their time. The research was approved by our Institutional Review Board.

Procedure

Upon arrival at the experiment location, each child and his or her parent/guardian was met by one of the experimenter team. Parents/guardians completed the extroversion questionnaire in a separate room. Most parents remained in the separate room while their children completed the study; however, sixteen parents accompanied their children to the study room. They sat 12 feet to their children's left with the experimenter in between. Parents could not see the telecommunications screen, but they could hear the conversation. Parents of children who completed the study successfully sat silently during the study. The child was allowed to select one of many stickers to help the experimenter decorate the apparatus, in order to let him or her warm up and become accustomed to the apparatus and environment. Then, the experimenter seated the child facing the apparatus with the curtain still down and read the storybook to prepare the child to play a game of pretend with the confederate either as a video or an animated character. Upon completion of the first half of the storybook, the experimenter asked if the child was ready and then whether the confederate was ready. After hearing agreement from both, she raised the curtain so that the participant and confederate were able to see each other.

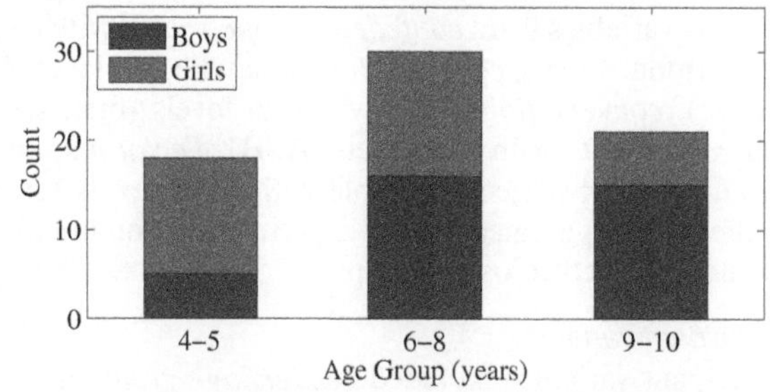

Figure 3. Participants by gender and age group.

Before starting the first task, the confederate engaged the participant in unstructured small talk, typically about the child's summer activities, age, and favorite school subjects, in order to make the child comfortable with the confederate and the apparatus. When the confederate believed that the child was comfortable, she began the first task. While the child made selections of food, the experimenter assembled the final product. When the child made his/her second selection, the confederate challenged the choice and offered her own suggestion. Upon completion of the first task, the experimenter closed the curtain so that the child could no longer see the confederate, showed the child the design, and completed the questionnaire with the child. Then, the experimenter verified that the confederate was ready to begin the next task and raised the curtain. For the second task, there was no small talk; the confederate asked the child if he or she was ready and then began the task. The confederate challenged the child on his/her second selection just as she had done in the first conversation. Again, the experimenter created the food design based on the child's selection, closed the curtain at the end of the task, showed the child the creation, and completed the questionnaire with the child. Finally, they completed the last three questions comparing both tasks and characters.

Measures

Independent variables were divided into experimental and participant variables. Experimental variables included appearance and motion manipulations. Participant variables included participant age, gender, and extroversion score. Dependent variables were split into conversation, gaze, gesture, and self-report measures.

We annotated the video recordings for child speech, gaze, and gesture using ELAN [28, 33], open-source software for annotating video and audio recordings. Each annotation has a start time, end time, and label or transcription. For each measure that involved annotated data, we had a primary annotator who annotated all of the data and a secondary annotator who annotated one third of each child's data. To evaluate interrater reliability, we calculated the percentage of aligned annotations and then calculated Cohen's Kappa (κ) for the aligned annotations. Percent alignment and κ are given below.

Experimental variables

Our main experimental variables included *confederate appearance* and *facial motion level*. Other experimental variables that we controlled in our analyses included *conversation topic*, *conversation order*, and *confederate*. The within-subjects variables were *confederate appearance* with two levels (cartoon, video), *conversation topic* with two levels (cake, sundae), *conversation order* with two levels (first, second), and *confederate* with two levels (A, B). *Facial motion level* was a between-subjects variable with three levels (damped, unaltered, exaggerated). The experimental conditions were counterbalanced across participants.

Participant variables

Participant variables included *gender, age group*, and *extroversion score*. Participants were divided into three age groups (four to five years old, six to eight years old, nine to ten years old) based on theories of cognitive development [25, 37]. Parents completed a short questionnaire to assess their child's level of extroversion. The parents' responses were averaged across the six questionnaire items to create a single *extroversion score* (Cronbach's $\alpha = .6712$).

Conversation measures

Conversation measures included *conversation length, number of utterances, number of words*, and *confederate influence*. The primary annotator transcribed all participants' speech, and the secondary annotator marked the times when participants spoke. Pauses between utterances had to be at least 500 ms long. The annotators had 82% alignment on their annotations; we did not calculate Cohen's κ because the secondary annotator did not transcribe speech. From the transcriptions, we calculated the *number of utterances* and *number of words* that each participant used. *Conversation length* was measured between when the experimenter asked the confederate if she was ready and when the curtain covered the screen. Because the first conversation included unstructured small talk, the start of the first task occurred when the confederate asked if the child was ready to begin the task. For *confederate influence*, we looked at when participants changed their selection based on the confederate's challenge. If the participant changed his/her original selection to the confederate's selection, we scored the confederate as influential. If the participant stuck with his/her original selection, we scored the confederate as not influential.

Gaze measures

Gaze measures included the percentage of time participants spent looking at the screen, *percent on-screen*, and the average length of each on-screen gaze segment, *average gaze length*. While *percent on-screen* gives a rough estimate of how much of the conversation participants watched the screen, the *average gaze length* gives an estimate of how long participants sustained their gaze at the screen. Annotators marked when participants were looking on- and off-screen. The annotators had 86% alignment of annotations, and they agreed on the annotation labels with perfect reliability (Cohen's $\kappa = 1$).

Gesture measures

Gesture measures included the *total number of gestures* and the *number of nods, shakes*, and *shrugs* each participant used. Gestures were only considered if they were communicative. For example, if a participant moved his/her head up-and-down to indicate "yes," the motion was counted as a nod; however, if the participant was simply bouncing in his/her chair, the head movement was not considered a nod. Annotators marked and labeled the beginnings and ends of gestures. The two annotators had 83% alignment, and they agreed on the labels with perfect reliability (Cohen's $\kappa = 1$).

Self-report measures

Self-report measures included *conversation score, appearance preference*, and *topic preference*. Participants were asked four questions after each task and another three questions after completion of both tasks, as described in the Questionnaires section of this paper. The first four questions asked participants to rate their conversations. The last three questions asked participants to compare their conversations. The ratings from the first four questions were combined to create a *conversation score* with good reliability (Cronbach's $\alpha = .6879$). The two questions, asking participants to select between the cartoon and video confederate, were combined to create the measure of *appearance preference* with good reliability (Cronbach's $\alpha = .7178$). The last question was used as an indication of participants' *topic preference*.

RESULTS

We conducted several ANalyses Of VAriance (ANOVAs) to investigate possible effects from the independent variables. Due to a lack of variability in *extroversion scores* across participants and the fact that no relationship was found between *extroversion score* and the dependent measures, we excluded *extroversion score* from further analyses. We also excluded *number of shakes* and *shrugs* from our analyses, as the median number of times these gestures occurred during conversation were 1 and 0, respectively. The *number of nods* and the *total number of gestures* were kept in the analyses. Although participants had strong preferences for appearance and topic, they did not alter their behavior to reflect these preferences. Interestingly, confederate appearance only affected the number of words children used.

Preliminary analysis

To determine which control variables to include in our main analysis, we first conducted a repeated measures ANOVA with *conversation topic* and *conversation order* as within-subjects variables and *confederate* as a between-subjects variable. Only *conversation length* was affected by these variables. Confederate B had significantly longer conversations than Confederate A, $F(1, 65) = 43.91$, $p < .0001$. Because the conversations were semi-structured and there were no significant effects of confederate on the number of utterances or words, the difference in conversation length was likely due to a difference in the confederates' rates of speech. Conversation length was also affected by conversation order, $F(1, 65) = 14.51$, $p = .0003$; however, conversation order and confederate did not create a significant interaction.

To understand the difference in conversation length between the first and second conversation, we look at the significant interaction of conversation order and topic, $F(1, 65) = 5.35$, $p = .0239$. Participants' second conversation was only longer than their first conversation if the second topic was ice cream sundae. From our analysis of self-report measures, we know that participants preferred the sundae topic to cake. We also

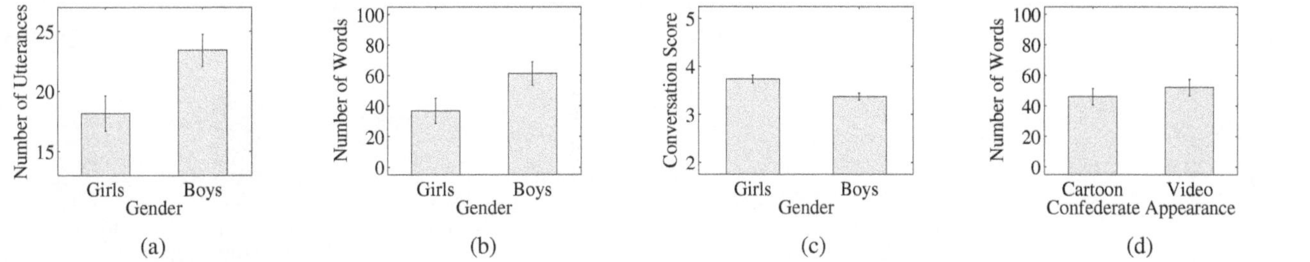

Figure 4. Main effects of gender on (a) number of utterances and (b) words, (c) conversation score, and of appearance on (d) number of words. All effects significant at $\alpha = .05$.

know that participants did not actually speak more about sundaes because we found no significant effect of topic on conversation length, nor did we find any differences in number of utterances or number of words. These results suggest that participants spent more time thinking about their responses if the second conversation was on their preferred topic. Participants were familiar with the conversation structure and the confederate by the second conversation so they may have felt less pressure to make their selections quickly. Because the control variables did not affect any of the behavioral measures except for conversation length, we did not include them in our main analysis.

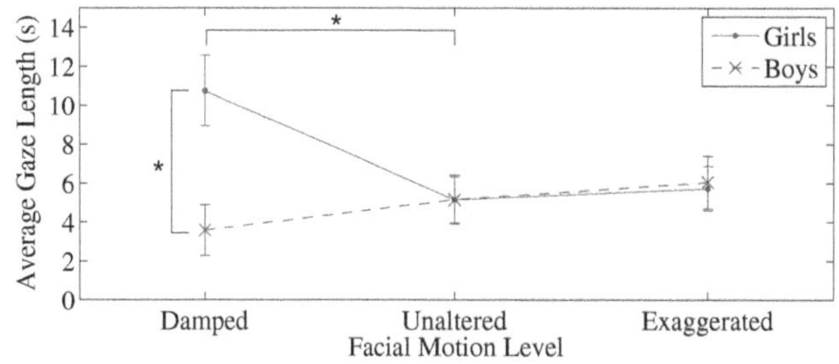

Figure 5. Interaction of facial motion level and gender on average gaze length. The * indicates significance at $\alpha = .05$.

Main analysis

We were most interested in how the experimental variables of *confederate appearance* and *facial motion level* would affect the dependent measures. Because many developmental changes occur between ages 4 and 10, we included the participant variables of *age group* and *gender* in our main analysis. We conducted a repeated measures ANOVA with *age group*, *gender*, and *facial motion level* as between-subjects variables and *confederate appearance* as the within-subjects variable. To analyze the data on appearance and topic preferences, we conducted a three-way ANOVA with age group, gender, and facial motion level as between-subjects variables.

Effects on conversation measures

We found that male participants had significantly more utterances than female participants, $F(1,55) = 6.27$, $p = .0153$. Similarly, male participants also used more words than female participants, $F(1,55) = 4.30$, $p = .0428$. On average, male participants used 25 more words than female participants. Although we had a disproportionate number of older boys, there were not significant interactions between gender and age for utterances or words, $F(2,55) = 1.81$, $p = .1731$ and $F(2,55) = .81$, $p = .4480$. Participants used significantly more words when speaking to the confederates by video than by cartoon character, $F(1,63) = 5.50$, $p = .0222$, but the difference was six words, on average (see Figure 4). We found no significant effects of our experimental or participant variables on confederate influence.

Effects on gaze measures

We found a significant interaction between gender and facial motion levels with participants' average gaze length, $F(2,55) = 3.89$, $p = .0264$ (see Figure 4). Female participants watched the damped cartoon character for longer periods of time than male participants, $F(1,55) = 8.67$, $p = .0047$. Female participants also watched the damped cartoon character for longer periods of time than the unaltered and exaggerated cartoon characters, $F(1,55) = 7.61$, $p = .0079$, and $F(1,55) = 5.49$, $p = .0228$, respectively (see Figure 5). We found no significant effects on percent of on-screen gaze.

Effect on self-report measures

We found a significant effect of gender on conversation score, with female participants rating the conversations higher than male participants, $F(1,55) = 10.43$, $p = .0021$. We also found a significant interaction of age group and gender with conversation score, $F(2,55) = 3.19$, $p = .0488$. The data illustrates that males and females converged on their conversation scores as age group increased, and that the largest difference between scores occurred between the 4- to 5-year-old males and females. The 4- to 5-year-old males rated their conversations significantly lower than the 4- to 5-year-old females, $F(1,55) = 14.66$, $p = .0003$ (see Figure 6).

We found no significant effects or interactions of age group, gender, and facial motion level on preferences. We did notice strong preferences across participants. We ran several Chi-squared tests to investigate these preferences. Participants who selected "both" instead of selecting a single topic or appearance were excluded from the analyses. Participants preferred the confederate in video to cartoon, $\chi^2(1, N = 54) = 21.41$, $p < .0001$. Participants also preferred speaking about sundaes to cakes, $\chi^2(1, N = 52) = 11.08$, $p = .0009$. If we include all participants and use "both" as a third category we still find a strong preference for video and sundae, $\chi^2(2, N = 69) = 29.30$, $p < .0001$ and $\chi^2(2, N = 69) = 14.87$, $p = .0006$, respectively.

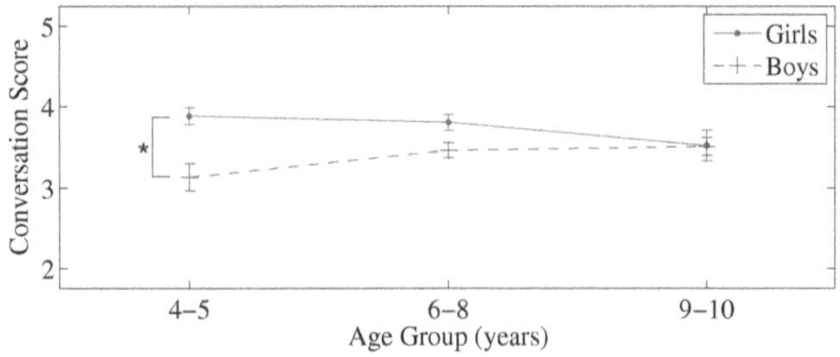

Figure 6. Interaction of age and gender on conversation score. The * indicates significance at $\alpha = .05$.

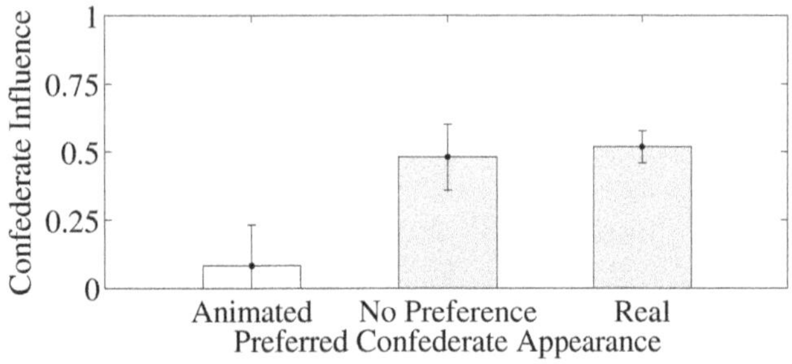

Figure 7. Main effect of participants' preference for confederate appearance on confederate influence.

Post-hoc analysis

Because participants had strong preferences for confederate appearance, we conducted a post-hoc analysis to ascertain whether or not participants' preferences influenced their behavior. We ran a repeated measures ANOVA with *age group*, *gender*, and *participant preference* as between-subjects variables and *confederate appearance* as a within-subjects variable. We found the same significant main effects of gender on number of utterances, number of words, and conversation score. We discovered a significant main effect of participant preference on confederate influence, $F(2, 53) = 3.39$, $p = .0413$ (see Figure 7). Participants who preferred the cartoon version of the confederate were less likely to be influenced by the confederate compared to the participants who had no preference or preferred the video version of the confederate, $F(1, 53) = 5.71$, $p = .0205$.

We also found a significant interaction between confederate appearance and participant preference with conversation score, $F(2, 63) = 3.69$, $p = .0305$ (see Figure 8). Participants who preferred the confederate in video rated their conversations with the animated confederate significantly lower than their conversations with the confederate in video, $F(1, 63) = 7.41$, $p = .0084$. In contrast, participants who preferred the animated confederate did not score their conversations significantly differently, $F(1, 63) = 2.22$, $p = .1409$, but this may be a reflection of the low number of participants (10) who preferred the animated confederate.

DISCUSSION

In our study, child participants conversed with an adult confederate who appeared as herself through video in one conversation and as a cartoon character in another conversation. Participants were aware that they spoke to the same confederate in both tasks even though she appeared different. We observed that some children were surprised that the cartoon character could see and respond to them. We also observed some children who were surprised by the confederate in the video condition, and some children who were not surprised by either condition. Statistically, the children did not converse, gaze, or gesture differently when speaking to the confederate through video and cartoon. The one exception was that participants used a few more words when in the video condition. Although our participants behaved similarly across conditions, they had a strong preference for the video condition.

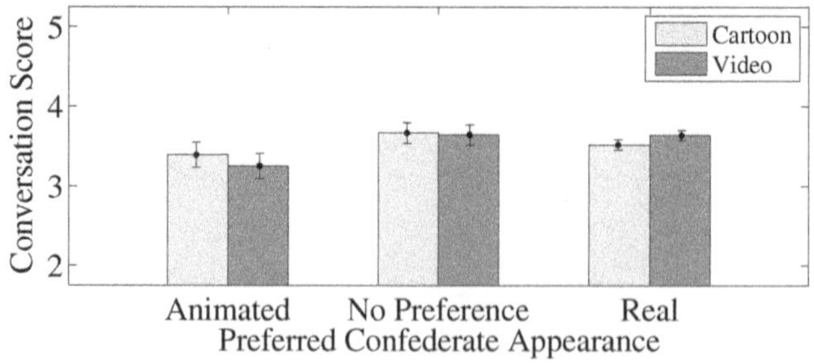

Figure 8. Significant interaction of participant preference and confederate appearance with conversation score.

We also altered the facial motion level of the cartoon character to see if it would influence participants' behavior. We found that facial motion level affected girls differently than boys, such that they had longer periods of on-screen gaze when the cartoon character's motion was damped. It is possible that the girls were more engaged with the task and therefore more attentive when the motion was damped because damped facial motion can be harder to understand [10, 22]. No other effects of facial motion level were found.

We found several effects of gender on participant behavior. Although female participants rated the tasks higher, male participants spoke more, both in number of utterances and words. The youngest girls also rated the tasks the highest, supporting the idea that they were the most engaged with the task.

Unlike prior studies [4, 29] that compared children's behaviors when conversing with an animated character to a person, our animated character was controlled in real time by the same person that participants spoke to through video. Prior studies used intelligent agents or Wizard of Oz techniques to control their animated characters, and comparison conversations were face-to-face. We limited confounds by designing our tasks to be as similar as possible. Participants had two conversations with the same confederate, engaged in two similar tasks (designing cakes and ice cream sundaes), and used the same apparatus to converse. The cartoon characters were even designed to have similar appearances to their respective confederates.

LIMITATIONS AND FUTURE WORK

There are some limitations to this work that we plan to address in the future. Our conversations were short and may not have allowed sufficient time for participants to adjust their behaviors. Different types of tasks, such as ones that require more trust and disclosure, may also cause children to alter their behavior based on their preferences. Future work should examine how longer and/or different types of tasks (e.g., storytelling, problem solving) could elicit different behaviors based on children's preferences.

We used adult female confederates and similar-looking animated characters in our study. Future work could explore the effects of confederate gender, age, and animated character appearance. Many of the animated characters children interact with are other children or non-human (e.g. Dora from *Dora the Explorer* and Daniel from *Daniel Tiger's Neighborhood*); therefore, a comparison of children's behaviors during interactions with adult, child, and non-human animated characters would also be interesting and informative. Our characters were rendered in a more realistic-looking style than many popular cartoon characters, and children may prefer more familiar and simplistic rendering styles. An examination of how children react to a character with different rendering styles would help answer this question.

Our cartoon characters were not perfectly realistic in their motion or in their appearances. We used 2D AAMs and 2D characters, which limited how our confederates and the characters could move. Specifically, 2D AAMs cannot track faces properly when certain features are obfuscated, such as when an eye disappears from view due to a head turn. Similarly, the characters were incapable of head rotation; therefore, they could not nod or shake their heads. Due to these limitations, we requested that our confederates limit their head motion. Although our confederates kept their heads mostly still, they still made some small nods and shakes, which are naturally occurring movements. The lack of these small movements in the cartoon condition may have influenced participant preference for the video condition. In the future, different tracking and animation techniques could be tested to verify our findings.

Our findings suggest that operators/animators could adjust a character/avatar's motion to increase a child's attention and to suit a child's facial processing ability. In the future, we intend to investigate how we can customize character/avatar appearance and motion to improve conversations with children who have facial processing deficits and social and communicative disorders, like those on the autism spectrum. Because animated characters created for children are often child-like and non-human, we believe future work should investigate the use of different types of animated characters. Along similar lines, animated characters are used for more than just short conversational tasks; therefore, exploring whether children might behave differently with real people and characters during other types of tasks would be useful.

CONCLUSION

We ran an experiment in which children conversed with an adult partner who appeared as herself and as a cartoon avatar via videoconference. We found that despite having strong preferences for confederate appearance, the children behaved similarly between conditions. In our study, we also examined how an animated character's facial motion level might affect children. According to Cassell and Tartaro [11, 12], embodied conversational agents in social settings should strive to elicit behaviors from users that are indistinguishable from the behaviors users would exhibit when with other real people. Our results indicate that, with child users, the goal of eliciting natural behaviors should be possible without needing perfectly realistic-looking human characters and head motion.

ACKNOWLEDGMENTS

We thank our participants and their families. We are grateful to Jill Lehman, Rachel Browne, Brooke Kelly, Randall Hall, Emily Jensen, Tomas Simon Kreuz, Peter Carr, Iain Matthews, Mo Mahler, Jimmy Krahe, Cole Heiner, and Melanie Danver. This work was funded by Disney Research and award R03HD068816 from the Eunice Kennedy Shriver Institute of Child Health and Human Development of the National Institutes of Health.

REFERENCES

1. Andrist, S., Pejsa, T., Mutlu, B., and Gleicher, M. Designing effective gaze mechanisms for virtual agents. In *Proc. CHI 2012*, ACM Press (2012), 705–714.

2. Baldwin, D., and Tomasello, M. Word learning: A window on early pragmatic understanding. In *Proc. Child Language Research Forum*. Chicago, IL, 2001, 3–23.

3. Bartneck, C., and Reichenbach, J. Subtle emotional expressions of synthetic characters. *International Journal of Human-Computer Studies 62*, 2 (2005), 179–192.

4. Black, M., Chang, J., Chang, J., and Narayanan, S. Comparison of child-human and child-computer interactions based on manual annotations. In *Proc. Workshop on Child, Computer and Interaction 2009* (2009).

5. Boker, S. M., Cohn, J. F., Theobald, B.-J., Matthews, I., Brick, T. R., and Spies, J. R. Effects of damping head movement and facial expression in dyadic conversation using real-time facial expression tracking and synthesized avatars. *Phil. Trans. R. Soc. B 364*, 1535 (2009), 3485–3495.

6. Borgers, N., de Leeuw, E., and Hox, J. Children as respondents in survey research: Cognitive development and response quality 1. *Bulletin de Méthodologie Sociologique 66*, 1 (2000), 60–75.

7. Borgers, N., Hox, J., and Sikkel, D. Response effects in surveys on children and adolescents: The effect of number of response options, negative wording, and neutral mid-point. *Quality & Quantity 38*, 1 (2004), 17–33.

8. Burleson, W., and Picard, R. W. Gender-specific approaches to developing emotionally intelligent learning companions. *IEEE Intelligent Systems 22*, 4 (2007), 62–69.

9. Calder, A. J., Rowland, D., Young, A. W., Nimmo-Smith, I., Keane, J., and Perrett, D. I. Caricaturing facial expressions. *Cognition 76*, 2 (2000), 105–146.
10. Calder, A. J., Young, A. W., Rowland, D., and Perrett, D. I. Computer-enhanced emotion in facial expressions. *Phil. Trans. R. Soc. B 264* (1997), 919–925.
11. Cassell, J. Embodied conversational agents: representation and intelligence in user interfaces. *AI Magazine 22*, 4 (2001), 67.
12. Cassell, J., and Tartaro, A. Intersubjectivity in human-agent interaction. *Interaction Studies 8*, 3 (2007), 391–410.
13. Cootes, T. F., Edwards, G. J., and Taylor, C. J. Active appearance models. *IEEE Trans. on Pattern Analysis and Machine Intelligence 23*, 6 (2001), 681–685.
14. Cootes, T. F., Wheeler, G., Walker, K., and Taylor, C. J. View-based active appearance models. *Image and Vision Computing 20*, 9-10 (2002), 657 – 664.
15. Costa, P. T., and MacCrae, R. R. *Revised NEO Personality Inventory (NEO PI-R) and NEO Five-Factor Inventory (NEO FFI): Professional Manual.* Psychological Assessment Resources, 1992.
16. Coulston, R., Oviatt, S., and Darves, C. Amplitude convergence in children's conversational speech with animated personas. In *Proc. International Conference on Spoken Language Processing*, vol. 4 (2002), 2689–2692.
17. Darves, C., Oviatt, S., and Coulston, R. Adaptation of users' spoken dialogue patterns in a conversational interface. In *Proc. International Conference on Spoken Language Processing*, vol. 1 (2002), 561–564.
18. de Melo, C. M., Carnevale, P., and Gratch, J. The impact of emotion displays in embodied agents on emergence of cooperation with people. *Presence 20*, 5 (2011), 449–465.
19. Grist, C. L., Socha, A., and McCord, D. M. The M5-PS-35: A five-factor personality questionnaire for preschool children. *Journal of Personality Assessment 94*, 3 (2012), 287–295.
20. Guadagno, R. E., Swinth, K. R., and Blascovich, J. Social evaluations of embodied agents and avatars. *Computers in Human Behavior 27*, 6 (2011), 2380–2385.
21. Hayes, D. *Anytime Playdate: Inside the Preschool Entertainment Boom, or How Television Became My Baby's Best Friend.* Free Press, New York, NY, 2008.
22. Hess, U., Blairy, S., and Kleck, R. E. The intensity of emotional facial expressions and decoding accuracy. *Journal of Nonverbal Behavior 21*, 4 (1997), 241–257.
23. Hyde, J., Carter, E. J., Kiesler, S., and Hodgins, J. K. Perceptual effects of damped and exaggerated facial motion in animated characters. In *Proc. IEEE International Conference on Automatic Face and Gesture Recognition 2013* (2013).
24. Kirkorian, H. L., Wartella, E. A., and Anderson, D. R. Media and young children's learning. *Children and Electronic Media 18*, 1 (2008), 39–61.
25. Knowles, A. D., and Nixon, M. C. Children's comprehension of expressive states depicted in a television cartoon. *Australian Journal of Psychology 41*, 1 (1989), 17–24.
26. Linebarger, D. L., and Walker, D. Infants' and toddlers' television viewing and language outcomes. *American Behavioral Scientist 46*, X (2004), 1–21.
27. Matthews, I., and Baker, S. Active appearance models revisited. *International Journal of Computer Vision 60* (2004), 135–164.
28. Max Planck Institute for Psycholinguistics, The Language Archive, Nijmegen, The Netherlands. ELAN. http://tla.mpi.nl/tools/tla-tools/elan.
29. Oviatt, S. Talking to thimble jellies: Children's conversational speech with animated characters. In *Proc. INTERSPEECH 2000* (2000), 877–880.
30. Read, J. C., and MacFarlane, S. Using the fun toolkit and other survey methods to gather opinions in child computer interaction. In *Proc. IDC 2006*, ACM Press (2006), 81–88.
31. Rideout, V. J., Vandewater, E. A., and Wartella, E. A. Zero to six: Electronic media in the lives of infants, toddlers and preschoolers. Tech. rep., The Henry J. Kaiser Family Foundation, 2003.
32. Scheck, A. M., L. Alvin Malesky, J., Grist, C. L., and McCord, D. M. Personality in preschool children: Preliminary psychometrics of the M5-PS questionnaire. *American Journal of Psychological Research 6*, 1 (2010), 134–156.
33. Sloetjes, H., and Wittenburg, P. Annotation by category: ELAN and ISO DCR. In *Proc. LREC* (2008).
34. Tam, J., Carter, E., Kiesler, S., and Hodgins, J. Video increases the perception of naturalness during remote interactions with latency. In *Proc. CHI EA 2012*, ACM Press (2012), 2045–2050.
35. Theobald, B.-J., Matthews, I., Mangini, M., Spies, J. R., Brick, T. R., Cohn, J. F., and Boker, S. M. Mapping and manipulating facial expression. *Language and Speech 52* (2009), 369–386.
36. Troseth, G. L., Saylor, M. M., and Archer, A. H. Young children's use of video as a source of socially relevant information. *Child Development 77*, 3 (2006), 786–799.
37. Widen, S. C., and Russell, J. A. Children acquire emotion categories gradually. *Cognitive Development 23*, 2 (2008), 291–312.
38. Zaman, B., Abeele, V. V., and Grooff, D. D. Measuring product liking in preschool children: An evaluation of the Smileyometer and this or that methods. *International Journal of Child-Computer Interaction 1*, 1 (2013), 61–70.

Involving Children in Content Control: A Collaborative and Education-Oriented Content Filtering Approach

Yasmeen Hashish
University of Manitoba
Winnipeg, MB
hashishy@cs.umanitoba.ca

Andrea Bunt
University of Manitoba
Winnipeg, MB
bunt@cs.umanitoba.ca

James E. Young
University of Manitoba
Winnipeg, MB
young@cs.umanitoba.ca

ABSTRACT
We present an approach to content control where parents and children collaboratively configure restrictions and filters, an approach that focuses on education rather than simple rule setting. We conducted an initial exploratory qualitative study with results highlighting the importance that parents place on avoiding inappropriate content. Building on these findings, we designed an initial prototype which allows parents and children to work together to select appropriate applications, providing an opportunity for parents to educate their children on what is appropriate. A second qualitative study with parents and children in the six to eight year-old age group revealed a favorable response to this approach. Our results suggest that parents felt that this approach helped facilitate discussions with their children and made the education more enjoyable and approachable, and that children may have also learned from the interaction. In addition, the approach provided some parents with insights into their children's interests and understanding of their notions of appropriate and inappropriate content.

Author Keywords
Children and technology; parental control strategies; collaborative content filtering.

ACM Classification Keywords
H.5.2. [User Interfaces]: User-centered design

INTRODUCTION
Many parents have concerns over media that their children may be exposed to, for example, books with adult content, highly violent movies, or even games that encourage gambling, evidenced by the range of content rating and labeling schemes available (e.g., PG13 vs. R for movies, or the ESRP video-game ratings). This concern is well grounded, as exposure to such content may impact childhood aggression and education [5,8]. Many parents have strategies for controlling content, such as monitoring access by placing computers and televisions in a common area in the house, using the internet together [18], or by employing blanket passwords on devices. One modern challenge is that there are an increasing number of devices connected to the internet, providing gateways to unfiltered content that many parents want to control.

There are a number of existing tools designed to help parents limit their children's exposure to inappropriate content, for example, Net Nanny, or CYBERsitter for PC web browsers, or child-friendly filtered versions of tablet software such as Netflix's children's area or Apple's pre-configured adult filter on the iPad. A common feature of these tools, however, is that they rely on sets of rules created and maintained solely by parents (or by companies) and are not designed with the intent of involving children in the process; as such, there may not be an opportunity to help the children understand the restrictions placed.

We present an alternative approach to content control which includes the child in the process of setting filters, thereby facilitating a collaborative and discussion-oriented parent-child opportunity for educating about issues surrounding appropriate and inappropriate content. This provides an opportunity for children to voice their opinion in decisions. For example, a child may want to point out that a game is popular with their friends' parents, thus inclining the parent to examine it more closely. This involvement of children in the process builds from pedagogy and psychology research showing how educating young children about rules and morals, and to some extent helping them form their own opinions, may be more effective than simply creating and enforcing rules without explanation [7,10]. Involving children also aligns with the Positive Youth Development framework, which suggests that providing structure, positive norms, and opportunities to be involved can support youth in making good decisions [20]. Finally, this has the added advantage of providing parents with a healthy way to communicate their opinions on media, which has been shown to have a strong impact on how children themselves see media [23].

Our work specifically targets content filtering on current-generation internet-capable smart phones and tablets. We selected this platform for our exploration as it is modern and usage is rapidly increasing [26,27], yet there are currently few content-control mechanisms. Application marketplaces also represent a clean and bounded notion of content, in comparison with, for example, a classic web

CHI 2014, April 26–May 1, 2014, Toronto, Ontario, Canada.

ACM 978-1-4503-2473-1/14/04...$15.00.
http://dx.doi.org/10.1145/2556288.2557128

browser, which provides access to a vast and heterogeneous set of material.

We present a new approach to content control that aims to include children in the content filtering process, and focuses on child involvement and education rather than control. We first present an open-ended study that explored children's technology usage patterns and parental opinions, with the results supporting the importance of content control in current-generation devices. We designed and implemented an initial software platform that serves as a prototype for educational content-control sessions and enabled us to conduct a follow-up qualitative study with parents and their children. Our findings show that parents consider the collaborative, educational approach to be an effective and engaging way to initiate conversations with their children, and that it provides a novel way to discuss topics which may otherwise be difficult to breach (or find time for), and that children learn (at least in the short term) from these sessions. Overall, we believe this kid-in-the-loop approach to content control has promise and can serve as an important part of modern internet-capable technologies.

RELATED WORK

Why families adopt technologies (or decide not to) has been broadly studied, for example, showing how family values and social class can shape attitudes and adoption [1,25]. There is also investigation of how new technologies can have an impact on the home and its social structures [18]. Broadly speaking, such work has indicated that parents have a great deal of concern over their children's exposure to inappropriate content, primarily pornography [21]. Our exploratory study provides some updated insight into a family's adoption patterns of current-generation technology, but more importantly, our work primarily focuses on actual interactions between parents, children, and technologies in contrast to broad patterns of behavior.

Work on technology usage regulation and content control in families has articulated parental strategies, for example, through discussions with children, co-use, or direct restriction such as passwords [3,17,18]. Co-use and interaction rules (e.g., not on sunny days) may be preferred over employing hard restrictions such as control software (e.g., for older children and teenagers [17]), in part due to a lack of trust in the robustness of the system [21]; our new approach encourages and scaffolds discussion between parents and their children on what is or not appropriate.

There is some evidence that low uptake of control software – only 33% according to a 2004 study – may be correlated with the age of the child, with more use for families with younger children [21]; this study also indicated that perceived ease-of-use of such tools may be a barrier. Further, commercially-available control software generally provides rule-oriented (sometimes query-like) control methods, for pre-configuration by parents [15], or machine-learning approaches such as automatically detecting adult images [2,14]. Work that has involved children in filtering content has looked at helping them form appropriate search queries [6,9], as opposed to involving them in content control. Our approach attempts to address all of these concerns: we target younger children and involve them directly, and aim to reduce parental barriers to filtering use by making filtering an interactive parent-child process.

Studying children's interactions with technology has been a common theme in sociology, psychology, and human-computer interaction; for example, children and television in general [13,24], how video games may promote exercise [11], or how internet use may impact psychological development [12]. Some explicitly involve children by including their attitudes and points of view as a part of the investigation [19]. Our work continues this theme by exploring how children use current-generation technologies and parents' attitudes toward them, and more specifically, how children can be involved in the content filtering configuration for current-generation technologies, and how this can impact education of appropriateness.

EXPLORATORY STUDY

We conducted an exploratory study to investigate current patterns of how children use technology, what kinds of current-generation technology they use (for example, dedicated or internet-capable toys), and the range of thoughts, opinions, and concerns that parents have about such technologies. In doing so, we provide updated insight into these issues; many prior studies pre-date the current smart phone and tablet trends (e.g., [3,15,16,18]). We explicitly did not target content control schemes, as a part of this evaluation was to determine if content control was indeed a strong current parental concern, thus motivating our current work, and so we let it emerge from the data. As the results below show, overall the idea of control – for appropriate content as well as appropriate use – is a very large concern and consideration for parents, and they have a range of strategies for dealing with this.

Study Design

We interviewed 12 parents (10 mothers, 2 fathers) of children 4-10 years old. Demographics are listed in Table 1. We recruited participants through snowball sampling and signs placed throughout our university. When possible, interviews took place at a participant's home to facilitate note-taking (7/12). Interviews lasted 20-45 minutes, participants received a $10 gift card, and the study was approved by our research ethics board. Data were collected via audio recordings, which were later transcribed.

Interview Questions and Data Analysis

We asked participants to describe specific examples of how their children used technology throughout the day. We used a semi-structured interview technique to investigate:

- What kinds of technologies are children interacting with, and, how are they using them?
- How do parents feel about the interactions their children have with technology?
- What, if any, challenges do the parents and their children face with respect to these technologies?

Participant Number	Occupation	Children's Ages and Genders
eP1	Daycare worker	5-yr old boy
eP2	Graduate student	8- and 10-yr old boys
eP3	University support staff	5-yr old girl, 8-yr old boy
eP4	Daycare worker	4-yr old girl, 9-yr old boy
eP5	Stay-at-home parent	7-yr old boy, 10-yr old girl
eP6	Graduate student	8-yr old girl
eP7	Unreported	8- and 10-yr old boys
eP8	Daycare worker	7-yr old girl
eP9	Daycare worker	9-yr old boy
eP10	Graduate student	7-yr old boy
eP11	University support staff	5-yr old girl
eP12	University professor	8-yr old boy 10-yr old girl

Table 1: Participants in the exploratory study ('e' indicates exploratory study).

We used affinity diagramming for data analysis [4], where we clustered and axial-coded related statements to uncover themes and commonalities in the parents' discussions.

Findings

Parents indicated that their children use a variety of devices ranging from those specifically manufactured for children (e.g., Leapster), to gaming platforms (e.g., Wii), to multi-purpose devices (e.g., tablets, laptops). Children also used their parents' smart phones. Overall, while parents were supportive of their children using technology, a major theme of discussion was how parents struggle with setting limits of use, for example, in terms of content types and amount of time. We elaborate on these concerns below.

Acceptable Use of Technology

A dominant theme in our data was that parents exhibited strong notions of what they consider to be acceptable uses of technology for their children. In addition, these notions were highly parent and family-specific. A common acceptable use that parents focused on was education:

> *I feel she does learn logical kind of skills [from Leapster], like matching games and things like that because those games are very educational. – eP3*

Parents' discussion of educational uses covered a range of areas, one of which was religious education:

> *He uses computer for his religious lessons... It is not about fun and playing games. – eP1*

Parents also approved of educational uses that support creativity or learning to work with others:

> *It is a building game [Mine Craft] so I can't be too upset about it. It requires a lot of imagination, [intuition] and creativity so I kind of feel better about them playing that versus a lot of other games that maybe wouldn't be as creative. – eP2*

> *[Any new device] has to be something that [the siblings] can share, or use together that's all – basically something that they can do together cooperatively. To me that's a big one. I just don't want to have them next to each other and doing like a parallel play, I want them interacting with each other and learning how to be brothers. – eP7*

In addition to education, another common acceptable use was technologies that engage children in physical activity:

> *[The Wii] is not just sitting and playing, there are games where they will get up and moving. – eP11*

Thus, while parents may be positive about and welcome some uses of technology by their (young) children, it is often for specific use cases, with the primary emphasis being on education and physical activity.

Strategies for Control

Parents heavily discussed a wide range of methods they employed to control how their children use technology, mirroring prior research on parental control strategies [18]; our results below outline how these strategies are manifested with current-generation technologies.

Supervised Use: A common strategy articulated by parents was to only allow children to use technology while under some form of supervision:

> *He doesn't use the laptop alone, never! – eP10*

> *They have a laptop but they only use it at the dining room table, so we're always around and usually we at least know what they are doing, if not what site exactly they are on. – eP12*

However, one parent commented that while supervision is required for certain devices, this adds overhead:

> *[The laptop] is too multi-functional to let them loose with it, it has to be where you're monitoring it and that's a lot of extra work to do. – eP2*

In this particular case, the parent attempts to avoid this overhead by choosing devices that require less supervision (that is, have fewer risky features).

Filtering: Some parents reported that they pre-filter content for appropriateness before giving access to their children, often providing the child with no opportunity for input:

> *You choose the songs and games you put inside [the iPod] so you are very confident they are suitable and this is what you want them to hear. – eP5*

Although one parent noted that they investigated with their children, providing an opportunity for education:

> *If they ask to go on a website we haven't heard of, we'll sit with them and check it out a little bit and make sure that we know something about it before they go on it. – eP12*

Software-Assisted Control: Parents infrequently described using software-based control solutions (such as parental controls in browsers), with the exception of using passwords. Parents indicated that they were aware of such control solutions; however, many commented on the difficulty of use or added overhead for shared devices:

> *I know there are those parental control things, but it's not that easy and it takes time to go and apply these settings. – eP5*

Thus, while a number of software-based solutions exist, they perhaps do not meet parents' needs.

Time Limitations: Many parents employed time limitations for their children; however, enforcing these limits was often challenging and stressful (e.g., led to arguing with children). For this reason some parents simply avoided purchasing certain devices to circumvent the issue:

> *When he has his own [DS], it'd be hard to take it from him. He'll be all the day just playing and not focusing on anything, so we decided not to buy one. – eP5*

Other parents developed creative solutions to avoid this, such as sharing ownership of a device – where others use it as well – as an indirect way of limiting time:

> *At the beginning we got the iPad for him as present and then because he spent so much time on iPad, so we said both his daddy and I have to use it. Just wanting to reduce the time he spends on it. – eP10*

Discussion

Parents in our study generally welcomed technology for their children and discussed the potential for positive impacts. At the same time, parents expressed concern over some of the dangers of technology use, such as inappropriate content or diminishing of physical and social activities. They further indicated a range of techniques for mitigating these concerns, and expressed some of the challenges of maintaining control. The emergence of these themes from our exploratory interviews motivates investigating new filter configuration methods, and combined with our goal of involving children in the decision process, supports our work in developing an approach to content control that facilitates an educational, discussion-oriented "kid-in-the-loop" process.

WE-CHOOSE CONTENT-CONTROL PROTOTYPE

We propose a new content control method that i) enables parents to involve children in the filtering process and ii) facilitates an educational approach to control. The long-term vision for our approach is to help children learn rules in an engaging setting, decreasing the ongoing parental management overhead, while at the same time giving parents a control mechanism that meets their needs. In this section, we describe a proof-of-concept prototype that we use to explore parents' and children's attitudes towards this alternative model of content filtering. We highlight that this is the first system we are aware of which includes the child in the filtering process, and that emphasizes educational discussion over simple rule setting. Below we outline how our approach was manifested through the We-Choose prototype.

We-Choose Prototype

Our We-Choose content filtering prototype is an Android application running on a tablet computer (Samsung GALAXY Note 8.0) that allows a parent and a child to work together to configure a filter for which applications the child has access to. We selected this platform as a modern relevant example: mobile devices with a central application repository (e.g., Apple Store, Google Marketplace, or Microsoft Store) are increasing in popularity, and there are currently very few content-control options available. In addition, the application-repository model provides a clear (although somewhat simplistic) cutting point for content: an application can either be marked as appropriate or inappropriate.

We targeted We-Choose primarily at children within the six to eight year-old age group, based on psychology literature that indicates this is when children are capable of reasoning about appropriate and inappropriate material [22], and are also able to start making generalizations [16]. However, we do not limit the approach to this age range.

Our We-Choose prototype is designed to facilitate an educational parent-child session about the appropriateness of content. We provide this in a two-part way: first, in *parent-child mode* parents and children work together to set content filtering rules and establish what is appropriate, and in *game mode*, children test their knowledge of what is appropriate. While game mode is primarily designed for the child, parents can continue to be involved, for example by providing discussion and explanation when the child is unsure about why something was or was not appropriate. Overall, we highlight that particular design decisions (e.g., selection of icons) are not the point of our research; rather, we simply aimed to construct a proof-of-concept of the overarching kid-in-the-loop approach that would enable us to run initial studies in this area.

Parent-Child Mode: Creating Filtering Rules Collaboratively

The parent-child mode follows a simple process: an application is presented on the device, and the parent and child together determine if it is appropriate. After this, another application is presented, until the parent and child together determine that they have had enough training and switch to game mode.

As Figure 2 illustrates, to help drive this discussion and decision, the application presentation includes: the application logo and name in the center, icons above the logo indicating the kind of content, a text description of the application at the bottom of the screen, and two bins used to classify the game: a green check box (as appropriate) or a red 'X' (as inappropriate). The parent and child can then assess the information, discuss why it may or may not be appropriate, and together classify the application.

While the parent can use the application's text description to help explain why it is bad or good, the young children targeted by our system (ages 6-8) may not be able to read the application titles and descriptions. As such, a key element of our prototype is the addition of icons, which (after a quick and simple explanation from their parents on what the icons represent) creates a way for the children to develop an opinion on an application they are not familiar with. Through the discussions, we anticipate that children

Figure 2: Parent-child mode showing an application for the parent and child to classify together. This particular application belongs to the action category, and has a high-maturity age rating (depicted by the stick figure).

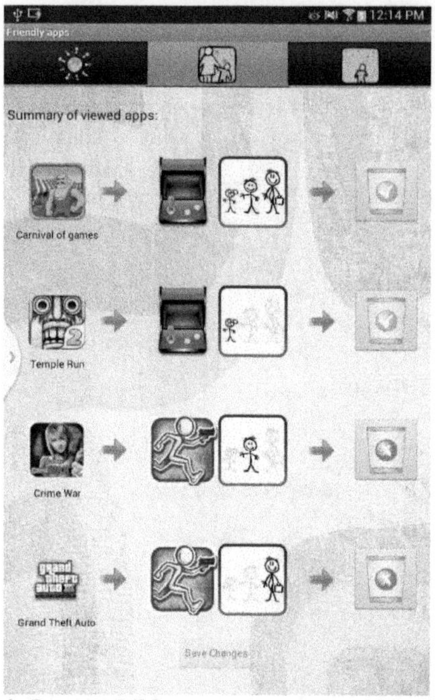

Figure 3: Parent-child summary screen, which displays a list of applications classified in parent-child mode.

can create associations between the topics of conversation and the icon shown. In our prototype, we have icons indicating appropriate age by relative size of a stick figure, as in Figures 2 and 3, which indicate everyone (all three people sizes in the icon), and a range from young to high maturity (indicated by the person size). Figure 3 illustrates the range of possibilities for this icon. We also included icons for the application category, which can be one of: action, arcade, puzzle, casual, gambling/casino, educational, sports, racing and adult (e.g., the "action" category in Figure 2 represented by a figure with a gun). These category and age-rating icons are intended to facilitate conversation about which subject matters or age group applications are considered appropriate for the child. For example, a parent could explain why an application with a gun (violence) may not be appropriate. They could also explain why the child is not able to use applications that have a high-maturity age rating. The same icons are used in the game mode explained below.

Users can also at any time view a summary screen (Figure 3) that contains a list of the applications that the parent and child has already seen and shows how they were categorized. This enables the users to refer to previous choices to compare and contrast as part of their discussion.

When the parent and child decide that they have had enough training, they can switch to game mode by clicking the "Let's try!" button (Figure 2, bottom).

Game Mode: Exploring What the Child Learned

Game mode tests the child's knowledge of the rules and provides additional discussion and learning opportunities for the child. In game mode, the child works through a number of additional example applications (not previously shown) in a manner similar to the parent-child mode; however, unlike previously, in game mode the child has to try to guess whether or not each application is appropriate for them. The expectation is that the child will retain some of the rules they learned previously with their parents. After guessing, feedback is provided as a happy or sad character animation (Figure 4) accompanied by a clapping or crying sound. Upon completion of all of the examples, the prototype displays all the applications that the child has gone through while playing the game, highlighting any incorrect choices (with a format similar to the summary screen shown in Figure 3). This screen can then be used by the parent and child for discussion.

The mode-oriented design of We-Choose enables parents and children to change back and forth between the modes to fit their own particular discussion and education style.

Implementation Details

We-Choose is a mockup of an application marketplace with a set of pre-coded (category, maturity) applications based on real Google Marketplace items. The internal filter-learning system was simply a mock-up for the purposes of enabling interaction within our proof-of-concept prototype. Through interaction with the parent-child mode, the system internally builds a simple set of binary rules where age ratings and categories are labeled as appropriate or not, based on how applications are rated during parent-child mode. Following, in game mode if any of the binary flags match the application (e.g., inappropriate category or age), it is classified as inappropriate. Conflicts (e.g., if an action game is rated as appropriate once and inappropriate another time) are not addressed. For a more advanced

Figure 4: Game mode showing the sad animated character (customizable according the child's preferences) in response to a childs misclassification.

implementation and future prototype, the learning algorithm itself would need to be properly addressed.

WE-CHOOSE EVALUATION

The primary purpose of our evaluation was to introduce the concept of kid-in-the-loop content filtering to a group of parents and children, through the use of our We-Choose prototype, and to learn about their impressions of our discussion and education-oriented approach. We recruited parents and their children and had them use our prototype to configure a content filter for roughly 20 minutes.

Participants

We recruited 13 sets of parents and children in the six to eight year-old age group via signs posted throughout our university campus and daycare, and in the local community. In all cases only a single parent participated (all mothers, Table 2). Parents received a $10 gift card and children received a small toy. The study was approved by our university's research ethics board.

Study Method

The procedure for each session was as follows. Participants were given a brief (~3 min.) explanation of the approach and the We-Choose prototype, including the concept of parent-child discussion mode (shown in Figure 2) and child-learning game mode (shown in Figure 4).

After participants completed a short practice session with each mode, we administered the main condition: we clearly explained to participants how they start with parent-child mode and could switch back and forth to game mode as they wished, and should not necessarily aim to try and classify all applications in parent-child mode. Participants were told to continue until they felt that they clearly

Parent Number	Occupation	Children's Ages and Genders
P1	Insurance agent	6-yr old girl
P2	Nurse	7-yr old boy
P3	Graduate student	8-yr old girl
P4	Unreported	6-yr old boy
P5	Unreported	6-year old girl
P6	University support staff	6-year old boy
P7	Unreported	6-yr old boy
P8	Graduate student	6-yr old girl
P9	Nursing-home worker/Graduate student	7-yr old boy
P10	Maid/Undergraduate student	Twin 6-yr old boys
P11	Stay-at-home parent	6-yr old boy
P12	Unreported	7-yr old girl
P13	Graduate student	7-yr old girl

Table 2: Participants in the prototype evaluation.

explained, and they felt the child understood, the rules they wanted to configure. We-Choose had 40 items that could be classified, 20 for parent-child mode and 20 for game mode.

We finished with a semi-structured interview with both the parent and child to investigate their impressions of our kid-in-the-loop approach to application selection and filter configuration, and to elicit feedback on the We-Choose instantiation. Each interview started by talking to the child (to mitigate the influence of parents' responses). One parent and child pair stopped part way through the game mode when the child became tired and irritable; however, the parent still participated in the interview. Each session lasted approximately 45 minutes.

Findings

We begin by describing parents and their children's responses to the approach, followed by a discussion of their interactions with We-Choose.

Attitudes towards the Kid-In-The-Loop Approach

All parents responded very positively to the collaborative content filtering approach, showing interest in using such a system if available. Below we discuss aspects that parents were particularly enthusiastic about.

Discussion Catalyst: Our We-Choose instantiation was successful in facilitating discussion and giving children an active voice in the content selection process, a point that parents indicated they liked about the system:

> *You can kind of set it and let them decide a little bit more so they have more choices. – P4, with 6yr boy*

Parents were appreciative of the opportunity for discussions with their children, with the interface providing context on what was considered appropriate and providing opportunities for corrections:

I'd be able to say and talk with them, 'why did you think this was ok?', 'this [application] tells me you chose the wrong answer here', 'how come you chose that?' and have a discussion and poke at the problem and see what goes on. – P10, with 6yr boy twins

Some parents believed that the benefits would go beyond the initial discussion session:

It was educative, because right now, when we leave this room we can talk about this and see there are some apps that are proper and some improper. – P13, with 7yr girl

Parents also saw opportunities to extend discussions on appropriateness to the whole family:

It also makes you sort of need to discuss what is appropriate and what is not appropriate and to sort of clarify the guidelines for the family. – P12, with 7yr girl

Two participants went on to discuss how the approach might encourage them to carve out time for more of this type of discussion time with their children:

It is often hard to find time to sort of address the values of the family or the beliefs of the family or moral and ethics. So if you have a chance to sit down and do something like this together then we can talk about it. I think it creates a dedicated time and space to do it, whereas everyone is busy all the time. Everyone is running here and there. – P12, with 7yr girl

I can use it when I'm ready to be present with it and really connect with them using this thing and use that opportunity to establish ourselves for a period of time so I know that the maintenance is done. – P10, with 6yr boy twins

In comparison to other education methods, such as the traditional sit-down conversation, some parents felt that our method would provide an easier and more fun way to teach their children the guidelines of what is appropriate:

It provides a conversation, it is a nice way, an easy way to bring up a topic in a way that is more visual and fun instead of me sitting there and telling him what we can and cannot do. – P6, with 6yr boy

Reducing the Content-Filtering Burden: Parents, as in our exploratory study, indicated the complexity of content selection and filtering:

I find it hard to sort through [application store] myself, I don't know if a 10 year old would be able to figure that out because often I'd look at that stuff and I'd be like 'I don't even know'. – P2, with 7yr boy

Parents also felt that the system could simplify the selection process, for example, by acting as a first-pass filter:

It seems to be like a filter, where it alleviates or eliminates all of the other apps that I wouldn't agree to her having anyway. – P1, with 6yr girl

Many pointed to the benefits of our particular design decision of using visual indicators for appropriateness:

I myself might not know if it is good for her or not, but having this thing, which gives more information if it is appropriate or not, will help the parent definitely. – P8, with 6yr girl

This system helps me quickly distinguish between the appropriate and inappropriate so that I can include some of the things that I may have not included. – P10, with 6yr boy twins

Diagnostic Tool: Participants reported seeing potential for using the kid-in-the-loop approach to gain insight into their children's comprehension of rules and what is appropriate, as well as their interests:

It was fun and it was really interesting for me to see her work away at this herself and I guess discovering that we sort of share these feelings about what is appropriate and what is not appropriate. – P12, with 7yr girl

I really enjoyed when I withdrew that they knew and that they were able to follow. – P10, with 6yr boy twins

It lets you know what your child is interested in. – P12, with 7yr girl

One parent also felt that it helped develop her confidence in her child's understanding:

Having something like that, with all the apps out there would really boost my confidence by showing him at this age how he can tell what is appropriate and what is not. – P6, with 6yr boy

Children's Reactions: While children were less vocal in the interviews than their parents, they also responded positively to the kid-in-the-loop approach. For example, expressing interest in the game or having their own voice:

I think that I like that game so that you can sort of choose your apps. – C2, 7yr boy

Another child commented that it was enjoyable to work with their parent:

I liked playing with my mom, because sometimes it is hard [to decide]. – C13, 7yr girl

Maintaining Final Approval: While parents were enthusiastic about the approach, many still indicated that they would not fully delegate control to such a system:

Because he still can't read, he could install something and get frustrated with it even if it is age appropriate [...] I'd prefer to know... just to give him a bit of a warning first, so even though it would be age appropriate for a range of kids, for him it may not be exactly what he was thinking. – P4, with 6yr boy

Part of this is due to the inherently subjective nature of what is appropriate:

At the final stage [before installation] I still want to see what [the child has chosen]... Even though some toys are made for the kids but we may think it is not okay for him to have it, it's the same for the apps. Sometimes the industry thinks it is good but we don't. – P9, with 7yr boy

As a middle ground, many proposed that automatically approved or child-selected applications could perhaps be added to a "pending" list for review:

If I could say 'you pick which ones you want' and then I approve, that is probably easier... probably a better way of doing it instead of just letting him go ahead. – P6, with 6yr boy

Reluctance to fully trust the resulting filters is not unique to our approach – similar attitudes have been expressed in prior studies on content filters and blocking software [21].

Explanation Styles and Discussion Strategies

Using video recordings of the sessions, we examined how parents explained and discussed application appropriateness with their children while using our prototype and approach. Most parents' explanations (9/13 parents) depended heavily on the application age ratings (the stick-figure icons shown in Figures 2-4), perhaps even more so with children who could not yet read. To explain the icon meanings to children, some parents spent time working through a reference sheet that we provided containing all icons used in the prototype:

> *This is a game that everybody should be able to play because all the people are highlighted. This means it is for little kids. This one, just by looking at the picture, [is] for medium maturity or kids that are probably [your brother's] age [10 years-old] and up. And then high maturity is really for like adults only because they took out the little ones. So you can look at that for a clue whether it is good for you. So if you look at these which ones should you be playing? – P5, with 6yr girl*
>
> *[C5 points at the "low maturity" age-rating icon]*
>
> *What else has a little kid? – P5*
>
> *[C5 points at the "everyone" age-rating icon]*
>
> *That's right because it means it is for everyone – P5*

Other parents instead used the context of a particular application – within We-Choose – to explain:

> *Is this a good game or not? – P10, with 6yr boy twins*
>
> *A good game – Twin1*
>
> *Why? – P10*
>
> *[C10 points at the "everyone" age-rating icon]*
>
> *See, it shows all of us – Twin1*
>
> *Who is this one good for? [Parent point at "low maturity" age-rating icon] – P10*
>
> *Me, for little kids – Twin1*
>
> *So what are you going to push? – P10*
>
> *Yes – Twin1*

The application categories (action, puzzle, gambling etc.), on the other hand, were not as heavily utilized by parents, with only three parents incorporating category extensively into their discussions, for example:

> *Pool break, this is playing pool. See this one [pointing to sports category icon] it is a sports game and this is for everyone it says, anyone can play it. – P7, with 6yr boy*
>
> *What does this [application icon] look like to you? You don't know? It looks like someone is looking through a gun. This looks like blood, and this guy here is running with a gun [pointing to action category icon], so I think no, that is not appropriate. – P12, with 7yr girl*
>
> *Here it says puzzle and that's good, go ahead. Anything that helps us think is good. – P13, with 7yr girl*

These explanations further illustrate how parents wanted their children to not only identify which categories are appropriate or not appropriate, they also wanted their children to understand why, and used the discussion as a means to communicate this.

We-Choose Use Strategies in the Parent-Child Mode

All but one set of participants completed the entire parent-child mode before their child started using the game mode (12/13). Most of the parents (9/13) actively involved their children while in parent-child mode, explaining the ratings and categories and asking their child to guess whether or not the application would be considered appropriate. Seven parents used this strategy from the start, while two parents worked through a couple of examples first before asking their child to guess. Three parents provided explanations as they went through the applications but did not ask their child to venture guesses as to their appropriateness.

One group moved back and forth to game mode before completing all examples in parent-child mode; when asked, this parent indicated she chose this strategy because she wanted to both keep her explanations fresh in her child's mind and keep her child engaged by giving her a chance to actively interact with the prototype:

> *I thought maybe it will be easier for her when I let her do her task just after it. I thought that if I talk and don't let her touch anything for a long time she would have said 'I don't want this' [...] It's a break for her that I give her a chance to touch it. – P8, with 6yr girl*

Interactions in the Game Mode

For the most part, parents let their children play the game mode completely by themselves, only occasionally stepping in to clarify misconceptions. For example, when C3 (8yr girl) made mistakes, her mom reminded her to look at the age-rating icon and use it to decide:

> *Just look at this picture here and if it is suitable for your age or not. – P3, with 8yr girl*

In the case of the twins, they played the game together, and worked collaboratively through their reasoning:

> *Is this one good for you guys or not good for you? – P10, with 6y boy twins*
>
> *No – Twin1*
>
> *[Twin1's name] look – Twin2*
>
> *[Twin2 points at "everyone" age-rating icon]*
>
> *Little people, big people, really big people – Twin1*
>
> *So is that a good one or not? – P10*
>
> *Yes – Twin1*

The children seemed to enjoy playing the game, despite the fairly basic design (e.g., no sophisticated plots, graphics or animation) and educational focus. Children enjoyed the rewards for good performance and appeared to take it very seriously. One child (C6, 6yr boy) wanted to change an answer he got wrong, and commented *"I'm good at this game!"* when he got a series of examples correct. C10 (Twin1, 6yr boy twins) happily exclaimed *"Mom, we keep getting it right*!" indicating that he was enjoying playing the game with his mom there to help. Another child (C4, 6yr boy) upon completion turned to his mom and the experimenter and asked: *"Can I play again?"*

The children performed very well in game mode: average 18.2/20 correct responses (stdev 2.9) with seven children classifying all applications correctly. For the children who got wrong answers, interviews revealed that they were also factoring in whether or not they thought they would like the application in addition to the appropriateness. For one child, who scored 11/20, we noted that the parent's rules about appropriateness were not consistent with our criteria (some of which were based on particular application preference) which appeared to be the source of confusion.

Discussion

Our results indicate that parents saw value in the discussion opportunity, above and beyond simply creating filters. This is a primary goal of our kid-in-the-loop approach: it provided context (real applications) within which meaningful discussions about rules and values can take place, as well as an excuse, opportunity, and fun way to discuss things which may be less interesting for the child or may be ignored otherwise. Although we concede that our results do not strongly inform us on how much children were actually in the loop, in terms of how much their opinions impacted the final filter configuration, our approach improves the chances of children learning and following rules by providing a discussion opportunity beyond parent-only filter configuration [7,10].

Although our work targets the configuration of content filters, this emerged as a secondary point (to the benefit of facilitating discussion) in our results. While some parents highlighted the time and effort saving potential, many indicated that they may not trust a filter that learns from the demonstrations. We note that despite this, these parents still indicated the value from an educational standpoint.

The We-Choose prototype successfully enabled initial interaction sessions where children and parents work together to configure and discuss content filtering. No problems arose that hindered interactions, and participant feedback was generally positive. We do note that families approached the interaction in a variety of ways (e.g., parent-child then game mode, going back and forth, or pre-learning icons) and We-Choose supported these differences; future work should likewise consider flexibility.

Overall, we believe that our results lend initial support to the kid-in-the-loop approach to content control and filtering. Although there remains work in investigating how exactly children enter the decision-making process, the discussion and education approach was well received by parents, who appreciated the facilitation of meaningful discussions with their children, and there was indication of at least short-term learning on behalf of the children (they learned their parent's rules during our session). There was also some indication that children themselves appreciated having some input into these control type decisions.

Although we target the specific task of content filtering, many of the benefits we found surrounding children being involved and families discussing collaboratively may apply to other interaction scenarios as well. As such, we believe our results support this direction as a promising one for future work, not only for configuring control and restrictions for children, but anywhere where parents and children may find themselves using technology together.

FUTURE WORK

As this project was an initial test-bed for kid-in-the-loop education and discussion-oriented content filtering, our positive results leave a rich breadth of future work.

This current work is limited in that it was an in-lab study where children may have been particularly well behaved given the official and public scenario. Moving forward, it will be important to investigate how such systems would be used during longitudinal deployments to homes. Further, while pedagogical foundations served as a motivation for this work, we only superficially investigated child learning, and future work should more rigorously explore how being "in the loop" may impact learning about appropriate content. As part of these questions, we need to investigate how culture and socio-economic status – factors which can impact technology use – would affect interaction. Further, while we targeted young children in our work, at least some parents saw benefits for older children. Exploring other age groups – and how this may change the requirements and mechanics – is an important direction for future work.

Part of our prototype design was to rely on visual representations of the content types and appropriateness. We selected these heuristically and while they appeared to work; future work should take a more structured approach to developing improved representations, for example, that cover additional dimensions such as length of play session, or theme (fantasy and dragons, etc.). Other child-friendly representations such as video, color schemes, and so forth, should also be explored. Similarly, our use of reward and feedback (through happy or sad animations) may have been somewhat simplistic, and it will be interesting to consider a more fine-grained setup, or how to maintain the reward benefit as the novelty of the animation wears off. For example, point systems (e.g., to unlock tools or games) could be explored.

Finally, we took a minimalist approach to the technical components of content-learning as our research was focused on the kid-in-the-loop discussion aspect and not on the adaptive technologies. Moving forward, it will be important to consider how content may actually be tagged in real marketplaces, how such tags may be represented through approaches such as ours, and how a system should properly learn based on a small number of examples.

CONCLUSION

In this paper we presented a novel approach to child-oriented content control for internet-capable devices, which keeps the child in the loop and emphasizes education and discussion over simply setting rules. We conducted an exploratory study with the results emphasizing the broad range of technologies that children today interact with as well as the importance parents place on maintaining appropriate content, and the high amounts of energy that parents expend to control content.

To test our approach and mitigate some of these issues, we designed and developed an initial kid-in-the-loop prototype based on a tablet PC with a marketplace application paradigm, and conducted a study to investigate how parents and children may react to and use such an approach. Our study results illustrate how discussion can be facilitated and how children can learn through this approach. Both parents and children in our study expressed a great deal of enthusiasm about the idea and our instantiation, and many parents provided suggestions of how it may be useful beyond our use case.

ACKNOWLEDGEMENTS

This work was supported by the GRAND Network Center of Excellence and the National Sciences and Engineering Research Council of Canada.

REFERENCES

1. Ames, M.G., Go, J., Kaye, J.J., Spasojevic, M., Road, P.M., and Alto, P. Understanding technology choices and values through social class. In *Proc. CSCW,* (2011), 55-64.
2. Arentz, W.A. and Olstad, B. Classifying offensive sites based on image content. *Computer Vision and Image Understanding 94*, 1-3 (2004), 295–310.
3. Van den Bergh, B. and Van den Bulck, J. Media use, perceived parental media guidance and supportive parent-child commmunication in fifth and sixth graders. *Communications 24*, 3 (2009), 329–350.
4. Beyer, H. and Holtzblatt, K. *Contextual Design: Defining Customer-Centered Systems*. Elsevier, 1997.
5. Chakroff, J.L. and Nathanson, A.I. Parent and school interventions. In *The Handbook of Children, Media, and Development*. 2008, 552–576.
6. Elliott, D., Glassey, R., Polajnar, T., and Azzopardi, L. Finding and filtering information for children. In *Proc. SIGIR,* (2010), 702-702.
7. Freedman, J.L. Long-term behavioral effects of cognitive dissonance. *Experimental Social Psychology 1*, 2 (1965), 145–155.
8. Gentile, D.A. and Walsh, D.A. A normative study of family media habits. *Journal of Applied Developmental Psychology 23*, 2002, 157–178.
9. Glassey, R., Elliott, D., Polajnar, T., and Azzopardi, L. Interaction-based information filtering for children. In *Proc. IIiX*, (2010), 329-334.
10. Goodman, J.F. Moral education in early childhood. *Early Education and Development 11*, 1 (2000), 37–41.
11. Graf, D.L., Pratt, L. V, Hester, C.N., and Short, K.R. Playing active video games increases energy expenditure in children. *Pediatrics 124*, 2 (2009), 534-540.
12. Greenfield, P. and Yan, Z. Children, adolescents, and the internet: a new field of inquiry in developmental psychology. *Developmental Psychology 42*, 3 (2006), 391-4.
13. Himmelweit, H.T. *Television and the Child.* Oxford 1970.
14. Hu, W., Zuo, H., Wu, O., Chen, Y., Zhang, Z., and Suter, D. Recognition of adult images, videos, and web page bags. *ACM Trans on Multimedia Computing, Communications, and Applications 7S*, 1 (2011), 1–24.
15. Jeon, W., Lee, Y., and Won, D. Analysis of content filtering software. In *Proc. HI*, (2011), 548–557.
16. Kail, R. V. and Zolner, T. *Children. A Chronological Approach*. Pearson, Education Canada, 2005.
17. Livingstone, S. and Helsper, E.J. Parental mediation of children's internet use. *Broadcasting and Electronic Media 52*, 4 (2008), 581–599.
18. Livingstone, S. Strategies of parental regulation in the media-rich home. *Computers in Human Behavior*, (2007), 920-941.
19. McKenney, S. and Voogt, J. Technology and young children: How 4-7 year olds perceive their own use of tcomputers. *Computers in Human Behavior 26*, 4 (2010), 656-664.
20. McNeely, C. and Blanchard, J. *The Teen Years Explained. Johns Hopkins*. 2009.
21. Mitchell, K.J., Finkelhor, D., and Wolak, J. Protecting youth online: Family use of filtering and blocking software. *Child Abuse and Neglect 29*, 7 (2005), 753-765.
22. Mohseni, N. The relations between moral and social development in 6 to 12 year old children. *Enfance 34*, (1981), 75–84.
23. Nathanson, A.I. Parent and child perspectives on the presence and meaning of parental television mediation. *J Broadcasting & Electronic Media 45*, 2 (2001), 201-220.
24. Schramm, W. *Television in the Lives of our Children*. Stanford University Press, 1961.
25. Yardi, S. and Bruckman, A. Income, race, and class. In *Proc. CHI*, (2012), 3041-3050.
26. Smartphone ownership 2013. http://pewinternet.org/Reports/2013/Smartphone-Ownership-2013/ Findings.aspx.
27. More kids can work smartphones than can tie their own shoes. http://www.theatlantic.com/technology/archive/2011/01/more-kids-can-work-smartphones-than-can-tie-theirown-shoes/70101/.

What did Spot Hide? A Question-Answering Game for Preschool Children

Anuj Tewari[1,2] & John Canny[1]
[1]Computer Science Division and Berkeley Institute of Design,
University of California, Berkeley, USA
[2]GE Global Research, 2623 Camino Ramon, San Ramon, California, USA
{anuj, jfc}@cs.berkeley.edu

ABSTRACT
Early literacy is critical to child development, and determines a child's later educational and life opportunities. Moreover, preschool children are incessantly inquisitive, and will readily engage in question answering and asking activities if given the opportunity. We argue here that question asking/answering technologies can play a major role in early literacy. We describe the design and evaluation of a conversational agent called Spot, with the goal of engaging children in a 20-questions game. Towards this goal, we conducted a feasibility study to determine if children's questions are "on-topic" and suitable for ASR/dialogue systems. We evaluated Spot's performance at conducting a game of 20-questions against that of a human partner.

Author Keywords
Games; Preschool literacy; question-answering; conversational agents.

ACM Classification Keywords
H.5.m. Information interfaces and presentation (e.g., HCI): Miscellaneous.

INTRODUCTION
Many national organizations recognize the essential role of early literacy in a child's later educational and life opportunities [28], [29], [30]. "The richness of nouns, modifiers, and past-tense verbs in their parents' utterances, their parents' high propensity to ask yes/no questions, especially auxiliary-fronted yes/no questions; and their parents' low propensity to initiate and use imperatives and prohibitions were more strongly predictive of the children's performance on the Stanford-Binet IQ test battery." Hart and Risley [18] note that early literacy is an enormous challenge and will require lengthy and regular language experiences for the child.

The greatest impact on child literacy will arguably come from intervention at pre-school ages [18]. Moreover, a growing body of research is also suggesting that pre-school children are voracious inquisitors. One recent study found that preschoolers ask approximately 80 questions/hour [8]. These questions are an essential part of language development: they provide primary experience with question construction, statement construction, explanation construction, complex tenses etc. At the preschool level, most questions are fact-based, e.g. "do fish fly?" although around age 3 there is a sharp increase in explanation-oriented questioning. Fact-based questions are readily answered by short statement responses. Children may ask follow-up questions, but in general the chain of conversation is short. Explanation-oriented questions seek richer answers with causal links or chains [13]. They will often be met with additional requests for more information, or a universal "why." Children have strong preferences for the form of the answer (a causal explanation vs. fact-based answer), although less so for content. Question-asking, not surprisingly, goes beyond literacy and is an integral part of children's cognitive development [7]. So attention to this activity may have benefits in cognitive development as well.

Children evidently need some form of linguistic engagement for many hours a week, with a language-able partner who can engage with them in age-appropriate language-learning activities. Since research in early child development suggests that for pre-school children question-answering serves as a frequent and heavily-utilized medium, this linguistic engagement can come in the form of interactive question-answering systems. Since children spend a significant amount of time playing alone, or out of home, there might be instances when they don't find an adult around to answer their questions. There might also be times, when the adult doesn't have sufficient information at hand to answer a child's question. This explains the need for expert interactive systems that can work as engaging question-answering agents.

ENVISAGED SOLUTION
We envision a projection system with a virtual character that acts as the question-answering agent. The aim is to create a virtual play space that can keep the conversation grounded in a context. Grounding is important because context specific speech recognition is more feasible than that in scenarios that lack context [36]. The virtual character (usually an animal),

CHI 2014, April 26 - May 01 2014, Toronto, ON, Canada

http://dx.doi.org/10.1145/2556288.2557205

rendered over a wide area using a projection system, will engage children in language games that use question-answering as the primary dialogue structure. For example, the character will show the child several objects, then hide one and ask the child to guess what it is by asking questions about it. The game engages children in language use, and also in concrete questions about things in the world and their properties. The envisaged solution is shown in Figure 1.

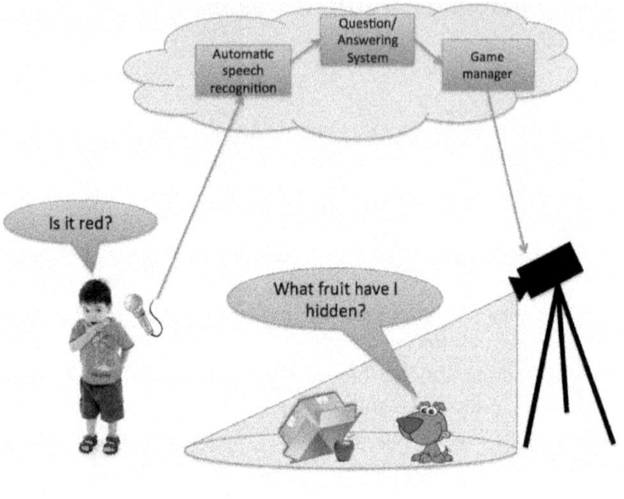

Figure 1: The envisaged solution

CURRENT WORK

In this paper we describe a two-phase study, one phase using a human language partner, and the second using a system which approximates figure 1. Rather than relying on speech recognition and dialog interpretation, we used a Wizard-Of-Oz system. The goal of the studies was to explore the feasibility of the envisaged solution: whether students would ask "on-topic" questions, whether the questions matched some templates, and whether they would be engaged by the game. Phase 1 involved 12 children studying at the same preschool, playing a 20-questions game with a familiar researcher. It contributed to answering the following research questions:

1. Are children's questions predictable and deterministic, when grounded in an activity like 20 questions?
2. Is the repair required in such a dialogue limited and feasible?
3. Is it possible to effectively "nudge" preschoolers to solve problems without disengaging?

Phase 2 involved the same participants as phase 1. Half of them played the game with the same researcher. The other half played the same with (wizard-of-Oz) Spot, an agent that we designed and implemented. Effectively, 6 children played just with the familiar human in both the phases and the remaining 6 first played with the human and then the agent. In phase 3, all the participants played with (non-wizard, fully automated) Spot. Phases 2 and 3 built on phase 1, and answered the following research question:

1. Using commonly used parenting styles in dialogues, how can we design an agent that can engage preschoolers in a familiar question-answering activity as effectively as a familiar human?

Effectiveness in this case is primarily restricted to question-answering efficiency, flow of communication and affect/engagement. Moreover, literature suggests that vocabulary accrues from language use [18]. It is not feasible to measure vocabulary richness, especially in constrained activities like question answering. Therefore, in this round of research priority was given to the volume of language use. We see the following contributions for this work:

- Testing the feasibility of question-asking/answering behavior in preschoolers, and if technology can be designed to support such behavior.
- Investigation of engaging preschoolers in context of language usage, using technology.
- Using common and effective parenting styles to design and develop a system for preschoolers.

RELATED WORK

With the growth of conversational technologies, the possibilities for integrating conversation and discourse in e-learning are receiving greater attention in both research and commercial settings. Conversational agents have been produced to meet a wide range of applications, including tutoring (e.g. [16], [19], [2]), question-answering (e.g. [10], [12], [34]), conversation practice for language learners, (e.g. [14], [1]), pedagogical agents and learning companions (e.g. [23], [33], [4], [11]), and dialogues to promote reflection and metacognitive skills (e.g. [17], [20]). Conversational agents build on traditional education systems, providing a natural and practical interface for the learner. They are capable of offering support for each individual, and recognizing and building upon the strengths, interests and abilities of individuals in order to create engaged and independent learners. However, the current interactive conversational tutors are geared more towards older children, who have a larger set of knowledge or skills than pre-school children and are easier to understand, and also focus on specific skills or domains.

The key difficulty in developing an agent for such a younger audience is maintaining children in their ZPD (Zone of Proximal Developent) [37]. The project CACHET examines the responses young children have to interactive conversational agents using electronic stuffed toys [25]. These toys are designed to speak, respond to touch via sensors, gesture with motors, and be linked to a PC wirelessly to provide support and feedback while a child plays games encouraging number and language learning [25]. Children were able to skillfully navigate through the games, however, and were adept at asking for help when they were aware of and were not irritated with the toy [25]. This technological adroitness suggests high potential for interactive agents for younger children.

There is also some recent reflective work in media psychology [22] and education [9] that critically analyses the results of experiments with pedagogical agents in general. Most such work calls for testing with younger audiences. Moreover, prior research has shown that projection systems can be effective mediums of interaction for younger children. This could either be for remote collaboration with other children [39] or communication via media with parents [38]. Overall, we did not find examples in the literature of systems that use projections of virtual agents to do question-answering based games for preschool children.

PHASE 1: FEASIBILITY STUDY

Participants

12 children (6 boys, 6 girls) participated in our feasibility study. The participants in the study were 4 and 5 year old children at a preschool in California. Previous research suggested that 3-year-old children would be too young for such an experiment [8]. The preschool that was chosen as the location for the study was a research preschool.

Equipment and setup

The study was conducted in a research room on the preschool premises, reserved for that purpose. The room was equipped with a one-way mirror and audio equipment that allowed a visual supervisor to monitor the study at all times. The presence of the visual supervisor was required by the preschool's protocols. During the study two researchers were present for all sessions, in addition to the child. The children could see the researchers, but not the visual supervisor. A video camera recorded the child's and researchers' activity at all times.

Method

The preschool consisted of two classrooms, namely east and west. As per preschool protocol, no child was allowed to be outside the classroom for more than 20 minutes in one session. No child could attend more than three study sessions in a week. Overall all participants attended one such session, and the entire phase 1 took three weeks.

Each classroom had a circle time from 10am every morning, which is when the researchers got to interact with the participants before starting the study. The research team attended several (>5) circle times to become familiar with the study participants. Familiarity was important because a large part of the study involved playing games with researchers on the team.

During the study each child attended a session individually. Before each session a researcher from the team went to one of the classrooms and invited participants to attend a study session. Out of the consenting children one was escorted to the study room. As stated above, the study session could not last more than 20 minutes.

Each session comprised of multiple question-answering exchange trials. Each child was shown photographs of two objects. After this both the photographs were shuffled, one was put away and one was retained. The child was told that the purpose of the game is to ask questions and figure out which object was being retained. The session started with a demo trial, where the two objects were cat and ball. In the demo trial, one of the researchers asked questions and another researcher answered. If the child did not understand the demonstration, it was repeated till the child was comfortable in contributing to the questions being asked. After the demo trial, 6 more trials followed. Each child was asked to identify the two objects at the start of each trial. For each question that a child asked, a truthful answer was given. After each question-answer pair, the child was asked if they wanted to ask more questions or were ready to guess. Sometimes the child would just guess without perceivably having enough information to make a guess.

Each child went through 7 pairs of objects, including the demo trial. For each trial, the stimulus pair of objects presented got more difficult. Increased difficulty meant increased similarity in the stimulus pair. For example, a cat and a ball are easily distinguishable, but a bicycle and a car are harder to differentiate. In formal terms, the more difficult stimulus pairs were closer to each other in terms of parts, functions and properties. A list of all the pairs is given in Table 1[8]. It should be noted that no object was repeated across two trials. This was done to level the amount of practice children receive with each object.

Target item	Low similarity	Moderate similarity	High Similarity
Phase 1	Book & Banana	Table & Bed	Apple & Orange
	Elephant & Spoon	Shoe & Hat	Bicycle & Car
Phase 2	Chair & Rose	Bear & Dog	Truck & Bus
	Flower & Kite	Chicken & Pig	Clock & Watch

Table 1: Object pairs used in the two phases

Data collection and analysis

After the study, all the videos were transcribed. Care was taken that critical incidents like questions, explanations, hints and off-topic conversations were recorded. Previous literature suggested that most of these questions fall in one of the three categories: parts of objects, functions of objects and properties of objects [8]. Six individual coders/raters were asked to classify the questions into one of the three categories. There was substantial agreement in the ratings (Fleiss Kappa: 0.71, kappa error = 0.0117, kappa C.I. (95%) = 0.7022, z = 60.5003, p = 0.0001). Analysis of these ratings was done to answer the research questions allocated to this phase.

Results

Children asked questions

Participants in our study seemed to be naturally primed to ask questions. They asked a total of 127 questions, which means an average of 11 questions per child in a span of 20 minutes.

It also turned out that the number of questions asked by a child was significantly correlated with the number of trials successfully solved (r(10) = 0.7, df = 8, $p<0.05$). In other words, children who asked more questions solved more problems. This jibes with previous research on the subject [8].

Questions had specific categories
Analysis of the coded data revealed that 80% of the questions asked by our participants were about the part, property or function of objects. The remaining 20% were guesses about what the object could be, example "Is it a cat?". Out of the non-guess questions, 46.5% were property related questions, 30.5% were function related questions and 23% were part related questions. Therefore, it was clear that most questions in such scenarios would deal with one of these three objects. This helped us create the database of possible questions expected by the agent.

Limited need for repeated explanation & tendency to guess without proper inference
Participants in our study needed limited explanation. On average researchers had to intervene only 1.67 times per child. This was generally in cases where a child responded in a manner that represented an inaccurate understanding of the game. In all such cases, one of the researchers would repeat the explanation of the game. All such cases helped us build conversational edge cases into the agent later. This is more formally known as repair/error-recovery in dialogue systems.

Children were adept at inferring the objects. In phase 1, they were able to successfully solve 80% of the trials conducted. Sometimes however, they would still try guessing the object without having enough information to solve the problem. This is in addition to the final guess that they would use to solve the problem. Overall 40 such inaccurate guesses were recorded across the 12 participants.

Off-topic dialogues and hint mechanisms
During the study, sometimes a child would talk about objects or contexts that were not grounded in the environment. Any such deviations from the task at hand were counted as an off-topic dialogue (average = 0.83, max =3). It was noticed that approximately 5% of the utterances by the participants were not grounded in the environment, and were counted as offtopic.

Sometimes (41 out of 476 statements, 8%) a child would find it hard to frame a question about two objects. Predictably, more than 70% of such cases happened for objects with high levels of similarity, namely: apple and orange, bicycle and car. In such cases, hint mechanisms were used to help them think of possible questions. Phase 1 was used to come up with effective hint mechanisms. The two types of hints (in that order, if required) that were used were:

- How are <object1> and <object2> different?
- Think about what <object1> has/does that <object2> does not or what <object2> has/does that <object1> does not?

It was important to keep the hints finite and deterministic as they would eventually be built into the agent. It turned out that hints were effective in what they were supposed to do. In about 90% of the cases of a child finding it hard to frame questions, a hint helped them. In cases where both the hints did not work, the trial was considered incomplete and the next trial was started.

Phase 1 helped us determine if building such a system is feasible, if children's questions are deterministic, if the repair required in dialogue is limited, if it is possible to effectively prod children of this age to solve problems without disengaging. The next section describes how the agent/system was built, given the feasibility study.

SYSTEM DESIGN

The system that was built, replicated the same task as in phase 1. An interactive agent in the form of a puppy dog character conducted the game sessions instead of a human. The character introduced the game, showed two objects, hid one and then played a 20-questions game till the child guessed the hidden object correctly. The character followed a script, the design of which is explained in the dialogue subsection.

System architecture

The system worked through modules shown in Figure 2. The speech recognition component of the system was wizard-of-Oz. Collecting audio data and corresponding transcriptions while we evaluate our system was the motivation for using wizard-of-Oz method [26]. So for everything that the child said, the wizard (a researcher) would transcribe the speech. Using the questions asked in phase 1, templates of possible questions were created. If the incoming utterance's transcription matched any of these templates, it was sent to a keyword search routine, else it was sent to an edge case handler that used redirections (explained in detail under "Dialogue"). This answer was either "yes, it does" or "no, it doesn't". If the keyword search routine was unsure of the structure, but sure of the semantics of the question, a yes/no response was given. If the question was an invalid (or incomprehensible) question, responses expressing soft disapproval were generated (explained earlier). Moreover, if the child found it hard to frame a question and there was silence for some time, the system would detect this and generate a hint. In cases where the wizard felt that the participant does not understand the activity, he would send a command directly to the agent logic and Spot would replay the explanation of the game.

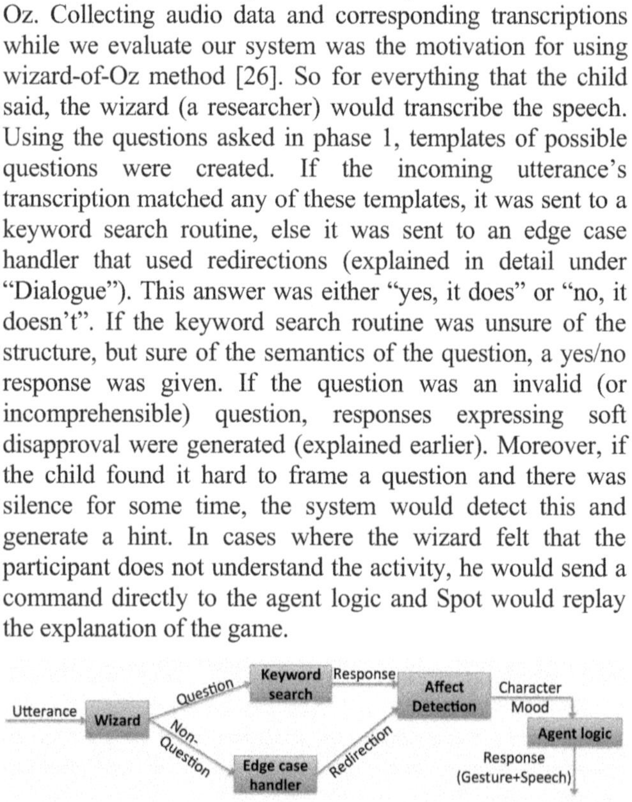

Figure 2: System architecture

Depending on the content of the response (from keyword search and edge case handler), appropriate affect features were generated and used to predict Spot's gestural response. The audio responses were pre-recorded audio. The voice used to record these responses was that of a female in her early 20s. The frequency range of her voice was deemed appropriate for Spot. Throughout the duration of the study no child commented on the voice texture, and all of them seemed comfortable.

Interface

In terms of the form that the agent could take, the need was for a character that is gender-neutral, engaging and likeable. A puppy character was employed to be the agent [21]. He was named "Spot", and will be referred to by that name henceforth.

Previous research also suggested that such agents should have lifelike characteristics [31]. To create engaging videos with minimal effort, we used Machinima from the SIMS Pets game. SIMS is a widely used "god" game that supports high-level control of characters, including non-human characters. Machinima is the process of using in-game recording facilities to record segments of game action under high-level control of the player [24]. A puppy character was created in the SIMS create-a-pet tool and machinima videos were recorded (with the inbuilt video capture in SIMS) with various different personality traits set. In the create-a-pet tool, depending on what personality is chosen the pet character responds through gestures. This was ideal for the study, as the character was supposed to respond to the child's questions, not just with speech but also through gestures.

Dialogue

Hart and Risely [18] argue that in particular three features add quality and engagement to such interactions. How we incorporated these features into the script that Spot followed while talking to children, is discussed in the following subsections.

Discourse Functions

These represent the kind of utterances used by parents. This refers to categorization of utterances in terms of the responses that they can prompt. Hart and Risely [18] argue that there are three levels of prompts that parents use as discourse functions. Therefore to make the child ask a question, we introduced three types of cues into Spot's script: a rule ("if you ask me a question, I will give you the answer"), a question ("can you ask me a question?"), and a demand ("go ahead, ask me a question").

Adjacency Conditions

These represent the relationship between utterances of the speaker and listener. This refers to categorization of sequence of utterances in an interaction. Hart and Risely [18] argue that this consists of initiations, response and floorholding. Spot's script contained initiations that can draw the child's attention if they deviate from the game. This involved saying things like, "Are you still there?", "Do you remember what the two objects were?". It should be noted that these questions are different from the ones mentioned under discourse, in that they are only posed if the child goes off-topic or gets distracted. Spot's script had a response to any question that was asked, even if it was off-topic. The instructions on how to play the game were split across multiple audio clips and played after pauses so that it feels like a continued conversation, and doesn't overwhelm the child.

Valence

Valence is the emotional tone given to interactions. It can be both, positive or negative. Hart and Risely argue that this comprises of prohibitions, approvals and repetitions. However, there was a possibility for Spot to be viewed as inappropriate if it explicitly disapproved any child behavior. Therefore, softer disapprovals were included into Spot's script. The script was designed to include things like, "That's not really the right question to ask. Do you want to ask something else?" or "Could you try that again?" Spot's script also contained affirmative feedback like, "That's right" and "That's great" to encourage further questioning. Spot used repetitions in the context of the question. Some examples that were included in the script:

Child: Does it <part/function/property>?

Spot: Yes it does/No it does not.

Child: Is it a/an <object>?

Spot: Yes it is an <object>/ No it is not an <object>.

In terms of the hint mechanism, Spot used the techniques tested in phase 1, if a child found it hard to frame a question. Although children did not deviate from the game frequently during phase 1, any dialogue system is incomplete without certain edge cases or redirections. Most chatbots use such redirections to direct users to topics within the chatbot's knowledge base. Redirections in Spot's script were encouraging and/or affirmative:

- "I like playing with you! Let's continue!"
- "This is my favorite game. Let's play my favorite game together!"

Gesture

Spot used a variety of gestures to convey meaning during a game session. These were mappings of the content of the response to specific gestures. Research suggests that gestures can be of four types [27]: iconic, deictic, metaphoric and beat. Iconic gestures represent object attributes, spatial relationships and actions. Such gestures were used to signal: affirmative or negative response to a question, right or wrong guesses and an invalid question. Spot nodded its head for an affirmative response and shook it for a negative response. For an invalid question Spot turned shy and stepped back. For a right guess Spot jumped and for a wrong guess shook his head and looked away. Deictic gestures involve connecting speech to location of objects, more specifically pointing. Spot used deixis to introduce objects during a trial, as shown in Figure 3 (A and B). Spot did not use any metaphoric and beat gestures as they might have been too complex to interpret, given the age of our participants. Moreover, beat gestures are just meant to keep the rhythm of the speech and convey no semantic meaning. In addition to using the aforementioned gestures, Spot also used speech bubbles to grab the child's attention whenever speaking.

Figure 3: A typical game session. Spot first identifies the two objects (A & B), then converts them into question marks (C). After that it hides one object in a box while the other one goes off the screen (D).

PHASE 2: 20 QUESTIONS (HUMAN + AGENT CONDITION)

Participant

Participants were the same as phase 1. Half the participants (6) were assigned to the human condition, and the other half were assigned to the agent condition.

Experiment

Phase 2 of the study followed a between subjects design. Participants from phase 1 were randomly assigned to the human and the agent condition. To make sure that two groups were not different to each other *a priori*, we conducted individual two-tailed t-tests on the data from phase 1. We tested the two groups for any significant difference in terms of the following parameters: total questions on property, total questions on part, total questions on function, total questions overall, total explanations required, total off-topic count, total hint, total questions successfully solved. None of the t-tests suggested significance, so there was no reason to believe that the two selected groups were different from each other in *a priori* question answering behavior (this was just a sanity check, as randomization should have already ensured this). Moreover, just like phase 1 in a particular session a child went through 7 trials including the demo trial. The object pairs used in the trials for phase 1 and phase 2 were completely different, and are summarized in Table 1.

The procedures in the human condition were the same as phase 1. The only change was that the human conducting the session tried to stick to the dialogue script designed for Spot, and deviated only if the child went off-topic or got confused. In simple words, the script was supposed to be overruled only if the conversation needed "repair", despite the strategies used in the script. The adherence to script was done so that the verbal exposure in the two cases (human and agent) is comparable. The deviations were allowed because parents in practice use a lot of strategies to engage children and technology cannot replicate all of those. Phase 2 was therefore designed to compare and contrast Spot's limited, deterministic but organized strategies against that of an actual person. It should be noted that even though the researchers conducting the study were not teachers or parents, they were significantly familiar to the participants because of exposure during circle time (explained above) and also during phase 1.

The procedures in the agent condition were very similar to the human condition, except that Spot was supposed to conduct the entire game session. As mentioned already Spot used a script to go through its dialogues. The part of setting up the game remained the same for all users. In each game session Spot introduced itself, explained the rules of the game step-by-step and then went through the trials with different object pairs. In any given trial, Spot would first show the two items, identify both of them, then convert them into question marks. After this, through some animation, one question mark would leave the screen and the other one will go into a box. All of this is depicted in Figure 3. Once the object was hidden, the child was expected to ask questions to figure out the hidden object. After this, the game took different conversational routes for different participants.

Environment and setup

The environment and setup for the human condition was the same, as phase 1 because the premises and the room used remained the same. However, for the agent condition we decided to project Spot on a wall using a projector. This was done because of multiple reasons. Firstly, having the character on a wall made sure that mona lisa effect exists and gets preserved in the room [5]. Secondly, research suggests children this age have higher depth of search for interactions that are less manual (touchscreens) [6]. Thirdly, projector offered the advantage of larger size and form-factor. The layout of the room can be seen in Figure 4.

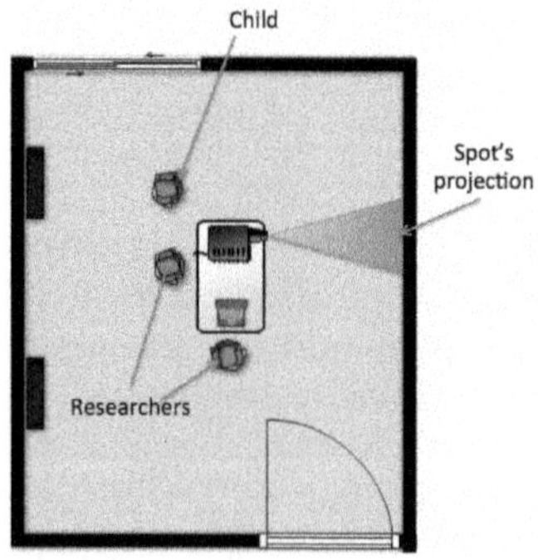

Figure 4: The layout of the research room, during the study session.

Data collection and analysis

In the same fashion as phase 1, all the video data from the study was transcribed. Again, six individual coders/raters were asked to classify the questions into one of the three categories: parts of objects, properties of objects and functions of objects. There was substantial agreement in the ratings (Fleiss'es (overall) kappa = 0.79, kappa error = 0.0117, kappa C.I. (95%) = 0.7840, z = 67.5126, p = 0.0001). An analysis of the ratings is contained in the next subsection.

Results

Question-answering experience

It was found that Spot was able to engage children in short conversational sequences, sometimes even better than the human condition. Across the 7 trials in the session, children in the human condition asked 55 questions and this number was 86 for the agent condition. A two-tailed t-test for the total number of questions asked, pointed towards statistical significance (p-value = 0.03, Cohen's d = 0.94). Analyzing the individual question categories, it was found that children asked more property (p-value = 0.046, Cohen's d = 0.83) and part questions (p-value = 0.01, Cohen's d = 1.49) in the agent condition. The numbers of questions on functions of objects were not significantly different. It should be noted that children asked more property questions for objects of increased similarity, and asked more part questions for objects that were easy to distinguish. This trend is predictable given prior research [8], and did not differ across conditions. However, children in the agent condition successfully solved more problems than the ones in the human condition (p-value = 0.03, Cohen's d = 1.3). We hypothesize that this is because of the increased number of questions in the agent condition, because children can effectively use questions as a means to solve such problems [8]. Children had limited tendency to guess without proper inference, which is consistent with phase 1. There were 28 such guesses in the human condition and 15 in the agent condition. The individual numbers of guesses in both conditions were not significantly different from each other (p-value = 0.25). It should be noted that the results from phase 1 were compared to the results from phase 2 for the human group. We did not find any significant difference in performance (across all recorded parameters) of the group assigned to the human condition, in phase 1 and phase 2.

The participants did not exhibit any significant learning effect, which is reasonable because the object pairs used in phase 2 were completely different from phase 1 and the activity at hand was not something that is unfamiliar to preschoolers [8]. Therefore, it is reasonable to assume that any change in the performance of the agent group across the two phases was caused by the introduction of the agent. Since the aim of this research was to design an agent that can produce question-answering experience that is comparable to interacting with a familiar human, these results are highly encouraging. All totals have been plotted in Figure 5.

Dialogue flow and quality

Handling redirections and offtopic conversations is an important characteristic of any question-answering system. Interactions with Spot, just like interactions in phase 1 did not deviate from the topic much. Children generally stayed focused and there was no significant difference in the number of offtopic dialogues in the human and agent condition (p = 0.813). Children only went offtopic 6 times in the human condition, and this number was 5 for the agent condition. In all the 5 cases of going offtopic, an edge case handler dialogue (explained above) by Spot was able to bring the child back to the original conversation.

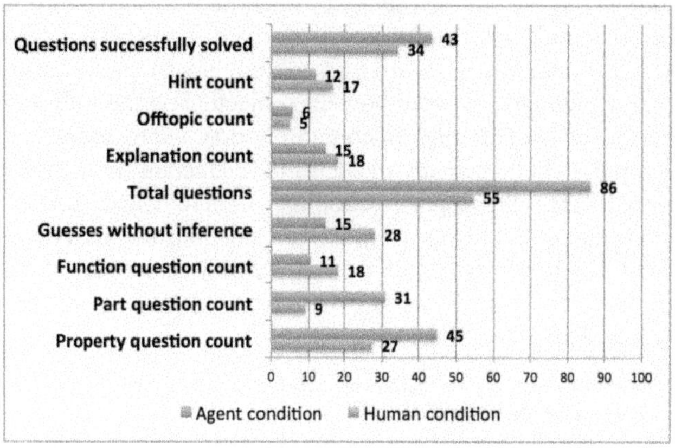

Figure 5: Graph with the total counts for all the measured parameters, for the two groups.

In terms of explanations, children in the human condition needed explanation 18 times and those in the agent condition needed it 15 times. Moreover, there was no significant difference in the number of times explanation was required by a child (p = 0.5). The total number of hints required by the group assigned to human condition was 17, and that required by the agent condition group was 12. However, there was no significant difference in the number of hints required individually (p=0.69). It is clear from these numbers that children follow a similar pattern as phase 1 in talking to Spot, and there was a limited need for explanation, hints and offtopic dialogue handling. Moreover, in all such edge cases Spot does as well as a familiar human, if not better.

Child's subjective experience

During the session, children appeared to enjoy the interaction with the agent. Some of them said things like "I want to ask more questions", "I really like when he jumps", "Spot is clever, but he lets me win." Three participants in agent condition wanted to go through more trials when the session ended. After the game session, children were interviewed for any immediate experience that they might want to share. All children who were a part of the agent condition, said they enjoyed the session. This observation was the same for human condition. We acknowledge that there might be participant response bias, but the ratings do point towards a positive user experience in the agent condition. It should also be noted that 8 out of the 10 participants in the agent condition said they want to play again. The rest said they want to play a different game with Spot. Some of these post-game session interview accounts also explain the quantitative results we have seen so far. Two out of the ten children in the agent condition reported that they wanted to know how much Spot knows and therefore asked a lot of questions, even when they were sure of what the hidden object was. Novelty factor could also have played a role in motivating children to ask more questions.

While playing the game, two children said things like "hey, when he says another one, I am doing it!" and "when he says play again, I play again!" Two children demanded playing more games with Spot, asking things like "can he play more games?" Three children said they liked Spot and the fact that he could talk. None of the participants paid attention to the fact that there was a wizard transcribing things that they said. Four children did wonder how the projection on the wall was being executed. During video transcription, we recorded and appropriately tagged any incidents of distraction. In both the human and the agent condition, children had limited tendency to look away or get distracted from the activity at hand. We hypothesize that the activity in itself was engaging to them, and they found it even more engaging when Spot helped them through it.

PHASE III: 20-QUESTIONS (FULLY AUTOMATED AGENT ON NEW KNOWLEDGE)

Given that phase 2 had helped understand the engagement that (wizard-of-Oz) Spot offers as compared to a natural interaction, the need was for another study to determine if the fully automated Spot would retain the same level of engagement over a new batch of object pairs (excluding the ones in Table 1).

Participant

Participants, procedures and environment setup were the same as phase 1 (and 2), except with a fully automated agent and new set of object pairs. It should be noted that all the 12 participants were recruited for this phase. The reason we did not do a human condition for this phase was to collect more data, and because we have already established the effectiveness of Spot's interaction against that with a real person. The contribution of phase 3 was to demonstrate that even a fully automated (non-wizard) system would still give similar performance. Moreover, we did not expect any learning effects, as the activity was a familiar one and something that preschoolers do on a daily basis [8]. Given that no learning effect was observed in phase 2 (stated above), there was no reason to believe in its existence for phase 3.

System

The system, as discussed so far was developed in a way that even if Spot doesn't understand the exact utterance of a participant, using edge case handling and hint mechanisms it would still be able to drive the conversation along the context, which in the case of 20-questions is constrained. For this phase, we substituted the wizard component in the system design with Google™ speech recognition. Given the simplicity of children's speech vocabulary, and the large spectrum of voice features our system was expected to work with, this was the most logical choice. Standard techniques like error lookup tables and Levenshtein distances for query matching were used to match incoming transcription to question templates, but discussion on those are outside the scope of this paper. However, such discussions have been reported by some related works [35].

Data collection and analysis

Just as in the case of the previous phases, all the video data from the study was transcribed. We observed substantial agreement in the ratings (Fleiss'es (overall) kappa = 0.85, kappa error = 0.012, kappa C.I. (95%) = 0.7650, z = 65.5126, p = 0.0001).

Results

Question-answering experience

It was observed that the automated Spot had very similar performance as the wizard-of-Oz Spot. If we cross-compared the human condition (phase 2), the agent condition (phase 2) and the automated agent condition (phase 3), against each other, the fully automated Spot's performance was not significantly different from the wizard-of-Oz agent. This seems logical, because Spot was already built to handle mismatches and errors, and Levenshtein distances in query matching, mostly handled any additional errors that speech recognition introduced. For example if the object in context was a cat, and the question asked was "does it meow?", the recognition routine would transcribe it as "does it mean now?". However, because of the use of edit distance, the keyword search routine would assume that the speaker intended to say, "meow". After transcription, it was also observed that 87% of the incoming queries were matched correctly with an intended response. In simple words, in 87% of the cases, the automated Spot was able to produce a response that the wizard would have generated. Moreover, in terms of the measured parameters, there was no significant statistical difference between the performance of the fully automated Spot and the wizard-of-Oz Spot from phase 2. Given that the object pairs were different, this may not be a fair comparison, but the contribution of phase 3 was to replicate performance similar to the agent condition in phase 2, for new object pairs, which clearly happened. To give a visual understanding of the results we have plotted the average values of the parameters for the two conditions from phase 2 and for the automated Spot from phase 3. We plot averages because there were 6 participants in each condition in phase 2 and all of them (12) were involved in the evaluation of the automated Spot in phase 3.

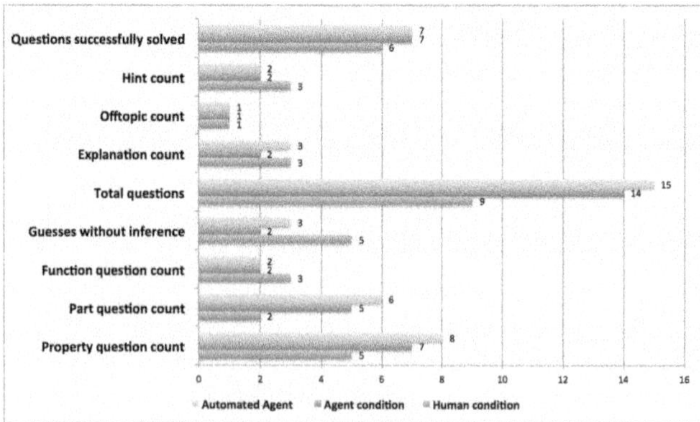

Figure 6: Graph with the averages for all the measured parameters, for the two groups from phase 2, and phase 3.

From Figure 6, it is easy to observe that the fully automated Spot replicates the performance of the wizard Spot from phase 2. And both these conditions are at least at par, if not better than the human condition.

DISCUSSION

Given the importance of question-answering in the early years of a child's life, our initial problem was to design a question-answering agent that could help preschool children with short question-answering sequences. Phase 1 of our study was dedicated to studying the feasibility of such a system, given how open-ended dialogues with preschoolers can be. Using 20-questions as an activity that can constrain question-asking behavior, we reached the following conclusions. Firstly, children's questions are predictable and deterministic, when grounded in an activity like 20 questions. Secondly, the repair required in such a dialogue is limited and feasible. Thirdly, it is possible to effectively prod preschoolers to solve problems without disengaging. In phase 2 and 3 of the study we designed and implemented a question-answering agent using commonly used parenting styles (in dialogues) and machinima videos. We found that children asked more questions and solved more problems in the 20-questions game with the agent, than if they play with a familiar human. Prior education research [8] suggests that the two observations might not be independent, as children use questions as tools to solve problems. Moreover, we found that the tendency to deviate from the task at hand was no more in the agent condition, than the human condition. And even in case of deviations, some standard edge case handlers built into the agent's script were able to take care of the redirection to original dialogue. We also found that children did not need significantly more hints or explanations in the agent condition, than they did in the human condition.

Even though our results were positive and demonstrated strong effects, there were a few limitations to our study. All the findings mentioned in the paper are restricted to a game of 20-questions and not to open ended question-answering. Open-ended conversational sequences are much harder to handle given current technological capability. Moreover, our participants were part of a research preschool and therefore had experience being a part of research studies. However, some of these limitations are essentially avenues for future investigation in this domain.

FUTURE WORK

We hope that contributions made in this paper can help shape the next steps in building question-answering systems (or more generally dialogue systems) for younger children. We think that another solution of the initial envisaged problem could be a "character" toy (instead of a projection) with speech recognition and synthesis capabilities. This could take the form of a plush toy or a favorite TV character. This could be a common internal platform (the electronics, microphone, speaker and batteries) that can be used with various external skins. Future work could compare the individual and relative effectiveness of these solutions against each other, in similar activities. We chose the particular game for this study to be "ASR-friendly". i.e. the dialog is highly contextualized around the objects that the child has seen. The question vocabulary is quite limited, and questions follow a limited number of templates. This could be extended to other forms of question-answering, in the future.

CONCLUSION

Despite the hype around how conversational systems (SIRI [3] and S-voice [32]) can make information more accessible, more rigorous research is clearly called for. In this paper, we have identified need and opportunities for question-answering based conversational games in the everyday lives of preschool children. Based on these insights, we have investigated how preschoolers ask questions in a constrained environment, and how we can build technology that can handle such questions and keep children engaged. We have demonstrated that such a system, if carefully designed, can at times perform better than a familiar human in the short-term. We hope that experiences and the challenges we have encountered will be beneficial to our colleagues who seek to conduct more rigorous, longer-term evaluations of such conversational applications under naturalistic conditions in similar environments.

ACKNOWLEDGEMENTS

We would like to thank the Early Child Education Program, the Child Study Centre (Berkeley) in particular for providing the necessary setting to conduct such a research experiment. This work would not have been possible without help from volunteers. We would like to thank Timothy Brown, Samantha Dove and Peiyi Ko, for their help in conducting pieces of the study.

REFERENCES

1. Abu Shawar, B. and E. Atwell, Fostering language learner autonomy via adaptive conversation tutors, in Corpus Linguistics. 2007: Birming- ham, UK.
2. Aleven, V., K. Koedinger, and K. Cross, Tutoring Answer Explanation Fosters Learning with Understanding, in Artificial Intelligence in Education. 1999, IOS Press: Amsterdam. p. 199-206.
3. Apple Siri: http://www.apple.com/ios/siri/. (Last accessed: Sept 19, 2012)
4. Baylor, A.L. and Y. Kim. Simulating Instructional Roles through Pedagogical Agents. International Journal of Artificial Intelligence in Edu- cation, 2005. 15(2): p. 95-115.
5. Boyarskaya E, Hecht H, "The Mona Lisa effect: Is it confined to the horizontal plane?" Perception 38 ECVP, 2009
6. Byrd D., van der Veen T., McNamara J. & Berg W. Preschoolers Don't Practice What They Preach: Preschoolers' Planning Performances With Manual and Spoken Response Requirements, Journal of Cognition and Development, 5:4, 427-449, 2004
7. Callanan M. and Oakes L. Preschoolers' questions and parents' explanations: Causal thinking in everyday activity. Cognitive Development, 7:213-233, 1992.
8. Chouinard, M. M. Childrens questions: A mechanism for cognitive development. Monographs of the Society for Research in Child Development, 72 (1, Serial No. 286), 2007.
9. Clarebout, G., Elen, J., Johnson, W.L., and Shaw, E. Animated pedagogical agents. An opportunity to be grasped? Journal of Educational Multimedia and Hypermedia, 11, 267286, 2002.

10. De Pietro, O. and G. Frontera, TutorBot: an application AIML based for Web-Learning. Advanced Technology for Learning, 2005. 2(1): p. 29-34.
11. Dillenbourg, P. and J. Self, People Power: A Human-Computer Collaborative Learning System in Intelligent Tutoring Systems. 1992, Springer-Verlag: Berlin-Heidelberg. p.651-660.
12. Feng, D., E. Shaw, J. Kim, and E. Hovy, An Intelligent Discussion-Bot for Answering Student Queries in Threaded Discussions, in 2006 International Conference on Intelligent User Interfaces. 2006, ACM Press: Sydney, Australia. p. 171-177.
13. Frazier B., Gelman S., and Wellman H.. Preschoolers' search for explanatory information within adult-child conversation. Child Development, 80:1592-1611, 2009.
14. Fryer, L. and Carpenter R., Bots as Language Learning Tools. Language Learning and Technology., 2006. 10(3): p. 8-14.
15. Goffin V., Allauzen C., Bocchieri E., Hakkani-Tr D., Ljolje A., Parthasarathy S., Rahim M., Riccardi G., and Saraclar M., "The AT&T WATSON speech recognizer," in Proceedings of IEEE ICASSP-2005, Philadelphia, PA, USA, 2005.
16. Graesser, A.C., N.K. Person, and D. Harter, Teaching Tactics and Dialog in AutoTutor. International Journal of Artificial Intelligence in Education, 2001. 12: p. 23-39.
17. Grigoriadou, M., Tsaganou G., and Cavoura T., Dialogue-Based Reflective System for Historical Text Comprehension, in Workshop on Learner Modelling for Reflection at Artificial Intelligence in Education. 2003.
18. Hart, B. and Risley, T. Meaningful Differences in the Everyday Experience of Young American Children, Paul H. Brookes, 1995.
19. Heffernan, N.T., Web-Based Evaluations Showing both Cognitive and Motivational Benefits of the Ms. Lindquist Tutor, in Artificial Intelli- gence in Education. 2003, IOS Press: Amsterdam. p. 115-122.
20. Kerly, A., Ellis, R. and Bull, S. CALMsystem: A Conversational Agent for Learner Modelling. Knowledge Based Systems, 2008. 21(3): p. 238-246.
21. Koda T. and Maes. P. Agents with faces: The effect of personification. In the 5th IEEE international workshop on Robot and Human Communication, 1996, pp. 189-194.
22. Kramer, N.C: Psychological Research on Embodied Conversational Agents: The Case of Pedagogical Agents. Journal of Media Psychology 2010. Vol 22(2): p. 47-51
23. Lester, J.C., B.A. Stone, and G.D. Stelling, Lifelike Pedagogical Agents for Mixed- Initiative Problem Solving in Constructivist Learning Environments. User Modeling and User-Adapted Interaction, 1999. 9: p. 1-44.
24. Lowood, H. High-performance play: The making of machinima. In A. Clarke & G. Mitchell (Eds.), Videogames and art: Intersections and interactions. London: Intellect.
25. Luckin R., Connolly D., Plowman L., and Airey S. With a little help from my friends: children's interactions with interactive toy technology. Journal of Computer Assisted Learning, Special issue on Children and Technology:165-176, 2003.
26. Makela K., Salonen E. and Raisamo R. Conducting a wizard of oz experiment on a ubiquitous computing system doorman. In Proceedings of the International Workshop on Information Presentation and Natural Multimodal Dialogue, pages 115–119, 2001.
27. McNeil D.l, Hand and Mind: The University of Chicago Press, Chicago IL, 1992.
28. NELP: National Early Literacy Panel (2008) Developing Early Literacy, National Institute for Literacy (NIFL), available from site www.nifl.gov
29. NFCL: National Family Literacy Organization, main site www.famlit.org
30. NIH: Clear Communication: An NIH Health Literacy Initiative http://www.nih.gov/clearcommunication/healthliteracy.htm
31. Pérez-Marín, D., Pascual-Nieto, I.: Conversational Agents and Natural Language Interaction. Techniques and Effective Practices, IGI Global, 2011
32. S-voice: http://www.samsung.com/global/galaxys3/ (Last accessed: Sept 19, 2012)
33. Shaw, E., W.L. Johnson, and R. Ganeshan, Pedagogical Agents on the Web, in International Conference on Autonomous Agents. 1999, ACM Press: Seattle, WA, USA. p. 283-290.
34. Taylor, K. and Moore, S., Adding Question Answering to an E-Tutor for Programming Languages, in AI-2006, 26th SGAI International Conference on Innovative Techniques and Applications of Artificial Intelligence. 2006, Springer: Cambridge, UK. p. 193-206.
35. Tewari, A., Brown, T., & Canny, J. (2013, January). A Question-answering Agent Using Speech Driven Non-linear Machinima. In *Intelligent Virtual Agents*(pp. 129-138). Springer Berlin Heidelberg.
36. Watson, AT&T: http://www.research.att.com/projects/WATSON. (Last accessed: Sept 19,2012)
37. Wood, D. Scaffolding, contingent tutoring and computer-supported learning. International Journal of Artificial Intelligence in Education, 12:280-292, 2001.
38. Yarosh S., Cuzzort S., Muller H., and Abowd G. 2009. Developing a media space for remote synchronous parent-child interaction. In Proceedings of the 8th International Conference on Interaction Design and Children (IDC '09). ACM, New York, NY, USA, 97-105
39. Yarosh, S, Inkpen, K.M., Brush, A.J. "Video playdate: toward free play across distance." Proc. CHI 2010, 1251-1260.

Rafigh: A Living Media Interface for Speech Intervention

Foad Hamidi
Department of Computer Science and Engineering
Lassonde School of Engineering, York University,
Toronto, Canada M3J 1P3
fhamidi@cse.yorku.ca

Melanie Baljko
Department of Computer Science and Engineering
Lassonde School of Engineering, York University,
Toronto, Canada M3J 1P3
mb@cse.yorku.ca

ABSTRACT
Digital media can engage children in therapeutic and learning activities. Incorporating living media in these designs can create feelings of empathy and caring in users. We present, *Rafigh,* a living media interface designed to motivate children with speech disorders to use their speech to care for a living mushroom colony. The mushrooms' growth is used to communicate how much speech is used during interaction. The main focus of the interface is to motivate children to use their speech as part of interaction.

Author Keywords
Living Media Interfaces; Speech Intervention; Embedded Computing.

ACM Classification Keywords
H.5.2. User Interfaces

INTRODUCTION
Embedded electronics allow for new ways to interact with living beings. A new wave of hybrid biological interfaces sometimes referred to as "moistmedia" [2], explore novel ways to engage users through combining digital and biological elements in design. Additionally, therapeutic digital activities have the potential to motivate users, especially children, to perform repetitive and otherwise boring tasks for long periods of time. We bring together these two ideas in an empathetic living media interface that focuses on caring as interaction goal in an interface to be used in the context of speech intervention and elicitation.

In the face of increasing urbanization and lack of contact with nature, it is important to design systems that facilitate a re-connection or at least dialogue around our interaction with living beings. Many children are naturally fascinated by animals and plants. By developing technology that encourages and builds on this fascination we can support children's relationship with nature and the environment around them. Additionally, this area provides opportunities to build-in caring and empathy into interaction; elements whose absence have been a cause of concern for the critics of computer games [1].

CHI 2014, April 26 – May 01, 2014, Toronto, Canada.
Copyright 2014 ACM 978-1-4503-2473-1/14/04...$15.00.
http://dx.doi.org/10.1145/2556288.2557402

The need for regularity in the care of living beings corresponds well with therapeutic and intervention applications for repetitive and regular use [17]. In this work, we present a design that requires children to take responsibility for taking care of living beings with regularity and by performing tasks that would benefit them therapeutically and aid with intervention.

Rafigh is an embedded tangible interface that uses a living mushroom colony as part of its display, where the growth rate of the mushrooms corresponds with the amount of speech practiced through the use of the interface. It is designed to motivate small children (ages 4-7) with speech disorders to use their speech to perform a series of digital activities that results in the irrigation of the mushrooms. We have chosen to use mushrooms as the living interface because of their relatively rapid growth rate that is suitable for engaging children (typically 6-10 days). Children who undergo speech intervention typically work with trained *Speech-Language Pathologists* (SLPs) who assign speech exercises to them and provide corrective feedback [9]. To inform our design we interviewed five SLPs who work with children and also performed a review of extant systems [9]. The results were incorporated into our design. We have used a holistic design method that emphasizes not only the therapeutic use of speech but also the promotion of knowledge about the environment and encouragement of family and community involvement.

In the next section, we review similar research projects that examine human-nature interaction through computational material. We will describe *Rafigh* next, including a discussion of its design rationale, and results of a series of SLP interviews that informed it.

BACKGROUND
Our fascination with nature is as old as humanity. Recently, digital designs have emerged that explore intimate digital-biological interaction scenarios. While there are relatively few research projects in this area, they cover a wide spectrum of interactions with nature. At the one end of the spectrum are biohacking projects that directly manipulate plant and animal biology, turning them into cyborgs and allowing control or monitoring of their activities (e.g.,

Cyborg Beetle [18]). On the other end of the research spectrum are projects that aim to foster nurturing and less hierarchical relationships with living beings through technology. For example, in the Botanicalls project, embedded sensors communicated information about a plant's well-being (e.g., moisture level, soil quality) via phone calls and Twitter messages, to plant owners [10].

Previous studies have shown that interacting with living pets can have positive therapeutic and educational benefits. Caring for pets has been shown to increase children's self-esteem [3]. Many parents admit that interacting with pets gives children valuable lessons about life events [15]. Other positive outcomes have included reduced levels of loneliness [5], stress and anxiety [19].

The *Time to Eat* project has examined the effectiveness of using virtual pets to promote positive behavior change, specifically health eating, in children [17]. During the period of use, virtual pets request to be fed regularly and encourage the children to eat breakfast with them. In a user study with 53 middle school children, it was observed that children who used the game ate breakfast more frequently. Children also expressed interest in and attachment to their pets in interviews. While having virtual pets can be beneficial in some contexts, we believe there is a qualitative difference between caring for a living being and a virtual one. A review of hybrid biological-digital games has identified several potential benefits, such as enabling care, education and interspecies awareness [14]. While the review focuses on games that interact with animals, the mentioned implications are relevant to this project.

A small number of projects have used living media to communicate information. *PlantDisplay* uses plant growth to display information about the owner's amount of daily communication with friends, collected through monitoring of phone call logs [13]. Plant growth is correlated with the amount of communication: the more the owner communicates the more the plant grows.

Babbage Cabbage uses live red cabbage as empathetic biological feedback display [8]. Each head of cabbage is viewed as a single organic pixel that can change color based on the pH level of an administered solution. Social and ecological information are communicated to a viewer of the system through a range of colors that the cabbage head displays. The same research group has developed an ambient empathic interface that uses DNA-transformed E. coli to communicate information through glowing microorganisms [6].

Spore consists of a self-sustaining rubber tree plant watered depending on the stock exchange value of a corporation [7]. Information about the rising or falling price of the company's stock controlled the amount of water that was given to the plant, thus affecting the health of the plant based on the activity of the company's finances. The project ended when the plant died of overwatering.

Meet Eater consists of a garden of plants watered based on activity on its Facebook page [12]. Activity on the plants Facebook page (i.e., receiving "likes") triggered a watering mechanism. The plant garden is used as an ambient display that can communicate about the plant's online social life via its health and growth. Similar to Spore, the plant got overwatered due to increased activity on its Facebook page.

Our system is different from other previous living media interfaces in several important ways: a) the growth and wellbeing of the mushrooms are mapped to the actions of the child (as opposed to an abstract form of data as in the cases of Spore, Babbage Cabbage and Meet Eater), b) the child is responsible for the well-being of the mushrooms and in this way is empowered and, c) the growth cycle of the mushrooms is short and eventually they are to be harvested (and potentially eaten) after a week of care, thus having a concrete and tangible outcome for the child in the short term that is different from caring for a plant over a long period of time.

RAFIGH: A LIVING MEDIA INTERFACE FOR SPEECH INTERVENTION

We present *Rafigh* (which translates to "companion" in Farsi), an empathetic living media interface for speech elicitation and intervention for children with speech disorders. Figure 1 shows *Rafigh*. The interface consists of a box designed to house a mushroom colony (with its growing side exposed), an irrigation system controlled by a wireless microcontroller and housing for an iPad.

Figure 1. *Rafigh* interface (left): the iPad is mounted on the left and the mushroom colony peers out of an opening on the right. The irrigation system (right) is a water pump activated by a microcontroller.

The child can interact with the digital activity on the iPad at any time but typically we expect them to use it at least once a day. The SLP can specify the number of repetitions and words needed for each child, determining the length of the interaction. The SLP can also input new images and audio for a word or phrase. Other parameters such as how often the activity should be done each day and how many repetitions requested for a word can also be specified. After a period of use, the child's recorded activities can be reviewed (via segmented and categorized video logs).

The software interface consists of a series of audio and image prompts that require the user to repeat names of familiar animals, fruits and vegetables. The current setup uses a set of words that contain common English phonetic sounds, but the prompts and images are customizable and can be changed by the SLP as needed for each client. Once the user finishes a set of exercises (that currently consists of 10 words but can also be customized), he or she is informed that the mushrooms will be "fed" (i.e., watered). The irrigation mechanism (shown in Figure 1) consists of an Arduino microcontroller and a small water pump originally designed for use in fish tanks. The mushrooms will be irrigated for durations calculated based on the amount of the child's input speech. Once irrigation starts, the mushrooms grow considerably every day (Figure 2).

Figure 2. *Rafigh* grows every day; after the second or third day, mushroom growth is clearly visible.

We have set three levels for the amount of water to be administered to the mushrooms based on how regularly and thoroughly the child repeats the set of exercise words and phrases: High, Medium and Low. High is activated if all words are repeated, Medium, if half the words are repeated and, Low, if less than half are repeated. Feedback is provided to the child after each repeated word.

The thresholds are set such that the mushroom colony will always live and grow no matter how little speech is used. While this might seem unintuitive as it provides positive feedback to the child even if they don't practice their speech, we made this decision based on the ethical principle of wanting to avoid the death of the mushrooms at any cost due to over- or under-watering (which can easily happen as is apparent from the case of earlier projects reviewed earlier). Thus, we provide the child with positive feedback through the growth and size of the mushrooms not its life and death.

We use a mushroom colony developed by the *Back to the Roots Company* and designed for educational purposes [2]. The mushrooms are edible and can be consumed by the child's family and friends after growth. Therefore, another aspect of the design is that it empowers the child through food production. The idea of incorporating a living being as part of the interface was inspired by our observation of several children who are family and friends and through informal conversations with theirs parents who told us that the children are generally interested in living beings and nature. While there is merit in including rewards such as badges and scores in games, we wanted to experiment with caring as a mode of interaction and the health of the living component and its growth as a form of alternative (possibly more meaningful) reward.

Rafigh's design is informed by interviews with five SLPs who work with children [9]. All of the SLPs agreed that developing a digital media toy for speech elicitation would be useful. Three SLPs regularly use props such as dolls and physical toys, as well as, images and flash cards to engage children. They emphasized that for young children (ages 4 to 7) having toys that can be grasped, touched and are durable is recommended. Tangible language intervention games have proven promising for children [11].

A key design idea was to focus on engagement rather than the generation and presentation of automatic feedback. All SLPs indicated that having no or little feedback that is consistent and accurate is preferable to having inconsistent or incorrect feedback, especially in the absence of the SLP who can mediate between the technology and the child. However, they recommended having a measure of progress so that not all speech is rewarded equally. This confirmed the results of a review of extant computational intervention systems that showed that the use of automatic speech recognition to provide corrective feedback to children is technically challenging and might backfire by providing incorrect and inconsistent feedback due to a lack of analysis capabilities of non-standard speech in current systems [14]. On the other hand, projects that focus on motivating and engaging speech rather than analyzing it automatically, have shown promising results [16]. Thus, we decided to use the interface to motivate and engage children to use their speech and record it for future analysis by a qualified SLP.

The recording of speech samples was recommended for other reasons as well: One SLP noted that capturing the child's natural speech (i.e., speech spoken in the absence of the SLP) would be helpful in assessing intervention needs. Our system is designed such that, once set, it can be used in the absence of the SLP. Another SLP records samples of her clients' speech during some of her sessions. She uses these samples for future comparison of intervention outcomes and analysis of speech in the absence of the client. In addition to recording speech, all the SLPs suggested that automatic tracking and record keeping of exercises are useful functions that a computational toy could provide, and that we have built into the design.

Another important recommendation by the SLPs was to make the application customizable as each client is unique. Given the multicultural context in which they work (Toronto, Canada), three of the interviewed SLPs recommended support for multilingual contexts. In addition to the customizations mentioned already, support for multiple languages will be incorporated into the future versions of the software.

The use of an iPad as part of the interface was initially motivated by the observation that two of the SLPs already use iPads to play games that engage speech. They believe the use of tablets will become more prevalent among SLPs and it is important to incorporate these tools into future designs. Surprisingly, they preferred activities that allowed for the engagement of speech through play but were not specifically developed for speech intervention and have simple interfaces (e.g., My PlayHome). One SLP commented that she prefers to use non-computational material during intervention because too much technology can be distracting for the children. We used a simple digital activity on the iPad and decoupled it as much as possible from the living media using modular design, so that, in the future SLPs could use a variety of games and activities of their choice to trigger the irrigation mechanism.

Another factor that led to the inclusion of the iPad was an unsuccessful experience with an earlier prototype that relied on LED lights and a bubble blower that were activated by input speech to engage the user. When one of the SLPs invited us to show it to one of her clients, a 4-year old boy with speech delays, the prototype failed to engage the child. We realized that we needed engaging video and audio components that a tablet such as the iPad can provide.

CONCLUSION AND FUTURE WORK

We have presented *Rafigh*, a living media interface for children with speech disorders that encourages them to use their speech to care for a living mushroom colony.

In future, we plan to conduct user studies with the interface and examine its usefulness and impact, not only in terms of speech intervention, but also in how it affects user satisfaction and experience. Additionally, we plan to explore its use for other applications such as second language learning and adult population speech intervention and speech banking.

REFERENCES

1. Anderson, C. A., Shibuya, A., Ihori, N., Swing, E. L., Bushman, B. J., Sakamoto, A., and Saleem, M. (2010). Violent video game effects on aggression, empathy, and prosocial behavior in eastern and western countries: a meta-analytic review. *Psychological Bulletin 136*, 2, 151.
2. Ascott, R. (2007). *Telematic Embrace: Visionary Theories of Art, Technology, and Consciousness by Roy Ascott.* University of California Press, Berkeley, CA.
3. Back to the Roots. http://www.backtotheroots.com
4. Bloch, L. R., and Lemish, D. (1999) Disposable Love The Rise and fall of a virtual pet. *New Media & Society 1*, 3, 283-303.
5. Calvert, M. M. (1989). Human-pet interaction and loneliness: a test of concepts from Roy's adaptation model. *Nurs Sci Q 2,* 4, 194–202.
6. Cheok, A. D., Kok, R. T., Tan, C., Newton Fernando, O. N., Merritt, T., and Sen, J. Y. P. (2008). Empathetic living media. In *Proc. DIS 2008,* ACM Press, 465-473.
7. Easterly, D. Bio-Fi: inverse biotelemetry projects. (2004). In *Proc. MM 2004,* ACM Press, 182-183.
8. Fernando, O. N., Cheok, A. D., Merritt, T., Peiris, R. L., Fernando, C. L., Ranasinghe, N., and Karunanayaka, K. (2009). Babbage cabbage: Biological empathetic media. *VRIC Laval Virtual Proceedings*, 363-366.
9. Hamidi, F., Baljko, M. (2013). Automatic Speech Recognition: A Shifted Role in Early Speech Intervention. In *Proc. SPLAT'13,* 55-61.
10. Hartman, K. (2006). Botanicalls: The plants have your number. http://www. botanicalls. com/.
11. Hengeveld, B., Hummels, C., van Balkom, H., Voort, R., and de Moor, J. (2013). Wrapping up LinguaBytes, for now. In *Proc. TEI 2013.* ACM Press, 237-244.
12. Isai, B., and Viller, S. (2010). Meet Eater: affectionate computing, social networks and human-plant interaction. In *Proc. OzCHI 2010,* ACM Press, 414-415.
13. Kuribayashi, S., and Wakita, A. (2006). PlantDisplay: turning houseplants into ambient display. In *Proc. SIGCHI 2006,* ACM Press, 40.
14. Lamers, M. H., and van Eck, W. (2012). Why simulate? hybrid biological-digital games. In *Proc. Applications of Evolutionary Computation 2012,* Springer Berlin Heidelberg, 214-223.
15. Levinson, B. The child and his pet: A world of non-verbal communication. (2001). *Ethnology and non-verbal communication in mental health 12,* 4, 63-83.
16. Mitra, S., Tooley, J., Inamdar, P. and Dixon, P. (2003). Improving English pronunciation - an automated instructional approach. *Information Technologies and International Development 1,* 1, 75-84.
17. Pollak, J., Gay, G., Byrne, S., Wagner, E., Retelny, D., and Humphreys, L. (2010). It's time to eat! Using mobile games to promote healthy eating. *Pervasive Computing 9*, 3, 21-27.
18. Sato, H., Berry, C. W., Casey, B. E., Lavella, G., Yao, Y., VandenBrooks, J. M., and Maharbiz, M. M. (2008). A cyborg beetle: insect flight control through an implantable, tetherless microsystem. In *Proc. MEMS 2008*, 164-167.
19. Wilson, C. C. (1991). The pet as an anxiolytic intervention. *J Nerv Ment Dis 179*, 8, 482–489.

A Comparative Study about Children's and Adults' Perception of Targeted Web Search Engines

Tatiana Gossen
Otto von Guericke University
Magdeburg, Germany
tatiana.gossen@ovgu.de

Juliane Höbel
Otto von Guericke University
Magdeburg, Germany
juliane.hoebel@st.ovgu.de

Andreas Nürnberger
Otto von Guericke University
Magdeburg, Germany
andreas.nuernberger@ovgu.de

ABSTRACT
In this paper we describe an eye-tracking study where we compare children's and adults' search behavior and perception of search interface elements on search engine results pages (SERPs) during an informational and a navigational search with Google and a search engine for children. Our first results indicate that children employ an exhaustive scanning strategy combined with cued visual jumps. Then they navigate to the next result page and only then modify their query. Adults only scan the first three results, following the F-shaped strategy, and immediately reformulate the query. Children pay less attention to textual summaries and more to thumbnails than adults do. Children take notice of a navigational menu with categories while adults do not.

Author Keywords
Search engine; User study; Eye-tracker; Children.

ACM Classification Keywords
H.3.3. **[Information Search and Retrieval]**: *Search process*; H.5.2. **[User Interfaces]**: *Evaluation/methodology*

INTRODUCTION
Many children have access to the Internet and explore the Web from a young age. The German 2010 KIM study [9] reports that about 60% of the children of ages six to thirteen use the Internet and 70% of them use search engines. Children exploit the Internet for entertainment, e.g. to play online games, but also to research for their school activities [6]. More than half of the children search the Internet predominantly alone [9]. Therefore, there are special search engines that aim to support children, e.g. *quinturakids.com*. Unfortunately, these search engine do not address children's cognitive, fine motor and other abilities and they have some usability issues [5]. To increase the usability of search engines for children, understanding their search behavior and interface perception is essential and can be achieved with help of user studies.

Previous research shows differences between kids and adults in their search behavior. However, these findings were mainly based on observational studies, e.g. [1, 8], or log file analysis, e.g. [6]. Furthermore, a recent study [7] found that kids' performance on children's interfaces is not better than on Google. However, the mentioned studies do not provide details about differences in children's and adults' perception of the search engines' interface elements during information seeking. In case there is no difference in perception, one could argue that standard search engines like Google have equally appropriate user interfaces for both user groups and no improvement is required. To complement existing findings, eye-tracking devices can be used. Eye-tracking provides information about users' eye positions and movements, i.e. information about what web interface elements caught users' attention, for how long and in which order.

There exist eye-tracking studies either about adults' or children web search behavior. For example, adults' reading behavior was studied across many different web sites and search tasks [10]. It was found that they follow a reading pattern in the shape of an "F". Dinet et al. [3] studied young users in the age from 10 to 17 and observed their search behavior on Google SERPs. They found that the visual exploration of young children is influenced by highlighted terms. Younger children tend to use a "cued visual jump"-strategy, i.e. after reading a highlighted keyword they jump to reading the next one. Whereas older children often exhaustively read search result's title, snippet and URL. To our knowledge, there exist no comparative study between children and adults perception of targeted web search engines. Therefore, we study the information seeking behavior not only on results pages of a standard search engine, but also on SERPs of a web search engine for children. Our main research question is: Do children and adults have different perception of web search interfaces? The answer to this question provides information whether there is potential in improving search engines' user interfaces for children and how to do this.

In this paper we describe the design and first results of an eye-tracking user study with children of primary school age and adults to study their seeking behavior and search engine perception during informational and navigational search (in terms of Broder's taxonomy [2]). The purpose of *informational search* is to find information about a topic. Children tend to employ informational search [6]. Meanwhile, most frequent queries of adults are *navigational* with the immediate intent to reach a particular website [6]. Therefore, we study both search variants. We focus on children in third and fourth school grade. At this time children already have enough reading and writing skills to perform a web search,

CHI'14, April 26–May 01, 2014, Toronto, ON, Canada

ACM 978-1-4503-2473-1/14/04...$15.00.
http://dx.doi.org/10.1145/2556288.2557031

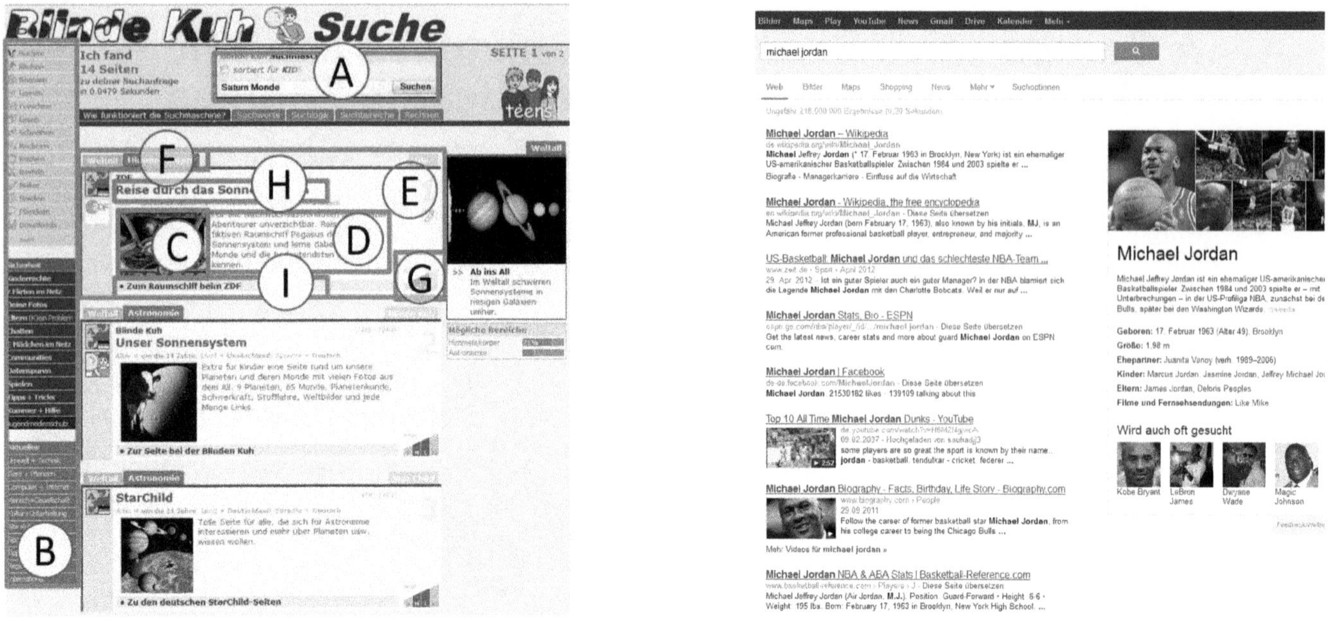

(a) Blinde-Kuh.de (b) Google.de

Figure 1. Screenshots of the studied search engine taken on 2012-12-18. Letters indicate different user interface elements of Blinde-Kuh.de.

however they are only superficially familiar with web search engines [9]. Therefore, they are an appropriate user group to study how intuitive search engines are. Druin et al. [4] also call these children "developing searchers" who have challenges with spelling, typing, query formulation and results interpretation.

STUDY DESIGN

In our study we used a German search engine for children *Blinde-Kuh.de* (Fig. 1a) and *Google* (Fig. 1b). Blinde-Kuh.de (BK) offers a keyword search (A) along with navigation in different categories provided on the left side (B). These categories lead to informational pages about the corresponding topic. BK returns at most ten results per page as a vertical list. Search results are separated through boxes in contrast to Google where no separation is done. Each BK surrogate contains a picture (C), textual summary (D), rank (E), information about the result's category (F), the target age group in categories "S", "M", "L", "XL" for children from six to thirteen (G) and does not use any keyword highlighting. To see the BK search result's page, one can click on the title (H), picture or a link below (I).

Within Participants Design was used in our study. In particular, we used a two-stage experimental design with two factors, type of web search engine (standard web search engine and children's web search engine) and search task type (informational and navigational). We also applied latin square design where each participant interacted with both search engines but in a different order to avoid different biases due to usage order, tiredness etc. We used two informational (Info) and two navigational (Nav) search tasks. Each participant was given one navigational and one informational task. However, due to differences in the provided results between the two search engines and to construct appropriate search scenarios, different search tasks with similar complexity were used for different search engines (see Table 1).

Procedure: We tested one participant at a time. Using a structured pre-interview, we gathered user's demographic data and Internet experience. Users were told that first they would receive search results for a query provided by the supervisor[1]. Thus, participants began on the same SERP, but were allowed to proceed in any way they chose. We used Tobii Eyetracker T60 that is integrated in a 17" monitor to gather the data. Each subject received a search task to solve within 10 minutes for each search engine. After each search task, we also asked the participants about their own assessment of the search task difficulty. At the end, a structured post-interview about users's preferences in search engines was performed.

The search tasks and corresponding initial queries used in the study are presented in Table 1. The scope of a task is designed so that it can be solved in a reasonable amount of time, but the solution is not trivial. Initial queries were selected such that they had at least two SERPs, and that the correct answer could be found in one of the first 20 results. For navigational tasks there was only one correct result web page. The initial SERPs contained significant SUI elements. We ensured the search consistency in order for the search conditions to be the same among all participants. In specific, the same SERPs were presented to the users using initial queries. As SUIs could be altered by the search engine owners, we fixed the first two SERPs for the pre-specified queries we used in our study[2]. After each session, the browser history

[1]Initial SERPs were necessary for the eye-tracking experiment to be able to compare users' gaze data and aggregate the results.

[2]This procedure was done for Google. The search engine for children was static.

was automatically deleted to avoid highlighting of previously clicked search results. All browser cookies were automatically deleted to disable the personalization of search results.

Participants: The user study was conducted in February 2013. We collaborated with a primary school in Biederitz (Germany) and used a separate school room there. 14 children participated in the study. Unfortunately, not all the eye-tracking data were valid as children are very agile and some of them moved too close to the monitor during the session so that the eye-tracker could no longer capture their eye movements. Our further analysis is based on 11 young users. They are between eight and eleven years old (9.27 on average, $\sigma = 0.79$), 64% were boys. 55% of the children are from third and 45% from fourth grade. 80% of fourth grade and 33% of third grade children use the Internet at least once a week. Thus, older children spend more time online. 63% of the pupils use the Internet without any supervision (83% of the third grade and 40% of the fourth grade), whereas the rest of the participants share the company of their parents or older siblings. 54% of the young participants use the Internet mostly to play online games and watch videos. 36% also search for information. 9% use the Internet only to search for information, for example, to do their homework. More than 80% are familiar with Google and 45% also know BK. Children like both Google and BK because they can provide "a lot of information."

Adults were recruited mostly from an academic context and tested in our lab. 17 adults also participated in the study. They were between 22 and 59 (29.81 on average, $\sigma = 8.93$). 65% were male. 70% of adults are students in computer science or working in the IT sector. This introduces one side effect. These adults can be considered as search experts, while the children are novices in web search. All the adults use the Internet every day without any supervision. 18% use the Internet only to search for information. The rest also use the Internet for other activities such as chatting etc. All the adult participants usually use Google to search for information. 29% of the adults use other search engines such as Yahoo, Bing or DuckDuckGo along with Google. Adults told us that Google is "concise and user-friendly," and it offers "a good balance between speed and quality of search results."

STUDY RESULTS

To analyze the users' perception of SERPs we created heat maps. Fig. 2 and 3 show several aggregated heat maps both for children and adults, i.e. accumulated number of fixations from all the selected test persons. Red color indicates the regions with a highest number of fixations and green the least, with varying levels in between. The heat maps show a difference between the children's and the adults' search behavior.

ID	Search task *(Initial Query)*
Info-1 *(Google)*	How many animals does the zoo in Magdeburg have? *(Zoo Magdeburg)*
Info-2 *(BK)*	What is the name of the largest Saturn moon? *(Saturn Monde)*
Nav-1 *(Google)*	Find the homepage of the photographer Michael Jordan. *(Michael Jordan)*
Nav-2 *(BK)*	Find the online-game page of ZDF Tivi portal. *(ZDF Tivi)*

Table 1. Search tasks and corresponding initial queries used in the study.

Both search engines: On both search engines, the adults only fixated on the first search results. The fixation areas get smaller for results ranked lower. This pattern is consistent with the F-shaped strategy [10]. In case the answer is not found within the first search results, the adults reformulated the query starting a new search. Young users exhaustively explored all the ten results and used the navigation buttons between results pages to continue further examination. We assume that navigation is easier for children than query reformulation due to children's low capacity for abstraction [11] that makes it difficult for children to create own queries. Children reformulated the query mostly on the second SERP.

The heat maps for children on both Google and BK contain relatively closely spaced, circular, color-highlighted areas, which are spread across all titles of the search results list. This scan pattern indicates a partial reading of the search results titles. Due to this reading style relevant information can be overlooked, so that children often navigate to the next SERP. Our findings are consistent with Dinet [3] who found a tendency towards a cued visual jump strategy of younger children, however we also found that children tend to scan the whole result list using jumps between highlighted words especially in titles. During navigational search the children paid more attention to snippets than during informational search both using Google and BK. This can be explained by the fact that navigation tasks are more difficult to solve and require an extensive reading of the snippet content [12]. Children paid more attention to media elements such as pictures and video elements embedded in a search result than adults.

Google: The Google search engine provides query suggestions placed on the bottom of the page. However, only children paid attention to query suggestions and adults did not. Furthermore, children employed visual-jump strategy from a highlighted word in the title to the next one available.

BK: In contrast to adults children looked at the navigational menu with categories on the surface of the BK. Some chil-

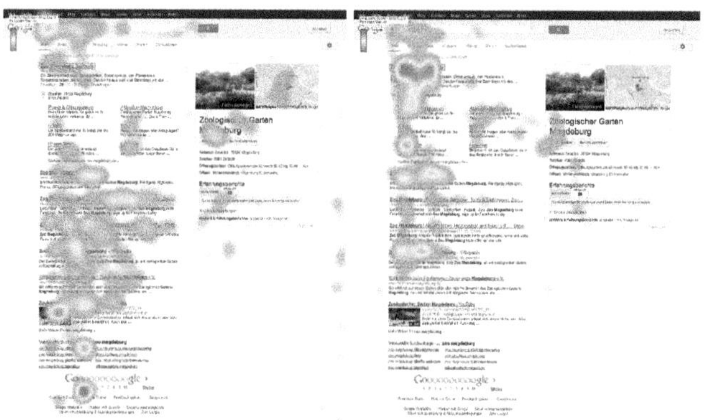

(a) children (b) adults

Figure 2. Aggregated heat maps for Google informational search.

(a) children (b) adults

Figure 3. Aggregated heat maps for Blinde-Kuh navigational search.

dren even clicked on the category "Games". This category was related to their navigational task to find the online-game page of the ZDF Tivi portal. Both children and adults had difficulties to determine what parts of BK results surrogates are clickable. Probably the box around a surrogate indicated that the whole area is clickable. In contrast to Google, BK also provides thumbnails for nearly each search result and uses no highlighting of keywords. The heat map of BK shows a Γ-shaped scanning strategy of children within a search surrogate as children tend to scan the title and look at the web page picture. Adults did not fixate on thumbnails as much as children did. Spotty and closely spaced, colored areas in the titles of search results indicate a partial reading of children the same as for Google. Children fixated informative words, e.g. "television broadcasting" in the title, but also in the snippet and the link of a search result.

CONCLUSION

We found differences in the perception of search engines SERPs between children and adults. Based on the findings of this study we provide the following suggestions to design better search user interfaces for children in the future. As the children paid attention to thumbnails and embedded media, these elements should be used in SERPs and provide relevance cues. As the children only partially read the results' snippets, it may be unnecessary to present a long text in each snippet of a search result. Instead snippets should be short and provide relevant typographical cues to avoid frustration of children when reading long texts and to help children in finding relevant information. As the children used navigational elements and at least looked at the menu with categories, these elements should be part of a search engine and support children who have difficulties to formulate a new query. In the future, we are going to analyze participant's efficiency, effectiveness and user preferences during the search and further eye-tracking parameters such as gaze plots.

ACKNOWLEDGMENTS

We would like to thank all participants of the user study.

REFERENCES

1. Bilal, D., and Kirby, J. Differences and similarities in information seeking: children and adults as Web users. *Information Processing & Management 38*, 5 (2002), 649–670.
2. Broder, A. A taxonomy of web search. *SIGIR Forum 36*, 2 (Sept. 2002), 3–10.
3. Dinet, J., Bastien, J. M. C., and Kitajima, M. What, where and how are young people looking for in a search engine results page?: impact of typographical cues and prior domain knowledge. In *Conf. IHM '10*, ACM (2010), 105–112.
4. Druin, A., Foss, E., Hutchinson, H., Golub, E., and Hatley, L. Children's roles using keyword search interfaces at home. In *Proc. of the SIGCHI Conf. on Human Factors in Computing Systems*, ACM (2010), 413–422.
5. Gossen, T., Hempel, J., and Nürnberger, A. Find it if you can: usability case study of search engines for young users. *Personal and Ubiquitous Computing 17*, 8 (2013), 1593–1603.
6. Gossen, T., Low, T., and Nürnberger, A. What are the real differences of children's and adults' web search. In *Proc. of the 34th int. SIGIR conf. on Research and development in Information Retrieval*, ACM (2011), 1115–1116.
7. Jochmann-Mannak, H., Huibers, T., Lentz, L., and Sanders, T. Children searching information on the Internet: Performance on children's interfaces compared to Google. *Towards Accessible Search Systems Workshop of the Int. SIGIR Conf.* (July 2010), 27–35.
8. Kammerer, Y., and Bohnacker, M. Children's web search with google: the effectiveness of natural language queries. In *Proc. of the 11th Int. Conf. on Interaction Design and Children*, ACM (2012), 184–187.
9. Medienpädagogischer Forschungsverbund Südwest. KIM-Studie 2010. Kinder+ Medien. *Computer+ Internet. Stuttgart* (2011).
10. Nielsen, J., and Pernice, K. Eyetracking web usability. New Riders, London, 2010.
11. Piaget, J., Inhelder, B., and Inhelder, B. *The psychology of the child*, vol. 5001. Basic Books (AZ), 1969.
12. Rele, R. S., and Duchowski, A. T. Using eye tracking to evaluate alternative search results interfaces. *Proc. of the Human Factors and Ergonomics Society Annual Meeting 49*, 15 (2005), 1459–1463.

Structuring the Space: A Study on Enriching Node-Link Diagrams with Visual References

Basak Alper
UC Santa Barbara
basakalper@gmail.com

Nathalie Henry Riche
Microsoft Research Redmond
nath@microsoft.com

Tobias Höllerer
UC Santa Barbara
holl@cs.ucsb.edu

ABSTRACT
Exploring large visualizations that do not fit in the screen raises orientation and navigation challenges. Structuring the space with additional visual references such as grids or contour lines provide spatial landmarks that may help viewers form a mental model of the space. However, previous studies report mixed results regarding their utility. While some evidence showed that grid and other visual embellishments improve memorability, experiments with contour lines suggest otherwise. In this work, we describe an evaluation framework to capture the impact of introducing visual references in node-link diagrams. We present the results of three controlled experiments that deepen our understanding on enriching large visualization spaces with visual structures. In particular, we provide the first tangible evidence that contour lines have significant benefits when navigating large node-link diagrams.

Author Keywords
Information Visualization, Network Diagrams, Navigation, Revisitation

ACM Classification Keywords
H.5.m. Information Interfaces and Presentation (e.g. HCI): Miscellaneous

INTRODUCTION
Exploring large visualization spaces that do not fit in the viewer's screen, such as a node-link diagram of several hundreds of nodes, raises orientation and navigation challenges [27]. Over the last decade, the human-computer interaction community has offered a plethora of interactive techniques to ease these tasks in large visualizations [8, 7, 29, 27, 23].

Enriching the space with additional visual elements such as grids [17] or contour lines [33] is an alternative approach. Such visual elements provide spatial landmarks which may help the viewer better grasp the dimensions of the space and provide memorable cues for better recognition and navigation [17] in large spaces.

Whether introducing non-data visual elements (such as a grid) hinders the readability of a visualization, and whether such elements play a beneficial role during an exploration are open-ended questions. While visualization practitioners strive to eliminate "chart junk" [34], prior work in psychology [12, 16] and empirical evidence presented by Bateman et al.[6] indicate that there may be benefits of even "seemingly useless" visuals in terms of memorability.

CHI 2014, April 26–May 1, 2014, Toronto, Ontario, Canada.
Copyright © 2014 ACM 978-1-4503-2473-1/14/04..$15.00.
http://dx.doi.org/10.1145/2556288.2557112

This paper aims to deepen our understanding on the utility of such visual enrichments within the context of visual representations of networks. Specifically, we study the effects of augmenting node-link diagrams with grid and contour lines. Both grids [5, 4] and contour lines [21, 13, 11] are commonly employed to enrich visualizations, however their relationship to the data differs significantly.

Grids are uniform structures independent of the data: two different datasets can be displayed on the exact same grid. In contrast, contour lines reflect an underlying property of the data such as a density measure, thus they present a unique pattern per dataset. Contour lines not only provide spatial landmarks enabling the use of spatial memory, but also reinforce data encoding by indexing elements topologically.

While a grid visualization has shown to be useful for navigation and revisitation of nodes in a node-link diagram [17], there is no conclusive evidence on the utility of contour lines. On the contrary, a controlled experiment by Tory et al.[33] on dot visualizations indicated that contours did not play a role on memorability.

Discrepancies in these results warrant further research. In this work, we describe an evaluation framework attempting to capture the impact of introducing additional visuals on the readability of node-link diagrams. In particular, we compare a uniform grid to contours generated from the data properties and investigate their potential role in helping the viewer build a mental model of the visualization space. Results of our controlled experiments shed a different light on previous results. We discuss the implications of our findings and reflect on key directions for further experimentations on the topic.

RELATED WORK
Grids are ubiquitous in a variety of charts that people use commonly such as scatterplots and bar charts. Their advocates argue that well-designed grids [5, 4] do not obstruct the primary visualization and serve as spatial references to compare relative positions of elements. For example, a grid in a scatterplot may help estimate the gap between two data points. However, we could not find any experimental results quantifying their benefits in visualizations.

Initial evidence by Ghani and Elmqvist [17] indicates that grids and other spatial landmarks may play a role in the formation of a mental model of large visualization spaces. Their study compared several designs for augmenting node-link diagrams, such as colored or textured grids and randomly distributed icons, while performing a revisitation task in a larger than screen node-link diagram. Their results show that solid colored grid cells increase performance when revisiting nodes. These findings suggest that grids play a role in the formation of a mental model of the space. However, the specific design used in this study contradicts suggested design guidelines [5, 4, 22]. The choice of employing grid cells with saturated solid colors may have improved revisitation performance at the cost of threatening the readability of the visualization.

Contour lines or topographic maps (contour lines with color filling and/or shading) are also commonly employed to enrich abstract data visualizations and node-link diagrams in particular [21, 13, 11]. Alluding to a geographic landscape featuring peaks and valleys, these representations enhance spatial metaphors. Fabrikant et al. argue that such "spatializations" act as fundamental sense makers for abstract domains because concepts about space are easily accessible to human cognition [15, 31]. However, they do not provide concrete evidence of spatial metaphors helping the viewer build a better mental model of the visualization space.

Tory et al. studied the benefits of 2D and 3D topographic maps for the readability of dot representations. Their first study dealt with the estimation of number of dots within a contour region [32]. They found that simple color coding was more effective than both conditions. A second study on memorability of dot representations [33], where subjects had to recognize previously seen dot distributions, also failed to show any benefit of 2D or 3D maps on memorability.

At the extreme end of the spectrum, Bateman et al.[6] have investigated the role of "chart junk", defined as seemingly not useful visual embellishments on the memorability of simple charts. These embellishments refer to illustrations or deformations that do not convey any information about the data, hence could be considered visual noise. The surprising results of their study suggest that such embellishments may provide richer spatial features that increase the memorability of charts. A recent study by Borkin et al.[10] support this argument by showing that visualizations with low *data-ink-ratio* and high visual density (more chartjunk) were more memorable than minimal, "clean" visualizations.

Other findings [9] on the topic suggest that there is a fine line between providing additional *data ink* (even if metaphorical) to increase memorability and engagement versus obstructing the data. These research pieces argue for conducting further studies in this area, carefully considering the design of visual embellishments and their impact on memorability and mental model.

In graph visualization domain, mental map preservation has been investigated in the context of dynamic graphs. However, work in this area focuses on the utility of layout preservation and animation rather than augmenting the representation with visual references [28, 1, 18].

Comparing and contrasting results across different experimental protocols, visual representations, tasks, datasets, and design of added visual enrichments proved extremely difficult. Conflicting outcomes of previous studies resorted in no clear answer whether or not augmenting a node-link diagram with additional visuals would help a viewer build a better mental model of the space. We refined a set of questions and propose a unified framework for evaluating the benefits and drawbacks of introducing enrichments to node-link diagrams.

EVALUATION FRAMEWORK

In this section we describe our rationale for assessing the role that visual structures such as grids and contours may play in the formation of a mental model. We seek answers to our high-level questions through low-level tasks performed in controlled settings.

Complementing visualizations with reference structures adds clutter that may hinder the readability of the primary visualization, and also contradicts guidelines of practitioners such as Tufte, advocating for *minimal ink*. Hence, assessing the potential negative impact of added visuals on readability of a visualization is crucial.

To address this question, we selected a low-level **readability task** on graph topology —*find common connections between two nodes*. We hypothesized that visual structures such as a grid and contours would interfere most with the links in node-link diagrams since their visual encodings are similar. Therefore, we selected an identify-common-neighbors task as outlined in [19], which requires participants to follow multiple links in the diagram.

A key reason for introducing visual references in a visualization is the idea that they can help the viewer form a better *mental model* of the space. Mental model is an overloaded term referring to concepts as diverse as the formation of an internal representation of a document collection and the formation of an internal 3D model of an object based on its 2D representation. In this paper, our definition of mental model is *an internal representation that one constructs about the spatial organization of objects*.

We believe that forming a mental model of the space involves at least two aspects of the spatial organization of visual elements: (1) *spatial structure*: gaining a sense of the relative positions of the elements in the visualization (i. e. grasping their distance and orientation to each other); (2) *spatial landmarks*: memorizing unique recognizable motifs in the representation that the viewer can refer to in order to navigate and orient himself in the space.

To measure the role of grids or contour lines in helping the viewer gain a sense of spatial structure and relative positioning of elements, we selected a **comparison task** — *determine if and how two graphs differ*. We conjectured that participants would make use of relative spatial encodings (e.g. the cluster to the left of the central grid cell) when performing a region-by-region comparison between two similar visualizations displayed alongside each other.

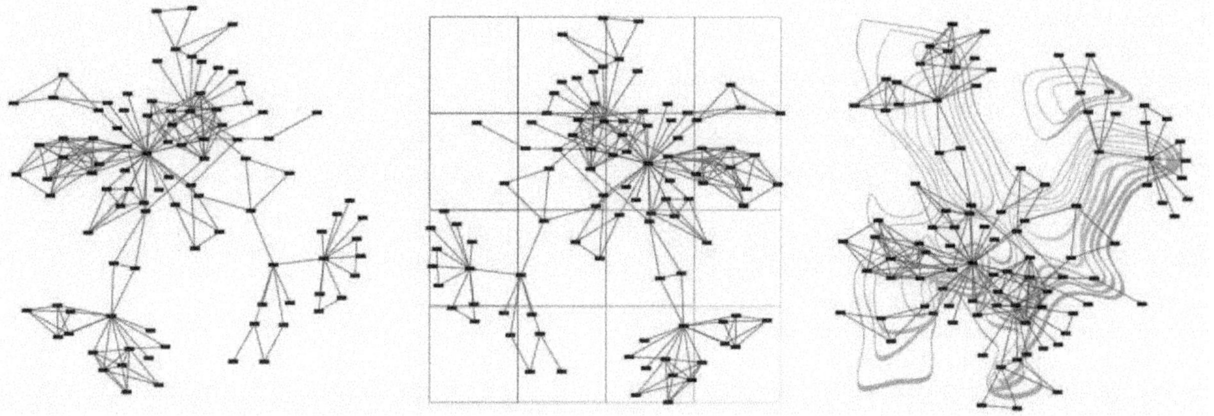

Figure 1. Example stimuli images from our controlled study evaluating user performance in revisiting previously highlighted nodes. Shown are the three visualization conditions used in the experiment: node-link diagram only, node-link diagram with grid, and node-link diagram with contour maps.

Gaining an understanding of recognizable and memorizable motifs in node-link diagrams is a research question in itself [26]. While a recall task such as drawing the diagram from memory may provide useful insights [26], it is not applicable for graphs with more than ten nodes. To measure the role of grids and contour lines in providing memorable spatial features, we devised a **revisitation task** — *revisit previously highlighted nodes*. We selected this task to build upon the previous work of Ghani et al.[17], recognizing it also as a plausible task that analysts perform [24, 30].

We also hypothesized that the construction of a mental model differs significantly depending on whether the whole visualization space can be seen in one view or not. While in the former case visual memory plays a more dominant role, spatial memory might have a stronger effect in the latter. For this reason, we suggest to perform the revisitation task under two different interaction conditions. We propose a first condition in which the viewer can only pan in the visualization space, thus never seeing the whole visualization space at once; and a second condition in which the viewer can acquire a view of the whole space with a zoom-out operation.

EVALUATION

We performed three studies for each task described above.

Techniques

We compared grid and contour lines and with a control condition of plain node-link diagram. Technique settings and data were adjusted for each of the separate experiments and are reported in each study section.

Node-Link-Only.

In this control condition, participants complete the tasks using a node-link diagram without any additional visuals.

Grid.

This condition augments the node-link diagram used in the previous condition with an underlying grid. We employ a modified version of the grid design proposed by Ghani et al.[17] which used strongly saturated solid colors for each grid cell. In realistic scenarios however, such colors may greatly interfere with the visual encoding of the primary data [35, 4], a disadvantage we believe overpowering the benefit of improved memorability in many visual analysis tasks. Thus, we opted for a grid representation consisting of empty frames rather than solid color regions. We assigned a distinct color to each grid cell as in [17], but used transparency as advised in [4].

Contours.

This condition augments the node-link diagram used in the control condition with contour lines. In the context of node-link diagrams, contour lines can be derived from several data properties such as node degree or node centrality. Similar to [21] we generate our contours starting with Delaunay triangulation of nodes in a given layout. Corners of each triangle are assigned a height value corresponding to the selected node property. We interpolate this height value within each triangle using barycentric coordinates. Given a set of iso-property values indicating where the contours should pass, our implementation of the marching squares [25] algorithm computes the set of points marking the boundary of the iso-value. We sample these boundary points and use piecewise Bezier curves to connect them.

Visual references such as grids and contours are designed to reside in a visual middle ground between the foreground of the primary data encodings and the background, such that they can be brought to the foreground when attended to, and pushed to the background otherwise [20, 4, 5]. Following the design guidelines suggested in [4, 5], we chose visual parameters to render the contours sufficiently discernible, yet minimize their interference with the primary visualization. Instead of a gray-scale representation, we opted for color coding to help distinguish nested contour lines. However, we selected a very narrow color palette, with minimal saturation and high luminance, allowing it to blend more with the white background of the node-link diagram. In addition, we utilized shadow-like offsets to emphasize unique contour shapes further, while making them more distinguishable from the simple stroke used for the links of the node-link diagram. Another motivation was to allude to a 3D landscape, featuring recognizable geographic formations such as peaks and valleys.

Experiment 1: Readability

This experiment investigates whether the presence of grid or contour lines compromises the readability of a node-link diagram by employing a common neighbors task. We performed a within-subject design with 3 Techniques × 2 Data Sizes × 4 Repeats. We recruited 9 participants, 3 females and 6 males, with a mean age of 33.8 years.

Data

For this study, we generated graphs using Eppstein and Wang's power law model [14]. The model is designed to ensure that the synthetic data generated follows a well-known property of the degree of node observed in many real networks [3]. We used two different sizes: 50 nodes and 75 links (small); and 100 nodes and 150 links (large). We generated 6 graphs per size for each repeat and training trials. Across techniques, we used the same graphs. In order to minimize learning effects, we flipped the layout horizontally and/or vertically for each technique.

Technique Settings

All graphs, regardless of their size, were scaled to fit in an area of 600 by 600 pixels, fitting on a standard computer screen and removing the need for interactive navigation that could impact the completion time. We opted for a legible but small visualization size to capture the potential effect of background interference with a high density of visual elements. From a series of pilots, we found that a grid of 3 by 3 provided a good compromise. For the contour lines, we experimented with several metrics and opted for using the node degree. We observed that this metric produced contours distinctive enough from each other, while not introducing too much clutter. We used the same color palette for coloring the contours and the grid lines. Figure 2 shows examples from visual stimuli used in our experiment.

Procedure

Given two highlighted nodes, participants had to select nodes that are connected to both of the highlighted nodes in a total of 24 trials. The order of techniques were counterbalanced across participants. For each trial we selected two random high-degree nodes which were not connected directly but had a minimum of two common neighbors. Due to the high connectivity requirements, the highlighted nodes were likely to appear at a busy region of the node-link diagram, where the visualization is more susceptible to interference with the background. Thus, the chance of capturing a potential effect of the background on the readability of the node-link diagram would be higher. The order of techniques were counterbalanced across participants. The participants selected the common neighbors by clicking on the nodes. After selecting all common neighbors, the participants were asked to confirm their answer by pressing a button. Participants were instructed to take breaks as needed after every trial while the visualization screen was blank.

Hypothesis

We hypothesized that **(H1)** Grid and Contours would decrease the readability of the representation and impact at least the completion time as they introduce additional visual clutter.

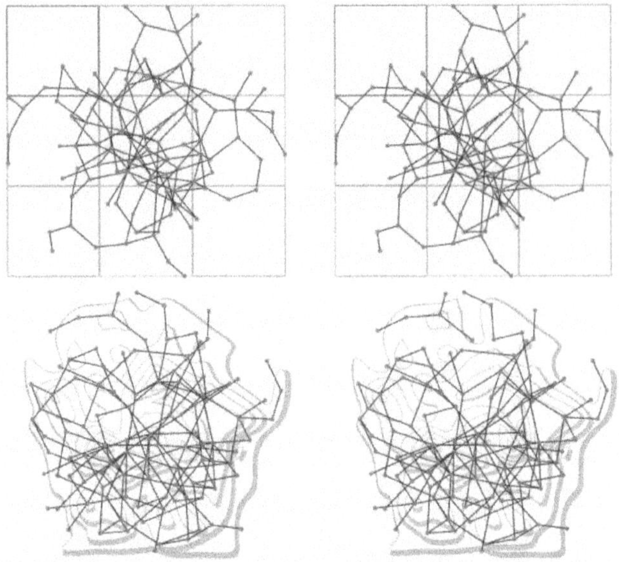

Figure 2. Examples of the visual stimuli used in the controlled studies on readability (Experiment 1) and comparison (Experiment 2). Only one of each pair of images was used in the readability study.

Results

Since accuracy results did not follow a normal distribution, we analyzed them using Friedman's non-parametric test. Friedman's test did not reveal any significant difference in accuracy between Node-Link-Only, Grid, or Contours. All techniques had a mean of about 90% accuracy (with 3.5% standard error). Pairwise comparisons of Wilcoxon's test Z values reveal weak effect sizes ($r < 0.1$).

We analyzed the completion time for correct trials only, using a Mixed Linear Model (MLM) that can handle missing values. We excluded the about 10% of incorrect trials. MLM did not reveal any significant difference in completion time, contradicting our hypothesis **(H1)**. All techniques had a mean of about 15 seconds (with 7 sec standard error).

We asked the participants to rate whether they found the Grid or Contours distracting for this task, using a 5-point Likert scale from 1 (not distracting at all) to 5 (very distracting). Grid received an average rating of 1.5 (SD=0.35), while the average rating for Contours was 2.3 (SD=0.47). In line with **(H1)**, the majority of participants (6 out of 9) preferred the Node-Link-Only condition for this task.

Experiment 2: Visual Reference

In this experiment participants were asked to identify presence and nature of differences between two seemingly similar graphs that are displayed side by side. We performed a within-subject experiment of 3 Techniques × 2 Data Sizes × 4 Repeats. This experiment was performed right after the Experiment 1 session by the same participants using the same data sets and visual stimuli.

Procedure

For each graph, we generated an altered version by randomly deleting a high degree node with all its connections. However, we avoided eliminating nodes with high betweenness centrality to ensure that the task was challenging enough. We created new contour lines for the altered graph since their node degree had changed. Half of the trials presented the exact same graph on both sides. Participants had to answer whether the graph on the right had a smaller, higher, or equal number of nodes and edges as the graph on the left by pressing one of the three buttons.

Hypotheses

We hypothesized that **(H2)** participants would be more effective to conclude if the two graphs are identical with Contours, where they can rely on these visuals for gauging the differences instead of carefully inspecting the node-link diagram. For quantifying the differences (larger or smaller), we expected that **(H3a)** Grid would yield better results than Node-Link-Only, as grid cells would enable participants to structure the space and inspect regions systematically. We also believed that **(H3b)** Contours would yield to better results than the two other techniques because the landscape built from data properties would guide participants' attention towards the region that is different.

Results

Since accuracy results did not follow a normal distribution, we analyzed them using Friedman's non-parametric test. The test revealed a significant difference between techniques for identifying if graphs are identical or not ($p < .05$). Pairwise comparisons using Wilcoxon's tests indicate that the Contours technique outperforms Node-Link-Only ($p < .05$) and Grid ($p < .01$) confirming **(H2)**. An estimate of effect size based on Z value reveals a medium effect size ($r \approx .3$) for both of these pairwise comparisons. Mean accuracy indicates that Contours are 10% more accurate than Node-Link-Only and 18% more accurate than Grid. Graph size did not yield to any significant difference between techniques.

We analyzed the results on completion time for correct trials only using a Mixed Linear Model (MLM) that can handle missing values. We excluded the 24% of incorrect trials (*i.e.* participants failed to recognize if the modified graph was identical, smaller or larger). MLM revealed an effect of Technique ($F_{2,16} = 5.29, p < .05$) and Size ($F_{1,8} = 41.49, p < .001$) on completion time. As expected, pairwise comparison revealed that participants performed 20% faster to identify changes in Small size networks, with a statistically significant difference ($p < .001$). Pairwise comparisons revealed that Contours led to significantly faster task completion times ($p < .05$) than the other two techniques. Mean completion time indicates that users performed the tasks 12% faster on average with Contours than with the two other techniques, confirming **(H3b)**. Contrary to **(H3a)**, Grid however did not produce more accurate or faster identification of differences between graphs compared to Node-Link-Only.

We asked participants to rate the usefulness of the Grid and Contours visualizations for this comparison task, using a 5-point Likert scale from 1 (not useful at all) to 5 (very useful). Grid received an average rating of 3.77 (SD=0.22), while the average rating for Contours was 4.45 (SD=0.24). 6 out of 9 participants preferred the Contours visualization, while the remaining 3 preferred the Grid visualization for this task.

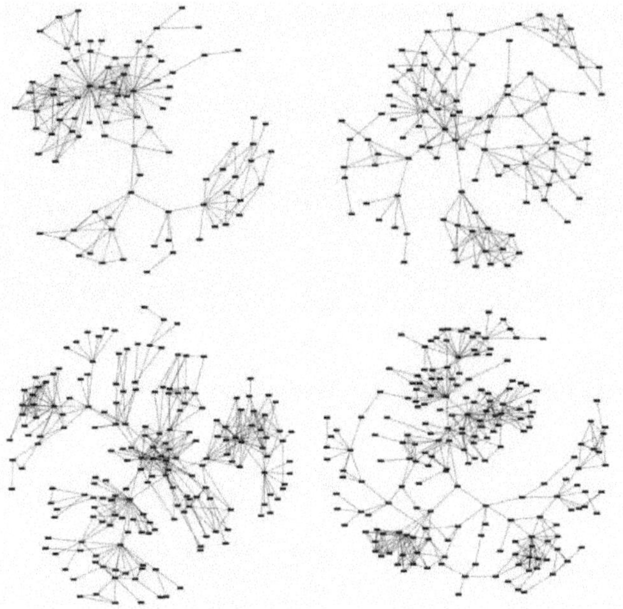

Figure 3. Examples from the small (top row) and large (bottom row) data sets used in Experiment 3.

Experiment 3: Revisitation

In this experiment, we investigated whether the Grid and the Contours visual reference structures aided users in forming a mental model of a visualization space. To assess the formulation of a mental model, we devised a task of revisiting previously highlighted nodes in a visualization space that is larger than the viewing window. We performed a 3 Techniques × 2 Data Sizes × 2 Interaction Methods × 3 Repeats within-subject design. We recruited 12 participants, 8 males and 4 females, with a mean age of 28.3 years.

Data

We used two data sizes in this experiment : 100 nodes and 150 links (small), and 150 nodes and 300 links (large). We decided against using a graph generator for this task because we did not have access to one that could produce graphs with distinguishable topological features (i. e. dense communities or hubs) as real graph often do [2]. We conjectured that this factor could bias our results as grid or contour lines are likely to play a more significant role when used to augment "featureless" visual spaces. Therefore, we generated our graphs from real social network data. Starting from a data set representing co-autorship relationships in a real social network, we randomly added and removed nodes and edges until the desired number of elements and sufficient distinctive topological features were achieved. We generated five graphs per size for each repeat and training trials. Examples are shown in Figure 3. Across techniques, we used the same graphs. In order to minimize learning effects, we flipped the layout horizontally and/or vertically for each visualization technique.

Technique Settings

In this experiment, participants had to perform the task in a visualization space that did not fit in view (unless specifically zoomed out in one of our conditions). We used a window size of 1000x1000 pixels over a 3000x3000 pixels canvas (small)

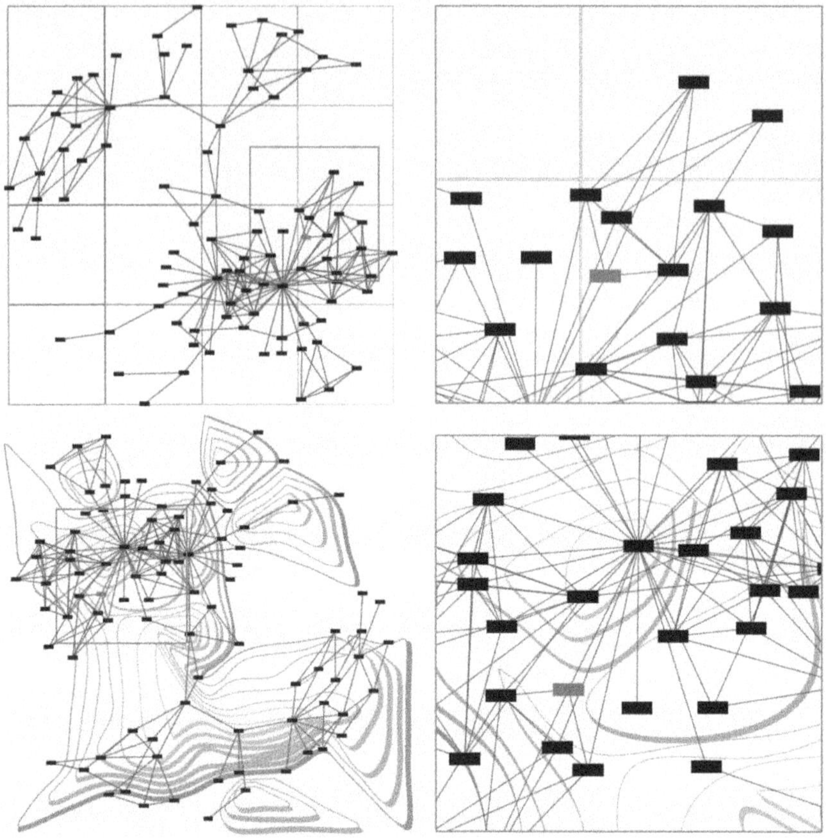

Figure 4. Examples from the Grid and Contour visualization stimuli images used in Experiment 3 (revisitation). The images on the left show the whole visualization space with a highlight of what can fit in the view in the pan and zoom-in conditions. The images on the right show the contents of the viewing window in detail.

or a 4500x4500 pixels canvas (large). We picked a grid cell size of 750x750 pixels ensuring that an entire cell and some portion of its neighboring cells would fit in the view, while avoiding a fine grid spacing. Thus, we used a 4x4 grid for the small data, and a 6x6 grid on the large one. We opted for using color on the grid lines as a secondary cue to encode relative positions of the grid cells (see Figure 4, top).

To generate contour lines, we used the betweenness centrality of each node. This metric produced a good compromise between the simplicity of the patterns (i.e. the number of distinct peaks) and the presence of distinguishable features (i.e. the variation in shape). See Figure 4, bottom for an example visual stimulus.

Navigation and Interaction

The participants used either pan or zoom to navigate within the visualization space. Dissociating navigation techniques is common practice [23] as it ensures similar navigation strategies between participants. Here, it also enabled us to observe different strategies while forming a mental model of the space. In the pan interaction mode, participants could not view the whole visualization but they could pan by dragging their mouse. In the zoom interaction mode, we designed a simple two-level zoom wherein participants could toggle between a zoomed-in and a zoomed-out state on right mouse button click as implemented in [23]. In the zoomed-out state, the whole visualization fit in the view. In this mode, when participants right-clicked, the visualization zoomed in, centering around the position of the mouse click. The scales used in the zoomed-in state and the pan mode were the same.

Procedure

We designed a revisitation task consisting of a learning and an execution phase, similar to [17]. In the learning phase, three random nodes were highlighted in sequence. The starting view was at the center of the visualization space in the pan mode, and at the zoomed-in state for the zoom mode. Participants had to navigate to find the highlighted node, collect information about its locality and click on it to view the next highlighted node. Once they clicked all three nodes, they viewed a blank screen for four seconds. After, the execution phase began with the starting view, where participants had to revisit the nodes (now dehighlighted) in the same order. They provided their answer by clicking on the node. Time to revisit a node was limited to 25 seconds, with a countdown appearing in the last 10 seconds. If the time expired, a pop up dialogue instructed them to proceed to the next node. We forced a ten second break after every trial, displaying a photograph to reset visual memory. We instructed them to take longer breaks if needed.

Participants completed 18 trials using pan, and another 18 using zoom interaction. We used the same visuals but highlighted a different set of nodes to limit learning effects. We counterbalanced the order of visualizations, but we kept the order of interaction methods fixed across participants, opting for presenting the most difficult condition (pan) first. We trained participants before each task and interaction mode, informing them about strategies they could utilize. We instructed them to collect sufficient information about the locality of a highlighted node before clicking on it in the learning phase while being as time efficient as possible. On average participants took about 70 minutes to complete the study. All participants were rewarded with a 25 dollar gift card, while the best performing participant was promised an additional 25 dollars.

Hypotheses

We expected that **(H4a)** participants would be least accurate with the Node-Link-Only condition, because the presence of Grid or Contours would provide additional visual references encoding the locality of a visited node. In addition, we expected **(H4b)** Contours to outperform Grid because, in contrast to the uniform visual characteristics of grids, contours provide unique visual structures in different parts of the visualization which would ease recall.

We hypothesized that **(H5)** in the zoom condition, differences between the Contours and Grid techniques may not be significant since participants could effectively memorize the exact row and column of the cell containing the node in the Grid visualization. However, we expected that **(H6)** in the pan condition, Contours would have clearer benefits over the other two techniques as they provide unique landmarks across space.

Finally, we did not expect **(H7)** to see any significant time difference across visualization techniques because we hypothesized that any possible gains provided by the visuals on recalling the location would be eclipsed by the interaction time required to navigate there.

Results

Since accuracy did not follow a normal distribution, we analyzed them using Friedman's non-parametric test, which revealed a significant difference among techniques ($p < .001$). Pairwise comparisons using Wilcoxon's tests showed that Contours outperformed Node-Link-Only ($p < .01$) and Grid ($p < .001$), confirming **(H4b)**. An estimate of effect size based on Wilcoxon's test Z value revealed medium effect size ($r \approx .3$) between Contours and the other two techniques, while the effect size between Node-Link-Only and Grid was small ($r < .1$). Mean accuracy indicates that Contours produced 7% more accurate results than Node-Link-Only and 16% more accurate results than Grid for revisiting previous nodes. Contrary to our hypothesis **(H4a)**, we did not find any significant difference between Grid and Node-Link-Only. When splitting results by interaction condition, Friedman's tests revealed significant differences in accuracy among techniques in both the zoom ($p < .05$) and pan ($p < .01$) conditions. Contours significantly outperformed Node-Link-Only ($p < .05$) and Grid ($p < .05$) using zoom, contradicting **(H5)**. In addition, Contours outperformed Grid ($p < .001$) but not Node-Link-Only in the pan condition, partially validating **(H6)**. Table 1 and Figure 5 summary the results.

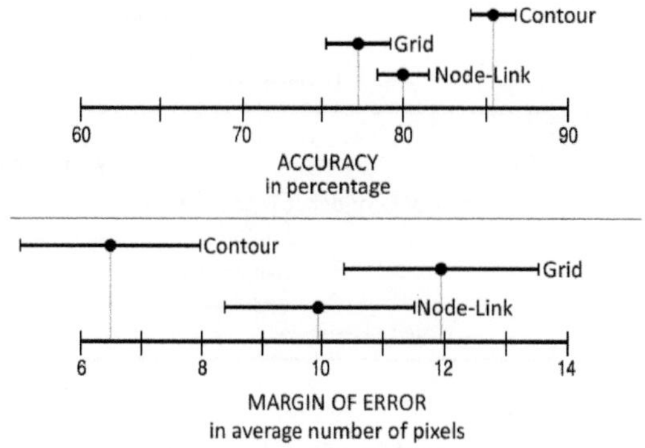

Figure 5. Accuracy and margin of error results for all three techniques in Experiment 3. Means and +/- standard error values are shown.

Technique	Pan and Zoom	Pan	Zoom
C x G x NL	($p < .001$)	($p < .01$)	($p < .05$)
C x G	($p < .001$)	($p < .001$)	($p < .05$)
C x NL	($p < .01$)		($p < .05$)

Table 1. Significant differences in accuracy across techniques and interaction conditions in Experiment 3. C: Contour, G: Grid, NL: Node-Link-Only

We analyzed the results on completion time for correct trials only using a Mixed Linear Model (MLM) that can handle missing values. We excluded 24% of incorrect trials. Inline with **(H7)**, MLM did not reveal any significant difference among techniques.

Subjective Ratings

After the controlled experiment, participants rated their confidence in their results using a 5-point Likert scale from 1 (not confident) to 5 (very confident). Mean confidence levels are provided in Table 2 and Figure 6. Since these ratings do not follow a normal distribution, we analyzed them using non-parametric tests. Friedman's test shows a significant difference in participant confidence between techniques for both pan ($p < .05$) and zoom ($p < .001$). Pairwise comparisons using Wilcoxon's test reveal that participants felt significantly more confident using the Contour compared to Node-Link-Only for both pan ($p < .05$) and zoom ($p < .01$). In the zoom condition, participants felt also significantly more confident using Contour than using Grid ($p < .05$).

We also asked the participants to give an overall preference ranking for the three visualization techniques. Friedman's test indicated a significant difference in preference among techniques ($p < .01$). Pairwise comparisons using Wilcoxon's test reveal that Contours were ranked significantly higher than both Node-Link-Only ($p < .001$) and Grid ($p < .05$). Indeed, 8 out of 12 participants ranked Contour as their favorite technique.

Finally, we also report on most recurrent participants' comments collected using a printed questionnaire. For Node-Link-Only, 5 out of 12 participants indicated that they felt their performance was dependent on the node to revisit and particularly easy for nodes on the periphery of the diagram. For the Grid, 5 out of 12 participants indicated that they were able to relocate the grid cell but that they forgot the exact position of the node within this cell. A few participants explained

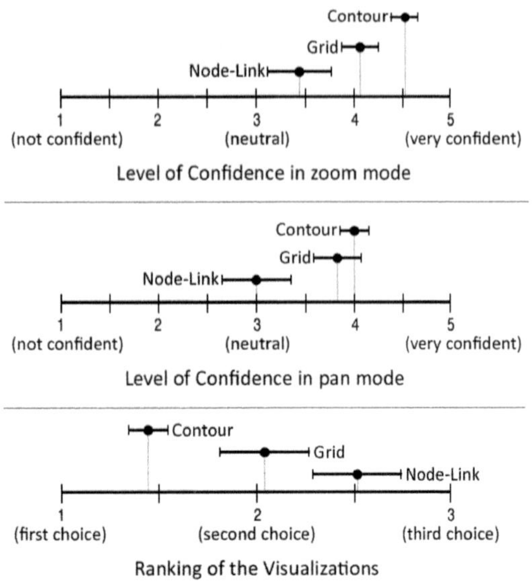

Figure 6. Subjective rating results for confidence levels in the zoom (top), and pan interaction modes (middle), as well as the overall rankings of the three visualization techniques (bottom). Means and +/- standard error values are shown.

Int.	Contours	Grid	Node-Link-Only
Pan	4 (SD=0.6)	3.83 (SD=1.02)	3 (SD=1.27)
Zoom	4.58 (SD=0.51)	4.16 (SD=0.57)	3.41 (SD=1.16)

Table 2. Average confidence levels indicated by the participants for each interaction mode per visualization technique. Standard deviations are provided in parenthesis.

that counting the grid cell was diverting their attention from the actual graph structure. For the Contour, 7 out of 12 participants indicated that they used contour shapes as spatial landmarks. For example, a participant commented that he "could see islands, coves and mountains to easily associate with geographic locations" and another explained that he "could find unique representative shapes... that represent objects in real life, for example, crown on a prince's head".

DISCUSSION

In this section we discuss the implications of our findings as well as address the key limitations of our studies to take into account in the future.

Implications for Design

Whispering Visuals

We followed the guidelines prescribed in [5] for the visual design of our grids and contour lines. Our readability study did not reveal any significant difference when additional visual structures were present. As the common neighbor task required participants to follow many links in the diagram that were overlapping these visuals, we feel confident that readability of the diagram was not hindered when suggested design guidelines were followed.

Structuring the Space with Grids

We were surprised that our results did not show any significant increase in performance using Grid versus Node-Link-Only. In particular, the results from our revisitation study seem to be in contradiction with previous studies reported in [17]. We explain these discrepancies by two major differences in the experimental setups. First, in contrast to the previous study, we selected a more "whispering" color palette. This choice may have downplayed the role of grids in helping user form a mental model of the space but ensured its readability as advised in [5, 4] and confirmed in our readability study. Second, we selected graph data featuring distinguishable topological structures, as we conjectured it was more common in real datasets. However, such features may have helped task performance more than the information provided by the grid. Experiments with representations that naturally contain less salient motifs (such as dot visualizations) may capture a stronger effect of a grid.

Unexpectedly, despite the lack of a significant increase in performance, the grid was consistently preferred over the control condition. Participants also reported a higher sense of confidence in their answers with the grid. These subjective impressions could point to benefits that we failed to capture with our current experimental settings. However, from our current findings, we also want to call for a careful consideration of their use in visualizations, as they might lead to a false sense of confidence.

Structuring the Space with Contour Lines

While many researchers experimented with augmenting visualizations with contour lines or topographic maps [33, 33, 15, 21, 13, 11], there has been no tangible evidence of their utility. On the contrary, advocates for *minimal ink* may caution against the use of these structures as they may obstruct readability. Our quantitative findings are the first to indicate that contour lines do not hinder readability (study 1), play a significant role in helping viewers structure the space (study 2), and form a mental model when navigating a large visualization (study 3). Our quantitative results from the controlled experiments as well as qualitative comments from the participants suggest that contour lines can provide a general outlook of the node-link diagram, helping viewers identify unique spatial landmarks to return to previously visited nodes. Our subjective ratings also concur with the increased performance as contour lines are consistently preferred. Based on these insights, we project that contour lines could ease navigation and orientation in an infinite zoomable and pannable canvas.

In our studies we manually selected the metric to generate the contours to ensure the presence of identifiable geometric features while minimizing interference with the primary visualization. While node centrality provided sufficient discernible characteristics for a social network type of data (study 3), we opted to use the degree metric for synthetic data generated using a power law distribution (study 1, 2). Non-graph data properties associated with the nodes can also be used. Thus, the metric to be used for contour generation is highly specific to the data.

Structuring the Space for Dynamic Visualizations

Enriching node-link diagrams with visual structures that reflect a data property is a double-edged sword. It may, as we illustrated in studies 2 and 3, help viewer's build a mental model of the representation. However, in contrast with a grid, these structures may also prove highly unstable when exploring a dynamically changing diagram. Contour lines could help grasp where the changes are, but if these are dramatic, they may rather disorient the viewer.

Study Limitations

In our studies we strived to devise realistic tasks while controlling many factors that could impact our findings. Consequently, as with all controlled experiments, there are key limitations that need to be taken into account when generalizing our results and designing further experiments.

Tasks and Sample Size

What a mental model exactly is and how to assess it is an open and challenging research question. Our evaluation framework is an attempt at characterizing several of the aspects that may be at play when viewers form a mental model of a visualization. However, other aspects could be taken into account. In particular, we did not include any recall [26] or recognition tasks [33] as we could not decide on a systematic way to operationalize them or interpret their results.

Our study is of a limited sample size. For the first two studies, where we recruited only nine subjects, arriving at definite conclusions is not possible. However, we can observe certain trends. For instance, due to very small effect size, only a much larger population could reveal a significant effect of visual enrichments on readability. Our study on identifying differences across similar graphs unexpectedly showed that grid visualizations might not be helpful for side-by-side comparison tasks. This trend calls for further investigations on the role of a grid as a reference cue.

Granularity of the Visual Enrichments

As mentioned earlier, we manually adjusted granularity settings such as the number of contour lines and grid cells after a series of pilot sessions, ensuring that a certain amount of contour or grid lines were always present, regardless of the scale. We still collected conflicting feedback from our participants: 3 commented that smaller cells would allow them to better structure the space; 2 argued for larger cells as they had difficulties remembering the cell positions. Participants also commented that while some contour lines did not appear to provide enough recognizable patterns in the pan and zoom-in modes, they became discernible as spatial landmarks in the zoom-out mode. While we had to fix granularity of both contours and grids for a manageable study size, future studies that focus on granularity as an independent variable are needed.

Semantics

In this study we did not address the particular role of the data semantics. However, we would like to acknowledge that semantics may play a major role in mental model formation, possibly eclipsing the gain provided by additional visual structures. However, this role would be highly dependent on the dataset itself and the participants' previous knowledge, interests and analysis skills, thus making this factor extremely difficult to control. We believe that studies in less controlled settings (ideally longitudinal ones where participants explore their own datasets) would be more adequate to evaluate the interplay between semantics and additional visual structures when a viewer is forming a mental model of the visualization.

CONCLUSION

In this paper, we proposed an evaluation framework to extend our knowledge on the impact of introducing visual references to node-link diagrams. Through three controlled studies, we collected evidence quantifying the benefits and drawbacks of two types of visual structures : grids and contour lines.

We discussed how our findings shed a new light on previous results in the literature. In particular, our results seem to indicate that when node-link diagrams present recognizable motifs, such as clusters, the benefits of grids for revisitation tasks [17] may not be discernible. Our studies are also the first ones to reveal tangible benefits of the use of contour lines to enrich node-link diagrams. Our experimental design attempts to capture how these visuals could help the viewer form a mental model of the visualization (by structuring the space and identifying spatial landmarks). Results indicate that contour lines play a significant role in these activities.

We believe that our results on the benefits of enriching visualizations with additional visual structures will inspire further research in this space, and the evaluation framework we propose will serve as a building block for further studies.

REFERENCES

1. Archambault, D., Purchase, H., and Pinaud, B. Animation, small multiples, and the effect of mental map preservation in dynamic graphs. *Visualization and Computer Graphics, IEEE Transactions on 17*, 4 (2011), 539–552.
2. Bach, B., Spritzer, A., Lutton, E., Fekete, J.-D., et al. Interactive random graph generation with evolutionary algorithms. In *Graph Drawing* (2012).
3. Barabási, A.-L., and Albert, R. Emergence of scaling in random networks. *science 286*, 5439 (1999), 509–512.
4. Bartram, L., Cheung, B., and Stone, M. C. The effect of colour and transparency on the perception of overlaid grids. *Visualization and Computer Graphics, IEEE Transactions on 17*, 12 (2011), 1942–1948.
5. Bartram, L., and Stone, M. C. Whisper, don't scream: Grids and transparency. *Visualization and Computer Graphics, IEEE Transactions on 17*, 10 (2011), 1444–1458.
6. Bateman, S., Mandryk, R. L., Gutwin, C., Genest, A., McDine, D., and Brooks, C. Useful junk?: the effects of visual embellishment on comprehension and memorability of charts. In *Proceedings of the 28th international conference on Human factors in computing systems*, ACM (2010), 2573–2582.
7. Baudisch, P., and Rosenholtz, R. Halo: a technique for visualizing off-screen objects. In *Proceedings of the SIGCHI conference on Human factors in computing systems*, ACM (2003), 481–488.

8. Bederson, B. B., and Hollan, J. D. Pad++: a zooming graphical interface for exploring alternate interface physics. In *Proceedings of the 7th annual ACM symposium on UIST*, ACM (1994), 17–26.

9. Borgo, R., Abdul-Rahman, A., Mohamed, F., Grant, P. W., Reppa, I., Floridi, L., and Chen, M. An empirical study on using visual embellishments in visualization. *Visualization and Computer Graphics, IEEE Transactions on 18*, 12 (2012), 2759–2768.

10. Borkin, M. A., Vo, A. A., Bylinskii, Z., Isola, P., Sunkavalli, S., Oliva, A., and Pfister, H. What makes a visualization memorable? *Visualization and Computer Graphics, IEEE Transactions on 19*, 12 (2013), 2306–2315.

11. Cao, N., Sun, J., Lin, Y.-R., Gotz, D., Liu, S., and Qu, H. Facetatlas: Multifaceted visualization for rich text corpora. *Visualization and Computer Graphics, IEEE Transactions on 16*, 6 (2010), 1172–1181.

12. Collins, A. M., and Loftus, E. F. A spreading-activation theory of semantic processing. *Psychological review 82*, 6 (1975), 407.

13. Cortese, P. F., Di Battista, G., Moneta, A., Patrignani, M., and Pizzonia, M. Topographic visualization of prefix propagation in the internet. *Visualization and Computer Graphics, IEEE Transactions on 12*, 5 (2006), 725–732.

14. Eppstein, D., and Wang, J. A steady state model for graph power laws. *arXiv preprint cs/0204001* (2002).

15. Fabrikant, S. I., and Skupin, A. *Cognitively plausible information visualization*. Elsevier, 2005.

16. Gambrell, L. B., and Jawitz, P. B. Mental imagery, text illustrations, and children's story comprehension and recall. *Reading Research Quarterly* (1993), 265–276.

17. Ghani, S., and Elmqvist, N. Improving revisitation in graphs through static spatial features. In *Proceedings of Graphics Interface 2011*, Canadian Human-Computer Communications Society (2011), 175–182.

18. Ghani, S., Elmqvist, N., and Yi, J. S. Perception of animated node-link diagrams for dynamic graphs. In *Computer Graphics Forum*, vol. 31, Wiley Online Library (2012), 1205–1214.

19. Ghoniem, M., Fekete, J.-D., and Castagliola, P. A comparison of the readability of graphs using node-link and matrix-based representations. In *Information Visualization, 2004.*, IEEE (2004), 17–24.

20. Gombrich, E. H., Gombrich, E. H., Gombrich, E. H., and Gombrich, E. H. *Art and illusion: A study in the psychology of pictorial representation*, vol. 5. Phaidon London, 1977.

21. Gronemann, M., and Jünger, M. Drawing clustered graphs as topographic maps. In *Graph Drawing*, Springer (2013), 426–438.

22. Heer, J., and Bostock, M. Crowdsourcing graphical perception: using mechanical turk to assess visualization design. In *Proceedings of the 28th ACM SIGCHI*, ACM (2010), 203–212.

23. Irani, P., Gutwin, C., and Yang, X. D. Improving selection of off-screen targets with hopping. In *Proceedings of the ACM SIGCHI conference*, ACM (2006), 299–308.

24. Lee, B., Plaisant, C., Parr, C. S., Fekete, J.-D., and Henry, N. Task taxonomy for graph visualization. In *Proceedings of the 2006 AVI workshop on BEyond time and errors: novel evaluation methods for information visualization*, ACM (2006), 1–5.

25. Lorensen, W. E., and Cline, H. E. Marching cubes: A high resolution 3d surface construction algorithm. In *ACM Siggraph Computer Graphics*, vol. 21, ACM (1987), 163–169.

26. Marriott, K., Purchase, H., Wybrow, M., and Goncu, C. Memorability of visual features in network diagrams. *Visualization and Computer Graphics, IEEE Transactions on 18*, 12 (2012), 2477–2485.

27. Moscovich, T., Chevalier, F., Henry, N., Pietriga, E., and Fekete, J.-D. Topology-aware navigation in large networks. In *Proceedings of the 27th international conference on Human factors in computing systems*, ACM (2009), 2319–2328.

28. Purchase, H., Hoggan, E., and Görg, C. How important is the "mental map"?–an empirical investigation of a dynamic graph layout algorithm. In *Graph drawing*, Springer (2007), 184–195.

29. Shoemaker, G., and Gutwin, C. Supporting multi-point interaction in visual workspaces. In *Proceedings of the SIGCHI conference on Human factors in computing systems*, ACM (2007), 999–1008.

30. Skopik, A., and Gutwin, C. Improving revisitation in fisheye views with visit wear. In *Proceedings of the SIGCHI conference on Human factors in computing systems*, ACM (2005), 771–780.

31. Skupin, A., and Fabrikant, S. I. Spatialization methods: a cartographic research agenda for non-geographic information visualization. *Cartography and Geographic Information Science 30*, 2 (2003), 99–119.

32. Tory, M., Sprague, D. W., Wu, F., So, W. Y., and Munzner, T. Spatialization design: Comparing points and landscapes. *Visualization and Computer Graphics, IEEE Transactions on 13*, 6 (2007), 1262–1269.

33. Tory, M., Swindells, C., and Dreezer, R. Comparing dot and landscape spatializations for visual memory differences. *Visualization and Computer Graphics, IEEE Transactions on 15*, 6 (2009), 1033–1040.

34. Tufte, E. R., and Graves-Morris, P. *The visual display of quantitative information*, vol. 2. Graphics press Cheshire, CT, 1983.

35. Ware, C. *Information visualization: perception for design*. Morgan Kaufmann, 2012.

Highlighting Interventions and User Differences: Informing Adaptive Information Visualization Support

Giuseppe Carenini, Cristina Conati, Enamul Hoque, Ben Steichen, Dereck Toker, James Enns*[1]
Department of Computer Science, *Department of Psychology
University of British Columbia, Vancouver, Canada
{carenini, conati, enamul, steichen, dtoker}@cs.ubc.ca, jenns@psych.ubc.ca

ABSTRACT
There is increasing evidence that the effectiveness of information visualization techniques can be impacted by the particular needs and abilities of each user. This suggests that it is important to investigate information visualization systems that can dynamically adapt to each user. In this paper, we address the question of *how to adapt*. In particular, we present a study to evaluate a variety of visual prompts, called 'interventions', that can be performed on a visualization to help users process it. Our results show that some of the tested interventions perform better than a condition in which no intervention is provided, both in terms of task performance as well as subjective user ratings. We also discuss findings on how intervention effectiveness is influenced by individual differences and task complexity.

Author Keywords
User characteristics, Adaptive Information Visualization.

ACM Classification Keywords
H.5.m. Information interfaces and presentation (e.g., HCI): Miscellaneous.

INTRODUCTION
Recent advances in visualization research have shown that individual user needs, abilities and preferences can have a significant impact on user performance and satisfaction during visualization usage (e.g., [6][14][19][33]). It is therefore important to investigate the potential of user-adaptive visualizations, i.e., visualization techniques and systems that support the provision of visual information personalized to each user's needs and differences.

The benefits of user-adaptive interaction have been shown in a variety of human-computer interaction tasks and applications such as operation of menu based interfaces, web search, desktop assistance, and human learning [22]. There are three key decisions that need to be made when designing a user-adaptive system: (1) what to adapt to, i.e., understanding which user features should be considered for adaptation, including stable, long-term user traits (e.g., cognitive abilities, personality, etc.), as well as transitory, short-term states (e.g., current task, cognitive load, attention); (2) when to adapt, i.e., understanding when it is appropriate and/or necessary to provide adaptive support to the user; (3) how to adapt, i.e., understanding how adaptation should be provided.

In this paper, we focus primarily on this latter question in the context of designing user-adaptive visualizations. In information visualization, the only research we are aware of targeting the question of how to adapt is on *recommending alternative visualizations* based on specific user, data, or task features (e.g., [16][18]). By contrast, in this paper we focus on adaptive interventions aimed at *improving the effectiveness of the visualization a user is currently working with*. In particular, we evaluate a set of four alternative *highlighting* interventions aimed at supporting analytical interaction by directing the user's attention to a specific subset of data within a visualization, while still retaining the context of the data as a whole [12].

Highlighting can be extremely useful in any scenario in which an agent (a system or a human) needs to communicate to a user *several* points about a possibly large and complex dataset. For instance, in a dataset of car sales, two key points could be that *"more cars were sold this year in China than in India"* and that *"Europe sales have been decreasing in the last 3 years"*. In these scenarios, the ability to highlight subsets of the data would naturally support a more effective communication. While the whole dataset can be compactly conveyed with an appropriate visualization, the information relevant to each point can be synchronously highlighted as the key points are sequentially expressed in language (written or spoken). For instance, in our example, *sales for China and India* would be highlighted first, followed by *sales for European countries in the last 3 years.*

The ability to generate highlighting interventions would be especially useful in computer-human communication, for instance, when a system has automatically analyzed and derived insights from a complex dataset (e.g., [5][30]), and needs to communicate this to a user. This functionality may also be beneficial to support a user in inspecting human-generated presentations combining visualizations with

CHI 2014, April 26–May 1, 2014, Toronto, Ontario, Canada.

ACM 978-1-4503-2473-1/14/04...$15.00.
http://dx.doi.org/10.1145/2556288.2557141

[1] Author order is alphabetical except for last author.

textual material, which are quite common in documents ranging from newspaper articles to scientific papers. If a system could track what part of the text the reader is currently reading, and infer the corresponding point made (as it is being investigated in [10]), such a system could use one (or more) of the interventions evaluated in this paper to highlight the relevant visualization elements [7].

The interventions that we evaluated in our study were inspired by the analytical interaction techniques presented in Few [12] and by a taxonomy of post-hoc strategies for visual prompts presented by Mittal [26]. While both [12] and [26] provide valuable descriptions and taxonomies of different techniques, to the best of our knowledge there is no formal evaluation of which interventions may be most useful, both in general and under particular task/user contexts. The user study presented in this paper aims to answer the following research questions on the effectiveness of the four interventions that we target:

1. Can highlighting interventions improve information visualization processing?
2. Is there an intervention that is the most effective?
3. Are questions 1 & 2 above affected by individual user characteristics, by task complexity, and by when the interventions are delivered?

Generally speaking, if we find an intervention that is the most effective, it should be used whenever a system needs to draw the user's attention to a subset of the data. However, if intervention effectiveness is found to depend on the task and/or the user, the results of our study could inform adaptive highlighting for visualization support.

RELATED WORK

Three key decisions are involved in supporting user-adaptive interaction: *what to adapt to*, *when to adapt* and *how to adapt*. Deciding *what to adapt to* involves identifying which individual user features influence interaction performance enough to justify adaptation. In visualization, there are already results on the impact of a number of user characteristics on user performance and satisfaction. For example, user performance across different visualizations and task types has been linked to the cognitive measures of perceptual speed and spatial visualization ([6][33][37]), as well as to the personality trait of locus of control ([19][40]). Also, the cognitive abilities of visual/verbal working memory, as well as visualization expertise, have been shown to impact user satisfaction [33].

Addressing the decision of *when to adapt* involves formalizing adaptation strategies that identify those situations in which the benefits of providing adaptive interventions outweigh their cost (e.g., disrupting the interaction). *When to adapt* has been extensively investigated in fields such as Intelligent Tutoring [39] or Availability Management Systems [22]. In visualization, to our knowledge, [16] is the only work that actively monitors real-time user behavior in order to infer the need for intervention, although [7] describes a user study designed to capture instances of user confusion during visualization.

Addressing the question of *how to adapt*, which is the focus of this paper, has been studied outside information visualization to support, for example, display notifications [2], or hints provision [27]. In information visualization, researchers have so far focused on adaptivity that relates to suggesting alternative visualizations based on specific user or task features [16][18]. By contrast, in this paper we focus on interventions that relate to the current visualization.

Highlighting interventions are the most relevant techniques to our goal of devising dynamic interventions, because by definition they can be added to an existing visualization as needed to emphasize a specific aspect. Our sources of inspiration for highlighting interventions were Few [12] and Mittal [26]. Mittal [26] was especially useful, as it presents a taxonomy of post-hoc strategies for visual prompts, which is based on a detailed analysis of previous InfoVis literature [3][25], and on the analysis of several thousand charts in newspapers, magazines and business/governmental reports.

USER STUDY

We conducted a user study to investigate the effectiveness of four different highlighting interventions that can be used to emphasize specific aspects of a visualization. We also look at how this effectiveness may be impacted by task complexity, user differences, and delivery time. To keep the number of conditions manageable, we only studied one visualization: bar graphs (see Figure 1 for an example). We focused on bar graphs for three reasons. First, bar graphs are one of the most ubiquitous and effective information visualization techniques. Second, there is already research showing that performance with and preferences for this basic form of visualization is influenced by individual differences such as perceptual speed, visual working memory, and verbal working memory [6][33][37]. Thus, it can be beneficial to investigate how to provide visual interventions for different users who may be working sub-optimally with bar graphs. Finally, as we argue at the end of the paper, results on bar graphs are likely to generalize to other information visualizations.

Experimental Tasks

Tasks were performed via dedicated software. Each task consisted of presenting the participant with a bar graph along with a textual question relating to the displayed data. Participants would select their answer from a horizontal list of radio buttons and click 'Submit' to advance to the next task (see Figure 1). The study questions related to comparing individuals against a group average (data points in the bar graph) on a set of dimensions (data series in the bar graph). Since all tasks require comparisons to the average, the corresponding bar was given a fixed color (black) and position (leftmost) across all tasks (see Fig. 1). In contrast, the color of the other bars was varied from task to task, and selected at random from a set of four color schemes optimized using ColorBrewer [20].

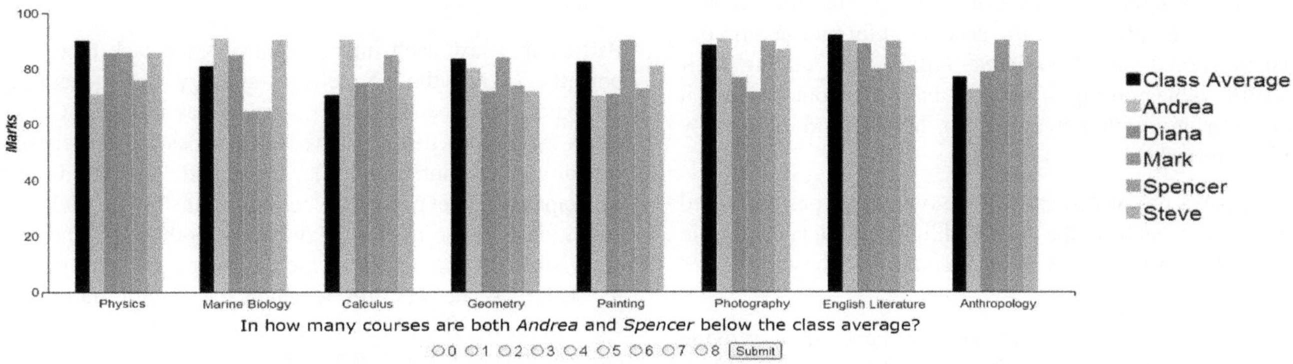

Figure 1. Example bar graph visualization as used in the experimental tasks.

For variety, the task questions were drawn from four different data sets: *i)* student grades by course; *ii)* movie revenue by city; *iii)* pet food nutritional values by vitamin and mineral content; and *iv)* company growth rates by business department. All tasks involved the same number of data points (six, including the average) and series dimensions (eight).

Task complexity was varied by making subjects perform two different types of task, chosen from a set of primitive data analysis tasks that Amar et al. [1] identified as "largely capturing people's activities while employing information visualization". The first task type was Retrieve Value (RV), described by Amar et al. [1] as "Given a set of specific cases, find attributes of those cases". This is one of the simplest task types in the Amar hierarchy, and thus it was selected to exemplify tasks of lower complexity. In our study, RV tasks required to retrieve a specific individual in the target domain and compare it against the group average (e.g., "Is Club Universe's revenue in Paris below the average movie revenue in that city?"). The second task type we chose was Compute Derived Value (CDV), defined in [1] as "Given a set of data cases, compute an aggregate numeric representation of those data cases". In our study, CDV tasks required users to first perform a set of comparisons, and then compute an aggregate of the comparison outcomes (e.g., "In how many departments is BioRestore above the average growth and Microfirm is below it? "). CDV tasks in our study are more complex than RV tasks because they require users to *i)* perform significantly more comparisons, *ii)* remember the comparison outcomes, and *iii)* compute an aggregate from the remembered comparisons.

Highlighting Interventions

Selected Interventions

Figure 2 shows the four highlighting interventions that were evaluated in the study, which are designed to guide a user's focus to a specific subset of data within the bar graph while still retaining the context of the data as a whole [12].

In our study, these interventions would highlight those bars that were relevant to answer the current question. For instance, the question "In how many cities are both Shark Swamp and Speed Freak above the average movie revenue?", the interventions would highlight the bars for Shark Swamp's revenue, Speed Freak's revenue, and the average movie revenue in each city. *Bolding* (Figure 2, top left) draws a thickened border around the relevant bars[2]. *De-Emphasis* (Figure 2, top right) fades all non-relevant bars. *Average Reference Lines* (Figure 2, bottom left) draws a horizontal line going from the top of the left-most bar (representing the average) to the last relevant bar, to facilitate comparison. *Connected Arrows* (Figure 2, bottom right) involves a series of connected arrows pointing downwards to the relevant bars.

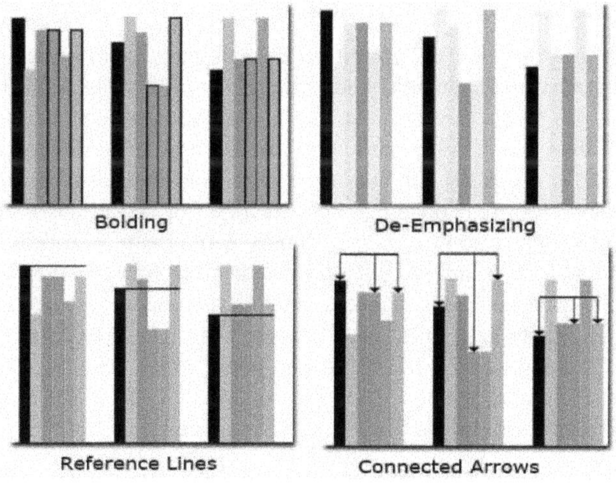

Figure 2. Interventions used in the study.

We focused on only four highlighting interventions to keep the number of conditions and trials within the limit of the available resources for this study. We selected the four interventions in Figure 2 because they were the most

[2] Notice that *Bolding* highlights the average only by thickening the bar, because of its black color. This is arguably not a serious confound, because the average is always relevant in the study tasks, and it was already made to stand out through its constant and distinctive color as well as a consistent leftmost position.

suitable to support our target tasks, as compared, for instance, to highlighting by *Color Change* (left out because color is already used to encode information in our visualizations), or to *Annotate Values*, i.e., adding their specific values on top of selected bars (left out because it can interfere with perceived bar height, and negatively affect our tasks).

Participants performed each of the two task types described earlier with each of the four highlighting interventions in Figure 2, as well as with *no intervention*, as a baseline.

Intervention timing

If highlighting interventions were to be used to provide real-time adaptive support, they would be superimposed on a visualization while the user is looking at it. This could possibly be disruptive, even if the adaptive system had a reliable mechanism to decide *when* the interventions should appear based on user needs. In this study, we wanted to evaluate the relative effectiveness of the selected interventions without this confound, as well as gain initial insights on whether this relative effectiveness changes when the interventions are provided dynamically. Thus, we added an experimental factor that varied *when* the interventions would be shown, consisting of two conditions, *Time zero* (T0) and *Time x* (TX).

In the **T0 condition**, the interventions are included in the bar graph from the beginning of the task, to evaluate them without the possible confound of the disruption that can be caused by a dynamic superimposition.

In contrast, the **TX condition** aims to gauge interventions' effectiveness when they are added dynamically. At the time of the study, however, we had no criterion implemented to decide when an intervention should appear based on a user's needs. Thus, we adopted a procedure designed to minimize the potential intrusiveness of an unjustified superimposition of visual prompts. Essentially, the idea is to add the visual prompts to the target bar graph as soon as the user has had a chance to look at both the bar graph and the related task question. This constraint is enforced in the TX condition by the following steps, which leverage the real-time gaze information provided by a Tobii T120 Eye-tracker installed on the experimental machine:

1. The bar graph appears, without the task question (and without intervention). It stays visible until a user has had a total of 5 eye fixations on the graph or more than 5 seconds have passed.
2. The graph disappears and the question text appears. The question stays visible until the user has had at least 6 fixations on it (2 fixations each in the first third, in the middle, and in the last third of the text), or more than 5 seconds have passed.
3. The graph reappears. At this point, the graph and question text are both visible.
4. After 500ms, the selected intervention is added. This slight delay aims to ensure that users recognize that the intervention is an added component to the graph they had seen so far.

Participants saw each intervention on each task type with both the T0 and the TX delivery strategy, thus generating 20 experimental conditions: 2 task types (RV vs. CDV), times 2 delivery times (T0 vs. TX), times 5 interventions (including no intervention). It should be noted that participants are expected to be slower in the TX delivery condition because of the delay before both graph and text are visible on the screen (which is necessary to complete the task). What we aim to understand with these two conditions is whether delivery time affects the *relative effectiveness* of the interventions.

User Characteristics Explored in the Study

The user characteristics investigated in this study include three cognitive abilities (perceptual speed, verbal and visual working memory), two measures of user visualization expertise with using bar graphs, as well as one personality trait (locus of control).

Perceptual speed (a measure of speed when performing simple perceptual tasks), visual working memory (a measure of storage and manipulation capacity of visual and spatial information), and verbal working memory (a measure of storage and manipulation capacity of verbal information) were selected because they were repeatedly shown to influence visualization performance or user satisfaction in studies involving bar graphs ([6][33][37]).

Besides cognitive abilities, the study in [33] also looked at the impact of visualization expertise, but results were inconclusive, possibly because they measured expertise via self-report questions asked *after* the experimental tasks. In this study, we aim to provide a more reliable investigation of the impact of user visualization expertise, not only on bar graph processing but also on the effectiveness of our visual interventions. We use two separate measures for expertise, captured in a pre-questionnaire: one that gauges user familiarity with simple bar graphs (*expertise-simple*) and one with complex ones (*expertise-complex*), elicited as described in the next section.

Locus of control (a measure of the degree to which individuals perceive outcomes as either a result from their own behavior, or from forces that are external to themselves) has been shown to impact user performance with visualizations other than bar graphs [19][40], e.g., list-like visualizations and visualizations with a strong containment metaphor. With this study we wanted to ascertain whether locus of control may also have an impact while interacting with simpler visualizations such as bar graphs and on the effectiveness of our visual interventions.

Study Procedure

62 subjects ranging in age from 18 to 42 participated in the experiment. We selected the number of participants by performing a power analysis [11] a priori on the parameters

of our experimental design, defined to detect a small effect size of at least $\eta_p^2 = .01$ with 0.8 power.

	Min	Max	Max Possible	Mean	Std. Dev.
Perceptual Speed	31	63	96	45.37	7.12
Verbal WM	3	6	6	4.69	.83
Visual WM	0	5.2	6.0	2.01	1.20
Locus of Control	3	22	23	11.40	4.18
Expertise - Basic	1	5	5	3.16	.772
Expertise - Complex	1	4	5	2.27	.813

Table 1. Descriptive statistics of user characteristics.

Participants were mostly recruited via dedicated systems at our university. This resulted in a variety of student participants from diverse backgrounds (e.g., Psychology, Forestry, Computer Science, Finance, Fine Art, German, Commerce). We also recruited 7 non-student participants such as a non-profit community connector, 3D artist, and air combat systems officer. Table 1 presents summary statistics on the user characteristics data collected from the study. A correlation analysis over our 6 user characteristics shows no significant correlations, except for a strong positive correlation ($r = 0.47$, $p < .01$) between *expertise-simple* and *expertise-complex*, and a weak negative correlation ($r = -0.27$, $p < .01$) between perceptual speed and locus of control. Because the expertise measures are highly correlated, we retain only *expertise-complex* as our measure of expertise for further analysis, given its higher variance.

The experiment was a within-subjects study, fitting in a single session lasting at most 90 minutes. There were 20 experimental conditions: 2 task types (RV vs. CDV), times 2 delivery times (T0 vs. TX), times 5 interventions (including no intervention). Participants were instructed to complete the tasks as quickly and accurately as possible. To account for within-subject variance, each participant repeated each condition 4 times, which is a well-established procedure in perceptual psychology experiments measuring performance in terms of time and accuracy [28][36]. Thus, there were a total of 80 trials per participant. To avoid participants getting bored, each of the four domains described earlier were randomly assigned to each task.

Participants began by filling out a pre-study questionnaire asking for demographic information as well as self-reported expertise with simple and complex bar graphs. *Expertise-simple* was elicited with the question *'How often do you look at simple Bar Graphs'*, followed by a basic bar graph with 8 bars (values for one series over 8 dimensions); *Expertise-complex* was elicited with the question *'How often do you look at complex Bar Graphs'*, followed by a graph with 48 bars (values for 6 series over 8 dimensions), as used for the experimental tasks. Both questions had five answer options: *i)* Never, *ii)* Rarely (several times a year), *iii)* Occasionally (several times a month), *iv)* Frequently (several times a week), *v)* Very frequently (several times a day). Participants then completed standard computer-based tests for Locus of Control [29], Verbal Working Memory [35], Visual Working Memory [15], and a paper-based test for Perceptual Speed [9]. Next, participants underwent a training phase to expose them to bar graphs, the study tasks, and the highlighting interventions. Then participants underwent a calibration phase for the eye-tracker, before starting the study trials. Participants then performed 40 of the 80 study trials, followed by a 5 minute break. After the break, the eye-tracker was re-calibrated and the participant performed the remaining 40 trials. The 80 trials were fully randomized in terms of experimental conditions (i.e., task complexity, intervention delivery time, interventions). The experimental software was fully automated and ran in a web-browser, with the visualizations and interventions programmed using the D3 visualization framework [8].

Lastly, participants took a post-questionnaire asking for their evaluations of each intervention's usefulness, as well as their relative preferences. The questionnaire included:

- 10 rating statements in the form of "I found the X intervention useful for performing Y tasks", for each intervention and task type (i.e., simple vs. complex). The statements were rated on a Likert scale from 1 to 5.
- 2 ranking statements in the form of "Please rank your preference of interventions for simple/complex tasks (order from 1 to 5) (1: most preferred, 5:least preferred)".

ANALYSIS OF TASK PERFORMANCE

We look at both task *completion time* and task *accuracy* as performance measures. *Completion time* was normally distributed (M=19.5s, SD=10.2), whereas task accuracy indicated a ceiling effect with 91.4% correct answers, possibly due to the tasks being generally easy to solve, or due to participants focusing on generating the correct answer, while sacrificing their time on task. The ceiling effect on accuracy arguably makes a separate analysis of this performance measure not very informative. We nevertheless did not want to discard accuracy altogether, because trials that were answered incorrectly should be penalized accordingly. We opted to use a combined score for task performance, known as Inverse Efficiency Score [34]. Given that participants repeated each experimental condition 4 times, *task performance* is calculated by averaging completion time for the trial repetitions that were performed correctly, and then dividing this score by the percentage of correct repetitions[3]. Task performance values thus calculated can be essentially interpreted as completion times penalized for incorrect trials (the lower the percentage of correct trials, the higher the adjusted average time on these trials). Thus, performance is reported in seconds and a higher score represents a lower performance.

[3] When there are no correct repetitions, leading to a divide-by-0 problem, the participant for that trial must be discarded from the analysis. In our study, only one participant's data was removed from the analysis for this reason.

We use a General Linear Model (GLM) repeated measures to analyze our performance data. We first run a 2 (task complexity) by 2 (delivery time) by 5 (intervention type) General Linear Model (GLM) repeated measures to investigate the effects of our experimental factors alone. Next, we analyze the effects of each of our five co-variates separately (perceptual speed, visual WM, verbal WM, locus of control, and expertise-complex), by running a GLM with the experimental factors and only that co-variate. Due to the high number of covariates in our study, this approach ensures that we do not overfit our models by including all co-variates at once. Each co-variate was discretized into three levels via a three-way split. *Low* represents the bottom quartile of the values distribution (i.e. lower 25%), *average* represents the values within the interquartile range (i.e., middle 50%), and *high* represents the upper quartile (top 25%). In the next sections, effect sizes (partial eta-squared) are reported as small for .01, medium for .09, and large as .25 [13]. All reported pairwise comparisons are corrected with the Bonferroni adjustment.

Results on Task Performance

Main Effects

We found main effects of task type, delivery time, intervention type, Perceptual Speed, and Verbal WM, as shown in Table 2.

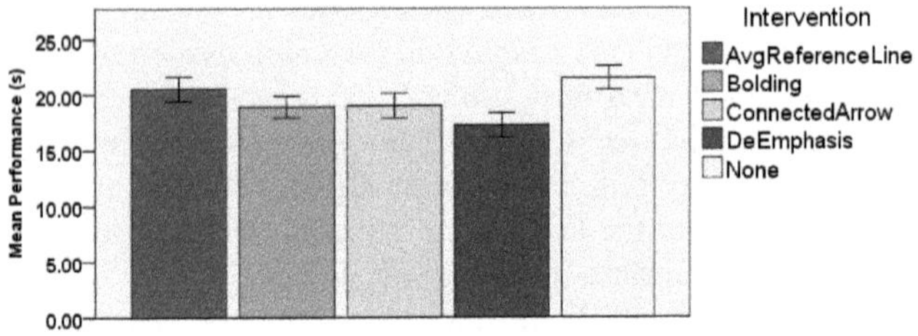

Figure 3. Performance score for each intervention. All bar graphs are shown with 95% confidence intervals.

Main Effect	F-Ratio	Effect Size	Sig. Value
Task Type	F(1,59) = 543.47	η_p^2= .902	p< .001
Delivery Time	F(1,59) = 1277.94	η_p^2= .956	p< .001
Intervention	F(4,236) = 44.44	η_p^2= .430	p< .001
Percep. Speed	F(1,58) = 10.02	η_p^2= .147	p < .01
VerbalWM	F(3,56) = 5.42	η_p^2= .225	p < .01

Table 2. Significant main effects on task performance.

The main effect of task type confirms the difference in complexity between the two task types in the study, with Compute Derived Value having longer task performance values (M=25.2s, SD=7.5) than the simpler Retrieve Value tasks (M=13.8s, SD= 5.3). The main effect of delivery time is to be expected because of the delay in answering the question generated by the TX condition, as discussed earlier. The average performance for TX was 22.7s (SD=7.8), as opposed to 16.3s (SD=8.2) for T0.

There was also a main effect of intervention type. As shown in Figure 3, performance was best for *De-Emphasis*, and worst for *None*, (i.e., no intervention provided). Pairwise comparisons show that interventions are significantly different from one another except for *Bolding* and *Connected Arrows*, and for *None* and *Avg. Ref. Lines*. This result indicates that all interventions, except for *Avg. Ref. Lines*, were helping users solve the selected tasks more efficiently than when they received no intervention. These results will be further qualified by interactions with task type and delivery time described in the next section.

The main effect and related pairwise comparisons for Perceptual Speed indicate that performance was similar for users with low Perceptual Speed (M=20.6s, SD=8.6) and average perceptual speed (M=20.3s, SD=9.3), whereas users with high perceptual speed were significantly better at completing tasks (M=17s, SD=6.7), hence confirming previous work [30]. The results for Verbal WM show similar directionality, except that the performance of users with low Verbal WM (M=24.1s, SD=12.0) was significantly worse than the scores of users in both the average group (M=19.4s, SD=8.4) and the high group (M=18.0s, SD=7.2). While [33] previously uncovered a link between Verbal WM and user preferences for different visualizations, and [32] has showed that low Verbal WM increases a user's gaze fixations on textual elements [30], our current result on Verbal WM is, to the best of our knowledge, the first to directly link this cognitive ability to task performance with information visualizations. The results for Perceptual Speed and Verbal Working memory will be further qualified by interactions with task type.

Interaction Effects

Table 3 shows a summary of the interaction effects.

Interaction Effect	F-Ratio	Effect Size	Sig. Value
Intervention*Task Type	F(4,236) = 8.65	η_p^2= .128	p< .001
Perceptual Speed*TaskType	F(1,58) = 8.64	η_p^2= .130	p < .01
VerbalWM*TaskType	F(3,56) = 5.79	η_p^2= .237	p < .01
VisualWM*TaskType	F(1,58) = 3.81	η_p^2= .062	p < .05
DeliveryTime* Intervention	F(4,236) = 7.56	η_p^2= .114	p < .01

Table 3. Significant interaction effects for task performance.

Intervention*TaskType: Figure 4 shows that, for both task types, *None* is the intervention with the worst performance and *De-Emphasis* the one with the best. Pairwise comparisons, however, show that for simple tasks (RV), all interventions are significantly different from one another and are better than *None*, whereas for complex tasks (CDV), *Avg. Ref. Lines* is no longer significantly better than *None*. A possible explanation is that *Avg. Ref. Lines* helps the comparisons with the average bar, but it does not highlight the elements to be compared as well as the other interventions, except in the case when they are contiguous to the average bar and to each other. This may become a greater disadvantage with the more complex comparisons involved in our CDV tasks.

Additionally, there are no-longer significant differences between *Bolding* and *De-Emphasis*, nor among *Bolding, Connected Arrows*, and *Avg. Ref. Lines,* indicating that for more complex tasks, the relative performance between the interventions is less pronounced. For instance, feedback we gathered from participants indicates that *De-Emphasis* can make it hard to see bar groupings. Even though *Bolding* and *De-Emphasis* can be considered conceptually similar (emphasizing relevant bars vs. de-emphasizing non-relevant bars), it is possible that for complex tasks, the fading of 'irrelevant bars' removes some contextual cues for sample grouping, which would help solve the tasks (e.g., when many bars in the middle of a group are faded out, the outermost bars of a group may look disconnected).

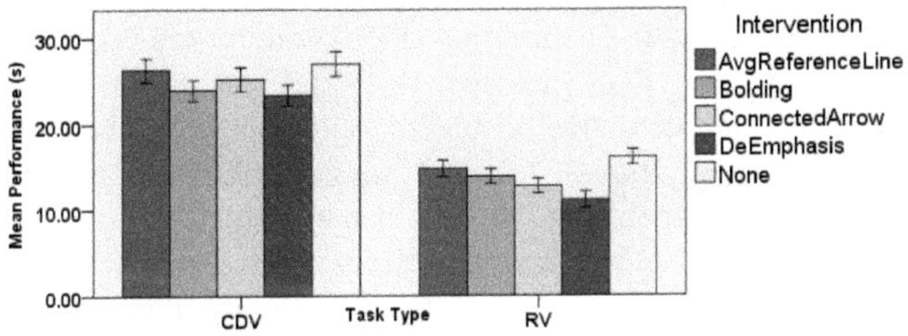

Figure 4. Interaction between Interventions and Task Type.

Perceptual Speed*TaskType, VerbalWM*TaskType, VisualWM*TaskType: There was no significant difference in performance with RV tasks for users with different values of Perceptual Speed, VerbalWM, and VisualWM. For CDV tasks, in contrast, users with higher values of these cognitive measures perform better. Figure 5 shows the interactions for Perceptual Speed and Verbal Working Memory.

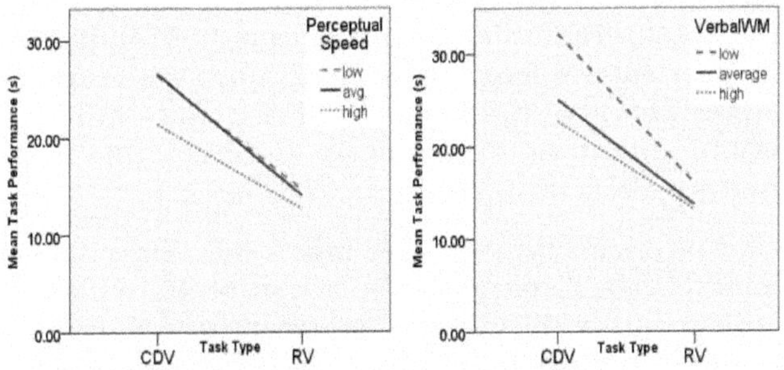

Figure 5. Interaction between: Perceptual Speed and Task Type (left); VerbalWM and Task Type (right).

The trends for Visual Working Memory are very similar to those in Figure 5. These results are likely due to the fact that CDV tasks requires processing and remembering more of the visual elements (bars, interventions, etc.) and more of the verbal information on the graph (i.e., legend items, labels, etc.). Thus, for CDV tasks, higher values of the cognitive measures may be having a stronger impact compared to RV tasks. The result for perceptual speed aligns with results in previous work [33], where it was also found that users with lower perceptual speed require more time to complete a complex task relative to their high perceptual speed counterparts. For visual and verbal working memory, this study is the first to connect these two cognitive traits to task performance (as opposed to user preferences) with a visualization, possibly because previous studies relied on tasks that were not complex enough to detect these effects.

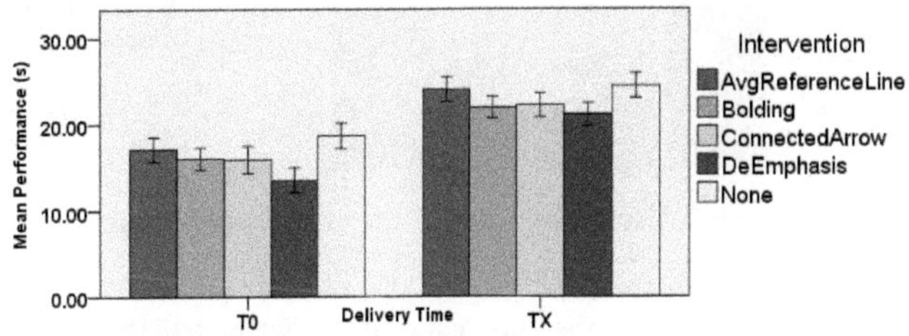

Figure 6. Interaction between Delivery Time and Interventions on task performance.

Delivery Time*Intervention: This interaction effect is shown in Figure 6 and indicates that for T0, *None* and *De-Emphasis* are, respectively, significantly worse and better than all other interventions (with no other significant differences). For TX, the difference between interventions are much smaller, with *Avg. Ref. Lines* no longer being significantly better than *None*, and *Bolding* and *Connected Arrows* no longer being worse than *De-Emphasis*. This result is important, because it suggests that when interventions are delivered dynamically, they may lose some of their value due to possible intrusiveness, and thus it is crucial to evaluate them in the right context of usage. On the other hand, even in the potentially intrusive TX condition, some interventions are still better than none, indicating that it is possible to provide dynamic adaptive interventions that can help improve effectiveness.

ANALYSIS OF SUBJECTIVE MEASURES

As we did for performance measures, we first ran a 2 (task type) x 5 (intervention) General Linear Model repeated measures on the usefulness *ratings* in order to investigate the effects of our experimental factors alone, followed by additional analyses on each of our five co-variates with the experimental factors. These ratings were corrected using the Aligned Rank Transformation (ART)-Tool [38] to make them suitable for parametric analysis. Results from this analysis are shown in Table 4. A similar set of analyses on the preference *rankings* yielded no significant results.

There was a significant main effect of intervention on usefulness ratings, shown in Figure 7. Pairwise comparisons reveal that all of the intervention ratings were significantly different from one-another (except for *Connected Arrows* and *Bolding*), and that all interventions were better than *None.*

Results	F-Ratio	Effect Size	Sig. Value
Intervention	$F(4,236) = 100.23$	$\eta_p^2 = .629$	$p < .001$
VisualWM* Intervention	$F(4,224) = 2.34$	$\eta_p^2 = .040$	$p < .05$

Table 4. Significant effects for intervention usefulness ratings.

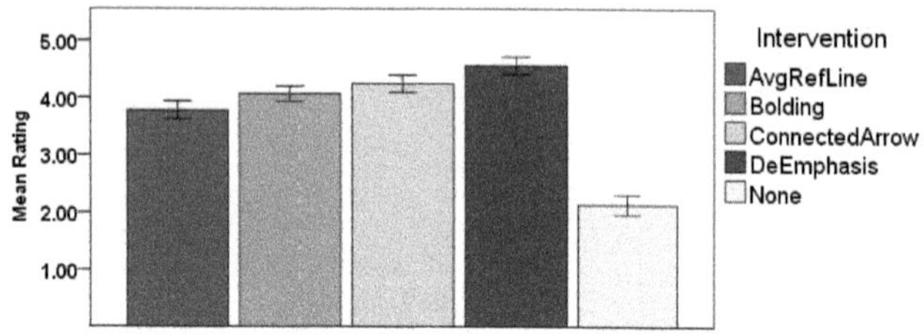

Figure 7. Usefulness ratings for each Intervention.

This main effect and the trends of the relative ratings between interventions correspond exactly to those for intervention on task performance found in the previous section (see Figure 3), showing a strong connection between objective and subjective effectiveness of the tested interventions. It is also worth noting that users found all the interventions more useful than no intervention, regardless of task type. This was not the case for task performance. There was, however, an interaction between intervention type and visual WM, as shown in Figure 8.

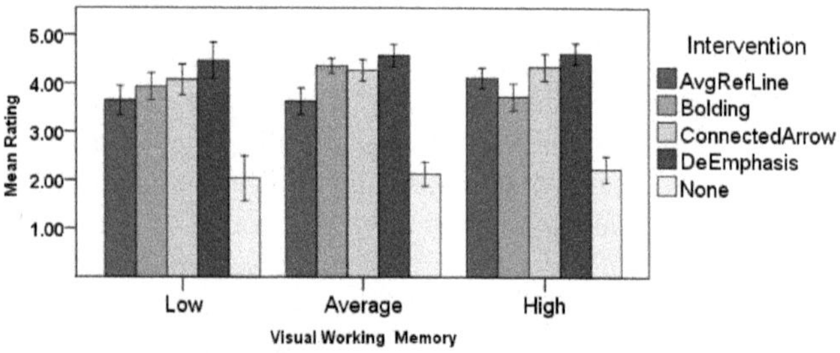

Figure 8. Usefulness ratings by VisualWM levels.

This is in line with previous work linking Visual WM to user subjective (preference) scores [32]. Pairwise comparisons show that users with either low or average Visual WM rated the usefulness of *Avg. Ref Lines* significantly lower than users with high Visual WM. A possible explanation for this result is that the added reference lines may have been 'visual distractors' for lower Visual WM users, given that the lines do not run only through the relevant bars, but also through any other bars between the average and the last relevant bar. We also find that users with average Visual WM rate *Bolding* significantly higher than users with either low or high Visual WM. While this finding further confirms the influence of Visual WM on subjective ratings, we currently do not have an intuition as to the directionality of the result.

DISCUSSION AND CONCLUSIONS

The goal of our study was to investigate the relative effectiveness of four visual prompts designed to support users in visualization processing by highlighting visualization elements relevant to performing target tasks. As we discussed in the introduction, this functionality can be extremely useful for scenarios in which users need to make a variety of inferences on a visualized dataset, and may benefit from having the most relevant subsets of graph elements emphasized in turn.

Although in our study, to keep the number of conditions manageable, we only considered one type of information visualization, i.e., bar graphs, there are at least three different arguments that support the potential generality of our results to other visualizations (but of course, generalizations should be eventually corroborated by empirical evidence). First, bar graphs are one of the most popular visualizations because they rely on length and 2-D position, the only two pre-attentive attributes that can be perceived quantitatively with a high degree of precision [12]. Thus, results on bar graphs can arguably generalize to other popular visualizations that rely on the same pre-attentive attributes, like line-graphs and scatter-plots. Second, since bar graphs are so effective and popular they have been used as building blocks of more complex visualizations. For instance, [17] recently presented LineUp, an interactive visualization supporting the very common and critical task of ranking items based on multiple heterogeneous. As another example, ValueCharts [4] is a visualization that has been applied to elicit user preferences in decision making in different domains, as well as a component of a sophisticated interface to query event sequences. We argue that our results may well generalize to these more complex and extremely useful visualizations based on bar graphs. Third, most of the interventions considered in the paper can be applied to other visualizations besides bar graphs. Thus, our results may well generalize also to these visualizations. For example, [24] demonstrated several example applications of reference line, bolding, and de-emphasis in pie charts and line charts in addition to bar graphs. Average reference lines have been used to visually compare individual marks to a predetermined value in various charts [26][24]. Bolding and de-emphasis form a perceptual group based on the Gestalt principle of similarity [24] and thus have been applied in various visualizations to relate items (e.g., TreeMap, Scatter Plot Matrix, Arc diagram [21]).

We now discuss the user study results with respect to our original research questions. In the study we wanted to ascertain (1) if highlighting interventions can improve visualization processing; (2) if there is a highlighting intervention that is the most effective, and (3) if questions 1 & 2 are affected by user characteristics, task complexity, and intervention timing. We investigated these questions in the context of performing visual tasks with bar graphs.

As for question 1, our results show that all the highlighting interventions we tested, except for *Avg. Ref Lines*, can improve visualization processing compared to receiving no interventions, both in terms of task performance and a user's perceived usefulness. Thus, these interventions should be further investigated as means of providing users with dynamic support during visualization tasks.

As for question 2, results show that no single highlighting intervention is the most effective in general. *De-Emphasis* always performed at the top, in terms of both performance and rated usefulness, but it was absolute best only with the simpler RV tasks, and when it was present from the beginning of the task (delivery condition T0).

Hence, we did find significant effects of task complexity and delivery time on intervention effectiveness (question 3). When considering task performance, there was no longer a significant difference between *De-Emphasis* and *Bolding* during complex tasks, or among *De-Emphasis*, *Bolding* and *Connected Arrows* when the interventions were delivered dynamically. For the long-term goal of providing adaptive highlighting interventions, this latter result suggests that future studies should focus on further investigating the effectiveness of *De-Emphasis*, *Bolding* and *Connected Arrows* in dynamic delivery conditions, and in particular in conjunction with delivery criteria based on actual user needs (e.g., at the onset of *confusion* as suggested in [7]). It is already a very encouraging result however, that delivering the interventions dynamically did not neutralize their effectiveness compared to no intervention, suggesting that their benefits outweigh their potential intrusiveness.

Still in relation to question 3, we also found an impact of user characteristics, in terms of an effect of Visual WM on ratings for perceived intervention usefulness. This result is in line with previous findings that Visual WM affects subjective ratings for visualizations [33]. Our results suggest that, if information on a user's Visual WM is available, higher perceived usefulness may be achieved by using *Bolding* as a highlighting intervention for users with average Visual WM.

Interesting effects of individual differences were also found when analyzing the interaction with task complexity for task performance. In particular, for each of the three cognitive abilities tested in the study, we found no significant difference in performance among participants with different levels of these abilities for simple tasks (RV). In contrast, for complex tasks (CDV) participants with high measures performed significantly better, indicating that complexity can significantly impact user performance depending on cognitive abilities. Similar results were found in previous work for Perceptual Speed [33], but this is the first study that extends them to Visual and Verbal WM, likely because of the increased complexity of our tasks.

The implication for user-adaptive visualizations is that participants with low-medium cognitive measures would benefit the most from help such as adaptive interventions. The fact that there were no interaction effects between cognitive abilities and the different highlighting interventions targeted in the study suggests that perhaps other types of interventions should be explored to help users with low-medium cognitive measures. For instance, previous work linking gaze patterns to performance when processing bar graphs [33], suggests that users with low Perceptual Speed may benefit from help in processing a graph's legend, whereas users with low Verbal WM may benefit from interventions that facilitate processing of the verbal elements of a graph.

Also to note, we did not find any significant results for the personality trait Locus of Control. A likely explanation is that most findings for this user characteristic were found when comparing list-like visualizations and visualizations with a strong containment metaphor [19], which were not the target of our interventions. We also did not find any significant results for the visualization expertise measures we collected from users. This could be due to the fact that some users were possibly biased when self-reporting their expertise, or that previous expertise was not a relevant factor with regard to a user's performance/preference with the visualization tasks administered in our study.

Our next step involves an analysis of user eye gaze behavior in order to verify and better qualify our findings, and to suggest further interventions for adaptive help. We also plan to run similar experiments on more complex visualizations and on a broader set of interventions.

REFERENCES

1. Amar, R.A., Eagan J., & Stasko, J.T. Low-Level Components of Analytic Activity in Information Visualization. 16th IEEE Info. Vis. Conf., 15-21, 2005.
2. Bartram, L., Ware, C., & Calvert, T. Moticons: detection, distraction and task. Int. J. Hum.-Comput. Stud. 58(5), 515-545, 2003.
3. Bertin, J. Semiology of Graphics. University of Wisconsin Press, 1983.
4. Carenini, G., Loyd, J. Valuecharts: Analyzing Linear Models Expressing Preferences and Evaluations. In Proc. of the working conf. on Advanced visual interfaces, 150–157, 2004.
5. Carenini G. & Rizoli L. A Multimedia Interface for Facilitating Comparisons of Opinions. Proc. 13th Int. Conf. on Intelligent User Interfaces, IUI 2009, 325-334.
6. Conati, C. & Maclaren, H. Exploring the Role of Individual Differences in Information Visualization. In Proc. Conf. on Advanced Vis. Interf., 199-206, 2008.
7. Conati, C., Hoque, E., Toker, D., & Steichen, B. When to Adapt: Detecting User's Confusion During Visualization Processing. Proc. 1st Int. Workshop on User-Adaptive Inf. Vis. (WUAV 2013), in conj. with UMAP 2013.

8. D3 javascript library. http:// http://d3js.org/.
9. Ekstrom, R., French, J., Harman, H. & Dermen, D, Manual from Kit of Factor-References Cognitive Tests. Educational Testing Service, Princeton, NJ, 1976.
10. Elzer, S., Carberry, S., & Zukerman, I. The automated understanding of simple bar charts. Artificial Intelligence Journal 175(2), 526-555, 2011.
11. Erdfelder, E., Faul, F., & Buchner, A. GPOWER: A general power analysis program. Behavior Research Methods, Instruments, & Computers, 28, 1-11, 1996.
12. Few, S. Now You See It: Simple Visualization Techniques for Quantitative Analysis, First Edition. Analytics Press, 2009.
13. Field, A., & Hole, G., How to Design and Report Experiments. Sage Publications, London, 2003.
14. Flatla, D.R., Gutwin, C. SSMRecolor: Improving Recoloring Tools with Situation-Specific Models of Color Differentiation. Proc. of Human factors in computing systems, CHI 2012, 2297-2306.
15. Fukuda, K., & Vogel, E.K. Human variation in overriding attentional capture. J. of Neurosc., 8726-8733, 2009.
16. Gotz D., & Wen, Z.. Behavior Driven Visualization Recommendation. Proc. Conf. on Intelligent User Interfaces, IUI 2009, 315-324.
17. Gratzl, S., Lex, A., Gehlenborg, N., Pfister, H., & Streit, M. LineUp: Visual Analysis of Multi-Attribute Rankings. Visualiz. & Comp. Graph., 2277-2286, 2013.
18. Grawemeyer, B. Evaluation of ERST – an external representation selection tutor. Proc. Conf. on Diagrammatic Represent. and Inference, 154-167, 2006.
19. Green, T. M. & Fisher, B. Towards the personal equation of interaction: The impact of personality factors on visual analytics interface interaction. In IEEE Visual Analytics Sc. and Technology, 203-210, 2010.
20. Harrower, M. & Brewer C. Colorbrewer.org: an online tool for selecting colour schemes for maps. The Cartographic Journal 40.1, 27-37, 2003.
21. Heer, J., Bostock, M., Ogievetsky, V. A Tour through the Visualization Zoo. Communications of the ACM, 53(6), 59-67, 2010.
22. Jameson, A. "Adaptive Interfaces and Agents" in Human-Computer Interface Handbook, eds J.A. Jacko and A. Sears, 305-330, 2003.
23. Kaptein, M.C., Nass, C., & Markopoulos, P. Powerful and Consistent Analysis of Likert-Type Rating Scales. Proc. Conf. on Human factors in Comp. Sys., CHI 2010, 2391-2394.
24. Kong, N., Agrawala, M. Graphical Overlays: Using Layered Elements to Aid Chart Reading. Visualization and Computer Graphics, 2631-2638, 2012.
25. Kosslyn, S.M. Elements of Graph Design. W.H. Freeman and Company, 1994.
26. Mittal, V.O. Visual Prompts and Graphical Design: A Framework for Exploring the Design Space of 2-D Charts and Graphs. Proc. AAAI/IAAI, 57-63, 1997.
27. Muir, M. & Conati, C.: An Analysis of Attention to Student – Adaptive Hints in an Educational Game. Proc. Intelligent Tutoring Systems, 112–122, 2012.
28. Palmer, E.M., Horowitz, T.S., Torralba A., Wolfe, J. What Are the Shapes of Response Time Distributions in Visual Search? J. of Exp. Psy.: Human Percep. and Perf., 37(1), 57-71, 2011.
29. Rotter, Julian B. Generalized Expectancies for Internal Versus External Control of Reinforcement. Psych. Monographs: General and Applied 80.1, 1-28, 1966.
30. Skytree Adviser. http://www.skytree.net/products-services/adviser-beta/faq/.
31. Steichen, B., Carenini, G., Conati, C. User-Adaptive Information Visualization - Using eye gaze data to infer visualization tasks and user cognitive abilities. Proc. Conf. on Intelligent User Interfaces, IUI 2013, 317-328.
32. Toker, D., Conati, B., Steichen, Carenini, G. Individual User Characteristics and Information Visualization: Connecting the Dots through Eye Tracking. Proc. Conf. on Human Factors in Comp. Sys., CHI 2013, 295-304.
33. Toker, D., Conati, C., Carenini, G., & Haraty, M. Towards Adaptive Information Visualization: On the Influence of User Characteristics. Proc. Conf. on User Model., Adapt., and Personaliz., UMAP 2012, 274-285.
34. Townsend, J. T., & Ashby, F. G. (1983). Stochastic modelling of elementary psychological processes. London: Cambridge University Press.
35. Turner, M. L., & Engle, R.W. Is working memory capacity task dependent? Journal of Memory and Language, 28(2), 127-154, 1989.
36. Van Zandt, T. How to fit a response time distribution. Psychonomic Bulletin & Review, 7(3), 424-465, 2002.
37. Velez, M.C., Silver, D., & Tremaine, M. Understanding visualization through spatial ability differences. Proc. of Visualization, 511-518, 2005.
38. Wobbrock, J., Findlater, L., Gergle, D., & Higgins, J. The Aligned Rank Transform for Nonparametric Factorial Analyses Using Only ANOVA Procedures. Proc. Conf. on Human Factors in Comp. Sys., CHI 2011, 143-146.
39. Wolf, B.P. Building Intelligent Interactive Tutors: Student-Centered Strategies for Revolutionizing E-Learning. Morgan Kaufmann Publishers Inc., 2008.
40. Ziemkiewicz, C., Crouser, R.J., Yauilla, A.R., Su, S.L., Ribarsky, W., & Chang, R. How Locus of Control Influences Compatibility with Visualization Style. Proc. of IEEE VAST 2011, 81-90.

Exertion in the Small: Improving Differentiation and Expressiveness in Sports Games with Physical Controls

Mike Sheinin and Carl Gutwin
Department of Computer Science, University of Saskatchewan
110 Science Place, Saskatoon, Saskatchewan, Canada
mike.sheinin@usask.ca gutwin@cs.usask.ca

ABSTRACT

Many sports video games contain elements such as running or throwing that are based on real-world physical activities, but the translation of these activities to game controllers means that the original physicality is lost. This results in games where players have limited opportunity to improve their physical skills, where there is little differentiation in people's physical abilities, and where skills do not change over the course of a game. To explore ways of adding these elements back into sports games, we developed two games with small-scale physical controls for running and throwing – one game was a simple running race, and one was a team-based handball-style game called Jelly Polo. In two studies (three track-and-field tournaments for the running game, and a four-week league for Jelly Polo), we observed the effects of physical controls on gameplay. Our studies showed that the physical controls enabled substantial individual differences in running and passing skill, allowed people to increase their expertise over time, and led to fatigue-based changes in performance during a game. Physical controls increased the games' challenge, complexity, and unpredictability, and dramatically improved player interest, expressiveness, and enjoyment. Our work shows that game designers should consider the idea of 'exertion in the small' as a way to improve play experience in games based on physical activities.

Author Keywords

Sports video games, physical controls, exertion games

ACM Classification Keywords

H.5.2. Information interfaces (HCI): Interaction techniques

INTRODUCTION

Many video games contain elements that are based on physical activities (e.g., running, throwing, jumping, or kicking), and sports games in particular are strongly based on physicality. Sports games have many complexities, and players can build up considerable amounts of expertise in them – but the nature of this expertise is usually very *un*like that of the original sport. This is because games must translate a real-world physical activity to an action that can be carried out with an Xbox-style game controller, and in the translation, the physicality of the original activity is lost.

CHI 2014, April 26–May 1, 2014, Toronto, Ontario, Canada.

ACM 978-1-4503-2473-1/14/04...$15.00. http://dx.doi.org/10.1145/2556288.2557385

For example, one main element of many real-world games is bodily movement such as running. Running in many sports video games is translated to a rate-controlled joystick action (i.e., press the stick to move the on-screen character) or a fixed-rate keyboard action (i.e., press and hold the WASD keys to move). This changes the activity of running from a repeated large-muscle action with substantial physical demands, to small fixed movements of the fingers and hand on a controller. In addition, this translation changes a complex multi-degree-of-freedom action to a simpler rate-controlled action where velocity is a function of the system rather than a function of player effort.

A second example involves throwing skill. In the real world, passing is a precision skill that requires substantial practice, but in many sports games, passing is translated into an action that is at least partially controlled by the computer (e.g., direction and distance are automatically set or adjusted so that a pass will go to a teammate).

These kinds of translations between physical activities and controller actions are present in almost all sports games (and many other avatar-based games as well). However, this approach presents three drawbacks for sports games:

- There is limited opportunity for expertise development. Although there are many ways for a player to increase their skill in a sports game, there is little opportunity for improvement of basic actions like running or throwing. In contrast, improvement in basic physical skills is a foundation for expertise in real-world sports.
- There is little differentiation between players in terms of basic actions like running and passing, and thus little opportunity to use these differences in the game. In contrast, success in real-world sports often revolves around individual differences (e.g., taking advantage of a mismatch with an opponent's physical capabilities, or setting up a team to capitalize on individual strengths and minimize individual weaknesses).
- Third, the artificial simplicity of controller actions means that there is no change in a player's physical capabilities over the course of a game. In real-world sports, effort-based factors such as fatigue clearly set apart better players and teams from weaker ones – e.g., many games are won and lost when the team with more endurance takes advantage of the other team's fatigue.

Overall, these drawbacks reduce the richness and realism of sports video games. Although some games can add other types of richness (e.g., difficulty levels for computer players, minigames such as fighting in a hockey game, or 'manager modes'), the core play experience of a sports game is often limited by these problems.

In this paper we investigate the idea of adding physicality back into controller-based movement in order to add expressiveness and player differentiation back into sports video games. We maintained the basic play environment, with standard controllers and settings, but added two kinds of physical control: *impulse-based movement*, where each physical action on the controller only moves the character a small amount (similar to taking a single step); and *high-precision throwing*, where control input has a detailed relationship to the direction and distance of a throw.

To test the idea of physical controls in sports video games, we developed two games and ran two studies. The first game was a track-and-field running game called Track and Field Racing (TaFR), where two players race each other in a simulated 100m, 200m, or 400m race. Players controlled the running movement by alternately pressing two keys on the keyboard, as fast as possible, with their first and second fingers. We ran three track meets with TaFR to see whether the physical controls led to individual differences and to performance changes over time. Our study clearly showed both of these effects – physical controls appeared to greatly increase the complexity and unpredictability of the game.

Our second game – called Jelly Polo – was a three-on-three top-down ball game loosely based on European Handball. Discrete movement in Jelly Polo involves repeatedly tapping the left joystick of a game controller in the desired direction; precise throwing involves pushing the right joystick in a particular direction and by a particular amount. To explore the effects of these controls on gameplay, we ran a four-week 'Jelly Polo league' with four persistent teams of three people. We found substantial evidence that the physical controls changed all three of the issues identified above: first, people's basic skills in discrete running and precise throwing increased over the four weeks; second, there was considerable individual skill difference across the twelve players, and both people and teams had to adjust to accommodate these differences; and third, fatigue played a major role in the gameplay – it directly affected player speed, and led to novel team strategies and exploitation of fatigue-based mismatches.

Our work builds on existing foundations of exertion-based interfaces (e.g., [12, 14, 17]), but looks specifically at 'exertion in the small,' with physical actions of hands and fingers. We make four novel contributions:

- we show that small-scale effort-based control can add considerable complexity and unpredictability to simple actions such as running and movement;
- we show that providing more expressive input provides increased opportunities for expertise (and differentiation in expertise) for both movement and throwing actions;
- we show that physical controls can add interest, challenge, and enjoyment to simple team games;
- we show that fatigue can be a valuable design principle that can dramatically change the way that gameplay evolves, and the ways that teams develop strategy.

Overall, our work suggests that designers of games based on physical actions (and sports games in particular), should consider 'exertion in the small' as an idea that can improve player experience and player satisfaction.

RELATED WORK

Exertion Interfaces and Exergames

A large body of work studies exertion interfaces and their use in games (e.g., [9, 11, 13, 15]). An exertion interface is one that requires some form of physical effort [11], and an exertion game (or exergame) is one in which the player purposely expends physical effort through an exertion interface [16]. These systems have two main goals: first, to create healthier lifestyles and reduce health problems associated with lack of exercise [15]; and second, to use the experience of exertion as a factor in game design – for example, bringing the idea of contact sports into distributed video games [13]. It is important to note, however, that health benefits or exercise (although common in many exergames) are not requirements for the genre.

The majority of previous work looks at full-body interfaces and substantial amounts of exercise and fatigue [11, 12, 14]. Full-body exergames can often be very tiring, and players can get fatigued after a short amount of time. Previous researchers have often accommodated player fatigue by adding elements to their systems that are outside the games themselves – for example, providing rest breaks, or reducing the length of game sessions [11]. One example of this is Mueller's Remote Impact [12] where players have to punch, kick and slam into a mattress on which is projected the silhouette of a remote player. The harder the impact the player can create, the more points they receive [13]. This design requires substantial exertion, and players need breaks in order to play for extended periods of time.

Mueller's taxonomy of exergames (Figure 1) divides the design space into exertion or non-exertion games, competitive or non-competitive exergames, parallel or non-parallel competitive exergames, and finally combat or object-based, non-parallel competitive exergames [16].

There is little work in this area that focuses on fatigue in non-full-body interaction, although a few projects have considered exertion that uses only a specific part of the body. For example, Mueller's MouseGrip system [17] is a low cost input device which fits in the hand and affords a squeezing action to produce exertion. This exertion interface is meant to be small and discreet so users can use it without taking up any extra space. The MouseGrip is intended to make mundane tasks more enjoyable and can even be used for simple games.

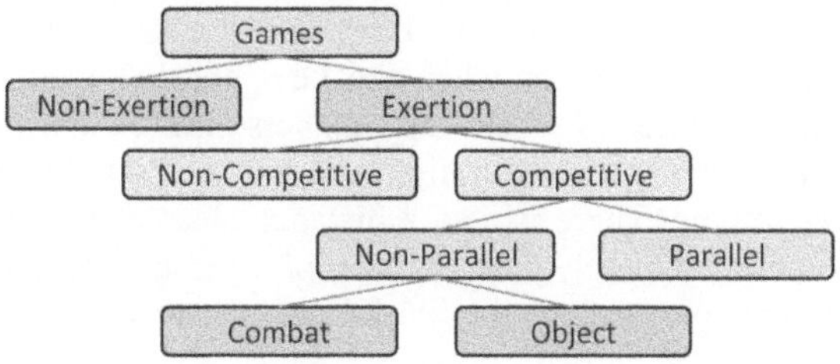

Figure 1. Exergame Taxonomy (adapted from [16]).

Commercial Exergames

Physical activity in commercial video games is now becoming common through the use of new input devices like the Nintendo WiiMote, the Xbox Kinect, and the Playstation Move. Several games make use of the capabilities of these devices for game mechanics such as swinging rackets or swords (e.g., "Wii Sports"), or jumping (e.g., "Kinect Adventures"). The "Mario & Sonic at the Olympic Games" title for the Wii uses physical control almost exclusively – for example, running events involve the player swinging both arms in a running motion as fast as possible. Other events like swimming are controlled in a similar fashion.

Some sports video games also have an option to use physical controls (e.g., Madden football for the Wii). However, this mode of interaction has not been very successful for the sports genre: for example, Madden'08 sold triple the number of units for Xbox as it did for Wii [4]. Nintendo also introduced their "All-Play" series of sports games in 2008 where all controls were physical. This series was not a market success, suggesting that sports gamers prefer traditional platforms and devices.

These commercial games are similar to previous exergame research in two ways. First, the physical activity involves large movements of the arms or legs – players must clear the space around them to play the game. Second, the activities generally involve short bursts of exertion rather than sustained effort – that is, quick-as-possible movements for a short amount of time that do not involve longer-term fatigue when done in isolation.

In contrast, our research focuses on *small-scale exertion*, which we define as exertion that uses small movements and small muscle groups – for example, fingers, hands, and feet. Small-scale exertion has the advantage that it does not require a large space, and can be integrated into traditional game settings where people use standard controllers and sit in groups in front of a display.

There are very few examples of this type of exertion interface in commercial games – but one game of interest is the "Olympic Games" series for the Xbox or Playstation platforms. Unlike the Wii version, here players can control the game with a standard controller. Running a race in "Beijing 2008" involves pressing two controller buttons back and forth as fast as possible (much like our TaFR game discussed below). Interestingly, a newer game in the series ("London 2012") changed the control style so that races are not as fatiguing: instead of pressing as fast as possible, the player must maintain a rhythm in their presses.

Sports Video Games and Electronic Sports

Sports video games – including titles like Madden Football, EA NHL and NBA, and FIFA Soccer – are the third-largest game genre by units sold (15.3% of all video games), with revenue of $US 1.8bn in 2012 [3, 8]. Despite this popularity, there is little research into sports games.

One large study was performed recently (2012) to find out who plays sports games. An online survey asked 1718 participants what kind of players play sports video games and their habits concerning sports in general. The survey found that 98.4% of sports video game players are males, mostly in their mid-20s. The study also supported a widespread belief that sports gamers are also sports fans with 93.3% self-identifying with this statement [19].

Research has also shown that playing sports video games can improve performance in the real-world sport counterpart [2]. In addition, previous knowledge of a sport can affect success in playing sports video games [10]. This research also states that not much work has been performed concerning individual differences, and this is an area that should be further explored.

Electronic Sports (eSports) is another area that has recently gained popular attention – eSports are professional sport-like competitions using video games that are broadcast over the Internet [1].These competitions are much like real sports, in that players train, gain expertise, and compete at high levels. Some research in the area of eSports is about new interaction techniques to help with high-level performance [6], and different broadcasting techniques to showcase the competition [1]. The most common genres played professionally are multiplayer online battle arena (MOBA), real-time strategy (RTS), fighting games, and first-person shooters [20]. There is little to no recognition of sports video games being included in the area of eSports; however, professional eSports players have recently been officially granted 'professional athlete' status by the U.S. government in order to obtain visas to play in the U.S. [5].

A CONTROL SCHEME FOR PHYSICAL ACTIONS

There are many possible ways to map movement control to the available capabilities of a computer input device. Researchers have defined several properties of devices and the input relationship, including the property sensed, state sensed, and number of dimensions sensed [7]. For example, a keyboard key senses only state (up/down) and a single dimension; a joystick on a game controller senses position in two dimensions, but no state.

We designed physical control schemes for two activities - movement and throwing. Movement was designed for both a keyboard (TaFR) and a game controller (Jelly Polo), and our goal was to mimic the physical effort needed to sustain movement in the real world. Real-world movement is based on repeated actions that provide a kinetic impulse to the body - taking one step moves the body by a certain amount. An impulse has both a direction and a magnitude, and the result of the impulse is an increase in velocity that fades over time. If another impulse is received before velocity reaches zero, higher velocities can be attained. Discrete versions of impulse-style controls were common in early handheld games (e.g., Mattel Football), where pressing direction buttons moved an on-screen character by one unit.

Impulse-based control can be implemented in several ways. On the keyboard used in TaFR, we used repeated alternating keypresses as the impulse signal - the magnitude of the impulse was fixed, and no direction was needed as the game involves a straight-line race. In Jelly Polo, we developed a more complex control scheme using the joystick of a game controller: each push of the joystick with the thumb represents a single impulse, with the amount of displacement providing the magnitude value, and the 2D position of the joystick providing the direction. Controller joysticks automatically return to centre, allowing the next impulse to be initiated immediately.

Precision throwing requires that the user control two values: direction and distance. The properties of a joystick can be mapped to these values (2D position to direction, and displacement speed to distance), and so we used the second joystick of the game controller for arm movement and throwing. We used a threshold-based release mechanism so the ball can be thrown without an explicit release switch.

STUDY 1: TRACK AND FIELD RACING

To explore effort-based repetitive actions as a gameplay mechanic, we created a two-player racing game, TaFR (Figure 2). In a TaFR race, two players run from a start line to a finish line; TaFR is an example of a parallel exergame (Figure 1). We note that this game was designed to explore particular issues in exertion interfaces, and is not intended as a real-world game that people would choose to play.

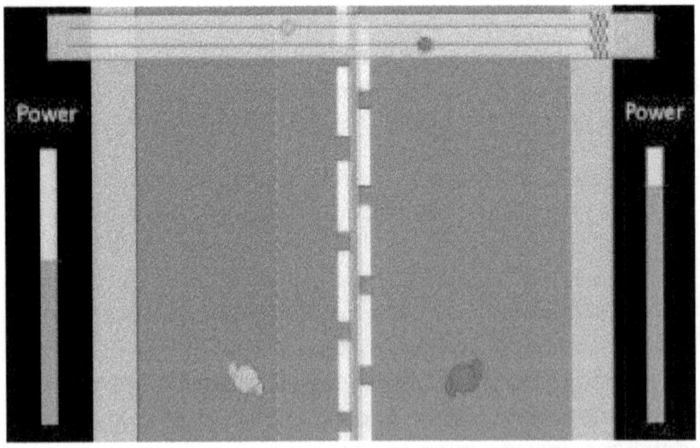

Figure 2. Track and Field Racing (TaFR).

To run in TaFR, players press two keys repeatedly (player 1 used the A and D keys; player 2 used left and right arrow keys). The faster the player presses the keys, the higher the player's power bar rises, and the faster the character runs. The power level has an upper limit, and decreases when the keypress rate drops, or when the keys are not pressed in alternating order. To run fast, players must consciously work to alternate fingers at high speed; this repetitive action causes fatigue. There is also a distance chart at the top of the screen, showing how far the players are from each other, and how far from the finish line they are.

Study Methods

We ran three double-elimination tournaments: one with short races (simulated 100m race), one with medium races (200m) and one with long races (400m). There were two brackets in each tournament. Each player started the tournament in the top bracket. Double elimination means that if a player wins, they move on to the next round. If they lose once, they move down to the bottom bracket. If they lose for a second time, they are eliminated.

Eight participants ran in all three tournaments. Participants were recruited from our research lab (2 female, 6 male), and were between 22 and 32 years old (mean 25.6). We recruited from our lab for convenience, but because we were only looking at low-level effects of exertion, there is little likelihood of any participant bias. Each participant ran between two and seven races. We held races one after another so participants did not have much time to recover; there was a five-minute break between races. For the first tournament (100m) we randomly entered the eight participants into the bracket. Performance in the 100m race determined seeding for the subsequent tournaments.

For each race, we kept track of the time between keypresses, the power level over time, and incorrect keypresses. We also kept track of race times, each player's keypress rate, and each player's average power level.

Results: TaFR

We used TaFR to investigate two issues: whether physical control over running led to individual differences in ability and to changes in performance over a race.

Movement and ability differences between players

We recorded players' running power over time – Figure 3 shows four results from the 100m race. As the charts show, people performed very differently in terms of several characteristics: acceleration, top speed, and consistency. For example, player A had faster acceleration and a higher top speed than player B (row 1 of Figure 3). Player C had the fastest top speed of all the players, and was also able to hit the maximum power possible in the game (row 2).

The performance differences arose both from basic differences in the physical capabilities of the players (finger speed and coordination) and from the amount of effort put into the race. The best players (e.g., Player C) could press the two-key sequence faster, could maintain a high press rate without losing coordination, and could continue at that high rate for the entire race. However, performance also depended on effort, in that players had to work hard to win races against opponents who had similar physical abilities.

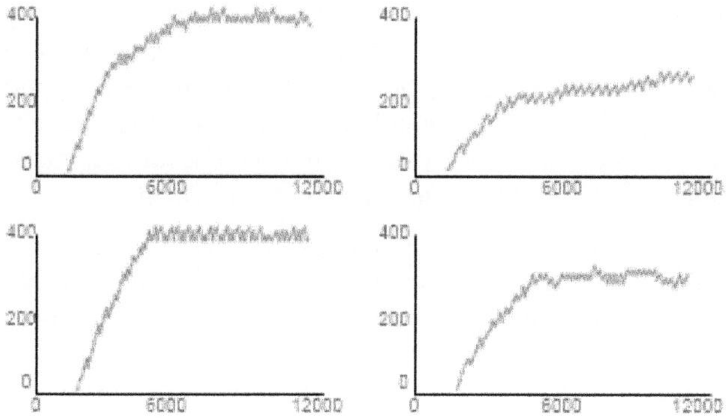

Figure 3. Power-over-time charts for two 100m races.

Changes in performance during the race

Figure 4 shows power-over-time charts from four additional races: 100m in rows 1 and 2, and 400m in row 3. These charts clearly demonstrate that players' performance changed over the course of a race (sometimes dramatically), due to fatigue or a desire to conserve energy.

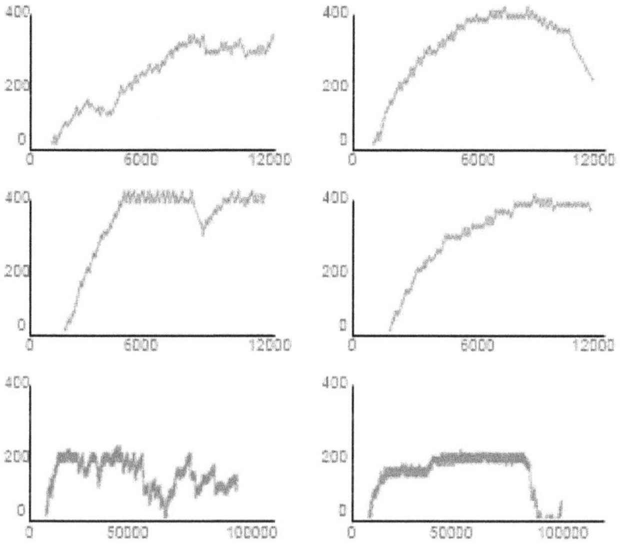

Figure 4. Power-over-time charts for example races (100m, 100m, 200m, and 400m).

In the 100m race (Figure 4, row 1), player 1 (left) is well behind the entire race because player 2 (right) can 'run' faster, with better acceleration and a higher top speed. Near the end of the race, player 2 slows down (falling power line) because he is so far ahead that he does not need to expend much effort to win the race.

In the second 100m race (row 2), player 1 (left) moves into an early lead, but partway through the race, becomes tired and has to rest his fingers (sharp dip in the power line). Player 2 (right) has been steadily increasing her speed, and so catches player 1. The approach of player 2 prompts player 1 to expend more effort again to match the increasing speed of the other runner. (Player 1 wins).

The 400m race (row 3) shows an extreme case of an early leader becoming fatigued and losing the race. Player 2 (right) had a substantial lead coming into the final part of the race – but then his fingers 'gave out' from fatigue (power line drops to near zero). Player 1 (left), who had been much less consistent, made a final desperate dash, passing player 2 near the finish line.

These episodes clearly demonstrate that physical controls – even something as simple as two-finger key pressing – can lead to considerable complexity in the way a race plays out. In particular, fatigue becomes an important factor in the race: players must conserve energy, must 'dig deep' to finish the race strongly, and can encounter catastrophic collapses that dramatically change the race's outcome. The TaFR game goes further in terms of fatigue levels than a real-world game would, but showed the effectiveness of the small-scale approach to exertion – and we built upon these lessons in a more realistic game called Jelly Polo.

STUDY 2: JELLY POLO

The second study explored the use of physical controls for both movement and precise throwing, in an environment more like a sports video game. We created a game called Jelly Polo in which two teams of 3 play a top-down 2D handball-style game for two 10 minute periods. Each player controls one character for the whole game. There are no set positions, players can freely move anywhere, and the team with the most goals at the end of the game wins. Jelly Polo is an object-based, non-parallel exergame (Figure 1).

There are two controls in Jelly Polo: the left and right joysticks on a standard controller. As described above, the left joystick is used for impulse-based movement; unlike most sports games, movement is not rate-based, and players cannot simply hold the joystick to one side to make the player move. In Jelly Polo, players must repeatedly flick the left joystick in the direction they want their character to move; a bigger flick results in a bigger impulse. There is no limit to speed, other than the human limitations on operating the controller.

The right joystick is used to control the character's arm. The arm is used to pass, shoot, steal, fake, and make saves. Unlike many sports games, players must flick the right joystick in the exact direction and speed to throw, requiring precision for passes and effort for hard shots.

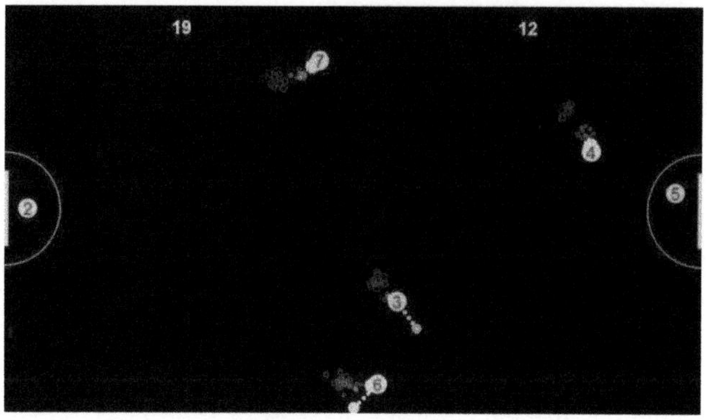

Figure 5. A game of Jelly Polo in progress.

Figure 6 shows an annotated action shot of Jelly Polo. Jelly 5 has the ball and is moving toward the other team's net. The bubble trail shows the direction of movement. Jelly 5 is also holding the ball away from the incoming defender (Jelly 6) and the goalie (Jelly 4). The defenders (6 and 4) hold their arms out in an attempt to steal the ball or save a shot. Arm position is independent of player movement.

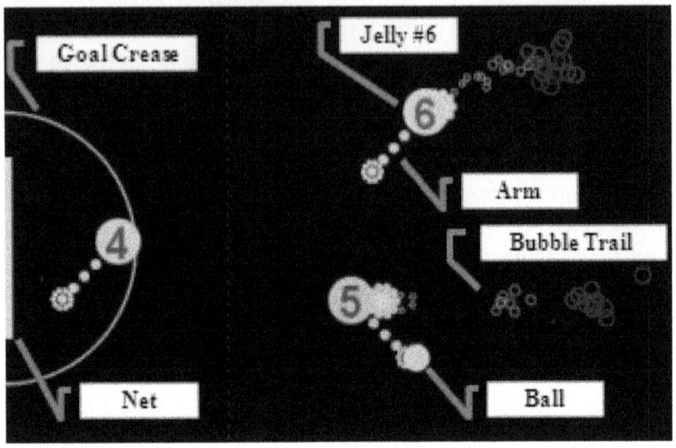

Figure 6. Jelly Polo close-up.

Study Methods

We ran a 4-week Jelly Polo League with 12 participants (4 teams of 3, 10 men and 2 women). Participants ranged in age from 19 to 36 (mean 25.3), and were recruited from within our research lab. Three participants played real-world sports on a regular basis (>3 hrs/wk). All participants had gaming experience (mean 11.7 hrs/wk), although only two participants played sports video games regularly, and only half had played games with physical controls (e.g., Wii Sports). We used participants from our lab because we needed to maintain consistent teams across the month-long study, because we wanted teams to become familiar with each other and discuss strategy between games, and because of the large time commitment (11 play sessions plus several interviews, totaling more than eight hours).

Games were played every Monday, Wednesday and Friday in a round-robin format. After two weeks of play (6 games per team), we had a one-week break, and then held a third week of games. 18 games were played in total (9 for each team). After the three weeks, each team was ranked by wins, and we held a two-round playoff (first vs. fourth, second vs. third, and the two winners played in the finals). The final used a best-of-three format – the first team to win two games was the winner. The finals had two 15-minute periods instead of the standard 10 minute periods.

For each game, we kept track of Goals, Assists, Shots, Saves, Steals, Own Goals, Passes, Face-Off wins, and Turnovers for each player. These stats were kept online. All games were videotaped for later analysis.

Results (Jelly Polo)

Jelly Polo games were fast, exciting, and extremely active, with high average-per-game numbers of Shots (184), Goals (34), Steals (164), Passes (78), and Saves (87). The teams were highly competitive, and games were rousing and noisy affairs. In addition to the overall success of Jelly Polo as a game, we also observed behavior and events that support our hypotheses about small-scale exertion. The sections below report our observations of expertise development, individual differences, and changes in performance.

Expertise development with physical controls

Player skills develop over time in all types of games – both in Jelly Polo and in more traditional sports. Here we focus particularly on the development of skill with the physical aspects of the game – impulse-based movement and precision throwing. We observed the development of several types of skills over the four weeks of the Jelly Polo league. Based on questionnaire results, 9 out of the 12 players stated that they had improved over time. In follow-up group interviews with each team, people discussed the ways in which they had seen improvement, and many of these areas were related to our interests in physical-based movement and passing:

- Movement – running speed, mobility (i.e., 'deking' around other players), ball handling (i.e., moving the jelly's arm around to protect the ball), and goalie movement (i.e., how to best block shots);
- Passing and shooting – directional and distance accuracy in throwing the ball, learning to use the walls for bank passes, and mastering trick shots (e.g., fast shots, or shooting in a different direction to movement);
- Strategy – both individual strategies such as choosing the time to make a rush, when to shoot, or when to attempt a steal; and team strategies such as who would play forward or defense, how to set players up for passes, and when to switch goalies.

One person mentioned that their performance did not improve as much as others in one area (they were not as fast as other players), but that they learned other skills that helped to make up for that limitation.

As an example of skill improvement in passing and throwing, Figure 7 shows a well-designed passing play (orange arrows indicate a pass, yellow arrows indicate movement, and the red arrow indicates a shot; red numbers indicate the order of the actions). In this play, Jelly 4 passes to 6 to keep the ball away from opponent 7. Then, Jelly 6 moves up with the ball, and Jelly 2 moves into position to take the pass. Jellies 3 and 5 move to intercept the ball carrier, leaving a lane open for 6 to pass to 2. With the defender and goalie out of place, 2 has an open-net shot.

Another example is diagrammed in Figure 8, in which one team completes a 'bank pass.' In this scene, the goalie (Jelly 7) has the ball. Opponents 4 and 6 rush him to try and steal it. Teammate 5, knowing that his team has clear possession of the ball, moves up field and sees that a bank pass is open. Before 4 and 6 can get to the goalie (7), he passes the ball off the wall and toward his teammate (5), leading to a breakaway.

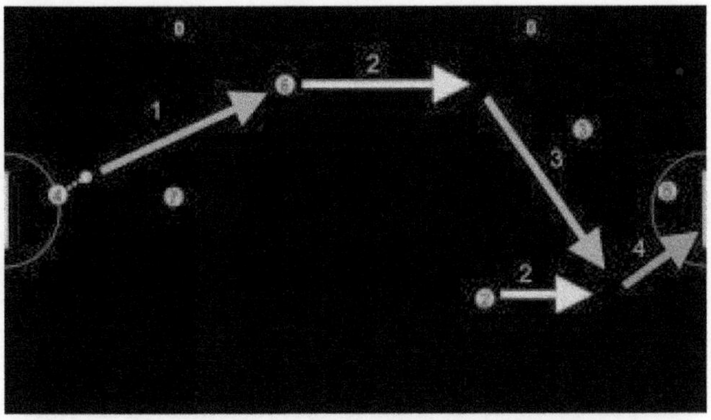

Figure 7. Jelly Polo 'One-timer' passing play.

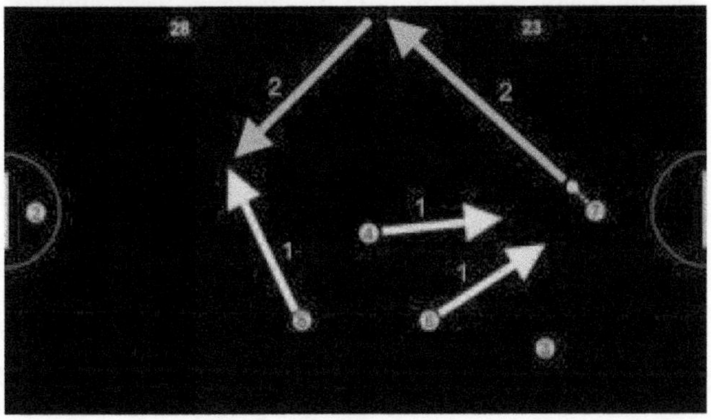

Figure 8. Jelly Polo bank pass.

The league had a one-week break in the middle of the season, and players also felt that their skills had degraded somewhat during that rest, suggesting that 'rust' from lack of practice occurred during the break.

Player stats, however, did not change dramatically as the league continued – for example, there were similar numbers of Goals, Assists, and Shots in the first half of the league (38, 12, 196) as in the second half (30, 9, 173). Discussions with players suggests that the lack of change to the stats is a result of the global increase in skill across most of the players – that is, players became better at defense as well as offense, and so individual stats did not improve even though the overall level of play was higher.

Individual Skill Differences Arising from Physicality

The addition of physicality to the Jelly Polo controls led to a wider range of skill levels in certain aspects of the game – particularly movement speed. It was very clear from observing games and from interviews that different Jelly Polo players had different top speeds. In the interviews, we asked who the fastest player in the league was. Three players received all of the votes (P5: 5 votes; P8: 4 votes; P11: 1 vote), showing that a small set of players had particularly good speed with the impulse-based controller. In the interviews and during the games, people also talked about speed differential in terms of their own abilities: for example, one person stated that for the faster players "even if I could keep up with some people, I still couldn't catch them;" another stated that "this feels like the opposite problem I have with soccer. I can kind of shoot OK [in Jelly Polo], but I can't run fast enough." After being caught on several plays, P3 said: "I can't move as fast as them!"

Figure 9 shows a situation where a player on a breakaway is caught by a faster opponent. Jelly 3 has an open path to the net, and is as fast as Jelly 4, but is much slower than Jelly 2. Even though he starts far behind, Jelly 2 catches up to Jelly 3 and breaks up the chance. This happened frequently in games – one participant noted "there were plenty of times where it would have been a breakaway if someone didn't charge back and cut you off."

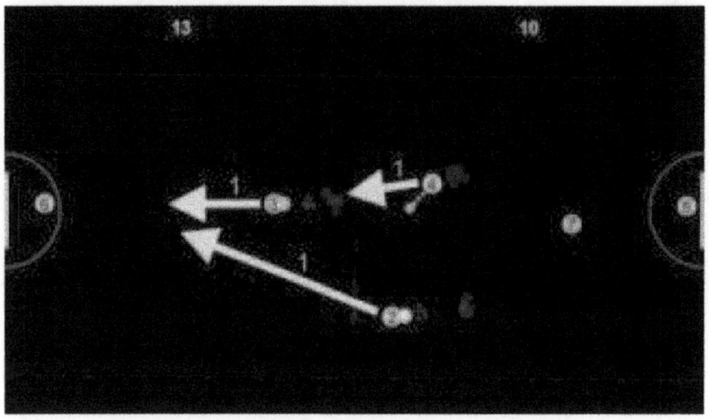

Figure 9. Jelly Polo caught on a breakaway.

Player speed also became a part of team strategy – teams had to adjust to accommodate particular players' abilities. For example, one player discussed having to defend against the speedy P5: "[he] is really fast, so it makes it hard because you can't catch up to him." P5's team sometimes made use of his speed by positioning him in the middle of the field where he could get breakaways. This forced other teams to change their strategy: one player said, "[we] had to keep one guy back to play defense on the cherry picker."

To check people's actual speeds with impulse-based control (but outside of a game situation) we carried out an informal race in which players moved as fast as they could across the playing field and back again (using impulse-based control). These races confirmed the wide range of speeds – the fastest player finished in 6.5 seconds, and the slowest in 11.4 seconds, with eight other players distributed between (see Figure 10).

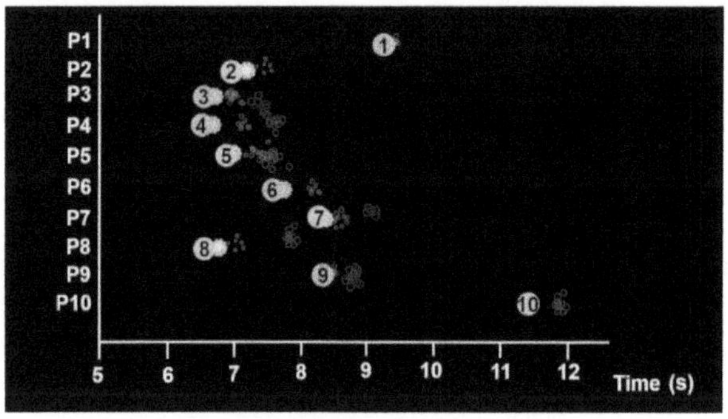

Figure 10. Jelly Polo race results.

We also looked for individual variance in the player stats, and there was clear evidence of differences in this data. For example, the stats showed large differences in Goals, Shots, Saves, and Steals (see Figure 11); this suggests that some players were better in particular roles (e.g., playing in net and making lots of saves, but with few goals).

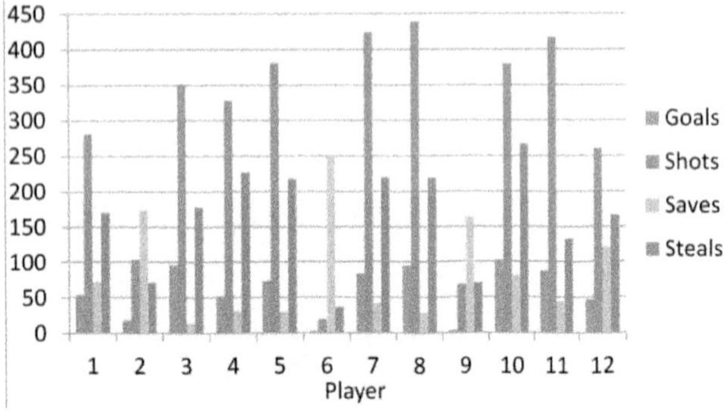

Figure 11. Individual player stats

Changes During Games Arising from Physicality

The largest difference that we observed between traditional games and Jelly Polo was in the way that the physical controls (i.e., impulse movement) led to changes in people's movement abilities over the course of a game. The main issue was fatigue – people got tired, particularly over the short term. The thumb-based control action required effort, and people could not perform at their maximum speed throughout the whole game. Players were able to 'sprint' with a burst of speed, but then would be unable to move as quickly until they had rested.

The effect of fatigue was clearly evident from game comments and interviews, and had a dramatic effect on both individual and team play. On an individual level, it was clear that people got tired, and that they had to adjust their play based on their fatigue level: one person stated "I got tired a bit if I sprinted back and forth, but I would usually recover before the game ended;" and P1 said "if it didn't have that [thumb-based movement] I would play offence and defense all the time; but I wouldn't go as far forward because I knew I had to go back on defense." Several people also talked about their thumbs getting sore during the game, and one player (P5) even worked so hard that he had his hand cramp up during a game: he yelled out "Cramp!" to tell his teammates that he would be out of the game for a few moments while he massaged his hand.

Several players changed their individual strategy to conserve energy. P1's comment above is one example; two other people stated that they played more in the middle of the field (e.g., "I tried to stay near the middle so I wouldn't have to run so far back and forth;" "I cherry-picked because it would give me time to rest so I could perform when I had to"), and another stated that in general "I tried to minimize movements" to maintain energy for short sprints.

Fatigue also played a major role in the way teams organized themselves. In most cases, the team's forwards had to work harder as they raced toward the other team's net or a loose ball, and so this role was generally much more tiring than playing defense. As a result, most of the teams adopted a strategy where they would switch players between forward and defense (or goalie) in order to give tired people a rest. As one person stated, "we switched off a lot so that made it [game fatigue] better." The switching-roles strategy was useful not only for resting, but also for taking opportunistic advantage of the other team's fatigue. As P10 stated, "if you had a chance to rest, then you could burst out and be faster than everyone. It was like you had the invincibility star. You could be faster than everyone else for a while." Another player found the same strategy, saying "by playing goal for a while I can kind of save up some steam, and then really go on a tear."

The idea that fatigue can be an important factor in the outcome of a game, and can play an important role in minute-to-minute strategy decisions during the game, is something that is taken for granted in real-world sports, but that is almost completely absent from sports video games. In addition, although other exertion games have thought about fatigue [11, 12, 14], there is little work done to use tiredness as a critical factor in the performance of the game itself. Finally, we saw evidence that the effort and physical difficulty of our movement mechanism actually made the game more enjoyable – it increased the complexity of the game play, it increased the degree to which teams had to coordinate their activities, and it added to the unpredictability of the game (e.g. through unexpected events like hand cramps). One player summarized this in the interviews by saying that "the interaction–like the constant clicking [i.e., impulse movement], and the effort you were putting into it, was what made it fun."

Expressive communication through physicality

Mueller discusses the idea of 'metagaming' [18] as part of exergames, and suggests that incorporating physicality into digital games can provide opportunities for additional bodily expression and communication. We found many instances of expression through physicality in Jelly Polo. Players would use their onscreen arm for a number of different expressions – spinning their arm around, 'high fiving' each other, or poking other players.

Players could also bounce off another player if they ran into each other. This body checking mechanism was rarely used during gameplay to gain an advantage over the other team, but was often used to taunt other players. This happened especially at half time or before the game began. Players would also chase one another around the screen at these times – either to play a game of keep-away with the ball, or to run away until the other player could make contact with them, like a game of tag.

FOLLOWUP: RATE-BASED JELLY POLO

We were interested in the degree to which players' enthusiasm for Jelly Polo was related to the physical movement controls, so we created a version of the game with rate-based movement. The game was the same as before (graphics, arm movement, and rules), but in this version players could simply hold the left joystick in any direction and your jelly would move in that direction. Two teams (six people) who played in the Jelly Polo league played one game with the rate-controlled version, and discussed the game, over a period of about an hour.

The players' response to the game was overwhelmingly negative. The first comment heard during the game was "It's terrible when you can't catch up to someone [by moving faster]." Players also complained about not being able to fake as well because the defense could stay on you so much easier now. One participant said "this sucks."

After the much-quieter-than-usual game, players were asked what they thought about the change in movement control. Players agreed that they disliked it: for example, P1 said "I thought it was really annoying." When asked to compare this version of Jelly Polo to the original, players pointed to both the overall excitement of the original, and to the physical basis for that enjoyment: one player said "way less exciting;" another stated "you don't have to put as much effort into it," and a third said "it doesn't force you to get as involved."

This exercise suggests that without the physicality added to the game, players did not have as much fun, and team strategies would not change as much because there was no fatigue factor. Without differentiation and changes over time, the game seemed unrealistic and less competitive.

DISCUSSION

Our studies provide four main findings:

- Physical controls allowed expertise development over time, particularly for precise passing in Jelly Polo;
- Impulse-based control of movement led to clear individual differences in player abilities, in both TaFR (keyboard input) and Jelly Polo (controller input);
- Physical movement control also clearly led to changes in player capabilities over time, with fatigue becoming a major factor in both in both game outcomes (TaFR) and game strategy (Jelly Polo);
- Physical control appeared to add to the complexity and unpredictability of Jelly Polo, leading to greater player expressiveness, enjoyment, and enthusiasm.

In the following sections, we consider reasons why physical controls had these effects, and discuss issues of generalizability and applicability to other games.

Explanations for results

There are several ways that physical controls added to the play experience of both TaFR and Jelly Polo. First, the added complexity of the gameplay with physical controls made a major difference in the play experience. In TaFR, physical control over running made an extremely simple system into a fun and challenging contest. The changes in races over time, and the last-minute reversals that occurred, added a level of interest that clearly aided the gameplay.

Second, the element of uncertainty that physical controls (and the resulting fatigue) added to these games was another important improvement. Mueller identified this benefit in terms of exergames more generally:

> *Uncertainty contributes to an element of suspense and facilitates surprise in games through random or chance events, which can play an important part in what makes a game engaging. [...] In conventional button-press computer games, any chance encounters need to be artificially introduced through explicitly programmed code [...] In exertion games, on the other hand, uncertainty can also arise through the body. The body's response to exertion is hard to predict for player and technology alike ("how long can I keep up?"), and the variety of bodily movements can cause even simple actions to go wrong (e.g. missing a free-throw in basketball or a short putt in golf). [15], p. 2653.*

Although Mueller was discussing larger-scale exertion games, our experience is that even small-scale physicality can provide exactly this kind of uncertainty, leading to enhanced enjoyment and interest in the game.

Third, the added level of commitment that exertion required appeared to enhance the play experience for players of both games. There were many comments heard during the races or during Jelly Polo games that would not have been out of place on a real-world sports field – this is best characterized by P10's exhortations to his teammates in the final Jelly Polo game: "DIG! DIG! DIG!". The physical requirements clearly meant something to the players, and changed the play experience from a casual encounter to a more personal contest. This element was clearly lacking from the rate-based version of Jelly Polo, and players quickly saw and understood the critical difference between these versions.

Fourth, the expressiveness of complex physical controls seemed to be an area that players greatly enjoyed. Players quickly and naturally made use of the full range of communicative capabilities of the Jelly characters. Although this kind of communication also occurs in commercial sports games, it is important to note that the physical control scheme added considerable range to what players were able to express.

Generalization

Here we consider two potential issues in using the ideas explored here more widely. First, it is important to consider the potential drawbacks of physicality in game controls, and we see two areas for further consideration. Physical controls are intended to be physically difficult (at least to some degree), and they may cause injury if overused. Even in our brief experience, we saw several sore thumbs, and it is not our intention to cause overuse injuries through the employment of small muscle groups like the hands and fingers. This issue may stand in the way of commercial adoption of our movement control schemes – but we note that early handheld games of the 1980s successfully used similar movement mechanisms.

Second, the increased range of expertise and the increased importance of fatigue raise the issues of game balance and inclusiveness. It is clear that as people become better and better at the physical actions of a game like Jelly Polo, the harder it becomes for a weak-thumbed novice to join in the game. Inclusiveness is an important aspect for game design – but our goal in this research was to try and increase the range of experiences that designers would be able to provide for players, rather than simplify controls such that all players become equal. There are other possibilities for balancing in a game such as Jelly Polo (e.g., adjusting impulse speeds), and we plan further studies to see whether these techniques undo the value of individual differences that were created by physical controls.

CONCLUSIONS AND FUTURE WORK

The physicality and complexity of real-world physical actions are often lost when sports are translated into sports video games. To explore the possibility of returning physicality to controller-based games, we developed two games that provide physical control over movement and precision throwing. Our studies of these games showed that physical controls led to substantial individual differences in running and passing skill, allowing people to increase their expertise over time, and leading to fatigue-based changes in performance during a game. Physical controls increased the games' challenge, complexity, and unpredictability, and improved player interest, expressiveness, and enjoyment. Our results show that the principles of exertion interfaces can also exist 'in the small,' and suggest that game designers should consider exertion as a way to improve play experience in games based on physical activities.

Our future work with these ideas will continue in three directions. First, we will continue to develop small-scale exertion interfaces like Jelly Polo, and evaluate the ideas over a longer time period. Second, we will develop physical controls for other games based on physical activities, such as MMORPGs or fighting games, and explore the ways that the ideas change in other domains. Third, we will further consider the issue of game balance, and explore methods for allowing a wide variety of people to play together, but without losing the complexity and uncertainty that physical controls are able to provide.

REFERENCES

1. Baek, W. Park, A. Kim, J. Jung, K. e-Sports live: e-sports relay broadcasting on demand. *Proc. Conf. on Human interface*, 2007, 685-693.
2. Dörrfuß, K. Bader, F. Wegener, R. Siemon, A. Schwake, J. Horman, F. Hieber, T. Schmid, U. Video Games can Improve Performance in Sports – An Empirical Study with Wii Sports Bowling. *KI 2009*.
3. ESA. *Essential Facts about the Video Game Industry*, www.theesa.com/facts/pdfs/ ESA_EF_2013.pdf, 2013.
4. Gamasutra. *Analysis: The Puzzling Case of Madden's Wii Sales*, 2008, http://www.gamasutra.com/php-bin/news_index.php?story=20434.
5. Gamespot. *US government recognizes League of Legends players as pro athletes*, www.gamespot.com/news/us-government-recognizes-league-of-legends-players-as-pro-athletes-6411377, 2013.
6. Hamilton, W. Kerne, A. Robbins, T. High-performance pen + touch modality interactions: a real-time strategy game eSports context. *UIST 2012*, 309-318.
7. Hinckley, K., Wigdor, D., Input Technologies and Techniques. *Human-Computer Interaction Handbook*, Jacko, J., ed., Taylor & Francis, 2010.
8. IBISWorld. *Sports Video Game Publishing*, 2012, http://clients1.ibisworld.com/reports/us/industry/default.aspx?entid=4860.
9. Larssen, A. Loke, L. Robertson, T. Edwards, J. Understanding Movement as Input for Interaction – A Study of Two Eyetoy Games. *OZCHI 2004*.
10. Marraffino, M. Lum, H. Sims, V. Chin, M. Halse, S., Lippman, B. So you Think you Know Football? Effects of Individual Differences on Video Game Performance. *Proc. HFE*, 55(1), 2011, 1516-1519.
11. Mueller, F., and Agamanolis, S. Sports over a distance. *Computers in Entertainment*, 3(3), 2005, 4-4.
12. Mueller, F. Agamanolis, S. Gibbs, M., Vetere, F. Remote impact: shadowboxing over a distance. *CHI EA 2008*, 2291-2296.
13. Mueller, F., Agamanolis, S., Vetere, F., Brute force as input for networked gaming. *OZCHI 2007*, 167-170.
14. Mueller, F. Cole, L. O'Brien, S. Walmink, W. Airhockey over a distance: a networked physical game to support social interactions. *ACE 2006*, 1133-1138.
15. Mueller, F. Edge, D. Vetere, F. Gibbs, M. Agamanolis, S. Bongers, B. Sheridan, J.G. Designing sports: a framework for exertion games. *CHI 2011*, 2651-2660.
16. Mueller, F. Gibbs, M.R. Vetere, F. Taxonomy of exertion games. *OZCHI 2008*, 263-266.
17. Mueller, F. Gibbs, M.R. Vetere, F. The mousegrip. *CHI EA 2009*, 3199-3204.
18. Salen, K. Zimmerman, E. *Rules of Play: Game Design Fundamentals.* The MIT Press, 2003.
19. Stein, A. Mitgutsch, K. Who are sports gamers? A large scale study of sports video game players. *Convergence*, 19(3), 2013, 345-363.
20. Wikipedia. *Electronic sports,* 2013, http://en.wikipedia.org/wiki/Electronic_sports.

"Healthifying" Exergames: Improving Health Outcomes through Intentional Priming

Frank X. Chen
Computer Science Department
Stanford University
fxchen@cs.stanford.edu

Abby C. King
Stanford Prevention Research Center
Stanford University
king@stanford.edu

Eric B. Hekler
School of Nutrition and Health Promotion
Arizona State University
ehekler@asu.edu

ABSTRACT
Exergames, video game systems that require exertion and interaction, have been rising in popularity in the past years. However, research on popular exergames shows mixed health benefits, potentially due to minimal energy expenditure and decreasing use over time. This paper presents a 2x2 experimental study ($N = 44$), using a popular exergame, where we vary the framing of intention (i.e., "Gameplay" or "Exercise") and feedback (i.e., "Health" or "No health") to explore their single and interactive impacts on perceived exertion, objectively measured energy expenditure, affect, and duration of usage in a single session. Our study showed that participants primed with exercise used the system significantly longer than those primed with game play ($M = 49.2 \pm 2.0$ min versus $M = 39.3 \pm 2.0$ min). We discuss our results and possible design implications based on our single-session experiment. We conclude with a discussion on the potential impact of focusing on "healthifying" exergames—highlighting an exergames' dual purpose as both a game and exercise—as opposed to gamifying health behaviors.

Author Keywords
Exergaming; Priming; Persuasive Technology; Fitness

ACM Classification Keywords
H.5.m. Information interfaces and presentation (e.g., HCI): Miscellaneous.

General Terms
Design, Human factors, Measurement

INTRODUCTION
A large body of research suggests insufficient physical activity increases the risk of chronic diseases and conditions such as cardiovascular disease and obesity [18]. Some commonly reported barriers to regular physical activity include cost, location, social anxiety, and lack of social support [15, 45]. The field of human-computer interaction (HCI) may offer valuable insights for individuals to overcome these barriers and reach the weekly recommended 150 minutes of moderate to vigorous intensity physical activity (MVPA) [37]. Video games for exercise, also known as exergames, have become increasingly popular (e.g., Wii Fit and Microsoft Xbox Kinect) [33]. Exergames can be used at a relatively low cost within a person's home to promote MVPA [22]. However, recent studies show mixed results for exergames in fostering sufficient levels of activity (e.g., MVPA) to confer health benefits [29, 36]. Furthermore, a three-month study of Wii Fit usage by eight families showed no significant health outcomes among its participants, potentially due to decreasing use over time [35].

Much of the current focus on exergames has emphasized game dynamics and feedback as the primary factors to be manipulated for promoting increased usage [34, 38]. However, previous work from psychology and more recently behavioral economics suggests that *priming* and *intentions* may have an impact on engagement and usage. Priming is a common technique in psychology whereby a researcher experimentally manipulates a stimulus to "prime" different responses from an individual. A meta-analysis suggests these techniques could positively influence health outcomes [5]. We contend that *intentional priming* has not received sufficient attention within the HCI literature. We propose intentional priming as a potential key design feature to be explored within exergames.

Our work fits into a growing body of HCI research focused on improving the translation of basic psychological/ behavioral economic principles into the design of behavior-change technologies (BCT) [21]. For example, Lee et al [25] conducted a series of randomized experiments on webpage design that incorporated lessons from behavioral economics on default options. Similarly, our research uses a randomized experiment to test basic psychological processes to inform improved BCT design. Specifically, our work focuses on exploring the impact of (1) priming for using an exergame (i.e., intention to use the system primarily as a game vs. as exercise) and (2) health feedback (i.e., providing a calorie counter or not, see Figures 1 and 2, workout mode includes the health feedback) on perceived energy expenditure, objectively measured energy expenditure, positive affect, and duration of use within a single session in an adult population. Our goal is to better understand the influence of these two mechanisms on exergame usage in a laboratory setting to inform later studies on more long-term use. We hypothesize that

CHI 2014, April 26 - May 01, 2014, Toronto, ON, Canada
Copyright 2014 ACM 978-1-4503-2473-1/14/04…$15.00.
http://dx.doi.org/10.1145/2556288.2557246

Figure 1. "Perform It" mode. Gaming feedback includes a point system, a multiplier (for a sequence of correct dance moves), and a glowing cue (for accuracy of dance move).

Figure 2. "Workout" mode. Health feedback includes a workout timer that persists between songs and a calorie counter.

exercise / health intention priming could increase energy expenditure and duration of use in a single session.

We begin with a review of (1) systems that provide feedback to encourage individuals to change behavior; (2) psychological research related to intentional priming. We follow with a description of our experiment and highlight key results. Finally, we discuss some design considerations that could be further explored in more long-term studies.

BACKGROUND

Exergaming Systems

An exergame drives physical activity through game play / feedback such as competition and the conference of points, tokens, and badges as mechanisms of feedback [1, 10, 11, 32, 34, 42, 47]. For this exergame to confer health benefits, at least two criteria must exist: (1) the exergame fosters sufficiently intense activity (i.e., MVPA, an activity intensity above 3 or more Metabolic Equivalent values or METs), and (2) the exergame fosters sustained usage resulting in an increased amount of MVPA that is maintained in the long-term.

Sufficient Intensity: In general, results are mixed with regard to the likelihood of an exergame facilitating MVPA. Specifically, researchers have found that among forty-six different Wii Fit activities, 67% were light intensity (less than three METs) and 33% moderate intensity physical activity (three to six METs) [29]. Furthermore, Bausch et al. found that the Wii Boxing and Wii Tennis games promoted 5.2 MET and 3.2 MET levels respectively, among young adults [7]. As such, some exergames can foster the appropriate intensity level but MVPA is not guaranteed.

Sustained Usage. The issue of sustained usage can be broken down into three related subdomains: length of bouts the game is played, total length of time played per week, and consistent use of the exergame in the long-term (e.g., using the system for several months to years to foster health benefits). Owens et al. [35] explored system usage of a Wii Fit within a home environment among eight volunteer families over three months. Results showed that the Wii Fit promoted sufficient duration of physical activity during the first 6 weeks (i.e., M = 21.5 ±9.0 min/day or 150.5 min/week) but usage dropped precipitously during weeks 7-12 (i.e., M = 3.9 ±4.0 min/day in the second 6 weeks). Not surprisingly, this study also found no health benefits. Similarly, Schwanda et al. interviewed 16 individuals on their long-term use of the Wii Fit [40] and found that all individuals reported significant decreases in usage over time; 7 reported decreased use due to a reduced motivation to accomplish goals, and the remaining 5 reported that they were not challenged by the exergame. Related to intentions, participants reported that the Wii Fit was "enough of a fitness tool to be useful [...] but it wasn't fun enough to be played regularly as a game." In sum, prior work suggests that some exergames promote a sufficiently high intensity level of physical activity to confer health benefits, but that this intensity level is not guaranteed across all games. Further, it may be possible to promote initial usage of an exergame, but that usage often drops quickly after only a few short weeks [17, 26, 27]. Building on this point, a core problem may be that many of these exergames are perceived as fitness tools rather than games, with the game-like elements "bolted on" and thus not deeply embedded in the user experience [23].

Intentions and Health

Within the health realm, the construct of intentions is an essential component of an important behavioral theory, the theory of planned behavior (TPB) [2]. Within TPB, an individual's intention to engage in a behavior was defined as a person's explicit intention to engage or not engage in an action, such as physical activity and much previous research suggests the predictive utility of explicit intentions on sustained engagement [4]. Research from psychology and behavioral economics provide insights on priming of intentions in the moment, which might be a particularly advantageous method for influencing intentions within an exergame.

Priming Intentions

Priming can occur through a variety of mediums such as text, visual cues, or audio files. For example, the Proteus Effect, a mechanism in which digital avatars are used to inspire future actions, is a form of priming that has been used to inspire exercise [49]. Another example outside of the technology realm is a study conducted by Crum et al.

In their study, room attendants in hotels were either primed to think or not think about the caloric expenditure of their everyday activity (i.e., cleaning a hotel) [13]. At baseline, 66.6% of these attendants reported not exercising regularly and 36.8% said they did not get any exercise at all, despite the fact that their job was a form of MVPA. Four weeks after the experimental intervention, both groups reported no behavior change (e.g., not starting an exercise regimen) but the experimental group showed a significant decrease in weight, blood pressure, body fat, waist-to-hip ratio, and body mass index relative to control. Further, this group perceived themselves as being more physically activity. These results highlight the possibility for priming to have an impact on behaviors that can impact health outcomes.

Beyond the potential subtle influence of priming on activity levels, priming can also influence mood. In a study on verbal priming for health, 48 young adults were given a 10-week exercise program [14]. The experimental group was informed that they were in a program to improve psychological well-being and given a fitness regime, while the control group was given just the fitness regime without a prime about the psychological benefits. Results suggested that the experimental group showed a greater increase in self-esteem and positive affect than the control group while both groups showed similar fitness benefits. Desharnais' experiment showed a significant difference for attitude.

We draw upon research from exergames and intentions/intentional priming in the creation of a novel experiment. We examine the use of priming an exergame to encourage health behavior change in a single session.

Hypotheses

Based on our review of the exergame literature, an exergame should elicit at least 3 METs to confer health benefits and the exergame should promote sustained use within a single session (i.e., supports at least 10 minutes but more optimally, at least 30 minutes per session of use), ideally over a long period of time (i.e., accruing 150 minutes per week of moderate intensity activity over several months to years). This pilot research explores if intentional priming may be important to consider in the design of exergames beyond just feedback. Support for intentional priming in this single session experiment would provide important justification for the far more resource-intensive efforts of exploring intentional priming on longer-term usage in subsequent research.

To explore these issues, we designed a 2x2 factorial experiment (Intention Prime Factor: "Game play" vs. "Exercise", Feedback Factor: "Health" vs. "No health") described in greater detail below. This experimental design allows us to parse out the individual and interactive impacts of intention priming and health feedback on perceived and actual energy expenditure, positive affect, and duration of usage within a single session. Based on our review of the literature, we hypothesize the following effects:

Hypothesis 1: The "Exercise" prime will result in significantly higher perceived and actual energy expenditure relative to the "Game" prime.

Hypothesis 2: The "Health" feedback condition will result in significantly higher perceived and actual energy expenditure relative to the "No health" feedback condition.

We hypothesize these effects based on the previous research suggesting that general health priming can have an impact on health outcomes. The likely mechanism for this would be either implicit (i.e., impact only on actual energy expenditure) or explicit (i.e., impact on both perceived and actual energy expenditure) influence of health priming on outcomes. As the health feedback mechanism is feedback about the health benefits of the exergame, we hypothesized that it would work similarly to the health intentional priming.

Hypothesis 3: The "Game play" intentional prime will result in significantly higher positive affect relative to the "Exercise" prime.

Hypothesis 4: The "No Health/Game Only" feedback condition will result in significantly higher positive affect relative to the "Health and Game" feedback condition.

We made these hypothesizes because games are usually leisure activities undertaken for the amusement of their players. When an exergame is thought to be "exercise" (either via intentional priming or via the feedback provided), the action may move from being an optional choice action to a required action. McGonigal writes, it is essential for any game, particularly serious games, to be perceived as a choice instead of a requirement to ensure the game remains fun and enjoyable [28]. Thus, priming an exergame to be exercise may come at the psychological cost of individuals perceiving exergames as a requirement rather than as a choice (and thus, less enjoyable).

Finally, we hypothesize the following related to duration:

Hypothesis 5: The "Game play" prime will result in significantly longer game play relative to the "Exercise" prime.

Hypothesis 6: The "No Health/Game Only" condition will result in significantly longer game play relative to the "Health and Game" feedback condition.

We made these hypothesizes based on the potential for the health priming and feedback to deleteriously impact the perception that the exergame is a requirement. If it is perceived as a requirement rather than a game, it is hypothesized that this reduced enjoyment will extend to reduced length of gameplay.

Figure 3. Photograph of experimental room and a participant in exercise intention prime. There are visual cues on the projector wall "Exercise Time" and "Have a Great Workout."

METHODS

Dance Central for Xbox Kinect

We chose Dance Central for Xbox Kinect for a number of reasons. It was one of the first video games released for the Xbox Kinect. The Xbox Kinect detects movement and maps skeletal movement as gestures to use as cues for navigation and gameplay. Based on this, the Xbox Kinect's controlling mechanism fosters full body movement. Particularly when complemented by the actions elicited from Dance Central, we believed that participants would likely engage in at least the 3 MET threshold. Further, Dance Central included the capability of activating and deactivating workout mode (See Figs. 2 & 3), thereby providing a useful parameter for exploring health feedback.

Development of the Priming Manipulation

We iterated upon our experimental procedure three times before the final study design. We used a limited set of participants (n = 8) whose data are not included in the final protocol. In our first iteration, we used a general frame of "stress relief" for recruitment purposes to mask the true purpose of the study, which appeared to work as a believable cover story. Further, we initially tried to prime only within the instructions given by mentioning either "exercise" or "game." Specifically, participants in the "game" intention priming condition were told to "play the Kinect Dance Central program to relieve some stress. The game is a very fun way to pass time and relax." Alternatively, participants randomized to the "exercise" priming condition were told to "exercise using the Kinect Dance Central program to relieve some stress. This exercise program is a great way to get some physical activity and relax." The study proctor gave all other oral instructions with references to the exergame as either "exercise" or "game." All participants in the first wave of participants described Dance Central as a game, not exercise even in the exercising priming condition, suggesting the likelihood that Dance Central is perceived first and foremost as a game. In our second iteration, we added contextual cues such as "Exercise Time" and "Have a Great Workout" near the screen for exercise priming (see Figure 3). In the second iteration of testing, we found better evidence for those in the exercise prime to think of using Dance Central as exercise. That said, some individuals appeared to be distracted based on the novelty of the situation for using the system. To counteract the novelty effects, in the third iteration we gave instructions prior to turning on the Xbox and added "Break It Down" session (i.e., a training session built into Dance Central) for performing basic dance moves on the easiest setting for all participants. In the third iteration, participants described the systems according to the appropriate primes in interviews. Specifically, individuals who were primed to view the system as a game reported Dance Central as a game. In contrast, those in the exercise priming condition described the system as primarily exercise.

Study Design

Participants were recruited via email, flyer, and online bulletin board postings for a "Kinect as a Stress Reliever study." Participants were excluded if they owned and / or regularly used the Xbox Kinect. No compensation was given for participation.

The lab experiment, which was approved by the appropriate institutional review board, consisted of one session in an empty room in the basement of a science building at the University. An Xbox, Xbox Kinect, and projector were placed on an end table near the middle of the room. The projector used a wall as a screen (Figure 4). A tape marking on the floor indicated where participants should stand (i.e., 8 feet away from the screen/Kinect sensor).

Before the experiment, the study proctor randomized each participant to one of four conditions based on the two experimental factors: (1) intention priming, and (2) feedback. After receiving informed consent, a study proctor instrumented the participant with a strap on the participant's chest (Zephyr Bioharness, described later). The participant then took a preliminary survey on their current affect.

Feedback Factor: For those in the health feedback condition, the study proctor changed the mode to "Workout mode" (see Figure 2). Those randomized to the no health feedback condition did not have the workout mode turned on.

Priming factor: The study proctor instructed the individual to use the system for at least 10 minutes to relieve stress but to exercise / play (depending on condition) as long as he / she liked and that the proctor would return in 60 minutes; if the participant wanted to finish early, he / she just needed to come to the room next-door to find the research proctor. The participant was asked to choose 1 of the 32 songs (at easy, medium, or hard difficulty settings) to "relieve stress" through "playing" or "exercising" depending on the priming factor.

No constraints were placed on the dance sequence or difficulty; thus, a participant could use the system with the exertion level and pace she / he desired. This freedom of choice was essential to allow the natural MET value for playing the game without any constraints because the level of difficulty would likely impact energy expenditure. A hard song usually required more complex and faster movements, thus, potentially increased energy expenditure. Further, no constraints were placed on how to use Dance Central to allow for differences between conditions on all outcome measures to be exhibited through the natural choices of the participants based on the experimental manipulations.

After the Dance Central session, each participant was asked to complete a survey and a semi-structured interview. The interview explored what the individual did during the session (e.g., "Tell me about your activity during the [game / exercise]") and their usual exercise habits (e.g., "What are your habits for exercise? Why do you exercise?").

Measurements

The primary measurements were perceived exertion, energy expenditure (EE), positive affect, and duration of session. The Borg scale for rated perceived exertion (RPE) [8] has been found to correlate to heart rate [9] in both anaerobic exercise routines [16] and aerobic exercise routines [44]. EE was measured using a device that measures heart rate, activity level (as measured via accelerometry), and respiration rate, called the Zephyr Bioharness [50]. Previously validated algorithms have been developed for translating heart rate, activity level, and respiration from the bioharness into METs on a minute-by-minute basis [3, 39]. As we were interested in the overall MET value for the entire session and because duration was being accounted for, we averaged the minute-by-minute MET estimates of energy expenditure into an average MET energy expenditure across the entire session. Positive affect was measured using the positive and negative affect schedule (PANAS) [48]), which is a well-validated measure for assessing moment-to-moment changes in positive affect. Duration of the session was measured via a stopwatch. We also included surveys related to exercise habits [46] and video game usage [41] as possible control variables.

Our semi-structured interviews were completed after the experiment to determine if our priming manipulation worked and to glean insights into intentions and feedbacks that may not be evident from the quantitative data.

Statistical Analysis

Descriptive statistics (i.e., means and standard errors) were calculated for all key study conditions. Pearson Product Moment Correlations were used to examine correlations between continuous variables. For predictions of positive affect, the key hypothesis focused on changes in positive affect after participating in the Kinect session. Because change scores tend to inflate standard error estimates [12], we used residualized change scores to control for any pre-session differences in positive affect.

RESULTS

Participants

Forty-four undergraduates, graduates, post-doctoral fellows, and staff participated in this one-session study ($M_{age} = 26.5 \pm 7.1$, 56.8% men). 70.4% of participants reported regular exercise. Age was not associated with RPE, actual EE, or duration in this sample (r-values < 0.25, p-values > 0.10). Through the remainder of this paper, we use shorthand to describe each participant <**Gender** (*M* for Male or *F* for Female), **Priming factor** (*G* for gameplay or *E* for exercise) × **Feedback factor** (*nH* for game only or *H* for health & game)>.

Intention Prime Manipulation Check

An important first step was to validate the priming. To determine this, participants were asked to describe their sessions during the semi-structured interview to explore whether they would describe the exergame according to their randomized frame (i.e., viewing the exergame as a game or exercise). Following the session, we found the responses in line with our experimental manipulation All individuals in the exercise and gaming priming , in response to the prompt, "Tell us about your session," described their sessions primarily according to their respective experimental manipulations. Eight participants in the exercise priming and three participants in the gameplay priming mention the dual benefits of exercise and gaming. It is important to note that the three individuals in the game priming condition that also mentioned the dual benefits of exercise and gaming exercised regularly. Examples of responses including:

> *"I played through many songs [...] I really liked and had a lot of fun. I found myself becoming very competitive, more than I had imagined I would [because I do not play a lot of games]." <M, G×nH>*

In comparison, one participant randomized to the exercise condition discussed fitness and routines:

> *"This could be one of the things I do to train. What you see a lot on dance teams is it's difficult to learn new routines due to lack of feedback on what I'm actually doing..." <F, E×nH>*

Finally, eleven individuals discussed the dual benefits:

> *"I think this is a great game. I typically run and do strength training and burn about 360 calories at the gym per session. You could have used a different game... It's still not as efficient as a workout at the gym." <M, E×nH>*

In this case, the participant, randomized to the exercise priming condition, talked about his session as a game and compared the Kinect exercise to routine gym exercise. As such, the participant recognized the activity as potentially serving dual purposes.

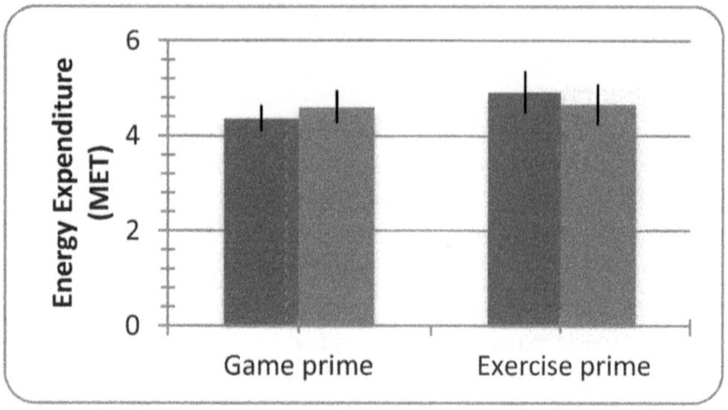

Figure 4. Energy Expenditure grouped by condition.
Grouped by: ■ "No Health" then ■ "Health" feedback

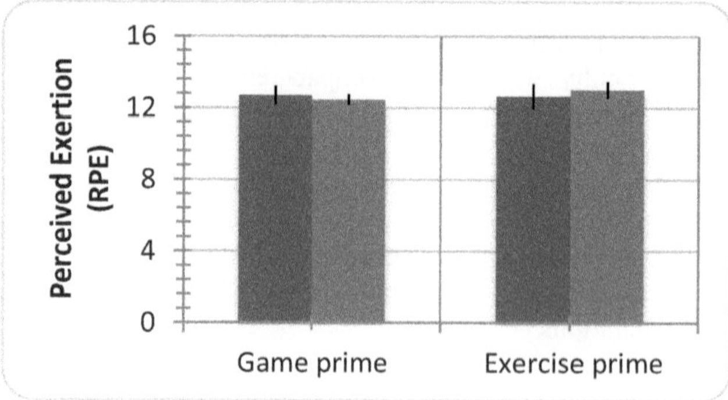

Figure 5. Perceived Exertion grouped by condition.
Grouped by: ■ "No Health" then ■ "Health" feedback

Energy Expenditure and Perceived Energy Expenditure

The grand mean for overall energy expenditure was $M_{MET} = 4.5 \pm 1.1$. Based on this, the average MET value for activity was within the moderate intensity realm, thereby suggesting that using Dance Central can result in meaningful physical activity [37]. Further, the grand mean for perceived exertion neared the "somewhat hard" realm (i.e., $M_{RPE} = 12.8 \pm 1.7$).

Analysis of variance (ANOVA) revealed no significant predictors of perceived exertion or energy expenditure (*p*-values>0.54, see Figures 4 and 5) across all conditions.

Positive Affect

ANOVA predicting residualized change scores of positive affect suggested a trend for feedback influencing change in positive affect ($F(1,43) = 3.62$, $p = 0.065$). Post hoc power analyses suggested a sample of 68 would have been required for statistical significance. All other variables (priming and the interactions of priming and feedback) were not associated with post-session positive affect (*p*-values > 0.29, see Figure 6).

Duration of Use

ANOVA revealed a significant effect of intention on duration of use ($F(1,43) = 6.6$, $p < 0.05$). Specifically, participants used the system significantly longer for the exercise priming condition ($M = 49.2 \pm 2.0$ min) than the gameplay condition ($M = 39.3 \pm 3.0$ min). This ran counter to expectations (see Figure 7). All other variables were not significant (*p*-values > 0.33, see Figure 7).

INTERVIEW RESULTS

In this section, we outline key themes that arose from the semi-structured interviews to provide context for the quantitative data and to provide further insights into potential design parameters within an exergame context.

Frame Exergame Use with Similar Prior Experience

Participants who had used the Wii Fit in the past ($n = 5$) contrasted the energy level difference of their use of other exergames against their use of Dance Central: some said it was "harder" and it was harder to "cheat" by only using their arms. A former Wii user <F, E×nH> highlighted the fine-tuned feedback compared to her mirroring videos streamed from the internet and the extra energy she used with this system as compared to the Wii where "you only move your hands."

> *"The level of energy to play games like the Kinect and Wii are interesting. When I first got Wii, I felt it was very tiring at first; then I learned how to conserve my energy and cheat the system. I could get very high scores and maintain it. At first I couldn't play for more than 30 minutes. Now I have learned to play and limit my movements to play for hours [on Wii]."* <M, G×H>

Participants with dance experience ($n = 3$, all female) described different affordances of using an exergame to learn dancing. A former competitive dancer <F, G×H> described being able to slow down complex movements in break-it-down mode and receiving feedback extremely useful; this personal feedback process is typically not accommodated in dance instruction courses with many people.

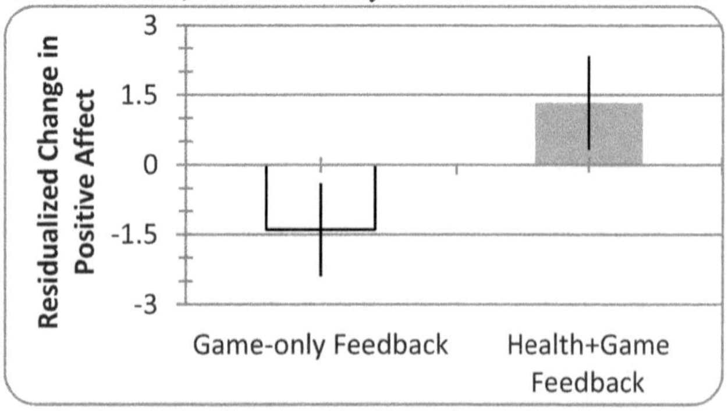

Figure 6. Residualized change scores in Positive Affect for game only feedback and Health Intention & Game Feedback.
Grouped by: ■ "No Health" then ■ "Health" feedback

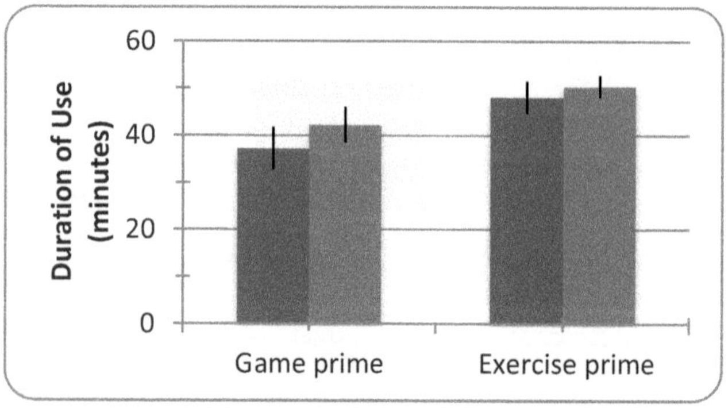

Figure 7. Duration grouped by condition.
Grouped by: ■ "No Health" then ■ "Health" feedback

> *"This could be one of the things I do to train. What you see a lot on dance teams it's difficult to learn new routines due to the lack of feedback on what I'm actually doing."* <F, E×nH>

In these interviews, prior experience (including whether the individual reports regular exercise) seemed to play a role in perceptions of the system. Future work could explore how prior experience influences measures such as exertion or positive affect compared to those who do not have these prior experiences. Unfortunately, we did not have a sufficient sample to explore these issues in more detail.

Use of Health Feedback in Exergames

One of our hypotheses was that visual health feedback (i.e., calories burned and time spent in the workout) would influence the time of usage and energy expenditure. Surprisingly, health feedback was not predictive of duration of use or energy expenditure in our experiment.

While most individuals mentioned the visual game cues as fun and exciting, no individuals mentioned the health feedback as particularly beneficial. In fact, one participant had a negative reaction to the exercise prime and health feedback that was in line with our original hypothesis.

> *"I did not use the feedback [...] I play sports. I don't run or lift weights. Exercise is boring, rather than doing something monotonous I like to play games."* <F, E×H>

While the health feedback in this study did not significantly impact measurements, health feedback (e.g., calories burned) is a common theme in many exergaming systems [42]. Future work might explore health feedback that is more deeply embedded in the activity itself and not "bolted on" [23].

Exergames as a nudge for further physical activity

Eight individuals from game priming and five from exercise priming, when asked about exercise reported a desire to start exercising again during the semi-structured interview. These participants reported the use of this exergame made them realize they needed to do more physical activity while others described the feeling in more specific contexts.

Focus on gaming cues

Eight participants reported appreciating the visual and auditory game-like incentives to succeed in their activity. For example, one participant mentioned:

> *"There is a lot of incentive to do well. It's a lot more fun when you do it well and when you can do the right moves. The feedback was really helpful to help me do well."* <M, E×nH>

Social Element

The design of this study purposefully left out social elements related to using Dance Central with others as that would have likely introduced a confound to the study. Interestingly, many participants volunteered insights on their play or exercise routines by giving unsolicited social information on how much their own behavior could have changed if there was social activity in the experiment.

Five participants talked about the importance of social context in the experiment without prompting. For example, "I wish I could play this as a team so there's more of a sense of cooperation or competition." *<F, E×H>*. Another participant *<F, E×H>* who was formerly on a dance team, noted that the social connections formed through dance helped relieve stress. Finally, one participant implied that the social elements would have been problematic and contrasted his session to other games he plays socially:

> *"I felt very relaxed while I played alone. If I played with others, I would feel pressured if I didn't dance as well as others."* <M, G×nH>

DISCUSSION

In this study, we explored how intentional priming and feedback may influence perceived and actual energy expenditure, changes in positive affect from using the system, and duration of usage in a lab-based single session experiment. Results of our study confirmed that Dance Central could inspire individuals to engage in moderate intensity physical activity. If Dance Central can also promote long-term usage, then these results suggest that Dance Central may be a useful tool for meeting national physical activity recommendations. Results also suggested that providing health feedback resulted in a trend for more positive affect compared to the game-only feedback. This result was counter to expectations as we hypothesized that a more pure game focus would elicit more positive affect. In addition, results also suggested that individuals randomized to the exercise priming condition used the system longer in a single session than those randomized to the gameplay condition. All other analyses (i.e., exploration on how priming or feedback predicted perceived exertion or energy expenditure) revealed no significant effects in this single session.

The determination that Dance Central can promote moderate intensity physical activity has an important implication for the broader realm of exergame research. Previous research has suggested that some Wii Fit games promote light but not necessarily moderate intensity physical activity [29, 36]. While the Wii Fit can be perceived as a starting point for inspiring individuals to start to become more physically active, individuals may not be able to sustain sufficiently high levels of intense physical activity for health outcomes using the Wii alone [40]. Our results for Dance Central, coupled with the full body movement required from the Kinect, suggest that the Kinect sensor system might more consistently foster the appropriate intensity of activity. However, future research with other Kinect games is required to confirm this point.

The key finding from our quantitative data suggested that individuals who were primed to think of the exergame as exercise used the system for a significantly longer period than those primed to use the system as a game in a single session. This was counter to expectations that were based on the hypothesis that priming the activity as "exercise" would implicitly change the experience of using Dance Central as a "want to" to a "have to" activity and thus reduce interest in using the system for a longer session. There are several parts to our data that suggest a somewhat more nuanced understanding of game design than our original hypothesis. In particular, eleven participants perceived the dual purpose of the exergame (i.e., as both exercise and a game). Further, many of the individuals within the exercise-priming condition stated in the semi-structured interviews that they wanted to "work out" for a long enough time to get their exercise in for the day and therefore not have to go to the gym later. It is important to note here that the vast majority of participants (70.4%) reported exercising regularly. Based on this, it appears that those individuals who are already active and primed to think about this as "exercise" may persist in using the system partially because it is fun but *also* to ensure they receive the health benefits. In contrast, those individuals who only perceived the system as a game likely stopped playing the game as soon as it was below some threshold of fun. As such, there was no added motivation beyond just enjoyment to ensure continued engagement. This explanation fits with other work from psychology showing that self-identity might be a driver for persisting in an action in the long term [43].

Counter to expectations, we did not find any significant impact of intention priming or feedback on perceived exertion or actual energy expenditure. It is plausible that this non-significant result was due to our small sample size. Indeed, if only looking at the patterns of the data, the results suggest that modestly more energy was expended within the exercise-primed group overall. Future research with a larger sample could be conducted to better explore the potential impact of intention on energy expenditure within a properly powered study (based on current effect size estimates, a minimum sample of 72 would have been required). Barring running a full study, our results suggest that an exercise intention and health feedback likely do not play an important role in increasing activity intensity, at least within a game that already promotes average MET values around 4.5. This suggests that game dynamics (e.g., full body movement that can be achieved within the Kinect) may be of primary importance for exergames to meet the moderate intensity threshold in a single session.

With regard to positive affect, our results suggest that receiving health feedback promoted a trend towards increased positive affect more so than the game-only feedback. This finding, while counter to initial expectations, makes sense within the context of our interview data and the duration findings. Specifically, our formative work coupled with our interview results both suggest that Dance Central is perceived primarily as a game. As such, providing health feedback may have been a mechanism for highlighting the dual benefits (i.e., fun and health) that could be achieved via Dance Central. Based on this, a design parameter to further explore is to more explicitly highlight its dual purpose of both fun and health.

Limitations

There were several limitations to the study. First, only individuals connected to a major university were recruited and the vast majority of these participants reported exercising regularly. As such, there are potential problems with generalizability. Further, this study utilized an in-lab single session experimental design. As such, no conclusions can be drawn about long-term usage. Finally, while the data support our intentional priming manipulation, there were some individuals from both the gameplay prime and exercise prime that discussed the dual purpose of the game. This does not run counter to our intentional prime, however, as each participant explicitly mentions their original primed condition before discussing the dual role of both exercise and gameplay in their session. It is important to note that all of the individuals in the gameplay priming condition that also discussed exercise were regular exercisers and enjoyed exercise. As such, it is not surprising that they might perceive the dual purpose of the activity. Further, for the exercise prime condition, it appeared that Dance Central was perceived primarily as a game with it only being perceived as exercise after a strong manipulation based on our formative work. As such, the greater number of individuals recognizing the dual purpose of exercise and play in the exercise prime (eight) compared to the gameplay prime (three), while not definitive, is an interesting outcome of our study.

Implications and Future Directions

The results from our work provide an intriguing counterpoint to common practices for developing exergames. An emphasis for many exergames is "gamifying" exercise through the addition of points, badges, competition, and similar gaming elements [6]. The implicit motive for "gamifying" exercise is that exercising needs to be more fun to promote engagement.

Our results raise some questions about the value of gamifying exercise, as it was the health feedback and exercise priming that improved enjoyment and usage. We believe that this may have occurred because of the strong game dynamics in Dance Central, which we then augmented with our "healthifying" elements (i.e., intentional priming and health feedback) to make the system a more successful exergame. Our results suggest that the design of an exergame may be improved if emphasis is placed first on good game mechanics that foster a specific behavior such as dancing in Dance Central and then supplemented with "healthifying" the game via strategies like intentional priming and health feedback. The goal of this healthification would be to highlight the dual benefit/motivations for engaging in the behavior (i.e., healthy and fun). This hypothesis requires additional research, particularly with longitudinal studies but this research does support the likely value of exploring this within more resource-intensive longitudinal studies.

CONCLUSION

This work explored the impact of intentional priming and health feedback on the use of an exergame, Dance Central, within a single session. Our experiment with 44 participants confirmed that this exergame could elicit moderate intensity physical activity. Results also suggested that priming the use of the system for exercise increased duration of use and that providing health feedback within the session elicited a trend towards increased positive feedback in a single session. These results were counter to expectations, but highlight a potential for placing more emphasis on "healthifying" engaging games over "gamifying" health behaviors. These results should be interpreted cautiously however, as the impact of "healthification" may change as the person uses the system over an extended period.

We believe that this "healthification" process may be particularly impactful for well-designed games because it can highlight the potential dual purpose of using the system (i.e., for both fun and health). Emphasizing this dual purpose in a highly engaging game may be key for eliciting greater positive affect and longer sustained use, as the person is achieving success in two realms, a "two birds with one stone," mentality. Future research should further explore this "healthification" concept to promote more long-term use of exergames, a key problem with current exergame systems.

ACKNOWLEDGMENTS

We would like to thank BJ Fogg, Scott Klemmer, and Erika Poole for thoughtful comments and feedback on this paper. Further, we thank Florian (Floyd) Mueller for his insights and feedback on experimental design. This research was supported by a Google Research Award (PI: King).

REFERENCES

1. Adams, M. A., *et al.* 2009. A theory-based framework for evaluating exergames as persuasive technology. *Persuasive '09,* Article 45.
2. Ajzen, I. 1991. The theory of planned behavior. *Organizational behavior and human decision processes*, 50(2), 179-211.
3. Albinali, F., Intille, S., Haskell, W., & Rosenberger, M. 2010. Using wearable activity type detection to improve physical activity energy expenditure estimation. *Ubicomp '10,* 311-320.
4. Armitage, C. J. and Conner, M. (2001), Efficacy of the Theory of Planned Behaviour: A meta-analytic review. *Brit J Soc Psychol*, 40, 471–499.
5. Baer, R.A. 2003. Mindfulness Training as a Clinical Intervention: A Conceptual and Empirical Review. *Clin Psychol: Sci Pract*,10(2), 125–143.
6. Baranowski, T., Buday, R., Thompson, D. I., & Baranowski, J. 2008. Playing for real: Video games and stories for health-related behavior change. *Am J Preven Med*, 34(1), 74-82.
7. Bausch L, Beran J, Cahanes S, Krug L. 2008. Physiological responses while playing Nintendo Wii Sports. *J Undergrad Kinesiol Res*, 3(2), 19-25.
8. Borg, G. 1985. *An introduction to Borg's RPE-scale.* Ithaca, NY: Movement Publications.
9. Borg, G., Hassmen, P., & Lagerström, M. 1987. Perceived exertion related to heart rate and blood lactate during arm and leg exercise. *Euro J Appl Physiol Occupat Physiol*, 56(6), 679-685.
10. Consolvo, S., McDonald, D. W., Toscos, T., Chen, M. Y., Froehlich, J., Harrison, B., Klasnja, P. & Landay, J. A. 2008. Activity sensing in the wild: A field trial of ubifit garden. *CHI'08*, 1797-1806.
11. Consolvo, S., McDonald, D.W., & Landay, J. 2009. Theory-driven design strategies for technologies that support behavior change in everyday life. *CHI'09*.
12. Cronbach, L.J., & Furby, L. 1970. How we should measure "Change" or should we? *Psych Bull*, 74, 68-80.
13. Crum, A.J. & Langer, E.J. 2007. Mind-set matters: exercise and the placebo effect. *Psychol Sci.*18(2), 165-71.
14. Desharnais, R., *et al.* 1993. Aerobic exercise and the placebo effect: a controlled study. *Psychosom Med*, 55(2), 149-154.
15. Dishman, R.K., Sallis, J.F., & Orenstein, D.R. 1985. The determinants of physical activity and exercise. *Public Health Rep*. 100(2), 158–171.
16. Egan, A. D., Winchester, J. B., Foster, C., & McGuigan, M. R. 2006. Using session RPE to monitor different methods of resistance exercise. *J Sports Sci Med*, 5(2), 289-295.
17. Eiriksdottir, E., *et al.* 2011. Assessing Health Games in Secondary Schools. An Investigation of the American Horsepower Challenge 2009-2010. *Georgia Institute of Technology Technical Report.* Atlanta.
18. Ezzati, M., Lopez, A. D., Rodgers, A., & Murray, C. J. (Eds.). 2004. *Comparative quantification of health risks: global and regional burden of diseases attributable to selected major risk factors* (Vol. 1). World Health Organization.
19. Finkelstein, S., *et al.* 2011. Astrojumper: Motivating exercise with an immersive virtual reality exergame. *Presenc Teleoperator Virt Environ*, 20(1), 78-92.
20. Fogg, B. J. (2009). A behavior model for persuasive design. *Persuasive'09*, Article 40.
21. Hekler, E. B., Klasnja, P., Froehlich, J. E., and Buman, M. P. 2013. Mind the Theoretical Gap: Interpreting,

Using, and Developing Behavioral Theory in HCI Research. *CHI'13*, 3307-3316.

22. Graves, L. E., Ridgers, N. D., Williams, K., Stratton, G., & Atkinson, G. 2010. Deakin Research Online. *J Physic Activ Healt*, 7, 393-401.
23. Isbister, K., Flanagan, M., Hash, C. 2010. Designing Games for Learning: Insights from Conversations with Designers. *CHI'10,* 2041-2044.
24. IGN. 2010. Dance Central Images. Internet. http://j.mp/ign_kinect Retrieved December 15, 2011.
25. Lee, M., Kiesler, S., and Forlizzi, J. 2011. Mining behavioral economics to design persuasive technology for healthy choices. *CHI'11,* 325-334.
26. Lin, J.J., Mamykina, L., Lindtner, S., Delajoux, G. and Strub, H. B. 2006. Fish'n'steps: Encouraging physical activity with an interactive computer game. *UbiComp'06,* 261-278.
27. Macvean, A., and Robertson, J. 2013. Understanding Exergame Users' Physical Activity, Motivation and Behavior Over Time. *CHI'13*, 1251-1260.
28. McGonigal, J. 2011. *Reality is broken: Why games make us better and how they can change the world.* Penguin Press.
29. Miyachi, M., Yamamoto, K., Ohkawara, K., Tanaka, S. 2010. METs in adults while playing active video games: a metabolic chamber study. *Med Sci Sports Exerc.* 42(6),1149-53.
30. Mueller, F., Vetere, F., Gibbs, M.R., Edge, D., Agamanolis, S., Sheridan, J.G., Heer, J. 2012. Balancing Exertion Experiences. *CHI'12*, 1853-1862.
31. National Center for Health Statistics. 2013. *Health, United States, 2012: With Special Feature on Emergency Care*. Hyattsville, MD.
32. Norman, G. J., Adams, M. A., Ramirez, E. R., Carlson, J. A., Kerr, J., Godbole, S., ... & Marshall, S. J. 2013. Effects of behavioral contingencies on adolescent active videogame play and overall activity: A randomized trial. *Game Healt*, 2(3), 158-165.
33. O'Loughlin, E. K., Dugas, E. N., Sabiston, C. M., & O'Loughlin, J. L. 2012. Prevalence and Correlates of Exergaming in Youth. *Pediatrics*, 130(5), 806-814.
34. Oinas-Kukkonen, H., Harjumaa, M. 2009. Persuasive Systems Design: Key Issues, Process Model, and System Features. *Commun Assoc Inform Syst*, 24, 28.
35. Owens, S. G., et al. 2011. Changes in Physical Activity and Fitness After 3 Months of Home Wii Fit™ Use. *J Strengt Condition Res*, 25(11), 3191-3197.
36. Peng, W., Lin, J. & Crouse, J. 2011. Is playing exergames really exercising? A meta-analysis of energy expenditure in Active Video Games. *Cyberpsychol, Behav Soc Network.* 14(11), 681-688.
37. Physical Activity Guidelines Advisory Committee. 2008. *Physical activity guidelines advisory committee report, 2008*. US Depart. Health and Human Services.
38. Purpura, S., *et al.* 2011. Fit4life: the design of a persuasive technology promoting healthy behavior and ideal weight. *CHI'11*, 423-432.
39. Rosenberger, M.E. 2011. Device Measuring Heart Rate, Respiration Rate, and Motion Accurately Estimates Activity Level and Energy Expenditure. *Med Sci Sport Exerc*. 43 (1): 63.
40. Schwanda, V., *et al.* 2011. Side effects and 'gateway' tools: advocating a broader look at evaluating persuasive systems. *CHI'11*, 345-348.
41. Sherry, J.L., Greenberg, B.S., Lucas, K., & Lachlan, K. 2006. Video game uses and gratifications as predictors of use and game preference. In P. Vorderer & J. Bryant (Eds.), *Playing computer games: Motives, responses and consequences*. Psychology Press.
42. Sinclair, J., Hingston, P., Masek, M., & Nosaka, K. 2010. Testing an exergame for effectiveness and attractiveness. *ICE-GIC'10*, 1-8.
43. Strachan, S. M., Woodgate, J., Brawley, L. R. and Tse, A. 2005. The Relationship of Self-Efficacy and Self-Identity to Long-Term Maintenance of Vigorous Physical Activity. *J Appl Biobehav Res*, 10, 98–112.
44. Sweet, T. W., Foster, C., McGuigan, M. R., & Brice, G. 2004. Quantitation of resistance training using the session rating of perceived exertion method. *J Strengt Condition Res*, 18, 796-802.
45. Tappe, M. K., Duda, J. L. & Ehrnwald, P. M. 1989. Perceived Barriers To Exercise Among Adolescents. *J School Healt*, 59, 153–155.
46. Taylor-Pillae, R.E. et al. 2010. Validation of the Stanford Brief Activity Survey: examining psychological factors and physical activity levels in older adults. *J Phys Act Healt*. 7(1):87-94.
47. Torning, K., & Oinas-Kukkonen, H. 2009. Persuasive system design: state of the art and future directions. *Persuasive'09*, 30.
48. Watson, D., Clark, L. A., & Tellegen, A. 1988. Development and validation of brief measures of positive and negative affect: The PANAS scales. *J Psychol*, 54(6), 1063-1070.
49. Yee, N., & Bailenson, J. 2007. The Proteus Effect: The Effect of Transformed Self-Representation on Behavior. *Hum Communic Res*. 33: 271–290.
50. Zephyr, Inc.. *Zephyr Bioharness.* http://www.zephyr-technology.com

Human Factors of Speed-based Exergame Controllers

Taiwoo Park[1], Uichin Lee[2], I. Scott MacKenzie[3], Miri Moon[4], Inseok Hwang[1,5], Junehwa Song[1]

[1]Dept. of Computer Science, KAIST, Korea

[2]Dept. of Knowledge Service Engineering, KAIST, Korea

[3]Dept. of Electrical Engineering and Computer Science, York University, ON, Canada

[4]Div. of Web Science Technology, KAIST, Korea

[5]Center for Mobile Software Platform, KAIST, Korea

{twpark, miri.moon, inseok, junesong}@nclab.kaist.ac.kr, [2]uclee@kaist.edu, [3]mack@cse.yorku.ca

ABSTRACT

Exergame controllers are intended to add fun to monotonous exercise. However, studies on exergame controllers mostly focus on designing new controllers and exploring specific application domains without analyzing human factors, such as performance, comfort, and effort. In this paper, we examine the characteristics of a speed-based exergame controller that bear on human factors related to body movement and exercise. Users performed tasks such as changing and maintaining exercise speed for avatar control while their performance was measured. The exergame controller follows Fitts' law, but requires longer movement time than a gamepad and Wiimote. As well, resistance force and target speed affect performance. User experience data confirm that the comfort and mental effort are adequate as practical game controllers. The paper concludes with discussion on applying our findings to practical exergame design.

Author Keywords

Exergame; Game Controller; Speed-based Control.

ACM Classification Keywords

H.5.2 [**Information Interfaces and Presentation**]: *User Interfaces-evaluation/methodology, input devices and strategies*

INTRODUCTION

Sports are an entertaining and engaging part of many people's lives, enhancing both athletic performance and physical condition. However, busy urban lifestyles make social sports difficult to participate in since they usually require a pre-determined schedule. Solitary exercises such as stationary cycling or running on a treadmill are popular alternatives; however, the monotonous and repetitive nature of these exercises present challenges to increasing people's motivation to exercise. Moreover, it may be hard to motivate people to exercise using rewards that are not immediately observable, such as better general health [14] and appearance.

CHI 2014, April 26 - May 01 2014, Toronto, ON, Canada
Copyright 2014 ACM 978-1-4503-2473-1/14/04...$15.00.
http://dx.doi.org/10.1145/2556288.2557091

Exergames – games involving physical activity – have shown potential to increase the enjoyment of repetitive exercise [24, 29, 39]. They usually involve new technology, such as an exergame controller that adds a gaming interface to exercise equipment. The transformed device serves as a medium to introduce fun factors such as *coordinated interactions* and *competition* to repetitive solitary exercises. The device also provides an opportunity for game developers to design interactive exergames similar to commonly enjoyed video games. We envision that new exergame controllers will emerge featuring rich interactivity and immersive game play.

Academia and industry strive to develop new exergames and game controllers. Yet, the design of an exergame is challenging. The reason is simple: Exergames require and promote exercise, unlike traditional video games which primarily seek to entertain. Mueller et al. describe the property of exergames as follows: "The outcome of exergames is predominantly determined by the physical effort" [26]. In contrast, designers of traditional games generally strive to minimize physical effort [33]. It is thus important to correctly understand exergames and to accumulate appropriate design knowledge – to guide designers.

Existing studies, however, are generally limited to exploring how exergame controllers influence the design of in-game content and user interaction. A deeper understanding of controllers will help designers predict, organize, and evaluate exergame experiences.

As our research goal, we evaluate an exergame controller to help designers accommodate characteristics and limitations of input devices in exergame design. We study human factors of speed-based exergame controllers (e.g., performance, comfort, effort) under two different types of tasks: a maintenance task (maintaining exercise speed) and a pointing task (moving between points). Also, we examine the user experience with a speed-based controller. The following contributions emerge from our investigation with bike-based exergame controllers:

- The performance of a steady-speed maintenance task is dependent on target speed and resistance force of an exercise device. Contrary to expectations, performance

Figure 1. Games which can be controlled by speed-based controllers: (a) shooter, (b) paddle game, (c) puzzle game, (d) action game. Players can relocate the avatar's position using (e) a stationary cycle or (f) a traditional controller.

does not proportionally degrade as the target speed and resistance force increase. The performance rather abruptly drops when these values exceed certain thresholds, even though they fall into the recommended aerobic exercise ranges. This finding implies that exergame designers should carefully select a proper speed range and consider a user's preferred resistance level to provide users with a consistent perception of controllability.

- The results of a pointing task show that speed-based exergame controllers follow Fitts' law but with a steeper slope than with other devices.
- Our interviews and questionnaire provide detailed reports about user experiences in using the speed-based controllers. These results help game designers anticipate players' performance and user experiences.
- We discuss a number of design implications in a case study of a practical game design. We show how exergame designers can consider the findings, such as speed mapping, object placement/control, and difficulty setting.

RELATED WORK

Novel game controllers permit new ways of interacting in exergames. A foot pad in Dance Dance Revolution by Konami [19] allows players to perform rhythmic stepping with music. In Remote Impact [25] and LightSpace by Exergame Fitness Co. [5], players punch or touch a large contact-sensing smart wall. Similarly, in Table Tennis for Three, users hit a virtual object on a smart wall with a ball [27]. Several exergames incorporate physiological sensors (e.g., heart rate) [24, 29, 39]; for instance, remote joggers exchange heart rate information for a balanced running experience.

Motion-based game controllers have recently received a great deal of attention following the release of popular gaming consoles such as Sony EyeToy, Nintendo Wii, and Microsoft Kinect. These devices can detect a player's body motion using cameras and motion sensors. The popularity of these gaming consoles has motivated the design of exergames such as Wii Fit, Wii Sports, and Kinect Sports. Researchers also designed and evaluated specialized exergames in particular contexts, such as rehabilitation [10, 15, 16] and social relationships [40].

Alternatively, exercise machines are widely used as exergame controllers. Exercise bikes are popular due to their familiarity and accessibility [36]. In 1983, Atari Interactive prototyped an exercise bike connected to a game console and devised prototype games such as a racing game. Similarly, AutoDesk developed HighCycle, which allows users to explore a virtual landscape using an exercise bike. Recent products include Cateye GameBike and PCGamerBike, which support the control of a variety of games (mostly racing games) on Sony PlayStation and personal computers. Fisher Price's Smart Cycle offers educational exergames for young children, with a control mechanism similar to the games shown in Figure 1a and 1d. Park et al. [31] recently demonstrated the potential of existing exercise devices as exergame controllers for repetitive body movements (e.g., treadmill running, cycling, rowing, rope jumping).

A large body of work focuses on developing new exergame controllers (e.g., smart wall) [5, 25] or evaluating well-known motion-based controllers such as Wiimote [28]. To our knowledge, a comprehensive study on fitness equipment-based controllers has yet to be reported. This study aims to bridge this gap and deliver practical game design implications. Our work complements other exergames studies on context (e.g., education [1], medical [12, 40]) and benefits (e.g., exercise effectiveness and adherence [41], social relationships [40], and cognitive function [9]).

SPEED-BASED EXERGAME CONTROLLERS

This work focuses on fitness equipment with repetitive physical movements, such as treadmills, indoor cycles/rowers, and elliptical trainers. Speed-based exergame controllers require continuous physical effort, a major departure from existing devices for games, such as a mouse or gamepad. The intensity of exercise (i.e., linear/angular speed) is used to realize one-dimensional speed-based movement control. On a stationary cycle, for instance, the angular speed (or pedaling speed) is mapped to the speed of an avatar. Speed is altered by pedaling faster or slower (Figure 1e). Such speed-based movement control differs from existing distance-based movement control in traditional pointing devices (e.g., mouse, Wiimote) where linear movement of the device is directly mapped to an avatar's movement.

As such, using speed-based exergame controllers requires a fresh look at the characteristics of game play. We compare and discuss the characteristics of traditional and speed-based controllers. For simplicity, we focus on two major aspects of control: *maintaining* the current state and *transitioning* to a different state.

For a maintaining activity, the player's goal is to keep the current game state. Examples include holding an avatar's

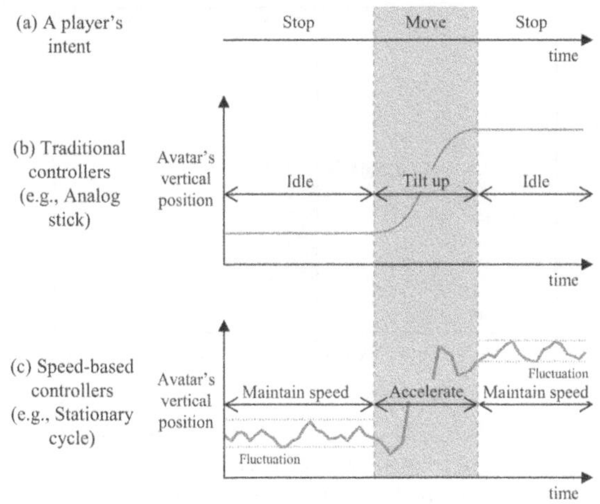

Figure 2. Control mechanism of traditional and speed-based controllers.

position in a scrolling game or maintaining the current speed and direction in a racing game.

For a transitioning activity, the player's goal is to change the game state, such as relocating an avatar to a different position or steering a vehicle to a new path. Typical traditional controller designs, such as buttons or joysticks, are effective in identifying the player's intent for either maintenance or transition. Examples include pushing a button (transition) or not (maintenance), or tilting a joystick (transition) or holding it at a fixed position (maintenance). Figure 1f illustrates the process of relocating an avatar along the vertical axis and holding its position by a traditional controller.

In contrast, the original design goals of speed-based controllers do not consider whether the player's intention is maintenance or transition. Instead, the goal is the precise and continuous measurement of the parameters representing a player's instantaneous exercising intensity. A common practice in designing speed-based exergames is to leverage the value of a speed-equivalent parameter as a 1-dimensional controller input, and translate it into a unique game state. An example is revolutions per minute (rpm) for a stationary cycle [38, 39]. Figure 1e illustrates an example of translating cycling rpm into the avatar's vertical position.

In the cases above, the controller requires the player to maintain physical exertion throughout game play. Even if the intention is maintenance, the player should continue pedaling at a consistent rpm. This characteristic is different from discrete inputs such as pressing buttons. Figure 2a depicts a time sequence of a player's intent while playing games from Figure 1: holding the avatar at position A, moving upward to position B, then holding at that position. Figure 2b and Figure 2c show the player's behavior history and the avatar's actual trace in the game when using a game pad and a stationary cycle, respectively.

RESEARCH QUESTIONS

The observations above have various implications regarding game play by a speed-based controller. To attain an in-depth understanding and derive unique design considerations of speed-based controllers, we formulate the following research questions.

RQ1. How precisely can players maintain the speed of speed-based controllers?

RQ2. Are there specific factors that account for performance during speed maintenance?

As shown in Figure 2c, a certain amount of error persists even when a player's goal is to maintain a specified speed. Here, a number of factors are at work, such as the limited precision of human motor output, the exercise intensity, and the mechanics of the exercise equipment. It was reported that even if a player intends to pedal at a constant rpm, the instantaneous torque is not consistent but increases while the pedals are being pushed, and vice versa [3]. In-depth understanding of the error characteristics and the achievable precision is important in exergame design (e.g., setting the tolerance level to classify the player's input as maintenance). However, this was not seriously investigated thus far in the context of game controllers.

RQ3. What are the differences and similarities for performance and comfort between speed-based controllers and traditional controllers?

Understanding the human factors of a new controller, such as performance and comfort, would assist in designing in-game challenges and in estimating the associated experiences [34]. Manipulating a speed-based controller requires a large displacement of limbs. This may decrease the performance of controlling tasks in terms of accuracy and agility compared to pressing buttons a few millimeters deep. Similarly, requiring the motion of massive body parts could quickly exhaust the users. This might have an adverse effect on user-perceived comfort. To evaluate the performance and comfort of a speed-based controller, we adopt a Fitts' law paradigm [6] to assess performance. This test is widely used in analyzing inter-device differences [4, 21, 22], as well as in predicting user performance while manipulating devices [37]. We measure performance and comfort levels and compare with traditional controllers including a gamepad and a Wiimote.

While examining characteristics of speed-based controllers, we also focus on learning effects, considering inexperienced game players with speed-based controllers. The results will be helpful for game designers to accommodate newcomers, for example, in providing a tutorial or incremental challenges [8, 33].

Device Prototype

We built a prototype of a speed-based controller using an exercise bike. See Figure 3. Our prototype monitors angular rotation speed using an optical rotary encoder and a photo interrupter (as suggested by [12, 30]). To smooth unwanted fluctuations in the detected signals, the sensor output is averaged over a sliding interval of 0.5 seconds. This provides a good sense of responsiveness combined with a sufficient resolution.

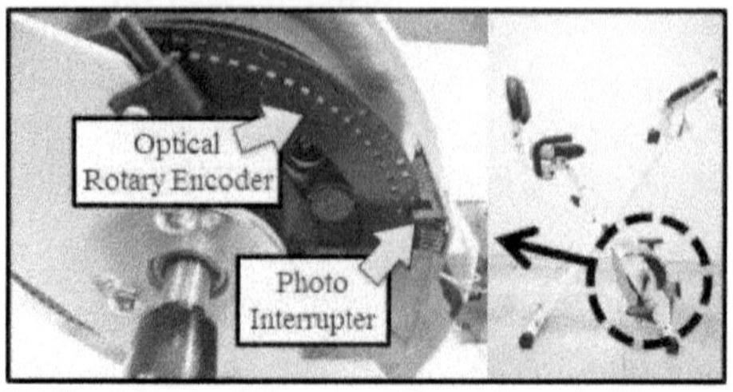

Figure 3. Hardware of the speed-based controller prototype.

STUDY 1: MAINTENANCE PERFORMANCE

Method

Our first experiment evaluates players' performance for speed maintenance; that is, holding a target speed. As stated earlier, speed-based controllers require players to maintain their speed to retain an in-game state. Considering the operation of exercise equipment, we focus on two factors that may affect maintenance performance: target speed and resistance force of an exercise bike.

Participants

Fifteen participants (6 females) were recruited on campus from an age group of 18 to 23. The average age was 20.8 (*SD* = 1.82). We advertised that the experiments may require physical abilities related to the operation of an exercise bike. Participants were compensated the equivalent of $10 US.

Apparatus (Hardware)

Input was via the exercise bike, which supports variable resistance in eight levels. Prior to the experiment, we carefully measured the resistance force of the bike (by referring to [23]) and found that the force ranges from 4.89 kp to 35.32 kp, under a 0.5 meter flywheel circumference.[1] Output was presented on a 24-inch display with a resolution of 1280 by 720 pixels.

Apparatus (Software)

The test software was developed in Microsoft XNA, a popular game development framework. The display included a vertical speed gauge showing the current speed and target speed as well as the time remaining. See Figure 4. The gauge range was from 50 to 130 rpm with each 10 rpm mapped to 90 pixels (3.75 cm). This range encompasses common pedaling rates in cycle training [2]. The target speed is indicated by an arrow on the left of the gauge. The remaining time appears at the top-right corner.

Procedure

Participants performed trials of a simple maintenance task. They were instructed to manipulate the bike to maintain the gauge level as close as possible to the target speed for 30 seconds. A beep sounded at the end of each trial.

Design

A 3 × 3 within-subjects design was used. Independent variables were target speed (f = 60, 90, and 120 rpm) and resistance force (r = 9.2, 14.3, and 19.4 kp, set by resistance levels 2, 5, and 8, respectively). All nine conditions were used and presented in random order until all trials were

[1]kp denotes kilopond, or kilogram-force, a gravitational metric unit of force.

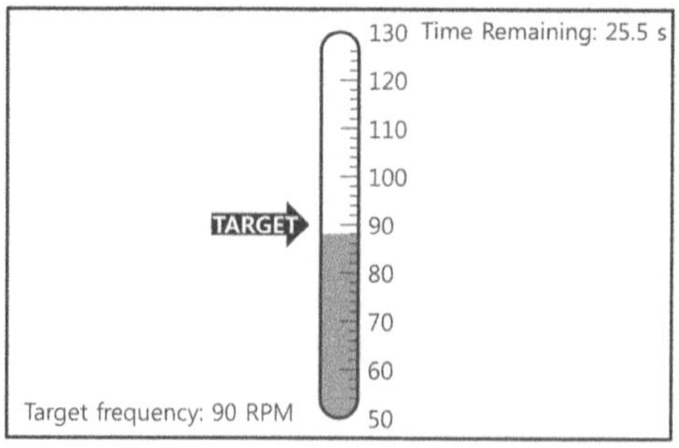

Figure 4. Screenshot of the maintenance test.

completed. The dependent variables were offset error and root mean square (RMS) error, both with units rpm. These errors capture the variation between participants' speed and the target speed. In detail, the offset error is calculated for each subject by averaging the differences of all sampled speeds (for the 30 seconds) from the target speed. Similarly, we obtained the RMS error by calculating the root of the squared mean of the differences.

Results and Discussion

The results for offset error and RMS error are shown in Figure 5. For offset error, the difference was statistically significant for target speed ($F_{2,117}$ = 20.16, $p < .001$). For RMS error, the differences were statistically significant, both for target speed ($F_{2,117}$ = 22.04, $p < .001$) and for resistance force ($F_{2,117}$ = 6.09, $p < .005$).

Note that the errors do not proportionally increase as the target speed increases. The error rate abruptly jumps when the target speed exceeds a certain value. The offset error is close to zero at 60 and 90 rpm, but is negative and relatively far from zero at 120 rpm, as shown in Figure 5a. The error is more prominent as the resistance force becomes higher. This indicates that with the highest workout combination (120 rpm at 19.4 kp) it was difficult for the participants to

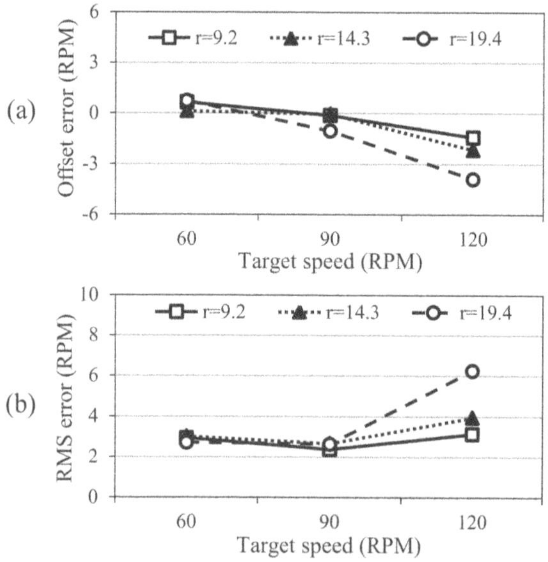

Figure 5. Error by target speed and resistance force. (a) offset error, (b) RMS error. (Note: the reported values are the means of the measures across all 15 participants. *r* is the resistance force of the exercise bike in kp.)

maintain the target speed. That is, if a player riding at 19.4 kp of resistance wants to use a range from 60 to 120 rpm, she may feel that controllability is not consistent throughout the range. Under the lowest resistance force (9.2 kp), a paired *t*-test indicated no statistically significant difference in the RMS error and the offset error.

We investigated the literature on exercise physiology to identify the major factors responsible for errors at higher target speed. The literature indicates that pedaling torque is not consistent throughout a revolution, thereby causing variability on pedaling speed [3, 35]. The causal relationship between the torque and speed could be significant when the resistance level is high [35]. We also found that the inertial load of the cycle crank and flywheel could affect the perceived difficulty in maintaining a target speed [13], and it is thus necessary to take into account these factors.

Thus, exergame designers should carefully select a speed range for game play in consideration of resistance force of the bike, to give users the perception of controllability over the range. We thus set the resistance force as 9.2 kp for the next experiment to facilitate maintenance performance. We also set the minimum target width of the pointing task to require a range larger than 8 rpm, based on the observation that the RMS error was lower than 4 rpm at this level of force.

STUDY 2: POINTING PERFORMANCE AND COMFORT

Method

We designed the second experiment to compare a speed-based controller with popular game controllers, namely, a gamepad and a Wiimote. We anticipated that a speed-based controller may increase the difficulty of control or lead to inconsistent performance. We adapted Natapov and MacKenzie's approach of testing a game controller with a pointing task and checking whether it follows Fitts' law [6], as with other non-keyboard input devices [21, 28]. Here, Fitts' law gives the time to move to a target (*MT*) as a function of the distance to the target (*A*) and the width (*W*) of the target [4]:

$$MT = a + b \log_2(\frac{A}{W} + 1), \quad (1)$$

where *a* and *b* are constant coefficients determined through linear regression. The logarithmic term is the index of difficulty (*ID*, in bits). We expected that the overall movement time of speed-based controllers would be longer than that of traditional game controllers.

Participants

The fifteen participants who took part in the first experiment participated in the second experiment a few days later. They were compensated the equivalent of $50 US.

Apparatus (Hardware)

The input devices included the exercise bike, an XBOX360 gamepad, and a Wiimote. See Figure 6. For clicking with the bike, we attached two push buttons on the handle bar and asked participants to push the buttons using their left or right index finger. To utilize the Wiimote's pointing feature based

Figure 6. Game controllers used for the pointing task – exercise bike, gamepad, Wiimote.

on infrared sensors, we attached a Wii Infrared Sensor Bar on top of the monitor. The output was presented on a 24-inch display. The distance between the display and eyes of a participant was fixed at 85 cm, with the height of the eyes fixed at the center of the display. The height of the display was adjusted, as necessary, for each participant.

Apparatus (Software)

The display showed a crosshair-type cursor, centered horizontally. See Figure 7. For the exercise bike, the vertical position of the cursor was directly mapped to the speed of the exercise bike; that is, 50 rpm at the bottom and 130 rpm at the top; with 10 rpm increments mapped into 90 pixels (3.75 cm).

For the gamepad, participants used the analog stick at the top-left corner. We used only the vertical component of the analog stick data. The analog stick can generate a continuous value from –1.0 to +1.0 via Microsoft XNA Input Device API, which is mapped to the tilted angle of the stick. We then mapped the value to incrementally change the vertical position of the crosshair on the screen. The maximum velocity of the cursor was ±900 pixels/s when the stick was fully extended.

For the Wiimote, we utilized GlovePIE (v0.36) software and a specialized script to convert the Wiimote data to mouse data. We then mapped the vertical position of the data to the vertical position of the cursor. For clicking, we used the customized push buttons for the exercise bike: 'A' button for the gamepad and both 'A' and 'B' buttons for Wiimote.

Task

A vertical version of a one-directional pointing task was implemented (by referring to [4, 17, 18]) using Microsoft XNA. See Figure 7. A trial starts when a participant clicks on the green home square, and ends when the participant clicks on the red target square. The time between these clicks is recorded as the movement time for a trial (*MT* in seconds).

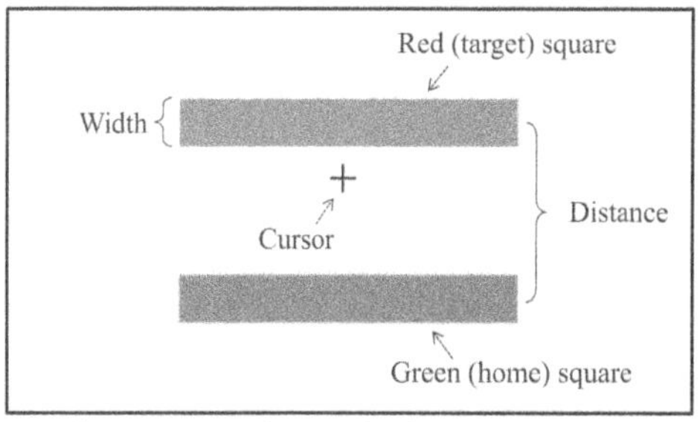

Figure 7. Screenshot of the pointing task. A participant is performing a trial, having just clicked the home square and moving toward the target square.

Combinations of width and distance were presented randomly. (The detailed settings of the combinations follow in the next subsection.)

Procedure

Participants were randomly assigned to one of three groups (5 per group). Each participant was tested with all three devices (one device per day, three days in total). The order of testing was counterbalanced using a Latin square. The total time for each participant ranged from 30 to 90 minutes per day for three days.

Before testing, the task was explained and demonstrated to participants. Participants were instructed to perform the task as quickly as possible while trying to avoid mistakes. They performed ten blocks of multiple combinations of target width and distance. The participants took 5-minute breaks between blocks to avoid fatigue.

Design

A within-subjects design was used with the following independent variables and levels:

- Input Device {Wiimote, Gamepad, Exercise Bike}
- Target Width {80 pixels, 120 pixels}
- Target Distance {200 pixels, 300 pixels, 400 pixels}
- Block {1 to 10}
- Trial {1 to 10}

Considering the maintenance performance of the exercise bike (within a range of target speeds ±4 rpm), we set the minimum width at 80 pixels, which represents about 9 rpm. This is large enough to contain the maintenance variability. The widths and distances yield Fitts' index of difficulty values from 1.42 to 2.58 bits.

A block consisted of 60 trials (10 trials for each width-distance combination × 6 combinations). The trials were presented in random order. A total of 600 trials were run (6 combinations × 10 trials × 10 blocks) for each participant, and thereby the total number of trials was 600 × 15 = 9,000.

Dependent variables were movement time (*MT*) for each trial and throughput (*TP*). Throughput is the rate of information transfer measured in bits per second (bps) [17, 18]. We also conducted an exit interview and administered a questionnaire to solicit participants' qualitative impressions and experiences with the test conditions.

Results and Discussion

Learning Effects and Movement Time

As mentioned above, the speed-based controller offers a manipulation mechanism unfamiliar to many game players. Thus, a learning effect was expected.

Figure 8 shows the results for movement time by input device and block. The Wiimote was the fastest device, the bike the slowest. The main effects were statistically significant for input device ($F_{2,420} = 533.27$, $p < .001$) and block ($F_{9,420} = 11.48$, $p < .001$). The input device by block

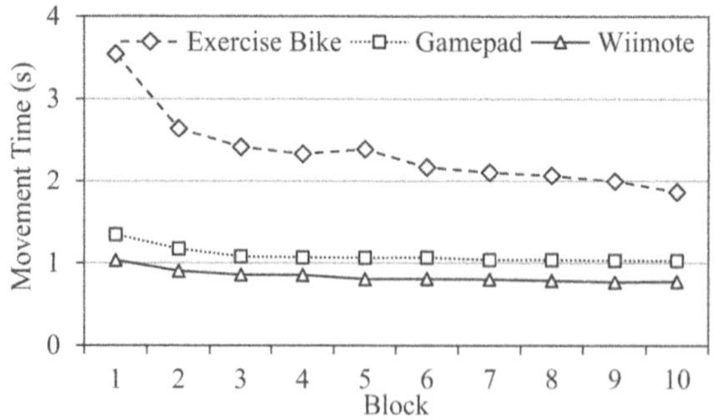

Figure 8. Movement time by input device and block.

interaction was also statistically significant ($F_{18,420} = 4.19$, $p < .001$).

We analyzed Helmert contrasts by following a previously reported approach [22]. The results showed that the block effect was not significant after blocks three and four for the gamepad and Wiimote, respectively. However, the speed-based controller showed significant differences as the number of blocks increases. The movement time of the speed-based controller improved substantially – from an initial value of 3.54 s to a final value of 1.86 s. Thus, there was clearly a much greater improvement for the speed-based controller than with the other two input devices.

It is worth noting the details of the block effect for the speed-based game controller. There were significant differences for movement time from blocks 1 to 6, but no significant differences from blocks 6 to 9. Finally, block 10 showed statistical difference from the former four blocks. Further studies on the learning effect will help identify whether the performance change in the last block occurred by chance. Subsequent analyses were based on means from the last block only because including blocks 6 to 9 did not yield significant changes.

Fitts' Law Models and Throughput

To test whether the exercise bike follows Fitts' law, we separately examined the six combinations of target widths and distances and the five distinct values of index of difficulties (*IDs*). This is shown in Table 1. For each combination, we computed the error rate (*ER*) and movement time (*MT*). Each dependent measure is based on 120 observations (12 participants × 10 trials per combination).

Figure 9 shows scatter plots and regression lines for the six *MT-ID* points for each input device. The prediction equations

Distance	Width	ID	Exercise Bike		Gamepad		Wiimote	
(pixels)	(pixels)	(bits)	ER(%)	MT(ms)	ER(%)	MT(ms)	ER(%)	MT(ms)
200	80	1.81	17.33%	1697	3.33%	1032	5.33%	729
200	120	1.42	6.00%	1302	1.33%	873	4.00%	655
300	80	2.25	11.33%	1959	3.33%	1130	6.00%	844
300	120	1.81	1.33%	1662	2.00%	925	2.67%	723
400	80	2.58	12.67%	2413	6.67%	1193	8.00%	915
400	120	2.12	5.33%	2150	2.00%	1032	0.67%	788
	Mean:	2.00	9.00%	1864	3.11%	1031	4.44%	776
		Throughput:	1.07 bps		1.94 bps		2.57 bps	

Table 1. Throughput calculations from the Fitts' law experiment.

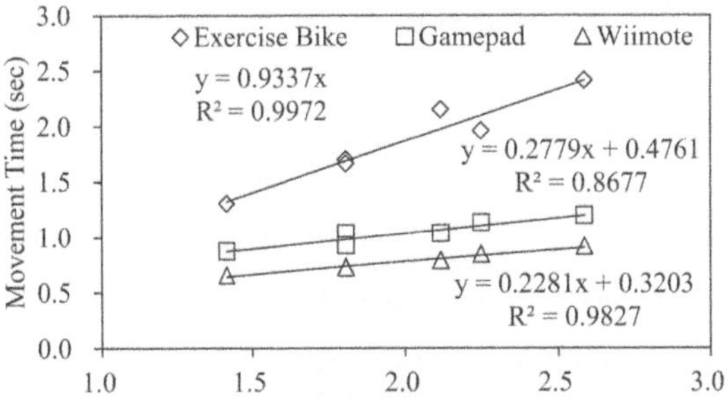

Figure 9. Fitts' law regression results for three input devices.

for *MT* as a function of *ID* are also shown. *R* squared values are high for all three input devices, including the exercise bike. The throughput (calculated by referring to [4]) was 1.07 bps for the exercise bike, 1.94 bps for the Gamepad, and 2.57 bps for the Wiimote. Note that our results for the Gamepad and Wiimote are comparable with previous results [28] of 1.48 bps and 2.59 bps, respectively.

Exit Interview and Questionnaire

The questionnaire was a modified version of the Device Assessment questionnaire [4]. There were 18 items on a wide range of human factors relating to effort, fatigue, and comfort. Responses were on a 5-point Likert scale. We used the questionnaire to guide the exit interviews while soliciting detailed explanations related to the participants' responses.

The means and standard deviations of the responses are presented in Table 2. A Freidman test revealed statistically significant differences with respect to the following attributes: force required for actuation ($H_2 = 16.68, p < .001$), smoothness ($H_2 = 11.88, p < .01$), physical effort ($H_2 = 17.38, p < .001$), difficulty of accurate pointing ($H_2 = 10.65, p < .01$), operation speed ($H_2 = 14.17, p < .001$), and overall usability ($H_2 = 14.63, p < .001$). The differences favored the gamepad on the physical effort, accurate pointing, and overall usability, and the Wiimote on the smoothness and operation speed. On the force required for actuation, the gamepad and Wiimote received the poorest ratings. No significant differences were found on the other questions regarding mental effort, operation speed, and general comfort. We did not find any statistically significant differences on comfort and mental workload, although it was noted that the speed-based controller was regarded as slightly less comfortable and required a greater mental workload than the Wiimote and the gamepad (in terms of average values). Overall, the reported levels of comfort and mental effort are adequate with respect to practical use as game controllers (comfort: *mean* = 3.07, *SD* = 1.03; mental effort: *mean* = 3.07, *SD* 1.39). The participants generally agreed that they could confidently maneuver the device after training. As expected, the required physical effort of an exercise bike is significantly higher (*mean* = 3.93, *SD* = 1.33) than existing devices (gamepad: *mean* = 1.60, *SD* = 0.63). Smoothness during operation is above the moderate level (*mean* = 3.13, *SD* = 0.83), which is slightly worse than that of existing devices (gamepad: *mean* = 4.27, *SD* = 0.70). Fast movements are easy to perform

	Question		Exercise Bike	Gamepad	Wiimote
1	Force (1:low – 5:high)	***	3.27(1.28)	1.47(.64)	1.47(.52)
2	Smoothness (1:rough – 5:smooth)	**	3.13(.83)	4.27(.70)	4.33(.98)
3	Mental effort (1:low – 5:high)	ns	3.07(1.39)	2.27(1.33)	2.13(1.36)
4	Physical effort	***	3.93(1.33)	1.60(.63)	1.87(.64)
5	Accurate pointing (1:easy – 5:difficult)	**	3.93(1.22)	2.33(1.11)	2.53(1.13)
6	Operation speed (1:fast – 5:slow)	***	2.40(.63)	2.33(.90)	1.40(.83)
7	Finger fatigue (1:none – 5:high)	ns	2.20(1.21)	2.80(1.21)	2.20(1.21)
8	Wrist fatigue	ns	2.67(1.50)	2.13(1.06)	3.40(1.40)
9	Arm fatigue	ns	2.40(1.40)	1.80(1.08)	2.73(1.10)
10	Shoulder fatigue	ns	2.07(.88)	1.47(.92)	2.27(.88)
11	Neck fatigue	ns	1.93(.70)	1.67(.72)	1.67(.90)
12	Foot fatigue	N/A	3.20(1.08)	N/A	N/A
13	Ankle fatigue	N/A	3.67(1.29)	N/A	N/A
14	Leg fatigue	N/A	3.53(1.30)	N/A	N/A
15	Knee fatigue	N/A	3.33(1.18)	N/A	N/A
16	Thigh fatigue	N/A	3.73(1.49)	N/A	N/A
17	General comfort (1:uncomfortable)	ns	3.07(1.03)	3.67(1.05)	3.80(1.08)
18	Overall usability (1:difficult – 5:easy)	***	2.93(1.03)	4.33(.82)	4.07(1.10)

***: $p < .001$, **: $p < .01$, ns: not significant

Table 2. Results of the Device Assessment Questionnaire. Shaded cells show the most favourable response (where statistical significance was attained).

(*mean* = 2.40, *SD* = 0.63), but accurate pointing was reported to be somewhat difficult, mainly due to the moderate level of perceived smoothness. Overall, the participants believed that when compared with traditional controllers, the exercise bike has a moderate level of usability (*mean* = 2.93, *SD* = 1.03).

In the following, we report user comments from the interviews. Consistent with the questionnaire results, many participants noted that the exercise bike required more physical effort to maintain speed than the gamepad or the Wiimote. One participant reported that it even required more mental workload, commenting, "*It was a bit hard to maintain a steady speed [with the cycle] and I had to pay significant attention.*" Maintaining steady speed requires careful coordination of one's bodily movements. One participant said, "*When I feel acceleration, I take some rest [to decelerate]. Then it significantly drops. It's a bit hard to control.*" Another participant complained that the controller has less control power: "*As it may be using body parts, the problem is not that I made any subtle mistakes but that acceleration control is hard to perform.*"

In addition, several participants commented on unfamiliarity: "*At the beginning it was really hard to point at the target. And it was difficult to figure out how to control the speed of the cycle.*" These comments highlight the importance of training and tutorial sessions to help users become accustomed to the controller.

The participants felt that approaching the target area is easy, but accurate pointing takes time and effort. One participant said, "*It's difficult to enter the rectangular area as the cursor keeps moving up and down. It is a bit hard to exactly point at the area.*" The fluctuation in speed comes from a series of repeated acceleration and deceleration activities as the user aims to reach the target speed range. Participants generally agreed that when compared with the gamepad and Wiimote, fine-grained movement control using the speed-based controller is more difficult, as one participant reported, "*When I operate the controller, I have to make one small movement after another, and such fine-grained control was a bit hard to make.*"

In addition, participants commented about asymmetries in physical efforts when making transitions between speed levels: "*There was no notable discomfort. It was easy to go down, but it was difficult to go up [during a pointing task]. It does not require a great effort, but it requires quite a lot of attention.*"

The importance of resistance level was pointed out by one of the participants who said, "*The resistance level was good [during the experiments]. But if the level is higher than the current level, there will be a smaller degree of freedom for acceleration, and it will be difficult to perform the task.*" These comments are consistent with our experimental results, and these aspects should be carefully reflected in the game design.

We collected several comments from the participants that the controllability could be influenced by individual fitness levels, particularly in terms of muscular endurance. One participant commented: "*In the final trial, I felt my legs a little bit tired, and I saw the cursor was sometimes not exactly moving as I intended.*" Another participant said: "*I think I could do better if I had better endurance for the entire session.*" We anticipate that further studies with subjects of different fitness levels would reveal how individual muscular endurance or strength levels would result in a degradation of controllability as trials progress.

EXERPLANET: A DESIGN CASE STUDY

To illustrate how our findings are applicable to practical exergame design, we designed a game called ExerPlanet. It belongs to the shooter game category. Action is viewed side-on, with the screen continuously scrolling horizontally. Other possibilities include action and puzzle games.

Game Description

As shown in Figure 10a, the player's spacecraft moves vertically while planets attack from a horizontal direction. (Note that vertical steering is commonly used in exergame design [7, 11, 36].) The spacecraft continually shoots missiles with the player raining fire on a planet until it is destroyed; a larger planet takes more time to destroy. Points are gained based on the size of the planet. The player seeks to avert a plane crash and to earn as many points as possible to improve their ranking on the leader board.

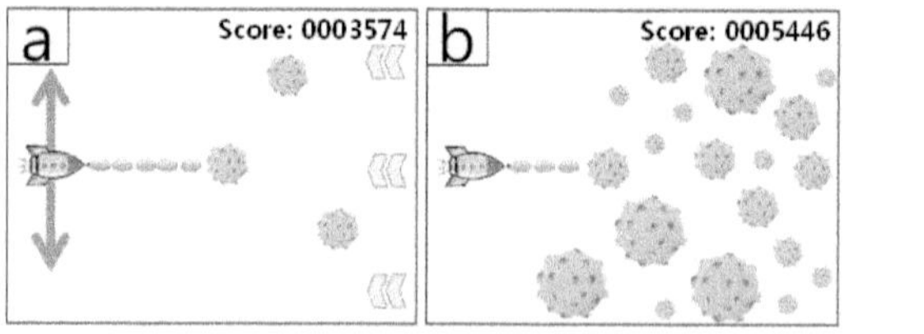

Figure 10. Screenshots of the sample game.

Detailed Examples: Level Design

The key factors on level design include the properties of a planet (i.e., size, position, speed) and the number of planets.

Planet location: A planet can move in a straight line. We set the speed range to maneuver a spacecraft from 60 to 120 rpm, with the resistance force fixed at 9.2 kp. According to our results, there was no significant maintenance variation under different speeds in the range (here, vertical location). This means that a planet's initial position can be randomly selected from the right side.

Planet size: When determining a planet's minimum size, the designer should carefully consider a controller's characteristics. In particular, we showed that a player's speed tends to fluctuate when performing a maintenance task; nonetheless, for a given target speed, the RMS error is within ± 4 rpm. This means that designers should configure the size of a planet by considering the range of RMS error, that is, 8 rpm; if the size is below this range, players may feel that the game lacks controllability.

Planet placement and speed setting. Consider a scenario where there are two planets on the screen. To allow a player to blast both planets, we should properly configure their placement and speed setting to allow sufficient time to destroy both planets. In other words, after blasting one planet, the player should be able to steer the spacecraft to successfully shoot and destroy the other planet. Our pointing task results show that the movement time approximately follows Fitts' law. This empirical model can be used to find the minimum time required to reach the target speed (or target height). For instance, changing from 60 rpm to 120 rpm takes about 4 seconds; thus, the designer can properly configure the planet placement and speed accordingly.

Player tutorial session: According to our results, the exercise bike requires some time for learning when compared with traditional pointing devices. The designer may want to introduce a tutorial level; the goal is to allow users to maneuver the controller skillfully. In addition, data from the tutorial can be used to understand a player's capabilities and provide for more personalized gameplay.

DISCUSSION AND LIMITATIONS

Designing Unique Physical Challenges in Exergames

As stated, providing a consistent sense of controllability throughout game play is important. Exergame designers, however, may intentionally adapt a speed range with inconsistent controllability, to create physical challenges.

For example, defeating a boss character in a game is supposed to be difficult. To avoid fire attacks from the boss character, players might be required to pedal at 115 to 125 rpm with a high resistance level. This challenge would be difficult for some players, as the average RMS error at 120 rpm was above 5 rpm. Employing physical in-game challenges can be one unique characteristic of exergame design. It is worth noting that the difficulty of challenges in traditional games is usually controlled by adjusting the complexity of mental tasks, e.g., to make players identify a specific hidden movement pattern of a boss character.

Exercise and Training Perspectives

When considering a player's energy expenditure, the game designer should carefully design or adapt in-game challenges to avoid exhausting a player quickly or failing to achieve a sufficient amount of exercise [14, 16, 39]. For example in the shooter game, it would help to distribute initial positions of planets—the higher the speed (proportional to a planet's height), the higher the energy expenditure.

From the training viewpoint, a maintenance task can be employed in exergames to help exercisers learn an effective pedaling method. It is known that maintaining a steady pedaling speed requires an even distribution of pedaling torque throughout a revolution [20, 35], and this is regarded as an efficient pedaling technique [3]. We envision that more training methods can be adapted in speed-based exergames and thereby effectively provide exercisers with better ways to physically train.

Limitations

We restricted our attention to an exercise bike. In general, existing fitness devices for repetitive exercises (e.g., running, elliptical training, rowing) share similar properties, as mentioned in [31, 32]. Our experiments can thus expand to other fitness regimes. Further user studies are needed to generalize our findings to other devices.

We intentionally limited our discussion on game design to action games (particularly shooter games) as many existing exergames belong to this genre [7, 11, 36]. Given our understanding of an exergame controller, exploring alternative genres such as role-playing and simulation would be an interesting avenue for future work.

Furthermore, we employed a group of participants in their 20s to promote internal validity of the experiments. Additional experiments with different age groups and physical capabilities are necessary to generalize the results.

CONCLUSION

We evaluated a speed-based exergame controller based on a stationary cycle with a maintenance task and a pointing task and derived the following results. First, the performance of a maintenance task is largely dependent on the difficulty level (e.g., target speed and resistance level), and maintenance error is approximately within a range of 10%. Second, the results of a pointing task with a directional constraint follow a Fitts' law model, but the slope is much steeper than for other devices such as a gamepad and Wiimote. Third, we provided detailed accounts of user experiences in using the exergame controller and illustrated how our findings can be applied to practical exergame design.

ACKNOWLEDGEMENTS

We thank Haechan Lee and Bupjae Lee for their assistance. This work was jointly supported by NRF grant funded by the Korea government (MSIP) (No. 2011-0018120), the IT R&D Program of MSIP/KEIT [10041313, UX-oriented Mobile SW Platform], and CMTC of the Agency for Defense Development [1415125561].

REFERENCES

1. Al-Hrathi, R., Karime, A., Al-Osman, H. and Saddik, A. E. Exerlearn Bike: An Exergaming System for Children's Educational and Physical Well-being. *Proc. IEEE ICMEW'12*, (New York: IEEE), 489-494.
2. Coast, J. R., Cox, R. H., and Welch, H. G. Optimal pedaling rate in prolonged bouts of cycle ergometry. *Med. Sci. Sports. Exerc*, *18*, 2 (1986), 225-230.
3. Davis, R. and Hull, M. Measurement of pedal loading in bicycling: II. Analysis and results. *J. Biomech., 14*, 12 (1981), 857-872.
4. Douglas, S. A., Kirkpatrick, A. E. and MacKenzie, I. S. Testing pointing device performance and user assessment with the ISO 9241, Part 9 standard. *Proc. CHI'99*, (New York: ACM), 215-222.
5. Exergame Fitness: Lightspace Play Wall. http://www.exergamefitness.com/products/item.php?show=lightspace_play_wall, accessed August 2013.
6. Fitts, P. M. The information capacity of the human motor system in controlling the amplitude of movement. *J. Exp. Psychol.*, *47*, 6 (1954), 381-391.
7. Frevola. http://frevola.com/, accessed August 2013.
8. Fullerton, T. *Game design workshop: A playcentric approach to creating innovative games*. Burlington, MA: Elsevier Morgan Kaufmann, 2008.
9. Gao, Y. and Mandryk, R. The acute cognitive benefits of casual exergame play. *Proc. CHI'12*, (New York: ACM), 1863-1872.
10. Gerling, K., Livingston, I., Nacke, L. and Mandryk, R. Full-body motion-based game interaction for older adults. *Proc. CHI'12*, (New York: ACM), 1873-1882.
11. Göbel, S., Hardy, S., Wendel, V., Mehm, F. and Steinmetz, R. Serious games for health: Personalized exergames. *Proc. Multimedia'10*, (New York: ACM), 1663-1666.
12. Guo, S., Grindle, G. G., Authier, E. L., Cooper, R. A., Fitzgerald, S. G., Kelleher, A. and Cooper, R. Development and qualitative assessment of the GAMECycle exercise system. *IEEE Trans. Neural Sys. Rehab. Eng.*, *14*, 1 (2006), 83-90.
13. Hansen, E. A., Jørgensen, L. V., Jensen, K., Fregly, B. J., and Sjøgaard, G. Crank inertial load affects freely

chosen pedal rate during cycling. *J. Biomech.*, *35*, 2 (2002), 277-285.

14. Haskell, W. L., Lee, I., Pate, R. R., Powell, K. E., Blair, S. N., Franklin, B. A., Macera, C. A., Heath, G. W., Thompson, P. D., Bauman, A. Physical activity and public health: updated recommendation for adults from the American College of Sports Medicine and the American Heart Association. *Med. Sci. Sport. Exer., 39*, 8 (2007), 1423-1434.
15. Hernandez, H. A., Graham, T., Fehlings, D., Switzer, L., Ye, Z., Bellay, Q., Hamza, M. A., Savery, C. and Stach, T. Design of an exergaming station for children with cerebral palsy. *Proc. CHI'12*, (New York: ACM), 2619-2628.
16. Hernandez, H. A., Ye, Z., Graham, T., Fehlings, D. and Switzer, L. Designing action-based exergames for children with cerebral palsy. *Proc. CHI'13*, (New York: ACM), 1261-1270.
17. *ISO 9241-9 Ergonomic requirements for office work with visual display terminals (VDTs) - Part 9: Requirements for non-keyboard input devices*, International Organization for Standardization, 2000.
18. *ISO 9241-411 Ergonomics of human-system interaction - Part 411: Evaluation methods for the design of physical input devices*, International Organization for Standardization, 2012.
19. Konami Dance Dance Revolution. 2005.
20. Korff, T., Romer, L. M., Mayhew, I., and Martin, J. C. Effect of pedaling technique on mechanical effectiveness and efficiency in cyclists. *Med. Sci. Sports Exerc., 39,* 6 (2007), 991.
21. MacKenzie, I. S. Fitts' law as a research and design tool in human-computer interaction. *Hum.-Comp. Int., 7*, 1 (1992), 91-139.
22. MacKenzie, I. S., Kauppinen, T. and Silfverberg, M. Accuracy measures for evaluating computer pointing devices. *Proc. CHI'01*, (New York: ACM), 9-16.
23. McArdle, W. D., Katch, F. I. and Katch, V. L. *Exercise physiology: Nutrition, energy, and human performance*. Philadelphia: Lippincott Williams & Wilkins, 2010.
24. Mueller, F., Vetere, F., Gibbs, M. R., Edge, D., Agamanolis, S. and Sheridan, J. G. Jogging over a distance between Europe and Australia. *Proc. UIST'10*, (New York: ACM), 189-198.
25. Mueller, F. F., Agamanolis, S., Gibbs, M. R. and Vetere, F. Remote impact: Shadowboxing over a distance. *Proc. CHI'08 Extended Abstracts*, (New York: ACM), 2291-2296.
26. Mueller, F. F., Edge, D., Vetere, F., Gibbs, M. R., Agamanolis, S., Bongers, B., and Sheridan, J. G. Designing sports: a framework for exertion games. *Proc. CHI'11*, (New York: ACM), 2651-2660.
27. Mueller, F. F. and Gibbs, M. A table tennis game for three players. *Proc. OzCHI'06*, (New York: ACM), 321-324.
28. Natapov, D., Castellucci, S. J. and MacKenzie, I. S. ISO 9241-9 evaluation of video game controllers. *Proc. GI'09*, (New York: ACM), 223-230.
29. Nenonen, V., Lindblad, A., Häkkinen, V., Laitinen, T., Jouhtio, M. and Hämäläinen, P. Using heart rate to control an interactive game. *Proc. CHI'07*, (New York: ACM), 853-856.
30. Ohmae, T., Matsuda, T., Kamiyama, K. and Tachikawa, M. A microprocessor-controlled high-accuracy wide-range speed regulator for motor drives. *IEEE Trans. Indus. Elec.*, 3 (1982), 207-211.
31. Park, T., Hwang, I., Lee, U., Lee, S. I., Yoo, C., Lee, Y., Jang, H., Choe, S. P., Park, S. and Song, J. ExerLink: Enabling pervasive social exergames with heterogeneous exercise devices. *Proc. MobiSys'12*, (New York: ACM), 15-28.
32. Park, T., Lee, U., Lee, B., Lee, H., Son, S., Song, S., and Song, J. ExerSync: facilitating interpersonal synchrony in social exergames. *Proc. CSCW'13*, (New York: ACM), 409-422.
33. Rollings, A. and Adams, E. *Andrew Rollings and Ernest Adams on game design*. Berkeley, CA: New Riders Publishing, 2003.
34. Schell, J. *The Art of Game Design: A book of lenses*. Burlington, MA: Elsevier Morgan Kaufmann, 2008.
35. Seck, D., Vandewalle, H., Decrops, N., and Monod, H. Maximal power and torque-velocity relationship on a cycle ergometer during the acceleration phase of a single all-out exercise. *Eur. J. Appl. Physiol. Occup., 70*, 2 (1995), 161-168.
36. Sinclair, J., Hingston, P. and Masek, M. Considerations for the design of exergames. *Proc. The International Conference on Computer Graphics and Interactive Techniques in Australasia and South-East Asia - Graphite'07*, (New York: ACM), 289-295.
37. Soukoreff, R. W. and MacKenzie, I. S. Towards a standard for pointing device evaluation, perspectives on 27 years of Fitts' law research in HCI. *Int. J. Human-Comput. St.*, 61, 6 (2004), 751-789.
38. Stach, T., Graham, T., Brehmer, M. and Hollatz, A. Classifying input for active games. *Proc. ACE'09*, (New York: ACM), 379-382.
39. Stach, T., Graham, T., Yim, J. and Rhodes, R. E. Heart rate control of exercise video games. *Proc. GI'09*, (New York: ACM), 125-132.
40. Theng, Y.-L., Chua, P. H. and Pham, T. P. Wii as entertainment and socialisation aids for mental and social health of the elderly. *Proc. CHI'12 Extended Abstracts*, (New York: ACM), 691-702.
41. Warburton, D. E., Bredin, S. S., Horita, L. T., Zbogar, D., Scott, J. M., Esch, B. T. and Rhodes, R. E. The health benefits of interactive video game exercise. *Appl. Physiol. Nutr. Metab*, 32, 4 (2007), 655-663.

Establishing Design Guidelines in Interactive Exercise Gaming: Preliminary Data from Two Posing Studies

Monica Zaczynski
Carleton University
Ottawa, Ontario
Monica.zaczynski@carleton.ca

Anthony Whitehead
Carleton University
Ottawa, Ontario
Anthony.whitehead@carleton.ca

ABSTRACT

Interactive gaming has demonstrated promise as a low-cost, at-home training and fitness instruction alternative. However, commercially available systems today are designed primarily for entertainment. As a result, the quality of instruction delivery and level of involvement may not meet the needs of a user.

This paper examines several issues including adapting for occlusion and lack of visibility; learning and orientation; and providing feedback to develop a set of design recommendations. While, the effect of visual delivery variation on performance was found to be inconclusive verbal delivery significantly improved performance. Additionally, verbal + haptic feedback produced the highest performance scores in comparison to other feedback types. With the additional support of qualitative data, these results, provide a strong foundation for future exploration of interactive training delivery that engages users, prevents injury and helps maintain fitness.

Author Keywords

Low-paced exercise training, Feedback, Haptic Feedback, Visual Delivery, Panning, Yoga, Wii Balance Board, Design Guidelines, Usability

ACM Classification Keywords

H.5.m. Information interfaces and presentation; Evaluation/ methodology, User-centered design.

INTRODUCTION

Fitness and training games have become increasingly more prevalent for interactive gaming systems. They are more convenient than joining an overcrowded class while offering dedicated monitoring from the comfort of home. Interactive games can be designed for a range of activity types and can provide reporting and progress data if game software collects body measurement information effectively. Current commercially available systems are not necessarily designed for focused fitness but rather for entertainment, and as a result, the quality of instruction delivery and level of involvement falls short for the needs of users [8,16].

Though current research on exergaming for fitness and rehabilitation has focused on refining the systems hardware – body measuring technology – [7,11] or searching for an appropriate blend of entertainment and following a prescribed regimen – the actual game design – [2,5,15], it seems the *quality* of the activity execution has not been given due attention – the effective marrying of hardware and software – [1,5]. Likewise, the user's self-efficacy associated with fully understanding what is expected is often overlooked. As much as a refined body measuring system and engaging game are important, paying attention to the users confidence in their own ability and understanding of expectations are essential to ensuring the level of interest and motivation that keep users motivated long term [3,13].

We will explore user understanding of pose presentation in low paced interactive training activities by examining elements that contribute to comprehension including occlusion and lack of visibility; learning and orientation and feedback. The goal of this paper is to document an ideal visual demonstration delivery that maximizes pose understanding and user self-efficacy, determine whether supplementary modalities are important for instruction, and determine if there is an ideal feedback delivery that promotes pose comprehension, confidence and motivation.

BACKGROUND & RELATED WORKS

Fitness instruction and yoga games are available for most interactive gaming systems today but are generally geared towards entertainment rather than accuracy. Games typically include a demonstration or training module preceding gameplay to teach users the action before they attempt to execute it themselves. Though this can mitigate the risk of injury, the quality of delivery can affect the comprehension of the action, which may increase the risk of injury. By allowing for a wide range of acceptable motion, interactive games accommodate for varying audience ability and evidently, understanding, at the expense of motion measurement precision. As a result, accepting a

CHI 2014, April 26–May 1, 2014, Toronto, Ontario, Canada.

http://dx.doi.org/10.1145/2556288.2557329

wider range of error in the name of keeping the game fun and entertaining [6].

During execution, game feedback is limited to informing users of incorrect positioning rather than offering a way to correct. In some cases, because of the game's method of motion capture, no feedback is provided at all. For example, at least three poses in the Nintendo's Wii Balance Board Yoga game do not even use the balance board, thus not collecting any motion information or having capability of providing feedback. Though this may be an appropriate design for entertainment it is not necessarily useful or well suited for exercise training like Yoga, where precision and accuracy are important.

At the core of this issue is the body-measuring machine itself. The method and amount of body information collected determines the gaming system's feedback capability. Commercially successful systems often use one or more types of sensors so that games can gather enough body information to create an engaging interaction or rapport with the user, however, this is not sufficient for providing constructive contextual feedback for the purpose of training. For example, the Nintendo Wii Balance board uses pressure sensors that are used to measure the user's center of balance and weight. Though balance is an important component to many poses and exercises in the Wii Fit game, it does not speak to the accuracy of the other elements of the pose, which are not collected. Two problems can occur here: firstly, since success is determined by only one measure – the weight distribution – pose accuracy, according to the game, may be achieved before the physical benefits from the other elements of the pose are attained, resulting in reduced effort by the user due to the game's affirmation. Secondly, inaccuracy of the other pose elements that are not measured can undermine the exercise itself and even lead to injury.

Confidence in one's ability is an important element to successfully complete a fitness routine [4,14]. However, due to limited body measurement collection, games offered for systems like the Wii Fit + Balance Board, Kinect, and PS-Move contribute to a patients' false sense of confidence. An inaccurate pose may produce encouraging words and praise from the game rather than constructive feedback, giving users an inflated sense of understanding and ability.

Engagement and system accuracy of the body-measuring machine are both important aspects, however; literature that we have discussed suggests that the effectiveness of information delivery is crucial to providing a successful and engaging experience. An effective demonstration is often formed by the instructor's experience; compiling elements that they found useful when learning it. When gaming is introduced, that element of ad hoc feedback from personal experience is lost and a host of new issues regarding visuospatial understanding and learning in a virtual 3D space surface. The aim of this study is to explore the variables that contribute to the *quality of execution* and user comprehension; this study will look at adapting for occlusion and lack of visibility, learning and orientation and providing feedback. We will examine each of these variables in detail next.

Adapting For Occlusion

For the purposes of this study, occlusion is defined as a visual obstruction that prevents the viewer from obtaining visual data required to complete an accurate mental image of the object being viewed. While in-person instruction has addressed occlusion on an individualized basis, training videos and interactive games to a certain extent have not. For example, Physiotherapists often provide patients with a sheet of printed exercises to perform at home. Like interactive pose systems, these 2-dimensional flat images try to illustrate the angle that best shows the body position, but occluded limbs or small body presentation errors may result in an incomplete mental image of the pose.

Designing a visual solution for providing multiple views or modalities without overwhelming the user and impairing their cognitive load can increase pose understanding and confidence and decrease the risk of injury.

Orientation & Self

Understanding and awareness of oneself with relationship to others is an essential part of imitation and kinesthetic learning [10]. Where body language and communication between self and instructor address these challenges in-person, a virtual instructor, virtual space and virtual avatar to represent self, produce new learning and interaction challenges. Maintaining the users' sense of orientation of self and environment in comparison to their virtual avatar and the virtual environment is essential to learning through visual imitation and comparison to the instructor [12].

While gaming systems have made it possible to offer a strategic angle change when necessary, the seamlessness of the demonstration can also impact a users sense of orientation. Daems et. al found that when participants were asked to select like-poses, being shown two images at rotation angles greater than 30 degrees in difference consecutively, resulted in increased response times when compared to angles of lesser degree separations [4].

A commonly mistaken solution to visual misinterpretation is to add additional graphical elements to assist with clarification; however, adding more visual elements can increase the cognitive load and can make understanding even more difficult. This study will examine both performance and user confidence and preference to ensure design considers overall experience.

Feedback

We define feedback as any visual, verbal or physical criticism of an individual's actions that lead them to achieve a target. While initial instruction usually demands the participant's full attention, effective feedback has to consider the interpretation factors described above while considering the user's context – which in some cases, they may be mid-activity.

Providing constructive feedback and not just listing inaccuracies is something game-based instruction has yet to offer. Feedback can be divided into three requirements; the gathering of body information by the hardware sensors, the software's interpretation of the information with appropriate response, and finally, how the response is delivered to the user through the game. While an ideal game design would marry the software and hardware capabilities effectively so that the system would be intelligently aware of the users' activity from body measurement and would adapt modally to suit the users capability. In reality, constructive feedback is very difficult, if not impossible to provide if detailed body information is not collected.

While a significant amount of literature in exergaming and gaming for physiotherapy has focused on developing more suitable methods of collecting and interpreting body information by the system [11,17] exploration has been limited when it comes to delivering meaningful (contextually but also in an appropriate modality) and constructive criticism.

DESIGN

We evaluated the aforementioned factors in two experiments. The first experiment was divided into two sections. The first section focuses on visual demonstration delivery to examine the impact of occlusion from view and also orientation and self when angles and views are augmented during demonstration. The second section focuses on supplementary modalities and their impact on comprehension. Our second experiment examines the impact of various types of feedback, comparing current types of feedback with hypothetical contextual ones that explore different modalities and combinations of modalities. We will expand on these design goals next.

STUDY 1: DEMONSTRATION DELIVERY

Methods

Participants were described the purpose of the study before beginning and signed a consent form confirming they understood. They were then verbally asked a number of introductory experience and demographic questions which were recorded on paper. Each participant used a 15' laptop to watch 2 sets of yoga pose demonstrations with five in each set, for a total of 10 different yoga poses

Demonstration videos were created for the study using Maya animation software to the specifications of the visual delivery required for the study. Poses, verbal description and pose elements, were derived from Nintendo Wii's Yoga game poses unless a particular pose was not available. In these cases a standard Bikram Yoga pose was used.

The conditions include:

Set 1

The first set of the demonstration delivery test focused on the visual delivery. Participants all saw the same poses in a random order matched with a random condition. All Participants saw all conditions. The conditions, illustrated in *figure 5*, include:

- Front: The most occluded view type.
- Front + Wide: The second begins with a frontal viewpoint then switches to the viewpoint that captures the widest visual area of the instructor – this view type offers an additional angle from the front angle to improve visualization of occluded areas.
- Front, Pan + Wide: The third begins with the frontal view, but will pan around the instructor to 40 degrees while they are performing the exercise. The viewpoint then switches to one that captures the widest visual area of the instructor – This view type offers a smoother transition between the same angles in the last view type.
- Front, Pan +Wide x1: Third but will offer an additional supporting viewpoint while the widest viewpoint is displayed – This view type reveals three angles throughout the demonstration, making occluded areas minimal.
- Front, Pan +Wide x2: This view type offers two additional images for a total of 4 angles throughout the demonstration making it the least likely to offer occluded areas. The amount of information displayed in this demonstration is what we anticipate will be a visual/cognitive peak.

Participants were able to watch the demonstration twice and were then asked to replicate the final pose using a flexible manikin. Both male and female manikins were available to participants. The final image of the demonstration was left on screen while the participant posed their manikin. To compensate for the lack of range of motion of the manikins and also to obtain a clearer idea of participant understanding of physical subtleties of the pose, participants were asked to verbally describe the elements of their posed manikin. With 6 years of regular Bikram Yoga practice, the researcher scored pose accuracy after each pose, based on a set of elements in the demonstrations. After each pose the researcher asked participants to verbally score their confidence in understanding, clarity of the demonstration and perceived pose accuracy on a 5-point Likert scale. Comments and criticism on experience were transcribed by the researcher using a laptop.

The second set of demonstration videos in the demonstration delivery test focused on verbal + visual vs. visual only delivery. Like the last set, participants were shown a visual demonstration in a consistent visual delivery on a 15' laptop. In this section, however, the poses were

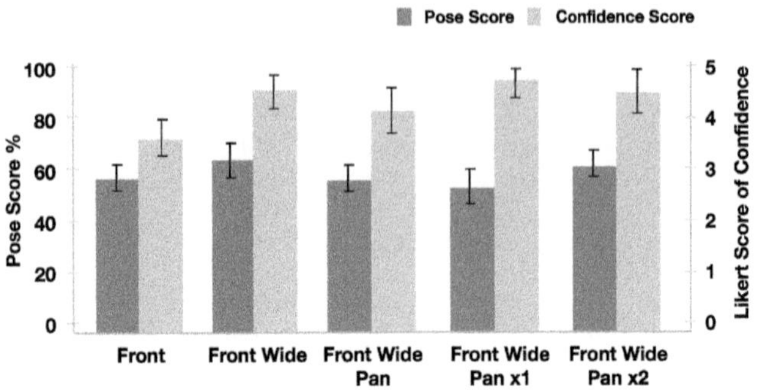

Figure 1 Mean Pose Scores (%) and Confidence Scores for Visual Delivery Conditions

provided in a random order with a random condition – with or without verbal description. Again, participants were able to watch the demonstrations twice and had to then pose and describe the manikin. They were able to see the final frame of the video while posing the manikin, just as in the first set. After each pose, they were scored by the researcher and asked the same questions as the previous set. Upon completing all 10 poses, participants completed a short exit survey about their preferences of visual and verbal delivery.

Hypotheses

We hypothesize that participants' comprehension score will be best when offered a single, short but continuous, multi-view demonstration that will ensure any obstructed or occluded pose elements are clarified (H1). Suggesting that too many additional images will be visually overwhelming to participants (H2) and that they will score lowest when presented with only a front view of the pose (H3).

From strictly qualitative data we predict confidence ratings will follow pose accuracy scores. We expect participants will feel most confident in their understanding of poses offering a single, short but continuous, multi-view demonstration (H4). Conversely, we predict participants will feel least confident when provided only a single view of a pose (H5).

Although visual delivery is important it is often not enough on its own to gain a comprehensive understanding of an exercise, particularly in situations where the user must avert their gaze to complete the pose correctly. Under these conditions we anticipate that participants would score higher and also rate confidence higher if they were provided with verbal description of the pose in addition to visual (H6, H7). Conversely, they would score lower when only provided visual demonstration (no verbal) (H8).

Participants

20 participants were recruited to complete the Demonstration Delivery portion (10 male, 10 female). The mean age of participants was 30 years old with a standard

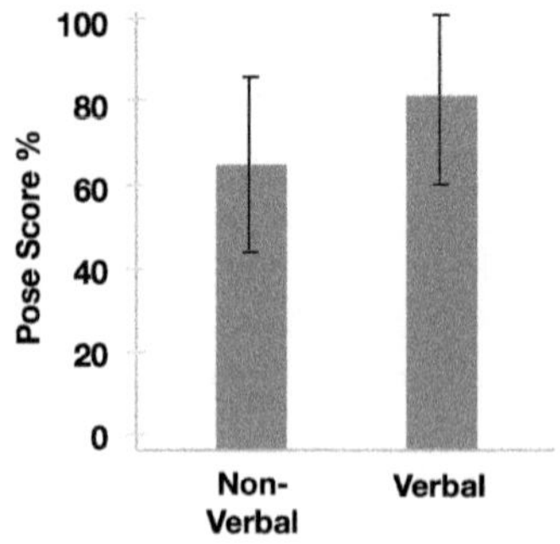

Figure 2 Mean Pose Scores (%) for Verbal Delivery Conditions

deviation of 7. On average, participants reported to be in above average physical health.

Results

We began by looking for an effect of visual demonstration on pose accuracy. In this case, we predicted that the single, short but continuous, multi-view demonstration or *Front, Pan + Wide* would elicit improved pose accuracy. *Figure 1* presents the mean pose accuracy scores and standard deviation across visual demonstration types. A repeated measure ANOVA did not reveal a significant relationship between pose score and visual demonstration conditions, $F\ (5,95) = .842, p > .05.$ *partial* $\eta 2 = .042.$

A paired-samples T-Test was performed on pose scores for verbal and non-verbal conditions. We discover that there is, in fact, a statistically significant effect of verbal conditions on pose score, $t\ (19) = 2.132, p = .046, d = 0.48$, where the verbal condition improved performance by 11%. It is clear from *figure 2* that participants performed better with verbal description than without.

User Feedback

A repeated measures ANOVA analysis did not reveal a significant relationship between confidence and visual demonstration conditions, $F\ (5,95) = .842,\ p > .05$, or perceived pose accuracy and visual demonstration, $F\ (4, 76)$

A repeated measures ANOVA analysis did not reveal a significant relationship between confidence and visual demonstration conditions, $F\ (5,95) = .842,\ p > .05$, or perceived pose accuracy and visual demonstration, $F\ (4, 76) = 1.121,\ p > .05$. However, when examining the mean Likert scores of participant-reported demonstration quality, we can see that the *Front* view type was scored much lower than the remaining types. In support of this observation, analysis using the Greenhouse-Geisser correction revealed a significant effect of demonstration quality preference on visual demonstration, ($F\ (2.853, 54.205) = 3.361, p < .027.$ *partial* $\eta 2 = .150.$). *Post-hoc* analysis with a Boneferroni adjustment further clarify the significant differences between the *Front* view and the other view types, suggesting participants found the *Front* view of lesser quality.

We then examined the responses to post-pose questions on confidence in understanding, quality of demonstration and perceived pose accuracy for the verbal section. A paired-samples T-Test was performed on each of the Likert questions with verbal vs. non-verbal conditions. We discover that there is a statistically significant effect of verbal conditions on confidence, $t\ (19) = 3.356,\ p = .003,\ d = 0.75$ and also quality of demonstration, $t\ (19) = 2.396,\ p = .027,\ d = 0.54$. This suggests that participants, not only prefer being provided verbal description to support a demonstration, they are more confident in their understanding when provided with it. We did not find any significant effect of verbal conditions on perceived performance.

Following analysis of collected quantitative data, we began exploring individual participant responses. These responses were transcribed and coded using a Grounded Theory method.

Categories were combined to form groups of 'negative comments' and 'positive comments'. From *figure 3* we can see that the *front view* produced the highest number of negative comments and, in fact, received significantly more comments relating to the visual inadequacy of the demonstration, specifically. *Panning view with 1 additional angle* received the least number of negative comments. Conversely, the *panning view with 2 additional angles* received the most amount of positive comments further supporting the notion that a panning view with additional angles is the most preferred type of visual delivery for 3D virtual demonstration.

At the end of the study, participants were asked to rate the most helpful type of visual feedback and the least helpful. The *panning view with 1 additional angle* was found to be the most helpful with a mean rating of 3.55, STD = 1.05. The *front view* was the least helpful with a mean rating of 1.35, STD = 0.99. Participants deemed the wide view angle – the most visible surface area of the instructor – more important than the other visual elements. A repeated measure ANOVA analysis revealed a statistically significant effect of demonstration deliveries, $F\ (4, 64) = 5.325,\ p < .001.$ *partial* $\eta^2 = .250$. *Post-hoc* analysis with a Boneferroni adjustment revealed that participants significantly prefered the *wide view* compared to the *front pan wide x2 (1.059 (95% CI,.156 to 1.961), p = .015)*. While additional views were, on average, less helpful than other visual elements. The exit questionnaire also further supported the trend that verbal delivery was very important to participants, receiving a mean rating of 4.65 on a Likert scale of helpfulness, STD = 0.67.

Discussion

Though we predicted a single, short but continuous, multi-view (pan) demonstration – Front, Pan + Wide – would perform best, statistical analysis found no significant difference in pose accuracy across each of the visual

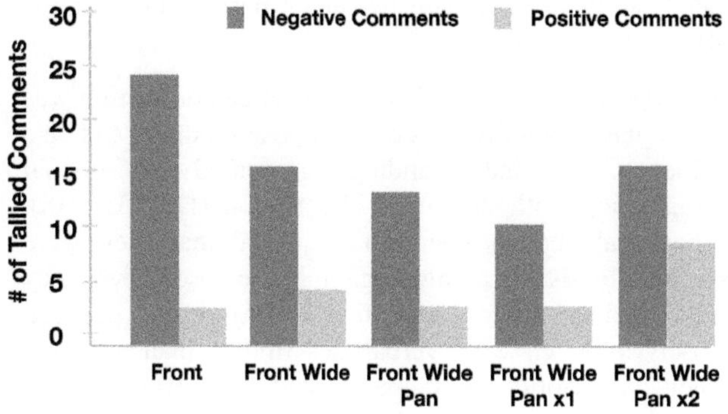

Figure 3 Grouped Negative & Positive Comments for Visual Deliveries

demonstration deliveries (H1, H2, H3). While not significant, the increase in mean pose accuracy from 1 additional image to 2 may indicate that we have yet to reach a peak of cognitive load. For the purposes of the experiment, we felt that two additional angles to the main demonstration would suffice as an example of excessive information but performance did not decrease (H2). In that case, further research exploring greater amounts of visual information to determine where the peak of cognitive load lies.

From questionnaire feedback and verbal account we can tell that participants were overall most positive about the panning view with 1 additional angle but most confident with 2 additional angles. While this is not what we expected (H4), in the absence of feedback, the additional views may have given participants a sense of confidence by offering additional points of reference to self-check their own pose accuracy.

The *front view* demonstration type provided a highly occluded perspective of the pose. While a high number of participants noted the poor visual quality of this feedback type this was not reflected in the pose accuracy scores. The front view was not found to have a significant effect on pose accuracy or confidence. Additionally, participants reported almost double the amount of negative commentary on the *front view* than any other visual delivery, specifically, more than double the amount of comments regarding the visual inadequacy. This seems to support the notion that, in the absence of feedback, the amount of reference points to self-check one's pose accuracy can impact the confidence and self-efficacy of a user. Future research in interactive gaming demonstration might assess the impact of varying amounts of visual information, including more than 2 additional angles, on performance and cognitive load and what that means for user confidence.

We found that some of our hypotheses were not confirmed. Participant scores were not found to have a significant difference between self-reported confidence in understanding (H5) or with perceived performance ratings (H4).

Verbal description to supplement visual demonstration was found to have a significant effect on pose accuracy and also confidence in understanding compared to visual demonstration with no verbal description (H6, H7, H8). From verbal account, participants noted that they were better able to visualize how to get into the pose, where they should feel a stretch and how to correctly position themselves better with verbal description than without. Without description participants said they were unsure about where they should feel the stretch and overall did not feel confident in their understanding. This was also reflected in high scoring of verbal delivery in the exit questionnaires.

STUDY 2: FEEDBACK DELIVERY

Methods

During the Feedback study, participants were tested on comprehension of yoga poses delivered by Nintendo's Wii Fit Yoga game and Balance Board. The intent of this experiment is to find an improved method of feedback delivery that can prevent injury during exercise in an at-home physiotherapy environment. Different types of feedback were assessed including visual, verbal, haptic and combinations of feedback.

Like the demonstration delivery study, participants were asked a number of introductory experience and demographic questions by the researcher. To complete the experiment, participant's interacted with Nintendo's Wii Fit Yoga fitness game and balance board. Six yoga poses were selected from the game and were delivered in demonstration mode (rather than play mode) in a random order. The researcher used the Wiimote to select the appropriate pose. The participants watched the demonstration once and executed the pose during the second demonstration along with the 2D instructor. During execution, participants received a randomly chosen feedback condition to help correct any pose errors. The feedback conditions included:

- No feedback: As a baseline.
- Mirror Feedback: To determine the effectiveness and value of a participant's own mirrored body as comparative feedback. Yoga studios and physiotherapy clinics often use mirrors to observe positioning and posture. Similarly, some gaming systems use on-screen avatars to offer users a method of visually comparing their position to the virtual instructor. The Mirror used was a long rectangular full body mirror. It was placed in front of the participant careful to not obstruct the demonstration.
- Wii Yoga's built-in graphic and verbal feedback: Mechanism measured by the balance board. To evaluate the effect of the combination of graphical and verbal feedback driven by limited body measurement information on participant performance and confidence.
- Custom verbal feedback: Delivered by the researcher that is detail-focused. Simulates the effect of a richer body measuring system and evaluate the importance of more comprehensive body measurement information on performance and confidence.
- Haptic feedback: Simulated by tapping participants on an incorrectly positioned area. This condition is meant to imitate the assistive touch of a physiotherapist putting a patient into the correct position and evaluate the effect of an alternate supporting modality, such as touch, on performance in a gaming environment.
- Haptic and verbal feedback: Combining the last two conditions to simulate the modalities utilized at an in-person session.

Feedback was based on the scored elements directly from the demonstration and was provided for the duration of the onscreen instruction – about 1 minute. Participants received feedback only when position was incorrect. Pose accuracy was scored by the researcher, based on a set of elements in the demonstrations. Participants then verbally scored their confidence in pose understanding before feedback and after receiving feedback as well as perceived pose accuracy on a 5-point Likert scale. Comments and criticism on experience were transcribed by the researcher using a laptop. Participants were not informed of their pose accuracy scores. Upon completing all 6 poses, participants completed a short exit survey about their preferences of feedback type. Participants were reminded that if a condition wasn't clear that they could be shown an example to assist in answering the questions.

Hypotheses

As we have discussed, feedback is an essential part of fully grasping a pose or activity. Using the mentioned modes of feedback, we anticipate that participants would perform best (H9) and feel most confident in their pose understanding (H10) when provided with customized verbal and haptic feedback that replicated feedback delivery offered by a physiotherapist. We also predict that because the Wii offers feedback only for a particular aspect of the pose, balance, and not necessarily the primary objective of the pose, Wii feedback with balance board would improve confidence but not performance score (H11).

Participants

A different group of 20 participants were recruited for the Feedback section (11 male, 9 female) of the study. The mean age of participants was 29 years old with a standard deviation of 5. On average, participants reported to be in above average physical health.

Results

We analyzed the collected measures by performing a repeated measures analysis of variance (ANOVA) using feedback types (6) x performance scores.

We began by looking for an effect of feedback on pose accuracy. In this case, we predicted that the customized combination of verbal feedback and haptic feedback would illicit improved pose accuracy. *Figure 4* presents the mean pose accuracy scores and standard deviation across feedback types. Here, we can already see a positive increase in pose accuracy for the three customized feedback types. Mauchly's test of Sphericity was applied to assess variance and covariance. This test was found to be significant [χ 2(14) = 42.436, p =.000, W=.084] suggesting that the assumption of sphericity was violated and groups do not demonstrate homogeneity. The Greenhouse-Geisser correction revealed a statistically significant effect of feedback conditions on pose accuracy, $F(2.900, 55.107) = 10.231, p < .0005$. partial $\eta^2 = .350$. *Post-hoc* analysis with a Boneferroni adjustment revealed that performance significantly increased from no feedback to verbal feedback *(.156 (95% CI, .004 to .307), p = .041)* , and from no feedback to haptic feedback *(.169 (95% CI, .009 to .329), p = .032*), and finally, the largest increase in performance from no feedback to the combination of verbal and haptic feedback *(.184 (95% CI, .032 to .336), p = .010*). Neither mirror feedback *(-.061 (95% CI, -.294 to .173*), p = 1.00), nor Wii graphic + verbal feedback *(-.048 (95% CI, -.274 to .179), p = 1.00*), had a significant increase in performance from no feedback.

User Feedback

We then looked at the Likert scores participants provided after each pose to determine if there is an effect of feedback on confidence and on perceived pose accuracy. Here, we predicted that the customized combination of verbal feedback and haptic feedback would improve confidence and also perceived pose accuracy, along side performance.

We began by examining confidence. *Figure 4* presents the mean Likert scores and standard deviation for confidence in understanding after feedback across each feedback type. There appears to be a lot of variability, but we can see the

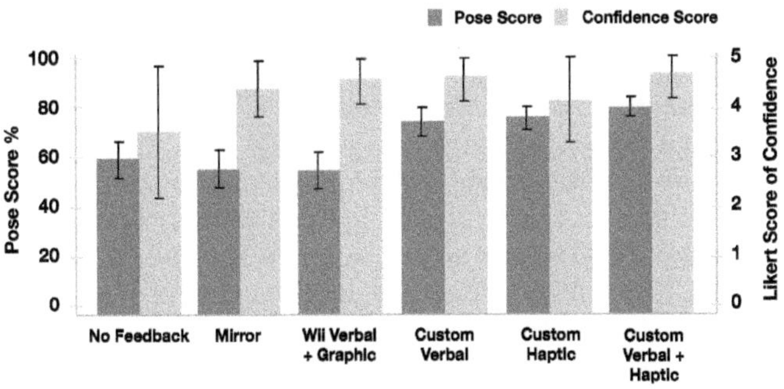

Figure 4 Mean Pose Scores (%) and Confidence Scores for Feedback Conditions

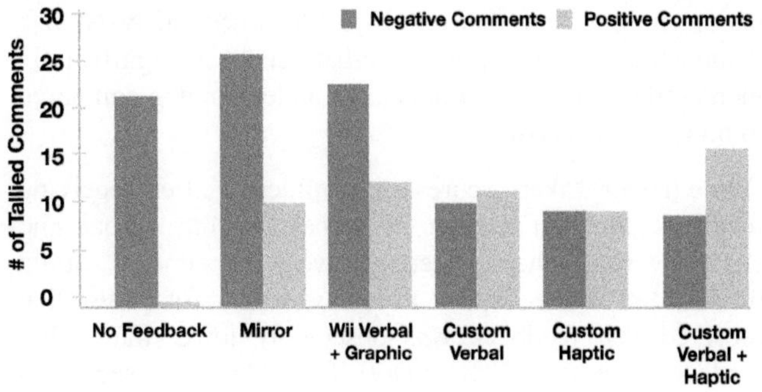

Figure 5 Grouped Negative & Positive Comments for Feedback Types

Wii graphic + verbal, custom verbal and haptic + custom verbal feedback types excel, but it should be noted that the Wii feedback seem particularly inflated after noting the poor performance scores for that feedback type. A repeated measures ANOVA revealed a statistically significant relationship between confidence in understanding and feedback conditions, $F(5, 90) = 5.671, p < .013$, partial $\eta^2 = .240$. Pairwise post-hoc tests, with Bonferroni corrected comparisons, showed that only verbal feedback resulted in a significant increase from no feedback.

We then inspected participant self-efficacy by examining the effect of feedback types on participant-reported Likert scores of perceived pose accuracy. Analysis did not reveal a significant effect of self-reported pose accuracy on feedback type, $F(5, 95) = .842, p > .05$, partial $\eta^2 = .042$.

We performed an exploratory investigation of individual participant responses. Categories were combined to form groups of 'negative' and 'positive' comments. *Figure 5* illustrates the disparity between the three custom feedback types (Custom verbal, Custom haptic, Custom haptic/verbal) had fewer negative comments, while custom haptic + verbal received more positive comments than any other feedback type.

Lastly, we examined the results from the exit questionnaire. A clear inclination for more customized feedback types with a particular preference for custom verbal + haptic feedback was noted.

Discussion

As predicted, participants scored higher on pose accuracy with more customized feedback. While custom verbal and haptic feedback, individually had a significant relationship with pose accuracy, haptic + verbal feedback received the highest mean score with 95% and a standard deviation of 0.090 (H9). Participant reports found that this was not only the preferred feedback type but was also found to make participants the most confident in their understanding of the pose. These findings demonstrate that a more customized type of feedback is necessary to ensure not only performance accuracy, which is essential for an at-home rehabilitation system, but also users' confidence in their understanding and their ability. Statistical analysis also demonstrated that haptic + verbal feedback significantly increased participant confidence in understanding compared to no feedback (H10).

While mean Likert scores in confidence after receiving feedback for Wii graphic + verbal, custom verbal and custom verbal + haptic feedback were the same, it should be noted that mean pose accuracy scores for poses that received Wii feedback was observably lower than other feedback types at 72%, SD=0.20 (H11). This seems to suggest that the Wii feedback makes users over confident in their actions even when they are not performing poses correctly. Users do not receive the benefits of the pose while not being aware of their inaccuracies and may lead to injury if over confidence leads to over exertion.

This trend was also found in verbal accounts where Wii feedback had the most commentary regarding feedback inadequacy, but also received the highest amount of reports for confidence. We speculate this is due to participants not being clear on how to interpret the system's feedback but then feeling confident in pose completion once the system congratulated them on a job well done. Here is an example of participants comments on the inadequacy of Wii feedback:

"I was confident in what I had to do but the feedback was unclear. I didn't know what to do to my body get myself into the correct position." - Participant 15

In the categorized verbal responses we can see that physical limitation was noted by participants a number of times (24). While this was not under review in our testing it is our belief that users shouldn't ever feel as though they cannot perform an action, particularly in a training scenario when the system should be better geared to a user's capabilities. The system should provide appropriate alternatives that still capture the major benefit of the pose. In a similar vein, research in the field of exergaming has explored adapting a game's difficulty to a user's heart rate [9]. Future research might explore the effect of pose alternatives and detection of user ability on confidence and pose accuracy.

CONCLUSIONS

In this paper, we examined elements that contribute to pose comprehension in a virtual 3D environment including occlusion and lack of visibility, learning and orientation, and feedback, in an effort to better understand what is necessary to achieve a high level of performance, confidence and motivation.

We evaluated these factors in two experiments. The first experiment was divided into two sections. The first section focused on visual demonstration delivery and determined that a panning view, which includes an angle that captures the greatest visible surface area of the instructor and additional angles is preferred though didn't greatly impact performance. The second section focused on supplementary modalities and established that verbal delivery improved performance and increased user confidence while being a favoured element in demonstration. Our second experiment established that more customized and contextual modes of feedback are necessary to improve feedback and increase user comprehension and confidence. While addressing our design goals, these evaluations offer a direction and set of guidelines for designing for training and fitness applications.

DESIGN RECOMMENDATIONS

The evaluation of these factors can be summarized into the following design recommendations for future research and design of interactive gaming systems for fitness and training:

1. **Multiple Visual Angle Demonstration**: When demonstrating a pose, we recommend that users be provided with multiple angles of a demonstration to help them resolve the visual information they require to understand a pose. Additional angles can provide more points of reference for the user to check their understanding or self-positioning. Panning can offer a seamless range of view without imposing a cognitive increase with a visual angle switch. Although there were no significant differences between pose accuracy or confidence and visual delivery methods, the inclusion of a wide view that incorporated the largest amount of visible surface area of the instructor, a panning view and also simultaneous additional angles were found to be preferred elements by users.
2. **Multi-modal Demonstration**: We observed that participants required verbal or clear descriptive language about what their body should be doing, where to feel the stretch, when to breathe etc., in order to complete their mental model of the pose but also to feel confident in their understanding on the pose being executed. Descriptive verbal delivery was found to have a significant relationship with pose accuracy and confidence in understanding. Instruction without verbal description was found to feel inadequate and lead to a lack in confidence. Some participants expressed the importance of analogies to help relate to the pose more effectively. This can help connect with users and can contribute to engagement.
3. **Clear Orientation Environment**: When providing a visual demonstration we recommend that instruction begins by establishing a clear orientation environment. This may include the ability to face the instructor away or towards the user or simple visual cues like a yoga mat. This allows the user to mentally clarify the relationship between their own body and the instructor. We observed that several users would miss an entire demonstration because they were cognitively engrossed in interpreting which hand or foot to use. Establishing a

clear orientation environment becomes especially important with complicated poses.

4. **Verbal Delivery as Supplementary**: Relating to the previous recommendation, when demonstrating a pose, we suggest that verbal delivery remain a supplementary modality to visual delivery. We observed that the use of direction (i.e., left and right) in description often lead to confusion. Visual delivery should be used as a point of reference or imitation while verbal delivery provides analogy, unobservable detail and establishes rapport with the user. Haptic feedback can also assist with directional instruction.

5. **Custom, Contextual feedback**: Though we can really only evaluate currently available fitness and training games that offer feedback, this feedback was found to be inappropriate for more performance focused activities like training and rehabilitation. When offering feedback for these situations, we recommend providing users with customized, contextual feedback to help them resolve errors. Custom, contextual feedback offers a direct solution to inaccuracy rather than just demonstrating inaccuracy and allowing the user to determine a solution. Custom, contextual feedback types, including verbal, haptic and a combination of these, were found to have a significant relationship with pose performance and were also highly preferred to commercially available, Wii system feedback or self-regulated modes of feedback such as a mirror or avatar of one's self.

6. **Multi-Modal Feedback**: Speaking further to the point of contextual feedback, we recommend that feedback be provided in a modality that compliments the orientation of the action. It is likely the user is mid-action when receiving feedback, in these cases, the system should adapt it is feedback modality to accommodate the user – provide haptic or verbal feedback if the user's eyes are averted, for example. It was noted that participants rated modalities that were ill-matched to the pose worse than more appropriate ones. Some participants did not even take advantage of the feedback provided because they weren't able to see it from the position they were in. In some cases, participants performed as though they had no feedback at all if they were provided with an ill-matched modality and even said they did not use or notice the feedback.

7. **Understand & Adapt For Capability:** Especially in training, the system's awareness of the user's capabilities is essential to ensuring poses are performed accurately and without injury. For this reason we recommend that the system be aware of user ability and provide alternative actions that still address the benefit of the pose without overexerting or discouraging the user. During analysis we found that participants often commented on their physical limitations when attempting the poses. Not feeling capable or able to complete a pose can lead to noncompliance. Providing participants with alternatives, that still address the gross benefit of the action, yet still offer a challenge, may make users feel confident while still performing the pose correctly, without risk of injury and working towards recovery.

While we recognize that many of these recommendations are not currently realizable and may still require a lot of technical exploration, we feel that by exploring user needs and submitting possible solutions we can begin the iterative journey to a well-designed application that exceeds the needs of the user.

LIMITATIONS & FUTURE WORK

This paper only addresses some of the many factors that contribute to action comprehension. The goal of this paper was to begin to build a foundational set of design guidelines for further research in the area where none exists.

We acknowledge the sample sizes of all studies were very small, limiting adequate power of these research studies. As a result many of these observations aren't fully supported statistically, however, we believe that qualitative feedback can, at a minimum, drive further investigation.

In the visual delivery section we chose a very general set of delivery types to reveal patterns that could be later explored. We feel we accomplished this. While we did not find a significant relationship between the deliveries we chose and pose accuracy future research in interactive gaming demonstration might assess the impact of varying amounts of visual information, including more than 2 additional angles, on performance and cognitive load and what that means for user confidence.

While we did find a significant effect of verbal + haptic feedback, suggesting the use of a haptic feedback system has implications. Haptic systems are typically comprised of a series of wearable bands with sensors and feedback mechanisms that need to be attached to the body in specific locations to ensure effective data collection and feedback. The challenge of repeatedly applying the haptic system is not only tedious but also difficult to perform accurately each time. Additionally, an ideal haptic solution would also consider ease of donning the system without assistance since users may be applying it themselves. Future exploration of the feasibility of haptic feedback to support interactive training would need to consider the context as well as performance and user confidence.

Beyond elements of these studies, exploration of learning styles and adapting for different user needs could also enrich the application of guidelines for rehabilitation in gaming systems.

REFERENCES

1. Anderson, F., Annett, M., and Bischof, W.F. Lean on Wii: Physical Rehabilitation With Virtual Reality Wii Peripherals. *Studies in health technology and informatics 154*, (2010), 229–34.
2. Burke, J.W., McNeill, M.D.J., Charles, D.K., Morrow, P.J., Crosbie, J.H., and McDonough, S.M. Optimising Engagement For Stroke Rehabilitation Using Serious Games. *The Visual Computer 25*, 12 (2009), 1085–1099.
3. Crook, P., Rose, M., Salmon, P., Stott, R., Peters, S., and Stanley, I. Adherence to Group Exercise: Physiotherapist-led Experimental Programmes. *Physiotherapy 84*, 8 (1998), 366–372.
4. Dishman, R.K. and Ickes, W. Self-motivation and Adherence to Therapeutic Exercise. *Journal of behavioral medicine 4*, 4 (1981), 421–38.
5. Flores, E., Tobon, G., Cavallaro, E., Cavallaro, F.I., Perry, J.C., and Keller, T. Improving Patient Motivation in Game Development for Motor Deficit Rehabilitation. *Proceedings of the 2008 International Conference in Advances on Computer Entertainment Technology - ACE '08*, (2008), 381.
6. Johnston, H. and Whitehead, A. Pose Presentation for a Dance-Based Massively Multiplayer Online Exergame. *Entertainment Computing 2*, 2 (2011), 89–96.
7. Kifayat, K., Fergus, P., Cooper, S., and Merabti, M. Body Area Networks for Movement Analysis in Physiotherapy Treatments. *2010 IEEE 24th International Conference on Advanced Information Networking and Applications Workshops*, Ieee (2010), 866–872.
8. Lange, B., Flynn, S., and Rizzo, A. Initial Usability Assessment of Off-the-Shelf Video Game Consoles for Clinical Game-Based Motor Rehabilitation. *Physical Therapy Reviews 14*, 5 (2009), 355–363.
9. Masuko, S. A Fitness Game Reflecting Heart Rate. *Advances in Computer Entertainment Technology 53*, (2006), 3–5.
10. Mitchell, R. Kinesthetic□Visual Matching and the Self Concept as Explanations of Mirror□Self□ Recognition. *Journal for the theory of social behaviour 27*, 1 (1997), 17–39.
11. Negrete, M.A., Matamoros, M., Olveres, J., et al. Nintendo Wii Remote and Nunchuck as a Wireless Data Subsystem for Digital Acquisition of Analog Physiologic Data Relevant to Motor Rehabilitation After Stroke. *2009 Pan American Health Care Exchanges*, (2009), 130–131.
12. Pinelle, D., Wong, N., and Stach, T. Heuristic Evaluation for Games: Usability Principles for Video Game Design. *Proceedings of the 2008 SIGCHI Conference*, (2008), 1453–1462.
13. Skelly, a. H., Marshall, J.R., Haughey, B.P., Davis, P.J., and Dunford, R.G. Self-Efficacy and Confidence in Outcomes as Determinants of Self-Care Practices in Inner-City, African-American Women with Non-Insulin-Dependent Diabetes. *The Diabetes Educator 21*, 1 (1995), 38–46.
14. Sluijs, E.M., Kok, G.J., and Zee, J. Van Der. Correlates of Exercise Compliance in Physical Therapy. *Physical Therapy 73*, 11 (1993), 771–782.
15. Sweetser, P. and Wyeth, P. GameFlow: A Model for Evaluating Player Enjoyment in Games. *Computers in Entertainment (CIE) 3*, 3 (2005), 1–24.
16. Taylor, M.J.D., McCormick, D., Shawis, T., Impson, R., and Griffin, M. Activity-promoting Gaming Systems in Exercise and Rehabilitation. *The Journal of Rehabilitation Research and Development 48*, 10 (2011), 1171.
17. Yong Joo, L., Soon Yin, T., Xu, D., et al. A Feasibility Study Using Interactive Commercial Off-the-Shelf Computer Gaming in Upper Limb Rehabilitation in Patients After Stroke. *Journal of rehabilitation medicine 42*, 5 (2010), 437–41.

The Department of Hidden Stories: Playful Digital Storytelling for Children in a Public Library

Gavin Wood[1], John Vines[1], Madeline Balaam[1], Nick Taylor[2], Thomas Smith[1], Clara Crivellaro[1], Juliana Mensah[3], Helen Limon[3], John Challis[3], Linda Anderson[3], Adam Clarke[4], Peter Wright[1]

[1]Culture Lab, School of Computing Science, Newcastle University, UK
[2] Eclectric Research Studio, University of Dundee, UK
[3] Newcastle Centre for the Literary Arts, Newcastle University, UK
[4] The Common People The Old School, Penrith, UK

{g.wood2; john.vines}@ncl.ac.uk

ABSTRACT

We detail the design of the Department of Hidden Stories (DoHS), a mobile-based game to support playful digital storytelling among primary school children in public libraries. Through a process of iterative design in collaboration with library staff and children's writers we designed DoHS to support the potential for playful storytelling through interactions with books. A deployment of DoHS with two classes of 8 to 10 years olds as part of their regular library visits revealed insights related to how to balance the expectations of a child-at-play and the requirement to further develop their creative reading and writing skills. Based on our experiences we recommend that designers create playful digitally based activities that encourage children to explore libraries and experience new interactions with physical books.

Author Keywords

Storytelling; play;children's library;augmenting books.

ACM Classification Keywords

H.5.m. Information interfaces and presentation (e.g., HCI): Miscellaneous.

INTRODUCTION

We describe the design and evaluation of Department of Hidden Stories (DoHS), a mobile-based game developed to support 8 to 10 year old children in playful digital storytelling and engagement with books in public libraries (Figure 1). DoHS is the result of a process where designers worked with a team of creative writers, library staff and children to explore how physical books found in public libraries could be linked with digital content. The resulting mobile phone game guided children as they explored the library and wrote fictional stories based upon the content of books they found. Their stories were captured on a phone and tagged to each book. By scanning a book's barcode, children visiting the library are able to access stories that were created earlier by others. In doing so, the game was designed to support children in new exploration and browsing activities in libraries, and provide new ways of linking physical books with child-generated digital content.

Figure 1. DoHS App – splash screen and barcode scanner

DoHS was designed in response to claims that modern public libraries are not particularly engaging places for young children to visit and explore books, and fewer children than ever are reading for enjoyment [10, 27]. Nevertheless, libraries are still considered important places for children. The significance of the library as a lifelong learning resource for children is emphasised in the UK through regular school organised library visits between the ages of 5–12 [17]. In response, DoHS was designed to explore how playful digital interactions within the library environment might facilitate children's engagement with their local library in new ways, potentially leading to sustained engagement with literature and libraries.

In developing DoHS, we explore ways in which digital technology can scaffold engagement with the library space and the physical books it houses. Traditionally there has been a disconnection between the provision of ICT and digital technologies in public libraries and the library's core resource of books. The use of digital technologies in relation to books is limited to search systems, providing links to book review sites and self-service loan services that have limited potential in terms of engaging children. Furthermore, DoHS is based upon the idea that playfulness is a core attribute to learning storytelling [1, 25], where

CHI 2014, April 26 - May 01 2014, Toronto, ON, Canada

ACM 978-1-4503-2473-1/14/04…$15.00.
http://dx.doi.org/10.1145/2556288.2557034

learning how to tell stories is fundamental to the development of a child's literacy skills [15, 23]. We take a pragmatic focus on the potential benefits such systems may have on learning by suggesting there is value in simply engaging children with libraries and books.

In this paper, we describe in detail the iterative design process that lead to the creation of DoHS through three key stages: i) collaborative design workshops between designers, library staff and creative writers to develop an initial set of simple playful activities and associated rules for children engaging with books in libraries; ii) the piloting of two initial card-based games with twenty 8-10 year old children; and iii) the deployment and evaluation of the digital DoHS game that incorporated insights from the first two stages. Primarily, based on our evaluation of DoHS we contribute a series of insights for the HCI community on how digital technologies can support playful interactions for 8-10 year old children within the space of a library and encourage their engagement with books. Secondarily, we carefully consider how our design process and our digital game structures a playful experience to promote creativity.

BACKGROUND: BENJAMIN ROAD LIBRARY

Our design work is centred on Benjamin Road Library, a state-funded public library located in the inner suburbs of a city in the north of England. It holds a large number of fiction and non-fiction books, DVDs, music, as well as a smaller selection of children's books catering for ages from 3 upwards. Benjamin Road is located in one of the city's poorest and ethnically diverse conurbations, and provides access to a number of core services for local residents. One half of the building is dedicated to services provided by the local social housing provider. Tenants arrive at the entrance to the library, take a ticket from an electronic dispenser, and wait in a large seating area until their number is called out. It is not uncommon for large families to arrive together and wait until it is their time to go to the counter. The bustling noise of people talking to one another and the occasional calling out of "*can number 123 please come to counter 3*" stands in stark contrast with public conceptions of the quiet library space. ICT provision has become important to public libraries over the last decades and this is also true for Benjamin Road. It has 20 PCs which can be booked an hour at a time by members of the public. On many of our visits to the library we observed machines in intensive use. Library staff would also run courses each day using these machines, such as curriculum vitae sessions for the unemployed, or lessons on how to use word processing software for the first time. The library has recently installed a self-service loan kiosk, albeit used rarely, with many preferring to visit the manned desk. The city's libraries had also just released an iPhone app that allowed people to search and request bookings for books and other services.

Our initial insights were formed from a series of visits to Benjamin Road and other community libraries across the city. Two team members also observed and participated in creative writing sessions organised by schools and libraries for children. Our observations were supplemented with semi-structured interviews with teaching staff who accompanied local school children on library visits and informal meetings with library managers and staff. During initial fieldwork it was clear that the technology provided within most libraries was limited to the use of the bookable desktop PCs. These would be used for a range of activities by library users, from general web browsing and searching for new jobs, to basic word processing. What was notable was the large number of young people (mostly teenagers) observed across libraries using these public computers to access social media (e.g. Facebook) and play free games online (e.g. MiniClip and ebaumsworld). Those visiting the library to use the PCs would rarely visit the book section. Indeed for the most part it appeared that computers were not used to directly engage with books at all. It was clear that in the specific context of Benjamin Road there was a distinct disconnect between the role that technology played and the children's section—the computers used adult seating, they default to adult book services such as book search, and were situated away from the children's library.

It became apparent on initial visits that while play and gaming seemed to be valued in terms of the use of ICT in the library, visits by groups of school children would neglect play as a means of exploring the library. Our meetings with library staff and school staff highlighted how visits to the library would be orientated around finding information from books that relates to specific elements of the national curriculum. Therefore, at an early stage in our engagements with Benjamin Road we considered challenging this view by exploring how play could be introduced into these visits and their associated activities to provide new ways for school children to interact with books, seek information and engage with the library.

Play and Storytelling

Play as a concept has been well explored by the HCI community [13, 18, 21, 23]. We find Verenikina et al.'s [30] work particularly influential in terms of how theories of play can be applied in games design. They highlight how play is spontaneous, self-initiated and a self-regulated activity where children are actively involved in creating their play and are in control of it. This definition of play shares characteristics with Caillois's *paidic* play (cited [18] and [13]) where play is open, ambiguous and affords self-expression. Cassel and Ryokai [6], Verenikina [30] and others [1, 4, 15] argue that fantasy and make-believe are key elements of play. Fantasy and storytelling can also be seen as core components of telling creative stories, and as such storytelling can also be seen as an inherently playful activity [1, 14]. By playing through storytelling it is also possible to attract children who lack confidence in their reading and writing and help engage the imagination [15].

Storytelling is well represented in the field of HCI and is often supported as a creative activity [4, 8, 11, 16, 22, 29].

We focus here on drawing and building upon work that is synergetic with the qualities of the library site we designed for. A number of systems have explored the design of engaging interfaces to encourage children to form stories and narratives in novel ways. In *Picture This!* [29] augmented toys are used to support children as they direct their own film narrative, while StoryMat [6] allows a child to move freely around an embroidered blanket as they record and recall oral narratives with physical tangibles. Pogo [8] and StoryRoom [22] are aimed at young children (5-6 and 6-8). These systems encourage children to play with tangible objects providing audio and visual cues as to how they should be used. Finally, there are examples of in-situ digital storytelling systems, such as Mobile Stories [12] and TellTable [4], where children explore the immediate environment as part of the creative process. Nevertheless, while TellTable was deployed in a children's library, this space was chosen as appropriate for children targeted by the deployment given it was a lively place, full of toys [4]. TellTable as such did not account for a child's use of the library or engagement with books.

During the Interactive Children's Library Project, Eriksson et al. [10] explored similar challenges to those we face at Benjamin Road. In the design of bibPhone [19] they created a bespoke artefact to allow spoken stories to be added as a new digital layer in the children's library. Eriksson et al. found that children enjoyed using bibPhone to listen to what others had recorded on the books. However, they concede that children were reluctant to make their own recordings. In contrast, StorySurfer [11] encourages children aged 7 and 8 to search for books by using physical play. Here, StorySurfer uses tangible blocks in an installation to get a child to think about the book they want to find. In contrast to bibPhone the emphasis of this study is on play within a bespoke installation, although it is still deployed in the children's library.

This prior work reveals that technology can provide opportunities to support creative play within physical space, as well as support children in searching the specific resources that a library holds. In DoHS we extend this work by not only examining how technology can support browsing and searching for new books, but also in how newly discovered books can support creative writing and storytelling activities.

DESIGN PROCESS

To begin exploring the potential of linking play and storytelling together in a library-based game, we held an initial exploratory workshop at Benjamin Road. The participants were the project team, which included two computer scientists, two games designers, an interaction designer, two creative writers, an English teacher, a children's book author and a member of library staff. The primary aim of the workshop was to develop a common understanding across the team about the potential for using games to engage children in reading and writing about books. The majority of the workshop was spent with the team working in three small groups and 'experience prototyping' [3] basic games that were acted out in the library. Each group used blank playing cards to make basic prompts that initiated playful interactions with the library's book collection. After prototyping and iterating their games, the groups reconvened to share ideas. Through further discussion and iteration, three approaches to using prompts were selected to take forward:

Finding books with specific qualities. A common approach was prompting players to find a book using simple criteria, such as retrieving a book that used a specific colour. This encouraged exploration of the library through a form of "treasure hunt". The envisioned use here was that child players would be encouraged to seek and touch books, even if this was just reading the cover, flicking through the pages, or reading the blurb on the rear.

Playing cards with characters, objects and places. A popular approach was also for games to start by dealing a random character that would be illustrated on a card. This character would take the role of the protagonist. After this, further cards could be dealt that described generic objects and places. These playing cards were inspired by children's trading card games like Pokémon and board games like Cluedo. The purpose of these cards would be to provide the starting elements of a story, from which books would be used to situate the characters, objects and places in.

Stories with fortunate and unfortunate events. One group added another set of playing cards that introduced unfortunate or fortunate events to the story. The cards themselves did not describe what the fortunate or unfortunate event was—instead, it was down to the player to find a book to inspire their own story about this change in fortune. For example, a player might start by describing a farmer living by a river. They could be given an 'unfortunate event' card. From browsing the library the child could find a book on volcanoes, inspiring them to write how a terrible fire engulfs the farmer's land. Next they might be dealt a 'fortunate event' card and inspired by a book on firefighting to write how their character uses the water from the river to fight the fire, and so forth. It was considered that these prompts would inspire the child players to collect multiple books in developing a story, winding through a series of changing fortunes. It was taken that this game challenged its player to solve a series of problems for a character through creative writing.

Card-based Playful Storytelling Games

Following the exploratory workshop, our design processes involved integrating the identified prompts into an initial card-based playful storytelling game. This game was to be piloted with groups of children aged 8 to 10 years on a school visit to Benjamin Road Library.

Reflecting upon the team's own experiences playing the games, it was decided that the pilot should include a short initial activity that would act as a 'warm up' to familiarise the children with the library and the facilitators before beginning the main activity. This game reflected the *finding books with specific qualities* rule, asking children to randomly choose a card from a pack of *object cards*. The game then prompted them to find a related book. The children were told that there was no right and wrong but they would be asked to explain their choice to the other children on their table. This initial exercise would last for 10 to 20 minutes before the children played the main game.

The second game introduced the children to the idea of writing new stories based on inspiration from books. Building on the games developed at the initial workshop, this game included a set of *character cards* and a set of *fortunately and unfortunately cards*. Characters included a doctor, pilot, captain and animals such as a polar bear, which were illustrated on the front of each card. Having a protagonist character was deemed to be particularly important since it can be the persona through which a child exerts themselves into the imaginary world of the game [26]. To focus each child on developing this starting character, we explained how they had become lost from the library and could only be saved by writing them into a new story. The instructions on how to select a character card were left deliberately ambiguous. This meant the children could choose randomly, pick one particular character over another, or even swap their selection with another child.

Once a child had selected a character, they were prompted: *"Where does your character's story begin? Go to the bookshelves and choose a book where your story starts..."* The intent here was that the first book they retrieved from the library would help define the 'qualities' for the beginning of their story, such as describing a particular place or location. Again, this prompt was intentionally open so as to encourage the child to freely explore their own ideas. Once they had made their selection the children would return to their table to begin writing their story. We covered the tables completely in paper, so the children's stories could take up as much room as they wanted. We provided a variety of pens and crayons so stories could be created with as much freedom and expression as possible.

Having started writing their story the children would then randomly choose a fortunate or unfortunate event card to continue their story and select another book. The game would continue like this with a succession of fortunate and unfortunate events encouraging the child to return to the library space and come into contact with more books. In order to support different learning styles and relax constraints as much as possible, we did not limit the number of cards children could take, or how much room they could use on the tables. However, the children were warned 10 minutes before the game ended to allow them time to complete their stories. After this the children reviewed all the stories together.

Figure 2. DoHS create mode main screens

Pilot Study

To test out these initial games we held two workshops at Benjamin Road Library with a total of twenty 8–10 year old school children who represented a wide range of literacy proficiency. The workshops were organised as part of their normal visits that occurred during their English classes. Two teaching assistants accompanied each group, while six members of the research team acted as facilitators. The workshop itself was held in a meeting room in the library, with the discussions on each table audio recorded and the stories documented with photographs. An additional researcher stayed in the library to make observations of the children's interactions with books and the library space in general. After each workshop the researchers shared their immediate observations and insights before revisiting the game design. This revealed a number of insights regarding how the children engaged with the game that could be taken forward in the design of a digital tool:

Keeping a physical drawing space: As children created their stories on paper they used large surface areas and drew boundaries around their work to differentiate it from the stories of others. They creatively used colour, different sizes of text and incorporated drawings into their stories. Digital storytelling systems (e.g. TellTable [4]) often use the convention of a digital canvas to allow drawing, writing and the import of media. It was clear here however that there would be value in using these traditional writing materials as part of the digital game.

Enabling darker themes: The use of character cards such as vampires, soldiers, etc. gave children the permissiveness to express stories without fear of being told off. In particular, it provided assurance that they could explore darker themes, which are important in childhood play since it lets children express real life events that may not be positive [23].

Swapping and sticking with characters: As we designed our game with collectable games such as Pokémon in mind, we let the children trade their cards. They took delight in swapping their characters with one another as they compared the merits of each card before, typically, returning to their original choice. This made us consider what would happen if the character was not allowed to be swapped, and whether this would impact on engagement.

DEPARTMENT OF HIDDEN STORIES

We designed DoHS as a two-part game based upon our experiences from the pilot study. The mobile game allowed children to create a digital archive in the library which we held securely online indexed by each book's ISBN number. We designed this archive so it could eventually be scaled beyond Benjamin Road and allow a larger population of children using DoHS at different libraries to discover each other's stories. We also designed the game with specific time-based interactions to provide additional prompts to the child and to carefully control the game's progression in order to stop children skipping tasks. These features would have been difficult to support in a card game, and responded to a number of observations from the pilot study where the children relied heavily on the facilitating researchers to prompt them at certain stages in the game.

In order to create these game features we implemented DoHS as an Android OS app connecting to a remote server. DoHS was developed to be used on any touchscreen Android device. For the purposes of our study, DoHS was installed on Google Nexus 4 mobile phones running the JellyBean operating system. The app presents two interaction modes: *create mode* and *discover mode*. Both interaction modes of the app used a skeuomorph of a book, with pages turned by curling the corner of the touchscreen. We hoped this would allow children to navigate the pages using a simple and appropriate interaction. Children can switch between modes freely, although for the purposes of the study these were treated as separate aspects of the game.

Create Mode

In create mode, children are guided in the creation of stories through step-by-step instructions that are delivered on a set of successive pages (see Figure 2). As per the card-based game, create mode starts by asking the child to help a character, who is lost in the library. This character is chosen randomly from 23 pre-assigned characters in the system. Next, the child is prompted to find and bring back a book from the library where their character's story may begin. At this stage they are asked to start writing and drawing the beginnings of their story using physical materials. Initially, we had envisaged that DoHS would contain a 'virtual canvas' that would allow players to enter text and make drawings either on a hand-held device or on a digital tabletop or surface. However, as noted it was evident from the pilot study that the children valued having a large, physical canvas on which to develop their stories. Therefore, rather than restricting the children to interacting with the small screen of a phone in constructing their story, we focused on supporting the capturing and sharing of these handwritten and drawn stories. Keeping the paper canvas also made the technology more reliable and achievable, which was important given the scalable vision of DoHS.

Once a child feels they have written enough to start their story, they can move on to the next stage of create mode. At this point DoHS asks them to scan the book's barcode and then capture the start of their story using the phone's camera. The image is associated with the book scanned.

DoHS then changes the fortune that the story should follow. We used the device's accelerometer to allow the child to shake a virtual dice to reveal either a fortunate or unfortunate turn of events. The child is then asked to find a new book to inspire this event and repeat the process of writing, drawing and capturing from the previous stage. This process continues iteratively until the child is given 10 minute advance warning to complete their story.

The game also gauges the activity of the child by looking at the last touch event and movement of the phone, which it detects through the motion sensors. If the phone has not been "used" for three minutes then the game awards the child a random object, which they can either use as inspiration and write into their story or ignore if they wish.

Discover Mode

Discover mode allows children to hunt for hidden stories created by other players and hidden in books around the library. DoHS prompts children to scan a book and displays any story segment that has been 'hidden' inside that book. By turning to the previous or next page in the app, the child can see which books other parts of the story are hidden in.

THE STUDY

DoHS was deployed in Benjamin Road Library in two further workshops with the same 20 children who had participated in the pilot study. As before, the children were accompanied by teaching staff. We used the dictation facility on each mobile phone as a way of documenting audio from the workshop, which enabled us to capture the children's conversations both in the workshop room and in the library space itself. This was supplemented by field notes from each researcher detailing interactions between children, teachers and facilitators as well as the children's use of the library space. DoHS also logged interactions with books for later analysis.

Over the course of the two 2-hour workshops, the twenty children collected 109 books. The books chosen by them to incorporate into their stories were diverse, ranging from non-fiction such as books on the geography of Asia, to fiction such as Alice in Wonderland and Dracula. The relative freedom that we provided for the children to explore the library also meant that there were instances where children picked books from the adult section, much to the bemusement and occasional concern of the teachers. 10 of the 109 books in total were used by both of the workshop groups.

To understand how the experience of creating stories and discovering books unfolded through playing DoHS, an inductive thematic analysis [4] was performed on the research data gathered from the workshop. This involved members of the team repeatedly listening to 20 hours of audio from the workshop and transcribing this data. Initially, the codes drawn from the data included examples

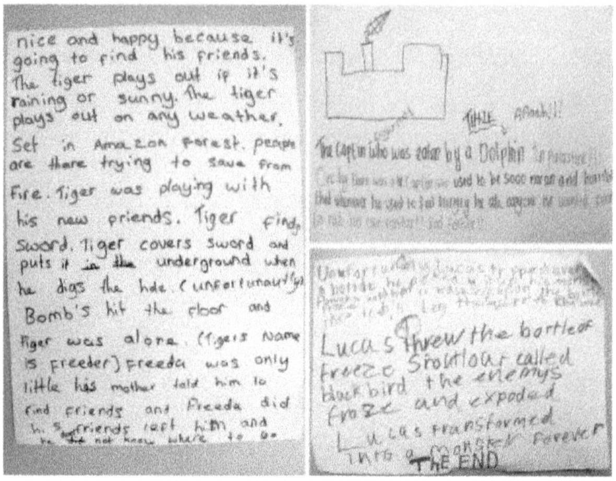

Figure 3. Various stories. (a) Tiger hides sword (b) Different coloured pens (c) The End

of emotion such as cruelty, control and humour which reflected details within the children's written stories. Through coder discussions these codes were grouped under the theme of 'self-expression' allowing the team to look at the wider picture of what was happening in the context of the library. In total, we grouped codes into five overarching themes: 1) *Browsing the shelves*, 2) *Incorporating books into stories*, 3) *Structuring stories*, 4) *Following and subverting rules*, and 5) *Self-expression*. These are described in the following section, where our child participants are given pseudonyms, the facilitating researchers labelled 'FT', and teaching assistant or teacher as 'TA'.

Browsing the Shelves

One goal of create mode was to support the children in exploring the resources of the library without direct facilitation from the research team or teaching staff. The vast majority of the children felt immediately comfortable leaving the confines of the workshop room and exploring the shelves for books within which their character might 'live'. Upon arriving in the library space it was clear that the children had very different approaches for searching for books to begin their character's story.

After establishing their characters a group of boys immediately ran through the library in search for specific types of books that they wanted to support the start of their story (in this case, Dracula for their vampiric character who began life as a doctor). Their interactions with the shelves were short, focused and chaotic—they had a strong sense of what type of book they were looking for and left as soon as they found it. Other children responded more cautiously to these initial explorations around the bookshelves. Chloe struggled to find a book about a tiger, *"Miss, I can't find a book with a tiger in."* Eventually Chloe is helped by a teacher to find the animal section where she looks for books that might contain tigers. Like the boys before, Chloe had a strong sense of what she wanted to find.

Although some browsing activities during create mode were jovial and vociferous, it was during the discovery mode where the children searched for books in ways that might be considered particularly unfitting of traditional library etiquette. To ensure as little disruption was caused to the library as possible, rather than return the books children used in their stories to the shelves we formed a temporary library shelf in the room where the workshop was held. At the end of the workshop the children were prompted to use discovery mode to explore these books and find where stories were hidden. This part of the workshop caused the most excitement and there were cries from the children, such as *"whoah! Whoah!"* in response to finding a story. In this activity we saw children browse the books randomly after an initial enthusiastic charge toward the shelves, as they dashed to get hold of anything that took their fancy. In one case the children discovered "Phenomenology of Perception". This book revealed some captures of the workshop room and the book itself, which had been brought to test barcodes after setting up the phones. This book caused real excitement as children realised they had found something secret and had got the better of the adults.

Incorporating Books into Stories

Along with diversity in browsing behaviour, there were also a number of critical differences in how children incorporated found material resources into their stories. Some children were inspired by imagery on covers or inside the book, while others used only the title of the book, or were inspired by the names of the book's characters. For example, Amber received the Tiger character, which she immediately named Freeda. Amber started by browsing for a book that would allow her to start adding details to Freeda's character. She was very deliberate in identifying a book, and although the nearby teachers made several suggestions she avoided taking their advice and picked up a non-fiction book on Asia: *"They will show me how to colour in a tiger."* On returning to the table, Amber continued to develop Freeda which led to a conversation with a researcher who mistakenly suggested that a tiger should be fierce and eat zebras. Amber was appalled by this idea and told the researcher decidedly that: *"They don't eat zebras"*. Amber was then happy to continue her story setting the scene that described a friendly and social tiger; Amber writes that the tiger *"was nice and happy because it's going to find his friends. The tiger plays out if it raining or sunny."* Later, after starting with this positive scene Amber received an unfortunate event. Reflecting on the pictures of lone Tiger's in the Asia book, she asks for confirmation from a nearby researcher: *"Something about being lonely. [...] I'm wondering if the tiger can have a friend that can maybe run away."* When she returns from browsing, she has found a book titled *"Slavery: from Africa to the Americas."* When asked why she had picked this booked, she explained: *"if you were a slave, you would be very lonely."*

Amber's example illustrated how some children responded to the some of the immediate qualities of the books or the rich imagery discovered inside. Others borrowed ideas from the actual text after reading some content. Harry was writing a super-natural story about an evil doctor surrounded by his evil minions. On returning from a browsing trip Harry had found a book about a black hole and explains to a researcher why he chose this book:

Harry: *In a black hole. A doctor went to see to it. Then some creatures from the black hole entered. If they come near you, you can get a rash.*

FT: *Why did you choose this book?*

Harry: *Because I don't know about black holes, so I picked up a book about black holes and read the blurb, and it's full of good ideas.*

Structuring Stories

Although the create mode provided specific prompts and activities for children to undertake in writing their stories, the ways in which the stories themselves could be structured were still left ambiguous as per our pilot game. We observed that children started to form their own ways of creating a narrative and structuring their stories. Watt's story structure [32] describes eight key story points such as 1) Stasis 2) Trigger, 3) The quest, 4) Surprise, 5) Critical choice, 6) Climax, 7) Reversal and 8) Resolution. In the children's stories we can find examples of many of these key points, for example, Chloe's story about a fierce tiger called Terry begins with an explanation of the stasis, or status quo: *"It all started with fright. In India there was a tiger called terry, was a fierce one. He was king of the jungle. He was a good hunter."* The stasis in the children's stories in our study is often followed by a trigger that sparks off the story. In Chloe's story, the trigger is the tiger whose bad fortune is compounded by heavy rain: *"But one day wasn't in shape, he was feeling awful"*, and *"Suddenly it was raining so much"*. In Jim's story there are examples of climax: *"The next week it was the day, the big day, it was world war 6"*. Following this, his story ends with some finality: *"Dan daan daaan! It is Kevin the solider! He got £50 million pounds and he was The King!!!"*.

Following and Subverting the Rules

As noted, the level of independence afforded by the create mode differed from child to child. Although none of the children appeared to struggle to act independently in creating their stories at one stage or another, it was clear that many were concerned about following the 'rules' of the game. Some were unsure of what the 'right' or 'wrong' way of starting their story would be, despite assurances from the researchers that there was no right or wrong. Some of the children felt being free to write anything was a misunderstanding, or an elaborate trick being played by their teachers and the researchers. They needed to know they were doing the "right" thing, that their story's direction and meaning was ok and made sense. They also needed assurance that the books were the right choice for the prompts they had received, for example James asked, *"Miss, I need to look for another book for fortunately again. It could be like... I could get the ghosts out of the house?"* Indeed, on some occasions the children's concerns about playing the game correctly were affirmed further by the intervening TA's who would question their stories and unwittingly undermine children's narrative decisions.

We also observed instances of how children upheld the game rules. Amber was so engrossed in writing her story that the game assumed that she was stuck since the phone had not been touched or moved for three minutes. The game presented Amber a new random object, in the hope it would help inspire her story. This object card happened to be a picture of a sword. At this point Amber sighed and dismissed the prompt on the phone. She exclaimed to the nearest researcher that Freeda was friendly and the tiger could not possibly be interested in the sword that had just been given to her. Amber's solution was to let her tiger decisively dispose of this unwanted object card (top-left in Figure 3a). She wrote: *"Tiger was playing with his new friends. Tiger finds sword. Tiger covers sword and puts it underground when he digs the hole."* Amber then returned to telling the story as if the event had not happened. This is notable because Amber could have ignored the object completely and pretended it hadn't happened, but instead she subverted the story itself to deal with this intrusion.

Although most of the children followed and seemed to enforce stricter rules on themselves than the game implied, there were also examples of where the 'rules' of the game were subverted. Unlike the card-based games, one rule here was that the child would have to use the randomly assigned character given at the start of the game. Some of the children had learned through self-exploration however that closing DoHS and restarting it would mean receiving a different character at the start of the game. On initial observation, it appeared that those children who restarted the app did so because they disliked their initial character:

Jack: *I'm changing mine!*

FT: *Are you trying to secretly change it by going back?*

Jack: *Yeah*

Jim: *I don't wanna be a nurse!*

After this exchange they continued restarting the game until both had the soldier character. The boys 'cheating' was not just because of their dislike for the nurse character as indicated. They were also seeking to write their stories together with the same characters—in this case a soldier, which they had learned from other children was one of the characters available in the game. In another example Andy wanted an unfortunate card instead of the fortunate card that they had been given. They were caught closing and restarting DoHS by a researcher, leading Andy to exclaim: *"We weren't cheating...!"*

Self-Expression

Finally, DoHS supported the children in expressing themselves creatively through their interactions with their peers and the stories they created. Some would express themselves simply by giggling or laughing while writing their story. In one example, Emily described how she was getting married in her own story, as she declared while giggling: *"I want a wedding book as I'm getting married to Justin Bieber!"*. Quite often humour was driven by unfortunate events occurring to the characters within the stories. On many occasions we witnessed stories being created where the characters would be punished in unlikely situations. The children would frequently express their humour at these stories through expressive language and theatrical laughter such as: "*hahahah.* [...] *the pilot broke his back so he's in hospital!"*

The children also expressed themselves through the ways in which they constructed their stories with the crayons and paper made available to them. As with the pilot workshop, the children quickly felt comfortable working on paper and as before used different crayons to represent aspects of their story. Three girls in one session all preferred to draw what their characters looked like to begin with when starting their stories. Others drew illustrations and added visual details to their stories as they were being created. Sometimes these appeared to be as a distraction from the game—often however it seemed out of self-directed enjoyment. One girl however became deeply frustrated, exclaiming: *"ah it's rubbish!"* and *"I can't draw at all"*. While most enjoyed writing in this way, it could be a frustrating process for those who felt less comfortable with their writing or drawing skills.

Self-expression also emerged through visceral acts of frustration when playing the game. Sometimes this frustration was born of programming bugs (such as DoHS not connecting to Wi-Fi correctly) or problems with scanning books because of damaged barcodes. The deepest frustrations however related to the prompts provided by the game. As we noted above, some children 'gamed' DoHS by finding ways to generate new characters if they disliked the initial selection the game provided. Lily however did not enjoy her selection (a 'captain') but was not aware of this 'trick'. She persevered with this character but stated on a number of times that she *"didn't like him"* and *"there's nothing I can do with him"*. Great frustration was also felt by those who were dealt the same event cards several times on a row. While frustrating, this led to huge cries of excitement when finally receiving the opposing card.

DISCUSSION

In designing DoHS we aimed to create a digital game that supported new modes of exploring and interacting with the core resources of the public library: its books. Rather than take an approach that prescribed children which books they should interact with, we looked at carefully prompting children to discover new or unusual books that could inspire them to create their own stories. These same books were then to be used as a resource to discover the stories participating children had created.

The British public library has traditionally not been a very playful space. This is highlighted in the ways in which digital technologies have typically been used here—to organise information, to act as digital archives, and to provide more efficient ways of locating books. Yet the act of reading, writing and being inspired by books can be an inherently creative and playful act [15]. This is particularly important to young children who lack confidence in their reading and writing skills. Although DoHS was oriented towards general engagement with books and not educational outcomes, our findings suggest that playful digital storytelling can support both curricular and extra-curricular interactions with books. We reflect on these findings in the following, noting implications for the design of future playful technologies in this context.

Starting stories with characters or prompts

As noted, the children browsed and searched for books in very diverse ways. It is clear that our decision to initiate their stories by responding to a randomly assigned character hugely influenced the beginnings of the story and the manner in which each child searched for their first books. As we saw in our themes, some children were very direct in how they searched for books to inspire their character. They would go straight to the appropriate section in the library, i.e. reference books or maps, looking for a specific book or browse books holding onto an idea of what they were looking for. The game provided the assurance the child needed by providing characters that they had preconceived ideas about. This selection of the character (even though it could be random) preloaded their tale as it made their writing prescriptive by effectively limiting their amount of free-expression. In some cases this led to children subverting the game (by restarting the app) as they sought new creative ways of getting around this prescriptiveness. We suggest that this subverting of the game was positive. It was a display of imagination and inherently not risk free; children did not know the repercussion to the game or what would happen if they were caught.

Rather than provide a complete character, our design could have borrowed a convention from games - a character builder. A character builder typically defines the character from a much smaller granularity. This may be a series of questions asking the child whether their character was mythical, real, what age they were, or if there character was an animal and so on. This would give the child more control in not only their character's development but also their story and place them in control of the play from the onset.

Letting the child take control of the structure

Related to the prior point, DoHS also heavily influenced the ways in which children constructed their stories over time in the provision of the fortunate and unfortunate events. The aim of providing these prompts was to leave a child to respond openly to what could be considered 'fortunate' or 'unfortunate'. Yet we saw occasions where children struggled to find inspiration for these events from books. This led to the teachers and researchers having to help.

One response to these issues might be to expand upon the range of prompts. We saw how some children's stories followed a story arc, and a set of prompts around these features may be one way to initiate more flexible and diverse responses from children. This could be taken further and provide a child with a set of arc elements to choose from, asking them questions such as: 'your character is surprised, tell us why'; 'a big event will happen in the future, what is it?' From here a child might build their story up in a still creative but more controlled manner.

Providing expressive places to play

A decision taken early on was to allow the children to use the tables covered in paper as the 'canvas' on which to construct their stories. This design decision was carried through to DoHS. As we saw, the children enjoyed making use of this large space and developed their own ways of expressing their stories within their own, unbounded, space. Having this space external to the phone also supported multiple interactions at once—it allowed a child to have their phone with its situated prompts, the book acting as inspiration and the space on which to construct the story laid out in front of them at once. As such, rather than being the centre of play, DoHS was scaffolding and supporting play in this existing physical environment.

Providing this large expressive space however did raise problems for the children, and in the latter workshop impacted negatively on the experience of DoHS. What was especially challenging was the disconnection between DoHS and the written material. In DoHS sharing a story was based upon photographing each phase of the story as it was being created and tagging this to a book. However, the children regularly had practical difficulties in using the phone's camera. They also struggled to get a sense of what part of their story to capture each time: should they capture just the last bit they wrote, or the entire story? Invariably they chose to capture it all each time, meaning their images became gradually harder to read on the devices display.

There are likely far better ways of capturing the written and drawn data the children created than as executed in DoHS. Prior work has explored the use of Anoto pens [31] or the Wacom Inkling [7] to translate handwritten into digital content. However, in practice these devices require further equipment and come with additional technical challenges. Furthermore, they would restrict the real estate of the canvas, which the children most appreciated. Instead, we might consider ways of providing new prompts in games like DoHS where the expressivity of photography for children [9] is harnessed further. We might imagine additional elements of the app that support the child in constructing their documentation of the story in creative and expressive ways—such as only revealing one part of their story, or providing hints to someone who discovered their story as to where the next part of their story may lie.

CONCLUSION

As with any study, there are limitations to our findings. While the children who participated in our workshops were diverse in ethnicity and literacy level, we were still limited to meeting the one class as two separate groups. This includes involving the same children in the pilot workshop and the digital DoHS workshop. Clearly this may have biased some of the responses from the children, who were indeed highly motivated to play DoHS after playing the pilot game. However, as our intention was to support an iterative design process and not a comparative study, involving these same children engendered a sense of ownership over the design of DoHS, and supported them in being able to comment on what was better (or worse) about DoHS in comparison to the initial card game.

While we do not seek to over generalise in our findings, our initial evaluation of DoHS is promising in terms of strategies for the design of new library spaces and services. Libraries and similarly schools are often considered institutions bounded by rules. Meyers [20], for instance, describes how preteens perceive the library as somewhere they are told to be *"SHHH!"*, and that *"Libraries are so-o-o-o quiet—they are creepy"*. These public perceptions impact on who uses the library and indeed how it is used [28]. Regardless of the library stating users no longer need to be quiet, this perception still widely exists, and as a result libraries remain quiet spaces. Some of the most compelling observations of children using DoHS relate to how they ardently ignored adults' suggestions for potential books and storylines. Additionally, while playing along with DoHS they found ways to usurp its rules of play and structure. By creating a simple game based on playful principles where children are put in charge of their own self-initiated, spontaneous and self-controlled play [30], we simultaneously created a context where children felt free to break a number of the institutional rules (both school and library) around them: no use of adult book sections, no running in the library, no shouting. Our library partners also remarked on how the children appeared to use the library space in ways that are not afforded by normal school visits, and have noted an increase in recurrent visits from our participants. We are continuing to develop DoHS across other libraries, employing playful design principles in the design of the library space to help people of all ages appropriate these spaces for lifelong learning that better suits a multitude of potential users. Rather than designing tools that are a focal point of play, we argue that we should design tools that act as conduits and mediators for play. In DoHS, we have illustrated how we can design playful interventions to promote such activities from an early age.

ACKNOWLEDGEMENTS

This research was funded by the AHRC Creative Exchange Knowledge Exchange Hub and the TSB ALIP 3/4 project

SALT (2377-25137). We would like to thank Benjamin Road Library and Tin Street School (not their real names) for their support, and Selina Sutton and Aftab Kahn for reading through drafts of this paper.

REFERENCES

1. Åkerman, P. and Puikkonen, A. Prochinima: using pico projector to tell situated stories. *Proc. MobileHCI '11*, ACM (2011), 337-346.
2. Arrasvuori, J., Korhonen, H. and Väänänen-Vainio-Mattila, K. Exploring playfulness in user experience of personal mobile products. *Proc. OZCHI '10*, ACM (2010), s88-95.
3. Buchenau, M. and Suri, J. Experience prototyping. *Proc. DIS '00*, ACM (2000), 424-433.
4. Braun, V. and Clarke, V., Using thematic analysis in psychology. *Journal of Qualitative Research in Psychology*, 3, (2006), 77-101.
5. Cao, X., Lindley, S., Helmes, J. and Sellen, A. Telling the whole story: anticipation, inspiration and reputation in a field deployment of TellTable. *Proc. CSCW '10*, ACM (2010), 251-260.
6. Cassell, J. and Ryokai, K. Making Space for Voice: Technologies to Support Children's Fantasy and Storytelling. *Pers. Ubiq. Computing*, 5 (3), 169-190.
7. Chiang, C., et al. Birds on paper: an alternative interface to compose music by utilizing sketch drawing and mobile device. *Proc. TEI '12*, ACM (2012), 201-204.
8. Decortis, F. and Rizzo, A. New Active Tools for Supporting Narrative Structures. *Personal & Ubiquitous Comput.* 6, 5-6 (2002), 416-429.
9. Durrant, A., Hook, J., McNaney, R., et al. Design to support interpersonal communication in the special educational needs classroom. *Proc. IDC '13*, ACM (2013), 46-55.
10. Eriksson, E., et al. Inquiry into libraries - a design approach to children's interactive library. *Proc. Design Inquiries* (2007).
11. Eriksson, E. and Lykke-Olesen, A. StorySurfer: a playful book browsing installation for children's libraries. *Proc. IDC '07*, ACM (2007), 57-64.
12. Fails, J., Druin, A. and Guha, M. Mobile Collaboration: Collaboratively Reading and Creating Children's Stories on Mobile Devices. *Proc. IDC '10*, ACM (2010), 20-29.
13. Gaver, B. Designing for Homo Ludens, Still. In: *(Re)searching the Digital Bauhaus*. Binder, T., et al. (eds.). London, Springer, 163-178
14. Garzotto, F. and Forfori, M. Hyperstories and social interaction in 2D and 3D edutainment spaces for children. Proc. HYPERTEXT '06, ACM (2006), 57-68.
15. Göttel, T. Reviewing children's collaboration practices in storytelling environments. Proc. IDC '11, ACM (2011), 153-156.
16. Hourcade, J., et al. KidPad: collaborative storytelling for children. *Proc. CHI EA '02*, ACM (2002), 500-501.
17. IFLA, *Guidelines for Children's Libraries Services*, IFLA, Edinburgh, 2003.
18. Lindley, E., S, Harper, R., and Sellen, A., Designing a technological playground: a field study of the emergence of play in household messaging. *Proc. CHI '10*. ACM (2010), P. 2351-2360.
19. Lykke-Olesen, A. and Nielsen, J. bibPhone: adding sound to the children's library. *Proc. IDC '07*, ACM (2007), 145-148.
20. Meyers, E. The Coolness Factor: Ten Libraries Listen to Youth. *The Journal of American Libraries* 30, 10 (1999), 42-45.
21. Monk, A., Hassenzahl, M., Blythe, M. and Reed, D. Funology: designing enjoyment. *Interactions*, (September 2002), 11-11.
22. Montemayor, J., et al. Tools for children to create physical interactive storyrooms. *The Journal of Comput. Entertain.* 2, 1 (2004), 12-12.
23. National Literacy Trust. *Literacy Guide for Secondary Schools 2012-2013*. National Literary Trust, London, 2012.
24. Pykhtina, O., Balaam, M., Wood, G., Pattison, S., Kharrufa, A. and Olivier, P. Magic land: the design and evaluation of an interactive tabletop supporting therapeutic play with children. *Proc. DIS '12*, ACM (2012), 136-145.
25. Ryokai, K. and Cassell, J. Computer support for children's collaborative fantasy play and storytelling. *Proc. CSCL '99*, International Society of the Learning Sciences (1999).
26. Salen, K. and Zimmerman, E. *Rules of play: Game design fundamentals*. Cambridge, MIT Press, 2003.
27. The Reading Agency. http://readingagency.org.uk/news/reading-facts003/
28. Usherwood, B. and Linley, R. New Library - New Measures: A Social Audit of Public Libraries. *The Journal of IFLA*, 25, (2), 90-96.
29. Vaucelle, C. and Ishii, H. Picture this! Film assembly using toy gestures. *Proc. UbiComp '08*, ACM (2008), 350-359.
30. Verenikina, I., et al. Child's play: computer games, theories of play and children's development. *Proc. CRPIT '03*, ACS, (2003), 99-106.
31. Vines, J., Blythe, M., Dunphy, P., Vlachokyriakos, V., Teece, I., Monk, A. and Olivier, P. Cheque mates: participatory design of digital payments with eighty somethings. *Proc. CHI '12*, ACM (2012), 1189-1198.
32. Watts, N. *Write a Novel and Get It Published: A Teach Yourself Guide*. London, Teach Yourself, 2010.

Visualizing Interactive Narratives: Employing a Branching Comic to Tell a Story and Show its Readings

Daniel Andrews and Chris Baber
Department of Electronic, Electrical and Computer Engineering
The University of Birmingham
Birmingham B15 2TT, United Kingdom
d.e.w.andrews@gmail.com, c.baber@bham.ac.uk

ABSTRACT
This paper describes the design and evaluation of a branching comic to compare how readers recall a visual narrative when presented as an interactive, digital program, or as a linear sequence on paper. The layout of the comic is used to visualize this data as heat maps and explore patterns of users' recollections. We describe the theoretical justification for this based upon previous work in narrative visualizations, interactive stories and comics. Having tested the comic with school boys aged 11-12; we saw patterns in the data that complement other research in both interactive stories and visualizations. We argue that the heat maps helped identify these patterns, which have implications for future designs and analyses of interactive visual and/or narrative media.

Author Keywords
branching comics; interactive stories; narrative visualization; story comprehension

ACM Classification Keywords
H.5.m.

INTRODUCTION
In 2013, DC Comics released a digital, interactive comic book, inspired by Choose Your Own Adventure books, for Apple's iPad [14]. Though branching comics have existed for some time [3], the success of tablet computers seems to have revived an interest in the opportunities that can be offered to audiences in comparison with traditional modes of presentation. Studies of such hypermedia have typically analyzed their user experiences. However, there has been relatively little exploration of the impact such presentations could have upon the comprehension of stories, and the implications this may have for the design of branching comics, or other interactive stories and visualizations.

Comics are a form of narrative visualization [29] and in fact derive from the earliest forms of visual communication [9, 18]. Whilst the study of comics has grown considerably in recent years, theorists have struggled to keep abreast with the technological advances that could impact the medium. Though user experience studies have previously been applied to related hypermedia, the study of comics could complement existing research by offering insight into the impact of interacting with narrative visualizations upon their comprehension. Subsequently, if there is an impact upon how users 'read' these representations, this data could provide insight into the impact interactions might have upon the comprehension of other visual information.

Previous work by Andrews et al. [3] integrated paper within a multi-touch interface to explore theories of both comics and interactive storytelling, and create an environment for authoring and reading branching comics. It was argued that comics are particularly useful for exploring interactive stories, as they can be employed to visualize where and how different interactive elements are embedded within a story. For example, a comic strip drawn on paper might have a series of panels containing drawings that could be freely interpreted by readers. These drawings would also contain gaps for other visual or textual elements such as characters, objects, dialogue or captions. When placed upon the multi-touch surface developed, users could drag and drop objects into corresponding gaps in the comic, which would trigger additional material to be projected into remaining gaps. By dragging different combinations of objects, users could therefore embellish the comic with additional material and explore different branches within the story.

Though these studies indicated that the separation of visual levels helped users comprehend how branching narratives could be authored, the impact of interaction upon the comprehension of visual branching narratives was not explored. Following this work, we now consider how readers respond to such narratives when delivered as interactive, digital presentations or printed sequentially on paper. Apart from exploring the impact of interacting with visualizations, this also contributes a method of exploring stories and narrative visualizations beyond user experiences.

In this paper, a comic design based upon a theoretical foundation employing abstraction levels [4] and visual narrative structure [9] is presented. We demonstrate how

CHI 2014, April 26 - May 01 2014, Toronto, ON, Canada

http://dx.doi.org/10.1145/2556288.2557296

branching comics can be presented in both interactive and linear form for the purposes of exploring differences between their readings. We then employ the same design layout of the comic in the visualization of its readings. It is argued that this facilitates both visualizing and evaluating interactive narratives, and identifying patterns for further analysis.

RELATED WORK

The work presented here combines approaches to visualization with those of interactive storytelling design and evaluation; bound by theories of comics.

Visualization

Segel and Heer [29] have used the analogy of storytelling to discuss a range of case studies comparing the strengths and weaknesses of different visualizing techniques. There is discussion over the dilemma of balancing author- or reader-led designs in data visualizations, and the different capabilities that users could, or should, be offered. This is a concern worth noting as it is similar to those of interactive storytelling theorists more generally, who are continually exploring the balance between the control of the author and the reader [5]. It is argued that some of the best data visualizations are those that provide their users with brief narrative overviews ('snippets') to facilitate comprehension [29]. Yet it seems that the level of detail given in these 'snippets' is created intuitively by the author(s) of these visualizations, having taken into account the method(s) of presenting the information and the opportunities offered to the user(s). A recent study integrating game mechanics into data visualization has indicated that such mechanics could be used to provide structure to an interactive visualization and would appear to align readers' attention in a manner which is different to visualizations which do not use such mechanics [10]. Whether similar effects can be seen in branching narrative interfaces is yet to be explored.

Interactive Storytelling

With the exception of video games [19, 22], visualizations have rarely been employed in Interactive Stories, though work has begun to emerge in this area. Experimental visualizations have been applied to a range of Choose Your Own Adventure (CYOA) books from the 1980s, for example, and to more recent digital experiments such as the interactive drama *Facade* [28]. In the case of the CYOA books, the visualizations are used to depict the structure of their content rather than to support or reflect their comprehension, whereas the visual information on *Facade* shows how users interact with the 'story space' depending upon the interface chosen.

Similarly, there seems to be a trend amongst evaluations of interactive stories to focus upon users' experiences rather than their comprehension of the stories (for examples, see [5, 15, 20, 25, 30]). This could be because the notion of 'story comprehension' is highly debatable, even before the equally contested term 'interactive story' is considered. Following formalists such as Propp [26] and structuralists such as Barthes [6], cognitive psychologists such as Rumelhart [27] and Thorndyke [31] have tried to give order to stories so that their content and reception could be studied. However, subsequent theorists have contested such approaches [7, 11, 13]. One of the reasons to question the notions of generic structures in stories (as these approaches imply) is that readers often respond to different aspects of stories and so bring different 'readings' to the same material. This returns us to the debate of author- and reader-led 'design' (in that an author-led approach might favor a Formalist method of having defined roles for characters responding to defined situations, whereas a reader-led approach might favor a more open-ended framework in which the reader is able to imbue the events and characters in the story with a range of features). Of particular interest in interactive storytelling, therefore, is the question of balancing a formal structure of the story (for instance, in which characters have properties and these properties respond to events) with a more open-ended presentation of the story itself, in which the reader is free to offer interpretations and hypotheses about character behavior and motivation [5].

Formalist structures or schemas have been used for the benefit of research to facilitate the production of computational models of narrative [1]. Finlayson's [12] *Analogical Story Merging*, for example, uses morphologies derived from Propp and others in a model to validate the existence or otherwise of story frameworks by 'merging' stories to identify their structural differences and similarities along these morphologies. In this case, the model is applied to some simple stories as well as a set of Shakespeare's plays. Whilst the output of the models may be inconclusive, at the very least they serve to show the practical application of such structures.

Aylett et al. [4] have discussed a system of *abstraction levels* in relation to emergent narrative and artificial intelligence which has been applied to previous work on branching comics [3]. It is argued that the social aspects of interactive storytelling, inspired by the table-top roleplaying game Dungeons and Dragons, are categorized to facilitate the development of a model towards managing emergent narrative in artificial intelligence. This uses the analogy of the Game Master; who would maintain an overview of the story, whilst permitting differentiation through player interactions at lower levels of abstraction. To specify what information should, or could, be contained within these levels of abstraction, the levels could be combined with existing models of narrative, such as story grammars. Whilst this is designed to determine the impact of interactions upon the levels within an emerging story, it could also help determine where, or how, these interactions can occur for authors of interactive stories.

Comics

As stated above, it has been previously argued that comics can help visualize where and how the specific details of interactive stories are implemented by incorporating them within the layout of comics [3]. This approach employs abstraction levels, and distinguishes the top level overview of the story, drawn directly on paper, with the lower levels of abstraction, modified by users' actions and projected underneath the paper via a multi-touch surface. It was argued that physically separating the top level from the bottom level(s) of branching comics in this way facilitated the rapid prototyping and evaluation of interactive stories. The impact upon the reading of such stories, and how this might compare with traditional presentations, was not explored.

Research into the reading of comics is a growing area, and much of the most recent work (at the time of writing) has been by Neil Cohn and his colleagues [8, 9]. When proposing a visual narrative structure, Cohn [9] divides comic strips into units, visualized as panels or combinations of panels and split into categories: Establisher, Initial, Prolongation, Peak and Release. These combine to form 'phases', which can form a self-contained narrative arc or be embedded within one another to create a broader arc. In this way, the notion of visual phases can be related to episodic narratives such as television programs. Many modern American television seasons tend to adopt an approach wherein each episode contains a self-contained arc, but contributes information as part of a broader arc: a model which has also inspired approaches to interactive game design [2]. Comic strips that allow users to embellish narrative arcs with additional phases, or manipulate the outcomes within embedded phases, could therefore be employed to visualize interactive narratives.

Experiments have suggested that, if they are semantically related, sequential panels that follow this structure are more easily comprehended than those that are ordered differently [8]. Irrespective of the validity of such a structure, however, questions remain regarding the impact that interaction and branching may have upon the comprehension of a visual narrative. Methodologies previously employed in the study of reading stories, traditional and interactive, could inform an approach to evaluating an interactive comic.

Methods

As Cohn [9] has described, previous experiments, the results of which support story schema, have used data from participants who were simply asked to recall stories. In an experiment comparing the recollections of adults and children, Mandler and Johnson [16] asked subjects to recall stories that were told orally, and employed procedures to ensure that stories' recollections were 'verbatim', and not simply summarizations. For the purposes of analyzing interactive stories, it may be useful to distinguish between verbatim and summarized accounts in relation to low level and high level accounts, respectively.

Since the end of the last century, readers' responses to literary texts started occupying increasingly more researchers; employing techniques ranging from questionnaires to 'think aloud' experiments, and combining quantitative and qualitative methodologies [21]. Qualitative methods such as interviews [20, 30], oral retellings [23], focus groups [24], retrospective protocols [15] and think aloud-, or protocol-, analysis [25] have also been used in the study of interactive stories. As stated previously, interactive stories seem to be most often evaluated in terms of the user experience rather than their comprehension, though it should be noted that the term 'interactive story' is a term that can be assigned to a range of media and texts. A comparison between interactive digital texts presented on CD-ROM and traditional printed texts by Pearman [23], for example, is noteworthy in that it did focus upon story comprehension of school children, and found that there were differences between the two modes of presentation. The method adopted categorized oral retellings against Morrow's 10-Point Scale of story comprehension, and found that the mean retelling scores of CD-ROM texts were significantly higher than those of traditional texts. The study found that illustrations in both formats facilitated engagement, which is worth noting in the context of evaluating visual narratives. However, the digital texts were embellished with rich multimedia content rather than branches. Therefore, whilst they did contain interactive 'hot spots' and illustrations, these texts do not compare directly with branching narratives.

Hypertext stories, on the other hand, which have previously been presented in comic form as hypercomics [3], could be regarded as the digital equivalent of choose-your-own-adventure books, and have more obvious parallels with the branching comic design employed in this paper. In their study of the re-readability of hypertext stories, Mitchell and McGee [20] employed a modified version of a Piagetan clinical interview, asking about initial reactions to the story and motivations for re-reading. The study found that users stopped wanting to explore additional branches after a period of exploration, which may have been due to the lack of an obvious purpose, or goal, of doing so.

The approach of Mitchell's and McGee's study was in keeping with similar studies of interactive stories, in that its focus was upon the experience of using the stories, rather than the possible impact that being able to choose which branches to read may have had upon their comprehension. Although the focus of our study is upon story recollections, the impact of interactions upon the users' experience(s) of stories could provide insight into the comprehension of branching comics. Mangen [17] has previously argued that the differences between texts presented on paper and screen are 'phenomenological', as there is a tangible difference between the 'visible' and the 'invisible' in the media. Books, for example, can be held and flicked through, meaning that, though the stories may not be visible on the pages until they are read, readers will have a sense of the length and body of the works through their physical presence. E-books, on the other hand, employ various techniques to simulate this indication of the invisible, such as thumbnail images of remaining or preceding pages. Comparing the comprehension of branching comics on paper and in digital form could contribute to this theory.

If the comprehension of visual narratives can be compared with the comprehension of visual data, as inferred by Segel and Heer [29], then perhaps the work of Diakopoulos et al. [10] may provide some insight into what can be expected of adding interactions to comics. Their methodology employed a system of logging each user's interactions as well as a questionnaire post-task to explore the impact of game mechanics within an interactive visualization. The study suggested that 'game-y' designs redistributed attention across the visualizations, rather than enhanced their comprehension. Though our study does not incorporate game mechanics, the results would confirm whether interactions related to branches can lead to equivalent effects.

RESEARCH QUESTIONS

Our research questions are as follows:

1) How can an interactive, branching comic, be compared with a traditional, paper-based version of the same comic?
2) Are there any differences between the readings of this comic when presented digitally or on paper, and if so, what does this mean?
3) How can we measure such differences?

Having explored a range of approaches and methodologies to studying comics, interactive stories, and visualizations, it seems that a methodology derived from these developments may be appropriate to this study. One of the useful aspects of employing branching comics as opposed to other branching media is that the layout of the comics can be easily employed to present the branches on both paper and screen. This also means that the comic can be used to visualize both the story and the data related to its readings.

COMIC DESIGN

The comic being tested had to contain sufficient branches that could be incorporated in an interactive comic, yet not so many that it could not be presented in a paper-based comic book. As part of a local project looking to explore attitudes in aviation travel, a prototype was devised based upon the concept of a father of two children travelling from the Midlands in the UK to visit his sister in Chicago in the U.S. One of the children can accompany him, and they have to decide which case to take, which airport to fly from, how to travel from the airport in Chicago, and which sights to see once they're in Chicago. The top level of abstraction (Level 0) was purely visual. Level 1 of the comic was depicted textually via captions across three panels narrating a few basic details about the trip. Relating this to Cohn's [9] structure, this would be a basic, self-contained arc, but with spaces for the arc to be embellished with additional narrative material. Level 2 of the comic was depicted via captions and dialogue bubbles, which were also prompts to the user to make decisions within the interactive comic.

Once Levels 1 and 2 were defined, it was possible to assign all of Cohn's [9] categories within the comic and distinguish between panels that were Establishers, Initials, Prolongations, Peaks and Releases (see Figure 1). Cohn defines the Establisher as being the panel which "sets up an interaction without acting upon it", which is what happens in panel 1 of our comic. In the next two panels, the tension of the broader narrative arc is initialized through the choice of which case to take on the trip and where to fly from. Cohn states that the Prolongation "marks a medial state of extension, often the trajectory of a path", which fits panels 4-7 of page 1 depicting the journey to the airport. The Peak of this comic is the arrival at Chicago, as depicted in panels 1-3 of page 2. The Release of the comic is provided in the final 2 panels, when the Father and his Sister part ways.

For such a short story, Level 3 was deemed to be the lowest level of abstraction. In the printed comic, the embedded phrases were already displayed, but in the interactive comic the user could embellish the arc with additional phases through their decisions. For example, whilst the choosing of an airport was part of the 'Initial' panel group, it would contain it's own phase of debating the airports' merits (Initial), travelling there (Prolongation) and going through security (Peak). Figure 2 shows one of the possible stories that could emerge through the combination of choices, and the impact these choices had upon the artwork and text. In the example shown, the decision to fly from Birmingham, which was more convenient but also more expensive, meant that the family could not afford to see more than two attractions whilst in Chicago. Had they flown from London, the flight would have been cheaper and they would have been able to see more attractions, but the journey over would have been longer and less pleasant. Carrying a big case meant the family could take back more souvenirs, but had more difficulty carrying it around (depending on the modes of transport chosen). In the end, regardless of the decisions made, the family always had a good time.

The story was designed to be reasonably balanced, and there were no 'ideal' scenarios envisioned during the authoring of the possible outcomes. The comic contained two pages and enough branches to accommodate sixteen possible variations. It was deemed that this would be sufficient for the presentation of the comic on paper, and suitable for a comparison between digital and traditional presentations. The paper-based version of the comic was printed on A4 paper single-sided, with each variation of the comic printed on each piece of paper and ordered randomly. The interactive comic was developed in Adobe Flash for use on a personal computer. The panels in the interactive comic were presented sequentially to the user, and flashing 'hot spots' were used to show that the user could make decisions that would impact the subsequent panels. For example, after the user selected one of the children in the first panel, the second panel's caption would display and both the big and small cases would start flashing, prompting the user to select one to continue the comic. Once the comic was finished a small reset button would display in the bottom right corner, which could be used to start from the beginning and attempt a new combination.

Figure 1: Abstraction levels 1 & 2 of the comic, and a possible application of Cohn's [9] visual structure (Est. = Establisher, Init. = Initial, Pr. = Prolongation, Pk. = Peak, Re. = Release)

Figure 2: One of the sixteen possible variations of the comic.
The numbers indicate the level of abstraction to which each textual element was assigned.

METHOD

The comic produced was not designed for adults or teenagers, but we had concerns about how the data would be obtained and analyzed if participants were too young. We decided that 11-12 year olds would be suitable for the study, which was conducted at an independent boys' school in Birmingham, UK, with 2 classes of 16 pupils consisting of this age range. Whilst narrowing the study to a specific gender and age group created an obvious limitation, we would argue that one benefit of using this approach is that it limits the number of variables to be considered in a comparative study of different media which, as we will argue, still produced noteworthy results.

Experiment Design

The experiment was done in a school computer lab during one of each class' lesson periods. Each class was divided into two groups of eight: one group to read the printed comic on paper and the other to use the interactive comic on a PC. Before beginning the experiment, the pupils were informed that what they were doing was not a test, that they were not being judged on any perceived measure of performance, and that they should stop reading or using the comics whenever they wanted. This was important due to the age of the participants, but was also deemed to be important for comparing attitudes towards the different media, and how these might impact the reading patterns.

The pupils were shown the paper copy of the comic and it was demonstrated to them that each piece of paper actually presented two pages of the comic side-by-side in order to avoid any confusion about the reading direction. It was also explained to them that the comic was actually the same story told slightly differently, and the comic was flicked through in front of everybody to illustrate this. It was deemed necessary to do this due to the time constraints of the experiment, as it may have taken the children a while to understand this of their own accord.

The desktop version of the comic also presented the two pages side by side on the computer screen, which the pupils were informed of prior to using the interactive comic. Following this introduction, the pupils were given fifteen minutes to use the computer version of the comic and read the paper version. Those using the desktop version of the comic did not have access to the paper version, and vice versa.

Due to the classroom settings in which the study was conducted, it was not possible to obtain 'talk-aloud' data or conduct individual interviews. We therefore adopted to use a simple questionnaire containing two open-ended questions, which were:

1) If you were to summarize the story to someone else, even taking into account its different versions, how might you describe it?
2) How might you describe your favorite version of this story to someone else?

These questions were deemed to be the simplest way of encouraging pupils to distinguish between what could be interpreted as 'high level' overviews of the story and 'low level' specific narratives. As this is a key aspect of our approach to authoring branching comics, we were interested in seeing whether this was reflected in the readings. It also meant that our approach was distinguished from prior methodologies where the recall of stories is encouraged to be as detailed as possible [16], as the summaries in our analysis are equally important. Prior to the experiment, we also went through these questions briefly with the classes and explained in more detail what the questions we were asking meant. Again, we felt that this was an important step to take given the age group we were working with. We also pointed out that, if the respondents did not have a 'favorite' version of the story, then they could just describe one that they remembered.

After doing the questionnaire, we invited participants to use the alternative version of the comic for the same period of time. Once this was done, we discussed the pupils reading experiences in a debriefing inspired by methods employed by Poels et al. [24]. The rationale for this was that, although user experiences were not the focus of this study, they could provide insight into observations made during the experiments or patterns identified in the readings.

Analysis

Following the experiments, we had to categorize the responses in some way to make the data meaningful. In general, the approaches outlined above that use qualitative data tend to involve coding responses against some predefined criteria, and revisiting the data to ensure that there is consistency in the categorization [15, 16, 20, 23]. As we were exploring a relatively new form of narrative visualization, we felt that an approach that incorporated the criteria we had already designed for the comic would be appropriate for this study. Visually, we assigned the responses provided in both the 'summary' and 'favorite' answers of the paper to heat maps against the layout shown in Figure 3. This layout provided a diagram representation of the comic, with separated compartments depicting where information, both visual and textual, was contained. The specific information given with the outcome of combined options was displayed as smaller containers within the diagram. For example, if the big case and London airport were chosen in panels 2 and 3, then in panel 5 of page 1 the big case (an anthropomorphic character in the comic) would point out how inconvenient it might be for the family to carry it such a long way. As this is one of four possible things that the dialogue balloon might have shown in this panel, it is displayed as a small container within the illustration of the bubble as 'Ldn/ BgC' (London / Big Case).

The diagram therefore provided a code to which responses could be assigned and visualized, and potential patterns identified. When analyzing the responses the majority of statements could be easily mapped against the diagram, as the information respondents provided was a direct reference to information contained in sections of the comic. For example, "They had to decide on a case" refers to the caption in panel 2 of page 1. More detailed statements were assigned to multiple containers in the visualization. For example, "They had to choose the closer but more expensive flight from Birmingham or the further away but cheaper flight from London" was a statement deemed have referred to containers from panels 3 and 4 of page 1 within the comic, which together contained this information.

As anticipated when asking for summaries of the story, some statements were vague and needed to be interpreted according to the visual structure of the comic. An example of this was "A family going on holiday to Chicago". This statement contains information pertaining to both the caption and the image of the family sitting down in the first panel. More ambiguous statements, however, needed to be carefully considered when aligning them to the comic diagram. One such statement was "It also tells us about the journey there and back", which was the kind of statement that occasionally came about in response to the paper comic. When coming across phrases like this, the order in which these sentences were written was considered when interpreting them. This sentence, for example, came after the description of having to choose the case and airport, but before the description of choosing sites at Chicago. It was therefore assigned to the group of panels that represented the 'Prolongation' of the journey to the airport and the panel depicting the journey from the airport.

RESULTS

Figure 4 shows the heat maps produced when the responses were assigned to the diagram. The visualization shows a clear distinction between the different representations of the story in the range of details given to summarize the paper comic in comparison with the digital version. In the readings of the digital comic, only two participants gave high level responses related to the 'Prolongation' panel group, two for the embedded journey panel within the Peak group, and five for the final 'Release' panel. The remaining responses related to descriptions around points of interaction (level 2 of the comic's design). By contrast, between two and ten high level statements related to each panel were identified in the paper-based readings, except for panels 4 and 5 of the first page where there was only one low-level mention of the distance to Birmingham airport. Other low-level responses were also given in the summaries of the paper comics, such as descriptions of places to visit in Chicago or how may souvenirs that could be taken, which contrasted readings of the digital comic.

Overall, there were fewer responses given in answer to question on low level 'favorite' accounts, which seems to be because most pupils did not repeat the process of writing out the same story again. One pupil merely wrote "The one where they get to see all 4 attractions" in response to this question, for example, in spite of the guidelines given prior to the experiment. Though the data are more limited than that of the summaries in this respect, there are some points that can be drawn from the visualization. It is apparent, for instance, that every single participant that used the interactive version of the comic stated that visiting four attractions in Chicago was their 'favorite' version of the story, whereas only six of the participants reading the paper version stated this. The visualization also shows that more participants (ten) reading the paper version of the comic stated that they preferred the case to be the correct size for the souvenirs compared with those reading the digital version (three).

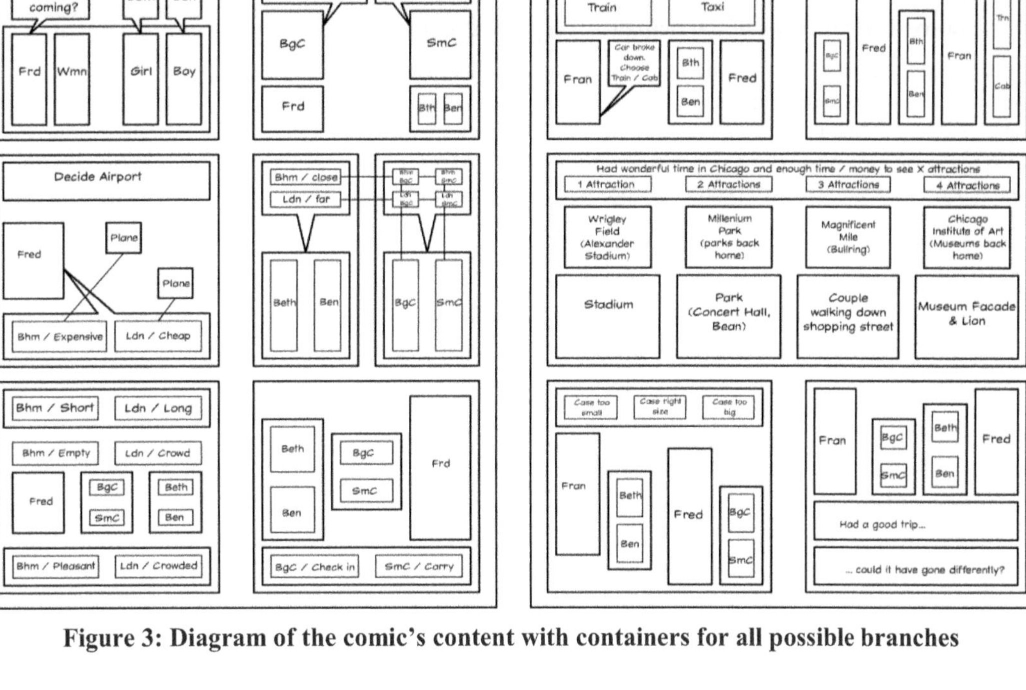

Figure 3: Diagram of the comic's content with containers for all possible branches

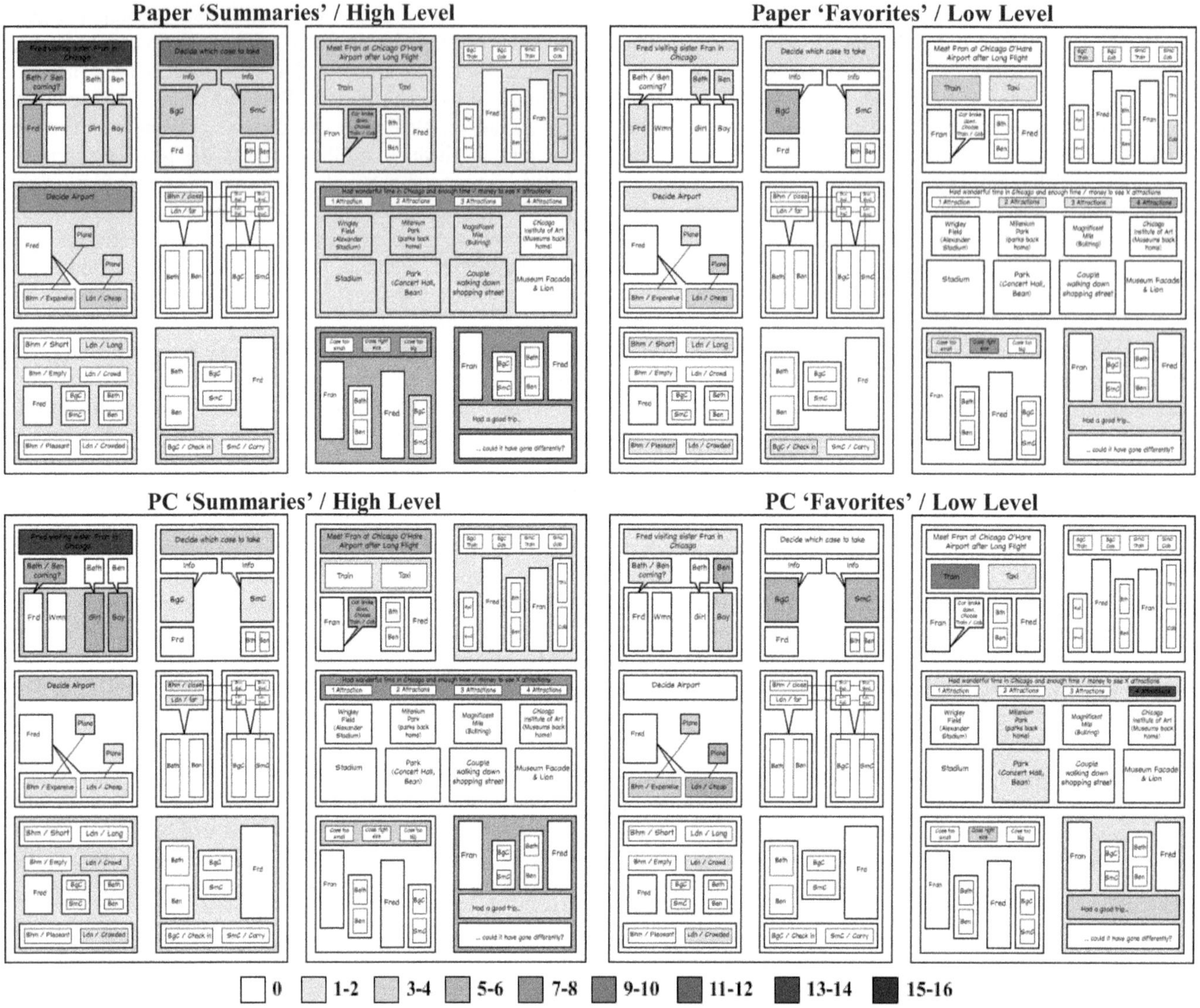

Figure 4: Heat maps of participants' responses to questions about the comics' content

Once these details are identified, the visualizations help determine other related statements. For example, the heat map of the paper version of the comic shows that the same number of participants who chose the big case (six) also wanted to see all four attractions. Although this does not necessarily mean that the same participants chose both these options, it does make sense given that this is one of the combinations that would allow the family to fit all the souvenirs in their suitcase.

A similar pattern can be seen when relating the preceding options chosen to the decision of the number of attractions to visit in readings of the digital comic. Twelve of the participants opted for the family to take the train from Chicago O'Hare airport in this version, compared to sixteen who preferred the version where all four attractions were visited. Again, given that it was necessary for the family to take the train in order that they could afford to see all the attractions (as it was cheaper than taking a taxi), it makes sense that the majority of participants would pick this.

It was noted during the experiment that more students opted to stop reading the digital comic sooner than the paper comic. In fact, several students from both classes wanted to continue reading the paper comic beyond the allotted time, but were politely asked to stop. The discussions following the experiment revealed that, in the digital comic, participants felt that it was not possible to see all the different branches, but the physical nature of the paper comic meant that the pupils knew when the end was and how to get there. Pupils therefore felt motivated to 'finish' the paper version of the comic, whereas the digital comic did not afford a finite endpoint.

DISCUSSION

The small sample size, specific age and gender group meant that the data was insufficient for statistical analysis. For an exploratory investigation, however, the qualitative data, visualizations and observations have helped identify patterns of reading. These patterns have immediate implications for related designs and warrant focused study.

In the digital version of the comic, the statements given by respondents which they deemed to be 'summaries' could be directly paired with captions that corresponded with points of interaction. The visualization shows that the summaries of paper-based comics given by pupils, on the other hand, contained a greater variance of high and low level statements. The implication here is that that, although our authored high level and low level elements in the design do not relate to readings of the paper-based comic, interaction can be employed in branching comic designs to narrow down focus in or around certain panels or groups of panels. This makes sense when referring to the work of Diakopoulos et al. [10] who found, as described earlier, that attention in interactive visualizations could be redirected with game mechanics. Although this study explored game-y designs specifically, the implication now is that even small amounts of interaction can guide responses to visual narratives.

Despite the relative lack of data in the 'favorites' heat maps, the patterns identified are still noteworthy when related to the data from the summaries. The fact that all respondents stated that they preferred the version of the comic where all of the attractions could be visited seems to suggest that the interactive comic was more goal-oriented that the paper comic. This corresponds with the work of Mitchell and McGee [20] who found that readers of hypertext were also looking for some sort of 'goal'. To a lesser extent our results indicate that some of the recollections of the paper-based comic may also have been goal-oriented, though the goal of having the correct case size was not in as many readings of the interactive comic. As the panel depicting the attractions visited is interactive in the digital comic, this indicates that interactions can direct goal-driven readings of visual narratives as well as attention more generally.

The preference for these 'goals' in both representations of the comic was inconsistent with the decisions made for the preceding options. This is quite striking in the case of the digital comic, wherein the decision of which airport to fly from had the most bearing on the number of attractions the family could visit, yet only a relatively small number of participants stated a preference here compared with the decision of transport from the airport in Chicago. This could be because of the limited responses to this question as described earlier. However, it may also relate to the notion of 'causal distance' as discussed by Urakami and Krems [32] in their analyses of hypertext documents. Causal distance refers to the amount of nodes between two events in a hypertext document which have a bearing upon one another. It is argued that the greater the causal distance between two nodes in a reading sequence the less likely it will be that readers will identify the relationship between them. The distance between the branch points in both the paper comic and the digital comic may therefore have affected whether pupils identified their correlation with one another. It is interesting to note that, whilst this was more prominent in the interactive comic, the same pattern could also be identified in the paper comic through the visualization of the data.

The observations made during the experiments have also revealed phenomena worthy of further exploration. They provided additional evidence to suggest that interacting with branching visual narratives can be related to navigating hypertext stories, as users chose not to explore all the branches in both our study and Mitchell's and McGee's [20]. When exploring the reasons behind this, the discussions after the experiment may also have provided evidence to support Mangen's [17] theory of the phenomenological differences between reading from paper and screen; as users seemed to respond to the physical affordance for the set of branches in the paper comic, which was missing from the digital version. It could be that designs that inform users of the number of branches to be explored in digital comics eliminate this difference, however. Further studies incorporating such designs could therefore be employed to explore the differences between presentations of branching comics in greater depth.

CONCLUSION

This study indicated that our comic in digital, interactive form was more goal-oriented than the paper-based version, and that the interactions embedded in the digital comic have the capability of directing these goals, as well as attention more generally. The implications for the design of visual narrative media are that interactions can be integrated at points where authors wish to direct attention, though it should be noted that this could be at the cost of attention elsewhere in the text(s). As causal distance may have been a factor in both the paper and digital comics, this should also be considered when designing such media if authors would like users to identify relationships between points in the narrative(s).

The visualizations of the data have facilitated the identification of these patterns, and it is noteworthy that our results correspond with those from other studies of related media. The possibility of there being phenomenological considerations that could affect these patterns has also emerged, which warrants further analysis. One of the recognized problems of evaluating interactive stories is that the conclusions may not to be applicable beyond the texts being analyzed [5]. Here, however, we have situated our work within other experiments in both interactive stories and narrative visualizations, and have identified comparable results.

Future studies can now be done around these specific phenomena incorporating a greater number of participants from more varied groups. Now that professional comics are being released in interactive, branching format as well as on paper [14] it would also be appropriate to study these in the context of our findings.

ACKNOWLEDGEMENTS

We would like to thank Mister Bradley Spencer and the participating pupils of King Edward's School Birmingham for their invaluable assistance.

REFERENCES

1. Abello, J., Broadwell, P., and Tangherlini, T.R. Computational Folkloristics. *Communications of the ACM 55*, 7 (2012), 60–70.
2. Adams, E. and Rollings, A. *Fundamentals of Game Design*. Pearson Prentice Hall, 2007.
3. Andrews, D., Baber, C., Efremov, S., and Komarov, M. Creating and using interactive narratives: reading and writing branching comics. *Proc. CHI 2012*, ACM Press (2012), 1703–1712.
4. Aylett, R., Louchart, S., Tychsen, A., Hitchens, M., Figueiredo, R., and Mata, C.D. Managing emergent character-based narrative. *Proc. INTETAIN 2008*, ICST (2008), 1–8.
5. Aylett, R., Louchart, S., and Weallans, A. Research in Interactive Drama Environments, Role-Play and Story-Telling. In M. Si, D. Thue, E. André, J. Lester, J. Tanenbaum and V. Zammitto, eds., *Interactive Storytelling*. Springer Berlin Heidelberg, 2011, 1–12.
6. Barthes, R. and Duisit, L. An Introduction to the Structural Analysis of Narrative. *New Literary History 6*, 2 (1975), 237–272.
7. Black, J.B. and Wilensky, R. An Evaluation of Story Grammars*. *Cognitive Science 3*, 3 (1979), 213–229.
8. Cohn, N., Paczynski, M., Jackendoff, R., Holcomb, P.J., and Kuperberg, G.R. (Pea)nuts and bolts of visual narrative: Structure and meaning in sequential image comprehension. *Cognitive Psychology 65*, 1 (2012), 1–38.
9. Cohn, N. Visual Narrative Structure. *Cognitive Science 37*, 3 (2013), 413–452.
10. Diakopoulos, N., Kivran-Swaine, F., and Naaman, M. Playable data: characterizing the design space of game-y infographics. *Proc. CHI 2011*, ACM Press (2011), 1717–1726.
11. Dundes, A. Binary Opposition in Myth: The Propp/Lévi-Strauss Debate in Retrospect. *Western Folklore 56*, 1 (1997), 39–50.
12. Finlayson, M.A. Deriving Narrative Morphologies via Analogical Story Merging. *Proc. Analogy 09*, New Bulgarian University Press (2009), 127–136.
13. Garnham, A. What's wrong with story grammars. *Cognition 15*, 1-3 (1983), 145–154.
14. Hudson, L. DC Releases a Choose Your Own Adventure-Style Digital Comic About Batman. *Wired*, (2013). http://www.wired.com/underwire/2013/12/choose-your-adventure-comic/.
15. Knickmeyer, R.L. and Mateas, M. Preliminary evaluation of the interactive drama facade. *Proc. CHI EA '05*, ACM Press (2005), 1549–1552.
16. Mandler, J.M. and Johnson, N.S. Remembrance of things parsed: Story structure and recall. *Cognitive Psychology 9*, 1 (1977), 111–151.
17. Mangen, A. Hypertext fiction reading: haptics and immersion. *Journal of Research in Reading 31*, 4 (2008), 404–419.
18. McCloud, S. *Understanding Comics: The Invisible Art*. HarperCollins, 1994.
19. Medler, B., John, M., and Lane, J. Data cracker: developing a visual game analytic tool for analyzing online gameplay. *Proc. CHI 2011*, ACM Press (2011), 2365–2374.
20. Mitchell, A. and McGee, K. Limits of rereadability in procedural interactive stories. *Proc. CHI 2011*, ACM Press (2011), 1939–1948.
21. Moissinac, L. Review of Psychonarratology: Foundations for the empirical study of literary response. *Narrative Inquiry 14*, 1 (2004), 231–234.
22. Moura, D., el-Nasr, M.S., and Shaw, C.D. Visualizing and understanding players' behavior in video games: discovering patterns and supporting aggregation and comparison. *ACM SIGGRAPH 2011 Game Papers*, ACM Press (2011), 2:1–2:6.
23. Pearman, C.J. Independent Reading of CD-ROM Storybooks: Measuring Comprehension with Oral Retellings. *The Reading Teacher 61*, 8 (2008), 594–602.
24. Poels, K., de Kort, Y., and Ijsselsteijn, W. "It is always a lot of fun!": exploring dimensions of digital game experience using focus group methodology. *Proc. Future Play 2007*, ACM Press (2007), 83–89.
25. Pope, J. Where Do We Go From Here? Readers' Responses to Interactive Fiction: Narrative Structures, Reading Pleasure and the Impact of Interface Design. *Convergence: The International Journal of Research into New Media Technologies 16*, 1 (2010), 75–94.
26. Propp, V. and Wagner, L.A. *Morphology of the Folk Tale*. University of Texas Press, 2010.
27. Rumelhart, D.E. Notes on a schema for stories. In *Representation and understanding: Studies in cognitive science*. Academic Press, New York, 1975, 211–236.
28. Sali, S. and Mateas, M. Using Information Visualization to Understand Interactive Narrative: A Case Study on Façade. In M. Si, D. Thue, E. André, J.C. Lester, J. Tanenbaum and V. Zammitto, eds., *Interactive Storytelling*. Springer Berlin Heidelberg, 2011, 284–289.
29. Segel, E. and Heer, J. Narrative Visualization: Telling Stories with Data. *IEEE Transactions on Visualization and Computer Graphics 16*, 6 (2010), 1139–1148.
30. Seif El-Nasr, M., Milam, D., and Maygoli, T. Experiencing interactive narrative: A qualitative analysis of Façade. *Entertainment Computing 4*, 1 (2013), 39–52.
31. Thorndyke, P.W. Cognitive structures in comprehension and memory of narrative discourse. *Cognitive Psychology 9*, 1 (1977), 77–110.
32. Urakami, J. and Krems, J.F. How hypertext reading sequences affect understanding of causal and temporal relations in story comprehension. *Instructional Science 40*, 2 (2012), 277–295.

FOCUS: Enhancing Children's Engagement in Reading by Using Contextual BCI Training Sessions

Jin Huang[1, 2], Chun Yu[1], Yuntao Wang[1], Yuhang Zhao[1], Siqi Liu[1], Chou Mo[1], Jie Liu[1], Lie Zhang[2], Yuanchun Shi[1, 3],

Pervasive Computing Division, Tsinghua National Laboratory for Information Science and Technology

[1]Department of Computer Science and Technology, Tsinghua University, Beijing, 100084, China

[2]Department of Information Art and Design, Tsinghua University, Beijing, 100084, China

[3]Department of Computer Technology, Qinghai University, Xining, 810016, China

{huangjin8808, yc2pcg, w.yuntaosea, zhaoyh630, lsqgonna, mochou9211, liujiejesse}@gmail.com

{zhlie, shiyc}@tsinghua.edu.cn

ABSTRACT

Reading is an important aspect of a child's development. Reading outcome is heavily dependent on the level of engagement while reading. In this paper, we present FOCUS, an EEG-augmented reading system which monitors a child's engagement level in real time, and provides contextual BCI training sessions to improve a child's reading engagement. A laboratory experiment was conducted to assess the validity of the system. Results showed that FOCUS could significantly improve engagement in terms of both EEG-based measurement and teachers' subjective measure on the reading outcome.

Author Keywords

Reading engagement; brain-computer interface (BCI); contextual reading

ACM Classification Keywords

H.5.2 [Information Interfaces and Presentation]: User Interfaces: Input devices and strategies, Evaluation/methodology, User-center design; K.3.1 [Computers and Education]: Computer Uses in Education.

INTRODUCTION

Reading is an important aspect of a child's development. Research shows reading outcome is highly dependent on the level of reading engagement [9]. On the other hand, Electroencephalography (EEG)-based Brain Computer Interface (BCI) provides a non-invasive method to measure engagement level. Recent advances in commercial EEG devices make it possible to augment the performance of daily tasks that require engagement, such as children's reading.

In this paper, we present FOCUS, an EEG-augmented reading system, which helps children to maintain engagement while reading. FOCUS inserts contextual BCI training sessions into the reading process by constantly monitoring children's engagement level. Once the engagement level is detected to be low, the system triggers a content-related BCI training session for the child to reengage. Utilizing this method, FOCUS ensures efficient reading through maintaining the high engagement level through the entire reading process.

To assess the validity of the design, we conducted a laboratory experiment with 24 primary school students. Results showed that with contextual BCI training sessions, both EEG-based measurement of reading engagement and teachers' subjective measure of the reading outcome could be improved. Our experiment provides empirical evidence that content-related contextual BCI training sessions can have a positive effect on improving the engagement level of reading for children.

RELATED WORK

Electroencephalography (EEG) is a well-studied method of non-invasive BCIs to measure the brain's electrical activity. The main EEG frequencies of humans are categorized into four wave patterns: Delta (0.5-4Hz), Theta (4-8Hz), Alpha (8-13Hz) and Beta (13-30Hz) [8]. Research has shown that these patterns are strongly correlated to human emotions and cognitive states [7, 8]. Eq. 1 [1, 6, 7] is widely used to estimate task engagement based on the amplitudes of $Alpha\ (\alpha)$, $Beta\ (\beta)$ and $Theta\ (\theta)$ waves. Note that this EEG measurement of engagement (EEG-engagement) is a ratio value without a unit.

$$EEG\ engagement = \frac{\beta}{\alpha + \theta} \qquad (1)$$

Currently, a typical EEG application is EEG biofeedback training: a treatment of ADHD (Attention Deficit Hyperactivity Disorder) children. During such treatments, children are asked to focus their attention on tasks, in the form of games, and to complete specific goals [5]. In this method, EEG biofeedback training works as a separate tool to improve children's attention ability for general tasks using an intensive and long-term training schedule.

Recent trends show that researchers have tried to use EEG-based engagement measure to augment learning activities.

CHI 2014, April 26–May 1, 2014, Toronto, ON, Canada.

PAY ATTENTION [7] designs an embodied story-telling agent, which uses a modulated spoken volume and gestures to attract users' attention when their engagement level drops. BRAVO [4] constantly analyzes users' brain activity, estimates their attention and meditation levels, and presents users with learning material that only results in high engagement. LET'S LEARN [1] is most relevant to our research. It is an EEG-augmented reading system using content-related videos grabbed from YouTube to improve users' engagement. However, this system has not been formally studied.

FOCUS

FOCUS is an EEG-augmented reading system. As shown in Figure 1, its hardware contains three main parts: a physical book, a commercial BCI device (Emotiv[1]) and a pico-projector.

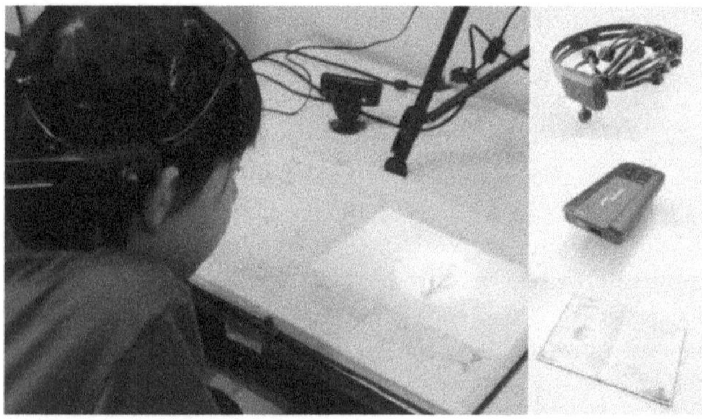

Figure 1. The FOCUS System

The book is specially designed with separate areas for lessons and BCI training sessions. With FOCUS, children wear Emotiv as they read. If the system detects low engagement levels, the system will trigger BCI training mode, and project a BCI training session onto the book.

The design of BCI training adopts the method of EEG biofeedback training [5]. The key principle is to improve children's engagement by making them focus their attention, and to imagine the state transition of an object related to the lesson. Notable here is that BCI training tasks are highly relevant to the content of the lesson. For example, in the reading section about seasonal characteristics of the spring, the BCI training task is to drive the process of an opening flower. To achieve this, children have to concentrate on imaging the "open" action, causing EEG-engagement to increase. Once the required engagement level is achieved, the goal of the task is completed. In this case, the flower opens. Children can then continue to read the succeeding section. Moreover, after each BCI training session, we provide children with virtual rewards such as a displayed image of smiling faces, hugs and praises projected onto the book.

For the purpose of our research, when estimating reading engagement with Emotiv, we only used O1 and O2 electrodes because these signals are highly relevant to visual attention [2] as well as reading engagement. To remove the noise of eye movements, eye blinks, muscle activities and line noise, we used an extended version of Independent Component Analysis (ICA) method [3]. Finally, the engagement level was obtained by averaging results from O1 and O2 based on Eq. 1.

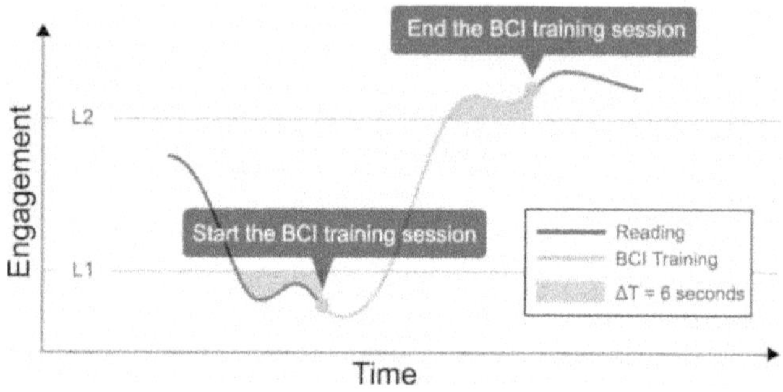

Figure 2. Engagement migration with FOCUS

We adapted different thresholds (L1 and L2) to determine low/high engagement for individual children. This is because EEG-engagement measured by Emotiv is user-dependent. To trigger a BCI training session, engagement level has to be continuously below the low engagement threshold (L1) for a particular time span (6 seconds). Similarly, the high engagement (L2) has to be maintained for 6 seconds in order to complete the goal. Figure 2 illustrates the migration of EEG-engagement for a typical BCI training session.

EXPERIMENT

The goal of this experiment is to assess the validity of the FOCUS design and to validate whether it can improve children's engagement level.

Participants

A total of 24 participants (14 girls and 10 boys) took part in this experiment. All participants were from a primary school. Their average age was 7.56 (SD=0.86) with a range from 6 to 8.5.

Design of lessons and BCI training sessions

Four lessons were designed. They were "Solar System", "Earth's Rotation", "Earth's Revolution" and "Earth's Climate". These lessons were selected from the Children's Encyclopedia, and were further adjusted with the help of a literature teacher from the same primary school to guarantee that four lessons were of the same difficulty level.

[1] Emotiv is a commercial EEG device. It exposes 14 electrode sensors with two bipolar reference electrodes spatially organized using the International 10-20 system exposed. Different from Emotiv, the medical device used in Pope's work [6] has more available electrode sensors, but these kinds of large-scale medical devices are much more expensive and complicated to use.

Correspondingly, four BCI training sessions were designed, consisting of planet zooming, rotating the Earth, making flowers bloom and making balloons rise. These training sessions can also help children to better understand the designed lessons. For instance, by zooming in on planets of the solar system, children can receive more detailed knowledge about the planets; rotating the Earth allows children to understand the process of change of the day-night cycle; blooming a flower enables children to observe one of the seasonal characteristics; and making a balloon rise helps children to understand that temperature decreases as altitude increases. Depending on individual engagement performance, it took 30-120 seconds to accomplish a BCI training task.

Task

Each participant took two lessons by following two reading modes: Contextual Reading and In-order Reading. In the Contextual Reading mode, the BCI training session was automatically triggered if the engagement level was detected to be low. If the BCI training session was not triggered (due to the participant maintaining a high level of engagement during the reading process), the lesson was removed from the analysis. In the In-order Reading mode, participants first read the lesson, and then performed the BCI training session. The purpose of designing these two reading modes was to ensure that the knowledge presented to participants was equal due to the fact that the BCI training session was content-related. We counterbalanced the order of presentation of two reading modes among participants.

Procedure

Before the experiment, we showed participants a video demonstration on how to complete a BCI task with Emotiv, and described the procedure of the experiment to them.

Before each lesson, we asked the participant a brief question related to the theme of the upcoming reading task to make sure that participants had no prior knowledge about the lesson. If they did, we replaced it with another lesson. An experimenter aided the participant in putting on Emotiv and ensured the device was connected properly. Then, a calibration process was conducted to determine thresholds of L1 and L2. For each participant, we asked him/her to perform three calibration tasks, including a 5-min resting, a 5-min reading and a 5-min BCI training session. We defined the average EEG-engagement of resting as L1, and defined L2 as the larger between the peak value of EEG-engagement of reading and the average EEG-engagement of BCI training. As expected, the average EEG-engagement of BCI training was highest ($M = 1.712$, $SD = 0.067$); the average EEG-engagement of resting was lowest ($M = 1.618$, $SD = 0.045$); the average EEG-engagement of reading was 1.674 ($SD = 0.043$).

After each lesson, participants were asked to retell the content of the lesson in detail (Recall Task) and to answer questions related to the lesson's content (Quiz Task). For each lesson, we summarized 10 key points and designed four questions with the help of the literature teacher. The experimenter counted the key points that the participants had mentioned, and rated a score from 0-5. In the quiz, participants received 1 point for each correct answer. At the end of the experiment, we had participants fill out a questionnaire to receive subjective feedback of FOCUS.

RESULTS

We utilized within-subjects one-way ANOVA to analyze the data. Results showed no statistically significant difference between the four lessons on both EEG engagement ($F(3,11696) = 1.35$, $p = 0.43$) and reading outcome (Recall: $F(3,39) = 2.14$, $p = 0.13$).

In total, 20 out of the 24 participants triggered BCI training sessions during the experiments. In average, a child experienced 1.20 ($SD = 0.83$) BCI training sessions, with 3 times at most. This result showed that children often lost reading engagement during the reading task.

EEG-Engagement of contextual reading ($M = 1.705$) was significantly higher than that of in-order reading ($M = 1.678$) ($F = 382.16$, $p < 0.001$). Figure 3 illustrates the average EEG-engagement values of two reading modes for each participant. We only compared EEG-engagement values in reading sections. Note that the only difference between In-order Reading and Contextual Reading was whether FOCUS triggered BCI training sessions when detecting the low-level engagement during the task. Therefore, the result proved that it was the contextual BCI training sessions that produced the positive effects on engagement level.

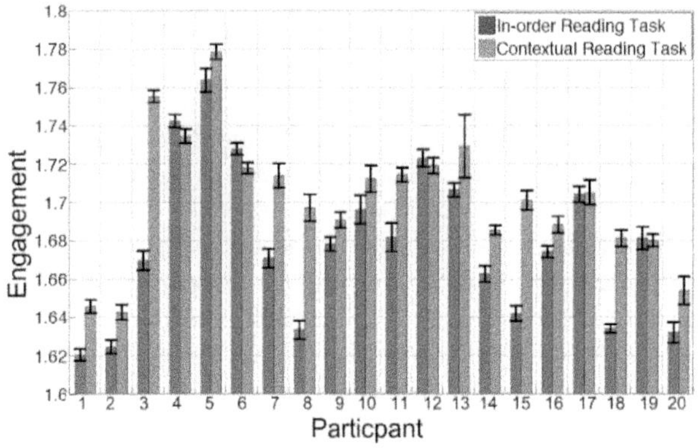

Figure 3. Comparison of EEG-engagement between In-order and Contextual Reading tasks (Error bars represent standard deviations)

Figure 4 illustrates teachers' subjective measure on children's reading outcome for Contextual Reading and In-order Reading. As expected, the scores of Contextual Reading were significantly higher than that of In-order Reading (Recall: $F(1,39) = 10.61$, $p = 0.002$, Quiz: $F(1,39) = 13.03$, $p = 0.001$). On average, recall score increases by 40.9% (0.90) and quiz score increases by 26.8% (0.725). The result shows that FOCUS could indeed improve reading outcome as a result of improving engagement.

We used five-point scale (1 = lowest, 5 = highest) in the post-experiment questionnaire, all participants showed great interest in FOCUS and preferred to read with contextual BCI training sessions (M = 4.00, SD = 0.79). They also reported no difficulty of completing BCI training sessions (M = 2.15, SD = 0.93). They even felt a sense of achievement to complete BCI training tasks with the power of their focused attention.

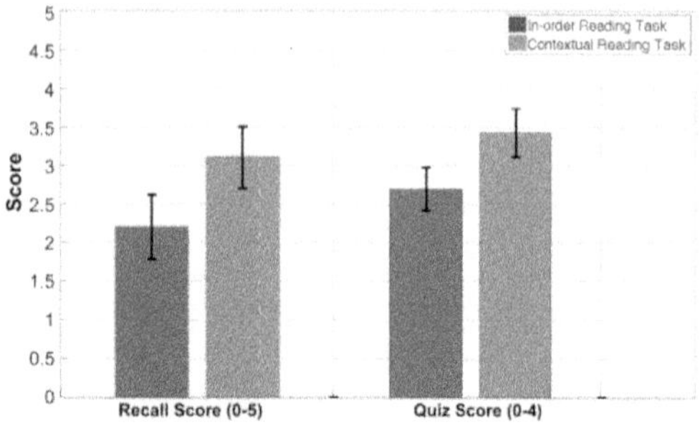

Figure 4. Comparison of reading outcome between In-order and Contextual Reading tasks (Error bars represent confidence intervals of 95%)

LIMITATION AND FUTURE WORK

The first limitation of our research is that the accuracy of EEG-based BCI devices is subject to the complex (or noisy) relationship between brain activity and EEG signals. Moreover, we used only O1 and O2 electrodes to measure engagement. These two electrodes are more reliable to pick up activity in the primary visual cortex. This means the engagement measured in this experiment is actually "visual engagement", not reading engagement, because reading engagement should be related to other cognitive activities such as thinking, remembering etc. Therefore, one assumption of our work is that visual engagement should be highly correlated with reading engagement for reading tasks.

Second, the BCI training sessions in the experiment were content-related. They actually played a partial role in instructing the knowledge (lesson content) to children. It is thus interesting to know whether a content-unrelated BCI training session would have a similar effect on improving engagement for the same reading task. If it does, it would be easier to apply our contextual BCI training method to a general reading task, because we would not have to customize BCI training session for different lessons.

In the future, we will refine and modify FOCUS for ADHD (Attention Deficit Hyperactivity Disorder) children, and further study how this contextual BCI training method can help them. Psychiatrists who specialize in ADHD treatment have suggested that we first study on children without ADHD. Our study has provided a first-hand understanding of children's reading performance, and it will serve as a basis for future studies and comparisons on ADHD children.

CONCLUSION

In this paper, we present FOCUS, an EEG-augmented reading system for improving reading engagement for children. Our experiment showed contextual BCI training sessions that were related to the lesson content could indeed help maintain reading engagement for children. Children's reading outcome could also be significantly improved by using FOCUS. In addition, children preferred the reading experience provided by FOCUS to an experience without the system.

ACKNOWLEDGMENTS

We thank all children from Tsinghua Primary School for taking part in the experiment and Minxing Xie from Tsinghua High School for taking care of them. This work is supported by National High-Tech Research and Development Plan of China under Grant No. 20131860089 and Natural Science Foundation of China No. 61272230.

REFERENCES

1. Andujar, M., and Gilbert, J. E. Let's learn! Enhancing User's Engagement Levels Through Passive Brain-Computer Interfaces. *Ext. Abstracts CHI 2013*, ACM Press (2013), 703-708.
2. Brefczynski, J. A., and DeYoe, E. A. A physiological correlate of the 'spotlight' of visual attention. *Nature Neuroscience*, Volume 2, 1999, 370-374.
3. Jung, T. P., Humphries, C., Lee, T.W., Makeig, S., McKeown, M.J., Iragui, V., and Sejnowski, T. J. Extended ICA Removes Artifacts from Electroencephalographic Recordings. *Advances in Neural Information Processing Systems*, 10:894-900, 1998.
4. Marchesi, M., and Ricco, B. BRAVO: A BRAin Virtual Operator For Education Exploiting Brain-Computer Interfaces. *Ext. Abstracts CHI 2013*, ACM Press (2013), 3091-3094.
5. Monastra, V. J., Lynn, S., Linden, M., Lubar, J.F., Gruzelier, J., and LaVaque, T. J. Electroencephalographic Biofeedback in the Treatment of Attention-Deficit/Hyperactivity Disorder. *Applied Psychophysiology and Biofeedback*, Vol. 30, No. 2, June 2005, 95-114.
6. Pope, A.T., Bogart, E. H., and Bartolome, D.S. Biocybernetic system evaluates indices of operator engagement in automated task. *Biological Psychology 40*, 1-2 (1995), 187-195.
7. Szafir, D., and Mutlu, B., Pay attention! Designing Adaptive Agents that Monitor and Improve User Engagement. In *Proc. CHI 2012*, ACM Press (2012), 11-20.
8. Teplan, M. Fundamentals of EEG Measurement. *Measurement Science Review*, Volume 2, Section 2, 2002, 1-11.
9. Wigfiel, A., Guthrie, J. T., Perencevich, K. C., Taboada, A., Klauda, S. L., Mcrae, A. and Barbosa, P. Role of Reading Engagement in Mediating Effects of Reading Comprehension Instruction on Reading Outcomes. *Psychology in the Schools*, Vol. 45(5), 2008, 432-445.

Sensing a Live Audience

Chen Wang[1], Erik Geelhoed[2], Phil Stenton[2], and Pablo Cesar[1]

[1]CWI: Centrum Wiskunde & Informatica
Science Park 123, 1098 XG Amsterdam
Netherlands

[2] Falmouth University
25 Woodlane, Falmouth, Cornwall TR11 4RH
United Kingdom

cw@cwi.nl, erik.geelhoed@falmouth.ac.uk, phil.stenton@falmouth.ac.uk, p.s.cesar@cwi.nl

ABSTRACT

Psychophysiological measurement has the potential to play an important role in audience research. Currently, such research is still in its infancy and it usually involves collecting data in the *laboratory*, where during each experimental session *one* individual watches a video *recording* of a performance. We extend the experimental paradigm by *simultaneously* measuring Galvanic Skin Response (GSR) of a *group* of participants during a *live* performance. GSR data were synchronized with video footage of performers and audience. In conjunction with questionnaire data, this enabled us to identify a strongly correlated main group of participants, describe the nature of their theatre experience and map out a minute-by-minute unfolding of the performance in terms of psycho-physiological engagement. The benefits of our approach are twofold. It provides a robust and accurate mechanism for assessing a performance. Moreover, our infrastructure can enable, in the future, real-time feedback from remote audiences for online performances.

Author Keywords

Audience engagement; Galvanic Skin Response.

ACM Classification Keywords

H.1; J.4 ; J.5;

INTRODUCTION

The primary motivation for the current study, and our research question, is to explore the viability of using Galvanic Skin Response (GSR) to monitor audience feedback during a live performance. We took GSR measurements of 15 people watching a live theatre performance simultaneously. The readings were synchronized with video recordings of the performance and the audience. The audience filled out questionnaires aimed to evaluate the emotions that the performance evoked. This resulted in a high volume of useful data of around 1680 data points for each participant.

CHI 2014, April 26 - May 01 2014, Toronto, ON, Canada

http://dx.doi.org/10.1145/2556288.2557154

Results indicate that our approach – gathering GSR data during the play - is valid, as such data accurately reflects the engagement of the audience members. Moreover, it proves to be a useful tool for temporally unfolding the experience of the public, as the reactions of the public can be mapped to specific events during the play. In principle, we can conclude that our solution of using GSR data for monitoring audience feedback is novel and very valuable.

The paper is structured as follows. First, we highlight the novelty of our approach, when compared to prior works. Then, we describe the methodology we use in the study, followed by the results that support our hypothesis. Finally, the results are analyzed and discussed, focusing on the most important implications for next-generation video-mediated performances.

RELATED WORK

Jennifer Radbourne details the importance of audience feedback through an extensive literature review and in-depth interviews [8]. The study justifies our hypothesis, as it shows that audiences are not primarily passive and that gauging the audience experience might provide an important measure of quality in the performing arts.

GSR measures excitation of the sympathetic nervous system and combined with other types of physiological and neurological, as well as self-report measures, have been applied in many areas of research, e.g. psychology, medical, gaming and education. Pejman et al. have explored how GSR data can be used for improving game design [6]; GSR sensors were also extensively used in research with hyperkinetic children [3]. For the purpose of this paper, we narrow the scope to audience feedback and how such measures open up new possibilities for interaction.

There are few studies using physiological measurements for learning about audience engagement per se (e.g. [1]). There seems to be more interest in *applying* sensor feedback *creatively*, e.g. to influence the outcome of a movie [2]. The most related work is the one from Celine Latulipe [5] who provides an extensive overview of research in this area. Her work draws on the empirical and theoretical work of Peter Lang [4], who describes a two dimensional space of different emotional states where one dimension runs from low to high (GSR) arousal and the other from low to high pleasure. Latulipe and colleagues explore how bio-feedback (in particular GSR) can be used to provide real-time visual feedback to performers. In interviews with dance and theatre experts the notion of "valence" is introduced, i.e. how GSR arousal validates audience response.

Nevertheless, all these studies involve experimental sessions in which a single person watches a video recording of a performance. We instead took GSR measurement into the "field", the natural habitat, and took collect the data of the audience simultaneously during the play. As such, we believe that our system supports ecological validity much better than the previous laboratory experiments.

METHOD

Seven females (mean age 28.29) and eight males (mean age 23.13) formed the audience for a 28 minute theatre performance. Their GSR was measured every second throughout, resulting in 1680 data points for each participant. Actors devised and performed a comedy that was aimed at audience participation and produced occasional "shocks" (e.g. a popping balloon) to elicit the occurrence of GSR spikes during the performance (fig. 1).

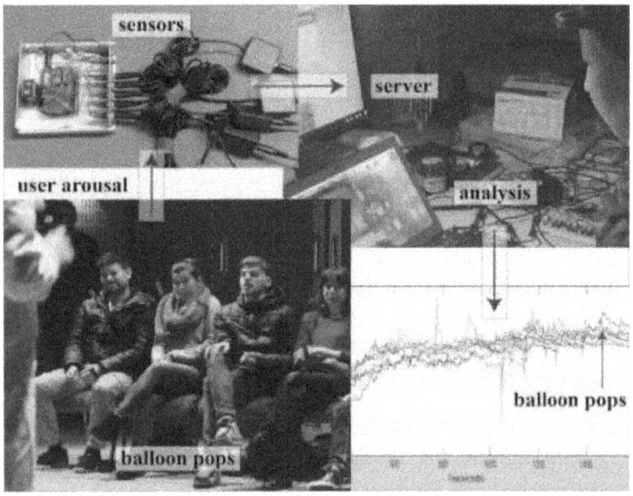

Figure 1: GSR system

For the results reported in this paper we used our own built sensors consisting of 1 Arduino UNO board and 1 Xbee wireless module (per five users), 1 47uF capacitor, 1 2Mohm resistor, and some aluminum foil. Two electrodes were placed in the users' palm: in the case of the Arduino, one was connected to the 5V and the other to one of the analogues. There is a parallel circuit built with the resistor and the capacitor between the analogue and the GND. Arduino analogue readings range from 0 to 1023: when the two electrodes are open, the readings should be always 0; when the two electrodes are closed without the users connected, the readings should be always 1023. This mechanism allowed us to test the noise level (no noise after several hours of checking).

In addition to the noise proof testing, another validation method we used was to observe the distribution of the readings from the sensors. The sensor data distributions saw typical linear patterns. Moreover, we applied the Filtering and Smoothing Matlab function in order to avoid the impact of hand movements during the experiment.

Groups of five sensors were each connected to one of three Arduino UNO boards (sample rate 1Hz). Xbee RF modules were used to create a wireless network such that the GSR data were sent directly to a laptop. This ensured the synchronization of all GSR readings. Cameras recorded the audience and the performance. Video streams were synchronized (post production) with GSR data.

Before the performance, participants filled out a short questionnaire asking about the type and intensity of the emotions they had experienced during the day. Afterwards participants filled out a similar questionnaire asking about emotions experienced during the play. The questionnaires were in the form of graphic rating scale [10]. and measured 100mm. Participants were asked to make a mark between two extremes, i.e. between "not at all" and "very much".

Participants were seated in one row with three sections of five seats each, arranged in a semi-circle around the stage. GSR modules were attached to the palm of the left hand. Before the performance started, participants took part in a meditation exercise to establish a baseline GSR level.

Questionnaires were analyzed using Analysis of Variance (ANOVA) and correlations. The synchronized GSR and video streams enabled us to relate events during the performance to corresponding GSR readings. GSR readings were analyzed using the Multidimensional Scaling (MDS) method [7]. Correlations and ANOVA had some limitations to do a complete interpretation of the readings. They are fairly suitable if the audience is being treated as a whole, but they cannot properly explain relationships – similarity and dissimilarity - between objects in a multi-dimensional space. In our case, we were interested in understanding the relationships between 15 objects (each audience member) GSR responses'. We calculated the dissimilarities between the objects using Pearson Correlation Coefficients, and two-dimensional scaling was chosen for scaling. After 30 iterations, the final configuration graphs were achieved and Kruskal's stress reported in the results.

RESULTS

Audience clustering

A MDS solution (fig. 2), based on correlations of GSR readings between audience members, shows how ten participants correlated closely (on average $r = .86$), showing an initial rise in GSR followed by a flattening towards the end of the performance (inset in fig. 2). In this plot the Kruskal's stress value is 0.06 (less than 0.15), indicating that the configuration of the 15 participants' GSR readings can be considered as reliable. Questionnaire results and brief interviews after the performance indicated that this group had been deeply engaged in the performance, reporting high levels of enjoyment.

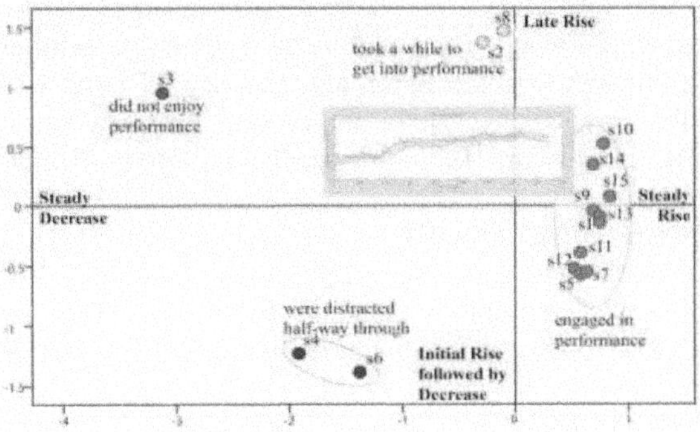

Figure 2: MDS Audience clustering based on GSR data

Five participants displayed different patterns. Two showed an initial rise in GSR followed by a decrease, i.e. after an initial engagement with the performance their attention waned; for one this was related to receiving sad news during the day. Two showed an initial lack of rise in GSR followed by an increase; they reported to be confused initially by the purpose of the play and as such it took them a while to get into the performance. One participant displayed a consistent drop in GSR and reported not liking the performance. These characteristics enabled us to label the extremes of the X and Y-axes.

Unfolding of the performance

For each minute, the GSR readings were averaged for each participant. Here MDS (Kruskal's stress: 0.05) yielded an almost chronological minute by minute unfolding of the play (anti-clockwise in fig. 3) up to minute 19. Using the video footage we were able to identify the clusters based on the content of the performance. Thus, initially the GSR readings are low (minute 1) followed by a steady rise (minute 2 – 19) after which the intensity of the GSR flattens (minute 20 – 28). The first part of the performance (minute 2 – 16, in red in fig. 3) built up to an active and physical participation during which the participants were asked to raise either their left or their right leg in response to (silly) questions by the actors. In minute 17 – 19 (in green) the results of a competition were revealed, where the relatively higher GSR readings might indicate anticipation. After that the audience was not required to interact as actively as they listened to a trumpet player (dark blue) and watched a juggling act (yellow). The Y-axis reflected levels of GSR intensity and the X-axis ran between low and high audience participation. Spikes were identified that corresponded to the intended "shocks", e.g. balloon popping, the sudden sound of a (badly played) trumpet.

The minute average GSR readings during this comic play correlated positively with participants being (very) cheerful (on average r = .62) and correlated negatively with participants being sad (on average r = -.60) at different stages of the performance, in particular from minute 16 onwards the average GSR readings showed strong correlations with audience's "cheerful" ratings.

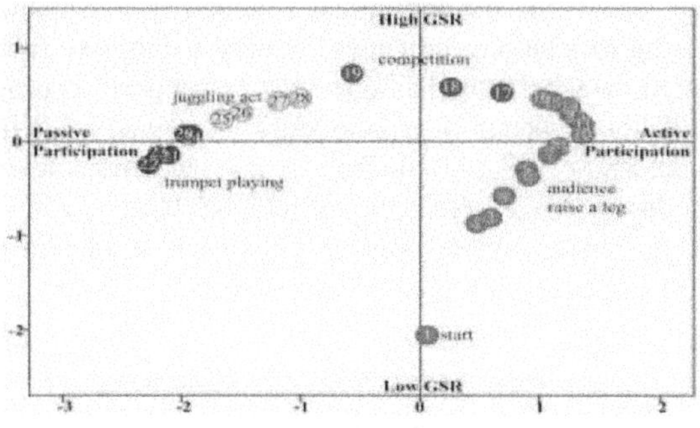

Figure 3: MDS minute by minute unfolding of the performance

Table 1 summarizes the significant differences between pre- (asking about their experiences during the day) and post-performance questionnaires. The ratings were given on a scale between "not at all" (= 0) and "very much" (=100). Thus participants rated that during the day, on occasion, they had a laugh with a mean intensity of 45 (Mean pre in Table 1) and they reported that the intensity of laughter generated by the performance was rated on average as 68.5 (Mean post), resulting in a significant difference, $F_{(1,14)} = 14.68$, $p = .002$. Similarly, for cheerfulness, the difference between pre-and post- ratings was significant, $F_{(1,14)} = 7.12$, $p = .018$. On average, participants had a reasonably cheerful day (Mean = 55) but these ratings increased to on average 74.5 after the performance. Lastly, although participants did not have a particularly sad day (with the exception of one participant) yielding a mean of 35, this was significantly reduced to a mean of 11.4 after the performance $F_{(1,14)} = 5.82$, $p = .03$. There were also significant effects for gender and whether a participant knew another participant sitting in their row or not. However, due to the low numbers in each "cell", we refrain from reporting these in this short paper.

Pre- and Post- Performance Questionnaires

Item	p	Mean pre	Mean post
Laugh	.002	45	68.5
Cheerful	.018	55	74.5
Sad	.03	35	11.4

Table 1: Significant differences between pre-and post-questionnaires

DISCUSSION

This paper describes an audience experience during a live theatre performance using a system to measure GSR of 15 people simultaneously. Psychophysiological measurement in audience research is usually carried out in a laboratory, where during an experimental session one individual watches a recording of a performance. There are advantages to such studies as a range of sensors can be used concurrently. However, being part of an audience is a group experience and it might not be straightforward to extrapolate from an individual's experience watching a recording to a larger audience watching a live performance. As such, we believe that our system supports ecological validity much better than laboratory experiments. It is not just an innovative contribution to audience research methods that makes this study of interest. We found that for most participants there was an unexpected and unusually high level of physiological closeness (GSR), which has not been reported before.

Analyzing the GSR data in conjunction with synchronized video recordings provided additional insights, e.g. we were able to link spikes in GSR to shock-effects during the performance. This validates the robustness and accuracy of our measurements. However, more interesting are the general (smoothed) shapes of audience engagement. We found that GSR readings of most of the audience followed a curve where in the initials stages readings were low and as the play progressed this increased steadily, reflecting an increase in engagement with the play across time. Returning to the notion of valence [5], low GSR does not necessarily imply a negative audience judgment, for peaks to happen troughs are essential, but it is informative to evaluate the overall shape of the response, as exemplified by the steady decrease in GSR of one participant who was not engaged by the play. In addition we could place the performance in a two dimensional space, not unlike Lang's [4] where one dimensions runs from low to high arousal and the other from low to high audience participation. Embedding the audience experience in how their day had been also showed how a performance can lift an audience out of the ordinary. Cheerfulness and enjoyment were the main (more) emotional components linked to the GSR data.

CONCLUSION AND FUTURE WORK

We are currently in the process of scaling up the system, taking advantage of small form-factor developments in wireless technology and GSR measurement. Heart rate and blood pressure might make useful additions.

There are some near future applications of a relatively low-cost system such as the one described here. In a "next-bench" type of fashion it can be used for further audience research. It makes it feasible for theatre companies to receive detailed (and time-stamped) early feedback during try-outs, to evaluate what works well and what does not or rather identify where audience engagement wanes.

In our work we are exploring how current video-mediated technologies can be used, and extended, for supporting novel interactive performances. In particular, our final goal is to provide the infrastructural components and support, so performing artists can reach a wider remote audience with their productions, but still maintaining the close relationship between the actor and the audience. Live performances of big productions are already streamed to cinemas and to homes. However, these present limited opportunities for audience interaction. Wearable physiological sensors have the potential to open a whole array of creative solutions to suite this aim, e.g. the aggregate response of those who are deeply engaged in a performance can be used to provide visual, auditory or even haptic feedback [9] to performers.

ACKNOWLEDGEMENTS

This work was supported in part by funding from the European Community's Seventh Framework Programme (FP7/2007-2013), grant agreement no. ICT-2011-287760.

REFERENCES

[1] S. Bardzell, J. Bardzell, and T. Pace. 2009. Understanding affective interaction: Emotion, engagement, and internet videos *IEEE Conference on Affective Computing and Intelligent Interaction*, 1-8.

[2] C. Grant. 2013. Many Worlds: The movie that watches its audience. *BBC News* http://www.bbc.co.uk/news/technology-21429437

[3] J.E. Hastings, R.A. Barkley. 1978. A Review of Psychophysiological Research with Hyperkinetic Children. *Journal of Abnormal Child Psychology*, 6(4): 413-447.

[4] P. Lang. 1995. The emotion probe: Studies of motivation and attention. *American Psychologist.* 50(5): 372–385.

[5] C. Latulipe, E.A. Carroll, and D. Lottridge. 2011. Love, hate, arousal and engagement: exploring audience responses to performing arts. *Proceedings of CHI*, pp. 1845-1854.

[6] P. Mirza-Babaei, L. E. Nacke, J. Gregory, N. Collins, and G. Fitzpatrick. 2013. How does it play better? exploring user testing and biometric storyboards in games user research. *Proceedings of CHI*, 1499-1508.

[7] G.P. Quinn, M.J. Keough. 2002. *Experimental Design and Data Analysis for Biologists*.

[8] J. Radbourne, K. Johanson, H. Glow, and T. White. 2009. Audience experience: measuring the quality in the performing arts. *International Journal of Arts Management*, 11(3): 16-29.

[9] S. Stenslie. 2013. Towards Telehaptic Performativity. *Remote Encounters: Connecting bodies, collapsing spaces and temporal ubiquity in networked performance.*

[10] H. Stone, J. Sidel, S. Oliver, A. Woolsey, and R. C. Singleton. 1974. Sensory Evaluation by Quantitative Descriptive Analysis. *Food Technology*, 28. 24-34.

Interface Design for Older Adults with Varying Cultural Attitudes toward Uncertainty

Shathel Haddad*
Department of Computer Science
shathel.haddad@gmail.com

Joanna McGrenere*
Department of Computer Science
*University of British Columbia, Canada
joanna@cs.ubc.ca

Claudia Jacova*
Department of Medicine
cjacova@pacificu.edu

ABSTRACT
This work reports on the design and evaluation of culturally appropriate technology for older adults. Our design context was Cognitive Testing on a Computer (C-TOC): a self-administered computerized test under development, intended to screen older adults for cognitive impairments. Using theory triangulation of cultural attitudes toward uncertainty, we designed two interfaces (one minimal and one rich) for one C-TOC subtest and hypothesized they would be culturally appropriate for older adult Caucasians and East Asians respectively. We ran an experiment with 36 participants to investigate cultural differences in performance, preference and anxiety. We found that Caucasians preferred the interface with minimal elements (i.e. those essential for the primary task) or had no preference. By contrast, East Asians preferred the rich interface augmented with security and learning support and felt less anxious with it than the minimal.

Author Keywords
Cultural design; uncertainty avoidance; experiment; computerized cognitive assessment; older adults

ACM Classification Keywords
H.5.2 [Information interfaces and presentation]: User Interfaces - Evaluation/methodology.

INTRODUCTION
Despite the multitude of software technologies that span the globe, interface design has largely remained framed in a western-centric perspective. Linguistic translation is not enough to provide cross-cultural flavor; it offers only a superficial solution where western culture remains deeply engrained in the design of international technology [18]. To truly design cross-cultural interfaces, we need to look beyond translation and restructure design to manufacture holistic, culturally appropriate user experiences. Cross-cultural usability, or "culturability" as suggested by Barber and Badre [1], rejects the dominant one-size-fits-all approach of international technology design in favor of one that promotes culturally adapted interfaces. Culturability delivers a culturally customized user experience to international consumers, and should hence be incorporated in the design vision of technology spanning multicultural user populations.

CHI 2014, April 26 - May 01 2014, Toronto, ON, Canada

ACM 978-1-4503-2473-1/14/04...$15.00.
http://dx.doi.org/10.1145/2556288.2557124

Investigating culturally informed design is an important step for developing Cognitive Testing on a Computer (C-TOC) – a computerized self-administered screening test for cognitive impairments intended for older individuals (55+) [2]. It is being designed initially for a clinic setting, with the goal of it eventually being taken at home. Canada is very multi-cultural; hence C-TOC's design must accommodate users' different cultural needs. Moreover, cultural differences should not create serious variations in user experience or skew test results. C-TOC can become an essential tool for all older adults as it will triage at-risk individuals to professionals quickly, and eliminate wait time for a comprehensive cognitive consultation in a clinic, which in Canada currently ranges from 6 to 24 months.

We are interested in the interplay between culture and older users' attitude to the uncertain interaction context of C-TOC. Cognitive testing intrinsically causes uncertainty as it raises health concerns in test-takers and possibly cultural stigma about cognitive competence and aging. Furthermore, the demands of self-administration or doubts about computer proficiency may contribute additional uncertainty, especially if cognitive impairment is already present. C-TOC users might feel uncertain as well about the protection of their data online. While our intention is not to tease apart the various contributors of uncertainty in the context of C-TOC, we feel it would induce anxiety. Experiencing some anxiety is expected in the context of cognitive testing, but excessive levels can reduce the size of working memory and distract from the primary task [9]. This could degrade performance and increase the likelihood of false positives. We speculate that cultural differences in attitudes toward uncertainty might produce varying user needs for anxiety appeasement and security reassurance for C-TOC users.

The contributions of this research include the design of two interfaces for one C-TOC subtest (the Symbol-Digit Matching test – Fig. 1), by using variation in information richness to accommodate two varying cultural attitudes toward uncertainty. In addition, we contribute an evaluation of our designs with older Western Caucasian and East Asian users where we observe cross-cultural usability differences. Finally, we provide guidelines for cross-cultural design for older adults in interaction contexts characterized by uncertainty.

RELATED WORK

We begin by describing prior research in cross-cultural differences in psychology and HCI. Next we cover three models related to cultural attitudes toward uncertainty: Hofstede's uncertainty avoidance, the theory of uncertainty orientation, and the theory of behavioral inhibition. Through triangulation of these theories, we hypothesized cultural profiles for Eastern and Western C-TOC users. We used Hofstede's uncertainty avoidance to guide cross-cultural design of two interfaces for a C-TOC subtest.

Prior to starting our discussion of culture, it is important to clarify that any cultural observations we present do not intend to generalize to all in the observed cultures, or pigeonhole people in rigid cultural categories. Instead, they should be viewed as observed cultural tendencies, similar to how gender differences in behavior also describe general tendencies, without implying that all women or all men behave the same way.

East is Not West: From Psychology to HCI

Research has found cultural differences in a myriad of social and cognitive phenomena [12]. The field of cultural psychology claims that the connection between mind and culture is bidirectional and intertwined, since cultures arise from the participation of minds in them and the mind develops from participating in a cultural context [12]. Cultures differ from one another in belief systems, social structure, heritage, and other measures that are tangible to culture observers. Cultural differences even persist at the level of basic cognitive and psychological processes. For example, Japanese have been found to perceive contextual information more readily than Americans [15]. Japanese have also been found to focus more on background items and reason holistically compared to Americans who focus on foreground items and reason analytically [19]. Other inter-cultural differences have been found in perception, low-level processing, reasoning, self-concept, concept of others and emotional responses [12]. Such strong evidence of the effect of culture on psychology implies a similar effect on human computer interaction, as some HCI literature had also found. For instance, Frandsen-Thorlacius et al. (2009) found that Danish and Chinese users differ in their perceptions of usability [11]. Similarly, Clemmensen et al. (2009) found that Easterners and Westerners differ in usability evaluations using the think-aloud method [6].

Most other HCI literature in cultural differences however is limited to detecting cultural differences or identifying cultural dimensions related to user experience, rather than designing culturally adapted interfaces and evaluating them. For example, one study investigated different cultural attitudes to electronic products and identified 10 cultural dimensions relevant to user experience [16]. Another surveyed cross-cultural differences in four countries regarding loyalty, trust, and satisfaction with existing local and foreign websites [8]. Yet another study evaluated attitudes toward mobile data services in three countries and found that users in a shared cultural context tend to like/dislike the same features [5]. Similar work has been done on preferences for mobile phone design where cultural differences were also identified [14, 27].

Little work exists that extends such surveys to provide heuristics for cross-cultural interface design. In one study, Aaron Marcus surveyed global websites and provided a set of heuristics for altering design components in response to cultural preference [17]. For instance, regarding the mental model of user interfaces, Marcus suggests that individualistic societies (e.g., Canada) prefer task-oriented models that highlight personal achievement, while collective societies (e.g., China) prefer role-oriented models that highlight connectedness and harmony. In a follow-up survey of 57 UI design experts from 21 countries, Marcus concluded that five cultural dimensions are most relevant to cross-cultural design: *Context, technological development, time perception, authority conception,* and *uncertainty avoidance* [17]. We focus on uncertainty avoidance in our work due to the relevance of uncertainty in the context C-TOC usability. While Marcus provided some guidelines for culturability beyond surveying, he did not discuss how it affects user preference or performance, nor did he evaluate cross-cultural designs.

Reinecke and Bernstein (2011) carried out an evaluation of cross-cultural design [22]. They designed Mocca, a task management application, and evaluated two interfaces for it: a fixed culturally neutral interface and an adapted one based on a cultural screening questionnaire. The neutral interface was created using the guidelines of American design since American designers and companies provide a large portion of websites and software solutions globally. The culturally adapted interface was generated by creating a cultural user profile, and then using it to modify the neutral interface. To create the cultural user profile, the system calculated weighted user scores of the Hofstede cultural dimensions based on the countries a user had lived in and the duration of residence in each. Next, and using design heuristics similar to Marcus' [17], the system modified the neutral interface to align with the cultural user profile. The findings showed that users preferred the culturally adaptive interface to the neutral one and performed better on it. Their results point to the importance of culturability when designing interfaces for multicultural user populations, as it does have an impact on user experience.

Hofstede's Uncertainty Avoidance

Uncertainty avoidance is one of the dimensions of the Hofstede cultural model [13]. This dimension describes society's attitude to uncertainty and tolerance of ambiguity. This is one of several cultural dimensions in the Hofstede model, the others being *Power Distance, Individualism versus Collectivism, Masculinity versus Femininity, Long-Term Orientation* and *Indulgence versus Restraint*. These dimensions were identified from a survey of cultural influences on workplace values that was run between 1967 and 1972. During that time, Hofstede worked at IBM and collected data from about 116,000 IBM employees from 40 countries in one of the most comprehensive cultural studies.

Hofstede found a cultural contrast in uncertainty avoidance between the East and West. Countries like the USA and Canada were found to be relatively less uncertainty avoidant, and more tolerant of new untraditional contexts. By contrast, countries like Japan and Korea were found to be more uncertainty avoidant, as they maintain more rigid behavioral codes and feel less comfortable with novelty.

The Theory of Uncertainty Orientation

The theory of uncertainty orientation by Shuper et al. asserts that people differ in how they feel in uncertain circumstances and how they resolve uncertainty [23]. It is similar to Hofstede's uncertainty avoidance. The theory stipulates that individuals fall on a spectrum between being *certainty-oriented* and *uncertainty-oriented*. Certainty-oriented individuals tend to react more apprehensively in uncertainty and seem to depend on others to resolve it. Uncertainty-oriented individuals, by contrast, feel fairly comfortable and oriented when confronted with uncertainty and tend to seek out information independently to resolve it.

There is evidence of an East-West cultural dichotomy in uncertainty orientation. Shuper et al. found that Canadians are significantly more uncertainty-oriented than Japanese [23]. Western cultures tend to be uncertainty-oriented since they are more individualistic, and tend to promote independence in resolving uncertainty. In contrast, Eastern cultures tend to be certainty-oriented because they are more collective in nature, promoting interdependence to deal with uncertain circumstances. These findings resonate with Hofstede's findings about the East-West contrast in uncertainty avoidance, as Japanese are significantly more uncertainty avoidant than Canadians.

The Theory of Behavioral Inhibition and Activation

The theory of behavioral inhibition and activation, by Carver and White, postulates that there are two separate neurological systems that regulate behavior [3]. The first system, the *Behavioral Inhibition System* (BIS), promotes inhibitive behavior to steer away from undesired situations. The BIS is triggered by cues of punishment, non-reward or novelty. It regulates experiences of anxiety, fear or frustration as a result of such cues. Individuals who possess a heightened BIS are more prone to anxiety and more inclined to be conservative in unfamiliar contexts. The second system, the *Behavioral Activation System* (BAS), motivates the individual toward coveted goals. The BAS is triggered by signals of reward and non-punishment, and generates positive feelings of hope and happiness. Those with a heightened BAS are consequently more willing to engage in unfamiliar or ambiguous contexts.

Once again, research in cultural psychology found evidence of a contrast between the East and West in behavioral inhibition. Tanaka and Yamauchi found that collectivism is associated with high behavioral inhibition [25]. This implies that collective cultures (e.g., China) tend to have more activated BIS, and are more vulnerable to anxiety in novel or uncertain situations. In comparison, individualistic cultures (e.g., Canada) possess less active BIS, and tend to feel less aversion and anxiety in uncertain situations.

DESIGN FOR ATTITUDE TOWARD UNCERTAINTY

Given the importance of culturability for the design of C-TOC, we ventured into the design of two cultural interfaces for one of its subtests (Fig. 1). We wanted one design to cater to the cultural needs of East Asian users (from Japan, China, and Korea), and the second to address those of Western Caucasian users of European descent. We chose these two cultural groups because they have been investigated extensively in cultural psychology literature, and because they constitute the largest two cultural groups in the major Canadian city where the study was carried out.

First, we created cultural user profiles for East Asians and Western Caucasians through triangulation of the three cultural theories above. We hypothesized that individualistic Western Caucasian users would generally be less uncertainty avoidant according to Hofstede's model, uncertainty oriented, and less behaviorally inhibited. By contrast, collective East Asian users would be more uncertainty avoidant, certainty oriented, and more behaviorally inhibited.

Second, we employed Hofstede's uncertainty avoidance to guide our design of the two cultural interfaces. Previous survey work in uncertainty showed that users who are less tolerant of it prefer efficient layouts of large amounts of information on the screen, clear labeling and secondary information about content [5] whereas those more tolerant of uncertainty prefer less information. Marcus had similarly found that web design in high uncertainty avoidance cultures is characterized by redundant cues to reduce ambiguity, and help systems that reduce user error [17]. In addition, Hofstede found a strong correlation between uncertainty avoidance and anxiety where high uncertainty avoidant cultures tend to be more susceptible to stress [13]. This shows that user preference for different levels of information richness might be due to culture, and has been linked to uncertainty avoidance. Similarly, one survey found Cypriots (high uncertainty avoidance) to be more nervous about e-commerce, and more demanding of security reassurance than Britons (low uncertainty avoidance) [10]. As a result, we postulated that it was important to provide high uncertainty avoidance users with further reassurance by enriching the interface with elements of learning support and security.

We designed a *Minimal* interface (Fig. 1 top) for Caucasian users, who are more tolerant of uncertainty. In this interface, we included only the task elements necessary for the primary task (central figure, nine small figures, nine numbered buttons, and instructions). The instruction does appear for the

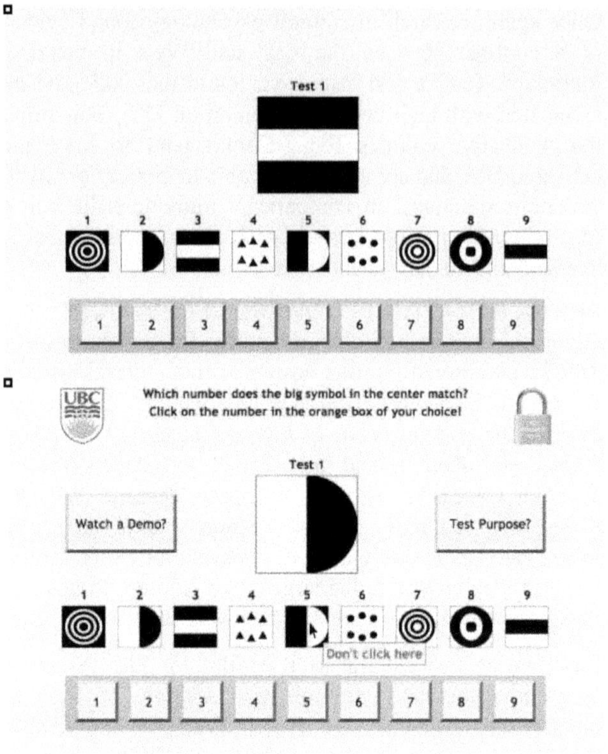

Figure 1. Minimal (top) and Rich (bottom) interfaces for the Symbol-Digit Matching test. In this test, the user clicks on the numbered button in the bottom row that corresponds to the image that matches the large central symbol. The instruction does appear initially in the Minimal interface, but disappears after the first trial.

first trial, but disappears for all subsequent trials to reduce information richness further. We hypothesized that this interface would be a better fit for Caucasians who are more comfortable with uncertainty. By contrast, it might seem information-deficient in a manner that could induce anxiety for East Asians.

For East Asian users, who are less comfortable with uncertainty, we designed a *Rich* interface (Fig. 1 bottom). This is a Minimal interface augmented in four ways: (1) *Instruction repetition* – instructions continue to appear in each trial of the task; (2) *Security elements* – a university logo and an information security icon are added in the top left and right corners respectively; (3) *Background information* – a test purpose button that when clicked produces a popup containing background information including test justification, description, and scoring scheme; (4) *Learning support elements* – hovering popups for the central figure, the small nine figures, and the nine numbered buttons. These popups reinforce the instructions by clarifying what the task elements are and how users should interact with them (e.g., "*do not click on small figures*", "*click on the numbered buttons*"). The interface also contains a demo button that links to a video showing how to do the task. We postulated that this interface would provide East Asians a higher sense of control over the environment, soothing anxiety about uncertainty. By contrast, its richness might feel like a distraction from the task to Caucasians.

We presented both prototypes to the C-TOC neurologists. They reassured us that the cognitive test integrity was preserved since both designs contain the primary task elements with identical dimensions and in the same layout.

EXPERIMENT

We conducted an experiment to investigate the effects of user attitude toward uncertainty for Caucasians and East Asians while taking a self-administered cognitive test. We evaluated our two interface designs of a C-TOC subtest with the two cultural user groups.

Methodology

Primary Task

The primary task was the Symbol-Digit Matching test (Fig. 1). This is one of the 15 tasks that together form the C-TOC testing battery under development. In this task, the user needs to look at a central large figure, and search for its match out of nine smaller figures arranged in a row below it. The user then submits his/her answer by clicking on the number that corresponds to the matching small figure. This task targets the cognitive functions of attention and information processing speed, and intentionally requires the user to click on a numbered button instead of the matching figure directly.

Distractor Task

We used a within-subject design in order to expose each user to both the Rich and Minimal interfaces. Given that the task was identical for both interfaces, we sandwiched a distractor task in between conditions to reduce carryover effects. We used a 2-back working memory task [21]. This task was a good distractor because: (1) it imposes a significant demand on (wipes) working memory, providing a considerable distraction between the two conditions, and (2) it has a fixed duration so that time spent between conditions is held constant across participants, avoiding a confounding effect.

Dependent Measures

We collected data for ten measures related to anxiety, preference, performance, use of support buttons and dimensions related to uncertainty.

For **anxiety**, we measured:

(1) *General anxiety* using the State Trait Anxiety Inventory [24], a 20-item questionnaire through which users self-report their current state by indicating their dis/agreement on a 4-point Likert scale with short statements such as "*I feel at ease*", and "*I feel indecisive*".

(2) *Interface-specific anxiety* using a 4-item block in the usability questionnaire (described below), adapted from the Unified Theory of Acceptance and Use of Technology (UTAUT) questionnaire [26] such as "*The interface was intimidating to me*" or "*I hesitated while doing the task for fear of making mistakes that I could not correct.*"

For **preference**, we measured:

(3) *Overall interface preference* via a question comparing the two interfaces at the conclusion of the study.

(4) *Usability preferences* using an 8-item usability questionnaire administered after completion of the task on each interface. This was partially adapted from the UTAUT questionnaire [26], and targeted the usability areas of effort expectancy, information richness, trust/confidence and security using 4-point Likert scale questions.

For **performance**, we measured:

(5) *Completion time*, the mean trial completion time on each interface averaged over 12 out of 15 trials. The first 3 trials were excluded as practice trials.

(6) *Response accuracy*: the correct selection of the small figure number that matches the central figure.

(7) *Error clicks* on interface elements that should not be clicked, such as the central figure or the small figures. Correct clicks include only the number buttons, the demo button or test purpose button in the Rich interface.

For **use of support buttons**, we measured:

(8) *Clicks on support buttons* (test purpose and demo buttons) in the Rich interface. (Fig. 1 bottom)

For **dimensions related to uncertainty of**, we measured:

(9) *Hofstede's uncertainty avoidance score,* calculated using the uncertainty avoidance portion of the Hofstede 2008 Values Survey Module, which solicits user opinion about statements such as "*Children must be taught to be organized and avoid ambiguity*".

(10) *Behavioral inhibition score,* measured using the behavioral inhibition part of the BIS/BAS scale [3], where users evaluate items such as "*I worry about making mistakes*".

Participants

After piloting the study with 6 young HCI research colleagues and 1 adult over 55, we recruited 20 Caucasian participants (mean age = 64.7 yrs., 14 female). They were from Canada (10), the USA (4), the UK (4) and Germany (2), and had lived in Canada an average of 51 years. We recruited 16 East Asian participants (mean age = 64.4 yrs., 10 female). One participant came from Japan, the rest from China. They had been living in Canada for an average of 40 years, and all had lived the first 18 years of their lives in East Asia. Research in cultural psychology suggests that our East Asian participants would identify more with Eastern culture despite living in the West for a long time since they had spent their formative years (pre-adulthood) in the East. For example, Cheung et al. found that Canadian immigrants from Hong Kong did identify with western culture the longer they were exposed to it, but only if exposure occurred during formative years [4].

All participants culturally self-identified as Caucasian or East Asian. They were all over 55 years old, free of diagnosed cognitive impairments, and comfortable with English. We recruited 20 Caucasian participants through flyers posted through the city, Craigslist advertising, and information booths setup in senior or community centers. These means were not sufficient to recruit our target of 20 East Asian participants over 55, which led us to rely on the personal networks of our research colleagues. Half of the East Asian sample (8/16) in the end consisted of individuals recruited through our research network. The difference in familiarity with the researcher in this sample proved to have some repercussions on our results, as we explain later.

Design

We used a 2x2 design with a single exposure to each interface condition. Our factors were *ethnicity* (between subject: Caucasian or East Asian), and *interface* (within subject: Rich or Minimal). Order of presentation of interface was fully counterbalanced.

Procedure

We met participants at a place of their choosing such as public libraries, coffee shops, community centers, and private homes. We told them that they would go through a self-administered computer application for about 30 minutes. We encouraged them to go through the application independently and to only ask for assistance as a last resort.

We began the prototype with instructions for interaction alongside an overview of the various components. Next, we administered the uncertainty avoidance and behavioral inhibition questionnaires. After that, we showed a 20-second video of a beach at sunset in order to calm users before exposure to the first interface condition.

We then presented the Rich or Minimal interface where users did a block of 15 trials with each interface. We administered the State Trait Anxiety Inventory immediately after exposure to the interface in order to get the most accurate measure of anxiety as a result of interaction. Next, we administered the usability questionnaire for the first interface condition. Next we presented the distractor cognitive task (users were not told it was a distractor). Users did two trials of this task. Next, we showed a relaxing video before presenting the second interface condition, followed by the anxiety inventory and the usability questionnaire. At the end of the prototype, we administered the interface comparison questionnaire.

A short open structure interview was conducted at the conclusion of the study to discuss user experience and comments. After that, participants were provided with a small monetary sum as compensation. The study administrator was a young male Middle Eastern researcher.

Apparatus

We used a MacBook Pro laptop with Mac OS X Lion 10.7.5 operating system. The experiment prototype was developed in HTML and JavaScript and was run on Mozilla Firefox 16.0.2. Participants interacted with the prototype using the laptop keyboard and a Logitech optical scroll mouse. Videos were hosted on YouTube.

Both the Rich and Minimal interfaces were implemented on an 800x600 pixel layout so no scrolling was needed. The primary task elements (central figure, nine small figures and nine numbered buttons) occupied identical positions on both interfaces and matched in size, color and resolution. The four additional elements in the Rich interface were placed in between the primary task elements so that spatial relationships were preserved in both interfaces.

Hypotheses

Our main hypotheses can be summarized as follows:

H1-Anxiety: East Asians will experience less anxiety with the Rich than the Minimal. Caucasians will experience less anxiety with the Minimal than the Rich, or no difference.

H2-Preference: East Asians will prefer using the Rich interface and Caucasians will prefer the Minimal interface.

H3-Performance: East Asians will perform better on the Rich than the Minimal. Caucasians will perform better on the Minimal than the Rich.

H4-Use of support buttons: On the Rich interface, East Asians will use support buttons more than Caucasians.

H5-Attitude toward uncertainty: East Asians will have higher uncertainty avoidance and behavioral inhibition scores than Caucasians.

RESULTS

After performing a preliminary ANOVA analysis, we surprisingly found that East Asians as whole experienced less general anxiety than Caucasians across interfaces ($p < .05$), contradicting the cultural theories. We suspected that differences in familiarity with the researcher for East Asians affected experience of anxiety, and possibly other measures of interest. As mentioned earlier, we had to resort to personal networks of our research colleagues to build our East Asian sample, as public recruitment had proved insufficient. Consequently, our East Asian sample consisted of two equal-sized subgroups differing in level of familiarity with the researcher administering the study: *East Asian Strangers* (recruited through public ads, n=8, 6 female, mean age=64.1 yrs, mean time in Canada=38.2 yrs.) and *East Asian Acquaintances* (recruited through networking, n=8, 4 female, mean age = 64.7 yrs, mean time in Canada=41.8 yrs.). On the other hand, Caucasians were all strangers to the researcher and none were recruited through personal networks.

Analysis on the East Asian sample showed that East Asian Strangers experienced significantly more anxiety on the Minimal than the Rich ($F_{1,14}$ = 3.99, $p < .05$), whereas Acquaintances felt relatively no anxiety on either interface. This difference in experience of anxiety confirmed the confounding effect of familiarity with the researcher on anxiety between East Asian Acquaintances on one hand (knew researcher indirectly) and the Caucasians or East Asian Strangers on the other (did not know researcher at all), so we decided to exclude the former from the analysis. In the primary analysis, which we describe next, we compare Caucasians to only those East Asians who shared the same level of familiarity with the researcher. Luckily, order of presentation of interfaces was counterbalanced for the East Asian Stranger subgroup.

Primary analysis: Caucasians vs. East Asian Strangers

We performed a 2x2 mixed model ANOVA using *ethnicity* (20 Caucasian and 8 East Asian) and *interface* (Rich and Minimal). All results reported here are effects of ethnicity and/or interface. Order of presentation had no significant effect on any of the results reported here.

All measures were checked for normality. Completion time and overall anxiety were positively skewed, so we performed a log transform prior to the ANOVA in order to normalize the data. Data of self-reported Likert-scale measures, such as usability questions, were also not normal. For those measures, we performed the Align Transform Rank (ART) procedure prior to the ANOVA in order to normalize the data and enable interaction analysis [28]. Since the data was transformed prior to analysis, the graphs of our raw data results do not show error bars.

Pairwise comparisons on significant interactions were performed using a Bonferroni correction to protect against type I error. We report on measures that were significant ($p < .05$). Additionally, we report observed power and partial eta-squared (η^2), a measure of effect size, where 0.01 is a small effect size, 0.06 is medium, and 0.14 is large [7].

General anxiety: East Asian Strangers were less anxious on the Rich than the Minimal, and were less anxious on the Rich than Caucasians. Scores on the State Trait Anxiety Inventory showed an interaction of ethnicity and interface ($F_{1,26}$ = 7.831, $p < .01$, η^2 = .231, power = .768). Pairwise comparisons showed that East Asian Strangers were less anxious on the Rich than the Minimal ($p < .05$), and that they were less anxious than Caucasians on the Rich ($p < .05$) (Fig. 2). This partially supported H1; no difference was found in interface-specific anxiety.

As mentioned earlier, East Asian Acquaintances showed no significant difference in general anxiety between interfaces (Mean/Std on Rich=3.8/1.8; Mean/Std on Minimal=4.7/1.3).

Overall interface preference: East Asian Strangers preferred the Rich interface, and Caucasians preferred the Minimal interface or had no preference. Responses to the overall preference question on the interface comparison questionnaire showed a significant main effect of ethnicity ($F_{1,26}$= 4.31, $p < .05$, η^2 = .142, power = .516). 5 out of 8 East Asian Strangers preferred the Rich to the Minimal. By contrast, 16 out of 20 Caucasians preferred the Minimal interface or had no preference. (Fig. 3a)

Qualitative comments revealed that 4 out of 8 East Asian Strangers weighed security elements in their preference for

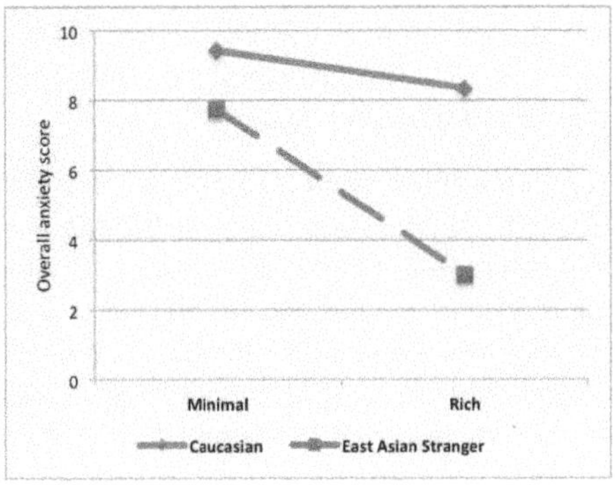

Figure 2. General anxiety score for Caucasians and East Asian Strangers. ($N = 28$)

the Rich interface, explaining that they rendered it more "*legitimate*" and "*professional*". By contrast, only 3 out of 20 Caucasians mentioned security as a factor influencing interface preference. Almost half (9 out of 20) specifically mentioned lack of perceived "clutter" as one of the reasons for their preference. Altogether, this partially supported H2. In order to understand these preferences, we looked at user feedback on the usability areas of effort expectancy, information richness, trust/confidence and security.

Usability preference (effort expectancy): East Asian Strangers found the Rich easier to use than the Minimal. In terms of the Minimal interface, Caucasians found it easier to use than East Asian Strangers. Responses to the question "*I found the test interface easy to use*" showed a significant interaction of interface and ethnicity ($F_{1,26} = 18.129$, $p < .01$, $\eta^2 = .393$, power = .984). Pairwise comparisons showed that East Asian Strangers found the Rich interface easier to use than the Minimal ($p < .01$), and that Caucasians found the Minimal interface easier to use than East Asian Strangers ($p < .01$). (Fig. 3b) Thus effort expectancy might be one factor that explains the overall preference finding above.

Usability preference (trust/confidence): Caucasians were more trusting of the research than East Asian Strangers, and trust was higher on the Rich interface. Responses to the question "*I have confidence in the legitimacy of the research team which designed the interface*" showed a main effect of ethnicity ($F_{1,26} = 7.501$, $p < .05$, $\eta^2 = .211$, power = .753), and a main effect of interface ($F_{1,26} = 7.158$, $p < .05$, $\eta^2 = .204$, power = .733) (Fig. 3c). This result proved important in understanding recruitment problems we had faced with East Asians and the variation in attitudes toward uncertainty between the two cultural groups, but cannot be used directly to explain the overall preference finding.

Usability preference (security and information richness): no effect of ethnicity on either. No quantitative difference was found in these two usability areas.

Performance: No effects of ethnicity on performance. Mean completion time showed no effect of ethnicity or interface. Data for response accuracy and error clicks showed a ceiling effect, where participants performed well on both interfaces with very few incorrect answer choices and few error clicks. H3 was not supported.

Use of support buttons: No quantitative evidence of ethnicity effect on use of support buttons. On the Rich interface, no participant clicked on the test purpose button, and only 1 East Asian Stranger clicked on the demo button, resulting in no significant difference with regard to use of support buttons. H4 was not supported quantitatively.

Qualitatively however, 5 out of 8 East Asian Strangers indicated they weighed support buttons in their interface preference, whereas only 2 out of 20 Caucasians indicated appreciation for this additional support.

Attitude toward uncertainty: no cultural difference found in uncertainty avoidance or behavioural inhibition scores, but the two scores were correlated. Contrary to H5, no significant difference was found between the two cultural groups in uncertainty avoidance score ($F_{1,26} = .860$, $p = .36$, $\eta^2 = .035$, power = .145) or behavioural inhibition score ($F_{1,26} = 2.319$, $p = .14$, $\eta^2 = .088$, power = .310), although East Asian Strangers scored higher on both. We reflect on the low observed power of these tests later. We computed the Pearson product-moment correlation coefficient for the two scores and found they were positively correlated ($r = .468$, $n = 28$, $p < .05$).

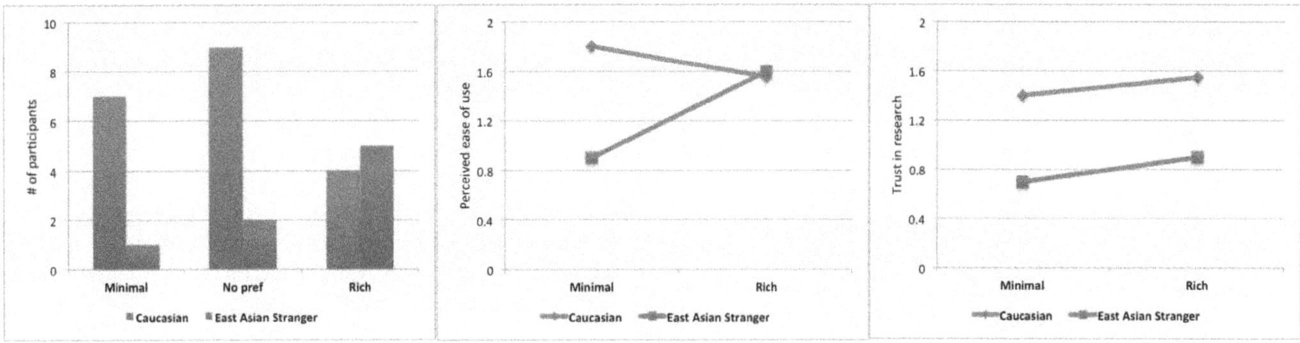

Figure 3. Caucasian and East Asian Stranger results for (a) overall interface preference (b) perceived effort expectancy (c) trust in research. ($N = 28$)

Summary of Hypotheses

H1-Anxiety: East Asians will experience less anxiety with the Rich than the Minimal. Caucasians will experience less anxiety with the Minimal than the Rich, or no difference. Partially supported. East Asians did have less general anxiety using the Rich than the Minimal. No differences in interface specific anxiety were found however. Caucasians experienced no difference in anxiety for the two interfaces.

H2-Preference: East Asians will prefer using the Rich interface and Caucasians will prefer the Minimal interface. Partially supported. East Asians preferred the Rich interface. However, Caucasians preferred the Minimal or had no preference.

H3-Performance: East Asians will perform better on the Rich than the Minimal. Caucasians will perform better on the Minimal than the Rich. Not supported; participants performed well on both interfaces.

H4-Use of support buttons: On the Rich interface, East Asians will use support buttons elements more than Caucasians. Not supported quantitatively; only one participant clicked on one button.

H5-Attitude toward uncertainty: East Asians will have higher uncertainty avoidance and behavioral inhibition scores than Caucasians. Not supported quantitatively, but low statistical power makes this result questionable.

Secondary Analysis using Uncertainty Avoidance Score

Since we did not get the expected mapping between ethnicity and Hofstede's uncertainty avoidance, we wanted to explore whether uncertainty avoidance had any effect on our primary dependent measures of anxiety and preference. We performed a secondary analysis using uncertainty avoidance (UA) grouping, ignoring ethnic group. The full sample was divided into groups based on their uncertainty avoidance score resulting in 3 groups for Low, Med and High UA. The average UA score was -4.2 for Low (n = 10), 0.9 for Med (n = 12) and 4.1 for High (n = 14). We chose this division over equal-sized groups since the latter would have resulted in individuals with the same UA score being placed in different groups. We performed a 2x2 mixed model ANOVA on the dependent measures of the primary analysis using *UA groups* (Low, Med and High) and *interface* (Rich and Minimal). We report on the same parameters as the primary analysis, with the addition of the Scheffé post hoc test when a main effect of UA groups is found. We report only on the measures that showed significant differences. These results should be seen as preliminary given that UA grouping was not a controlled factor in our experimental design.

Usability preference (security): High UA users noticed the university logo more than low UA users. Responses to the question "*I noticed the logo of the University on the webpage (of the Rich interface)*" showed a main effect of UA grouping ($F_{1,33} = 4.52$, $p < .05$, $\eta^2 = .215$). Post hoc analysis showed that high UA users noticed the university logo more readily than the low UA users ($p < .05$). Most high UA users (11 out of 14) indicated they noticed the university logo, whereas most low UA users (7 out of 10) indicated they were either not sure or that they did not notice it at all.

Usability preference (information richness): Low UA users found interfaces to have unnecessary information more so than high UA users did. Responses to the fill-in-the-blank question "*The information provided in the interface was {not enough, just right, too much} to do the task*" showed a main effect of UA grouping ($F_{1,33} = 3.23$, $p < .05$, $\eta^2 = .155$). Post hoc analysis showed that low UA users felt interfaces had "*too much information*" more than high UA users ($p < .05$).

Interface-specific anxiety: High and Medium UA users felt more anxious during the task than low UA users. Responses to the question "*I felt anxious while doing the task*" showed a main effect of UA grouping ($F_{1,33} = 3.71$, $p < .05$, $\eta^2 = .184$). Post hoc analysis showed that on both interfaces, low UA users felt less anxious than both high and med UA ($p < .05$ for both). No difference was found in general anxiety.

DISCUSSION

Reflection on results

Preference: We detected a cultural difference in preference that partially met our hypothesis. In terms of usability areas, we detected a cultural difference in effort expectancy and trust, but not in information richness or security. Perhaps having only one item in the usability questionnaire for each of these areas limited our power to detect a quantitative difference. Qualitatively, however, we found evidence of a cultural contrast. East Asians indicated weighing security elements in their preference for the Rich interface, even though they were iconic of security and not functional. On the other hand, Caucasians indicated that the lack of perceived clutter tipped their preference toward the Minimal interface. This implies that varying information richness to align with cultural attitude toward uncertainty likely has merit.

Performance: Our performance hypothesis was not supported, as we found no significant difference in performance between ethnicities or interfaces. This is actually good news for C-TOC as having cultural variations in performance could have serious implications on its integrity as a cognitive test. On the other hand, doing 30 trials of a cognitive task may not have provided enough time to allow for variations in performance; going through the full cognitive test battery would be more taxing and might create a larger variation in performance, especially with other C-TOC subtests that have a richer answer space. Moreover, our participants were likely less preoccupied with the implications of cognitive testing than "real" C-TOC test-takers will be, as we focused on usability in our study rather than the cognitive aspects of C-TOC.

Use of support buttons: Our hypothesis about use of support buttons did not receive quantitative support either, as we witnessed only one East Asian participant clicking on the demo button, and no one clicked on the test purpose button. In retrospect this is not surprising, as participants may have thought that their time "off task" would count towards their performance. Our qualitative findings do show that a greater proportion of East Asians than Caucasians appreciated such elements and weighed them in their preference of the Rich interface. This implies that these elements provided a sort of cognitive cushion [20], reassuring users by their presence. This aligns with our design vision that the richness of the interface provides East Asians with a sense of control over the interaction environment through support elements, soothing anxiety about uncertainty.

Anxiety: We detected a cultural difference in general anxiety that matched our hypothesis. While Caucasians exhibited no difference in anxiety on the two interfaces, East Asians were less anxious on the Rich interface than the Minimal. Again, it is possible that security and support elements appeased their anxiety on the Rich interface, as qualitative comments showed that East Asians weighed those elements in their preference for the Rich interface. On the other hand, these elements seemed less valuable to Caucasians, and did little to alter their anxiety experience on the two interfaces.

Reflection on cultural attitude toward uncertainty

Our hypothesis about differences in uncertainty avoidance score between Caucasians and East Asian Strangers was not met. This was surprising, but could be explained partially by the low observed power of our statistical test (.145). It may also be a result of our participants belonging to the subculture of East Asians who had spent their formative years in Asia, but lived in Canada afterwards (compared to those who lived in Asia all their lives). However, we gleaned from our informal conversations with participants that East Asians are less comfortable with uncertainty. First, we learned that East Asians in general have less affinity to participate in research given our findings on confidence in research (Fig. 3c). Second, we noticed that East Asian participants were generally more apprehensive of the study context than Caucasians. For instance, 3 of the East Asian Strangers in the study asked for proof of identity before meeting the researcher, while no Caucasian asked for any such information. This implies a stronger aversion to uncertainty among East Asians than Caucasians.

Our struggle in recruiting East Asian participants over a long period of time indicates that they might indeed avoid participating in research. We began recruiting from both cultural groups simultaneously using public advertisements. While we succeeded in reaching our Caucasian quota of 20 after only about 1.5 months, it took 3 months to recruit 8 East Asian participants in a city where they constitute about 25% of the population. Expanding our public recruitment artillery, by setting information tables or participating in activities with seniors to build rapport, did little to help. The futility of public recruitment with East Asians led us to consider contacting acquaintances of our research network. We still could not reach our East Asian quota of 20 within a reasonable timeframe. This struggle to reach our East Asian recruitment target further implies relative discomfort in unfamiliar contexts.

As with all research, we faced the problem of self-selection to participate, but this had a larger impact on East Asian recruitment, as this group was relatively less accessible in our cultural investigation. The reason we suspect Hofstede managed to detect a difference in uncertainty avoidance scores between the East and West was that he had the rare opportunity of avoiding the problem of self-selection; he was an IBM researcher requesting international IBM employees to participate in work-mandated research. By contrast, we lacked that privilege.

In sum, this suggests that our findings related to Hofstede's uncertainty avoidance are conservative. This is due in part to the intrinsically challenging dilemma of studying uncertainty avoidance: how can we investigate a phenomenon whose presence in a culture discourages participation in research in the first place? The East Asian Stranger participants we recruited were probably less uncertainty avoidant than the average East Asian person whom we struggled to recruit because the latter avoids participating in research altogether.

Design implications

We provide some design guidelines for C-TOC, and similar multicultural design contexts for older adults characterized by uncertainty. For older East Asians, we recommend information rich interfaces augmented with security elements and learning support. We found that such elements are especially important when anxiety is likely during interaction. Our secondary analysis showed that high UA users are more likely to feel anxious, and are more tolerant of information richness than low UA users. For older Caucasians, minimal interfaces are more appropriate, as these users mainly attend to the primary task elements. Catering to cultural preferences may increase willingness across cultures to use C-TOC. We imagine C-TOC could develop to become a cultural adaptive interface similar to Mocca [22], where a culturally adaptive version would be presented after collecting a modest amount of cultural data.

CONCLUSION AND FUTURE WORK

Our design and evaluation of cultural interfaces show that there is some validity in culturability. Varying the information richness of an interface based on uncertainty avoidance impacted the experience of two ethnic groups with differences on 1) interface preference, 2) perceived effort expectancy, and 3) anxiety. East Asians leaned towards an information rich interface on all these measures whereas Caucasians showed no difference or leaned towards information minimal. The cultural difference in UA was not detected, but the test was underpowered. Catering to cultural preferences – in the case of C-TOC at least – may increase the likelihood to use a technological solution across cultures. However, it proved hard for us to attribute the cultural preference to one measure of attitude toward uncertainty, such as Hofstede's uncertainty avoidance, as it was deficient on its own in explaining the cultural variation.

We envision other paths to further this research. *Translating the study prototype* might expand the pool of recruitment as we found a population of older East Asians who could not manage the level of conversational English of our prototype. Finally, *running the study online remotely* could help us mitigate the recruitment challenges we faced. While it might result in a less controlled study environment, it could extend our reach to users across cultures.

REFERENCES

1. Barber, W., & Badre, A. (1998). Culturability: The merging of culture and usability. *Proc. of the 4th Conference on Human Factors and the Web*, 1–14.
2. Brehmer, M. M. (2011). Usability and the effects of interruption in C- TOC: Self-Administered Cognitive Testing on a Computer. *M.Sc thesis*. University of British Columbia.
3. Carver, C. S., & White, T. L. (1994). Behavioral inhibition, behavioral activation, and affective responses to impending reward and punishment: The BIS/BAS Scales. *Journal of Personality and Social Psychology*, *67*(2), 319–333.
4. Cheung, B. Y., Chudek, M., & Heine, S. J. (2011). Evidence for a sensitive period for acculturation: Younger immigrants report acculturating at a faster rate. *Psychological Science*, *22*(2), 147–152.
5. Choi, B., Lee, I., Kim, J., & Jeon, Y. (2005). A qualitative cross-national study of cultural influences on mobile data service design. In *Proc. of CHI 2005* (pp. 661–670).
6. Clemmensen, T., Hertzum, M., Hornbæk, K., Shi, Q., & Yammiyavar, P. (2009). Cultural cognition in usability evaluation. *Interacting with Computers*, *21*(3), 212–220.
7. Cohen, J. (1973). Eta-squared and partial eta-squared in communication science. *Human Communication Research*, *28*, 473–490.
8. Cyr, D., Bonanni, C., & ilsever, J. (2004). Design and e-loyalty across cultures in electronic commerce. In *Proc. of 6th Int'l Conference on Electronic Commerce* (pp. 351–360).
9. Darke, S. (1988). Anxiety and working memory capacity. *Cognition & Emotion*, *2*(2), 145–154.
10. De Angeli, A., & Kyriakoullis, L. (2006). Globalisation vs. localisation in e-commerce: cultural-aware interaction design. In *Proc. of the Working Conference on Advanced Visual Interfaces* (pp. 250–253).
11. Frandsen-Thorlacius, O., Hornbæk, K., Hertzum, M., & Clemmensen, T. (2009). Non-universal usability?: A survey of how usability is understood by Chinese and Danish users. In *Proc. of CHI 2009* (pp. 41–50).
12. Heine, S. J. (2007). *Cultural Psychology* (1st ed.). W. W. Norton & Company.
13. Hofstede, G. (1980). *Cultures Consequences : International Differences in Work-Related Values* (Abridged.). SAGE Publications, Inc.
14. Jhangiani, I., & Smith-Jackson, T. (2007). Comparison of mobile phone user interface design preferences: perspectives from nationality and disability culture. In *Proc. of the 4th Int'l Conference on Mobile Technology, Applications, and Systems* (pp. 512–519).
15. Kitayama, S., Duffy, S., Kawamura, T., & Larsen, J. T. (2003). Perceiving an object and its context in different cultures: A cultural look at new look. *Psychological Science*, *14*(3), 201–206.
16. Lee, I., Choi, G. W., Kim, J., Kim, S., Lee, K., Kim, D., Han, M., Park, S., An, Y. (2008). Cultural dimensions for user experience: cross-country and cross-product analysis of users' cultural characteristics. In *Proc. of the 22nd British HCI Group Annual Conference on People and Computers: Culture, Creativity, Interaction - Volume 1* (pp. 3–12).
17. Marcus, A. (2010). Cross-cultural user-interface design for work, ho play, and on the way. In *ACM SIGGRAPH ASIA 2010 Courses* (pp. 5:1–5:160).
18. Merritt, S., & Bardzell, S. (2011). Postcolonial language and culture theory for HCI4D. In *Proc. of CHI 2011, Extended Abstracts* (pp. 1675–1680).
19. Miyamoto, Y., Nisbett, R. E., & Masuda, T. (2006). Culture and the physical environment. *Psychological Science*, *17*(2), 113 –119.
20. Nekrasovski, D., Bodnar, A., McGrenere, J., Guimbretière, F., & Munzner, T. (2006). An evaluation of pan & zoom and rubber sheet navigation with and without an overview. In *Proc. of CHI 2006* (pp. 11–20).
21. Owen, A. M., McMillan, K. M., Laird, A. R., & Bullmore, E. (2005). N-back working memory paradigm: A meta-analysis of normative functional neuroimaging studies. *Human Brain Mapping*, *25*(1), 46–59.
22. Reinecke, K., & Bernstein, A. (2011). Improving performance, perceived usability, and aesthetics with culturally adaptive user interfaces. *ACM Trans. Comput.-Hum. Interact.*, *18*(2), 8:1–8:29.
23. Shuper, P. A., Sorrentino, R. M., Otsubo, Y., Hodson, G., & Walker, A. M. (2004). A theory of uncertainty orientation. *Journal of Cross-Cultural Psychology*, *35*(4), 460 –480.
24. Spielberger, C. D., Gorsuch, R. L., & Lushene, R. E. (1970). Manual for the state-trait anxiety inventory. Retrieved from http://ubir.buffalo.edu/xmlui/handle/10477/2895
25. Tanaka, A., & Yamauchi, H. (2004). Cultural self-construal and achievement goal. *Hellenic Journal of Psychology*, *1*, 221–237.
26. Venkatesh, V., Morris, M. G., Gordon B. Davis, & Davis, F. D. (2003). User acceptance of information technology: Toward a unified view. *MIS Quarterly*, *27*(3), 425–478.
27. Walsh, T., Nurkka, P., & Walsh, R. (2010). Cultural differences in smartphone user experience evaluation. In *Proc. of the 9th International Conference on Mobile and Ubiquitous Multimedia* (pp. 24:1–24:9).
28. Wobbrock, J. O., Findlater, L., Gergle, D., & Higgins, J. J. (2011). The aligned rank transform for nonparametric factorial analyses using only anova procedures. In *Proc. of CHI 2011* (pp. 143–146).

Social Dependency and Mobile Autonomy – Supporting Older Adults' Mobility with Ridesharing ICT

Johanna Meurer
University Siegen, Germany
Information Systems
johanna.meurer@uni-siegen.de

Martin Stein
University Siegen, Germany
Information Systems
martin.stein@uni-siegen.de

David Randall
University Siegen, Germany
Information Systems
david.randall@uni-siegen.de

Markus Rohde
University Siegen, Germany
Information Systems
markus.rohde@uni-siegen.de

Volker Wulf
University Siegen, Germany
Information Systems
volker.wulf@uni-siegen.de

ABSTRACT
Alternative mobility modes for older adults are increasingly important for economic, ecological and social reasons. A promising option is ridesharing, defined as use of the same vehicle by two or more people traveling to a common destination. In particular, mobile computer supported ridesharing provides a promising way to enlarge older adults' mobility choices in addition to private driving and public transportation options. In order to understand the opportunities and obstacles of ridesharing from the point of view of elderly people, we conducted an interview study in order to examining ridesharing experiences. It turns out that 'mobile independence' and 'decisional autonomy' are key issues for mobile wellbeing. This partially conflicts with common ridesharing concepts. Hence, we further analyze older adults' strategies dealing with these conflicts and show that these strategies offer departure points for the design ridesharing solutions, which are better suited to the demands of older adults.

Author Keywords
Dynamic Ridesharing, Elderly, Design, Ethnography, Social Experiences.

ACM Classification Keywords
H.5.m. Information interfaces and presentation (e.g., HCI): Miscellaneous.

INTRODUCTION
In 2000 about 13% of the total U.S. population were over the age of 65. By 2025, the number of older Americans will have more than doubled, so that nearly every fourth person will be over the age of 65. In Europe, China or Japan this effect will be even more dramatic, because migration is not as high as in the US. All but the most fortunate senior citizens will be confronted by an array of medical and other constraints on their mobility even as they continue to seek an active community life [17]. Many older adults drive but still face mobility barriers, or suffer from physical or medical problems [22]. Then there is a large number of elderly people who live in regions that are underserved with public transportation infrastructure [17]. Debates on providing transportation for the elderly in gerontology, transport studies, health research and urban studies do not always capture the complexity of their situations. Based on the complex and diverse mobility situation and needs of the elderly we suggest a ridesharing system that is flexible enough to address the heterogeneous contexts of older adult mobility. Ridesharing provides not only an alternative mobility infrastructure, but also includes a social network that allows personal help when needed, or can support social inclusion. Despite its great potential, ridesharing presents quite a new topic for gerontological mobility research and we know little about developing ridesharing ICT for the elderly. This provides motivation for a qualitative study on 21 older adults' attitudes and experiences towards ridesharing in a German mixed density area consisting of rural and urban spaces.

In the following we will draw a detailed picture of the mobility situation of older adults and we will give reasons to focus on ridesharing solutions for this particular user group (section two). Then we will provide an overview of related work on ridesharing systems in HCI research (section three), followed by a discussion (section four), arguing that research about ridesharing for the elderly is under-rehearsed. After outlining the methodological framework (section five), findings will be presented. Ridesharing needs, problems and strategies for coping with challenges of older adults provide innovation seeds for design implications that will be outlined at the end (section six).

CHI 2014, April 26 - May 01 2014, Toronto, ON, Canada

http://dx.doi.org/10.1145/2556288.2557300

IMPROVING OLDER ADULTS' MOBILITY WITH RIDESHARING

According to Ziegler et al. older adults' mobility can be understood along three dimensions in gerontology, transport studies and health research of western societies [37]: (1) as quantified movements through space and time, (2) as dependent on preconditions like the available infrastructure and (3) as subordinate to individual physical mobility status. In the following we will see how these dimensions address ridesharing and how it supplements older adults' mobility.

Measuring mobility

The first research dimension deals with counting mobility trips on a daily or weekly basis, measuring the distances the elderly cover and the transport modes they choose (e.g. [7]). Although older adults make 22% fewer trips overall after retirement, studies show that those over 65 make a greater percentage (roughly 90%) of their trips with a car than younger people do [22]. Further, older people typically have very active post-retirement lifestyles until they are 85, and take as many as 23% more non-work trips than people under 65. In particular, older adults at retirement often have much more spare time. Older adults drive often to sports clubs, make visits, go to sightseeing tours, or just go for a walk or undertake a shopping spree. Thus older adults often undertake activities along with others, and often in informal ridesharing arrangements. Studies show that about half of all trips are done in cars with at least two persons, the driver and at least one passenger [24]. In addition the percentage of trips in cars made by those over age 65 without a license is almost as high as licensed drivers. This means that informal ridesharing is already a very common and also very important transport mode among the elderly, that supports that older adults who do not drive [23].

Mobility preconditions

The second research string addresses the unequally distribution of options for older people in relation to different transport modes [17]. As the majority of older adults in western countries will increasingly live alone in suburban or rural communities, access to public infrastructure becomes increasingly problematic for this cohort. Thus the private car becomes crucial to sustain individual mobility. In addition Fobker and Grotz point out that incomplete knowledge about public transport services is a significant barrier preventing older adults from using alternative transportation modes as well [7] and explains why a good social network becomes of great importance to compensate for the absence of a car. Coughlin, for instance, discovered that older adults who are embedded in a good social network are more likely to give up driving because informal ridesharing opportunities exist [5]. In this context Lord emphasizes the adaptation of lifestyle through 'mutual aid' and 'community based' help [13]. Again others argue that such structures should be institutionalized to increase the benefits [27], [6]. One way of doing so could be a ridesharing system based on existing social networks.

Mobility and health

Existing research tends to focus on bodily or cognitive impairments in later life, causing difficulties in undertaking the basic mobility activities of daily life [3]. In particular Rosenbloom criticizes the fact that most research on older adult mobility focuses on those with the most obvious and severe disadvantages, those who do not drive or who are severely disabled [22]. She shows that disability rates have in fact been falling among all cohorts of the elderly for decades, caused by a combination of good nutrition, improved health care, better education, and higher incomes. Most elderly people, she argues, will be in overall good health until they reach age 80 or older (apart from smaller problems, like vision problems at night, problems of carrying heavy bags or coping with crowded streets) [22]. Thus, life from 60 to 80 can no longer be regarded as *residual life* time, but is characterized by *late freedom,* posing new challenges, and creating new development tasks and design options. However, driving is still the easiest physical task for older adults. Long before they lose the ability to drive, older people may be unable to board or ride public transit, or to walk to a bus stop. Thus, it is not surprising that the fear of losing the driving license is widespread among older adults [24].

In summary, ridesharing practice is a common and deeply established mode in the elderly's daily travel. In particular, ridesharing can address the needs of those who have never had a car or a license, as well as those who have driven well into their senior years, but now are unable to do so and have poor access to public transport.

SUPPORTING RIDESHARING

Ridesharing systems became popular in the 1970s to cope with the challenge of increasing environmental awareness, oil prices and transport collapse. People at that time joined together in ridesharing communities using slip-boxes in order to exchange offers and demands [9]. Since that time ridesharing research in information systems and HCI has undergone a change in perspective, shifting from logistical concerns towards questions of social acceptance.

Matching demands and offers

The precondition for matching a driver with one or more passengers is that their mobility patterns are as congruent as possible, given travel time and route convergence. The prevalent research focus emphasizes the challenge of finding appropriate algorithms for matching rides. While there is no standard method to determine the best ride-matching method, several approaches have been developed along different foci of activity-based behavior [30], [29]. Meanwhile agile and real-time matching became key components for a successful ridesharing system. Location aware Internet-enabled mobile phones allow very short notice or even en-route notification. This constitutes the technical basis for flexibility among spatial, time, role and route dimensions [9]. Another factor for intelligent matching operations is to improve the modal choice of transport [29]. Increasingly, attention is being paid to the question how the use of online social networks can contribute to solving problems of meeting potential sharers, coordination, and logistics [8], [15].

Reducing transaction costs

Reducing costs has been a major element in ridesharing research since its onset. In HCI, the focus has widened to include transaction costs. In the case of commuting, transaction costs are very low, because commutes are based on routinely established practices that do no longer need a lot of coordination work [9]. However, with the arrival of more flexible, agile ridesharing systems, handling transaction costs, becomes a much more challenging issue. For example Hansen et al. [10] focus on community based-toolkits and ICT as means to reduce transaction costs by lowering the complexity of the selection of and the navigation to meeting points. Largely in line with this perspective is the work of Xing et al. who take meeting points into consideration and call for 'multi-modal travel planning systems', including information about public transportation to offer optimal meeting points [36]. Several approaches, such as those presented by Brereton et al. [4] or Wash et al. [32] focus on the improvement of communication processes, comparing informal and formal systems.

Accounting for social acceptance

The arrival of dynamic and flexible ridesharing systems precipitated a discussion in HCI research on issues of social acceptability. Pioneering work was done by Brereton et al. [4], Allen [2], and Ozenc et al. [19], who argue that ridesharing systems can reach a wider mass of users if social challenges concerning personal preferences of commuting choice and social interaction are solved. They point out that it is necessary to understand that riding, meeting with people and participating at an event are related activities and hence a broader view of the social situation in which people travel and meet is needed. Further Ghelawat et al. [8], [4] pinpoint that agile rather than static matching programs need to arrange ridesharing based on extended social networks. Wessels et al. [33] show that online social networks provide users with the ability to share daily travel activities by publishing information using a personal profile and have the additional function of showing relationships between people. Thus, designing for participation in local social ridesharing has to deal with the question of designing networks of relations between people in order to understand how to better support ridesharing relations. Yet in using social networks systems and further using tracking and data mining technologies in combination with personal information, concerns about issues like *trust*, *privacy* and *security*, which are situated in social practices, are raised [16], [21], [33].

Hence, with the arrival of agile, flexible ridesharing systems, design decisions can no longer be addressed separately from concrete social and cultural perspectives. However, increasing interest in social issues like trust, privacy, safety or social interaction has not addressed ridesharing specifically. Mobility behavior is still considered as a derived demand, based on the spatial and temporal characteristics of the performed activities.

DISCUSSION

Economic pressure on the public sector and the low incomes of older adults create a need for developing new mobility options in the near future. Currently, supporting elderly people to use ridesharing is a blind spot in gerontology and HCI research: While gerontology articulates the challenge of supporting independent living, it has yet missed to investigate new opportunities offered by mobile and ubiquitous computing. In contrast, while transportation and mobility research gains importance in HCI research, the elderly are not thus far addressed and hence their interests are typically neglected when it comes to the design of mobile ridesharing systems. This blind spot might result from the stereotyped view that older adults are not technology savvy: a largely unwarranted assumption given that mobile phone users are getting older [17].

Further, our literature review shows that understanding older people's mobility is mainly framed by a transportation perspective. The dominant topic is the overcoming of mobility barriers through increasing the numbers of mobility activities, providing infrastructure, and improving the health situation of older adults to enhance the ability to move from A to B in physical space. Others, however, argue that this view does not guarantee mobility without problems or an increased quality of life. For instance, authors like Ziegler et al. [37], Kaiser [11], and Steg [28], stress that we need to take subjective meanings of mobility more into consideration. In this new understanding, mobility is more than just a means to reach destinations but contributes significantly to older people's wellbeing and quality of life. In addition, we need to consider social and cultural factors which act as barriers to choice for older adults when they examine viable means of travel [6], [23].

This new understanding implies that HCI research on ridesharing for older adults should not focus on transportation issues only. Instead we should broaden the investigation to the elderly mobility experiences, wellbeing and subjective attitudes to ridesharing. Although existing literature draws a realistic picture about older adults' mobility activities, patterns, and transportation mode preferences, qualitative research which takes values, fears and desires into account and uncovers current mobility practices is still lacking [7]. Sensitized by the above-made arguments, the research question of how ridesharing is experienced by older adults is our primary research issue.

METHODOLOGY

Addressing this question we conducted an interview study. Interviews can provide detailed insights into the subjective life-worlds of individuals and therefore were chosen to investigate subjective attitudes, meanings and interpretations towards mobility in general and daily ridesharing in particular.

We chose problem-centered interviews [34] for the data collection, because they aim at focusing on experiences, perceptions and reflections in relation to specified issues. On the basis of a question guide, therefore, we asked interviewees to reflect on and expand our themes in any way they chose. The semi-structured interviews were accompanied by a short questionnaire with the function to complement the study with additional biographical and socio-demographic background information about the interviewees. The questions asked were loosely structured around a topic list about the living arrangements within daily mobility routines and the way they dovetailed (or not) with available infrastructure like possessing a car, using public transport, or other forms of mobility like ridesharing. We were further interested in mobility choices, preferences and habits.

Asking questions in a problem-centered interview provides some structure, but also provides for an open, iterative, and reflective response by both parties to the interview. Interviewers relied on reflective questioning and probing, prompting participants to provide additional detail, clarification and exemplification. Hence, we kept interviews as open as possible in order to gain individual insights in the issue of older adults' ridesharing experiences. The interviews were conducted in participants' homes by one of the researchers, audio-recorded and transcribed verbatim afterwards. The duration of interviews was driven by interviewees, and thus varies in length from 45 minutes to two and a half hours.

The initial contact with participants was made through various local senior organizations. We selected a heterogeneous group of seniors (N=21) in relation to gender, age, local infrastructure, and in the transport systems typically used, in order obtain a wider spectrum of ridesharing and mobility experiences. Table 1 provides an overview of the interviewees according to relevant categories. Pseudonyms are used to ensure participants' anonymity and confidentiality.

The region that participants come from has about 100.000 inhabitants in western Germany. One characteristic of this area is that it includes both urban and very rural areas. The only public transportation option available is bus, or train (mainly for inter-city travelling). The bus service is very limited, especially in rural areas. Additionally, the landscape is very hilly and diverse; meaning that travelling from one location to another can mean very indirect journeys. Thus, the focus in this study lies on an area with limited public transport system, that is close to the real life context of most older adults.

All interviewees were still mobile and take actively part in social events and life in general. They agreed to participate on a voluntary basis and no financial compensation was offered. Further, all of the interviewees committed to collaborating in a three-year project, commencing with these initial interviews. The overall project aim is to develop a mobility platform for older adults that follows a participatory design approach [35]. Participants from the outset were aware of the research aim of building a ridesharing platform customized for older adults needs and are overall positively positioned toward mobile ridesharing solutions.

In the analyzing process we used MAXQDA[1] software. First, interview transcripts were organized into different content parts to organize the data with the help of different code groups. Second, the data was analyzed under three leading question headings: first, what makes daily mobility actually a valuable experience; second, how is ridesharing experienced; and third, what are the strategies people use to organize their ridesharing practice? In the following we will report on our findings on these issues.

Table 1 Characteristics of interview participants (N = 21)

Category	Characteristics	Number of Respondents
Sex	Male Female	5 (26%) 16 (74%)
Age	58-70 years 70-80 years (Average: 69 years)	11 (53%) 10 (47%)
Marital status	Married or living with a partner Widowed/ Single/separated	12 (58%) 9 (42%)
Housing tenure	Owned Rented	13 (63%) 8 (37%)
Self-rated technical competence	More good More bad	6 (26%) 15 (74%)
Population density	Low density High density	11 (53%) 10 (47%)
Travel Modes*	Own car Public transportation Walking Regularly involved in Ridesharing	17 (84%) 5 (21%) 8 (42%) 9 (47%)

* Multiple answers are possible

FINDINGS

Two categories turned out to be of particular significance for the experience of mobile wellbeing in older adults' lives: *independence* and *decisional autonomy*. However, both dimensions were viewed as constraints on ridesharing arrangements, but constraints, which nevertheless could be overcome with the adoption of various strategies.

Mobile independence and decisional autonomy

Participants consistently raised two issues, which we call 'mobility independence' and 'decisional autonomy' in relation to their daily experiences of mobility. Every interviewee referred to at least one of the two issues, but in most cases both arguments were referred to several times. Both arguments are illustrated in the following in more detail.

[1] http://www.maxqda.com/ (last view: 01.01.2014)

Maintaining independence from others: every participant mentioned mobility independence at least once during the interview. The following quote provides an insight into a typical answer given by one interviewee to the question of what mobility means to them:

'It (mobility) means being very independent and able to go to places. The bus services up here are really good and I'm really happy and that is important. You don't need anybody because the (bus) connections are excellent and you can get anywhere you like really quickly. That is very important for me. Yes, this is really very important to me', (Mrs. Thomson, 76).

For Mrs. Thomson, who lives in a single-household in a suburban area without a car, her mobility experience is directly interwoven with her understanding of mobile independence. Hence, the mobility she mentions is concerned with the ongoing maintenance of her individual independence. Thus, by independence she means being able to manage her daily mobility by utilizing her own resources in accordance with her abilities and without depending on others. It is this understanding of independence as 'doing things alone' on the basis of one's own physical and cognitive abilities that turned out to be the dominant meaning of independence. Hence, our interviewees point out that it is not just about reaching the destination but 'managing to get there', re-affirming their own capacity to do so. This issue of desired independence is well attested to in the gerontological literature. Plath [20], for instance, argues that the high value placed on independence can be understood against the backdrop of a society that is strongly influenced by liberal, individualist values, and is incorporated on the individual level. For older people, their status is a negotiated one. Declining physical prowess may mean that they are seen to be more dependent by others but on the basis of our evidence they are also fiercely determined to maintain independence.

Maintaining decisional autonomy: Although decisional autonomy relates to mobility independence, it is distinct from it. Quotes like following clearly express this position:

'Yes, a great deal [mobility means] everything. Everything... the decision too, just the thought of it even I CAN go, if I want... that is so important, you know? Even if I might not actually go anywhere but just... yes, just to know that if I wanted to go anywhere, I can just go to the garage, get in my car and drive off... and yes, I am scared of the day when that might not be the case any more', (Mrs. Martinez, 77).

Mrs. Marinez lives with her husband and two cars in a more rural area. Mobility is important for her as a means of maintaining and enhancing travel opportunities, rather than the travelling itself. In this way mobility is seen as a means of being autonomous in and through the capacity to make decisions about where, when and how to travel on one's own. Decisional autonomy refers to the way in which older people seek to maintain and maximize their choices. This issue of autonomous decision-making is in line with the findings of Sheller [25], or Urry [31] who show that decisional and executional autonomy are key aspects of our perception of freedom and that more mobility is widely considered a symbol and facilitator of that freedom. However, many of the interviewees stated fear of an uncertainty about the future:

'Well, err, I mean it's always just a question of time isn't it, how long you might still be able to drive a car. It might be over really quickly, you never know do you. It's something I think about of course; of course not all the time, but it is an important point', (Mrs. Harris, 75).

Mrs. Harris lives with her husband in a very rural area with two cars and demonstrates in this sequence her awareness about potentially rapid change in their mobility situation. Hence, while decisional autonomy is in general an important factor in mobile wellbeing, most participants also stated a fear of losing that autonomy in older age. Although all of the participants are still more or less satisfied with their current mobility, they also see it as endangered. Maintaining decisional autonomy 'while one can' seems to be tied up with making the most of current capacity in the knowledge that it may well be diminished in the future.

Independence and decisional autonomy in different transport modes

The concepts of *independence* and of *decisional autonomy* are interwoven but can be separated from each other on an analytical level. Their relative importance depends on the various transport modes being used.

Using private resources

People usually depend on a variety of resources to support mobility, including the car, bike, motorcycle or any other kind of vehicle that is appropriate for the person's surroundings. In our case the examples deal mainly with car usage. The 80-year old Mr. Moor who resides in a very low-density location area describes the advantages of car driving like this:

Interviewer: *'And you still drive don't you?'*
Mr. Moore: *'Of course, I always drive by car. It means a lot because it means I'm able to get out when I want. Although the bus stop is right before our house, the bus stops only twice a day when we are lucky (smiling). You need a car in order to do all the daily errands or if you want to get out in an emergency or anything like that, or go out to the theatre'*, (Mr. Moor, 80).

The car affords self-reliance in respect of both decisional autonomy and independence. In using the car, this interviewee can go to places he would not be able to reach by foot or by bus anymore. Thus, in keeping with Ziegler et al. [37] and Schwanen et al. [24], cars can function as 'compensation tools' to protect individual independence when physical functioning declines. Interestingly, Mr. Moor explains how he uses his 'car driver' capacities to occasionally extend a courtesy to older adults who cannot drive and whom he picks up when he sees them on his way. Thus he refers to the widespread belief that cars are the only transport mode that can provide people with the mobility and autonomy required to live a late modern life [31], and refers to the inequalities of having a car or not. In his understanding (*'You need a car in order to do all the daily errands')* it is necessary to offer rides to those who cannot otherwise manage their errands. Multiple studies – mostly set in car-dominated societies such as the USA and Australia – point out that being able to drive in later life is strongly related with self-reliance and independence [2]. On the other hand losing the driving license raises the prospect of a dependency which most older people strongly resent and wish to avoid [1]. Thus, as Mr. Moor describes, car driving brings a responsibility with it for the others who have no car or cannot drive (any more).

Decisional autonomy connects to one's ability to plan for oneself how to undertake journeys of whatever kind. Hence, decisional autonomy is highly connected with possessing a car. Driving means having the option of being mobile whenever one wants or needs [31]. This is in accordance with studies that examine driving cessation, where older people construct driving cessation as a loss of executional spontaneity [1]. Although decisional autonomy is also an important value for the younger ones, driving the own car can be particularly important for the older adults who more often live in low-density areas or have problems using public transportation. This is also stated in the interviews, when addressing the car as a *sine qua non* of mobility autonomy:

'I've got to have the feeling I can get in and drive off. [...] but I don't really NEED my own car, I don't use it every day. But I want it to be there, waiting in front of the door so it's there when I need it', (Mrs. Jackson, 64).

Mrs. Jackson who lives in a more urban location with good transport links sees the car as a symbolic representation of decisional autonomy. Further many participants stated that the car is the only transport mode, which allows translating immediate wishes into actions without the need for any detailed travel planning. Thus, the car is perfect for autonomous decision-making. The car allows the 'ageing car driver' spontaneity, independence and sense of control that cannot be replicated by other transport modes.

Using public transportation

With regard to public transportation, some interviewees also see independence in using buses, as is stated in the following:

'my mobility... as long as I can still walk to the bus stop, use the bus, I'm happy. It's my independence. I'd like to remain independent actually. And for me that means the bus. Not the car, because I don't own one', (Mrs. Martinez, 77).

Mrs. Martinez refers to the car as the transportation mode of choice but clarifies that taking the bus allows her to feel independent as well, since there is no need to ask for support. Interestingly, public services of this kind are not perceived as autonomy reducing, but as an infrastructural 'right'- a service that are all entitled to use and - given the fact that one pays to use the service- which confers no particular sense of obligation. By and large, our interviewees had no difficulty in planning journeys in such a way that they fitted in with timetable constraints. They often reported noting or accessing information about return journeys on the back of the hand, in short notes, or by using route leaflets, so they could refer to them as needed and react more flexibly to contingencies. Thus, decisional autonomy is restricted in the case of public transportation because timetables and routes restrict the flexibility of people's mobility. Regardless, mobility depends of course very much on people's residential location and its traffic connections. This pertains not only to the distance to the nearest bus stop, but also the frequency of buses during different times of the day and days of the week.

Using private resources publicly - Ridesharing

Ridesharing, by definition, entails a degree of mutual dependency. Driver and passenger depend on each other in several respects, for instance, in matching logistical concerns like time of departure, pick up places and return. Further, people have to cooperate by negotiating some agreement about the 'intensity' of interaction - is one expected to talk? How much? Laurier, for instance, showed that both parties have to find a way defining and negotiating their mutual relationship [12]. Further, Sherlock compares the roles of passenger and driver with the roles of being a good 'host' and a good 'guest' [26]. Thus while guest and host are background 'politeness' categories to driver and passenger they are resources for moral assessment of each person's conduct during the journey. These kinds of relationship are, of course, not those found between family members or between longstanding, good friends. There, such issues are more or less settled as habitual. Hence, there does appear to be some asymmetry of decisional influence depending on these roles. The following sequence gives a good glimpse in typical statements about the 'guest' and 'host' role:

[Talking about sharing regular rides with her neighbor and going to a particular bar] 'Of course I depend on the driver. If the driver wants to go to Xbar, drinking a coffee, I have to follow if I want or not. I don't like the Xbar. And in return when driving on Saturday to the market I would not go to Xbar. Then people can decide whether they want to go to Xbar or drive back home with me', (Mrs. White, 58).

There seems to be a mutual understanding that passengers as good guests have a duty to orient towards driver's habits as Mrs. White states who lives in a single household and possess her own car and often practices ridesharing as driver and as co-driver. She explained further that she would expect to accommodate driver wishes in respect of start times for instance, and would not expect equal consideration from the driver. Hence, there is a mutual understanding that passengers should make few demands on drivers largely because there is a sense of having been 'invited'. Drivers, in short, are perceived as having more rights in negotiating the arrangements.

Further, several interviewees expressed personal issues within decisional autonomy in ridesharing situations. Since the ride opportunity is not entirely predictable with respect to time, route, etc., the potential passenger has to deal with a considerable amount of uncertainty. Relying on someone else means lining activities up with the schedule of others, at least to some extent. The following sequence illustrates an issue that was stated by participants quite often and can be seen as a result of the passengers' loss of decisional autonomy:

'[With ridesharing] you've just got to follow suit, no matter how or when she's driving. I have to watch what anyone's doing, I can't look (when shopping) where I want and how long I want and what I want. Thus, I prefer to do it alone, you know [...] That's all those things, no, well it is (on my own) more independent', (Mrs. Williams, 73).

This respondent practices ridesharing regularly, but shows an awareness of this unequal relationship. The passenger has to adjust to the driver without even knowing what exactly s/he is adjusting to. In contrast to public transport, decisional autonomy is reduced for passengers because they are less able to plan independently. Thus, and in summary, the analysis has shown that ridesharing is characterized by participants with attitudes that fit uneasily with basic needs of mobile wellbeing: namely independence and decisional autonomy.

Organization of ridesharing practice

As we already mentioned above, however, ridesharing is quite popular among older adults and frequently used. This is because they adopt a range of strategies to cope with these demands that makes sharing rides a more pleasurable travel mode.

Preserving independence

As already mentioned above, the 'guest' and 'host' analogy in ridesharing practice, including gratitude, can cause a feeling of dependence on the driver, in contrast to using a bus, or renting a car. However, interviewees reported about a practice that can be described as 'lift giving' and 'gift giving', that can lower the experience of dependence.

'To square things you can take some flowers or a plant to say thank you now and again. They (the drivers) don't want anything but just to say thank you, you can get some flowers. Just a little plant. But I don't do it so often because they don't want you to. Like they say, it doesn't matter whether three people are in the car or four', (Mrs. Thomson, 64).

This woman lives in a single household directly into the city center. Although she possesses her own car, she regularly practices ridesharing with a woman who picks her up for errands and other routine chores. Giving a little gift like a flower or spending money on a coffee involves gift giving [14], and hence constitutes a form of reciprocity. Informal gift exchange economies are sometimes romanticized as being more social than the 'cold' value exchange economies, where one acquires a commodity or service by paying the price. However, gift exchange economies do not come for free, but involve quite complex and unspoken rules, governing timing, appropriateness and emotionality. The aforementioned roles of 'host' and 'guest' establish a particular kind of reciprocal social relationship, different in their implication from those of family member or paid service provider. The statement from Mrs. Thomson shows that people are aware of this underlying reciprocal paradigm of ridesharing and in consequence develop strategies in order to maintain their independence. Concerning this, Nicolini [18, p. 62], for instance, pointed out that 'reciprocating a gift too soon is bound to look like a payment, therefore negating the disinterested nature of the original act and creating embarrassment; conversely, delaying the reciprocation too much is bound to be understood as ungratefulness'. Establishing reciprocity needs to be socially negotiated and is difficult to establish in such ambivalent circumstances. Given the central importance of the moral order in these arrangements, it is obvious that the relation between driver and passenger can vary across a number of dimensions. The degree to which one can impose on another will depend to extent on the degree of familiarity both parties share. Sons, for instance, have a different set of obligations towards mothers than they do towards their drinking buddies. Casual friends are very different in status from 'good' friends. In each instance, the kind of reciprocity that might be entailed is very different.

As already stated, there is, in some circumstances, a great reluctance to impose someone when asking for rides. In particular, the intricacies of asking relatives and friends for rides were discussed with regard to the increasing level of dependence caused by asking for a ride too often. In particular it turned out that the interviewees are very careful when family members are involved. Statements like the following are frequently found in our sample:

'No, no, no, no, no, no, no! I don't want to pester anyone if I can help it. I always see to it that I can manage by myself, if possible', (Mrs. Gracia, 78).

Mrs. Gracia, one of the more 'fragile' users who lives with her daughter in a remote rural area and has no driving license, nevertheless expressed an aversion to asking family members for a lift. She further indicated that this was because she wished to avoid exploiting 'obligations' and preferred asking friends because some form of reciprocity was easier to negotiate. This wish not to impose is fairly consistently expressed in our sample. In sum, interviewees stated two strategies that provide some relief from the sense of dependency in ridesharing situations. This is to make use of the principle of reciprocity and to establishing a flexible economy that can be adapted to the specific kind of relationship between driver and passenger.

Preserving descicional autonomy

An aspect of ridesharing that is surprisingly common is that in many cases ridesharing arrangements are predicated on a common activity, such as club visits, going to the theater or cinema, or visiting friends. Ridesharing arrangements connected through a shared activity have the advantage that participants can more easily orient to the obligations entailed in an activity like shopping, club visits, going to theater or cinema or visiting friends. Hence, there are two kinds of activities that are particularly well suited for ridesharing: regular activities and spontaneous ridesharing invitations. In the first case travelling together not only enhances the experience in these circumstances, but has a pragmatic element, as well. The coordination of ridesharing within regular activities is much easier because it is based on similar, anticipated, commitments, as the following quote from Mrs. Thomson reporting about her ridesharing experiences, illustrates:

'*Well yes, they're fixed... well, there's a group of us who do things together... sometimes we drive to the cinema ... and erm yes, then you just ask do you want to go this evening or maybe tomorrow and then one person says, yes, listen I'll drive or [someone else says] I'll drive...That's what it's like'*, (Mrs. Thomson, 64).

Hence, there are some trips that are more suitable for ridesharing than others. However, in the case of regular mutual activities the activity has fixed borders. No negotiation about start and end time is necessary and there are few uncertainties caused by different interests (as long as all parties agree to limit the trip to the joint activity). Interviewees like the Mrs. Thomson report on developed routines for coordinating regular shared rides, such as meeting points and times. Thus, while single trips have to be coordinated with all parties in detail, regular ridesharing trips can be planned on a long-term basis and thus do not have negative impacts on decisional autonomy. The second kind of activity, spontaneous invitation, also has no negative consequences. Such unforeseen ride offers are valued as a win rather than a loss of decisional autonomy. In summary, constraints on decisional autonomy are reduced in ridesharing situations when certain kinds of activity are in question: Spontaneous ride offers that can provide a welcomed opportunity, or regular rides providing a long-term and routine planning opportunity.

CONCLUSION

This focus on the experiences of older adults' mobility and ridesharing, we argue, provides new insights into the ridesharing practices of this particular user group and can inspire ridesharing design.

Elderly ridesharing practice

Although the interview study was conducted with a heterogeneous group of older adults that differ in age (from 58-80 years), gender, marital status, or population density, they all have a positive attitude towards ridesharing and think that a mobile ridesharing system would improve their mobility situation. Like the literature suggests [23] informal ridesharing is a common and frequently used travel mode. In our sample of 21 older adults about the half of the interviewees make regularly use of ridesharing, but all are experienced with this particular kind of travel mode, more or less frequently.

In our study we followed authors like Ziegler et al. [37], Kaiser [11], and Steg [28] who emphasize the need to take subjective meanings of mobility into consideration, but specifically in relation to older adults' ridesharing experiences. One of the major observations was that although ridesharing can be a good transportation alternative either for the older adults who live in low-density areas, or have problems using public transportation, or the car, it seems not to be motivated by such issues. Hence, lacking infrastructure or a bad health condition does not primarily cause the indigence for a lift. Moreover, ridesharing takes place when people share the same destinations and particularly when undertaking joint activities. Further, findings show in accordance with the literature that mobile independence and decisional autonomy are central values for older adults' mobility experience [13]. However, it was astonishing to see, that particularly ridesharing is problematic because of these points, but is a quite popular and common transport mode at the same time. This gives reason to search for strategies older adults use to organize their ridesharing practice.

We discovered that interviewees regularly indicated negotiated, delicate ways in which principles of reciprocity are mediated in the driver-passenger relationship, and that this is used as a means to maintain independence in ridesharing contexts. This delicacy, contrary to the existing ridesharing literature on payment systems (which tends to the view that the main issue is providing adequate motivation for the driver [2]), suggests that a much more careful analysis of motivational elements is needed when dealing with older people. Establishing a balanced reciprocity between both parties of the driver and passenger is based on their relationship and the kind of ridesharing conducted. Further passengers are more likely to accept ride offers instead of asking for one, in order to keep their independence.

Like the desire for mobile independence, decisional autonomy, understood as flexible movement, turned out of special importance for the older adults, too. It means having the capacity to make decisions about where, when and how to travel on one's own. This makes the car, where possible, a preferred option that allows the older driver spontaneity, independence and sense of control that cannot be replicated by other transport modes. Although ridesharing creates some difficulties in relation to decisional autonomy, as we have seen, there are circumstances where autonomy is subordinate to other factors. Two in particular seem to outweigh this need. Firstly, spontaneous ride offers are easily accepted and secondly long-term ridesharing arrangements based on a regular and organized schedule are welcome.

Although we have no comparison with younger reference groups, there are some suggestions in the data that older adults interpret independent mobility and decisional autonomy in their own way. Hence, our interviewees point out that it is not just about reaching the destination but 'managing to get there', re-affirming their own capacity to do so, as long as they are able to do so. For the older adults independence and decisional autonomy are values that may be diminished in the near future, and thus, gain of importance.

Insights on ridesharing ICT

Our analysis demonstrates that HCI research on ridesharing for older adults should address ridesharing as a social practice rather than a transportation mode shifting people from place A to B. While ridesharing turned out to be a desirable objective in general, its practical implementation depends on a set of social issues, which relate to decisional autonomy, and to independence. These issues should be applied in ridesharing design additionally to issues discussed in literature already like trust [16], privacy [21], or security [33].

It would be naive to imagine that such insights lead directly to design decisions. Rather, we see these conclusions as aiding in the construction of the design space. That is, they point to the kinds of issue that need to be taken into account both in terms of possible constraints on design and in terms of avenues to explore. Thus and for instance, an examination of the concept of 'independence' and what it means for older adults has implications for the kind of payment system we might envisage. In most existing platforms, reciprocity is established exclusively via financial balancing. Among older adults, the issue of reciprocity and its concomitant obligations is nuanced, not only with respect to what payment might be negotiated as appropriate but also to when such payments might be made, if at all. As we have intimated, older people have a range of experiences in respect of their social networks, patterns of friendship and family relations. These subtle arrangements should be addressed by the design, giving the users the right to determine the kind of ridesharing conducted and what kind of reciprocity should be conducted. Beside classical paying systems, one can think for example on regular ridesharing journeys with an alternating driver where the system might remember users on the joint activity and the driver.

Further, there is a self- evident demand for mobile autonomy in our sample, but this is mediated by particular kinds of social activity with particular kinds of people. Joint activities which implicate friends and others in existing networks and which are geared to regular, repeated and routine activities are likely to be facilitated by ridesharing arrangements. Of course, to function adequately, such systems would need to provide a simple means for older people to delineate and limit who ride offers might be made to and in what circumstances. Additionally, such facilities enable participants to solve the issue of return journeys and to lower coordination effort in general, since people attend the same event and time and destination are usually tied to the event itself whilst at the same time supporting existing social networks and minimizing uncertainty. Otherwise, spontaneous ride offers can provide a welcome opportunity for traveling. In this case the design should be orientated towards easy and fast design solutions for offering rides and the design should incorporate features that help to create awareness about offers.

Lastly, ridesharing should be integrated into a pool of other mobility opportunities that do not exclusively depend on private ridesharing arrangements, but are integrated with public transport and other infrastructures that assure certain reliability. Ridesharing is of limited value to older passengers if it does not allow them to plan for contingent circumstances or changed plans. Such an integrated multi-modal platform would be of most value if it provided information not only about ridesharing opportunities but also about other modes of transport. Ridesharing, in this perspective, is one part of an enlarged mobility option that maximizes independence and decisional autonomy.

In sum, the focus on older adults' ridesharing experiences originates in joint activities, and offers orientation, reciprocity, and multimodality as design inspirations. Findings show that matching demands, transaction costs and social acceptance should not be addressed separately, but are related to each other in and through the social practice of ridesharing and the social situation in which people travel and meet.

ACKNOWLEDGMENTS

We thank all interviewees for their participation, our student assistants for transcription work, our local partners for their support in addressing participants and the University Heidelberg. Further we thank Gunnar Stevens for helpful comments and the BMBF for funding this project.

REFERENCES

1. Adler, G. and Rottunda, S. Older adults' perspectives on driving cessation. Journal of Aging studies 20, 3 (2006), 227–235.
2. Allen, J.L. human-center ridesharing-A sustainable solution. CHI, ACM, (2009).
3. Beswick, A.D., Rees, K., Dieppe, P., et al. Complex interventions to improve physical function and maintain independent living in elderly peoples. The Lancet 371, 9614 (2008), 725–735.
4. Brereton, M., Roe, P., Foth, M., Bunker, J.M., and Buys, L. Designing participation in agile ridesharing with mobile social software. Proc. of OzCHI (2009), 257–260.

5. Coughlin, J.F. Technology and the Future of Aging. Journal of Rehabilitation Research and Development 38, 1 (2001).

6. Dumbaugh, E. Designing Communities to Enhance the Safety and Mobility of Older Adults. Journal of Planning Literature 23, 1 (2008), 17–36.

7. Fobker, S. and Grotz, R. Everyday mobility of elderly people in different urban settings. Urban Studies 43, 1 (2006), 99–118.

8. Ghelawat, S., Radke, K., and Brereton, M. Interaction, privacy and profiling considerations in local mobile social software. Proc. of OzCHI (2010), 376–379.

9. Handke, V. and Jonuschat, H. Flexible Ridesharing: New Opportunities and Service Concepts for Sustainable Mobility. Springer, 2012.

10. Hansen, E.G., Gomm, M.L., Bullinger, A.C., and Moslein, K.M. A community–based toolkit for designing ride–sharing services. International Journal of Innovation and Sustainable Development 5, 1 (2010), 80–99.

11. Kaiser, H.J. Mobility in Old Age Beyond the Transportation Perspective. Journal of Applied Gerontology 28, 4 (2009), 411–418.

12. Laurier, E., Lorimer, H., Brown, B., et al. Driving and 'Passengering': Notes on the Ordinary Organization of Car Travel. Mobilities 3, 1 (2008), 1–23.

13. Lord, S., Després, C., and Ramadier, T. When mobility makes sense: A qualitative and longitudinal study of the daily mobility of the elderly. Journal of Environmental psychology 31, 1 (2011), 52–61.

14. Mauss, M. The Gift: The Form and Reason for Exchange in Archaic Societies, trans. WD Halls. New York and London: WW Norton, (1990).

15. Mirisaee, S.H., Brereton, M., and Roe, P. Bridging the representation and interaction challenges of mobile context-aware computing: designing agile ridesharing. Proc. of OzCHI, ACM (2011), 221–224.

16. Mirisaee, S.H. A human-centred context-aware approach to develop open-standard agile ridesharing using mobile social networks. Proc. of OzCHI (2010), 445–448.

17. Mollenkopf, H., Marcellini, F., Ruoppila, I., Széman, Z., and Tacken, M. Enhancing mobility in later life. Ios Press, Amsterdam, 2005.

18. Nicolini, D. Practice Theory, Work, and Organization: An Introduction. Oxford University Press, 2013.

19. Ozenc, F.K., and Morris, J.H. Adapt-a-ride: understanding the dynamics of commuting preferences through an experience design framework. Proc. of Designing Pleasurable Products and Interfaces, (2011), 61.

20. Plath, D. Independence in Old Age: The Route to Social Exclusion? British Journal of Social Work 38, 7 (2008), 1353–1369.

21. Radke, K., Brereton, M., Mirisaee, S., Ghelawat, S., Boyd, C., and Nieto, J.G. Tensions in developing a secure collective information practice-the case of agile ridesharing. In Human-Computer Interaction–INTERACT 2011. Springer, 2011, 524–532.

22. Rosenbloom, S. The Mobility Needs of Older Americans. Taking the High Road, TRB, (2004), 227–54.

23. Scheiner, J. Does the car make elderly people happy and mobile? European Journal of Transport and Infrastructure Research 6, 2 (2006), 151–172.

24. Schwanen, T., Banister, D., and Bowling, A. Independence and mobility in later life. Geoforum 43, 6 (2012), 1313–1322.

25. Sheller, M. and Urry, J. Mobile Transformations of `Public' and `Private' Life. Theory, Culture & Society 20, 3 (2003), 107–125.

26. Sherlock, K. Revisiting the concept of hosts and guests. Tourist Studies 1, 3 (2001), 271–295.

27. Silvis, J.B. Connecting Social Networks, Ridesharing, and Mobility: A Spectrum of Seniors' Behavior. ProQuest, 2008.

28. Steg, L. Car use: lust and must. Instrumental, symbolic and affective motives for car use. Transportation Research Part A: Policy and Practice 39, 2 (2005), 147–162.

29. Steger-Vonmetz, D.C. Improving modal choice and transport efficiency with the virtual ridesharing agency. 2005. Proc. of IEEE, IEEE (2005), 994–999.

30. Teodorović, D. and Dell'Orco, M. Mitigating traffic congestion: solving the ride-matching problem by bee colony optimization. Transportation Planning and Technology 31, 2 (2008), 135–152.

31. Urry, J. Mobilities. Polity, Cambridge, UK; Malden, MA, 2007.

32. Wash, R., Hemphill, L., and Resnick, P. Design decisions in the RideNow project. Proc. of GROUP (2005), 132–135.

33. Wessels, R., Pueboobpaphan, R., Bie, J., and van Arem, B. Integrating online social networks with ridesharing systems. (2010) www.pooll.nl/wpcontent/uploads/2010/02/Paperv5.pdf. Online [Last accessed on 1/01/14].

34. Witzel, A., and H. Reiter: The Problem-centred Interview. *Qualitative Social Research.* Vol. 1. No. 1. 2000.

35. Wulf, V., Rohde, M., Pipek, V., and Stevens, G. Engaging with practices. Proc. of CSCW (2011), 505–512.

36. Xing, X., Warden, T., Nicolai, T., and Herzog, O. SMIZE: a spontaneous ride-sharing system for individual urban transit. Springer (2009), 165–176.

37. Ziegler, F. and Schwanen, T. I like to go out to be energised by different people. Ageing and Society 31, 5 (2011), 758.

From Checking On to Checking In: Designing for Low Socio-Economic Status Older Adults

Ingrid Arreola[1], Zan Morris[1], Matthew Francisco[1], Kay Connelly[1], Kelly Caine[2], Ginger White[1]

[1]Indiana University
919 E 10th St; Bloomington, IN 47408
{inarreol,morris22,connelly,giwhite}@indiana.edu

[2]Clemson University
McAdams Hall; Clemson, SC 29634
caine@clemson.edu

ABSTRACT

In this paper we describe the design evolution of a novel technology that collects and displays presence information to be used in the homes of older adults. The first two iterations, the Ambient Plant and Presence Clock, were designed for high socio-economic status (SES) older adults, whereas the Check-In Tree was designed for low SES older adults. We describe how feedback from older adult participants drove our design decisions, and give an in-depth account of how the Check-In Tree evolved from concept to a final design ready for in situ deployment.

Author Keywords

Aging in Place; Older Adults; Caregivers, Peer production.

ACM Classification Keywords

H.5.m. Information interfaces and presentation (e.g., HCI): Miscellaneous.

INTRODUCTION

The population of older adults around the world is growing faster than the number of people available to help provide care for them [5]. While previous research [e.g., 8-9,11] has investigated how technologies can be used to help older adults age-in-place, much of this research has been conducted with higher socio-economic status (SES) participants. In this paper, we focus on designing technologies specifically for low-SES older adults. We define low-SES as older adults whose household income is at or below 200% of the federal poverty line (for 2012 this was an annual income of $20,000 or less [4]). We focus on this special population for a variety of reasons including that the area is under-researched, members of this population typically report worse health status, have more limitations on their physical functioning, have poorer overall health outcomes and generally have fewer resources with which to deal with these limitations [1-2]. Thus, there is an opportunity for our designs to have significant impact.

CHI 2014, April 26 - May 01 2014, Toronto, ON, Canada.
Copyright 2014 ACM 978-1-4503-2473-1/14/04...$15.00.
http://dx.doi.org/10.1145/2556288.2557084

In this paper, we describe the design evolution of a remote sensing technology through three iterations, describing how each instantiation was adapted to meet the specific needs of the target population of rural and urban-dwelling low-SES older adults. The technologies we describe are part of a larger suite of tools designed for a single household installation, which includes an older adult-centered method for receiving short messages, a magnet board for easy data entry, and tools for privacy controls. The focus of this short paper is on two of the other technologies in this suite: the Presence Clock and the Check-in Tree.

CHECKING ON: AMBIENT PLANT & PRESENCE CLOCK

The ambient plant (Figure 1a) was designed to connect older adults to their remote caregivers while respecting the privacy of both parties. A set of paired plants allows each party to gauge the activity of the other (as detected by a motion sensor) on their local plant (as displayed by LEDs). One difference between this and other similar technologies (e.g., the digital family portrait [9]) is that activity monitoring is displayed reciprocally, meaning that a caregiver can see activity from the older adult and the older adult can see activity from the caregiver.

The ambient plant was tested in situ in one pair of homes with one older adult and one caregiver for 2 weeks, and was evaluated in a focus group study with 65 older adults in which participants interacted with a variety of prototypes in a living lab and provided feedback [8]. In general, participants described how they thought using the technology would help them feel more connected to a caregiver, and caregivers felt that they would feel comfortable that the older adult was active, and not in need of assistance. On the other hand, participants expressed concern with "missing" the other person's motion since the LED lights on the Ambient Plant were only shining when the paired plant sensed activity. This led us to the design decision that we needed to include some type of activity history in the display.

The Presence Clock (Figure 1b) extended the idea of sharing motion information between paired objects with a historical display. Each clock is made from an existing analog desk clock modified with a motion sensor mounted on top. The sensor transmits detected motion to its paired clock. Each clock had 48 yellow LEDs placed around the clock face with each LED corresponding to a single 15 minute interval, affording both an easy representation of

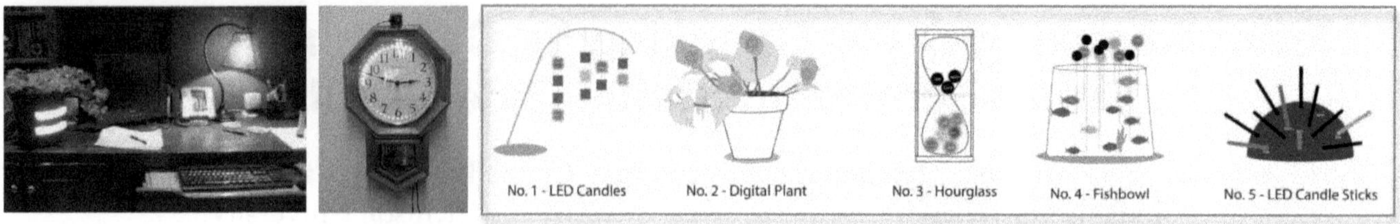

(a) (b) (c)

Figure 1: (a) Ambient Plant (b) Presence Clock (c) Check-in design ideas

current activity, as well as a historical account of motion detected over the last 12 hours.

Previous researchers evaluated the Presence Clock in the homes of 4 older adults and their informal caregivers as part of a larger study of a suite of technologies [12]. In these studies, the clock was well received by both older adults and their families. Comments were similar to comments about the Ambient Plant with respect to enhanced feelings of connection.

SOCIO-ECONOMIC STATUS

In our current research, we are focused on understanding how technologies can be designed to assist low SES older adults in both urban and rural settings. We conducted day long (i.e., eight hour) contextual observations in the homes of eight low-income, community-dwelling, older adults [13]. The contextual observations explored participants' physical environment (i.e., house, neighborhood and town), regular social interactions and daily routines. Unlike their higher-SES counterparts, the lower-SES older adults did not necessarily have a single informal caregiver.

Previous work in HCI [e.g., 6, 9] has focused on designing for higher-income older adults where technologies support a one-to-one (caregiver-to-older adult) relationship. In our work, similar to findings in work with another low-SES population (asthma patients [7]), we found that the low-SES older adults in our study had a much richer ecosystem of family members, service providers and peers who often served as informal caregivers.

The low-SES participants we observed relied heavily on their peer-group for a variety of needs, including socializing and running errands:

P1: "When I first moved in, the guy around the corner used to take me to stores and stuff like that, and cash my check. Every time I'm going to go to the grocery store I get him to go and take me."

However, these same participants also described how they were loathe to burden the traditional one-to-one informal caregiver: a family member. Participants described how individual family members were already struggling to take care of their families (including small children), and often multiple jobs. These findings suggest that we need to reconsider the model of care for which we design, from a one-to-one caregiver-to-older adult model to a peer-to-peer model in which older adults help care for each other.

The peer approach has many advantages. By replacing the individual caregiver with a peer group, each older adult has more eyes watching for them in case there is a problem. There is also less social stigma associated with asking about the day-to-day business of peers. This allows for less friction in terms of communication and may enhance activity within a community. Finally, strong peer groups are a strong motivation for older adults to be more active in their community, both physically and mentally, which can lead to a healthier lifestyle. This structure allows older adults to maintain their independence, which is a value that is highly important for older adults [11].

CHECKING-IN: CHECK-IN TREE

To generate ideas for a peer-based check-in system, we revisited findings from the contextual observations we conducted with low-SES older adults, spent time sifting through and categorizing designs from catalogs and stores that sell objects to older adults, and held weekly design sessions where we asked researchers to generate ideas. We also recruited a small group of older adult to serve as informal consultants [n=3].

We noted that older adults often devise a check-in system in which they can indicate to a neighbor that they have gotten up in the morning (e.g., turn on/off the porch light) and the neighbor agrees to call if they are not up by a certain time [10]. This system only works if someone nearby is willing and able. However we found that many low-SES older adults lack both a willing, co-located neighbor and reliable transportation, making it difficult to physically check-in on each other. In our designs we sought to remove some of these constraints and extended the idea of a morning check-in to utilize peers in a remote check-in prototype, allowing older adults who are not immediate neighbors to check on each other.

We developed five design ideas for a daily check-in display (Figure 1c) that show check-in information for a small group. Since we did not yet have information about the properties of the social groups of participants for these initial designs, we left some flexibility with respect to size of the group, but generally used 4 to 12 as our initial range of group sizes. From these five designs we brainstormed how we could build each one and do so at the scale required for our future field studies. Designs 2 – 4 (Figure 1c) proved to be very difficult to build since they involved parts with either complex movements (3 and 4) or simple

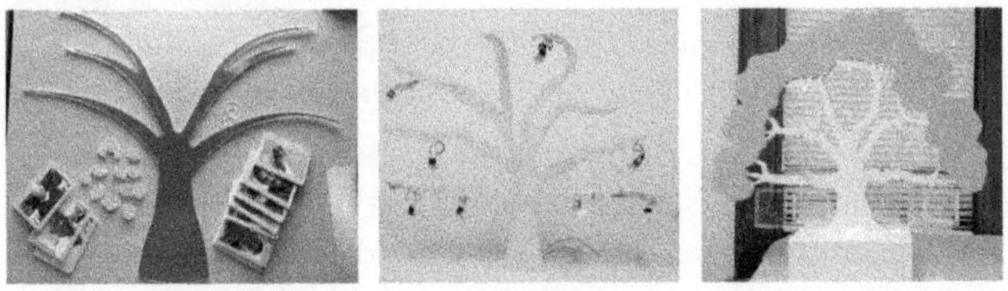

(a) (b) (c)

Figure 2: Three iterations of prototypes: (a) foam core, (b) tree without leaves, (c) final prototype.

movement but complex construction (2). We decided that an interesting grouping of non-moving lights that represent group members such as with designs 1 and 2 represented the best balance of building requirements and design constraints. At this point we began breadboarding the circuits, researching wireharness materials, working out costs, and developing an online control system for lights.

Check-In Tree

The final check-in prototype is a tree holding 8 picture frames (Figure 2c). Similar to the Ambient Plant, a tree may spark positive, healthy sentiments for the users. Trees are often used to represent families and to depict an individual's lineage. In our case, we use the tree to invoke the concept of a community and a sense of connection to peers. This tree design proved to be most well liked by our design team and had a straight- forward implementation.

In the final design, older adults have their own Check-In Tree, with a picture of everyone in their peer group, including themselves, hanging on a branch. Each picture has its own LED. In the early hours of the morning, all LEDs start to pulse gently. When an older adult gets up for the day, they press a button at the base of the tree to indicate that they are up (i.e. "checking-in"), causing the LED associated with their picture to switch from pulsing to on. This change is propagated to all of the trees in the group. In this way, an older adult simply needs to glance at their Check-In Tree to tell whose LED is still pulsing, and thus know who has not checked in that day. Having the LEDs pulse when someone has not checked in draws attention to those older adults who need to be checked on in person or by phone. The Check-In Tree empowers older adults to use and develop their knowledge of each other's daily routines and special circumstances, reducing unnecessary stress caused by false alarms in alert systems.

Finally, the Check-In Tree also has a switch for older adults to indicate when they will not be home for extended periods. When an older adult turns the switch off, the LEDs associated with their picture will turn off on all of the connected trees. In addition, all of the LEDs on the Check-In Tree in their home will also turn off, so they are incentivized to keep their trees on when they are home.

Evolution of Tree Form

Unlike other research (e.g., [14]) that focuses primarily on the aesthetic of a user's home and the relationship between the user and their possessions, we built several prototypes that allowed us to investigate functionality, aesthetics, cost, and a simplified construction process.

(a) (b) (c)

Figure 3: Three types of trees: (a) Oak, (b) Willow, (c) Juniper

The first prototype (Figure 2a) was a foam board construction of two tree types and two photo frame designs. Several challenges arose, including that the branches needed to hold picture frames. We developed a design that would allow frames to hang from branches and supply power, ground, and two data wires to each LED module. Foam board allowed us to evaluate affects of different branch layouts on the position of electronics and tree frames. It also gave us a sense of scale and size.

The second prototype was a 20" wide tree cut from 5/8" plywood (Figure 2b). This frame had several benefits: it could easily house the wires to power the LEDs; the thickness of the wood made hanging tree frames easy; grooves for LEDs controlled the direction of the lights; and the channels designed to hold wires made for an easy template to measure wires and solder them to their LEDs.

At this point, we further explored the aesthetics of the prototype by constructing three different types of trees (Figure 3): an oak, a willow, and a juniper. The picture frames were made with acrylic glass with an etched border to diffuse the light from the LED. For the frame border, we selected one simple design based on the ability of our CNC router to cleanly etch the pattern. We also explored the placing of the frames on the tree, hanging them below the branches like fruit.

Based on feedback within our research group and from our older adult consultants, the oak tree was selected as the final design. At this point in the design process, there were many fine-tuning details considered to make the tree look more aesthetically pleasing to the user and to finalize the functionality. The base was designed with the button and switch for easy user interaction. There were several iterations of LED placement, frame placement, and shape of leaves. Originally, the oak tree had a few tiny leaves and was overall very bare. One older adult consultant worried the points of the branches posed a safety issue; therefore, the leaf clumps were added to address safety issues and improve aesthetics. We sought to meet the aesthetic desires of older adults, identify ways to attach personal meaning (as suggested by [6]) to the devices, and increase the possibility that the technology would help participants achieve greater independence with each iteration. Finally, a back covering was added to hide the wire harness.

DISCUSSION

All three prototypes (Ambient Plant, Presence Clock and Check-In Tree) were created with a user-centered design process and tailored to the needs and desires of the target populations while fitting within a tight budget and short schedule for construction. Our research showed that reciprocity was greatly valued in these prototypes, and we sought to preserve that in the peer-based technology.

The nature of the shared data in the Presence Clock (i.e. real-time and historic presence) was less appropriate for a low SES population because they were unlikely to have a single informal caregiver. Instead, our participants relied more on peer support, which radically changed our design.

One design choice was to have each older adult's Check-In Tree include their own picture. Prior research suggested that older adults often liked to look and see what others could see about them [3]. The Presence Clock had this capability through a special tablet interface. The Check-In Tree includes this functionality within the prototype itself.

Once design choice of particular importance was to make the daily check-in a manual input (push the button), instead of an automatic one. We hope that by incorporating an interaction with the tree as part of their daily routine, older adults will feel more connected to their peers. However, this extra burden may reduce use of the tree, particularly for those older adults who have limited mobility. We have designed the tree such that the button interaction can easily be replaced with a motion sensor to automatically "check-in" an older adult if we find use is low or burdensome.

Another important design decision related to mobility was to design all three prototypes to blend in to a home's décor so that older adults will place them in commonly occupied spaces, such as a living room. This will encourage older adults to view and interact with these prototypes on a regular basis, even as their mobility declines.

Finally, the tree was designed with cost, ease of construction, and reusability/adaptability in mind. We are currently building 18 trees to be used for this research and as a platform for testing other ideas. The wooden tree can be filled with different circuits and different LEDs quite easily. It can be repainted and there is plenty of space for adding more ornamentation. It can be reprogrammed and adapted to further fit the needs of different user populations.

ACKNOWLEDGMENTS

This material is based upon work supported by the National Science Foundation under Grant No. IIS-1117860. We thank Meisi Huang for helping to create early tree designs.

REFERENCES

1. Balfour, J. L., & Kaplan, G. A. Neighborhood Environment and Loss of Physical Function in Older Adults: Evidence from the Alameda County Study. *American Journal of Epidemiology 155*, 6 (2002).
2. Cagney, K. A., Browning, C. R., & Wen, M. Racial Disparities in Self-Rated Health at Older Ages: What Difference Does the Neighborhood Make? *The Journals of Gerontology Series B: Psychological Sciences and Social Sciences 60*, 4 (2005) S181-S190.
3. Caine, K. E., Zimmerman, C. Y., Schall-Zimmerman, Z., Hazlewood, W. R., Camp, L. J., Connelly, K. H., Huber, L. L, & Shankar, K. DigiSwitch: A device to allow older adults to monitor and direct the collection and transmission of health information collected at home. *Journal of Medical Systems 35,* 5 (2011).
4. census.gov/hhes/www/poverty/data/threshld/index.html
5. Fleming, K. C. Evans, J. M. & Chukta, D. S. Caregiver and Clinician Shortages in an Aging Nation. *Mayo Clinical Proceedings 78*, 1026–1040 (2003).
6. Forlizzi, J. DiSalvo, C.F., Gemperle, F. Assistive Robotics and an Ecology of Elders Living Independently in Their Homes. *Human-Computer Interaction 19*, 1-2 (25-59) (2004).
7. Jeong, H.Y., Hayes, G.R., Yun, T-J, Sung, J-Y Abowd, G.D., and Arriaga, R.I. Act collectively: opportunities for technologies to support low-income children with asthma. In *Proc BCS Conf. on Human-Computer Interaction*, British Computer Society, (2011) 413-420.
8. Lorenzen-Huber, et al. Privacy, technology, and aging: A proposed framework. *Ageing International 36*, 2 (2011), 232-252.
9. Rowan, J., Mynatt, E. Digital family portrait field trial: Support for aging in place. In *Proc. CHI 2005*, ACM Press (2005), 521-530.
10. Rowles, G. D. & Bernard, M. *Environmental Gerontology: Making Meaningful Places in Old Age* (2013).
11. Rubinstein R., Kilbride J., Nagy S. *Elders Living Alone: Frailty and the Perception of Choice.* New York: Aldine de Grutyer, 1992. Print.
12. Shankar, K., Camp et al. "Aging, Privacy, and Home-Based Computing: Development of a Framework for Design." *IEEE Pervasive Computing*. December, 2012.
13. White, G., Connelly, K., Caine, K. Opportunities for ubiquitous computing in the homes of low SES older adults. *Ext. Abstracts Ubicomp* (2012).
14. Ylirisku, S. et al. Designing web-connected physical artefacts for the 'aesthetic' of the home. In *Proc. CHI 2013*, ACM Press (2013), 909-918.

Invisible Connections: Investigating Older People's Emotions and Social Relations Around Objects

[1]Kate Vaisutis, [1]Margot Brereton, [2]Toni Robertson, [3]Frank Vetere, [2]Jeannette Durick, [3]Bjorn Nansen, [1]Laurie Buys
[1]Queensland University of Technology, Brisbane {k.vaisutis, m.brereton, l.buys}@qut.edu.au
[2]Faculty of Engineering and Information Technology, University of Technology, Sydney{toni.robertson, jeannette.durick}@uts.edu.au
[3]Dept of Computing and Information Systems, The University of Melbourne{f.vetere, nansenb}@unimelb.edu.au

ABSTRACT
The advent of the Internet of Things creates an interest in how people might interrelate through and with networks of internet enabled objects. With an emphasis on fostering social connection and physical activity among older people, this preliminary study investigated objects that people over the age of 65 years viewed as significant to them. We conducted contextual interviews in people's homes about their significant objects in order to understand the role of the objects in their lives, the extent to which they fostered emotional and social connections and physical activity, and how they might be augmented through internet connection.

Discussion of significant objects generated considerable emotion in the participants. We identified objects of comfort and routine, objects that exhibited status, those that fostered independence and connection, and those that symbolized relationships with loved ones. These findings lead us to consider implications for the design of interconnected objects.

Author Keywords
Ageing; Internet of Things; Social Relations; Objects; Socio-material relations; Tangible Interaction

ACM Classification Keywords
H.5.. Information interfaces and presentation (e.g., HCI): H.5.3 Group and Organization Interfaces

INTRODUCTION
Applications for the Internet of Things (IoT) have been conceived of from an informational, machine-to-machine or monitoring perspective, with little regard to the people around the "things" (objects). Since people collect and interrelate around and with objects throughout their lives, we adopt a human-centred perspective to understand how objects currently foster social relations and physical activity and we explore the implications of these socio-physical relations with regard to the design of new technology that promotes ongoing social interaction in older adults.

It is well documented that humans benefit from having ongoing social connections. Continued socialization decreases the likelihood of becoming depressed, which in turn reduces the impact on the health system [5]. With the ageing population forecast to increase to 25% of the population in the next 30+ years, it is important to investigate ways to facilitate and extend independent living and foster social engagement. The paper aims to understand how this may be better facilitated through networks of people and their objects.

OUR RELATIONS WITH THINGS
Csikszentmihalyi [6] suggests there are 3 key reasons why we need things (objects): they give us the illusion of power; they serve as an extension of the self and they give permanence to the meaningful relationships in our lives. He suggests that "most of the things we make these days do not make life better in any material sense but instead serve to stabilize and order the mind." (p. 22)

Theories of socio-material relations articulated in the Social Studies of Science, Suchman [17], Orlikowski [16], Latour [13] have demonstrated how objects and social relations are mutually constituted. Our houses, offices, coffee pots, guns etc. materialize the relations between us. We inhabit and use objects and they in turn shape our interactions and our agency as we shape theirs.

Tangible and Embodied Interaction research [e.g. 7] has recognized the importance of understanding our embodied interaction with the physical world of materials, objects and other beings. Early work in tangible interaction emphasized the possibility of coupling digital and physical representations [11], while later work recognized the interweaving of the material/physical and the social aspects of interaction from a design perspective [10]. Some design work in domestic settings such as the history tablecloth [8] and the magic box [18] have investigated interesting properties of internet enabled objects. However, research has largely been based on discrete tangible and embodied

CHI 2014, April 26 - May 01, 2014, Toronto, ON, Canada.

ACM 978-1-4503-2473-1/14/04...$15.00.
http://dx.doi.org/10.1145/2556288.2557314

systems and has not examined multiple networked objects embedded in everyday lives. As a precursor to this study the "habituated objects" that support the habits and routines of an elderly person were investigated [4].

Leonardi et al., [15] considered the functional and emotional geography of older people's homes and concluded that new technologies should fit this landscape. For example, safety-related technologies are more acceptable in the bathroom than the bedroom, which is seen as a more intimate and emotionally laden space. Other studies [1] [2] [9] support the notion that the domestic space is a complex, changing environment with multiple variables that need to be considered when designing technology to assist the patient/resident with their at home healthcare/ rehabilitation programs.

The significance of exploring our relationship with our objects in the domestic environment has also been highlighted in the context of home archiving [12]. Van den Hoven et al [19] examines the ways in which everyday memories might be captured, stored and retrieved through the use of digital media. However the memories being digitally recorded are not specifically associated with everyday objects used in everyday life.

In this paper we investigate the social and physical relations around objects that are regarded as significant by older people in Australia. Through broadening our understanding of these relations we consider the implications for the design of Internet of Things technology that promotes social and emotional connection for older people.

METHODOLOGY

We explored the role of objects and social relations in place through contextual interviews [3] in the homes of 6 older Australians. The participants were over 65 years old and consisted of 4 men and 2 women from diverse backgrounds and life experience. They had lived in their respective homes from 2 up to nearly 40 years.

The participants were contacted by telephone to confirm their willingness to participate and were asked, at this time, to consider what might be their significant objects. This provided them the opportunity to think about their response ahead of the interview. "Significant" was framed as being really useful, provides pleasure or has sentimental value.

The interviews were audio recorded and the objects were photographed in place. Where permissible the objects were also video recorded. The original intention was to have the participant video the objects so that they could have control over what was recorded. This also meant that the participant would be behind the camera (not in front) thus protecting their identity and respecting their privacy. However, in practice, it would have been insensitive to ask this of them due to physical limitations of the different individuals and/or their home environment. One participant had recently undergone surgery, another used a walking frame, another lived in studio type accommodation and another was protective of her domain and didn't want to be the subject of a "show and tell" scenario.

Interviews were loosely structured and were steered by the thread of conversation and the items within the home. Nevertheless, a rough plan of questioning was devised in order to try to understand the significance of chosen objects and the way in which they supported social relations and physical activity.

The conversation started by looking at the physicality of the object; its purpose, positioning and the reason behind its significance. We explored whether the object connected them in any way to another person (past or present) and inquired about their personal relationship with the object and whether or not it currently promoted social or physical interaction. We also collected some general details about their current communication habits and use of technology.

FINDINGS

The interviews commenced in areas of the home open to visitors, usually the kitchen table or living room. However, as the participants relaxed into the interview and it was suggested we take a closer look at a specific object 'in place' they were happy to move around their homes and as we went more objects came to mind.

Some of the most revealing aspects of the contextual interviews were points where people clearly became emotional, preferred to gloss over or avoid discussion, indicated that they really preferred not to have photos or video taken, or where they declined to participate in workshops that would follow on. What was surprising and valuable about conducting interviews about significant objects in the context of the home was the insight into the emotions and privacy concerns that are revealed when the participants discuss their belongings.

In most cases there wasn't anything in particular that they didn't like about their homes. However, in one case, the dishwasher was mentioned; it was no longer in the home but was still openly disliked showing that there were also emotions attached to the memory of objects that were no longer there. Whilst the types of objects that were highlighted as being significant were varied, themes around what the objects mean to its owner emerged. The themes are not mutually exclusive. Examples are given below:

Objects of Independence: The car, the shoe horn, the laundry basket on wheels

One participant had quite practical significant objects that included a shoe horn, a set of steps, a handy vac and a miniature screwdriver. The connection he has with them was demonstrated through his enthusiasm. The shoe horn not only promotes physical activity by enabling him to put on his shoes without bending over, it also fosters social connection with his grandchildren through its use as a walking stick and a sword in their role play. His expression of disappointment at the thought of something happening to it and the fact that it also accompanies them on holiday further reinforced evidence of this emotional attachment.

Another participant described the importance of her car for supporting her independence. It not only represents a link to social connections like going to her weekly choir practice and minding her grandchildren but also facilitates the mundane routine physical activities like grocery shopping and attending doctors' appointments. When she talked about the cars she has had in the past she did so with pride and passion. However, the emotion tied up in the object parked in her carport at this stage of her life was sadness. Her current health situation does not permit her to drive and her dependence on others for transportation leaves her feeling really inadequate.

Objects of routine and comfort: The coloured bowls, the coffee filter, the tea-pots and the kettles.

Some participants identified objects that supported their daily routines such as at mealtimes and making tea. One conversation with a couple (who preferred not to be photographed) was held around the kitchen table. As the interview progressed it became apparent this was the neutral shared area in their home. He had prepared the objects he wished to discuss next and they were 3 different coloured bowls. The participant said playfully, "Would it be known or unbeknownst to other people" (he nods at his partner) he uses "the yellow one for cereal, the green one for salad and the other one for hot food". "Oh, well, now I know!" an admission from the partner of twenty years.

It was interesting to discover that little idiosyncrasies of daily habits and attachments to objects are not always known to family members, regardless of the length of time they had shared together. Discoveries of this nature through conducting interviews in context provide valuable insight into the relationships people have with each other, their shared spaces and their shared objects.

Here, privacy is an important consideration for the design process but so too is an understanding of the desire for playful secrecy in the partnership.

Objects of tradition, status and prestige: The Merc, the ipad, the collectors' items

Some objects clearly symbolized tradition, status or prestige. The car in this instance was more than just a method of getting around. The participant recalled a trip to Tasmania with the Mercedes Benz Club, only at that particular time he owned a Volvo. He laughed as he recalled that his car was the only one on the ferry that wasn't a Merc. The emotional connection he has with the object extends much further than the object itself.

In other situations it wasn't the object itself but how it was positioned that promoted social interaction; conversation pieces like a 'grey nomads' camping book and collectors items laid out on the coffee table and pictures or clocks on the wall. These objects connect people with others and to particular times in their lives.

In some instances the story attached to the object is what adds to its significance and this might easily be lost if the inheritor does not value or share the story. One man spoke about a remnant piece of furniture from the 1974 flood that was cherished because it survived.

Objects symbolizing relationships with loved ones: The Tiki, Toucan

On another occasion it was the words that weren't spoken that indicated the depth of emotion associated with the objects. One man, who lived alone with very few belongings, selected two ornaments as being significant; a "Tiki" (a Polynesian and Maori wooden carving of humanoid form) and a "Toucan" bird. The man described how they symbolize his daughter and granddaughter and as such he feels a connection to them through the objects in an emotionally safe, structured way. He indicated that he wants more contact with his daughter and is open to the possibility that through internet technologies the objects might allow him some form of connection with his daughter that may be asymmetric in nature. This indicates considerable scope and a framing for a personal and intimate design (provided the desire for connection is reciprocated) in relationships that may harbor both the desire for connection but also guardedness about connection due to the history of the relationship.

Objects for creativity or relaxation: a piano, a stereo/ entertainment system

Some participants freely expressed joy and enthusiasm as they explained what their chosen objects meant to them. The stereo was not simply a device on which to play music but a reminder of the speech he gave at his daughter's wedding. Through the discussion the object was identified as being key to facilitating dancing, laughter and social connection at family get-togethers.

DISCUSSION:

Our investigation found that whilst the majority of the objects expressed as being significant are not currently explicitly associated with communication (excepting mobiles, ipads etc.) many of them are routinely used in social interaction and others facilitate physical activity. Others harbor significant memories.

During the process of finding out more about the objects deep emotion was revealed. People have strong emotional attachments to their things. They use objects in their routines and through their use, however mundane, they are wrapped into life-stories and become intertwined and connected in the intricacy of their owners lives. It is undoubtedly possible to add interactive capabilities to many objects through the Internet of Things and participants indicated they saw possibilities for networked objects to facilitate communication. However design of such technology needs to be framed by an understanding of:

- The underlying emotions that are attached to and the social relations that are facilitated by objects;
- The kind of communications desired (if any and with whom) and how this might be best facilitated by objects;
- How memories associated with objects might be enhanced with technology;
- The need to respect privacy, safety and trust; and
- The circumstances in which objects might be better left alone and not networked so as not to interfere with memories and relationships.

A practical consideration is people's concerns about what happens to all of their objects when they die. There is the desire to pass on the knowledge and memories but apprehension that objects will be a burden that no-one would find interesting. However, in many instances, knowing the history of an object adds to its significance.

CONCLUSION

In this paper we aimed to provide insight into some of the issues that need to be considered when designing technology that promotes social interaction for older adults. Through conducting contextual interviews in a small sample of older adults we were able to observe the types of objects they consider significant and gain valuable insight into the emotional attachment they have with them. What is clear from the investigation is that objects that satisfy emotional needs are diverse and idiosyncratic presenting a challenge for design. As a first step it might be worth designing enhancement of specific objects for specific relationships and individuals rather than attempting to design more generic networked communicative objects. People have strong emotional attachment to the objects in their home environment and that ultimately needs to be respected in the design process.

ACKNOWLEDGMENTS

We sincerely thank the participants and the Australian Research Council for Discovery Grant DP1111999.

REFERENCES

1. Aarhus, R., Ballegaard, SA. Negotiating Boundaries: Managing Disease at Home, *CHI 2010,* ACM Press, (2010)
2. Bagalkot, N., Sokoler, T., Unboxing the tools for physical rehabilitation: embracing the difference between the clinic and home, *NordiCHI 2012,* ACM Press (2012)
3. Beyer, Hugh, Karen Holtzblatt. *Contextual design: defining customer-centered systems*. Elsevier, (1997).
4. Brereton, Margot. Habituated objects: everyday tangibles that foster the independent living of an elderly woman. *interactions* 20, 4 (2013), 20-24.
5. Buys, L., *Active and Productive Ageing: What is the Real Experience of Australians?* Research Bulletin (2005) 1(1)
6. Csikszentmihalyi, M. Why we need things. *History from things: Essays on material culture*, (1993) 20-29.
7. Dourish, P. *Where the action is: the foundations of embodied interaction*. MIT press (2004).
8. Gaver, W., Bowers, J., Boucher, A., Law, A., Pennington, S., & Villar, N. The history tablecloth: illuminating domestic activity. *Proc. Designing Interactive Systems* 2006 (Vol.26, No.28, pp.199-208).
9. Gronvall, E., Verdezoto, N., *Beyond Self-Monitoring: Understanding non-functional Aspects of Home-based Healthcare Technology*. UbiComp 2013,
10. Hornecker, E., & Buur, J. Getting a grip on tangible interaction: a framework on physical space and social interaction. *Proc.CHI 2006* ACM Press 2006 p437-446
11. Ishii, H., & Ullmer, B. Tangible bits: towards seamless interfaces between people, bits atoms. CHI'97 (pp. 234-241). ACM Press 1997.
12. Kirk, D., & Sellen, A., (2010). *On Human Remains: Values and Practice in the Home Archiving of Cherished Objects* ACM Trans Comput.- Hum Interact. (Vol. 17, Issue 3, p1-43).
13. Latour, B. (1999). *Pandora's hope: essays on the reality of science studies*. Harvard Uni Press. p 179
14. Leonardi, C., Mennecozzi, C., Not, E., Pianesi, F., Zancanaro, M., Gennai, F., & Cr istoforetti, A. *Knocking on elders' door: investigating the functional and emotional geography of their domestic space.* Proc. CHI 2009 ACM (2009).
15. Mueller, F. F., Vetere, F., Gibbs, M. R., Kjeldskov, J., Pedell, S., & Howard, S.. *Hug over a distance.* Proc CHI 2005, ACM (2005).
16. Orlikowski, W. J. (2007). Sociomaterial practices: Exploring technology at work. *Organization studies*, *28*(9), 1435-1448.
17. Suchman, L., *Human-machine reconfigurations: Plans and situated actions*. Cambridge University Press (2006)
18. Vetere, F., Davis, H., Gibbs, M., & Howard, S. (2009). The Magic Box and Collage: Responding to the challenge of distributed intergenerational play. *Int Journal of Human-Computer Studies, 67(2), 165-178.*
19. Van den Hoven, E., Sas, C., & Whittaker, S., (2012) *Introduction to this Special Issue on Designing for Personal Memories: Past, Present, and Future.* Human-Computer Interaction 2012 (Vol 27, pp 1-12)

Always Somewhere, Never There: Using Critical Design to Understand Database Interactions

Melanie Feinberg, Daniel Carter, Julia Bullard
School of Information, The University of Texas at Austin
1616 Guadalupe St., Suite 5.202, Austin, TX 78701 USA
feinberg@ischool.utexas.edu; carter.daniel.w@gmail.com; julia.a.bullard@gmail.com

ABSTRACT
Structured databases achieve effective searching and sorting by enacting sharply delineated category boundaries around their contents. While this enables precise retrieval, it also distorts identities that exist between category lines. A choice between Single and Married, for example, blurs distinctions within the Single group: single, perhaps, merely because same-sex marriage is not legal in one's locality. Sociologists Susan Leigh Star and Geoffrey Bowker describe such *residual* states as inevitable byproducts of information systems. To minimize residuality, traditional practice for descriptive metadata seeks to demarcate clear and objective classes. In this study, we use critical design to question this position by creating information collections that foreground the residual, instead of diminishing it. We then interrogate our design experiments with solicited critical responses from invited experts and student designers. Inspired by the anthropologist Tim Ingold, we argue that our experiments illuminate a form of interacting with databases characterized by notions of wayfaring, or inhabiting a space, as opposed to notions of transport, or reaching a known destination. We suggest that the form of coherence that shapes a wayfaring database is enacted through its *flow,* or fluid integration between structure and content.

Author Keywords
Design; criticism; classification; metadata; collections

ACM Classification Keywords
H.5.m. Information interfaces and presentation (e.g., HCI): Miscellaneous.

INTRODUCTION
Categories are indispensable elements of language and thought. Without categories, we couldn't refer to dogs as one group of similar animals, and cats as another group. To reduce ambiguity in communication, categories with clear boundaries are best. It's not difficult to separate cats and dogs. It's harder to separate tall and short; when does short end and tall begin? To enable effective searching of structured databases, systems of attributes and values are designed to avoid these areas of relative indeterminacy. In the case of tall and short, we might avoid potential miscommunication by using exact measurement ranges instead of verbal descriptions.

But clear and usable classification systems also flatten and distort complex realities. It might seem straightforward to distinguish relationship status by separating single and married people. But these simple categories mask a wide variety of experience. Within the Single category, we might find people with committed same-sex partners who cannot legally marry in their locality, people who have been divorced multiple times, and so on. The Married category, as well, might include couples in open relationships, or who live separately, or who enact marriage in various non-prototypical ways. Such examples illustrate the notion of residuality, a phenomenon of classification articulated by Star and Bowker [15]. The residual encompasses everything that doesn't quite fit into a category system. A residual state might be absent, inadequately expressed, or split between existing categories. Star, for example, writes about her own chronic pain, a state that can be described as neither "sick," in terms of a diagnosed illness, nor "well" in terms of lived experience. In a category system where "sick" is associated with conditions of clear etiology, chronic pain is residual. More generally, the residual represents the persistent vagueness, ambiguity, and invisibility that databases, and the classificatory systems that structure them, attempt to eliminate by establishing neatly differentiated relationships.

In this project, we use critical design experiments to highlight the residual instead of minimizing it, contradicting typical design practice for descriptive metadata. We created three "transformations" of a small digital video library to enact three separate approaches to highlighting residuality. We extended this design work by collecting critical responses to our transformations from both invited experts and from students in a course on collection design.

We target two research questions:

- How can a digital information collection foreground the residual?

CHI 2014, April 26 - May 01 2014, Toronto, ON, Canada
Copyright 2014 ACM 978-1-4503-2473-1/14/04...$15.00.
http://dx.doi.org/10.1145/2556288.2557055

- What is the interaction, or reading, experience of such a collection?

Our work makes several contributions to HCI. First, reflection upon our design experiments and the associated critical responses enables us to illuminate an alternate form of interacting with databases, one characterized by notions of wayfaring, or inhabiting a space, as opposed to notions of transport, or reaching a known destination [10]. We argue that residuality emerges through this wayfaring mode of interaction, and we contend that wayfaring databases are characterized by *flow,* or fluid integration between structure and content. In our experiments, flow is a property of a database's descriptive infrastructure (that is, metadata), and not its interface. In emphasizing the category systems that support database interactions as the focus of design, we surface an element of HCI that is less commonly addressed as such. Moreover, we suggest that the wayfaring mode of interaction illuminated through our experiments also constitutes a form of "design-after-design," or creative appropriation of the designed artifact as design material. Our concept of flow can be understood as a type of "infrastructuring," to use a term introduced by Binder and colleagues, to encourage design-after-design [2].

Our study also demonstrates a productive synthesis of critical design and interaction criticism. We suggest this combination is especially appropriate when the character of the artifact class (here, a database) is itself under scrutiny. The active reading demanded by criticism is also, we propose, a form of infrastructuring for subsequent design.

In the following sections, we first present conceptual and methodological foundations in more detail. We then introduce our study design and transformation experiments. After summarizing key findings, we put forth a refined account of our transformations, as enabled through analysis of the critical responses we received, in conjunction with anthropologist Tim Ingold's ideas of wayfaring.

CONCEPTUAL UNDERPINNINGS

We see residuality described by Star and Bowker as related to Gloria Anzaldua's idea of mestiza consciousness, a life experience that fuses divergent aspects of identity through the crossing and recrossing of border states. In her classic work of feminist theory, *Borderlands/La Frontera: The New Mestiza,* Anzaldua uses personal history to depict a mode of existence that is enacted both outside and between traditional categories of culture, class, and ethnicity. Anzaldua describes, for example, her status as a Chicana (American of Mexican descent) from the Rio Grande valley in Texas (on the border with Mexico), raised in an agricultural, socially traditional community, who is also a poet, scholar, feminist, and lesbian. The knot of categories that Anzaldua herself embodies incorporates ambiguity, conflict, and indeterminacy, a condition that Anzaldua terms *mestiza consciousness.* For Anzaldua, the term *mestiza* extends beyond ethnic heritage to involve the mixing of culture, class, language, and other extended elements of identity. In mestiza consciousness, Anzaldua reorients the residual, making it central.

Anzaldua evocatively describes mestiza consciousness in terms of the Aztec goddess Coatlicue, who includes both creator and destroyer aspects. The "Coatlicue state" involves operating in what Anzaldua calls pluralistic mode; the new mestiza embodies a path between oppositions, a path that incorporates a specific history of travel but has no endpoint. In the domain of classificatory infrastructure, mestiza consciousness implies a continual process of understanding what a category like Single or Married can mean: what it is to be Married, to not be Married, to sort of be Married, or to once have been Married, all as a specific, ephemeral event. Our goal to understand and exploit this complex state as a design resource complements and extends work to incorporate ambiguity, open-endedness, contradiction, and plurality into HCI, and to more generally understand HCI in terms of experience [8, 14].

Mestiza consciousness can also be seen as a rhetorical strategy. In *Borderlands,* the reader's path echoes the mestiza's path: Anzaldua includes historical background and scholarly exegesis mixed with poetry and personal anecdotes, even dreams. Anzaldua also uses multiple languages, juxtaposing English with a variety of Spanish dialects. The reader must work through material that can be frustrating, even irritating, in its violations of traditional rhetorical coherence. Eventually, the reader must release conventional expectations in order to perceive the structure of Anzaldua's thought and progress in understanding.

Borderlands suggested that our goal to foreground residuality in an information collection also needed to incorporate experimental forms, potentially in a disquieting way. Accordingly, in pursuing our theoretical investigation through design, we were not focused on what people typically want, need, or like when interacting with information systems. Instead, our transformations bent conventional structures in order to, following Anzaldua, reorient the residual, making it central. In transforming categories like Single and Married, for example, we might use Stable and Unstable. The latter are more ambiguous and tenuous; we can see how a relationship might include elements of both, and might shift over time. (Although mestiza consciousness and residuality are not equal, their overlap is extensive enough, given our research goals, that we use the term *residuality* to incorporate both notions for the remainder of this paper.)

METHODOLOGICAL UNDERPINNINGS

The creation of provocative artifacts to interrogate received ideas is a hallmark of critical design. Critical design produces experimental artifacts that transgress cultural norms and provoke reevaluation of those norms. Dunne, for example, describes design proposals to make apparent the invisible electro-magnetic fields that are emitted by household objects, such as televisions and computers [7]. Dunne calls these proposals "value-fictions," whose goal is not to satisfy user needs but to explore the enactment of alternate value states, to "stimulate discussion in a way that a film or a novel might."

Shaowen Bardzell and colleagues describe critical design as a form of research inquiry [5]. They summarize the design and deployment of two artifacts created to spur questioning of gender roles. With their "significant screwdriver," using the artifact generates a visual representation of the work performed with it, which can then be shared as a greeting card. This action recasts "handyman" tasks as an expression of caring. Similar to [7], the outcome of [5] centers on the interaction experience as a means of questioning received values. The significant screwdriver reveals attitudes associated with household work, and it suggests implications for feminist and critical design. Its goals are less focused upon hand tools as a class of objects.

Although not labeled as critical design, a number of conceptually aligned studies consider the artifact more directly, as well as the values underlying the artifact [13]. In reviewing the deployment of critical design in HCI, Bardzell and Bardzell claim that such studies, using the example of Dalsgaard and Dindler's interactive peephole projects, also constitute a form of critical design [4, 6]. [4] contends that Dalsgaard and Dindler evolve both an understanding of the peephole as an interactive form and an understanding of user engagement in general. Critical making, another complementary approach, uses the process of designing, building, and using an artifact to explore theoretical questions [12]. The outcome of critical making is reflection upon these processes; the design product provides the catalyst for this reflection.

Some critical design projects, such as [6, 7] rely on designer reflection to interpret and build knowledge from the designs. Other efforts, including [5, 13] conduct user studies to assess their design experiments. These studies include both user and designer reflections as research data. Although it has not been extensively coupled with critical design, information criticism has been proposed as a rigorous, systematic means of generating new understandings from scholarly "reading" of artifacts in HCI [3, 11]. The sustained accounts produced through criticism complement reflections from designers and users.

STUDY DESIGN

Our research goals combine an interest in residuality itself, in the expression of residuality through the classificatory infrastructure of databases, and in the interaction, or reading experience, of using a database that highlights the residual. Accordingly, our study design melds critical design, critical making, and interaction criticism. We aim to learn from:

- The process of making experimental designs.
- Our own reflections on the designs themselves.
- Responses contributed by informed critics.

We use critical responses rather than a more traditional user deployment because our experiments are based on a particular theoretical orientation, and not aligned with user needs, wants, or preferences. Moreover, our interests include understanding the information database itself, as a class of artifacts. This goal aligns with that of criticism; a literary critic may use detailed readings of particular poems, for example, to develop a more general scholarly argument about poetry. The critic, also, often incorporates the work of previous critics into these arguments. We too propose to learn about information databases through our own readings and those of other critics.

Our research plan therefore includes these elements:

- Develop design experiments that enact residuality through descriptive infrastructure (classification schemes and other metadata).
- Write structured reflections that address the authoring activity and the created product.
- Solicit critical responses to the design experiments from both subject experts and student critics.
- Synthesize and interrogate the responses to produce an integrated account of our work.

The following sections describe these elements more fully.

Design experiments

To ensure productive comparability between design experiments, we created three "transformations" of an existing digital video collection. The initial collection contained 50 short videos, gathered from a variety of sources, in the general domain of "Texas" as a subject area. The original Texas collection was created in 2010 to be used in teaching and research, and its descriptive infrastructure was designed to follow traditional design principles of neutrality and objectivity—that is, to restrict the emergence of residuality. The original Texas collection was created with the Open Video Digital Library Toolkit (OVDLT), an environment that includes a wide array of customizable metadata elements [9]. These include:

- Browsing categories (a group of descriptors, or index terms [such as Politics, Lecture, or Gulf Coast] identified with a broader category label [such as Subject, Genre, or Location]).
- Titles, brief summaries, and abstracts of content.
- Roles associated with the video or its metadata record (such as a director or metadata cataloger).
- Dates associated with the video or its metadata record (such as the video's original broadcast or the date the record was created).
- Freeform tags.

Figure 1: On the left, the home page of the original Texas collection. Each labeled browsing category (Texas, Genre, Goal, and so on) has an associated group of descriptors. On the right, a video metadata record shows assigned descriptors.

- "Collections," or selected subsets of annotated videos to express a theme.

Figure 1 shows some of these elements for the original Texas collection. Our three transformations took copies of this original collection and manipulated them as possible with the OVDLT tools. Accordingly, all three transformations and the original collection include the same 50 videos. Layout and interface features are standardized by the OVDLT. Only the descriptive infrastructure (browsing categories and associated descriptors, titles and abstracts, collections, and other metadata elements) was changed. Each of the three researchers took responsibility for one transformation.

Here in Texas (Figure 2) addresses the relationship between a stereotypical idea of Texas as positioned against its reality, filtered through an authorial persona's perspective as a non-native Texas resident. Some browsing categories reference Texas concepts that are not represented in the collection's current videos. For example, descriptors such as Despair and Armadillos are included in the category Somewhere in Texas, but are not assigned to any resources.

Kaleidoscopic Texas, shown in Figure 3, juxtaposes three descriptive approaches—three facets of a kaleidoscope. These include an "objective" perspective, a contrasting "subjective" perspective, and quoted material from the original collection. Kaleidoscopic Texas subverts traditional classificatory principles, such as a consistent level of abstraction in sibling descriptors, to call attention to the artificiality with which such distinctions are maintained. The Technique category, for example, includes descriptors such as Montage, Nostalgia, and Animation, which refer to very different kinds of technique.

Post-Texas Index, shown in Figure 4, describes video elements as "objectively" as possible but from an atypically high level of abstraction. The context that endows the videos with meaning is stripped away. Both political rallies and the exhortations of football coaches to their players are described, for example, as "men speaking."

Multiple forms of reflection on the design experiments

Each researcher wrote a summative reflective essay that distilled design goals as well as the process of enacting those goals. These reflections encapsulated each designer's sense of significant themes from the making experience.

For the first set of critical responses, we arranged for 11 experts to contribute a brief essay (approximately 750 words) that addressed the two research questions. Seven invited respondents were academics with expertise in aligned fields: classification research, infrastructure studies, digital libraries, and HCI. Four invited respondents were information professionals working in libraries and archives. Invited participants were provided with background about the project goals, including a concise introduction to residuality. They were also given access to the original Texas collection. Invited respondents received $75 gift cards. Respondents were instructed to address one, two, or three transformations in their responses, as they wished. Invited participants did not know which researcher was responsible for any individual transformation. Most invited respondents chose to remain anonymous, but some requested to have their contributions identified by name.

For the second set of responses, 14 master's students in a semester-length course on digital collection design were assigned a 3,000-word essay addressing the two research questions. As part of their course activities, the students learned about traditional classificatory practices, as well as

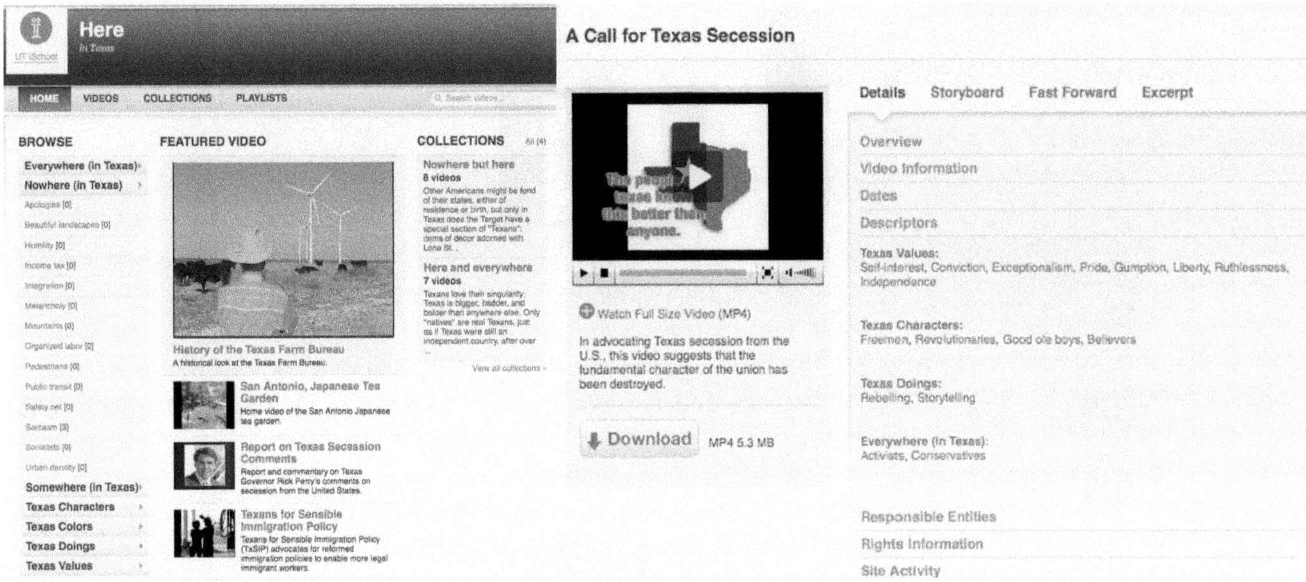

Figure 2: On the left, the Here in Texas home page. The Nowhere browsing category includes concepts that "do not" exist in Texas, although one descriptor is assigned to 3 videos in the collection. On the right, a metadata record shows assigned descriptors.

residuality. The students were also instructed in critical design and interaction criticism. As with the invited respondents, students could address one, two, or all three transformations in their essays, and they had access to the original Texas collection. This essay assignment was positioned as preparatory to a design project in which students created their own transformations of a different video library. Students were encouraged to engage deeply and critically with the transformations as a means to inform their subsequent design activities. Students did not know who had created the transformations.

FINDINGS

In addition to the three design transformations, this project yielded the following data:

- Structured essays and notes from the researchers.
- Eleven invited responses.
- Fourteen student responses.

These materials were exceedingly diverse in content, structure, and assessments. The invited responses, in particular, were wide-ranging. Some were oriented around immediate impressions, while others were dense scholarly reflections (for instance, one response was grounded in the French theorists Deleuze and Derrida). Some were loose and informal, while others put forth more polished theories. While the student responses incorporated more sustained arguments, they too represented disparate areas of focus.

Because we were soliciting criticism, which is oriented towards unique insight, we anticipated this variety, and we did not code our materials for pervasive themes, as is often useful for interviews and other forms of experience reporting. Instead, we used the responses as provocations to evolve our thinking on the transformations, as begun through the process of making them and continued via our own initial reflections on the completed products.

In the remainder of this section, we summarize selected observations from our three data sources. Then, in the following section, we provide an extended account of our experiments, as enabled by these observations. We have selected the findings included here to demonstrate the progress of our ideas; while they represent only a small fraction of our data, they show how each source contributed to our eventual understanding of the experiments and their significance as critical design interventions. We emphasize that our process was not intended to be replicable, and that our goal is to achieve insight, not to prove a hypothesis.

In our initial reflections around the process of making, we, the designers, were challenged by two concepts: coherence and authenticity. The experiences of the residual as articulated by Star and Bowker and Anzaldua demonstrate that a simple category like Married is ambiguous, fluid, and complicated, that its apparent coherence is a reductive simplification. But Star and Bowker and Anzaldua's goal is not to enact chaos but to propose an alternate form of coherence, a more complex one, as exhibited through the initially strange but ultimately cohesive rhetorical structure of Anzaldua's book. In their accounts of residuality, this alternate coherence derives from an authenticity of character, as expressed via distinct authorial personas.

Certain sections of Star and Bowker's article, for example, are written as signed first-person narratives, replete with both stylistic distinctions and vivid biographical details. Both Star and Anzaldua recount not only particulars of their residual experience but the difficult process of communicating that experience, which for both involved

Figure 3: On the left, the Kaleidoscopic Texas home page. The Era category mixes time period types, such as Cold War, Later Twentieth Century, and Globalization. On the right, a video metadata record shows assigned descriptors.

wrenching emotional states. The actual truth of such personal anecdotes is immaterial; the authenticity of authorial voice makes them *feel* true and provides a rationale, or explanation, that lends coherence to the expression of residuality. We, as designers of information collections, struggled with this dense relationship between residuality, coherence, and authenticity. Was an "authentic" voice the only way to find coherence in the residual?

The Here in Texas author did adopt that sort of character-focused approach, and that transformation was entwined with the intersecting specificities of an authorial persona. The Post-Texas Index author, however, relied on consistency of concept to maintain coherence: the transformation maintained a high level of abstraction in description, retaining conventional syntax while avoiding conventional semantics. The coherence for Kaleidoscopic Texas came from the distinctiveness of the three separate kaleidoscope facets: an "objective" perspective, a "subjective" perspective, and quoted material from the original collection itself. In our initial reflections, we felt that all three transformations were equally authentic in their commitment to these different approaches to coherence; that is, they all seemed to provide a focused rationale for their particular expressions of residuality. While these forms of authenticity were different, our design reflections led us to conclude that all three transformations were equally coherent and expressive of the residual.

The critical responses caused us to reevaluate our ideas about authenticity and coherence, and we provide just a few of the remarks that provoked this reevaluation. We had not expected our respondents to address the composition of the original Texas collection in any depth; we provided it as a backdrop to read the transformations against, but we didn't imagine that it would inspire comment, as it was typical and nondescript. But many respondents did address the original collection. Several invited respondents dismissed the original collection as "boring," a term that surprised us. A retrieval-oriented database like the original collection is more often seen as something to be used, not bored or intrigued by. It would be weird to call your local library "boring"; it just wouldn't seem like a germane assessment. It would be like calling the supermarket boring. "Boring" struck us. The student respondents described the original collection more like we expected: "accessible," "familiar," and "useful," and not "boring." However, the student respondents who looked at the original collection in depth tended to become frustrated: although it seemed easy to understand at first, individual descriptive decisions could seem arbitrary. While the Here in Texas and Kaleidescopic Texas collections were sometimes described as inscrutable, frustrating, or annoying, they were seldom called "boring." But the Post-Texas Index was occasionally so designated. Post-Texas, too, was most variously described: sometimes it was boring, sometimes it was the most strange, sometimes most successful, and sometimes least successful.

The appraisals of boredom in the responses spurred us to notice references to modes of attention. A non-boring collection might be described positively in terms of being inviting, intriguing, or clever, or negatively in terms of being annoying or frustrating. But a non-boring collection seemed to require a different form of attention than a boring one. If a collection was deemed both inscrutable and boring, respondents didn't try to figure it out. But non-boring collections seemed more likely to be actively read, or interpreted, in addition to being used. Several student essays organized their thoughts in terms of finding tools for this reading in the transformations that they engaged with. A "boring" collection didn't have such tools. Modes of

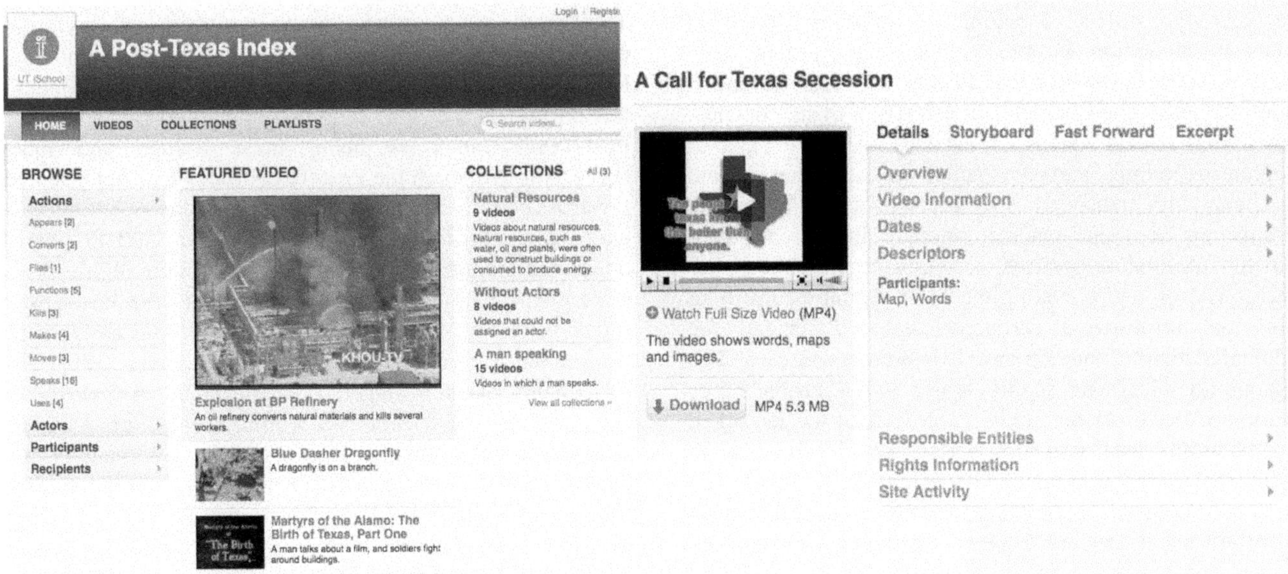

Figure 4: On the left, the Post-Texas Index home page. By emphasizing a high level of abstraction, the collection shows hidden commonalities, such as the prevalence of "speaking" as an action. On the right, a metadata record shows assigned descriptors.

attention also surfaced in the relationship between metadata structure and "content," or the videos themselves. When collections were not boring, attention was more often focused on the integration between structure and content, and not on particular videos or decisions about them.

What did boring mean? Were the different modes of authenticity in our three transformations not equally coherent in their expression of the residual? The next section describes the revised understanding of our experiment that these questions motivated.

DISCUSSION: WAYFARING THE DATABASE

We gradually realized that our transformations were most interesting in enabling us to understand and problematize "normal" database interactions against them. We began to associate residuality less with "unique" characteristics like ambiguity and fluidity and more with a mode of interaction that encouraged the reader's engagement with these characteristics. In other words, the notions of reading and the residual, which had been separate for us at the beginning of our project, started to blur. Our two research questions became commingled: it seemed like a collection might foreground the residual not through *being different* so much as through *being read differently*.

Our ideas gained shape as we examined them in conjunction with the concept of wayfaring put forth by anthropologist Tim Ingold in his 2007 book *Lines* [10]. Ingold's work defies pithy encapsulation, but a pervasive theme involves the contrast between wayfaring and transport as modes of travel. Transport involves getting from one point to another; the goal of transport is arriving at the destination. Wayfaring involves inhabiting a landscape; wayfaring is about where you are, as opposed to where you might, should, or will be. Ingold elaborates:

While on the trail, the wayfarer is always somewhere, yet every somewhere is on the way to somewhere else. The inhabited world is a reticulate meshwork of such trails, which is continually being woven and life goes on along them. Transport, by contrast, is tied to specific locations. Every move serves the purpose of relocating persons and their effects, and is oriented to a specific destination. The traveller who departs from one location and arrives at another is, in between, nowhere at all. [10, p. 84]

Ingold contends that contemporary Western society views reading and writing through the lens of transport; reading is about getting to the end, and writing is about laying out a plan for the reader to arrive there. But older ideas of reading incorporated more of a wayfaring orientation; for medieval monks, Ingold says, words were footsteps or waymarkers, and "every text, story, or trip is a journey made rather than an object found." Accordingly, a text is a place to be inhabited, not "a space to be surveyed" by extracting its pertinent facts [10, p. 13 and p. 16]. When reading is like wayfaring, it is always particular and never finished; there is no transcendent or universal meaning. In fact, reading is no longer about meaning, at least, not in the sense of figuring out an answer to the question posed by the text. Instead, reading is more like taking a walk. When you "go for a walk," you aren't going somewhere, you are just walking. The walking experience is the point, not the destination (which is often right back where you began). Ingold describes the oral storytellers of the Khanty people in Siberia as continuing their performances after everyone in their audience is asleep; the end doesn't matter, the experience does, for as long as one is able to listen.

Ingold doesn't consider databases when he talks about these two modes. But pervading conceptions of databases as mechanisms for efficient information retrieval and access are clear expositions of reading as transport. A typical database interaction is most often about getting to a predetermined destination as quickly as possible, and a useful database enables efficient extraction of its contents. The attributes and values of database structure exist to promote searching and navigation (a term that Ingold associates with transport); structure works like a vehicle, getting you from one place to another. Indeed, the ideal goal for information systems, according to the philosopher Patrick Wilson, is in locating the "best textual means to an end," the information resources that will enable the accomplishment of one's plans [16]. Wilson was careful to separate this ideal from reality, which is that our databases return what we describe, not necessarily what we need. The gap between need and description is what makes us dissatisfied with databases that do exactly what we ask. If I query the Epicurious recipe database for cakes, and none of the results seem enticing, I am frustrated, even though the results are correct, given my request. In Wilson's characterization, the ideal (and impossible) system would recognize that my need was for an indulgent and yet comforting dessert, and would supply me with the perfect recipe—for pecan pie, not cake at all. Upon receiving this "textual means" to satisfy my real need, I would disengage with the system and continue with my plans.

Ingold, we think, would describe this dissatisfaction differently. Ingold suggests that we build our environments generally "for occupation," a state of being suggested by the transport mode of travel, and not for "habitation," that suggested by wayfaring. We invariably find ourselves trying to inhabit that which we have built to occupy, however, and this disjunction causes frustration. Databases like Epicurious are oriented toward providing us lists of the cakes we think that we want, obeying our commands; they are not oriented toward taking us on a food journey where we start with cake and end somewhere else, with pecan pie, or even with oysters or zucchini, somewhere unrelated to our "needs." We sometimes enjoy "taking a walk" from cake to zucchini in a database, and yet we also tend to feel like doing so is merely wasting time. One of the invited respondents in our study, for example, mused in his narrative that he "should" have been searching the transformations, writing "Why am I bothering to explore the structure of the collection before I dive in and do a search?" Several invited respondents felt like they "should" have had a task to perform with the transformations, instead of "simply poking about," as one respondent remarked; another wondered if "a more effective way to structure this test would be to pose questions to the subjects." The unmarked, habitual mode of database interaction is about transport, about getting from one point to another, finding answers and moving on. We don't as readily interact with a database as wayfarers, following its mesh of trails as they snake over the landscape, intersecting in unpredictable ways. Or when we do, it feels slightly illicit.

Thinking about our transformations in terms of wayfaring enabled several realizations. We could now understand how both the original collection and the Post-Texas Index could be "boring" at the same time as some respondents saw the Post-Texas Index as being most strange and most successful. Although the Post-Texas Index was not oriented towards effective information retrieval as we typically understand it, it was nonetheless, in a certain sense, optimized for a transport mode of interaction. While there were plenty of individual idiosyncrasies in the Post-Texas Index in terms of descriptor instantiation and assignment (an invited respondent wondered, for example, "Why was the Obama mashup tagged as Appearance in the Action category? By what rationale would a video of a family interacting with animals receive the tag Woman?") the overall concept was unified and relatively easy to discern. In terms of "getting the point," or seeing an end goal to the transformation, these irregularities could be glided across in a way similar to the original Texas collection. When one looked closely at the original collection, as some of our respondents did, it was equally full of idiosyncrasies. A student participant, for instance, questioned why old footage of cowboys in 1898 was assigned the Report descriptor in the Genre category: what made this a report? Despite the care with which the original Texas collection had been crafted, such debatable decisions occur throughout any such database. But we are less likely to notice them, because the metadata infrastructure associated with retrieval seems familiar and unexceptional. The set of attributes used for the original Texas collection— Texas subjects, locations, genres–were easily recognizable routes to the "end" of document retrieval. The form of coherence enacted through each of these databases, in other words, was oriented towards moving *over* the content landscape to reach a destination: either a set of results, for the original collection, or a recognition of the arbitrariness of description, for the Post-Texas Index. Both of these databases were "boring" because their structure seemed like a map: framing the content by identifying potential destinations, but nonetheless resisting *integration* between route and underlying terrain. Post-Texas was most strange, for some, because its goal was not retrieval. Post-Texas was most successful, for some respondents, because it could nonetheless be associated with an identifiable goal, and the idea of success therefore more easily attached to it.

In contrast, Here in Texas and Kaleidoscopic Texas suggest wayfaring through a traveled landscape, with the descriptive infrastructure functioning as a meshwork of existing trails, or previous journeys, through the content. As such, these collections have no apparent end. The feelings of being lost or frustrated that some of the respondents noted (one student called Kaleidescopic Texas "a perfectly functioning dilemma generator," and an invited respondent said that "even after spending some time...I am still confused") can be traced to this lack of straightforward goal. As another example, participants quite naturally associated the available interaction tools, such as browsing categories and filters, with a transport orientation of extracting content to specifications, and some respondents were puzzled when these tools didn't work as expected with Here in Texas and Kaleidescopic Texas. For instance, an invited respondent wondered about the Texas Colors browsing category used in Here in Texas, asking "Why would anyone want to search on colors?" In transport mode, descriptors support identified user needs and tasks by delivering the closest textual means to those ends, and associating color with a video doesn't align with that conception, particularly with the approach taken in Here in Texas, where color was sometimes applied literally (assigning Denim when people in the video wore jeans) and sometimes metaphorically (using Red for a conservative political orientation) and sometimes in both ways (assigning Green to indicate associations with money and for green landscapes). A student respondent similarly remarked that difficulty in "decoding" the Texas Colors category would make it challenging to "use the data," that is, to find videos on command.

But other participants saw a different form of coherence in elements like Texas Colors, one in which the structure was integrated with the content, as a path is integrated into a landscape (in contrast to a map, which is only a conceptual overlay upon the landscape). When Ryan Shaw, an invited respondent, examined his reactions to descriptors that had no items associated with them, he realized that the original Texas collection and Here in Texas suggested different responses to the same mechanism. In describing his experience with the original Texas collection, Ryan reflected upon the appearance of a Food descriptor with no assigned videos: "This irritates me. Why list a category with zero matching items? That's bad practice." Subsequently, when exploring the Here in Texas collection, Ryan encountered a whole set of no-item descriptors associated with the broader category Nowhere in Texas. This time, he had a different reaction to the same device, allowing in this case "Why list a category with zero matching items? When you want to make a point about what's missing." Ryan does not retract his statement that categories with zero matching items are bad practice. Instead, he connects Here in Texas with a different mode of interaction and accordingly, different utilization of tools like descriptors and their display. Ryan further observed that the videos embedded within Here in Texas seemed to have transformed from those he had been "deeply bored" with in the original collection, commenting that "I find it hard to believe that the original Texas collection contained the same videos."

We suggest that Ryan was responding to the *flow* enacted by the Here in Texas collection, in which the metadata structure weaves a series of paths around and through the content, creating a merged environment for the reader to wander. The Nowhere in Texas descriptors for Here in Texas constitute one such route. This path provides access to very little of the collection's data, as all but one descriptor is empty. Instead, the Nowhere in Texas descriptors form a sort of promontory, offering a view, not of the collection's meaning in general, but of what the collection *meant to a specific previous reader, the Here in Texas author.* This view participates in the current reader's own evolving perception of the greater terrain of the database, which cannot be separated from the previous reader's—the author's— wandering footsteps. The flow of metadata structure both around and through the database content serves here like the hand, or ductus, of a scribe's writing; it comprises evidentiary traces of the author's activity through the database. While the videos themselves are not physically altered in the flow, just as a word does not change when it is written in a manuscript, they are nonetheless suffused by the flow, and they appear different, as Ryan experienced. (So too might the word "love" be unchanged and yet different when written by a child on a handmade Valentine card.)

We propose that databases oriented toward a wayfaring mode of interaction exhibit a different form of coherence than databases oriented toward a transport mode of interaction, and that this wayfaring form of coherence is characterized by flow. If the wayfaring mode of database interaction is more like reading a database than searching, or using, one, then flow is a means of following its story. Flow provides a rationale to contextualize apparent inconsistencies, deviations, and obscure judgments in the integrated environment (structure commingled with content), just as the sense of "an end" did so with a transport mode. Here, flow transmutes potential bewilderments by showing how they contribute to the story of the collection author's travels. The sense of "story," here, though, is not coextensive with a simple plotline but more like a saga in the oral tradition, where many adventures take place, and relationships between events, characters, and places emerge over multiple tellings. Flow builds up through subsequent interactions: it helps the reader understand "where" one currently is, but also how that "where" is related to both other "places" along the trail of the tale, as well as other "times," or other walks along the database paths.

When we conceive of wayfaring coherence in terms of flow, we can also better comprehend the role of authenticity in the expression of residuality. We now see authenticity as emerging through flow, through the entanglement of paths—an experience similar to the "pluralistic mode" of Coatlicue transition that Anzaldua both describes and enacts. As the reader wends through the database, authenticity arises when the story occasioned through the reader's travels seems *motivated,* even when events initially seem disconnected or abrupt. That motivation may coalesce through the realization of a character, as with the Here in Texas authorial persona, or it may coalesce through other forms of explanation, as with the three facets of Kaleidescopic Texas. Authenticity informs the residual in that it may encompass ambivalence, inconsistency, and change, but it is also not haphazard or mistaken. The authentic expression of residuality demonstrates, through flow, its wayfaring form of coherence.

To summarize, no transformations were "more" residual than any other database, including the original Texas collection, in terms of being more ambiguous, fluid, or indeterminate. However, the original collection and Post-Texas Index, in "having an end" and supporting a transport mode of interaction, disguised the residual to an extent (except when scrutinized, and individual decisions emerged as problematic). Here in Texas and Kaleidescopic Texas, on the other hand, revealed—and explained—residuality through flow, instigating a wayfaring mode of interaction.

CONCLUSION

We suggest that flow, as we describe it, constitutes a form of "infrastructuring" to support design-after-design, or ongoing reappropriation of materials in extended design conversations, as performed by users [2]. In *Design Things,* the A. Telier group relates infrastructuring to participatory design, in which the designer's work shifts from producing artifacts with users to facilitating the sociomaterial conditions that enable ongoing conversation between users and their environments. Flow represents the process that a database author took to develop an interpretation, or reading, of the database content. In travsersing the paths established by the initial author, guided by the infrastructure of flow, database readers come to their own understanding of the underlying terrain, potentially to forge new paths. Our work here extends the idea of infrastructuring into the mundane, everyday context of metadata design and application, and we equally extend the concept of design-after-design to the perhaps even more mundane context of database interactions. We suggest that metadata infrastructures to facilitate wayfaring constitute a productive site for design activities in HCI; the thoughtful and provocative design of category systems like those we engage in this study can serve to enhance user agency and re-imagine forms of user participation in meaning making.

Our work also contributes to HCI in demonstrating a productive synthesis of critical design and interaction criticism. Had we relied only on our own process of making and our initial associated reflections, our ideas would not have progressed to thoughts of transport and wayfaring. Moreover, by asking respondents to criticize our transformations, and not use them, we opened up the object of our participants' attention. Many respondents crafted real arguments inspired by the transformations, instead of just relating likes and dislikes. In both substance and scope, these arguments challenged our own initial interpretations of our work and propelled our thinking.

Indeed, just as we have come to see database flow as providing infrastructure for wayfaring interactions, we are also beginning to formulate critical reading as providing infrastructure for critical design and innovation, and our future work will explore this integration, via the new transformations subsequently created by the student critics in our study.

ACKNOWLEDGMENTS

We thank all our respondents for their perceptive and insightful contributions, and the anonymous reviewers for thoughtful advice. We especially thank Kristen Hogan, who initially suggested an integration of classification design and mestiza consciousness.

REFERENCES

1. Anzaldua, G. (2012). *Borderlands/La Frontera: the new mestiza.* (4th ed.). San Francisco: Aunt Lute Books.
2. A. Telier. (Binder, T., et al.) (2011). *Design Things.* Cambridge, MA: MIT Press.
3. Bardzell. J. (2011). Interaction criticism. *Interacting With Computers, 23,* 604–621.
4. Bardzell, J. and Bardzell, S. (2013). What is critical about critical design? *Proc. ACM CHI 2013,* 3297–3306.
5. Bardzell, S., et al. (2012). Critical design and critical theory: The challenge of designing for provocation. *Proc. ACM DIS 2012,* 288–297.
6. Dalsgaard, P., and Dindler, C. (2009). Peepholes as a means of engagement in interaction design. *Proc. Nordes 2009: Engaging Artifacts.*
7. Dunne, A. (2006). *Hertzian tales.* Cambridge, MA: MIT Press.
8. Gaver, W., Beaver, J., and Benford, S. (2003). Ambiguity as a resource for design. *Proc. ACM CHI 2003,* 233–240.
9. Geisler. G. Open Video Digital Library Toolkit. (Available at http://www.open-video-toolkit.org/)
10. Ingold, T. (2007). *Lines.* London: Routledge.
11. Lowgren, J. and Stolterman, E. (2004). *Thoughtful interaction design.* Cambridge, MA: MIT Press.
12. Ratto, M. (2011). Critical making. *The Information Society,* 27(4), 252–260.
13. Sengers, P. Boehner, K., David, S., and Kaye, J. (2005). Reflective design. *Proc. AARHUS 2005,* 49–58.
14. Sengers, P. and Gaver, W. (2006). Staying open to interpretation. *Proc. ACM DIS 2006,* 99-108.
15. Star, S.L., and Bowker, G. (2007). Enacting silence: residual categories as a challenge for ethics, information systems, and communication. *Ethics and Information Technology,* 9, 273–280.
16. Wilson, P. (1978). *Two kinds of power.* Berkeley, CA: University of California Press.

Reading Critical Designs: Supporting Reasoned Interpretations of Critical Design

Jeffrey Bardzell
Indiana University
Bloomington, IN 47401
jbardzel@indiana.edu

Shaowen Bardzell
Indiana University
Bloomington, IN 47401
selu@indiana.edu

Erik Stolterman
Indiana University
Bloomington, IN 47401
estolter@indiana.edu

ABSTRACT
Critical Design has emerged as an important concept in HCI research and practice. Yet researchers have noted that its uptake has been limited by certain lacks of intellectual infrastructure—theories, methodologies, canons and exemplars, and a community of practice. We argue that one way to create this infrastructure is to cultivate a community adept at reading—that is, critically interpreting and making reasoned judgments about—critical designs. We propose an approach to developing close readings of critical designs, which are both evidence-based and carefully reasoned. The approach highlights analytical units of analysis, the relevance of design languages and social norms, and the analytical contemplation of critical aspects of a design. It is intended to be relatively easy to learn, to try out, and to teach, in the hopes of inviting more members of the HCI community to engage in this practice. We exemplify the approach with readings of two critical designs and reflect on different ways that a design might serve a critical purpose or offer a critical argument about design, society, and the future.

Author Keywords
Critical design; criticism; design theory; interpretation; art

ACM Classification Keywords
H.5.m. Information interfaces and presentation (e.g., HCI): Miscellaneous

INTRODUCTION
The notion of *critical design* has received much attention in HCI and design research. And yet in our experience, many conversations about critical design suggest quite a bit of confusion about what it is, what counts as a critical design, what could be seen as good critical designs, etc. There have over the years emerged some attempts to define critical design. Dunne and Raby, who coined the term as it is used today, say that critical design "rejects how things are now as being the only possibility, it provides a critique of the prevailing situation through designs that embody alternative social, cultural, technical, or economic values" [17, p.58]. Malpass characterizes critical design as "a move away from commercial design towards a conceptual, discursive, inquisitive and often provocative role […] where the object and medium of design are used as a form of inquiry" [29, p.2]. Mazé and Redström write that "design, amended as 'conceptual' or 'critical', may counter conventions of utility and efficiency, profit and taste" [30, p.3].

CHI 2014, April 26 - May 01 2014, Toronto, ON, Canada
Copyright 2014 ACM 978-1-4503-2473-1/14/04···$15.00.
http://dx.doi.org/10.1145/2556288.2557137

Yet understanding a concept in abstract and being able to use it meaningfully in everyday practice are two different things. As a community we often face designs, such as critical designs, that challenge our "normal" design frames of reference, but that still have qualities that make the design intriguing. Critical designs challenge existing assessment schema and even if intrigued we may find it difficult to have a serious and insightful discussion about their potential value, meaning, and role. Bardzell et al. argue that it is not clear how to do critical design or how to know if one has done it well [4]. This might be because, as [30] write, critical design practice lacks a coherent "discourse around criticality" or much by way of "an intellectual basis" (p.7). If critical design is to be accessible to the broader design and HCI communities, more work needs to be done to develop theory and methodologies to support it. In the present work, we argue that the field would be well served if it improved its ability to insightfully "read" (i.e., critically interpret) critical designs, that is, to construct and critique design arguments about critical designs. We offer and then demonstrate a practical approach to doing so.

Challenges for Practitioners
All critical design researchers, practitioners, and students have to make pragmatic decisions as they propose new critical designs or even engage existing ones. Is critical design likely to help us do what we want to do in a given project? What would constitute a good collection of (critical) design exemplars for a given project? How can the technologies, practices, norms, and/or ideologies we wish to explore be expressed in the language of design? During brainstorming, sketching, and prototyping phases, how do we know if

we're on the right track? How do we assess or evaluate critical designs? What sorts of effects do we expect, want, or need a critical design to have?

We are not alone in seeking support for the everyday practices of critical design. For instance, DiSalvo advocates serious critical design assement, because it

> *informs broad arguments in design studies. Specifically, through assessment, claims made concerning the effects of design are made accountable; enabling broader arguments to be made, or refuted, regarding the value and place of design in increasing societal awareness, and motivating and enabling political action [12, p.62].*

DiSalvo proposes a number of criteria to support such assessments, including, among others, "How and how well are the aesthetic characteristics of possible future conditions portrayed?" and "Do the projections evidence an intimate understanding of how complex ideas are transformed into products, services, and artifacts?" [p.61] Similarly, in [2] we turned to critical theory to offer an account of "criticality" intended to support assessments of the criticality of designs, stating that whether something is a critical design is "a value judgment for which one has to provide good reasons" [p.3304]. Both of these approaches are helpful, but neither unpacks many of the basic analytic and critical tasks that underlie such high-level judgments. We argue that such judgments are made within the context of a hermeneutic community and its practices.

Hermeneutic Communities and Art-Based Practices

Critical design is often characterized as an art-based approach to design research [26], because it is genealogically connected to art movements (e.g., the situationists and conceptual art), often resembles contemporary artworks in form and meaning, and is frequently exhibited in showrooms in the style of, and often within the walls of, art museums. As with art, the social function of critical design is characterized as engendering debates and changing perspectives about important social issues [2,18,26].

Yet—and this is crucial—the presentation of art to the public is mediated by a field of experts, guided by shared understandings of the field's history, theory, and practice. These experts identify canons of exemplars, histories of movements and innovations, diverse approaches to interpreting works, etc. The same is increasingly true of traditional design fields as well, especially architecture. Whether someone is an expert is largely defined in terms of how well she or he has mastered these canons, histories, theories, and approaches; expertise can be acquired by professionals and hobbyists alike, in different degrees, and from different positions (e.g., as artists, critics, curators, fans).

In short, surrounding an art domain is a fluid and dynamic hermeneutic community that performs curatorial, educational, and interpretive functions that shapes how the community as a whole understands the art domain (obviously with plenty of debate) as well as how individuals come to enter that community (e.g., as students, apprentices, and hobbyists). This community and its practices amount to a kind of intellectual infrastructure enabling the continuation, innovation, and dissemination of its art form. However, as Mazé and Redström [30] note, critical design lacks much of this infrastructure, which explains some of the difficulties the HCI and design communities have had in taking it up as a practice and which also suggests an agenda for the HCI research community to help cultivate this practice more broadly.

The Porcupine Dress

Many of these issues can be see unfolding with an example. Porcupine Dress (fig. 1) is one in a series of "Defensive Dresses" created by Amisha Gadani [20]. Most of the time, it looks like a fairly ordinary dress. However, if its wearer feels threatened, she can bend forward in a gesture of self-protection, causing a set of porcupine quills to raise on her back. How are we to understand such a design? Most of us have fairly immediate reactions: e.g., we are intrigued or repelled. Yet often these reactions are fuzzy: we can feel strongly that the design is brilliant, terrible, boring, etc., and yet have trouble saying exactly why.

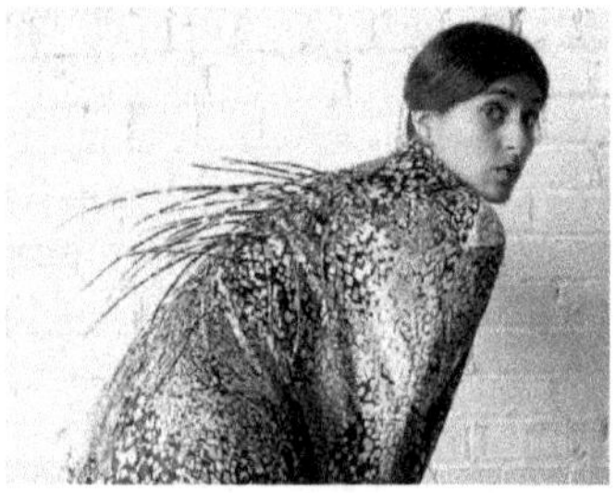

Fig. 1: Porcupine Dress (Amisha Gadani)

From childhood, we have been trained in practices of *interpretation* that seek to bring an analytical clarity that explains our hitherto strong but fuzzy reaction [33]. For example, we have been taught to categorize cultural works, so most of us looking at this dress will activate that hermeneutic skill to say that this is a dress, a work of art, a kind of statement, a design, a weapon, etc. Each of these classifications then activates norms and conventions that we can use to further understand the dress. As a dress, we might consider whether it is flattering, comfortable, goes with our other clothes, viable in the marketplace, etc. As a work of art, we might consider what it means, what the artist was trying to say with it, what art works it references or is similar to. We might read the dress-as-art as an awareness-raising *social statement* seeking to drive home the felt vulnerability of being a woman in today's cities. Or we might just Google it to see what the artist herself says, hoping that she will just tell us what it means:

> *The second in my series of defensive gowns, the Porcupine Dress allows the user to imitate the defensive quill-*

erecting behavior of a porcupine. Over thirty oven-baked, hand-painted quills prick up when the wearer detects a threat and bends their back in almost fetal position. In this way the user braces themselves for the possibility of an attack while simultaneously decreasing the probability of an attack by the sudden and alarming display. Created for the Geek Arts and Green Innovators Festival at the Pittsburgh Glass Center, this piece is designed to camouflage to a cocktail party and to erect it's quills when I'm intimidated. [20]

Though it offers helpful descriptive information, the statement says comparatively little about what the dress *means*; that is left to the viewer. (It is a convention of the art community that artist statements leave a certain amount of interpretation up to the viewer.)

However, viewers from different hermeneutic positions are likely to read this design in different ways. For example, a fashion editor might focus on a detail, such as the sleeve, and consider the historical and social connotations of its particular form and how it contributes to the dress's overall fit within this season's trends for a particular demographic. An art historian, in contrast, might consider the dress as part of a history of representations of animals in postmodern art so as to argue that the dress reflects a social trend in which earlier conceptions of humans' relation to nature as one of mastery and control are replaced with a newer conception that sees mimicking nature as key to our security.

If we take up a traditional design perspective, which as summarized by [27] entails viewing an artifact according to the three "mediations" of functionality, meaningfulness, and economy, we might ask why a consumer might want a "defensive dress"; we infer that it reflects and comments on the social problem of violence against women. In this way, we might read the dress as a *design proposition* that everyday commercial clothing should protect our bodies not just from the elements, but also from human social ills. This proposition raises many interesting—and generative—questions. How well does the dress protect the wearer? Can (or should) the dress injure an attacker? Is it machine washable? What sort of fashion statement would a woman wearing this dress be making about herself? Are there other everyday designs that could be made more defensive? Would the marketplace respond to this dress by offering clothes that better protect attackers? What other social ills we could protect ourselves from through defensive clothing? Do we as a society really want to address violence against women through defensive clothing?

We use the Porcupine Dress example to show that to a certain extent all of us have some ability using these hermeneutic strategies (e.g., to categorize, to make associations, to imagine or look up the artist's intent, to reason about it based on its context). But the example also suggests that some perspectives may be far stronger at generating certain kinds of insights and questions than others. All of which leads to this question: *What sorts of categorizations, associations, questions, insights, norms, judgments, etc., should be part of a critical designer's hermeneutic toolkit?*

Contribution and Roadmap

The purpose of this paper is to offer practical strategies for our community to read critical designs. Doing so should contribute towards the longer-term goals of developing collections of exemplars, histories, theories, evaluative norms, and other resources needed to help establish a communal literacy with critical design. We will present and exemplify the analytical strategies by which we have sought to read critical designs, to develop collections of examples, to categorize them, and to improve our understanding critical design's potentials. We believe this work can help support the following:

- Reading existing critical designs insightfully and generatively in a way that the community can understand, appreciate, and evaluate
- Making design choices in critical design processes, such as design problem framing and assessment
- Developing appropriate empirical strategies for deployments and exhibitions
- Supporting our own and also the public's evolving understanding of (critical) design arguments about the role(s) of design and our futures

In the next section, we account for the origins of our approach, including our intellectual assumptions and the history of its development. Following that, we present the critical design assessment approach itself, divided into three interrelated stages. Finally, through a close reading of a critical design, we demonstrate how our approach supports reasoned conversations about critical designs, how our approach helps us deal with borderline cases, and how it suggests the possibility of thinking more ambitiously about criticality and design.

DEFENSIBLE DESIGN JUDGMENTS

The approach we have taken is akin to ways that scholars in the humanities go about making critical judgments (as theorized in the humanities [5,7,9,19] and HCI and design [1,11,23,30,31,32]. Critical judgments typically have two key features: they are defended with arguments (comprising both verifiable evidence and reasoning), and they assert that others should agree with them [25] (which does not imply the empirical fact that others necessarily do). In everyday life, we make such judgments all the time, and the fact that we do so is neither a mystery nor controversial: a local theatre makes decisions about which plays to put on and asserts that a local public ought to come see them. A schoolteacher chooses readings for various reasons and in doing so asserts that they are appropriate readings for the students.

Design, likewise, is a knowledge practice that depends on judgments accompanied by arguments that seek assent. Critical judgments about designs are frequently generative

[31], that is, they help designers think in new ways [30], imagine alternative futures [12], frame design problems in new ways [10], and consider new material possibilities. Design judgments also have analytical benefits; for example, they can be used to assess designs in progress [27], and they can also reveal how designs construct for us qualities of life that we might want to develop or intervene upon [15]; they can help us interpret why a design succeeded or failed, or the ways in which a design was innovative; they can help us understand whether and how a design has critical qualities or critical functions in society [2,30]. To be effective, they must persuade stakeholders (at least to a degree), and to do that, they must incorporate evidence and arguments.

Success Criteria

A critical-analytical approach to reading critical designs is positioned to support knowledge production and decisionmaking about design in practical ways. We argue that any approach to reading critical designs can itself be assessed on how well it meets both of the following primary criteria:

- It should make it possible and as easy as reasonably possible for people to *articulate* and also to *justify* specific analytical judgments, that is, to offer evidence and arguments sufficient to persuade others.
- It should be oriented towards *pragmatic utility* over philosophical purity, by serving in a generative capacity and/or by supporting choices that designers, design researchers, project managers, design educators, etc., already make and need to make on an everyday basis.

As a secondary criterion, the assessment approach should scale to support most members of the design community, including design students, practitioners, and researchers (though the support it affords may require some practice and may support different members of the community in different ways).

Development Process

We developed our approach as part of our ongoing research on critical design. Our approach also builds on prior research we have done in critical design, design theory, and critical approaches to HCI [2,4], and a number of critical design research activities in particular, as follows.

Critical Design. Working with designers, fine artists, and technologists, we have been developing and deploying a collection of critical designs, which has forced us to confront practical questions about which design directions are better than others and to be able to justify our choices.

Critical Design Inventory. We constructed an inventory of over 350 critical designs (broadly construed) into two books, using existing reference works, web searches, personal recommendations, etc. These have been fundamental to our analytic work on critical design, including different strategies of categorizing these designs.

Design Critiques. We selected small groups of critical designs from our inventory (usually 5-10 at a time to enable close reading) and collaboratively developed arguments about ways in which they are critical. One common outcome of these critiques was that candidate framings, distinctions, norms, and so forth began to emerge. We then tried out these emerging framings and norms on different designs to test their broader applicability and fruitfulness.

Analytical Frameworks. Building on our design critiques and reviews of critical design literature [2,4,12,15,17,28, 29,30], and related topics, including speculative design [14], adversarial design [13], research through design [22,34], and constructive design [26], we prototyped several analytical frameworks, which we tested on ourselves, our students, and visiting academic and industry researchers to assess whether the frameworks were helping them generate judgments that are both rationally defensible and practical.

READING CRITICAL DESIGNS

We now begin articulating our approach to reading critical designs. We present our approach as a structured way of guiding and supporting the analytical process, as follows:

1. Identify a unit of analysis to work from (typically a part of a whole design, such as its UI; a design considered as a finished product; or a collection of related designs).
2. Situate that unit of analysis in relation to extant conventions and norms.
3. Isolate the *critical* aspects of the design as a focus of thought and attention.

Like any critical approach, the successful use of this approach is dependent on the practitioner: as critic Pauline Kael writes, "it takes extraordinary intelligence and discrimination and taste to use any theory in the arts" [24]. This means that though we present our approach as if it is a linear procedure, it cannot necessarily be deployed in such a fashion. Nonetheless, our presentation is intended to facilitate the learnability and memorability of the approach.

Identify the Unit of Analysis

We see two basic reasons why, based on the current literature, it is so difficult to determine whether a design is a critical design. First, as presented in key texts by Dunne and Raby, critical design and affirmative design are defined relationally in an overly simplistic binary, a problem already critiqued in [2]. Second, the unit of analysis is usually taken for granted to be the design as a completed product (e.g., [2,4,26,28,30]). This second assumption runs counter to criticism as it has been practiced for millennia. For instance, we talk about the use of metaphor separately from the narratological structure of a novel; we talk about screenwriting distinctly from cinematography. Not only can we talk about parts of works distinct from (or as constituting) their wholes, but we can also talk about collections of works, e.g., Hitchcock's suspense films. This same reasoning applies to designs, including critical designs, as follows:

- *A part of a design.* A part of a design could include a meaningful (and usually intuitively accessible) subset of its total functions (such as the steering system of a car), of its physical form (such as the legs of a dresser), of its appearance (a product's color palette), etc.
- *A design as a finished product.* This is typically what we mean when we say "a design" in everyday language. The physical composition makes this unit stand out as the typical unit of analysis. However, to chose this as the unit is as much a judgment and decision as any of the other units.
- *A given collection of designs.* A collection of designs is any grouping of designs, including designs introduced as part of a group, such as Gadani's Defensive Dresses, the collections designers construct as a part of design research [6], and designs that are shown together as part of an exhibition. [8] also proposes *portfolios* as an organizing framing for collections of a design studio's work.

The notions of "part", "product" or "collection" should not here be read as concepts that reference given entities; what one designer might identify as a whole design might be seen as a part or a collection by another, etc.

By opening up critical interpretation of critical design to different units of analysis, it becomes possible and more or less inevitable that conflicting judgments will be made about the same design. For example, a subset of a design's total functions might be read as critical, while the design as a part of a collection may be read as affirmative. We view the possibility of conflicting judgments about the same design as desirable and a crucial refinement to the present literature, because it would bring critical design assessment more in line with related critical practices, e.g, of interaction criticism and even film and digital media criticism.

Identify Appropriate Norms/Conventions

Coming to understand human works—be they art or design—requires that we have interpretative skills in place beforehand. These skills typically include basic categorization schemes and with them, norms and expectations. Our understanding of *Oedipus Rex* is made possible in large part because of our awareness of the conventions of ancient Greek dramatic tragedy—including notions of *katharsis*, tragic reversal, the function of the chorus, historical knowledge, and so forth. Our point is that to understand a work, we must also understand it as a certain *kind* of work. The same applies to design. To understand any given shoe, we must first appreciate shoes, including the ways that they protect us, communicate our personalities in social situations, fit with our outfits, etc. Fashion and consumer magazine and television industries exist to support and promote understandings and consumer behavior surrounding shoes.

What sort of work, then, is a critical design? We argue that all critical designs are composed from design languages found in one or more types of everyday design. Farkache's Come a Little Bit Closer Bench is a bench. Dunne & Raby's Teddy Bear Blood Bag Radio is a radio, a blood kit, and a children's toy. Gaver et al.'s Drift Table is a table, a screen, and an interactive peephole. These designs are all obviously many other things as well, but to understand them at all, we must first figure out what kinds of designs we think they are—tables, helmets, toasters, clocks—because this categorization invokes a collection of norms, conventions, and expectations: benches and tables are sturdy, sized at a human scale, comfortable (with predictable limits, e.g., the hardness of seating surfaces), expressive (e.g., a bed in a hospital is recognizably different from a bed in a historical museum or a modernist furniture showroom), etc.

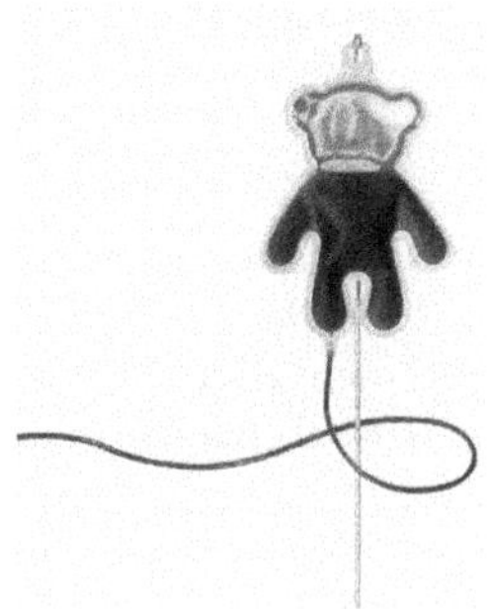

Fig. 2: Teddy Bear Blood Bag Radio (Anthony Dunne & Fiona Raby)

But insofar as they are *critical*, critical designs also comment on, subvert, reinterpret, exaggerate, juxtapose, or otherwise introduce one or more twists (also known as *tropes*) on the standard design. Tropes are imperceptible if we do not understand the conventional form of the design first. For example, a conventional radio is powered electrically, which in today's terms, typically means either a battery or plugging into a wall outlet. However, in researching alternative energy sources, designers Dunne and Raby came across a meat-eating robot in a university project. Speculatively imagining that decomposing organic matter as an electrical source were to become mainstream, they designed Teddy Bear Blood Bag Radio, which is a radio for children that is powered by blood extracted from their pets [16, Fig. 2]. The resulting design features a number of tropes: the blood bag is shaped like a teddy bear, because it is a children's radio; the radio is powered by organic matter, which has been extracted from of all sources a pet; this decomposing organic matter is blood, whose red is revealed as aesthetically pleasing. One can imagine any number of responses to this critical design, but much of the meaning emerges from the tensions between conventions of behavior and taste (such as how designs usually represent childhood) and the shocking norms elegantly inscribed in this design.

In short, reading a critical design, once its unit of analysis has been clearly identified, involves two steps. First is to classify it in relation to everyday design languages, and second is attending specifically to the tropes that make it a *critical* design. Following [9], we stress that we do not mean "classification" in a universal sense; rather, we think of classification as a pragmatic stance that we appropriate in a given situation in order to understand a work richly and usefully. For example, Teddy Bear Blood Bag Radio is not only a radio: it is also a teddy bear and a blood bag kit. As a blood bag, it is a medical product; as a teddy bear, it is an animal and a doll; as a radio, it is an electronic product, or an entertainment product, or part of a music ecology—the list goes on. Each of these is more or less amenable to reading from different hermeneutic perspectives. In other words, there is no "correct" classification; classification itself is an expert judgment contingent on a particular situation, and the "best" classification is the one that is most generative of whatever design thinking or sociocultural critique the analyst is engaged in.

We see this classificatory activity as unfolding into two separate but related tasks, as follows.

1. *Classify the unit of analysis in relation to design types or genres to which we judge it in this instance to belong.* As we have just shown, once this classification is made (e.g., Teddy Bear Blood Bag Radio as a medical device, a doll, or an element of a music ecology), very different sorts of norms are invoked leading to different sorts of insights and claims. It can be conventional or affirmative from one perspective, critical from another, and downright absurd from another.
2. *Classify the unit in relation to one or more contingent perspectives.* Designs can only be viewed by someone somewhere, so this task is about disclosing that sensemaking point of view and unpacking its consequences. Considering Teddy Bear Blood Bag Radio as a clinical interior designer has different implications than, say, a modern art lover viewing it in an art museum or a parent of a hospitalized child. Historical contingencies are also paramount: a telephone from the 1970s reads differently today than it did then. Such contingencies are not merely details; they are the conditions of possibility for the design to mean anything, to anyone.

Interpreting the criticality of a design depends, therefore, on how a given analyst in a given situation with given practical needs activates the hermeneutic skills of focusing on one or more parts of the design and considering them in relation to a set of extant conventions and norms. Without articulating this combination of sensemaking perspective or standpoint, a set of design particulars, and a set of extant semiotic structures (such as signifying conventions and their accompanying categories and norms), it is extremely difficult to construct, let alone express to others, a sophisticated understanding of a design. It is obvious that in many cases this articulation is a complex task that requires considerable effort and skill in constructing critical arguments. This may also be one reason why HCI has not seen many well-developed readings of specific critical designs (aside from their designers' own accounts), in spite of the benefits such readings would bring in terms of revealing and clarifying canons, categorizations, norms, etc.

Isolate Specifically Critical Aspects of the Design

The preceding sections have summarized many of the core strategies of design criticism or interaction criticism [1]. But the emphasis of the present research is specifically *critical* designs—including works explicitly presented as "critical designs" and works not presented as critical designs but whose critical function merits our consideration anyway. The challenge, then, is not to try to interpret the design "in itself" or "as a design," but specifically as a "critical design." We have argued that to be a critical design, a work must also be relatable to conventional designs; the criticality becomes visible in the twist or commentary that the critical design makes on the traditional design. Thus the analytic challenge is to understand the particular ways that a critical design can differ from the more conventional designs that they simultaneously embody and critique.

The basic strategy that we propose is to analyze relevant qualities of the design—now understood analytically as a unit of analysis set in relation to an appropriate set of norms and conventions as seen from a contingent perspective—in relation to criticality. In [2] we define the criticality of a design as follows:

> *a design research project may be judged "critical" to the extents that it proposes a perspective-changing holistic account of a given phenomenon, and that this account is grounded in speculative theory, reflects a dialogical methodology, improves the public's cultural competence, and is reflexively aware of itself as an actor—with both power and constraints—within the social world it is seeking to change.*

This formulation attempts to answer the question of the particular ways that specifically critical stances or qualities are made manifest. However, we discovered in our own practice that it can be difficult to work with as-is and might undermine the usability of our approach. Thus we adapted its five complex criteria into four simpler ones, hopefully without sacrificing too much of its analytic power.

	Changing perspectives	Proposals for change	Enhancing appreciation	Reflectiveness
Topic				
Purpose				
Functionality				
Interactivity				
Form				
Materiality				

Table 1. Matrix of Common Argument Types

We have iteratively constructed an inventory of argument types to support the argument that "X is/is not performing a critical function" where X is (once again) the selected unit of analysis set in relation to an appropriate set of design norms and conventions from a particular perspective or contingent situation. We offer 24 such sample arguments, which emerge from a matrix comprising *6 design dimen-*

sions and *4 dimensions of criticality* (the latter 4 as adapted from [2], Table 1). Of course, we do not propose that these are the only arguments that could be made; we certainly do not want to reify this list as the necessary and sufficient conditions of critical design. Rather, they are offered as an *inventory of supports*, that is, a scaffold that functions in a similar way that many literary theories scaffold critical analysis of literary texts: to facilitate and guide, not to determine or cause, the active and creative process for forming analytical judgments and assessments.

In the matrix of common argument types, the rows correspond to interaction design dimensions, while the columns correspond to dimensions of criticality. Each row and column is explained below, but simply: each row or column supports a particular perspective when analyzing designs. For example, we can ask if a design changes perspectives (column 1), and we can ask that question in relation to its topic, its purpose, its functionality, etc. (i.e., the rows).

We begin our explanation with the rows:

- *Topic/problem space*. This refers to the human domain in which the design serves, intervenes, participates, etc. Example: an ATM is in the domain of banking.
- *Purpose*. This refers to the central purpose of the design *qua* design, that is, its rationality considered as a whole. Example: an ATM's purpose is to provide to individual bank account holders useful and secure access to their bank records.
- *Functionality*. This refers to the discrete capabilities or things that the design can do or can enable its user to do. Example: an ATM's functionality includes authentication, balance inquiries, account transfers, withdrawals, deposits, etc.
- *Interactivity*. We define this mainly as input/output with a human. Example: an ATM's interactivity includes a range of simple, well defined linear tasks accomplished using a numeric keypad with a few function keys, a screen, a credit card slot, a cash dispenser, etc.
- *Form*. This refers to its specific instantiation: of all the ways such a design could have been formed, structured, styled, and/or made available to human awareness, what specific ways was this actually formed, etc. Example: an ATM's form includes drive-up versus walk-up, color vs. monochrome screen, size and feel of buttons and other elements, branding, etc.
- *Materiality*. This refers to the physical materials out of which the design is made, including what makes it available to human perception and consciousness, the qualities of that perception, how it is physically interacted with, etc. Example: an ATM's materiality includes the metal, glass, and plastic out of which it is formed as an ATM.

Assessing a work's "criticality" is known to be difficult. Appropriating and simplifying [2], we suggest the following four dimensions or aspects of criticality as different scaffolds for assessing the ways in which a design performs a critical function, expresses criticality, etc. Below, "the user" can refer to the end user of the design, or any stakeholder, or even a design researcher, depending on the contingencies in play.

- *Changing perspectives*. The design presents a framing or point of view that is new, coherent, and interesting enough to help the user perceive the particulars of a domain according to a new schema.
- *Proposals for change*. The design embodies a provocative proposal for an alternative way of being; the proposal is grounded in possibility, cannot be easily dismissed as "science fiction," and the user can imagine her or himself in its universe.
- *Enhancing appreciation*. The design contributes to the user's appreciation of or judgment on design's role(s) in a sociocultural issue of significance, by making the user more perceptive, imaginative, or aware of the complexity (political, symbolic, etc.) of a domain.
- *Reflectiveness*. This can be understood in two senses. One is the sense of encouraging user reflectiveness, that is, facilitating the user's shift from direct perception and action to a more reflective or self-aware stance. The other is the design itself embodying reflectiveness, for example, by revealing or foregrounding the tropes by which it distinguishes itself from design conventions as the rhetorical devices that they are.

We stress that we do not recommend attempting to evaluate a design in relation to all 24 types of argument, or even worse, counting checked boxes in the matrix to make a quantitative claim that designs with at least 12 checked boxes are critical, or that one design is more critical than another because it has more checked boxes. We simply propose that if a design intuitively feels critical, then it is likely that at least one of these types of argument will help bring analytical clarity to that intuition, allowing a more reasoned contemplation.

READING TEDDY BEAR BLOOD BAG RADIO

We have now presented our approach to reading critical designs as a hermeneutic process of identifying reasons to support judgments (or often clarify intuitions) about the critical function, effects, or argument of a design. We argued in the introduction that such a low-level strategy was needed as a precursor step of higher-level assessment strategies as outlined in DiSalvo [12] and Bardzell and Bardzell [2]. In this section we demonstrate how the approach we have just outlined interfaces with these higher-level assessment strategies and supports critical judgments about critical designs.

From Inventory of Arguments to an Analytical Judgment

If in [2] we were right in asserting that whether something is a critical design is "a value judgment for which one has to provide good reasons," then the interpreter of critical designs needs to provide good reasons. So one practical use of our approach is to support the generation of reasons, which we propose take the following logical form:

> *{X}* is critical inasmuch as *{a detail or quality pertaining to one of its design dimensions}* performs, exhibits, or embodies *{a criticality dimension}*.

Again, the design dimensions and criticality dimensions correspond to rows and columns in our matrix, respectively. Let us return, by way of demonstration, to Dunne and Raby's Teddy Bear Blood Bag Radio (Fig. 2). Of it, we can say,

> ***Teddy Bear Bloodbag Radio*** is critical inasmuch as ***blood*** *{from the design dimension 'Materiality'}* is presented as ***an aesthetic decoration*** *{from the criticality dimension 'Changing perspectives')*

We use the logical form of the sentence to emphasize the levels of specificity we are able to achieve in this kind of analysis, linking *evidence* (i.e., the material blood is a key part of the design's visual form) and *argument* (i.e., the use of blood as a design decoration goes against conventional representations and connotations of blood and therefore is critical). However, it is rhetorically tedious to continue using the logical form, so we express the rest in plain English (and we note that we did use the matrix to help generate these).

- The blood bag radio is critical because the child-pet relationship is proposed to be one of exploitation for human-only entertainment, a proposal that challenges us to reflect on how we, and our children, view pets.
- It is critical because a blood-extraction and storage kit is presented as a subsystem for an electronic music player.
- Using alternative energy sources is presented as something for children to do; it is not just an "adult" problem.
- The blood bag is aesthetically stylized (unlike conventional blood bags) as a child's doll.
- The music player is foregrounded as a device needing to be powered, something we easily forget.
- The concept of electronic wiring is reframed: no longer a copper conduit, it is now a blood conduit.
- The blood bag's teddy bear form is so over the top that it calls attention to itself as a rhetorical device.
- Blood Bag Radio features one of the key themes of its collection, "Is This Your Future?," by proposing the consumption of body materials in children's everyday practices.
- The banality of the horror represented in this future design is a call for sustainable behavior change today.

Each of these statements constitutes a reason or brief argument. We can group them together to construct, defend, or criticize an overall judgment concerning the critical function, effects, or argument of the design. There is no simple measure of when a collection of reasons meets the burden of achieving sufficient critical mass to support the claim that "X is/is not performing a critical function." Of course, the point at which a critical mass is achieved is itself a judgment call. Presumably, critical mass is achieved when one believes that the judgment could credibly demand assent from others, or at least provoke constructive further discussion and analysis.

Supporting Higher Level Critical Design Readings

We believe the bullet list of reasons in the previous section is sufficient to support the analytical judgment that Blood Bag Radio is indeed a critical design and that others ought to agree with that judgment for the reasons we provided. But this is just the beginning, not the end, because it has set us up for a new and carefully reasoned conversation about whether we think that Teddy Bear Blood Bag Radio is a *successful* critical design, i.e., whether we judge it to be a good critical design, and if so whether we would consider it an exemplary or even canonical critical design. For now, we are less interested making such judgments and more interested in demonstrating how the preceding analysis supports the construction of the kinds of reasoned interpretations that can underlie such judgments.

One might argue that even granting a future in which decomposing organic matter is used as a source of electricity, this design is too absurd to take seriously. That is, there is no plausible future in which Teddy Bear Blood Bag Radio could be a commercial design. Following science fiction theorists in distinguishing between "cognitive speculation" and "mere fantasy," in which the former is speculation grounded in a rigorous understanding of the past and present and used to project possible futures, and the latter is mere escapism [see 3], this radio seems to be more on the order of fantasy than serious speculation, and therefore the design *qua* critical design is unsuccessful.

Alternatively, one might argue that placed in a science museum gallery targeted at 7-14 year olds, Blood Bag Radio demands a level of critical reasoning that is not developmentally appropriate to children in that age group. Children will not understand that its flouting of medical device, entertainment device, home pet care, and design visual language conventions are intended to make a complex, symbolic argument about energy use in the possible future. Because the children are likely to miss these points, one might argue that the design *qua* critical design is unsuccessful.

Some of these issues could be further pursued with an empirical component. On the question of whether the blood bag radio is inappropriate for 7-14 year old museum-goers, we might ask, well how *did* the children (and their parents) at the museum actually react to this design? Did it, and if so where did it, generate worthwhile conversations: between parent and child, among curators, in the design research community? Empirical results are unlikely to conclusively resolve debates about the meaning of Blood Bag Radio, but the sorts of reasons our approach generates do interface well with empirical questions and results and can help stimulate reasoned discussions.

Such reasons could also be very helpful in critiquing with DiSalvo's assessment questions, as mentioned earlier. For example, DiSalvo encouraged those assessing critical designs to ask, "How and how well are the aesthetic characteristics of possible future conditions portrayed?" [12, p.61]. Many of the reasons we provided about the blood bag radio are about the presentation of aesthetic characteristics of future conditions. For instance, the decorative use of (actual) blood red is an important element of the radio's visual language, but it only makes sense if today's connotations of blood—illness, hospitalization, catastrophe—are no longer extant. The design also proposes a medicalization of domestic devices and environments, albeit with a whimsical sense of style. The depicted banality of children extracting blood from pets to power a radio can be read as a dystopian take on today's consumer fetish for electronic devices.

Pushing this interpretation further, one might argue that the blood bag radio tells us more about the present than about the future. It is difficult to imagine this radio as a commercial design in any reasonably expectable future. But as a metaphor of how consumerism twists us into a society of people that not only reaps environmental destruction to serve its consumer electronic fetish, but which also trains its children to do the same, the design is powerful. It works rhetorically in a way comparable to the symbolic retribution (*contrapasso*) in Dante: the torments of the damned in the *Inferno* both reenact and also reveal the truth about the sin. Because of the power of this metaphor, one might argue that the design *qua* critical design is successful.

What is Critical about Critical Designs

Is Blood Bag Radio's complex metaphor embodied in an improbable design, then, "design criticality"? Surely it is one form of it. But there are others: Goldsmiths' Drift Table [21], in contrast, is not only conceptually plausible in the present but has in fact been deployed in real situations and appreciated for what it is, a result that would be very hard to imagine with the Blood Bag Radio. Drift Table playfully embodies notions surrounding digital environments, the sociability of coffee tables, and the user experience of ambiguity, critiquing both prototypes and visions of the future emerging from university and industry IT labs. Yet Drift Table is not as metaphorically allusive to the implications of everyday cultural logics taken to extreme conclusions the way that Blood Bag Radio is.

As with Blood Bag Radio, it is also hard to imagine Porcupine Dress [20] actually being used in its ostensible intended sense. But unlike Blood Bag Radio, we would not say so because it is too dystopian. Rather, we would argue that it is an ambivalent design that prompts us to reflect on violence towards women, to consider fashion design's potential roles in the present and future of that social ill, and to consider how biomimicry can inform interactive fashion in highly provocative and generative ways. It raises many interesting questions about what we want from a design, but like the Drift Table it stops short of providing any clear answers.

So there is more than one way for a design to serve a critical function. A design can propose a future that that is different enough from what we would have extrapolated that it surprises us—and we desire it. It can reveal the horrifying implications of a contemporary practice. It can defamiliarize the present to render contingent that which we always thought was just natural, and open up hitherto unthought design possibilities. It can make us more empathic towards the lives and experiences of others. It can produce a design image that is gently troubling, neither utopian nor dystopian, but which nags at us to take it seriously. At a minimum, we believe that developing readings using arguments from our inventory (and arguments like them) will facilitate the construction of critical design curated collections, histories, categorizations, and above all a shared literacy for these designs that at best exists in nascent form in HCI.

CONCLUSION: ASSESSING OUR APPROACH

It is clear to us that our approach, as well as any other intending to present a detailed strategy of understanding a particular practice, runs the danger of supporting conformity. In this specific case that would be somewhat ironic because critical design usually is supposed to resist dominating systems of norms. We have taken this danger seriously. We have repeatedly stated that our approach is to be understood as a *support* for, not a recipe for, judgment making, and moreover that it is the pragmatic contingencies, not the transcendent truth (whatever that is), that are the ultimate ground of design meaning and value, and therefore that our approach supports the *engendering* of—not the resolution of—spirited yet reasoned debates about critical design.

Early on we presented two primary success criteria by which to judge our approach. The first criterion was that our approach must "make it possible and as easy as reasonably possible for people to *articulate* and also to *justify* specific analytical judgments." The second criterion was that "it must be oriented towards *pragmatic utility* over philosophical purity" by serving practicing designers and critics in a concrete and practical way in their everyday work.

We believe our approach explains and through this paper exemplifies specific, teachable, and learnable skills needed to engage in reasoned debates involving the criticality of designs. As our demonstrative analyses of Porcupine Dress and Blood Bag Radio in particular—show, the sorts of reasons that our approach helps generate do interface well both with empirical studies and existing critical-analytic approaches proposed in the research literature. They support a number of different assessment purposes, including how a design is seen to serve a critical function, understanding the criticality of any design, and (eventually, with more studies) supporting the ongoing development of theory on the criticality of design. The approach can also be used on sketches and prototypes to help guide critical design processes. Likewise it can be applied to understand the criticality of formally grouped or ad hoc collections of designs as a form of research for design. The approach can also help clarify the particular ways in which designs are intended to be critical, which can support the design of empirical studies (e.g., thoughtfully constructed deployment studies and exhibitions) of critical designs. Above all, we are confident that our approach fulfills the more modest goal to support productive dialogues around the notion of criticality and critical designs.

ACKNOWLEDGEMENTS

This research was funded by NSF IIS Creative IT (#1002772) and the Intel Science and Technology Center for Social Computing. We thank Carl DiSalvo, David England, Jodi Forlizzi, Shad Gross, Lone Koefoed Hansen, Youngsuk Lee, Stephanie Louraine and our reviewers.

REFERENCES

1. Bardzell, J. (2011). Interaction criticism: An introduction to the practice. *Interacting with Computers 23*(2011), 604-621. Oxford University Press.
2. Bardzell, J., and Bardzell, S. (2013). What is critical about critical design? *Proc. of CHI'13*. ACM Press.
3. Bardzell, J., and Bardzell, S. (2013). "A great and troubling beauty": Cognitive speculation and ubiquitous computing. *Personal and Ubiquitous Computing*
4. Bardzell, S., Bardzell, J., Forlizzi, J., Zimmerman, J., and Antanitis, J. (2012). Critical design and critical theory. *Proc. of DIS2012*. ACM Press.
5. Barnard, M. (2001). *Approaches to Understanding Visual Culture*. Palgrave.
6. Blevis, E. (2012). The PRInCiPleS design framework. In J. Carroll (ed.). *Human-Computer Interaction Series (1)*20, 143-169. Springer.
7. Bogost, I. (2008). *Unit Operations: An Approach to Videogame Criticism*. MIT Press.
8. Bowers, J. (2012). The logic of annotated portfolios: Communicating the value of "research through design." *Proc. of DIS2012*.
9. Carroll, N. (2009). *On Criticism*. Routledge.
10. Cross, N. (2006). *Designerly Ways of Knowing*. Birkhäuser.
11. Coyne, R. (1995). *Designing Information Technology in the Postmodern Age: From Method to Metaphor*. MIT Press.
12. DiSalvo, C. (2009). Design and the construction of publics. *Design Issues 25*(1), 48-63.
13. DiSalvo, C. (2012). *Adversarial Design*. MIT Press.
14. DiSalvo, C. (2012). Spectacles and Tropes: Speculative Design and Contemporary Food Cultures. *The Fiberculture Journal 2012 (20)*, 109-122.
15. Dunne, A. (2006). *Hertzian Tales: Electronic Products, Aesthetic Experience, and Critical Design*. MIT Press.
16. Dunne, A. & Raby, F. Design for Debate. Convivio Web-Zone 203: http://daisy.cti.gr/webzine/Issues/Issue-%203/Art%20and%20Design/
17. Dunne, A., and Raby, F. (2001). *Design Noir: The Secret Life of Electronic Objects*. Birkhäuser.
18. Dunne, A., and Raby, F. (2013). *Speculative Everything*. MIT Press.
19. Eagleton, T. (2008). *Literary Theory: An Introduction*. University of Minnesota Press.
20. Gadani, A. (2010). Porcupine Dress. http://amishagadani.com/Work/porcupine/
21. Gaver, W., Bowers, J., Boucher, A., Gellerson, H., Pennington, S., Schmidt, A., Steed, A., Villars, N., Walker, B. (2004). The drift table: Designing for ludic engagement. *CHI EA'04*. ACM Press.
22. Gaver, W. (2012). What should we expect from research through design? *Proc. of CHI'12*.
23. Greenberg, S. and Buxton, B. Usability considered harmful (some of the time). *Proc. of CHI'08*.
24. Kael, P. (2005 [1965]). The idea of film criticism. In Wartenberg & Curran (eds.), *The Philosophy of Film*. Malden, MA: Blackwell, 108-17.
25. Kant, I. *Critique of Judgment*. (1987 [1790]). Indianapolis: Hackett.
26. Koskinen, I., Zimmerman, J., Binder, T., Redstrom, J. and Wensveen, S. (2011). *Design Research through Practice*. Burlington, MA: Morgan Kaufmann.
27. Kuutti, K. (2009). HCI and design: Uncomfortable bedfellows? In Binder, Löwgren & Malmborg (eds.) *(Re)searching the Digital Bauhaus*. Springer, 43-59.
28. Lee, Y. & Lee, K. (2010). Design research and the complexity encountered in people's critical thoughts. *Proc. of DRS'10*.
29. Malpass, M. (2010). Perspectives on critical design: A conversation with Ralph Ball and Maxine Naylor. *Proc. of DRS'10*.
30. Mazé, R., & Redström, J. (2007). Difficult forms: Critical practices of design and research. *Proc. of IASDR'07*.
31. Nelson, H. and Stolterman, E. (2012). *The Design Way*. MIT Press.
32. Schön, D. (1984). *Reflective Practitioner*. Basic Books.
33. Taylor, C. Interpretation and the sciences of man. *The Review of Metaphysics 25*(1), 3-51.
34. Zimmerman, J., Forlizzi, J., and Evanson, S. (2007). Research through design as a method for interaction design research in HCI. In Proc. of CHI'07. ACM Press.

Designing for Slowness, Anticipation and Re-visitation: A Long Term Field Study of the Photobox

William Odom[1], Abigail Sellen[2], Richard Banks[2], David Kirk[4], Tim Regan[2], Mark Selby[3], Jodi Forlizzi[1], John Zimmerman[1]

[1] HCI Institute, Carnegie Mellon University, Pittsburgh, PA, USA, wodom@cs.cmu.edu
[2] Microsoft Research, Cambridge, UK, { asellen, rbanks, timregan }@microsoft.com
[3] Mixed Reality Lab, University of Nottingham, Nottingham, UK, psxms3@nottingham.ac.uk
[4] Culture Lab, Newcastle University, Newcastle, UK, david.kirk@ncl.ac.uk

ABSTRACT
We describe the design, implementation and deployment of Photobox, a domestic technology that prints four or five randomly selected photos from the owner's Flickr collection at random intervals each month. We deployed Photobox in three homes for fourteen months to explore how the slow pace at which it operates could support experiences of anticipation and re-visitation of the past. Findings reveal changes in attitude toward the device, from frustration to eventual acceptance. Participants drew on the photos to reflect on past life events and reactions indicated a renewed interest for their Flickr collection. Photobox also provoked reflection on technology in and around the home. These findings suggest several opportunities, such as designing for anticipation, better supporting reflection on the past, and, more generally, expanding the slow technology research program within the HCI community.

Author Keywords
Slow Technology; Home; Interaction Design; Design

ACM Classification Keywords
H.5.m. Information interfaces and presentation (e.g., HCI): Miscellaneous.

INTRODUCTION
The convergence of social, cloud, and mobile computing has made it increasingly easy for people to create, store, and share digital content. These new technologies have enabled people to create vast collections of their life experiences—a valuable resource for connecting with others and reflecting on one's own life. As an example, the social media service Facebook hosted roughly 210 billion photos in 2011, making it the largest single photographic archive in the world [10]; and this archive continues to grow.

These huge archives pose new challenges for HCI. As the archives grow larger, they become increasingly invisible, lacking the material presence that might enable people to notice and engage with the archive in the course of their everyday lives. It is also difficult for people to grasp just how big their archives are. And, because they do not take up physical space, people feel less inclined to curate their collections and conserve domestic storage space [23]. In parallel to these emerging issues, there has been a growing concern within HCI to develop new approaches enabling people to experience their personal digital content in more succinct, accessible, and meaningful ways [e.g., 29, 31].

While people are amassing more diverse kinds of virtual possessions [23], this paper focuses on digital photos, one of the most enduring and expansive contemporary forms of personal content. We wanted to investigate new forms of interaction that potentially enable meaningful experiences with photo collections by making them more material and by building in support for self-reflection and re-visitation of the past. In addition, we wanted to investigate the use of *slow technology* [12], and how this contrasting concept could challenge the idea of domestic technology being always on and accessible. Following this work, we wanted to explore how slowness might grow anticipation and create an interaction pace that supports self-reflection.

Figure 1. H1's initial installation. Photobox sits on top of table, while the laptop rests in plain sight underneath.

CHI 2014, April 26–May 1, 2014, Toronto, Ontario, Canada.

http://dx.doi.org/10.1145/2556288.2557178

To investigate these issues, we created *Photobox,* a domestic technology that prints four or five randomly selected photos from the owner's Flickr collection at random intervals each month (see Figure 1). We then deployed this device in three homes for fourteen months, using it to open a critical dialogue with households about the increasing digitization of their photo archive and about the experience of living with slow technology.

The field study revealed an interesting change in attitude around slow technology, from frustration to appreciation. Participants drew on the photos to reflect on past life events and celebrate (or let go of) aspects of earlier life stages. Reactions also indicated a renewed interest and appreciation among participants for their Flickr photo collection. Finally, Photobox provoked reflection on the role of technology in the home and even prompted subtle changes in routine.

This paper makes two contributions. First, it provides new insights on how slow technology can build anticipation and influence perceptions of value and meaning for digital collections of photos. Second, it provides a rare example of how a long-term deployment can be used to understand how the experience of a technology can change over time.

BACKGROUND AND RELATED WORK

Related work falls into three areas: material possessions and photographs; intersecting HCI research on reflection and reminiscence; and slow technology and anticipation.

Material possessions play important roles as triggers for personal and shared memories, signifying our evolving sense of self and relationships with others over time [1]. Csikzentmihalyi and Rochberg-Halton [4] describe how possessions become meaningfully integrated into one's life through the processes of reflecting on the past and prospectively looking forward toward one's idealized goals. Many others across the social sciences and humanities have investigated the roles material artifacts play in supporting memory, reflection and reminiscence [e.g., 20]. In this context, physical photographs have received particular attention. While initially emerging as a way to visually capture family histories in the late 19th century, photos have become a resource for individual identity construction and communication [37]. Photos can viscerally remind people of who they once were in a way that invites comparison and highlights how they have changed [see 1].

The shift to digital technology greatly expanded the practice of personal photography [30]. Van House [36] describes how this shift produced rapid increases in the everyday production, consumption, storage, and sharing of photos. Online services have created additional opportunities for people to share photos as a resource for self-presentation and expression [e.g., 35].

However, these collective shifts also produced unintentional consequences. Digital photos lack the enduring presence and "casual durability" of paper photos [36, p. 129], requiring more maintenance and effort to experience them. They can also become fragmented across several devices and online places, making them difficult to browse, search and retrieve [23]. Importantly, digital photo collections are prone to rapidly grow out of control, leaving people overwhelmed, which further complicates efforts to curate, organize, preserve and reflect on them [29, 31, 36].

The increasing prevalence of personal digital content affected by these issues, along with a growing interest in HCI toward designing for contexts of everyday life, has led to a stream of work exploring how reflection and reminiscence might be better supported. A core theme researchers have focused on is personal archiving practices [e.g., 16]. Another body of work has investigated the creation of new technologies to attach digital content to physical mementos [e.g., 29, 34], and ways to capture and explore image-based and audio recordings [e.g., 28, 31]. Most recently, Cosley and colleagues [3] demonstrated the potential value for re-experiencing social media to support reminiscence. Nonetheless, it remains unclear how to manage personal digital content as collections rapidly become larger, more diverse, and more fragmented.

Considering the rapid rate of digital photo production, we see an opportunity to explore how consumption might be slowed down. In their seminal article on *slow technology*, Hallnäs and Redström argue that the increasing presence of technology in contexts outside of the workplace require interaction design practice to move beyond creating tools to make people's lives more efficient to "*creating technology that surrounds us and therefore is part of our activities for long periods of time*" [12, p. 161]. These authors outline an agenda aimed at designing relationships with computational artifacts that will endure and develop over time, in part through supporting experiences of reflection on these things. Over a decade later, there has been a resurgence of work in the area [11, 18, 19, 24, 25, 26, 32, 33].

We also see an opportunity for connecting slow technology with the experience of *anticipation.* While this topic has rarely been tackled head on in HCI, McCarthy and Wright's [21] elegant description of anticipation in the context of felt experience is a noteworthy exception. They describe anticipation as occurring in two temporal phrases; the first before an experience has happened, while the second occurs during the experience as one actively reflects on whether their expectations have been unmet, met, or exceeded [21, p. 64]. We want to explore how slowness might open a space for anticipation over time, and how this might affect people's perceptions of their digital photo collections.

Collectively, these strands of research have made important contributions to understanding how interactive technologies could better persist in people's lives over time and how experiences of reflection and reminiscence might be supported. They also reveal how new problems are emerging as the rapid growth and fragmentation of personal digital content threatens its ability to be a valuable resource for reflection. Our work attempts to bring these strands of research together. We want to investigate how technologies might be designed to slow the consumption of digital photos and support experiences of reflection and re-visitation of the past. A secondary goal is to investigate how slow technology might fit within (or complicate) households' existing practices, and, more generally, their experiences living with slow technology. Beyond work that has gone before, we do this by grounding discussion around a fourteen-month deployment study of the Photobox prototype in three separate households.

METHODOLOGY

We designed the Photobox with the goal of exploring how slowing down the consumption of digital photos and making them material could generate anticipation, while also providing pause for reflection on and re-visitation of elements in the archive. We also aimed to investigate how these qualities could shape the perception of the digital photo archive in general. Specifically, we wanted to create a technology that might challenge the always-on-and-accessible qualities of many contemporary consumer devices. We intended to create a design artifact, which had a form that did not demand attention from its owner(s) nor require participation to enact its function. Our methodology drew on several approaches including speculative design [6], reflective design [32], technology probes [14] and research through design [39].

Process, Rationale and Implementation

The process leading to the development of the Photobox consisted of the following. We reviewed theoretical literature and empirical studies (a sample of which are noted in the prior section). We then ideated many design concepts and progressively refined and clustered several conceptually related sets to construct an understanding of the overall design space. We then engaged in iterative development and critique of the design concepts themselves to arrive at the final design (see [24] for more detail on our design process).

We intended the Photobox form to appear familiar to other non-digital cherished things, aiming for its material aesthetics to evoke a sense of warmth associated with older domestic artifacts. We settled on the final design because of its distance from contemporary 'technology' (i.e. oak compared to plastic). The two main components of Photobox are an antique oak chest and a Bluetooth-enabled Polaroid Pogo printer (which makes 2"x3" prints). We decided on using a chest that had already gathered a healthy amount of patina as it seemed to symbolize a well-aged artifact that could support the idea of re-visiting past experiences whose materials could inspire a sense of perceived durability [27]. To this end, we decided to use a printer to make digital photos material, contrasting the potential durability of paper prints with digital files.

We augmented the oak chest with an upper panel to hide the technological components (see Figure 2). The printer was installed behind the upper panel with a 3D-printed acrylic case securing it to a small opening in the panel (to allow a photo to drop onto the central platform of the box). This helped integrate all technology used to print photos into a form that enabled it to be opened up and later put away. This choice was influenced by prior work articulating the value of *designing technologies to be put away* [25].

Figure 2. Clockwise from top left: Augmented writing box (open) refitted with wood panels and brass lining; 3D printed acrylic case for printer; Printer power supply hidden in upper panel; Power cord exiting rear of box through brass fixture.

Every month the Photobox prints four or five photos randomly pulled from its owner's Flickr archive. To do this, at the beginning of each month, the participant's Flickr archive is indexed. The .NET Photobox service application we developed then enacts the following set of procedures (which we call *layered randomness*). It randomly makes a binary decision to print either four or five photos that month. Then, it randomly selects four (or five) photos from the index and generates four (or five) randomly selected 'future print timestamps', which specify the print time and date for each photo. Each photo is uniquely associated with a timestamp respectively. When the date and time arrive associated with a time stamp, the matching photo is printed. This application runs on a laptop that communicates wirelessly with the Photobox printer via Bluetooth. Members of our research team lived with the three Photobox prototypes for a four-month period to debug the system prior to deployment and to develop a general sense for how many photos should be printed each month.

Photobox's behavior was intentionally designed to be autonomous, not requiring input from the user. This choice was partly influenced by prior work describing how ceding autonomy to a system can enable new ways for people to meaningful experience their digital content [17] and, more generally, open a space for pause and contemplation [38]. We could have curated a special selection of photos from a person's collection to appear in their Photobox. However, randomness was selected to introduce a potentially unfamiliar and disruptive machine behavior. We wanted to explore how people might confront a technology delving into their personal archive and how their perceptions might change over time.

Participants, Data Collection and Analysis

We recruited three households from a large Midwestern city in the United States to participate in our study (9 people in total). This approach clearly has limitations; for example, it makes the results hard to generalize to a wide population of users. Similar to the aim and ambition of the seminal technology probes paper [14], and several field studies since then [e.g., 7, 8, 13], we want to initially focus on a smaller selection of households to gain a richer descriptive understanding of the space as a whole to inform what might be salient issues for future research and practice. We recruited participants through flyers, word of mouth and online advertisements. All participants were familiar with technology, owned digital cameras, and at least one member of each household owned a Flickr account with unlimited storage. No households had children. In the remainder of the paper, we use pseudonyms to describe household members.

Household 1 (H1) consisted of Tim (aged 48, bookstore clerk) and Britt (42, librarian), a married couple who had lived in their current home for ten years. Tim and Britt shared their Flickr account, contributing photos to it nearly equally; they had approximately 4,500 photos in their 7-year-old archive at the start of the study. **Household 2** (H2) consisted of five roommates (two female, three male): Heather (31, massage therapist), Zack (28, grocery store employee), Thomas (30, technician), Jenn (29, postal service employee), and James (29, barista). They had been living together for 18 months. Heather was the sole owner of the Flickr account and several of her roommates are featured in many photos in it. She had approximately 2500 photos in her 5-year-old archive at the start of the study. **Household 3** (H3) consisted of Samuel (35, insurance salesman) and Shelly (34, legal clerk), a couple who had been living together in the same apartment for nearly two years. Samuel was the sole owner of his 6-year-old Flickr account. He had approximately 3000 photos in it at the start of the study.

Participants owning the Flickr accounts used in this study all reported similar shifts in interaction with that service over time. Initially, they had been active members in the Flickr community, using the service to support social relationships, and as an outlet for self-expression (these trends in behavior match findings from prior research on Flickr [35]). However, over the past several years all account owners had become much less active in the Flickr community. At the time of this study, participants' primary use of their Flickr accounts was as storage for their digital photo collections (approximately between five to sixty photos were uploaded each month). Consequently, our participant pool helped support our goal of exploring how people might more meaningfully re-visit their photo archive on a general level.

We recruited participants with large Flickr photo archives for a few key reasons. First, these large archives would enable us to provide participants with glimpses into past experiences that stretched over several years. During preliminary research, we found many people's locally-stored photo archives were fragmented across various hard drives and physical media (e.g., DVDs). As a result, we decided against using locally stored digital photographs, as the effort required to make these archives cohesive would have complicated our goal to easily introduce a prototype into the home. Second, at the time we created the Photobox prototypes, the Flickr API emerged as the most flexible and robust option for the .NET application we developed.

We aimed to collect rich accounts from participants about the rhythms and activities of the home through semi-structured interviews that took place bi-monthly. This interview schedule included an introductory interview when installing the Photobox and a final interview at the end of the deployment. During our initial home visit (which lasted 2-3 hours), the research team aimed to develop an understanding of members' everyday lives, common domestic activities, perceptions of their photo collections, and technology-usage trends. Household members gave us a home tour and decided where the Photobox should be installed (all Photoboxes were installed in or near living rooms). We deliberately gave brief descriptions of the Photobox, noting it will occasionally print a photo from the owner's Flickr archive. We wanted participants to develop their own interpretations over time. We did not explicitly encourage participants to interact with the prototype and all were aware they could drop out of the study at any time.

The printer embedded in our prototypes was limited to holding ten pieces of paper, requiring us to visit each household bi-monthly to re-load each Photobox. These sessions were advantageous for us to probe and record household members' unfolding experiences with the Photobox in a reasonably structured, yet informal manner. These sessions typically lasted 60-90 minutes. At the conclusion of the study, we visited each household to collect the prototype and conduct in depth interviews with participants (these sessions lasted 2-4 hours). We commonly referenced prior field notes and recordings capturing participants' earlier experiences to explore possible changes in attitudes toward the Photobox, and to better understand changes in experience with it over time. We also paid attention to possible changes in attitude toward Flickr archives, emergent interpretations of the prototype, and how it potentially affected domestic practices.

All interview sessions over this fourteen month period were audio recorded, producing 40+ hours of content. Relevant segments of recordings were transcribed. Researchers also took field notes and documentary photographs during each interview. Field notes were reviewed immediately following each interview, and tentative insights were noted in reflective field memos [9]. We held weekly meetings to discuss emergent findings. Analysis of the data was an ongoing process. After each home visit, we conducted preliminary analysis, searching for emergent (and shifting) patterns across recordings field notes and photos to draw out underlying themes [22]. We coded raw data documents with these themes. We also created conceptual models and affinity diagrams to reveal unexpected connections and differences among households. In what follows, we present several descriptions and examples taken from field observations that help illustrate the themes.

FINDINGS

Despite the relative simplicity of the Photobox, it provoked a range of reactions across households—many of which were characterized by initial frustration and disappointment, which slowly shifted towards acceptance, and pleasurable anticipation. In what follows, we first describe how this *trajectory of appreciation* [7] unfolded across our three households, with particular attention to when the transition from disappointment to acceptance occurred. We then describe ways in which the Photobox shaped participants' perceptions of their digital photo collections. Finally, we detail insights into participants' reflections on living with slow technology.

Experiences over time: from frustration to acceptance

Gaver et al. [7] describe acceptance of new technology prototypes as moving across a *trajectory of appreciation*. A new technology may initially be embraced with excitement because it is novel. As novelty wears off and expectations are potentially unmet, people may become frustrated or disillusioned. Over time, the technology will normalize into a state of understanding—it is either abandoned or accepted. If accepted, people's experiences with it may improve as they develop ways to work around the difficulties they faced, and eventually the technology can integrate into everyday life.

While individual trajectories understandably varied, all three households followed a similar path: a period of initial excitement in the first few weeks, followed by tensions that emerged around a lack of control over the prototype, and, eventually key moments of acceptance as the Photobox settled into everyday life. In what follows, we briefly describe these stages.

The first four to eight weeks were characterized by excitement that tended to overshadow disappointment. While participants were aware the Photobox would only occasionally print a photo, it was common for them to check the box everyday (often several times). For example, Britt-H1 reflects on her experience during this period of the study: "*It's this new thing here* [points to dining room]. *It looks interesting, kind of antique. It's lovely. And, the photos it's popping out, we haven't seen most of them in so long. ...it's intriguing when we get one. But, it does make me want to have another one and another one. ...I guess I don't mind too much not being able to push a button and make it pop another one out. I am peeking in on it all the time. Sometimes there won't be one for a week! Or longer!*"

The optimism and creeping tension voiced in Britt's reflection is exemplary of discussions with households in the first two months of the study. Between months three to six tensions continued to surface, often leaving participants conflicted. They were usually delighted to receive a new photo, but struggled to come to terms with a lack of control over the Photobox's slowness. During the final interview, Samuel (H3) reflects on his experience in month four: "*At the time I think I didn't even realize how many images wash over me everyday. I'm so used to seeing photos on the internet, just clicking through them rapid fire* [makes rapid clicking sound], *it became hard to wait. ...When it did* [print] *I'd get excited but also well I'd get kind of tense. I'd be like 'When's the next one coming? What's it gonna be? When should I look next? Why is it doing this to me?!*"

In another case, Heather (H2) reported confronting her roommates about taking her photos as a way of rationalizing why they were not appearing as frequently as she initially desired: "*At that point, I think I was projecting my craving to see more little bits of my life onto my roommates.*" In general, as a matter of coping with these struggles, this period of the study was characterized by participants' efforts to 'make sense' of the prototype and, in some cases, the study as a whole. Accordingly, during this period, we encountered a range of speculations from participants about the Photobox. Tim (H1) appeared briefly convinced his Photobox would only print photos of people wearing hats, while Heather (H2) considered her Photobox may be predicting her love life after a photo of her ex-lover was consecutively followed by one of her current

Figure 3. From left to right. H1's Photobox after the laptop was moved under a living room couch (in month six of the study). H2's Photobox kept alongside many electronics and entertainment technologies. H3's Photobox kept near the kitchen and living room.

boyfriend. Interestingly, Samuel (H3) became temporarily skeptical of the study, mentioning he had at one point considered that the prototype was actually designed to track his movements through the house. Collectively, these descriptions help illustrate a period in which participants attempted to make sense of the device and, in some cases, balance their expectations with its slowness.

However, as the study progressed, we observed these tensions began to fade across households in different ways. During the final interview, Britt and Tim (H1) reflect on an important decision they made in month six: "Britt: *At first we were excited to show it to people and get the photos. Then, it became kind of a drag because, you know, we want to use it, but we can't do anything. I'd be walking through into the kitchen and be thinking 'When is the next one coming?' ...Then we moved the computer under a* [living room] *couch. ...That made it* [Photobox] *less like a focal point in the dining room. ...it became a lot easier to not worry about it but also not forget about it.* Tim: *Yea after the laptop was gone I didn't have to come and see the little lights on it and wonder what it's doing. ...It eased things up. It became a lot more comfortable for us.*"

While members in H2 and H3 made no material changes to their Photoboxes, they did note shifts in perception. Samuel describes how returning from a two week vacation in month seven caused him to critically rethink his perspective: "*The surprise of getting a photo was great but I had this, I don't know, sense that I should have some ability to make it print. ...Sometimes I'd have these thoughts like why am I not telling it when to? I guess it's what I'm used to doing. ...When we got back* [from vacation]. *...I opened it up and found three photos, one was of a different trip,* [from] *back when we first met. That's when I felt like I 'got it.' It's going to do its thing. It can take care of itself. That way of thinking about it changed things for me. I don't have other things that do stuff on their own. From then on, it started to take on a personality. It's independent and takes its time, but it's going to print something for me.*"

Somewhat similarly, Heather (H2) discusses how her perception of Photobox as a "technology" had to change before it could be completely integrated into her life: "*Even though it's using a laptop and getting on my Flickr, I had to let go of any idea that it's like our other gadgets. ...*[laughs] *it's not too typical that I have to* ***wait*** *for technology. That took time to get used to.* Zack: *But it's also not asking you for anything.* Heather: *Yes you're exactly right and I think that's one reason why it's cool. ...why I want to keep it.*"

Collectively, these reflections illustrate how participants' perceptions of the Photobox changed over time as it transitioned from a perplexing and, at times frustrating, device, to one that was eventually understood and integrated into the home. In the next section we describe how the Photobox facilitated interactions with households' Flickr archives. All of the remaining observations and reflections are taken from interviews after these points of transition had occurred.

Anticipating re-encounters with the archive

While households were initially frustrated by the slow rate of photos being printed, over time they appreciated how this pace created time to reflect on an individual image and the memories it triggers. The photos printed by the Photobox served as resources for reflecting on past life events and celebrating (or letting go of) aspects of earlier life stages. In the final exit interviews, participants reflected on their earlier experiences and how perceptions of the Photobox changed over time. For example, Samuel (H3) describes his experience during the final six months of the study: "*I'd take some time, a few minutes, and think about the people or the place in the picture. And I'd be focusing on the other stuff not in it too. ...What was going on in my life then, where I was at.*" Samuel later compared his experiences with the Photobox and his photo albums: "*I think I started to understand why it didn't print many* [photos]. *...Made them more special but also more easy to take in, in passing. ...*[It's] *kinda similar and kinda different to* [looking at] *a photo album. ...With* [my photo albums], *I have to make time and get absorbed in them. I get a lot out of it. But, realistically I don't do it much. ...The box created that same sort of feeling but without having to prepare to get too deep. I could look in, think for a minute then go about my day. ...since I never knew what was coming, there's no way I could prepare and now that I think about it, that's one reason it kept being exciting. ...It has certainly reinvigorated my* [Flickr] *account.*"

Similarly, Heather and Jenn reflected on how the Photobox provoked curiosity among members in Household 2: "Heather: *Eventually, the whole not knowing when it would print or what it would print made me curious for sure. It made me realize how I lose track of what's up there* [on Flickr], *even though I uploaded it at some point. That got me pretty interested about what might be coming next.*

Jenn: *We were all a little curious ...wondering who might be in the next photo. Sometimes we'd all be here and looking at the photos and asking her about them. Like, why one of us was in one but someone else wasn't? I think we learned a great deal about her past. Maybe more than she wanted us to!*

Heather: *That's probably true! ...Overall it's been an interesting experience. We'd never be sitting around my tiny laptop laughing about my photos like we did.*"

More generally, the randomized, non-linear approach to re-visiting Flickr photos appeared well accepted across households. For example, Britt (H1) draws a comparison between the randomization and her own experience of remembering: "*We'll get a photo of a concert we went to and that'll make me think of a person I went with, and then I'm thinking about something else we did together. ...so I remember experiences but not always in the order they happened. I like how this had that going on.*" Randomization was also commonly described as a key quality contributing to the building of anticipation. Following Britt's reflection in this same interview, Tim's remark characterizes a sentiment we encountered across participants: "*It could've printed anything from seven years ago to last month. There's a lot that happened in that span of time, so we were usually surprised at what we'd find.*"

Collectively, these reflections help illustrate how, over time, the Photobox supported experiences of anticipation, reflection, and meaningful interactions with participants' Flickr archives. However, occasionally participants encountered photos representing memories they wanted to forget; they were typically unaware these photos were still in their archive. While these examples included things such as images of now stolen possessions (e.g. bicycle, musical instruments); the two most compelling examples involved Samuel (H3) and Heather (H2) receiving photos of previous lovers, which they both they discarded the printed photo and deleted these images from their Flickr archives.

Transitioning the online archive from digital to material

A core aspect of Photobox's design is its ability to make 2"x3" material copies of Flickr photographs. We wanted to explore how participants might react to the transition from the digital to material, and explore any differences in perception between the two. In general, participants highly valued the material affordances of the paper copies, particularly in terms of (i) how a sense of age could be more richly captured over time as well as (ii) how they could be more easily integrated into everyday life. For example, Heather (H2) describes the material wear occurring on a subset of photos kept in her wallet and, at times, under her pillow (see Figure 4): "*Some of them* [prints] *represented special moments in my life. When I'd get one of those, I'd think 'this is a good omen.' Sometimes I'd slip one under my pillow at night. ...I'm not exactly going to put my laptop under my pillow!* [laughs] *...They started to crease and bend from the humidity and me jumbling them around. ...It's part of their history. That's something I'm obviously not going to get with the photos in my* [Flickr] *account.*"

In reflecting on the physical prints received from Photobox, Britt and Tim (H1) noted a re-emergence of their practice of curating photos on the fridge: "Britt: *Back when we developed our photographs, we'd have a rotating group of them on the fridge, like a lot of people did. When the change to digital came, we stopped printing them out almost entirely. ...*Tim: *Yeah so if you remember our fridge before, it didn't have many photos on it. Maybe a few from wedding invitations and some postcards. That's pretty much it. ...Having* [material] *copies got us back into it. We change them around as more come in and decide our favorites. ...It opened up a familiar way of using photos but kind of updated to our* [Flickr] *collection.*"

Interestingly, Samuel describes how the Photobox was able to support a richer way of re-visiting his digital photo collection, without compromising the value of online redundancy: "*It is extremely important to me. That's one reason I still use Flickr, to back it up. If our apartment burned down or flooded, god forbid, it would be saved. ...It took some getting used to, but I liked how it* [Photobox] *gave me little reminders about what's in there. Every once in a while I'd go back to check out some of the other photos online from around that time period or call a friend I hadn't seen in a long time that was in one of them that printed. ...It was the best of both worlds. I knew all of them were backed up* [online]*, but I also had some right here. I didn't have to deal with trying to organize them better. Or, even figure out where to start* [re-visiting them]."

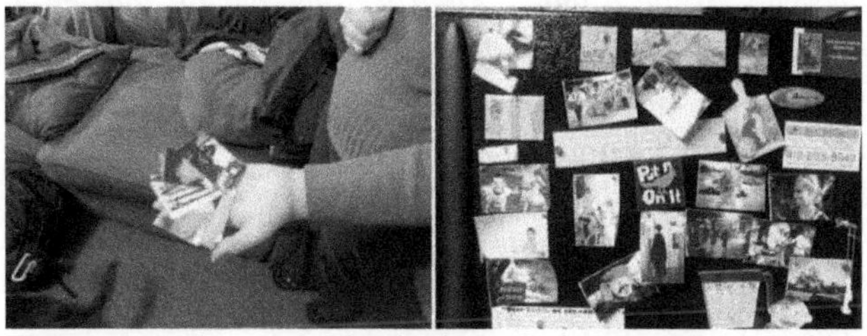

Figure 4. Left, a valued selection of photos, some of which Heather kept under her pillow from time to time. Right, a rotating curation of Flickr prints on Britt and Tim's refrigerator.

Collectively, these reflections help illustrate how, in different ways, Photobox enabled participants to have richer interactions with the photographs in their Flickr archive. These ranged from supporting material wear over time to the re-emergence of everyday photo curation in the home. Samuel's reflection provided insights into how the device supported a need for ensuring the redundant backup of his archive as well as his desire for richer, less overwhelming experiences with his digital photo collection.

Living with slow technology

Beyond experiences with the printed photos, households discussed living with the device itself. Drawing from our final bi-monthly and closing interviews, we briefly describe how the long-term experience of living with Photobox provoked participants to critically think about the role of technology in their everyday lives.

During these discussions some of our participants described how, over time, the relative slowness of our prototype provoked them to consider the rate at which other domestic technologies operate. Tim (H1) describes how undemanding it was compared to other devices in his home: "*Sometimes I am overrun. ...the sound of the TV and my phone, texts and notifications. Things to do and people to get back to on it* [motions to iPad]. *...it's creative in getting away from all this. ...I like how it's a technology but it does stuff in a simple way. ...*[it] *wasn't yelling at me.*"

Similarly, Heather critically considers her technological habits and describes a recent change in her routine: "*It made me think about how quickly things are moving these days. Like I check Facebook four or five times a day, clicking through all kinds of stuff. Like what's all that information doing to my brain?? ...I thought about changing things up some. ...I took a break from Facebook recently. Don't know how long it'll last* [laughs] *but I thought why not try it out.*"

Interestingly, Samuel (H3) makes a comparison between his experience of reading a Sunday newspaper and Photobox: "*I let my subscription to the Times expire a few years ago. Now I read everything online. I jump around* [from] *site to site on Google News. I'll have* [Google] *chat going too. It's fun, don't get me wrong, but it does feel different than when I was reading the paper. ...It's a calm feeling. I didn't expect it* [Photobox] *to make me think about that, but every once in a while it did. ...Finding a few photos, looking at them in an involved but laid back way reminded me of it.*"

Participants also described how the background nature of the Photobox contrasted with other domestic technologies. For example, Britt (H1) likens the presence of Photobox to other material artifacts in her home: "[It's] *in the backdrop of our life, not distracting, just there. ...like many of the things we keep out on the mantle or put up on the wall.*"

Collectively, these reflections help illustrate how the Photobox provoked some participants to critically consider the role of technology in their everyday lives and, in Heather's case, make a subtle change to her routine. They also highlight how participants, such as Samuel and Britt, drew on experiences and metaphors in which digital technology was conspicuously absent to describe their interactions with and perceptions of Photobox.

DISCUSSION AND IMPLICATIONS

It is clear that photographs hold a significant place in people's lives. However, the transition of photo collections from physical to digital brings new complications as they grow to increasingly unmanageable sizes and become more difficult to curate. A key contribution of our study is to reveal how technology might open up new opportunities for engaging with large and growing digital photo collections by making them more material and by building in support for re-visitation of the past through slower interaction.

Experiences of living with slow technology provoked participants to broadly reflect on the role of technology in their everyday lives. The Photobox was ultimately successful at opening up new experiences for participants with their photo collections, and in some cases, older photo curation practices re-emerged. These findings highlight the complexity bound to designing for reflection, re-visitation, and anticipation, and the challenge of enabling meaningful experiences with domestic technology that overrides user control. In what follows, we present several research and design considerations for the HCI community that emerged from our work.

Designing for anticipation

A core goal of our study was to explore how a design might build anticipation. It appeared the combined design choices of slow pacing and *layered randomness* were effective. Participants could not easily develop expectations about how many photos the device would print each month, when they would print, and what glimpses into their life they might provide. While these aspects of the Photobox design ultimately led to valued experiences, they were also the source of much frustration as participants struggled to recalibrate their expectations of living with a potentially worthwhile technology they had little control over. This highlights the complexity of designing for anticipation: people's desire to be in control and the enjoyment that can emerge if control is ceded to the system in a meaningful way. Balancing these two concerns harmoniously is difficult and unpredictable.

However, we found the Photobox provoked anticipation around receiving new photos, and that people generally connected these prints to three main themes: a person or social relationship, a specific life stage, and even an interpreted thematic sequence (e.g., Heather's past and current romantic relationships). Each of these themes suggest interesting spaces for designers to explore in the future when considering metrics to mine and re-present elements in valued digital archives.

More generally, the topic of anticipation has been described in HCI research as an important thread of felt experience [21]. However, little work has directly explored how these notions could be applied to the design of new technologies for reflection on the past. Our study contributes to this small but potentially important area of future HCI research. In particular, developing more meaningful ways to support the experience of ceding control to an interactive system in the context of re-experiencing one's digital content marks a clear space for future research in the HCI community. We imagine research on the relationship between autonomy and reflection [8, 13, 38] could be leveraged in support of this direction.

Designing for re-visitation and reflection

The study has also revealed how making digital photos materially present in the home played an important role in supporting re-visitation and reflection around this personal content. Printing the photos enabled participants to better incorporate material versions of their digital photos into their everyday lives. In some cases, this led to ritualized uses of the print outs (e.g., Heather putting 'good omen' photos under her pillow at night) as well as the re-emergence of prior practices of curating photos in the home (e.g., Tim and Britt's refrigerator). Interestingly, Samuel described how receiving material copies of his Flickr photos enabled him to "have the best of both worlds", where he simultaneously experienced the comfort of cloud-based storage and redundancy along with the manipulability and intimacy of physical photos. Clearly there are opportunities for increasing the presence of digital photos through new digital display technology. However, Samuel's reaction subtly highlights how people may not currently be experiencing the richness of combining physical form with the placeless, reproducible qualities that digital archives can provide.

These findings suggest a future opportunity for the HCI community to explore more diverse ways that new technologies might re-present different elements of people's ever growing—and increasingly online—collections of personal content. We imagine this approach could be applied across different kinds of archives and potentially clustered around digital histories of social relationships or events. For example, new interactive systems could be designed that create databases composed of electronic messages, photos, and location histories shared between two friends or those that characterize a specific life stage. Elements from such archives could be made present in everyday life to support reflection on these past experiences. Further, new systems could directly gather feedback from people to explore the extent to which different combinations of digital content are likely (and unlikely) to evoke aesthetic, meaningful experiences over time. This direction could provide a step toward enabling interactions with systems that subtly influence their behavior without ceding control to the user. Nonetheless, in some cases our participants did have negative experiences as they re-visited old photographs, which they had materially (and psychologically) expunged from their everyday lives. This marks an important implication to consider in the design of new systems aimed at support re-visitation of past experiences.

The Photobox successfully opened up new opportunities for participants to experience their expansive Flickr archives in slower, more succinct and meaningful ways. However, it is important to acknowledge that if left for six months or a year, our prototype itself could easily create a proliferation of digital prints that could induce overwhelming experiences. Importantly, in the aim and ambition of technology probes [14], our goal was not to engineer a solution to the problem of digital content proliferation. Instead, we hoped to further develop the design space for future exploration by HCI researchers and practitioners.

Slow Technology Future Research Considerations

Another goal of our study was to explore people's experiences living with slow technology over an extended period of time. While participants initially struggled with the unfamiliar pacing and (in)action of our prototype, over time they began to embrace these constraints and accept the Photobox as they reconfigured their perceptions of how this device played a role in their home.

The Photobox provoked participants to critically consider the role of technology in their everyday lives and, in Heather's case, prompted a subtle, if not temporary, change in her routine. These findings illustrate how the pacing of the interaction not only opened a space for reflection on participants' pasts, but also on their current domestic technological practices. Photobox was eventually accepted as a *background technology*—one that could be closed up and fade away, not demanding nor requiring the owners' attention. Building on recent values-oriented calls for design initiatives that help constrain people's choices [33], our study suggests an opportunity for future research to explore how new technologies could be created that similarly embrace unfamiliar constraints, operate on their own, and potentially enable people to make sense of (and draw on as resources) in their own time, when desired.

However, it is important to point out that the slow technology design space poses several practical and methodological challenges. For example, it is unclear how long deployments ought to last. Fourteen months was an appropriate scaling for this study considering the rate at which the Photobox created new photos. However, the amount of time and resources required for such a study may not always be at research teams' disposal.

The slow technology design space presents an under-engaged yet fruitful opportunity area for future research in the HCI community. Our study provided a glimpse into how long term deployments of slow technologies can open unique opportunities to explore designing for anticipation, mindfulness and reflection. It has clear links to ongoing initiatives exploring how more enduring forms of technology can be designed and how this might shape people's (or future generations') experience over time [e.g., 5, 15, 26, 27]. On a broader level, we see our study as a case building on and expanding prior research [2, 6, 8, 11, 12, 18, 19, 32] articulating how embracing values alternative to the more dominant focus of efficiency and usability can critically nurture and expand future research in the HCI. We hope this research will inspire the community to explore designing slow technology in the future as they increasingly focus on the intimate contexts of everyday life.

ACKNOWLEDGMENTS

We thank our subjects for their long-term participation and the reviewers for their encouragement and feedback.

REFERENCES

1.Belk, R. 1990. The Role of Possessions in Constructing and Maintaining a Sense of Past. *Advances in Consumer Research,* 17, 669-676

2.Blythe, M., Overbeeke, K., Monk, A., Wright, P. 2003. *Funology: From Usability to Enjoyment.* Springer Press.

3.Cosley, D., Sosik, V., Schultz, J., Peesapati, S., Lee, S. 2012. Experiences With Designing Tools for Everyday Reminiscing, *Human–Computer Interaction*, 27, 175-198

4.Csikszenthmihalyi, M., Rochberg-Halton, E. 1981. *The Meaning of Things: Domestic Symbols and the Self.* Cambridge University Press.

5. Friedman, B., Nathan, L. 2010. Multi-Lifespan Information System Design: A Research Initiative for the HCI community. *Proc. of CHI '10*, 2243-2246.
6. Gaver, B., Martin, H. Alternatives: Exploring Information Appliances through Conceptual Design Proposals. In *Proc.of CHI '00,* 2000, 209-216.
7. Gaver. W., Bowers, J. Boucher, A., Law, A., Pennington, S., Villar, N. 2006. The History Tablecloth: Illuminating Domestic Activity. *Proc. of DIS '06.*
8. Gaver, W., Sengers, P., Kerridge, T., Kaye, J., Bowers, J. 2007. Enhancing ubiquitous computing with user interpretation: field testing the home health horoscope. *Proc. of CHI '07*, 537-546.
9. Glaser, B., Strauss, A. 1967. *Discovery of grounded theory: strategies for qualitative research.* Sociology press.
10. Good, J. 2011. How many photos have ever been taken? http://1000memories.com/blog/94-number-of-photos-ever- taken-digital-and-analog-in-shoebox
11. Grosse-Hering, B., Mason, J., Aliakseyeu, D., Bakker, C., Desmet, P. 2013. Slow Design for Meaningful Interaction. *Proc. of CHI '13*, 3431-3430.
12. Hallnas, L., Redström, J. 2001. Slow Technology: Designing for Reflection. *P. Ubi. Comput. 5,* 201-212.
13. Helmes, J., Taylor, A., Cao, X., Höök, K., Schmitt, P., Villar, N. 2010. Rudiments, 1, 2, & 3: design speculations on autonomy. *Proc. of TEI '11*, 145-152.
14. Hutchinson, H. et al. 2003. Technology probes: inspiring design for and with families. *Proc of CHI '03.*
15. Karapanos, K., et al. 2009. User experience over time: an initial framework. *Proc. of CHI '09*, 729-738.
16. Kaye, J. et al. 2006. To have and to hold: exploring the personal archive. *Proc. of CHI '06*, 275-284.
17. Leong, T. et al. 2008. Abdicating choice: the rewards of letting go. *Digital Creativity, 19,* 233-243.
18. Leshed, G., Sengers, P. 2011. "I lie to myself that I have freedom in my own schedule": productivity tools and experiences of busyness. *Proc. of CHI '11.*
19. Mazé, R., Redström, J. 2005. Form and the Computational Object. *Digital Creativity*, 16(1), 7-18.
20. McAdams, D. 2001. The psychology of life stories. *Review of General Psychology*, 5(2), 100-122.
21. McCarthy, J., Wright, P. 2004. *Technology as Experience.* MIT Press.
22. Miles, M. B., Huberman, A., M. 1994. *Qualitative Data Analysis.* Thousand Oaks, CA: Sage.
23. Odom, W et al. 2013. Fragmentation and Transition: Understanding Perceptions of Virtual Possessions among Young Adults in South Korea, Spain and the United States. *Proc. of CHI '13*, 1833-1842.
24. Odom, W., Selby, M., Sellen, A., Kirk, D., Banks, R., Regan, T. 2012. Photobox: on the design of a slow technology. *Proc. of DIS '12*, 665-668.
25. Odom, W., Banks, R., Durrant, A., Kirk, D., Pierce, J. 2012. Slow Technology: Critical Reflection and Future Directions. *Adjunct Proc. of DIS'12*, 816-817.
26. Odom, W. Banks, R., Kirk, D., Harper, R., Lindley, S., Sellen, A. 2012. Technology Heirlooms? Considerations for Passing Down and Inheriting Digital Materials. *Proc. of CHI '12*, 337-346.
27. Odom, W., Pierce, J., Stolterman, E., Blevis, E. 2009. Understanding why we preserve some things and discard others in the context of interaction design. *Proc. of CHI '09*, 1053-1062.
28. Petrelli, D., Villar, N., Kalnikaite, V., Dib, L., Whittaker, S. 2010. FM radio: family interplay with sonic mementos. *Proc. of CHI '10,* 2371-2380.
29. Petrelli, D., Whittaker, S. 2010. Family memories in the home: contrasting physical and digital memories. *Personal and Ubiquitous Computing*, 14, 2, 153-169.
30. Sarvas R., Frohlich D.M. 2011. *From snapshots to social media: The changing picture of domestic photography.* Springer Press.
31. Sellen, A. et al. 2007. "Do life-logging technologies support memory for the past?: an experimental study using sensecam." *Proc. of CHI '07*, 81-90.
32. Sengers, P., Boehner, K., David, S., Kaye, J. 2005. Reflective Design. *Proc. of CC '05,* 49-58.
33. Sengers, P. 2011. What I learned on Change Islands: reflections on IT and pace of life. *interactions* 18, 40-48.
34. Stevens, M, Abowd, G., Truong, K., Vollmer, F. 2003. Getting into the Living Memory Box: Family archives and holistic design. *Personal Ubiq.Comput.,* 7, 210-216.
35. Van Dijck, J. 2010. Flickr and the culture of connectivity: Sharing views, experiences, memories. *Memory Studies,* 1-15.
36. Van House, N. 2011. Personal Photography, digital technologies, and uses of the visual. *Visual Studies*, 2.
37. Walker, A. 1989. Photo albums: Images of time and reflections of self. *Qualitative Sociology*, 12, 155-182.
38. Woodruff, A. Augustin, S., Foucault, B. 2007. Sabbath Day Home Automation: "It's Like Mixing Technology and Religion". *Proc. of CHI '07,* 527-536.
39. Zimmerman, J., Forlizzi, J., Evenson, S. 2007. Research through design as a method for interaction design research in HCI. *Proc. of CHI '07*, 493-502.

Generating Implications for Design through Design Research

Corina Sas
Lancaster University
Lancaster, UK
corina@comp.lancs.ac.uk

Steve Whittaker
University of California
at Santa Cruz
Santa Cruz, CA, USA
swhittak@ucsc.edu

Steven Dow, Jodi Forlizzi, John Zimmerman
Carnegie Mellon University
Pittsburgh, PA, USA
spdow, forlizzi, johnz@cs.emu.edu

ABSTRACT
A central tenet of HCI is that technology should be user-centric, with designs being based around social science findings about users. Nevertheless a repeated but critical challenge in design is translating empirical findings into actionable ideas that inform design, or generating *implications for design*. Despite various design methods aiming to bridge this gap, knowledge informing design is still seen as problematic. However there has been little empirical exploration into what design researchers *understand* by such design knowledge, the *functions* and *principles* behind their creation. We report on interviews with twelve expert HCI design researchers probing the roles and types of design implications, and the process of generating and evaluating them. We synthesize different types of design implications into a framework to guide their generation. Our findings identify a broader range than previously described, additional sources and heuristics supporting their development as well some important evaluation criteria. We discuss the value of these findings for interaction design research.

Author Keywords
Design knowledge; Implications for design; Design research.

ACM Classification Keywords
H.5.m. Information interfaces and presentation (e.g., HCI): Miscellaneous.

INTRODUCTION
A central tenet of HCI is that technology should be user-centric, with designs being based around social science findings about users. Nevertheless an outstanding challenge in interaction design is translating empirical findings into ideas or knowledge that inform design, aka generating *implications for design* [10,11,23]. This has led to a *perceived gap* between empirical studies and design [1,10,11,20,23,26,28]. In the HCI field, design researchers often attempt to bridge that gap by describing how empirical findings might influence system explorations. For those who follow this practice, implications are crucial, yet difficult to create and not well understood. This is reflected in a surprising lack of empirical studies investigating implications, although there are critiques of their perceived abstract quality [33]. This gap between fieldwork and design is a paradox given the wealth of practical design methods developed to mine empirical findings to generate actionable design suggestions. Examples include contextual design [4], activity-based prototyping [17] or design sketches [28].

This paper presents interviews with *design researchers* who employ user-centric design methods. These researchers have evolved practices to bridge the gap because their research products involve building research prototypes that are motivated by fieldwork. We explore these researchers' understanding of implications for design and the principles behind the practice of generating them. One goal is to help other design researchers bridge the gap through a better understanding of *different types of implications* commonly employed, the *sources* for generating them and *criteria* used for evaluating them. We also provide theoretical and practical implications of such knowledge for HCI researchers designing and building prototypes. While previous work has focused on the theoretical debate about the relationship between ethnography and design [13], our work takes a more pragmatic approach to bridging the gap from qualitative fieldwork studies to design. Increased understanding of the largely tacit and challenging *process of generating implications* should enable design researchers to refine design methods and improve resulting technologies. We analyze interview data to address the following questions:

- *What types of design implications* are generated through fieldwork? Are they predominantly communicating devices or are there new types such as abstract functionalities of classes of systems?
- *What sources* of information are used in generating design implications? Are implications predominantly informed by fieldwork data, human science theories and design practice, or are there other sources yet to be discovered?
- *How* are implications for design *generated*? What heuristics do people employ? Are implications generated after the analysis of fieldwork data, or during it?
- *What* are the main *characteristics* of design implications and how are they *evaluated*? Do they meet the validity criteria of scientific knowledge, or more specific criteria related to design practice?

CHI 2014, April 26 - May 01 2014, Toronto, ON, Canada
Copyright 2014 ACM 978-1-4503-2473-1/14/04…$15.00.
http://dx.doi.org/10.1145/2556288.2557357

We report an empirical study involving interviews with twelve experienced design researchers. Our contribution consists of a vocabulary to discuss various *types of design implications, their sources and evaluation criteria.*

RELATED WORK

Types and Sources of Design Implications

Implications for design are a specific type of design knowledge for which prior work has referenced three contrasting sources such as *fieldwork-, design-, and human science-informed design knowledge.* These three different approaches and their specific types of design knowledge are reviewed below including a mixture of fundamental HCI-textbook knowledge, with more detailed accounts of the lesser known ones. While we acknowledge the distinct value of each of these three approaches, this paper focuses mostly on the design implications derived from qualitative fieldwork as it is more commonly employed in user-centered design. Additional hermeneutical [34] and aesthetic [17] approaches to design are beyond the scope of this paper.

Fieldwork-Informed Design Knowledge

Requirements

Requirements gathering is a common HCI method for generating design knowledge, but it has been critiqued for its failure to capture the richness of social settings [10,11,23]. Requirements are highly specific design knowledge derived from fieldwork to support a situated design for that setting. They are intended to capture system goals and functionalities that lead to incremental improvements to existing systems in well-understood contexts. Requirements are highly prescriptive and implementable but are difficult to generalize beyond the settings where they have been explored.

Thick Descriptions

Ethnographic methods emerged to address the limitations of requirements gathering methods and are typically used in settings where complex social factors are at play. The explicit aim of ethnographic methods is the understanding of socialities, and more elusively to explore how technology may address their key social issues [22]. They typically use analytic methods that generate rich descriptions of social settings, while the process of deriving technical implications from these descriptions is complex and controversial [22]. Controversies concern whether ethnographies should be strictly descriptive or should speak to technology implications [13]. There is limited consensus about how ethnographic work should be expressed as design knowledge, or how that knowledge might be evaluated.

Communicating Devices

Design knowledge also serves to communicating succinctly to designers the essential fieldwork findings, i.e. personas and scenarios. *Scenarios* capture narratives describing users' activities in terms of system goals, and users' context of activity [8]. They are described in user-language and tend to be highly situated. Scenarios are versatile concepts which characterize various points on the continuum from fieldwork to design. Carroll [8] identified several functions they could serve, from mere descriptions supporting requirements analysis, to envisionment of conceptual models. Cooper's [9] *personas* represent archetypal users who manifest critical concrete behaviors, abstracted from multiple users along with engaging personal details to bring the character to life. Their value is partly derived from people's ability to engage meaningfully with fictional characters [19]. Beside provoking and inspiring, personas emphasize situated rather than generalized users, increasing designers' understanding and empathy.

Sensitizing Concepts

Sensitizing concepts highlight relevant social aspects concerning technology use. The term is borrowed from the social sciences [5], to describe new, intriguing, and underdeveloped observations about significant social problems that new technologies should address [10,23]. They serve as interpretative devices for the exploration of empirical instances and for abstracting their common features. More specifically, such concepts provide rich descriptions of socialities that capture key situational features and social interactions [13,33], which potentially orient designers towards key problems [23]. Sensitizing concepts also challenge assumptions about design [23,33], and provide new design research agendas [10]. The abstract nature of sensitizing concepts promotes generalizability but this is counterbalanced by a lack of clarity and limited specification of technologically implementable knowledge [10]. Despite their valuable contributions, ethnographers have repeatedly documented how sensitizing concepts are notoriously difficult to translate into specific or prescriptive design implications [10,23,26,28,33]. Finally, proponents of sensitizing concepts do not discuss explicitly their evaluation. In the design context, an implicit criterion is generativity, i.e. the extent to which they lead to novel designs.

Conceptual Models

Conceptual models introduced by Norman [27], capture users' understanding of a computer system. They are generated at the ideation stage of design to translate requirements into abstract user-centric descriptions of the system [3]. They tend to be generalizable, as alternative conceptual designs allow for a wider exploration of the design space. Conceptual models can also be generated through reflection on developed systems to extract the core features of their success, as further described.

Practice-Informed Design Knowledge

Design Concepts

A different approach to generating design concepts is to critically analyze successful systems to try to replicate their successes using related design concepts [7]. Early examples of successful designs included WYSIWYG desktop metaphor and document editors where important digital objects were rendered on the screen, behaving approximately like real world objects allowing direct manipulation of those objects [24]. More recent design concept approaches include Höök's *strong concepts* [21], which are general properties that multiple systems might possess. In Höök's work these properties include *social navigation*: socially enabling applications to show for example how users have traversed an information space. A different approach has been taken by Gaver [17], who suggests that designs be motivated by their *ambiguity,* as they are deliberately underspecified. Because of their focus, the relation between design concepts and prior empirical fieldwork is unspecified. Although the goal of design concepts is clearly to devise systems that are intended to motivate rich interaction experiences, neither Gaver nor Höök provide motivating fieldwork that maps concepts or principles to originating user behaviors. In the same way, no explicit criteria are developed for evaluating design concepts, although the implicit criterion seems to be whether concepts are generative: leading to multiple new instances of the design concept.

Design Heuristics

Heuristics are simple design-oriented rules of thumb to guide practical system design. Although their exact provenance is unspecified they seem to be derived from designers' expertise and reflections on successful prior practice of system building [12]. Unlike design concepts, their goal is to incrementally improve the design of specific systems, rather than to generate new systems. While less abstract than design concepts and usually depicted in terms of technology properties, heuristics can still vary in their level of abstraction but maintain their generalizability for a class of technologies. They serve as general orienting principles for system design: e.g. Nielsen's first principle of visibility of system status, or Schneiderman's reversibility principle. There have been various critiques of usability heuristics and their application, from being unreplicable or conflating important with more trivial types of system faults [18]. Nevertheless these techniques are commonly used in practical contexts when developing interfaces or interactive experiences and there is a specific system to be evaluated.

Other approaches to design, informed by practice consist of critical design [16], research-through-design [15,36], or material-driven design [34]. Additional types of knowledge derived from practice include *design deliberations around issues* arising during the design process consisting of responses proposed and their rationale [29], or *patterns* capturing proven solution to a specific design problem which together allow for the development of a pattern language [2].

Human Science-Informed Design Principles

A rather different approach to generating design knowledge is to derive *design principles* from prior social science theory. Carroll [6] identified *claims* about users' needs that could be informed by social and behavioral theories. Design principles provide high level technology goals [3,12] and tend to be abstract and general, i.e. widely applicable to a broader class of systems. Design principles also tend to be described in people- rather than technology-language, and need to be interpreted by designers to either develop new system types or incrementally improve existing systems. Principles are often evaluated by ascertaining the utility of systems designed after applying the principles. However the mapping between principles and their application to system design can be indirect, making their exact utility difficult to determine. A classic example of human science inspired design principles is the application of Fitts' law concerning perception and action, which has been successfully used in the design of many different types of pointing and input devices. Social sciences have also been used in the design of community systems, exploiting concepts of social capital, self-presentation, and social loafing.

METHOD

We examined the different types of design implications by employing a common HCI method of interviewing *experts,* in this case design researchers. For example, Zimmerman and colleagues [36] also interviewed researchers to explore the sources and outcomes of design research. We interviewed twelve experienced design researchers working in HCI, 9 with at least 10 years of experience, and 6 over 20 years, including 2 ACM SigCHI Academy members. Two non-random sampling techniques were employed. Through purposive sampling, invitations were sent to 25 design researchers, with recognized positions in the field, i.e. h-index above 10, and their expertise in qualitative research methods. A subsequent snowball sampling emerged, with 4 researchers being referred by the initially invited ones. The sample consists of 8 researchers working in academia and 4 in industry research labs, with 8 having experience of working in both sectors (Table 1). Eight participants work in the UK, 3 in the US, 1 in The Netherlands, and the sample was gender balanced, with research interests in memory technologies, interaction design, UX and CSCW. Each study participant was rewarded with a gift voucher worth £40.

#	PhD area	Years expertise	Current position
P1	Cognitive Sciences	25	Principal Researcher
P2	Cognitive Sciences	22	Professor
P3	Computer Science	24	Senior Researcher
P4	Interaction Design	22	Associate Professor
P5	Information Systems	20	Associate Professor
P6	Cognitive Psychology	20	Senior Researcher
P7	Informatics	15	Professor
P8	Design	14	Associate Professor
P9	Education	10	Professor
P10	Computer Science	9	Associate Professor
P11	Communication Science	7	Associate Professor
P12	Psychology	5	Researcher

Table 1. Participants' profiles

All participants have experiences in designing and building HCI prototypes, so that their own definitions of design implications are derived through years of practice. All participants have strong expertise in qualitative research methods including ethnography, interviews, diary studies, contextual inquiry as well as evaluation of deployed systems. The interviews lasted from 45 to 120 min (average 65 min), and were semi-structured around a set of core questions. We asked participants: *What are design implications?* and *What are their most important roles*? We also asked: *Are there different types of design implications?* and how are they generated: *Could you describe* the *process of generating them from fieldwork studies? Are there any specific information sources you use? Are there fieldwork findings that are more useful to generating implications than others and why?* We also explored the main characteristics and criteria used for evaluating design implications.

The interviews were completely transcribed, and over 1300 quotes capturing implications were thematically coded and analyzed. The analysis was intensely iterative and collaborative. A conceptual framework developed from prior literature provided initial categories of types of design knowledge and their information sources. This was further refined as new codes emerged to capture specific abstract types of implications, and additional sources, heuristics and evaluation criteria. The authors met at least weekly for over two months to discuss and revise the coding scheme and ensure its validity and reliability.

RESULTS

Types of Implications for Design

An important finding is a broader set of design knowledge capturing design implications beyond descriptions, requirements, principles and sensitizing concepts, to include more innovative ones such as meta-abstractions and instantiations. In contrast with ethnographic research emphasizing "thick descriptions" and HCI textbooks highlighting communicating devices, i.e. personas and scenarios, our findings show limited evidence of these types but a strong interest in "short descriptions" of fieldwork data. Our findings reveal a taxonomy of implications for design consisting of short descriptions (27%), prescriptions (18%), abstractions and meta-abstractions (23%), sensitizing concepts (18%), and instantiations (14%) and their weights in the overall data (totaling 100%). While descriptions are linked to the design problem explored through the fieldwork, and prescriptions are linked to the design solution, the last four types capture design concepts developed to specifically bridge the gap between the fieldwork and design.

Design Concepts as Abstractions of Technology Functionalities

Abstractions of technology functionalities capture *general functionalities* of an existing class of technologies (P1,P2,P4,P5,P6,P8,P10,P12). They are shaped as suggestions for interpreting more abstract technology goals captured by sensitizing concepts. For example, abstractions capture more technologically-oriented information such as interaction modes or system components: *"looking at how people read from paper, you can come up with a set of guidelines like "to support the reading of multiple documents when you are building systems for electronic reading". Another general one would be "to support note taking or the ability to annotate as people read"* (P1).

A particular type of abstraction is *meta-abstractions* focusing on the key aspects of a *new class* of technologies. They differ from abstract functionalities by moving beyond existing technologies, towards discovering new classes. Meta-abstractions offer "*a conceptual framework of reference for a new class of technologies [because] it's not about the design of the specific technology but about the whole space like a narrower field within HCI*" (P1). Usually, products of a large body of work, meta-abstractions are particularly visionary, enabling shifts in HCI research areas. They aim of *transforming* thinking about current technologies (P1,P6,P12), by challenging design assumptions and helping designers gain new perspectives: *"it's about challenging people's assumptions and [being] critical of some of the more conventional approaches to building these kinds of systems"* (P1). For this, they need to be inspiring and motivating: *"they not just teach how to think about a class of technology but inspire building new concepts"* (P1).

Design Concepts as Instantiations of Abstractions

Instantiations take the form of possible design concepts embodying an abstract property or feature (P2,P5,P6,P9). Their main aim is to support the understanding of the related abstraction: "*We've collected all this data [...] and here are three ideas about systems that might allow people to socially network in several ways; and you would actually describe prototypes that could be implemented"* (P2). Instantiations or design exemplars should also stimulate designers to think about the abstract principles they embody to further explore the design space: "*you could take those principles and generate a whole bunch of different types of systems that adhere to those principles but are innovative and make other people think"* (P2). Such exemplars are described predominantly verbally, and are not actual design solutions, but may act as *placeholders* within the design space. However they can be realised in working exemplar prototypes. Working exemplars are inspirational as they can be directly understood and used by technologists: *"We built systems based on early papers, and system builders have come up to me and said: "I love the xxx system, it was a big inspiration" or "I thought this was really interesting. I wanted to do something like this"* (P2). These systems could then serve as design concepts for others who are interested in building similar systems.

Both abstractions and instantiations express underlying design principles derived from fieldwork data, but manifest these differently: as *guiding principles* or as *concrete examples*. Abstractions of functionality use fieldwork to derive *general principles* that systems should possess, without specifying actual instances of systems. In contrast, instantiations specify *concrete exemplar systems* that could be or have been built. They are intended to be generative of designs that actually get built.

Sensitizing Concepts as Socially-Oriented Design Concepts

Sensitizing concepts offer a preferred form of generalized design knowledge for moving beyond the situatedness of requirements (P1,P7,P8,P10,P11). Described in user-oriented language, they capture abstract design knowledge.

They tend to state technology goals generated to meet specific social needs. For this, sensitizing concepts focus on the key aspects of social behaviors identifying key features of the design space, such as: "*high level things in terms of a social arrangements impacting design, configurations of families for example and their interrelationships and power structures; and try to articulate them as features of a design space to orient towards*" (P10). These social aspects relate to technologies by suggesting a range of social values, such as "*different types of moral and ethical sensibility, value constructs to take into account*" (P10). Sensitizing concepts often capture intriguing, underdeveloped social concepts which lack clear definition. Thus, they are more open and inspirational than abstract functionalities but less technologically actionable. Therefore, they require additional work from designer to interpret and apply them to specific settings: "*I often worry that some implications are too general to give any good guidance from a practical perspective*" (P1). Sensitizing concepts are also intended to challenge designers to reflect on how to implement them, and to support the advance of design thinking as they: "*might inspire designers or make them think more broadly about a better technology*" (P1). Abstractions can be employed to explore aspects of the sensitizing concepts that could become technologically actionable. The following example suggests that the sensitizing concept of *privacy* can be operationalized into abstract functionalities of a specific system: "*if you're building a system concerned with health, then privacy of data is a key consideration so you might state some abstract functions relating to privacy that that class of system should have*" (P2).

Succinct Descriptions for Communicating Core Findings

The most frequent type of design implications derived from fieldwork data consists of *short descriptions* as summaries of key empirical findings capturing constraints characterizing the problem space that can be used to inform the design space. Often the initial step in the development of the other types of design knowledge, short descriptions are derived through synthesis and abstraction of rich interview- or ethnography-based data: "*[to summarize thick description] you need to be able to communicate the most salient parts of it*" (P9). They can be user values, context, tasks or concerns expressed through a couple of paragraphs or visual aids. Short descriptions have several roles such as communicating the most relevant findings to allow designers' understanding of the problem context, and inspire them to explore new solutions. More specifically, they serve as communication devices, offering: "*a language for communicating ideas*" (P12). Communication focuses on the key fieldwork findings for understanding the design setting, as "*their main goal is the understanding of a particular phenomenon*" (P11). Such short descriptions also provide explanations for the saliency of the findings and their potential relevance to design: "*it's useful to illustrate **why** a certain finding is important and implications of design is sort of one way of concretizing those*" (P6). By promoting such understanding, short descriptions may inspire designers to frame the problem or focus on unexplored issues: "*making clear what are still open issues which may give some inspiration for designs, but are not yet detailed enough to start the design*" (P11). The above roles are enabled by the short descriptions' properties of being succinct and highly situated. These strengths are counterbalanced by their limited amount of knowledge that can be technologically implemented or generalizable across settings.

Prescriptions as Requirements for Specific Implementations

Another common type of design knowledge is concrete suggestions for simple implementations. These are very specific, prescriptive and easy to implement (P1,P6,P7,P10,P12). Similar to user requirements, prescriptions capture key system properties suggesting how they could be implemented in a particular design: "*very specific design features that would be very easy to address*" (P6). Not surprising, they are highly situated and actionable: "*something very specific that people can take on board and implement right away*" (P1), and have limited power to generalize to settings different that the one investigated.

Examples of Design Implications

Below are examples for the different types of design implications related to the concept of *social awareness* (Table 2).

Design implication	Example
Sensitizing concept	An influential example is *social awareness* [14], capturing understanding of the activities of others in the context of groupwork, i.e. seamless mediated interaction and sharing of documents. This spawned a huge amount of subsequent research that sought to further empirically characterize social awareness and to build technologies that would support it [25].
Abstraction & Meta-abstraction	An *abstract functionality* of social awareness is extending awareness of remote objects to gestures at, and around them [25]. An example of *meta-abstraction* related to social awareness is extending the collaborative tasks from desktop and shared displays to a different class of technologies, i.e. shared tangible interfaces [35].
Instantiation	An *instantiation* of the abstract property of seamless mediated interaction and sharing of documents was the Agora system itself [25], as one possible design solution.
Prescription	A specific requirement of Agora system was the need for a high resolution shared screen used in conjunction with desk cameras for capturing users' gestures at remote locations [25].

Table 2. Examples of design implications for social awareness

Sources for Generating Implications for Design

An important finding is that in generating design implications, design researchers draw from additional *sources* of information than previously mentioned. These new sources include emerging technology, important social categories and corpus of previous design implications.

Emerging Technology Context

A new, important source for generating design implications consists of the technology context (P1,P2,P3,P6,P7,P10,P11). Participants repeatedly pointed out that such context is critical for framing the fieldwork and observed social phenomena (P2, P3): "*my sense of the technology is already determining what kind of stuff I would be looking at and human situations I am interested in*" (P3). This also includes an awareness of the technological space in terms of shortcomings and possibilities*: "being aware of the technology landscape is very important"* (P1), with technology affordances being implicitly used as a lens for analyzing the data: "*there is an understanding of the basic technological capabilities beforehand"* (P6). In an attempt to overcome lack of technical expertise, social scientists may engage in generating design implications with deliberate disregard for technological constraints: "*without having the technology in mind but rather thinking about what experience should be facilitated"* (P11). This is a critical finding suggesting that even when lacking awareness of the technological context, technology is a significant lens for observing and interpreting data. Such technology context may play different roles from framing ideas to narrowing the scope of the fieldwork (P3,P7,P10): *"[to] a specific techno arena that you are exploring through fieldwork, otherwise that is very ungrounded and you have a difficult time in making implications"* (P10). Technology as a source for generating implications is an important finding suggesting a critical factor in evaluating what are important observations in the emerging technology context. This is different from other technology oriented approaches such as those based on design concepts [17,21]. Our participants were not focusing on successful prior designs but on the general context of emerging technologies. These observations are interesting because the process of generating design knowledge can be seen here as being run backwards, so that technology context is used to frame interpretations of the fieldwork data which are then expressed as technology-oriented design implications.

Social Categories: Social Values, Space and Time

Another source of information for generating design implications includes aspects of the socialities, such as social values: "*focused on different audiences, types of ethical sensibility or value constructs"* (P10). These may be data driven, or solely informed by general aspects of social science. They could also include the broader context with reference to social locality and time: "*if you are in a park [is important that the technology] is portable so that is a finding [motivating you] to imagine possibilities"* (P4), like *"what would you say about time in relation of your project that other designers should know about?"*(P8).

Previous Fieldwork-Informed Corpora of Design Implications

Sets of previous fieldwork-informed design implications offer another source for generating new design implications. In this way, researchers could scrutinize, build on and further extend them: "*implications need to be framed in such a way that I can use them as a basis for my own research, that I can build on them and that might be either to ratify or actually critique them"* (P10).

Fieldwork Data

Less surprising is that relevant fieldwork findings are the most common source of design implications. This aligns with the standard view on fieldwork-informed design knowledge. What is interesting, is the specific findings acting as sources, such as people's behaviors and preferences (P2), challenges that people face (P5)*;* consistent themes throughout the data (P2)*;* emotionally charged themes (P3,P4); unexpected findings (P4,P7) or expected things that did not show up (P8).

Design Practice

Design implications can also capture lessons learned *after* the evaluation of technologically implemented design solutions (P1, P10, P11): "*We developed a system and then we evaluated it and within that work the implications for design really got better"* (P10). This source for generating design knowledge is arguably the most difficult to tap into, because of the challenges of building the designed systems in the first place, and the difficulties of evaluating them in real settings: "*making the argument that this tool will work in real situations is extremely difficult to show"* (P7). Such evaluation builds on actionable knowledge embedded in the designed technologies. Apart from design concepts, another specific type of design knowledge tapping into this source is meta-abstractions. They tend to be the result of a sustained research effort within a domain, consisting of a substantial body of work. This could include iterative fieldwork, development and evaluation of prototypes which facilitates a continual revision of the design knowledge and increases confidence in their validity and generalizability: "*We have done a lot of work in our group about different types of xxx technologies, and therefore if you think about these as a class then you can start to sketch out a conceptual framework which will take people thinking about it much more broadly and diversely"* (P1).

Human Science Theories

Consistent with other theory-based approaches to HCI, some participants focused on human science theory when developing design knowledge. These kernel theories are usually outside the HCI area and include social science theories of human behavior or "*biological underpinning*" (P2): *"you have a sort of an inkling that is interesting and you need to go to some kind of social or human theory to figure out what is the literacy of these specific examples"* (P3).

How Do Researchers Generate Implications for Design?

In generating design implications, researchers are guided by several heuristics. These are employed during analysis of fieldwork data, after analysis, or even before designing the fieldwork study.

Heuristics for Generating Design Implications

Our participants employ several heuristics when generating design knowledge, including identifying and using prior examples of good implications (P8), as well as distancing from the data to take new perspectives. Awareness of cutting edge technologies helps to frame thinking while opening up new possibilities for design: *"the designer in our group regularly sends a newsletter where he kind of scours the web looking for new ideas, technologies, wacky things people are working on [...] having that as another set of inputs into the process is really helpful because it gets you out of the rut of thinking of the same old technologies and ideas"* (P1). It is an important point that design implications involve more than collecting rich user data. They involve characterizing the technology space, then combining that with the user data. This is critical in order to move beyond 'the same old technologies'. Participants also identified various mapping tactics that help bridge the gap from fieldwork data to design practice. A common form of mapping is from observed behavior to sensitizing concepts (P2,P11), from observed behavior to abstract functionalities and instantiations (P1,P2), and from technology affordances to sensitizing concepts (P6).

After Analysis of Fieldwork Data

Throughout the process of generating design knowledge, design researchers employ two contrasting approaches to the order of fieldwork data analysis and generation of implications for design. One approach favors the traditional process of generating design knowledge following analysis of the fieldwork data. Participants gave numerous accounts of this classical "fieldwork first" approach emphasizing the importance of first completing the data analysis before thinking about design implications (P5,P10,P11,P12): *"it follows on from having done full analytical work"* (P10).

During Analysis of Fieldwork Data

A rather different approach argues for exploring design implications during data analysis (P1,P4,P6): *"it goes hand in hand because while I analyze my data and I see these themes emerging, that automatically triggers an idea of what is the implication for design"* (P4). In this respect, this may influence the data reporting and analysis process, as considering design implications during analysis offers an additional lens for identifying the salient findings: *"[my analysis] is done with an eye towards design and technology [...] something is interesting because it has some technological implication in which case I might draw that out"* (P1). This second approach however, does not abandon the first "fieldwork first" approach, because participants acknowledged that design implications can be further improved once the findings are properly summarized: *"[The fieldwork findings] might be informed by an understanding of the kinds of implications that you want [...] but it becomes easy to think about implications after articulating a clear set of findings"* (P10). This quote stresses the iterative nature of the process of generating implications for design.

Before Designing the Field Study

A few participants employed an even more radical approach by considering design implications before planning the fieldwork: *"implications are actually the starting point of research, as in many cases the researcher has an idea"* (P7). For example, people may start from specific technology ideas for which they would like to explore relevant social settings: *"The study was motivated by the idea of a graphical user interface that would allow to look at your digital mementos [...] In the end, a design implication was that the screen was not the right thing to do but I was aware what I wanted to find in the end."* (P4). However, despite having prior technological framings, participants stressed the importance of staying open to counterintuitive fieldwork data. *"I have technology in mind when I select the people and the situations but when I go out, I'm usually just trying to get people to talk and trying to see what they do"* (P4). Various research methods contribute differently to the generation of design implications. Therefore, this approach of considering implications before planning the fieldwork allows for an explicit selection of the study methodology which could offer the most relevant fieldwork data: *"if you get to the end of your study and think about implications, you have probably left it too late [...] I think about it right throughout the whole process as I set up experiments or observations"* (P6).

Evaluation Criteria of Implications for Design

A particularly interesting finding is that implications for design must address quality criteria pertaining to both scientific and design practice. These criteria consist of validity, generalizability and originality, as well as generativity, inspirability and actionability. Such criteria are particularly important but seldom met satisfactory by the generated implications for design. Although some people employ implicit criteria (P4,P10,P12), the importance of evaluating design knowledge is strongly acknowledged and the value of explicit criteria particularly emphasized (P6,P8,P7,P10,P11).

Empirical Validity

An important characteristic of design knowledge is empirical validity, supported through explicit accounts of how such knowledge is grounded in fieldwork data, or acquired through reflection on the evaluation of developed technologies. Being grounded in fieldwork data legitimates and provides rationale for design knowledge (P10,P11): *"You should be able to trace back from implications and see how that's grounded"* (P10). This requires articulating the explicit connection to the data: *"those implications are self apparent [...] you need to be appropriate in terms and not making overly bold claims"* (P6).

Testing design knowledge after implementation is perceived by some participants as the most important evaluation criterion, offering the strongest form of empirical validity (P2,P10,P12): *"We developed a system and evaluated it and within that work the design implications really got better [...] the ability to build on implications is definitely a benchmark for evaluation; that's where one might find their value: in the extent someone could build on"* (P10), as it provides the ultimate test: *"building the system and evaluating it; that's the way that you can tell whether or not you've got the principles right"* (P2). This suggests that implementing and testing design knowledge allows for the revision of design implications. It also builds on the idea that design implications are hypotheses whose value can be best evaluated through empirical tests: "*implications are like hypotheses and the next thing in that process is to build a system that tests those hypotheses*" (P12). A few participants also mentioned comparing their design implications against previous ones within an area, to ensure their consistency: "*you are looking at different sources of literatures to see what kind of implications other people came up with*" (P8). This also supports further critique, revision and extension of the existing body of design implications within a given area.

Theoretical Validity
Theoretical validity is supported through explanatory theories from human and social sciences. However, these sources for grounding design knowledge are seldom made explicit in the writings documenting their generation process. This criterion explicitly positions design implications as scientific knowledge that can be argued for, critiqued and revised: "*check back to literature to see if you have support for your implications or not*" (P8)*;* as well as built on*: "how the implications support the theories and concepts which are already out there"* (P11) so that design researchers could "*take the most salient findings and compare them to the spaces within the literature to point out how the implications that you are devising are relevant within the larger research space"* (P10).

External Validity: Generalizability
Participants felt strongly that an important aspect of design implications is their generality when applied to settings beyond the fieldwork (P5,P6,P10). The challenge here resides in the differences between the settings which can reduce the applicability of implications (P5,P6). The issue of generalization from a single case study in qualitative research has been well studied and weaker forms have been accepted such as *naturalistic generalization* to similar settings [32] and *generalization through aggregation* of findings from multiple studies [31].

We found that participants employ both these forms with the former being the more frequent choice. In this case, abstractions are the preferred type of design implications as they promote generalization of findings from the situated fieldwork to other similar settings: "*findings are very specific to your research question and then the implications are perhaps extrapolated slightly further from that to a more generalizable design space"* (P10), "*across a range of different [settings]"* (P5). This suggests that an important property of abstractions is that they need to speak to multiple contexts, looking for example to "*cut across different people, different households*" (P1). In our data, there was however limited evidence regarding the exploration of the similarities of these settings.

Generalizations through aggregation of findings from independent studies was suggested through meta-abstractions on the basis of one's substantial body of work: "*it takes a lot of activity in a domain [...] those design implications didn't come from a single user study, they came from multiple user studies, building multiple very different prototypes and kind of seeing what worked and what didn't work. So exactly where those abstract principles came from?"* (P2). Such generalizations are the basis of meta-abstractions, and the aggregation is implicit. If such input from the previous body of work is made explicit, then the external validity of the generated implications could be strengthened.

Originality
Participants also emphasized the importance of originality, or developing implications that inform the design of novel technologies: "*they describe a phenomenon that people didn't know about and could say: "You could build systems in this area, I hadn't thought about before"* (P2). Ensuring originality is challenging, as generating design implications is difficult and supporting their novelty even harder (P7). Participants identified differences in the ability to generate original design implications relating to the maturity of the research area (P10), with newly emerging areas being better suited (P2). It also helps if there is general interest so that design implications can be built on by others: "*you want multiple people to act on implications for design and sociologically, you need to have a bunch of people who are interested in something"* (P2). People identified three sources of originality such as developing design implications that address a gap within the existing body of work*: "identifying the salient findings and marking them against the gaps in the research"* (P10)*;* those which offer new perspectives on technology design: "*tell a story that hasn't really been told so far"* (P1); or those which explore new research areas: "*At the time when we started doing that work it really wasn't a topic within HCI and we were able to start talking about those issues where other people haven't before"* (P1). However, originality must also be tempered by usefulness, particularly when implications aim to inform the design of novel technologies: "*Novelty is also a bogus criterion because we could think of any number of bad novel systems*" (P2).

Generativity
The exploration of new research areas for developing original design implications, points to another important criteria to evaluate design implications, namely their generativity. We defined this as the ability of design implications to create and open up new design spaces: "*when implications for design appear really open and visionary, then I think that designers feel more freedom to become creative"* (P11), and make them think differently: "*when it comes to implications I'm looking for things that can inspire people to think in a different way*" (P7). The generativity of design implications also relates to their ability to inform and inspire multiple instances of designs: "*there are five or ten systems I could build from the abstract principles"* (P2).

Inspirability
Design implications should also be inspirational in terms of motivating designers to explore them further or commit to implementing them: "*That's interesting, I can think about*

some good concepts based on this" (P11). Being stimulating, interesting, provocative and engaging are all qualities that could contribute to the inspirational value. The right level of abstraction and ambiguity is also expected to open the design space: "*something at a high enough level that can be inspiring [...] giving people room to apply it to their own systems"* (P12). This implies that abstractions and sensitizing concepts are more inspirational than prescriptions, as they allow space for designers' creativity.

Actionability

Technological actionability implies that design implications are described in terms of technology properties, so that they can be implemented or: "*acted upon by technologists"* (P2). Some participants expressed strong views on the importance of this quality; *"I think that is fundamental that implications can be implemented: at least for part of them, there is something that you can act upon [...] implications for design means something that is practical, something that you can really operate on and I don't mean writing ideas for designs or design concepts but things that you can use in practical terms and it will give directions in that sense"* (P4). For this, they need to be technologically feasible today or in the nearby future: *"they should be implementable and they shouldn't be too futuristic"* (P12). If design knowledge is not technologically actionable, it should be at least socially actionable by addressing the larger social setting where technologies are, could, or should (not) be employed. Such implications can be linked to technology by addressing aspects which may support or hinder technology adoption (P3), or specific technology goals: "*You can imagine some sort of design intervention, which would be about awareness raising or about starting a political campaign to increase resources"* (P9).

IMPLICATIONS FOR INTERACTION DESIGN RESEARCH

We now discuss the main findings and contributions of this work, highlighting several issues that design researchers may orient to while generating design implications. We suggest that researchers might benefit from understanding the different types of design implications, what constitutes support for generating them, how that knowledge needs to be actionable, general and inspirational. We also believe that the field can benefit from having a common language to characterize different types of design implications. Not least, the same criteria might be used to evaluate publications.

Awareness of Different Types of Abstract Design Concepts

Our findings reveal the prevalence of fieldwork-informed design concepts and a more nuanced understanding of this. Such design concepts are captured through four distinct types of design implications, i.e. abstract functionalities of new systems within existing technology classes, instantiations of such functionalities through design exemplars, sensitizing concepts as socially-oriented design concepts, and the new type of knowledge captured by meta-abstractions through abstract functionalities of new classes of technologies. More than half of identified design implications are represented by such design concepts. This is particularly important as design concepts are the only type of design knowledge that can be found on both sides of the gap, i.e. fieldwork and design practice. Subsequently, the more effort goes into generating these types of design implications, the greater the chances of better bridging the gap from fieldwork to design practice.

Awareness of Technology Context and Social Categories

In terms of generating design implications, our findings extend previously identified sources such as fieldwork data, design practice and human science theories. A striking finding is the emphasis on the value *of technology context*, described as the awareness of affordances and limitations of existing and in particular cutting-edge technologies. Another novel source for generating design implications is existing HCI work and in particular *the corpus of design implications* developed in a specific HCI area. We found limited reference to human science theories as a source of generating implications, but strong evidence for the use of *specific social categories* such as social values, norms, time and place. While our findings show limited references to the practice-informed design implications, this has been emphasized as a particularly relevant source for generating or revising meta-abstractions.

Awareness of Heuristics for Generating Design Knowledge

The process of generating implications extends the traditional approach of developing implications *after* concluding fieldwork analysis [1,10,11]. In contrast, novel ways of generating design implications occur *during* the fieldwork analysis, or even by considering implications *while* planning the fieldwork study. This latter approach captures the importance of technology context not only as a source of design implications but also in preparing and selecting social settings to be explored, if they are to more successfully inform the generation of design implications.

Provide Evidence to Support Validity of Design Implications

Another important outcome is that design implications aim to meet the validity criteria of scientific knowledge. However, current practice provides limited evidence for validity. Our findings reveal a large range of sources of design implications which can not only support the generation process but also its scrutiny and critique. Sensitivity to these sources of information and researchers' efforts for making them explicit are much needed to strengthen the validity of design implications. For example, empirical validity could be substantiated by grounding design knowledge in the fieldwork data or even better by building and evaluating previously designed technologies. Theoretical validity is supported by grounding the design knowledge in social sciences theories. External validity could be claimed by exploring the similarities between multiple settings or making explicit the findings from multiple studies employed as design resources.

Specify Generalizable Actionable Knowledge

Our findings also point to the importance of actionable knowledge embedded in the implications for design. The more situated and concrete this knowledge is, the closer to requirements it gets. But requirements lack both abstraction and ability to generalize. A specific useful combination of two types of design implications supporting design practice, is abstract functionalities combined with their instantiations. This combination is actionable because it provides concrete design concepts through instantiations. Moreover, it is also generalizable because the abstraction can be applied across multiple situations. Together, this combination provides a powerful device for bridging situated and general settings.

Provide Inspirational and Generative Power

A specific new value of design implications is that they should *call for action*, motivating designers to engage in their exploration. We need to generate implications that are engaging, compelling designers to explore them further by fostering broad divergent thinking. Future work should explore the characteristics of *compelling* implications and how they could support creative thinking or designers' emotions and values [22].

CONCLUSIONS

The main contribution of this work is *a participant derived taxonomy* to describe design implications. The taxonomy offers a framework for reflecting, debating and conversing within this challenging area, as well as documenting values that different types of design implications might serve. Various heuristics supporting the process of generating implications and a set of criteria for evaluating such knowledge offer much needed insight into a current and relevant research topic.

ACKNOWLEDGMENTS

This work was supported by EC DESIRE (2008-215446) and the Swedish Govern. Agency for Innovation Systems to the Mobile Life VinnExcellence Centre, in partnership with Ericsson, Microsoft, Nokia, IKEA and the City of Stockholm (2011-03460).

REFERENCES

1. Ackerman, M.S. The intellectual challenge of CSCW: the gap between social requirements and technical feasibility. *Human.-Computer Interaction. 15*, 2 (2000), 179-203.
2. Alexander, C., Ishikawa, S., & Silverstein, M. (1978). *A Pattern Language: Towns, Buildings, Construction*.
3. Benyon, D. R., Turner, P. & Turner, S. *Designing Interactive Systems*. Pearson Education, London, UK, 2005.
4. Beyer, H., and Holtzblatt, K. *Contextual Design*. Morgan Kaufmann, San Francisco, CA, USA, 1998.
5. Blumer, H. What is wrong with social theory? *American Sociological Review 19*, 1 (1954), 3-10.
6. Carroll JM, ed. 1991. *Designing Interaction: Psychology at the Human-Computer Interface*. NY: Cambridge Univ. Press
7. Carroll, J. M. & Kellogg, W. A. Artifact as theory-nexus: hermeneutics meets theory-based design. *Proc.*CHI 1988. ACM (1989), 7-14.
8. Carroll, J.M. (ed) *Scenario-Based Design: Envisioning Work and Technology in System Development*. 1995.
9. Cooper, A. *The Inmates are Running the Asylum*. SAMS, 1999.
10. Crabtree, A. and Rodden, T. Ethnography and design? *Proc. IAISCR* (2002) 70-74.
11. Crabtree, A., O'Brien, J., Nichols, D., Rouncefield, M., and Twidale, M. Ethnomethodologically informed ethnography and information systems design. *JASIST*, *51*, 7, (2000), 666-682.
12. Dix, A., Finlay, J., Abowd, G.D. and Beale, R. *Human-computer interaction*. Pearson Prentice, New York, NY, USA, 2004.
13. Dourish, P. Implications for design. *Proc.CHI 2006*, ACM (2006), 541-550.
14. Dourish. P. and Bellotti.V. Awareness and coordination in shared workspaces. *Proc. CSCW 1992*. ACM (1992), 107-114
15. Fallman, D., Design-oriented human-computer interaction. In *Proc.CHI* 2003, ACM (2003), 225-232.
16. Gaver, B., & Martin, H. Alternatives: exploring information appliances through conceptual design proposals. In *Proc. CHI 2000*, ACM (2000), 209-216.
17. Gaver, W.W., Beaver, J., & Benford, S. Ambiguity as a resource for design. In *Proc. CHI 2003*. ACM (2003), 233-240.
18. Gray, W. D., & Salzman, M. C. (1998). Damaged merchandise? *Human–Computer Interaction*, *13*(3), 203-261.
19. Grudin, J. and Pruitt, J. Personas, participatory design and product development: an infrastructure for engagement. In *Proc. PDC 2002*, (2002), 144-161.
20. Haynes, S. R. and Carroll, J. M. (2008). Theoretical Design Science in HCI: A Practical Concern? *Artifact*, 1(3), 159-171.
21. Höök, K. and Löwgren. J. 2012. Strong concepts: Intermediate-level knowledge in interaction design research. *ACM ToCHI*. 19, 3, 23.
22. Hughes, J.A., O'Brien, J., Rodden, T., Rouncefield, M., and Blythin, S. Designing with ethnography: a presentation framework for design. *Proc. DIS 1997*, ACM (1997), 147-158
23. Hughes, J.A., Randall, D., and Shapiro, D. Faltering from ethnography to design. *Proc. CSCW 1992*. ACM (1992), 115-122.
24. Johnson, J., Roberts, T. L., Verplank, W., Smith, D. C., Irby, C. H., Beard, M., & Mackey, K. (1989). The Xerox star: A retrospective. *Computer*, *22*(9), 11-26.
25. Luff, P., Heath, C., Kuzuoka, H., Yamazaki, K., and Yamashita, J. Handling documents and discriminating objects in hybrid spaces. *Proc. CHI 2006*. ACM (2006), 561-570.
26. Macaulay, C., Benyon, D. and Crerar, A. Ethnography, theory and systems design: from intuition to insight, *IJHCS 53*, 1, (2000), 35-60.
27. Norman, D. A. and Draper, S. W. *User Centered System Design: New Perspectives on HCI*. Erlbaum, Hillsdale, 1986.
28. Paay, J. (2008). From ethnography to interface design. *Handbook of Research on User Interface Design and Evaluation for Mobile Technology*, 1-15.
29. Rittel H, Webber M. 1973. Dilemmas in a general theory of planning. *Policy Sci.* 4: 155–69
30. Sas, C and Zhang, C. Do emotions matter in creative design? *Proc. DIS 2010*. ACM (2010), 372-375.
31. Schofield, J. W. (2002). Increasing the generalizability of qualitative research. *The qualitative researcher's companion*, 171-203.
32. Stake, R. E., Trumbull, D. J. (1982). 1 Naturalistic Generalizations.
33. Taylor, A. (2009). Ethnography in Ubiquitous Computing. In *Ubiquitous Computing Fundamentals*, 203-236. Chapman & Hall.
34. Vallgårda, A., & Redström, J. Computational composites. In *Proc.CHI 2007*. ACM 2007, 513-522.
35. Yamashita, N., Kaji, K., Kuzuoka, H., and Hirata, K. Improving visibility of remote gestures in distributed tabletop collaboration. *Proc. CSCW 2011*. ACM Press (2011) 95-104.
36. Zimmerman, J., Stolterman, E., and Forlizzi, J. An analysis and critique of Research through Design: towards a formalization of a research approach. *Proc. DIS 2010*. ACM (2010), 310-319.

Investigating the Effects of Encumbrance on One- and Two- Handed Interactions with Mobile Devices

Alexander Ng, Stephen Brewster and John Williamson
Glasgow Interactive Systems Group
School of Computing Science, University of Glasgow
Glasgow, United Kingdom, G12 8QQ
a.ng.1@research.gla.ac.uk, stephen.brewster@glasgow.ac.uk, jhw@dcs.gla.ac.uk

ABSTRACT
In this paper, we investigate the effects of encumbrance (carrying typical objects such as shopping bags during interaction) and walking on target acquisition on a touchscreen mobile phone. Users often hold objects and use mobile devices at the same time and we examined the impact encumbrance has on one- and two- handed interactions. Three common input postures were evaluated: two-handed index finger, one-handed preferred thumb and two-handed both thumbs, to assess the effects on performance of carrying a bag in each hand while walking. The results showed a significant decrease in targeting performance when users were encumbered. For example, input accuracy dropped to 48.1% for targeting with the index finger when encumbered, while targeting error using the preferred thumb to input was 4.2mm, an increase of 40% compared to unencumbered input. We also introduce a new method to evaluate the user's preferred walking speed when interacting - *PWS&I*, and suggest future studies should use this to get a more accurate measure of the user's input performance.

Author Keywords
Target acquisition; mobile interactions; one- and two-handed input; encumbrance.

ACM Classification Keywords
H.5.2. [User Interfaces]: Input devices and strategies.

INTRODUCTION
One of the benefits of modern touchscreen mobile devices is that they give users a vast array of features and applications that can be used while on the move. Mobile phones can be used in both portrait and landscape orientations and allow users to interact with the device using either one or both hands (text entry, for example). However, in mobile contexts, users are unlikely to be interacting only with their mobile devices as other activities may also be consuming the user's attention, for example moving through the environment and carrying objects such as personal gear and shopping bags. Therefore, a user study was conducted to examine the effects of *encumbrance* and *mobility* on both one- and two-handed interactions with touchscreen mobile phones. Interacting when encumbered has not received much attention from researchers but users often hold and carry cumbersome objects [17,19] or perform manual tasks [21] during interaction and these can cause usability problems. There is currently a lack of interaction techniques to support users when they are encumbered and the results from the experiment presented in this paper will help researchers understand the problems of encumbrance while walking and motivate designers to develop more efficient and effective input techniques to support users when they interact in this way. Our study examines the effects of carrying two shopping bags while using a mobile phone and walking. It is a typical manual task that people perform in their everyday lives and one that can have a significant impact on usability as the user has to struggle between holding both the objects and the device while trying to aim at the touchscreen to input accurately.

To investigate the effects of encumbrance and mobility on both one- and two- handed interactions, three different input postures were evaluated: two-handed index finger, one-handed preferred thumb and two-handed both thumbs while the user was walking and carrying a bag in each hand. The three input postures (see Figure 1) were selected because they are common ways to hold and use touchscreen mobile devices [9,12]. Furthermore, no previous study has compared the impact of encumbrance between the input postures. The one-handed preferred thumb posture is the traditional method of input on mobile phones before the introduction of touchscreen interfaces. Users could press the physical buttons with relative ease because they were within the thumb's reach. However, the introduction of larger touchscreen mobile devices meant that the thumb has more screen space to cover which results in greater thumb movement, especially for those interface components located opposite the preferred hand. This may force the user to change phone grip to reach the onscreen items or switch to a two-handed posture to input more effectively. Two-handed input divides interaction activity between both hands and there are two broad types. In the two-handed index finger posture, one hand holds the device (usually in the non-dominant hand) in a portrait orientation while the

CHI 2014, April 26 - May 01, 2014, Toronto, ON, Canada.
Copyright 2014 ACM 978-1-4503-2473-1/14/04...$15.00.
http://dx.doi.org/10.1145/2556288.2557312

other hand is used for input, for example tapping with the index finger or performing 'pinching' gestures using both the thumb and the index finger. The other common two-handed grip holds the phone in landscape orientation and input is made by both thumbs. There is no problem reaching items on the screen as, for a typical sized mobile phone, the thumbs can fully cover the screen. Interaction is faster than one thumb or the index finger since two digits are ready for input with the device firmly held in both hands [1]. Furthermore, for some input tasks, interface components can dynamically adjust for better input when the device is held in landscape orientation (wider keys for text entry, for example).

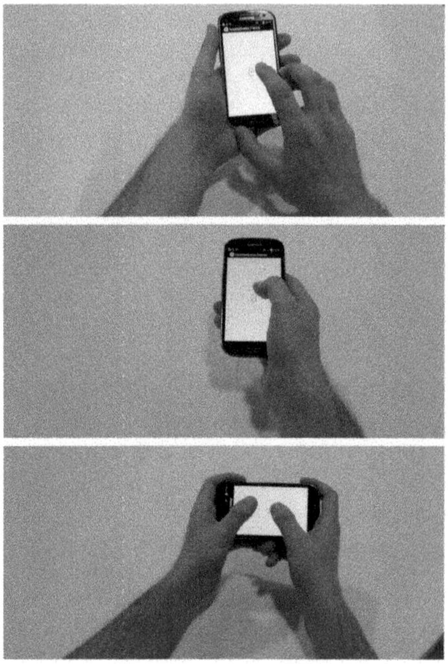

Figure 1. Three common input postures: two-handed index finger (top), one-handed preferred thumb (middle) and two-handed both thumbs (bottom)

BACKGROUND

The Effects of Encumbrance

In one of the earlier studies that investigated encumbrance and its effects on interaction, Ng, Brewster and Crossan [18] extended the work of Crossan *et al.* [6] by examining the practicality of using wrist-based gestures to point on a mobile phone while the user was encumbered. The results showed that holding a bag while performing wrist rotational gestures caused input accuracy to significantly decrease when compared to unencumbered. However, performance while carrying a box under the arm was similar to holding no objects as users were able to steady their forearm against the box which suggested that different types of encumbrances had a varied impact on usability.

Later, Ng, Brewster and Williamson [19] conducted a study which investigated the impact of encumbrance on mobile interactions. Prior to their main experiment, an observational study was carried out in three public settings to identify the common objects that users held and carried during interaction with mobile devices. During six hours of observation, they saw people carrying 878 objects, 554 of these were being held when users were interacting. Approximately 46% of the objects they observed were bags and 36% were boxes (the remaining objects included umbrellas, cardboard cups and pushchairs). Their data showed that using mobile devices while carrying objects is a frequent occurrence and therefore is an important use-case that should be studied to help users interact effectively. The results from their target acquisition experiment showed users were significantly less accurate at targeting on a touchscreen phone when either carrying a bag in the hand or holding a box under the arm while walking compared to unencumbered and standing still. Furthermore, there were significantly more hand movements and instability when the dominant hand or arm was encumbered compared to the non-dominant side. Users only selected targets using the two-handed index finger input posture in this study.

In a follow-up study, Ng and Brewster [20] investigated the trade-off between encumbrance and preferred walking speed (PWS) when targeting using the two-handed index finger posture. Input accuracy is often improved when the user's walking speed slows down [3]. Similar to [19], the results showed that carrying a bag or a box while maintaining the preferred walking speed (PWS) caused significantly more error than unencumbered and in a stationary position. Targeting error increased by as much as 112% while walking at the PWS and carrying a bag. This shows some of the problems that can occur when trying to use a mobile device when walking and encumbered. In this case, however, users were only carrying one bag or box so interaction is likely to be even worse when more items are carried while on the move.

Oulasvirta and Bergstrom-Lehtovirta [21] looked at physical multitasking during interaction by examining how performing common daily activities that require the user's hands influenced input performance on both desktop and mobile devices. Twelve physical tasks covering a range of different hand grips were assessed including holding differently sized objects ranging from a ballpoint pen (small), cigarette packet (medium) to a basketball (large) while either performing a pointing task on a laptop or text entry on a mobile device. Other objects were also assessed such as using a pair of scissors that required a more intricate and complex finger grip. The results from the text entry experiment showed one-handed typing on the mobile phone while holding an object (such as a mug) caused the user to input less accurately when compared to two-handed typing. This study did not look at mobility which could have compounded some of the problems they found. Ng *et al.* [19] observed users holding similar smaller-sized objects such as cups when using mobile devices in public settings.

Mainwaring, Anderson and Chang [17] conducted an ethnographic study across three major cities to examine the types of objects that young professionals carried in their everyday activities and how those items were used in the urban environment. The so called 'mobile kits' – the objects that the observed participants carried daily – included mobile technologies (phones, cameras and iPods), books, wallets and keys. Similar to [19], they found the participants across all three cities frequently carried different types of bags to transport their belongings. Jain [10] observed female users and found they typically carried their mobile phones in a handbag along with other personal belongings to prevent pick-pockets or items tumbling out. One of the subjects, who was constantly on her mobile phone for work (to purchase goods, arrange meetings with colleagues) while having to carry heavy and bulky boxes had interaction issues as she struggled to multitask. Perry *et al.* [24] investigated the role of technology and artefacts to support mobile workers (those who are not limited to an office space) and found users to carry objects ranging from PDAs and laptops to paper-based objects such as notebooks, working files and folders. These studies highlight the wide range of objects and situations that can encumber users and the need to understand how performance is affected so that we can design better interaction techniques to support them. Sherry and Salvador [26] commented that ordinary users may not have the skills or experience to perform multiple activities in a uniform and synchronised manner and suggested that, as interface designers, we need to understand the situations that users experience on a daily basis and develop more efficient and stress-free ways of interacting with computing devices.

One- and Two- Handed Interactions

Observational studies have been conducted to examine the common ways that users interact with mobile devices. Karlson, Bederson and Contreras-Vidal [12] studied one-handed interaction by conducting a field study in an airport to examine user behaviour with mobile devices. Their observations suggested that 60% of users engaged with their mobile phone in a one-handed posture when walking. A follow-up survey suggested 45% of participants would use one hand only for all device interactions compared to 19% for two-handed interactions. Users were also seen to carry objects during input but encumbrance was not examined specifically in their study. More recently, an investigation by Hoober [9] who made over 1000 observations of users in different public settings including bus stops and cafes found that 49% of people used their mobile phone in the one-handed preferred thumb posture, while 36% held the device in the two-handed index finger position to input. The remaining 15% of users held the device in the two-handed both thumbs posture. This shows the need to evaluate the effects of encumbrance on thumb-based input on mobile devices that previous studies [18,19] did not examine.

Studies have also been conducted to investigate and improve both one- and two- handed interactions. Parhi, Karlson and Bederson [22] examined target size for single thumb-based interaction and recommended target size of at least 9.2mm for discrete selections and slightly bigger target size of 9.6mm for continuous targeting. This study, however, did not evaluate one-handed thumb input while encumbered or walking. Later, Perry and Hourcade [23] extended the work of Parhi *et al.* [22] by examining one-handed thumb targeting and walking but unencumbered. The results from their study showed that users were more accurate and quicker at tapping with the preferred hand. Also, users preferred to select targets that were located in the centre of the device as they were subjectively easier but accuracy was actually higher for targets at the edge of the screen, especially for those targets near the input hand. Surprisingly, there were no significant differences in performance between standing and walking (participants walked at their normal pace in a hallway). Karlson and Bederson [13] tried to address the issues caused by one-handed thumb interaction and developed ThumbSpace which allowed users to configure the preferred screen area to select difficult to reach onscreen objects. Participants preferred to use the application for targets that were biomechanically difficult for the thumb to reach. Boring *et al.* [4] used the thumb's contact area to allow users to input efficiently on a touchscreen in the one-handed preferred thumb input posture. The results indicated that the technique worked well for small targets.

Kim *et al.* [14] used capacitive touch sensors on a prototype device to detect different hand grip positions which included the one- and two- thumb input postures. Later, Goel *et al.* [8] managed to use the built-in inertial sensors from a mobile phone to infer the user's hand posture while in a stationary position. The results showed that their application could accurately distinguish between the one-handed thumb and two-handed index finger input postures. The two-handed both thumbs position was not assessed. Azenkot and Zhai [1] compared text entry performance using the index finger, one thumb and both thumbs on a touchscreen device. Their results showed that typing with both thumbs was significantly faster than one thumb or the index finger. However, error rate was significantly higher for text entry using both thumbs which indicated a speed-accuracy tradeoff. Later, Goel *et al.* [7] examined the user's touch pattern to distinguish between the three input postures to improve text entry. Yin *et al.* [27] also used hand posture to enhance text entry on touchscreen keyboards and reported that their method could differentiate single finger and two thumbs typing with an accuracy of 86.4%.

The studies discussed here have all compared input performance of the common hand postures that users adopt when interacting with mobile phones. Some researchers have also examined the effects of mobility. However, no previous studies have looked at the impact of encumbrance and mobility on all of the three common input postures. The studies that have examined encumbrance ([19,20]) only evaluated targeting using the index finger. Therefore, we conducted an experiment to compare the effects of encumbrance while walking using three typical input postures to see how targeting performance on a touchscreen interface is affected.

EXPERIMENT

A within subjects experiment was designed to test the impact of carrying a bag in each hand while walking at a constant speed around a pre-defined route and performing target selections with a touchscreen mobile phone held in three common input postures.

Encumbrance Scenario

A typical supermarket carrier bag was chosen to evaluate the impact of encumbrance because it is a common object that people carry often in their daily lives [17,19]. The participants in our experiment held one bag in each hand to simulate situations where the user is carrying multiple objects. The bags were identical and the dimensions (cm) were approximately 33 x 48 x 6 (w x h x d). Each bag weighed 1.6 kilograms to replicate the effects of holding a realistic object yet keep the amount of fatigue and strain on the participants to a minimum. Figure 2 shows a participant carrying the bags during interaction.

Figure 2. A participant carrying the bags during one- (right) and two- (left) handed input.

Measuring and Maintaining the PWS

A pre-defined oval route (Figure 3) was created to examine encumbrance and mobility. The route was marked out using plastic cones in a spacious and open room and measured 20m in total length and was 1.2m wide. Participants were instructed to keep within the path during the experiment.

Three versions of each participant's preferred walking speed (PWS) were recorded before the experiment began:

PWS – Each participant was instructed to walk around the route for five laps at a pace that he/she would normally walk. The total amount of time required was recorded and the average walking speed was calculated, denoted as *PWS*. This is the standard measure of PWS [25]. No mobile device was used nor bags carried.

PWS&E – The first step was repeated but participants carried one bag in each hand to measure any change in PWS due to encumbrance. The calculated walking speed is denoted as *PWS&E* and gave us a baseline for walking speed when encumbered.

PWS&I – The first step was repeated again but participants also performed a targeting task on a smartphone to measure walking speed during interaction (but unencumbered), denoted as *PWS&I*. This gave us a baseline for walking performance when interacting. All participants performed the task in the two-handed index finger posture for consistency (this is the most commonly used input posture in mobility studies [3,19,20]). Although the same targeting task was used in the main experiment, targets for each condition were randomly ordered to keep bias and learning effects to a minimum.

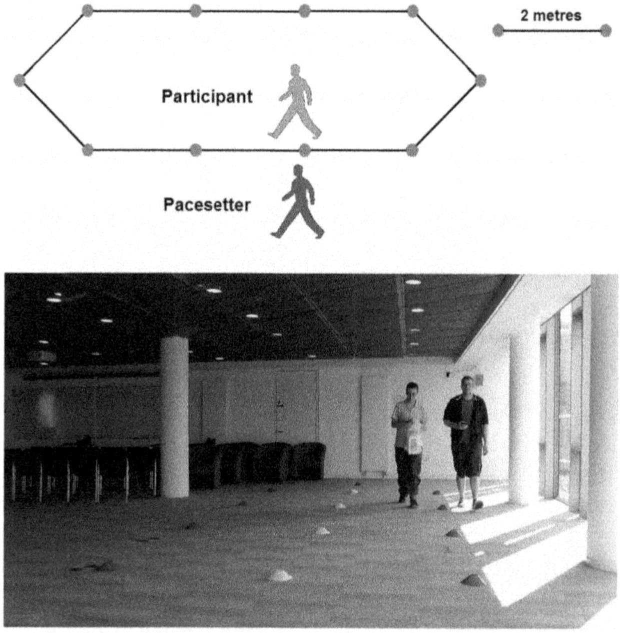

Figure 3. The pre-defined oval route marked out by plastic cones (red dots) is shown in the top image. The distance between each cone is 2m. During the experiment, the participant (green figure) maintained their PWS by walking side-by-side with the pacesetter (blue figure). Part of the actual route is displayed in the bottom image.

Once the walking speeds had been calculated, the experiment began and each participant walked at their individual PWS&I for each input posture condition. Participants walked side-by-side with a pacesetter who walked at the calculated PWS&I by using a metronome application that ran on a HTC One X phone. At the end of the experiment, the PWS and PWS&E were both measured again to assess any fatigue caused by interaction and carrying the bags.

We chose the approach of controlling walking speed, which is unusual for mobile evaluations, as it meant we could remove one variable from our results. In studies where walking speed is not controlled (e.g. [2,15,16,19]), participants can trade-off input performance and walking speed. It can be then difficult to understand these choices and therefore make recommendations based on the results. If we control walking speed then we can isolate the effects of targeting accuracy, error and selection time. The question then arises as to what walking speed should be used. In this paper, we chose a new measure: PWS&I, or the walking speed that a user naturally walks when using a device. Other studies have used different approaches; Kane *et al.* [11] do not explicitly state the walking speed they used but they trained a pacesetter to walk at a constant speed across all participants, rather than being based on a user's own normal walking speed. Ng *et al.* [20] used each participant's PWS, but this is not the speed at which a user would walk when using a device. So, in our study, we used PWS&I so that we could see the effects of encumbrance when interacting on the three input postures.

Experimental Task

The task was to select a series of targets one at a time on a touchscreen mobile phone as quickly and as accurately as possible. There were nine target positions evenly spaced in a 3 x 3 grid, as shown in Figure 4.

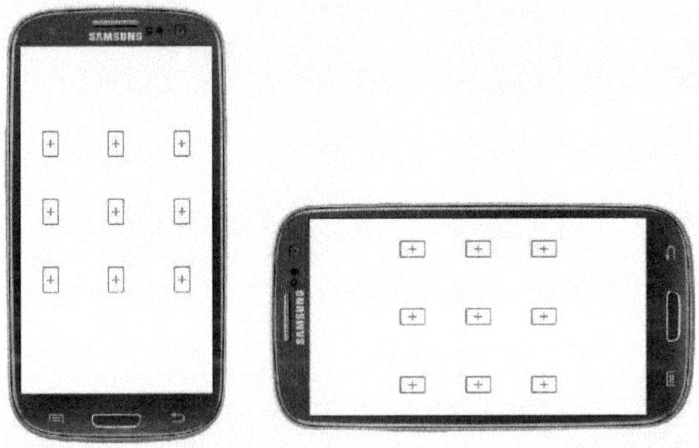

Figure 4. The targeting task ran on a Samsung S3 phone. The positions of the targets are shown in both orientation modes.

The centre and outer targets were selected in an alternate sequence - every second selection was an outer target – and the order of the outer targets were randomized for each block. Each outer target was selected ten times which resulted in 160 target selections per block and there were two blocks for each condition. Like Crossan *et al.* [5], there was a random interval ranging from 0.5 and 1.5 seconds between a selection and the next target being shown to negate any rhythm created between the participant's walking and onscreen targeting. A Samsung Galaxy S3 smartphone with a touchscreen resolution of 720 x 1280 pixels (~12 pixels/mm) was used. Each target was 60 pixels (5mm) wide and 96 pixels (8mm) long with the central crosshair measuring 30 pixels (2.5mm) in both directions. This is the size of a key on the standard keyboard for this phone. The device was held in portrait orientation for both the two-handed index finger and one-handed preferred thumb input postures. The device was used in landscape mode for the two-handed both thumbs posture with the bottom end of the device always to the right for consistency (see Figure 4). Participants were given a short training phase at the start of the experiment to familiarise with the targeting task in each input posture.

Participants

Eighteen participants (11 males) recruited from the university took part in the experiment. The mean age was 25 years (SD = 3.519) and all participants preferred using their right hand for interaction (despite one individual being left-handed). Sixteen participants owned and used a touchscreen mobile phone daily while two users occasionally used touchscreen phones. Participants were paid £6 for their participation.

Experimental Design

The participants performed the targeting task either unencumbered or carrying a bag in each hand for each of the three input postures which resulted in a total of six conditions. Each condition was conducted while walking at the PWS&I by following a pacesetter around the route. A within-subjects design was used and the conditions were counterbalanced. The Independent Variables were type of encumbrance (2 levels - unencumbered and carrying the bags) and input posture (3 levels - two-handed index finger, one-handed preferred thumb and two-handed both thumbs). The Dependent Variables were target accuracy, target error and selection time. Target accuracy was measured as the percentage of successful target selections; the position pressed on the touchscreen was either within the target border or not. Target error (in millimetres) was the absolute distance from the centre of the target to the recorded touch down position. Selection time (in milliseconds) was the duration from the display of the current target to the instance that a press down event was logged.

The main hypotheses of the experiment were:

H1: Participants will be significantly less accurate at target selection when encumbered compared to unencumbered, while walking at their PWS&I;

H2: Participants will be significantly less precise at target selection when encumbered compared to unencumbered, while walking at their PWS&I;

H3: Participants will take significantly more time to target when encumbered compared to unencumbered, while walking at their PWS&I;

H4: Target selection using both thumbs will be significantly more accurate, precise and quicker than input using one thumb or the index finger when encumbered;

H5: The PWS will be slower when encumbered or interacting with a mobile device than walking alone.

RESULTS

Each participant completed 12 blocks of targets – six condition and two blocks per condition. There were 160 targets for each block giving a total of 1920 targets per participants and 18 participants resulted in a total of 34,560 targets for the whole experiment. To filter out unintentional selections, targets that took less than 100 milliseconds to select were removed from the data. As a result, 23 targets were eliminated from the final data set. Two-factor repeated-measures ANOVAs with type of encumbrance (2 levels) and type of input posture (3 levels) as factors were conducted to analyse accuracy, error and selection time.

Target Accuracy

The ANOVA for target accuracy showed a significant main effect for encumbrance, $F(1,17) = 87.880$, $p < 0.001$. *Post hoc* pairwise comparison with Bonferroni corrections showed that the participants were significantly more accurate when unencumbered compared to carrying the bags (mean difference = 11.702, $p < 0.001$). There was no significant main difference between the three input postures $F(2,34) = 2.113$, $p > 0.05$. A significant interaction was observed between the factors, $F(2,34) = 3.757$, $p < 0.05$. Encumbrance caused accuracy to significantly decrease for each input posture when walking. Based on these results, hypothesis H1 is supported. Figure 5 illustrates the mean target accuracy for each condition. The graph shows the participants were more accurate at targeting when unencumbered than carrying a bag in each hand for each input posture.

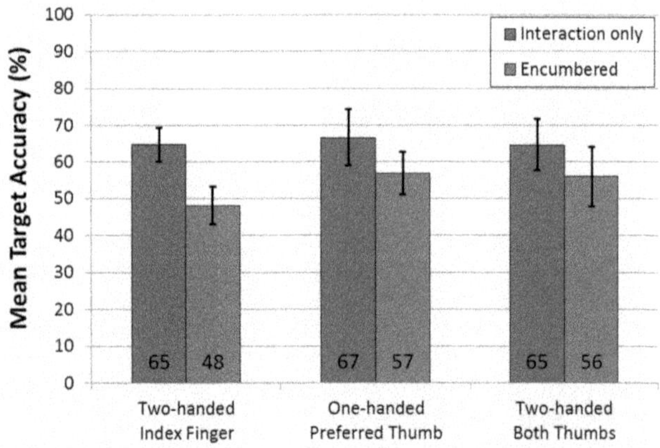

Figure 5. The mean target accuracy (%) for each condition. The blue and red bars illustrate the unencumbered and encumbered conditions respectively. Error bars denote 95% CI.

Target Error

The ANOVA for targeting error showed there was a significant main effect for encumbrance, $F(1,17) = 32.753$, $p < 0.001$, where error was significantly higher when the user was encumbered than unencumbered (mean difference = 0.941). There was no significant main effect for input posture, $F(2,34) = 0.481$, $p > 0.05$. The interaction between the two factors was not significant, $F(2,34) = 0.857$, $p > 0.05$. Based on these results, hypothesis H2 is supported. Figure 6 shows the mean targeting error for each condition. Error was evenly matched when users were unencumbered. As target selections got more physically challenging (by carrying the bags at the same time), error increased for each input posture.

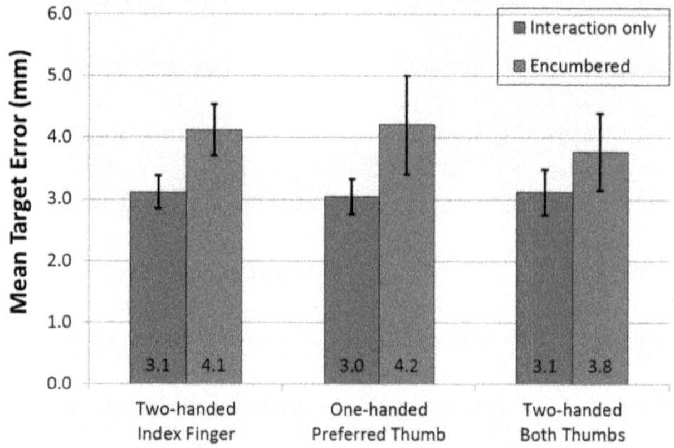

Figure 6. The mean target error (millimeters) for each condition. Error bars represent 95% CI.

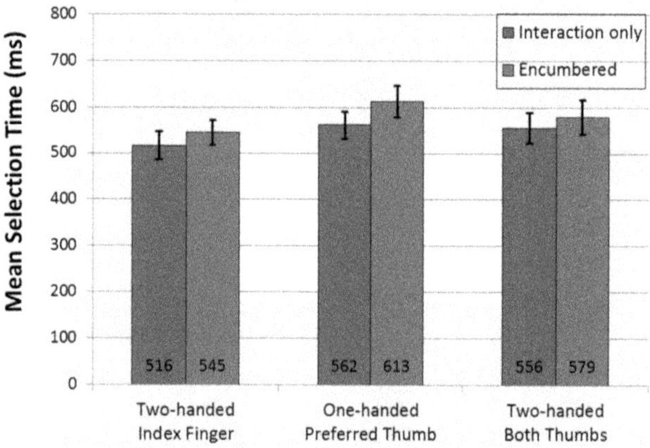

Figure 7. The mean selection times (milliseconds) for each condition. Error bars represent 95% CI.

Selection Time

The ANOVA for selection time showed a significant main effect for encumbrance, $F(1,17) = 11.672$, $p < 0.05$, where target selections took significantly longer when carrying the bags than interaction only (mean difference was 34.6 ms). There was a significant main effect for input posture, $F(2,34) = 13.646$, $p < 0.05$. *Post hoc* pairwise comparisons with Bonferroni corrections showed a significant difference between all pair combinations, except between the two thumb-based input postures. Target selection using the one-handed index finger posture was significantly quicker than the one-handed preferred thumb and two-handed both thumbs poses. Input using both thumbs was not significantly quicker than the preferred thumb. A significant effect was also observed for the interaction between the two factors, $F(2,34) = 3.924$, $p < 0.05$. Encumbrance caused significantly slower selection time for each input posture than unencumbered. The biggest negative effect was on the one-handed preferred thumb posture when encumbered. Figure 7 shows the mean selection times for each condition. Target selection took the longest in the one-handed preferred thumb posture when encumbered. Based on these results, hypothesis H3 is supported. However, hypothesis H4 is rejected since there was no significant difference between the input postures for accuracy and error. Furthermore, input was quicker when the index finger was used to target.

Performance of Individual Target Positions

The performance of each individual target position for the three input postures is shown in Figure 8, Figure 9 and Figure 10. The results for the two-handed index finger input posture showed that error was evenly matched for each target position when unencumbered and encumbered. The variability in taps for each target location is greater when encumbered (as shown by the larger red ellipses), especially the targets on the left of the first and second rows. Encumbrance caused accuracy to decrease for all target positions, with accuracy dropping to 41% for the target in the top left corner.

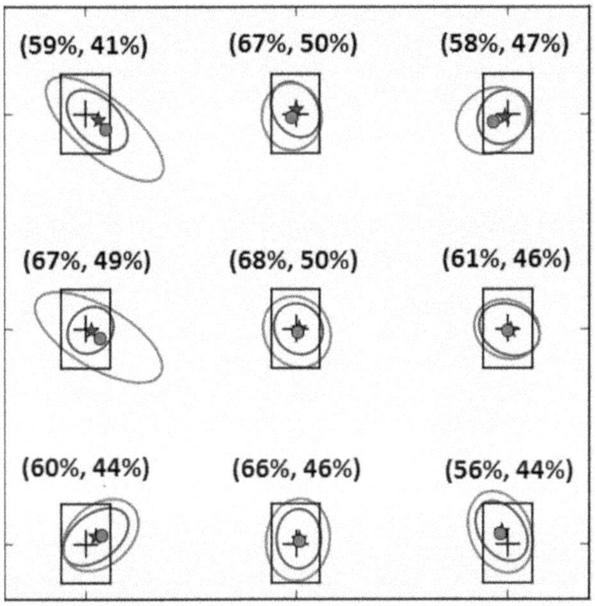

Figure 8. The mean and covariance of the x and y targeting error for each target position when unencumbered (blue) and encumbered (red), for the two-handed index finger input posture. The figures above each target show the accuracy (%) when unencumbered (left) and encumbered (right).

The results for the one-handed preferred thumb input posture show greater variability in tapping performance between unencumbered and carrying the bags. The four targets (middle and right targets on the second and third rows) had similar error when unencumbered and encumbered. All participants used their right thumb to input therefore these targets were the closest. There was a greater difference in error between tapping when unencumbered and encumbered for the other five target positions as these targets required more thumb movement to reach. The left target on the first row was affected the most when encumbered as it had the highest mean error and lowest target accuracy of 31%. The ellipse for the target in the top-left corner when encumbered also highlights a much greater spread of taps than the other target positions which suggest participants had the most difficulty to select the target that was the furthest away from the thumb.

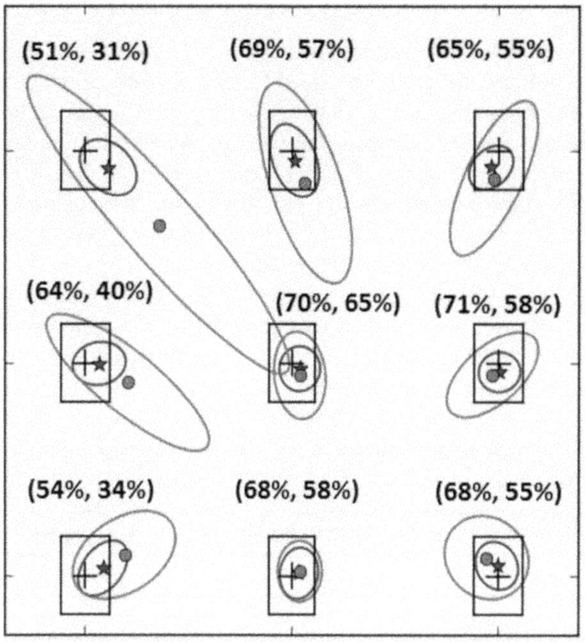

Figure 9. The mean and covariance of the x and y targeting error for each target position, for the one-handed preferred thumb input posture.

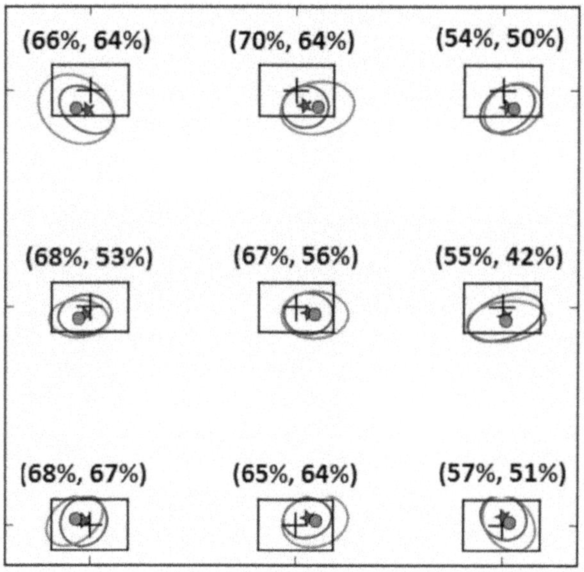

Figure 10. The mean and covariance of the x and y targeting error for each target position. for the two-handed both thumbs input posture.

The tapping performance for the two-handed both thumbs input posture showed that error was evenly matched for all target positions between unencumbered and encumbered. The mean errors for the three targets in the middle column illustrate an offset to the right which may suggest that the participants mainly used their right thumb to tap those targets. Target accuracy for the three targets in the right column was lower than the three targets in the left column for both unencumbered and encumbered, despite all participants preferred using their right dominant hand to input.

Comparison of Walking Speeds

We wanted to compare the different classes of walking speed discussed earlier to see how they differed as no previous study has measured the walking speed when encumbered but not interacting. The mean walking speeds for PWS, PWS&E and PWS&I recorded at the start of the experiment are shown in Table 1. A one-factor ANOVA with walking speed as factor (3 levels) showed a main effect, $F(2,34) = 52.281, p < 0.01$. *Post hoc* pairwise comparisons with Bonferroni corrections showed that the participants walked significantly slower when interacting (PWS&I) than walking and encumbered, and walking alone. There was no clear difference between PWS and PWS&E (given the objects we chose for our study). Therefore, hypothesis H5 is partially supported.

Walking Speed	Mean (km/h)	SD (km/h)
PWS	4.9	0.5
PWS&E	4.9	0.6
PWS&I	4.1	0.4

Table 1. The mean PWS (top row), when encumbered (middle row) and during interaction only (bottom row).

DISCUSSION

The results from the experiment showed that targeting performance on a touchscreen interface was significantly affected when users were encumbered by carrying a bag in each hand and walking at their PWS&I across three common input postures. Target accuracy was evenly matched between the three input postures when users were unencumbered. However, once the users were encumbered, accuracy decreased; the two-handed index finger input posture dropped by 16.7% compared to 9.9% and 8.7% for the one- and two- handed thumb input methods respectively. We anticipated that using both thumbs would be more accurate than the preferred thumb and the index finger. However, there were no big differences between the input postures which suggest the method of input does not greatly affect interaction for target accuracy when encumbered.

The results for targeting error showed that users were significantly less precise when encumbered compared to unencumbered. Like target accuracy, the mean error was similar for each input posture when unencumbered. However, the one-handed preferred thumb input posture was affected the most when carrying the bags, as error increased by 40%. For two-handed input, error increased by 32.3% and 22.6% for the index finger and both thumbs input postures respectively. There were no significant differences between the three input postures, as targeting error was similar when unencumbered or carrying the bags. If input precision is important, then no one posture can be clearly recommended for input when encumbered and walking. Furthermore, two-handed tapping might not result in more precise targeting than one-handed input. This shows that we need to take encumbrance into account when designing new interaction techniques for mobile devices.

The results for selection times showed users were significantly slower at targeting when encumbered compared to holding no objects. However, the differences were marginal - the biggest reduction of 51ms was caused in the one-handed preferred thumb posture. This posture also resulted in the slowest mean selection time when the user was encumbered. The user is effectively performing three manual tasks in one hand only: holding the device, attempting to target and carrying the bag, which makes interaction slower and more difficult. In the two-handed postures, the activity is divided between both hands with less cost to performance. The two-handed both thumb input posture was significantly faster than using the preferred thumb but significantly slower than the two-handed index finger posture. We anticipated that users would be faster at targeting when using both thumbs due to the advantage of having an extra digit to input. This suggests when the user is encumbered and walking, there is a speed-accuracy trade-off when using both thumbs to target. Azenkot and Zhai [1] reported a similar finding when they compared these three input postures for static text entry on a mobile device.

We also examined each individual target position for a more in-depth analysis of user's performance for each input posture. There was a greater distribution of taps for each target position when encumbered compared to unencumbered for the two-handed index finger input posture. The mean error between unencumbered and holding the bags was similar for each target position despite a greater difference in target accuracy. Users were least accurate at selecting the left target in the first row when encumbered and using the index finger to target. Since all participants preferred using their right hand to interact, there was likely to be a bias effect on the user's starting position to input. Targets on the left side of the device would therefore require more finger movement to select. Those targets might have been more difficult to reach when encumbered.

Like the two-handed index finger input posture, there was greater variability of taps for each target position when encumbered compared to unencumbered, for the one-handed preferred thumb posture. The targets that were closest to the thumb used for input were selected more accurately and precisely when encumbered than those that were further away and biomechanically difficult to reach. This was illustrated by the poor performance of the left targets in the first and third rows where accuracy dropped to 31% and 34% respectively. Users who have smaller thumb lengths would have had more difficulty to reach the targets located the furthest distance away from the thumb. Also, participants might have had difficulty adjusting their hand grip to reposition the device in an attempt to select those targets that are biomechanically challenging to tap when using the preferred thumb to input and holding the bag as well.

The distribution of taps for each target position was similar between unencumbered and holding the bags for the two-handed both thumbs posture. Target accuracy was evenly matched for the targets on the first and third rows. There was a greater difference in accuracy between unencumbered and encumbered for the targets on the second row. Interestingly, the targets on the right column were less accurate than the targets on the left column, which suggests holding a bag in each hand affects the user's dominant hand more than the non-dominant hand. Ng *et al.* [19] showed similar findings and reported that when the user's dominant hand or arm was encumbered, performance dropped significantly more than holding objects in the non-dominant side. However, users in their study only used the index finger to input.

The walking speeds calculated in our experiment allowed us to examine the effects of encumbrance and interaction on the user's PWS. The participants managed to carry the bags (weighing 1.6 kg each) without a major impact on walking speed – PWS and PWS&E were similar. However, as anticipated and shown in previous studies [2,3], the PWS&I dropped by 16.3% when compared to PWS. For comparison, Ng *et al.* [19] reported a similar decrease in walking speed of 16.7% when users were targeting on a touchscreen mobile phone, while Bergstrom *et al.*[3] found users to drop their PWS by 24% during interaction when on a treadmill. The targeting error when walking at PWS&I for the two-handed index finger input posture was 4.1mm. Ng *et al.* [20] used the same targeting task as ours and reported an error of 5.8mm when using the index finger to target but walking at the PWS. The mean walking speed from their study was 4.8km/h which suggests walking faster may overestimate the decline in performance. We recommend using PWS&I in future mobile studies for a more accurate representation of the user's input performance when walking.

We were also interested to see if users could maintain their walking speed at the end of the experiment because the results would give some indication of the fatigue caused by prolonged periods of interaction while encumbered and walking. The participants took an average of 18.3mins (SD = 1.9) to complete all six conditions. Once all of the targeting tasks were complete, the PWS and PWS&E were both measured again for each participant, both giving a mean walking speed of 4.9 km/h once again. This showed that participants were not significantly fatigued during the study and that they could walk with the bags without any problems. The mean distance walked to complete all 12 blocks was 1480.2m (~67 laps of our route). This suggests that fatigue may not have been a confounding factor that could have affected the user's targeting performance, although, the user's physical condition should always be taken into consideration. Participants in our experiment were only carrying 3.2kg during the study and it is likely that heavier items would cause more fatigue, a bigger impact on PWS and potentially more encumbrance problems.

Researchers and designers should consider the targeting errors from our experiment when defining the size of keys, buttons and other interface components. We recommend a radius of at least 4.2mm for small components to allow users to input more accurately when encumbered and walking. Input posture should also be considered when developing new techniques to help users input more accurately when carrying cumbersome objects while on the move. The results from our experiment showed that when unencumbered, there were no big differences between the postures in any of our metrics. The two-handed both thumbs input posture was generally the most suitable method to use when both hands were encumbered. So, a recommendation from our study is when using a mobile phone encumbered switch to the two thumbs posture! Also, if mobile devices could accurately detect the input posture then applications could automatically correct some of the input errors that are likely to occur to assist the user to interact with the touchscreen in a more efficient manner. For example, dealing with the large target distributions that occur around the left and top edges of the screen when using the one-handed preferred thumb input posture. Goel *et al.* [8] showed promising results when using built-in sensors in a mobile phone to predict the user's hand posture in a static position. Future studies should investigate if a similar technique can be used to correctly detect the different input postures while the user is encumbered and walking.

CONCLUSIONS

The study presented in this paper shows that researchers should consider the effects of encumbrance and mobility when designing new input techniques and applications. Encumbrance is often overlooked yet people frequently hold and carry objects such as shopping bags, boxes and umbrellas, which can make interaction less accurate, slower and more difficult while on the move. The results from our experiment have shown that input accuracy decreased while both targeting error and selection time increased significantly when carrying a bag in each hand during interaction. In general, encumbrance caused targeting performance to significantly decline for both one- and two- handed input. We compared three common input postures and showed the difference in targeting performance for each posture when the user was encumbered and walking. No previous studies have made this comparison. We introduced a new method to evaluate the user's walking speed; the preferred walking speed when interacting - *PWS&I*. This is the walking speed at which users walk on the ground when using mobile devices. Future studies should use this method when assessing interaction while walking to get a better reflection of the user's input performance.

Encumbrance as a research topic is still at its early stages yet usability issues are evident, therefore it deserves more focus from researchers in the HCI community. Users are frequently challenged with physical encumbrances that can make using mobile devices awkward and error prone. If more effective and efficient interaction techniques are developed, then the large number of applications and services available on smartphones will be more usable in a much wider range of contexts, which will be beneficial for users.

REFERENCES

1. Azenkot, S. and Zhai, S. Touch behavior with different postures on soft smartphone keyboards. *In Proc. MobileHCI 2012*, ACM Press (2012), 251–260.
2. Barnard, L., Yi, J.S., Jacko, J.A., and Sears, A. An empirical comparison of use-in-motion evaluation scenarios for mobile computing devices. *International Journal of Human-Computer Studies 62*, 4 (2005), 487–520.
3. Bergstrom-Lehtovirta, J., Oulasvirta, A., and Brewster, S. The effects of walking speed on target acquisition on a touchscreen interface. *In Proc. MobileHCI 2011*, ACM (2011), 143–146.
4. Boring, S., Ledo, D., and Chen, X. The fat thumb: using the thumb's contact size for single-handed mobile interaction. *In Proc. MobileHCI 2012*, ACM Press (2012), 207–208.
5. Crossan, A., Murray-Smith, R., Brewster, S., Kelly, J., and Musizza, B. Gait phase effects in mobile interaction. *Ext. Abstracts CHI 2005*, ACM Press (2005), 1312–1315.
6. Crossan, A., Williamson, J., Brewster, S., and Murray-Smith, R. Wrist rotation for interaction in mobile contexts. *In Proc. MobileHCI 2008*, ACM Press (2008), 435–438.
7. Goel, M., Jansen, A., Mandel, T., Patel, S., and Wobbrock, J.O. ContextType: using hand posture information to improve mobile touch screen text entry. *In Proc. CHI 2013*, ACM Press (2013), 2795–2798.
8. Goel, M., Wobbrock, J., and Patel, S. GripSense: Using built-in sensors to detect hand posture and pressure on commodity mobile phones. *In Proc. UIST 2012*, ACM Press (2012), 545–554.
9. Hoober, S. How Do Users Really Hold Mobile Devices? 2013. http://www.uxmatters.com/mt/archives/2013/02/how-do-users-really-hold-mobile-devices.php.
10. Jain, S.S.L. The means of mobility. *Journal of Consumer Culture 2*, 3 (2002), 419–438.
11. Kane, S.K., Wobbrock, J.O., and Smith, I.E. Getting off the treadmill: evaluating walking user interfaces for mobile devices in public spaces. *In Proc. MobileHCI 2008*, ACM Press (2008), 109–118.
12. Karlson, A., Bederson, B., and Contreras-Vidal, J. Understanding single-handed mobile device interaction. *Tech Report HCIL*, (2006), 02.
13. Karlson, A. and Bederson, B. ThumbSpace: generalized one-handed input for touchscreen-based mobile devices. *In Proc. INTERACT 2007*, Springer-Verlag (2007), 324–338.
14. Kim, K., Chang, W., Cho, S., and Shim, J. Hand grip pattern recognition for mobile user interfaces. *In Proc. IAAI 2006*, AAAI Press (2006), 1789–1794.
15. Kjeldskov, J. and Stage, J. New techniques for usability evaluation of mobile systems. *International Journal of Human-Computer Studies 60*, 5-6 (2004), 599–620.
16. MacKay, B., Dearman, D., Inkpen, K., and Watters, C. Walk 'n scroll: a comparison of software-based navigation techniques for different levels of mobility. *In Proc. MobileHCI 2005*, ACM Press (2005), 183–190.
17. Mainwaring, S.D., Anderson, K., and Chang, M.F. Living for the global city: mobile kits, urban interfaces, and ubicomp. *In Proc. UbiComp 2005*, Springer-Verlag (2005), 269–286.
18. Ng, A., Brewster, S., and Crossan, A. The effects of encumbrance on mobile gesture interactions. *In Body, Movement, Gestures & Tactility in Interaction with Mobile Devices Workshop, MobileHCI 2011*, (2011).
19. Ng, A., Brewster, S., and Williamson, J. The Impact of Encumbrance on Mobile Interactions. In *In Proc. INTERACT 2013*. Springer-Verlag, 2013, 92–109.
20. Ng, A. and Brewster, S. The relationship between encumbrance and walking speed on mobile interactions. *Ext. Abstracts CHI 2013*, ACM Press (2013), 1359–1364.
21. Oulasvirta, A. and Bergstrom-Lehtovirta, J. Ease of juggling: studying the effects of manual multitasking. *In Proc. CHI 2011*, ACM Press (2011), 3103–3112.
22. Parhi, P., Karlson, A.K., and Bederson, B.B. Target size study for one-handed thumb use on small touchscreen devices. *In Proc. MobileHCI 2005 2016*, ACM Press (2006), 203–210.
23. Perry, K. and Hourcade, J. Evaluating one handed thumb tapping on mobile touchscreen devices. *In Proc. GI 2008*, (2008), 57–64.
24. Perry, M., O'hara, K., Sellen, A., Brown, B., and Harper, R. Dealing with mobility: understanding access anytime, anywhere. *ACM Transactions on Computer-Human Interaction (TOCHI) 8*, 4 (2001), 323–347.
25. Pirhonen, A., Brewster, S., and Holguin, C. Gestural and audio metaphors as a means of control for mobile devices. *In Proc. CHI 2002*, ACM Press (2002), 291–298.
26. Sherry, J. and Salvador, T. Running and grimacing: the struggle for balance in mobile work. *Wireless world*, (2002), 419–438.
27. Yin, Y., Ouyang, T., Partridge, K., and Zhai, S. Making touchscreen keyboards adaptive to keys, hand postures, and individuals: a hierarchical spatial backoff model approach. *In Proc. CHI 2013*, ACM Press (2013), 2775–2784.

Modeling the Functional Area of the Thumb on Mobile Touchscreen Surfaces

Joanna Bergstrom-Lehtovirta[1], Antti Oulasvirta[2]
[1]Helsinki Institute for Information Technology HIIT, Aalto University
[2]Max Planck Institute for Informatics and Saarland University

ABSTRACT
We present a predictive model for the functional area of the thumb on a touchscreen surface: the area of the interface reachable by the thumb of the hand that is holding the device. We derive a quadratic formula by analyzing the kinematics of the gripping hand. Model fit is high for the thumb-motion trajectories of 20 participants. The model predicts the functional area for a given 1) surface size, 2) hand size, and 3) position of the index finger on the back of the device. Designers can use this model to ensure that a user interface is suitable for interaction with the thumb. The model can also be used inversely – that is, to infer the grips assumed by a given user interface layout.

Author Keywords
Predictive model; functional area; thumb; touchscreen.

ACM Classification Keywords
H.5.m. Information Interfaces and Presentation (e.g. HCI): Miscellaneous

INTRODUCTION
This paper addresses a challenge unique to interaction with hand-held touchscreens: not all of the surface can be reached with the thumb of the hand that holds the device. We call this area the *functional area of the thumb*. The larger the display and the smaller the user's hand, the smaller this area is in proportion to the total display area. If an interaction element is beyond the thumb's immediate reach, the user must change grip in order to reach it. The cost of changing the grip is particularly high if the other hand has to be recruited for the task. Frequent grip changes can be detrimental to mobile interaction, wherein users must also devote attention to their surroundings.

This is not a new problem. Designers have long been aware of it and developed estimates of the functional area (see Figure 1). However, such heuristics are only rough approximations of a complex phenomenon. The human hand has approximately 26 degrees of freedom [14], and grip styles [11, 19] and hand sizes [7, 8] vary. Moreover, users are known to adjust their grip or even switch type of grip when walking, changing body posture, or manipulating other objects in the hand [2, 3, 21, 23]. The dynamics and variability of grips call for more systematic investigation of the functional area of the thumb.

http://dx.doi.org/10.1145/2556288.2557354

This paper models the functional area of the thumb in interaction with a hand-held device. "Functional area" here denotes the continuous area on the touchscreen surface that the input finger (in our case, the thumb) can extend to while the hand is gripping the device. Interaction with any interface element falling within this area is possible without a change in grip.

The model is a quadratic equation that yields a parabola for the extrema of thumb motion. We derive this form through an observation that, although the free movement of the thumb is three-dimensional, the motion trajectory on a surface is two-dimensional. The thumb motion on a surface can be predicted from index-finger position, because the index finger and the thumb are linked. The model assumes that the index finger is maximally extended on the back of the device. Therefore, the estimate yielded is conservative: If the index finger is *not* extended, the real area lies somewhere within the predicted one.

The approach is generalizable: The model covers all grips in which the rest of the fingers are on the back of the device and the thumb operates on the screen surface. The model also accommodates grips with several orientations, users with various hand sizes, and devices of varying screen dimensions (including thickness). We discuss three applications:

1. Given statistics on the most probable grips, hand sizes, and screen dimensions, or even intuition as to these, the model can inform the designer of where best to place interface elements.

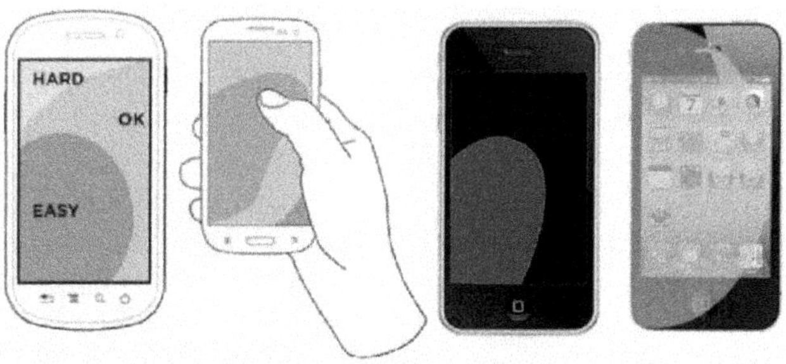

Figure 1. Designers (referred to from left) have previously used heuristic estimates for the functional area of the thumb [30, 13, 5, 6].

2. Given the positions of interface elements, the model can predict the grips that can cover them conveniently. This can be used in gauging whether a design is likely to be suitable for thumb-based interaction.
3. The model can be used to refine adaptive interfaces that use on-device grip-sensing [4, 10, 29].

PREVIOUS WORK

The general problem we examine is how grasping an object affects the ability to provide input on its surface. Relevant work has been carried out in kinesiology and biomechanics, alongside HCI.

Kinesiology and Biomechanics

Existing kinesiological or biomechanical models of object manipulation are not directly applicable to our case, because separate modeling is typically used for each of the two key elements: prehensile movements, for grasping [19], and non-prehensile movements, for aiming or gesturing [14].

The concepts of *functional space* and *workspace* have been used in kinesiology and biomechanics to refer to the possible postures of the thumb but not with the kinds of constraints typical of the case of touchscreens. Kuo et al. [17] tracked *unconstrained* motion of the thumb to compute its 3D workspace. The results cannot be directly applied to touchscreen interaction, because screen surface constrains thumb motion. Li and Tang [18] tracked the coordination of thumb joints during opposition of the thumb and the index finger . Their results imply a parabolic form of motion of the thumb when opposed to the palm.

Human–Computer Interaction

Previous work can be categorized by research interest: 1) informing the placement of interface elements, 2) evaluating the effects of interface element's position on grip and performance, and 3) adapting interfaces to the grip.

Firstly, the grip affects the performance of thumb input on the front-facing surface. Oulasvirta et al. [24] compared the performance of six distinct grips in a tapping task, to find the most efficient one. The grips were distinguished by the orientation and by where the edge and corner of the tablet device contacted the hand. Odell and Chandrasekaran [22] measured the thumb's reach on a tablet. They controlled one dimension of the grip in relation to the device: the position of the hand along the tablet's edge. Users performed a reaching task with two grip positions, palm on the side or on the corner of the device. The results of these studies cannot be directly applied to our case, because the grips studied address only a subset of the possible cases.

Secondly, the positions of interface elements have been found to affect grip and performance. Parhi et al. [25] studied the effect of target size in one-handed touch input, and Park and Han [26] investigated the effect of interface-element position and size on performance. Both studies suggest that performance of thumb input improves closer to the center of the screen. Trudeau et al. [28] investigated a tapping task with a 12-key grid, showing that location significantly affects the user's grip in terms of joint positions in relation to the mobile device. That is, users change their grip to reach the target. They further suggested that interface elements should be presented near the thumb's resting position instead of close to the limits of the functional area. The model presented here contributes to this line of work with its suggestion as to the area a thumb can reach without a grip change. Our model is not aimed at predicting the performance gradient within the area. However, the conclusion of Trudeau et al. can be combined with our model for a heuristic: UI elements should not be placed close to the predicted extrema of the thumb's reach.

Finally, recent work has looked at adapting interfaces by means of on-device sensors that can predict the user's grip. Goel et al.'s GripSense [10] distinguishes between index-finger and thumb input and between the left and right thumb. Input fingers can also be distinguished via tracking of the touches on the screen [1, 9, 31]. Kim et al. [16] distinguish among eight task-specific grip classes, such as "Call" or "SMS single-handed". Taylor and Bowe [27] use a capacitive sensor grid and accelerometer to characterize five grips on a hand-held object. Cheng et al.'s iGrasp [4] predicts the grasp position on the two sides of the device. It can sense the position with 1 cm accuracy and adapts the keyboard type and position on a tablet touchscreen. To our knowledge, these techniques do not predict the functional area of the thumb and are limited to locally specified grip classes or to a single dimension defining a grip. However, they do demonstrate the advantages of grip-based layout adaptation. Our aim is to cover all grips wherein the other fingers hold the device from the back while the thumb acts upon the screen.

BACKGROUND: ANATOMICAL CONSTRAINTS TO THUMB MOTION

The model is aimed at predicting the thumb's functional area for any grip wherein the other fingers are at the back of the device. To this end, we make a simplifying assumption: The position of an extended index finger at the back of the device constrains the position of the parabolic curve that describes

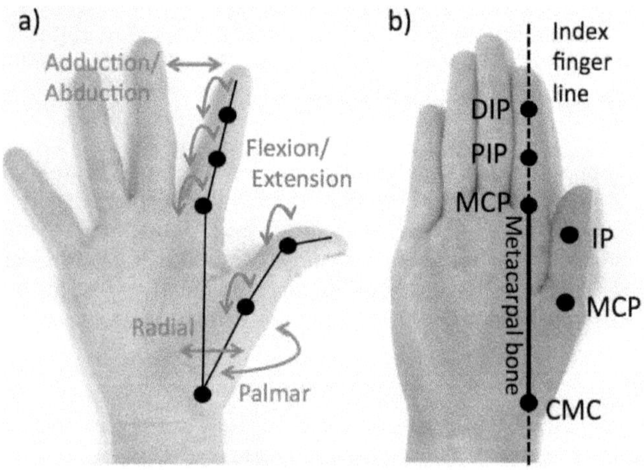

Figure 2. a) Terminology used in the model for joint motions: "adduction" and "abduction" (in red) and "flexion" and "extension" (in green); b) joint names and the "index finger line": a line that connects the adducted index finger and the metacarpal bone.

the extrema of the thumb's motion on the front surface. The logic is as follows: i) the distance of the index finger's tip from the edge of the device limits the maximal distance of the thumb tip from that edge and ii) the extrema of the motion of the thumb, when contacting a surface, lie on a parabolic curve. In other words, if one "pushes" the index finger (beneath the device) *further from* the edge, the thumb's tip moves *toward* that edge. Therefore, if we know the position of the tip of the index finger on the back of the device, we can predict the thumb's functional area on the screen side.

The Kinematic Chain, Linking Thumb and Index Finger

We work from the fact that the tip of the index finger is linked in a predictable manner to the base of the thumb and the tip of the thumb. The joints and joint articulations of this chain are introduced in Figure 2.

Starting at the index finger, the chain consists of the following joints and ranges of motions (see Figure 2):

1. The index finger's distal interphalangeal (DIP), proximal interphalangeal (PIP), and metacarpophalangeal (MCP) joints. The DIP and PIP joints allow extension and flexion of 65° and 110°, respectively. The MCP joint allows 85° flexion and active hyperextension of approx. 30°–40°. In addition, the MCP joint can abduct up to 30° from the midline of the hand. However, abduction becomes difficult or impossible when the MCP joint is flexed. [14]
2. The index finger's MCP and the thumb's carpometacarpal (CMC) joints are connected by a metacarpal bone in the palm.
3. The thumb's flexion/extension in rotatory planes are enabled by the CMC joint. The thumb's CMC is a saddle joint, and its palmar abduction ranges to about 45° and radial abduction to 60°. [14]
4. The thumb's MCP joint flexes to approximately 55° and hyperextends to 10°. The thumb's interphalangeal (IP) joint flexes to 70°–80° and hyperextends to 15°–20°. [14, 20]

Parabolic Motion Trajectory on a Surface

Because of the link described above, when the hand is *gripping* the mobile device, the position of the extended index-finger tip on the back determines the extrema of the thumb-tip position on the screen. The assumption that the thumb is fully extended allows us to model a grip via a single parameter: the distance of the index finger's tip from the edge of the device. What we still need to know is the thumb's workspace.

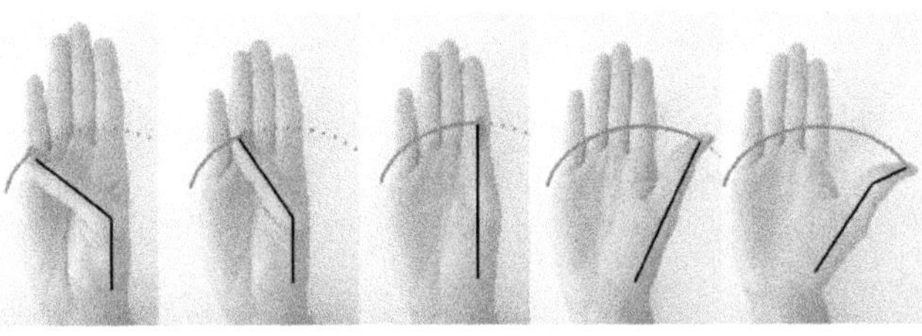

Figure 3. The ulnar–radial (in the figure, left–right) motion of an extended thumb on a surface defines the extrema of the functional area, here illustrated with a parabola.

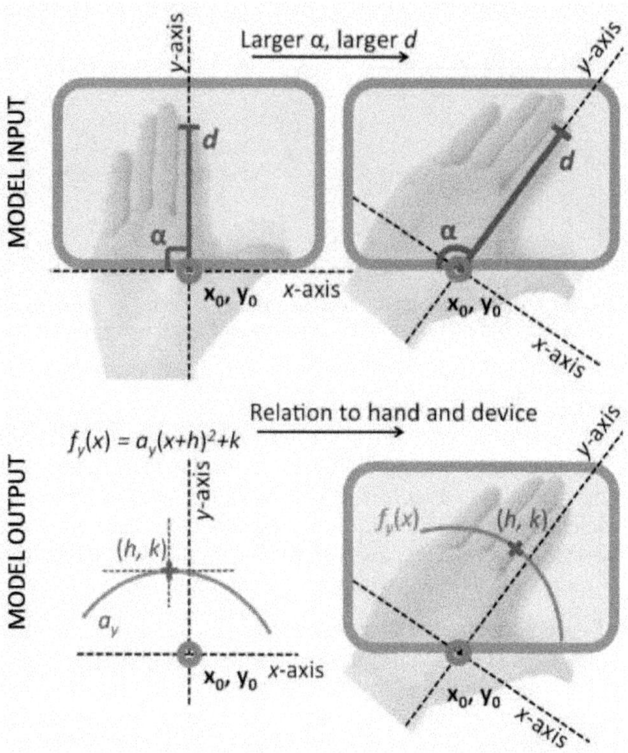

Figure 4. The model's coordinate system: the y-axis is defined by the index finger, and the red circle points to the origin defined by the y-axis crossing the device's edge. α is the rotation. The model input is d, the distance of the index finger's tip from the origin. The output is the quadratic model $f_y(x)$ and its coefficients.

Although the thumb's unconstrained 3D motion covers an irregular volume [17], the maximum of its reach on a surface appears parabolic. This knowledge has been used in consideration of the opposition of the thumb against the other fingers [18].

Figure 3 illustrates the rough form of the thumb tip's motion from the ulnar (Figure 3, left) to radial (Figure 3, right) side when the thumb opposes the other fingers. In summary, the assumption that a surface limits the motion allows us to model the motion in two dimensions. We later confirm the parabolic shape with empirical data.

OVERVIEW OF THE MODEL

In this section, we introduce the input parameters and then present the model and its coefficients.

Throughout, we assume a coordinate system that is *hand-centric*; that is, the index finger line is the *y*-axis in the model (see Figure 4). The model assumes an extended, adducted ("straight") index finger. The *origin* (x_0, y_0) is at the intersection of the *y*-axis and the edge of the device (see Figure 4). The *x*-axis is orthogonal to the *y*-axis at (x_0, y_0).

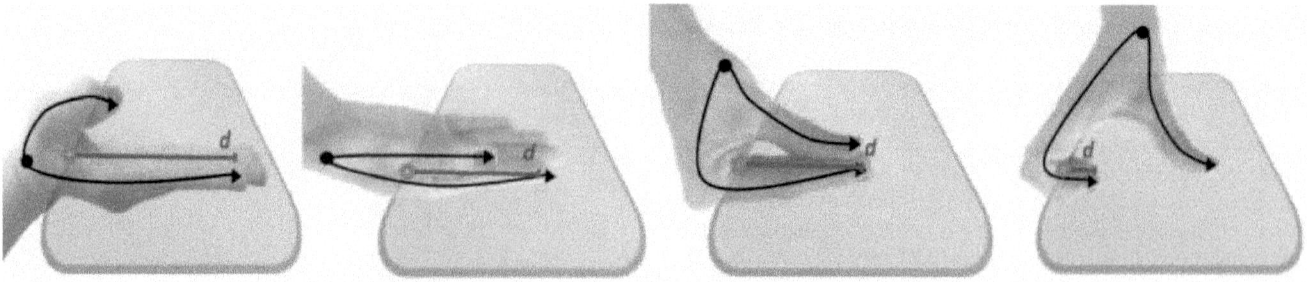

Figure 5. Illustration of effects of index-finger distance d: "Pushing" the thumb further along the surface simultaneously "pulls" the index finger from the back. d is the distance of the index finger from the edge closest to the thumb.

Index-Finger Distance d

In the model, *index-finger distance*, denoted as d, is the distance between the index finger's tip on the back surface and the origin (see Figure 5). d is assumed to affect the coefficients of the quadratic model because the index-finger tip physically connects to the thumb CMC joint and thereby strongly affects the pivot point for the thumb tip's motion.

Figure 5 shows that decreasing index-finger distance d on the back (from left to right) transforms the grip, giving the thumb CMC joint (indicated by the black dot) more space to move. When the touchscreen is held firmly in the palm and the four other fingers support the device over their full length, this "power grip" restricts CMC joint motion and only the MCP and IP joints of the thumb can move (see the first and second panes of the figure). In contrast, we can see (in the third and fourth panes) that when the device is balanced on the same digits in a precision grip, the CMC joint and the whole thumb from there on can move more freely.

Hand Size s

The user-specific dimensions of the index finger and the thumb necessarily affect the position and size of the thumb's functional area. However, it is not known which of the many measurements of the hand's anatomy is the best predictor. For example, one candidate might be finger span – the distance between an extended index-finger tip and thumb tip against a surface. We later test eight common hand measurements and apply the best scaling factor in the model.

Hand Orientation α

When the device is in the hand, α is the angle between the horizontal edge of the device and the hand's axis of orientation (the y-axis). Figure 4 shows an example wherein $\alpha \geq 90°$.

The Quadratic Model

We describe the parabola of the thumb's motion on the touchscreen as a quadratic function, $f_y(x)$. We use the *vertex form* instead of the *standard form*[1]:

$$f_y(x) = a_y(x + h)^2 + k \quad (1)$$

[1]The standard form of a quadratic function is $f(x) = ax^2 + bx + c$.

The effects of the coefficients a_y, h, and k are illustrated in Figure 6 and describe the following features of the parabola:

- a_y: Curvature, or the speed of decrease from the vertex (function's maximum). Our model opens downward (toward the thumb's base), so $a \leq 0$. A larger a (closer to 0) indicates slower decrease, and a smaller a indicates faster decrease (a tighter curve).
- h: The x-coordinate of the curve's maximum.
- k: The y-coordinate of the maximum.

The coefficient a_y expresses curvature, and coefficients h and k refer to the position of the vertex in x and y coordinates, respectively. Figure 4 illustrates the coefficients of the quadratic model in relation to the axes, the hand, and the device.

The coefficients a_y, h, and k in Equation 1 are assumed to depend on d. The dependencies are analyzed later with the collected data. For the time being, these are referred to as unknown functions $f_{a_y}(d)$, $f_h(d)$, and $f_k(d)$.

$$f_y(x) = f_{a_y}(d)(x + f_h(d))^2 + f_k(d) \quad (2)$$

DATA COLLECTION

Thumb-motion data were collected via a touchscreen, enabling us to do the following:

1. Validate the quadratic form (Equation 1) by analyzing its fitness to the data
2. Find a normalization parameter for hand size s from correlations of eight hand measurements and the maximum values in the motion data (coefficient k)
3. Model the coefficients describing the curvature ($f_{a_y}(d)$) and the maxima ($f_h(d)$ and $f_k(d)$) of the quadratic model (Equation 2) against index-finger distance d

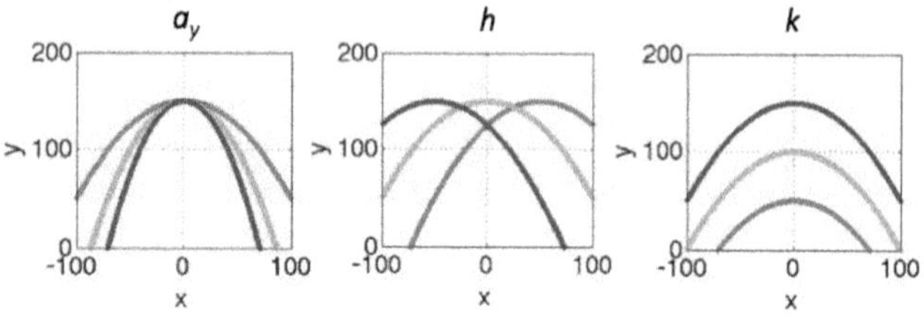

Figure 6. Illustrations of quadratic function coefficients.

In the study, 20 participants were asked to extend the thumb to its extrema on a touchscreen and perform a continuous movement that marks the limits of functional areas. We controlled the distance of the index finger d at the back of the device in 11 increments, while the touchscreen tracked the trajectory of the thumb in the front. The task was performed with the right hand, and the orientation of the index finger α was kept constant (at a right angle).

Participants

Data were collected from 20 subjects, eight of them female and 12 male, with a mean age of 29.4 years. The span between the index finger and the thumb ranged from 161.0 mm to 220.0 mm, with a mean of 189.7 mm and SD of 14.4 mm. Mean hand length varied between 147.0 mm and 200.0 mm, with a mean of 181.2 mm and SD of 12.0 mm. The data also include samples from the 5th and 95th percentiles of the anthropometric data reported in previous work [7]. Also, the mean of male and female samples fit within the standard deviation range of the anthropometric mean from the earlier work. Therefore, the sample can be considered representative.

The participants received a movie ticket as compensation for their time.

Apparatus

An iPad Mini was used to track the thumb touches on the screen (on the left in Figure 7). The iPad Mini has a wide enough screen for tracking of the thumb's full motion when the index finger (y-axis) is placed in the middle of the device's back. This device is also lightweight and has a thin profile that does not obstruct movement. The screen width is 120 mm (768 pixels) and height 160 mm (1024 pixels). The total width of the device is 134.7 mm, total height 200 mm, and thickness 7.2 mm.

An Interlink Electronics round force-sensing resistor (FSR) of 0.2-inch diameter was placed every 15 mm along the back of the device (see Figure 7, right). The first block, 0–15 mm, placed the center of the sensor 7.5 mm from the edge. The FSRs were powered by an Arduino Uno, rev. 3. Analog resistance was also measured on the Arduino analog input pins and computer-logged via the Arduino serial port. The analog force values were scaled to 0–1023. A > 0 force was required to indicate the index finger as touching the correct position, and 10 $k\Omega$ resistance was employed to ground the values.

Experiment Design

The experiment followed a within-subjects design wherein the value of index-finger tip distance d was adjusted to vary from small (d_1 = 7.5 mm) to maximum (d_{11} = 157.5 mm). d was increased in 15 mm increments, from the nearest edge to the greatest distance d with which the thumb tip could still reach the screen. The order of approach (from nearest to farthest end) was counter-balanced across subjects by rotation.

Task and Procedure

The participants were asked to position the tip of the index finger on the sensor with a given number (Figure 7, right). The index finger was kept straight on the sensor line (orthogonal to the device's edge) so that the finger also touched a sensor on the edge. The moderator monitored sensor values during the reach action, to ensure that the index finger was held in the correct d position, and the task was repeated if the finger slipped.

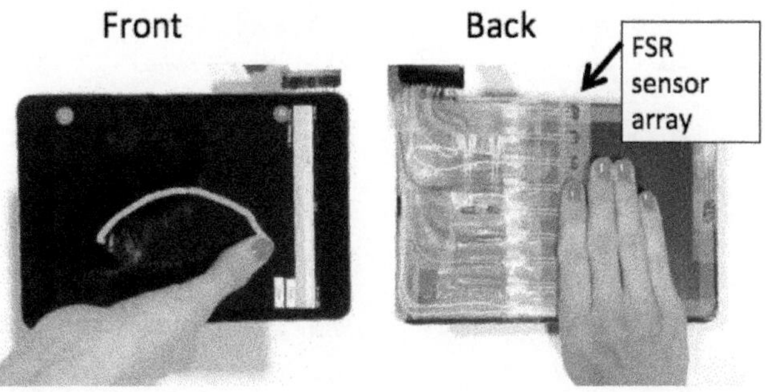

Figure 7. Data collection: Participants were requested to extend their thumb motion on the front surface to their extreme reach (left). The position of the index finger (d) was controlled by fingertip placement on a numbered sensor on the back side (right).

The task was to extend the thumb's reach as far as possible with one continuous movement toward the edges of the device while keeping the tip of the index finger in the d position (Figure 7, right). Participants were asked to hold all of their other fingers together (adducted, as in Figure 2, right). For measurement of extreme reach without device mass affecting performance, the participants were allowed to support the device with the left hand. Also, subjects were allowed to hold the device in any position, globally, by tilting or rotating it. The trajectory of the thumb motion was shown on the screen during the task (in Figure 7, represented by the blue line on the left).

The tasks were performed with the screen held horizontally to record as wide a motion as possible. However, with larger hands, some tasks were performed vertically if that was needed – i.e., when the reach at d was observed to extend beyond the opposite edge, the screen was shifted to vertical orientation to allow for and track the extended reach.

Participants were allowed four practice rounds for holding the index finger still and seeing the touch trajectory on the screen. They were asked to start the thumb reach from the left (ulnar) side and finish on the right (radial) always, only performing a single, continuous movement. One such movement was considered a task. The speed of the movement was not important: participants were told that determining maximum reach was the primary goal. After the practice rounds, hand measurements commenced. The experiment consisted of as many as 11 tasks, depending on the greatest distance the participant could reach on the screen. The experiment took approximately 20 minutes.

PARAMETER ESTIMATION

In this section, we validate the assumption that the shape of the thumb's extreme reach on a surface is described by a quadratic equation (Equation 1). Secondly, we identify a hand-size measurement for the normalization parameter (s). Thirdly, we model the relationship of d to the functions $f_{a_y}(d)$, $f_h(d)$, and $f_k(d)$ of Equation 2.

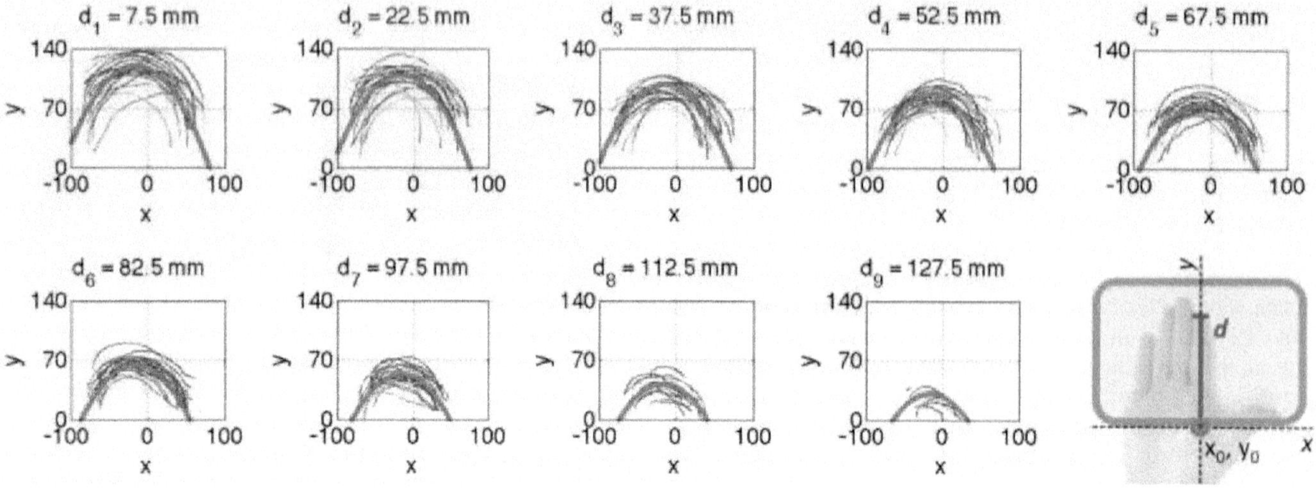

Figure 8. Observed vs. predicted functional areas. Trajectories in blue show original motion data from the 20 participants after normalization. The model's prediction is shown in red. The parameter d is illustrated on the right.

The dataset consists of, in all, 160 motion trajectories. All 20 participants reached seven distances (up to d_7, or 97.5 mm), 14 reached d_8 (112.5 mm), and six reached d_9 (127.5 mm). None reached the 10th or 11th d location. Data points with the same x-value but a y-value lower than another point were filtered. This procedure removed accidental touches by other fingers or other parts of the thumb or palm from the data.

The Quadratic Form of the Functional Area

We used non-linear regression and a least-squares approach to find the parameters a_y, k, and h of Equation 1 for every trajectory individually. This tests whether there exists a quadratic function that describes the shape of the trajectory. We later return to modeling every trajectory with a single model.

The average fitness of these is $R^2 = 0.958$ with a minimum of $R^2 = 0.822$ and maximum of $R^2 = 0.998$, suggesting that the limit of the thumb's functional area is parabolic.

Normalization with Finger Span (s)

To discover a predictive normalization parameter s for hand size, we tested the correlations between the maximum of the thumb trajectory (k) and eight hand measurements: 1) the distance of the index finger's tip from the knuckle (MCP joint) and 2) from the base of the thumb, 3) the distance from thumb tip to knuckle (MCP joint) and 4) to the base of the index finger, 5) hand span between abducted thumb tip and little finger's tip, 6) finger span between extended thumb tip and index finger tip (against a table surface), 7) angle between the abducted index finger and thumb, and 8) the hand length (from wrist to tip of the middle finger).

Significant correlation was found for no other hand measurement than finger span. The correlation with finger span is not surprising, since it is equivalent to the maximum reach from the tip of the index finger to the tip of the thumb in one plane. The finger span showed a significant correlation ($r = 0.687, p_{mean} = 0.029$) for all but the greatest (9th) distance. However, only six of the 20 participants reached that distance, so there are few data. For the first eight distances, the correlation was strong ($r = 0.701, p_{mean} = 0.004$).

We will use finger span s as a normalization factor for k, because it shows strong correlation and is easy to measure for input to the final model.

Functions $f_{a_y}(d)$, $f_h(d)$, and $f_k(d)$

From an anatomical point of view, the quadratic function's coefficients for curvature ($f_{a_y}(d)$) and maximum ($f_h(d)$ and $f_k(d)$) depend on the d value as discussed above (e.g., Figure 5). To determine this relationship more precisely, we measured the correlation of d with a_y, h, and k.

However, we found that the curvature parameter a_y ($r = 0.064, p = 0.642$) and the x-coordinate of the maximum h ($r = 0.195, p = 0.489$) do not correlate with d. The mean value of curvature was $a_{y\ mean} = -0.013$, with an SD of 0.007. The mean of the vertex's x-coordinate was $h_{mean} = -15.996$, with $SD = 11.612$, suggesting that the maximum point of the functional area was located, on average, at -16.00 mm from the y-axis.

This observation simplifies the model, because we use the mean values thus obtained as constants for a_y and h. The coefficient k was correlated significantly with distance d ($r = 0.996, p = 0.000$), and the relationship needs to be modeled in the function $f_k(d)$.

Coefficient Function $f_k(d)$

The coefficient k is the maximum value of the quadratic function. As presented above, k correlates strongly with index-finger distance d, and the finger span s correlates strongly with k.

Here we model the function $f_k(d)$ and test its fitness. Because the finger span equals the maximum reach between the thumb tip and the index finger's tip on a surface, subtracting s from d should indicate "ideal" maximum reach k: $f_k(d)_{ideal} = (s - d)$. By "ideal," we mean that no device is gripped such as would restrict the motions. However, in a touchscreen-input task, the index finger is on a surface opposite the surface where the thumb is, and the position of the CMC joint (the pivot) varies in three dimensions. Because the index-finger–thumb chain must travel around the edge of the screen (see Figure 5), the real k must be equal to or less than the ideal k (which is on a single surface).

$$f_k(d)_{ideal} = (s - d) \geq f_k(d)_{real} \tag{3}$$

Ideal ks were calculated for all of the data individually, in accordance with the participant's finger span. These values were then utilized in fitting of a linear function ($f_k(d)_{real} = a_k d + b_k$) to the difference between the ideal k and performed maximum value k:

$$\begin{aligned} f_k(d) &= (s - d) - (a_k d + b_k) \\ &= s - d(1 + a_k) - b_k \end{aligned} \tag{4}$$

The coefficient values for the linear fit are $a_k = -0.257$ and $b_k = 64.655$, with a mean $R^2 = 0.931$. Now the model $f_k(d)$ can be used for predicting the maximum value k of the thumb's functional area for any d and s.

MODEL FITNESS AND VALIDATION

In this section, we present the final model, test its fitness, and estimate its prediction error with cross-validation.

Adding the model of the maximum ($f_k(d)$ from Equation) 4 to the quadratic model in Equation 2 gives us the final model for the functional area of the thumb:

$$\begin{aligned} f_y(x) &= a_y(x + h)^2 + f_k(d) \\ &= a_y(x + h)^2 + s - d(1 + a_k) - b_k \end{aligned} \tag{5}$$

The goodness of fit of the final model was obtained by comparing the predicted curves with the trajectories from the data. Both the trajectory data and the predicted curves were averaged over the participants in the nine distance (d) conditions. Averaging the model means simply utilizing the average finger span (s = 189.7 mm). The error estimate for the individual-level predictions is given with the cross-validation.

The model predictions (with a mean of s) for different distances (d_1 to d_9) are illustrated in red in Figure 8. The fitness of the model with the average reaches for the nine distances is R^2 = [0.936 0.981 0.980 0.949 0.968 0.991 0.956 0.867 0.909], with a mean R^2 of 0.949.

Cross-validation and Error Estimation

Leave-one-out cross-validation was used to estimate prediction error for new data. Cross-validation is a standard procedure in machine learning to avoid overfitting and to assess generalizability to new instances.

The model (Equation 5) was trained on n–1 (i.e., 19) observations from the original sample of 160 trajectories and tested against the remaining, unseen sample. This was repeated such that each observation in the sample was used exactly once in the test data.

The estimated R-squared values for the model for the nine distances (from d_1 to d_9) are R^2 = [0.669 0.703 0.680 0.756 0.730 0.750 0.678 0.550 0.602], with a mean $R^2 = 0.6799$. The root mean squared error describing the estimated error of the model at the actual distance in millimeters (from first to ninth) are RMSE = [20.977 21.970 20.737 16.959 16.352 13.499 11.545 11.640 10.538], with a mean RMSE of 16.024.

A closer examination of the RMSE suggests that the estimated error is approximately equal to the width of a finger's tip [8]. Such error can result from, for example, the touchscreen's sensing properties or user strategies in touching the display with a different part of the thumb tip [12], and it can be considered negligible.

APPLICATION EXAMPLES

In this section, we demonstrate two example applications: 1) predicting the functional area of the thumb and 2) evaluating grip coverage. In the examples, we use the coefficients obtained above for Equation 5: $a_y = -0.013$, $h = -15.996$, $a_k = -0.257$, and $b_k = 64.655$.

Case 1: Functional Area Inferred from Grips

In the first case, we consider the task of predicting the functional area when given assumptions about the users. This emulates the case wherein the designer knows the average hand size of the user and uses the model to estimate the functional area of a grip for a particular device.

The protocol for this case is described in Table 1. Following this protocol, we provide two examples: a female user group with an oblique, one-handed grip on a smartphone and a user group of Oulasvirta et al. [24] with bimanual grip on a small tablet.

Female Users of a Smartphone

We consider a particular smartphone, the Nokia Lumia 900, which is 68.5 mm wide and 127.8 mm high. In line with Table 1, the first step is to determine the finger span. A female user has a finger span of s = 184.25 mm in this example[2]. Then we determine the grip. The grip in this example has the fingers extended on the opposing edge from the thumb, as if the user were reading the screen and firmly holding the device with the palm and fingers bent around the sides (on the left in Step 2). However, because we will need the parameters for the extended fingers, we estimate d with the extended non-grasping index finger posture (on the right in Step 2). Step 3 then establishes the position of the hand. The origin (x_0, y_0), where the y-axis crosses the edge, is on the long side of the device and, thus, $(width, height) = (127.8, 68.5)$. This point is 50 mm from the bottom corner, so the x-axis is limited by the edges of the device to [-50 77.8] (Step 3). In Step 4, the model is oriented according to the angle α between the index finger line and the edge of the device. In this example, $\alpha = 110°$. The distance of the index finger's tip from the opposing edge is estimated from a grip wherein the index finger would be straight and extended (as described for Step 2, right) and along the y-axis (Step 5). Here we use d = 80 mm. Finally, the model parameters are inserted in Equation 5, the model axis oriented according to α, and the results limited on the basis of the device dimensions $(width, height)$.

[2]The mean finger span of female participants in the study.

Table 1. Protocol for estimating functional areas for a design case

Step	Task	Example
1	Obtain or estimate the finger span of the target user group by measurement or by consulting anatomical tables [7, 8].	
2	Obtain information about the grip, via estimation, direct measurement, or consulting of statistics [15].	
3	Obtain the origin (x_0, y_0) of the grip by the index finger line (y-axis). Also, set x-axis orthogonal to y-axis at the origin.	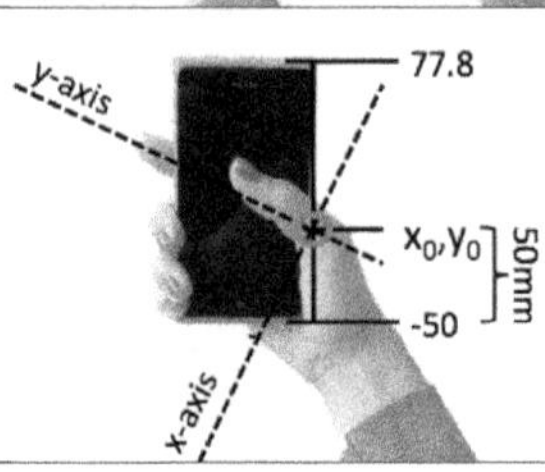
4	If the hand is rotated, obtain or estimate α.	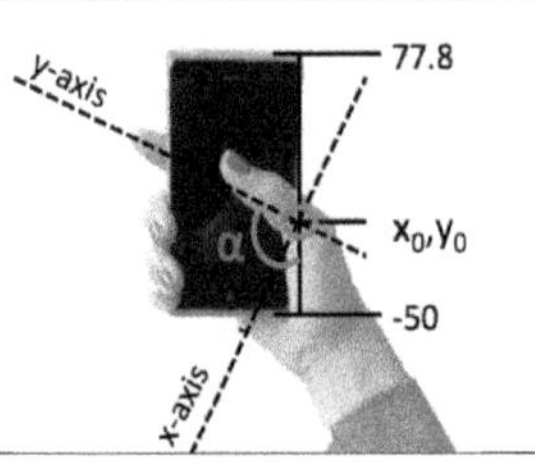
5	Measure or estimate d for the grip.	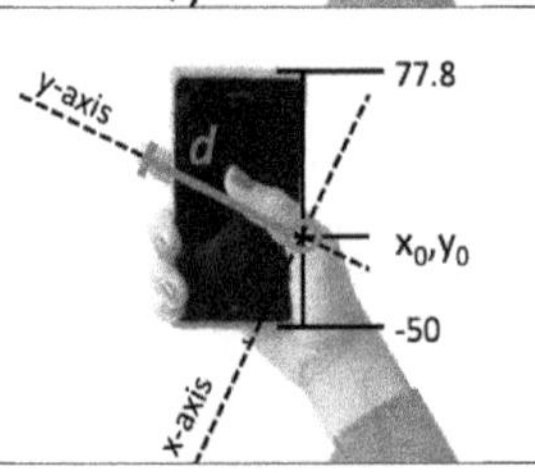
6	Insert parameters in Equation 5, rotate (blue line illustrates $\alpha = 90°$ and red line $\alpha = 110°$), and plot the model output appropriately for the device.	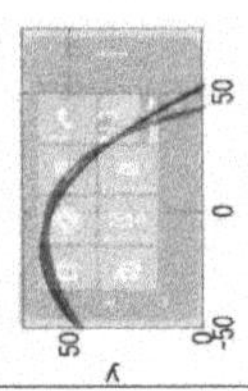

The figure accompanying Step 6 in Table 1 illustrates the outcome for this example in red (the model with $\alpha = 90°$ is shown in blue). We observe that, for example, the call button cannot be reached with this user's finger span without a change in grip.

Users of a Tablet Device

We obtained the hand-size data from Oulasvirta et al. [24] for comparison of the model-based predictions with their findings. The mean hand size in Oulasvirta et al.'s data is s = 188 mm. Grip 1, which performed best in their grip study, is illustrated in their figures 2 and 3 [24]. Not all grip parameters needed for the model are reported upon, but Grip 1

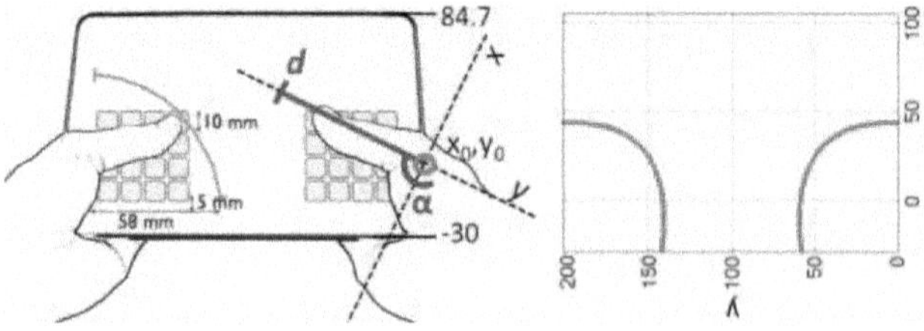

Figure 9. Left: Two-handed grip from Oulasvirta et al.'s work [24] analyzed with the model parameters. Right: The model's prediction of the functional area.

seems to be oriented at roughly 45° relative to the edge of the device, so we use $\alpha = 135°$. Moreover, we estimate that the origin is 30 mm from the bottom corner and set d to 80 mm. The model input and output are illustrated in Figure 9.

Oulasvirta et al. [24] report that the width of the active region with this grip is 57.6 mm. Our model predicts this well: the function (Figure 9, left) crosses the bottom edge of the device at 57.9 mm.

Case 2: Grip Coverage Inferred for a Layout

The model can also be applied to the evaluation of interfaces. Here we give an example of *grip coverage*: the permissible grips assumed by positions of interface elements. Utilizing the model of the thumb's functional area, we parameterize the grip by the index finger's position on the back of the device. The larger the covered area, the better the layout supports interaction and allows changing one's grip. The area could be weighted on the basis of a known frequency distribution for grips, but for the purposes of this example we treat all grips equally.

Grip coverage refers to the combination of the areas that the function of the index-finger distance d covers on the back surface. The function of d in x is $f_d(x)$ (now the interface-element position y is fixed), and we obtain it from Equation 5:

$$y = a_y(x+h)^2 + s - f_d(x)(1+a_k) - b_k$$
$$f_d(x) = \frac{a_y(x+h)^2 + s - b_k - y}{(1+a_k)} \quad (6)$$

The area is now calculated simply as a combination of the areas under the functions of d evaluated from the four sides, in line with the procedure presented in Table 2.

The Call Button of a Smartphone

For the next example, we determine the grip coverage for the call button in the Nokia Lumia 900 default start menu. We follow the protocol in Table 2. The first step is to choose a finger span for the model. In this example, we use s = 170 mm. In this model of device, the button chosen for evaluation (at the center when the device is held vertically) is (x_{pos}, y_{pos}) = (19.5 mm, 89.0 mm) (Step 2). In Step 3 (again, see Table 2), we start from the side ("bottom") from which the item position is determined and proceed through all four sides, inserting the limits and item position on the basis of the viewing side. Finally, the combination of the plotted areas indicates all possible index-finger positions on the back.

Table 2. Protocol for determining grips that can be used to interact with a given use-interface element

Step	Task	Example
1	Obtain or estimate the finger span of the target user group.	
2	Obtain the element position (x_{pos}, y_{pos}) and device dimensions ($width, height$) such that the x-axis is scaled from $x = 0$ to $x = width$ and y-axis from $y = 0$ to $y = height$. Calculate the areas from four sides in the following.	
3	From the "top" and "bottom" edges, calculate the area from 0 to $width$: firstly, set $x = width - x_{pos} - x$ and $d = y_{pos}$, and, secondly, set $x = x_{pos} - x$ and $d = height - y_{pos}$. From the "left" and "right" edges, calculate the area from 0 to $height$: firstly, set $x = y_{pos} - x$ and $d = x_{pos}$, and, secondly, set $x = height - y_{pos} - x$ and $d = width - x_{pos}$. Finally, calculate the combined area.	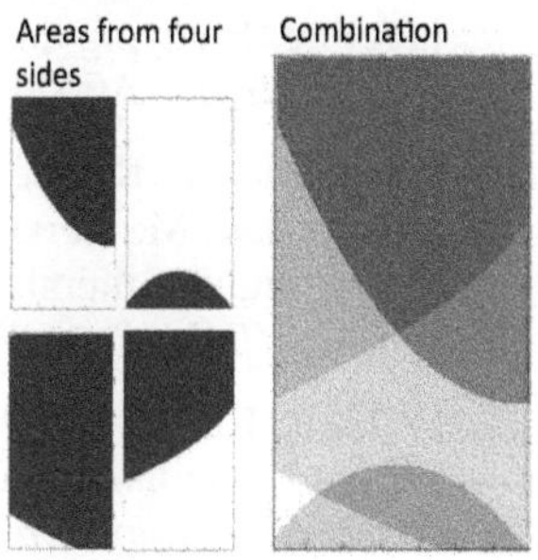

DISCUSSION

The functional area of the thumb in the interface region has been important for designers, who have previously taken heuristic approaches (see Figure 1). Some of these heuristics are special cases of our model, but various of them make implausible assumptions. The first heuristic on the left in Figure 1 corresponds to a special case in which the screen is smaller or hand size is greater than in our sample. On the other hand, in the second heuristic, the grip seems similar to that in our example. However, our data show that the thumb could not have reached the opposite upper corner. The third and fourth heuristic make contradictory suggestions as to what the thumb can reach. We hold that the functional area of the thumb is too complex to be captured by such heuristics.

We have proposed a novel mathematical model that predicts the functional area of the thumb on a touchscreen surface for given hand size, device dimensions, and grip. The model needs only one input parameter to describe the grip, the distance of the index finger from the edge (d), and another for the hand size, (s), and it returns a parabola that describes the limit of the functional area. The model can inform the design of input interfaces operated with the thumb.

The model can be used to address practical problems in interface design. Its application requires that the designer have some existing knowledge of, for example, statistics, or at least intuition about the probable dimensions of the device, grips, or interface layout. The model can then be used to 1) predict the functional area for a device and grip and 2) evaluate an interface layout for its grip coverage. Bimanual cases can be analyzed as well, if both hands are modeled separately.

We have shown that, no matter its simple form, the modeling approach can yield a high fit, with trajectories collected from 20 participants. We could predict the reachable area of a grip reported upon in a previous study [24]. Cross-validation suggested an error related to fingertip size [8]. The prediction accuracy achieved is sufficient for interfaces with medium-sized and large elements, but more work is needed to cover smaller elements, especially close to the limits of the functional area.

The model assumes that the fingers at the back are extended. Our casual observation is that this is often the case, and a power grip is needed for a firm hold, especially when the user is walking. We note also that a possible source of error exists in the adduction/abduction of the fingers at the back. However, when those fingers are kept together and the MCP joint of the index finger flexed, as is often seen in holding of a mobile device, there is virtually no adduction/abduction.

The model should also be improved to deal with devices with different form factors. At present, the model can take into account thickness: for a "chunky" device, the d parameter can be increased in line with the thickness of the device. For example, with an index-finger distance of 30 mm and device thickness of 60 mm, the input to the model can be approximated to d = 90 mm. However, the joint angles introduce complexity to this scaling, and user data must be collected to verify the approximation. While rounded corners of devices are not dealt with, corner grips can be estimated through rotation of the axes in the manner illustrated here.

Although the results support the potential of this modeling approach, more work is needed, to validate it further. We plan to collect a larger sample, with a broader distribution of device form factors, to adjust the model's constant coefficient values.

ACKNOWLEDGMENTS

A modeling tool will be released for practitioners on the project's Web site. This work was supported by the Helsinki Doctoral Programme in Computer Science - Advanced Computing and Intelligent Systems, Max Planck Center for Visual Computing and Communication and by the Cluster of Excellence on Multimodal Computing and Interaction at Saarland University.

REFERENCES

1. Azenkot, S., Wobbrock, J. O., Prasain, S., and Ladner, R. E. Input finger detection for nonvisual touch screen text entry in Perkinput. In *Proc. GI '12*, Canadian Information Processing Society (2012), 121–129.

2. Azenkot, S., and Zhai, S. Touch behavior with different postures on soft smartphone keyboards. In *Proc. MobileHCI '12*, ACM (2012), 251–260.

3. Bergstrom-Lehtovirta, J., Oulasvirta, A., and Brewster, S. The effects of walking speed on target acquisition on a touchscreen interface. In *Proc. MobileHCI '11*, ACM (2011), 143–146.

4. Cheng, L.-P., Liang, H.-S., Wu, C.-Y., and Chen, M. Y. iGrasp: Grasp-based adaptive keyboard for mobile devices. In *Proc. CHI '13*, ACM (2013), 3037–3046.

5. Clark, J. Designing for touch (section "Rule of thumb"). `http://www.netmagazine.com/features/designing-touch`.

6. Curtis, D. 3.5 inches. `http://dcurt.is/3-point-5-inches`.

7. Department of Defense, Human Factors Engineering Technical Advisory Group. Human engineering design data digest. `http://www.dtic.mil/cgi-bin/GetTRDoc?AD=ADA467401`.

8. Garrett, J. W. The adult human hand: Some anthropometric and biomechanical considerations. *Human Factors: The Journal of the Human Factors and Ergonomics Society 13*, 2 (1971), 117–131.

9. Goel, M., Jansen, A., Mandel, T., Patel, S. N., and Wobbrock, J. O. ContextType: Using hand posture information to improve mobile touch screen text entry. In *Proc. CHI '13*, ACM (2013), 2795–2798.

10. Goel, M., Wobbrock, J., and Patel, S. GripSense: Using built-in sensors to detect hand posture and pressure on commodity mobile phones. In *Proc. UIST '12*, ACM (2012), 545–554.

11. Guiard, Y. Asymmetric division of labor in human skilled bimanual action: The kinematic chain as a model. *Journal of Motor Behavior 19* (1987), 486–517.

12. Holz, C., and Baudisch, P. Understanding touch. In *Proc. CHI '11*, ACM (2011), 2501–2510.

13. Hoober, S. How do users really hold mobile devices? `http://www.uxmatters.com/mt/archives/2013/02/how-do-users-really-hold-mobile-devices.php`.

14. Jones, L. A., and Lederman, S. J. *Human Hand Function*. Oxford University Press, 2006.

15. Karlson, A., Bederson, B., and Contreras-Vidal, J. Understanding single-handed mobile device interaction. *Handbook of research on user interface design and evaluation for mobile technology* (2006), 86–101.

16. Kim, K.-E., Chang, W., Cho, S.-J., Shim, J., Lee, H., Park, J., Lee, Y., and Kim, S. Hand grip pattern recognition for mobile user interfaces. In *Proc. AAAI '06*, vol. 21 (2006), 1789–1794.

17. Kuo, L.-C., Chiu, H.-Y., Chang, C.-W., Hsu, H.-Y., and Sun, Y.-N. Functional workspace for precision manipulation between thumb and fingers in normal hands. *Journal of Electromyography and Kinesiology 19*, 5 (2009), 829–839.

18. Li, Z.-M., and Tang, J. Coordination of thumb joints during opposition. *Journal of Biomechanics 40*, 3 (2007), 502–510.

19. Napier, J. R. The prehensile movements of the human hand. *Journal of Bone and Joint Surgery 38*, 4 (1956), 902–913.

20. Neumann, D. *Kinesiology of the Musculoskeletal System: Foundations for Rehabilitation*. Mosby Elsevier, 2010.

21. Ng, A., Brewster, S. A., and Williamson, J. The impact of encumbrance on mobile interactions. In *Proc. INTERACT 2013*, Springer (2013), 92–109.

22. Odell, D., and Chandrasekaran, V. Enabling comfortable thumb interaction in tablet computers: A windows 8 case study. In *Proc. HFES '12*, vol. 56, SAGE Publications (2012), 1907–1911.

23. Oulasvirta, A., and Bergstrom-Lehtovirta, J. Ease of juggling: Studying the effects of manual multitasking. In *Proc. CHI '11*, ACM (2011), 3103–3112.

24. Oulasvirta, A., Reichel, A., Li, W., Zhang, Y., Bachynskyi, M., Vertanen, K., and Kristensson, P. O. Improving two-thumb text entry on touchscreen devices. In *Proc. CHI '13*, ACM (2013), 2765–2774.

25. Parhi, P., Karlson, A. K., and Bederson, B. B. Target size study for one-handed thumb use on small touchscreen devices. In *Proc. MobileHCI '06*, ACM (2006), 203–210.

26. Park, Y. S., and Han, S. H. Touch key design for one-handed thumb interaction with a mobile phone: Effects of touch key size and touch key location. *International Journal of Industrial Ergonomics 40*, 1 (2010), 68–76.

27. Taylor, B. T., and Bove, V. M. The bar of soap: A grasp recognition system implemented in a multi-functional handheld device. In *CHI '08 Extended Abstracts*, ACM (2008), 3459–3464.

28. Trudeau, M. B., Young, J. G., Jindrich, D. L., and Dennerlein, J. T. Thumb motor performance varies with thumb and wrist posture during single-handed mobile phone use. *Journal of Biomechanics 45* (2012), 2349–2354.

29. Wagner, J., Huot, S., and Mackay, W. BiTouch and BiPad: Designing bimanual interaction for hand-held tablets. In *Proc. CHI '12*, ACM (2012), 2317–2326.

30. Wroblewski, L. Responsive navigation: Optimizing for touch across devices. `http://www.lukew.com/ff/entry.asp?1649`.

31. Yin, Y., Ouyang, T. Y., Partridge, K., and Zhai, S. Making touchscreen keyboards adaptive to keys, hand postures, and individuals – a hierarchical spatial backoff model approach. In *Proc. CHI '13*, ACM (2013), 2775–2784.

Coordination of Tilt and Touch in One- and Two-Handed Use

Theophanis Tsandilas[1,2] fanis@lri.fr **Caroline Appert**[2,1] appert@lri.fr **Anastasia Bezerianos**[2,1] anab@lri.fr **David Bonnet**[2,1] bonnet@lri.fr

Inria[1] - Univ Paris-Sud & CNRS[2] (LRI)
F-91405 Orsay, France

ABSTRACT
Our goal is to enhance navigation in mobile interfaces with quick command gestures that do not make use of explicit mode-switching actions. TilTouch gestures extend the vocabulary of navigation interfaces by combining motion tilt with directional touch. We consider sixteen directional TilTouch gestures that rely on tilt and touch movements along the four main compass directions. An experiment explores their effectiveness for both one-handed and two-handed use. Results identify the best combinations of TilTouch gestures in terms of performance, motor coordination, and user preferences.

Author Keywords
Mobile devices; Tilt; Touch; Gestures; Touchscreen;

ACM Classification Keywords
H.5.2 [Information Interfaces and Presentation]: User Interfaces - Graphical user interfaces;

INTRODUCTION
Motion sensors such as accelerometers and gyroscopes offer a new space for the design of mobile interaction techniques that combine *touch* and *tilt*. Several previous approaches [1, 13] have studied motion-based gestures, but they depend on recognizers of rather exaggerated movements or explicit mode-switching techniques. We address this limitation by combing the two modalities, touch and tilt, as part of a single TilTouch gesture. TilTouch gestures do not interfere with simple touch and tilt actions. Thus, users can activate them within the flow of common navigation tasks without having to perform additional actions to switch between modes.

Our approach lies within the Sensor Synaesthesia design space [6], but we focus on directional drags rather than static touch. We empirically study the effectiveness of TilTouch gestures in terms of both user performance and preferences. We also investigate the extent to which users can control tilt and touch as integral input dimensions [7]. We study the use of the gestures for both one and two hands as each use is subject to different symmetries and requires the coordination of different limbs. We show that the same set of TilTouch gestures can be effective for both one- and two-handed use.

CHI 2014, April 26 - May 01 2014, Toronto, ON, Canada
Copyright 2014 ACM 978-1-4503-2473-1/14/04...$15.00.
http://dx.doi.org/10.1145/2556288.2557088

RELATED WORK
We can distinguish between two main forms of touch gestures for activating commands in mobile interfaces: free-form gestures, such as alphabetical ones [9], and directional marks inspired by marking menus [8]. According to Bragdon *et al.* [3], simple marks are more accurate than free-form gestures.

Tilt input has been used for navigation in sequential lists, two-dimensional spaces, and menus containing few items, typically three to four [10, 12]. Rahman *et al.* [11] have empirically studied the number of possible subdivisions along each main tilt direction around the wrist. They found that error rates are never below 5% on average, even for the smallest sets (four items) that they considered, and increases fast with the size of the set. Other projects considered more elaborated motion gestures like DoubleFlip [13] and JerkTilt gestures [1]. In the newest mobile devices, tilting automatically adjusts the view orientation of a device to portrait or landscape to fit its physical orientation [2, 5].

The Sensor Synaesthesia design space [6] combines tilt and touch to create richer interaction sequences. Specifically, it proposes tilt and touch interactions for discrete or continuous commands, however touch remains at a fixed screen location. The work also only reports on subjective feedback from an informal user evaluation. Thus, combined tilt and touch has never been studied before through a formal experiment.

COMBINING TOUCH WITH TILT
Our goal is to facilitate command invocation while users perform navigation tasks. By combining drags and tilts, we can enhance the number of available gestures but also avoid the use of explicit mode-switching. To that end, we explored how a TilTouch gesture should be defined such that it does not interfere with existing navigation gestures. We conducted a preliminary study to determine the angular range of unintentional tilts that occur during common drag and swipe actions. 10 participants interacted with three representative mobile interfaces: a large 2D view, a vertical list of 50 items, and a horizontally aligned view of five screens. We analyzed a total of 3935 events of navigation or directional-drag gestures and defined unintentional *relative tilt* angles to be in the range of $[-18, 18]$ degrees, where tilts are measured relatively to the initial orientation of the phone when the finger starts touching the screen. This range corresponds to less than 0.2% of false positives and does not hinder the activation of intentional TilTouch gestures. We also set the minimum drag distance for activating a gesture to 7 mm. When these criteria are met, we detect the dominant direction of the tilt ($tiltDir$) and the drag ($dragDir$) to recognize the TilTouch gesture $\langle tiltDir, dragDir\rangle$. The command associated with this combination is executed after lifting the finger.

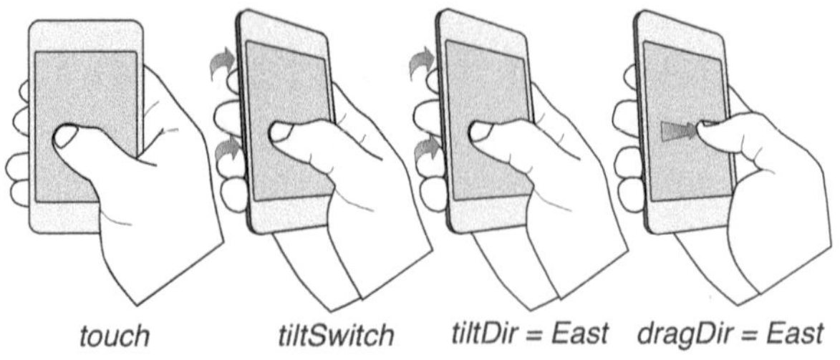

Figure 1. $\langle tiltDir, dragDir \rangle = \langle East, East \rangle$ **gesture performed with one hand. Here, the user starts with a tilt followed by a touch action.**

Our goal is to keep the shape of gestures as simple as possible while providing a reasonable number of accessible commands. Therefore, we only consider the simplest touch marks and tilt angles along the four cardinal directions: $North$, $South$, $East$, and $West$. Combining such simple gestures along the touch and tilt modality results in a total of 16 commands. Figure 1 illustrates an example where the user performs an $\langle East, East \rangle$ gesture.

TilTouch gestures are especially useful as quick triggers of commands, e.g., copy-paste, make a call, and add a bookmark on a map. The technique requires the sequential or parallel control of two input modalities. We envision that novice users will start discovering the gestures by controlling tilt and touch in sequence. However, we expect that with practice, expert users will be able to internalize a single action and use the two input channels in parallel, combining the two gestures into a single interaction chunk [4]. As other directional gestures, TilTouch gestures have drawbacks: drags are limited near screen edges, and screen visibility is reduced both by the finger and the tilt. Yet, our low threshold value of relative tilts ($\pm 18°$) minimizes this problem.

EXPERIMENT

We conducted a lab study where participants performed TilTouch gestures in conjunction with regular drags. Our goals were to find: (1) which TilTouch gestures are more effective; (2) whether the same gestures are appropriate for both single and two-handed use; and (3) whether users can control the two input modalities in parallel.

Participants and Apparatus

24 volunteers (7 women), 22 to 45 years old participated in the experiment. 23 were right-handed, one was mixed-handed. Participants interacted with a 4.3-inch 480×800 pixel Samsung Galaxy S2, running our software implemented in Java under Android 2.3.3.

Task and Conditions

The experimental task consisted of two sub-tasks:

Pre-task (Figure 2-(a-b)). First, the user drags a ring of 160-pixel diameter over another 40-pixel target ring. The direction of this sliding movement randomly varied circularly around the center of the screen. The pre-task represents a usual drag navigation task that interlaces with TilTouch gestures.

Main task (Figure 2-(c-d)). Then, the user completes the main task by performing a TilTouch gesture. As shown in Figure

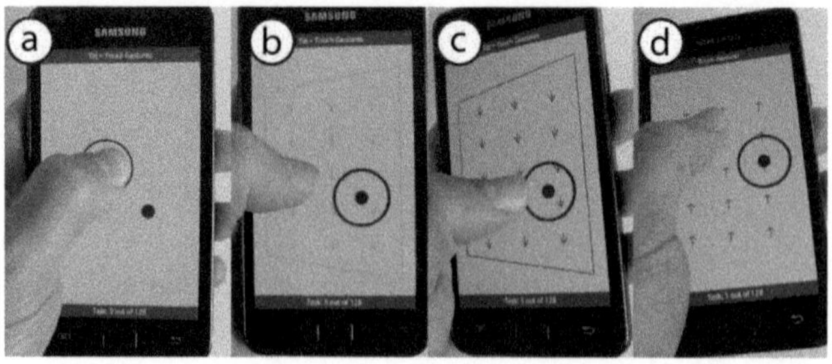

Figure 2. An experimental task for *directional-tilt* gestures. (a) Pre-task: The user starts sliding a ring over a circular target; (b) The pre-task has been completed; (c) Main task: The user tilts the device to the indicated direction while dragging the finger. (d) Main task for *free-tilt* gestures: visual instructions are only provided for the direction of the drag.

2, instructions about the target direction of the tilt and drag movements are constantly displayed on the screen. The drag direction is indicated with a flock of arrows while the tilt direction is shown with a trapezoid frame that represents the view of the device in perspective.

To assess the overhead due to selecting a given tilt direction, we tested two **types of gestures**:

Free Tilt. Participants were asked to perform a directional drag according to a suggested direction in conjunction with a tilt in *any* tilt direction. No tilt direction was indicated.

Directional Tilt. Participants were asked to perform both a directional drag and a directional tilt according to a suggested combination of TilTouch directions. We tested all the 16 possible settings of combined cardinal directions, e.g., tilting to the $North$ and dragging to the $West$.

We also tested the two **typical mobile uses**:

One hand. Participants completed the tasks with their right hand and used their thumb to touch the screen. The tilt and the drag movement were both performed by the same hand.

Two hands. Participants hold the device with their left hand but used the index finger of their right hand to touch the screen. The tilt movement was performed by the left hand while the drag movement was performed by the right hand.

Design, Procedure and Measures

We followed a mixed full-factorial design, with mobile use being a between-participants factor, and the remaining variables as within-participants factors. We analyzed 6144 tasks:

$$\begin{aligned} & 2 \text{ mobile uses} \times 12 \text{ participants} \\ \times\ & 2 \text{ types of gestures} \times 8 \text{ blocks} \\ \times\ & 4 \text{ drag directions} \times 4 \text{ tilt directions} \end{aligned}$$

In addition to these tasks, each participant completed 24 practice tasks for each type of gestures. The tasks were grouped into eight blocks of 16 tasks (4 drag directions $\times$ 4 tilt directions) presented in a random order. As no tilt direction is enforced for *free tilt* gestures, each participant performed four replications of each drag direction in each block.

Before the beginning of the session, participants filled out a pre-study questionnaire eliciting demographic information

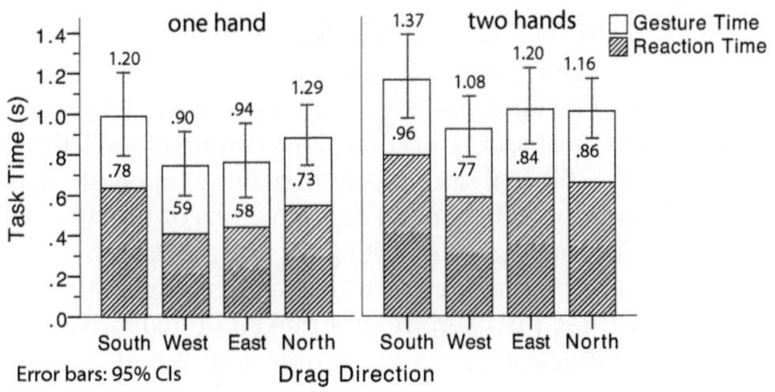

Figure 3. ***Free Tilt*: Effect of drag direction**

and their experience with smartphones and touch-enabled mobile devices. They were asked to interact in a standing position and always use their preferred hand. After the end of the session, participants answered a post-study questionnaire. They were asked to evaluate each of the 16 combinations of tilt and touch directions by using a 5-level Likert scale. The whole procedure lasted 30 to 40 minutes.

We measured the *Task Time* to complete the main task, which includes the *Reaction Time* to prepare a gesture and the *Gesture Time* to execute it. We considered two errors: accidental activations of TilTouch gestures during the first subtask (*PreTask Error*), and activations of the wrong direction, either tilt or drag (*Gesture Error*). In both cases, the user had to restart.

Results

For the analysis of the time measures, we conducted ANOVAs with mobile use treated as a between-participants factor, and type of gesture, block, drag direction and tilt direction treated as repeated measures. For the analysis of errors and user ratings, we used non-parametric tests.

Effect of Mobile Use and Type of Gesture. The difference for the overall *Gesture Time* was not significant between the two mobile uses ($p = .65$). However, taking a closer look reveals that participants had a higher *Reaction Time* ($F_{1,22} = 6.73$, $p = .017$) in a two-hand use. This indicates a higher amount of planning to coordinate control.

A comparison between *free-tilt* and *directional-tilt* gestures shows that constraining tilt direction has a great cost to user performance. This cost was significant for both *Reaction Time* ($F_{1,22} = 27.18$, $p < .001$) and *Gesture Time* ($F_{1,22} = 10.03$, $p = .004$). Similarly, *Gesture Error* was higher for *Directional Tilt* ($Z = -4.2$, $p < .001$), raising from 1.0% $[0.5\%, 1.6\%]$ to 8.4% $[6.6\%, 10.2\%]$[1]. A 71% of the latter errors were due to incorrect tilts. Interestingly, the error rate was lower for two-handed use ($Z = -2.03$, $p = .045$). Considering only directional tilts, it was 10.5% $[8.0\%, 13.1\%]$ for one hand and 6.3% $[3.7\%, 8.8\%]$ for two hands. *PreTask Error* was generally low, with a mean value of $.5\%$ $[.0\%, 1.1\%]$.

Effect of Drag and Tilt Direction. We first examine users' strategies for *Free Tilt*. For 80% of the tasks executed with one hand and 67% of the tasks executed with two hands, the direction of tilt and drag was the same. However, this strategy was not consistent among all the participants. One participant (one hand) almost always chose an $East$ tilt. A second (two hands) always tilted $South$, while a third (two hands) always tilted $North$. Three other participants (two hands) used a $North$ tilt for their $South$ drags.

[1]We report 95% confidence intervals (CIs) of the means in brackets.

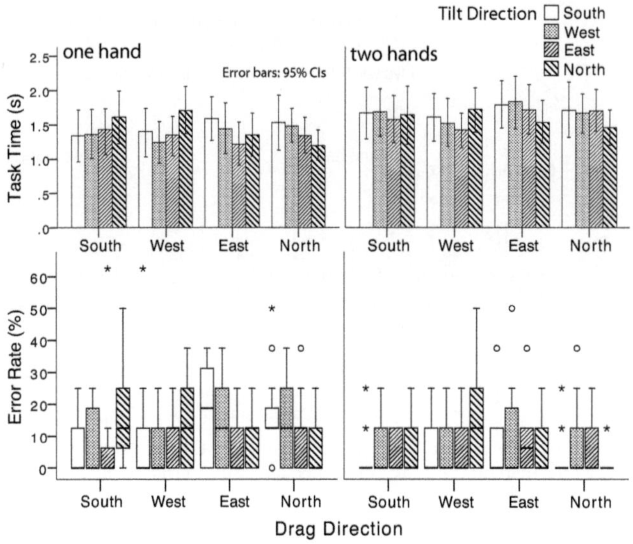

Figure 4. ***Directional Tilt*: *Task Time* and *Gesture Error* for the 16 TilTouch combinations. Circles and asterisks in the box plots represent mild and extreme outliers, respectively. Dark lines represent medians.**

For *Free Tilt*, the dragging direction had a significant effect on *Task Time* ($F_{3,66} = 6.18$, $p = .001$). As shown in Figure 3, the $West$ direction was the fastest and the $South$ direction was the worst. We found no significant interaction between dragging direction and conditions ($p = .74$). Differences were consistent for both one hand and two hands. Pairwise comparisons with Bonferroni's correction showed a significant difference between $West$ and $South$ ($p < .001$) and between $East$ and $South$ ($p = .021$). Differences were mostly due to reaction times. Our interpretation is that planning the tilt for the $South$ drag direction is possibly harder.

For *Directional Tilt*, we did not observe any effect of drag ($p = .65$) or tilt direction ($p = .18$) on *Task Time*. The effect of their interaction was significant though ($F_{4.5,99.1} = 2.95$, $p = .003$). Figure 4 shows the detailed results for the two mobile uses. By inspecting both task times and error rates, we see that certain tilt and drag combinations were particularly problematic: $\langle North, West\rangle$ for both conditions, and $\langle North, South\rangle$, $\langle South, East\rangle$, $\langle West, East\rangle$, $\langle South, North\rangle$ and $\langle West, North\rangle$ for one hand. In corroboration with observations on free-tilt gestures, combinations with same tilt and drag directions had the best performance. This was especially true for one-handed use. Overall, $North$ tilts were more compatible with $North$ and $East$ drags, while $South$ tilts were with $South$ and $West$ drags.

Subjective Ratings. The tilt direction had a significant effect on participants' rating ($\chi^2(3) = 15.61$, $p = .001$). Pairwise comparisons with adjusted p values showed that $East$ tilts received a significantly higher score than $West$

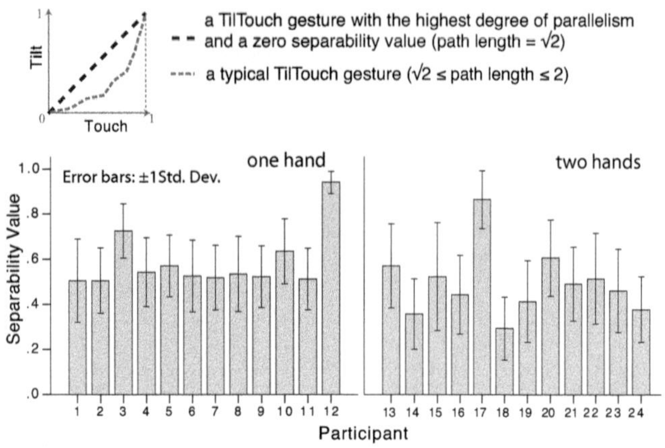

Figure 5. The normalized TilTouch space (top). Separability values for each participant (bottom). Presented only for *directional tilts*.

tilts ($p = .003$). $West$ tilts generally received low ratings for two hands as opposed to $East$ tilts, which were highly ranked. The drag direction did not have any significant effect on ratings ($\chi^2(3) = 4.26$, $p = .24$), but the effect of the combined tilt and drag direction was significant ($\chi^2(15) = 100.43$, $p < .001$). Participants gave high ratings to gestures with the same tilt and drag direction. Interestingly, participants using two hands rated $\langle East, West\rangle$ higher than $\langle West, West\rangle$. Other gestures received low scores for both conditions: $\langle North, West\rangle$, $\langle South, East\rangle$, $\langle South, West\rangle$, $\langle West, South\rangle$, and $\langle West, North\rangle$. Surprisingly, $\langle North, South\rangle$ was highly rated under one-hand use despite its poor performance. Overall, participants considered opposite tilt and drag directions easy to perform.

Degree of Parallelism. We analyzed the degree of parallelism of the tilt and touch input channels. To that end, we plotted the collected TilTouch gestures in the normalized tilt+touch space shown in Figure 5 (top). The path length of a TilTouch gesture exhibiting the highest degree of parallelism is $\sqrt{2}$ while a TilTouch gesture with no parallel control has a length of 2. By normalizing the path length of each TilTouch gesture, we obtain the *Separability* measure $\in [0, 1]$: the less parallel the control over the two input channels the higher the value of *Separability*.

Figure 5 shows its distribution across participants for *directional tilts*. Its mean value ranged from .29 (Participant 18) to .94 (Participant 12), who executed the tilt and the drag gesture always in sequence. We found a positive correlation between mean *Separability* and mean *GestureTime* (Pearson correlation $= .621$, $p = .001$). The mean value of *Separability* was .59 $[.49, 70]$ for one hand and .49 $[.40, 59]$ for two hands, but this difference was not statistically significant ($F_{1,18} = 2.20$, $p = .16$). We found a significant effect of both drag direction ($F_{3,54} = 3.36$, $p = .025$) and tilt direction ($F_{3,54} = 3.6$, $p = .023$) on *Separability*. Their interaction effect was also significant ($F_{4.6,82.3} = 4.73$, $p = .001$). Pairwise comparisons with Bonferroni's correction showed that $West$ drags resulted in significantly more parallel movements than *North drags* ($p < .05$). Finally, we observed low separability values for tilts and drags of the same direction for both conditions.

DISCUSSION AND CONCLUSIONS

We have studied combined touch and tilt gestures for one- and two-handed interaction with mobile phones. Our findings suggest that most users can control the two input modalities in parallel ($40 - 50\%$ of optimal parallelism) under both mobile uses. We observed that not all combinations of tilt+touch are effective. TilTouch gestures along the same direction result in lower error rates, are more intuitive, and are highly preferred by users. $East$ tilts were highly ranked. Finally, we found that $North$ tilts were more compatible with $North$ and $East$ drags, while $South$ tilts with $South$ and $West$ drags. These results are consistent between one- and two-handed use. This is an important finding suggesting that designers can use the same set of usable TilTouch gestures for both hand configurations. Future work needs to explore appropriate visual guides that assist in the discovery and effective use of such gestures.

Acknowledgments. This work was partly funded by ANR-11-JS02-004-01.

REFERENCES

1. Baglioni, M., Lecolinet, E., and Guiard, Y. Jerktilts: using accelerometers for eight-choice selection on mobile devices. *ICMI '11*, ACM (2011), 121–128.
2. Bartlett, J. Rock'n'scroll is here to stay. *Computer Graphics and Applications, IEEE 20*, 3 (2000), 40–45.
3. Bragdon, A., Nelson, E., Li, Y., and Hinckley, K. Experimental analysis of touch-screen gesture designs in mobile environments. *CHI '11*, ACM (2011), 403–412.
4. Buxton, W. A. S. Human-computer interaction. Morgan Kaufmann Publishers Inc., San Francisco, CA, USA, 1995, ch. Chunking and phrasing and the design of human-computer dialogues, 494–499.
5. Hinckley, K., Pierce, J., Sinclair, M., and Horvitz, E. Sensing techniques for mobile interaction. *UIST '00*, ACM (2000), 91–100.
6. Hinckley, K., and Song, H. Sensor synaesthesia: touch in motion, and motion in touch. *CHI '11*, ACM (2011), 801–810.
7. Jacob, R. J. K., Sibert, L. E., McFarlane, D. C., and Mullen, Jr., M. P. Integrality and separability of input devices. *ACM Trans. Comput.-Hum. Interact. 1*, 1 (1994), 3–26.
8. Kurtenbach, G., and Buxton, W. User learning and performance with marking menus. In *Proc. CHI '94*, ACM (1994), 258–264.
9. Li, Y. Gesture search: a tool for fast mobile data access. *UIST '10*, ACM (2010), 87–96.
10. Oakley, I., and Park, J. A motion-based marking menu system. *CHI EA '07*, ACM (2007), 2597–2602.
11. Rahman, M., Gustafson, S., Irani, P., and Subramanian, S. Tilt techniques: investigating the dexterity of wrist-based input. *CHI '09*, ACM (2009), 1943–1952.
12. Rekimoto, J. Tilting operations for small screen interfaces. *UIST '96*, ACM (1996), 167–168.
13. Ruiz, J., and Li, Y. Doubleflip: a motion gesture delimiter for mobile interaction. *CHI '11*, ACM (2011), 2717–2720.

28 Frames Later: Predicting Screen Touches From Back-of-Device Grip Changes

Mohammad Faizuddin Mohd Noor[*†], Andrew Ramsay[*], Stephen Hughes[‡], Simon Rogers[*], John Williamson[*] and Roderick Murray-Smith[*]

[*]School of Computing Science, University of Glasgow
{noorm,adr,srogers,jhw,rod}@dcs.gla.ac.uk

[†]Universiti Kuala Lumpur
Malaysian Institute of Information Technology
mfaizuddin@miit.unikl.edu.my

[‡]SAMH Engineering
Blackrock, Ireland
stephenahughes@gmail.com

ABSTRACT
We demonstrate that front-of-screen targeting on mobile phones can be predicted from back-of-device grip manipulations. Using simple, low-resolution capacitive touch sensors placed around a standard phone, we outline a machine learning approach to modelling the grip modulation and inferring front-of-screen touch targets. We experimentally demonstrate that grip is a remarkably good predictor of touch, and we can predict touch position 200ms before contact with an accuracy of 18mm.

Author Keywords
capacitive; touch; back-of-device; machine learning;

ACM Classification Keywords
H.5.2. User Interfaces: Input devices and strategies

INTRODUCTION
Touch input has become the dominant form of interaction with mobiles. There have been a number of proposed enhancements to touch interaction recently described to overcome input space constraints and extend the capabilities of touch, including hover tracking, full finger pose estimation and back-of-device/around-device interaction. Standard front-of-device touch is, however, likely to remain the most common modality for the forseeable future, because of its direct link between control and display. In this paper we explore how back-of-device sensors can improve front-of-device interaction by predicting the contact of fingers *before* they reach the touchscreen. This is based on the observation that, when holding a phone single-handed, it is impossible to target with the thumb across the whole display without adjusting grip (Figure 1). This paper explores *implicit* back-of-device interaction for the purpose of estimating front touch position. We focus on finding structures in the hand grip modulations and correlating these with touch actions. We use standard machine learning techniques to do prediction, forming a regression model which predicts x, y position and expected time of contact t from a capacitive sensor time series. As well as being an interesting result in its own right, this could be applied to extend user interfaces (e.g. with mid-air "taps") or to improve error correction (e.g. as a more robust measure of finger "slip"), and it has immediate and compelling application to reducing latency in mobile applications.

CHI 2014, April 26–May 01, 2014, Toronto, ON, Canada.

http://dx.doi.org/10.1145/2556288.2557148

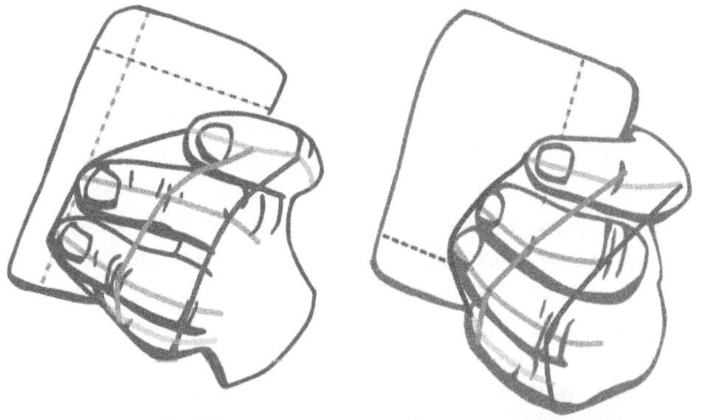

Figure 1. Grip changes as the thumb targets different areas. Thumb target shown as dashed crosshairs. Notice the change in the contours of the phalanges and finger tips (solid lines).

Use case: Preloading content
Off-device, cloud-based processing offers many opportunities for mobile interaction. One of the key issues holding back cloud applications is extended UI latency. Retrieving content over a wireless link introduces a substantial necessary latency; even a fast connection may have latencies of 100-200ms. This level of delay is very noticeable, and can disrupt the rhythm of an interaction. Prediction of touch events could be used to identify interface components a user was about to touch, and preload the content associated just ahead of time The accuracy of this touch prediction determines how much content needs to be downloaded (e.g. just for one button push or for four nearby buttons?) and thus the feasibility of the preloading.

Use case: Feedback Responsiveness Enhancement
Another potential application of touch contact prediction is enhancing auditory and tactile touch feedback. Existing feedback solutions can increase user confidence that touches have been registered, but introduce latency of their own (e.g. audio buffering delay). A delay of just 30ms between touch and response is clearly apparent. By predicting touch contact

times, audio or vibrotactile feedback can be queued to trigger exactly on the predicted touch time. This requires high predictive accuracy, but only at the fraction of a second immediately preceeding a touch.

RELATED WORK

In order to overcome occlusion problem, new interaction technique using back of the device has been proposed. This is by using a see through mobile device that allows direct touch input to be made precisely [11]. Apart from the occlusion problem, back of device interaction also has shown to be useful in increasing privacy by preventing *shoulder-surfing* [7], and to overcome *fat finger* problem in small devices [1]. Back of device interaction also allows the creation of grasp-based technique that could predict users' intention by the way they hold the device [6]. The Bar of Soap is a multifunction prototype device that used grasp interaction to switch between several hand-held modes [10]. Similarly, HandSense discriminates between different ways of grasping a device which can be used as interaction cues in both explicit and implicit ways [12]. The use of back of device sensing also allows mobile devices to be more adaptive to the dynamic nature of user interaction such as soft keyboard positioning in iGrasp [3] and screen orientation in iRotate [2]. Besides capacitive technology, users' hand postures also can be inferred using combination of built-in sensors found on most commodity mobile phones [4]. Alternatively using active acoustic sensing, rough positions of touch and different postures of touch on solid object can also be estimated [8].

EXPERIMENTAL SETUP

(a) Back view (b) Front side view (c) PCB view

Figure 2. Overview of the prototype device used in the experiment. The sensor pads are marked in yellow in (c).

Current smartphones do not typically have grip sensing around the device, and so we fabricated a custom prototype system (shown in Figure 2a). The prototype based around a Nokia N9, which has been modified to include around device sensing using a 0.1mm thick flexible PCB, interfaced directly to the phone's internal I2C bus with custom electronics. The prototype has 24 capacitive sensors distributed around the back and sides of the device (Figure 2c) to capture user's hand grip. We use 2x AD 7147 programmable touch controllers. The total size of this prototype is fractionally larger than the device itself, with dimensions of 116.5 mm x 61.2 mm x 12.1 mm and a weight 135 g. The N9 prototype has a screen density of 251 pixels per inch (ppi). Capacitive sensing technology is used because it is a well proven touch sensing technology which is practically implementable on mobile devices. The flexible PCB solution gives us a prototype which is almost identical in form factor to a standard mobile device. The prototype is configured to sample data at $50Hz$. The capacitive sensing has a raw bit conversion depth of 16 bits. It is subsequently filtered, offset removed and scaled to fit in an 8 bit container in software. A Python application was developed on the prototype to coordinate the data acquisition.

Data acquisition

In order to collect touch grip samples, 20 users were recruited locally (12 male and 8 female, age $25-40$). For each user, we recorded 250 unique touch targets with each hand, while seated on a chair, in front of their desk. We are not interested in how the users initially pick up the phone, therefore the recordings begin when the phone is held by the users. We used 5 sessions for each hand, each with 50 targets, for 500 targets in total, alternating hand between each session, for 250 targets for each hand. Each hand therefore has an equal number of touches. This is to ensure that we are not observing only a single grip pattern, but a range of plausible grips for each user. It is worth mentioning that each session was separated by a 5 minute break to minimise the repetition effects. The experiment required the user to touch random targets distributed randomly on the prototype screen using their thumb, while holding the phone single handed. A half second delay is used between targets to encourage the user to return to a rest pose before next target is shown. Audio feedback is given if the user touches the target correctly. A legitimate touch requires a stable thumb contact within the minimum target area for at least 60ms. The target area used in our setup is 1 cm in diameter or 98.8 pixels on our device. We recorded timestamps, both target and touch coordinates (x, y) in pixels and capacitive readings from the back of the device into the prototype's internal storage for subsequent off-line analysis.

Analysis methods

From the recorded samples, we performed Principal Component Analysis (PCA) to visualise the structure of the capacitive signal coming from the back of the device. In particular, we are interested to see whether there is a correlation between grip (back of device) and touch target (front of device). We used Canonical Correlation Analysis (CCA) to study this relationship. Drawing the results from CCA, we performed regression to see if touch target predictions can be made from the way the device is being grasped.

Canonical Correlations Analysis (CCA)

CCA [5] measures linear correlation between two multidimensional datasets. In our case, we have a 24-dimensional vector describing the capacitive sensor values at a given time point, $\mathbf{s}$ and a 2-dimensional vector defining the target the user was aiming for $\mathbf{x}$. CCA finds projection vectors, $\mathbf{a}$ and $\mathbf{b}$ such that for a set of $n = 1 \ldots N$ observations (sensor-target pairs), $u_n = \mathbf{a}^T \mathbf{s}_n$ is maximally correlated with $v_n = \mathbf{b}^T \mathbf{x}_n$. Typically, CCA finds M pairs of projection vectors, $(\mathbf{a}_1, \mathbf{b}_1), \ldots, (\mathbf{a}_M, \mathbf{b}_M)$ where M is equal to the dimensionality of the smaller data space (in our case, 2). The first pair

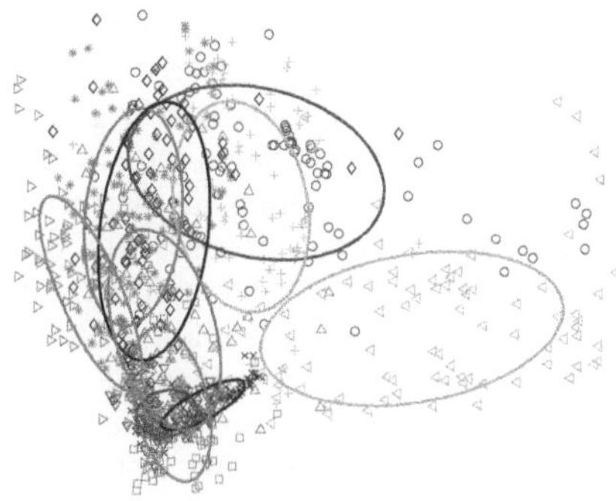

Figure 3. Principal component analysis of capacitive sensor values, s from 10 users for right hand during the touch. Each colour/symbol combination represents one user. For simplicity, only 100 samples are shown from each user. It is clear that users have quite distinct grip patterns.

of projection vectors provide the most correlated linear combinations and the second pair define the most correlated linear combinations that are orthogonal to the first, etc.

Gaussian Process Regression

Our final goal is to predict the intended target location $\mathbf{x}$ using the back of device sensors $\mathbf{s}$, which is naturally viewed as a regression task. Gaussian Process Regression (GP) [9] is a flexible, non-parametric approach to regression analysis. To define a GP, we define a prior mean regression function (in our case; $f(\mathbf{s}) = 0$) and a prior covariance function that defines the smoothness of the regression function. We train a separate, independent GP for each co-ordinate axis. In this work, we use the popular Gaussian covariance function. We used the `gpml` GP package for Matlab. In all experiments, the data are split into independent training and test sets. The hyper-parameters are optimised by maximising the marginal likelihood on the training data (see [9] for details).

RESULTS

We start by identifying the structure of hand grip data during the touch. We used Principal Components Analysis (PCA) on hand grip to project the 24-dimensional capacitive values, $\mathbf{s}$ to two-dimensional space. This allows us to observe patterns in the data. Figure 3, shows the first two components from right hand data from all users, and we can see that most of the users have different ways of holding the phone during touches. This diversity suggests that any model based from hand grip may have poor generalisation ability and is likely to be user-specific.

Canonical correlation analysis

In order to understand the correlation between grip and touch, we use CCA to measure the linear relationship between capacitive sensors, $\mathbf{s}$ and touch targets, $\mathbf{x}$. CCA provides 2 bases, one for each variable, that are optimal with respect to correlation. The plot of correlation coefficients in Figure 4 shows that the two variables are correlated.

Prediction of touch targets

Based on the touch-grip examples, we train the GP to predict touch targets before finger contact. We use root-mean-square error (RMSE) in millimetres to evaluate prediction error (Figure 5) and compare our results with a baseline defined by RMSE of always guessing the centre of the screen (an uninformed guess). To predict touch target before time of contact, we train the GP using grip data prior to the touch contact and measure the RMSE of the prediction on a separate test set. Figure 6 show the error against time before contact.

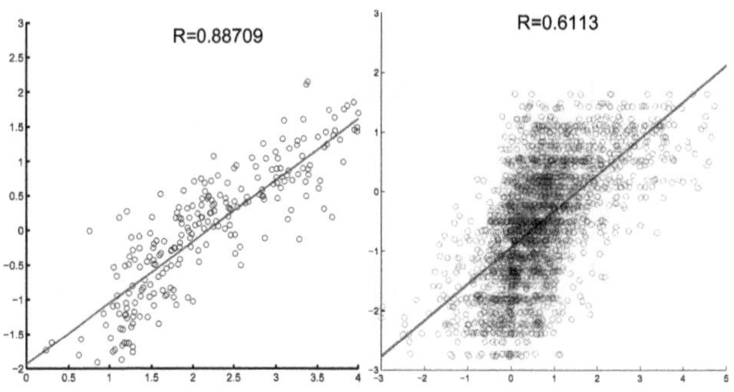

(a) Individual (b) Pooled

Figure 4. (a) shows an example of single user canonical correlation analysis. (b) Analysis based on 100 random samples pooled from every user. x and y axes correspond to first canonical components of s and x respectively. There is clear correlation between the back-of-device sensor values and the touch position.

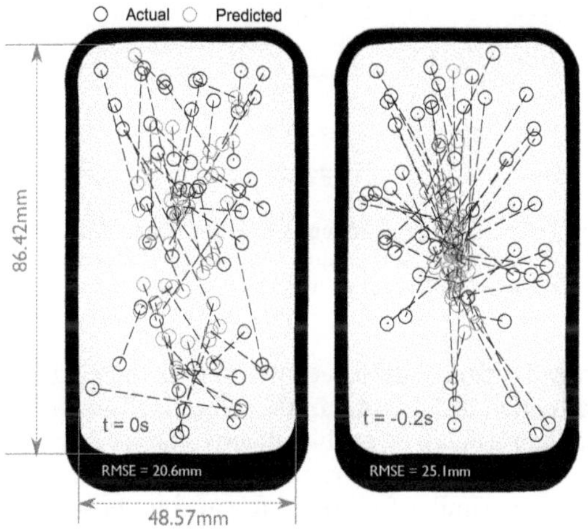

Figure 5. Example of touch target predictions for a random user, right hand at $t = 0$s and $t = -0.2$s. Black markers correspond to real targets and red markers correspond to predicted targets.

Prediction of contact time

To predict the time the finger will make contact with the display, we extend the feature vector to include the first time derivative (estimated using an order-4 Savitzky-Golay filter). We train a new GP with the resulting 48-dimensional feature vector. As Figure 7 shows, we can estimate time of contact accurately just before touch, with reasonable estimates up to 0.5 seconds before contact.

DISCUSSION

The results show that there is a surprisingly strong correlation between grip modulation and touch target, and we can predict touch contact position reasonably well several hundred milliseconds before touch. This is accurate enough to estimate

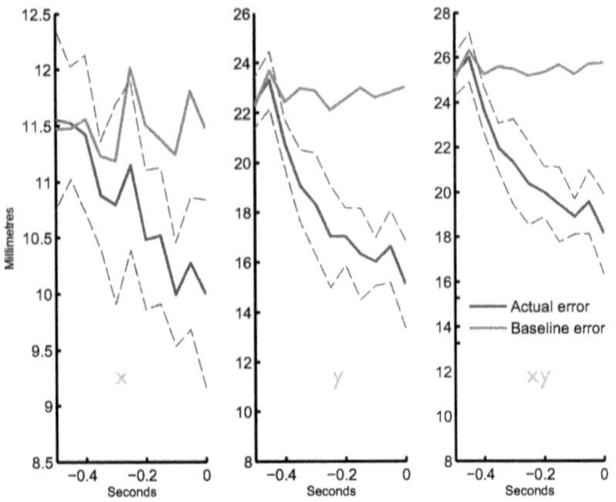

Figure 6. RMSE of touch target predictions including ± standard error before touch contact for right hand averaged across 10 users. Left and middle panels correspond to prediction error for x and y axes and right panel corresponds to combination error of x and y axes.

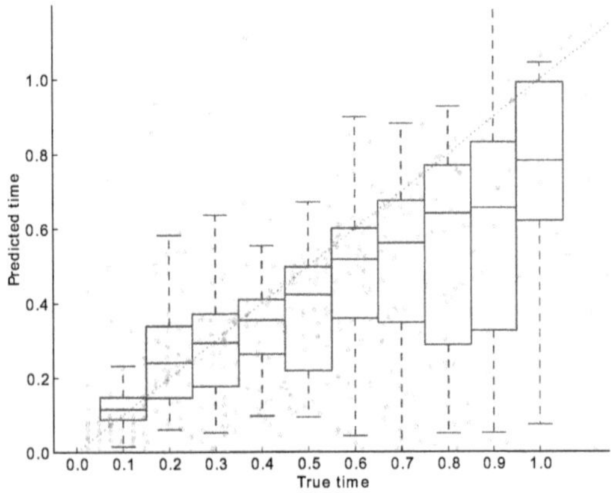

Figure 7. Predicted time of contact against actual time of contact, for all users, right hand, 1000 samples. The system can predict contact time with in a fairly small interval, even half a second before a touch.

the broad region of the screen user is targeting (e.g. to identify which cell in 3x3 division of the screen is being touched), and more than enough to enable effective preloading of content. Time-of-contact is also remarkably predictable. Prediction accuracy is similar for both left and right hand use, regardless of the user's handedness. We have focused on a specific targeting paradigm in this study – touching randomised abstract targets with one thumb. The grip dynamics of tasks with a known target positions (e.g. typing) may be different; this remains to be investigated. Other interaction poses, such as two-thumb interaction and single-finger tapping, are also likely to have substantially different grip models. Although our results suggest that the model may not be suitable for generalisation, however it could be possible to establish a group of people (based on clusters), and generalise the model based on this group.

CONCLUSION

The grip manipulations required to touch targets on a mobile touch screen have a distinct signature. Our methods are able to use this to predict finger contacts with a degree of accuracy that could enhance a wide range of mobile applications by reducing apparent latency. Gaussian process regression is efficient in learning a compact and robust mapping from a fairly low-resolution grip sensor to target positions and contact times. Although we used user-specific grip models a system using a pooled model combined with a small individual training sample may provide adequate performance without requiring a lengthy enrolment process. The use of back-of-device interaction for explicit interaction is a well explored area. Implicit interaction with whole device sensing offers opportunities to transparently enhance standard interaction techniques and build devices with responsiveness and precision beyond that which is possible from standard surface contact sensing.

ACKNOWLEDGEMENTS

We thank Nokia for funding the back of device hardware as part of the project "Human Emotional Communication in the field of Quality and Rapport".

REFERENCES

1. Baudisch, P., and Chu, G. Back-of-device interaction allows creating very small touch devices. *CHI '09* (2009), 1923.
2. Cheng, L.-P., Hsiao, F.-I., Liu, Y.-T., and Chen, M. Y. iRotate grasp. In *UIST Adjunct Proceedings '12* (2012), 15.
3. Cheng, L.-P., Liang, H.-S., Wu, C.-Y., and Chen, M. Y. iGrasp. In *CHI '13* (2013), 3037.
4. Goel, M., Wobbrock, J., and Patel, S. Gripsense: Using built-in sensors to detect hand posture and pressure on commodity mobile phones. In *UIST '12* (2012), 545–554.
5. Hotelling, H. Relations between two sets of variates. *Biometrika 28* (1936), 321–377.
6. Kim, K., Chang, W., Cho, Sung-jung Shim, J., and Lee, H. Hand grip pattern recognition for mobile user interfaces. *IAAI '06* (2006), 1789–1794.
7. Luca, A. D., von Zezschwitz, E., Nguyen, N. D. H., Maurer, M.-E., Rubegni, E., Scipioni, M. P., and Langheinrich, M. Back-of-device authentication on smartphones. In *CHI '13* (2013), 2389.
8. Ono, M., Shizuki, B., and Tanaka, J. Touch and activate: Adding interactivity to existing objects using active acoustic sensing. In *UIST '13* (2013), 31–40.
9. Rasmussen, C. E., and Williams, C. *Gaussian Processes for Machine Learning*. MIT Press, 2006.
10. Taylor, B. T., and Bove, V. M. The bar of soap: a grasp recognition system implemented in a multi-functional handheld device. *Ext. Abstracts CHI'08* (2008), 3459–3464.
11. Wigdor, D., Forlines, C., Baudisch, P., Barnwell, J., and Shen, C. Lucid touch. In *UIST '07* (2007), 269.
12. Wimmer, R., and Boring, S. HandSense: discriminating different ways of grasping and holding a tangible user interface. *TEI '09* (2009), 16–19.

Probabilistic Palm Rejection Using Spatiotemporal Touch Features and Iterative Classification

Julia Schwarz Robert Xiao Jennifer Mankoff Scott E. Hudson Chris Harrison
Human-Computer Interaction Institute
Carnegie Mellon University, 5000 Forbes Avenue, Pittsburgh PA 15213
{julia.schwarz,brx,jmankoff,scott.hudson,chris.harrison}@cs.cmu.edu

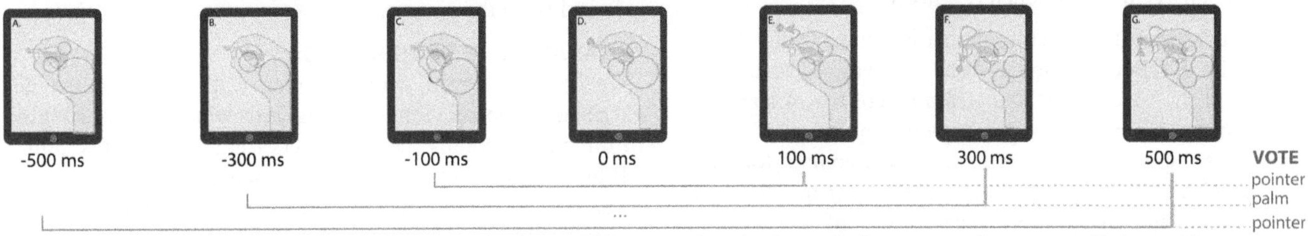

Figure 1. An illustrated example of touches present at different points in time relative to a touch contact of interest (D, green dot). Touch points due to palms (hollow circles) are often ephemeral, large, and have low velocity. Our approach extracts features and performs classification of each touch point at several points in time (blue lines), using different sized time windows (red). In this example, we show how the classification for the green dot only changes (purple text) as the window size changes.

ABSTRACT

Tablet computers are often called upon to emulate classical pen-and-paper input. However, touchscreens typically lack the means to distinguish between legitimate stylus and finger touches and touches with the palm or other parts of the hand. This forces users to rest their palms elsewhere or hover above the screen, resulting in ergonomic and usability problems. We present a probabilistic touch filtering approach that uses the temporal evolution of touch contacts to reject palms. Our system improves upon previous approaches, reducing accidental palm inputs to 0.016 per pen stroke, while correctly passing 98% of stylus inputs.

Author Keywords: Palm rejection; touchscreen; tablet computing; touch interaction; pen and stylus input.

ACM Classification Keywords: H.5.2 [Information interfaces and presentation]: User Interfaces

INTRODUCTION

Tablet computers are often called upon to emulate classical pen-and-paper input. However, most touch devices today lack palm rejection features – most notably the highly popular Apple iPad tablets. Failure to reject palms effectively in a pen or touch input system results in ergonomic issues [3], accidental activation and unwanted inputs, precluding fluid and efficient use of these input systems. This issue has been well explored in the academic literature (see e.g., [10,11,12,22]).

CHI 2014, April 26 - May 01 2014, Toronto, ON, Canada

ACM 978-1-4503-2473-1/14/04 $15.00. http://dx.doi.org/10.1145/2556288.2557056

The contributions of this work are three-fold. Foremost, we describe a novel, probabilistic approach to palm rejection. Our system requires no initial configuration and is independent of screen orientation and user handedness. Second, we review contemporary palm rejection implementations and compare our approach against two applications in a user study, offering the first publicly available comparison of such systems. Through our user study, we show that our implementation offers equal or superior performance to these applications.

We prototyped our approach on an Apple iPad 2 running iOS 6 – a platform without native palm rejection or stylus input. Our approach, however, is platform agnostic and will work on any system that reports multiple touch contacts along with location and touch area.

SPATIOTEMPORAL TOUCH FEATURES

Our work began with a series of observations of stylus use on tablets. We identified five properties that distinguished palms from pointer (i.e., finger or stylus) inputs: 1) the touch area for palms tends to be large, whereas pointers have small tips; 2) on most touchscreens, the large palm contact area is segmented into a collection of touch points, which often flicker in and out; 3) these palm points tend to be clustered together, whereas the pointer is typically isolated; 4) stylus touches have a consistent area, unlike palms, which change in area as they deform against the screen; and 5) palms generally move little, while pointer inputs tend to have longer, smoother trajectories.

Another insight was that there was often significant context that existed before a touch point appeared on the screen. For example, when dotting an 'i' the stylus touch might only exist for 50ms – however, the palm might have been on the display for several seconds beforehand. As our approach records all touch data, we can look backwards in time to make a more confident classification.

Using our observations as a starting point, we derived a series of features that characterize touch points of interest and their relationships to neighboring points[1]. These features are computed over touch event sequences corresponding to a particular touch contact (which we will eventually need to categorize as either a stylus or part of a palm) and occurring over windows of time, centered at t=0 (i.e. birth of the touch point). We expand the time window symmetrically about t=0, ensuring that data from before and after the initial touch event are included (Figure 1).

Each touch event has a centroid position and a radius (indicating the maximum distance from the centroid to the perimeter of the touch area). Our features consist of statistics (mean/stdev/min/max) computed over sequences of touch events corresponding to a particular touch contact for each time window. We calculate these statistics for the radius of each event and speed and acceleration of consecutive events. Additional features include the total number of events in the sequence and mean/stdev/min/max calculated over the Cartesian distances between the centroid of the touch event at t=0 and all touch events in any concurrent sequences (belonging to other touch contacts). All of these features are rotation and flip invariant. This should minimize the effect of device and hand orientation, as well as handedness, on classification.

Similar features have been used for other applications, including finger angle estimation [25], thumb-driven interactions [1] and more generally, finger pose estimation [20]. Wang and Ren provide a more complete overview of possible finger properties and related work [24].

To better understand which features discriminate palm from stylus, we performed feature selection on our training dataset (11,373 instances collected from 3 people) using correlation-based feature subset selection [8] with best first search, provided in Weka [9]. We found that min distance to other touches, number of touch events, and min/mean/max/stdev of touch radius to be most valuable[1].

ITERATIVE CLASSIFICATION AND VOTING

Our algorithm records all touch events reported by the touchscreen. After a touch point has been alive for at least 25ms, the system classifies the touch as either "pointer" or "palm". If a touch terminates before 25ms has elapsed, it is classified using all available data. At 50ms after birth, another classification is performed. For every 50ms thereafter, up to 500ms since birth, this classification repeats – each time contributing a single "vote". A temporary touch type, either pen or palm, is assigned based on the majority of the votes accumulated thus far. After 500ms, or if the touch point disappears (whichever comes first), voting stops, and the final vote is used to assign a permanent classification. Note that the vote implicitly encodes a confidence score that can be used in probabilistic input systems (such as those described in [21]).

One benefit of our iterative classification approach is that it allows our system to show immediate feedback to the user. The system initially shows its best guess (roughly 98% accurate, see Figure 2) and refines this later as more information becomes available. For example, if a touch is initially guessed to be a pen, the application will render a stroke on canvas. If this guess is later changed, the stroke is removed from the canvas.

TRAINING THE CLASSIFIERS

We trained eleven decision trees using the features described in the previous sections with window sizes ranging from 50 to 1000ms (i.e. classifiers triggered at 25ms, 50ms, 100ms, 150ms, etc. up to 500ms; see Figure 1). Each tree was trained using touch features from all window sizes up to the maximum window size. For example, the classifier triggered at 200ms uses features obtained from window sizes of 50, 100, 200, 300 and 400ms (windows are symmetric, centered on t=0). We used Weka [9] to train our decision trees using the C4.5 algorithm [19].

We collected training data using a custom iOS application. For each training instance, a 1cm radius dot was randomly placed on the screen. Users were told to place their palms on the screen however they saw fit, such that they could draw a stroke of their choosing starting in this circle. This procedure allowed us to collect labeled pointer and palm point data. In total, we captured 22,251 touch event instances (of which 2143 are stylus strokes) from five people using a variety of hand poses, tablet orientations, and handedness.

To estimate the effectiveness of our iterative approach, we split our data into 11,373 training instances (from 3 people) and 10,878 test instances (from 2 others). Figure 2 shows test accuracy over increasing time windows. Classification at t=1ms is included to approximate instantaneous classification. Accuracy improves as window size increases, plateauing around 99.5% at 200ms. We continued classification out to 500ms for experimental reasons, but as Figure 2 shows, the main gains occur in the first 100ms. This result underscores the importance of leveraging temporal features and also delaying *final* classification.

As shown in Figure 2, performing classification instantly (at t=1ms) yields a classification accuracy of 98.4% (kappa=0.79). This is sufficiently accurate that real-time graph-

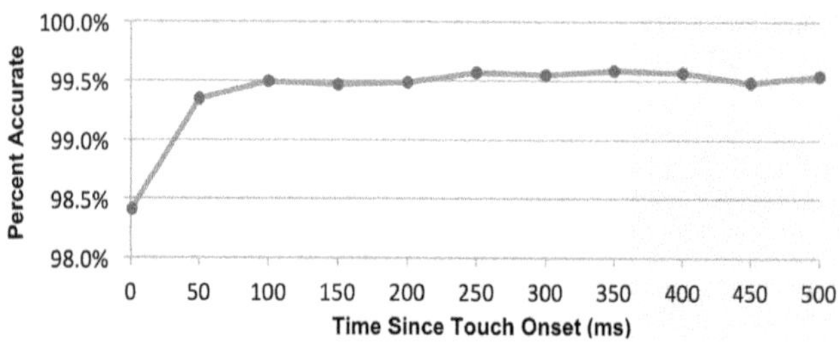

Figure 2. Classification accuracy (true positives) over different durations of time. Leftmost point is at t=1ms.

[1] See `calc_features.cpp` and `classify.cpp` in the supplementary material for information about features and implementation details.

ical feedback can be rendered immediately while only occasionally requiring later reversion. Reclassifying at 50ms reduces errors by 44%. By continuing iterative classification and voting up to 100ms, accuracy increases to ~99.5% (kappa=0.94), cutting the error rate by a further 29%.

RELATED SYSTEMS

Many palm rejection approaches – utilizing hardware, software, and combinations of the two – have been created, which we now review to position our work.

Hardware Approaches

The most reliable way to disambiguate stylus input from human input is to use special hardware. For example, ultrasonic transducers can be placed at the periphery of a screen to sense ultrasonic pulses emitted by an active pen (see e.g., [16]). It is also possible to use an infrared emitting pen and two or more cameras to triangulate the planar position on a screen (see e.g., iPen 2 [13]). The Jot Touch [14] uses a passive capacitive tip, which simulates a finger touch. The pen itself is powered and pressure sensitive, sending data to the device over Bluetooth. With timing information, it is possible to associate touch events with pen down events.

Another approach, popularized by Wacom, uses resonance inductive coupling [5], which uses a special pen and sensor board that operates behind the conventional capacitive touchscreen. This technology is used in devices such as the Microsoft Surface and Samsung Galaxy Note. Similarly, Gauss-Sense [15] uses a grid of Hall effect sensors behind the touchscreen to sense the magnetic tip of a special pen. LongPad [7] used a grid of infrared proximity sensors and computer vision to separate palm and finger inputs. Finally, advanced capacitive touchscreens can differentiate passive styli by looking at contact size and capacitive properties [2].

Even with special hardware for stylus support, simply distinguishing pen from finger is insufficient if the finger can still be used for input. In this case, unwanted palm touches may still be interpreted as finger touches in the absence of the pen. Thus, software is still needed to reliably distinguish pens and fingers from palms, which the above solutions do not address.

Software Approaches

Although special styli tend to offer excellent precision, a significant downside is the need for a special purpose accessory, which is often platform-specific. Further, additional internal hardware is often required to support these pens, adding to the build cost, size and power draw of mobile devices. Thus, a software-only solution, which can be easily deployed and updated, is attractive. Further, software solutions offer the ability to disambiguate between finger and palm input. However, without an innate way to disambiguate touch events, software solutions must rely on clever processing or interaction techniques.

For optical multi-touch devices, one approach is to identify palm regions visible from the camera image [6]. On mobile devices with capacitive screens, the task is more challenging, since applications generally do not have access to a hand image, or even the capacitive response of the touch screen. Instead, applications must rely on information about touch position, orientation (if available), and size. There are dozens of applications in the iOS and Android app stores that claim to have palm rejection features. Unfortunately, implementations are proprietary, precluding direct analysis.

One method applications employ is to specify a special 'palm rejection region' where all touches are ignored [17], though this is unwieldy. Unfortunately, palm touches outside the input region can still provide accidental input (e.g. accidental button presses). Vogel *et al.* [23] makes use of a more sophisticated geometric model to specify the rejection region, providing a five-parameter scalable circle and pivoting rectangle, which captures the area covered by the palm better than a rectangular region.

A second approach uses spatiotemporal features – looking at the evolution of touch properties and movement over a short time window. We hypothesize that applications that first draw, then remove strokes, must wait some period of time before detecting accidental touches. Two applications exhibiting this behavior include Penultimate [18] and Bamboo Paper [2]. Both applications require the user to specify information their handedness and use the tablet in a fixed orientation, neither of which our method requires. Additionally, Penultimate requires users to specify one of three handwriting poses they use.

USER STUDY

To assess the performance of our palm rejection approach, we compared against Penultimate and Bamboo Paper. As of September 2013, both of these apps have been featured in the Apple App Store, and were subjectively judged by the authors to have the best palm rejection out of 10 candidate applications tested.

We recruited 10 participants from our lab (3 female, one left-handed, mean age 29), who were paid $5 for their time. Users were provided a passive, rubber-tipped stylus, which is the most popular style for use with the iPad. The task was to replicate 15 symbols presented on cards. Participants were instructed to draw each symbol with a single stroke. If the application missed the stroke, they were told to continue to the next symbol. They were allowed to rest their hands on the screen, and to lift, slide and otherwise reposition their palm however they saw fit during drawing.

Six symbol sets, representing a variety of 1D and 2D shapes (the letter 'S', a circle, a dot, a horizontal and vertical line, and the letter 'L'), were presented in random order. This procedure was repeated for the three applications – Bamboo, Penultimate, and our own – in a random order. Bamboo and Penultimate were each configured for the user's handedness and preferred handwriting pose before the experiment; our application did not require configuration.

After each symbol set was drawn, the experimenter recorded the number of strokes that were successfully drawn (true positives), as well as the number of extraneous strokes (typically under the palm) that were drawn (false positives).

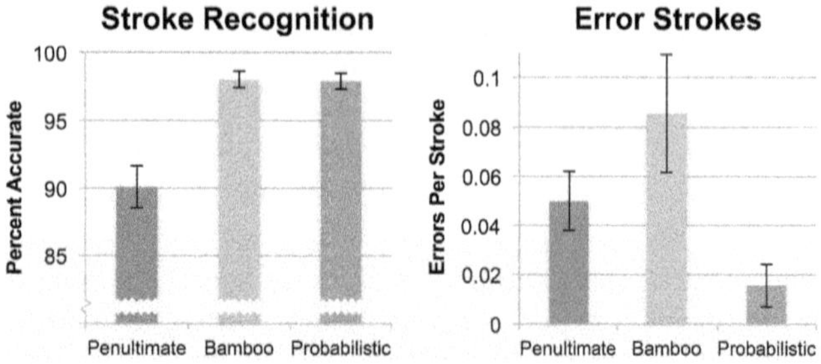

Figure 3. Stroke recognition accuracy and errors per stroke results from our study. Error bars reflect standard error.

This procedure provided 90 stroke attempts per user per application, for a total of 2,700 strokes. We did not record true/false positives for palm classification because it was not feasible to collect ground truth palm data.

RESULTS

Our approach has a true positive rate of 97.9%, compared to Bamboo's 98.0% and Penultimate's 90.1% (Figure 3). This outcome is not significantly different from Bamboo Paper, but both Bamboo and our approach are significantly more accurate than Penultimate ($p < 0.05$). Statistical significance was assessed by running a repeated measures ANOVA ($F_{2,18} = 20.53$, $p < 0.05$), followed by a Tukey HSD test.

Additionally, our approach has fewer false positives than Bamboo and Penultimate: 0.016 errors/stroke vs. 0.086 and 0.050 respectively (Figure 3). The difference between our approach and Penultimate was not significant, though our false positive rate was significantly lower than Bamboo (Tukey HSD $p < 0.05$; ANOVA $F_{2,18} = 5.09$, $p < 0.05$).

Although our system performs with accuracy equivalent to Penultimate, it does not require information about hand position (unlike Penultimate). We believe two things contributed to this robustness: we collected training data that represented a wide range of poses; and, as mentioned above, we designed our feature set to be hand invariant.

CONCLUSION

In this work, we described a palm rejection technique utilizing temporal features, iterative classification, and probabilistic voting. We demonstrate the efficacy of our solution with an evaluation, which showed improvements over popular applications considered to be the current state of the art. Finally, our approach provides a basis for future research efforts in palm rejection.

ACKNOWLEDGEMENTS

This work was funded by NSF Grant IIS1217929, and fellowships from Microsoft Research, Google and Qualcomm.

REFERENCES

1. Boring, S., Ledo, D., Chen, X., Marquadt, N., Tang, A. and Greenberg, S. The fat thumb: using the thumb's contact size for single-handed mobile interaction. In *Proc. MobileHCI '12*, 39-48.
2. Bamboo Paper. Wacom. http://bamboopaper.wacom.com.
3. Camilleri, M., Malige, A., Fujimoto, J., Rempei, D. (2013). *Touch Displays: the effects of palm rejection technology on productivity, comfort, biomechanics, and positioning.* In Ergonomics. Taylor & Francis Group.
4. ClearPad™ Series 3. http://synaptics.com/solutions/products/clearpad
5. EMR® Technology. Wacom. http://www.wacom-components.com/english/technology/emr.html.
6. Ewerling, P., Kulik, A, Froehlich, B. Finger and hand detection for multi-touch interfaces based on maximally stable extremal regions. In *Proc. ITS '12*, 173-182.
7. Gu, J., Heo, S., Han, J., Kim, S. and Lee, G. LongPad: a touchpad using the entire area below the keyboard of a laptop computer. In *Proc. CHI '13*, 1421-1430.
8. Hall, M.A. Correlation-based Feature Subset Selection for Machine Learning. Ph.D. Thesis, 1998. Hamilton, New Zealand.
9. Hall, M., Frank, E., Holmes, G., Pfahringer, B., Reutemann, P. and Witten, I.H. The WEKA data mining software: an update. *SIGKDD Explorations*, 11(1), 10-18.
10. Hinckley, K. and Sinclair, M. Touch-Sensing Input Devices. In *Proc. CHI '99*, 223-230.
11. Hinckley, K., Wigdor, D., (2012). Input Technologies and Techniques (Chapter 9). In The Human-Computer Interaction Handbook, 3rd Edition, published by Taylor & Francis.
12. Hinckley, K., Yatani, K., Pahud, M., Coddington, N., Rodenhouse, J., Wilson, A., Benko, H., and Buxton, B. Pen + touch = new tools. In *Proc. UIST '10*, 27-36.
13. iPen 2. Cregle Inc. http://www.cregle.com/pages/pressure-sensitive-stylus-for-your-imac-and-ipad.
14. Jot Touch. Adonit . http://adonit.net/jot/touch
15. Liang, R., Cheng, K., Su, C., Weng, C., Chen, B. and Yang, D. GaussSense: attachable stylus sensing using magnetic sensor grid. In *Proc. UIST '12*, 319-326.
16. MyNote Pen. http://mynote.eu/mynotepen-en.html.
17. Notability Ginger Labs. http://www.gingerlabs.com.
18. Penultimate. Evernote. http://evernote.com/penultimate.
19. Quinlan, J. R. *C4.5: Programs for Machine Learning.* Morgan Kaufmann Publishers, 1993.
20. Rogers, S., Williamson, J., Stewart, C. and Murray-Smith, R. AnglePose: robust, precise capacitive touch tracking via 3D orientation estimation. In *Proc. CHI '12*, 2575-2584.
21. Schwarz J., Hudson S., Mankoff, J. and Wilson, A.D. A framework for robust and flexible handling of inputs with uncertainty. In *Proc. UIST '10*, 47-56.
22. Steimle, J. (2012). Survey of Pen-and-Paper Computing. In *Pen-and-Paper User Interfaces* (pp. 19-65). Springer Berlin Heidelberg.
23. Vogel, D., Cudmore, M., Casiez, G., Balakrishnan, R. and Keliher, L. Hand occlusion with tablet-sized direct pen input. In *Proc. CHI '09*, 557-566.
24. Wang, F. and Ren, F. Empirical evaluation for finger input properties in multi-touch interaction. In *Proc. CHI '10*, 1063-1072.
25. Wang, F., Cao, X., Ren, X. and Irani, P. Detecting and leveraging finger orientation for interaction with direct-touch surfaces. In *Proc. UIST '09*, 23-32.

Orientation Matters: Efficiency of Translation-Rotation Multitouch tasks

Quan Nguyen
German Research Center for Artificial Intelligence (DFKI)
quan.nguyen@dfki.de

Michael Kipp
Augsburg University of Applied Sciences
michael.kipp@hs-augsburg.de

ABSTRACT
The translation and rotation of objects with two fingers is a well-explored multitouch technique. However, there are some unsolved questions regarding the optimal conditions under which this technique functions best. Does it matter in which direction the movement is oriented? Does parallel or sequential performance of the two operations work best? This study attempts to answer this question using a typical Fitts' Law setup but with varying translation-rotation orientation combinations. The results show that right-oriented movements were faster and easier than left-oriented ones. Movement combinations which went in different directions (translation right, rotation left, and vice versa) were found more tiresome and resulted in more strategy switches compared to equi-directional combinations. Our findings can inform positioning decisions in interaction design and contribute to theoretical adjustments to Fitts' Law.

Author Keywords
Multitouch interaction techniques; Fitts Law; 2D translation and rotation

ACM Classification Keywords
H.5.2. User Interfaces: Evaluation/Methodology: Input Devices and Strategies.

INTRODUCTION
Research on multitouch interaction techniques has resulted in many significant findings, especially for fundamental operations like translation and rotation, either in two dimensions (cf. Rotate'N Translate [7]) or three dimensions (cf. Sticky Fingers [3], Screen-Space [10], DS3 Depth-Separated Screen Space [9]).

However, there are open questions regarding the optimal usage conditions and execution strategies. Translation and rotation can be either performed in parallel or sequentially which is often examined with matching or docking tasks. Parallel execution is essential for applications where multiple degrees of freedom must be orchestrated (e.g. in real-time character animation) [6, 13, 14]. However, in other contexts studies suggest that a clear separation of translation and rotation, i.e. performing the operations sequentially, is more intuitive and easier to use [9, 12]. Most studies evaluate the interaction with specific tasks or applications such as moving or translating images or other objects [10] or controlling and moving an arm of a virtual puppet [6]. This context specificity makes it hard to generalize the results.

In contrast, several studies devised abstract task designs based on the original work by Fitts. The aim was to extend or adapt Fitts' law for special conditions (e.g. from 1D to 2D or for finger touch input) [1, 8, 2]. Hoggan et al. conducted a study where the angle, direction, diameter (distance between index-finger and thumb), and position of rotations were systematically manipulated [5].

Stoelen and Akin show that rotation and translation have the same difficulty and complexity which may indicate that parallel execution is efficient [11]. They used a magnetic sensor system instead of multitouch. In this study, 12 out of 13 participants performed the combined movements in parallel, and 1 performed them strictly serially. A reason for the often parallel excution could be the fixed configuration in terms of movement direction: translation was always to the right, rotation always counter-clockwise. It is possible that changing the orientation of these operations (translation to the left, rotation clockwise) modulate the results which may in turn explain the inconsistent research finding with regard to parallel vs. sequential execution.

Our study intends to fill a gap in existing work by systematically examining the effects of combining translation and rotation under varying conditions and looking at execution strategies by the users. We took Stoelen and Akin's experimental design and varied movement direction. We evaluated performance, subjective impression and choice of strategy. We consider our work a puzzle piece in the search for theoretical models that explain and predict such conditions.

CHI 2014, April 26–May 1, 2014, Toronto, Ontario, Canada.

ACM 978-1-4503-2473-1/14/04..$15.00.
http://dx.doi.org/10.1145/2556288.2557399

EXPERIMENT
We designed an experiment where participants had to move objects to a target position using 2-finger translation (left or right) and rotation (clockwise or counterclockwise), where the index finger was assumed to be the pivot for rotation. For investigating the effect of different movement orientations we devised four variants of the basic task (Fig. 1):

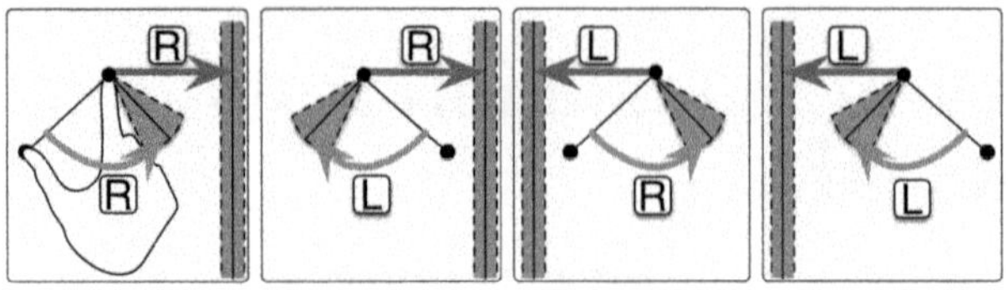

Figure 1: Four tasks - the blue arrow shows the translation direction, the red one the rotation direction

(a) *RR*: Translation right, rotation right (counterclockwise)

(b) *RL*: Translation right, rotation left (clockwise)

(c) *LR*: Translation left, rotation right (counterclockwise)

(d) *LL*: Translation left, rotation left (clockwise)

Here, 'rotation right' means that the thumb moves to the right (same for 'rotation left') which makes sense when comparing whether translation-rotation is performed in the same direction (equi-directional: RR, LL) vs. in different directions (counter-directional: RL, LR).

Apparatus

We used a 22-inch multitouch screen (3M model M2256PW) with 1680x1050 pixels and <6ms touch response time, positioned in front of the subject on a low table. The screen was tilted 50 degrees relative to a vertical display which was found optimal in a pre-study about visibility and comfort.

Participants

16 participants (7m, 9f), aged 21–31, were recruited via notice boards, Facebook (public announcements per messages and posts in groups and own Facebook timeline) and email lists and were paid 8 EUR. One was left handed, all others right handed. The left-handed one used the mouse with his right hand. In our questionnaire participants reported having experience with single- or multitouch devices. Eight used such devices often or very often, the other eight rarely or very rarely.

Experimental Design

In our experiment participants had to move an object (circle plus line) into a target translation zone and rotation zone, both colored green. The object had to be dragged with the index finger into the green target translation zone, depicted by a center line with dashed boundary lines. We define the distance as shortest path from the circle to the center line. For rotation, a line that is attached to the circle had to be rotated with the thumb into a green rotation zone (see Fig. 1).

All participants performed all four task variants. We generated 16 different task configurations (two distances, two target rotations and two tolerance levels). We decided to use only two values for translation and rotation to keep the experiment feasible. A similar design was used by Hoffman et al. [4] and Stoelen and Akin [11] who also used 16 configurations. The difficulty of each configuration (Table 1) was measured using the Index of Difficulty (ID) with the Shannon formula because it always gives a positive rating for the index of task difficulty [8]. Each participant did 256 trials (each configuration repeated 4x). Trial order was balanced across subjects using a Latin Square design.

Translation			Rotation		
Distance	Tolerance	ID	Angle	Tolerance	ID
$\pm$ 12.7 cm	0.8 cm	4.08	$\pm$ 50°	4°	2.18
$\pm$ 4.8 cm	0.8 cm	2.81	$\pm$ 50°	12°	1.12
$\pm$ 12.7 cm	1.6 cm	3.16	$\pm$ 130°	4°	3.35
$\pm$ 4.8 cm	1.6 cm	2.00	$\pm$ 130°	12°	2.02

Table 1: Configurations with ID (index of difficulty).

Procedure

First, all participants completed a practice phase with 48 trials. In the actual study, 256 configurations were presented in 4 blocks of 64 trials each with a 15-second break between blocks. Participants could make additional breaks at any time.

The subjects were instructed to perform the task as quickly and as error-free as possible. During practice the error rate was displayed to make the participants more aware of their current performance and to motivate them to reduce errors. During the actual study, the error rate was not displayed.

A trial was started when the finger touched the cursor on the multitouch screen. Then, the color of the objects on screen changed from white to blue when the first finger touched the first cursor. They became green when the second finger touched the second cursor. Time measurement started when objects were actually moved. In the pre-studies we fixed the finger distance but the participants wished for more flexibility because a fixed distance can lead to uncomfortable poses so that users would unintentionally lift their finger before task completion which then counts as an error.

One trial ends as (1) **success**: object is in the target zone when fingers are lifted. A green check mark appears and a high tone is played. (2) **error**: object is outside the target area when fingers are lifted off. A red cross mark appears and a low tone is played, (3) **interruption**: a finger is lifted without moving the cursor. A yellow exclamation mark appears and a "boing"-sound is played. The interruptions were logged but were not counted as errors to avoid counting unintentional interruption. Some participants e.g. touched the cursors and lifted the finger immediately to dry their fingers.

In case of error/interruption the participant repeated the trial. After the experiment, the participants completed a questionnaire. Each session took between 25–60 min.

Hypotheses

This experiment was designed to test two hypotheses:

1. Interactions with translation to the right are faster than ones with translation to the left

2. Interactions with the same direction for translation and rotation (equi-directional) are faster than interactions with different directions (counter-directional)

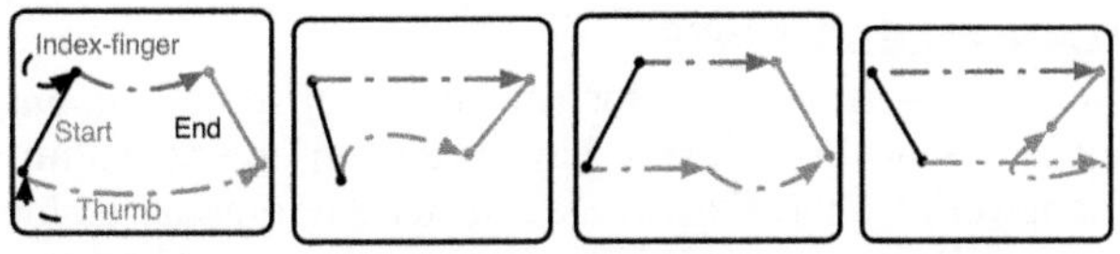

(a) RR (b) RL (c) RR (d) RL

Figure 2: Expected strategies for parallel (2a, 2b) and sequential (2c, 2d) execution with translation first for movements with translation to right. We expected the mirrored version of these strategies for movements with translation from right to left. The black line indicates the start position of index-finger (top) and thumb (bottom). The green line represents the end positions.

On top of this, we wanted to explore the strategies the participants would use to perform the tasks. We expected two main categories (see Fig. 2):

1. Parallel strategies (2a, 2b)
2. Sequential strategies: with the two subcategories *translation first* (2c, 2d) and *rotation first* (looks like 2c, 2d but with reversed direction of the arrows).

Results

Performance

Task RL was performed fastest (M = 2.45s, SD = 0.85), followed by RR (M = 2.51s, SD = 0.77). Slowest was LL (M=2.89s, SD=1.08) after LR (M=2.60s, SD=0.96). A multivariate analysis of variance MANOVA on execution time shows a significant main effect for translation direction, with right-oriented translation being faster than left-oriented ones, $F(1,15) = 15.01, p < .001, \eta^2 = 0.50$. Neither the main effect for rotation nor the interaction between translation and rotation were significant, both $Fs(1,15) < 2.59, ps > .13, \eta s^2 < 0.15$.

Used strategies

To identify the used strategies motion paths were manually analyzed and discussed with at least two people. We agreed on five strategies (examples in Fig. 3). Remember that, by default, participants should use the index finger for translation and the thumb for rotation (around the index finger).

1. *Parallel*: parallel execution of translation and rotation.
2. *Parallel-Changed-Pivot*: rotation was performed around the thumb instead of the index finger, achieving translation and rotation simultaneously with little effort.
3. *Sequential-Trans-Rot*: translation of both index finger and thumb and a final rotation around the index finger.
4. *Sequential-Rot-Trans*: first a rotation, then the translation.
5. *Sequential-Rot-Trans-Rot*: a rotation, a translation and a final rotation.

Distribution of strategies

The main strategy for LL was the sequential strategy *Sequential-Rot-Trans* (52% of all trials for LL were performed with this strategy). For configurations with a small rotation *Parallel* was preferred (51%), and for large rotations *Sequential-Trans-Rot* was the most common strategy (62%). For RR the participants worked more in parallel and used the strategy *Parallel* in 56% of the trials. However the second most common case for RR was *Sequential-Rot-Trans* (26%).

For the counter-directional movements RL and LR the participants switched more between strategies. The main strategies for RL and LR were *Parallel-changed-Pivot* (42%), *Parallel* (18%), *Sequential-Rot-Trans* (42%). In contrast *Sequential-Trans-Rot* and *Sequential-Rot-Trans-Rot* was used very rarely (4% and 0.2%). In LR *Parallel* was used five times more often for short translation movements (20%) than for long translation movements (4%).

The most commonly used strategy for long distances in RL was *Parallel-Changed-Pivot* (60%). In contrast *Parallel* was used just in 8%. But for short distances *Parallel* was the most used strategy (42%) and *Parallel-Changed-Pivot* the second fewest (26%).

Strategy switching

As an indicator for task complexity we measured the average number of different strategies a user would utilize per task across trials. For the counter-directional RL, for example, participants used 2.48 strategies on average. In contrast, for the equi-directional RR they just used 1.7 different strategies. The complete order was 1. RL (2.48), 2. LR (1.94), 3. LL (1.77) and 4. RR (1.70). In a one-tailed t-test the counter-directional tasks RL and LR showed significantly more strategy switching than the equi-directional tasks LL and RR ($t(15) = 3.79, p < 0.005$).

DISCUSSION

This experiment indicates that right-oriented movements were performed faster than left-oriented movements. One possible explanation for this phenomenon could be the right-handedness of all participants except for one and also the habit of reading and writing from left to right. To our surprise the participants used two strategies we did not expect:

1. *Parallel-Changed-Pivot* (see Figure 3a) was used for counter-directional tasks RL (43%) and LR (51%). Changing the pivot finger to rotate around the thumb may have been more economic in certain configurations.
2. *Sequential-Rot-Trans-Rot* (see Figure 3b) was used in a few cases.

Right-oriented movement are also found easier and less tiresome than left-oriented ones. In the questionnaire, participants found that LL was the hardest and most tiresome task, followed by LR. RL and RR were the easiest and least tiresome tasks. For RR the participants used mostly parallel strategies, whereas for the other cases the used sequential strategies. It seems to be clear that right-oriented movements yielded better performance and subjective judgment than left-oriented ones.

In terms of strategies, an interesting observation is that *Sequential-Trans-Rot* was used just in 8% of the trials. On the other hand *Sequential-Rot-Trans* was used in 35% of the

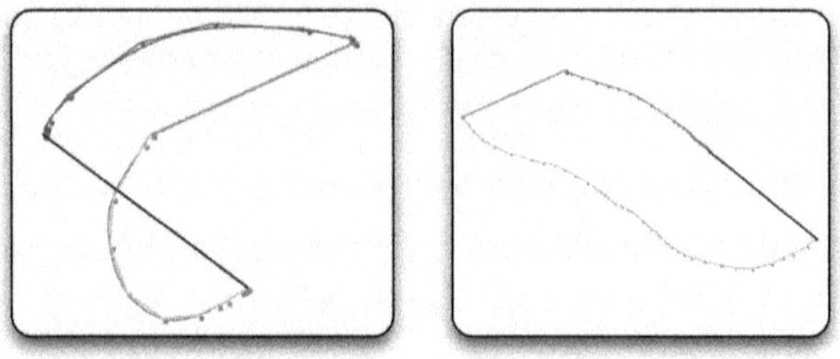

(a) *Parallel-Changed-Pivot* in a LR-movement (b) *Sequential-Rot-Trans-Rot* (RR)

Figure 3: Path of the unexpected used strategies.

trials. It seems to be preferable to rotate first. Looking at strategy switching, counter-directional movements showed much more switching. This could be an indication for the higher complexity of this kind of task so that participants are uncertain which strategy is the best one.

CONCLUSION AND FUTURE WORK

Our study explored the conditions under which a combined translation-rotation movement with a common 2-finger multitouch technique performs well and which execution strategies are used. We found two effects. First, right-oriented movements were performed faster and perceived as easier than left-oriented ones. Second, counter-directional combinations (translation right, rotation left, and vice versa) were found more tiresome by users and resulted in more strategy switches compared to equi-directional combinations.

These findings could guide interaction designers when deciding on placement of interactive elements, or make performance predictions about existing interfaces. Adaptable interfaces could use our results to automatically adjust interface elements, their parameters (rotation gain) or the view perspective to optimize conditions for translation-rotation.

How can these findings be used to adjust Fitts' law? We suggest to introduce a weights α that modifies the Index of Difficulty (ID) part of the formula (similar to [1]). α indicates the difficulty of movement direction with $\alpha > 1$ for left movements and $\alpha < 1$ for right movements.

$$MT = a + b\, log_2 \sqrt{\alpha \left(\left(\frac{A_t}{W_t}\right)^2 + \left(\frac{A_r}{W_r}\right)^2 \right)}$$

with A_t for translation distance and W_t for translation tolerance (A_r and W_r for rotation), assuming equal difficulty for translation and rotation. We intend to investigate the precise relationship between translation and rotation difficulty in the future.

Another future issue is the question of how handedness influences our findings which can only be held valid for right-handed people for the moment.

ACKNOWLEDGMENTS

We thank Angela Mahr for her help with some data analysis. Parts of this research have been carried out within the framework of the Excellence Cluster Multimodal Computing and Interaction (MMCI), sponsored by the German Research Foundation (DFG) and the Software Campus sponsored by the German Federal Ministry of Education and Research (BMBF), grant "01IS12050".

REFERENCES

1. Accot, J., and Zhai, S. Refining Fitts' law models for bivariate pointing. In *Proc. CHI*, ACM (2003), 193–200.
2. Bi, X., Li, Y., and Zhai, S. Ffitts law: Modeling finger touch with Fitts' law. In *Proc. CHI*, ACM (2013), 1363–1372.
3. Hancock, M., ten Cate, T., and Carpendale, S. Sticky tools: Full 6dof force-based interaction for multi-touch tables. In *Proc. ITS*, ACM (2009), 133–140.
4. Hoffmann, E. R., Drury, C. G., and Romanowski, C. J. Performance in one-, two- and three-dimensional terminal aiming tasks. *Ergonomics 54* (2011), 1175–85.
5. Hoggan, E., Williamson, J., Oulasvirta, A., Nacenta, M., Kristensson, P. O., and Lehtiö, A. Multi-touch rotation gestures: Performance and ergonomics. In *Proc. CHI*, ACM (2013), 3047–3050.
6. Kipp, M., and Nguyen, Q. Multitouch puppetry: Creating coordinated 3d motion for an articulated arm. In *Proc. ITS*, ACM (2010), 147–156.
7. Kruger, R., Carpendale, S., Scott, S. D., and Tang, A. Fluid integration of rotation and translation. In *Proc. CHI*, ACM (2005), 601–610.
8. MacKenzie, I. S., and Buxton, W. Extending Fitts' law to two-dimensional tasks. In *Proc. CHI*, ACM (1992), 219–226.
9. Martinet, A., Casiez, G., and Grisoni, L. The effect of dof separation in 3d manipulation tasks with multi-touch displays. In *Proc. VRST*, ACM (2010), 111–118.
10. Reisman, J. L., Davidson, P. L., and Han, J. Y. A screen-space formulation for 2d and 3d direct manipulation. In *Proc. UIST*, ACM (2009), 69–78.
11. Stoelen, M. F., and Akin, D. L. Assessment of Fitts' law for quantifying combined rotational and translational movements. *Human Factors 52* (2010), 63–77.
12. Veit, M., Capobianco, A., and Bechmann, D. Influence of degrees of freedom's manipulation on performances during orientation tasks in virtual reality environments. In *Proc. VRST*, ACM (2009), 51–58.
13. Wang, Y., MacKenzie, C. L., Summers, V. A., and Booth, K. S. The structure of object transportation and orientation in human-computer interaction. In *Proc. CHI*, ACM (1998), 312–319.
14. Zhai, S., and Milgram, P. Quantifying coordination in multiple DOF movement and its application to evaluating 6 DOF input devices. In *Proc. CHI*, ACM (1998), 320–327.

MotionMontage: A System to Annotate and Composite Motion Takes for 3D Animations

Ankit Gupta *, **Maneesh Agrawala** †, **Brian Curless** *, **and Michael Cohen** §
*University of Washington †University of California, Berkeley §Microsoft Research, Redmond
{ankit,curless}@cs.washington.edu maneesh@cs.berkeley.edu mcohen@microsoft.com

ABSTRACT
We present *MotionMontage*, a system for recording multiple motion takes of a rigid virtual object and compositing them together into a montage. Our system incorporates a Kinect-based performance capture setup that allows animators to create 3D animations by tracking the motion of a rigid physical object and mapping it in realtime onto a virtual object. The animator then temporally annotates the best parts of each take. MotionMontage merges the annotated motions into a single composite montage using a combination of dynamic time warping and optimization of a Semi-Markov Conditional Random Field. Our system also supports the creation of layered animations in which multiple objects are moving at the same time. To aid the animator in coordinating the motions of the objects we provide spatial markers which indicate the positions of previously recorded objects at user-specified points in time. We perform a user study to evaluate the perceived quality of the montages created with our system and find that viewers (including both the original animators and new viewers) generally prefer the animation montage to any individual take.

Author Keywords
Active visual feedback; Depth camera; Animation; Montage;

ACM Classification Keywords
H.5.2. Information Interfaces and Presentation: User Interfaces; I.3.6. Computer Graphics: Methodology and Techniques

INTRODUCTION
It is common practice in the movie industry to capture multiple takes of the same shot. Such re-takes allow the director to capture variations in the dialogue, and try out different positioning of the actors and camera angles. In performance-based 3D animation, a director may ask the animator to perform multiple takes in order to test different styles of motion (e.g. a more energetic performance versus a somber performance) and to find the most appropriate style for the shot.

CHI 2014, April 26 - May 01 2014, Toronto, ON, Canada.
Copyright 2014 ACM 978-1-4503-2473-1/14/04$15.00.
http://dx.doi.org/10.1145/2556288.2557218

Figure 1. A user working with the MotionMontage system to record multiple takes of a 3D animation.

In film, there are instances of a single shot requiring many takes; for example, one shot in the movie "The Shining" was reported to have needed 148 takes before the director, Stanley Kubrick, was satisfied [13].

Our work explores the concept of multiple takes for performance-based 3D animation. We focus on novice users who do not have any experience with high-end animation editing software such as Maya. We leverage 3D Puppetry [9] and DuploTrack [8], two recent Kinect-based performance capture systems that allow novices to easily create 3D animations by tracking the motions of rigid physical toys and mapping those motions in real-time onto virtual objects. However, one significant drawback of all such performance-based 3D animation systems is that they require the user to discard a take if any aspect of the motion was incorrect or undesired and then repeat the motion from scratch, hoping the next one will be just right. Yet, each take may contain some parts that are better than others even if no complete take is satisfactory. Since most novice users have little prior experience in creating animated stories, they may require a large number of takes to reach a desired animation, leading to fatigue and frustration in generating such re-takes.

We present *MotionMontage*, a system that allows novice animators to combine multiple takes into a desired result, called the *montage*. The animator records the motion of one object at a time, as shown in Figure 1. The takes may vary in style or trajectory of the motion. Our system allows the animator to annotate each take continuously through time based on their like or dislike of various parts of the take. The system then merges the best parts of each annotated take into a single composite montage using a combination of dynamic time warping and optimization of a Semi-Markov Conditional Random Field. The user can repeat the process for the same object to further refine the montage or to animate other objects.

Our system also allows animators to create layered animations in which multiple objects are moving at the same time. Although the animator must perform the motion of one object at a time, our system plays back all of the motions together. To aid the animator in coordinating the motions of the different objects, we provide spatial markers indicating the positions of previously recorded objects at user-specified points in time. The animator can place multiple markers for one or more objects to help plan the motion of the current object.

The key contribution of the paper is our technique for combining multiple takes of an object's motion into a motion montage using a simple annotation-based interface. We report on a formal user study that validates that the animation montage is generally perceived to be better than any individual take, both from the point of view of lay users who created the animations, as well as others who only viewed the animations.

RELATED WORK

Our system for combining multiple takes of performance-based 3D animations builds on several areas of prior work.

Performance-Based Animation Capture

In film, high-end motion capture systems are often used to capture performance-based animations. These systems are designed to accurately track human bodies or objects, but usually require complex hardware setups and/or attaching markers to the tracked objects [21, 6]. More recently, researchers have begun developing low-cost marker-less performance capture systems that work with video cameras or 3D cameras. Video puppetry [4] tracks the motions of paper cutouts using an off-the-shelf video camera and allows users to create 2.5D animations. Researchers have similarly used the Kinect 3D camera to track the human body [20], hands [20], as well as rigid physical objects [9, 8]. However all these methods require the user to repeatedly record motion takes till she is happy with one take. However the user may like different parts of different takes and there is no easy mechanism in these systems to intelligently combine takes based on user feedback. Our MotionMontage system presents a simple interface to annotate the recorded takes and uses a novel algorithm to combine these takes into the montage. Our system leverages the 3D object tracking algorithm of DuploTrack [8] as well as the performance-capture interface of 3D Puppetry [9] to record the takes.

Motion Synthesis and Blending

There have been several efforts to synthesize new motions by applying constraints or leveraging sets of motion capture recordings. Gleicher et al. [7] propose a formulation for synthesizing a motion sequence respecting a set of spacetime constraints. They pose it as a global optimization over a high-dimensional motion space. The optimization is non-convex and grows in complexity as the number of constraints increases. Our problem could also be modeled as this kind of global optimization with the spatial constraints coming from users' annotations and temporal constraints coming from an alignment method like Dynamic Time Warping [14]. Instead, we exploit the structure of our problem to propose a much simpler solution which leads to a one-dimensional optimization that can be solved in realtime. Further, unlike Gleicher et al. [7], our method is guaranteed to closely follow the original takes and the annotations.

Arikan et al. [3] use a database of motion sequences (captured using standard motion capture systems) to synthesize a new motion sequence. Each frame in the motion sequences is first tagged with actions like walk, run, jump etc. The user then specifies the desired action tags on a timeline and the system computes an optimal sequence of motion frames satisfying the tags. Their algorithm is based on representing the motion frames as a complete graph and then finding an optimal path in that graph using dynamic programming [12]. In our case, the motion sequences are semantically bound to a script and also vary in length of time. A complete motion graph would include a lot of transitions that violate the temporal and semantic structure of the sequences. Instead, we use temporal warping to align all the motion takes and then work with a graph that respects the temporal and semantic ordering of the frames. Further, the montage in our graph is non-Markovian in contrast to Arikan et al. due to an additional path constraint that we found necessary for editing the takes. Hence we propose a different solution in this paper based on performing an inference in a semi-Markov Conditional Random Field (CRF). We also visualize and describe these differences in the supplementary video.

Kovar et al. [11] look at the problem of blending multiple, annotated, human motion capture clips. They propose techniques for temporally and spatially aligning the clips and then apply a per-frame weighted average to blend them. We have found that taking weighted averages of existing takes gives undesirable results. For example, if a user happens to give high weight to two distinct motions that overlap in time, then the average at their overlap will not resemble either of the original motions. Instead, we focus on piecing together sections from the original takes, respecting user annotations to the extent possible, while finding good places to transition between the takes. Our work also differs in how we warp the user's annotations and unwarp the montage at the end. Our approach better preserves the original intent of the user and the original speeds of the recordings.

Interactive Compositing of Photos and Videos

Our work on compositing multiple motion takes is inspired by Agarwala et al.'s [2] *Interactive Digital Photomontage* sys-

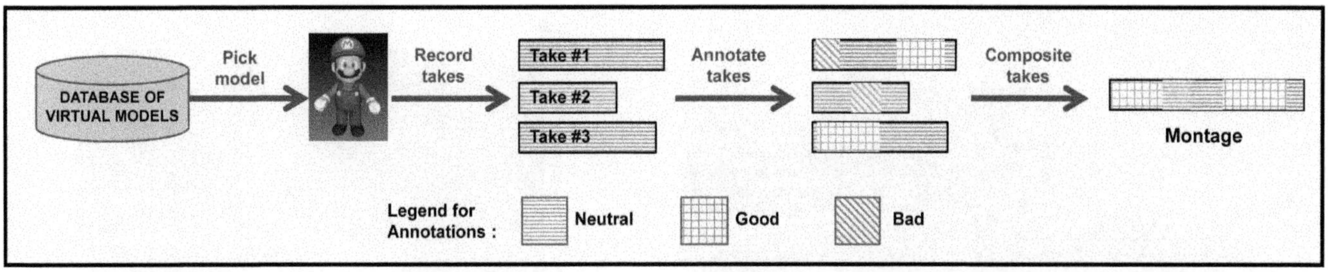

Figure 2. System functionality. The user chooses a virtual object from a pre-loaded database and records one or more motion takes for the object. He then annotates the takes and the system combines them into a montage, which can be longer than any of the original takes. The process can be repeated for subsequent objects.

tem for combining the best parts of a set of photographs. In that work, the user roughly annotates the parts of each photograph that are desired in the composite and the system uses a combination of graph-cut optimization [5] with gradient domain blending [15] to automatically generate the composite image. Ruegg et al.'s [17] *DuctTake* system extends the approach of Agarwala et al. [2] to compositing multiple videos. Our system similarly allows users to annotate the desired parts of each motion take, and automatically combines them into a motion montage. Since we are working with 3D motion data rather than images or video we use very different methods for optimizing the final composite.

SYSTEM SETUP AND INTERACTION

Our MotionMontage system allows the user to record 3D animations involving multiple objects, one at a time. We first discuss animating a single object, and then discuss differences in this procedure for animating multiple objects.

Figure 2 gives an overview of the system. The user first chooses a virtual object from a pre-loaded database. He then records one or more takes for the object, based on a script, by moving a physical object, called a *proxy*, in the 3D space in front of him. The tracked motion of the proxy is mapped in realtime onto a virtual object on a screen. The next step is to annotate each take. The user marks the parts of the take he likes and those he dislikes. The figure shows three discrete levels of annotations although there is a continuous scale. After annotating the takes, the system combines the best parts of each one into a montage animation.

The user can then repeat the process to animate additional virtual objects, and the system combines the montages of all objects to create the final animation. In the remainder of this section, we describe the details of the hardware setup and the various interactions described above. The supplementary video shows the effects of all these interactions in detail.

Hardware Setup

Figure 1 shows the hardware setup of our system. The interaction area is divided into two regions - a *Play area* and a *Like box*. The user acts out the story using the proxy in the Play area. The Like box is used as a slider by moving a green block inside it. The screen in front of the user shows the rendered virtual object in the tracked pose of the proxy. This hardware setup is based on Gupta et al.'s [8] DuploTrack system.

Setting up the Scene, Proxy and Virtual Objects

The user first chooses a virtual background scene. The background scenes are created by placing freely available 3D objects, downloaded from the internet. The play area on the table is mapped to an area in the background scene as in 3D Puppetry [9].

Unlike in 3D Puppetry, the user can use any rigid physical object as the proxy, as long as a model of the proxy is available. In our system, the user constructs the proxy with Duplo® blocks using the DuploTrack system [8], which then provides the model of the proxy to be used in tracking. The proxy can then be used to control the motion of a selected virtual object again chosen from a set of rigid virtual objects downloaded from online 3D databases. When recording a take, the system uses the color+depth image feed from a Kinect camera, segments it to remove the irrelevant pixels and performs real-time pose tracking of the proxy. The tracked motion is mapped one-to-one to the virtual object and rendered on the screen in front of the user in realtime. We have adapted the segmentation and tracking algorithms from DuploTrack [8]. There is a slight lag in the tracking currently, as seen in the supplementary video. In the future, this could be addressed by using a faster tracking algorithm, such as the one developed for 3D Puppetry [9], which uses both image features and 3D geometry to perform realtime object tracking.

Recording a Take

The user starts recording a take by pressing a key on the keyboard. He then acts out the motion with the proxy and ends the recording by pressing a key again. The user can record multiple takes with this process. These takes may vary in length. However, the assumption is that all the takes follow the same template story, and vary primarily in motion style. Arrow keys allow the user to scroll through the takes and review them.

Annotating the Takes

The user annotates each take to indicate their level of satisfaction with each part of each take. Annotations are made in realtime – while the take is playing the user moves a green Duplo block left or right in the Like box to indicate the degree of like or dislike for the corresponding part of the take. The Like box acts as a slider, ranging from -5 to $+5$, with the block serving as the thumb of the slider. We track the position of the block using the same tracking algorithm as for the proxy. The user annotates the whole take in one play-through.

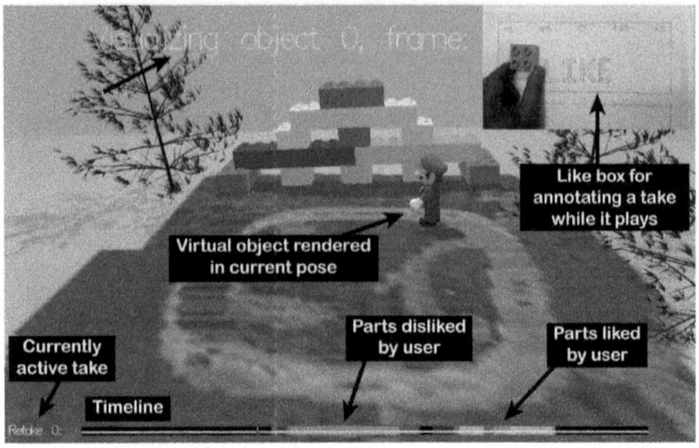

Figure 3. Annotating a take. While the take plays on the screen, the user moves a green block in the Like box (top right). The system localizes the position of the block and annotates the take with the corresponding slider value. Disliked and liked parts of the timeline are illustrated with red and green, respectively. The degree of like or dislike, is reflected by the brightness of the color.

Figure 3 shows a screenshot of the user annotating a take with this process.

When annotating a take, the user sees a motion, judges it, and then physically moves the green Duplo block. There is a natural time delay between the actual time of the motion and the placement of the green block in its intended position. To compensate for this lag, we shift the recorded annotations back in time by 0.3 seconds. This value is based on the average human reaction time [1] plus an empirically added delay for block movement. We found that this value worked well in practice for all our users.

The user repeats the annotation process for all the takes that he wants to composite for the montage. He then triggers the montage creation by pressing a key and the system generates the montage in realtime.

COMPOSITING THE TAKES INTO THE MONTAGE

In this section, we discuss the formulation for merging m annotated motion takes into a single motion recording called a *montage*. We denote the lth take as T_l and its annotation as a function a_l where $T_l(t)$ and $a_l(t)$ give the pose and annotation values respectively, at frame t. The like-dislike annotation values lie on a continuous scale of -5 (dislike) to 5 (like). We further decompose the pose $T_l(t)$ into a rotation quaternion and a translation vector, $T_l(t) = (q_l(t), x_l(t))$.

The goal is to create a montage that utilizes the best parts of each take without introducing noticeable artifacts due to frequent switching between takes. The latter constraints mean we should transition between takes where the different takes agree as much as possible, and we should also avoid frequently flipping from one take to another.

To determine the best set of switching points from one take to another, we first align all the takes in time. We temporally warp all the takes independently to match a single reference timeline. After warping, specific segments of each take are selected to create the montage on this timeline. Finally, we unwarp the timeline so that each segment will be played at

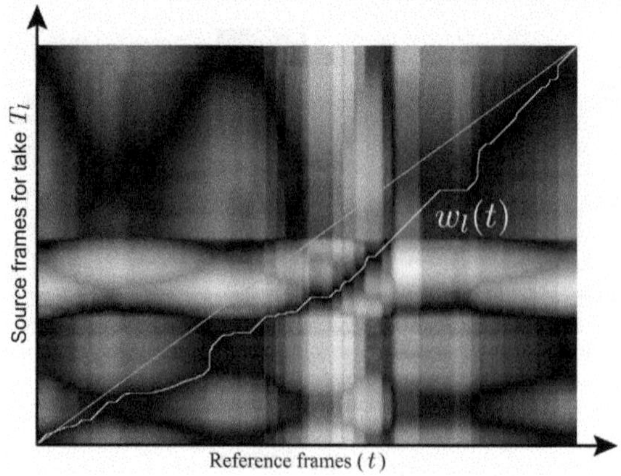

Figure 4. Dynamic Time Warping (DTW) finds an optimal warp function, $w_l(t)$, from the frames of the reference take, T_1 (x-axis), to the frames in the source take, T_l (y-axis). The values at each point in the quadrant represent the match of pose between the corresponding frames in the reference and the source takes. Darker color shows better pose match. The yellow path is optimal warp function computed by the algorithm while the green path shows the naive linear-scaling-based warp.

its original speed, and then blend between adjacent segments over short intervals to create the final montage. We note that unwarping the timeline is important to respect the user's intentions with respect to timing.

Temporal Warp of the Takes

We use a Dynamic Time Warping (DTW) [14] algorithm to align all the takes in time. For simplicity, we arbitrarily choose the first take as the reference, and warp all other takes to its timeline.

Formally, we consider take T_1 to be the *reference* take and then compute a monotonically increasing function w_l from the reference take's timeline to the timeline of each *source* take T_l. We can write each warp function w_l as a mapping,

$$w_l : \{1, ..., ||T_1||\} \rightarrow \{1, ..., ||T_l||\} \quad (1)$$

which is monotonically increasing,

$$t_1 > t_2 \Rightarrow w_l(t_1) \geq w_l(t_2) \quad (2)$$

and matches the start and end frames of reference and source,

$$w_l(1) = 1 \text{ and } w_l(||T_1||) = ||T_l|| \quad (3)$$

We solve for an optimal w_l by minimizing the cost of bringing each reference frame into alignment with a source frame summed over all frames t:

$$w_l^* = \underset{w_l}{\operatorname{argmin}} \sum_t C_{\text{match}}\left(T_1(t), T_l(w_l(t)) \right) \quad (4)$$

The matching cost C_{match} measures the difference between two poses. For two poses $A_1 = (q_1, x_1)$ and $A_2 = (q_2, x_2)$:

$$C_{\text{match}}(A_1, A_2) = ||q_1 - q_2||_2 + \lambda||x_1 - x_2||_2 \quad (5)$$

We set λ to 2.5, based on experimentation.

Figure 4 shows a visualization of the matching cost and the optimal w_l. We use the standard DTW algorithm [14] to solve this problem. Graphically, it finds a monotonically increasing path that tries to stay in the darker regions of the diagram in Figure 4. The resulting path, $w_l(t)$ lets us warp $T_l(t)$ to a new warped take, $T'_l(t) = T_l(w_l(t))$ that follows the reference timeline.

We also need to warp the respective annotations to the reference timeline. This requires special care. Consider the case where $w_l(t)$ is constant for a duration of $N_{w_l(t)}$ frames. This corresponds to a horizontal, flat region of the curve in Figure 4. In this case, the annotation $a_l(w_l(t))$, which applies to only one frame in the source take, will have an influence over $N_{w_l(t)}$ frames in the warped space. As a result, during later optimization over the warped timeline (described in the next section), this annotation will have extra influence because it is artificially sustained by the warp. In this case, we should down-weight the annotation by $1/N_{w_l(t)}$ for each frame in the set that maps to $w_l(t)$.

Conversely, where the slope of $w_l(t)$ is steep, the warped sequence can skip from one source frame to a distant next source frame when moving from frame t to $t+1$ in the reference timeline and thereby skip past all source annotations in between. To ensure that the annotations on such skipped influence on the final result we add all of their influences together and store the sum as the warped annotation.

Formally, we compute the warped annotations as follows:

$$a'_l(t) = \begin{cases} \sum_{t'=w_l(t)}^{w_l(t+1)-1} a_l(t'), & \text{if } w_l(t+1) - w_l(t) > 0 \\ \frac{1}{N_{w_l(t)}} a_l(w_l(t)), & \text{if } w_l(t+1) = w_l(t) \end{cases} \tag{6}$$

Another way of thinking about this is that we are (intelligently) scaling the annotation values so that the summation of the warped annotations $a'_l(t)$ over $||T_1||$ frames of the reference timeline is the same as the summation of the unwarped annotations $a_l(t)$ over $||T_l||$ frames of the (unwarped) source timeline. We have found this scaling to significantly improve the quality of results over naively warping the annotation functions.

Merging the Takes

We now have m warped, annotated takes T'_l's, each comprised of $n = ||T_1||$ frames. We first compute a warped montage, M', such that each frame of the montage comes from a corresponding frame in one of the m takes. M' can be denoted in shorthand as $\{l_1, l_2 ... l_n\}$ where $l_t \in \{1, 2...m\}$ is the take selected for time $t \in \{1, 2...n\}$. (Strictly speaking, the montage is a sequence of poses $\{T'_{l_1}(1), T'_{l_2}(2), ...T'_{l_n}(n)\}$.) We now define the overall cost function for a montage:

$$C_T(M') = \sum_{t=1}^{n} C_d(t, l_t) + \mu \sum_{t=1}^{n-1} C_s(t, l_t, l_{t+1}) \tag{7}$$

The total cost C_T is the sum of two terms: a data cost, C_d, and a smoothness cost C_s. We set $\mu = 100$ based on experimentation.

C_d is the cost of frame t coming from take l_t and is based on the annotation functions, where a higher annotation rating translates to lower cost. Specifically, for a given frame t and take l we define this cost to be:

$$C_d(t, l) = -a'_l(t) \tag{8}$$

The smoothness cost C_s favors temporal coherence by discouraging transitions between takes in regions where their poses are dissimilar. At frame t, it is computed by considering time windows in the takes T_{l_t} and $T_{l_{t+1}}$, centered around the unwarped location of t, and summing up the cost of matching the poses in those windows. Specifically, given frame t and given two takes l and k, we define the cost to be:

$$C_s(t, l, k) = \sum_{h \in \mathcal{W}} C_{\text{match}}\left(T_l(w_l(t) + h),\, T_k(w_k(t+1) + h - 1)\right) \tag{9}$$

Note that we are comparing poses of the unwarped takes, as the final composite will be comprised of sequences of unwarped takes between which we want smooth transitions. We set the window $\mathcal{W}$ to the range $[-7, ..., 7]$, suitably truncated when the window goes out of bounds in either of the two takes. C_{match} is the same cost function as in Equation 5. Here we choose $\lambda = 0.8$ based on experimentation.

We can solve for the optimal warped montage, M'^*, by minimizing the total cost:

$$M'^* = \underset{M'}{\operatorname{argmin}}\, C_T(M') \tag{10}$$

This formulation is equivalent to an inference problem over a Markov chain, which can be solved exactly using the dynamic-programming-based Max-Sum algorithm [10].

However, we have found that optimizing this objective, despite the smoothness term, can occasionally lead to sections of the montage that have rapid, frequent flipping between annotated takes. To address this problem, we impose a minimum length on contiguous frames with the same label in the montage.

Specifically, we can rewrite the warped montage M' as a sequence of subsequences, $\{M'_1, M'_2, ...\}$, such that each subsequence of frames or *segment* $M'_j = \{l, l, ..., l\}$ comes from a single take l. We then impose the constraint that the length of each segment M'_j must be greater than a threshold d, set to 60 frames in our experiments. We hereon refer to this constraint as the *Segment Length Constraint* and discuss its quantitative and qualitative effect in the results of the user study.

The formulation for the optimal montage M'^* now becomes,

$$M'^* = \underset{M'}{\operatorname{argmin}}\, C_T(M') \tag{11}$$

$$s.t. \quad ||M'_j|| > d, \quad \forall j \tag{12}$$

This formulation is equivalent to a Semi-Markov Conditional Random field that can be solved exactly with another dynamic-programming-based algorithm [18]. The computational complexity of the algorithm is $O(n^2 m^2)$ where again n is the number of frames and m is the number of takes.

Unwarping the Montage

We now have an optimal warped montage M' of length n frames where the frames come from the warped takes. We next unwarp the montage to preserve the original speed at which the takes were recorded. We consider the span of frames for each segment M'_j in the warped montage and replace it with the corresponding interval of frames, M_j from the original take. Each corresponding interval is determined by the corresponding mapping function w_l. Thus, the unwarped montage, M, is a sequence of intervals of poses from the original takes T_l's.

Motion Blending

As a last step, we blend the poses around the transitions between takes in M to ensure temporal coherence. We consider a window of length 15 frames centered at each transition point and blend the poses using a linear weighting scheme. For blending, we use linear interpolation of the translation vectors and spherical linear interpolation of the rotation quaternions [19].

CREATING MONTAGES FOR MORE THAN ONE OBJECT

When animating more than one object, the user can record the takes of the first object at his preferred speed. However, the motion of any new object typically have to be synchronized with those of a previous object. Hence after recording the first object, the motions of all previous objects are played in realtime on-screen as the new object's motion is recorded. This approach is similar to the layered animation recording approach of 3D Puppetry [9]. In the end, all the takes for new objects are of the same length. They can then be annotated and composited into the montage by the same process as described above, skipping the time warping stage.

Recording motion for a current object while the previously recorded motions of other objects play on the screen can be difficult since the user has to plan the current object's motion based on where other objects will be in future. For example, if the two objects are supposed to touch each other, they may end up passing by each other without touching or perhaps intersecting each other.

We provide *spatial markers* to alleviate this problem. The user adds a spatial marker for an object by navigating to a frame in the timeline of the object's montage and pressing a key. The spatial marker appears as a grey version of the object in that pose of the montage. It is also marked on the timeline as a pink bar. Figure 5 shows the usage of spatial markers in a sample script. Please see the supplementary video to see the use of the markers in action. To avoid visual clutter, we do not allow two markers for the same object to be placed within 60 frames of each other. We chose this empirically. The user can remove the markers by clicking on them and pressing a key. Spatial markers can serve as a sparsely sampled motion trail for an object where the user chooses the sampling.

SYSTEM PERFORMANCE

The system runs in realtime on a desktop PC with two 6-core 3.33GHz Xeon processors and uses at most 400MB of RAM. To achieve this performance, the implementation is

Figure 5. Mario (left, with red hat) is supposed to hit the Monster's head (right) in the script. The user adds a spatial marker for the Monster's position at the supposed time of the hit (3D replica in grey) to help plan Marios motion. The markers position in time is shown as a pink bar on the timeline.

multithreaded with separate threads for processing the camera feed, tracking and rendering. The algorithm for merging the takes usually operates in realtime. In our experiments, the length of a take is on the order of a few thousand frames (few minutes at 30fps) and the typical number of takes on is about 10. Computing a montage at this scale takes under a second.

USER STUDY: SINGLE OBJECT MONTAGE

MotionMontage combines takes in a way that tries to preserve the parts most liked by the animator and discard the disliked parts, while keeping the whole animation temporally coherent. We conducted a user study to understand the performance of the system in two ways. First, we observed users creating and annotating the original takes. Second, we evaluated whether the montage is indeed perceived to be better than the original takes. We also analyzed the effect of the Segment Length Constraint in the animators' montages.

Phase 1: Creating animations

The goal in the first phase was to familiarize the participants with using the system, then have them record takes and create a montage for a story script. We call the participants of this phase the *animators*.

Introduction to System

The animators were first given an introduction to the hardware setup and the capabilities of the system. We then demonstrated the process of recording takes, annotating them, and creating a montage for a simple script –

Mario

"Mario is happily walking around the park. He first takes a round in a clockwise direction and then turns back and takes a round in an anti-clockwise direction."

Figure 6 shows a screenshot of this story. After the demo, the animators were asked to practice using the system by acting out this script, thus familiarizing themselves with the system.

Task Design

After the demo, we asked the animators to record three takes for the following script –

Figure 6. A screenshot of the demo script - *Mario*.

Figure 7. A screenshot of the script - *Soldier takes a Break*.

Soldier takes a Break

"A soldier is guarding a castle by marching in front of it, back and forth. "This is so boring", he thinks. The weather is nice and he decides to take a walk around the castle's pathway. He looks around to see if anybody is watching him. Nobody else is there, so he starts his casual stroll. Slowly he becomes more and more carefree. Jumping around with joy, he does not notice a banana peel that is lying on his path. He steps on the banana peel, slips and falls down. He gets up slowly with effort and limps towards back to the castle. The monotonous routine starts again, guarding the castle by marching in front of it, back and forth, now with a limp. He finds it very hard to walk now and stops marching after reaching the other end."

Figure 7 shows a screenshot of this script. The animators were shown a sample path of the soldier and the goal was to record takes which roughly followed this path, while acting out the story script. We encouraged participants to try different motion styles on each take to better express the script. After recording the takes, the participants first viewed each take and then annotated them in a second viewing. The system used the annotated takes to create a montage. To conclude, the animators filled out a short questionnaire about their experience with the system.

Participants

Twenty participants (ten female, ten male, ages 20 to 30) volunteered to create animations with our system. None of them had prior 3D animation experience. The study took about one hour for each participant. At the end of this phase, we had 3 takes and 1 montage for each of the 20 animators.

Phase 2: Comparing animations.

A week after the first phase we ran the second phase of the experiment. The goal in phase 2 was to compare the quality of the animations recorded in the first phase. We refer to the participants in this phase as *scorers*. Note that some of the scorers were also the animators in the first phase.

Task Design

We asked the scorers to perform binary comparisons between a montage and one of its takes recorded by a randomly chosen set of 10 animators. The scorers first read the script which the animators had acted out. In each comparison, the scorer watched one of the three takes and the montage in a random order. The scorer then selected the animation they would have preferred if they were the script's director. Note that scorers only rated one of the animator's takes against the montage instead of ranking all 3 takes and the montage. We designed the task this way to reduce visual fatigue for the scorer. If a scorer was also an animator in Phase 1, we made sure that he did not do a binary comparison for his own animations.

In addition, if the scorer was also one of the animators, we added a second task. We asked them to rank all four animations (3 takes and 1 montage) that they created, ranking them from 1 to 4 (1 being the best) after watching them in a random order. This approach gave us a complete ranking of the animations from the animator's own perspective.

Participants

42 participants (21 female, 21 male, ages 20 to 30) volunteered for this phase. Of these, 20 were the animators from Phase 1. Each scorer's study lasted for about 50 minutes. At the end of the phase, we had 420 comparison samples, or 7 samples per comparison between a take and a montage for each animator. Additionally, we had each animator's ranking of their own takes and resulting montage.

Results

We analyze the results of the experiment in four ways. First, we present a quantitative analysis of the perceived quality of the montages from the animators' perspectives. Second, we present a similar analysis for the perceived quality of the montages from scorers' perspectives. Third, we present some qualitative feedback from the animators about their experience with the system. Finally, we present a brief discussion about the effect of the Segment Length Constraint on the montages.

Animators' perspective

We analyze animators' rankings of their own animations (Take 1, Take 2, Take 3, Montage). Figure 8 shows the that the average rank of the montage, averaged over all the animators, is much better than any of the three takes. We run a Friedman test with *rank* as an ordinal variable and *animation* as a nominal variable. *animation* is found to have a statistically significant impact on *rank*, $\chi^2(df = 3, N = 20) = 26.88, p < 0.0001$. Thus, we can conclude that the animators

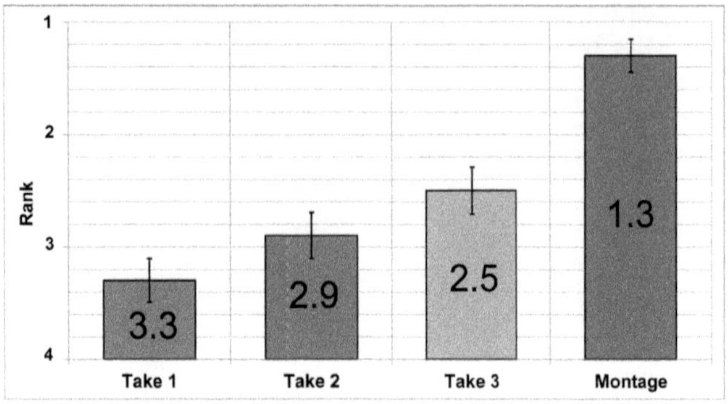

Figure 8. Average ranks for the takes (shown in the order originally recorded) and the resulting montage, as reported by animators evaluating their own work, averaged over the animators.

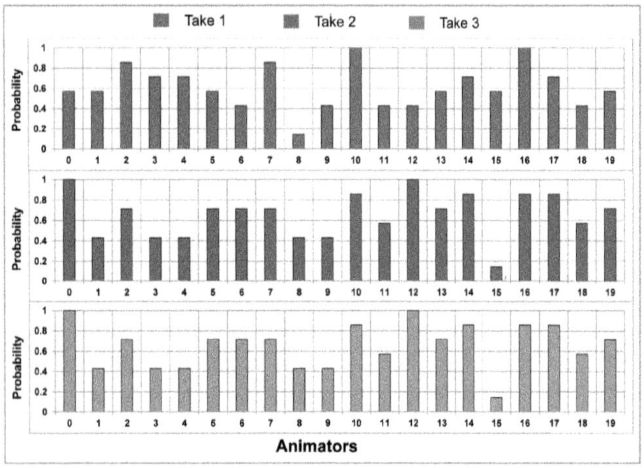

Figure 9. Probability that montage is better than a take for animators.

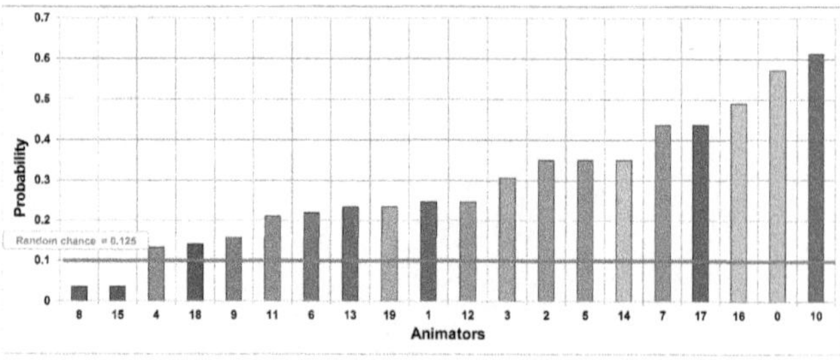

Figure 10. Probability that montage is better than all the takes for animators. The red line is the probability for random chance, 0.125.

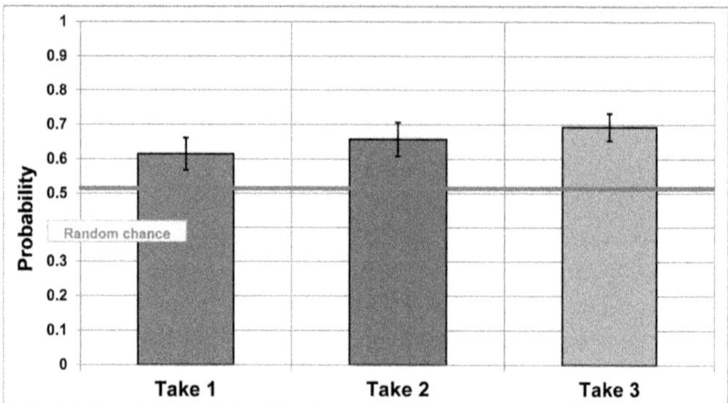

Figure 11. Probability that montage is better than a take (in the order they were recorded).

significantly prefer their montages to any of their individual takes.

Scorers' perspective

Next, we analyze how scorers rate other people's animations, to see if they generally prefer montages to original takes. We first compute how frequently the montage is perceived to be better than an individual take. The proportion of the scorers who voted for the montage vs. each of the 60 takes is shown in Figure 9. For further analysis, we denote the fraction of the ratings that chose the montage for animator i better than take j as m_{ij}, i.e., if $m_{ij} = 1.0$ then all 7 scorers rated the montage better, and a score of 0 has the opposite meaning.

We test three hypotheses.

H1. The average probability of an animator's montage being better than a take is greater than random chance, i.e., $\mu(m_{ij}) > 0.5$. A one-tailed single sample t-test indicates that the probability of the montage being better ($\mu = 0.6457$, $\sigma = 0.133$) is significantly greater than 0.5 ($t(19) = 5.18$, $p < 0.0001$).

We note that this t-test may be biased by the fact that we had only 7 binary samples to compute each m_{ij}. Hence we also test if the outcome of a binary comparison between the montage and a take is random. A chi-squared test over the set of all 420 binary comparisons indicates that the chance of montage being better than a take is not random ($p < 0.0001$).

H2. The probability of the montage being better than all the three takes for an animator is greater than random chance. This probability for an animator i is given by $(m_{i1} * m_{i2} * m_{i3})$, and we denote it as b_i. Thus the hypothesis can be restated as $\mu(b_i) > 0.125$. Figure 10 shows the probabilities b_i's for individual users. For all but 2 of the animators, the probability is higher than random chance. We first use a *goodness of fit* test and confirm that the b_i's follow a normal distribution. Then we perform a one-tailed single sample t-test; the results of this test indicate that the probability of the montage being better than all the takes ($\mu = 0.299$, $\sigma = 0.126$) is significantly greater than 0.125 ($t(19) = 4.555$, $p < 0.0002$).

H3. The probability of the montage being rated better than an individual take significantly depends on the order of the takes, i.e. m_{ij} is related to j. Figure 11 shows the average probability and standard errors of the montage being better than individual takes averaged over animators. We conduct a mixed-model analysis with take j as the fixed effect, user i as random effect and probability m_{ij} as the observed variable. The analysis indicates that there is no significant effect of the order of take on the probability of montage being better, ($F(2, 38) = 0.8277, p = 0.4448$). We also validate the correctness of this analysis by running a *goodness of fit* test on the residuals and verify that they are indeed normally distributed. Hence we reject this hypothesis.

Qualitative feedback

All the users said that they liked the capability of recording multiple takes for the story, since they did not have any prior animation experience and wanted to try out different styles. They were excited about the ability to annotate different parts of the takes and that the system could combine the takes for them. A few users suggested that the method of annotations required patience as they had to watch whole animations while annotating them. Further, they had to mentally remember the different parts from takes that they wanted to appear in the montage and annotate the takes accordingly. This leads to an interesting future direction of research of developing ways to summarize and visualize the takes together.

Effect of the Segment Length Constraint

The Segment Length Constraint in computing the montage ensures that the minimum length of a contiguous set of frames taken from a take must exceed a minimum threshold. This threshold was empirically chosen to be 60 frames, i.e., a time duration of 2 seconds. The goal of this constraint was to prevent quick take transitions in the montage.

For half the animators, the optimized montage contained no quick transitions even without the constraint. For the other half, adding the constraint avoids such segments but results in a montage with a slightly higher cost. However, the increase in the cost was found to be less than 1% in all the 10 cases. Hence the proposed algorithm is able to enforce the Segment Length Constraint without significant penalty.

Results summary and discussion

The results suggest that both the animators and the scorers significantly preferred montages. It is interesting to note that the average rank assigned by the animator is affected by the order in which takes were recorded. The rank is better for a take that was recorded later. We speculate that the animators, who were creating animations for the first time, grew better at acting out stylized motions with subsequent takes. However, the non-animator scorers' preference for the montage over the takes does not depend on their order to a statistically significant degree. This result does not support the conclusion that overall animation quality increases as animators gain more experience. We do not have a hypothesis for this difference and leave the understanding of visual or psychological perception in such animations to future work.

CONCLUSION AND FUTURE WORK

We have presented a system, MotionMontage, which allows users to record 3D animations involving multiple objects, one object at a time. The user can experiment with different motion styles and trajectories and record multiple takes for each object. The system allows the user to temporally annotate each take to indicate which parts of which takes are considered better or worse. The system then uses a novel formulation to combine these annotated takes into a montage. The same process can be performed sequentially for all the objects in the animation. The recording of takes for more than one object is handled via the traditional layered animation approach. We provide spatial markers to help the user see the recorded motions of other objects while recording the current object's motion.

We also reported on a user study to qualitatively and quantitatively measure the efficacy of MotionMontage from the animators' and the scorers' perspectives. The results indicate that the montage is significantly preferred over the original takes by both. In the supplementary video, we also show some multi-object animations created by a few users. The users found the system intuitive and indicated that the spatial markers helped them to record object interactions better in the animation.

We have identified a few directions for future work.

Better animation recording setup.

The users of our system suggested demarcating the physical volume of play area. This would prevent a user from moving the controller outside the volume which leads to loss of tracking. In addition, the current system uses a standard (and cumbersome) mouse-driven interface to adjust the camera's viewpoint on the screen; however, we could instead use a tracked object to adjust the camera.

Currently, a big challenge while recording the animations is to correctly handle the interactions between the animated object with the virtual scene props and with previously animated objects. The spatial markers can help to some extent, but the lack of physical proxies for other objects makes it hard. Allowing users to use physical proxies or automatically inferring the user's intent from the recording can alleviate this challenge and suggests an interesting avenue for future work.

To further improve the richness of the 3D animation, we are interested in enabling articulated 3D characters in the animation. Difficulties in mapping the articulation of physical objects to a character's motion will require new, intuitive puppetry interfaces.

The current interaction design of MotionMontage can be extended to a multi-modal interface involving voice, gestures, multiple physical controller objects, etc. Using multiple modalities may provide more natural interfaces but may make the system more complex to use. In the future we would like to explore this multi-modal interaction space and try to find a good trade-off between user empowerment and intuitive, easy-to-use interfaces for creating 3D animations.

Exploration of the annotation setup.

We enabled the users to annotate a recording easily by manipulating a physical slider while the recording played in realtime. The users may find it hard to keep up with the realtime pace of the recording and hence we added a lag in the annotations based on the human reaction time. However, this is just a heuristic. There can still be parts of the recording where the annotations are slightly delayed or ahead in time, specially in case of fast paced recorded motion. Our algorithm creates a montage which transitions smoothly between the takes while respecting these rough annotations. We also tried a keyboard and mouse-based interface which allowed users to select parts of different takes, play the selected parts, and then annotate them. This interface gives more control to the user and hence more accurate annotations. However, this process can become tedious for lay users. Hence we chose a simpler interface that results in rough annotations and focused more attention on developing an algorithm which combines these roughly annotated takes into the montage. In the future, it will be interesting to study the design of different annotation interfaces and their effect on the montage.

Enable audio recordings.
We would like to add the capability of recording audio voiceovers in the system. Currently, audio can be added afterward using standard audio-video processing software. However, some users indicated that they were actually humming and speaking in their mind while acting out the story, and would have liked to record audio while animating. Rubin et al. [16] have recently developed tools for editing and merging multiple audio takes of a story; it would be interesting to combine their tools with our motion editing interface.

In sum, we have presented a novel system that allows novice users to explore their creativity through the medium of 3D animated stories. We learned from our user studies that such animation creation systems can empower the user while being intuitive, with easy-to-use interfaces. We believe that MotionMontage is a small step in this direction and hope that our work motivates more researchers to explore this domain.

REFERENCES

1. Human benchmark - reaction time statistics. www.humanbenchmark.com/tests/reactiontime.
2. Agarwala, A., Dontcheva, M., Agrawala, M., Drucker, S., Colburn, A., Curless, B., Salesin, D., and Cohen, M. Interactive digital photomontage. In *ACM SIGGRAPH 2004 Papers*, SIGGRAPH '04, ACM (New York, NY, USA, 2004), 294–302.
3. Arikan, O., Forsyth, D. A., and O'Brien, J. F. Motion synthesis from annotations. *ACM Trans. Graph. 22*, 3 (July 2003), 402–408.
4. Barnes, C., Jacobs, D. E., Sanders, J., Goldman, D. B., Rusinkiewicz, S., Finkelstein, A., and Agrawala, M. Video puppetry: a performative interface for cutout animation. In *ACM SIGGRAPH Asia 2008 papers*, SIGGRAPH Asia '08, ACM (New York, NY, USA, 2008), 124:1–124:9.
5. Boykov, Y., Veksler, O., and Zabih, R. Fast approximate energy minimization via graph cuts. *IEEE Trans. Pattern Anal. Mach. Intell. 23*, 11 (Nov. 2001), 1222–1239.
6. Dontcheva, M., Yngve, G., and Popović, Z. Layered acting for character animation. In *ACM SIGGRAPH 2003 Papers*, SIGGRAPH '03, ACM (New York, NY, USA, 2003), 409–416.
7. Gleicher, M. Motion editing with spacetime constraints. In *Proceedings of the 1997 symposium on Interactive 3D graphics*, I3D '97, ACM (New York, NY, USA, 1997), 139–ff.
8. Gupta, A., Fox, D., Curless, B., and Cohen, M. Duplotrack: a real-time system for authoring and guiding duplo block assembly. In *Proceedings of the 25th annual ACM symposium on User interface software and technology*, UIST '12, ACM (New York, NY, USA, 2012), 389–402.
9. Held, R., Gupta, A., Curless, B., and Agrawala, M. 3d-puppetry: a kinect-based interface for 3d animation. In *Proceedings of the 25th annual ACM symposium on User interface software and technology*, UIST '12, ACM (New York, NY, USA, 2012), 423–434.
10. Koller, D., and Friedman, N. *Probabilistic Graphical Models: Principles and Techniques*. MIT Press, 2009.
11. Kovar, L., and Gleicher, M. Flexible automatic motion blending with registration curves. In *Proceedings of the 2003 ACM SIGGRAPH/Eurographics symposium on Computer animation*, SCA '03, Eurographics Association (Aire-la-Ville, Switzerland, Switzerland, 2003), 214–224.
12. Kovar, L., Gleicher, M., and Pighin, F. Motion graphs. In *Proceedings of the 29th annual conference on Computer graphics and interactive techniques*, SIGGRAPH '02, ACM (New York, NY, USA, 2002), 473–482.
13. LoBrutto, V. Stanley kubrick: a biography. Da Capo Press, Incorporated (1999), page 430.
14. Myers, C. S., and Rabiner, L. R. Comparative Study of Several Dynamic Time-Warping Algorithms for Connected-Word Recognition. *The Bell System Technical Journal 60*, 7 (1981).
15. Pérez, P., Gangnet, M., and Blake, A. Poisson image editing. In *ACM SIGGRAPH 2003 Papers*, SIGGRAPH '03, ACM (New York, NY, USA, 2003), 313–318.
16. Rubin, S., Berthouzoz, F., Mysore, G. J., Li, W., and Agrawala, M. Content-based tools for editing audio stories. In *Proceedings of the 26th annual ACM symposium on User interface software and technology*, ACM (2013), 113–122.
17. Ruegg, J., Wang, O., Smolic, A., Gross, M., Auzinger, T., Guthe, M., and Jeschke, S. Ducttake: Spatiotemporal video compositing. *Computer Graphics Forum (Proceedings of EUROGRAPHICS 2013) 32*, 2 (May 2013).
18. Sarawagi, S., and Cohen, W. W. Semi-markov conditional random fields for information extraction. In *In Advances in Neural Information Processing Systems 17* (2004), 1185–1192.
19. Shoemake, K. Animating rotation with quaternion curves. In *Proceedings of the 12th annual conference on Computer graphics and interactive techniques*, SIGGRAPH '85, ACM (New York, NY, USA, 1985), 245–254.
20. Shotton, J., Fitzgibbon, A., Cook, M., Sharp, T., Finocchio, M., Moore, R., Kipman, A., and Blake, A. Real-time human pose recognition in parts from single depth images. In *Proceedings of the 2011 IEEE Conference on Computer Vision and Pattern Recognition*, CVPR '11, IEEE Computer Society (Washington, DC, USA, 2011), 1297–1304.
21. Sturman, D. J. Computer puppetry. *IEEE Comput. Graph. Appl. 18*, 1 (Jan. 1998), 38–45.

History Assisted View Authoring for 3D Models

Hsiang-Ting Chen[1,2], Tovi Grossman[1], Li-Yi Wei[3], Ryan Schmidt[1], Björn Hartmann[4], George Fitzmaurice[1], and Maneesh Agrawala[4]
[1]Autodesk Research
[2]The University of Tokyo / JST ERATO Igarashi Design Interface Project
[3]The University of Hong Kong [4]University of California, Berkeley

ABSTRACT
3D modelers often wish to showcase their models for sharing or review purposes. This may consist of generating static viewpoints of the model or authoring animated fly-throughs. Manually creating such views is often tedious and few automatic methods are designed to interactively assist the modelers with the view authoring process. We present a view authoring assistance system that supports the creation of informative view points, view paths, and view surfaces, allowing modelers to author the interactive navigation experience of a model. The key concept of our implementation is to analyze the model's workflow history, to infer important regions of the model and representative viewpoints of those areas. An evaluation indicated that the viewpoints generated by our algorithm are comparable to those manually selected by the modeler. In addition, participants of a user study found our system easy to use and effective for authoring viewpoint summaries.

Author Keywords
3D model; editing history; viewpoint authoring

ACM Classification Keywords
H.5.2 User Interfaces: Interaction Styles

INTRODUCTION
Recent years have witnessed significant progress in 3D modeling and 3D printing. As the technologies are becoming essential to the industries and even people's daily life, the demand of high quality 3D models also increases rapidly. This trend has resulted in a variety of 3D model libraries and websites where 3D modelers can share models they created.

Understanding each model through 3D navigation can be a time-consuming and confusing experience. Thus, to achieve efficient browsing of large 3D model data sets, it is necessary to have visual summaries that can concisely show important aspects of the 3D models. An effective visual summary usually consists of static viewpoints and animated fly-throughs of the model. However, manually creating such views can be a long and tedious process.

CHI 2014, April 26 - May 01 2014, Toronto, ON, Canada

ACM 978-1-4503-2473-1/14/04...$15.00.
http://dx.doi.org/10.1145/2556288.2557009

As a result, automatic viewpoint selection [10, 14] has been an active area of research in the Computer Graphics community. However, the associated algorithms that have been developed typically consider only the final geometric models. Such algorithms may ignore features of the model that an author spent a particular amount of effort on during

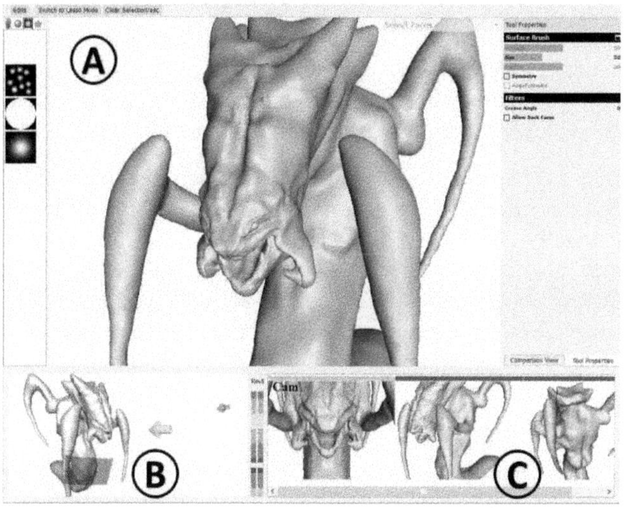

Figure 1. The proposed view authoring environment integrated in a 3D modeling software: (A) the main modeling window, (B) the authoring panel visualizing authored views in the spatial context, and (C) the navigation panel showing the authored views in the temporal sequence.

the modeling process. Furthermore, it is not clear how to integrate these automatic techniques into a modeler's view authoring process in practice.

Alternatively, the HCI literature has investigated techniques for navigating along constrained view paths and view surfaces to obtain effective overviews of 3D models [1, 2]. However, these systems require predefined constrained views. The authoring of such views, either manually or automatically, remains an open problem.

Recent work has demonstrated the utility of instrumenting a 3D modeling environment for visualizing editing operations and model differences [6, 7]. Guided by a set of observations and interviews, we hypothesize that enhancing such instrumentation to also include the camera history could be useful for authoring viewpoint summaries. In particular, the workflows used to create a model may be indicative of the important parts of the models and the viewpoints from which these important parts should be viewed. By recording and analyzing these workflows, it may be possible to derive effective summary views.

In this paper, we contribute a history assisted view authoring and navigation system for 3D modelers (Figure 1). Our system stores a model's editing and viewpoint history along with discrete versions of that model. By analyzing the history and the model, our system can suggest informative view points, animated view paths and view surfaces of the selected model region. These can be used for automatic visual summaries of 3D objects or in our interactive view authoring environment where modelers can select and customize such summaries.

Our system produces an interactive summary of the 3D model, allowing viewers to easily navigate between authored views and along view paths or surfaces, and even compare different versions from the model's revision history. Alternatively, our system can also automatically arrange the authored views into user-defined layout templates for a static brochure or catalogue-like display.

In a first study, we compare the viewpoints generated by our algorithm to those generated by Secord et al [12], and to manually created views by 3D modelers. The results show that our algorithm selects viewpoints with comparable quality to manual selection. In a second qualitative user study of our interactive system, participants expressed high enthusiasm and a desire to incorporate the system into their daily workflows.

PREVIOUS WORK

3D Navigation

Many existing techniques have attempted to simplify 3D navigation, which is often a challenge for inexperienced users [1, 2]. ShowMotion [2] replaces static camera bookmarks with pre-authored animated shots, and StyleCam [1] supports constrained navigation along pre-authored camera paths. Both works greatly improve users' viewing experience of a 3D model. However, these systems only consider the viewers of the 3D model and it is unclear how a modeler can author the required views. For example, ShowMotion [2] assumes pre-authored viewing motions and StyleCam [1] pre-authored surfaces and paths. Our work bridges the gap by assisting the modeler to author such viewpoints, view paths, and view surfaces.

3D Viewpoint Selection

At the core of our system is the viewpoint selection algorithm. Previous work [10, 14] infers the importance of viewpoints based on the visible geometric attributes of a given 3D surface. Secord et al. [12] summarizes existing techniques, and generates weightings of the various criteria explored in the literature such that the fitted model can predict people's preferred views. By additionally considering the editing history of a 3D model, our approach could potentially create viewpoint selection results that better convey the original author's intentions.

Tsang et al. [16] and Singh et al. [15] mine viewpoint data from users viewing a model after its creation. The collected data is used to summarize viewing behaviors [16] or assist in the future presentation of the model [15]. In contrast we instrument the authoring environment so that viewpoint information can be captured, and informative viewpoints can be inferred as soon as the model is created.

Capturing and Utilizing Workflow Histories

Numerous systems have been proposed to automatically record users' workflows within a software application. Captured interaction history and workflows have been shown to be useful for creating step-by-step tutorials [4, 8] or allowing users to explore and replay editing history of a document [3, 6, 9]. Our work on viewpoint summarization demonstrates a previously unexplored way to utilize captured workflows: to select views and create model summarizations.

INITIAL INSIGHTS AND OBSERVATIONS

A core problem related to our work is the automatic selection of informative viewpoints of a 3D model. Our premise is that the behavior of modelers as they create the model can provide useful cues for viewpoint selection. To better understand the validity of this premise, and gain other insights for guiding our work, we conducted multiple interviews and observation sessions with professional 3D modelers. This section summarizes the details of these sessions and some of the insights gained from them.

Interviews and Observation Sessions

We conducted three separate 45-minutes interview sessions with three 3D modelers. Two of the participants were internal to our institution, and one was externally recruited.

There were five additional observation sessions with the two internal modelers. Each session is 1 hour long of 3D sculpting [11] followed by 20 minutes of discussions. An observer took notes during the sessions, and the modeling processes were screen-captured for later reference.

Cameras Oscillate between Sculpting and Inspection Positions

We observed a camera movement pattern consistent across modelers, where they oscillate between sculpting at camera position A, move to position B for inspection, then move back to position A for further editing.

Such oscillation patterns are a necessity in sculpting tools. Typically, the 3D viewpoint which allows the modeler to precisely position a brush (*sculpting view*) is looking directly down the normal of the sculpting region. Yet the best view for assessing the effect of the brush (*inspection view)* is typically perpendicular to the plane normal.

Since these oscillations are often used for inspection, capturing and analyzing the inflection point of these oscillations may allow us to infer preferred viewpoints for specific areas of the model.

Sculpting Brushes are Short and Localized

We also observed that modelers tend to sculpt with short brush strokes localized to surface features, e.g. eyes and mouth, rather than long winding brushes across an entire surface. Presumably this is because 3D sculpting is largely a process of accumulating small additions and removals of local details. Similarly, modelers tend to work in a spatially- and temporally-coherent fashion.

Both observation and interviews confirmed that modelers tend to focus on one area of the model at a time, before moving on to the next. This indicates that we may be able to segment the 3D model into meaningful parts and to identify important regions, for the purpose of viewing or summarization, based on a modeler's editing history.

Complexity Does Not Imply Importance

Generally it has been assumed that geometric complexity (e.g. curvature variation) correlates well with importance [12, 14]. However, in 3D sculpting, we sometimes observe the exact opposite. Geometrically complex regions such as hair, scales, and textured skin are often quickly created by irregular scribbling of the sculpting brush, whereas very smooth regions that define the overall form (e.g. the shapes of hips, thighs, and shoulders) often require much more careful attention. These smooth "features" are usually marked as unimportant by geometric analysis, but are considered important by the modeler.

View Authoring is an Iterative Process

We observed that when authoring static views, the modelers first quickly selected many candidate views, followed by gradual pruning and refinement. Similarly, when authoring animated views, the modelers first assigned rough control points and then refined the paths and surfaces in detail. Such iterations between selection and refinement happened frequently throughout the view authoring process.

From our interviews we learned that the process could be tedious, spanning from several minutes to more than an hour, if animated views for walk-throughs or fly-bys were included. In general, the modelers welcomed aids for automation but also showed strong demand of some level of manual control over the final results.

OVERVIEW OF OUR SYSTEM

The observations and insights in the previous section motivate us to build a view authoring system that interactively suggests candidate static and animated views to the modeler during the view authoring process.

The core of the system is an automatic view suggestion algorithm driven by the modeler's own editing history. It is based on the observation above that there are significant amount of regularity in the camera movements and sculpting strokes and they may provide useful information for modelers' view authoring that is not readily apparent in the final 3D model. In particular, the oscillating camera movements suggest the existence of representative view clusters while the localized brushes suggest the possibility of segmenting the 3D model into meaningful components.

In the following sections, we first introduce the user interface of our authoring and viewing environments, followed by algorithm and implementation details.

VIEW AUTHORING USER INTERFACE

As a prototype system, we instrumented the 3D sculpting tools in the MeshMixer [11] modeling software for recording the editing history, and integrated the authoring environment inside MeshMixer.

Our view authoring system supports both authoring and viewing modes across three main categories of view widgets: view points, view paths, and view surfaces (Figure 2, as inspired from [1]). As an author, a user can generate a summary of the model through a series of informative viewpoints, constrained view paths and surfaces, and comparison views across versions of the model in its editing history. As a viewer, the user can easily inspect and navigate the model with the aid of these authored views.

System Interface

Figure 1 shows the user interface of our system, which consists of three main components: the *main window*, the *overview panel*, and the *navigation panel.*

Main Window (Figure 1A)

The *main window* (Figure 1A) of MeshMixer is used to display the 3D model. It is also the main area for inspecting the 3D model and for authoring the views.

Overview Panel (Figure 1B, Figure 2)

The purpose of the overview panel is to show all authored views within the spatial context of the current 3D model. Different visualizations are used to represent viewpoints, view paths, and view surfaces (Figure 2).

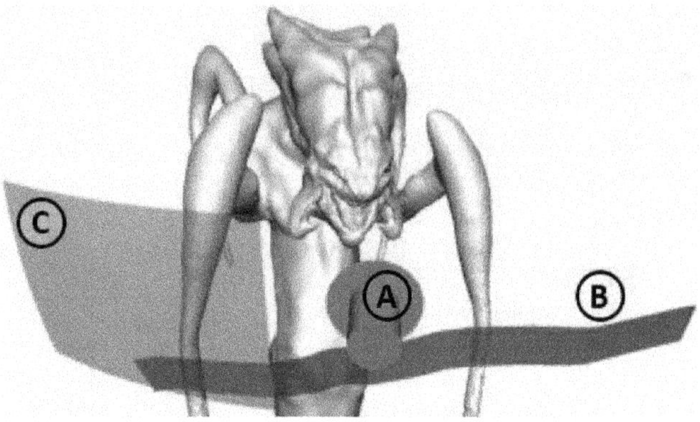

Figure 2. The overview panel contains a proxy of the 3D model and authored views. These can include (a) viewpoints, (b) view paths, and (c) view surfaces.

Navigation Panel (Figure 1C)

The *Navigation Panel* allows the user to navigate between authored views. This panel consists of two parts: a color-coded *version slider* on the left and a thumbnail list of authored views on the right.

The version slider allows users to navigate through previous versions of the model that were manually saved by the modeler or automatically saved by the system based on user-specified elapsed time and operation count. Each version has its own unique color code, and the corresponding model version will be displayed in the main window as the user drags the slider.

The thumbnail list shows the representative images of all authored views with a color-coded stripe indicating the corresponding versions. Double clicking on the thumbnail item loads the corresponding view and version into the main window, and highlights the corresponding view widget (i.e. the viewpoint arrow) in the overview panel.

Authoring Environment

In the following paragraphs, we use a 3D hydra model as an example to walk through the view authoring scenario and explain individual features of our system.

Manual Viewpoint Authoring

The modeler can inspect the 3D model in the *main window* with standard camera controls. When viewing the model from a desired viewpoint, the modeler can store the viewpoint. This authored viewpoint will then be added to both the *overview panel* and the *navigation panel.*

Authoring Region-Specific Viewpoints

Per our initial observation of the iterative authoring process, the modelers might desire a list of view candidates they can choose from and customize. Thus our system provides the function of interactive candidate viewpoint generation for a user-specified region of interest. First, the modeler specifies a region of the 3D model by directly painting the region on the surface of the model using the triangle selection function in MeshMixer (Figure 3). A list of viewpoints associated with the specified region is then displayed in the main window.

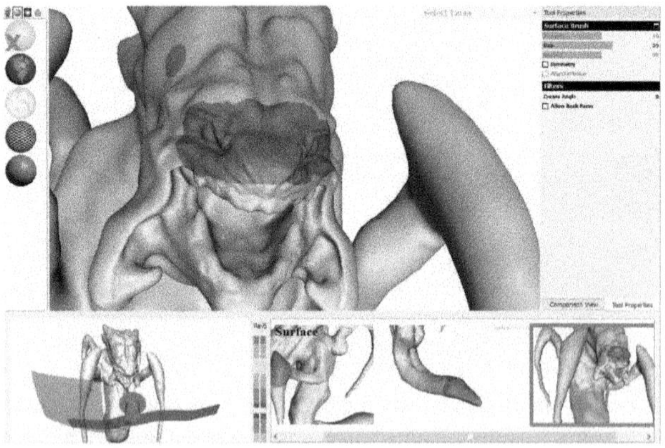

Figure 3. Region-specific view authoring. The orange colored region is the selected region of interest. Our system then suggests viewpoints, view paths, or view surfaces.

Authoring Region-Specific View Paths and View Surfaces

The *region-specific* view authoring mechanism also allows for efficient authoring of 3D view paths and view surfaces. The modeler can first specify a region of interest, as described above, then invoke the context menu to have the system automatically suggests multiple candidate view surfaces and view paths.

Suggested view surfaces are 3D spherical patches that spatially constrain the viewing camera for easier navigation. Suggested view paths are 3D paths consisting of a series of camera viewpoints. Once a candidate is chosen, the modeler can adjust the size of a view surface and the position and length of a path by dragging the mouse.

Automatic Global Viewpoint Suggestion

Alternatively, our system can also fully automatically generate the candidate views of the entire 3D model (Figure 4). The modeler can directly use the generated result to save the view authoring time or select the favored views and customize them.

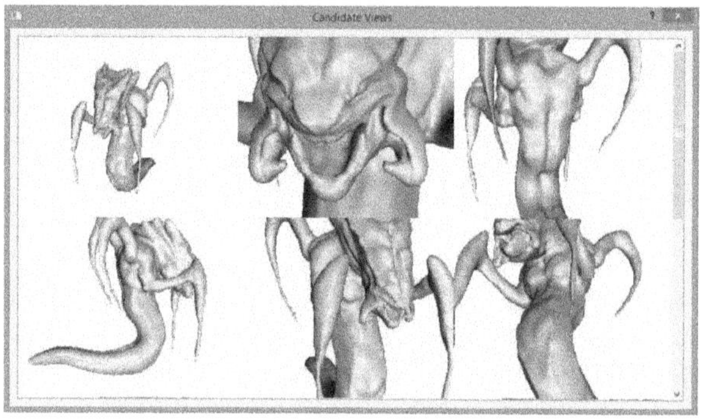

Figure 4. Candidate view-points picked by our automatic viewpoint selection algorithm.

Authoring Views for Different 3D Model Versions

The additional temporal dimension embedded in the editing history enables the modeler to revisit previous model states in the modeling process and associate authored view with the version. The arrow in the overview panel used to visualize the viewpoint is color-coded to represent its associated version.

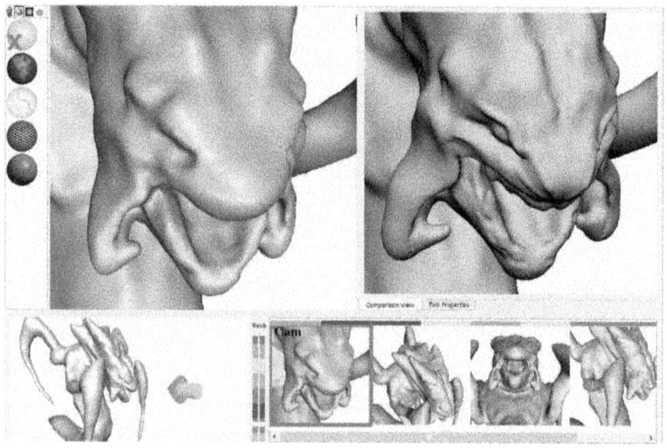

Figure 5. Comparison view function that shows the same viewpoint of two 3D model versions side-by-side. The arrow in the overview panel has two colors representing each version.

Authoring Comparison Views between 3D Model Versions

Our system also provides a *comparison view* function, which allows the modeler to display two different 3D model versions side-by-side (Figure 5). A context menu is used to toggle the comparison view mode on and off. Once enabled, the user can drag the *version slider* to set the versions being displayed.

In a comparison view, the camera navigation of both versions is synchronized, so that the modeler can easily compare specific areas of the model across versions. This function is particularly helpful when the modeler would like to highlight the evolution and differences of a 3D model in the modeling process. The views authored within these *comparison views* are displayed in the overview panel as a two-color arrow, which corresponds to the color codes of the two versions (e.g. the purple/green arrow in the *overview panel* in Figure 5). Selecting any two-color arrow from the overview panel will bring up the associated side-by-side comparison view into the *main window*.

Editing History Visualization

To further facilitate view authoring, our system can visualize various aspects of the editing history, including time spent on each surface region and the camera paths. By accumulating the sculpting time spent on surface regions we can render a time map on the surface (Figure 6a), while for camera history we create 3D ribbons along the camera paths (Figure 6b). Note that the homogeneous colors around features, such as the eyes, the wings and the chest, support our observation that brush operations tend to be localized. The modeler can author views while the editing history visualization is displayed.

The sculpting history may consist of thousands of operations, thus we also provide a region-specific history filter function (Figure 6b). The modeler can then navigate between the filtered camera positions.

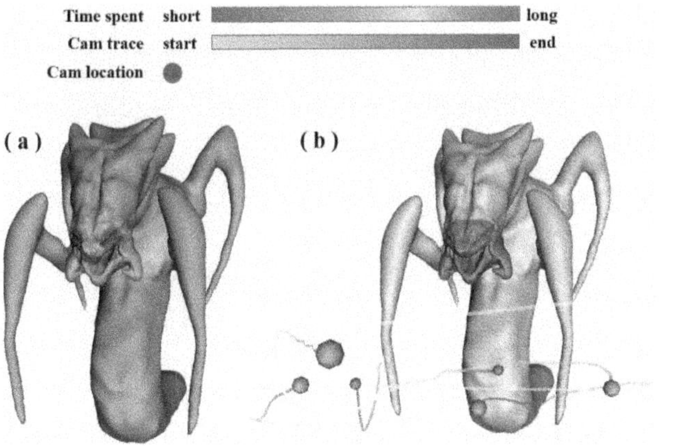

Figure 6. Visualizations of history data. a) A heat-map shows the time spent on each vertex in the model. b) A visualization of the camera history while editing the highlighted face region.

NAVIGATION EXPERIENCE FOR VIEWERS

The authored viewing information and associated representative thumbnail images are stored as meta-data of the 3D model. Figure 7 shows a sample authored result. This can be used to create an interactive navigation environment for other viewers.

In our current prototype, we reuse MeshMixer as the viewer for the viewing information. However, since the information is tool independent, it can be easily adopted by other 3D modeling systems [1, 2].

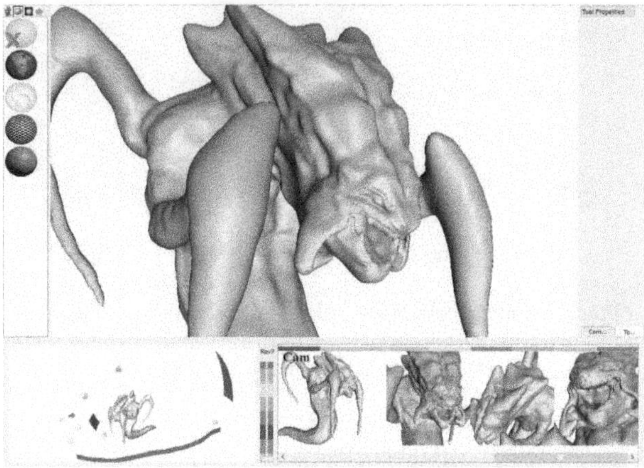

Figure 7. Views authored by the modeler using our system.

A viewer can explore the model using both the *navigation* and *overview panel*s. For example, the viewer can double click on a preview thumbnail in the navigation panel, which will load the associated version and viewpoint into the main window. When the viewer selects a pre-authored path or surface, the user can perform the associated constrained navigations of the model, e.g. follow the authored view path or drag the main camera on the authored surface. This allows the viewer to easily insect the model and experience high-quality views that the modeler has created.

Exporting 2D Image Collages

To further enhance the portability of the authored viewing experiences, our system provides the ability to export the authored views as a collage of representative 2D images. Our system pre-renders the authored views and arranges them according to pre-defined template layouts. The tool is particularly useful in helping modelers showcase their work on printed mediums or devices with low graphics capability. Our system provides two kinds of collages: *summary collage* and *progress collage*.

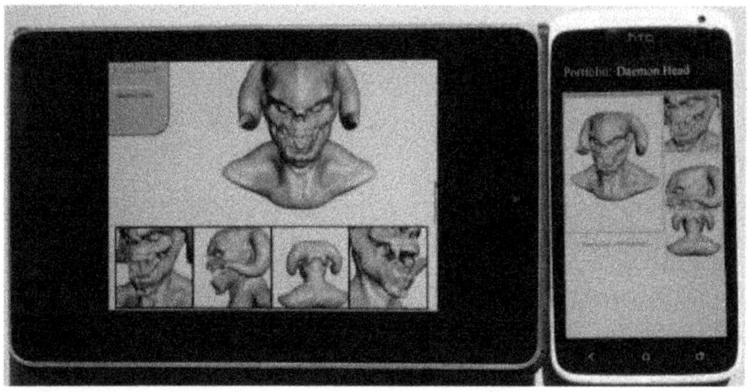

Figure 8. Summary collages on a tablet and a smart phone.

A *summary collage* presents a collection of rendered views that had been created in the authoring environment (Figure 8). Predefined templates are used for the layout, consisting of equally-sized tiles, or a central primary view supplemented with smaller secondary views. Users can drag along individual thumbnails to browse views pre-rendered along the authored view-paths and view surfaces.

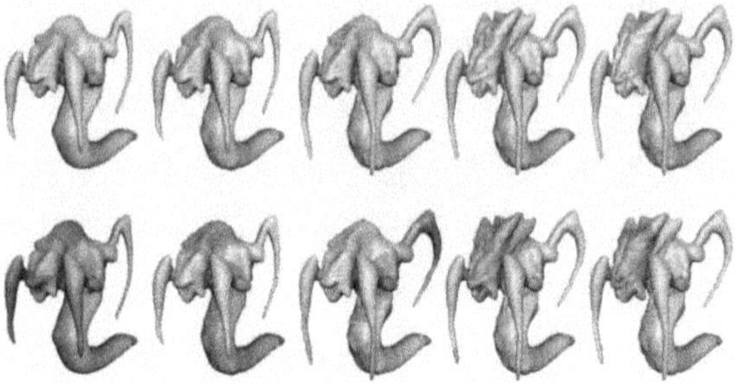

Figure 9. Temporal review using *progress* collage. Top row shows progress of the modeler sculpting a hydra. Bottom row shows time map of each version.

A *progress collage* is meant to be used for design review and workflow summarization. The *progress collage* displays a series of version snapshots from a fixed viewpoint (Figure 9). In each snapshot the surface is colored using a heat-map based on the accumulated editing time difference from the previous snapshot. This visualization enables users to rapidly assess which areas of the model have been changed between versions.

ALGORITHM AND IMPLEMENTATION

In this section we elaborate more on the instrumentation of MeshMixer and the algorithms used to construct candidate viewpoints, view paths, and view surfaces.

Editing History Instrumentation

The editing history recorded by our instrumented MeshMixer comprises of a complete log of the two most significant interactions in a 3D sculpting tool: interactive sculpting brush strokes, and 3D camera manipulations.

For each sculpting brush operation we store: a unique operation ID, elapsed time of the stroke, a list of the affected vertices, and the current camera viewpoint.

For the camera history we store all intermediate cameras (location, look-at, and up vector) during each camera transformation operation, as well as the elapsed time of the entire camera manipulation.

Region-Specific View Suggestion

Our system interactively suggests candidate views based on the region specified by the modeler. The following paragraphs describe the algorithms that generate candidate viewpoints, view paths, and view surfaces.

Candidate Viewpoint and View Path Construction

Our approach is motivated by the camera oscillations discussed in our initial observations. The captured *sculpting views* and *inspecting views* tend to form dense, disjoint clusters whose weighted centers we interpret as candidate viewpoints for the surface region specified by the modeler. From these candidate views, we interpret the associated oscillating camera traces as candidate view paths.

Given the modeler-specified region, we identify *sculpting views* as those camera positions where the modeler applied a sculpting brush to that region. We then apply spatial clustering to these views to pick representative ones. Our algorithm takes a set C of sculpting-view cameras, and builds an octree based on the camera positions. We then compute the accumulated camera time in each cell by summing the camera times in its sub-tree, and search for the dominant cell bottom-up until we find the one whose accumulated time is the largest among cells at the same octree level and is over 70% (T_l) of the total time. Finally, we calculate the weighted average center (based on time) of the viewpoints in the dominating cell, and select the camera in C that is closest to the weighted center. We denote this camera viewpoint c_{sculpt}, the representative sculpting-view for the specified region.

To identify *inspection views*, viewpoints used by the author to assess the model, we search for camera manipulations which occur between two sculpting operations applied to the same segment. We treat these as inspection operations. For each such camera manipulation, the sequential camera positions create a 3D piecewise-linear curve L. We compute the opening angle at each vertex (camera position) of L, and choose as a turning point, c_{turn}, the vertex with largest opening angle (Figure 10). For a given region, we take the 3D cameras associated with all of the turning points and then apply the same clustering technique described above to extract the inspection-view, $c_{inspect}$, for a segment.

Note that the camera controls between sculpting might not always be inspections. However, the experiment results seem to show that the modeler tend to stay on non-inspection cameras position much shorter and our algorithm is capable of identifying meaningful $c_{inspect}$. Furthermore, the goal is to provide suggested views for users to refine and choose and thus 100% accuracy is not necessary.

Iterating the procedure described above, we can extract multiple sculpting views and inspection views. We then treat these extracting views as candidate viewpoints and the oscillating camera traces these views belong to as candidate view paths of the specified region.

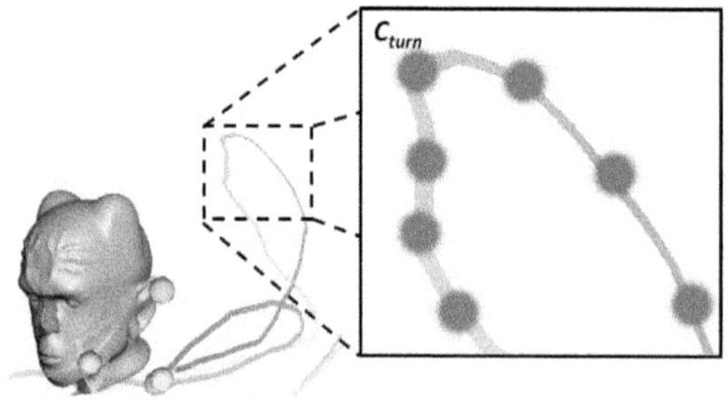

Figure 10. *Cturn* is the turning point of the oscillation camera movement pattern.

Candidate View Surface Construction

We hypothesize that a view surface that covers a cluster of sculpting views would be a good candidate for inspecting the selected region. Given a surface region of a 3D model, we calculate the average center v_{center} of the surface vertex and obtain its dominating octree cell of sculpting views and representative sculpting-view c_{sculpt} with the algorithm described above. Next, we construct a spherical patch with the center at v_{center}, radius as $||c_{sculpt} - v_{center}||$, and spanning angles that cover the octree cell.

Global Viewpoint Suggestion

In addition to suggest views for user specified regions, our system can also automatically segment the 3D model into meaningful surface regions and suggest good viewpoints for each of them. This allows our system to recommend global viewpoints that summarize the entire 3D model.

Per our initial observations, the modelers sculpt sequentially and locally. This leads to a feature-centric approach - we explicitly segment the surface into (potentially overlapping) regions based on the editing history and then rank them by an importance factor.

We first define a segment as a region in which each vertex has been given a roughly similar amount of attention - measured by accumulated sculpting time, by the modeler. We then extract segments via standard greedy region-growing [13]. To create a segment *S*, we first choose as the segment *seed* the vertex v_s with the largest accumulated sculpting time $T(v_s)$. We then incrementally include vertices v adjacent to *S* which have a $T(v)$ similar to the average accumulated sculpting time for S, denoted as $T(S)$. Specifically, we add v to S if $||T(S) - T(v)|| < T_2 = 0.3*T(S)$. The set S is then removed from the candidate set and we repeat the above process until either the required number of segments are found, or all vertices have been consumed.

Finally, we apply a refinement post-process. For each modeling operation that affects any of the vertices contained in segment S, we grow S to include all vertices of that operation. This is based on the previous observation that brush strokes tend to be local and stay on same feature.

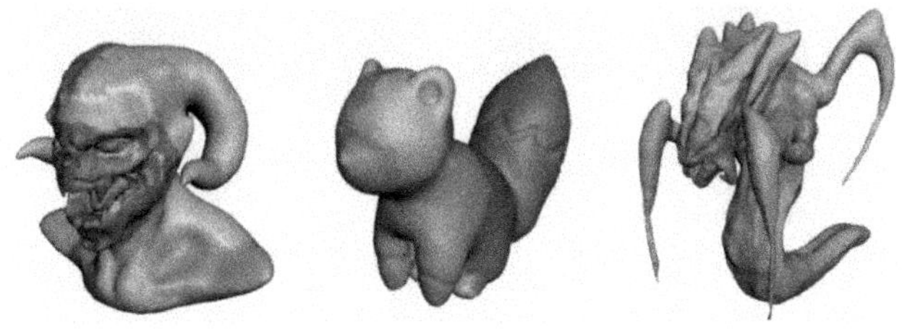

Figure 11. Segments generated by our algorithm.

Given surface segmentation, we then collect the c_{sculpt} and $c_{inspect}$ for each segment, as described above, and treat them as the initial candidate viewpoints.

Discussions

Compared to previous algorithms whose computational cost is related to the geometric properties (e.g. surface curvature, surface variance, and silhouette length), the cost of our algorithm is related to the length of editing history and dominated by the cost of the octree construction. Our prototype system is deployed as a CPU based implementation which constructs the octree in real-time for the models used in the paper (Table 1). For complex models with longer editing history, a faster GPU implementation might be needed to achieve good performance.

The two threshold values in camera clustering (T_1) and region growing (T_2) can be interactively adjusted by the users. The results will be visualized on-the-fly as in Figure 6 and Figure 11. In our current system, we hand-picked the value of $T_1 = 0.7$ and $T_2 = 0.3$ for all results in the paper.

It is also worth noting that previous work [12] assumes a 2 DoF camera model, where cameras lying on a fixed-radius sphere facing the center of the model. On the contrary, our framework extracts cameras from the editing history and preserves the 6 DoF camera model.

VIEWPOINT SELECTION ALGORITHM EVALUATION

The practical benefits of our view authoring system strongly rely on a premise that the history-assisted viewpoint selection algorithm generates viewpoints suitable for understanding the modeling process and the workflow history. In particular, it is important to verify the underlying assumption that good editing views are correlated with good display views.

To check this premise, we compare our automatic global viewpoint suggestion algorithm to two alternatives: viewpoints generated automatically by the state of art method in Secord et al. [12] and viewpoints hand-specified by the original 3D modeler. Note that it is not our goal to outperform the manual selections. Instead, we hope to get close to the quality of manually generated viewpoints with the advantage of a time saving automatic approach.

3D Models

We recruited a 3D modeler to create three 3D models from a sphere using our instrumented version of MeshMixer. Table 1 provided a summary of the 3 models. These models had varying levels of complexity and geometry features. For example, the hydra model had fine-grained details that would have required careful close-up viewing and editing while the squirrel model had a smooth shape suitable to be viewed far away.

name	daemon	squirrel	hydra
preview	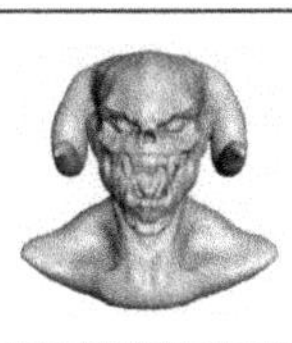	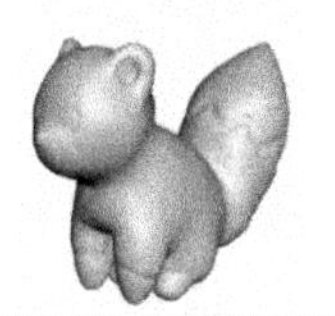	
minutes	52	30	55
vertices	67,418	27,902	130,658
editing op	1,566	420	1,022
camera op	738	247	425

Table 1. The 3D models created by a modeler for our study, using our instrumented version of MeshMixer.

Viewpoints

Once the 3D models were created, we generated 5 best views of each model using three different methods: our automatic viewpoint selection algorithm (*History Assisted*), Secord et al.'s automatic algorithm using linear-5b measure [12] (*Secord et al.*), and viewpoints hand-picked by the 3D modeler (*Modeler*).

For the algorithmic approaches we used the 5 top-ranked views for each 3D model. For the manual approach, we instructed the 3D modeler to "assume you are going to showcase your model on a website where one can only upload 5 images per model". It took the modeler about 15 minutes to pick all 15 static images. Figure 12 shows some viewpoints generated by these three methods. Please refer to the appendix file for complete materials.

Participants

To evaluate the viewpoints, we recruited 10 professional 3D modelers for the study, with up to 12 years of experience ($\mu = 5$ and $\sigma = 3.5$).

Procedure

In the beginning of the session, we briefly introduced our system and study to the participants. Then we gave the participants a chance to briefly inspect each of our three models in MeshMixer. Participants then carried out 2 tasks.

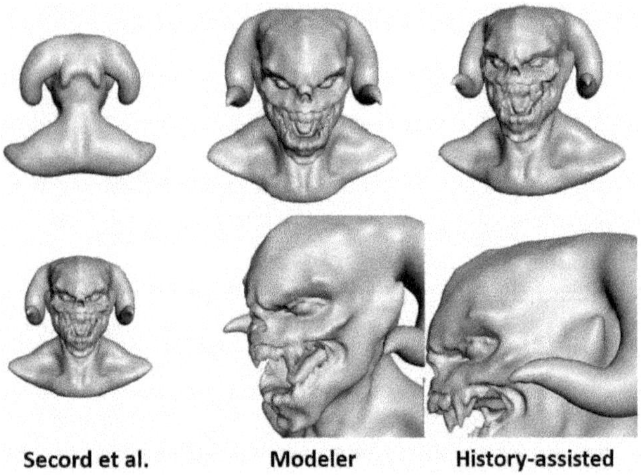

Figure 12. Sample viewpoints generated for the Daemon model for each of the three techniques.

Task 1 – Single View

The goal of the first task was to evaluate the quality of individual viewpoints. For each model, we showed the 15 images generated by the three techniques, one at a time, in random order. For each image, two questions were asked:

1. *The image conveys the information of (a) shape, (b) detail, or (c) shape + detail (pick one from these three)*
2. *I will take a picture of this 3D model from this angle*

Task2 – Multiple View

The goal of the second task was to evaluate the quality of viewpoints under the scenario of multiple image selection. For each model, we showed the participants 15 images at once in a 3×5 grid, and instructed them to pick five, under the assumption that they intended to showcase these models on a 3D forum.

On average, two task took approximately 30 to 40 minutes to finish. In the end of the session, we briefly interviewed the participants about the reasons for their ratings.

Evaluation Results and Discussions

Unless otherwise stated, we analyzed non-parametric participant data (Likert scale in case 1 and image count in case 2) with the Friedman test and pair-wise comparisons with the Wilcoxon signed-rank test.

Figure 13 shows the result of the first question in task 1. Although there is no statistically significant difference among the data, the responses indicated that our approach covers similar combination of shape and detail to the manual approach. These results are consistent with a visual inspection of the viewpoints generated by the three algorithms (Figure 12). It can be seen that the *Secord et al.* viewpoints provide more overall shape yet less detail due to its 2 DoF camera model.

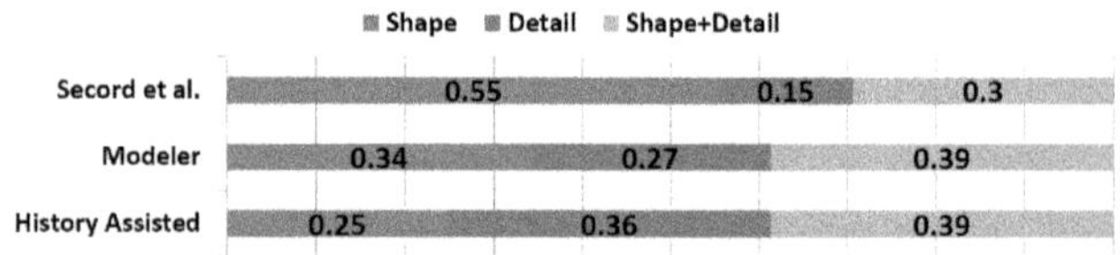

Figure 13. The result of first question in task 1. Each graph bar shows the percentages of participant labeling.

Figure 14 shows the result of the second question. The average rating for the *history assisted* viewpoints (3.24) is significantly higher than the *Secord et al.* viewpoints (2.80) ($p<0.05$). There was no significant difference between the *modeler* and *history assisted* methods.

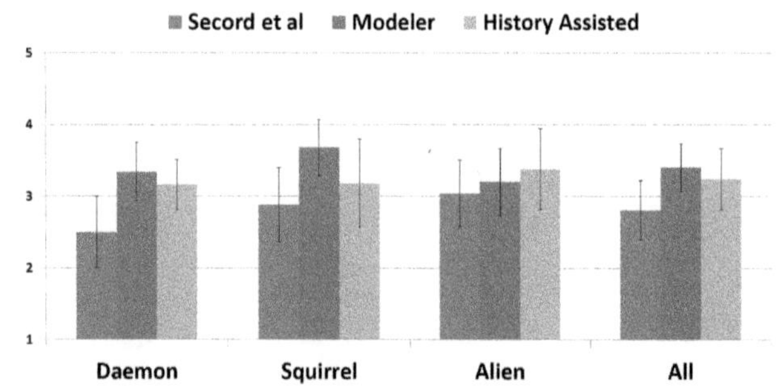

Figure 14. Average rating (from 1 to 5) for viewpoints in task 1. Error bars show 95% CI.

For task 2, we measured the average number of images picked from the three different methods. The averages were 1.3 (*Secord et al.*), 1.833 (*modeler*), and 1.867 (*history assisted*). Our algorithm had the highest rate of being picked by participants, but there were no significant differences among the three groups ($p=0.38$).

In summary, the results showed that good views from the editing history are indeed correlated with good display views. The viewpoints generated by our algorithm are similar in quality to those handcrafted by the 3D modeler, with the advantage of being automatic. As such, our algorithm does provide a suitable method for automatically selecting viewpoints, as used in our view authoring system.

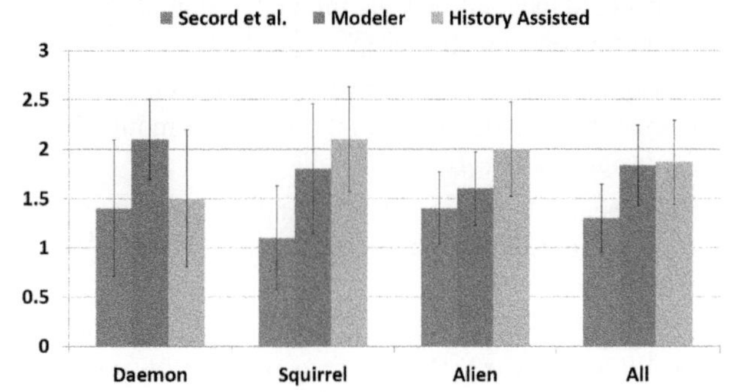

Figure 15. Average number of selected images in task 2. Error bars show 95% CI.

In addition, our study demonstrates the limitations of using existing automated techniques for assisting modeler's viewpoints authoring process. While Secord et al. [12] has been shown to be effective for modeling crowd preferences, its simplified 2 DoF camera model might miss certain viewpoints preferred by the modeler, e.g. close-up views or views not pointing to the center of objects.

In the post-interview, we found that even when two participants gave the same view an equal score, the provided reasons could differ dramatically. For example, for the bottom right image of Figure 12, a participant rated it as 5 because it showed the shape of the horn, while another rated it as 5 because it showed a clear silhouette of the head. It suggested that people could observe the same 3D model for different personal purposes, and it is difficult, if not impossible, to have a single automatic algorithm to cover everyone's preference. This reiterates the findings in our initial interview sessions, where the 3D modelers welcomed the automatic assistance on the view authoring while also considered the manual adjustment/modification over the final result necessary.

VIEW AUTHORING SYSTEM EVALUATION

The second user study was designed to provide a qualitative evaluation of the entire view authoring system, and to gain insights, observations, and feedbacks.

Participants and Materials

To evaluate the authoring system, we recruited three professional 3D modelers, two computer graphics researchers, and one architecture researcher. We used the same 3D models and editing histories in Table 1.

Procedure

The evaluation sessions began with a 20 minute walkthrough of the view authoring system. We first demonstrated individual features of our system, and then asked the participant to complete related short tasks. There were a total of 24 short tasks, such as "add a view path for the body region", and "add a comparison view for the head region for version 3 and version 5".

After the walkthrough and short tasks, we replayed the sculpting video of the "hydra" model (~1hr) at 5× speed to the participants. We then asked them to author views of the model using viewpoint, comparison view, view path, and view surface, at least once.

We replayed the modeling process before the view authoring session to allow participants to get a sense of the modeler's workflow and the viewpoints that were used. We did not ask the participants to perform the 3D sculpting on their own, mainly because it could take too much time.

At the end of the study, an interview was conducted and the participants filled out a questionnaire regarding individual features of the system.

Evaluation Results and Discussions

Overall, the participants were enthusiastic about the system, and considered it a potentially useful component in a modeler's toolset. Participants were all able to complete the provided tasks without difficulty.

Figure 16 summarizes the subjective ratings of our system. Overall, responses were quite positive. When asked about their favorite functions, participants were enthusiastic about the access to previous versions, the comparison view function, and the time map. In particular, the comparison view function received very positive comments from the professional modelers. P2 commented that when looking for critiques from peer modelers or asking for help on detailed topology issues, it is common for 3D modelers to post before-and-after image pairs on a forum.

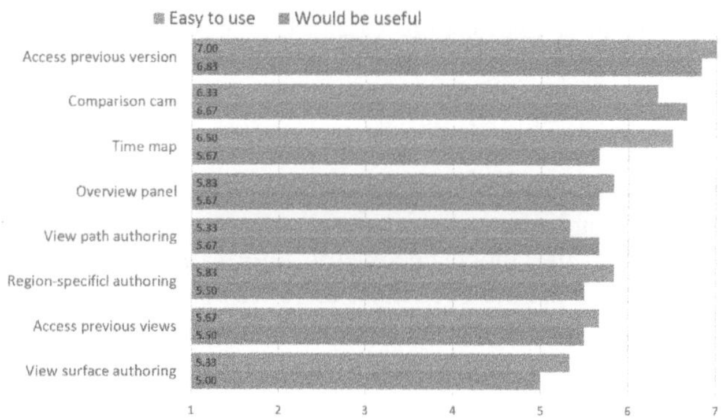

Figure 16. Subjective rating on system features.

One professional modeler (P1) particularly liked the time map function and commented that it would be very useful for workflow management. He stated that he usually works on multiple projects at the same time, and sometimes he might overlook some detailed regions on a 3D model. The time map function could serve as a good reminder about progress. Another modeler (P2) also commented that the combination of the time map and version slider could be very useful for an art director to track modelers' progress.

However, participants did express concern about learning so many new functions in such a short session. We believe this may have contributed to the lower scores for the view authoring functions, as they were less familiar concepts to the participants. Still, participants did comment that the regions-specific authoring techniques would be very useful in certain scenarios. One 3D modeler (P1) commented that the region-specific authoring function is particularly useful for parts that are difficult to inspect, e.g. the tongue inside the mouth, and the architect (P6) commented that the automatic construction of local view paths would be a time-saver for detailed inspection.

Compared to their previous view authoring experiences in 3D modeling software, the responses were quite positive. Participants were excited about the additional temporal information provided by our system and thought it would be beneficial to have candidate views suggested during the authoring process.

DISCUSSIONS AND FUTURE WORK

We focus mainly on 3D digital sculpting users and tools. We are interested in extending our methodology to other categories of 3D modeling tools. Our work does rely on the assumption that the 3D modeling tool has been instrumented at a very detailed level. The internal data model in MeshMixer is a straightforward triangle mesh; however the geometric representation in other tools might be more complicated.

Currently our system is designed for scenarios where the modeler sculpts a single 3D object from scratch. However, some 3D objects or 3D scenes (such as mechanical assemblies or architectural models) incorporate a large number of objects or import 3D assets from a database. Our instrumentation needs to be extended to handle deletion and creation of parts, copy-and-paste, and so on. A merge algorithm that can handle editing histories from multiple objects might also be needed.

Finally, we focus our current method only on the editing and viewing history of a 3D model. However, this does not mean that the model geometry information should be ignored. We believe even more effective view selection and navigation systems can be designed by considering both the final model and its editing history. We hope our work can inspire future work in this fruitful research direction.

CONCLUSION

We propose a history assisted view authoring system for 3D models. Our system provides modelers the ability to traverse and author the camera views, paths, and surfaces across different model versions. We introduce the *region-specific view authoring* technique where candidate views are automatically calculated based on the specified surface region. At the core of the view authoring system is a unified algorithm framework for 3D model segmentation and automatic view selection based on the editing history. Our user studies show that the quality of the viewpoints generated by our algorithm is comparable to ones manually selected by the modeler, and the authoring system elicits a high level of interest from potential end-users.

REFERENCES

1. N. Burtnyk, A. Khan, G. Fitzmaurice, R. Balakrishnan, and G. Kurtenbach. (2002). Stylecam: interactive stylized 3d navigation using integrated spatial & temporal controls. *ACM UIST*. 101–110
2. N. Burtnyk, A. Khan, G. Fitzmaurice, and G. Kurtenbach. (2006). Showmotion: camera motion based 3d design review. *ACM I3D*. 167– 174
3. H.T Chen, L.Y Wei, and C.F Chang. (2011). Nonlinear revision control for images. *ACM Trans. Graph*. 30, 4, Article 105
4. P.Y Chi, S Ahn, A, Ren. B, Hartmann, M. Dontcheva, W. Li(2012). MixT: Automatic generation of step-by-step mixed media tutorials. *ACM UIST*. 93-102.
5. M. Christie and P. Olivier. (2009). Camera control in computer graphics: models, techniques and applications. *ACM SIGGRAPH ASIA Courses*. 3:1–3:197
6. J. D. Denning, W. B. Kerr, and F. Pellacini. (2011). Meshflow: Interactive visualization of mesh construction sequences. *ACM Trans. Graph*. 30, 4, Article 66.
7. J. D. Denning and F. Pellacini. (2013). Meshgit: diffing and merging meshes for polygonal modeling. *ACM Trans. Graph*. 32, 4, Article 35.
8. F. Grabler, M. Agrawala, W. Li, M. Dontcheva, and T. Igarashi. (2009) Generating photo manipulation tutorials by demonstration. *ACM Trans. Graph*. 28, 3, Article 66.
9. T. Grossman, J. Matejka, and G. Fitzmaurice (2010) Chronicle: Capture, exploration, and playback of document workflow histories. *ACM UIST*, 143–152.
10. C. H. Lee, A. Varshney, and D. W. Jacobs. (2005). Mesh saliency. *ACM Trans. Graph*. 24, 3, 659–666.
11. R. Schmidt and K. Singh. (2010). MeshMixer: an interface for rapid mesh composition. *ACM SIGGRAPH Talks*, Article 6.
12. A. Secord, J. Lu, A. Finkelstein, M. Singh, and A. Nealen. (2011). Perceptual models of viewpoint preference. *ACM Trans. Graph*. 30, 5, Article 109.
13. A. Shamir. (2008). A survey on mesh segmentation techniques. *Computer Graphics Forum*, 27(6):1539–1556.
14. P. Shilane and T. Funkhouser. (2007). Distinctive regions of 3d surfaces. *ACM Trans. Graph*. 26, 2, Article 7.
15. K. Singh and R. Balakrishnan. (2004). Visualizing 3d scenes using non-linear projections and data mining of previous camera movements. *AFRIGRAPH*. 41–48.
16. M. Tsang, N. Morris, and R. Balakrishnan. (2004). Temporal thumbnails: rapid visualization of time-based viewing data. *AVI*. 175–178.

FrameBox and MirrorBox: Tools and Guidelines to Support Designers in Prototyping Interfaces for 3D Displays

Nora Broy[1,2,3], Stefan Schneegass[3], Florian Alt[1,3], Albrecht Schmidt[3]

[1]University of Munich
Media Informatics Group
Amalienstraße 17
80333 Munich, Germany
firstname.lastname@ifi.lmu.de

[2]BMW Group
Research & Technology
Hanauer Straße 46
80992 Munich, Germany
Nora.NB.Broy@bmw.de

[3]University of Stuttgart
VIS
Pfaffenwaldring 5a
70569 Stuttgart, Germany
firstname.lastname@vis.uni-stuttgart.de

Figure 1: We present two tools for stereoscopic 3D (S3D) user interface prototyping: The FrameBox (left) is made of laser-cut acryl and allows for inserting UI elements painted on transparency films into several slots (x and z position). Paper clips can be used to adjust the y position. The MirrorBox (right) uses semi-transparent mirrors to reflect UI elements painted on transparency films. An iPad is used as a backlight.

ABSTRACT
In this paper, we identify design guidelines for stereoscopic 3D (S3D) user interfaces (UIs) and present the MirrorBox and the FrameBox, two UI prototyping tools for S3D displays. As auto-stereoscopy becomes available for the mass market we believe the design of S3D UIs for devices, for example, mobile phones, public displays, or car dashboards, will rapidly gain importance. A benefit of such UIs is that they can group and structure information in a way that makes them easily perceivable for the user. For example, important information can be shown in front of less important information. This paper identifies core requirements for designing S3D UIs and derives concrete guidelines. The requirements also serve as a basis for two depth layout tools we built with the aim to overcome limitations of traditional prototyping when sketching S3D UIs. We evaluated the tools with usability experts and compared them to traditional paper prototyping.

Author Keywords
Prototyping; Stereoscopic 3D; User Interfaces

ACM Classification Keywords
H.5.2 User Interfaces: Prototyping

ACM 978-1-4503-2473-1/14/04?$15.00. http://dx.doi.org/10.1145/2556288.2557183

INTRODUCTION
3D displays are nowadays widely available for entertainment in cinemas or home environments. While the need for glasses is likely to be a major hindrance for their uptake, we believe that the advent of auto-stereoscopy leads in the near future to 3D displays becoming ubiquitous, for example in mobile phones, public displays, and cars. This provides novel means for designing user interfaces and exploiting the third dimension, including the opportunity to present information on different depth layers. Prior work shows that depth combined with other salient cues (e.g., color, motion) can improve the performance of visual search tasks [1, 8]. For instance, frequently used applications on mobile phones could be grouped together, using depth as an indicator for the most recently launched application. In security-critical environments, like the automobile, where users need to be able to quickly and accurately perceive information, a comprehensive visual structure can help to immediately identify important information.

To build such interfaces, there is an increasing need to provide basic design guidelines to sketch and arrange graphical user interface (GUI) elements. Building such S3D interfaces is in many ways challenging. For example, designers need to cater to the fact that elements cannot equally be perceived in different locations in 3D space and that a minimum distance needs to be maintained between elements so that users can easily distinguish which element is shown further to the front [4]. Hence, this paper puts a strong emphasis on understanding how the user can be supported in prototyping successful and usable S3D interfaces.

To do so, we identify requirements for layering information in 3D space. We study related literature and complement our findings by conducting a laboratory study which investigates object arrangement on different depth layers. We found that (a) positioning information on more than six layers significantly decreases user performance for depth-related search tasks; (b) that grouping objects can reduce error rates and task completion times for depth-related search tasks; and (c) that maximizing the distance between layers improves user performance when distinguishing information on different depth layers. These findings, together with the results from related work, serve as a holistic foundation to understand the requirements of layered S3D UIs.

At the same time, tools are needed that provide means to arrange items in 3D space. Within the field of user-centered design, low-fidelity prototyping is a powerful means to quickly and easily prototype new interfaces. Well-established techniques such as paper prototyping, however, cannot easily be adopted for S3D UIs as they do not support the positioning of UI objects in 3D space. As a solution we report on the design and development of two depth layout tools for prototyping S3D UIs. The design of the MirrorBox and the FrameBox (Figure 1) was informed by many of the requirements identified in the first part of our work.

We evaluate the prototypes and the generated guidelines in the context of two concrete use cases – S3D mobile phones and S3D dashboards in cars. Feedback from expert users suggests that the proposed prototyping tools are superior to ordinary paper prototyping as they encourage observation of the collected guidelines, support collaboration, and increase creativity as well as the perceived fidelity.

The contribution of this paper is threefold:

- First, we describe requirements for the design of layered S3D UIs, based on a literature review and a lab study.
- Second, we report on the design and development of the prototyping tools FrameBox and MirrorBox.
- Third, we present findings from an evaluation of the prototypes and guidelines by means of two expert focus groups.

RELATED WORK

In this work, we focus on interfaces for S3D displays. In general, the term 3D user interface is related to spatial input [3] and less to the graphical output of the UI. Therefore, we use the term S3D user interface to emphasize our research interest concerning the depth layout of the UI's visual output. We revisit related work from other application areas on 3D displays and provide an overview of prototyping tools.

S3D User Interfaces

3D displays are becoming increasingly popular as traditional 2D displays are being replaced by their 3D counterparts. They are deployed in a variety of contexts (e.g., mobile phones or laptops). Prior work explored the benefits of S3D displays. A detailed review of the performance benefits of S3D is presented by McIntire et al. in [15]. In the field of mobile phones, S3D displays increase UX [6, 26]. Broy et al. propose a concept for enhancing menu structures of a car infotainment system with S3D [5]. They show that the S3D presentation is more compelling and comprehensive than the 2D version. Prior work also shows how to use the third dimension for information visualization. In particular, it is used for medical applications [28], CAD tools [16], gaming [14, 21], as well as for navigation in virtual environments [3].

Prototyping

Prototyping constitutes an important step in the user centered design process of graphical user interfaces to build usable systems. It is applicable in different stages of the design process, ranging from early sketching on paper (low fidelity) to an almost implemented product (high fidelity) [20].

Prototypes, particularly in the early stage of designing UIs, are an important way to communicate and discuss ideas and requirements [2]. For this purpose, paper prototyping is often used as one of the most popular techniques. Snyder defines paper prototyping as a method of brainstorming, designing, creating, testing, and communicating user interfaces [24]. Due to the convenience of this approach, people at all stages of the development process and with diverse backgrounds can participate in the process, including designers, usability engineers, programmers, and end users.

As a system matures, increasing fidelity helps to improve the validity of evaluation through preliminary user studies [13]. Software toolkits have been developed for diverse application domains, including ubiquitous computing environments [13], location-aware applications [12], or mobile projectors [30]. In addition, hardware toolkits [11, 22] have been developed to rapidly prototype interactive devices and tangible UIs.

Discussion

The variety of application areas for S3D UIs shows the potential regarding tools for prototyping 3D depth layouts. Engaging interfaces that extend beyond straightforward user perception activities can particularly benefit from these tools. In particular, we see large potential in considering core challenges in S3D UI design and addressing them via tools that guides users during the design process. In the following, we present a requirements analysis before reporting on the development and evaluation of the tools proposed in this work.

LAYERED 3D - EXPLORING REQUIREMENTS

At the outset of our work, we aimed to understand fundamental challenges that affect the design of feasible S3D UIs. Previous work uncovered a number of aspects related to content design that strongly influence the quality of S3D UIs. In the following, we collect guidelines from previous work to facilitate design decisions for high quality layered S3D UIs.

Comfort Zone: Prior work found that excessive parallaxes reduce the viewing comfort due to accommodation and vergence mismatches [10]. Hence, a comfort zone needs to be determined in which it is easily possible for the user to perceive information. As a rule of thumb, Lambooji et al. recommend limits for retinal disparities of 1° with respect to Panum's fusion area [10]. However, there are studies that reveal more conservative values (e.g., [31]).

Show Content Behind the Screen Layer: Prior studies recommend the use of positive disparities for information display. Hence, the main content should be positioned behind the screen. Negative disparities can cause longer task completion times [4] and visual discomfort [14, 19].

Minimal Distance: Stereoscopic depth is a super acuity which allows a depth difference assessment of 40 arc-sec. Broy et al. explored the minimal distance between two depth layers that allows for quick separation [4]. They suggest a threshold of 2.7 arc-min.

Careful Use of Monocular Depth Cues: Monocular depth cues can support the spatial impression of stereoscopic visualizations, particularly in virtual environments [14]. However for abstract content (e.g., icons) that is likely to appear in layered information interfaces, monocular depth cues should be applied carefully so that scenes do not become unnecessarily complex, for example, through shadows. Moreover, focal blur can reduce user performance in judging depth and perceived quality of the system [17].

Use of Text: It is advisable to display text parallel to the screen surface, since perspective distortions reduce readability. Stuerzlinger et al. found a sharp decrease for rotations larger than 60 degrees [25].

Highlight Objects by Combining Salient Cues: Combining salient features for highlighting objects has been shown to decrease search times [1, 8]. Hence, S3D UIs should employ a foremost layer that depicts urgent information, such as warnings and notifications.

In summary, our analysis of prior work provided us with a rich set of requirements that we used to inform the design of our depth layout tools. The complex nature of S3D UIs suggests that the tools should be able to guide the user towards the optimal UI design process. At the same time, they help us to create guidelines for layered S3D UI design. However, there is a considerable lack of knowledge on how to structure and group information presented in 3D space, which is crucial for creating UIs for 3D displays [29]. Hence, we aim to close the gap through the subsequent user study.

STRUCTURING INFORMATION IN S3D UIS

We conducted a user study to evaluate how information can be structured and grouped in a 3D layered UI. In particular, we are interested in user performance when identifying grouped objects on one depth layer while several other (distractor) layers are present. We investigate how the number of layers, the distance between those layers, and the x- and y-distance between grouped objects impact task completion times and error rates for a depth-related search task. For this search task, participants have to identify two related objects among several distractor objects. The relation between the objects is defined by their depth position, meaning that objects on one depth layer belong to one group.

We investigate the following hypotheses:

H1: Smaller numbers of depth layers increase user performance in identifying grouped objects via depth.

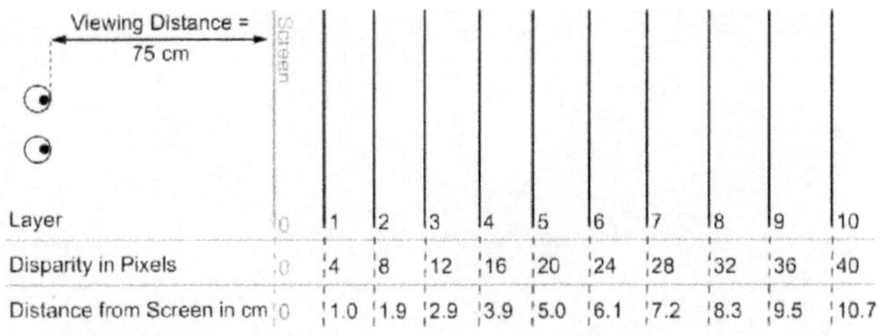

Figure 2: Layer positions applied in the user study. The distances between the screen layer and each depth layer are given in pixels and cm.

H2: Grouping objects additionally via x and y axes reduce error rates and task completion times for a depth-related search task.

H3: By increasing the distance between depth layers, user performance also increases.

Apparatus

For presenting information layers with different depth positions, we employ the 3D display of a notebook equipped with NVIDIA 3D Vision 2 shutter technology. We use a resolution of 1280x480 on a diagonal of 10.5". As a depth range we use parallaxes up to 40 pixels and as a minimum distance between two depth layers we use 4 pixels, as has been suggested by prior work [4]. According to Mahoney et al., information presentation should focus on the area behind the screen [14, 19]. Hence, we do not consider negative parallaxes in our study. Figure 3 visualizes the examined positions for the depth layers. The values are calculated with respect to our setup (pixel pitch = 0.196; viewing distance = 750 mm).

As we foresee text and icons to be important parts in informative UIs, we use binocular disparity as depth cue to structure information. In contrast to monocular cues (relative size, shadows, lighting, occlusion), binocular disparity neither changes the size of object (which is important for readability) nor does it make parts of the scene invisible.

Tasks

The participants had to solve two tasks during the experiment. First, we use a depth-related search task to gather insight into user performance when deciding on depth relationships between objects presented with the 3D display. We presented one object labeled with a number on each depth layer and, in addition, a reference object on one of the depth layers, showing a red square (Figure 3). The task for the participant was then to find the object placed on the same depth layer as the reference object (we refer to this also as the target object). All objects were squares with a height and width of 90 pixels. Note, that due to the lack of monocular depth cues it is not possible to identify the target object in Figure 3–top. For the purpose of simplicity, we rendered the scene in a 3D perspective (Figure 3–bottom).

Second, a distractor task prompted the participant to switch their visual focus to a large distractor display placed behind the 3D display. We applied the additional distractor task to increase the difficulty of the depth-related search task and to satisfy requirements for real world applications that involve

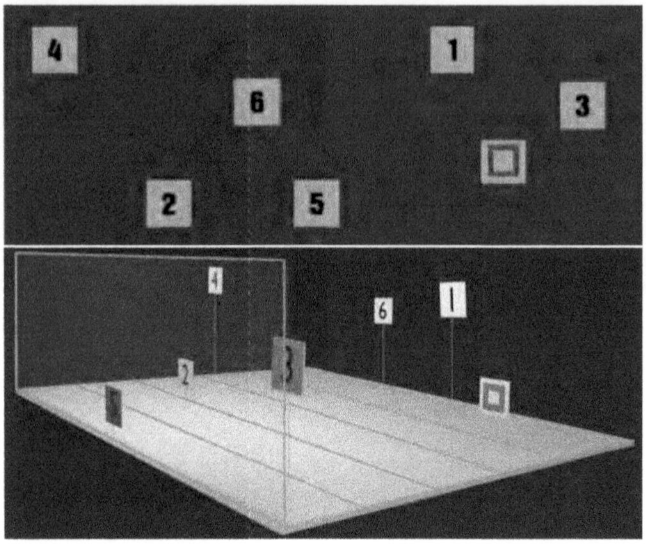

Figure 3: The search task in front view (top) and perspective 3D (bottom). In this example, the numbered squares occupy six layers while the reference object is located at the same depth layer as object *1*.

accommodation switches commonly occurring in pervasive display environments (e.g., automotive or mobile applications). The distractor task required the participant to focus and read a word depicted on the distractor display aloud. The words are composed of two or more simple, unrelated nouns (e.g., *daybreakhazard*) that force the participant to focus cognitively and visually on the distractor display.

Study Design

The study was designed as a repeated measures experiment. We altered three independent variables:

Depth Layers: We expected that the number of depth layers impacts user performance. Since one object is shown on each layer, we assumed that higher numbers of depth layers decrease user performance. Therefore, we tested the impact of 4, 6, and 8 layers.

XY-Distance: Based on the law of proximity, we expected effects on user performance for varying x- and y-distances between the target and reference object. We investigated small (5-15% of the screen's diagonal), medium (35% - 45%), and large distances (65% - 75%) for this study.

Z-Distance: The distance between two layers can be maximal (the layers are linearly distributed within the depth budget) or minimal (the layers are distributed 4 pixels next to each other starting with the screen layer). We thought that the z distance impacts the user performance.

Beside these independent variables, the depth position of target and reference objects can have a potential influence on user performance. Hence, we tested every possible layer position for target and reference square over all conditions. This resulted in (4*3*2) + (6*3*2) + (8*3*2) = 108 depth judgment tasks that every user has to solve. We grouped the conditions by blocks of depth layers. To avoid sequence effects

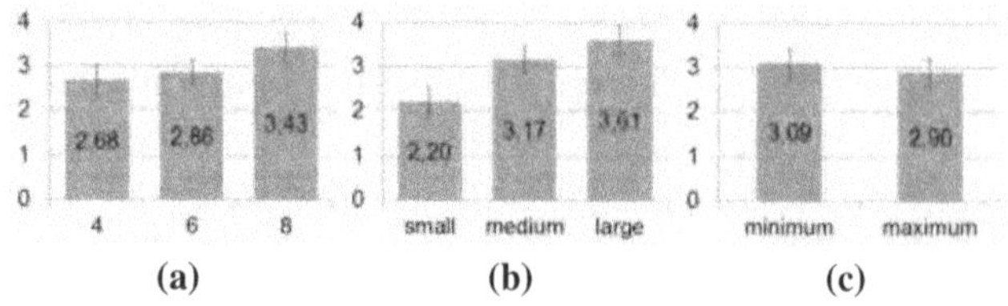

Figure 4: TCT mean values and standard errors as error bars for (a) depth layers, (b) xy-distance, and (c) z-distance. An ANOVA shows significant main effects for depth layers, xy-distances, and z-distance.

we counterbalanced the presentation of these blocks. The order of the xy- and z-distance conditions was randomized for each block. We measured task completion times (TCT) and recognition rates (RR) for the depth judgment task. Beside these objective measurements, the users rated the perceived difficulty of the task.

Recruiting, Setup, and Procedure

For the conducted study we recruited 30 participants through mailing lists. As participants arrived they were briefed on the study purpose and procedure. Prior to the study, we tested visual acuity with a Snellen test [23] and stereo vision with Random Dot Stereograms (RDSs) [9]. Participants passing both vision tests qualified for the study. They proceeded by completing a demographic questionnaire. Afterwards, the participants were seated 75 cm in front of the shutter display and 200 cm in front of the distractor display, respectively. We used a chin rest to ensure the same viewing distances across conditions and participants. After a training session (12 tasks), the participant started with the first task of the respective depth layer block by pressing the space key on the provided keyboard. After the participants detected the target object, they pressed the space key and read aloud the number shown on the target object. The difference between these button press events was measured as TCT. Next, the participant performed the distraction task. This procedure was repeated for all three blocks. After each block, the participants completed the questionnaire evaluating the difficulty of the task.

Results

In total, 30 participants (6 female, 24 male) aged between 20 and 53 ($M = 29.0$, $SD = 6.9$) took part in this study. All participants have normal or corrected to normal visual acuity and passed the stereo vision test.

Task Completion Time

Figure 4 shows mean and standard errors of TCT for depth layers, xy-distances, and, z-distances. We used a three-way analysis of variance (ANOVA) with repeated measures to investigate statistical differences. There are statistically significant differences for TCT concerning the number of depth layers, $F(2,58) = 13.877$,$p < .001$,$r = .548$, the xy-distance between target and reference object, $F(2,58) = 59.926$, $p < .001$, $r = .814$, and z distance between depth layers, $F(1,29) = 4.361$, $p = .046$, $r = .317$. We used pairwise t-tests with Bonferroni corrections for post-hoc analyses. For the number of depth layers the t-tests reveal statistically significant effects between 4 and 8, $T(29) = -5.564$, $p \leq .001$,

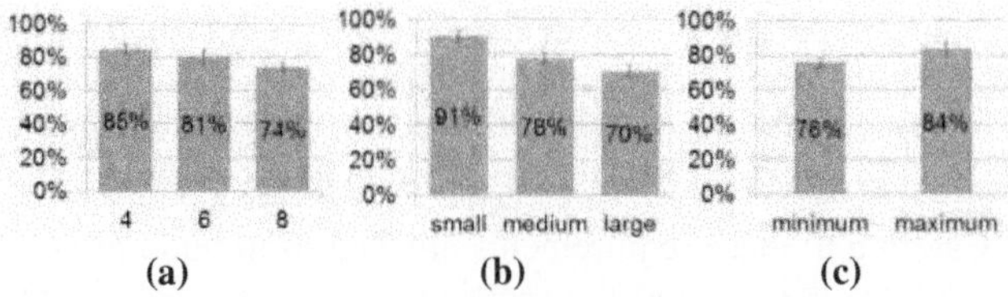

Figure 5: RR mean values and standard errors as error bars for (a) depth layers, (b) xy-distance, and (c) z-distance. An ANOVA shows significant main effects for depth layers, xy-distances, and z-distance.

Depth Layers	Mean	Standard Deviation
4	3.567	1.612
6	4.067	1.388
8	4.500	1.614

Table 1: Means and standard deviations for subjective ratings of difficulty depended on depth layers. Difficulty was rated on a seven point Likert scale from one (very easy) to seven (very difficult).

as well as 6 and 8 layers, $T(29) = -4.242$, $p \leq .001$. The comparison of 4 with 6 layers is not statistically significant, $T(29) = -1.047, p = .911$. Concerning the xy distances, the pairwise t-tests reveal significant differences between all distances, all $p \leq .001$. The results show that the TCT depends on the number of depth layers, xy-distance, and z-distance between the depth layers.

Recognition Rate

Figure 5 depicts mean and standard errors of the recognition rate (RR) for depth layers, xy-distances, and, z-distances. Analyzing the RR, a repeated measures ANOVA shows statistically significant differences for the number of depth layers, $F(2, 58) = 20.486$, $p < .001$, $r = .628$, xy-distance, $F(1.687, 48.913) = 49.033$, $p < .001$, $r = .785$, and z-distance, $F(1, 29) = 30.230$, $p < .001$, $r = .702$. Mauchly's test shows that the assumption of sphericity is violated for xy-distance, $X^2(2) = 7.859$, $p = .02$, and, therefore, the degrees of freedom are corrected using Huynth-Feldt estimation of sphericity. In accordance to the results of TCT, pairwise t-tests with Bonferroni corrections show statistically significant differences for comparing 4 with 8, $T(29) = 6.475$, $p \leq .001$, and 6 with 8 depth layers, $T(29) = 4.090$, $p \leq .001$. Again, 4 versus 6 depth layers reveals no statistical significance, $T(29) = 2.263$, $p = .094$. Moreover, all pairwise comparisons of xy-distances are statistically significant, $p < .001$. Thus, the number of depth layers, the xy-distance, and the z-distance influence the RR.

Subjective Ratings

The participants rated the perceived difficulty of the depth-related search task after each depth layer block. The difficulty scale ranges from 1 (very easy) to 7 (very difficult). Mean values and standard deviations for the ratings after each depth layer block are listed in Table 1.

A Friedman test reveals statistically significant differences for the subjectively rated difficulty regarding the variation of depth layers, $X^2(2) = 13.640$, $p = .001$. Pairwise comparisons using Wilcoxon tests show significances between 4 and 6 layers ($p = .039$) as well as between 4 and 8 layers ($p = .006$). In general, participants state that it is easier to solve the task if the target and reference pair is placed at the foremost or backmost depth layer. Furthermore, the task is perceived as easier if no objects are located between the target and reference layer in terms of the object's x- and y-position on the screen.

Implications

The described study investigates the influence of the number of depth layers, their differences in depth as well as the influence of xy-distances for grouping and structuring information on depth layers. The results let us derive several implications facilitating design decisions for developing S3D UIs.

Information Layers

Our results show that an increasing number of depth layers decreases user performance in terms of TCT and RR. Moreover, the subjective ratings concerning the task difficulty support the findings. Therefore, we can accept hypothesis H1.

An explanation for this finding is provided by the Hick-Hyman law [7] (increasing the number of choices will increase the decision time) as well as the feature integration theory of Treisman [27] (combining features leads to a serial search meaning increasing distractor objects increase search time). However, Nakayma and Silverman found that the conjunction of two salient features with one being stereoscopic depth remains a parallel search [18]. The results of Nakayama and Silverman are based on two depth layers, meaning that each of the two layers allows for parallel search.

Our study shows that the decrease in performance is not statistically significant between 4 and 6 depth layers, although we observed a minimal performance decline. Hence, we assume that six information layers are still suitable for distributing information in 3D space, while 8 layers decrease user performance significantly. Based on these results, we recommend a maximum number of 6 information layers for designing a S3D layered UI.

Proximity in the Third Dimension

As our findings suggest, the xy-distance between objects plays a major role for grouping information via depth. As user performance significantly decreases for increasing xy-distance between target and reference object, we accept H2.

Therefore, we recommend using the entire depth budget behind the screen layer for information structuring. Besides a proper depth layer position of user interface elements, x- and y-locations have to be considered carefully. In general, the Gestalt psychology provides laws for grouping elements through specific characteristics. The law of proximity explains the performance reduction for increasing xy-distances and proves valid for the examined depth layers.

Moreover, we found that the law of proximity is also valid for the z-dimension. Maximizing the distance between depth layers within the comfort zone improves user performance. Hence, our study also confirms hypothesis H3. Nevertheless, this effect is absent for small x- and y-distances between grouped objects.

Discussion and Limitations

In this study, we explore performance in the entire 3D space. We deliberately opted to address various applications areas and maximize internal validity. Thus, we created a rather abstract task (i.e., selecting objects on the same screen level), used abstract content, and kept object parameters (e.g., color, size, and position) constant. We acknowledge that applying our findings to specific areas with different TCTs, like automotive UIs, would need further investigation in the future and is outside the scope of this study.

As our results show, the chosen task constitutes a complex visual search task that requires TCTs longer than 2 seconds. In fact, there are many real world applications to which this artificial task is not directly applicable. For example, the automotive domain requires tasks that are interruptible and do not need immediate responses for infotainment related applications. However, this abstract task allowed for precise measurements and gives us insights into the effect of spatial structuring along the z dimension.

Prior work found that perception of information works best behind the screen level. Hence, we decided to focus our study on this area of the screen. This is a limitation of the study and findings may not generalize to the area in front of the screen.

DEPTH LAYOUT TOOLS FOR PROTOTYPING S3D UIS

In the previous section we explored the core requirements for designing and prototyping S3D UIs. With the tools presented in this section, we aim to provide a means for designers to adhere to these requirements.

The third dimension makes it particularly challenging to use existing, state of the art, prototyping techniques for 2D user interfaces. As has been stressed earlier, paper prototyping has been shown to be highly useful in early stages of the development process [2] but is clearly limited when trying to arrange UI elements in 3D space. Hence, we built tools that can overcome the flat nature of paper for prototyping S3D layered UIs. The core idea is to augment paper prototyping in a way that maximizes the artistic freedom of the designer while providing implicit guidance towards usable products. In the following, we summarize the requirements and determine physical dimensions for tools that can support low fidelity prototyping in 3D space.

Viewing Distance and Depth Budget First of all, designers need to identify the distance between the viewer and the screen on which the UI is being presented. Usually this distance is defined by the context in which the UI is to be used. For example, in cars the usual distance between driver and dashboard is 75 cm. The viewing distance then determines the depth budget in which UI elements should be positioned to provide a comfortable viewing experience. Prior work showed this range to be 17.9 arc min to the front and 35.9 arc min to the back of the screen level [4].

Target Interface Dimensions The second requirement is the envisioned size of the target interface (width and height), for example a public display, a mobile phone, or a dashboard. Together with the viewing distance and depth budget it then allows for calculating width, height, and depth.

Number and Position of Depth Layers The depth layer positions and their number depend (a) on the distance of the viewer from the screen, which determines the available space (comfort zone) in z-direction and (b) of the minimum depth distance (3.6 arc min, see previous section).

Catering to these requirements allowed us to build prototyping tools that support the user in creating UIs, that (1) minimize the visual discomfort S3D can potentially cause and (2) allow different depth layers to be quickly and accurately distinguished. In this section, we describe two novel prototyping tools – the FrameBox and the MirrorBox. Both tools were designed to be used for arbitrary S3D UI design tasks and to map the specified requirements in the best possible manner.

FrameBox

The core idea behind the FrameBox is to allow users to work with a large variety of materials, including paper, films, and 3D mockups created with a laser printer, and to spatially position the different elements. Hence, we designed a cubic box made of acrylic glass with a number of slots that represent the different depth layers and allow for positioning UI elements on the z-axis in discrete steps. Within each slot, UI elements can be easily moved in the x-direction. Positioning on the y-axis can be achieved by means of paper-clips. In accordance to the specified requirements, we built a series of FrameBoxes for different application areas. One FrameBox was aimed for the design of automotive UIs and two for the design of mobile phones UIs (one for landscape and one for portrait mode).

The automotive FrameBox is based on the dimensions of a conventional freely programmable instrument cluster (12.3") and a typical viewing distance of 750 mm. The viewing distance allows for positioning UI elements 44 mm to the front of the screen and 107 mm to the back of the screen to maintain the comfort zone. This results in the following dimensions of the FrameBox for an instrument cluster application: 293 x 110 x 151 mm (WxHxD).

For the mobile FrameBox we chose the size of the Samsung Galaxy S4 (5") and a typical viewing distance of 350 mm. These values result in a comfort zone of up to 21 mm to the front and 50 mm to the back of the screen. Hence, the dimensions of the FrameBoxes are 111 x 62 x 71 mm.

All FrameBoxes were built using a laser cutter. The laser cutter templates are available for public use from our website[1]. As material we used transparent acrylic glass. A red line references the screen layer and makes positioning in front of or behind the screen easy for the designers (Figure 6).

MirrorBox

As a second prototyping tool, we designed the MirrorBox. We use a number of semi-transparent mirrors in the front and a surface-coated mirror in the back to allow users to see the mirrored image of a UI element projected from below (Figure 7). The mirrors are aligned one after another on top of a light source. Transparency films can be used to design UI elements, which are then sliced between the mirrors and the light source to make them visible to the user inside the MirrorBox.

[1]Templates: `http://www.hcilab.org/p/3Dprototyping`

Figure 6: Frame Boxes for automotive and mobile phone applications (portrait and landscape).

Figure 7: The MirrorBox with an iPad as a lighting source.

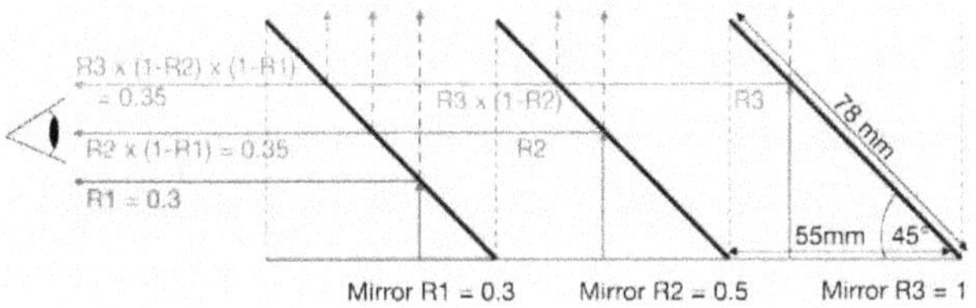

Figure 8: Principle of the Mirror Box: Mirror arrangements with reflectivity R1, R2, R3.

We constructed a multi-purpose MirrorBox consisting of 3 mirrors with a size of 125 x 78 mm. The mirrors are arranged behind one another and are horizontally tilted by 45 degrees. In this way, the mirrors generate three virtual layers by reflecting UI elements from below. We use a tablet as a lighting source. The mirrors have different reflectivity to provide the viewer with a similar brightness for all three virtual layers. The rear mirror reflects almost 100%, the mirror in the middle has a reflectivity of 50% and the foremost mirror has 30% reflectivity. This results in a total reflectivity of between 30% and 35% for each virtual layer (Figure 8). Since the mirrors are tilted by 45 degrees, the virtual images have a height of 55 mm. The distance between the layers is 55 mm. The outer dimensions of the MirrorBox are 125 x 55 x 165 mm.

EVALUATION

To evaluate the potential of our depth layout tools, we conducted two hands-on workshop sessions with experts in two fields, namely, automotive UIs and mobile phone UIs. We compared our approaches with paper prototyping, which is commonly used in early stages of development [2].

Procedure

As participants arrived, we first gave them a brief introduction on S3D UI design. We particularly focused on the guidelines explained earlier. The introduction took 10 minutes and slides were given to the participants as printouts for later reference. Then, the tasks for the hands-on phases were explained. We instructed the participants with a horizontal and a vertical prototyping task, depending on the workshop topic.

In the subsequent hands-on phase, participants were separated into two groups and asked to work on the tasks by means of three prototyping techniques. First, both teams used paper prototyping. As material we provided paper and post-its in different sizes and colors as well as colored pens. They were told that they had 15 minutes to work on the tasks and then had to present their ideas within no more than 3 minutes to the other group. After the presentation, one group was assigned the FrameBox and one group was assigned the MirrorBox and again given 15 minutes to work on the tasks. To each group, we also showed a brief concept video of the respective tool[2]. We told them that they can reuse and integrate their ideas and the ones of the other group. In addition to the paper prototyping material, we also provided them pieces of transparency films in different sizes and pens to write/draw on the film. After another 3 minute presentation, groups were asked to switch the depth layout tools and watch the other concept video. After 15 minutes we concluded the hands-on phase with another brief presentation. In total, each group created three prototypes, one with each prototyping tool (Figure 9).

Following the hands-on phases, participants were provided with a questionnaire that assessed their design skills, asked them to rank the tools, and to provide qualitative feedback. After that we entered a 30 minutes discussion phase led by two researchers. During the discussion phase, participants were asked to comment on strengths and weaknesses of the techniques, particular questions that came up during the hands-on phase, and observations made by the researchers.

Workshops

Design of S3D UIs is rapidly gaining importance in a lot of different areas. In two workshop sessions, we focused on automotive UIs and mobile phone UIs. The main reason for choosing these areas is that we envision 3D displays being commonly used in these contexts in the near future.

Automotive UIs are characterized by the fact that they draw the attention of the driver and, hence, direct the driver‘s sight off the road which must be critically minimized. This workshop session ran with nine members of the HCI department of BMW, grouped into two teams of four and five participants, respectively. All were experts in creating 2D UIs but nobody had designed a UI for a 3D display before. We refer to these participants as P1–P9 in the results section. The horizontal task for this session was to design a 3D dashboard for a car. In addition they were asked to integrate a conceptual navigation system within the dashboard that would provide guidance between two cities (vertical part).

[2]The concept videos are available from the ACM Digital Library and from `http://www.hcilab.org/p/3Dprototyping`.

Figure 9: Prototyping Workshop – After the two groups of participants received a brief introduction to S3D prototyping, they had to paper-prototype a 3D dashboard (1). After that groups used the MirrorBox (2) and the FrameBox (3) to refine their prototypes. After each session, groups presented their results (4) before filling in a questionnaire (5) and engaging into a discussion.

Mobile phones are ubiquitously used and the number of apps available is constantly growing. Many apps are used on the go and, thus, an easy to understand and use interface is important. This workshop session ran with six under- and post-graduates with backgrounds in either computer science or design, grouped in two teams with three participants each. All are experienced in developing applications for mobile devices. We refer to these participants as P10–P15 in the results section. The horizontal part of this session was to design the main screen of a mobile phone. For the vertical part, they had to design a widget that can be placed on the main screen.

Results

We collected results from the questionnaire and the discussion to get insights into how our concepts performed for creating low fidelity 3D prototypes. In addition, we report on observations made during the workshops.

A ranking of the three prototyping techniques shows that most participants favored the FrameBox (11 participants), followed by the MirrorBox (5) and paper prototyping (5). Further findings are grouped around four dimensions that we consider to be particularly important for prototyping tools, namely, expressiveness, usability, effort, and creativity. In the questionnaire, participants ranked the three prototyping techniques from one (best) to three (worst) to address these dimensions.

Expressiveness

Prototypes are often used to obtain early insights into concepts and, thus, the prototype needs to provide means for expressing and communicating the main idea. We explicitly asked participants whether they considered the prototype to have a high expressiveness. Answers show that participants attributed the highest expressiveness to the FrameBox ($Mdn = 1$), followed by MirrorBox ($Mdn = 2$), and paper prototyping ($Mdn = 3$). We performed a Friedman analysis of variance (ANOVA) that shows statistically significant differences between the three tools, $\chi^2(2) = 14.000, p = .001$. As follow up tests, we used three Wilcoxon tests for pairwise comparison with a Bonferroni correction applied. The Wilcoxon tests show statistically significant differences for FrameBox and paper prototyping, $Z = -3.226$, $p = .001$, as well as for MirrorBox and paper prototyping, $Z = -2.586$, $p = .010$. The differences between MirrorBox and FrameBox is not statistically significant, $Z = -1.355$, $p = .175$.

The discussions reflect these findings and provide further insights. Participants stated that "ideas are hard to communicate" (P4) using paper prototypes alone. Due to the two dimensional nature of paper "3D space is difficult to imagine" (P15), and it is "not sufficient for presenting the use of the z axis" (P5, P8, P9, P10, P13, P15). In contrast, FrameBox as well as MirrorBox represent the depth layers unambiguously and clarify depth positions. Participants feel the capabilities of the MirrorBox to be limited by just providing three layers, whereas "FrameBox offers a greater scope" (P7).

Usability

Prototyping in user-centered design is often done with users that are not prototyping experts. Thus, it is important that the tools are easy to use. We asked all participants whether they agree that the tools are easy to use. They rated paper prototyping best ($Mdn = 1$) followed by FrameBox ($Mdn = 2$) and MirrorBox ($Mdn = 3$). We performed a Friedman test (ANOVA) that shows statistically significant differences between the tools, $\chi^2(2) = 9.170, p = .010$. Using Bonferroni corrected Wilcoxon tests to follow up on this finding reveal statistically significant differences between the MirrorBox and FrameBox, $Z = -2.441$, $p = .015$, and between MirrorBox and paper prototyping, $Z = -2.565$, $p = .010$.

Participants believe the main reason for this to be that paper prototyping "is a well-known approach" (P10). Similarly, participants considered positioning elements on the layers to be very easy for the FrameBox (P2, P3, P8, P15). Creating depth layers as well as modifying their x, y, and z direction is perceived to be quick and easy. In contrast, positioning layers using MirrorBox is considered to be tricky since overlapping snippets impede each other. In addition, correctly positioning the transparency films (mirror-inverted) is considered to be confusing by some participants. Switching the depth position of layers is perceived as fast and easy.

Effort

Prototyping is particularly beneficial in iterative design processes. Hence, refined versions are frequently tested which suggests that the effort to create a prototype should be minimal. When asked how they rate the effort to create a prototype with each tool, participants rate paper prototype best ($Mdn = 1$), followed by the FrameBox ($Mdn = 2$) and the MirrorBox ($Mdn = 2$). The Friedman ANOVA shows no statistically significant differences, $\chi^2(2) = 2.393, p = .302$.

In the discussion, participants argued that paper prototyping is "good for first sketches and considerations" since it allows users to "generate and check out ideas quickly" (P9, P10, P14). Paper prototyping is considered to be effortless which "makes it easy to reject first sketches" (P10). The FrameBox supports less effortful design of realistic 3D impressions, whereas the MirrorBox is rated as more complex and sometimes even annoying, since the layers inside the small box are difficult to perceive without being positioned directly in front of it. Participants also felt that this makes collaboration among team members more difficult. This matches with our observations that the prototypes sparked quite a different amount of collaboration and discussion. With the MirrorBox, one member of the design team usually takes the task to position elements while the others draw the elements. For the FrameBox all participants design elements and position them themselves.

Creativity

Prototyping sessions are often performed in stages where design decisions are not made yet. Thus, the tool should not hamper the creativity of the user. Asked if the tools fully support the user's creativity, all three tools are rated equally good ($Mdn = 2$). A Friedman ANOVA shows, no statistically significant differences, $\chi^2(2) = 1.019, p = .601$.

The discussion showed that "paper prototyping fosters the flow of creativity due to starting from scratch on white paper" (P3, P12) and "offers the highest degree of freedom" (P13). Prototyping with paper and using the FrameBox fosters communication and collaboration. Participants feel inspired by the visual effect from the backlight and the mirrored layers of the MirrorBox. However, the mirror box somewhat "restricts the design space" (P4, P5, P8, P11, P12).

DISCUSSION

This paper provides (a) basic guidelines for designing user interfaces for 3D displays, that were gathered through a literature review and complemented by a laboratory study, and (b) prototyping tools supporting the design process for S3D UIs. We used the guidelines for the design of the presented tools and for instructing the participants during the workshops.

In the workshops, we were able to observe that the participants make use of the presented guidelines to fulfill their tasks. While the MirrorBox restricts the depth layout to only three depth layers, the FrameBox provides participants much more artistic freedom. Nevertheless, the participants stick to the guideline by using no more than six depth layers while prototyping with the FrameBox. Hence, this guideline can easily be followed by the users even if the tool does not explicitly implement this rule. For paper prototyping, we noticed that the participants have difficulties in observing the comfort zone as well as the minimal recommended distance between depth layers. Consequently, it is beneficial to integrate these guidelines in the tool in a way such that the designers can take the available depth relations into account. Furthermore, the participants propose an iterative process which involves a first concept draft based on paper prototyping and a later refinement using the FrameBox.

The conducted workshops show that our tools complement the strengths of paper prototyping – particularly low effort and support for creativity – with high usability and means for expressiveness. Our workshop participants try to cope with the fact that paper prototyping makes it difficult to position elements in 3D space. This comes at the cost of increased effort. For example, participants spend a considerable amount of time during the paper prototyping session making post-its 'stand' behind each other to reflect several layers or try to build 3D objects using paper. In contrast, the positioning of elements in 3D space is supported by MirrorBox and FrameBox. The use of our tools allows participants to concentrate on ideas, exploring the positioning of objects, adjusting fonts, and object size. The participants like to use paper prototyping in combination with the FrameBox as it has a low barrier for participation in the prototyping process but supports the spatial arrangement and the integration of 3D objects well. In contrast, the MirrorBox narrows the depth layout to three layers and does not allow the integration of 3D objects.

Furthermore, we have seen in the workshops that the prototyping tools help to effectively communicate design decisions within the team and to outside observers. The participants report that it is easier to understand the idea of the other group as they presented their results with the MirrorBox or FrameBox in contrast to seeing the results just as a paper prototype. This finding is supported by the results of the questionnaires regarding the expressiveness of the approaches. A low barrier for participation and the expressiveness is especially important for the UI development process as it often involves developers with different backgrounds.

Participants also express a clear interest in increasing the fidelity of the MirrorBox. While in our case, the iPad is only used as backlight, they suggest using an external monitor or tabletop surface that would allow users to sketch UI elements and display them immediately on the iPad.

Finally, we see potential in augmenting our tools with 3D elements, for example, from a 3D printer. In the automotive workshop we observed participants that exploit ways of modeling 3D objects. One group used the upper back part of the sticky notes to attach interface elements to paper. Another group used transparent scotch tape to create objects like mountains or buildings for the navigation system.

CONCLUSION

In this paper, we identify guidelines for creating UIs for 3D displays. Furthermore, we present MirrorBox and FrameBox, two display layout tools for prototyping S3D UIs. First, we provide an in-depth assessment of the requirements for building such user interfaces. Second, we report on how we designed the tools and evaluated them by means of two workshops with usability engineers. Third, we provide detailed information on how to adopt our idea to arbitrary UIs. Files to rebuild the tools are available from our website. In our evaluation, we show that our prototyping tools are, according to many aspects, superior to paper prototyping when it comes to designing for 3D displays as they increase creativity, usability, and expressiveness. For future work, we aim to apply the approach to high-fidelity prototyping.

ACKNOWLEDGEMENTS

We thank Carl Oechsner for his help during the user study. The research leading to these results has received funding from the European Union Seventh Framework Programme [FP7/2007-2013] under grant agreement no. 600851.

REFERENCES

1. Alper, B., Höllerer, T., Kuchera-Morin, J., and Forbes, A. Stereoscopic highlighting: 2d graph visualization on stereo displays. *IEEE Trans. Vis. Comput. Graph. 17*, 12 (2011), 2325–2333.
2. Baskinger, M. Cover story: Pencils before pixels: a primer in hand-generated sketching. *interactions 15*, 2 (Mar. 2008), 28–36.
3. Bowman, D. A., Kruijff, E., LaViola Jr, J. J., and Poupyrev, I. *3D user interfaces: theory and practice*. Addison-Wesley, 2004.
4. Broy, N., Alt, F., Schneegass, S., Henze, N., and Schmidt, A. Perceiving layered information on 3d displays using binocular disparity. In *Proc. PerDis 13*, 61–66.
5. Broy, N., André, E., and Schmidt, A. Is stereoscopic 3d a better choice for information representation in the car? In *Proc. AutoUI '12*, 93–100.
6. Häkkilä, J., Posti, M., Koskenranta, O., and Ventä-Olkkonen, L. Design and evaluation of mobile phonebook application with stereoscopic 3d user interface. In *CHI '13 EA*, 1389–1394.
7. Hick, W. E. On the rate of gain of information. *Quarterly Journal of Exp. Psych. 4*, 1 (1952), 11–26.
8. Huhtala, J., Karukka, M., Salmimaa, M., and Häkkilä, J. Evaluating depth illusion as method of adding emphasis in autostereoscopic mobile displays. In *Proc. MobileHCI '11*,
9. Julesz, B. *Foundations of cyclopean perception*. University of Chicago Press, 1971.
10. Lambooij, M., IJsselsteijn, W., and Fortuin, M. Visual discomfort and visual fatigue of stereoscopic displays: A review. *Journal of Img. Tech. and Sci. 53* (2009), 1–14.
11. Lee, J. C., Avrahami, D., Hudson, S. E., Forlizzi, J., Dietz, P. H., and Leigh, D. The calder toolkit: wired and wireless components for rapidly prototyping interactive devices. In *Proc. DIS '04*, 167–175.
12. Li, Y., Hong, J. I., and Landay, J. A. Topiary: a tool for prototyping location-enhanced applications. In *Proc. UIST '04*, 217–226.
13. Liu, L., and Khooshabeh, P. Paper or interactive?: a study of prototyping techniques for ubiquitous computing environments. In *CHI '03 EA*, 1030–1031.
14. Mahoney, N., Oikonomou, A., and Wilson, D. Stereoscopic 3d in video games: A review of current design practices and challenges. In *CGAMES* (2011).
15. McIntire, J. P., Havig, P. R., and Geiselman, E. E. What is 3d good for? a review of human performance on stereoscopic 3d displays. In *Proc. of Head- and Helmet-Mounted Displays XVII*, vol. 8383, SPIE (2012).
16. McWorther, S. W., Hodges, L. F., and Rodriguez, W. E. Comparison of 3-d display formats for cad applications. In *Stereoscop. Displ. and Apps II*, SPIE (1991).
17. Mikkola, M., Boev, A., and Gotchev, A. Relative importance of depth cues on portable autostereoscopic display. In *Proc. MoViD*, MoViD '10, ACM (New York, NY, USA, 2010).
18. Nakayama, K., and Silverman, G. H. Serial and parallel processing of visual feature conjunctions. *Nature 320*, 6059 (1986), 264–265.
19. Nojiri, Y., Yamanoue, H., Ide, S., Yano, S., and Okano, F. Parallax distribution and visual comfort on stereoscopic HDTV. In *Proc. IBC* (2006), 373–380.
20. Rogers, Y., Sharp, H., and Preece, J. *Interaction Design: Beyond Human-Computer Interaction*, 3 ed. John Wiley & Sons, New York, 2011.
21. Schild, J., Bölicke, L., LaViola Jr., J. J., and Masuch, M. Creating and analyzing stereoscopic 3d graphical user interfaces in digital games. In *Proc. CHI '13*,
22. Schneegass, S., Pfleging, B., Kern, D., and Schmidt, A. Support for modeling interaction with automotive user interfaces. In *Proc. AutoUI '11*, 71–78.
23. Snellen, H. *Probebuchstaben zur Bestimmung der Sehschaerfe*. Nabu Press, 2010.
24. Snyder, C. *Paper prototyping: The fast and easy way to design and refine user interfaces*. Morgan Kaufmann, 2003.
25. Stuerzlinger, W., and Wingrave, C. A. The value of constraints for 3d user interfaces. In *Virtual Realities*, Springer (2008), 203–223.
26. Sunnari, M., Arhippainen, L., Pakanen, M., and Hickey, S. Studying user experiences of autostereoscopic 3d menu on touch screen mobile device. In *Proc. OzCHI '12*, 558–561.
27. Treisman, A. M., and Gelade, G. A feature-integration theory of attention. *Cog. Psych. 12*, 1 (1980), 97–136.
28. van Beurden, M. H. P. H., Hoey, G. V., Hatzakis, H., and IJsselsteijn, W. A. Stereoscopic displays in medical domains: a review of perception and performance effects. In *Human Vision and Electronic Imaging*, vol. 7240, SPIE (2009).
29. Ventä-Olkkonen, L., Posti, M., and Häkkilä, J. How to use 3d in stereoscopic mobile user interfaces: Study on initial user perceptions. In *AcademicMindTrek '13*, ACM (New York, NY, USA, 2013), 39:39–39:42.
30. Weigel, M., Boring, S., Steimle, J., Marquardt, N., Greenberg, S., and Tang, A. Projectorkit: easing rapid prototyping of interactive applications for mobile projectors. In *Proc. MobileHCI '13*,
31. Yeh, Y.-Y., and Silverstein, L. D. Limits of fusion and depth judgment in stereoscopic color displays. *Human Factors: Journal of the Hum. Fac. and Erg. Soc. 32*, 1 (1990), 45–60.

Direct Drawing on 3D Shapes with Automated Camera Control

Michaël Ortega[1], Thomas Vincent[2]
[2]UJF-Grenoble 1 / UPMF-Grenoble 2 / Grenoble-INP / [1]CNRS / INRIA
[1,2]Laboratoire d'Informatique de Grenoble, UMR 5217 F-38041, Grenoble, France
firstname.lastname@imag.fr

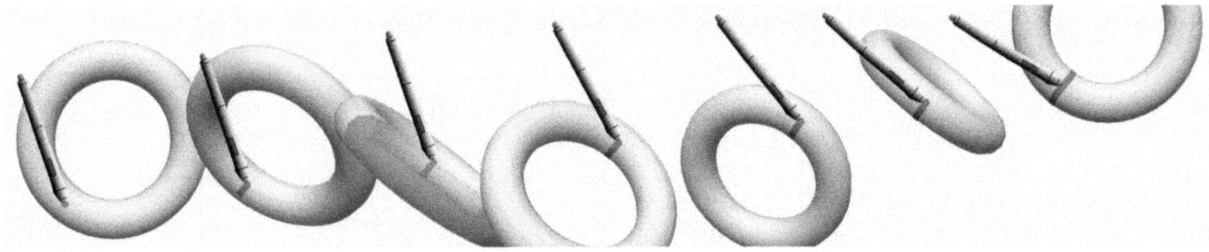

Figure 1. With Automated Camera Control for Drawing (*ACCD*), the small radius of a torus can be drawn in a single continuous curve.

ABSTRACT

We present ACCD, an interaction technique that allows direct drawing of long curves on 3D shapes with a tablet display over both multiple depth layers and multiple viewpoints. ACCD reduces the number of explicit viewpoint manipulations by combining self-occlusion management and automated camera control. As such it enables drawing on occluded faces but also around a 3D shape while keeping a constant drawing precision. Our experimental results indicates the efficacy of ACCD over conventional techniques.

Author Keywords

3D interaction technique; 3D painting; camera controls.

ACM Classification Keywords

H.5.2. Information Interfaces and Presentation: User Interfaces - Interaction styles, Input devices and strategies.

INTRODUCTION

Drawing on 3D shapes is a generic elementary action for performing various tasks: 3D models painting [5], 3D sculpture [14], sketch-based 3D objects modelling [10], mesh segmentation [3], specification and control of navigation in 3D environments [6]. In WYSIWYG interfaces, drawing consists of mapping 2D input strokes into curves on the 3D shape.

The status-quo configuration uses a tablet display for direct drawing, and a standard projection (pinhole camera metaphor) for a "realistic" representation of the shape [1]. Drawing is performed with stylus strokes on the tablet display, while viewpoint manipulation is done with separated tools (rotation, pan and zoom). However, this configuration requires the users to frequently switch between drawing and viewpoint manipulation.

Indeed, some parts of the 3D shape might not be reachable from a single viewpoint: (1) faces occluded by the object itself (i.e., ***self-occlusion***); and (2) ***back faces***. Viewpoint manipulations are required to access such faces. Moreover, the ***drawing precision*** depends on (1) the distance from the viewpoint to the shape, and on (2) the angle between the line of sight (viewpoint direction) and the normal of the surface [12]. Controlling this precision during drawing thus requires even more viewpoint manipulations. This number of viewpoint manipulation can be very high for complex 3D shapes, leading to tedious and time-consuming drawing task.

Furthermore, switching between viewpoint manipulation and drawing results in discontinuities at the junctions of the different sub-curves. For example, in 3D sculpture tools, like Pixologic ZBrush [14], the dig out tool is controlled by user strokes on the 3D shape. The junctions of those strokes result in visual gaps that the user must correct afterwards. Minimizing the number of strokes required to draw a single long curve is therefore key to avoiding visual gaps and hence reducing the correction step.

This paper presents *ACCD* (Automated Camera Control for Drawing), a new approach that minimizes the number of explicit viewpoint manipulations, and so the number of strokes while drawing long curves over both multiple layers and multiple viewpoints on 3D shapes. To do so, *ACCD* integrates self-occlusion management and automated camera control for accessing back faces and controlling the drawing precision.

CHI 2014, April 26–May 1, 2014, Toronto, Ontario, Canada.

http://dx.doi.org/10.1145/2556288.2557242

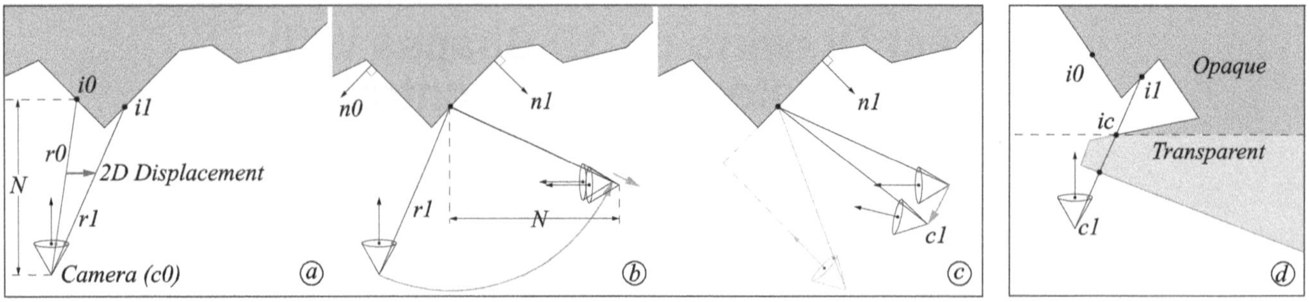

Figure 2. Computing the new position and orientation of the camera: *(a)* A new intersection *i1* is computed from the new position of the stylus. *(b) n0* and *n1*, the normals from the faces, give the angle of camera rotation around *i1*. The camera is rotated and translated to keep the distance to the shape (*N*) constant. *(c)* The camera rotates about 10% of the angle needed for having the line of sight orthogonal to the shape. *(d)* When self-occlusion occurs, a clipping plane is computed at *ic* (first intersection from *i1* to *c1*) and the occluding part of the shape is renderered transparently.

RELATED WORK

To address self-occlusion, Fu et al. proposed *LayerPaint*, a multi-layer approach [5]. They proposed a layer-aware drawing technique that allows to access self-occluded faces. Also, users can display a layer above another, and draw on it. However, back faces remain unreachable. Moreover, changing the layers order could be disturbing as it breaks the users' depth perception. In this paper we propose a transparency-based approach rather than a layer-based approach to self-occlusion.

To address the back-faces issue, some commercial softwares use the *UVMap* technique [7]. This technique displays all the parts of a shape by unfolding it on a single 2D plan. However, with complex shapes:
- context is lost, the shape is displayed outside its 3D scene;
- understanding the new representation requires a high cognitive load, which is even higher for untextured shapes;
- most of the 3D shapes cannot be unfolded in a single 2D one: It has to be cut in pieces, preventing drawing continuity.

According to Schmidt *et al.* [12], the drawing precision depends on both the distance between the viewpoint and the shape (*D*) and the angle between the line of sight and the shape normal (*A*). The lower are *D* and *A*, the higher is the precision. Controlling *D* and *A* with the status-quo configuration requires frequent viewpoint manipulations, which is tedious and time-consuming. Balakrishnan *et al.* [2] proposed to delegate the viewpoint manipulation to the non-dominant hand. Both drawing and viewpoint control can then be done in parallel. In our evaluation, we compare *ACCD* with this bimanual approach for direct drawing and viewpoint manipulation.

Automated camera control has been explored to assist different tasks in 3D environments [1, 4, 9, 11, 13, 15]. The most complete study has been presented by Kahn *et al.* [8] with the *Hovercam* technique. *Hovercam* proposes to ease navigation around 3D objects at constant and close proximity by integrating camera controls into a single 2D gesture. Thus it allows to access back faces while keeping *D* constant and trying to minimize *A*. However, this technique is designed for mouse-based interaction and it does not support the direct mapping of stylus inputs on the tablet display.

To sum up, existing techniques does not address self-occlusion, back-faces and drawing precision issues at once. Also, some techniques are not adapted to tablet display.

ACCD

To reduce the number of viewpoint manipulations and to keep a rather constant drawing precision, the *ACCD* approach provides self-occlusion management combined with automated camera control inspired by the *HoverCam* technique [8].

Self-Occlusion

In ACCD, the self-occlusion management uses a GPU approach that interactively changes the transparency while the viewpoint changes. No pre-computation is needed, and the principle is simple (illustrated in figure 2d). For a camera position (*c1*), ACCD looks for intersections with the 3D object along the segment [*i1-c1*]. The closest intersection to *i1* (*ic*) is used for separating the 3D scene into two parts. Camera frustum is changed, and the part of the scene from *ic* to *c1* is rendered in a texture. Then, the other part of the scene is rendered (adapting camera frustum too), and finally the texture is transparently superimposed.

Camera movements

Figure 2 shows an overview of the 4 main steps of the *ACCD* computation. The whole computation is done for each 2D stylus displacement on the screen. The first step consist of computing the new *intersection point* (*i1*) on the object from the 2D displacement (figure 2a). *ACCD* takes the intersection between the object and *r1* (the ray defined by the camera position and the final position of the 2D displacement). The camera is rotated around *i1* of an angle defined by *n0* and *n1*, the normals of the previous and the current intersection faces (figure 2b). Next, the camera is translated to keep the distance to the object constant, and to keep *i1* under the current stylus position. Finally, the camera is rotated once more to have its viewpoint direction orthogonal to the current face. Yet, the rotation is not done at once (figure 2c). It only takes a percentage of the complete movement (10% in our implementation), and the orthogonality is only obtained after a few 2D displacements. This allows to smooth the transitions between the 3D object faces.

Clutching on screen sides

Because of the constraint of direct manipulation, the 3D object does not stay centered on the screen during the drawing. Manual translations of the camera has to be integrated in the process of drawing, without breaking the continuity of the curve. This is done with a translation mode, controlled by a switch button. It allows the user to translate the camera position along the projection plan, while keeping the drawing cursor under the stylus. Then, it is possible to switch between drawing and translating without lifting the stylus.

EVALUATION

In this experiment we evaluated three approaches to combine viewpoint's manipulation with long curves drawing over both multiple layers and multiple viewpoints on a 3D shape. The goal of this experimentation is to evaluate whether or not the user takes advantage of ACCD to improve curve continuity. To quantify this, we mainly measured both the number of strokes (NS) and the number of viewpoint manipulations (NVM) required by each technique. With all these techniques, drawing is performed with stylus strokes on the screen of a tablet display. Yet, the viewpoint manipulation control differs:

- **One-handed** (*One-H*): Viewpoint rotations (arcball) are available as a quasi-mode triggered by a tablet display shortcut key (on the edge of the tablet display) and controlled with the stylus.
- **Bimanual** (*Biman*): Viewpoint rotations (arcball) are controlled with finger strokes on the screen, with the non-dominant hand. It is therefore possible to draw and rotate the viewpoint in parallel.
- **ACCD**: As described above. Viewpoint is automatically controlled during the drawing. For the clutching issue, viewpoint's translations are available as a quasi-mode triggered by a screen shortcut key and controlled with the stylus.

As we wished to focus on viewpoint control, all three techniques benefited from the same self-occlusion management.

Procedure, Apparatus and Participants

We asked participants to draw long strokes along a guiding path on the surface of different 3D shapes with the three techniques. Participants were standing-up and holding the stylus in their dominant hand. We decided to do so as the sitting posture can constraint participants' gestures.

For each of the three techniques, participants first freely practiced on an **infinity loop** object (figure 3a). Then they performed guided drawing tasks on three different 3D models (figure 3-[b-d]) presented in the following order:

- A **Sphere** as a simple convex shape;
- A **cut Cylinder** as a more complex shape with concavity and thus possible self-occlusion; and
- A **Trefoil Knot** with a very long guiding path.

For the Sphere and the Cylinder, participants first performed 5 training tasks with a large brush (1cm on screen) and then 5 trials with a smaller brush (0.5cm on screen). As the Trefoil Knot was much longer, participants performed only 2 trainings with the large brush, and 2 trials with the smaller one.

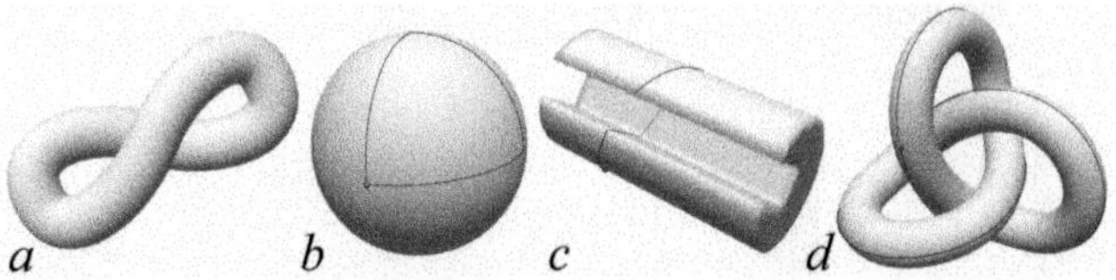

Figure 3. Models used for the evaluation: (*a*) The training "infinity loop"; *b*, *c*, and *d* were successively presented for each technique. The guiding path is the black line. Starting and ending points are reds spheres.

Participants were instructed to keep the guiding path within the brush while drawing. After each trial, participants were informed of the percentage of the guiding path that lies outside the path they drew. We asked them to try to keep this percentage around 5%. This aimed at having a consistent accuracy across participants.

Presentation ordering of the three techniques was counterbalanced across participants using a Latin-square. For each participants, we recorded 36 drawing tasks. The experiment was about one hour long.

Twelve right-handed novices (from 22 to 42 years old) participated in our experiment. We used a Wacom Cintiq 24HD Touch multi-touch and stylus sensitive screen (resolution: 1920x1200, pixel pitch: 0.27mm). We developed an OpenGL-based ad hoc application for this evaluation.

Results

The analysis of variance below were performed separately for each 3D shape on the mean aggregated by participants with participant as a random factor and *Technique* as a factor. Means were compared using Tukey's HSD tests. We discarded 5 unfinished trials (accidental application closure by participants) from the 432 recorded drawing tasks.

Performances

Average *Completion Time* (CT) were 29.8s for the *Sphere*, 20.3s for the *Cylinder* and 82.5s for the *Knot*. *Technique* had a significant effect on CT only for the *Sphere* (see table 1) where *ACCD* was found significantly faster than both *One-H* ($p<.0001$, mean difference=9.49s, SE=2.57) and *Biman* ($p<.05$, mean difference: 6.50s, SE=2.57).

3D Curves Continuity and Regularity

The *Technique* factor had a significant effect on both the *Number of strokes* and the *Number of viewpoint manipulations* (see table 1 and figure 4).

The *Number of strokes* (NS) was found significantly smaller with *ACCD* than with the two other techniques for both the *Cylinder* and the *Trefoil Knot* (all with $p<.0001$). For the *Sphere*, *ACCD*'s NS was only significantly smaller than *Biman*'s NS (with $p<.01$).

The *Number of viewpoint manipulations* (NVM) was found significantly lower with *ACCD* than with *Biman* on all 3D shapes (all with $p<.0001$). *ACCD*'s NVM is also significantly lower than *One-H*'s NVM on the *Cylinder* ($p<.0001$) and the *Knot* ($p<.05$). *One-H*'s NVM was significanlty lower than *Biman*'s NVM for the *Sphere* ($p<.05$).

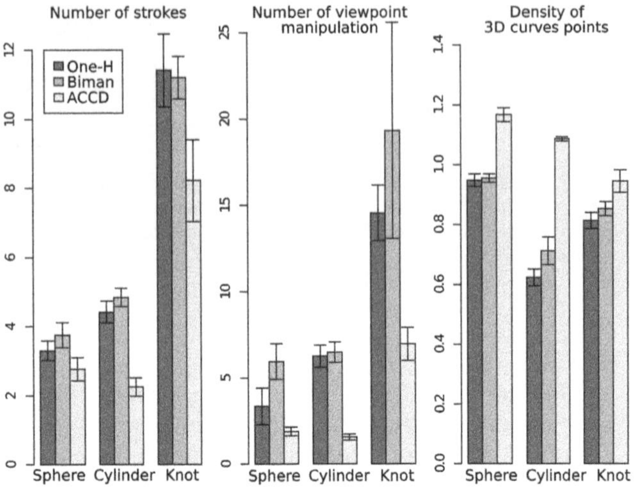

Figure 4. Means and 95% confidence intervals: (Left) Number of strokes (NS); (Middle) Number of viewpoint manipulations (NVM); and (Right) Density of input points of the 3D curves (ρ).

We also explored the effect of *Technique* on two measures of drawn curves regularity and found significant effects. First, the *Density of input points* on the 3D curve (ρ) was found significantly higher with *ACCD* than with the two other techniques for all 3D shapes (with at least p<.001). The only significant ρ difference between *One-H* and *Biman* was found for the *Cylinder* (though with p<.05). Second, the *Standard deviation of the distances between input points* along the 3D curve (σ_d) was found significantly smaller with *ACCD* than with the two other techniques for the *Sphere* and the *Cylinder* (with at least p<.01 but for the *ACCD-Biman* comparison on the *Sphere* where p<.05). For the *Knot*, *ACCD*'s σ_d was only significantly smaller than *One-H*'s σ_d (p<.05).

User Preference

We asked participants for their preferred technique, 9/12 participants said it was *Biman* and 7/12 said *ACCD*, but none answered *One-H* (multiple answers allowed). Those measurable results are consistent with participants' comments. All participants were comfortable using *ACCD*, and no participant complained about the camera rotations. Only one participant found clutching of *ACCD* annoying. Another participant said that *Biman* needs more training than *ACCD* and two further participants clearly preferred *ACCD*, as the technique avoids jumps between different parts of the same shape. Some participants expressed the need for occasional explicit control of the viewpoint while drawing with *ACCD*. This could be useful for occasionally reorienting the 3D shape in a more convenient way, to draw in more comfortable directions and to avoid hand occlusion.

Table 1. F and p values of the analysis of variance of the *Technique* effect on CT, NS, NVM, ρ and σ_d for each 3D shape.

	Sphere		Cylinder		Knot	
	$F_{2,22}$	p<	$F_{2,22}$	p<	$F_{2,22}$	p<
CT	7.14	.01	1.44	.26	1.14	.34
NS	5.76	.01	34.59	.0001	15.17	.0001
NVM	7.28	.01	44.36	.0001	7.91	.01
ρ	60.63	.0001	115.96	.0001	19.13	.0001
σ_d	7.46	.01	15.30	.0001	3.57	.05

CONCLUSION AND FUTURE WORK

The evaluation provides encouraging results on the benefits and potential of *ACCD*. First, *ACCD* reduces the number of strokes performed to draw a curve on a 3D shape. This indicates that it allows to draw longer curves in a single stroke. Thus it requires less switching between drawing and viewpoint control. Secondly, *ACCD* provides a higher density and more homogeneity of input points along the drawn curve. This indicates that it provides a more constant drawing precision. Third, it tends to be faster than the other techniques even if this was only significant for the *Sphere* 3D shape. These three points show that *ACCD* improves drawing continuity.

An outcome of our experiment was that occasional explicit viewpoint control would be helpful to reorient the viewpoint while drawing with *ACCD*. *ACCD* could be extended with explicit finger strokes based viewpoint rotation. The user would then rotate the viewpoint with its finger with the current drawing brush position as the pivot point.

ACKNOWLEDGMENTS

This work was supported by the FUI project 3DCI (AAP14); the ANR/JST AMIE project; and Région Rhônes-Alpes. LIG is partner of PERSYVAL-Lab (ANR–11-LABX-0025).

REFERENCES

1. Bae, S.-H., Balakrishnan, R., and Singh, K. Ilovesketch: as-natural-as-possible sketching system for creating 3d curve models. In *Proc. of UIST*, ACM (2008), 151–160.
2. Balakrishnan, R., and Kurtenbach, G. Exploring bimanual camera control and object manipulation in 3d graphics interfaces. In *Proc. of CHI*, ACM (1999), 56–62.
3. Chen, X., Golovinskiy, A., and Funkhouser, T. A benchmark for 3d mesh segmentation. In *Proc. of SIGGRAPH*, ACM (2009), 73:1–73:12.
4. Foskey, M., Otaduy, M. A., and Lin, M. C. Artnova: Touch-enabled 3d model design. In *Proc. of VR*, IEEE (2002), 119–.
5. Fu, C.-W., Xia, J., and He, Y. Layerpaint: a multi-layer interactive 3d painting interface. In *Proc. of CHI*, ACM (2010), 811–820.
6. Hagedorn, B., and Döllner, J. Sketch-based navigation in 3d virtual environments. In *Proc. of SG*, Springer-Verlag (2008), 239–246.
7. Hormann, K., Levy, B., and Sheffer, A. Mesh parameterization: Theory and practice. In *SIGGRAPH Course Notes* (2007).
8. Khan, A., Komalo, B., Stam, J., Fitzmaurice, G., and Kurtenbach, G. Hovercam: interactive 3d navigation for proximal object inspection. In *Proc. of Interactive 3D graphics and games*, ACM (2005), 73–80.
9. Ortega, M. 3D object position using automatic viewpoint transitions. In *Proc. of CHI*, ACM (2013), 193–196.
10. Owada, S., Nielsen, F., Nakazawa, K., and Igarashi, T. A sketching interface for modeling the internal structures of 3d shapes. In *Proc. of Smart graphics*, Springer-Verlag (2003), 49–57.
11. Phillips, C. B., Badler, N. I., and Granieri, J. Automatic viewing control for 3d direct manipulation. In *Proc. of I3D*, ACM (1992), 71–74.
12. Schmidt, R., Khan, A., Kurtenbach, G., and Singh, K. On expert performance in 3d curve-drawing tasks. In *Proc. of SBIM*, ACM (2009), 133–140.
13. Veit, M., Capobianco, A., and Bechmann, D. Cros: A touch screen interaction for cursor manipulation on 2-manifolds. In *Proc. of VRST*, ACM (2012), 97–100.
14. ZBrush. http://pixologic.com/zbrush.
15. Zeleznik, R., and Forsberg, A. Unicam - 2d gestural camera controls for 3d environments. In *Proc. of I3D*, ACM (1999), 169–173.

Interactively Stylizing Camera Motion

Neel Joshi, Dan Morris, and Michael F. Cohen
Microsoft Research
{neel, dan, mcohen}@microsoft.com

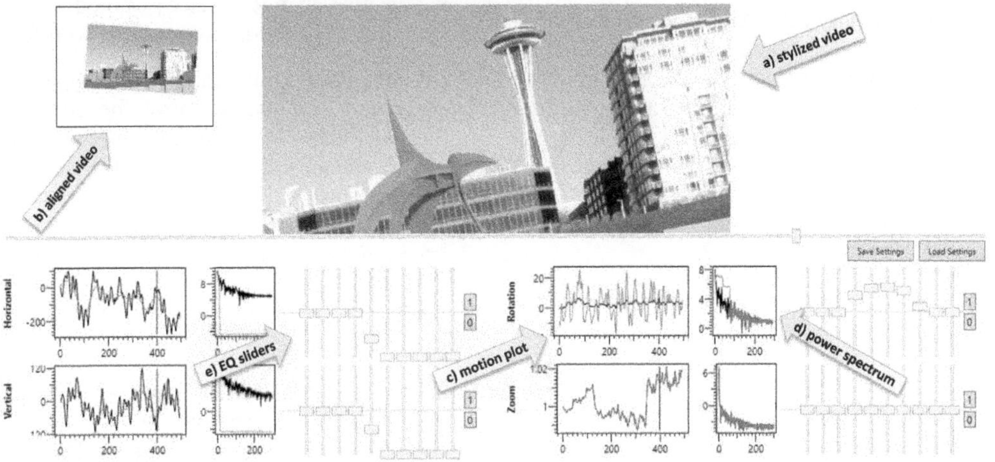

Figure 1. A user can modify camera motion style in real time by manipulating sliders which modify the power spectra for each camera motion parameter. The UI shows a) the input video with the current stylized motion applied and b) the video aligned to the global canvas. There are sub-panels for the motion parameters: x and y translation, rotation, and scale. Each sub-panel has c) a plot of the original and stylized motion and d) power spectrum and e) a 10-band equalizer (EQ). In the motion plot, the bold line is the original path and the finer gray line is the stylized path. Here we have dampened the mid and low frequencies for the x and y motion and amplified the mid frequencies for rotation.

ABSTRACT
Movie directors and cinematographers impart style onto video using techniques that are learned through years of experience: camera movement, framing, color, lighting, etc. Without this experience and expensive equipment, it is very difficult to control stylistic aspects of a video. We introduce a novel approach for post-hoc editing of one specific aspect of cinematography – camera motion style – via an equalizer-like set of controls that manipulates the power spectra of a video's apparent motion path. We explore free manipulation of apparent camera motion as well as the transfer of motion styles from an example video to a new video to create a wide range of stylistic variations. We report on a user study confirming the ability of non-expert users to create motion styles.

Author Keywords
Camera motion editing; video stylization

ACM Classification Keywords
H.5.2 [Information Interfaces and Presentation]: User Interfaces - Interaction styles;

INTRODUCTION
Our emotional responses to a film are guided by a composition of acting performances, staging, sound effects, scoring, and cinematography.

CHI 2014, April 26–May 1, 2014, Toronto, Ontario, Canada.

ACM 978-1-4503-2473-1/14/04 ...$15.00.
http://dx.doi.org/10.1145/2556288.2556966

One of the more visceral aspects of a film is *camera movement*. Camera movement is a powerful tool used by filmmakers to establish pace, point of view, or rhythm in a scene – it can be used to draw the viewer into the action or to convey a disconnect between audience and characters. Camera motion, as a stylistic choice, is often so powerful that it can be the primary memory of a film or video – movies such as "The Blair Witch Project" and "Cloverfield" evoke feelings of tension and chaos, while Alfred Hitchcock's "The Rope" is remembered for the "continuous take", and "The West Wing" for its long "walk-and-talk" shots.

While camera movement is well-understood, its artistic control is challenging. This ability is typically restricted to professional cinematographers and directors, because it requires experience, careful planning, and often costly equipment (Steadicams, tracks, etc.). For example, the director of "Cloverfield" created the movie's signature shakes and swoops with a custom rig that would be prohibitively expensive for amateur videographers. Furthermore, even if one is able to film with a desired style, there are few tools for changing the apparent motion *after* the fact without reshooting.

Video stabilization is a well-known methodology that manipulates a moving crop window to remove much of the apparent motion of the camera. We extend the stabilization paradigm to impart many other motion styles. Specifically, we present an application that allows one to adjust the relative frequency characteristics of the camera motion using a paradigm similar to graphic equalization (EQ) in audio editing. Just as an EQ on a mixing panel can be used to change the prominence of certain tones to balance instruments or give a song a "concert feel" or "studio sound", our tool can amplify or dampen the frequency components of camera motion to change its perceived style. Our contributions include 1) an interactive tool for editing apparent camera motion by manipulating frequency content and 2) a method for automatically setting the editing parameters from another video clip.

To the best of our knowledge, this is the first time that an equalization-like interface has been used for controlling camera motion. We demonstrate the creation of a variety of camera motion styles using our interactive app. We also report on a user study in which participants were asked to create four specific styles of motion. Most users were able to quickly impart the requested styles, and the quality of their created styles was confirmed by a separate set of scorers who correctly labeled the resulting videos with the four styles.

PREVIOUS WORK

Video stabilization is the removal of undesirable high-frequency motion, often resulting from the instability of handheld cameras. This is a special case of motion stylization that has received significant attention [2]. Current stabilization systems minimize user interaction by design and do not generalize to other forms of motion stylization. We leverage previous work in stabilization to re-synthesize a video given a modified camera path, but we provide novel, interactive approaches for generating that camera path.

The notion of interactive motion stylization has been addressed in other areas of computer graphics with similar goals: to enhance a non-expert's creative control over a video artifact. However, that work primarily addresses stylization of human motion animation and does not address video camera motion. Neff et al. [4], for example, provide an intuitive parameterization of kinematic chains for interactive motion editing in animation. Our work aims to provide a similar parameterization of *camera paths* for video motion.

The transfer of styles from one artifact to another has also been addressed in the computer animation literature: Hsu et al. [3] present an approach to learning and transferring stylistic components of an animation sequence to a new animation, without disrupting the non-stylistic content of the target. This in part inspired our "Stylizing Camera Motion by Example" approach to capturing the stylistic dynamics of an existing video. This aspect of our system also draws on the audio domain, where the multi-band equalizer is common and has been exploited for stylistic transfer (e.g., the Match EQ feature of Apple's Logic Studio[1], which transfers equalizer settings from a reference recording).

STYLIZATION FRAMEWORK

The goal of our work is to modify stylistic elements of camera motion interactively. It has two components: 1) inferring camera motion from a video clip and 2) modifying the motion in a stylistically meaningful way. The first step is essential for stylizing camera motion, however it is not our focus, and we use existing methods. Our contributions address the second component: stylistically meaningful motion editing.

Modeling Camera Motion

We build on video stabilization methods for recovering camera motion. Though in reality the camera may have moved and rotated in three dimensions, we use 2D transformations (translation, rotation, and scale) for modeling the camera motion. This simplification assumes that the effect of camera motion on the scene can be modeled as a time-varying set of rigid image transformations. It does not model depth or perspective changes. As was noted in [2], despite these assumptions, the model works quite well for most videos.

As our goal is to interactively manipulate stylistic elements of camera motion, we have the additional constraint that the parameters of the motion model should be concise and understandable to a user. Thus we use a *similarity* motion model, which models camera motion as a time-varying set of transformations, S_t, that decomposes to four values: $[x_t, y_t, \theta_t, s_t]$, representing x and y translation, in-plane rotation, and global image scale. In cinematographic terms, these map to pan, roll, and zoom (or forward/backward dolly).

Recovering the apparent camera motion from a video amounts to inferring the sequence of transformation for each frame that best maps that frame to a base frame. The alignment is computed by extracting image features for each frame and performing a search between frames to find matching features. A feature is determined to be a match if the descriptor distance of the best match is sufficiently different from that of the second-best match (a.k.a. the ratio test). To avoid locking onto scene motion, the tracks are analyzed to distinguish foreground motion from background static features by using a RANSAC (RANdom SAmple Consensus) method to find the largest set of inlier tracks such that a single temporal sequence of similarity transforms can map all background features to their positions in the base frame. The transforms are then decomposed into x and y translation, rotation, and scale.

Modifying Camera Motion

The next section, the focus of our work, will address generating a new, stylized camera motion path based on our interface. First, we briefly discuss how we will apply that new path to render a stylized video. We assume that the stylization engine has output a desired motion path $S'[t, 0]$, which can be decomposed into $[x'_t, y'_t, \theta'_t, s'_t]$.

Given $S[t, 0]$ as the transform in the original video between any frame (t) and the first frame (0), represented by $[x_t, y_t, \theta_t, s_t]$, and the modified transform $S'[t, 0]$ from the stylized motion path $[x'_t, y'_t, \theta'_t, s'_t]$, a frame in the stylized sequence can be computed by warping the frame based on the difference between $S[t, 0]$ and $S'[t, 0]$. This is equivalent to warping the image to the base (first) frame's coordinate system and then applying the inverse transformation to map to the stylized sequence.[2]

Any transformation other than the identity will create unknown regions around the video border. The final result is thus cropped to eliminate the unknown regions (we use a fixed crop to 80% of the original video size). This also sets bounds on how much the stylized motion can vary from the original.

Stylizing Camera Motion Interactively

The question of how to modify and/or transfer camera motion style is really a question of what aspects of camera motion are

[1] http://apple.com/logicpro

[2] Any frame can serve as the reference frame; we use the first frame.

"story vs. atmosphere" or "substance vs. style". Editing operations, such as stabilization, do affect camera movement style in some sense, but provide no artistic control for achieving a particular style.

While there is an informal understanding in cinematography of what aspects of camera motion are stylistic, there is no mathematical description of camera motion style that we are aware of. Thus, drawing on inspiration from audio and image editing, we use a frequency-based equalization approach to edit camera motion style. Our approach is analogous to using a graphic equalizer in audio editing. Just as on a mixing panel an EQ can be used to change the prominence of certain tones or instruments to change the "feel" of a song, our camera motion equalizer is an interactive method to amplify, dampen, or transfer the frequency components of camera motion to create a desired look and feel.

Just as an audio equalizer can operate independently on the left and right channels of a stereo audio signal, we break our motion signal into the four channels of x (horizontal) translation, y (vertical) translation, in-plane rotation θ, and scale s. For each channel, we compute a frequency-space representation using an FFT (Fast-Fourier Transform) and then multiply or add power to bins in this frequency representation as a function of user-driven sliders corresponding to frequency bands. An inverse FFT is then used to generate the output motion paths. Our bins are logarithmically spaced in frequency, with the bin size increasing as the frequency increases; this is also common practice with audio equalizers. Our EQ does not modify the DC component of the signal; in other words, we aim to manipulate the style of movement, not to completely re-position the camera post-hoc. Just as in audio, where other tools are used to change the fundamental notes or melody, our work would complement other tools for changing the fundamental camera motion path, such as motion transformations and key-framing in Adobe Premiere[3].

The user-provided values are between 0 and 2 for each bin, where a value of 1 returns the original motion. From 0 to 1, we treat the value as a simple multiplier in the frequency domain. Thus these values dampen frequencies in the original signal. For example, setting all values to zero creates a stabilized video. Values above 1 result in an additive operation instead of a multiplicative operation. The system switches from multiplicative to additive because multiplication would have little to no effect when the original magnitude of a frequency in the motion path is at or near zero. By adding to the magnitude, we can add frequency content that was not originally present. This allows us to stylize stationary videos, such as those filmed on a tripod, in addition to hand-held videos.

Stylizing Camera Motion by Example

In some cases, a user may have another example video whose style they want to match. For this case, we provide an automated approach to set the EQ sliders from an example. The user loads the example into the application, and we calculate the EQ values that will scale or add (as appropriate) to the power in each band so the input video has the same average power in each band as is present in the example.

[3]http://www.adobe.com/products/premiere.html

INTERACTIVE SYSTEM

The app (Figure 1) is designed to be simple yet expressive to help users quickly change camera motion style. It reflects three primary design decisions: 1) camera motion is parameterized by x and y translation, in-plane rotation, and scale; 2) stylization of motion is done by manipulating a multi-band equalizer independently for each motion parameter; 3) edits occur in real time and the effect is seen immediately.

The main panel shows the input video with the current stylized motion applied. When a video is loaded, the equalizer sliders are set to 1; thus when the video is first played, the video motion appears unchanged. In the top-left, we show the video aligned to the global canvas, to show how the current frame relates to the others in space.

The bottom panel has four sub-panels for each motion parameter (x, y, θ, s). Each panel has a plot of the original and stylized motion, a plot of the original and stylized power spectrum, and a 10-band equalizer (Figure 1). The equalizer control has shortcut buttons to set all sliders to "1", which yields the original, unmodified motion, and "0", for no motion at all. The effects are applied in real time, at 30 fps, when running on a 2.67 GHz PC.

USER STUDY

We conducted a preliminary study to assess both the efficacy and usability of our system for modifying apparent camera motion. Ten participants (5 female and 5 male) used the system to modify existing videos. Participants were first asked whether they have used video editing software "never" (n=1), "a few times" (n=6), or "regularly" (n=3). Participants were also asked whether they have used graphic equalizers (as found in most music player apps) "never" (n=3), "a few times" (n=5), or "regularly" (n=2). Thus, although participants all had some technical background, the range of familiarity with video editing and with equalizers varied widely.

A session began with approximately three minutes of training. We then presented each participant with one of six 10- to 20-second videos to modify. They were asked to create four modified videos that exhibited each of four styles: (1) Bouncy: as if the videographer had a bounce in their step, (2) Earthquake: as if the videographer was filming during an earthquake, (3) Boat: as if the videographer was on a boat in stormy seas, and (4) Steadicam: as if the camera was moving in a controlled, stable way. Participants were given 12 minutes total to complete the four videos and were allowed to complete the styles in any order and revisit them as desired.

In a second 12-minute task, participants were given a new video and were asked to create four versions, but this time they were asked to *match* four stylized "target" versions of the video. As before, participants could work in any order and revisit their styles or watch the target videos as desired.

The studies aimed to validate two hypotheses: (1) non-expert users can create multiple styles that exhibit the meaning of descriptive labels, and (2) non-expert users can re-create styles based on visual examples.

In a second phase of the study, we recruited seven scorers to match the four videos created by the each of the initial participants in their first task (40 videos total) to the text labels. Each scorer was presented with a panel of four videos, randomly arranged into a 2x2 grid, representing the four videos from one of the participants. They were asked to assign the four labels (Bouncy, Earthquake, Boat, Steadicam) to the videos. They then went on to four more videos from another participant and continued this task until all ten sets had been labeled. Thus we had seven labels for each of the 40 videos.

User Study Results

We use the labels assigned by our scorers to assess whether the study participants were able to create meaningful styles. Given that sets of four videos were presented simultaneously, the probability of randomly getting all 4 in a set correct is 1 in 24, or 4.17%. Of the 70 sets labeled, 53 (or 76%) were all labeled correctly. One can also assess accuracy at the individual-video level; the odds of labeling any video correctly on its own is 1 in 4, or 25%, and the scorers correctly identified 86% of the videos. These results support hypothesis (1): non-experts were able to create meaningful styles using our tool.

In the second task, participants matched a pre-recorded video created with our system. In this case, we automatically classify the sets by numerically comparing the power spectra of the pre-recorded videos with those created by our participants. For example, if user video U1 is matched to target video T1, we compute the L_2 error between the power spectra of U1 and T1. Four user-generated videos are matched to the set of target videos to minimize the sum of L_2 errors across the four matches. Even this simple approach results in 8 in 10 (80%) of the participants' sets being labeled correctly, vs. a 4.17% random chance. Looking individually at each video in the automatically labeled sets, 90% are correctly labeled, vs. a 25% random chance. This supports the hypothesis (2): non-expert users can re-create styles based on visual examples using our tool.

General Study Observations

Based on survey comments, the second task was somewhat frustrating for some. Although most converged quickly to a video similar to the target, many were still not satisfied. It became clear there were two different mental models employed. For some, who adopted a "frequency space" view, getting the stylistic aspects correct was enough. Others, who were more frustrated, were trying to also match the "phase", i.e., they wanted the apparent camera motion to go up or down exactly when the target video's motion went up or down. This is clearly a more difficult task and not as well-supported by our tool. As our primary goal is to allow exploration of motion "style" and not perform the matching problem, we do not see this as a flaw, but it does inform the way one would communicate the equalization metaphor to a broad audience.

Another issue relates to the ease of immediately understanding changes in the higher-frequency vs. lower-frequency sliders. Not surprisingly, changing a high-frequency slider results in an almost immediate response. However, changes in low-frequency sliders are reflected with some inherent latency; for example, it takes at least a second to see the addition of 0.5Hz sinusoidal motion to the video, and in practice the perceived latency is higher, as it is compounded with other low-frequency motion. This led to what we observed to be some users "thrashing" when setting the low-frequency values. Here, the analogy to audio EQ breaks down, since even low-frequency changes are immediately noticeable (the lowest relevant frequency for audio EQ is typically 20Hz).

Yet, even with some latency, the effect is still much more immediately perceived than with current alternatives, and we believe users could master the interface quickly via real-time trial and error. However, further study is warranted. Admittedly, the number of sliders we used (40) may be intimidating to some users and perhaps fewer sliders would work just as well. We focused on evaluating the overall efficacy of our approach; however, there are open questions such as how many sliders are ideal and how efficient are users with these sliders.

DISCUSSION

We have used our work to create many different styles as seen in our supplementary video. The video also includes results from our method to automatically set the equalizer controls using example videos and some results from our user study.

We have presented an interface for manipulating apparent camera motion style based on an *equalizer* (EQ) interface inspired by those used to balance audio frequency components. The EQ values can be set manually or automatically. We believe having a familiar metaphor for doing *anything* to camera motion is novel and exciting, and our approach is easier and faster than the current approach of key-framing individual motion changes. For example, consider creating our shaky "Earthquake" style for a 20-second video. The user would need to create a key frame for each change in direction, so vertical shaking alone at 10 Hz would require creating 400 key frames. Our system requires moving just one slider.

For future work, it would be interesting to consider other interfaces for global editing of camera motion, e.g., "direct manipulation" [1] approaches could be be used for camera motion editing, as they would allow a quick, broad specification of a motion path. It would be interesting to combine our method with such an approach or with key-framing interfaces.

REFERENCES

1. Dragicevic, P., Ramos, G., Bibliowitcz, J., Nowrouzezahrai, D., Balakrishnan, R., and Singh, K. Video browsing by direct manipulation. In *Proceedings of CHI '08* (2008), 237–246.
2. Grundmann, M., Kwatra, V., and Essa, I. Auto-directed video stabilization with robust l1 optimal camera paths. In *Proc IEEE CVPR 2011* (2011).
3. Hsu, E., Pulli, K., and Popović, J. Style translation for human motion. *ACM Trans. Graph. 24*, 3 (July 2005), 1082–1089.
4. Neff, M., and Kim, Y. Interactive editing of motion style using drives and correlations. In *Proceedings of the 2009 ACM SIGGRAPH/Eurographics SCA* (2009).

Stimulating a Blink: Reduction of Eye Fatigue with Visual Stimulus

Tarik Crnovrsanin
University of California, Davis
tecrnovrsanin@ucdavis.edu

Yang Wang
University of California, Davis
ywang@ucdavis.edu

Kwan-Liu Ma
University of California, Davis
ma@cs.ucdavis.edu

ABSTRACT
Computers make incredible amounts of information available at our fingertips. As computers become integral parts of our lives, we spend more time staring at computer monitor than ever before, sometimes with negative effects. One major concern is the increasing number of people suffering from Computer Vision Syndrome (CVS). CVS is caused by extensive use of computers, and its symptoms include eye fatigue, frequent headaches, dry eyes, and blurred vision. It is possible to partially alleviate CVS if we can remind users to blink more often. We present a prototype system that uses a camera to monitor a user's blink rate, and when the user has not blinked in a while, the system triggers a blink stimulus. We investigated four different types of eye-blink stimulus: screen blurring, screen flashing, border flashing, and pop-up notifications. Users also rated each stimulus type in terms of effectiveness, intrusiveness, and satisfaction. Results from our user studies show that our stimuli are effective in increasing user blink rate with screen blurring being the best.

Author Keywords
CVS; Blink Detection; Blink Stimulus; User Study;

ACM Classification Keywords
H.1.2. User/Machine Systems: Human factors

INTRODUCTION
Computers have greatly influenced how we interact with the world. More of the population are finding themselves in front of computer than ever before [41]. This long-term use of computers can have to negative effects on one's health. The symptoms range from headaches, fatigue, blurred vision, eye strain, dry/irritated eyes to difficulty focusing, which are all signs of Computer Vision Syndrome (CVS). The formal definition of CVS is a group of eye and vision-related problems that result from prolonged computer use. The symptoms are mostly caused by tightening of the inner eye muscles which decrease the blink reflex. Not surprisingly, many computer users are affected by CVS. Studies show at least 14-23% [41] and upwards of 70% [7] of computer users have CVS related problems.

CHI 2014, April 26–May 1, 2014, Toronto, Ontario, Canada.

http://dx.doi.org/10.1145/2556288.2557129

A contributing factor to CVS is a reduced blink rate when using computers for extended periods of time. The spontaneous eye blink rate (SEBR) is reduced significantly from 15-16 blinks per minute in conversation to 5-6 blinks per minute during computer use [19, 33]. The problem is exacerbated as our eyes open up wider when looking at the computer screen, increasing tear evaporation.

Computer users can fight against CVS by developing good habits that help prevent the symptoms. These preventative strategies are a mixed bag. Methods that require one time setup such as computer screen being placed at least 20 inches and viewing angle of 15 degrees lower than the horizontal level are easy to implement and work well for most symptoms. Unfortunately, methods that help with dry eye require frequent attention from the user, such as the 20/20/20 rule [12] (for every 20 minutes of computer use, users should look at something 20 feet away for 20 seconds). These methods are not practical as users have a difficult time taking regular breaks when they are focusing on their work.

Dry Eye Syndrome (DES) is often overlooked but studies have shown that DES has significant impact on quality of life [32, 27]. DES causes itchy or burning eyes, discomfort wearing contact lenses, increased sensitivity to light or excessive tearing and in extreme cases, blurred vision [2, 38]. The recommended treatment for DES is to blink more [38] or replace with artificial tears [2, 6]. Artificial tears can be expensive over prolonged use and do not solve the cause of the problem. Blinking more is a good idea but it is hard for the user to pay attention to their own blink rate throughout the day.

Researchers have studied methods for helping individuals with DES. There are software packages that help users manage their exercises and rest brakes [30, 1, 34]. They usually measure activity level by keyboard and mouse interaction, which does not correctly represent user's behavior with activities that do not use input, such as reading or watching a movie. Researcher have also worked on stimulating a blink[28], but these methods require special hardware to work and do not take the person's blinking into account. Therefore, they are not practical for daily use. There are systems that detect blink, but these applications are mostly used for fatigue detection [13, 42] and not for preventing the problem in the first place.

To help the user with DES, it is necessary to create a system that can not only detect blinks but also apply a stimulus when the users had not blinked for an extended period of time. In this paper, we present a prototype application that does this using only the monitor and a standard monitor-mounted webcam. The idea is to increase the user's blink rate when using a computer and thereby help reduce occurrence of dry eyes. To test the effectiveness of our prototype, we conducted two user studies. Our first user study looks at different media types and their effect on blink rate. Does looking at text, image or video cause different rates of blink? We then conduct a second user study to see if our prototype can increase users blink rate and which stimulus methods work the best.

The contributions of our work can be summarized as follows:

- The design and evaluation of a prototype system that leverages the state of the art vision-based object detection algorithm for human-computer interaction;
- The development of a set of stimuli taking into consideration both the habit of computer usage and the human blink mechanism;
- The design, conducting, and presentation of a qualitative user study which confirmed that the human blink rate can be improved based on these stimuli.

RELATED WORK

Our work relates to human blinking mechanism and its application in Human-Computer Interaction (HCI). Though eye-based interfaces have been widely studied in the CHI community, there is a lack of work on how to relief CVSs based on blinks.

Human Blinking Mechanism

Blinking is a common facial motion that consists of rapid closing and opening of the eyelids. It can be further classified into spontaneous, reflexive and voluntary blinking [16]. Most blinks are triggered unconsciously, reflecting a person's emotional or cognitive state [4]. Reflexive eye-blinks, on the other hand, are elicited in response to a variety of environmental stimuli [31], such as loud noises and flashing lights. Blinks can also be voluntarily, like as in clinical experiments where test subjects were instructed to blink as fast as possible after a verbal command is given [8].

There are many factors that affect blink rate. Studies reveal that SEBR largely depends on the type of tasks being conducted. Different tasks have different visual demands. As depicted in Table 1, the reading-SEBR (as in reading books) is lower than the primary gaze-SEBR, and they are both lower than face-to-face conversational-SEBR [14]. Primary gaze is an act that subjects directing their gaze to a distant target adapt with their habitual palpebral aperture. Skotte et al. [35] found similar results when conducting active visual tasks where the SEBR decreased to an average of 5 blinks per minute compared to the average of 15 blinks per minute for the passive computer tasks.

Other factors include environmental and visual condition, such as viewing angles on the screen and lighting conditions around the computer. The room temperature and humidity can also affect blink. Blink rate fluctuates when changing gaze direction [18], during line change [23], or squinting [29].

Type of tasks	SEBR (blinks per minute)	Source
Reading	1.4 - 14.4	[14]
Primary gaze	8.0 - 21.0	[14]
Conversation	10.5 - 32.5	[14]
Active visual tasks	avg. 5	[35]
Passive visual tasks	avg. 15	[35]

Table 1: The SEBR is largely dependent on the type of tasks being conducted; the more the user is focused, the less is the SEBR.

However, present results show that there is no significant influence to the change in SEBR given the above factors [22].

Finally, the various media (e.g. text, image, video with audio, etc.) with distinct features (e.g. static vs. dynamic, organized vs. random, simple vs. complex, etc.) used in different computer tasks may also impact blink rate. However, we have found no comprehensive study from this perspective.

Blink Detection and Its Application in HCI

Computer users are often engaged in various visual tasks. The intensive use of our eyes results in decrease of SEBR and eye fatigue. Several utilities [30, 1, 34] have been developed to notify computer users to blink voluntarily. These utilities try to follow the 20/20/20 rule and notify the user to rest regularly. For fragmented tasks, regular breaks may help restore and relax the accommodative system, thereby preventing eye-strain [26, 17]. However, when dealing with long-lasting tasks that require more concentration, people tend to compensate for interruptions by working faster. This comes at a price of experiencing more stress, higher frustration, time pressure, and effort [25].

Miura et al. [28] introduced an LED timer device and evaluated the eye blink rate on non-dry eye subjects and dry eye patients. According to their study, the reflexive eye-blink rate (REBR) was higher in tasks with the device properly set up. One defect of their experiment setting is that the LED timer device can only be programed to flash based on a predefined time interval (4 seconds in their study).

To actively detect blinking event in real-time, vision-based eye detection systems have been implemented for both desktop [13, 3, 42] and mobile devices [20]. A general eye-blink detection algorithm starts with detection based-on facial biometrics. The eye region is then extracted to reduce the dimension of data used to detect and quantify eye-blinks. The ability to detect eye-blink in real-time makes fatigue detection, anti-spoofing recognition and other general HCI tasks possible [10, 21, 24, 37]. However, none of these previous systems provided provided an effective solution to increase the REBR.

DESIGN

Here, we describe the design of the hardware and test environment configuration, blink detection algorithm, the stimulation mechanism used to support the user study, as well as the limitations of the design.

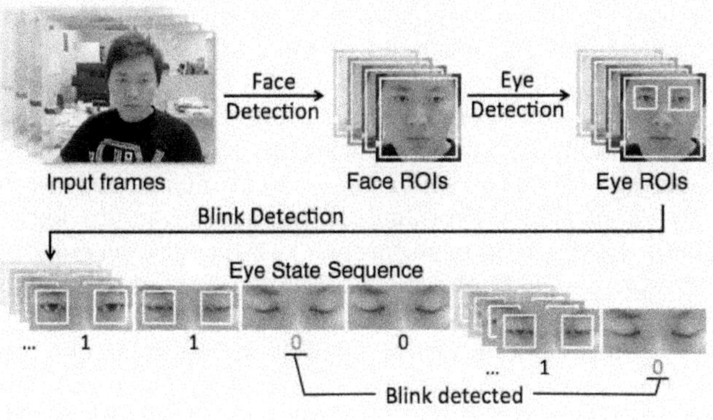

Figure 1: The workflow of the blink detection algorithm. For each input image frame, the facial and eye regions of interest are extracted in succession. Eye blink events are then being detected based on the sequence of historical eye-opened state.

Hardware and Test Environment

Our blink detection and stimulation system is configured using a personal computer together with a consumer affordable web camera with 720p (1280*720) video acquisition capability (most of the latest laptops, smart phones and tablets have a 720p front facing camera). This gives us enough resolution for detection of subtle changes on the face. The camera is set on top of the computer screen facing the user. To ensure the whole face region is obtained, the user is seated 50 to 60 cm away from the display.

Eye Blink Detection

An overview of the eye blink detection algorithm is depicted in Figure 1. We use an eye blink detection algorithm similar to the one described in [13] using OpenCV [9] due to its high accuracy (over 95%). In out implementation, we counted double-blinks as one blink instead of two, which led to even lower false-positive rate (less than 0.4%). We determined our false-positive rate by counting blinks manually from the recorded videos in our study and compared it to our system results. The video frames are obtained at 30 frames per second. For each video frame, a cascade of boosted classifiers is applied. The cascade classifier was trained using a few hundred sample images for identifying human faces. After the facial regions have been extracted, a second set of cascade classifiers is applied to detect opened-eyes, yields the corresponding positions of opened-eyes within the facial region. Geometrical constraints are also used to verify candidate eye regions to avoid mis-detections.

Since eye blinking consists of rapid closing and opening of the eyelid, we can detect a blink event by recording the sequence of historical eye open-states. We can also use this sequence to trigger stimuli after a target interval of time. Both of these tasks are accomplished using Algorithm 1, where s denotes the eye open-state at a certain time stamp, and 1 and 0 denote the opened-eye and closed-eye states, respectively. This simple algorithm is capable of detecting long-closing voluntary eye blinks as well as double-blinks.

Algorithm 1 Blink event detection and stimulus triggering based on historical eye-open states

```
n ← 0 // # frames eyes are open
initialize k // minimum # frames eyes are open
initialize limit ∈ [4s, 8s] // fatigue limit
while incoming video frames do
  s ← is eye opened ? 1 : 0
  if s = 1 then
    n = n + 1
    if n > limit then
      trigger stimulus
    end if
  else
    if n > k then
      blink event detected
      n = 0
    end if
  end if
end while
```

Stimulating a Blink

A stimulus response is triggered when the user has not blinked for a certain timespan - the fatigue limit. Previous studies used a constant time of 4 seconds in accordance to the average blink rate of 15 blinks per minute [28]. When we conducted our pilot study, we found two problems with this fatigue limit. First, people started to expect the stimulus response. This stems from the fact that individuals do not blink at a constant rate, and therefore using a constant time feels unnatural. Second, users found it bothersome and annoying to have stimulus applied so frequently. This makes sense, as each person has a different blink interval and the interval can change based on external factors [41]. We decided to use a interval of time instead of constant time, thereby making harder to expect the stimulus. We conducted several pilot studies to find the correct interval of time. The fatigue limit should be set such that blinks could be triggered frequently enough for the eyes to be moisturized, while not disturbing the user. We found setting the interval between 4 and 8 seconds after the blink, worked well.

For our study, we implemented four blink stimulation mechanisms: Flash, blur, flashing border, and pop-up notification. Flash and blur stimuli are designed to trick the eye into blinking, while flashing border and pop-up notifications provide a reminder to blink.

The flash stimulus makes use of the fact that when a person blinks, there is a flicker that occurs. Instead of using extra hardware as suggested in Miura et al. [28], a flash stimulus can easily be implemented using the computer screen. The flash stimulus waits until the fatigue limit is reached and clears the screen to white for a predefined time interval $t_{interval}$. The $t_{interval}$ is chosen such that it is long enough to be noticed by our visual system but not long enough to be considered to be intrusive. We found white to work well for our given task as it was more effectively at getting a blink response, though other colors can work. A drawback of the flash is that the user could miss the stimulus since it only happens once.

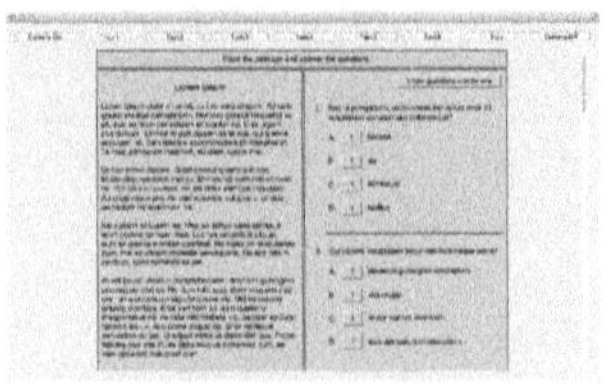

(a) User interface

(b) Blur stimulus

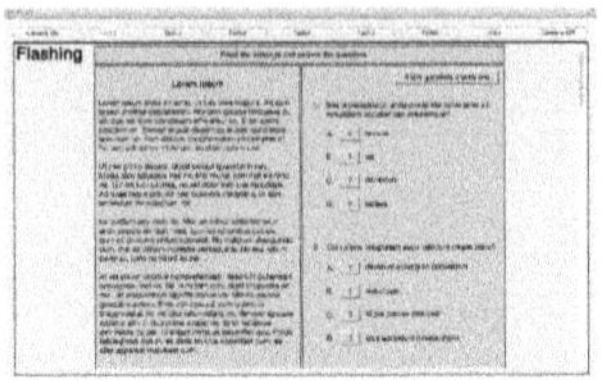

(c) Flashing border stimulus

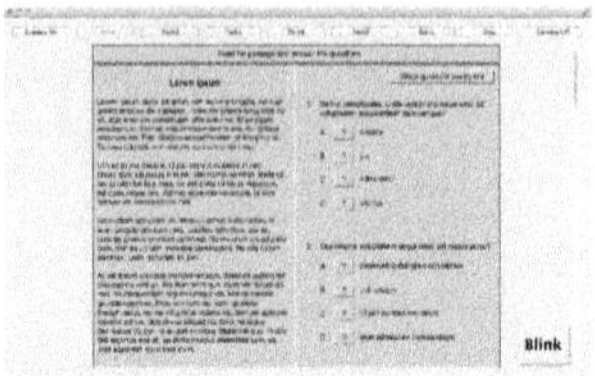

(d) Pop-up notification stimulus

Figure 2: Three of the four stimuli used in our study. The camera and task control button are found on top of the user interface (Text are replaced to avoid copyright issues).

The blur stimulus tries to mimic how our eye sight behaves when our eyes get dried. Once the stimulation event is triggered, a Gaussian blur filter is applied to the screen as the task is being conducted. As shown in Figure 2(b), this effect tricks the user into thinking their eyes have lost focus, thereby stimulating a blink. The Gaussian weights are calculated accordingly to the Gaussian function with standard deviation of 2.7. The blurring effect is carried out in two passes, first horizontally and then vertically to guarantee least memory fetches. We slow down the transition of the blur, making it less disturbing for the users to finish their tasks. The drawback of the blur is the user has to respond with a blink or they will be unable to continue working. This similar problem can occur if the blink detection does not capture the user's blink, thus causing the user to waste time trying to clear the blur effect.

The flashing border stimulus is the middle ground between the blur and the pop-up notification effect. When the fatigue limit is reached, the border of the task window will flash, until the user blinks to clear the effect. A demonstration of the flashing border stimuli is depicted in Figure 2(c). Unlike the blur stimulus, the border flashing does not prevent the user from completing the task and thus acts more like a notification. Nevertheless, some users might find the flashing border quite annoying and distracting.

The pop-up notification stimulus as the name implies creates a pop-up window in the bottom right corner of the screen. This window is purposely kept in the peripheral vision as to not disturb the user, as shown in Figure 2(d). This method is used in most of the eye fatigue relief software packages. It suffers from two drawbacks, the user can easily choose to ignore it and because it is in the periphery, and it tends to draw the attention of the user away from their tasks.

Logging

Our system integrates two logging mechanisms to make sure the desired data is properly collected. First, the blinking and stimulating events are logged in time stamped text. The blink rate of each task-stimuli combination is calculated accordingly. Given that under certain circumstances, e.g. when the user is too close to the screen that his or her eyes cannot be captured by the camera, or the eye tracking algorithm does not work properly due to the position and angle of the glasses, it is possible that part of the blinks event might not be detected by the detection algorithm. In addition to the text log, the screen shots of users performing tasks are also recorded. To prevent critical blink screen shot from being smoothed out in videos, we chose a static image log instead. The images logs are outputted at the frequency of 30 to 100 milliseconds per image, which is fast enough to store information for checking blinks event afterwards.

Limitation of Our Design

One limitation of the system is that the camera cannot be set right in front of the user's sight. When conducting different tasks, the eyes of the users are focusing inside the area of the computer screen. It is possible for the user to be too close to the screen and part of his or her face is not captured by the camera. This will result in miss detection of the eye blinks.

USER STUDIES

We want to test how effective our system is, but before that we need to know how different media type affect blink rate. Hence Study 1 will seek to find out what kind of media type lead to the lowest blink rate (because this is the highest risk task for developing CVS) and with that in mind Study 2 will see how the various stimuli described above influence blink rate (on this bad blink-rate task).

Study 1 (Media Type User Study)

This user study tries to find a task with the lowest blink rate, as these are more likely to exacerbate CVS symptoms. We do this by seeing if the blink rate changes depending on what computer task is being performed. Specifically, we were interested in seeing which media type has the lowest blink rate and if there is variance within the media types. The lowest blink rate should have the most impact on dry eyes and is therefore the best media type to use for Study 2.

Participants and Apparatus

We asked 13 participants (5 females), ranging from age 25 to 31, with a mean of 27.7. The participants had normal or corrected vision and used the computer on average 8 hours per day. The experiment was conducted in a well lit room. The study took between 20 to 30 minutes for each subject to complete.

The study was conducted on a 27 inch display with 1920x1080p resolution and a camera installed on top of the monitor. The task themselves were on a smaller resolution (1880x980p) window to fit the necessary buttons for switching to the next task. We asked the user to sit at least 50cm away from the monitor and make sure the monitor was at least 15 degree below the horizontal level.

Task

The user study comprises six computer tasks, two in each media type. We chose a passive and active version of each media type to see if there is variance within each media type.

Dumery et al. [15] found subjects blink rate drops soon after they started the task. Therefore, each task was kept short, ranging form three to five minutes to complete, enough time to capture the SEBR. Before we describe each of the task, we should define what are passive and active tasks in the context of this user study. An active task elicits/requires more attention from the user to complete a task than a passive task.

Text tasks: For the passive text task, the subjects were asked to read a set of paragraphs on a general topic. A Wikipedia page on Principle Component Analysis was used because all subjects are familiar with the topic. For the active text task, the subjects were asked to read a passage, displayed on the left, and answer questions on the passage on the right (an example is depicted in Figure 2(a)). This requires more attention as the user has to go back and forth between the passage and the question to answer them correctly.

Image tasks: We asked the user to do a memory test for the passive image task. The user was shown a set of equally sized images for 30 seconds. The user was then asked to pick out those images from a collection 20 images. The memory test was repeated twice with an increase in the number of images the user had to remember. In the case of the active image task, the user was given two images side by side and asked to spot the difference between them. Memorizing a set of images uses more mental power. The user thinks of ways to associate the images or create a rich context by adding together auditory, visual and other information to the image. In either case, the user was spending more time making the necessary connections than staring at the images. Spot the difference is a good active task because it requires the user go back and forth between two set of images. Blinking actually makes detecting the difference harder as it disrupts iconic memory (discussed later) [36].

Video tasks: The passive task was to watch a presentation, while for the active task, the user watched an action trailer. Trailers are designed to grab the attention of the viewer, showing series of clips to entice the viewer into watching the movie. They have 2 to 3 minutes to sell the audience on the movie. On the other hand, talks are more slowly paced and provide more content. A talk is more about what is being said than what is being shown. Therefore, the visual content is not as important as in the trailer.

It should be noted, that we did not track how well they completed each task, since it has no relevance to our study.

Procedure

We used a within-subject design. Each user was asked to fulfill a quick survey before starting the study. The survey covered basic question such as age and gender, as well as questions about their vision and computer usage.

Before starting the task, the participants saw a live feed of themselves with the eye detecting software enabled and were asked to make sure the software could detect their face, as shown in Figure 1. The user started a task by clicking on one of the task buttons as shown in 2(a). Once a task was completed, the task button is grayed out. The tasks were given in a random order assigned by the computer. A camera was mounted on top of monitor to capture blink rate. Images frames were recorded in case the blink events are not properly detected. The users were asked to always stare forward and not to touch their face as it will affect the blink capturing software. Between tasks, the user is given a small break and shown live feed to check positioning. An experimenter recorded observations, rating and follow-up interviews.

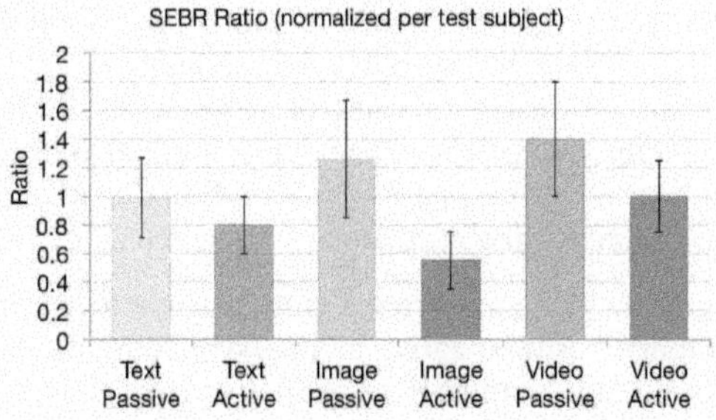

Figure 3: The SEBR ratio over the average SEBR per test subject for each of the six tasks. Error bar: standard deviation.

Results

To make sure false-positives were not counted, captured video data was manually counted and compared against our system. False-positives occurred less then 0.4% across both studies and were removed from the dataset.

Figure 3 summarizes the results from Study 1. The ratio was acquired by taking the absolute SEBR of each task over the average SEBR per individual. We used One-way analysis of variance(Anova) to analye the SEBR ratios. We found a significant effect of media types for SEBR ratio ($F_{5,13} = 4.6282, p = 0.001$). Posthoc Tukey analysis shows a pairwise difference between image active and image passive ($p < 0.001$) as well as video passive ($p < 0.001$). There was also a pairwise difference between text active and video passive ($p < 0.05$).

Discussion

When we looked at the SEBR, we noticed some individual had higher or lower baseline. For instance, one participant had SEBR of 20.57 for passive image and 10.42 for active image, while another had a SEBR of 5.3 for passive image and 1.94 for active image. There is a clear difference between the passive and active image, though just averaging the SEBR on each task would create quite bit of variance. This pronounced variance is typical for averaged SEBR measurements. Blinking in real-life settings depends on a large number of parameters([14, 40, 39]), which may influence the SEBR positively or negatively and contribute to the observed large variation in SEBR within normal population. This is why we chose to use the ratio of absolute SEBR of each task over the average SEBR per individual as it was a better indicator.

Study 1 has shown that active image computer tasks have the lowest SEBR ratio. This might be due to the fact that an active image task uses iconic memory to complete the task. Iconic memory is known as a very brief (less than one second), precategorical, high capacity visual memory. The problem with iconic memory is that automatic and voluntary blinking disrupts the information stored in iconic memory [36]. Therefore, blinking during the task becomes a disadvantage and reduces subjects' performance. This could also explain why stimuli that force the user to blink are found to be more intrusive, especially if the blink does not get detected.

Skotte et al. [35] conducted a similar study to see if there is a difference between active and passive computer tasks. We can not directly compare the studies as they consider watching a video to be a passive task. They defined video as a passive task because it does not require interaction with the computer. For the active computer task, they used Birch et al.'s [5] simulated work task. The task presents a graph to the subject and they have to reconstruct the graph, in the correct location, by selecting and linking a set of equally distributed points together. Birch et al.'s simulated work task is quite similar to the spot the difference task and can be considered an active image task. In both, the subject is processing a small area of an image or graph at a time, going back and forth, and looking at what is supposed to be there or not (for the graph, it is an edge and for the image, it is a missing object). Comparing our image active task with the passive video task, we obtained results similar to that of Skotte et al.'s study.

Stimulus User Study

The stimulus user study tests to see which methods are more effective in stimulating a blink response from the user. We are also interested in the user opinion of the stimulus. Did they find the stimuli annoying and how effective did they feel the stimuli were? We used the active image task for our task as it had the lowest blink rate.

Participants and apparatus

We asked 13 participants (5 females), ranging from age 24 to 33, with a mean of 27. The participants had normal or corrected vision and used the computer on average of 8 hours per day. The experiment was conducted in the same location as the first experiment and under the same conditions to avoid introduction of any new variables. The study took each subject approximately 30 minutes to complete.

Task

This user study asked each user to complete a set of tasks and measured how often they blink per minute (SEBR) during each task. If the user did not blink for a designated amount of time, a stimulus was triggered. There are four stimulus types plus one control. Our previous user study showed that active image task has the lowest SEBR, and therefore we chose to use that for all of the tasks. We want to mimic the situation where the software can assist the user in remembering to blink.

The five types of stimuli are Flash, Blur, Flashing Border, Pop-up notification, and control. The Blur stimuli causes the screen to slowly Blur until the user blinks. This method, unlike the rest, forces the user to blink or else the image becomes unreadable after a while. The flashing stimuli administers a quick white screen flash (15ms). The Flashing Border pulses from white to black. The pop-up notification method works as it sounds, by causing a pop-up window to appear

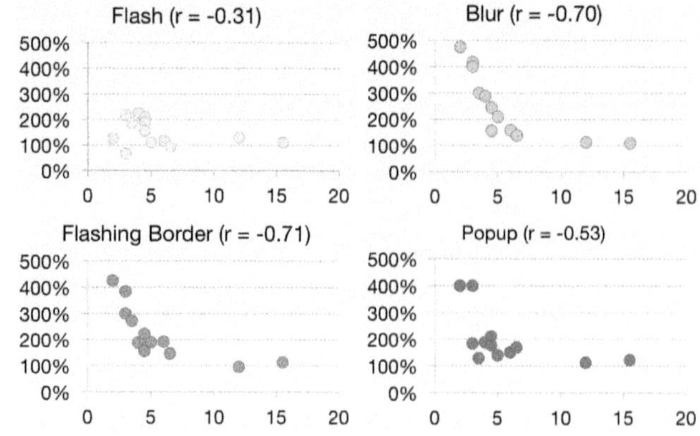

Figure 4: Comparing the four types of stimulus. The x-axis is the users sorted based on their SEBR obtained from the non-stimulus condition. The y-axis encodes the rate (in terms of percentage) of increase for stimulus blink rate over the non-stimulus condition. The plots indicate that all four stimuli helped to increase the blink rate compared to the non-stimulus condition, as almost all the ratios are greater than one. Blur and Flashing Border have a negative correlation to SEBR.

in the lower right corner of the screen to remind the user to blink. The control has no stimulus.

Procedure

We used a within-subject design. Subjects were asked to fill a quick survey about their computer usage and vision. We gave each subject 5 minutes to get accustomed to each type of stimulus before starting on the tasks.

The subject was presented with a series of spot the difference tasks and spent between 3 to 5 minutes on completing each task. The tasks were given in random order. The users were asked to always stare forward and not to touch their face as it will affect the blink capturing software. After each task, the users were asked to rate each stimulus based on effectiveness, distraction, and satisfaction. We were curious to see if there was a difference between perceived effectiveness versus the qualitative measure. The rating was done on a 1 to 5 scale where 5 equals very effective, very distracting, and very satisfied. An experimenter recorded observations, rating, and follow-up interviews.

Results

As with Study1, video data was compared against our algorithm. False-Positives were removed from the dataset.

Figure 4 shows the four stimuli where the x-axis is the users, sorted by their SEBR from control test. Y-axis is the ratio of the stimulus blink rate over SEBR. The larger the x value is, the higher the SEBR. Almost all ratios are larger than 1, which indicates all four stimuli help to increase the blink rate compared to the control. The results for the Blur and Flashing Border stimulus also reveal a pattern of negative correlation; that is, users with lower blink rate tend to have higher blink rate increase, when these two stimuli are applied.

All four stimuli increased subjects' SEBR. Flash stimulus was the least effective as the stimulus rate was higher than

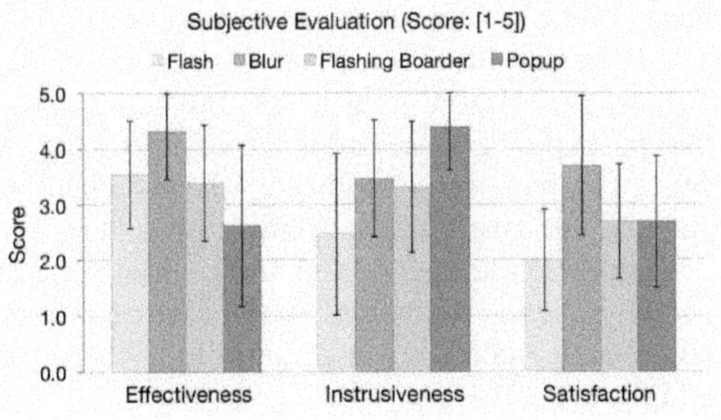

Figure 5: Subjective evaluation of the four types of stimulus. The higher the value, the better performance a stimuli has, where 5 = very effective, not intrusive at all and very satisfied.

the blink rate for several of the subjects. As expected, individuals that had higher control SEBR had the lowest increase in blink rate and stimulus rate.

Subjective results

Figure 5 shows the results of the user feedback. We used Kruskal-Wallis ANOVA. The result ($H = 10.45, df = 3, p < 0.05$) indicated a significant difference in effectiveness. Mann-Whitney U test showed a pairwise difference between Blur and Pop-up ($p < 0.005$, z = 2.82) where Blur ($\mu = 4.31$, $\sigma = 0.85$) was more effective than Pop-up ($\mu = 2.62$, $\sigma = 1.45$). The result for intrusiveness ($H = 12.94, df = 3, p < 0.005$) indicated a significant difference as well. The Mann-Whitney U test revealed that Pop-up ($\mu = 4.38$, $\sigma = 0.77$) is less intrusive than Flash ($\mu = 2.46$, $\sigma = 1.45$ with $p < 0.005$, z = 3.1), Blur ($\mu = 3.46$, $\sigma = 1.05$ with $p < 0.05$, z = 2.23), and flashing boarder ($\mu = 3.31$, $\sigma = 1.18$ with $p < 0.05$, z = 2.31). The result ($H = 11.42, df = 3, p < 0.01$) also indicated a significant difference for satisfaction. The participants found Blur ($\mu = 3.69$, $\sigma = 1.25$) to be more satisfying than Flash ($\mu = 2.00$, $\sigma = 0.91$ with $p < 0.005$, z = 3.05) and Flashing Border ($\mu = 2.69$, $\sigma = 1.03$ with $p < 0.05$, z = 2.05).

We asked users what they thought of each stimulus. Half felt the Flash was annoying, while only one liked Flash because it was quick and did not block the content. One individual commented that the Flash made him feel uneasy. An interesting comment was made by two individuals about how once they got used to the flash, it lost its effectiveness.

Blur received more positive comments. Several users liked the steady change effect because of the way that it cleared the screen. However, several subjects could not clear the Blur in the first try and thus found Blur effect annoying. This can be fixed by using a more robust detection system.

Users found the Flashing Border to be less noticeable than the flash. One user mistook it as a system alert. We also received several suggestions to change the border color according to the background color, so flashing would be more noticeable.

Two users liked the Pop-up stimulus because it was something they were used to. Almost half of the users commented they wanted the pop up window to be in the center, suggesting a need to have the option to select the position of the Pop-up.

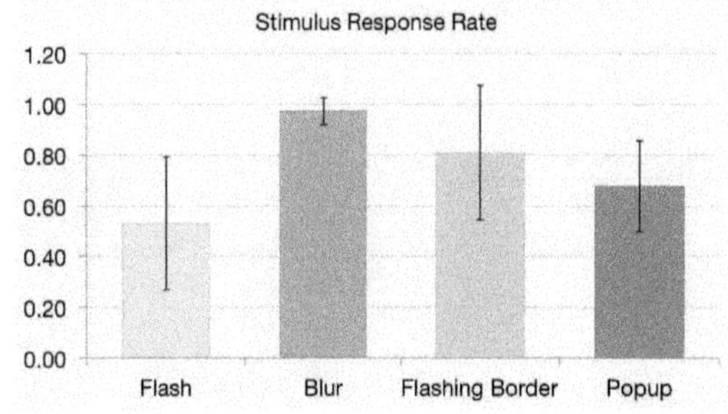

Figure 6: Response rate of each stimuli. Y-axis: the ratio of number of stimulated blinks over the number of stimulations.

A few users mentioned they found the Pop-up not intrusive because it was out of sight.

Stimulus response rate

We kept track of whether the user responded to a stimulus or not. A response to the stimulus was counted if there was a blink between two stimulations (4 to 8 seconds). This was done because some stimuli are persistent such as the Blur, Flashing Border, and Pop-up notification. Note that we started the timer again right after the stimulus was applied, independent of them being persistent or not.

Figure 6 summarizes the results of the response rate. We used a one-way ANOVA with Tukey. We found a significant effect of stimulus for response rate ($F_{3,13} = 6.5768, p < 0.005$). Pairwise comparison revealed Blur had a better response than Flash ($p < 0.005$) and Pop-up ($p < 0.0001$).

Stimulus response time

We logged the time taken for the user to respond to a stimulus. It should be noted, we ignored cases where the stimulus was triggered but the user did not respond. We used a one-way ANOVA with Tukey. Figure 7 summarizes the results for response time ($F_{3,13} = 1.6964, p = 0.1904$), showing no significant results for any of stimulus. It took individuals 1.5s ($\sigma = 0.86$) to blink after the flash, 2.13s ($\sigma = 0.37$) for Blur, 1.69s ($\sigma = 0.67$) for Flashing Border and 2.24s ($\sigma = 1.03$) for Pop-up. The variance for the Blur stimulus was smaller because the time interval from the blurring being noticed to the content being unreadable was small.

DISCUSSION AND FUTURE WORK

The results from our Study 2 indicate all of our stimuli helped to increase blink rate. The lower the blink rate, the more the stimuli helped. This makes sense as having a low blink rate means a stimulus is triggered more often and thus going to be more effective.

Though all the stimuli helped, not all were liked. Between the survey and user feedback, it is clear that Flash was the least liked. This is very interesting as Flash is the shortest stimuli. This might be explained by the way Flash is delivered. Blur has a steady change while Flashing Border and Pop-up are sudden but happen on the peripheral. Flash, on the other hand, happens suddenly and covers the entire screen, which might cause individuals to lose focus.

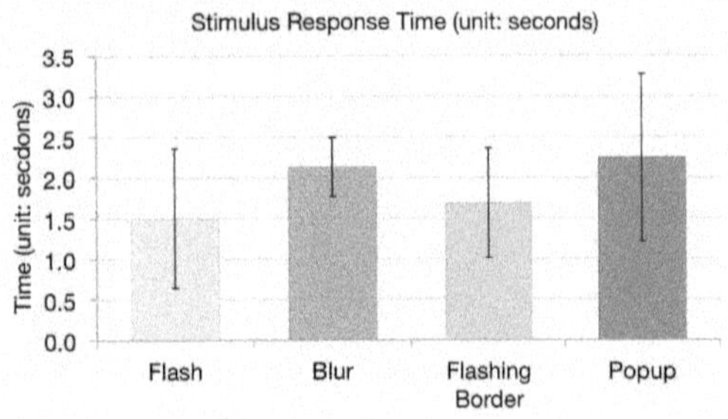

Figure 7: Response time of each stimuli. Y-axis: the response time in second. Error bar: standard deviation
. The Flash stimuli has the lowest response time in average. All except the Blur stimuli have large standard deviations.

We were surprised to see that there was no clear winner among the stimuli. We expected stimuli that were supposed to trick the eye into blinking, such as Blur and Flash, to do better. In some cases Blur did do better such as being better than Pop-up in effectiveness. A potential reason why Blur and Flash did not do clearly better than the other stimuli is because they failed to trick the eye. As we can see from the response time in Figure 6, it took on average 1.5 to 2 seconds to blink after a stimuli was applied. For Flash it is safe to say that most of the blinks were voluntary; otherwise, the response time would be close to 0 seconds. It is a bit harder to tell if the blinks were reflexive or voluntary for Blur stimulus as it takes time for the Blur effect to be seen by the users.

Being able to detect a blink plays a huge role in how intrusive the subject feels a stimulus method is. This affects methods that require the blink to be detected to reset, such as the Blur and Flashing Border. Even with a 95% detection rate, some blinks may not be registered. If this happens more than once during a specific task, subjects may become flustered with the stimulus, as it is preventing them from completing the task. This explains why certain methods have higher variances than others. It also explains why certain methods are highly effective in stimulating a blink (the subject has to blink multiple times to register a blink) but at the same time are very intrusive to the subject. It is difficult for us to determine the impact on performance as we did not gather task performance data. Hence, it's unclear from Study 2 how the different blink stimulation techniques might impact task performance. Unfortunately, this is not easy to fix, as any system will have margin of error. However, improving the detection rate will reduce the chance of multiple negative detections occurring within a small time interval.

We noticed from the pilot study that the size of the screen area occupied by the task affects blink rate considerably, especially in video and image tasks. Reducing the font size could produce the same results in the text tasks. For instance, reducing the size of the image task to half the screen drops the blink rate by at least half. We surmise that trying to focus or do comparison on a smaller image requires more concentration. In some cases, the subjects would lean forward in order to see greater detail. This prevents users from maintaining a proper viewing distance from the screen, possibly exacerbating CVS.

Another possible reason why screen size can affect blink rate is due to large amplitude saccades. Saccades are fast movement of the eye. Large screens require more and/or larger saccades to inspect and saccades are often (87.5%) followed by blinks [11]. This same study found a correlation between head movement and large amplitude saccades (more then 10°). Therefore, the size of the screen has to be relatively larger to elicit head movement. In the case of our studies, all the tasks were centered so large amplitude saccades did not play a big role.

Combining with existing techniques

Our system is not meant to replace existing utilities or fatigue detection systems [10, 21, 24, 37], but works alongside them as a first line of defense. First, our system would increase blink rate and help with alleviating some of the effects of dry eyes. When the system detects the user is suffering from fatigue, it can suggest the user to take a break or recommend any set of utilities [30, 1, 34]. Combining both sets of approaches would be straight forward as our system uses the same method of blink detection as the fatigue system.

Limitations of Our System and Studies

Different parameters: Each stimulus has parameters that can be tweaked, such as size, duration, location, and intensity. Also, there are other tweaks suggested by the test subjects. We did not want to add these variables to Study 2 as they would over complicate the study and our goal was simply to show that our stimulus worked. Further studies are necessary to see how tweaking such parameters affects the effectiveness and perceptions of the stimuli.

Glasses: Wearing glasses can affect the system's ability to detect blinks. If the user is staring directly ahead, then there is no effect on the detection. However, the blink rate drops if the glasses' frame blocks the user's eyes. This can also affect people's perceptions of the stimuli, specifically those which require the system to detect blinks to reset the effect.

Screen size: One limitation of our system is that the size of the screen affects how well the stimuli work. The greater the field of view the screen covers, the more likely the subject is to respond to the stimulus. This implies that mobile use of our method would be less effective. However, from our Study 1, attention effects blinks per minute as well. Therefore, another would need to be conducted to see what kind of effects a smaller screen size has on the stimulus methods.

Different types of blink: Our studies only looked at blink as a whole and did not take into account different types of blink. Further studies are needed to see if our stimulus methods cause a reflexive or voluntary blink.

Long term effects: We would also like to run a longer study to determine the long term effects of our system. Can the system help someone with dry eyes? Is training viable, and if so, what effect does that have on the different stimulus methods?

Implication for building a system

In our study, we learned few important guidelines to help create these systems. User frustration and interruption of workflow play a big role in individuals adopting these systems.

Detection systems will never be perfect. Touching one's face, movement and glasses will all reduce the chance for the blink to be detected and increase user frustration. This is especially a problem for methods like Blur that prevent the user from continuing their work. The problem stems from not being able to determine where the eyes are. Once eyes are found the detecting process is highly accurate. Therefore, our suggestion is when the face is not detected, to clear the effect and not start fatigue limit until the face is detected. This has potential of reducing effectiveness but will also reduce user frustration, which is more important.

No single stimulus is the best. Our Study 2 found a large variance in which stimulus subjects preferred. This variance can be attributed to both detection rate and subject preference. Some liked the effect taking up the entire screen, while others wanted something less intrusive. Since one method is not necessarily better than the rest, the system should let the user decide what type of stimulus they want to use.

Do not be afraid to experiment with other stimuli. The goal of our paper was to show that software-induce stimuli work. There are other stimuli that can be tried. For instance, instead of blurring the entire screen, the effect can start from the edge of the screen and slowly move toward the center or where the eyes are focused. Another possible idea is to track eye movement and apply effect to peripheral vision.

Stimulus responses do not have to be just for blinking. As we mentioned before that proper viewing angle and distance can help with CVS. Though when working on a tough problems it is easy to slip out of these proper position. If the camera is stationary, it is possible to detect the location and size of the head. With this information, the user can have stimulus response applied, such as Pop-up, to let them know when they slip out of the proper position.

CONCLUSION

We present a prototype system that tracks a user's blink rate and administers a stimulus to trigger the user to blink when the user has not blinked for a while. Our system is unique in that it stimulates a blink response by only using the screen itself. We considered a range of different stimulus methods that can be used to cause a blink response. We conducted two user studies. The first user study determined that active images have the lowest blink rate. We used these results to conduct a second user study to access our system. The results of this study indicate that it is possible to prompt a blink response with our stimulus methods. Our methods use a standard setup that can be found on any modern laptop. Therefore, a full system of our prototype can be created to help individuals alleviate dry eyes symptoms. Our findings can help others build future blink stimulus systems.

ACKNOWLEDGMENTS

We thank all the volunteers, and all publications support and staff, who wrote and provided helpful comments on previous versions of this document. This research was sponsored in part by the UC Davis RISE program.

REFERENCES

1. Protect your vision. `http://www.protectyourvision.org/`.
2. Acosta, M., Gallar, J., and Belmonte, C. The influence of eye solutions on blinking and ocular comfort at rest and during work at video display terminals. *Experimental Eye Research 68*, 6 (1999), 663 – 669.
3. Arai, K., and Mardiyanto, R. Eye based hci with moving keyboard for reducing fatigue effects. In *2011 Eighth International Conference on Information Technology: New Generations*, IEEE (Apr. 2011), 417–422.
4. Bacher, L. F., and Smotherman, W. P. Spontaneous eye blinking in human infants: a review. *Developmental psychobiology 44*, 2 (Mar. 2004), 95–102.
5. Birch, L., Juul-Kristensen, B., Jensen, C., Finsen, L., and Christensen, H. Acute response to precision, time pressure and mental demand during simulated computer work. *Scandinavian Journal of Work, Environment & Health 26*, 4 (Aug. 2000), 299–305.
6. Biswas, N. R., Nainiwal, S. K., Das, G. K., Langan, U., Dadeya, S. C., Mongre, P. K., Ravi, A. K., and Baidya, P. Comparative randomised controlled clinical trial of a herbal eye drop with artificial tear and placebo in computer vision syndrome. *Journal of the Indian Medical Association 101*, 3 (Mar. 2003), 208–9, 212.
7. Blehm, C., Vishnu, S., Khattak, A., Mitra, S., and Yee, R. W. Computer vision syndrome: a review. *Survey of ophthalmology 50*, 3 (2005), 253–62.
8. Bologna, M., Agostino, R., Gregori, B., Belvisi, D., Ottaviani, D., Colosimo, C., Fabbrini, G., and Berardelli, A. Voluntary, spontaneous and reflex blinking in patients with clinically probable progressive supranuclear palsy. *Brain : A Journal of Neurology 132*, Pt 2 (Feb. 2009), 502–10.
9. Bradski, G. *Dr. Dobb's Journal of Software Tools* (2000).
10. Caffier, P. P., Erdmann, U., and Ullsperger, P. Experimental evaluation of eye-blink parameters as a drowsiness measure. *European journal of applied physiology 89*, 3-4 (May 2003), 319–25.
11. Cardona, G., and Quevedo, N. Blinking and Driving: the Influence of Saccades and Cognitive Workload. *Current eye research* (Oct. 2013), 1–6.
12. CRC Press, Anshel, J. *Visual Ergonomics Handbook.* 2005.
13. Divjak, M., and Bischof, H. Eye Blink Based Fatigue Detection for Prevention of Computer Vision Syndrome. *MVA2009 IAPR Conference on Machine Vision Applications* (2009), 350–353.
14. Doughty, M. J. Consideration of Three Types of Spontaneous Eyeblink Activity in Normal Humans: during Reading and Video Display Terminal Use, in Primary Gaze, and while in Conversation. *Optometry and Vision Science 78*, 10 (2001), 712–725.

15. Dumery, B., Grounauer, P., and Toi, V. V. Eyestrain, Blink Rate and Dry Eye Syndromes of Video Display Terminal Users. *The Third International Conference on the Development of Biomedical Engineering in Vietnam* (2010), 270–273.

16. Evinger, C., Manning, K., and Sibony, P. Eyelid Movements Mechanisms and Normal Data. *Investigative ophthalmology & visual science 32*, 2 (1991), 387–400.

17. Fenety, A., and Walker, J. Short-Term Effects of Workstation Exercises on Musculoskeletal Discomfort and Postural Changes in Seated Video Display Unit Workers. *Physical Therapy* (2002), 578–589.

18. Folk, C. L., Leber, A. B., and Egeth, H. E. Made you blink! contingent attentional capture produces a spatial blink. *Perception & psychophysics 64*, 5 (July 2002), 741–53.

19. Freudenthaler, N., Neuf, H., Kadner, G., and Schlote, T. Characteristics of spontaneous eyeblink activity during video display terminal use in healthy volunteers. *Graefe's archive for clinical and experimental ophthalmology 241*, 11 (Nov. 2003), 914–20.

20. Han, S., Yang, S., Kim, J., and Gerla, M. Eyeguardian: a framework of eye tracking and blink detection for mobile device users. In *HOTMOBILE'12* (2012), 6–6.

21. Heishman, R., and Duric, Z. Using eye blinks as a tool for augmented cognition. *Foundations of Augmented Cognition* (2007), 84–93.

22. Helland, M., Horgen, G., Kvikstad, T., and Aars, A. *Do Background Luminance Levels or Character Size Effect the Eye Blink Rate During Visual Display Unit (VDU) Work Comparing Young Adults with Presbyopes?*, vol. 4566. Springer Berlin Heidelberg, 2007.

23. Karson, C. N., Berman, K. F., Donnelly, E. F., Mendelson, W. B., Kleinman, J. E., and Wyatt, R. J. Speaking, thinking, and blinking. *Psychiatry research 5*, 3 (Dec. 1981), 243–6.

24. Królak, A., and Strumio, P. Eye-blink detection system for humancomputer interaction. *Universal Access in the Information Society 11*, 4 (Oct. 2011), 409–419.

25. Mark, G., Gudith, D., and Klocke, U. The cost of interrupted work: more speed and stress. In *Proceedings of the SIGCHI Conference on Human Factors in Computing Systems*, CHI '08, ACM (New York, NY, USA, 2008), 107–110.

26. Mclean, L., Tingley, M., Scott, R. N., and Rickards, J. Computer terminal work and the benefit of microbreaks. *Applied ergonomics 32*, 3 (June 2001), 225–37.

27. Miljanović, B., Dana, R., Sullivan, D. a., and Schaumberg, D. a. Impact of dry eye syndrome on vision-related quality of life. *American journal of ophthalmology 143*, 3 (Mar. 2007), 409–15.

28. Miura, D. L., Hazarbassanov, R. M., Yamasato, C. K. N., Silva, F. B. E., Godinho, C. J., and Gomes, J. A. P. Effect of a light-emitting timer device on the blink rate of non-dry eye individuals and dry eye patients. *The British journal of ophthalmology 97*, 8 (Aug. 2013), 965–967.

29. Nakamori, K., Odawara, M., Nakajima, T., Mizutani, T., and Tsubota, K. Blinking is controlled primarily by ocular surface conditions. *American journal of ophthalmology 124*, 1 (July 1997), 24–30.

30. Pampana, V., and Chandran, R. Eye pro. `http://classlesoft.in/eye-pro`.

31. Rushworth, G. Observations on blink reflexes. *Journal of neurology, neurosurgery, and psychiatry*, 1906 (1962).

32. Schaumberg, D. a., Sullivan, D. a., Buring, J. E., and Dana, M. Prevalence of dry eye syndrome among US women. *American Journal of Ophthalmology 136*, 2 (Aug. 2003), 318–326.

33. Schlote, T., Kadner, G., and Freudenthaler, N. Marked reduction and distinct patterns of eye blinking in patients with moderately dry eyes during video display terminal use. *Graefe's archive for clinical and experimental ophthalmology 242*, 4 (Apr. 2004), 306–12.

34. Shelter Publications, I. `http://www.stretchware.com/`.

35. Skotte, J. H., Nø jgaard, J. K., Jø rgensen, L. V., Christensen, K. B., and Sjø gaard, G. Eye blink frequency during different computer tasks quantified by electrooculography. *European journal of applied physiology 99*, 2 (Jan. 2007), 113–9.

36. Thomas, L., and Irwin, D. Voluntary eyeblinks disrupt iconic memory. *Perception & psychophysics 68*, 3 (04 2006), 475–488.

37. Trutoiu, L. C., Carter, E. J., Matthews, I., and Hodgins, J. K. Modeling and animating eye blinks. *ACM Trans. Appl. Percept. 8*, 3 (Aug. 2011), 1–17.

38. Tsubota, K. Tear dynamics and dry eye. *Progress in Retinal and Eye Research 17*, 4 (1998), 565–596.

39. Wolkoff, P., Nø jgaard, J. K., Troiano, P., and Piccoli, B. Eye complaints in the office environment: precorneal tear film integrity influenced by eye blinking efficiency. *Occupational and environmental medicine 62*, 1 (Jan. 2005), 4–12.

40. Wolkoff, P., Skov, P., Franck, C., and Petersen, L. N. Eye irritation and environmental factors in the office environment-hypotheses, causes and a physiological model. *Scandinavian Journal of Work, Environment & Health 29*, 6 (dec 2003), 411–430.

41. Yan, Z., Hu, L., Chen, H., and Lu, F. Computer Vision Syndrome: A widely spreading but largely unknown epidemic among computer users. *Computers in Human Behavior 24*, 5 (Sept. 2008), 2026–2042.

42. Yang, F., Yu, X., Huang, J., Yang, P., and Metaxas, D. Robust eyelid tracking for fatigue detection. In *Image Processing (ICIP), 2012 19th IEEE International Conference on* (2012), 1829–1832.

Smart Photo Selection: Interpret Gaze as Personal Interest

Tina Walber
WeST Institute
University of Koblenz, Germany
walber@uni-koblenz.de

Ansgar Scherp
Kiel University, Germany
Leibniz Information Center for Economics, Kiel, Germany
mail@ansgarscherp.net

Steffen Staab
WeST Institute
University of Koblenz, Germany
staab@uni-koblenz.de

ABSTRACT
Manually selecting subsets of photos from large collections in order to present them to friends or colleagues or to print them as photo books can be a tedious task. Today, fully automatic approaches are at hand for supporting users. They make use of pixel information extracted from the images, analyze contextual information such as capture time and focal aperture, or use both to determine a proper subset of photos. However, these approaches miss the most important factor in the photo selection process: the user. The goal of our approach is to consider individual interests. By recording and analyzing gaze information from the user's viewing photo collections, we obtain information on user's interests and use this information in the creation of personal photo selections. In a controlled experiment with 33 participants, we show that the selections can be significantly improved over a baseline approach by up to 22% when taking individual viewing behavior into account. We also obtained significantly better results for photos taken at an event participants were involved in compared with photos from another event.

Author Keywords
Photo selection; eye tracking; usage-based image selection.

ACM Classification Keywords
H.5.2 User Interfaces: Input devices and strategies

INTRODUCTION
The large number of personal digital photos makes the management of one's photo collection an increasingly challenging task. Users easily take hundreds of photos during vacation or personal events such as weddings or birthday parties. Often, selections of "good" photos are created to reduce the amount of photos stored or shared with others [5, 7, 13, 16]. While users enjoy certain photo activities like the creation of collages for special occasions such as anniversaries or weddings, these tasks are seen as "complex and time consuming" for normal collections [5]. In order to alleviate this situation, different approaches that allow for the automatic selection of a subset of photos from a large collection have been developed in the past. *Content-based approaches* initially used pixel information of the photos to compute exposure, sharpness, and other photo properties in order to determine a photo subset [24, 23, 3, 25, 26]. These approaches were followed by *context-based approaches*, which exclusively or additionally analyze the contextual information of the photos. This information could be technical parameters of the digital still camera, such as capture times or GPS coordinates, or information gained from social networks like blogs [10, 22, 12, 15]. While acknowledging the achievements made by content- and context-based approaches, we claim that they miss the most important factor in the photo selection process: the user's interests. Capturing the user's interests is important as the human photo selection process is assumed to be guided by very individual factors and is highly subjective [20].

Rodden and Wood showed that photo collections are browsed frequently [16]. However, the frequency of browsing decreases over time. Thus, the viewing of photos usually happens shortly after the capturing or downloading to a computer. We present a *usage-based approach* [18], where the very individual viewing behavior of the user is captured and used in the selection process. We record the user's eye movements while viewing a photo collection. Fixations in the gaze paths show the moments of the highest visual perception and indicate the user's attention. Different eye tracking measures have been used to identify important photos. They consider for example the duration of fixations, how frequently a photo is fixated, and the pupil reaction. Photos with high measure values are assumed to be the most interesting to the user and thus should be part of a selection. Our approach is reasonable as we expect a higher availability of eye tracking hardware in the future, as indicated by recent developments in the directions of less expensive professional hardware and eye tracking with low-cost hardware like webcams.

In our experiment participants first viewed a collection of photos and then manually created personal selections. The manual selections served as ground truth and allowed for the evaluation of different selection approaches. As we assume that the eye movements are strongly influenced by interest, we also investigated if the personal relevance of viewed photo sets influences the quality of the gaze-based photo selection results. To this end, we showed photos of an event the user took part in or in which the user knew the participants ("home collection") and photos of an event the user was not personally involved in ("foreign collection"). Also, the different selection tasks for manual selection are compared (selections

CHI 2014, April 26–May 1, 2014, Toronto, Ontario, Canada.

ACM 978-1-4503-2473-1/14/04..$15.00.
http://dx.doi.org/10.1145/2556288.2557025

for private collection, for friends and family, and for publication on social networks). The results of our experiment show that photo selection criteria are often subjective and manually created selections are diverse. The usage-based approach, taking the individual user interest into account, significantly improves the automatically created photo selections based only on content and context information [10, 25, 26] by up to 17%. Considering only photo sets of the home collection, we even achieve an improvement of up to 22%. The three different tasks for manual selection had only little influence on the performance of the usage-based approach. The related work is discussed below. Subsequently, we describe the experiment design and the applied methods for creating photo selections. We compare the participants' behavior when viewing and selecting photos and show the distribution of the selected photos. Finally, the gaze selection results are presented and discussed before we conclude the paper.

BACKGROUND LITERATURE

Approaches for the automatic creation of photo selections typically use low-level image features (content-based information) and/or photo meta data (context-based information). For example, Chu and Lin [3] selected representative photos by identifying near-duplicate photos. Xiao et al. [25] presented a semiautomatic collage creating tool that makes a selection of photos purely based on content-based information, such as color histograms, sharpness, and near duplicates. Li et al. [10] created summaries of photo collections based on time stamps and facial features. Sinha et al. [22] introduced a framework for generating representative subsets of photos from large personal photo collections by using multidimensional content and context measures like GPS coordinates or tags. Rabbath et al. [15] used content and context information from blogs to automatically create photo books.

Eye tracking technology can be used as an explicit input device. The users explicitly control software by moving their eyes as presented, for example, in the evaluations of gaze interaction by Mollenbach et al. [11] and Sibert and Jacob [21]. We differentiate our approach from gaze-controlled approaches as the user is not asked to control his or her gaze in interacting with the system, e.g., by fixating on a photo to select it or by concentrating only on the "best" photos. In contrast, we obtain information from users freely viewing the photos without concrete instructions. Several approaches use eye tracking to identify attractive or important images in a search results list and use this information as implicit user feedback in improving the image search, e.g., [6, 8, 9]. From these works, we know that it is possible to use gaze information to detect images relevant to a given search task. Support vector machines have been applied on eye tracking data together with content-based features to rank images [14]. Santella et al. [19] presented a method for image cropping based on gaze information. Their goal was to find the most important image regions in order to exclude these regions from cropping. This approach does not have the goal of creating selections of photos. However, it shows that relevant information on the user's interest can be obtained from gaze.

It can be assumed that eye tracking will be available to the average user in the near future. One reason for this assumption is the rapid development of sensors in IT hardware: While the cost for eye tracking devices was about USD $35,000$ just two years ago, embedded and low-cost solutions are available now for less than USD 100[1]. Nowadays, eye trackers can also be developed using low-cost hardware. San Agustin et al. [17] compared a commercial eye tracker and a webcam system. The results for the webcam system are satisfactory and comparable to the commercial system, although still with limitations concerning the comfort of use. This rapid development in eye tracking hardware will allow using gaze information in everyday tasks like photo viewing.

EXPERIMENT

We developed an experiment application that allowed the participants to view and select photos from a collection $C = \{p_1, p_2, ...p_n\}$. In the first part of the experiment, eye tracking data was collected from the participants while viewing photos. Subsequently, ground truth data was collected by asking the participants to manually create three personal selections of these photos.

Participants

A total of 33 participants (12 of them female) completed the first part of the experiment. Twelve were associated with a research lab A in North America and 21 with institute B in Europe. Members of institute A and institute B did not know one another. Their age ranged between 25 and 62 years (M: 33.5, SD: 9.57). Twenty of them were graduate students and 4 postdocs. The remaining 9 participants worked in other professions, such as secretaries or veterinary assistants. Eighteen of the 33 participants (7 of them female) completed the second part of experiment. Six of them were associated with institute A and 12 of them with institute B. Their average age was 31.7 (SD: 8.74).

Materials

The experiment photo collection C consisted of two collections of photos taken during two social events, one organized by each of the two research institutes the participants were associated with. The activities during the events included teamwork situations, group meals, as well as leisure activities like bowling and hiking. Event A lasted half a day and event B three days. The photos were taken by different people: three people for collection C_A and two for collection C_B. The photos were not preselected but taken directly from the camera. Only two extremely blurry photos were removed. The photo collection of the participants' own institute is called "home collection" and the other one "foreign collection" (cf. Figure 1). Collection C_A (photos were taken during the event of institute A) consisted of 162 photos and C_B 126 photos. The photo collection $C = C_A \cup C_B$ was split chronologically into sets of nine photos $c_i = \{p_{i \cdot 9+1}, ..., p_{i \cdot 9+9}\}$. Each set c_i contained only photos of one of the collections. The complete collection of 288 photos was thus split into 32 sets (18 sets of C_A and 14 sets of C_B).

[1] http://www.tobii.com/eye-experience/ (last visited Jan. 5, 2014)

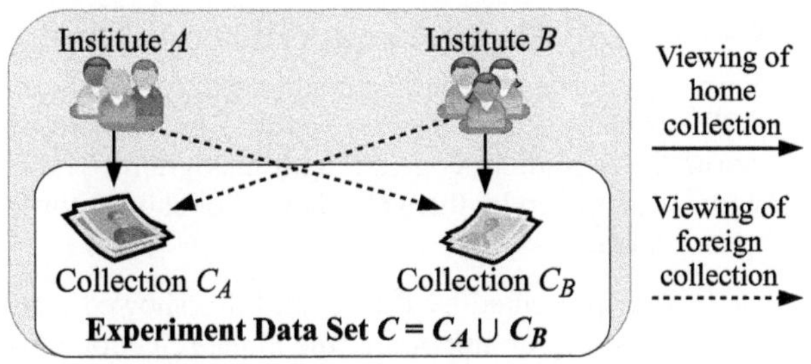

Figure 1. Structure of the experiment data set.

We assumed that the photos of the home collection are of higher personal interest for the participants than the photos of the foreign collection. This assumption is supported by results from the questionnaire. The participants were asked to indicate how interesting the two photo collections were using a Likert scale from 1 ("Not interesting") to 5 ("Very interesting"). For the home collections, the question was answered with an average of 4.36 (SD: 0.6) and for the foreign collection with an average of 2.72 (SD: 1.14). A chi-square test was applied for testing the significance of the differences as the data was not normally distributed (shown by a Shapiro-Wilk test of normality with $p < .001$ for the home set ratings and $p < .018$ for the foreign set ratings). The chi-square test showed a statistically significant difference between the answers, $X^2(5, N = 66) = 34.594, p < .001$.

Apparatus

The experiment was performed either on a 22-inch or a 24-inch monitor for the two research groups (cf. section Participants). The participants' gazes were recorded with a Tobii X60 eye tracker at a data rate of 60 Hz and an accuracy of 0.5 degree. The distance between the participants and the computer screen was about 60 cm. The setup (including a laptop, the eye tracking device, and a standard computer mouse) was the same for both groups.

Procedure

The experiment consisted of four steps, one viewing and three selection steps. In the first step ("Photo Viewing" in Figure 2), the participants were asked to view all photos of collection C with the goal "to get an overview." Eye tracking data was recorded only during this photo viewing step. Thus, unlike other item selection experiments [2], we clearly separated the viewing step from the selection steps. This was crucial to avoid an impact of the selection process on the viewing behavior. The order in which the two collections C_A and C_B were presented to the participants in the experiment was alternated. No time limit was given for viewing the photos. The participants were told that they would afterward, in the second step, create selections of the photos. No details about the selection process were given at this stage of the experiment.

Each photo set c_i was presented on a distinct page; the photos were arranged in 3×3 grids in the center of the screen. The photos' maximum height and width were set to 330 pixels, corresponding to about $9°$ at the visual angle. The minimum distance between the photo was 22 pixels ($0.6°$). By clicking on a button, the next set of nine photos was presented. The photos in each set c_i were arranged in random order, whereas the sets themselves and the order of the sets remained the same to preserve the chronological order of the events.

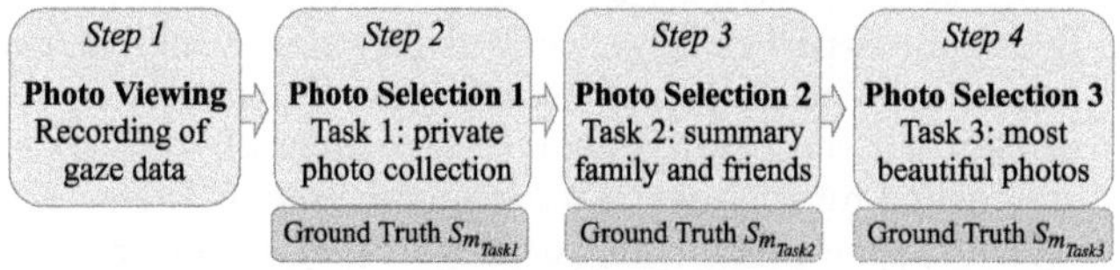

Figure 2. Experiment setup with the photo viewing step and the three selection steps.

After having viewed all photos, the participants were asked to select exactly three photos of each set c_i in the second step ("Photo Selection 1" in Figure 2). The photos were selected by means of a drag-and-drop interface as depicted in Figure 3. The same sets as in the viewing step were again presented to the participants, but the photos were rearranged in a new random order. The participants were asked in this second step to select the photos as they would do for their private photo collection. We gave no specific instructions regarding the selection criteria for choosing the photos. Thus, the participants could apply their own (perhaps even unconscious) criteria. Also, in the third and fourth steps ("Photo Selection 2" and "Photo Selection 3" in Figure 2), the participants performed manual selections. In the third step (Task 2), the participants were asked to "select photos for their friends or family that provide a detailed summary of the event." The fourth step (Task 3) was to "select the most beautiful photos for presenting them on the web, e.g., on Flickr." In the experiment steps 3 and 4, the users performed the manual selections only for the photo sets belonging to their home collections, not the complete collection C. Eighteen of the participants completed these tasks. The manual selections served as ground truth in the later analysis. Finally, the participants filled in a questionnaire. It comprised questions about demographical user data (age, profession), the experiment data set, and the experiment task as well as a rating on different selection criteria.

Figure 3. Photo selection interface with one selected photo.

METHODS FOR CREATING PHOTO SELECTIONS

The aim of the photo selection methods is to create a subset $S \subset C$ that best suits the user's preferences. The capabilities of each method are evaluated by comparing the calculated selection with the manual selection for each set c_i created during the experiment. A "perfect" selection would be a selection identical to the manual selection. The photos C were displayed in sets of nine photos c_i. Selections of $j = 3$ photos are created for each set. An overview of the different photo selection approaches is shown in Figure 4. They are presented in detail in the following sections. We start by describing the content-based and context-based measures for photo analysis used in our baseline system. Subsequently, we present the eye tracking based measures and then the combination of different measures by means of logistic regression. Finally, we describe the calculation of precision P for comparing the selections with the ground truth selections $S_{m_{Task1}}$, $S_{m_{Task2}}$, and $S_{m_{Task3}}$.

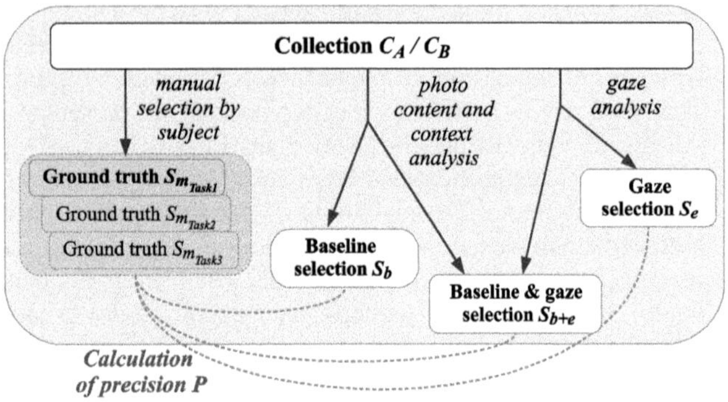

Figure 4. Overview of the investigated photo selection approaches and calculation of precision P.

Content and Context Analysis Baselines

We make use of six measures as baselines that analyze the context or the content of photos. An overview is shown in Table 1. The measures are motivated from related work, and details on their implementations can be found in the cited papers.

No	Measure	Description
1	concentrationTime	Photo p was taken with other photos in a short period of time [10]
2	sharpness	Sharpness score [25]
3	numberOfFaces	Number of faces
4	faceGaussian	Size and position of faces [10]
5	personsPopularity	Popularity of the depicted persons [26]
6	faceArea	Areas in pixels covered by faces

Table 1. Baseline measures based on content and context analysis.

The first measure, (1) concentrationTime, relies on the assumption that many photos are taken within a short period of time when something interesting happens during an event [10]. This measure is context-based as the information when a photo was taken is obtained from the photos' meta-information. Li et al. [10] created a function f_k indicating the number of photos taken for a point in time. By means of the first derivation of this function, a temporal representative value for each photo is calculated. The next four measures are content-based as they analyze the photos' content at pixel level. The photos' quality is considered in measure (2) sharpness by calculating a sharpness score as presented by Xiao et al. [25]. The score is calculated as $Q = \frac{strength(e)}{entropy(h)}$ with $strength(e)$ as the average gradient edge strength of the top 10% strongest edges and $entropy(h)$ as the entropy of the normalized gradient edge strength histogram. The edge strength is calculated by the well-known Sobel operator from computer vision.[2]

Related work, presented by Boll et al. [18], showed that depicted persons play an important role in the selection of photos. The four measures (3) to (6) are based on the analysis of depicted persons. Measure (3) numberOfFaces simply counts the number of faces on a photo. The detection of faces is done using OpenCV's Haar Cascades[2]. Also, measure (6) faceArea is based on this calculation. It considers the size in pixels of the photo areas covered by human faces. A Gaussian distribution of the face areas as proposed by Li et al. [10] is considered by measure (4) faceGaussian, identifying photos with large depicted faces in the photo's center. Measure (5) personsPopularity considers a persons' popularity in the data set as presented by Zhao et al. [26]. It assumes that faces appearing frequently are more important than the ones appearing less often. The calculation is performed by the OpenCV's face recognition algorithm and considers persons appearing in each set c_i of nine photos. This measure is context-based as well as content-based.

Gaze Analysis

Human gaze paths consist of fixations and saccades. Fixations are short time periods when the gaze is focused on a specific point on the screen. Saccades are the fast movements between the fixations. Most of the visual perception takes place during the fixations. Thus, we mainly analyze these parts of the gaze paths. Fixations are extracted from the raw eye tracking data by applying a fixation filter. This preprocessing is performed with the fixation filter offered by Tobii Studio[3] with the default velocity threshold of 35 pixels and a distance threshold of 35 pixels. A visualization of a sample gaze path can be found in Figure 5. Fixations are visualized as circles, and the diameter indicates the duration of a fixation.

The obtained fixations are analyzed by means of eye tracking measures. Each measure assigns a value to each photo p. An overview of all measures can be found in Table 2. Measure (7) fixated determines if a photo was fixated or not. Measure (8) fixationCount indicates how often a photo was fixated. Measures (9) to (12) consider the durations of fixations on a photo. Measures (13) to (15) are based on "visits." A visit is a series of fixations on a photo. Measure (16) saccLength considers the saccade lengths before fixating a photo. The three measures (17) to (19) rely on the size of the user pupil while fixating a photo. Related work shows that the pupil size can vary with emotional reactions [1]. This reaction could appear more often for interesting photos. To compensate the inaccuracy of the eye tracking data, fixations in the surrounding of 11 pixels ($0.3°$ at the visual angle) of a photo are also

[2] http://opencv.org/ (last visited Sept. 17, 2013)
[3] http://www.tobii.com (last visited Sept. 18, 2013)

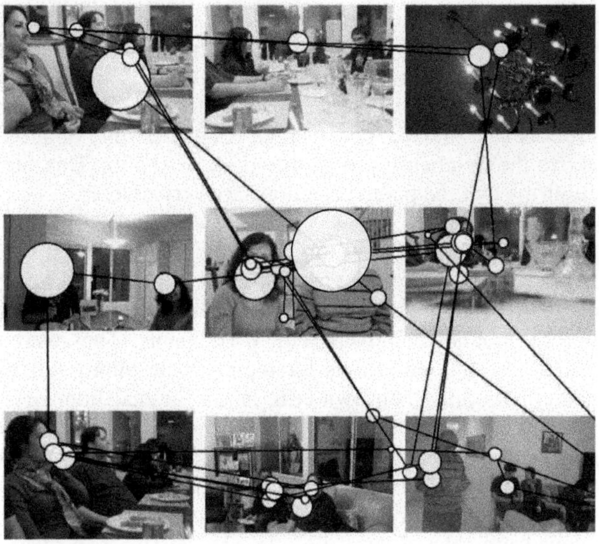

Figure 5. Visualization of a gaze path on a photo set.

considered as being on a photo (the smallest distance between two photos is 22 pixels, or 0.6°).

No	Measure	Description
7	fixated	Indicates if p was fixated or not
8	fixationCount	Counts the number of fixations on p
9	fixationDuration	Sum of the duration of all fixations on p
10	firstFixationDuration	Duration of the first fixation on p
11	lastFixationDuration	Duration of the last fixation on p
12	avgFixationDuration	Average of the durations of all fixations on p
13	maxVisitDuration	Maximum visit length on p
14	meanVisitDuration	Mean visit length on p
15	visitCount	Number of visits within p
16	saccLength	Mean length of the saccades before fixating on p
17	pupilMax	Maximum pupil diameter while fixating on p
18	pupilMaxChange	Maximum pupil diameter change while fixating on p
19	pupilAvg	Average pupil diameter while fixating on p

Table 2. Eye tracking measures for photo p.

Combining Measures Using Logistic Regression

Different combinations of the content-based and context-based measures and eye tracking measures are investigated. To this end, all measure values are normalized per set c_i by subtracting the mean of the nine values per set and dividing it by the standard derivation σ. The measures are combined by means of a model learned from logistic regression as presented by Fan et al. [4]. The data of all users is split into a training set and a test set. About 15% of the data are selected as test data, which correspond to five sets of nine photos for every user as test data and 27 sets of nine photos as training data. The test sets are randomly chosen. Only complete sets c_i are selected for training and testing, respectively. When analyzing subsets of the data (e.g., when analyzing only the photos that are part of the home collection for each user) less data is available. The test data size is reduced to three sets of nine photos. The model is trained with the training data of all 33 users. That corresponds to $33 * 27 * 9 = 8,019$ training samples, when using the whole data set C. This number reduces to 3,699 samples when training the model only with those photos of the home sets. 1,998 samples were used when performing the training for the data from the experiment steps 3 and 4, which were completed by less participants. The default parameter settings of the LIBLINEAR library [4] are used for training. For every analysis, 30 iterations with different random splits are performed and the average results of all iterations are presented in this paper.

Three different measure combinations are investigated. Selection S_b takes only the baseline measures (1) to (6) into account. For the selection S_{b+e}, all 19 measures are considered in the logistic regression. For S_e exclusively the gaze measures (7) to (19) are used in the learning algorithm. The logistic regression predicts a probability of being selected for each photo in set c_i of nine photos. The three photos with the highest probability are chosen for the selection and compared with the ground truth selections $S_{m_{Task1}}$ to $S_{m_{Task3}}$.

Computing Precision P

For comparing a computed selection to the ground truth, the percentage of correctly selected photos of all selected photos is calculated (precision P). This calculation is conducted for each set c_i. Precision P for a selection approach is the average precision over all sets c_i. As three of nine photos are selected, a random baseline selecting three photos by chance would have an average precision of $P_{rand} = 0.\bar{3}$.

USERS' PHOTO VIEWING AND SELECTION BEHAVIOR

In this section, we first investigate the users' photo viewing times and photo selection times in our experiment. Subsequently, the distribution of the manual photo selections of our participants is presented. Finally, we show the users' rating regarding the importance of different photo selection criteria.

Viewing and Selection Times

The sets c_i of nine photos were viewed on average for 12.6 s (SD: 11.9 s). The shortest viewing time was below a second and the longest 121.1 s. The viewing times were on average higher for the sets belonging to the home collection with 13.3 s (SD: 12.2 s) compared with 11.8 s (SD: 11.5 s) for the foreign collection. These values are calculated from the time the participants looked at the photo viewing pages in the experiment application. The distribution of the viewing times significantly deviated from a normal distribution (shown by a Shapiro–Wilk test of normality with $p < .001$ for the home set and foreign set, respectively). Thus, we applied a Mann–Whitney U test in comparing the viewing durations for the sets belonging to the home collection and the foreign collection. The result is that the viewing durations are significantly longer for the home sets compared with the foreign sets ($U = 138462, Z = -3.194, p = .001$).

The average selection time per set was 20.9 s (SD: 11.6 s) for Task 1. The selection times were slightly shorter for the foreign sets with an average of 20.1 s (SD: 10.5 s) compared with those of the home collection with an average of 21.7 s (SD: 12.6 s). Like the viewing times, the distribution of the selection times also significantly deviated from a normal distribution (shown by a Shapiro–Wilk test with $p < .001$ for the home set and foreign set, respectively). Applying a Mann–Whitney U test on the selection durations showed that the differences are not statistically significant ($U = 125877, Z = -1.013, p = .311$). The selection process clearly took longer than the viewing step (+66%). Although the selection process was different from selections usually performed in daily life, it shows that the selection of photos is more time-consuming than the viewing.

The participants rated how difficult the creation of the selection was on a Likert scale from 1 ("It was hard to select the photos") to 5 ("It was easy to select the photos"). The ratings were performed separately for the home collection and the foreign collection. The results show that the ratings were on average higher for the home set with 3.85 (SD: 0.94) versus 3.06 (SD: 0.94). Shapiro–Wilk tests revealed that the data was not normally distributed ($p < .001$ for the home set ratings and $p < .015$ for the foreign set ratings). A chi-square test was applied, which showed that the difference is significant ($\alpha < 0.05$) with $X^2(4, N = 66) = 9.714, p < .046$.

Distribution of the Users' Manual Photo Selections

In Figure 6, the numbers of selections for all photos are displayed. On average, every photo was selected 3.7 times. The highest number of selections was 24. Approximately 75% of the photos were selected five times or less. Thus, most of the photos were selected only by a minority of the participants. We conclude that photo selections were very individual in our experiment and confirm results from previous work [20].

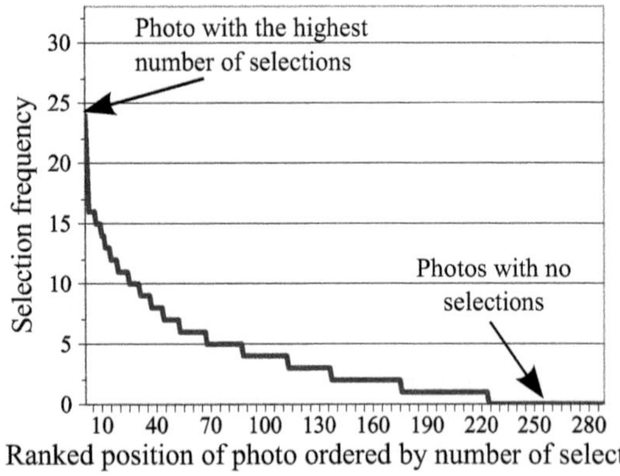

Figure 6. The number of selections for all photos in data set C, ordered by the number of selection.

Cohen's kappa k was calculated for all possible user pairs with $k = \frac{q_x - q_r}{1 - q_r}$. In this formula, q_x is the observed agreement between two users. This corresponds to the percentage of photos that were selected by both users. The value $q_r = 0.556$ is the probability of a by-chance agreement of two users on their photo selections. As the number of selected photos is high compared with the total number of photos per page (we select three out of nine), the value for q_r is already quite high. The obtained results for Cohen's kappa comparing all user selections have a minimum of $k = 0.5$ and a maximum of $k = 0.757$. The average Cohen's kappa over all users is $k = 0.625$. The average result lies only about 12% above the by-chance probability of $q_r = 0.556$. This further confirms that the photo selections are very diverse.

Ratings of Photo Selection Criteria

In the second experiment step, where a manual selection was created for Task 1, no specific criteria regarding the selection of photos were given to the participants. They were just asked to create selections for their private photo collection and could apply their own criteria. In the questionnaire, we asked the participants to indicate how important different criteria were for their selections. Nine criteria were rated on a five-point Likert scale. Additionally, the users were given the option to add criteria as free text. The selection criteria were taken from related work [22, 18, 25, 7, 16]. An overview of the criteria rated by the participants can be found in the following list:

1. Attractiveness — the photo is appealing
2. Quality — the photo is of high quality (e.g., it is clear, not blurry, good exposure)
3. Interestingness — the photo is interesting to you
4. Diversity — there are no redundant pictures
5. Coverage — all locations/activities of the event are represented
6. Depiction of the persons most important to me
7. Depiction of all participants of the event
8. Refreshment of the memory of the event
9. Representation of the atmosphere of the event

Figure 7 shows the results of the ratings on a Likert scale between 1 ("Not important") and 5 ("Very important"). The criteria are ordered by their mean results. One can see that some of the criteria have a wide range of ratings, from 1 to 5. Every criterion has at least one rating with five points.

The criteria were classified as "rather objective" (striped bars) and "rather subjective" (solid bars), expressing if a criterion is an objective measure and could (theoretically) be calculated by computer algorithms. Although this classification could be a subject of discussion, it serves the goal to better understand the nature of selection criteria. In Figure 7, we can see that three of the five criteria with the largest range in the answers (8, 4, 6, 7, 5) belong to the objective criteria. Also, the two criteria with the lowest mean results are rather objective criteria. It is remarkable that the two criteria with the highest average rating and the smallest deviation, *3. Interestingness* and *1. Attractiveness*, are rather subjective criteria. Also, four of the five highest-rated criteria are subjective. Eight participants provided additional criteria as free comments like "the picture makes me laugh" or "the photo is telling a story." All criteria added by the participants were very subjective.

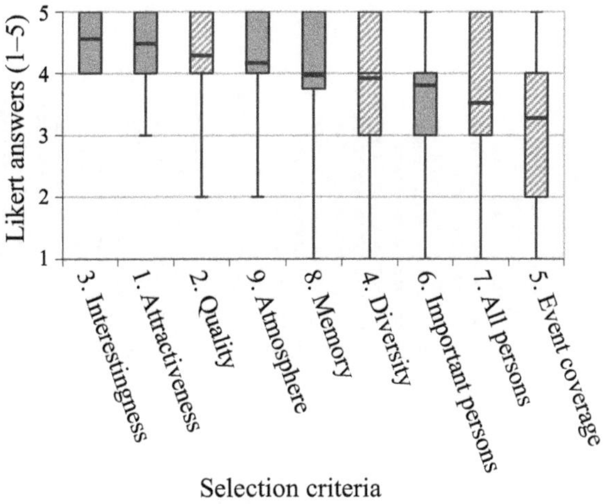

Figure 7. Selection criteria sorted by mean value.

Figure 8. Sample photos with the highest and lowest results for three of the baseline measures.

GAZE SELECTION RESULTS

We present the results for selections based on single measures, followed by the results from combining the measures with machine learning. Subsequently, we show the influence of personal interest in the photos in the selection results. Finally, the weak influence of different selection tasks is shown.

Selection Results for Single Measures

Figure 8 shows some sample photos with the highest and lowest measure results for three baseline measures. The samples show that the measures basically succeeded in analyzing the content of the photos. For example, the first row shows the most blurred photo (left) and the photo with the highest sharpness (right). But it also shows the limitations of today's computer vision approaches as, e. g., the photo with the highest number of faces is determined with 7 faces, although almost 20 people are captured in this shot. Please note that for measure (4) faceGaussian the examples with the lowest result of 0 (no faces) are not considered in this overview.

As described in the previous section, we randomly split the data set into a training set and a test set in 30 iterations. For the analysis of the performance of single measures in this section, no training was needed. Thus, the training data set was not considered, but for ensuring compatibility to the following sections, we applied the measures only on the test data sets. Figure 9 shows the average results for each user over the 30 iterations. Precision P was calculated by using only a single measure for creating the selections of the test data sets. The photos in the selections were the three photos with the highest measure values. The results strongly vary between $P = 0.202$ and $P = 0.56$ for different users and measures. Of all baseline measures, (6) faceArea performed best with a mean precision of $P = 0.365$. One can see that the face-based baseline measures (3) to (6) show high variances in precision P. (2) sharpness delivered a mean result that lies with $P = 0.344$, which is close to random selection with $P_{rand} = 0.\overline{3}$. It is interesting that photo quality as a selection criterion was ranked very high by the users (third important measure, see previous section), but the sharpness score, considering the photo quality, did not deliver good results. On average, 29.3 fixations were recorded per set (SD: 19.97). The average fixation number per photo is 3.25 (SD: 3.15). The highest median precision results are obtained by the three eye tracking measures (9) fixationDuration ($P = 0.419$), (13) maxVisitDuration ($P = 0.42$), and (14) meanVisitDuration ($P = 0.421$). The pupil-based eye tracking measures (17) to (19) did not deliver good results. They are close to the precision results for a random selection $P_{rand} = 0.\overline{3}$ or even slightly below for (19) pupilAvg with $P = 0.32$.

Selection Results for Combined Measures

We combined the measures by means of logistic regression. Pairwise Pearson correlation tests showed that all correlation coefficients were below 0.8. Thus, the correlations between the single measures were not too high, and we, therefore, decided not to exclude measures from the logistic regression. We obtained the best average precision result of $P = 0.428$ for S_{b+e}, the selections created based on baseline measures and eye tracking measures. The result for S_e (only eye tracking measures) is $P = 0.426$ and $P = 0.365$ for S_b (only baseline measures). Using gaze information improves the baseline selection by 17%. The results of all users averaged over 30 iterations are shown in Figure 10. Statistical tests were applied on the average precision values obtained from the 30 random splits for each user for investigating the significance of the results. A Mauchly's test showed that sphericity had been violated ($X^2(2) = 27.141, p < .001$). Consequently, the nonparametric Friedman was used for the analysis. We found that the differences between the three selections are significant ($\alpha < 0.05$) for P with $\chi^2(2) = 49.939, p < .001$, $n = 33$. For post hoc analysis, pairwise Wilcoxon tests

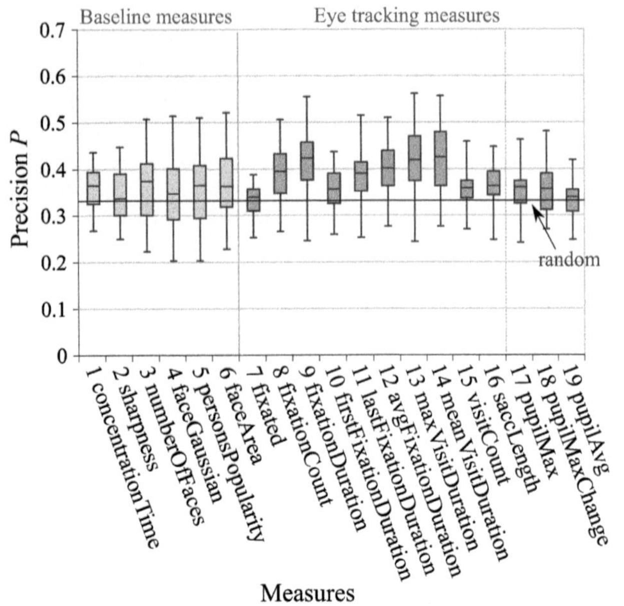

Figure 9. Precision results for all users averaged over 30 random test sets when selecting the photos based on single measures.

were conducted, with a Bonferroni correction for the significance level ($\alpha < 0.017$). The tests showed that baseline selection S_b was significantly outperformed by the gaze including selections S_{b+e}, $Z = -4.297, p < .001$, and S_e, $Z = -3.600, p < .001$. No significant difference was detected between S_{b+e} and S_e, $Z = -0.019, p < .496$.

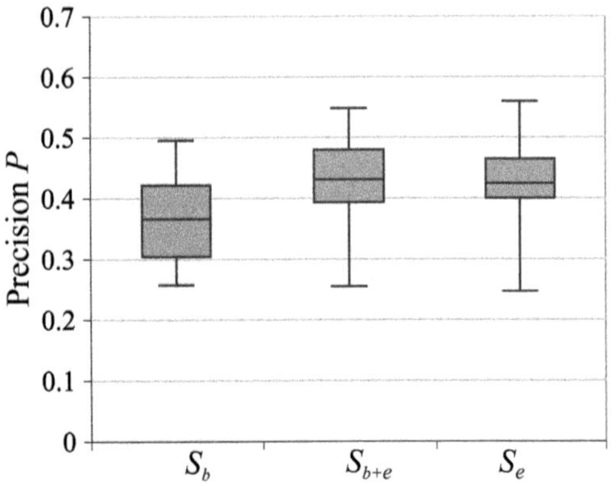

Figure 10. Precision results for all users averaged over 30 random splits obtained from combining measures by logistic regression. The results are based on baseline measures S_b, eye tracking measures S_e, and all measures S_{b+e}.

Figure 11 shows the results for the 30 random splits for one single user. Precision results are between $P = 0.267$ and $P = 0.6$ and show the strong influence of the training data and test data splits. The user selected for this example is the one with the precision result closest to the average precision over all users.

Influence of Personal Involvement

For each user, we distinguished between photo sets c_i that were part of the home collection and those that were part of

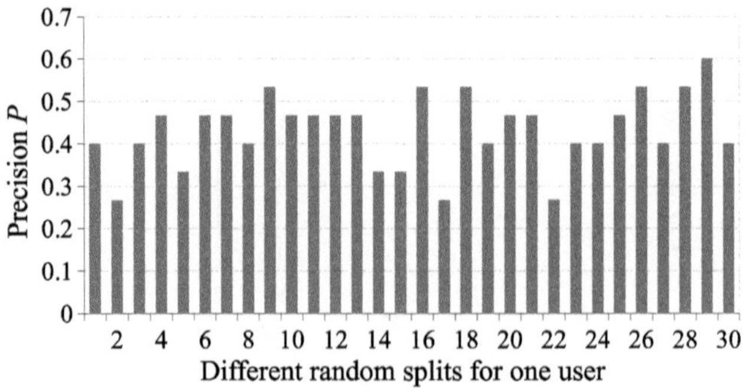

Figure 11. Precision results for S_{b+e} over 30 different random splits for one user.

the foreign collection as described in the section Experiment. Precision of selection S_{b+e} was calculated separately for both collections. The results can be found in Figure 12. They show that P results for the foreign photo set have a larger range, and the average precision is lower with $P = 0.404$ compared with $P = 0.446$ for the home set. Comparing the precision result for the home sets with the results for S_b leads to an improvement of 22%. A Wilcoxon test showed a significant difference between the precision values of all users for the home and foreign photo sets, $Z = -2.842, p < .004$.

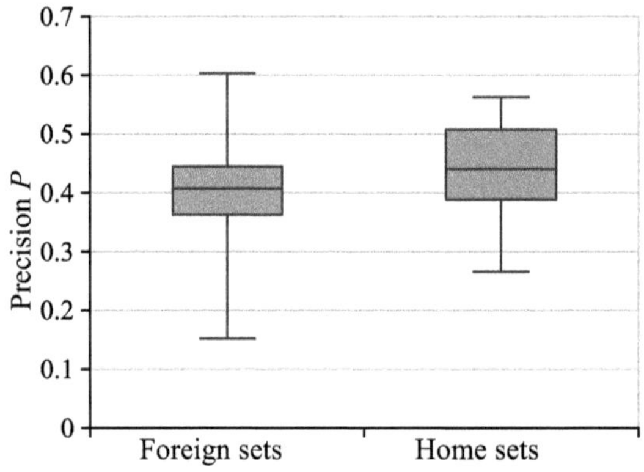

Figure 12. Results for S_{b+e} for foreign and home sets.

Influence of the Selection Task

In the experiment, the participants were first asked to create a "selection for their private photo collection" (Task 1). Subsequently, we asked them to perform further selections for the task: "Select photos for giving your friends or family a detailed summary of the event" (Task 2) as well as "Select the most beautiful photos for presenting them on the web, e.g., on Flickr" (Task 3). The participants created the selections in Task 2 and Task 3 only for the photo sets of personal interest (the "home sets"), which were taken during the event they participated in.

As we were interested in the differences between the performances of the automatic selection compared with these three manual selections, we computed the precision results of the selections under each task (Tasks 1 to 3). The results are shown in Figure 13. The average precision results for the 18 participants that took part in this part of the experiment are $P = 0.456$ for Task 1, $P = 0.432$ for Task 2, and $P = 0.415$ for Task 3. A Friedman test revealed no statistical significance between the three tasks with $\alpha < 0.05$ for P, $\chi^2(2) = 0.778, p < .678, n = 18$.

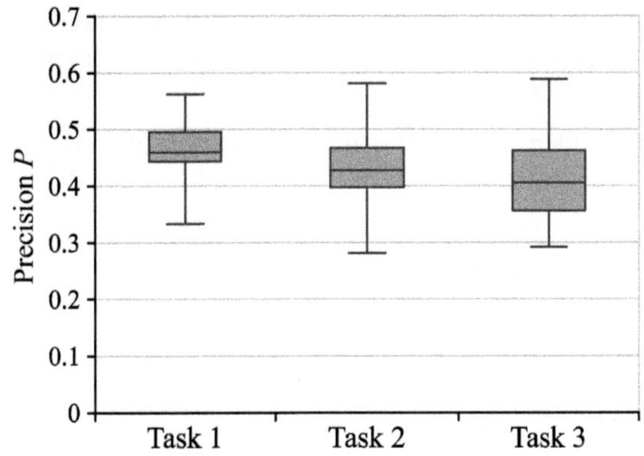

Figure 13. Results for S_{b+e} for different selection tasks.

DISCUSSION

This work has two main contributions. (1) We found that users created highly individual photo selections based on very individual selection criteria. From the analysis of the selection criteria, we conclude that the criteria judged by the users as most important are rather subjective. At the same time, the more objective criteria which could at least theoretically be calculated by algorithms, such as the number of faces depicted or the sharpness of a photo, are less important to most users. In addition, the manually created selections are very diverse; only few photos were selected by most of the users. Thus, there is no "universal" selection that fits the preferences of all users. (2) We found that previous attempts to automatically select photos solely based on content information and context information are not sufficient. Rather, a system supporting users in automatic photo selections by applying eye tracking data significantly outperformed these approach by 17%. Considering only photo sets that were of personal interest, the improvement increased to 22% over the baseline approach. Thus, our approach performed better for photos that are personally related to the user viewing them. The overall best selection result with a mean precision of 0.428 were obtained when combining all measures (content, context, and gaze) by machine learning. It is noteworthy that a single eye tracking measure already delivered competitive results with a mean precision of 0.421 without any machine learning.

In our experiment application, users viewed sets of nine photos and navigated through the sets by clicking on a "Next" button to avoid scrolling. This viewing behavior is different from real life photo viewing, where it is more likely that photos are viewed in a file viewer environment or in full screen mode. It could be that the analysis of viewing behavior in these settings has to be adapted. Bias effects like the concentration on the first photo of a page would be necessary to be considered.

The results strongly vary between users and between different partitions of the data into training set and test set for the machine learning. It is possible that this effect depends on the users and their individual viewing behavior or on the characteristics of the viewed photo sets. For example, for sets including many interesting and good photos the viewing behavior is less obvious, because it is likely that several photo are intensively fixated, and it is more difficult to create a selection.

Automatic approaches, even when including gaze data, may probably be not sufficient for a "perfect photo selection," because of the complexity of human decision processes. We think that the decision on how much support a gaze-based system should offer has to be made by the user. Assistance in the creation of selections by suggesting photos is an option as well as applications that fully automatically create photo selections for the user without additional interaction. One participant in our study concluded: "Dealing with only half of the photos of a collection would already be an improvement."

The viewing and the selection times were longer for photo sets of personal interest. At the same time, the ratings from the questionnaire showed that the selection was rated as being less difficult for the photos of personal interest. This indicates that on the one hand, users like viewing photos of personal interest, but on the other hand, the selection process seems to be even more time-consuming for these sets. Our approach delivers significantly better results for photo collections of personal interest than for photo sets of less personal interest. With other words, the prediction of the photo selections performs better when the photos' content is personally related to the users. This suggests that our approach could work even better in real life with users viewing photos of strong personal interest, e. g., one's wedding, summer vacation, or a family gathering, compared with the data set in this experiment, which is taken from a working group situation. Finally, we compared the results for different manual selections created under different selection tasks. We found that the results are about the same. This result indicates that the information gained from eye movements can be useful in diverse scenarios where photo selections are needed.

Based on our results, others features such as photo cropping based on gaze data [19] may be integrated into future research. The results of our findings may be implemented in authoring tools such as miCollage [25] to enhance an automatic photo selection for creating multimedia collections. We hope that our approach enhances research in the direction of helping users in their photo selection tasks and allowing them to spent more time on the pleasurable aspects of creating photo products like slide shows or collages.

Acknowledgments. The research leading to this paper was partially supported by the EU project SocialSensor (FP7-287975). We thank Chantal Neuhaus for implementing the baseline system and all volunteers for participating in our study.

REFERENCES

1. Bradley, M. M., Miccoli, L., Escrig, M. A., and Lang, P. J. The pupil as a measure of emotional arousal and autonomic activation. *Psychophysiology 45*, 4 (2008), 602–607.
2. Brumby, D. P., and Howes, A. Strategies for guiding interactive search: An empirical investigation into the consequences of label relevance for assessment and selection. *Human-Computer Interaction 23*, 1 (2008), 1–46.
3. Chu, W.-T., and Lin, C.-H. Automatic selection of representative photo and smart thumbnailing using near-duplicate detection. In *MULTIMEDIA*, ACM (2008), 829.
4. Fan, R.-E., Chang, K.-W., Hsieh, C.-J., Wang, X.-R., and Lin, C.-J. LIBLINEAR: A library for large linear classification. *JMLR 9* (2008), 1871–1874.
5. Frohlich, D., Kuchinsky, A., Pering, C., Don, A., and Ariss, S. Requirements for photoware. In *Computer supported cooperative work*, ACM (2002), 166–175.
6. Hajimirza, S., and Izquierdo, E. Gaze movement inference for implicit image annotation. In *Image Analysis for Multimedia Interactive Services*, IEEE (2010).
7. Kirk, D., Sellen, A., Rother, C., and Wood, K. Understanding photowork. In *CHI*, ACM (2006), 761–770.
8. Klami, A., Saunders, C., De Campos, T., and Kaski, S. Can relevance of images be inferred from eye movements? In *MIR*, ACM (2008), 134–140.
9. Kozma, L., Klami, A., and Kaski, S. GaZIR: gaze-based zooming interface for image retrieval. In *Multimodal interfaces*, ACM (2009).
10. Li, J., Lim, J. H., and Tian, Q. Automatic summarization for personal digital photos. In *Pacific Rim Conf. on Multimedia*, IEEE (2003), 1536–1540.
11. Mollenbach, E., Stefansson, T., and Hansen, J. P. All eyes on the monitor: gaze based interaction in zoomable, multi-scaled information-spaces. In *Intelligent user interfaces*, ACM (2008), 373–376.
12. Naaman, M., Yeh, R. B., Garcia-Molina, H., and Paepcke, A. Leveraging context to resolve identity in photo albums. In *JCDL*, M. Marlino, T. Sumner, and F. M. S. III, Eds., ACM (2005), 178–187.
13. Neustaedter, C., and Fedorovskaya, E. Understanding and improving flow in digital photo ecosystems. In *Proceedings of Graphics Interface 2009*, Canadian Information Processing Society (2009), 191–198.
14. Pasupa, K., Saunders, C., Szedmak, S., Klami, A., Kaski, S., and Gunn, S. Learning to rank images from eye movements. In *Workshops on Human-Computer Interaction* (2009).
15. Rabbath, M., Sandhaus, P., and Boll, S. Automatic creation of photo books from stories in social media. *TOMCCAP 7*, 1 (2011), 27.
16. Rodden, K., and Wood, K. How do people manage their digital photographs? In *CHI*, ACM (2003), 409–416.
17. San Agustin, J., Skovsgaard, H., Hansen, J., and Hansen, D. Low-cost gaze interaction: ready to deliver the promises. In *Extended abstracts on Human factors in computing systems*, ACM (2009), 4453–4458.
18. Sandhaus, P., and Boll, S. Social aspects of photobooks: Improving photobook authoring from large-scale multimedia analysis. In *Social Media Modeling and Computing*. Springer, 2011, 257–277.
19. Santella, A., Agrawala, M., DeCarlo, D., Salesin, D., and Cohen, M. Gaze-based interaction for semi-automatic photo cropping. In *CHI*, ACM (2006), 771–780.
20. Savakis, A. E., Etz, S. P., and Loui, A. C. Evaluation of image appeal in consumer photography. In *Electronic Imaging*, SPIE (2000), 111–120.
21. Sibert, L. E., and Jacob, R. J. Evaluation of eye gaze interaction. In *CHI*, ACM (2000), 281–288.
22. Sinha, P., Mehrotra, S., and Jain, R. Summarization of personal photologs using multidimensional content and context. *Multimedia Retrieval* (2011), 1–8.
23. Tan, T., Chen, J., and Mulhem, P. Smartalbum - towards unification of approaches for image retrieval. In *ICPR (3)* (2002), 983–986.
24. Wenyin, L., Sun, Y., and Zhang, H. Mialbum - a system for home photo managemet using the semi-automatic image annotation approach. In *MULTIMEDIA*, ACM (2000), 479–480.
25. Xiao, J., Zhang, X., Cheatle, P., Gao, Y., and Atkins, C. B. Mixed-initiative photo collage authoring. In *MULTIMEDIA*, ACM (2008), 509–518.
26. Zhao, M., Teo, Y. W., Liu, S., Chua, T.-S., and Jain, R. Automatic person annotation of family photo album. In *Image and Video Retrieval*. Springer, 2006, 163–172.

Pupil Responses during Discrete Goal-directed Movements

Xianta Jiang[1,2] M. Stella Atkins[2] Geoffrey Tien[2] Roman Bednarik[3] Bin Zheng[4]
[1]Zhejiang University, Hangzhou, China, jxt@zju.edu.cn
[2]Simon Fraser University, Burnaby, BC, {xiantaj, stella, gtien}@sfu.ca
[3]University of Eastern Finland, Joensuu, Finland, roman.bednarik@uef.fi
[4]University of Alberta, Edmonton, AB, bzheng1@ualberta.ca

ABSTRACT
Pupil size is known to correlate with the changes of cognitive task workloads, but how the pupil responds to requirements of basic goal-directed motor tasks involved in human-machine interactions is not yet clear. This work conducted a user study to investigate the pupil dilations during aiming in a tele-operation setting, with the purpose of better understanding how the changes in task requirements are reflected by the changes of pupil size. The task requirements, managed by Fitts' index of difficulty (ID), i.e. the size and distance apart of the targets, were varied between tasks, and pupil responses to different task IDs were recorded. The results showed that pupil diameter can be employed as an indicator of task requirements in goal-directed movements—higher task difficulty evoked higher valley to peak pupil dilation, and the peak pupil dilation occurred after a longer delay. These findings contribute to the foundation for developing methods to objectively evaluate interactive task requirements using pupil parameters during goal-directed movements in HCI.

Author Keywords
Pupil diameter; goal-directed movement; movement-evoked pupillary response; Fitts' Law.

ACM Classification Keywords
H.5.2 [Information interfaces and presentation]: User Interfaces- *Evaluation/methodology*

INTRODUCTION
The extent of achievement of a complex task critically relies on the task requirements while performing the task, since the human mental capacity is a finite resource [5]. This especially holds true in goal-directed movements with high task requirements. For example, surgeons undergo higher mental workload in a minimally invasive laparoscopic surgery than in open procedures [3], since the task requirements in laparoscopic surgery are higher than in open surgery, due to the long tool shaft and the lack of depth information when projecting the scene inside the body to a 2-D screen. Therefore, it is highly desirable to objectively and continuously measure the task requirements as a surrogate for mental workload of the users during goal-directed movements. Such a method would allow indirect evaluation of the performance during the procedure.

CHI 2014, April 26 - May 01 2014, Toronto, ON, Canada

http://dx.doi.org/10.1145/2556288.2557086

Pupil size has been well proven to correlate with the information processing load in a variety of cognitive tasks [2], but has not been thoroughly explored in the field of HCI [16]. In order to apply pupillary indicators to task workload in the field of HCI research, pupil size changes during goal-directed movements should be explored first. For example, how do the pupil size changes correlate with the level of the task difficulty in an eye-hand coordination movement? Only a few works have been published in this research area, and to a very limited extent. One of the pioneer fundamental works was done by Richer and Beatty [24], who found that the pupil dilated as a function of the complexity of finger movements. However, this is not a real situation of goal-directed movement; the participants in this 1985 study simply flexed their fingers while looking at a blank screen for the purpose of pupil size recording.

This work aims to explore the pupillary responses during a discrete goal-directed movement with the task difficulty level clearly defined by Fitts' law [8] (the size and distance between targets were varied corresponding to difficulty level) to quantify the pupil dilation during movements. The findings from this study constitute the foundation for constructing methods towards objectively measuring the task requirements during complex goal-directed movements. Such measurements can be used for adjusting proactive responses of user interfaces, for instance in medical educational simulations.

RELATED WORK

Mental Workload and Measurement Methods
Past research introduced three main categories of mental workload measurement techniques: subjective rating scales (self-assessment), performance measures (including primary and secondary task measures), and psychophysiological measures [10]. The subjective rating methods are easy to perform, and they only require the

operator to answer survey questions about the mental stress associated with a task. However, the answers to the survey questions are affected by the operator's working memory and have a bias to the task difficulty [26].

The subjective shortcomings may be avoided by using a secondary task to the primary task where decreased secondary task performance means increased mental workload caused by the primary task. However, there may be extra workload caused by the secondary task that affects the performance of the primary task.

Although psychophysiological measures have the advantage of eliminating the possibility of subjective distortions and generally do not interfere with task performance, most of them present an intrusion, as they need sensors attached to the user. Modern eye-tracking systems can monitor the eye movements remotely. Pupil size data are a by-product of virtually all psychophysical experiments which use eye tracking and are thus available without adding any further technology to the experiment.

Pupil Dilation as an Indicator of Mental Workload

With advances in eye-tracking technology, pupil diameter can be recorded remotely and its subtle changes have been proven to indicate the cognitive task load [19].

The pioneer work exploring pupil size changes relating to mental workload and task difficulty was done by Hess and Polt [13] in a mental arithmetic experiment. The authors found that the pupil size of the subjects gradually dilated along with the time elapse of presentation of a multiplication problem and reached a peak immediately before the production was orally reported; then constricted rapidly back to the original size. The mean pupil dilation was also found to be a function of the level of difficulty of the problem. Following this work, extensive studies have shown that the changes of pupil size reflect mental workload and the level of difficulty in different tasks, e.g., mental arithmetic tasks [4], recall or memory tasks [11, 22], and visual search tasks [23].

Pupil size also responds to the critical event during information processing, which is called Task-Evoked Pupil Response (TEPR), appearing at the event onset with a short latency (averaging between 100ms and 200ms), and terminating rapidly following the completion of the event [2]. The TEPR has been employed as an approach to capture and evaluate the mental workload changes during a variety of tasks [2].

Pupillary Responses to Mental Workload in HCI

In the HCI domain, Iqbal et al.[15] employed pupil diameter as an objective indicator of mental workload in interactive tasks including route planning and document editing, purporting to find proper moments for low cost interruption; they found that the pupil diameter is relatively low during task boundaries, which are suitable for interruption with lower mental workload.

Richer and Beatty [24] examined the pupil responses to simple movement, the self-paced finger flexion. The authors found the typical pupil dilation pattern to a simple movement is that pupil dilates at around 1.5s before the movement and peaks afterwards at around 0.5s. This pupil dilation pattern was confirmed by other works [21, 23]. For example, in a visual target search study, Privitera et al.[23] found a quite similar pupil dilation pattern to that in Richer and Beatty's finding when the participants successfully detected a target and responded with a key-press.

However, in goal-directed interactive movements, such as aiming at a target and selecting a menu item, the tool may move continuously, which may evoke a different pupil response pattern. Such phenomena, if confirmed, would have important implications. For example, interactive environments could continuously adjust the presented information to accommodate the workload of the user in real-time. Design guidelines for fundamental movements of a tool could be objectively evaluated, and training and simulation systems could be developed with specific tasks toward the improvement of motor and aiming skills.

In the field of eye-hand coordination in health care training, Jiang et al. [17] investigated the pupil changes in a simulated laparoscopic task, and found that the pupil dilates faster during the execution of higher task difficulty subtasks, such as dropping a peg into a tiny cup, than during the execution of tasks with lower difficulty, such as touching a centrally located home position with the operating tool. However, the difficulty level for each of the tasks was not well defined in this study.

Marshall [20] reported the Index of Cognitive Activity (ICA) that is capable of capturing subtle cognitive changes from pupil metrics, and was used to predict the expertise of surgeons, together with other eye metrics [25]. However, details of the pupil response to motor tasks were not reported.

In summary, previous research confirmed that pupillary response reflects the internal cognitive processing. If we want to build interactive systems that accommodate various types of user's workload and respond to it, it is fundamental to investigate the relationships between the pupillary response and the varying task demands.

A handy conceptualization of task requirement is to apply Fitts' law's index of difficulty. Because no knowledge is available about the relationships between the motor goal-directed interactive tasks, the objective assessment of their difficulty, and the respective pupillary response, we conducted the study reported here.

Our hypothesis was that increased index of difficulty would result in distinguishable patterns of pupillary response. Confirmation of such a hypothesis would mean establishment of new measurements of the difficulty of fundamental motor tasks in HCI.

USER STUDY

To examine the pupil's responses to task difficulty, we designed a goal-directed aiming task using a laparoscopic grasper, in order to answer the question: do pupil size changes correlate with increases of task requirement during goal-directed movements?

Experiment Design

The task was to move the grasper horizontally to touch the circles printed on a paper inside a laparoscopy training box (see below for details), while the eyes of the user were looking at the projection of the inside of the box on a display screen, as shown in Figure 1. Three pairs of target circles with combinations of variable size and distance between targets were designed with three indices of difficulty (ID). The detailed parameters of the target circles are illustrated in Figure 2. The formula for calculating ID is as in Equation 1 [8]:

$$ID = -\log_2 \frac{W}{2A} \qquad (1)$$

where W is the diameter of the target circle and A is the distance between the pair of targets.

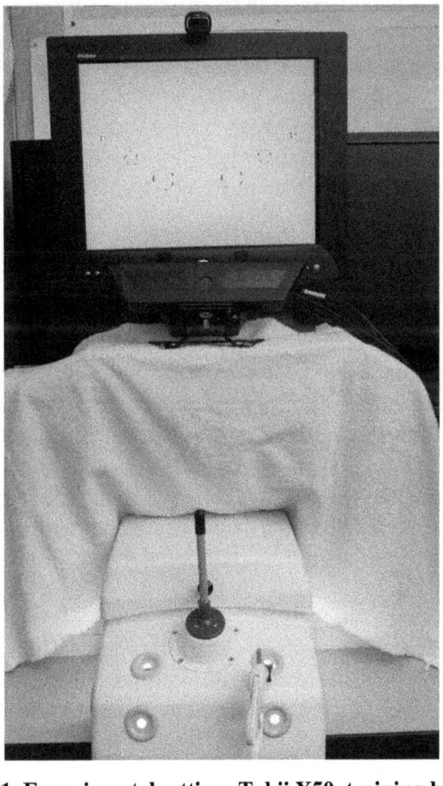

Figure 1. Experimental setting; Tobii X50, training box, and web camera.

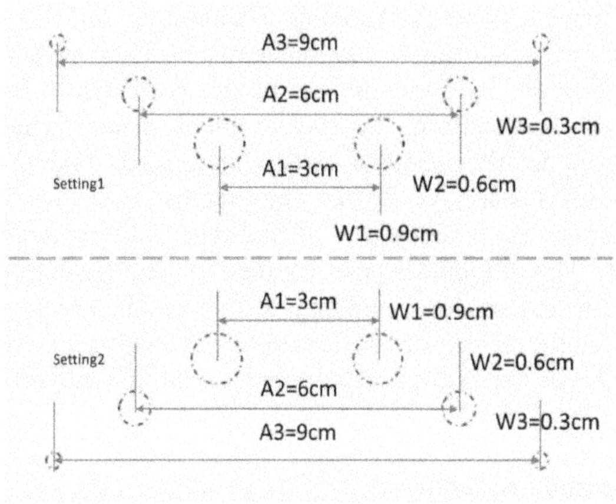

Figure 2. Illustration of target patterns (the pairs of target circles on the paper inside the training box showing on the screen as in Figure 1). One group of subjects executed bottom up from the easiest task to the hardest task and then back to the easiest task (shown in the upper panel); another group of subjects executed bottom up from hard to easy tasks and then back to the hardest task (lower panel). A1 to A3 represent the distances between targets and W1 to W3 represent the sizes of the targets of ID1 to ID3.

In our experiment, we employed the following settings: ID1=2.7 bits/response (W1=0.9cm, A1=3cm) denoted here as Easy, ID2=4.3 bits/response (W2=0.6cm, A2=6cm) denoted here as Middle, and ID3=5.9 bits/response (W3=0.3cm, A3=9cm) denoted as Hard.

Since the frequency of pupil response to a movement is typically lower than 0.5Hz [21, 23, 24] and the frequency of the Fitts' tool movement under laparoscopic environment is usually around 0.5Hz [6], in order to avoid overlap of the pupil dilation curve, we used discrete Fitts' pointing [9] by waiting 10s before each tooltip move. Such discrete goal-directed movements and related eye-hand coordination are elementary parts of any human-computer interaction and arise in the vast majority of our interactions with surrounding objects.

Participants and Apparatus

Twelve participants (four females) were recruited to the study, including ten graduate students, one undergraduate student, and one staff member from a local university. All were right-hand users and had normal or corrected-to-normal vision. None of them were previously trained in any surgical procedures.

The task was performed using a surgical training box for laparoscopic procedures (Laparoscopic Trainer, 3-D Technical Services, Franklin, OH). Subjects held a surgical grasper at a standing pose about 60cm from the eye-tracker. The tips of the grasper were black taped to keep its color consistent with the shaft, and make image processing easier. The scene of the work area inside the training box was illuminated and captured at 30Hz by a built-in camera and projected to a 17" display. The eye movements of the participants were recorded simultaneously using a remote eye-tracker (Tobii X50, Tobii Technology AB). A web camera was attached on the top center of the display frame recording the face expressions of the participants for the purpose of identifying eye blinks and lost data. The eye-tracker and the cameras were integrated using Tobii software, Clearview 2.7.0. The setting was physically isolated to keep the effect of ambient lighting relatively stable. The brightness and contrast of the display were constant and set to a moderate level to make the pupil to work at the center of the length-tension curve of the iris muscle, for the best pupil response to the task requirement [23].

Tasks and Procedure

The task was to move the surgical tool to point to the circles printed on a piece of paper at the bottom of the training box. This was a discrete pointing task, so that participants had to wait 10 seconds before each move to the next circle. Specifically, a trial consisted of 16 discrete movement steps, each separated by 10s, with the execution sequence shown in Figure 3. The trial started by placing the tooltip on the right bottom circle for 10s, then moving the tool to the left bottom circle (step (1)), and ended by stopping the tooltip on the right bottom circle for 10s after step (16). Only the 12 horizontal moves were used for analysis.

The participants were instructed to move the tool and hit the target as accurately and as fast as possible; once the target was hit, 10s were counted before moving to the next target. Each trial took about 180s.

Each participant read and signed the consent form before entering the study, and then read the instructions. The participants practiced the task for a few minutes, until they were ready to begin. Each participant performed two blocks, each containing three trials with 20s break between trials. To achieve counterbalance, each block used either task setting 1 (from easy to hard as shown in top panel in Figure 2) or task setting 2 (from hard to easy as shown in bottom panel in Figure 2). Half of the participants started with setting 1 and the other started with task setting 2. We did not consider other ordering options like executing from middle difficulty to hardest to easiest, because the ANOVA results showed there was no significant difference in movement time between the two groups, and no interaction effect of ID and group order.

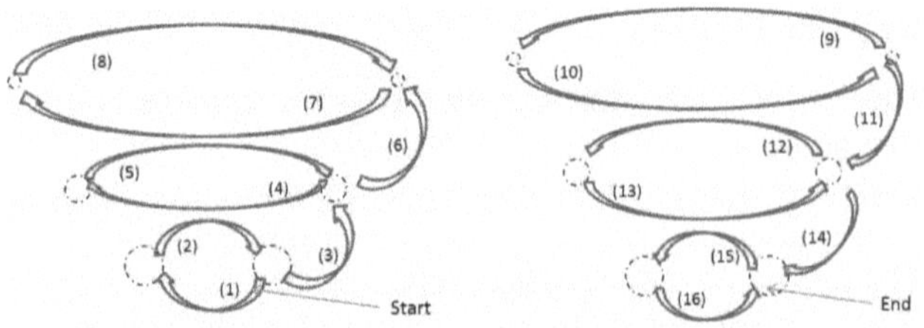

Figure 3. Execution sequence of a trial (target setting 1), steps shown in parentheses. The arrows represent tool movement from one circle to another; before each tool movement, the tool stops on the circle for 10s.

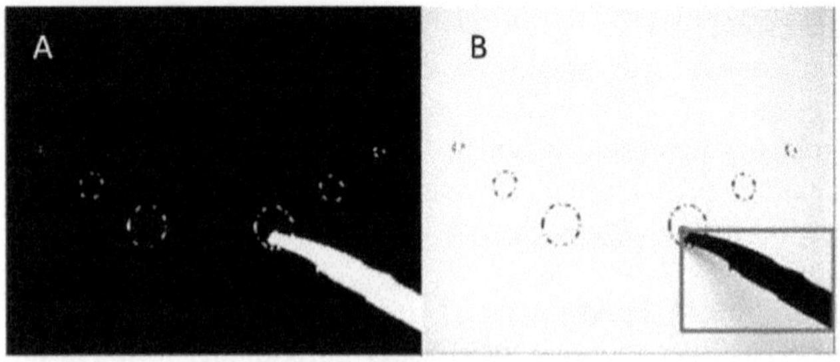

Figure 4. Key steps in detecting tooltip from surgical videos. Panel A shows the binary-thresholded image with mostly the tool left. Panel B shows the recognized tool (in red rectangle) and tooltip (the blue dot).

Data analyses

The task video recorded at 30Hz and resolution of 352×288 pixels by the camera attached to the training box, and the text files containing eye movements (50Hz) were exported from Tobii Clearview for the offline analysis. The tooltip position and eye movements were calculated and then synchronized for subsequent analysis.

Location of the tooltip

We developed a customized video processing algorithm written in Visual C++ (Microsoft Visual Studio, Microsoft Corporation) to derive the position of tooltip automatically. The algorithm involved three major steps. First, the RGB video was read in frame by frame and transferred to gray scale image format, and then binary-thresholded into black and while image format, where mostly only the tool was left in the image as shown in Figure 4A.

Second, the biggest connected object was searched and identified as the tool, as shown within the red rectangle in Figure 4B.

Third, the coordinates of the left top corner of the tool rectangle was used as tooltip position, as the tool was always consistently north-west orientated. The determined tooltip position was the blue dot shown in Figure 4B. The tooltip positions (x and y coordinates in pixels) together with timestamps were stored in a text file for further analysis. The tooltip data were smoothed with a running-average-filtered using equally weighted four samples window.

Identification of moments of tooltip leaving and arriving

Some critical moments of tooltip movements—the moments when the tooltip started to move (tooltip-start) and reached (tooltip-reach) the target—were detected by another customized algorithm, written as a Matlab script. The algorithm first finds the absolute tooltip movement peak velocity along the x-axis during a move, and then detects backward and forward respectively for the moments of tooltip-start and tooltip-reach, by checking whether the x-axis absolute velocity is lower than a threshold. The velocity thresholds for detecting the tooltip-start and tooltip-reach moments were empirically determined, since

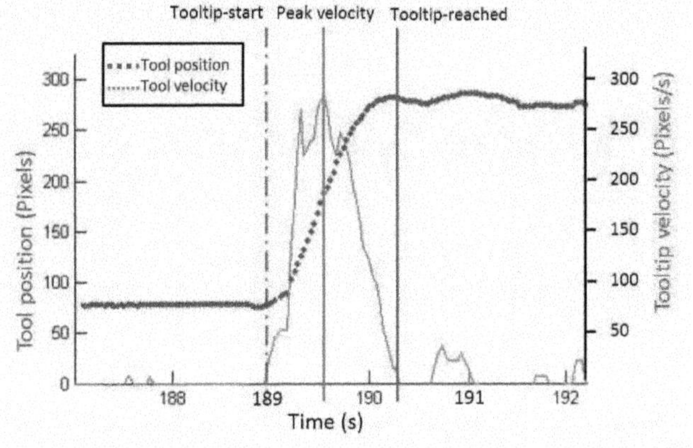

Figure 5. Kinematics of tool movement (subject 01, trial 01) during a typical horizontal movement between circles. The blue curve is the tooltip position in pixels along the horizontal line between the circles, and the red curve is the velocity of tooltip.

there are abrupt changes of tool velocity at the moments of tooltip-start and tooltip-reach. The tooltip-start and tooltip-reach thresholds were both set to 30pixels/s. The moment of tool-reach detected by the algorithm is the moment that the tool quickly arrives at a position above (but not necessarily touching) the target circle. An example of kinematics of tool movement is shown in Figure 5.

Pupil data processing and segment extraction

Segments of missed pupil data shorter than 440ms were interpolated, since they might have contained blinks. Then a Butterworth low-pass filter with a cutoff frequency of 4Hz was applied to the pupil diameter data, since frequency above 2Hz of the pupil is considered as noise [24].

The pupil diameter data sequences were extracted from a 7-second window starting 3 seconds before and 4 seconds after every tooltip-start. The 7-second window is motivated by considering the extra movement time (about 1s-2s) before the tool leaves in our study compared with others who noted pupil increases start 1.5s before the stimulus [21, 23, 24] and the pupil continuous to dilate afterwards to a peak value in a few seconds e.g. 3s-window in [23] 4s-window in [24] and 5s-window in [21]. Relative pupil diameter changes in the window were derived by subtracting each sample from a baseline pupil diameter which was the mean of the pupil size during the first second of the window. All the data in the windows were aligned at the tooltip-start (3 seconds into the window), and the mean pupil diameter change was calculated for each time point in the window across all horizontal tooltip moves from all trials. Assuming there are m moves from all trials of all subjects and each move has n samples in a 7-second window, $X = \{x_{ik}, i = 1...m, k = 1...n\}$ is the matrix of pupil diameter values in the 7-second windows across all tooltip moves of all trials of all subjects. The mean pupil diameter change of each time point in the window is in a vector $\overline{X} = \frac{\sum_{i=1}^{m} x_{ik}}{m}, k = 1...n$. Similarly, the mean pupil diameter changes were calculated across all moves from all trials for each ID. The mean pupil diameter changes in the 7-second window were drawn in a graph for visual analysis.

To examine segments where significant differences occurred in the 7-second window between the three IDs, the graphical significance testing approach [12, 23] was employed. This method applies a paired t-test to the same time point sample and examines all the p-values along the time axis to determine which segments of the curves are significantly different. Due to the temporal autocorrelation of pupil waveform, we considered a series of more than 4 consecutive samples (80ms) with p-values $< .05$ as significantly different [23].

RESULTS

A total of 72 trials were recorded (12 participants, each performed 6 trials). Three trials were excluded from analysis due to low ratio of total fixation time over total execution time (TF/TT), since we have observed that the quality of the eye movement data cannot be guaranteed when TF/TT is lower than a certain value (less than about 70%). From the 69 valid trials, there was window data for 828 movements available (each trial has 6 ID executions as each ID has been executed twice, with each ID execution having 2 moves—from right to left and left to right). However, we discarded 20 windows due to mis-operation such as when the participant moved the grasper to a wrong target. Therefore we have 808 valid movements.

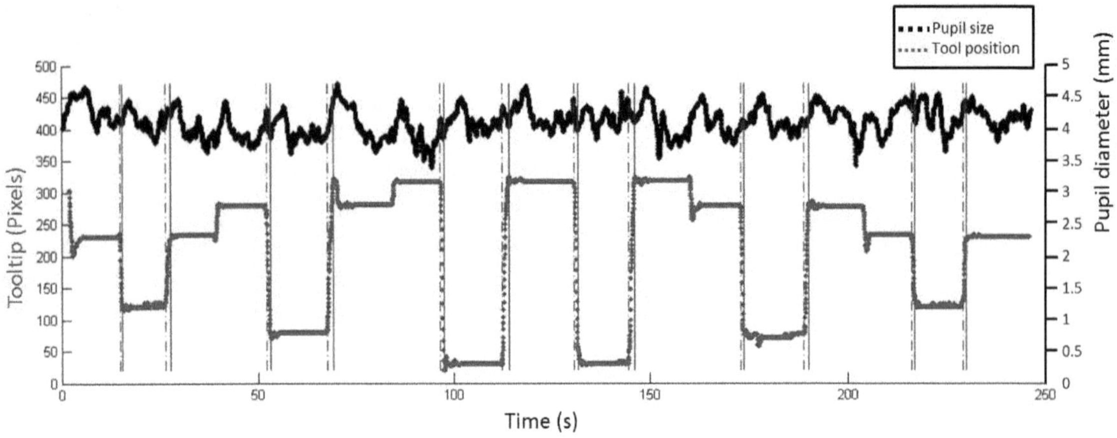

Figure 6: Example of tooltip movement (blue) and pupil size (black) over time for a complete trial (subject 01, trial 01). The blue curve is the tooltip position in pixels along the horizontal line between the circles. The dash and solid vertical lines represent the moments of tooltip-start and tooltip-reach.

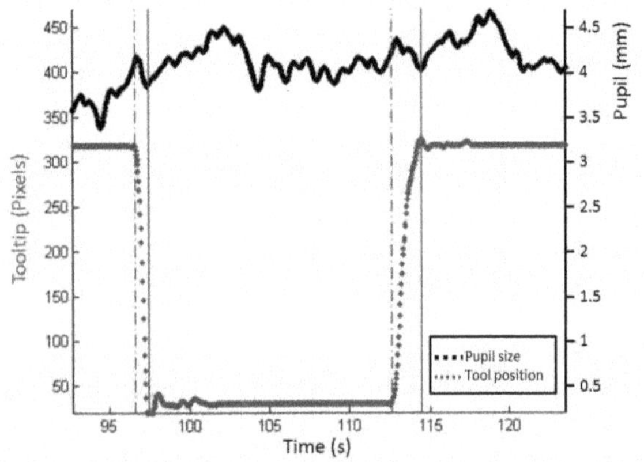

Figure 7. Blow up of a segment (95s-120s) from Figure 6, showing how the pupil size (black curve) increases when tool movements occur. The blue curve is the tooltip position in pixels along the horizontal line between the circles. The dash and solid vertical lines represent the moments of tooltip-start and tooltip-reach.

Figure 6 shows an example of pupil size aligned with horizontal tooltip movement over time for a complete trial. The pupil responses to the tooltip movement are actually recognizable in the graph, although there are several more fluctuations which might relate to pupil unrest. Figure 7 shows a blow-up of a segment of the trial data from Figure 6; there are significant dilations when the tool moves.

Performance

The mean movement time (MT) is the mean transportation time between tooltip-start and tooltip-reach for all horizontal movements. The mean MT for all IDs is 1.0±0.3s, and the MT changes as a function of ID, i.e., the mean MT increases when the difficulty level increases (Figure 8). There is significant main effect between three IDs in terms of mean MT ($F_{(2,805)} = 209.868$, $p < .001$). Post Hoc test (Tukey HSD) shows that the differences between

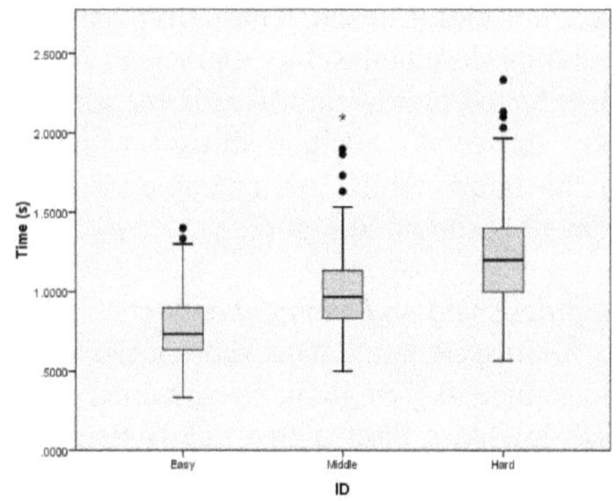

Figure 8. Box-whisker plot for Mean movement time for each ID.

pairs of the three IDs are significant ($p < .001$), with mean MT of Easy, Middle, and Hard IDs being 0.8±0.2s, 1.0±0.2s, and 1.2±0.3s respectively.

Pupil Diameter Changes

Descriptive analysis

Figure 9 shows the mean changes of pupil diameter during horizontal tooltip movements over a 7-second window. The data is averaged across 808 valid moves of 69 trials from 12 subjects. For clarity, error bars are drawn every 400ms rather than drawn for every time sample (at 50Hz).

Figure 10 shows the means of pupil size changes in the 7-second window for three IDs. The three ID curves share a common pupil change pattern as shown in Figure 9, i.e., all of them dilate in response to the movement preparation and execution in a relatively long period from about 1.5s before tooltip-start and peak about 1s after the tool is reached, corresponding to movement preparation and execution [23, 24]. There is also a small constriction 200ms after the tooltip starts to move, between the moments of tooltip-start and tooltip-reach.

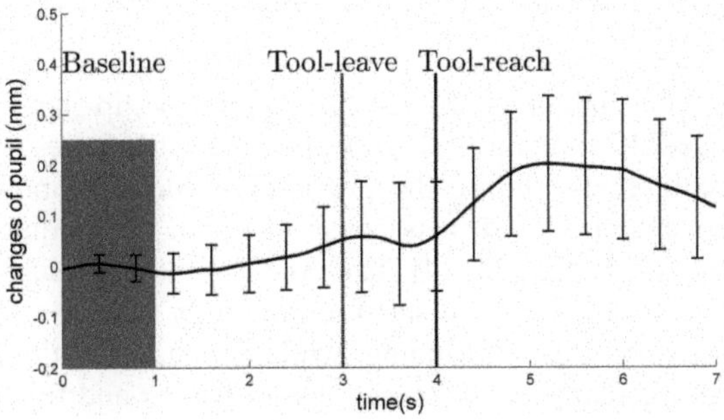

Figure 9. Mean pupil diameter changes for 808 valid moves of 69 trials from 12 subjects. Data were aligned over a 7 second window 3 seconds before the tooltip-start. The baseline is defined as the mean diameter of the pupil over the first second of the window, and the solid black curve is the mean pupil diameter change from the baseline over time. The black vertical dashed line is tooltip-start where all the data are aligned and the vertical solid black line is the average tool-reach time. The error bars for 1 std. dev. are drawn every 400ms.

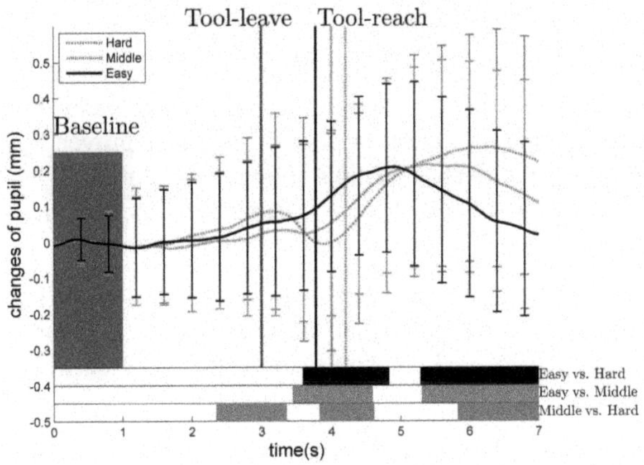

Figure 10. Mean pupil diameter changes against different IDs; data are aligned over a 7-second window around tooltip-start. The vertical dash black line is the tooltip-start and other three solid color vertical lines represent the tooltip-reach moments of three IDs respectively. The three colors of bars at the bottom indicate significant differences in pupil dilation between Easy, Middle and Hard ID with black representing Easy vs. Hard, pink representing Easy vs. Middle, and green representing Middle vs. Hard. The error bars for 1 std. dev. are drawn every 400ms.

However, major differences can be observed between the three IDs. First, during 2-3s in Figure 10, the pupil dilation for the Hard ID (green curve) is more than Easy (black) and Middle (pink) ones. Second, during tool moving, the pupil of the Hard ID constricts the most among three IDs and the pupil of the Easy ID constricts the least. Third, the peak value and duration from valley to peak pupil size of the three ID curves are different: the Hard ID has the highest peak and longest duration and the Easy ID has the smallest peak and the shortest duration.

Furthermore, the increase of pupil size from the valley (between 3s and 4s along the time window in Figure 10) to its peak correlates to IDs: the easy task (black curve) increased about 0.13mm (0.07mm at valley to 0.2mm at peak), the middle task (pink curve) increased about 0.18mm (0.02 to 0.2mm), and the hardest task (green) had the largest increase of about 0.27mm (-0.01 to 0.26mm). Also, the valley to peak duration can be observed to be different between IDs.

Statistical Analysis

Graphical significance testing was applied between the pupil size change curves for the three IDs, with the results as shown in the bottom bars in Figure 10. For each time point, the paired *t*-test was performed in two IDs each containing samples from the 69 trials.

Significant differences in pupil size between Easy ID and Hard ID are shown in black bars (upper row) in Figure 10. The first significant time period is located at 3.7s to 4.9s along the time window, where the Hard ID pupil curve (green) is at its local valley while the Easy ID curve (black) has already recovered from a short period of constriction. The second significant time period starts at the intersection of Hard ID curve and Easy ID curve (at around 5s) to the end of the window.

The pink bars (middle row) in Figure 10 show similar significant differences between Easy ID and Middle ID, only with the first bar starting a little bit earlier (3.5s to 4.6s in time axis).

The green bars (bottom row) in Figure 10 show significant differences between Middle ID and Hard ID. There are three major significant time periods: the first one (2.3s to 3.4s along the time window) where the pupil dilates more during the hard ID than the Middle ID, the second one (3.8s to 4.6s along time window) where the pupil constricts more during the Hard ID than the Middle ID, and the third one starts after 5.8s along the time window.

According to three color bars in Figure 10, significant differences between all three IDs can be found in two major time periods: one is around tool-reach where the hardest ID has deeper pupil constriction than easier ones, and another area is after the peak, where the hardest ID has bigger pupil diameter than the easier IDs.

ANOVA shows there is significant difference in the pupil size increase from valley to peak between IDs ($F_{(2,805)} = 44.754$, $p < .001$). Post Hoc test (Tukey HSD) also shows that the mean increase of pupil size from valley to peak is significantly different ($p < .001$) between Easy (0.3±0.2mm), Middle (0.4±0.2mm), and Hard ID (0.5±0.2mm).

ANOVA shows there is significant difference in the duration of the pupil dilation from its valley to peak size between IDs ($F_{(2,805)} = 91.938$, $p < .001$). Post Hoc test (Tukey HSD) shows that the duration from valley to peak is significantly different ($p < .001$) between Easy (1.6±0.7s), Middle (2.1±0.9s), and Hard ID (2.7±1.1s).

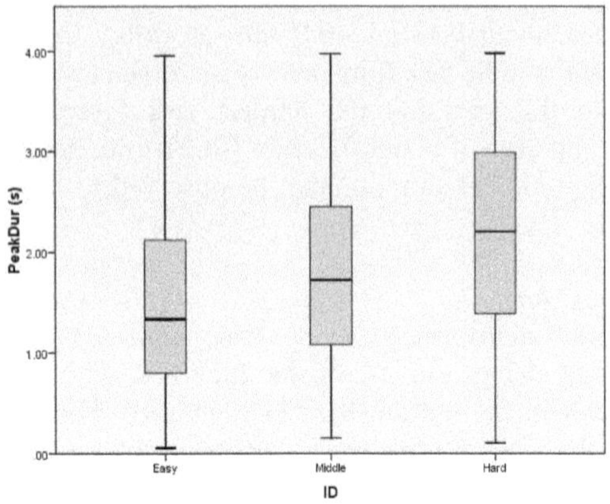

Figure 11. Box-whisker plot for Mean duration from tooltip-reach to the moment where the pupil peaked in size for three difficulty IDs.

Figure 11 shows the duration from tooltip-reach to the moment where the pupil peaked in size for each ID, up to 4s after the tool-tip reach. There is significant main effect between three IDs in terms of this duration ($F_{(2,805)} = 30.558$, $p < .001$). Further Post Hoc test (Tukey HSD) shows that this duration for the Hard ID (2.2±1.0s) is significantly ($p < .001$) longer than that of Easy (1.6±1.0s) and Middle (1.8±0.9s), and the Middle ID is significantly longer than that of Easy ID ($p < .01$).

DISCUSSION

Our work is the first one in the HCI literature that relates pupillary response and task difficulty measured by Fitts' Law. Previous research investigated either movement time (MT) and task difficulty, or pupillary response and mental workload. The present study bridges these two directions and uncovers new knowledge about the relationships between tool-movement difficulty and respective pupillary response. Previous work [15] conducted investigations for cognitive tasks; this study however, examines and takes the results to the motor domain of HCI.

The performance measures exhibited expected behavior—the MT correlated perfectly to the increase of the ID, as shown in Figure 8. Therefore, Fitt's ID is a good measure for the task requirement in this study. Although it would be interesting to see if the differences hold if the movement time is normalized by distance and then compared across the three difficulty levels in this study, we did not do that since our other research [18] showed the pupil dilations and the movement time in goal-directed movements still respect Fitts' Law, by only changing the target distance or target size.

The pupil response to simple goal-directed movement tasks was shown by our data, and furthermore, the different task IDs elicited different pupil responses. Thus our hypothesis, that increased index of difficulty would result in distinguishable patterns of pupillary response, was confirmed.

The pupil dilation started 1.5s before tooltip-start and continued 2s afterwards (Figure 9) and clearly reveals the task requirement during the preparation and execution of the movement. Our data is consistent with the finding of previous works [21, 23, 24]. The time that the pupil starts to dilate (1.5s before tooltip-start) in this study is same as that of Richer and Beatty's finding, while the peak duration (2s after tooltip-start) is longer than that of Richer and Beatty's (0.5s). The likely reason is that we have a tool movement time around 1s, while Richer and Beatty's is only a simple finger flexion.

The pupil constricts slightly between tooltip-start and tooltip-reach (Figure 9), which is the time when the tooltip moves speedily to a target. During the initial phase of the aiming movement, the eye gaze usually saccades to the target ahead of tooltip for the visual guidance [1, 7]; the saccade causes the pupil constriction. Our results show that longer travel distances require longer saccades, causing deeper pupil constriction, as shown in Figure 10.

The two significantly different time periods for pupil size (the pupil constriction around the tool-leave movement, and the peak pupil size after the tool-reach) were proven by the graphical significance testing shown in Figure 10, where the three pairs of IDs (Easy vs. Hard, Easy vs. Middle, and Middle vs. Hard) all show significant differences.

Although the peak pupil size of Easy and Middle ID shows similar amplitudes in Figure 10, the increase of pupil size from valley to peak is significantly different between all three IDs.

Furthermore, the delay of peak pupil dilation (represented by the duration between tooltip-reach and peak pupil size, as shown in Figure 11) was correlated with the three IDs, i.e. the Hard ID has the longest delay, and the Middle ID has the middle one. This is consistent with the finding of previous work [24].

The 7s window approach of averaging many repetitive task epochs to show the pattern of pupil size change may not be able to measure task requirement in real-time. However other features introduced here, such as the valley to peak pupil size dilation, the valley to peak duration, and the duration between the moments of tool-reach and peak pupil size, can be employed to classify the task difficulty of each targeting step alone using techniques such as machine learning. The ANOVA results showed that all these features have strong ($p < .001$) ability in distinguishing the three difficulty levels of task requirement.

For real-world application, several steps should be carefully considered. First, the critical moment of the movement (the moment the tool/hand starts to move or reach) should be accurately detected as a timing marker of the movement event that the pupil responses to. Usually tool-leave is more promising as a movement event marker than tool-reach since in a complex movement such as surgical tasks [17] the tool may need extra actions at the end of movements such as grasping or releasing an object. One effective and robust way to detect tool-leave and tool-reach is to first find the moment of peak velocity of the tool movement and then search backward and forward to get tool start and reached moments, as presented here.

Second, the features of pupil size change should be extracted within a window in the vicinity of the movement start. The window size should be properly defined according to the property of the application, since if the window is too small or too wide, useful pupil information may be excluded, or false pupil information introduced.

Third, the baseline of pupil diameter used for deriving each relative pupil diameter change in the window should be carefully chosen. In the present discrete movement study, the selection of the position of the baseline is quite straightforward, using the period between 2s to 3s before the tool-leave moment, which is near the end of the 10s waiting time and is right before the pupil starts to dilate. However in a real-world motor task where the movements may occur consecutively without a clear waiting time between them it may be a challenge to select the position of the baseline.

The luminance of the screen was well controlled to induce a mean pupil diameter of 4.1mm (±0.8mm) which falls in the center of length-tension curve of the iris muscle, enabling the pupil to capture the cognitive changes well. ANOVA results show that there was no significant difference between three IDs in terms of mean pupil size in baselines of the moves in each ID.

The results have important implications for the design of interactive systems and training and simulation environments. First, we showed that elementary task demands can reliably be measured in real-time. With the availability of low-cost eye-tracking sensors, it will be possible to embed such pupil size estimations in a variety of user interactive tasks and have intelligent systems to monitor the second-to-second workload of a user. Therefore, not only internal processing load can be estimated, but also the motor-level component of workload can now be incorporated into the interaction design.

Second, the method by which we measured the task requirements using pupil diameter in a discrete elementary task, that is the ID-to-pupil mapping in this motor-coordination task, could be further applied to complex tasks which can be decomposed into several elementary tasks [14], and is a subject for future research.

Third, if we monitor and model the pupil over short intervals, such as the 7-second intervals as done here, we can make accurate predictions about the difficulties user experience. This contributes to building more intelligent interfaces both for general HCI and for surgery procedures, for example for automatically evaluating and monitoring the task workload in a very fine resolution during image-guided procedures.

CONCLUSION

The results of this study answered positively the proposed question that the pupil response pattern is distinguishable for different levels of task difficulty. The pupil diameter increase for harder task IDs has a higher valley to peak value and longer delay.

Knowledge gained from this study contributes to the understanding of how pupil responses indicate the changes of task requirement during a goal-directed movement. The research opens an opportunity for us to develop valid methods of measuring task load using pupil parameters in HCI.

ACKNOWLEDGMENTS

We thank the Natural Sciences Research Council of Canada (NSERC), Royal College of Physicians and Surgeons of Canada (RCPSC) Medical Education Research Grant, and all the volunteers in the case study.

REFERENCES

1. Abrams, R.A., Meyer, D.E., and Kornblum, S. Eye-hand coordination: oculomotor control in rapid aimed limb movements. *Journal of Experimental Psychology: Human Perception and Performance 16*, 2 (1990), 248-267.

2. Beatty, J. Task-evoked pupillary responses, processing load, and the structure of processing resources. *Psychological Bulletin 91*, 2 (1982), 276-292.

3. Berguer, R., Smith, W.D., and Chung, Y.H. Performing laparoscopic surgery is significantly more stressful for the surgeon than open surgery. *Surgical Endoscopy 15*, 10 (2001), 1204-1207.

4. Bradshaw, J. Pupil size as a measure of arousal during information processing. *Nature 216*, 5114 (1967), 515-516.

5. Cassenti, D.N. and Kelley, T.D. Towards the shape of mental workload. *Proceedings of the Human Factors and Ergonomics Society Annual Meeting 50*, 11 (2006), 1147-1151.

6. Chen, H.-J. and Lin, C.J. The investigation of laparoscopic instrument movement control. *Lecture Notes in Engineering and Computer Science 2198*, 1 (2011), 1309-1313.

7. Elliott, D., Helsen, W.F., and Chua, R. A Century Later: Woodworth's (1899) Two-component Model of

Goal-directed Aiming. *Psychological Bulletin 127*, 3 (2001), 342-357.

8. Fitts, P.M. The information capacity of the human motor system in controlling the amplitude of movement. *Journal of Experimental Psychology 47*, 6 (1954), 381-391.

9. Fitts, P.M. and Peterson, J.R. Information capacity of discrete motor responses. *Journal of Experimental Psychology 67*, (1964), 103-112.

10. Gawron, V.J., *Human Workload*, in *Human Performance, Workload, and Situational Awareness Measures Handbook, Second Edition*. 2008, CRC Press. 87-230.

11. Goldinger, S.D. and Papesh, M.H. Pupil dilation reflects the creation and retrieval of memories. *Current Directions in Psychological Science 21*, 2 (2012), 90-95.

12. Guthrie, D. and Buchwald, J.S. Significance testing of difference potentials. *Psychophysiology 28*, 2 (1991), 240-244.

13. Hess, E.H. and Polt, J.M. Pupil size in relation to mental activity during simple problem-solving. *Science 143*, 3611 (1964), 1190-1192.

14. Hoeks, B. and Levelt, W. Pupillary dilation as a measure of attention: a quantitative system analysis. *Behavior Research Methods 25*, 1 (1993), 16-26.

15. Iqbal, S.T., Adamczyk, P.D., Zheng, X.S., and Bailey, B.P. Towards an index of opportunity: understanding changes in mental workload during task execution. In *Proc. CHI 2005*, ACM Press (2005), 311-320.

16. Iqbal, S.T., Zheng, X.S., and Bailey, B.P. Task-evoked pupillary response to mental workload in human-computer interaction. *Ext. Abstracts CHI 2004*, ACM Press (2004), 1477-1480.

17. Jiang, X., Zheng, B., Tien, G., and Atkins, M.S. Pupil response to precision in surgical task execution. *Studies in Health Technology and Informatics 184*, (2013), 210-214.

18. Jiang, X., Zheng, B., Tien, G., Bednarik, R., and Atkins, M.S. Pupil dilations during target-pointing respect Fitts' Law. In *Proc. ETRA 2014*, ACM Press (2014), In press.

19. Klingner, J., Kumar, R., and Hanrahan, P. Measuring the task-evoked pupillary response with a remote eye tracker. In *Proc. ETRA 2008*, ACM Press (2008), 69-72.

20. Marshall, S.P., Method and Apparatus for Eye Tracking and Monitoring Pupil Dilation to Evaluate Cognitive Activity. 2000: United States.

21. Moresi, S., et al. Response preparation with adjacent versus overlapped hands: A pupillometric study. *International Journal of Psychophysiology 79*, 2 (2011), 280-286.

22. Otero, S.C., Weekes, B.S., and Hutton, S.B. Pupil size changes during recognition memory. *Psychophysiology 48*, 10 (2011), 1346-1353.

23. Privitera, C.M., Renninger, L.W., Carney, T., Klein, S., and Aguilar, M. Pupil dilation during visual target detection. *Journal of Vision 10*, 10 (2010), 1-14.

24. Richer, F. and Beatty, J. Pupillary dilations in movement preparation and execution. *Psychophysiology 22*, 2 (1985), 204-207.

25. Richstone, L., et al. Eye metrics as an objective assessment of surgical skill. *Annals Surgery 252*, 1 (2010), 177-182.

26. Zheng, B., Cassera, M.A., Martinec, D.V., Spaun, G.O., and Swanstrom, L.L. Measuring mental workload during the performance of advanced laparoscopic tasks. *Surgical Endoscopy 24*, 1 (2010), 45-50.

Collocating Interface Objects: Zooming into Maps

Jon May
School of Psychology
University of Plymouth
Plymouth, PL4 8AA, UK
jon.may@plymouth.ac.uk

Tim Gamble
Department of Psychology
University of Bath
Bath, BA2 7AY, UK
t.gamble@bath.ac.uk

ABSTRACT
May, Dean and Barnard [11] used a theoretically based model to argue that objects in a wide range of interfaces should be collocated following screen changes such as a zoom-in to detail. Many existing online maps do not follow this principle, but move a clicked point to the centre of the subsequent display, leaving the user looking at an unrelated location. This paper presents three experiments showing that collocating the point clicked on a map so that the detailed location appears in the place previously occupied by the overview location makes the map easier to use, reducing eye movements and interaction duration. We discuss the benefit of basing design principles on theoretical models so that they can be applied to novel situations, and so designers can infer when to use and not use them.

Author Keywords
Zooming; collocation; maps; cinematography; eye-tracking; cognitive models.

ACM Classification Keywords
H.5.2. User Interfaces: Theory and methods

INTRODUCTION
Interactive maps are everywhere nowadays, and map use has become routine [5]. Ramblers and drivers no longer have to battle with unwieldy sheets of paper, compromising breadth of representation against level of detail, with the crucial junction lost in the fold of the map, and the new road not even shown. Up to date cartographical information is now instantly accessible on computers, cars and handheld devices that are wirelessly connected to the internet, accurately positioned by GPS [9]. Relevant objects or businesses can be highlighted and irrelevant detail removed from the view, and the maps can be drawn at whatever level of detail the user requires for their current goal, zooming in from a low detail overview to successively more detailed local views of an area [3].

CHI 2014, April 26 - May 01 2014, Toronto, ON, Canada
Copyright 2014 ACM 978-1-4503-2473-1/14/04...$15.00.
http://dx.doi.org/10.1145/2556288.2557279

Such flexibility comes at a cost, however, because the representation on the device cannot necessarily be the same as that on a paper map. A paper map is a designed representation of reality. It has been constructed by a skilled practitioner to take advantage of the map readers' attentional and perceptual processing, to allow them to selectively attend to certain classes of information in alternation [4]. Enormously successful, cartographic conventions have not developed overnight, and their evolution has relied upon developments in printing technology as well as the skill of the cartographer. In moving from a static, paper to dynamic, electronic representations, with far smaller screens and lower resolutions than are achievable in print, cartography faces a challenge. Allowing classes of information to be hidden or revealed adds interactional overheads to the design and use of a map that are absent when the map design takes advantage of selective attention. Changing between different scales of map as the user zooms in and out requires design decisions to be made about how successive views should be related. Designing an interactive map becomes a problem in human-computer interaction, prone to the same conflicting demands as other computer interface designs [5]. Technological change makes trade-offs between speed, capacity and mode of delivery difficult to anticipate. Fashions in implementation flourish and designers imitate more often than they innovate.

One thing that does not change, however, is the mental architecture of the map reader. It has previously been argued [2] that computer interface design should be a science as much as a craft, and should benefit by a principled understanding of the tasks users undertake, in order to capitalise upon the mental resources available for interaction. Early in the development of computer based maps, Moellering noted that 'when one begins to work with interactive display systems and particularly animations ... displays must be considered in a dynamic setting' [12]. Some researchers (for example, Young and Clanton [17]) have since advocated that interface designers learn from the dynamics of film editing, and should manage changes in their interfaces in the same way that film editors manipulated temporal and spatial jumps in films. May and Barnard [10] argued that rather than naively imitate cinematographic editing conventions, designers needed to understand why these conventions worked for films, and to create parallel changes in their interfaces based upon that understanding. Film editing had evolved as a craft skill, and its rules of thumb were situated within the domain of camera angles, lighting, and narrative, as sets of 'dos and don'ts', with no real account of why certain practices worked and were 'filmic', while others were 'unfilmic'. While the work of researchers such as Kraft [6,7] had shown that conventions in film cutting did have a sound psychological basis, their domain specific nature made it hard for designers to know what it was they were to apply to their interfaces.

May and Barnard [10] presented a theoretical analysis of cinematography based upon Barnard's Interacting Cognitive Subsystems (ICS) model of cognition [1], and made several extrapolations to interface design, including one scenario of a tourist information system combining large-scale and detailed views of a locale to help people find places of interest and plan routes. The problem posed was how to combine these two representations. In contrast to ingenious and novel combinations of fish-eye views, magnifying lenses and multiple simultaneous displays, it was argued that to be like a film the map interface should cut directly from an overview to a detailed view, without any swooping animation (as advocated in the context of data spaces by Mackinlay, Card and Robertson [8]).

The cognitive model of film watching that was proposed assumed that the main task of someone watching a film was to follow the narrative (in ICS terms, at the propositional and implicational levels of representation), and that any requirement imposed upon them to search the screen for relevant material (in ICS terms, at the object and propositional levels of representation) interfered with this task, detracting from their immersion in the story and making them aware of the surface detail at the expense of the story. Similarly, it was argued that in using a computer interface to carry out a task, any requirement for users to search the screen to relocate elements following a scene change would interfere with their main task, making the system less usable. Subsequent work on task-switching [13] makes a similar point, that interleaving two tasks adds cognitive overheads in terms of time and error compared to completing them in sequence.

In the context of map use, May & Barnard argued that the point that the user clicked on in the overview was where they were interested in for their task, and would be where they were still looking immediately after any screen change, and so the detailed view of the point clicked should be redisplayed in the same physical position on the screen: a principle they called collocation, as opposed to translation of the point of interest to a different spatial location. At that time, 1995, there were few such interactive maps readily available, but they noted the similarity between zooming-in with a map and with graphics packages. All but one of the graphics packages surveyed broke the collocation principle: they did a variety of things, often inconsistently, but most often they would translate the clicked element to the centre of the new view. The exception was Adobe Illustrator, the vector based partner of Adobe Photoshop (although in a subsequent release, it too joined the 'move to centre' camp).

One problem with the theoretically based principle of collocation was that there was no empirical evidence that filmmakers actually did make use of it. May, Dean and Barnard [11] gave a more detailed account of the cognitive model of film watching, and reported an eye-tracking study in which participants watched a commercially released film in its entirety. They measured the amount that observers moved their gaze location in the frames immediately after each of ten classes of cuts, and found that there was minimal eye movement in cuts where the cut zoomed-in to a detail, followed a moving actor or object, showed objects whose position was predictable, or showed the result or consequence of an action, or showed novel unexpected objects. In all of these circumstances, filmmakers had succeeded in collocating salient regions of the screen before and after cuts, so that the viewers did not have to move their eyes to locate something on the screen to comprehend the unfolding narrative. In five other classes of cut, large eye movements were found. Based on these findings, May *et al.* specifically argued that map interfaces should make use of collocation when zooming in and out to help map users rapidly locate the topic of their enquiry without having to search the screen for it. They also made recommendations about interactions where collocation would not be necessary, but where structural changes in the display might guide a user to the novel information, while leaving previous information visible to provide a context or history of the interaction. Such a situation, where translation would be better than collocation, might arise in the use of hierarchical databases, for example, where an object or name makes sense in the context of superordinate information and might be ambiguous or difficult to parse without this context remaining on the screen.

Despite this research, the translation convention was subsequently adopted for several computer-based maps, and in a recent evaluation of map interfaces, colocation was not even considered as an option [16]. There are clearly reasons why the translation convention was adopted, other than imitation or the re-use of open source code. Computationally, all that needs to be returned to the map server are the absolute co-ordinates of the clicked location and a scaling factor (either of the current or of the new view), as can be seen by inspecting the URLs, which generally include a latitude, longitude and level parameter. Without knowing where within the previous image the clicked location was, the obvious place to put it in the new view is in the centre. If the user is going to zoom in further, then it will remain at the centre. It could even be argued that such interfaces are consistent, which has become a watchword of design guidelines, and hence easy to learn and use.

However, translation also has disadvantages, from the point of view of the user. If they have been looking in one point on the screen, the place they are interested in is now not there, and they have to search for it. If the new representation is stylistically different to the original, as is often the case with maps of different scale, then it is not an easy task to re-orient oneself to the new view and to relocate the place name of interest. If one has not clicked on the actual place, but on or near its name, which is usually to one side of the place, then the actual location desired will not be in the centre of the screen, and if its name has been repositioned on the new view it may be anywhere within the screen, depending upon the scaling factors. If one is unfamiliar with a geographical region, as is often the case when using a map, each wrong place name one reads gives no help; serial search is all that is possible. On the other hand, translation has some advantages for the programmer, because to collocate the result with the original map, two additional parameters need to be returned to the server to indicate the relative location of the point of interest within the first map, so that it can re-occupy that position in the new map. In essence, the decision between the two modes of presentation appears to be a contest between ease of use and ease of programming.

From a psychological point of view, the only way that a move-to-centre translation algorithm could be of benefit to map readers rather than to map programmers, is if the widespread adoption of the convention has been learnt by the general public and so they expect to look in the centre of maps as a result of an interaction with a place on the periphery. This is the question that is set out to be answered with the three experiments reported in this paper. By contrasting an interface using collocation with the same design but using translation, it should be possible to see if the theoretically principled recommendations provided any advantage for users, or whether they had grown used to the convention and by knowing where to look would be able to interact as easily with the translated interfaces.

EXPERIMENT 1

Method

There were 26 participants in the study, all of whom were paid £5 for their participation. They were told that the study was investigating eye movements people made while zooming into maps, but not that either method of zooming was of particular interest.

The two interface techniques of collocation and translation were presented to the participants as different computer systems, both using maps. One was a traffic control system, in which their task was to locate traffic monitors; the other was a gas supply system and their task was to locate gas meters. The interface was written in RealBasic and run on a 2.7GHz G5 Mac using a 20" NEC Multisync 2080UX+ LCD monitor at 1024 x 768 pixel resolution, viewed by participants from a static operator's chair with headrest (to minimise head movement) at a distance of approximately 75 cm. Each map was 297mm square, subtending approximately 22 degrees, with the centre of the screen approximately level with the participants' eyes.

Thirteen scenarios were created, using Ordnance Survey maps of different cities in Britain (the maps were obtained from the Edina Digimaps service under an educational license). Each scenario began with a text message asking participants to locate a target in a specific named location within a city, e.g. 'There is a traffic monitor located near Walkley in Sheffield. See if you can find it'. On clicking OK, the screen cleared and a start button was displayed centrally. When clicked, an overview map of 1:50,000 scale was displayed and the participant had to find and click on the specific local placename (e.g., Walkley). Following the click, a 1:25,000 scale map of the area clicked on was displayed, and the participants had to relocate and click on the placename, to be shown the final 1:12,500 map (produced by rescaling the OS 1:10,000 map). This final map had a target symbol (a black diamond 4mm high and wide) embedded within it, upon which the participant had to click to complete a trial. The target was placed in the area that the participant had been asked to search, but was not systematically located in relation to the place name on that view. If at any point the participant clicked on a region not containing the target area, they could 'zoom out' to the previous map using option-click.

Twelve of the scenarios were divided between two experimental blocks. In one block the maps were collocated such that the geographical location under the mouse cursor was identical before and after the click, notwithstanding the change in scale. In the other block the conventional translation approach was used, such that the geographical location clicked on the first map was placed in the centre of the second map (Figure 1). The remaining scenario was used as a practice trial before each block.

The traffic monitor and gas meter cover stories were balanced over experimental conditions, and the order of the conditions was also balanced over participants. The twelve scenarios were presented in a Latin square design over participants, such that after twelve participants each scenario had been used in each serial position within each condition.

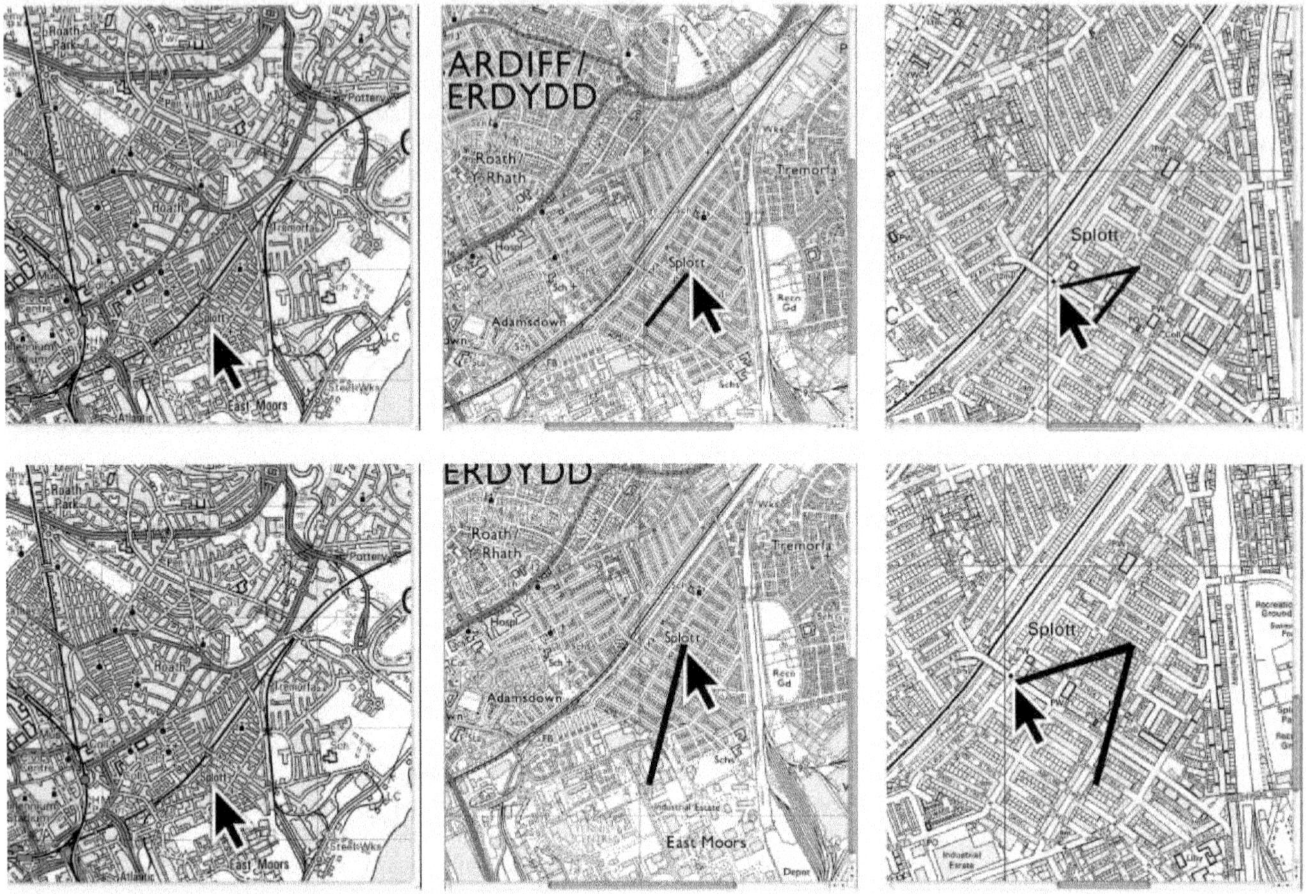

Figure 1: In the collocate condition (upper row) the geographical detail clicked on is positioned under the cursor on the new, higher scale map. In the translate condition (bottom row), the clicked detail is moved to the centre of the new map. In both conditions, the task is to *find* a place name in the first map (the Splott area of Cardiff), *relocate* it in the second map, and *select* a diamond shaped target symbol in the third map. The arrow cursors have been exaggerated for clarity, and indicate the point that is about to be clicked, and the lines show the path traversed. Note that the location of the place name relative to the street layout varies from map to map. Maps (c) Crown Copyright/database right 2008. An Ordnance Survey/EDINA supplied service.

Each participant was tested individually. Participants' eye movements were recorded using a SensoMotoric Instruments iView X eye tracker, which requires no head restraint or worn head position tracking device, thus making the situation as naturalistic as possible. The screen coordinates of each participants' gaze location were logged every 20 msec for the duration of the experiment. The presentation computer recorded reaction times for each experimental event.

Results

Reliable eye tracking data could not be obtained for four participants. Of the 22 remaining participants, ages ranged from 18y 9m to 27y 2m, and three were male. Eleven completed the study in each order (i.e., Collocate-Translate or Translate-Collocate). Raw eye tracking data was analysed using the BeGaze software, with parameters defined to detect fixations with a minimum duration of 80 msec and a maximum dispersion of one- sixth the screen height. This reduces the raw data to a series of fixations (where the pupil is relatively stationary), saccades (where the pupil is moving) and blinks (where the pupil is not detectable for several frames). If the software reported more than three blinks in a step, the data was discarded as unreliable, because the software does not distinguish between true blinks and episodes where the pupil cannot be detected due to tracking problems such as head movement. Trials in which the participant used the zoom-out function to step back were also discarded. Over the 264 trials from the 22 participants, data was rejected from 39 of the Find steps, 14 of the Relocate steps, and 18 of the Target steps (9% overall).

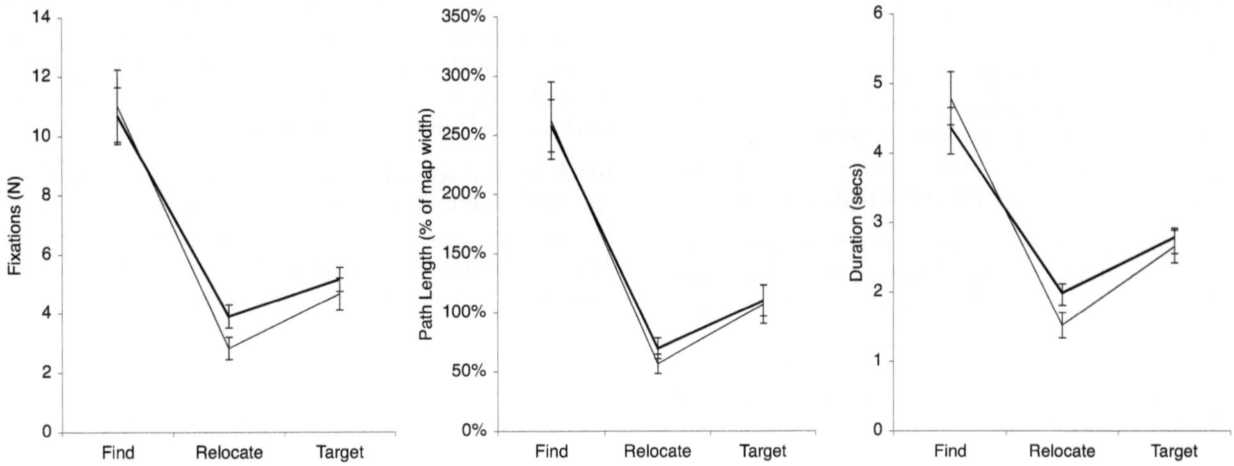

Figure 2: The two interfaces performed identically on the *find* and *target* steps, but the translate interface (bold line) required more gaze fixations, a longer search path, and took longer to complete on the critical *relocate* step, than did the collocated interface (narrow line). Bars indicate one standard error.

From the resulting analyses, the number of fixations, their total path length (expressed as a percentage of the width of the map), and the overall duration of each step in each trial was obtained (Figure 2). These three dependent variables were entered into a MANOVA with the factors of condition and task step. There was no overall effect of condition (Pillai's trace $F(3,19)=0.69$), but there was an effect of task step (Pillai's trace $F(6,82)=13.5$, $p<.001$, $\eta_p^2=.497$) and an interaction (Pillai's trace $F(6,82)=2.60$, $p=.023$, $\eta_p^2=.160$).

Univariate tests showed no overall effects of condition for any of the three measures (all Fs<1), but significant effects of task step for all three (Fixations $F(2,42)=52.6$, $MSE=12.3$, $p<.001$, $\eta_p^2=.715$; Path lengths $F(2,42)=58.5$, $MSE=1.06$, $p<.001$, $\eta_p^2=.736$; Durations $F(2,42)=70.9$, $MSE=1.27$, $p<.001$, $\eta_p^2=.771$), and interactions of condition with task step for Fixations ($F(2,42)=3.60$, $MSE=5.64$, $p=.036$, $\eta_p^2=.146$) and Durations ($F(2,42)=5.04$, $MSE=0.85$, $p=.011$, $\eta_p^2=.194$), with a non-significant interaction for Path lengths ($F(2,42)=2.80$, $MSE=0.67$, $p=.07$, $\eta_p^2=.118$).

To interpret the interactions, one-tailed paired t tests were then conducted between the two conditions in each task step. There were no differences between the two conditions in the Find step (Fixations $t(21)=1.22$; Path-length $t(21)=1.05$; Duration $t(21)=1.72$; all $p>.10$) or for the Target step (Fixations $t(21)=1.17$; Path-length $t(21)=0.15$; Duration $t(21)=0.34$; all $p\geq.10$), but on the Relocate step the translate interface required more fixations (Col=2.76, Trans=3.89, $t(21)=2.36$, $p=.014$), longer path lengths (Col=65%, Trans=105%, $t(21)=2.59$, $p=.009$), and took longer to complete (Col=1.54s, Trans=2.00s, $t(21)=2.22$, $p=.019$).

Discussion

The two interfaces did not differ on the initial Find step, where participants were searching for the name for the first time, nor on the Target step, where they were searching for the diamond symbol, but they did differ on the crucial Relocate step. At this point in the task, participants had already found the name and clicked on it on the first map, and had to find and click it again. The conventional translation approach of presenting the clicked point in the centre of the new view required more and longer eye-movements and took participants longer to execute than the advocated principled approach of collocating the position on successive maps. This difference exists even though the translation approach is consistent, because the clicked point is always in the same physical screen position in the new view and so participants could simply make a single change in gaze direction. Instead, they are not able to make use of this consistency, having to search for the place name again.

The lack of benefit of collocation on the target step supports the proposed argument because the diamond was fixed on the map, and not collocated with the place name or the location clicked by the user. In practice, the locate step required visual search in both interfaces.

It could be argued that this version of a map-searching task does not give much benefit to the consistency of the translation approach because with only three levels of map to search through, there is only one critical trial upon which this consistency can be used: the transition from the second map (in which the clicked point has been translated to the centre) to the final map. The next experiment extends the task to a five level task, so that having selected a point on the first map, and having had it translated to the centre, subsequent clicks on maps two, three and four should also be close to the centre of the map, potentially making a translation approach more useful, and in practice, more like a collocation approach.

EXPERIMENT 2

Method

There were 25 participants in this experiment, and each was paid £10 for their participation. They were told that the study was investigating eye movements people made while navigating computer-based maps. The experiment was conducted using the same equipment as Experiment 1.

Twenty-four map-reading scenarios were created using Ordnance Survey maps of the Plymouth area, with which none of the participants were familiar. Each scenario began with a text message instructing participants to locate a local place name in a numbered region of Plymouth. Participants read this instruction aloud. On clicking OK, an 250mm square overview was displayed, based on a 1:50,000 scale map, upon which the numbers 1 to 12 had been superimposed in a clock face arrangement (Figure 3). After clicking on or near the relevant number, a twice as detailed view of a quarter of the original map was displayed. Clicking on this displayed a third level view, again twice as detailed, and so this time of 1/16th of the original map. Clicking on this presented a fourth (1/64th) and finally a fifth level (1/256th) view. The first three levels were all based on the same 1:50,000 scale map, level four on a 1:25,000 scale map, and level five on a 1:12,500 scale map (rescaled from the OS 1:10,000 map). When the target place name had been clicked in the fifth level map, a congratulation message was displayed. If at any time a click would have resulted in the place name being off-screen, an error message was displayed and the trial was restarted from the instruction message (this meant that the zoom-out function did not have to be made available).

The place names used as targets were spurious, being taken from a different region (Northumberland) and added to the maps so that while they were in roughly the same geographical location on each map, their actual position and typeface varied in the same way that real place names varied in typeface and position on the three original maps used. Participants undertook two sessions (approximately three months apart), each of 24 trials divided into two blocks. One block in each session used the Translate method of zooming in, so that the new view was centred upon the location represented by the point clicked in the previous level; and the other block used the Collocate method, so that location represented by the point clicked in the previous level was presented in the same relative location within the new map window.

Block order was balanced over sessions and participants, so that half experienced Translate first followed by Collocate in the first session, and then Collocate followed by Translate in the second session. The twenty four scenarios were balanced so that half were used in the translate condition in session one and the collocate condition in session two, while the others were used in the collocate condition in session one and the translate block in session two. Within each block, the order of trials was rotated over participants in a Latin square, so that each target appeared at least once at each position in the block.

Results

Three participants were unable to return for the second session, and eye-tracking data from one participant was too poor for analysis. This left 21 participants' data for analysis (6 males; age range 20-36 years, median 24 years). Of these 1008 trials, 48 (5.2%) were repeated due to errors, with one participant making 8 errors (17%); the next worst made 4 errors (8%). Errors were more frequent in the second session (n=29) than the first (n=19), the reverse of a practice effect, but were more likely near the start of a block (number of errors per four trials: 17; 10; 5; 7; 5; 4). They were also more frequent in the Translate condition (n= 30) than in the Collocate condition (n=18). A binomial test gives a probability of .056 of observing 18 outcomes or fewer out of 48.

For each of the five steps in each trial, three measures were computed as in the previous experiment: the number of fixations, the total path-length, and the duration of each step. For each participant, a mean for these measures was computed over the twelve trials in each block, resulting in a 2x2x5 repeated measures design with the factors of Session, Method, and Step.

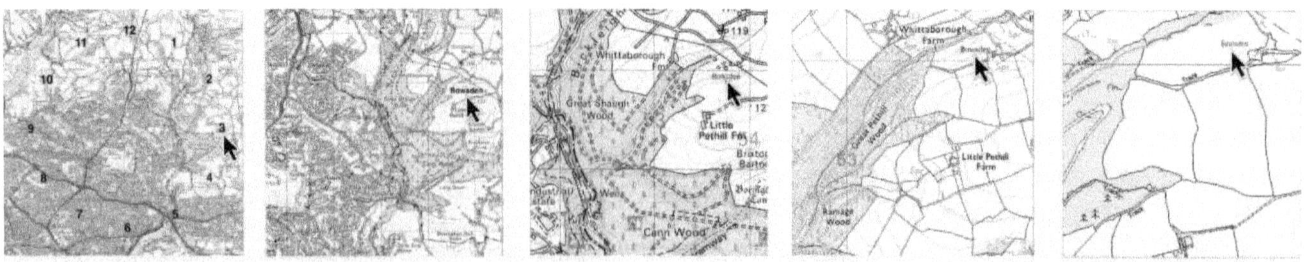

Figure 3: In the second experiment, participants had to locate a place name that had been added to five increasingly detailed maps such that its appearance and geographical position varied from map to map, as real place names do on different scale maps of the same region. In this example, the task is to locate Bowsden using the collocated interface. The cursor has been exaggerated for clarity. Maps (c) Crown Copyright/database right 2008. An Ordnance Survey/EDINA supplied service.

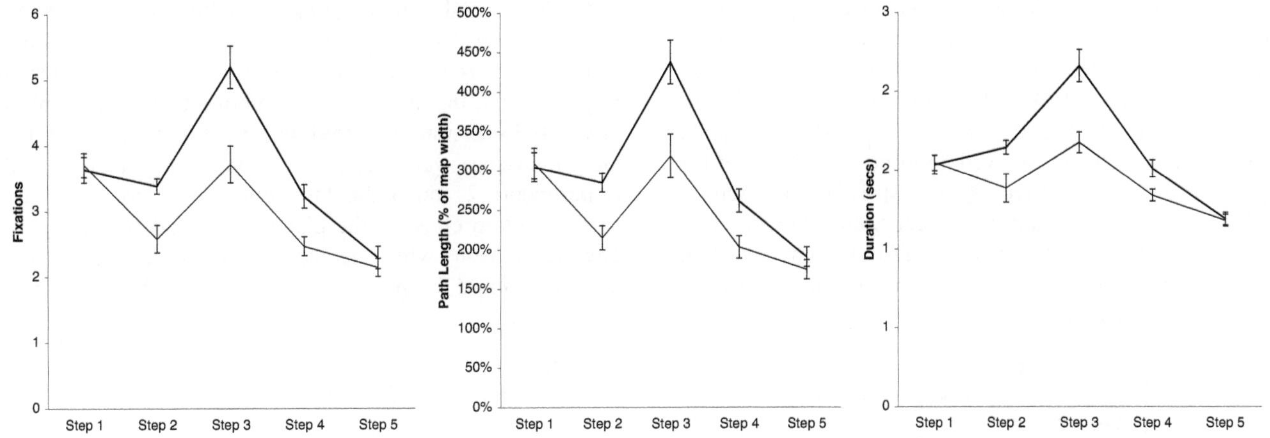

Figure 4: The Translate method (bold line) required a longer path length, more fixations, and took more time than the Collocate method (thin line) for steps 2, 3 and 4 of the map task. The initial steps (locating the number on the clock face) and the final steps did not differ (bars indicate one standard error).

The three dependent variables of path-length, fixations and duration were entered into a MANOVA, and multivariate tests showed that all factors and interactions produced significant effects (Figure 4). Because of the effects of Session factor, separate MANOVAs were then conducted upon each sessions' data, in a 2x5 repeated measures design. The effects of Method, Step and their interaction were significant in both of these analyses. Five further MANOVAs were then conducted upon each Step, pooled over both Sessions, with the single factor of Method. The multivariate tests showed no differences between the conditions for Step 1 ($F(3,18)=0.211$, $p=.887$) or Step 5 ($F(3,18)=1.16$, $p=.352$). Steps 2, 3 and 4 showed significant differences between the methods (Step 2 $F(3,18)=4.75$, $p=.013$; Step 3: $F(3,18)=10.9$, $p<.001$; Step 4 $F(3,18)=8.29$, $p=.001$), with the Translate condition resulting in longer path-lengths, more fixations, and longer durations for each of these three steps (Figure 4). Univariate tests within each of these MANOVAs showed the same pattern of effects for all three dependent variables.

Discussion

Despite the consistent placing of the clicked points at the centre of the screen following a transition to a new map, the translation interface is used less efficiently than the collocated interface, where the new point is in the same physical location as the old point, wherever this is on the screen. This is despite the fact that the place names themselves are not in exactly the same positions on successive maps, so that some search is required in both interfaces. The need to move gaze from the clicked location back to the centre is an impediment to the usability of the translation interface.

While watching participants use the maps, it became apparent that the typefaces used for the spurious place names did not look like the simple serif and sans serif faces used for real names on the original map (Table 1). This could have made them stand out more from the background, perhaps giving some advantage or disadvantage to one of the interfaces that might not be apparent in a real map. In fact, the differences between the typefaces might explain why the difference between the two interfaces is larger for Step 3 than for Steps 2 or 4. Step 2 is the first step on which the place name has to be found, and it was in a Helvetica Bold face. It then changes to Times Normal on Step 3, and on Step 4 to Georgia Normal. The appearance of the name is thus quite different between the second and third steps, but quite similar between steps 3 and 4. The change from Georgia Normal to Palatino Italic on step 5 is also quite different, although both are serif faces, and here the interfaces performed equivalently. We therefore ran the task again using different typefaces, changing between Times and Helvetica on each step, and including one change from normal to italic, one between two italic faces, and one from an italic to a normal face.

EXPERIMENT 3

Method

Twelve participants, all postgraduate students (8 males and 4 females; age range 21:5 to 33:11, median 28:5), took part in this experiment. They were paid £5 for their assistance. This experiment used the same materials and design as Experiment 2, except that the typefaces used for the spurious place names were altered to make them more like those of other names on the maps and the changes more systematic over different steps in the task (Table 1).

Results

Error rates in this experiment were very low, with only five trials needing to be repeated. Three of the errors were made by one participant, who also took abnormally long to complete several steps of the Translate task (over a minute in one case), and so his data were excluded. The three dependent measures of fixations, path-length and duration were computed for each of the five task steps in both conditions, as in the previous experiments. A MANOVA showed a main effect of condition $F(3,8)=10.8$, $p=.003$, $\eta_p^2q=.802$, Step $F(12,120)=8.1$, $p<.001$, $\eta_p^2=.448$, and their interaction $F(12,120)=2.28$, $p=.012$, $\eta_p^2=.186$. Separate MANOVAs at each step showed no effects of condition for Step 1 $F(3,8)=0.51$, Step 4 $F(3,8)=1.74$ or Step 5 $F(3,8)=0.58$, but significant effects for Step 2 $F(3,8)=10.8$, $p=.003$, $\eta_p^2=.802$ and Step 3 $F(3,8)=10.8$, $p=.003$, $\eta_p^2=.802$). One-tailed t tests showed that all three measures differed for Step 2 and Step 3.

Level	Experiment 2	Experiment 3
Step 2	**Helvetica Bold**	Times Normal
Step 3	Times Normal	*Helvetica Italic*
Step 4	Georgia Normal	*Times Italic*
Step 5	*Palatino Italic*	Helvetica Normal

Table 1: The typefaces used in experiment three were chosen so that they were more consistent than those in experiment two, were more like the faces used for real place names on the OS maps, and the differences between successive maps were equivalent.

Discussion

This experiment provides a close replication of the previous findings, despite the changes in typeface. The advantage of the collocated interface is the same on steps 2 and 3 (when the place name changes from a sans-serif normal to a serif italic face), but declines on step 4 to become non-significant (when the place name changes between two italic faces). In all three experiments, the initial and final steps do not differ. The initial step, of course, is in fact the same for both interfaces, because the place name has not yet been found and so there is nothing to collocate. On the final step in Experiment 1, the target was a symbol rather than the place name, and was not collocated with the point clicked and so the interfaces are again equivalent. However, in Experiments 2 and 3 the last four task steps all require participants to click on the place name, and so there is no obvious reason why the advantage of the collocated interface should disappear so consistently in the last step.

One possibility is that the low level of detail on these final maps makes it easy to re-orient on the place name, so that the searching required by the translated interface becomes trivial.

GENERAL DISCUSSION

The three experiments showed a consistent benefit for collocating the point of interaction with its result in a map interface. In summary, this is what May, Dean and Barnard [11] predicted, but which the designers of some online maps have not implemented. While it would be nice if the conventional design of maps were to change as a result of this work, it would also be good if it leads to a better understanding of how principles and theory can be used to guide design decisions in interface design. This research has followed a path from anecdotal observation (that film editors seem to control the position of elements within the frame) to a cognitive model of film watching (in which any demand for visual search interrupts the comprehension of narrative), to empirical data supporting the model (in terms of eye movements following cuts in a commercial film), and applied it to interface design (in the form of

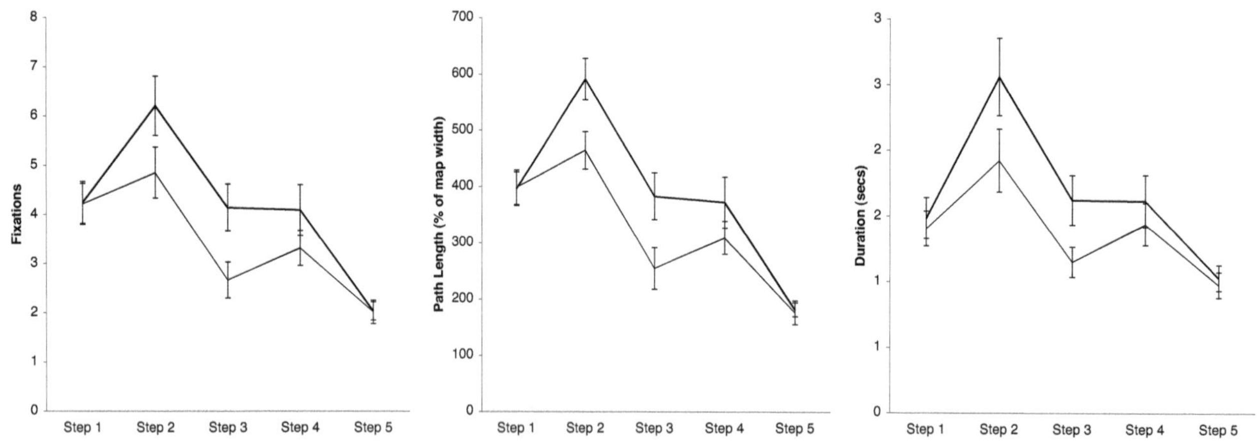

Figure 5: Changing the typefaces of the place names shown in experiment three did not remove the advantage of the collocated interface (thin line) over the translated (bold line) interface for the intermediate steps of the task (bars indicate one standard error).

contextualised but generic principles such as collocation). Here it has been shown that this principle does what the theoretical model says it will do, making it easier for a map user to understand what they are looking at when they click to zoom-in to a map. This paper is not so much an argument about the design of interfaces for maps, but about the utility of theoretically based principles for interface design. It also shows that the participants in this study were not benefitting from having learnt a consistent translation principle, despite its widespread adoption.

In the case of maps, it is not as if the designers are unaware of the confusion caused by the unfilmic, move-to-centre translation. Most online maps now try to guide the user's gaze to the new, central location by making use of a form of animation, interpolating four or five views of the initial map progressively moving a little each frame so that the clicked point moves toward the centre of the screen, before then displaying the new map. Whether intentionally or not, they are following the suggestion of Mackinlay, Card and Robertson [9] that the user should be supported in relocating points of view by moving them through virtual space rather than jumping directly from point to point; see Shanmugasundaram and Irani for an experimental study exploring this technique [15]. They are making their interfaces resemble fictional interfaces such as the 3D hologram viewer used by Deckard in Ridley Scott's film 'Blade Runner' [14]. This is not how film editors create their own material, however, because the experience of watching uncut footage shot while the cameraman is moving through a scene is not only time consuming but often nauseating, when the viewer's bodily and visual sensations do not correlate. Cutting directly between two different viewpoints can work, if collocation is used, as filmmakers do know, and as interface designers should know.

The collocation principle applies to more than map interfaces. It should also work whenever the user wants to move directly from one object to another, as yet unrepresented, object, and where the previous view is now superfluous. Clicking on an entry in a table of contents in a word-processor can allow you to jump to that heading in the body of the text, but the heading is rarely located on-screen in the same position as was the corresponding entry in the table of contents, and must be searched for.

Overall, this series of three experiments has shown that the advantage of collocating maps over the conventional approach of translating them to the centre is robust, supporting the argument that the design principle derived from the analysis of film cutting techniques can be used to improve interface design. Future work needs to show that the advantage of collocating is not generic, but depends upon the task being performed. There is some indication here that collocation does not always improve performance, when the search is simple in the final step, for example. May, Dean and Barnard [11] found that collocation was not used in film editing in situations where the location of the topic of interest was predictable and when the occurrence of the cut could be anticipated, as when two actors were talking to each other. In such conversational scenes, cuts would alternate between views of the two actors faces, on alternate sides of the screen. The resulting sequence resembled the view of the actors one would have if standing next to them while they were talking, moving ones gaze between them, prompted by the dialogue. Another class of cut in which collocation did not occur were 'over the shoulder' cuts, where an actor would be seen doing something before a cut, and the camera would then show the result of their action from behind them, with the rear of their head and a shoulder occupying a corner of the frame. Such framing of the action serves to provide a context, linking the results of the action to the person responsible, and also allowing one to see it from their point of view.

Extrapolating to computer interfaces, a similar lack of benefit from collocation should be found when context is important, or when translation of focal point after a screen change is predictable. Earlier in this paper, it was suggested that a scenario that might benefit from the retention of contextual information would be searching through a hierarchical database, where one is successively refining the category within which one is searching. Instead of replacing the initial set of categories with a second, finer-grained subset, a translated interface would place the new subset off to one side, with the original selection still visible so that the result of the interaction is contextualised by the super-ordinate category name. This form of interface is in fact used in Apple's iTunes Column Browser view, in which three panes arranged horizontally contain genre, artist and album titles. When nothing has been selected, each pane shows all of the information in the Library. Clicking upon a genre in the leftmost pane refines the content of the other two panes so that only artists and albums within that genre are now listed. Clicking again upon an artist further refines the album list to only those albums by that artist within that genre.

In a future study, databases could be contrasted that work in a similar manner to this, with the new information appearing alongside previous windows of information, with collocated designs where the new information replaces the previous window. If the collocation principle was working simply because it minimised eye movements, then the collocated versions of the databases should similarly benefit, because the new information is physically located close to the previous focus of attention. If, however, collocation worked in the Maps interfaces because it was concordant with the users' task, then it should not be as useful here, because the task involves successively moving through a data structure in a predictable manner, with detail unfolding on each operation. A translated design in which the new window opens to the right of the previous window will be contrasted with a collocated design in which the new window opens where the old window was, and the old window appears to the right. The collocated design thus removes the sense of moving successively through the data while retaining the availability of contextual information.

From a psychological point of view, the model of interface use and the ICS account of cognition can be used to reason about the cognitive consequences of changes to the task, such as the use of verbal material of increasing ambiguity (increasing demand upon a propositional-morphonolexical loop). Without the link between the principle and its theoretical derivation, such extrapolation and extension would be impossible and the guidance to designers would become rapidly out-dated, as new devices are developed, and novel tasks digitized. It also provides a link between the applied domain of human-computer interaction and computational models of visual search, (see, for example, Zelinsky [18]), where top-down models in which search is driven by object based information are simulating human behaviour with increasing accuracy.

ACKNOWLEDGMENTS

This work was supported by the UK Engineering and Physical Sciences Research Council grant EP/C515528/2.

REFERENCES

1. Barnard, P.J. Interacting cognitive subsystems: A psycholinguistic approach to short-term memory. In A. Ellis, (ed.), *Progress in the Psychology of Language, Vol. 2,* Erlbaum: London (1985), 197-258.
2. Bellotti, V., Blandford, A., Duke, D., MacLean, A., May, J. and Nigay, L. Interpersonal access control in computer-mediated communications: A systematic analysis of the design space. *Human Computer Interaction 11*, (1996), 357-432.
3. Burigat, S., Chittaro, L. & Gabrielli, S. Navigation techniques for small-screen devices: an evaluation on maps and web pages. *International Journal of Human-Computer Studies, 66,* (2008), 78-97.
4. Garlandini, S. & Fabricant, S.I. Evaluating the effectiveness and efficiency of visual varables for geographic information visualization. In K.S. Hornsby, C. Claramunt, M. Denis & G. Ligozat (Eds) Spatial Information Theory COSIT2009, *Lecture Notes in Computer Science 5756,* (2009), 195-211.
5. Harrower, M., & Sheesley, B. Designing better map interfaces: A framework for panning and zooming. *Transactions in GIS, 9(2)*, (2005),77-89.
6. Kraft, R.N. The role of cutting in the evaluation and retention of film. *Journal of Experimental Psychology: Learning Memory and Cognition, 12*(1), (1986), 155-163.
7. Kraft, R.N. Rules and strategies of visual narratives. *Perceptual and Motor Skills, 64*, (1987), 3-14.
8. Mackinlay, J.D., Card., S.K., & Robertson, G.G. Rapid controlled movement through a virtual 3d workspace, In *Proceedings of Siggraph'90*, (1990), 171-176.
9. Manson, S.M., Kne, L. Dyke, K.R., Shannon, J. & Eria, S. Using eye-tracking and mouse metrics to test usability of web mapping navigation. *Cartography and Geographic Information Science, 39(1),* (2012), 48-60.
10. May, J., & Barnard, P.J. Cinematography and interface design. In K. Nordby, P. Helmersen, D.J. Gilmore, & S. Arnesen (Eds.), *Human-computer interaction: Interact'95,* Chapman and Hall (1995), 26-31.
11. May, J., Dean, M.P. & Barnard, P.J. Using film cutting techniques in interface design. *Human-Computer Interaction, 18* (2003), 325-372.
12. Moellering, H. At the interface of cartography and computer graphics. *Proceedings of the 2nd annual conference on computer graphics and interactive techniques,* Bowling Green Ohio, June 25-27, ACM Press (1975), 256-259.
13. Monsell, S. Task switching. *Trends in Cognitive Sciences, 7,* (2003), 134-140.
14. Scott, R. (Director). Blade Runner [MotionPicture], United States: Warner Brothers (1982).
15. Shanmugasundaram, M. & Irani, P. The effect of animated transitions in zooming interfaces. *Proceedings of the working conference on Advanced visual interfaces '08*, ACM Press (2008), 396-399.
16. You, M., Chen, C.-W., Liu, H. & Lin, H. A Usability Evaluation of Web Map Zoom and Pan Functions. *International Journal of Design, 1(1)* (2007), 15-25.
17. Young, E., & Clanton, C. Film craft in user interface design. Tutorial presented at the *InterCHI'93* conference, Amsterdam (1993).
18. Zelinksy, G. J. Eye movements during target acquisition. *Psychological Review, 115(4)* (2008), 787-835.

Showing Face in Video Instruction: Effects on Information Retention, Visual Attention, and Affect

René F. Kizilcec[1], Kathryn Papadopoulos[2,3], Lalida Sritanyaratana[2]

Department of Communication[1]
Stanford University
kizilcec@stanford.edu

HCI Group[2]
Stanford University
lalida@google.com

Customer Experience[3]
Citrix
kathryn.papadopoulos@citrix.com

ABSTRACT

The amount of online educational content is rapidly increasing, particularly in the form of video lectures. The goal is to design video instruction to facilitate an experience that maximizes learning and satisfaction. A widely used but understudied design element in video instruction is the overlay of a small video of the instructor over lecture slides. We conducted an experiment with eye-tracking and recall tests to investigate how adding the instructor's face to video instruction affects information retention, visual attention, and affect. Participants strongly preferred instruction with the face and perceived it as more educational. They spent about 41% of time looking at the face and switched between the face and slide every 3.7 seconds. Consistent with prior work, no significant difference in short- and medium-term recall ability was found. Including the face in video instruction is encouraged based on learners' positive affective response. More fine-grained analytics combining eye-tracking with detailed learning assessment could shed light on the mechanisms by which the face aids or hinders learning.

Author Keywords

Audiovisual Instruction; Multimedia Learning; Eye-tracking.

ACM Classification Keywords

K.3.1. Computers and Education: Computer Uses in Education, Distance learning.

INTRODUCTION

Do you remember those educational TV programs your science teachers showed in class? Audiovisual instruction is not a novelty of the 21st Century; it has been around for many decades, whether in classrooms, on TV, or for corporate training. However, the increasing ubiquity of broadband Internet access has fueled the rapid proliferation of audiovisual educational material in the last few years. In 2012, 32% of higher education students took at least one course online [1]. And with the recent development of online asynchronous computer-mediated communication platforms for educational content, access to education, mostly in the form of audiovisual instruction, continues to extend far beyond traditional academic institutions.

One of the largest providers of massive open online courses (MOOCs), Coursera, went from zero to 2.9 million registered users from more than 220 countries in their first year of operation [38]. The majority of courses offered by Coursera and other online education providers, including corporate training providers, are built around audiovisual instruction. Hundreds of hours are spent preparing, recording, and editing original video lectures for a typical online course [20]. Research on how to effectively design audiovisual instruction undoubtedly has the potential to improve the educational experience of millions of people today.

A major concern with online courses has been the sense of isolation that many learners report and that can hinder their ability to learn [29]. Recent ethnographic findings suggest that video-based courses facilitate a richer interaction between learners and the instructor, who reportedly seems more present and real to learners; moreover, learners in such courses find the learning experience similar to face-to-face instruction [4]. The influence of instructional media, such as video lectures, on learning has been the topic of the "media effects" debate between Clark, who holds that the choice of medium has no influence on learning outcomes [7, 8], and Kozma, who argues that carefully matching media with learners and instructional goals can lead to more effective learning experiences [21, 22]. Kozma emphasizes the importance of attributes of various media over the specific media themselves; for instance, the extent to which social cues can be embedded in a medium.

A number of studies in multimedia learning research have investigated multiple channel presentation and the resulting phenomenon of split attention [13, 27, 34]. Similarly, research on instruction in physical classrooms has explored the attention division between the professor and blackboard or slides [33]. Following this line of research and observing that an increasing number of online instruction is presented as full-screen lecture slides with a small embedded video overlay of the instructor speaking (Figure 1), we investigate the effects of the instructor's face in video instruction on visual attention, information retention, and learner affect.

CHI 2014, April 26–May 1, 2014, Toronto, Ontario, Canada.

ACM 978-1-4503-2473-1/14/04..$15.00.
http://dx.doi.org/10.1145/2556288.2557207

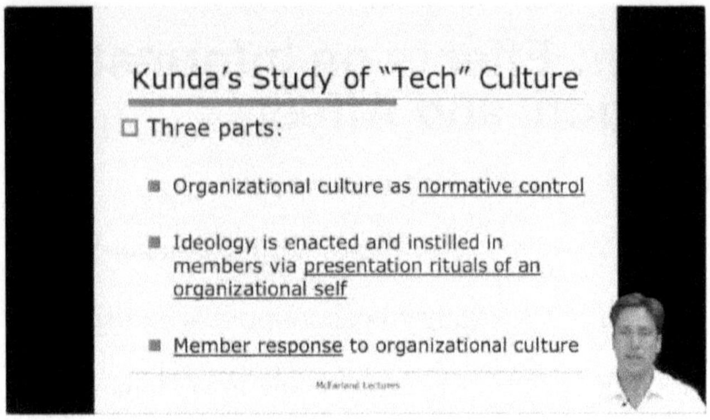

Figure 1. Example of video instruction with lecture slides in the background and a picture-in-picture of the instructor's face.

BACKGROUND

Cognitive Processing, Learning, and Affect

Meaningful learning occurs when cognitive processing of instructional material is moderate: too little processing results in subpar learning, while too much processing can lead to cognitive overload, potentially inhibiting learning [28]. We can use Baddeley's Theory of Working Memory [2] as a lens to understand cognitive processes in multimedia learning. It posits that separate processing units are employed for different input modalities: one area of working memory, called the visual-spatial 'sketchpad', stores visual input while another area, the phonological loop, stores auditory information. According to this model, the video of the instructor's face would compete for visual-spatial cognitive resources with the slide content while the instructor's narration is processed separately though potentially supported by non-verbal information encoded in the instructor's face (e.g., gestures and facial expressions).

Clark and Mayer [6] present a series of empirically established principles to reduce cognitive load in the design of multimedia instruction. For instance, if the content of the presentation is overloading the visual channel, some of the information should be moved to the auditory channel for processing. Extraneous material should be removed, as it may interfere with the resource allocation for processing the important learning materials. And instructional design that induces switching between materials that are presented through different modalities (text, pictures, etc.) may increase cognitive load. The design of much audiovisual instruction has been informed by such insights from multimedia learning theory. Prior research in the multimedia learning tradition on the instructor's face has investigated its effect on learning (perceived, and recall and transfer ability), perceived social presence, cognitive load, and self-reported affective measures (e.g., usefulness and comfort) [15, 24, 25]. The present study is the first that combines information recall and affective measures with information on how learners watch a video lecture with and without the instructor's face.

At first sight, the instructor's face might be considered 'extraneous', as all lecture-relevant information is encoded on the slides and in the narration. As a result, the additional extraneous processing could hinder cognitive processing of important information and ultimately hinder learning. A more positive view on the face is put forward by Clark and Mayer [6] who emphasize the effectiveness of social cues from the instructor, because they trigger social responses in the learner [32] and encourage deeper engagement with the lecture content. Wang et al. [39] report higher learning outcomes as a result of learners responding with politeness to a pedagogical agent, because they treat it as a social actor. Moreover, learners who worked with pedagogical agents with a human voice and that exhibit more natural, human-like gestures, facial expression, and eye gaze performed better on knowledge transfer tests than learners working with a less humanoid agent [26].

Experimental evidence on the effect of including the instructor's face in lecture videos, however, does not support the predictions of this social argument. Mayer's [25] image principle, which summarizes multiple studies' insignificant findings for learning outcomes (e.g. [30]), states that adding a picture or video of the instructor to multimedia instruction does not necessarily support learning. The image principle has also been confirmed in more recent studies. Homer, Plass, and Blake [15] found no significant difference in recall and transfer knowledge as a result of adding a small video of the speaker to a video of slides from a conference talk with narration. Nevertheless, learners who saw the speaker's face did not report a greater sense of social presence than those who did not see the speaker, which might suggest that the social cue was too weak to induce positive social responses in learners. In light of the conflicting views on the effect of the instructor's face on learning outcomes, we pose the following research question:
RQ1: Are recall scores higher, lower, or equal if the instructor's face is present in the lecture video than when it is absent?

Beyond learning outcomes, there is also competing empirical evidence on learners' affective response to the instructor's face in video lectures. Consistent with predictions from the "media equation" [32], greater perceived social presence in online learning environments has repeatedly been associated with increased learner satisfaction and perceived learning (see [9] for a review). However, in a recent investigation into affective responses to the instructor's face, learners with low technological efficacy reported lower perceived learning, social presence, and video usefulness when the face was present [24]. Moreover, Homer et al. [15] report higher levels of cognitive load for learners who saw the video of the speaker; too high cognitive load is bound to damage the learning experience. Given the conflicting evidence on learner's affective response to the face, we pose the following research question:
RQ2: Do learners prefer audiovisual instruction with or without the instructor's face? How do learners rate the experience with and without the instructor's image on a set of descriptive adjectives?

In a large literature on individual differences in learning, preferences for the modality of information presentation (written, spoken, visual aids, etc.) have been studied extensively. While individuals may choose representations that align with their preferences, the literature is mixed on whether or not im-

provement in actual learning occurs [10]. For instance, when a foreign-language story was supplemented with visual aids (e.g., relevant pictures), students with a visual preference understood it better, while those with a verbal preference understood it better with a written translation of the text [31]. Although Homer et al. [15] found no effect of information preference on learning outcomes, they did find the presence of the speaker's face to affect viewers' cognitive load. Specifically, those who preferred visual information reported higher cognitive load without the speaker's video, while those who preferred verbal information experienced higher load with the video. A higher level of cognitive load indicates additional cognitive processing that could either support learning (germane cognitive load) or hinder learning (extraneous cognitive load) [36]. Based on this evidence for individual differences in preferences for information presentation, we formulate the following hypothesis:
H1: Preferences for information presentation moderates the effect of the presence of the face on recall ability.

Visual Attention and Faces

Eye-tracking generates a wealth of information but it can be challenging to identify what information is processed and retained based on people's gaze. The eye-mind hypothesis [18] suggests that there exists a link between human gaze and attention, positing that people process the information that they visually attend to.

Historically, the transfer of knowledge among humans has been mediated primarily through face-to-face communication. Preferential looking studies have confirmed people's innate tendency to attend to faces over, for example, scrambled faces or blank stimuli [12]. The human attraction to faces has been shown to already develop in infants who attend favorably to faces and face-like configurations [17]. From early on, people are attracted to stimuli that promote social interaction and communication [11]. Consequently, we would expect showing the instructor's face in video lectures to have a profound impact on learners' allocation of attention. We therefore pose the following descriptive question: What proportion of time do learners spend looking at the face when it is present? And for how long do they dwell on the face and the slides?

Eye-tracking research on multimedia learning is only in its beginnings, but strongly encouraged by previous work to gain insights into what learners attend to, for how long, and in which order [37]. In a line of eye-tracking research on the spatial contiguity principle, which asserts that placing words near corresponding graphics promotes learning, transitions between words and graphics were interpreted as evidence for integrative cognitive processing, which occurs when information from the visual and auditory channels in working memory are integrated [16, 34, 14]. Schmidt-Weigand et al. [34] found that learners transition around 0.22 times per second between a graphic and corresponding written text in an animation on lightning formation. Similarly, the instructor's face competes for visual attention with content presented on the lecture slides, which induces split visual attention. Although the text shown on the slides does not describe the face, the instructor who is represented by the face tends to refer to information on the slides in speech and gesture. This prompts the learner to engage in similar eye movements to integrate information from the two sources, though it is unclear how this behavior compares to the spatial contiguity case. Thus, we pose the following descriptive question: How frequently do learners transition between fixating on the face and the slide content when the face is present?

Finally, in the case of split visual attention, where learners transition between competing visual stimuli, the tension, and thus the transition rate, that develops between the stimuli is likely higher in learners who prefer learning from visual than verbal information. Accordingly, we hypothesize:
H2: The transition rate is higher for learners who prefer visual than verbal information.

METHODS

Participants

Undergraduate and graduate students (n=22; 11 female; aged 18 to 24) were recruited from the participant pool of a major U.S. university. It was ensured that none of the participants were knowledgeable on the topic of the video lecture. Participants were awarded 1 unit of course credit upon completion of the study.

Experimental Design

This study used a 2 (face, no face) x 7 (repetitions) repeated-measures design. Participants were randomly assigned to watch a video lecture in which a video of the instructor is either present or absent in 3 or 4 of the 7 video segments. This yielded 4 segments in which the face was present for a random half of the participants but absent for the other half, and 3 segments for which it was reversed. To estimate the average causal effect of the instructor's face on information recall ability, we compute the difference in recall test scores between participants who watched lecture segments with the face and those who watched them without.

Materials

Stimulus

The stimulus was presented as a video with audio. The video starts with a 30 second resting period (black screen with white text "Resting Period") followed by 14 minutes 18 seconds of continuous instruction on a topic in organizational Sociology by Professor Dan McFarland. In the instruction period the instructor's face alternates between being present and absent approximately every 2 minutes (coinciding with slide changes), yielding a total of seven segments (four with face in one order, three with face in the other order). When the face was present, participants viewed a lecture video with a picture-in-picture (PiP) video of the instructor's face in the lower right corner. When it was absent, there was no PiP of the instructor's face in the lecture video, only lecture slides.

Eye tracker

Eye position was measured in x-y coordinates of the display monitor using the SensoMotoric Instruments (SMI) iView X RED tracker. The device was mounted to the bottom of the computer monitor on which the lecture video was displayed.

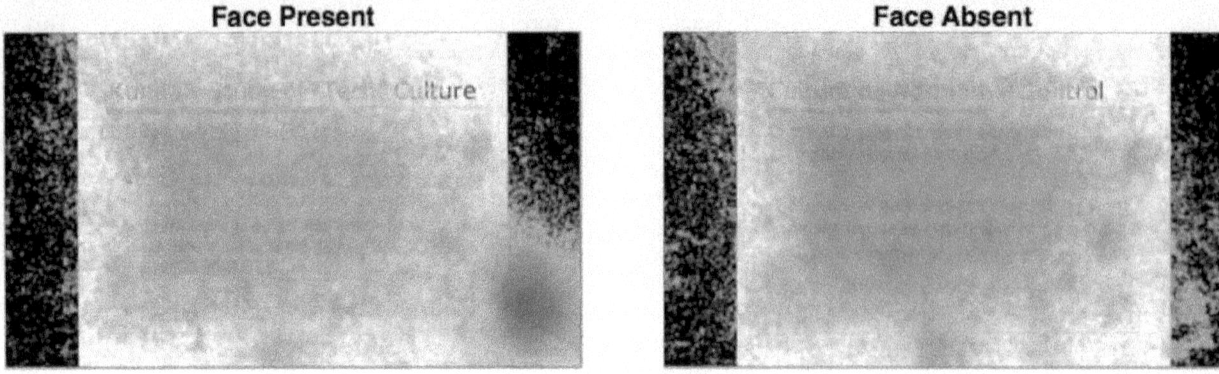

Figure 2. Heatmap of visual attention aggregated for all segments where the face was present or absent with exemplary screenshot in the background.

It operates at a distance of 60 - 80cm and has a high accuracy of 0.4 degrees. Its contact-free setup allows for free head movement of 40cm x 20cm at 70cm distance.

Questionnaires

The pre-stimulus questionnaire contained questions on gender, age, amount of experience with video lectures, prior subject knowledge, and preference for information presentation in educational contexts (two sentence-completion items from the index of learning styles questionnaire [35]: "I prefer to get new information in i. pictures, diagrams, graphs, or maps, ii. written directions"; "I like teachers who i. put a lot of diagrams on the board, ii. spend a lot of time explaining.").

The post-stimulus questionnaire contained questions on participants' affective response to lecture segments with and without the instructor's face. Participants were asked to rate what parts of the lecture video they liked better: the parts where the instructor's face was present or absent on a 10-point bipolar scale. Participants also rated how well each of a list of adjectives describes their lecture experience when the face was present and separately for when the face was absent. Adjectives included 'helpful', 'useful', 'frustrating', 'annoying', 'confusing' and were rated on a 10-point bipolar scale from "describes very poorly" to "describes very well".

Knowledge Recall Tests

Two tests were administered to measure participants' ability to recall information from the lecture. The short-term recall test was administered following the post-stimulus questionnaire about three minutes after watching the lecture. A medium-term recall test was administered five days after watching the lecture. Both recall tests contained the same 19 questions presented in random order, consisting of seven multiple choice (MC) and twelve select-all-that-apply items. In order to reduce variance from guessing, participants were instructed to select the "I don't know" (IDK) answer option if they did not know the correct answer.

Test scores were computed by awarding one point for each correct MC answer and one point for each correctly selected or unselected choice option in select-all-that-apply questions, zero otherwise. Questions that were answered IDK also received zero points. All scores were normalized by the total number of possible points.

Procedure

After granting consent, the experimenter escorted the participant to the eye-tracking room, which contained a chair facing a large computer monitor. The participant completed the pre-test on a laptop in the absence of the experimenter. The experimenter returned to remove the laptop and instructed the participant to pay attention to the lecture as there would be a short quiz on the material afterwards. The experimenter then turned off the lights in the room, exited, and checked the participant's eye position in the experimenter room. The participant was instructed via radio to alter the chair position until their eye level was centered to the monitor. Before the video stimulus started, participants were asked to follow a dot on the screen with their eyes for calibration. Calibration was repeated until satisfactory accuracy levels were achieved.

The participant watched the stimulus without pauses and was not allowed to take notes. Once the lecture was over, the experimenter turned on the lights and handed the participant a laptop to complete the post-test. After completion, the participant was asked to guess the purpose of the study and was then debriefed on the experiment. Most participants thought the study was conducted to inform video lecture design and mentioned the instructor's face. Five days later, the participant received an email with a link to the medium-term recall test to complete on the same day.

RESULTS

Affective Response

All participants' ratings of which video segments they preferred were strongly in favor of showing the face, with 15 out of 22 participants extremely preferring segments with the face. This clearly addresses the first part of research question RQ2. All eight participants who prefer learning from visual information extremely preferred the face, while responses from those who prefer learning from verbal information were more varied but still positive.

To answer the second part of RQ2, a factor analysis on participants' ratings of how well each adjective applies to their experience was performed, yielding two factors: one on educational value (helpful, useful) and the other on learning experience (frustrating, annoying, confusing). Participants indicated that the sections of the lecture video where the face was present were more helpful and useful, $t(21)$=5.58, p<0.001, Cohen's D=1.19, while the sections without the face were more frustrating, annoying, and confusing, $t(21)$=4.36, p<0.001, D=0.93. Furthermore, participants who self-reported to prefer learning from verbal rather than visual information more strongly indicated that sections with the face were more helpful and useful, $t(18)$=2.19, p=0.04, D=0.9.

Visual Attention

In this section we present insights from the eye-tracking data on how participants watched the lecture video. Figure 2 shows a heatmap of where participants looked during segments when the face was present and when it was absent. An example of a lecture slide with and without the face is shown in the background to provide context. It stands out that the face receives considerable visual attention when it is present. In fact, when the face was present, participants spent 41% of time looking at it on average (median=39%, SD=14.5%, ranging from 9% to 60%).

Visual attention is typically measured in the form of fixations, which describe durations of around 500 milliseconds that a person spends looking at a small area on the screen. At times when the instructor's face is present, visual attention is split between the face and the lecture slide content. Table 1 summarizes the average number of fixations, the average fixation length, and average median fixation length (in seconds). While the number of fixations does not differ significantly, participants dwelled for longer periods on the face than on the lecture slide content, even though the area of the face is smaller than the slide.

It is worth noting that participants' self-reported preference for information presentation was not significantly associated with their lecture watching behavior. In particular, participants who reported to prefer learning from written materials did not spend more time looking at the slide content than those who reported to prefer visual materials, $mean_{\text{visual}}$=40.6%, SD_{visual}=15.1%, $mean_{\text{written}}$=42.7%, SD_{written}=13.9%. To investigate how frequently learners transition between fixating on the face and the slide content when the face is present, we computed the transition rate (transitions per second) following Schmidt-Weigand et al. [34] (using the previous definition of a fixation as lasting at least 500 ms). We find that participants transition 0.27 times per second on average (SD=0.09, median=0.28, ranging from 0.11 to 0.49) which is considerably higher than transition rates reported by Schmidt-Weigand et al. [34]. Moreover, we hypothesized that a preference for visual versus verbal information would induce higher transition rates (H2). The data supports this hypothesis with visual-preference learners switching 1.3 times more frequently than those with a verbal preference, $t(20)$=2.0, p=0.060, D=0.88.

Table 1. Mean (and SD) of fixation count and length while the face is present.

Target	Count	Length	Median Length
Instructor Face	57.0 (27.0)	11.5s (5.4)*	2.9s (2.0)*
Lecture Slide	58.4 (23.0)	2.7s (1.4)*	1.7s (0.8)*

* significantly different at p<0.05

Information Retention

Scores on the short-term recall test were approximately normally distributed with mean 0.588 and standard deviation 0.163, ranging from 0.273 to 0.832. Scores on the medium-term recall test were left skewed (probably due to question familiarity) and distributed with $mean$=0.532, SD=0.233, ranging from 0.105 to 0.857. Average test scores were not significantly different at the 5% level between test and retest, $t(21)$=1.87, p=0.075, D=0.40, but there appears to be a downward trend in scores.

To investigate the research question of whether the instructor's face affects recall (RQ1), each answer option was coded by whether the face was present or absent when the relevant information was presented in the lecture. As participants were randomly assigned to a stimulus order, half the participants answered questions for which the face was present, while the other half answered the same questions but did not see the face. As a result, there is no issue of question-level confounding for this comparison.

Two repeated-measures MANOVAs were performed to simultaneously test short- and medium-term recall scores repeated over stimulus segments. The first MANOVA compares scores for odd segments (1, 3, 5, 7) in which participants assigned to stimulus order 1 saw the face and the rest did not. The second test is performed for even segments (2, 4, 6) in which participants assigned to order 2 saw the face and the rest did not. Both tests yielded a significant repetition effect (i.e. scores changed over segments), but no significant main effect or interaction (with the segment number) associated with the presence of the face, $F(2,19)$=0.275, p=0.76, 95% CI=[-0.193, 0.322] for odd segments, and $F(2,19)$=0.709, p=0.50, 95% CI=[-0.759, 0.211] for even segments. A power analysis was performed to compute the required effect size that could be detected with 95% confidence given 80% power, with 22 participants and four repeated measures, and a 0.2 correlation between repeated measures: a medium to large effect size f of 0.4 is detectable under these circumstances.

Figure 3 illustrates test scores for each segment with 95% confidence intervals (clipped to [0-1]) by whether the participant watched the segment with or without the instructor's face. Notably, confidence intervals between groups overlap considerably for all segments. This provides strong evidence that whether or not the face is present has no effect on recall ability, neither immediately after the lecture, nor five days later (medium-term recall). Moreover, we find no evidence in support of hypothesis H1 that learning preferences moderate the effect of the face on learning.

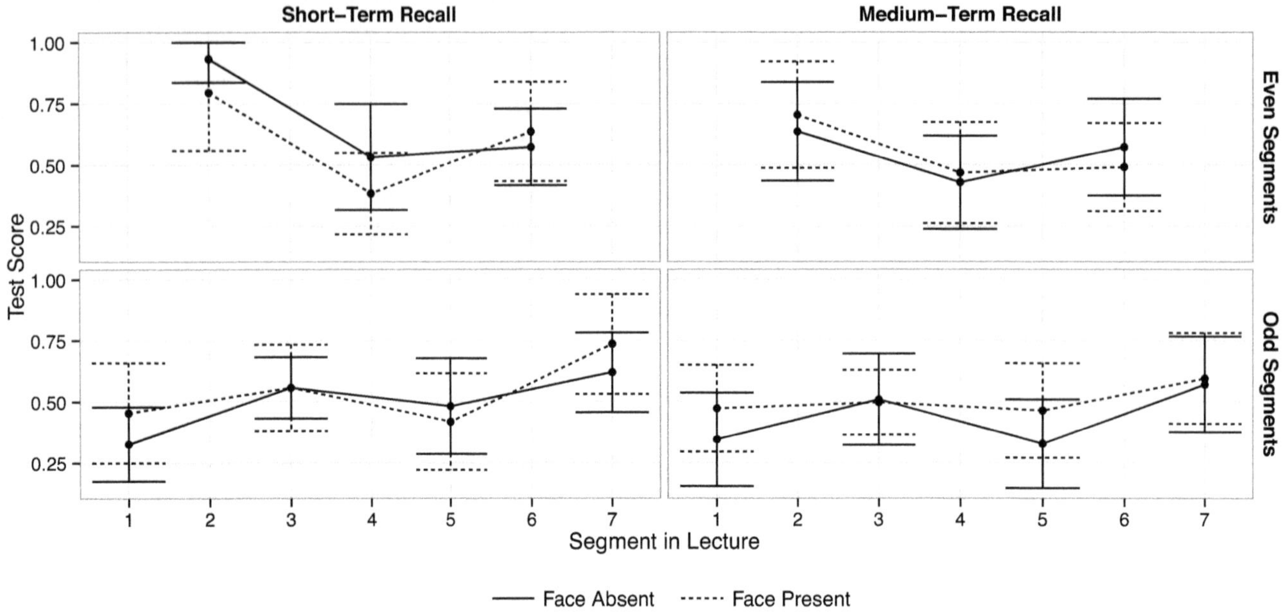

Figure 3. Average test scores with 95% confidence intervals by recall type for each segment comparing scores with the face present and absent.

DISCUSSION

The present study suggests that although learners strongly prefer video instruction with the instructor's face and their watching behavior is profoundly changed by including the face, they do not perform significantly better or worse on knowledge recall tests compared to without the face. This finding simultaneously reflects the established null results for learning outcomes as summarized in the image principle [25] as well as established positive affective responses to social cues in learning environments [9]. This positive affective response to the face is likely to boost learner motivation, which positively affects the amount of time learners are prepared to devote to learning [5]. Beyond learning and affect, this investigation is the first to uncover how the presence of the face changes learners' viewing behavior: on average, learners spent 41% of time looking at the face when it was present and transitioned between looking at the face and slides every 3.7 seconds. Despite being a relatively coarse characterization of learners' watching behavior, it emphasizes the great impact on visual attention of including the instructor's face. These findings suggest that a more fine-grained analysis of individual learners' watching patterns combined with detailed learning assessments could provide very rich insights into how the instructor's face might aid or hinder learning.

The comparison of individual differences in learning preference (learning from visual versus verbal information) produced two insights. First, seeing the face was rated as more useful by those who prefer learning from verbal information, which is not surprising, as although the face is visual (an image), it conveys non-verbal information which supports the processing of verbal information, thus alleviating the amount of cognitive load. According to this view, the face is largely processed in the verbal channel, because it shows the instructor speaking, which encourages lipreading and provides other non-verbal information. Second, as hypothesized, learners who prefer learning from visual information transitioned more frequently (by a factor of 1.3) between the face and slides than those with a verbal preference. The transition rate can be a measure of the amount of integrative processing learners engage in, though a high transition rate could also signify difficulties integrating the information [14]. Learners probably switch between the face and the slides to compare the instructor's narration to what is illustrated or written on the slides.

Our findings speak in favor of presenting the instructor's face in video instruction from a learner affect perspective, but are subject to certain limitations. Our study participants–undergraduate and graduate students–represent an appropriate sample for a study on lecture videos in a brick-and-mortar university setting, but are less representative of the population of lifelong learners and corporate trainees who rely heavily on video instruction. Moreover, the study was conducted in a highly controlled environment, which might have induced demand characteristics that affected participants' performance and watching behavior. Specifically, participants were told they would be tested on the material in the lecture video, which may have led to increased apprehension and desire to be a 'good participant'. Participants were told that their eye movements would be recorded, which may have induced unnatural lecture-watching behavior. Mayer and Moreno [28] suggest that if both visual and auditory channels are overloaded, segmenting (adding breaks) may reduce cognitive load. In our study, the lecture video was shown without the opportunity to pause, rewind, or take notes, which might have induced higher levels of cognitive load than would have been experienced without such constraints. Although an authentic video lecture from a MOOC was employed as a stimulus in this study, the generalizability of our findings is constrained by significant variation in video length and other attributes of audiovisual instruction between online courses.

Our study observed a specific type of interaction with video instruction, namely one where learners attentively follow the lecture content because they expect to be tested afterwards but are not taking lecture notes. Historically, this type of engagement has been very common, but online learning opportunities, such as MOOCs, have created space for less performance-oriented types of engagement, for example auditing or exploring a course [19]. A majority of MOOC learners do not take the course with the intention of performing well on tests, which we might expect to be reflected in a less conscious effort to remember lecture content, more frequent pausing, and casual note-taking, if any. The variety in how learners interact with audiovisual instruction poses a challenge for the design of video instruction to facilitate personalized learning experiences.

Future work could attempt to distinguish between patterns of lecture watching and how instructional design affects learners differentially depending on their objectives. This line of research could shed light onto how video instruction can be customized to learning objectives. The present study employed knowledge tests for short- and medium-term recall memory as well as a measure of affect toward the lecture experience. Future research should use measures that go beyond information recall and assess deep understanding and conceptual knowledge in combination with eye-tracking measures to determine how including the instructor's face might aid or hinder learning. Finally, a longitudinal field experiment in which learners' interactions with video instruction and test performance is observed over time for thousands of learners in a MOOC could provide valuable insights on the effects of the instructor's face and other design elements in video instruction.

CONCLUSION

The unique contribution of this paper is to combine eye-tracking with affective and information recall measures to inform instructional design decisions by providing empirical evidence for the effects of a widely used but understudied design element: the instructor's face in video instruction. Our findings plausibly generalize to a group of potential learners within the usual constraints of the instructor's lecture style and the lecture topic presented in the video stimulus. A missing piece in the cost-benefit analysis for the instructional design decision on the instructor's face in video lectures is the financial and opportunity cost of filming and editing it. While further research into the long-term effects of including the instructor's face under more realistic circumstances are needed, this investigation could only uncover an affective benefit of the face.

Many institutions employ the picture-in-picture instructional format in their video lectures using expensive recording equipment and editing software [3]. Moreover, training instructors and teaching staff on its usage, as well as allocating time for editing, is a time-consuming addition to the course production process. For instance, the University of Pennsylvania estimates production costs for an online course at around $50,000, with videography as its top expense [23]. Considering that adding the instructor's face to lecture slides has no apparent effect on recall ability, further research into its effect on learning beyond recall is required to evaluate whether course producers should incur the cost of adding the face.

ACKNOWLEDGMENTS

We are grateful to Stanford's Office of the Vice Provost for Online Learning for supporting this research and Dan McFarland for allowing us to use his lecture video as our experimental stimulus. We would also like to thank Dean Eckles, Scott Klemmer, Clifford Nass, Andreas Paepcke, Candace Thille, and our CHI review committee for their helpful feedback.

REFERENCES

1. Allen, I. E., and Seaman, J. *Changing Course: Ten Years of Tracking Online Education in the United States.* ERIC, 2013.

2. Baddeley, A. Working memory. *Science 255*, 5044 (1992), 556–559.

3. Bixhorn, A. How moocs are evolving with video technology. *eCampus News* (September 2013).

4. Borup, J., West, R. E., and Graham, C. R. Improving online social presence through asynchronous video. *The Internet and Higher Education 15*, 3 (2012), 195–203.

5. Bransford, J. D., Brown, A. L., Cocking, R. R., et al. *How people learn.* National Academy Press Washington, DC, 2000.

6. Clark, R. C., and Mayer, R. E. *E-learning and the science of instruction: Proven guidelines for consumers and designers of multimedia learning*. Wiley. com, 2011.

7. Clark, R. E. Reconsidering research on learning from media. *Review of educational research 53*, 4 (1983), 445–459.

8. Clark, R. E. Media will never influence learning. *Educational technology research and development 42*, 2 (1994), 21–29.

9. Cui, G., Lockee, B., and Meng, C. Building modern online social presence: A review of social presence theory and its instructional design implications for future trends. *Education and Information Technologies* (2012), 1–25.

10. Dunn, R. S., and Dunn, K. J. *Teaching secondary students through their individual learning styles: Practical approaches for grades 7-12*. Allyn & Bacon, 1993.

11. Farroni, T., Johnson, M. H., Menon, E., Zulian, L., Faraguna, D., and Csibra, G. Newborns' preference for

face-relevant stimuli: Effects of contrast polarity. *Proceedings of the National Academy of Sciences of the United States of America 102*, 47 (2005), 17245–17250.

12. Goren, C. C., Sarty, M., and Wu, P. Y. Visual following and pattern discrimination of face-like stimuli by newborn infants. *Pediatrics 56*, 4 (1975), 544–549.
13. Hartman, F. R. Single and multiple channel communication: A review of research and a proposed model. *Audiovisual communication review 9*, 6 (1961), 235–262.
14. Holsanova, J., Holmberg, N., and Holmqvist, K. Reading information graphics: The role of spatial contiguity and dual attentional guidance. *Applied Cognitive Psychology 23*, 9 (2009), 1215–1226.
15. Homer, B. D., Plass, J. L., and Blake, L. The effects of video on cognitive load and social presence in multimedia-learning. *Computers in Human Behavior 24*, 3 (2008), 786–797.
16. Johnson, C. I., and Mayer, R. E. An eye movement analysis of the spatial contiguity effect in multimedia learning. *Journal of Experimental Psychology: Applied 18*, 2 (2012), 178.
17. Johnson, M. H., Dziurawiec, S., Ellis, H., and Morton, J. Newborns' preferential tracking of face-like stimuli and its subsequent decline. *Cognition 40*, 1 (1991), 1–19.
18. Just, M. A., and Carpenter, P. A. A theory of reading: From eye fixations to comprehension. *Psychological review 87* (1980), 329–354.
19. Kizilcec, R. F., Piech, C., and Schneider, E. Deconstructing disengagement: analyzing learner subpopulations in massive open online courses. In *Proceedings of the Third International Conference on Learning Analytics and Knowledge*, ACM (2013), 170–179.
20. Kolowich, S. The professors who make the moocs. *Chronicle of Higher Education 59*, 28 (2013), A20–A23.
21. Kozma, R. B. Learning with media. *Review of educational research 61*, 2 (1991), 179–211.
22. Kozma, R. B. Will media influence learning? reframing the debate. *Educational technology research and development 42*, 2 (1994), 7–19.
23. Lewin, T. Students rush to web classes, but profits may be much later. *The New York Times 6* (January 2013).
24. Lyons, A., Reysen, S., and Pierce, L. Video lecture format, student technological efficacy, and social presence in online courses. *Computers in Human Behavior 28*, 1 (2012), 181–186.
25. Mayer, R. E. Principles of multimedia learning based on social cues: Personalization, voice, and image principles. In *The Cambridge handbook of multimedia learning*, R. E. Mayer, Ed. Cambridge University Press, New York, NY, 2005, 201–212.
26. Mayer, R. E., and DaPra, C. S. An embodiment effect in computer-based learning with animated pedagogical agents. *Journal of Experimental Psychology: Applied 18*, 3 (2012), 239.
27. Mayer, R. E., and Moreno, R. A split-attention effect in multimedia learning: Evidence for dual processing systems in working memory. *Journal of educational psychology 90*, 2 (1998), 312.
28. Mayer, R. E., and Moreno, R. Nine ways to reduce cognitive load in multimedia learning. *Educational psychologist 38*, 1 (2003), 43–52.
29. Moore, M. G. Independent study. *Redefining the discipline of adult education 5* (1980), 16–31.
30. Moreno, R., Mayer, R. E., Spires, H. A., and Lester, J. C. The case for social agency in computer-based teaching: Do students learn more deeply when they interact with animated pedagogical agents? *Cognition and Instruction 19*, 2 (2001), 177–213.
31. Plass, J. L., Chun, D. M., Mayer, R. E., and Leutner, D. Supporting visual and verbal learning preferences in a second-language multimedia learning environment. *Journal of educational psychology 90*, 1 (1998), 25.
32. Reeves, B., and Nass, C. *How people treat computers, television, and new media like real people and places*. CSLI Publications and Cambridge university press, 1996.
33. Rosengrant, D., Hearrington, D., Alvarado, K., and Keeble, D. Following student gaze patterns in physical science lectures. In *AIP Conference Proceedings*, vol. 1413 (2012), 323.
34. Schmidt-Weigand, F., Kohnert, A., and Glowalla, U. A closer look at split visual attention in system-and self-paced instruction in multimedia learning. *Learning and Instruction 20*, 2 (2010), 100–110.
35. Soloman, B. A., and Felder, R. M. Index of learning styles. `http://www2.ncsu.edu/unity/lockers/users/f/felder/public/ILSdir/ILS-a.htm` (2004).
36. Sweller, J. Cognitive load theory, learning difficulty, and instructional design. *Learning and instruction 4*, 4 (1994), 295–312.
37. van Gog, T., and Scheiter, K. Eye tracking as a tool to study and enhance multimedia learning. *Learning and Instruction 20*, 2 (2010), 95–99.
38. Waldrop, M. M., and magazine, N. *Massive Open Online Courses, aka MOOCs, Transform Higher Education and Science*, March 2013.
39. Wang, N., Johnson, W. L., Mayer, R. E., Rizzo, P., Shaw, E., and Collins, H. The politeness effect: Pedagogical agents and learning outcomes. *International Journal of Human-Computer Studies 66*, 2 (2008), 98–112.

Supporting Learners in Collecting and Exploring Data from Immersive Simulations in Collective Inquiry

Michelle Lui[1], Alex Kuhn[2], Alisa Acosta[1], Chris Quintana[2], James D. Slotta[1]

OISE / University of Toronto
252 Bloor Street West,
Toronto, Ontario M5S 1V6 Canada
{michelle.lui, alisa.acosta}@utoronto.ca,
jslotta@oise.utoronto.ca

School of Education
University of Michigan
610 East University
Ann Arbor, MI 48109 USA
{kuhnalex, quintana}@umich.edu

ABSTRACT
Digitally augmented physical spaces (e.g., smart classrooms) offer opportunities to engage students in novel and potentially transformative learning experiences. This paper presents an immersive rainforest simulation and collective inquiry activity where students collect observational data from the environment and explore their peers' data through large visualization displays and personal mobile devices. Two iterations of the design were tested, which resulted in higher quality student explanations constructed. Images were found to be an important source of evidence for the explanations, more so than text-only evidence. We also found that patterns of collective ideas influenced student performance, and that visualizations, as ambient or plenary displays, supported both teacher and students in reviewing patterns of collected data.

Author Keywords
Digitally augmented physical spaces; smart classroom; science inquiry; visualizations; large displays; multi-device environments; mobile computing

ACM Classification Keywords
H.5.2 [Information Interfaces and Presentation]: User Interfaces - Interaction styles; K.3.1 [Computer Uses in Education].

INTRODUCTION
The design and research of technology-enhanced environments can offer new opportunities for learning and instruction for K-12 science. The primary goals of these environments are to help students develop deep understanding of complicated concepts while also attaining scientific reasoning, critical thinking skills, and collaboration and communication skills [19]. In scientific inquiry, an established approach advocated by educational research, students typically investigate a phenomenon and draw conclusions about it. Instead of mastering disconnected facts, this approach places a heavy emphasis on posing questions, gathering and analyzing data, and constructing evidence-based arguments (e.g., [4, 10, 12]). However, in traditional inquiry-based learning, students typically work autonomously as individuals, pairs or, at most, in small groups. Current means of supporting inquiry instruction with technology also tend to isolate students, often confining them to work together on single machines [29].

In recent years, researchers have begun to reconsider the role of the physical learning environment and to experiment with learning activities in digitally augmented physical spaces (i.e., mixed-reality environments). These spaces offer new ways of engaging students with science concepts that have traditionally been taught or addressed through more passive forms of instruction. By coupling digital content with more familiar forms of physical engagement, students are prompted into active learning, which encourages students to think, reflect, and drive their own understanding [22]. Early efforts of digitally augmented physical learning spaces have shown positive outcomes in facilitating creativity and reflection (e.g., [1, 6, 25]). It has been suggested that coupling digital augmentation with physical spaces promotes active learning by increasing the students' awareness of the activities and information presented, provides a richer experience by bridging various perspectives between the physical and digital worlds, and engages students through a juxtaposition of familiar actions with unexpected digitally augmented results [22].

This paper explores a new form of digitally mediated "smart classroom," [30] where students are supported with personal learning devices that guide their exploration of an immersive simulation (Figure 1). The environment is responsive to student observations (recorded on mobile devices), with real-time emergent visualizations that serve to capture and aggregate student observations for knowledge building and discourse.

Our research is concerned with the design of inquiry activities that complement and define such immersive environments, where students are engaged as a whole class, jointly negotiating problems and working towards a common goal. In this form of inquiry-based learning, called

CHI 2014, April 26 - May 01, 2014, Toronto, ON, Canada.

ACM 978-1-4503-2473-1/14/04...$15.00.
http://dx.doi.org/10.1145/2556288.2557162

Figure 1. Students engaging in EvoRoom inquiry activity.

"collective inquiry," the entire classroom of students is treated as the focus of interaction design. Collaborative inquiry—a related form of inquiry-based learning—in contrast, tends to focus on interactions between pairs or small groups of students (e.g., [29, 26]). In collective inquiry, students are encouraged to think deeply about materials and develop their own understandings, but with an emphasis on collective knowledge or progress over individual contributions. Students are responsible for generating and building upon each other's ideas, ultimately developing and depending upon their own community knowledge base [21, 28]. Our motivations for using digitally augmented physical spaces for advancing a collective epistemology is to leverage more natural forms of social interactions afforded by such spaces, to enhance collaboration and authenticity of the learning experience.

While considerable research has addressed the design of digitally augmented physical spaces, few projects have investigated rich, immersive experiences for inquiry-based learning, and none have investigated collective inquiry in digitally augmented physical spaces. This paper explores how the physical space of the room can serve to mediate students working as a knowledge community to collect data, support the visualization of the community's aggregate data, and facilitate inquiry activities, including discussions of data. Specifically, this paper considers the following research questions over two design iterations:

RQ1: How do we support learners in collecting observational data from immersive simulations in a way that promotes scientific reasoning?

RQ2: How do real-time visualizations on large shared displays support learners and teachers in assessing and discussing the aggregated observational data?

BACKGROUND

Digitally Augmented Physical Spaces for Learning

Much of the prior work on using embedded, ubiquitous computational media to support learning is based on the pioneering work of Wilensky and Resnick, who argued for the use of pervasive, non-desktop technologies that engage learners with the physical environment [35]. The concept of participatory simulations [3], where students themselves become the elements of the simulation (e.g., with the use of physical manipulatives), demonstrates this idea using role-playing activities. Colella [3] for example, gave students wearable transmitting badges, transforming them into potential virus carriers with the mission of greeting as many classmates as they could without getting "sick."

The Hunting of the Snark [25] combines the use of mobile technology with the physicality of the classroom environment. Young children (ages 6-10) investigate a virtual creature by exploring a variety of physical spaces the creature might be located (e.g., cave where it sleeps). Location tracking devices, pressure pads, and other sensor technology is used to engage pairs of children in interacting with the creature (which responds with sounds) and exploring its characteristics. The children in the study generated theories about the Snark (i.e., describing its emotional state), and were found to engage in various forms of collaboration to creatively experiment and explore ways of interacting with the Snark [23].

The Embedded Phenomena (EP) framework leverages the physicality of the classroom, carefully "mapping" a persistent scientific simulation onto the walls or floor of the room in the form of location-specific computer "portals" [16]. Students monitor and manipulate the simulation and gather evidence to solve a problem or answer a question. The use of EP was associated with greater learning gains compared to students who experienced an analogous "non-embedded" curriculum (i.e., the simulation activity was replaced with an exercise on desktop computers) in a quasi-experimental, within-teacher study [17].

Another example of digitally augmented learning spaces is that of SMALLab, where high school students studied geologic evolution by collaboratively constructing and monitoring the earth's crust, investigating uplift and erosion over time [2]. Using various input devices (e.g., glowballs, Wii remotes, wireless game pads) and a projected interface on the ground, groups of students were responsible for building, maintaining or evaluating a cycle of the geologic clock. The intervention resulted in significant achievement gains, demonstrating the promise for further research regarding face-to-face interactions in a computationally-augmented physical space, and distributed roles through a generative process that unfolds over time [2].

The examples above illustrate the potential of such innovative technologies for learning. However, there remains a need to understand how digitally augmented physical spaces can contribute to collective approaches in classroom learning. In particular, we are concerned with how to capture knowledge, as it emerges in real-time, including aggregate or summative aspects (i.e., "wisdom of the crowd") as well as discrete knowledge elements—all the while carefully balancing face-to-face interactions

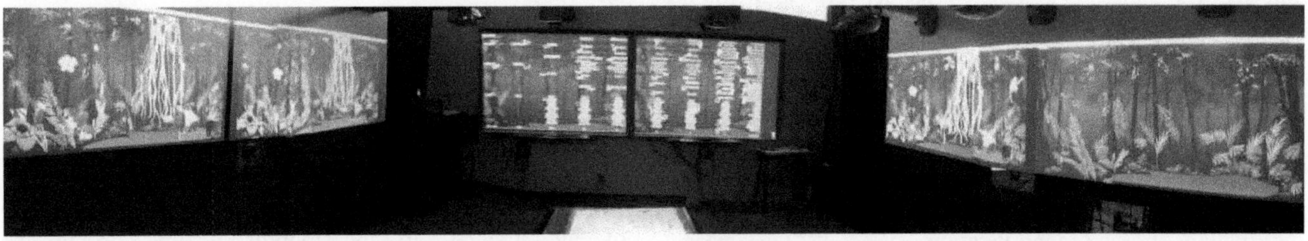

Figure 2. EvoRoom configuration. Consisting of six projected displays (three per side) and two interactive whiteboards (middle).

within inquiry activities. One important challenge involves designing interfaces that capture and represent student contributions, and making them accessible to peers.

Capturing and Visualizing Student-Collected Data

Researchers have used a variety of technology solutions to support learners in collecting and sharing their observations with peers. Several researchers have identified the need for visualizations to give users an overview of data while also supporting requests for details on demand [27]. In the Participate project, data was collected by and shared amongst students (ages 13-15). Using Google Earth and graphing software in conjunction with GPS enabled data collection equipment and mobile phones, students explored visualizations of large numerical datasets [36]. This research found that student generated data was an engaging source of discussion and inquiry in later classroom activities. Fraser's SENSE project, in which students (ages 10-14) collect environmental data in the field and share this information with their peers on returning to the classroom, found the process of viewing data from another class helped students reflect and understand new perspectives [7].

The Zydeco project [11] used a mobile app to support students in collecting data from the field and found that students were able to collect data from informal environments and have the students successfully evaluate and utilize their personal and peer-collected data to construct science explanations. Students were able to review and filter their data set by the different ways the data was annotated (title, tags, questions the data was collected under, and media types present in the data).

Interestingly, none of the projects described here employed large displays for the visualization of student data. Rather, they relied on teacher-led class discussion based on the display of aggregated data presented on individual devices.

The use of physically shared displays for Computer-Supported Cooperative Work (CSCW) has been advanced in the development of single display groupware (SDG) [31, 33]. SDG emphasizes face-to-face interactions, enabling multiple co-located users to collaborate via a single shared display using multiple (and simultaneous) input devices. Early applications in educational settings, such as KidPad [5] and Give and Take [9] investigated how small groups of children could work together creating stories and solving puzzles respectively. More recent efforts focus on supporting larger groups of children (e.g., [18] who engaged up to 32 students), or groups of children playing collaborative learning video games [8].

With the proliferation of personal mobile devices, a natural extension of the design solution to support co-located collaboration are multi-device environments (MDEs), where multiple personal and shared devices are connected with specialized underlying software architecture [34]. Large shared displays from such environments have been shown to improve collaboration by promoting group awareness and communication processes [34], suggesting possible applications for collective inquiry. This paper investigates the use of large shared displays to advance collective knowledge work.

EVOROOM

In order to understand how digitally augmented physical spaces can contribute to collective approaches in classroom learning, our research group at the University of Toronto developed a "smart classroom" research environment at a partner secondary school. Previous reports described the smart classroom technology framework [28], and learning outcomes in its application in mathematics and physics activities [14, 32].

EvoRoom represents the first instantiation of immersive simulations designed for the smart classroom environment. Students are situated in the rainforest of Borneo through two sets of large projected displays (achieved by stitching together three displays) that students examine during collective inquiry activities designed in parallel with the immersive simulations (Figure 2). Two interactive whiteboards are located at the front of the room. The simulation files are networked and controlled with a custom application that allows the teacher to manage the time spent in each portion of the activity, controlling the pedagogical flow within the room.

EvoRoom was co-designed [20] with a teacher to fit seamlessly within a broader secondary school biology curriculum, in topics of evolution and biodiversity. Running for 10 to 12-weeks, the integrated curriculum includes in-class activities, homework, a field trip to the zoo, and two collective inquiry activities with immersive simulations.

To date, a pilot study and two design iterations of EvoRoom have been developed and tested. During the collective inquiry activities, students take on the role of "field researchers," and work individually, in small groups, and as a whole-class to complete tasks delivered to them on their personal tablet computers. The tablets help to place students in small groups, scaffold their activities, collect observations, and give real-time updates and resources. Student observations and reflections are aggregated and displayed on the interactive whiteboards in real-time. In the first design iteration, a custom EvoRoom tablet application was developed to support the collection of student observations. In the second iteration, Zydeco [24] was used to collect and review student observations, as it offered more data collection and sharing capabilities.

The first collective inquiry activity focused on evolutionary concepts. Students gathered evidence of evolution by observing changes in life forms as the simulation advanced across two hundred million years. Findings from the pilot study and the first design iteration of this activity were previously reported. Early designs of EvoRoom were found to engage students, and curricular scaffolding in the first full implementation was tied to increased variation and complexity in student ideas about evolutionary topics [13].

The present paper focuses on the second collective inquiry activity, on the topic of biodiversity. Prior to the activity, students wrote predictions about how changing an environmental factor (e.g., tsunami, earthquake, low rainfall) for a single season could change the biodiversity in Borneo over a five-year time span. In the immersive environment, students were presented with four different versions of the Borneo rainforest ecosystem. The activity challenged them to explore the differences between these four rainforests and to locate the rainforest that resulted from the variable they explored in their predictions, using the following digitally mediated interactions:

1. Engaging with immersive simulation: Students go up to the walls and find evidence about changes to the ecosystem that might have taken place;
2. Engaging with mobile devices: Students make observations and record their findings using tablet computers. Students also work in small groups, with interactions scaffolded by their tablets;
3. Engaging with real-time emergent visualizations: Student and teacher interactions form around large emergent displays of student observations.

We have previously described early designs of EvoRoom [13], including how the immersive simulation and collective inquiry activities impact student ideas about evolutionary concepts. Here, we report on a second iteration of the collective inquiry activity on biodiversity. This work builds on previous reports on student learning by: 1) examining how student interactions with personal devices and large emergent displays are associated with learning outcomes, and 2) their implications on how specific design features might impact the learning experience.

METHOD

Our core design team, consisting of two researchers and a high school biology teacher collaborated using a co-design methodology to create the simulation, inquiry activity and interactive materials [20]. Our co-design partnership began a year prior to the first enactment. Meeting approximately once per week during the academic school year, we considered important design elements and outlined our overall strategy. In the months leading up to the enactments, design meetings widened to include two technology developers, and (in the second trial) three additional researchers.

Participants included students (ages 14-16) from four class sections of Grade 11 Biology taught by our co-design teacher. The first iteration included 45 students. The second trial occurred in the following academic year, included 54 students. All of the participants (99 students) entered the study with no prior experience of the immersive simulation.

In both trials, video and audio recordings served to capture patterns of interactions within the room. All student artifacts were collected for analysis. Two members of the research team coded students' observation notes, with discrete "observations" serving as a unit of analysis. The observations were judged for whether they could potentially be useful to the investigation or not [11]. An example of a useful observation is: *"The jambu tree, rafflesia, and ginger are all missing."* An example of a scientifically unproductive observation is: *"Scorched earth indicative of magic."* The quality of students' final explanations were analyzed using the Claim-Evidence-Reasoning (CER) grading rubric [15], which was modified slightly to fit the context (Table 1).

TRIAL 1 DESCRIPTION

Prior to visiting EvoRoom, students worked in groups of two or three to complete their predictions assignment on

Claim	Evidence	Reasoning
0: Nothing/not a claim	0: No evidence	0: Reasoning absent, non-sensible, or fails to connect evidence to claim.
1: Claim is incomplete or not related to the question	1: Does not provide relevant evidence	1: Provides reasoning that links the claim and the evidence by repeating the evidence
2: Makes a complete claim related to the question	2: One relevant evidence	2: Explains why evidence supports the claim, but does not address all aspects of

Table 1. Modified Claim-Evidence-Reasoning rubric.

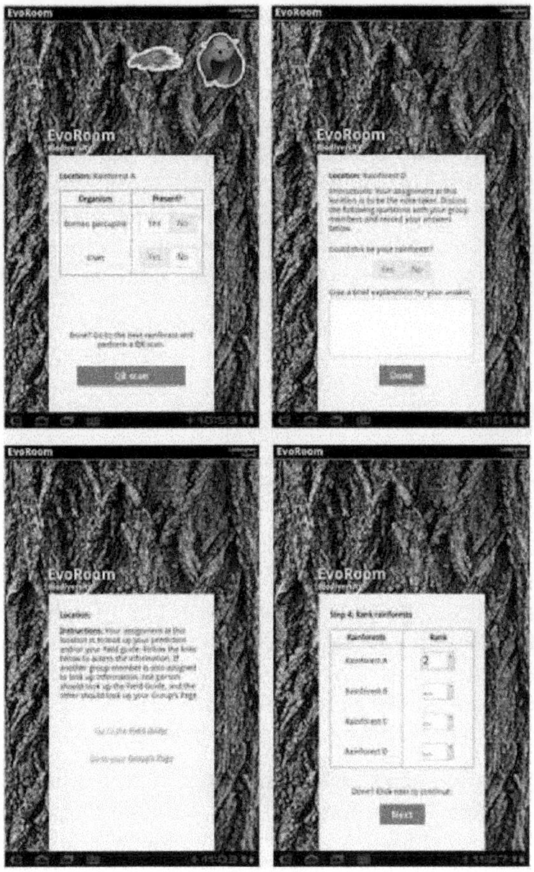

Figure 3. Custom tablet interface from trial 1.

their class website. Each group also commented on at least two predictions made by other groups.

Four sessions (each with different students) were run, with 10 to 12 students split into four groups. Each student was provided a tablet computer with a custom designed application that supported navigation through the activity while scaffolding students to work together and to collect data throughout the session (Figure 3).

The activity was designed for a 75-minute class period, including several data collection steps where students examined the organisms in each of the four rainforest stations, eliminating rainforest stations that they felt did not result from their factor, and discussing their findings with other groups. Using the tablets, students contributed written explanations to simple questions (e.g., *"Could this be your rainforest?"*). All of the groups' decisions and notes were displayed on the interactive whiteboard at the front of the room. Once data collection was complete, students ranked the four rainforest stations according to which was most likely caused by their assigned factor. Students explained their group's choice by answering follow-up questions (e.g., *"What is your strategy in ranking the rainforests? Describe your process"*). The aggregated results were shown on the interactive whiteboards, and were also used by the teacher in their classroom the following day, for a final discussion.

TRIAL 1 RESULTS

Scaffolded data collection

To evaluate how learners collected observational data from immersive simulations, we examined the characteristics of their initial hypotheses, which were written about each rainforest station as a group. A total of 146 discrete observations were coded from 65 notes, with each group contributing an average of 9.1 observations (SD=2.2). Inter-rater reliability (IRR) was performed on 20% of data, where 92.3% agreement (Kappa=0.90, $p<0.001$) was achieved. 145 (99%) of the observations were coded as being potentially useful indicating that students tended to be engaged in the task.

Overall 6 out of the 16 total groups correctly identified the rainforest stations that were associated with their assigned environmental factor. In one session, all four groups correctly identified their climatic scenario. Generally, students who made the correct match used a specific strategy, such as process of elimination or identifying a set of characteristics that matched their predictions. The explanations for the groups' final choices were evaluated, with average scores of 6.0 of 8 (SD=1.4). IRR was performed on 20% of data, where 100% agreement was achieved. A one-way ANOVA was conducted to evaluate the relationship between the groups' CER scores and their identification accuracy, which found that students who correctly identified rainforest stations received significantly higher CER scores than groups who incorrectly identified the rainforest stations, $F(1, 14)=7.30, p<0.02$.

Interactions supported by emergent visualizations

85% of students referred to the visualizations at the interactive whiteboards (Figure 4. Students also interacted with the whiteboard to obtain further details of the data being displayed, which was done by one student in three of four sessions and four students in one session. The teacher interacted with the interactive whiteboard the most, with an average of 8.3 interactions per session (SD=2.9). She reviewed and organized student work, using the displays to monitor student progress.

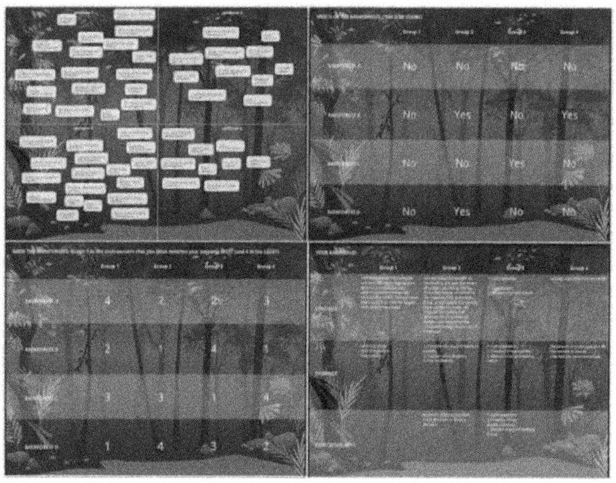

Figure 4. Emergent visualizations from trial 1.

Additionally, ad hoc discussions were observed between the teacher and students near the interactive whiteboards. When the teacher was located at the boards, students would approach, either curious about the display, or wanting to consult with teacher. They would engage in discussion, with the teacher often gesturing towards the boards and using them as an aid to answer the students' questions. When students independently walked up to the displays without the teacher's presence, their group members often joined them and engaged in their own discussion. In most such cases, the teacher then joined the group discussion.

DESIGN ITERATION

Scaffolded data collection

For the second iteration, an important goal was to encourage more thoughtful interaction with the immersive simulation. We felt that in the first trial, while we were satisfied with the number of observations contributed and the general quality of observations, we had hoped for more accurate identification of the rainforest stations. One idea we wished to explore further was taking photos of the immersive visuals, as a mode of data collection, which could potentially support students in making more intentional comparisons between the rainforest stations.

Design change 1: Allow students to collect evidence in the media of their choice (e.g., photo, video, audio note, text note) and include a "control" version of Borneo (with no environmental impact), to promote more thoughtful comparisons of the immersive simulation.

From the first trial, when we examined students' recorded explanations regarding how they chose the rainforest (i.e., strategy, supporting evidence used, additional information), we noticed that the nature of the evidence ranged from lists (e.g., *"No water. Trees losing leaves. Low flora and fauna."*), to detailed explanations for all stations observed (e.g., *"Rainforest A has too much water. Rainforest B seems hot and hazy, hotter than rainforest D, and if there was an extreme increase in temperature, so B is higher than in our preference. Rainforest C has abundant life and has a lot of biodiversity, so if there was a slight increase in temperature, the plants could possibly flourish more"*). In some of the responses, we were unable to determine the evidence underlying their explanation (e.g., *"Looking at plant life and animal life"*). This prompted us to revise the data collection design to require students to explicitly link one or more of their (or their peer's) observations within their final explanations.

Design change 2: Have students link observational data in their final explanation as evidence, and structure observations using annotations (e.g., title, tags, questions) that denote environmental factors (e.g., high rainfall) and station identification (e.g., station A) for students to sort the data.

Interactions supported by emergent visualizations

The emergent visualizations presented in the first trial were in the form of ambient displays, which students could review on their own. However, we noted that not all students reviewed the front board and thus did not consider the collective data their peers had collected.

The feedback from the teacher was that the interactive whiteboard was a useful resource for spontaneous and planned discussions. Hence, for the second trial we set aside time for the students to formally review the visualization and have a group discussion, facilitated by the teacher, to help everyone benefit from reviewing the collective work.

Design change 3: Inclusion of a teacher-facilitated data review step with emergent visualizations to support students in understanding their collective knowledge base.

Incorporating Zydeco with EvoRoom

Zydeco offered several features we hoped to incorporate in our tablet application: 1) the ability for students to collect observations in a variety of media forms (e.g., images, audio, written notes); 2) the scaffolding of data collection and analysis of observational data through the use of annotations; and 3) the ability to link existing observations to student explanations. We opted to incorporate Zydeco into the second design iteration rather than make significant changes to our existing custom application.

An extension of Zydeco to visualize student-collected data on the interactive whiteboards was designed and developed for the second trial. A trade-off from this was that separate tablets were needed to drive the interactivity of the boards (limiting access to the those handling the tablets).

TRIAL 2 DESCRIPTION

As in the first iteration, students in trial 2 were assigned an environmental factor and wrote predictions about its effects on biodiversity in Borneo. Students visited EvoRoom in cohorts of 13 to 14 students and were again split into four different groups of three or four members. Within the 75-minute class period, students used a handheld computer to collect evidence concerning which rainforest station showed the effects of their group's assigned environmental factor. The teacher facilitated a data review session that revealed students' initial ideas, which was followed by students constructing explanations about their final decision. Each group displayed their work and presented their findings. At the end of the session, the teacher revealed the correct answers (i.e., which station resulted from which environmental factor) and held a deeper discussion about environmental impacts and biodiversity.

TRIAL 2 RESULTS

Scaffolded data collection

193 data objects were collected, with an average of 12.1 pieces of data collected by each group (SD=5.6). The majority (89.1%) contained an image, with less than half of all data collected containing text notes (42.5%). Of the data collected, those observations with accompanying descriptive text (in either text note or title) or audio (either in the audio note or video entry) were judged in a similar

fashion as in trial 1, where each discrete unit of observation was counted. 190 observations were coded, with each group contributing an average of 11.9 observations (*SD*=8.3). It was interesting that three groups in the same session made fewer than five observations, tending to only take photographs of areas and verbally discuss their observations but did not record it. 97.9% of the observations were categorized as potentially useful. IRR was performed on 20% of data, where 87.2% agreement was achieved (Kappa=0.83, p<0.001).

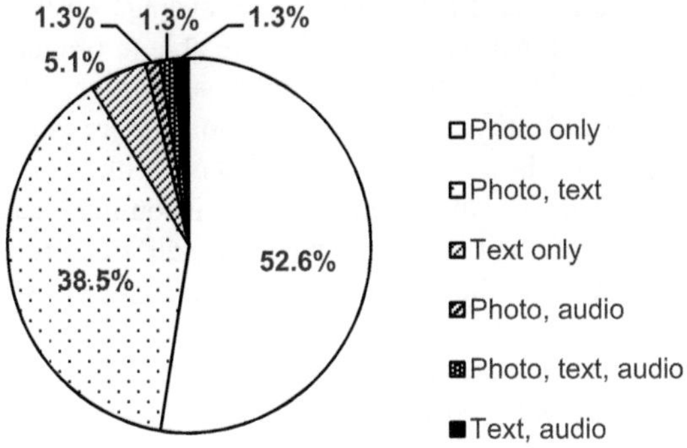

Figure 5. Composition of data objects used as evidence.

Similar to the results in the first trial, 6 out of the 16 total groups correctly identified the rainforest stations and in one of the sessions all four groups correctly identified their environmental factor. However, students' final explanations scores were higher in trial 2, averaging 7.6 of 8 (*SD*=0.6), with no significant relationship between identification accuracy and CER scores (as in trial 1). IRR was performed on 20% of data, where substantial agreement was achieved (Kappa=0.71, p<0.01). It should be noted though that in the session for which all four groups correctly identified their factors, all groups achieved perfect scores for their final explanations.

Of all the data objects that were collected, 40.4% were later used as evidence to support the explanations. Most of the of the evidence used to support claims included a photo (93.6%), compared to less than half which had a text note attached to the data object included as evidence (46.2%; Figure 5). One group mentioned that they only took photos because they had previously conducted a lot of research on the different environments and were looking for characteristics in the photos they knew would be in each environment. Another group fixated on certain traits they knew their scenario should have, and went looking for any observational evidence that exhibited those traits. For example, high rainfall would result in an environment with more water and greater biodiversity, and so they took photos of any elements of the displays with plentiful water.

Interactions supported by emergent visualizations

Only the teacher's use of the emergent visualization was analyzed in the second trial, since the teacher used a separate tablet to drive the interactivity of the boards. In each of the four sessions, the teacher used the filtering options of the emergent visualization to ensure that students were collecting evidence for all stations and tagging evidence properly (Figure 6). During the data discussion, the teacher used the visualization's filtering functionality to review the groups' work. For example, toggling the visibility of "earthquake" observations and hiding all others revealed only those associated with earthquakes. In the visualization, the observations were organized according to the rainforest stations the observations were about. In this way, the teacher was able to notice preliminary trends (e.g., *"station B and C could be low rainfall"*). The teacher also expanded the data objects to reveal detailed information (e.g., text note, annotations), reading out examples or examining larger images. After the data discussion, students accessed the collective set of data objects from their own tablets (Figure 7).

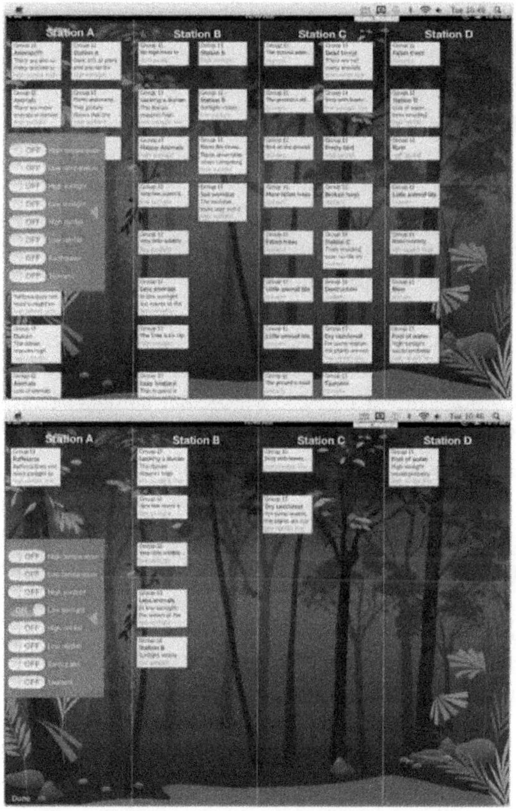

Figure 6. Emergent visualization used in trial 2.
Unfiltered (top) and filtered by "low sunlight" (bottom).

To understand how students used their session's collective information, we examined the students' final choice with the pattern of collected observational data tagged with their particular climate scenario. 13 of 16 groups (81.3%) chose a station associated with the highest number of data objects tagged with their environmental factor. In the students' final explanations, two of the three remaining groups indicated that they considered the collective data, but had reasons to believe that the more popular choice was incorrect.

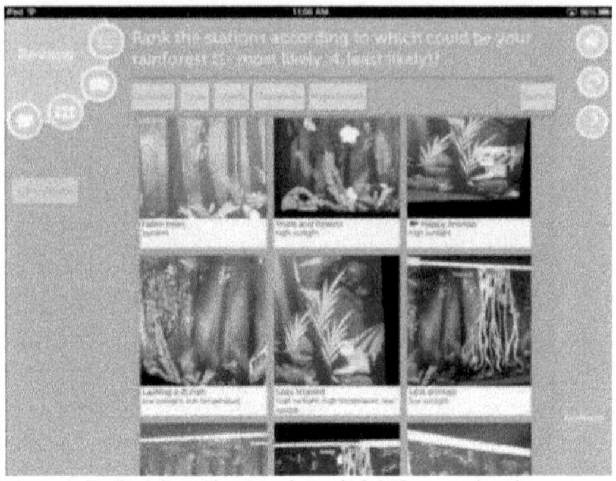

Figure 7. Tablet display in trial 2 for reviewing peer-collected observational data.

However, in these three cases, their final choices as well as the stations associated with the highest number of data objects tagged with their scenario were both incorrect. The highest number of data objects was annotated with the correct environmental factor and rainforest station in only 8 of 16 instances (50% collective accuracy).

DISCUSSION

Scaffolded Data Collection

The first design change allowed students to collect evidence in the form of photographs, video or notes. The decision was made to promote more thoughtful interactions with the immersive simulation, however the students in trials 1 and 2 achieved the same level of accuracy. There were also comparable numbers of text-based observations, recorded per group in the two trials, as well as comparable numbers of written observations that were deemed useful. However, there were a number other reasons that led us to believe that this was a positive change.

In trial 2, the majority of observations collected contained photographs. While the number of text-based observations in the two trials was comparable, there was an additional set of photographic observations in trial 2, which meant that a great deal more observations were made in the second trial. Further, a majority of trial 2's explanations (94%) relied on data objects that contain images as evidence (a form of observational data not used in trial 1), which points to its effectiveness in the immersive environment. This was somewhat surprising since we anticipated some dependence on written observations to serve as evidence, indicating that while written observations were useful to some, other students found images informative. This may be because the annotations accompanying the images supplied students with sufficient information about the observed. It could also be that the highly visual immersive simulation environment lent itself to image-based observations. By enabling access of information through different senses, we hoped to increase the awareness of students being in the immersive space, which would have provided a richer basis for reflection [22].

The CER scores of students' final explanations was another outcome that distinguished trial 1 from 2. Despite the same level of accuracy attained, the CER scores for explanations in trial 1 were lower than those in trial 2. It was also interesting that the CER scores in trial 1 corresponded with the accuracy of the students' final choice, but the same was not observed in the second trial (due to the higher average CER scores). This indicated that more students were able to produce well-reasoned claims with appropriate supportive evidence. Incorrectly identified rainforest stations were sometimes accompanied by strong explanations with appropriate evidence. This was the case if students' incoming ideas about the impact of their environment factor differed from what was presented as the correct answer. As such, the students' inability to identify rainforest scenarios only served to highlight false assumptions and possible rigid thinking, unrelated to their observational data collection. Thus, the pedagogical goal of this activity was not focused on the correct identification of rainforest stations, but rather on scientific reasoning from a collective inquiry process.

The second design change allowed students to structure observations using annotations and explicitly link data in their final explanation as evidence. For the most part, students successfully annotated the observational data. In cases where tags were not properly assigned, the teacher noticed the problematic observations in the emergent visualization and asked students to revise their notes.

In trial 1, although observational data was collected, the data were only accessible from the front boards, which were not as easy to examine. Nor did everyone review them. This led us to believe that the observations themselves were largely ignored when students constructed their explanations, although the experience of collecting the observations likely supported them in making their final choices. In trial 2, we had students spending more time reviewing the evidence they had collected through their tablets, filtering through large data sets using annotations (e.g., by searching "low sunlight") and structuring their explanations such that they had to attach existing pieces of observations to their claims. This way, we were able to see if there was any relationship between the kinds of observations that were used as evidence and their claims. As noted above, we saw an improvement in CER scores in trial 2 over trial 1 when observational data served as evidence to students' final explanations. This result may be attributed partially to both design changes—from more intentional data collection and thoughtful interaction with the immersive environment, as well as explicitly linking student observations to support their explanations.

Interactions Supported by Emergent Visualizations

In the first trial, emergent visualizations designed to show larger patterns of early ideas fostered ad hoc discussions when used as ambient displays. The third design change in trial 2 was a teacher-facilitated data review step with the visualizations to help more students consider the collective knowledge base. The data review discussion revealed patterns of early ideas that students had, however many students had false assumptions, which permeated through to the data they collected. Showing these early patterns (that had an average accuracy rate of 50%) potentially affected students' final choice and overall accuracy.

It was interesting that in both trials there was one session where all the groups selected the correct rainforest station for their assigned factor. In the other sessions, the accuracy ranged between 0% and 50%. In the session with the highest accuracy rate in trial 2, the collective pattern shown during the data review step was essentially correct (i.e., the highest number of data objects was annotated with the correct environmental factor for each of the four rainforest stations), which likely contributed to the high accuracy rate. While showing a correct collective pattern translated to a higher accuracy rate, showing incorrect collective patterns was associated with lower accuracy. It is true that technology can help the teacher and students reveal their assumptions and have this information corrected, but it should be presented in a manner that encourages students and teacher to advance the discussion. For example, collective knowledge could be positioned to students as a body of work to be revised and built upon, rather than a "completed" state of knowledge. Future designs could benefit from providing more support and guidance in encouraging students to think about what the collective set of observational data mean for their own question in the investigation, and how this may be built upon and be used in their explanation. Large shared displays, such as the emergent visualizations, have been used as status displays to promote group awareness, while those that replicate content from personal devices have been shown to improve efficiency of collaboration by facilitating conversational grounding [34]. Our work contributes to this body of research on MDEs by advancing the design of large shared displays that serve to display both status information, as well aggregated content from numerous participants' devices (i.e., emergent visualizations).

We found that as ambient displays, the visualizations supported teachers in monitoring student progress both in terms of tasks completed, as well as depth of thinking. For students, they grounded conversations, and the formation of physical foci for ad hoc discussions with group members and with the teacher. They served as real-time representations of the collective knowledge, demonstrating emergent patterns, and served as presentation displays for plenary discussions.

Limitations

One limitation of our work may be the over-reliance on student handheld computers, which could actually serve to disrupt naturally occurring collaborations (i.e., as students are distracted by the specific mediations of the handheld environment). Another is related to the cost of the innovation. We are cognizant that our project consists of a unique system not typically found in classrooms today, and knowing the potential costs, we have tried to set it up with hardware that schools may already have (e.g., projectors, interactive whiteboards)—with the hope that they will become more available for the uses outlined in the current paper.

CONCLUSION

This work explored how student collected data from immersive simulations and how large visualization displays supported teachers and students in reviewing the students' collective work. It presents one of the first studies on collective inquiry through the use of immersive simulations to engage students in a traditionally challenging scientific domain through several levels of interaction (i.e., individual, small group, and whole class). It also serves as an example of a digitally augmented physical space and MDE that incorporates the use of personal devices, mixing one-to-one screen experiences with collective immersion via several large-screen displays of dynamic content and shared displays of emergent visualizations of collective knowledge work. With respect to our specific research questions, we found that:

1. Including photographs of the immersive simulations was important to students' data collection, when large collections of observational data are structured with tags or other annotations (RQ1).
2. Emergent visualizations afforded naturalistic social interactions when placed as ambient displays, but require the design of explicit interactions, to ensure active engagement of all participants. (RQ2).
3. The patterns of collective ideas presented influenced student performance, either positively or negatively, depending on the accuracy of the pattern shown. This suggests the need for careful design, including real-time monitoring and input from the teacher (RQ2).

This work revealed a number of opportunities for refinement of the EvoRoom activities and technology supports, particularly concerning how to design collective knowledge building experiences in digitally augmented physical spaces. Future research will explore additional technologies and form factors for supporting student-to-student, student-to-teacher, and student-to-whole-class interactions, and design opportunities for such interactions to influence student inquiry.

ACKNOWLEDGMENTS

We are grateful to our partner teacher María Niño-Soto for her extensive contributions. We thank members of the EvoRoom and Zydeco team and student volunteers for time given to the project. We also acknowledge Lana Yarosh, who gave helpful guidance to our preparation of the final version of this paper. The work reported here was funded partially by the Social Sciences and Humanities Research Council of Canada Grant 410-2008-2125 and the National Science Foundation Grant DRL-1020027. Any opinions and findings expressed herein are those of the authors and do not necessarily reflect those of the funding agencies.

REFERENCES

1. Bell, M., Chalmers, M., Barkhuus, L., et al. Interweaving mobile games with everyday life. *Proc. CHI 2006*, ACM Press (2006), 417–426.
2. Birchfield, D. and Megowan-Romanowicz, C. Earth science

learning in SMALLab: A design experiment for mixed reality. *J. of CSCL 4*, (2009), 403–421.

3. Colella, V. Participatory simulations: Building collaborative understanding through immersive dynamic modeling. *J. of the Learning Sciences 9*, 4 (2000), 471–500.
4. de Jong, T. and van Joolingen, W.R. Scientific discovery learning with computer simulations of conceptual domains. *Review of Educational Research 68*, 2 (1998), 179–201.
5. Druin, A., Stewart, J., Proft, D., et al. KidPad: A design collaboration between children, technologists, and educators. *Proc. CHI 1997*, ACM Press (1997), 463-470.
6. Facer, K., Joiner, R., Stanton, D., et al. Savannah: Mobile gaming and learning? *J. of Computer Assisted Learning 20*, (2004), 399–409.
7. Fraser, D.S., Smith, H., Tallyn, E., et al. The SENSE project: A context-inclusive approach to studying environmental science within and across schools. *Proc. CSCL 2005,* ISLS (2005), 155–159.
8. Infante, C., Weitz, J., Reyes, T., et al. Co-located collaborative learning video game with single display groupware. *Interactive Learning Environments 18*, 2 (2010), 177–195.
9. Inkpen, K., Booth, K.S., Gribble, S.D., and Klawe, M. Give and take. *Proc. CHI 1995*, ACM Press (1995), 258–259.
10. Krajcik, J.S. and Blumenfeld, P.C. Project-based learning. In R.K. Sawyer, ed., *The Cambridge Handbook of the Learning Sciences*. Cambridge University Press, New York, 2006, 317–334.
11. Kuhn, A., McNally, B., Schmoll, S., et al. How students find, evaluate and utilize peer-collected annotated multimedia data in science inquiry with zydeco. *Proc. CHI 2012*, ACM Press (2012), 3061-3070.
12. Kuhn, D., Black, J., Keselman, A., and Kaplan, D. The development of cognitive skills to support inquiry learning. *Cognition and Instruction 18*, 4 (2000), 495–523.
13. Lui, M. and Slotta, J.D. Immersive simulations for smart classrooms: exploring evolutionary concepts in secondary science. *Technology, Pedagogy and Education*, (2013), 1–24.
14. Lui, M., Tissenbaum, M., and Slotta, J.D. Scripting collaborative learning in smart classrooms: Towards building knowledge communities. *Proc. CSCL 1*, ISLS (2011), 430–437.
15. McNeill, K.L. and Krajcik, J.S. Supporting grade 5-8 students in constructing explanations in science: The Claim, Evidence, and Reasoning framework for talk and writing. *Pearson Allyn & Bacon*, (2011).
16. Moher, T. Embedded Phenomena: Supporting science learning with classroom-sized distributed simulations. *Proc. CHI 2006*, ACM Press (2006), 691–700.
17. Moher, T., Wiley, J., Jaeger, A., et al. Spatial and temporal embedding for science inquiry: An empirical study of student learning. *Proc. ICLS 2010*, ISLS (2010), 826–833.
18. Moraveji, N., Inkpen, K., Cutrell, E., and Balakrishnan, R. A mischief of mice: Examining children's performance in single display groupware systems with 1 to 32 mice. *Proc. CHI 2009*, ACM Press (2009), 2157–2166.
19. National Science Foundation. *Preparing the Next Generation of STEM Innovators*. 2010.
20. Penuel, W.R., Roschelle, J., and Shechtman, N. Designing formative assessment software with teachers: An analysis of the co-design process. *Research and Practice in Technology Enhanced Learning 2*, 1 (2007), 51–74.
21. Peters, V.L. and Slotta, J.D. Scaffolding knowledge communities in the classroom: New opportunities in the Web 2.0 era. In M.J. Jacobson and P. Reimann, eds., *Designs for Learning Environments of the Future*. Springer, Secaucus, NJ, 2010, 205-230.
22. Price, S. and Rogers, Y. Let's get physical: The learning benefits of interacting in digitally augmented physical spaces. *Computers & Education 43*, (2004), 137–151.
23. Price, S., Rogers, Y., Scaife, M., et al. Using “tangibles” to promote novel forms of playful learning. *Interacting with Computers 15*, 2 (2003), 169–185.
24. Quintana, C. Pervasive science: Using mobile devices and the cloud to support science education. *interactions 19*, 2012, 76–80.
25. Rogers, Y. and Muller, H. A framework for designing sensor-based interactions to promote exploration and reflection in play. *International Journal of Human-Computer Studies 64*, 1 (2006), 1–14.
26. Rogers, Y. and Price, S. The role of mobile devices in facilitating collaborative inquiry in situ. *Research and Practice in Technology Enhanced Learning 3*, 3 (2008), 209–229.
27. Shneiderman, B. The eyes have it: A task by data type taxonomy for information visualizations. IEEE Comput. Soc. Press (1996), 336–343.
28. Slotta, J.D. Evolving the classrooms of the future: The interplay of pedagogy, technology and community. In K. Makitalo-Siegl, F. Kaplan, J. Zottmann and F. Fischer, eds., *Classroom of the Future: Orchestrating collaborative spaces*. Sense, Rotterdam, 2010, 215–242.
29. Slotta, J.D. and Linn, M.C. *WISE science: Web-based inquiry in the classroom*. Teachers College Press, 2009.
30. Slotta, J.D., Tissenbaum, M., and Lui, M. Orchestrating of complex inquiry: Three roles for learning analytics in a smart classroom infrastructure. *Proc. LAK 2013*, ACM Press (2013), 270–274.
31. Stewart, J., Bederson, B.B., and Druin, A. Single display groupware. *Proc. CHI 1999*, ACM Press (1999).
32. Tissenbaum, M., Lui, M., and Slotta, J.D. Co-designing collaborative smart classroom curriculum for secondary school science. *J. of Universal Computer Science 18*, 3 (2012), 327–352.
33. Tse, E. and Greenberg, S. Rapidly prototyping Single Display Groupware through the SDGToolkit. *Proc. AUIC 2004*, ACS (2004), 101-110.
34. Wallace, J.R., Scott, S.D., Lai, E., and Jajalla, D. Investigating the role of a large, shared display in Multi-Display Environments. *CSCW 20*, 6 (2011), 529–561.
35. Wilensky, U. and Resnick, M. Thinking in levels: A dynamic systems approach to making sense of the world. *J. of Science Education and Technology 8*, 1 (1999), 3–19.
36. Woodgate, D., Fraser, D.S., Gower, A., et al. Using mobile and pervasive technologies to engage formal and informal learners in scientific debate. In T.T. Goh, ed., *Multiplatform E-Learning Systems and Technologies: Mobile Devices for Ubiquitous ICT-Based Education*. Information Science Reference, Hershey, PA, 2010, 196–214.

Learning to See the Body: Supporting Instructional Practices in Laparoscopic Surgical Procedures

Helena M. Mentis[1,3], Amine Chellali[2,3], & Steven Schwaitzberg[3]

[1]Department of Information Systems
UMBC
Baltimore, MD
mentis@umbc.edu

[2]IBISC Laboratory
Département de Génie Informatique
Université d'Evry-Val-d'Essonne
Évry, France
amine.chellali@ibisc.fr

[3]Department of Surgery
Cambridge Health Alliance / Harvard Medical School
Cambridge, MA
sschwaitzberg@challiance.org

ABSTRACT

Learning the performance of physically manipulating instruments in minimally invasive surgeries is an impetus for the development of surgical training simulators. However, an often-overlooked aspect of surgical training is learning how to see the body through various imaging mechanisms. With this study, we address the ways in which surgeons demonstrate and instruct residents in seeing the body during minimally invasive surgical procedures. Drawing on observations and analysis of video recordings of minimally invasive surgical operations, we examine how particular anatomy and movement within the body to see and conceptualize that anatomy are made visible by the instructive practices of the surgeon. We use these findings to discuss further directions for minimally invasive surgical training through mechanisms for making the body visible during situated surgical training and surgical training simulation systems.

Author Keywords

Surgery; training; movement; vision; gestures

ACM Classification Keywords

H.5.m. Information interfaces and presentation (e.g., HCI): Miscellaneous.

INTRODUCTION

In modern day surgical interventions, medical imaging has come to play an increasingly important role, particularly with it enabling minimally invasive procedures. These are procedures that enter the body through small incisions or existing body orifices. Although the procedure itself may be longer than an open-procedure, the patient benefits of performing a minimally invasive surgery include the reduced risk of hemorrhaging, reduced pain, shortened recovery time, and reduced exposure to infections.

CHI 2014, April 26 - May 01 2014, Toronto, ON, Canada

http://dx.doi.org/10.1145/2556288.2557387

In order to conduct these surgeries, alternatives to 'direct vision' of the anatomy are required – these could include fluoroscopic X-rays or, as in this paper, a laparoscope. This method of visualizing the body is referred to as 'indirect vision'. New 'indirect' digital visualization technologies in minimally invasive surgery alter what it means to see the body [7] in that they present information that could not have otherwise been seen, information in a different manner or representation than had been seen before, or new ways for the surgical team to see the body together.

Moreover, these digital representations require further work in perceiving and acting upon the information presented. Many studies of medical image use discuss the negotiations around and interpretation of images in clinical and surgical work [1, 24, 29, 30, 44] and that vision is situated and interactional (see [15, 16, 18, 23, 41, 46, 52]); that the information one must glean from an image is not self-evident and work must be done (alone with the image or in conjunction with others) in order to use the images in practice. Seeing the body during surgery is a complex process of resolving the digital body as it is represented on the screen with what one knows from prior study and what one learns through interaction and explorations of the body. Surgeons bring their past experiences into alignment with their sensory stimuli in order to interpret what is before them and address contingencies of the surgical work [43] [38]. Learning the practice of surgery is reliant on the ability of the trainer to teach a resident to resolve the body before them with the abstract representations of anatomy they have learned from books and diagrams.

One mechanism of achieving this is through dissection –the process through which the internal body is made visible and identifiable in relation to abstract representations [24]. This method of viewing the body is a part of the training and visual learning of human anatomy that a surgeon must undergo – to see the body as parts that are separable from the whole body [44]. However, in order to perform a dissection, one must be able to identify anatomy through the representation before them. It is an iterative process of seeing and acting; one that requires an effective medical gaze.

As we argue in this paper, simply viewing an image does not directly translate to a surgeon acquiring an effective medical gaze in minimally invasive surgery. Much guidance is needed in interpreting and working with that image towards the particular goals of the surgery. Koschmann has particularly been integral in showing the importance of the interpretive nature of seeing in surgery and the effect it has over action [32, 33]. However, the general attention around training programs and the development of simulations for training residents in the conduct of minimally invasive surgery has focused on the learning of skill in manipulating instruments and manipulating objects with those instruments. Much less discussion has been on the trainee's ability to make useful images and, more importantly, how to see into the body through this constrained view. For instance, learning how to identify where to look next, what one is seeing before them, and where the object they want is located in reference to where they are now are just a few of the visual abilities a new surgeon must acquire before being deemed proficient in this new method of surgery. This missing concern for how one learns to view and work with and within these images reflects, ironically, a cultural habit of the Western sciences to privilege vision as the most important perceptual sense [25]. The assumption is that what is seen in the video is self-evident – that it is what one would see if they were looking directly into the body and thus, their knowledge from one form of visual representation to the other is easily transferable.

With this paper, we want to show the considerable work surgeons engage in in order to use the images effectively in practice and consider the ways in which surgical training is accomplished, specifically in how surgeons instruct trainees in how to see the body through indirect vision. Examining these occasions when instruction is provided exposes not only how a trainee's knowledge and skills are manifest, but also how practitioners 'situate' learning in their own practice. We aim to expose the techno-mediated practices of surgical instruction and learning in using endoscopic video. This is important due to the increasing use of images in minimally invasive surgery and opportunities for design of mechanisms for interaction around those videos, but also more broadly for our understanding of how image and video seeing practices (in any domain) are not without work and require learning, experience, and training as well.

We pull from the field observations and video recordings of twelve 'naturally occurring' surgical operations for our analysis. From our findings, we aim to address the question of the future directions for minimally invasive surgical training systems as well as consider referencing mechanisms to enable trainees and trainers to observe and perceive together in situ in order to attain technical mastery.

The Challenges of Seeing in Minimally Invasive Surgery

There are a number of barriers and artifacts of use that must be overcome in order to make the leap from open surgery to closed surgery utilizing 'indirect vision' – more than simply learning how to use a new set of instruments to manipulate the body [49, 50].

For instance, there may be a difference in orientation between one's relationship to the body and the direction the imaging device is oriented. As opposed to an open abdominal operation where the surgeon looks down at their hands, instruments, and the workspace, in a laparoscopic operation the camera's line-of-sight is usually different from the surgeon's natural line-of-sight. The surgeon must compensate for artifacts such as a rotated view of the scene or the instrument tips moving in a different direction. Typically this entails a form of mental rotation of the scene by the surgeons in order to compensate [17, 6].

In addition, the scale of the visual may be well beyond that which would normally be encountered in an open surgery [54]. Due to these visual differences, there can be an unnatural linkage between movement of, for instance, instruments and its visual consequence. Surgeons must learn to see and manipulate the objects together through repeated trials to adapt the scale of their movements to match the scale of the objects on the display [11, 12]. Although magnifying the view scale of an operation can enhance fine movement control by making objects easier to see and actions more precise [34, 11], it has also been shown that the discrepancy in the visual and physical speed of movement may interfere with the user's normal visual control of action [53].

These are simply a few issues that begin to require training for surgical trainees. Beyond these issues of magnification and orientation of movement, trainees need to learn to interpret the information that is before them in order to identify anatomy. The difference in the ability to interpret what is being seen in an image quickly and accurately can be seen in the difference in attention between experts and novices. Studies of pilots [31], chess players [8], and computer programmers [3] have all shown the difference in expert attention of the scene due to their skilled experience, including shorter fixation durations due to ease in information processing [3] and limited fixations on less relevant information [8]. More relevant for our purposes, Eivazi et al [10] showed that expert surgeons' gaze would focus on the point of anatomy of importance, would not frequently change, and, once focused, would exhibit longer fixations than novices. In addition, they employ fewer fixations on the instruments being used in a procedure indicating the focus of attention should be on the anatomy being worked on, not the instruments doing the work.

Specifically with regards to minimally invasive surgery and laparoscopic images, this paper's domain and representation of interest, Law et al [36] showed that novices tend to look at the instrument tip rather than at the target and Tien et al [51] showed that experts were able to split their attention between the laparoscopic display and other vitals monitors. Thus, novices, through repeated practice as well as through guided instruction, must learn to, on the one hand, be able to attend to multiple sources of information and, on the other hand, be able to attend to the most important aspects of the field of view by filtering out the unimportant aspects.

These are the challenges and opportunities for training resident surgeons to see – to teach them to overcome the barriers of using images that may distort the field of observation and to teach them what to fixate on and what is meaningless for the work at hand.

Training the Surgeon to See

What we can ascertain from these findings is that trainees need to be provided with the resources to be able to learn how to see the representations of the bodies before them. It is not simply self-evident what is and is not important to perceive and interpret. Our question then is how surgeons provide 'tacit guidance' [45] and how 'professional vision' is gained within the surgical environment [15] in order to understand the practice of 'situated learning' [35].

A number of sociological studies have discussed how learning is integrated into surgical practice. For instance, Bosk [5] described how surgeons carve out the room for situated learning experiences while at the same time ensuring the patient's risk is minimal. In addition, Mondada [40] showed that surgeons consciously display their actions towards other surgeons and residents in the use of the endoscopic video. More recently, Svensson, Heath, & Luff [47] investigated the training of residents during surgery and identified the skilled practices of a surgeon in identifying and crafting moments for sharing insights. However, these findings do not specifically address learning to see the body in digital representations or implications for designing situated instructional learning systems. How does a surgeon provide the resources to residents to perceive and act on the images that are part of complex medical procedures?

With this study, we intend to contribute to the burgeoning corpus of HCI research concerned with the interplay of embodied movement, talk, and the use of instruments at hand [37, 21] by elucidating how surgeons instruct trainees in how to see the body. Our findings can benefit the field of minimally invasive surgery in design implications for making the body visible during situated surgical training and training simulations. But they can also more broadly contribute to the growing number of studies that address how image and video seeing practices (in any domain) are not without work. Previous work in HCI and CSCW literature such as [1], [27], [38], [39], and [42] have highlighted the interest in studies of video and imaging interaction in surgical environments as well as the long history of interest in video studies by Heath and Luff [19, 20] and John Tang [26, 48]. Our work aims to contribute to this corpus of HCI research by addressing the training practices that can guide a novice in how to perceive the images as an expert.

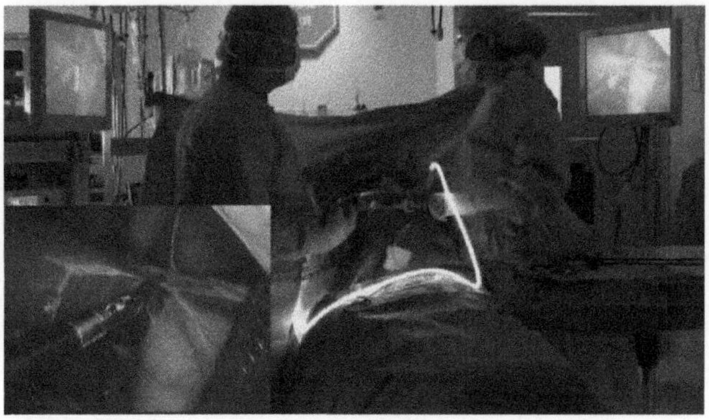

Figure 1. External Surgery Video Overlaid with Internal Laparoscopic Video

LAPAROSCOPIC SURGERY FIELDWORK

This study was conducted within the context of residency training in minimally invasive laparoscopic surgeries in the sub-specialty of general surgery. In the United States, after a student has graduated from a medical school, they continue on with their training through residencies. A residency is under the supervision of fully licensed physicians in a particular sub-specialty of medicine. This is the stage of career training where a student gains in-depth experiential practice of their chosen branch of medicine. In order to practice as a surgeon after they complete their residency, they must pass a board certification test indicating their mastery of basic knowledge and skills. Since 2009, the American Board of Surgery (ABS) required that all general surgery residents successfully complete the Fundamentals of Laparoscopic Surgery exam to be eligible to take the ABS Qualifying Exam in Surgery for certification.

One of the more significant aspects of the surgical residency is the opportunity to observe and assist senior surgeons in the operating room. In teaching hospitals, senior members of the surgical team have the responsibility to enable trainees to learn from the case. This may involve showing how to perform particular procedures to a resident or providing the resident with the opportunity to perform an incision or suture under the supervision of the surgeon.

Data Collection and Analysis

The examples presented in this paper are from fieldwork in the surgery department of a teaching hospital in the Northeast US. At that site, we employed observations and open-ended interviews – both of which we video recorded for further analysis in addition to our field notes. During the observations, we were in the surgical theatre with freedom of movement to observe the operations and the use of the images. We also had the opportunity to ask questions of the surgeons at appropriate moments during the surgery regarding image use.

A total of twelve (12) laparoscopic cholecystectomies (gallbladder removal) were observed for a total of approximately 33 hours. (The removal of the gallbladder

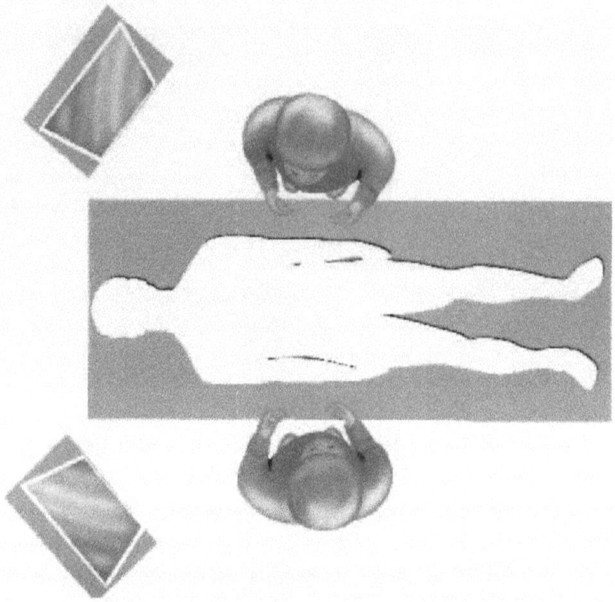

Figure 2. Example Orientation of Surgeons and Laparoscope Displays around Patient Table

during a typical laparoscopic cholecystectomy procedure is described in Jones et al. [28].) The observed cases included three different surgeons (four surgeries of each surgeon) and six different fourth year residents in different combinations of the two groups. The video collected included both the external video captured on a handheld video camera and the internal video captured by the laparoscopic recorder. For data analysis purposes, we combined the two video windows into a synced picture-in-picture format, which allowed us to simultaneously review the surgeons' actions both in and out of the body (Figure 1). As a further step in data collection and validation, the surgeons were presented with findings and given opportunities for comment during interviews.

The focus of the analysis presented here is on how the attending surgeon instructed the surgery resident to successfully view the body through the use of instruments, talk, and the laparoscope. An inductive bottom-up data analysis approach was used in which the authors examined their field notes and then the videos for themes around moments of instruction. The resulting themes led to the findings presented here and subsequent literature informing the discussion of those findings.

Laparoscopic Surgery

Laparoscopic surgery is a minimally invasive surgery that uses small incisions in the abdomen to insert instruments and cameras in order to perform procedures such as a cholecystectomy. In order to perform these procedures, the surgeon must be able to see the operative field. In most cases, a laparoscope is used for this purpose. A laparoscope is a rigid tube that houses optical components such as prisms and lenses aligned to form a lens system. There is also a separate channel made of glass fibers for transmitting light. A cable then connects the tube to a monitor providing high-resolution images to the surgeons. A laparoscope may have a 0°, 30°, or 45° lens angle to allow for viewing around objects. The view angle is steered by the light cord post and the direction of view is opposite the scope post - to look down, the light cord is steered up and to look up, the light cord is steered down.

Typically, there will first be multiple incisions and ports inserted into the abdomen: at least two for instruments and one for the laparoscope. This means that at least three hands are actively holding and manipulating instruments at the same time. Consequently, laparoscopic procedures require coordination between at least two surgeons. These surgeons may stand on opposite sides of the table, facing one another, which yields equal access to the manipulation of the instruments and camera (see Figure 2). In order to facilitate this physical arrangement, two monitors are used to display the laparoscopic video; one is placed on each side of the head of the bed, angled towards one of the surgeons. Thus, each surgeon has a different orientation to the video in relation to their orientation to the body as well as their orientation to the instrument and camera movements. In particular, the surgeon not manipulating the camera has an inverted view of the field of work. This means additional mental rotation, which could be significant if the novice is in this position.

General surgery residents in their fourth or fifth (and final) year typically perform the surgery with the senior surgeon assisting. Thus, they are also the one to hold and maneuver the laparoscope. This means that they can control what they are looking at and if the senior surgeon wants to change that view, they must take control of the laparoscope.

FINDINGS

For the following, we will discuss three ways that a surgeon helps the fourth year resident to see the body and, more importantly, how this training is integrated into surgical practice. The situations described are indicative of these training moments, but are by no means the only occurrences witnessed.

Revealing Anatomy

The laparoscope is used in minimally invasive surgery in order to see the anatomy within the body. However, 'seeing' the body through the laparoscopic video is not a matter of simply looking at the video monitor. Many of the training moments engaged in by the surgeon and the residents were in identifying anatomy in the view. The process of guiding trainees to begin to determine where and in what orientation their camera and instruments were in the body with relation to what they see was a crucial first step.

> *After inserting the laparoscope into the first port, the attending surgeon turns to the two residents and begins to question them on what they see.*
>
> *"Where are we?" [a short pause] "I know where we are, where do you think we are?"*

There is no response. They are both looking intently at the monitor as the attending moves around the camera.

"Where are we?" He asks again. "Laparoscopy is about recognizing what you see."

The resident points to the screen. "I don't understand what..."

The attending begins to explain, "We are below [posterior] to the omentum. When you see the bowel and not the peritoneum you know you are below and you need to recognize that so you don't mess your patient up."

As the surgeon points out, laparoscopy is about seeing the anatomy within the view. It first requires one to know where in the body they are. But in order to do that a surgeon needs to sometimes make a determination based on what he sees. In this example, the surgeon reveals where they have entered the internal body by pointing out the crucial wayfinding structures. He is explaining how seeing and orienting is sometimes about the context of the view.

Being able to identify various anatomy and orientation is also crucial for the first step of a laparoscopic surgery: the insertion of ports in the abdomen. A port for the camera is the first to be created. This port is used for insulfation of the abdomen and then the camera is inserted in order to guide the placement of the other ports. Thus, the camera port is inserted through direct vision while the other ports are guided by the camera through indirect vision.

After the first port is inserted into the belly button, the laparoscopic camera is inserted and maneuvered around by the attending surgeon as the resident looks on.

The resident points to the screen behind him. "It could go here."

The surgeon nods, says, "Yep. Let's go a little bit lower than usual only because the liver is coming down further", and points the camera at the liver.

The surgeon then palpates with his free finger the abdomen at the proposed insertion point and moves the camera internally up to that point. As he takes his finger away, the resident replaces it with his own finger and begins to palpate the abdomen so he can see with the camera where the insertion point would be on the internal abdominal wall.

The surgeon nods on seeing this method of identification and says, "Yes right there."

This process of palpating in order to see the resulting movement of tissue is a mechanism of connecting one's orientation and movement on the outside of the body to the resulting location on the inside of the body (Figure 3). The first step sets the stage not only with the ideal location of ports for conducting the surgery, but also with a working

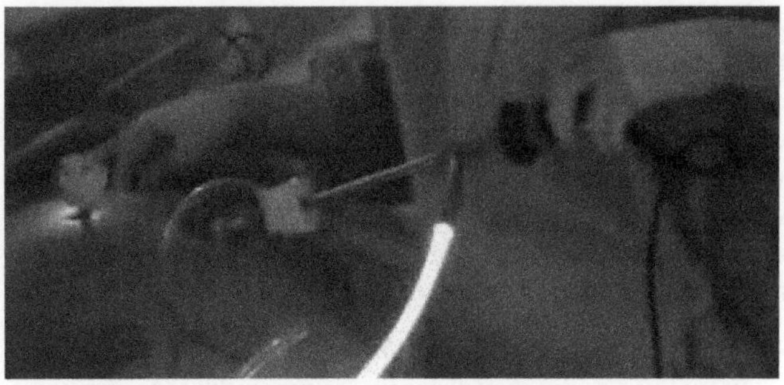

Figure 3. Palpating and Orienting

map between what the surgeons know about the mapping of the body and what they now see on the video screen.

Throughout a surgery, the process of explanation, deictic referencing, and dissection makes anatomy emerge from the chaos of tissue; not in actual physical presence – there is often no change in the view as it were – but rather in how the visual information begins to take on new meaning.

The attending takes his dissector and begins to probe at the connective tissue covering. "If this is the common bile duct that means the window [space between the cystic duct and common duct] goes this way." He begins to probe with the dissector where he indicated the window would be and a space opens quite easily to reveal the window.

The resident nods during the explanation and then, when the window appears, utters, "Oh yeah. Yeah."

The attending continues with the dissection, "And this might be the artery." He uses the dissector to hook and hold up the elongated tissue.

The resident again nods with a "yeah".

"You know, what she really has is a tiny gallbladder stuck right onto the common bile duct."

This final comment completed the reveal of the anatomy as he was explaining the reason why this particular patient's anatomy looked different from what the resident had seen before. Prior experience was, in this case, interfering with the resident's vision of the tissue before her. Through the surgeon's explanation and guidance, he slowly showed her what she could not see before.

As we said before, in order to identify anatomy, there is the need sometimes to see the context. Oftentimes we saw a resident pull back the camera to see again where they were or, in this example, explain to the surgeon that they needed context, *"Can I just pull it away to get some perspective for a second?"* Context is necessary and if it can not be determined from the current view, surgeons show the residents that changing the view can help with identification, *"Let's see what we've got. Come back for a second and let's see where we think we are."*

Anatomy needs to be continually revealed to the trainee throughout the surgery as the body moves around considerably due to dissection. In the following two examples, the resident does not see what the surgeon sees, which results in surgical errors. What is evident is that the surgeon thought that the resident had the same understanding of where structures were in relation to where the work was being conducted.

As the resident is burning through connective tissue to dissect the cystic duct from the common duct, he lingers on the electrosurgical instrument's energy switch for a few seconds. The surgeon begins to scold, "Watch it, watch it – you have to learn to pulse electrocautery so it doesn't burn everything." He pulls the tissue a bit and then points out, "You see that? You see how close you are here?" He pulls the tissue more taught and then points to the blood indicating the artery was nicked.

...

The resident is using the electrosurgery instrument to remove tissue and expose the ducts. The surgeon sees the side of his instrument get too close to the artery and tries to stop the resident. "Don't don't don't!" But he was not effective and the back of the instrument hits the artery and bleeding begins. "I was just going to say that's the artery." Later he explains, "Use the hook to tease it off. This is the one place you can't back into because you are two close to it."

In the first example, even though the resident had already identified the artery, he 'lost sight' of it in his focus on removing tissue from over the cystic duct. In the second example, the resident is not aware of the closeness of his instruments to other structures – structures which moments before he had demonstrated seeing.

As you can also see in the first illustration, the use of pulling tissue into focus is a technique often employed by the surgeons. A surgeon may not have control of the laparoscope, but he does have readily at his disposal the instruments currently in his hand being used for traction.

As a resident uses the electrosurgery instrument to remove tissue, he exposes a node. He moves in to remove more tissue and the surgeon interrupts him saying, "Stay a little bit higher." The resident moves the instrument up slightly and hovers, "Here?" The surgeon continues by explaining, "See you are off of the ... [pulls the tissue taught to display the node better] if you stay on top of the nodes ... see it?" The resident affirms and continues with removing tissue above the node. When he is done the surgeon starts to move the tissue around so the other side is visible and holds the tissue taut. "Come back around the other way now."

In all of the examples, the surgeon is revealing anatomy to the trainee in order for the resident to see what the surgeon

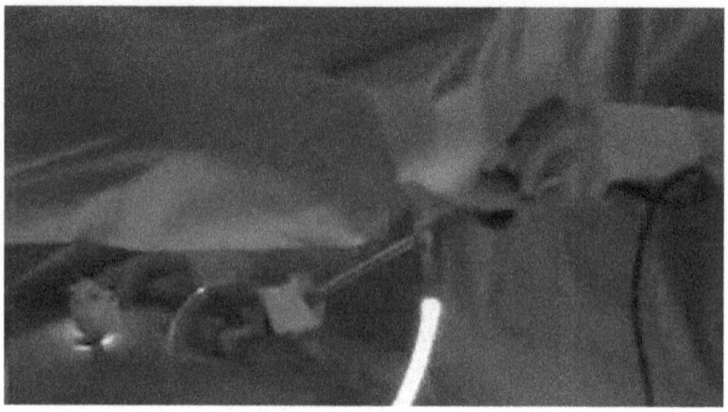

Figure 4. Guiding the Hand.

sees in the images. These situated learning moments do not take much time from the task at hand, but they do require the ability of the surgeon to demarcate where attention should be. Surgeons do this through the use of the instruments at their disposal, the video screen strategically placed behind them within reach to point to, or, as in the next section, by moving the camera itself.

Guiding the Hand to Train the Eye

There are many examples of when the surgeon finds a need to control the camera view in order to reveal anatomy. As we can see in the next two examples, oftentimes he or she grabs the hand of the resident so the resident continues to have proprioceptive awareness of the instrument's movements (Figure 4).

The surgeon tells the resident, "You need to move your post so you can see." He turns to the medical student next to him to ask her to take the retractor he is holding in his right hand. He then reaches across the table and begins to slowly turn the post all the way to the left and then he puts his hand over the residents and moves the camera view to the right in order to center the area of work again. He then proceeds to explain, "OK, so we need to open up down here."

The attending reaches across and grabs the hand of the resident that is guiding the electrosurgical instrument. She then moves his hand to point to a particular part of the anatomy while she explains, "So if you select the line over here...".

Guiding the hand, however, does not always mean 'hands-on' guidance. Much guidance is through verbal explanation or even pointing at the video screen behind them (Figure 5). Either way, guidance of the hand needs to be coupled with an explanation of why the eye should be looking at the images in that manner.

The surgeon explains to the resident, "Open up this some more up here [points to the video screen behind him]. Just get underneath this and go up both sides of it so you don't burn it." Shortly after this instruction the resident's instrument gets too close to the gallbladder and burns it, resulting in bile seeping out. The surgeon tsks, sighs, and then says, "So what I

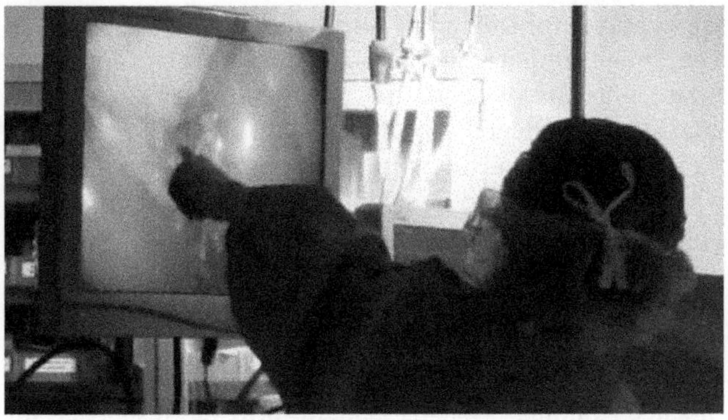

Figure 5. Guiding the Eye.

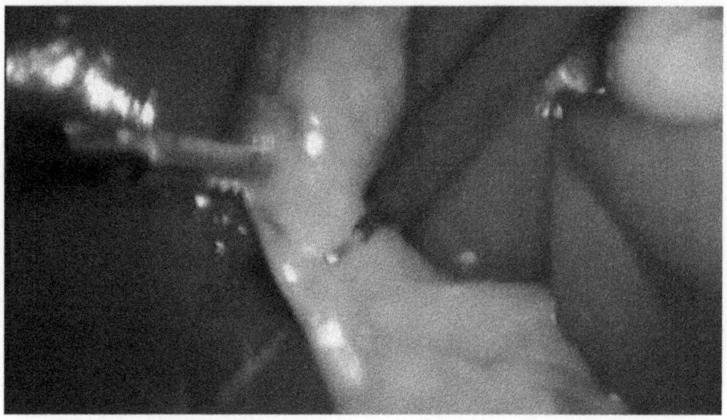

Figure 6. Demarcating a Line with the Instrument Tip.

meant was go underneath it so you don't burn the gallbladder."

This 'why' was a crucial part in understanding the instruction the resident was receiving. The 'why' encompassed what the surgeon saw as a potential collision point. But the resident did not see the 'why', but only the instruction received.

Finally, residents often learn from the surgeons that they can visually guide their instruments to a point in the body. It is the method that surgeons first use to help residents get their bearing and to ensure they do not veer off course and nick something unintentionally. Until a resident feels comfortable moving inside the body without seeing where they are going they will continue to do this when they are in control of the laparoscope. They will move the camera out to see the instrument entering and then follow the instrument to the site of work. This is not something that they will always need to do as is evidenced by a young resident doing this for a surgeon and him finally explaining, *"You don't have to come in and out for me."*

Envisioning What is Not Seen

Elucidating what is to be seen in an image is one thing but oftentimes what needs to be seen is actually not there. There may be conceptual aspects of the view or else things that are hidden from view.

At the start of the dissection step of a laparoscopic surgery the attending pauses and asks the resident, "Have we done a gallbladder together?" He replies in the affirmative and so she continues, "Yeah? So you know I like to select an imaginary line below it?" The resident again replies in the affirmative and continues for her, "So we are not going to cross [he traces a line across the artery and ducts with the electrosurery instrument]" and in unison they both say, "...this line right there."

In this case, what is being envisioned on the image is in actuality not present; however that imaginary line will guide the action taken throughout the surgery (Figure 6).

It is not always evident what anatomy is before them. Oftentimes the surgeon has to make inferences as to what is before him and where anatomy may be hiding. And this has implications on what actions will be taken.

As the resident is removing tissue early in the dissection process, the surgeon quizzes him, "So where do you think the artery is? Are you over it?" The resident pauses and looks at the screen. Then he begins, "The artery is riiighht...here." He starts to trace what he believes to be the arterial line. The surgeon indicates to move to the next phase of the surgery, "OK so you are past it."

In this example, the resident needed to stop to determine if he had passed the artery based on what he can see before him. This required an inference of the location based on the location of ducts and the liver along with the contours of the tissue.

Sometimes envisioning has to do with envisioning how actions will affect one's space for maneuvering. This is often evident in where to place the ports, but it is also evident in how tissue moves during the procedure.

As the cystic duct has been dissected away from the common duct, the resident asks the surgeon to move the tissue, "Can we see the artery back there – I think it [the artery] is right there [points to screen]." He then turns to the scrub nurse and asks, "Can I get a Maryland [dissecting forceps]." However, the surgeon stops the resident there and explains that that is not the best idea right now. "If it starts bleeding then you have to open." After they make the cut on the cystic ducts, the surgeon continues on to explain again why waiting was necessary. "See it springs away [from the common duct] quite a lot. So if I get into any trouble now I still have some room to maneuver with my laparoscopic tools."

Movement of the tissue explains why revealing anatomy was a continual occurrence throughout the surgery, but it also is an effect of dissection that must be envisioned in order to understand how the view will change after an action is undertaken.

Coming back around to the beginning of a laparoscopic surgery, envisioning what is not there is an important part of determining the best place for ports and instruments, requiring one to imagine the lines and movement in a confined space.

> *After looking around the interior of the abdomen and determining the case will be complicated due to an inordinate amount of connective tissue, the surgeon begins, "So let's think about where you want to put it." The resident points to a point on the external abdomen wall with her finger, "Probably right here" and begins to palpitate that point so they can see the resulting indentation on the laparoscopic video. "OK", says the surgeon. "Lower than usual", explains the resident. The surgeon continues, "That's going to be...", he moves the laparoscopic camera to first point to the proposed entry point and then to the internal organ area, "...parallel to the liver. I agree." The resident continues to explain her proposal, "I want to have some perspective. I don't want to be right on top." The surgeon affirms, "Yes good."*

Thus, 'seeing' an image often means envisaging information out of what they can see – whether that is how instruments will line up with anatomy, how tissue will move after an action is taken or an imaginary demarcation that cannot be crossed.

DISCUSSION

Our work has aimed to demonstrate the situated learning [35] that occurs in minimally invasive surgery in order to train surgical residents to perceive and appropriate digital representations of the body. We show that seeing a medical image during minimally invasive surgery is not an endpoint: it requires interaction and discussion. Our video recordings, augmented by conventional fieldwork, have enabled us to consider how seeing practices and training residents to see are accomplished through the interplay of embodied gesturing, talk, and the use of various instruments at their disposal. The revelations and guidance form a critical element of gestalt that enables an emergent perception of the area of work represented in the images. These are not achieved simply through moments of looking, but by virtue of seeing as the presentation unfolds. They enable an emergent repertoire of knowledge in how to see and act within 'indirect vision'.

Instructing one to see has to be positioned with regard to the proper performance of the task at hand. In fact, this is the only way one can 'see' in order to perform the task. The perception and determination of location of ducts and arteries, and the trainee's ability to comprehend why and where action is occurring are accomplished in and through the interaction between the surgeon, the trainee, and the images. The interaction provides the trainees with access to, and a way of seeing, the anatomy through the images. The trainee does not relate to the images in a merely representational manner, that is, as a disembodied gaze – he is an active participant.

Implications for Design of Surgical Training Systems

The broad implication here is that learning to create meaningful images and use them as a part of surgical practice is an integral aspect of minimally invasive surgical training. As it stands now, this training is primarily gained while observing and assisting a senior surgeon in the operating room. This situated learning embodies the seeing practices and highlights the tight interlink between seeing and action. For surgical instructional system designers, it highlights the need for further training beyond simply the motor skills associated with minimally invasive surgery. Situated training systems should provide resources for surgeons to allow students to 'see' what the senior surgeon sees.

This relates to our ongoing interests in developing situated interactive instructional systems for laparoscopic surgery. What we have learned is that a trainee needs to be able to seamlessly interact in a fashion to work out what he sees. Oftentimes this is done in the image itself, but the question is if we can provide an overlay or a secondary display to augment training to provide this interaction. Currently, there is no mechanism for aligning endoscopic views to contextualized anatomic identification and trajectory guidance. Alongside the real-time laparoscopic video display one could provide a guidance system. This system would provide 3D models of the chest and abdominal cavity that could be rotated, panned, and zoomed by both surgeons from either side of the table through gesture and voice control in order to view and interact with the 3D shape and structure of the anatomy of the chest and abdominal cavity. In addition, an infrared sensor would monitor the location and rotation of the laparoscopic camera tube in the hands of the surgeon and highlight the field of view on the 3D model. Although potentially leading to additional work for the senior surgeon, providing further information to residents and allowing that information to be accessed by the trainee or the senior surgeon for elucidation could improve the ability of residents to learn how to see the body in images and use them more effectively in their surgical practice.

Furthermore, the availability of senior surgeons can be an obstacle to repeated training in this situation. An interesting alternative can be a training system that includes guiding aids to simulate the practice of 'situated learning'. These guiding aids aim to reproduce the three learning situations observed in our study. For instance, virtual landmarks displayed on the novices' screen while interacting with a virtual body, can help them focus on the most important aspects of the field of view in a specific scenario. This metaphor represents the deictic referencing used by experts to attract the novices' attention. Moreover, the haptic guidance metaphor [13] can be adapted to direct the novices' hands through specific visual information while manipulating the camera. This metaphor was previously used to teach motor skills. In this situation, it can be used to replace the expert's hand guidance observed in our study.

Moreover, these interaction metaphors can be supplemented by contextual (verbal or textual) information for further explanations to the novices about context while they interact with the system.

CONCLUSION

Learning how to see and use intraoperative imaging systems for minimally invasive surgery requires a continually interactive process between the images, the instructor, and the instruments at hand. In our studies of this situated learning practice, we have found that the 'seeing' of images is an embodied process achieved through a coordination of visual information about the body and instruments and explorative actions with instruments on and in the body. The importance of the seeing process contrasts with the popular notion that surgical trainees simply need to view the images; instead, our intention has been to lay a foundation for the innovation of surgical training simulations and instructive systems for situated learning.

ACKNOWLEDGMENTS

We thank the surgeons and staff for allowing us to observe their work and answer our questions. This work was partially supported by the National Institute of Medicine (NIH NIBIB 2R01 EB005807-05A1, 1R01 EB010037-01, 1R01 EB009362-01A2, 1R01 EB014305-01A1).

REFERENCES

1. Aanestad, M. (2003). The camera as an actor: Design-in-use of telemedicine infrastructure in surgery. *Computer Supported Cooperative Work, 12*(1), 1-20.
2. Alač, M. (2008). Working with brain scans: Digital images and gestural interaction in fMRI laboratory. *Social Studies of Science, 38*(4), 483-508.
3. Bednarik, R. (2012). Expertise-dependent visual attention strategies develop over time during debugging with multiple code representations. *International Journal of Human-Computer Studies, 70*(2), 143-155.
4. Bohan, M., McConnell, D.S., Chaparro, A., Thompson, S.G. (2010). The effects of visual magnification and physical movement scale on the manipulation of a tool with indirect vision. *Journal of Experimental Psychology: Applied, 16*(1), 33-44.
5. Bosk, C. (1979) *Forgive and Remember: Managing Medical Failure*. Chicago: University of Chicago Press.
6. Breedveld, P. & Wentink, M. (2001). Eye-hand coordination in laparoscopy – An overview of experiments and supporting aids. *Minimally Invasive Therapy and Allied Technologies, 10*(3), 155-162.
7. Burri, R.V. (2008) Boundary work and symbolic capital in radiology. *Social Studies of Science, 38*(1), 35-62.
8. Charness, N., Reingold, E., Pomplun, M., & Stampe, D. (2001). The perceptual aspect of skilled performance in chess: Evidence from eye movements. *Memory & Cognition, 29*(8), 1146-1152.
9. Dolezal, L. (2009). The remote body: The phenomenology of telepresence and re-embodiment. *Human Technology, 5*(2), 208-226.
10. Eivazi, S., Bednarik, R., Tukiainen, M, Fraunberg, M., Leinonen, V., Jaaskelainen, J.E. (2012). Gaze behaviour of expert and novice microneurosurgeons differs during observations of tumor removal recordings. *ETRA*, 377-380.
11. Ellis, R.D., Cao, A., Pandya, A., Composto, A., Chacko, M., Klein, M.D., & Auner, G. (2004). In optimizing the surgeon-robot interface: The effect of control-display gain and zoom level on movement time. *HFES,* 1713-1717.
12. Ferrel, C., Leifflen, D., Orliaguett, J.P., & Coello, Y (2000). Pointing movement visually controlled through a video display: Adaptation to scale change. *Ergonomics, 43,* 461-473.
13. Feygin, D., Keehner, M., & Tendick, F. (2002). Haptic Guidance: Experimental Evaluation of a Haptic Training Method for a Perceptual Motor Skill. *Proc. of HAPTICS*, 40-47.
14. Gallagher, S. (2005). *How the body shapes the mind.* Oxford: Oxford University Press.
15. Goodwin, C. (1994). Professional vision. *American Anthropologist, 96*(3), 606-633.
16. Goodwin, C. (2000). Practice of color classification. *Mind, Culture, and Activity, 7*(1-2), 19-36.
17. Hanna, G.B., Shimi, S.M., Cuschieri, A. (1998). Task performance in endoscopic surgery is influenced by location of the image display. *Ann. of Surg., 227*, 481–4.
18. Heath, C. & Hindmarsh, J. (2000). Configuring action in objects: From mutual space to media space. *Mind, Culture and Activity, 7*(1-2), 81-104.
19. Heath, C.C. & Luff, P. (1991). Disembodied conduct: Communication through video in a multi-media office environment. *Proc. of HFES*, 99-103.
20. Heath, C.C. & Luff, P. (1992). Media space and communicative asymmetries: Preliminary observations of video-mediated interaction. *HCI, 7*(3), 315-346.
21. Heath, C.C. and Luff, P. (2000) *Technology in Action.* Cambridge: Cambridge University Press.
22. Hindmarsh, J., Reynolds, P. and Dunne, S. (2011). Exhibiting Understanding: the body in apprenticeship. *Journal of Pragmatics, 43* (2), 489-503.
23. Hindmarsh, J. & Heath C. (2000). Embodied reference: A study of deixis in workplace interaction. *Journal of Pragmatics, 32*, 1855-1878.
24. Hirschauer, S. (1991). The manufacture of bodies in surgery. *Social Studies of Science, 21*(2), 279-319.
25. Ihde, D. (2002). *Bodies in Technology*. Minneapolis, MN: University of Minnesota Press.

26. Isaacs, E. & Tang, J. (1994). What video can do and cannot do for collaboration: a case study. *Multimedia Systems, 2*(2), 63-73.

27. Johnson, R., O'Hara, K., Sellen, A., Cousins, C., & Criminisi A. (2011). Exploring the potential for touchless interaction in image-guided interventional radiology. *Proc. of CHI.*

28. Jones, D.B., Maithel, S.K., & Schneider, B.E. (2006). Laparoscopic Cholecystectomy. In Jones DB, Maithel SK, & Schneider BE (eds) *Atlas of Minimally Invasive Surgery*, Cine-Med, Inc.,Woodbury (CT), pp 12-39.

29. Joyce, K. (2005). Appealing images: Magnetic resonance imaging and the production of authoritative knowledge. *Social Studies of Science, 35*(3), 437-462.

30. Kaplan, B. (1995). Objectification and negotiation in interpreting clinical images: Implications for computer-based patient records. *Artificial Intelligence in Medicine, 7*, 439-454.

31. Kasarskis, P., Stehwien, J., Hickox, J., Aretz, A., & Wickens, C. (2001). Comparison of expert and novice scan behaviors during vfr flight. *In Proceedings of the 11th International Symposium on Aviation Psychology.*

32. Koschmann, T., LeBaron, C., Goodwin, C., & Feltovich, P. (2011). "Can you see the cystic artery yet?" A simple matter of trust. *Journal of Pragmatics, 43*(2), 521-541.

33. Koschmann, T., LeBaron, C., Goodwin, C., Zemel, A. and Dunnington, G. (2007) Formulating the 'Triangle of Doom', *Gesture*, **7**, 1,97–118.

34. Langolf, G.D., Chaffin, D.B., & Foulke, J.A. (1976). An investigation of Fitts' law using a wide range of movement amplitudes. *Journal of Motor Behavior, 8*, 113-128.

35. Lave, J. and Wenger, E. (1991) *Situated Learning: Legitimate Peripheral Participation.* Cambridge, MA: Cambridge University Press.

36. Law, B., Atkins, M.S., Kirkpatrick, A.E., & Lomax, A.J. (2004). Eye gaze patterns differentiate novice and experts in a virtual laparoscopic surgery training environment. *Proc. of ETRA,* 41-48.

37. Luff, P.K., Hindmarsh, J. J. and Heath, C.C. (eds) (2000) *Workplace Studies: Recovering Work Practice and Informing System Design.* New York and Cambridge: Cambridge University Press.

38. Mentis, H.M. & Taylor, A. (2013). Imaging the Body: Embodied Vision in Minimally Invasive Surgery. *Proc. of CHI,* pp. 1479-1488.

39. Mentis, H.M., O'Hara, K., Sellen, A., & Trevedi, R. (2012). Interaction proxemics and image use in neurosurgery. *Proc. of CHI,* 927-936.

40. Mondada, L. (2003). Working with video: how surgeons produce video records of their actions. *Visual Studies, 18*(1), 58-73.

41. Nishizaka A. (2000). Seeing what one sees: Perception, emotion and activity. *Mind, Culture, and Activity, 7*(1-2), 105-123.

42. O'Hara, K., Harper, R., Mentis, H.M., Sellen, A., & Taylor, A. (2013). On the naturalness of touchless: Putting the "interaction" back into NUI. *TOCHI, 20*(1), pp. 5:1-5:25.

43. Pope, C. (2002). Contingency in everyday surgical work. *Sociology of Health and Illness, 24*, 4, 369–84.

44. Prasad, A. (2005). Making images/making bodies: Visibilizing and disciplining through magnetic resonance imaging. *Science, Technology & Human Values, 30*(2), 291-316.

45. Prentice, R. (2007). Drilling surgeons: the social lessons of embodied surgical learning, *Science, Technology and Human Values*, *32*(5), 534–53.

46. Suchman, L. (2000). Embodied practices of engineering work. *Mind, Culture and Activity, 7*(1-2), 4-18.

47. Svensson, M.S., Luff, P., & Heath, C. (2009). Embedding instruction in practice: Contingency and collaboration during surgical training. *Sociology of Health and Illness, 31*(6), 889-906.

48. Tang, J. & Isaacs, E. (1993). Why do users like video? Studies of multimedia-supported collaboration. *Computer Supported Cooperative Work, 1*(3), 163-196.

49. Tendrick, F., Bhoyrul, S., & Way, L.W. (1997). Comparison of laparoscopic imagin systems and conditions using a knot tying task. *Computer Aided Surgery, 2,* 24-33.

50. Tendrick, F., Jennings, R., Tharp, G., & Stark, L. (1993). Sensing and manipulation problems in endoscopic surgery: Experiment, analysis and observation. *Presence: Teleoperators and Virtual Environments, 2,* 66-81.

51. Tien, G., Atkins, M.S., Zheng, B., & Swindells, C. (2010). Measuring situation awareness of surgeons in laparoscopic training. *Proc. of ETRA,* 149-152.

52. Ueno, N. (2000). Ecologies of inscriptions: Technologies of making the social organization of work and the mass production of machine parts visible in collaborative activity. *Mind, Culture, and Activity, 7*(1-2), 59-80.

53. Van Doorn, R.R.A., Unema, P.J.A. (2005). Effects of adaptation to altered display gain on the control of single aimed movements. *Motor Control, 9,* 3-22.

54. Van Wynsberghe, A., & Gastmans, P. (2008). Telesurgery: An ethical appraisal. *Journal of Medical Ethics, 34*(10), e22.

Information-Building Applications: Designing for Data Exploration and Analysis by Elementary School Students

Tia Shelley, Leilah Lyons, Tom Moher, Chandan Dasgupta, Brenda Lopez-Silva, Alexandra Silva
University of Illinois at Chicago, Chicago, IL
851 S. Morgan (M/C 152), Chicago, IL 60607 USAcm
tshell2, llyons, moher, cdasgu2, brendita, asilva2 @ uic.edu

ABSTRACT
The propagation of Inquiry Based Learning has lead to many more elementary students interacting with authentic scientific tools and practices. However, the more problematic realities of scientific data collection, such as noise and large data sets, are often deliberately hidden from students. Students will need to confront these realities and be able to make skillful data scoping decisions in order to make sense of ever more prevalent large datasets. We dub software designed to support these activities Information-Building Applications (IBAs). This paper presents the design considerations that went into building an exemplar IBA, PhotoMAT (Photo Management and Analysis Tool), a brief user study to show how the solutions enacted by following these principles are taken up by actual students, and a discussion of how the design considerations identified by our work might be applied to another IBA.

Author Keywords
K-12 Science Education; Learner Centered Design; Information-Building Applications

ACM Classification Keywords
H.5.2. User Interfaces

INTRODUCTION
This paper presents the design considerations for a new class of tool, Information-Building Applications (IBAs), the design rationale and development process underlying an exemplar IBA, a mobile software tool, PhotoMAT (Photo Management and Analysis Tool), students' experience with this tool within a curricular unit - Neighborhood Safari, and a discussion of how the design considerations we identified in our work might be applied to another IBA.

With the rise of educational software, many tools that support data collection [e.g., 27] or help students form more complete data analysis [e.g., 23] have been developed. But these tools often focus on working with data types that have been vetted in advance or data sets that have been cleaned up and "sanitized" for students. The rationale behind this was to keep classroom focus on the processes of data collection or data analysis, so in these cases, each data element carries with it useful informational content. Unfortunately, this prevents learners from getting experience with confronting the conceptual challenges involved in how one converts raw data (which may be ill-structured, involve duplicate entries, involve spurious entries, involve noisy entries or may be missing entries) into useful information. We dub this process "information building." We propose here that to develop their information-building skills, students can and should interact with "unsanitized" data sets, that is, those that include non one-to-one relationships between data and information. We also propose that students can be supported in this endeavor with a new class of applications: Information-Building Applications (IBAs). While sharing some characteristics with existing educational data collection and analysis tools, the driving goal of IBAs dictates the need for different design strategies for viewing, categorizing, sorting, and sensemaking with "raw" data sets. In this paper we describe the design of a specific IBA, PhotoMAT, to illustrate these design strategies.

PhotoMAT was designed to support learners' investigations of backyard animal behavior and works with image sets obtained using fixed-position field cameras ("camera traps") that capture "bursts" of images in response to motion within their visual field. Camera traps have become a standard tool of contemporary wildlife research practice, commonly used to support studies of population diversity, habitat and dietary preference. Working with these image sets can be challenging for young learners. In areas of abundant wildlife, a camera deployment over several days may produce hundreds of bursts. This number of images can increase dramatically by inattention (typical among novices) to non-wildlife trigger sources such as wind-blown leaves, people, and pets (incidental motion). These situations create a "big data" challenge for young learners that are not readily addressed using common photo management tools. More fundamental still is the challenge of effecting a transition from children's cultural framing of images as art ("nature pictures") to a framing of image sets as raw data requiring interpretation and transformation into abstract representations of information. This transformation is essential for conducting analyses of habitat and dietary preference and demands the determination of relative

CHI 2014, April 26–May 1, 2014, Toronto, Ontario, Canada.

ACM 978-1-4503-2473-1/14/04...$15.00.
http://dx.doi.org/10.1145/2556288.2557294

frequency of wildlife sightings across (segments of) image sets. By identifying the potential misunderstandings and designing PhotoMAT to support the correct interpretations, we can reshape these misunderstandings instead as learning opportunities for students.

We will explore how the problems of "messy data" can be ameliorated by user interface design decisions in our exemplar tool, PhotoMAT, in this paper. We focus on how each of the above noted characteristics of these large data sets can be presented to students in ways that support their transformation of raw data in scalar representations of relative frequency. We propose generalized notions for how to deal with each of the characteristics based on our experiences with our exemplar, and describe them alongside a hypothetical IBA for use in a different domain area. From there, we share the experiences of students who used PhotoMAT as part of a classroom unit to illustrate how IBAs support science practices in the classroom.

RELATED WORK

Inquiry Learning

Researchers have highlighted the importance of having a classroom environment that fosters a culture of inquiry that is uncommon in the traditional science classroom practices [16, 19]. Inquiry learning asks students to find solutions to real problems by asking and refining questions, designing and conducting investigations, gathering and analyzing information and data, making interpretations, creating explanations and drawing conclusions [15, 17, 18]. For each stage of the inquiry process, there have been many pieces of educational software developed to support that stage [e.g., 23, 26]. These tools often assume cleaned data though, and rarely involve large quantities of data that students need to sort through to find information. Alongside an inquiry learning perspective, we also wanted to align our activity with disciplinary practices, and worked to both situate the practices in the meaningful context of the students' own interests and to simplify the practices appropriate to the developmental level of the students[5].

Existing Image Management Tools for Camera Traps

An initial survey of existing image management tools illustrates the need for the category of information building tools. Existing image management tools do not tend to have a way to distinguish images that are useful and images that are not useful, typically relying on a lack of tagging or labeling to indicate that the image should be discarded. For example, DeskTEAM, which was designed for expert scientists to use for the classification of camera trap images focuses allows for one label to be applied to an image by typing in a text box to the side of the image, with an additional text box to record the quantity of the animal, but has no way to mark an image as empty of interest [6]. Camera Base, also designed for scientists, adds the additional feature of allowing images from two cameras to be shown at the same time, allowing for multiple viewpoints of an area, a tactic that is sometimes used by scientists in order to better capture animal movement [27]. Neither tool was designed to be used by children, something exemplified by the level of abstraction required to label an entire image as a particular animal, and by the lack of image status labels. For PhotoMAT to be distinguished from these tools, we needed to start at a more concrete level of analysis and then move to abstraction, a path which we describe in the design rationale segment.

Science Learning and Big Data Exploration

Contemporary perspectives of science learning emphasize the importance of developing understandings of disciplinary practices as complements to understandings of domain phenomena [4]. An important element of science practice is the use of discipline-specific instrumentation to support investigations of phenomena that don't yield to observation by the naked eye. Effective instrument use requires the development of understandings of their operation, and of their affordances and constraints with respect to the nature of the investigations that they can support. This requires that learners have structured opportunities to work with scientific instruments iteratively and experience both success and failure during learning activities [24]. In the case of camera traps, an important part of that learning comes from experiencing the impact of improper deployment: the manual processing of datasets with low signal (wildlife images) to noise (incidental motion) ratios. In addition to this experience, it is critical for learners to gradually acquire higher-order or abstract information out of concrete instances [8], a skill typically ascribed to domain experts [2]. Piaget [22] was of the view that students gain abstract knowledge indirectly from one's activities by reflecting on such activities. They start from being content focused (i.e. referring to concrete examples) and gradually proceed to become content-free (i.e. abstracting rules from those concrete examples) [7]. However, skepticism exists regarding viewing expertise and knowledge development as a simple shift from concrete to abstract [29]. Simons and Keil [26] suggested that abstract ideas should guide the elaboration of the concrete data. These arguments suggest the need for seamlessly switching between abstract and concrete focus depending on the students' needs and level of understanding.

This seamless switching, which we argue is a critical piece of Information-Building Applications, is particularly important in cases of large datasets. Expert data analysts move fluidly between different levels of understanding data [9]. Data visualization experts emphasize the need to manipulate the data view, typically by zooming out to view aggregate patterns or zooming in to view low-level details [11]. The notion of "drilling down" to view low-level details doesn't actually advocate a return to concrete data for data visualization experts, however, but instead to a closer view of the data abstraction. We propose that information-building applications are the first to emphasize the need to pass between abstraction (frequency counts of animal appearances) and concrete data (camera trap images).

Aggregate views of data are important since they enable students to look beyond the data and make inferences about the underlying populations or processes represented by the data samples [9]. However, children commonly view data simplistically and do not notice aggregate and emergent features of data sets [10, 12, 13]. Software tools like TinkerPlots [14] have been used previously to help students focus on the aggregate view. TinkerPlots software helped students in grouping together data points having specific ranges of values and chunk them into "bins". This facilitated ease of data exploration with large datasets [9]. While data exploration software like TinkerPlots serve to acquaint students with statistics, it is intended to be used with a "sanitized" data set where each data point provides information. In our context, many of the data points lack information (e.g., empty images triggered by wind-tossed branches), highlighting the need for a specialized tool. The design of this tool should also scaffold switching between the individual data points (i.e. pictures with specific metadata information) and the complete dataset to understand the frequency of observations of the animals. In addition to scaffolding students' need to explore data and chunk them into categories, our tool should support the students in scoping their own problem space (i.e. which chunks to look at) and extracting abstract information from these chunks to answer their problem.

PILOT IMPLEMENTATIONS AND STUDIES

Our research project did not initially set out to create "information building applications" – we identified the need for such software via our early pilots. We wanted to be able to support two kinds of investigations that could be conducted using a single camera: (a) "natural experiments" in which learners investigated differential outcomes due to variations in time (e.g., day vs. night, dry vs. rainy) and (b) experiments in which manipulations were introduced sequentially (e.g., using different kinds of bait on different days). These two classes of experiments are the primary classes used by practitioners using a single camera in the field, lending authenticity to the tasks we wanted to support. In order to support these studies, simple aggregate frequencies were inadequate; students needed to be able to obtain frequencies conditioned by time constraints, a process we'll describe in the section on representations.

We performed two pilot studies to determine the feasibility of students making use of camera trap data in classrooms. Our first pilot made very minimal use of software: the native image-viewing capability of Mac OS was used to inspect the camera trap photos, and Microsoft Excel was used for recording observations. We gave our first volunteer, a high-performing middle-school student, the basic task of recording unique animal sightings. Our volunteer reported that sorting through the image files was inconvenient, because the file names were unwieldy and she would often lose track of which images she had already processed. Moreover, we noticed that when the learner encountered images of the same animal (originating from a multi-image burst), she recorded each image as a new sighting, indicating that she struggled with realizing that a current image and a prior image were actually evidence of the same animal. We knew that we would need additional image management support: a tool which would allow users to move seamlessly from image to image, would allow them to mark which images had been processed, and which would allow users to see images not singly, but as part of a "stream" of data so that they had the appropriate context when recording their observations.

During the second pilot with a grade 5 class of 56 students, we utilized a commercial solution for photo management, Flickr, as it supported image browsing, tagging, and filmstrip views of images. We continued to use Excel to manage counts. Additional details from this pilot can be found in our previous study [21]. When students brought back their images, they used classroom laptops to upload the images to the Flickr account we created for the activity. We had intended for students to use the Flickr "filmstrip" image browsing feature and the tagging feature to assist with their analyses, as those features would support the image-to-image browsing and image marking activities we deemed necessary. In practice, however, the students did not use these features as we asked them to, instead reverting to using Flickr much as regular users do, to quickly find a "good picture" using the gallery view to get to the images of animals (or in some cases, friends) that they had captured. The ease of being able to browse images allowed students to be satisfied with their camera placements even if they had many images that lacked content, because they could still access the interesting images. We were concerned that this did not help students acquire a perspective that resembled how scientists regard camera trap images, and that such an interface may well push the students even further away from perceiving the images as part of a stream of evidence.

These pilot studies revealed that presenting images within a stream or set is not sufficient for helping students treat them as information within a context that has meaning of its own; they still saw images as singular "trophies." This perspective prevented learners from acquiring a disciplinarily authentic attitude towards the data and how they are interpreted. Learners need to see bursts as evidence of individual sightings, and individual sightings as part of a larger pattern of events, as scientists do. Scientists also use their results to improve their future data collection – they actively seek to reduce "bad data." We saw no such awareness in the students, an indication that they need to be encouraged to reflect on how a better experimental methodology could result in fewer spurious images. Students clearly needed help in considering how raw data could be transformed into useful information, and existing tools did not supply appropriate affordances for helping learners gain this perspective. This led us to conclude that we needed to design our own Information-Building Application.

DESIGN CONSIDERATIONS FOR IBAS

Our failure to effectively appropriate existing software to suit our curricular needs drove us to design and build our own custom Information-Building Application (IBA), which we dubbed PhotoMAT. We will focus on how the PhotoMAT tool was designed to support students as they build information from the data generated by camera traps, while revealing ways in which IBAs support students by managing some of the characteristic management problems associated with large data sets (namely: ill-structured data; irrelevant data that is generated spuriously, noisily, or via duplication; and missing data) and how IBAs can help bridge abstract and concrete representations. Our research goals only required us to build one IBA, but to better elucidate the characteristics of IBAs as a class of applications, in this section we will describe the design considerations for our IBA alongside a hypothetical IBA. This hypothetical IBA, Whether The Weather, would be used with a meteorology curriculum to perform similar data filtering and analysis tasks.

Structuring Ill-Structured Data via Grouping

A common problem faced by scientists who grapple with large data sets is the need to reorganize, sort, label, or otherwise give meaningful structure to data (many large sets of data are collected as continuous, undifferentiated streams). Data restructuring can take many forms, but at its core involves transforming data points from concrete instances into meaningful abstractions: no longer just measurements, they become measurements of a specific *something* relevant to the scientist's inquiry.

The data students are presented with in Neighborhood Safari are ill-structured: they are a collection of images, with only timestamps to suggest some ordinality. Depending on the students' inquiry questions, they would need to restructure this stream of images using different abstractions: labeling the images by types of animals present, numbers of animals present, types of bait present, the times of day of the images, or so on. We wanted to support a variety of student-designed research questions by allowing students to determine the structure of their data. This led us to deciding against designing the labels to be used in advance, opting instead to support user-defined ("folksonomy") tags in PhotoMAT. Each time a user creates a new tag type (e.g., "squirrel" or "peanut bait" or "morning"), it is added to the list of labels PhotoMAT provides for learners to use. Once labeled, the students can focus their analyses on the structured data, for example, determining which species were present when peanut bait was out.

Similarly, in Whether the Weather, the initial data recovered would be a set of numbers paired with time stamps. This data doesn't allow students to answer meaningful questions until it is abstracted in some way. For example, students may be interested in knowing if the amount of rainfall that reaches the microclimate is affected by how windy that location is. To perform this analysis, students would not label each data point as is done in PhotoMAT – but there is still a need to separate out the anemometer and rain gauge readings for rainy days from the rest of the data stream. To help structure this data, the IBA could help students group the sampling points using the data's own properties (e.g., by filtering the data by rain gauge readings above 0) or by using external information (e.g., selecting only data from days when weather reports called for rain). Rather than operating on all anemometer readings, students would only be working with the abstraction of "anemometer readings on rainy days."

Allowing learners to build bridges between concrete and abstract perspectives on data is a key scientific practice. With PhotoMAT a labeling is the operation used to begin building this bridge, while in Whether the Weather a filtering operation is used, but in both cases the operations help students see how raw data can be transformed into useful information when it is meaningfully abstracted. Thus, allowing students to add structure to the data is a core feature of IBAs.

Dealing with Irrelevant Data through Pre-aggregation, Persistent Labels and Appropriate Costs

Another common problem faced by scientists working with large data sets is how to deal with large amounts of data that do not speak to the inquiry question. Some educational researchers argue that to help learners engage in authentic scientific practices less-relevant tasks should be streamlined [5], and so many scientific inquiry applications often remove irrelevant data without any learner awareness of or involvement in the process. We argue that grappling with irrelevant data is in fact a core learning task when dealing with large data sets, but we also argue that the processes for that removal and the degree of learner involvement in those processes may differ depending on the source of the irrelevant data. Irrelevant data can be spurious, meaning that it was caused by unforeseen circumstances or by poor experimental data collection procedures, or could be a result of noise or duplication arising from the fundamental characteristics of the measurement tools. Here we work through several cases of irrelevant data and discuss how an IBA might handle them

Spurious data from camera traps can be caused by factors both natural (wind causing plants to move across the frame) and due to experimental set-up (e.g., poor camera placement near high-traffic areas). Real scientists care about spurious data because it incurs real costs: collection costs, storage costs, and analytic costs. Our prior trials showed that students were not troubled by excess spurious images, which was worrisome because it removed one of the major drivers for improving experimental data collection.

In order to encourage students to want to improve their data collection, we opted to motivate their concern by attaching some sort of cost to spurious data. With PhotoMAT we used two primary tactics for this: students labeled images with no animals "Nothing", and students could only progress through the image files sequentially (that is, we chose not to provide a gallery to view thumbnails of the images). Navigating sequentially through their dataset using the arrows on the right and left of the image helped them to better understand the contexts that could produce spurious data. By linking a small cost (in the form of the time spent labeling bad images) to spurious data, students would also be motivated to prevent those contexts. With Whether the Weather, a temperature sensor placed in direct sunlight could generate spurious data. The prior strategy of attaching a manipulative cost to each data point would not work here, as the volume of data points would be too high. In this case, the IBA could be structured to prevent students from using any data collected during a given day if the number of outliers is too high – thus inducing a cost to the student, who would be motivated to reposition the temperature sensor so that it is less exposed to the sun. Notice that in both of these examples the students have the ability to easily correct the data collection procedures that resulted in the irrelevant data.

Contrast this with a case of duplicate data. Duplicate data is the norm for camera traps, which capture a series of images (1 image per 3 seconds on our equipment) in a "burst". Bursts allow biologists (and students) to see what happens just after the sensor is triggered, which provides context for what triggered the sensor. Our first pilot suggested that children would label each image within a burst, which would triple the frequency counts. Allowing students to apply single labels to multiple images poses new challenges concerning the "persistence" of the label, however – if, for example, the first two frames contain a squirrel and the last frame contains a cat, the labeling would fail to highlight the species-species interaction if the "squirrel" label persists only across the first two images.

To address these issues within PhotoMAT, we developed two strategies: "pre-aggregation," a strategy to help children see each "burst" as a unified piece of information by playing the "burst" as a continuous stilted animation (like an animated GIF); and persistent labels, which once placed, would persist across each image in the pre-aggregated data set. To emphasize the persistent nature of the labels, we used an interface design that intentionally treated them as on-screen "objects" in their own right: users drag a label onto the burst, and it persists in that location while the burst continues to animate underneath (see Figure 1). The persistent labels allow users to specify cardinality (e.g., if the user saw two squirrels, s/he could drag the "squirrel" label onto the image twice) while also enabling the learner to move labels into proximity to the animal in question (thereby resolving ambiguities with respect to which animal was being counted, see Figure 1). A combination of pre-aggregation and persistent abstract labels clearly conveys that there need not be a one-to-one mapping between individual observations and more abstracted information.

Duplicate data is less likely with Whether the Weather, but sensor noise may produce irrelevant data points. Here, pre-aggregation may involve the IBA precomputing simple averages over 5 minute windows, to provide slight smoothing. The "raw" data reading fluctuations for each smoothed segment should still be illustrated, however; perhaps by displaying both the raw and the smoothed line graphs. Since Whether the Weather would focus on how the climate affects longer-term phenomena like plant growth, abstract labels for Whether the Weather may have even more persistence: pegged to whole days ("rainy day") or even weeks ("warming trend"). Giving learners some control over the degree of smoothing (e.g., from 5 to 30 minutes) and over the label persistence time would help them understand how measurements become information.

Figure 1. The Label Screen of PhotoMAT, with two birds in one frame, each bird labeled by a student.

Note that in these two cases of duplicate and noisy data, learners have little control over improving the data collection procedures, so no costs are associated with the bad data points. Rather, where duplicates and noise are features of the instruments students use and not of their measurement techniques, we suggest that IBAs can use pre-aggregation as a first-step process of abstraction to help students grapple with irrelevant data, and that persistent abstract labels can further help them realize that a measurement is not automatically a piece of information. It is important to make the data representation match the unit of analysis, as by turning related sequences of images into animations, or days of temperature readings into trends. We claim that IBAs should always make students aware of the presence of irrelevant data, even if processing it is scaffolded for them, as awareness of the possibility of irrelevant data is a core part of data literacy. Second, we argue that in circumstances where learners have control over the amount of irrelevant data it may be wise to more actively involve learners in processing it, which requires more learner effort. In these cases, the purpose of the extra effort is not to improve retention[1], but to motivate learners to improve aspects of their data collection practice.

Acknowledging Missing Data via Time-scaled Overviews

An important perspective for students to acquire regarding large data sets is that just because large volumes of data are being collected, data important to making interpretations may still be missing (owing to equipment failure or limitations). Scientists are careful to consider whether missing data may affect their analyses, and are as attentive to spans of no data points as they are to outliers. We wanted to support students in critically thinking about what data might be missing. With PhotoMAT our main support for this was the abstract overview representation of the data points presented at the bottom of the Label Screen (See Figure 1). There are clear gaps between the dots, representing the time passing between each observation. Scaling the overview of observations by time (Figures 2 and 3) gives students the opportunity to question if absence of data in these spaces is really an absence of information.

In Whether the Weather, students may expect to face missing data as well. If a sensor is blocked or if it lacks power during a certain time, it may not report for a period of time. Similar to the technique used with PhotoMAT, we would expect to leave visual space in any representation of trends of measurements to express the lack of data during a certain time period. Showing the absence of data within IBAs via time-scaled overviews emphasizes missing data.

Supporting Information Abstraction Rigor with Concurrent Bifocal Mapping

Scientists are highly aware that the information they analyze comes from measurements and observations, and that the quality of their analysis hinges on the rigor with which they interpret the original measurements. When scientists notice an oddity in their analysis, one of the first steps often taken is to go back to the original data, to make sure no mistakes were made in processing it for analysis. Recall in our review of existing science inquiry applications, students are never faced with the need to question the data they are working with, even though this is a core part of authentic scientific practice. When data is given to students in a fully-abstracted form (e.g., in a spreadsheet) it may not occur to them (and it may be inconvenient for them) to go back and double-check that the abstracted information is correct.

Rather than represent data as numerical lists or tables, then, with PhotoMAT we chose a representation that depicts animal sightings along a graphical timeline. Each species label is represented along a separate timeline, using circles to reflect the time of the observations. This representation reflects both the cardinality of species-specific observations (with a "total count" provided at the end of each timeline) and affords students visual access to temporal variability, both within and across species. (In Figure 2 we see a clear pattern of "clusters" of sightings, with different species appearing at different times during the data capture period. For example, the cat is never sighted with other species.)

One of the primary differences between experts and novices, is the ability of experts to notice abstract qualities of a problem-space over the surface-level details that novices tend to prioritize [2]. To assist students in making connections across the abstract timeline data and the concrete data point, touching a dot on the timeline causes a small version of the photo burst linked to it to appear at the top of the screen, and begin to animate through the burst images. On the surface, this action seems to parallel the manipulation of data view by experts in data visualization [10], but in reality, the use of this affordance is very different. Rather than students "drilling down" into the data to gain more detail, as is often done in data visualization, this inspection activity serves instead to reinforce for students the connection between the abstract representation and the original data. This representation, which we call concurrent bifocal mapping, equally privileges both the individual data point and the gestalt view. This reinforcement of the data-information relationship is a key property of information-building applications. We expect that bifocal concurrent mapping would be of great use in the hypothetical Whether the Weather IBA when learners are varying the size of the "smoothing windows" – by interactively seeing how many data points are being aggregated into a informational abstraction learners can begin to build a sensitivity to how aggregation boundaries affect information.

Bifocal concurrent mappings such as these are critical to IBAs, allowing users to move back and forth between abstract and concrete representations and reconsider assumptions they had made earlier when abstracting their data. These mappings also support student discovery of how bad data collection can lead to bad analyses, since they can easily confirm their unmodified source data.

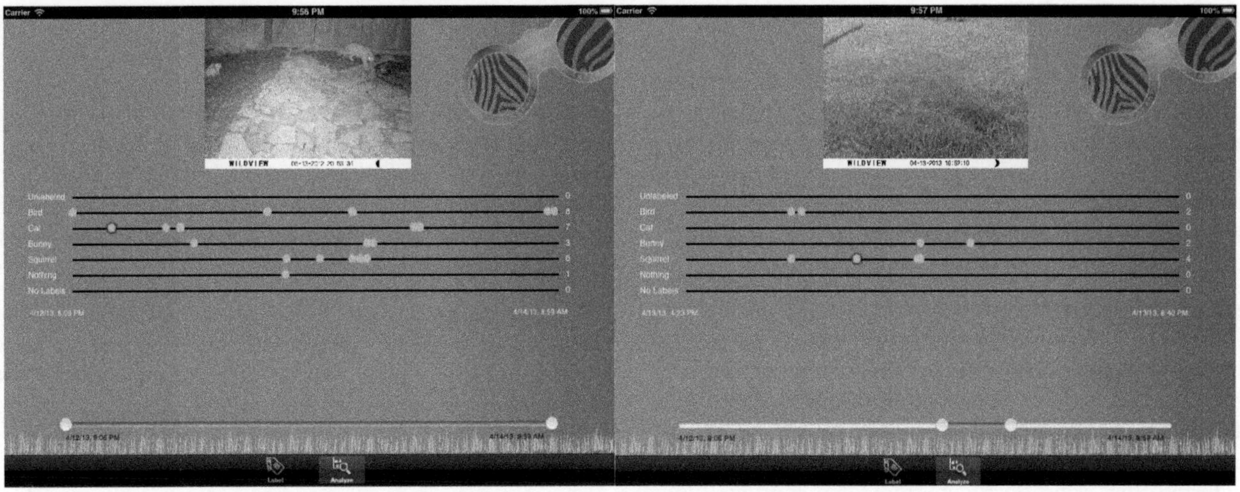

Figure 2. Left: PhotoMAT's Analyze screen, with a complete timeline visible, spanning a three day time period. Each dot represents a single instance of an animal spotting. Right: The same set of data, scoped to a single evening's observation.

Scoping Data via Adjustable Scaling

One important practice in dealing with large data sets is scoping the data to discover unique and interesting segments of the data, or to eliminate data that is not relevant to a particular research question. Trends that seem meaningful at one level of scale might appear inconsequential at other levels of scale. We wanted the students to be able to play a more active role in choosing a scale for their data that would be relevant to their investigations, especially the one-camera investigations as described earlier. Thus, we also provided a mechanism that would allow users to constrain the species- specific timelines to specific time periods. The slider control at the bottom of the right side of Figure 2 allows users to select the starting and ending times visualized by the species timelines. Based on the same data set as the left side, the right side of Figure 2 shows a view of animal observations constrained to four hours in the evening, which reveals the number of dots seen on the Squirrel line more clearly. Being able to fluidly manipulate the starting and ending periods and see how the data points "scrunch up" or "stretch out" implicitly communicates that frequency can only ever be defined relative to a bounded interval.

Since Whether the Weather requires that students compare the summative effect of microclimates across different yards, the same widget for interactively scoping a visualization of data points across time may not be the most appropriate. However, a similar tool for scoping the breadth of smoothing periods, as mentioned above, may serve a similar goal.

By providing mechanisms to help students perform adjustable scaling tasks, IBAs can allow students to manipulate the data they collect to better reflect their research questions. IBAs can thus support questions at multiple scales within their structure.

PHOTOMAT IN PRACTICE

20 fifth-grade students from a suburb of a large Midwestern city participated in our final study over a period of 5 weeks. Our research team visited the classroom 11 times over this period, for approximately 50 minutes per visit. Throughout the study period, we video recorded the classroom sessions, and audio recorded small group work sessions. We recorded other classroom observations via unstructured notes. Students filled out worksheets each time that they took the cameras home where they stated their questions, described their experimental set ups, and described how they would use the information they found to answer their questions. When they completed analysis of their data set, they completed an additional worksheet

Study Iteration	Average Photos per camera
Neighborhood Animal Diversity	154 images (51 bursts)
Independent Research Questions	260 images (86 bursts)

Table 1. Table detailing the average number of photos retrieved by camera in the two iterations where students placed cameras in their backyards.

The worksheet answers were analyzed for how students used PhotoMAT to construct their answers. We also collected log files from PhotoMAT, which included time-stamped data for the type and position of all tags placed or removed, all new tags created, each time students switched between the label and analyze view, each time a student used one of the dots in the analyze tab to view an image, and each time a student moved one of the handles on the timeline slider. At the conclusion of the study, we conducted structured interviews with groups of students about their experiences with PhotoMAT to both assess their comfort with the tool and elicit design recommendations from the students. We expected that some students would demonstrate a growth in competency of using camera traps through using PhotoMAT, since they would be confronted with their errors. We also expected that those students that took up PhotoMAT would demonstrate this through their discourse around the tool and their own analysis would illustrate an understanding that there was not a one-to-one relationship between data and information.

RESULTS

We wanted to determine if the children could successfully use PhotoMAT to convert data into information, could then easily move between abstract and concrete representations of the data, and could use their results to inform their future instrument use. We specifically wanted to know if they would take advantage of the supports we placed for structuring the data, learning from the spurious data, dealing with the duplicate data, and visualizing missing data.

Students' Ability to Structure Data

We coded the labels that students placed in the final round for accuracy. Of 396 labels, 86% accurately represented the wildlife. Some students were able to use this abstract information to make unprompted interpretations their results, as evidenced by the answers of student worksheets. For example, one group of students noted that one thing they learned is that "the amount of people effects how many animals (are captured)." They had processed the concrete data (63 photos of humans, 38 photos of birds, but no pictures with birds and humans in them) into an abstract form (labeled photos) and noted that the two label categories never overlapped. Without performing the labeling process, or having access to the label timelines, the group may not have noticed this lack of intersection.

Additionally, students were comfortable making the leap back from frequency notation to the original data. 13 of the 18 students who used PhotoMAT during the diversity question and independent research sessions used a point on the timeline representation in the analysis screen to navigate back to that image to either look at in full screen, add additional labels to that screen or add additional notes. This illustrates that students took advantage of the bridge between abstract and concrete representations of the data as a way to deal with the ill-structured data.

Students' Responses to Irrelevant Data

We saw evidence that students learned from the spurious data experienced during the learning activities to improve their instrument use. We intentionally designed PhotoMAT to require that students label non-informational images with a "nothing" tag, so students who captured spurious data would have the opportunity to reflect on the effectiveness of their camera placement. In the first iteration of data collection, 63% of the tags students added to their images were the "nothing" tag. During the second investigation, only 28% of tags placed on the image were "nothing" tags, showing that students took more care when placing the cameras. Students also reported on worksheets after reviewing their data what they would do differently the next time. Several students noted on their worksheets in the first round that next time they would put it in a different place because they got too many pictures of people. Without processing the images into information, it is unlikely that the students would have seen development in the field science practice of using camera traps to capture images of wildlife.

We had also been concerned about how students would respond to duplicate data, mistakenly assuming a concrete, one-to-one correspondence between an image and a piece of information, especially if an animal moved from frame to frame. Students were interviewed in groups of three post-intervention, how they had been grouped throughout the intervention period. When asked to explain how to label an image, each group accurately demonstrated how they would create a new label if needed, and then drag that label on top of or near the animal in the image, thus providing structure to the data. In the interviews, all five interview groups treated the bursts as a single piece of information, explaining that if an animal moved from frame to frame, they just put the label near the animal in one frame of the animation. Since students did not struggle with seeing bursts as a unit of analysis, we believe that the burst aggregation and persistent label strategies for dealing with duplicate data were successful.

Students' Response to Missing Data

In general, students did not critically consider the spaces between observations as opportunities for missing data. This suggests that our design proposal of simply leaving visual space may not be enough, and that IBAs that wish to specifically call attention to missing data may need to not just leave space but to actively highlight those spaces or times that lack observations.

Appropriation of Information-Building Affordances

Of the five groups that completed the independent research question portion of the study, two groups were able to answer their research questions. (Of the groups that were unable to answer their questions, two had one or more group members forget to put up cameras, and one failed to place the bait that they needed. We plan to add another round of investigation to the curriculum to allow groups to recover from these kinds of oversights). Of the two groups that succeeded, one group set up three cameras in one backyard, each with a different kind of bait in front of it to determine squirrel food preferences. The students performed their analysis by loading the labeled data from the three cameras onto three different tablets running PhotoMAT, and comparing the visualized frequencies on the three analysis screens. Further evidence that they correctly interpreted these visualizations was in their final report, where they described both their set-up and how they found the answer to the research question they had proposed; and in their final presentation, where they cited the higher frequency of squirrel photos in front of the cracker bait as evidence that squirrels like crackers the best. The other successful group investigated if rabbits would be out at night. In their worksheet, they described their analysis approach thusly: "We will put the timeline at night and see if there are any rabbits." Here, the group used the affordance to change the scope of the data to highlight only nighttime periods to analyze their question (although no other groups used this feature in their analysis, 20 students took advantage of the ability to scope their data by zooming in or zooming out).

CONCLUSIONS AND FUTURE WORK

This paper has presented two exemplars of the class of tools we call IBAs, and highlighted the rationales behind design considerations for IBAs with these exemplars. Our results show that the design considerations we highlighted for IBAs can function in practice, with the exception of highlighting missing data. Our immediate future work will address this problem, looking to alter both the curriculum and PhotoMAT design to better highlight the import of missing observations. We also wish expand the class of questions that students can ask from looking only at questions of diversity and frequency over time to looking at other classes of questions. This specifically includes adding video support so that students can ask questions about animal behaviors. Adding this new medium for data should help us refine the design considerations identified here. We anticipate that IBAs can be developed for supporting students in explorations of many problem domains with large sets of messy data. By investigating these design challenges in other domains, more generally applicable design strategies can be evolved for the broader class of Information-Building Applications.

The primary contribution of this work is the design and preliminary assessment of an exemplar of an under-explored class of tools: information-building applications. While the literature on inquiry learning is replete with tools that support data collection [26] or scaffold data analysis [23], there has been little attention given to the conversion and manipulation of raw data into information. "Messy" data is typically hidden from students. And yet, learning to grapple with "messy data" is an important and consequential skill with the rise of "big data." By introducing a new class of tools, Information Building Applications, we hope to highlight an area that warrants future research, and can ultimately promote data literacy in education.

ACKNOWLEDGMENTS

The authors wish to thank the rest of our research term for their participation in running the studies. This work was supported in part by National Science Foundation award #1124495.

REFERENCES

1. Bjork, R.A. (1994). Memory and metamemory considerations in the training of human beings. In J. Metcalfe and A. Shimamura (Eds.) *Metacognition: Knowing about knowing*. (pp.185-205). Cambridge, MA: MIT Press.
2. Chi, M. T., Glaser, R., & Rees, E. (1981). *Expertise in problem solving*. Pittsburgh: Learning Research and Development Center, University of Pittsburg
3. Czeskis, A., Dermendjieva, I., & Yapit, H. (2010). Parenting from the Pocket : Value Tensions and Technical Directions for Secure and Private Parent-Teen Mobile. *SOUPS: Symposium on Usable Privacy and Security*.
4. Duschl, R. A., & Gitomer, D. H. (1991). Epistemological perspectives on conceptual change: Implications for educational practice. *Journal of research in science teaching, 28*(9), 839-858.
5. Edelson, D. C., & Reiser, B. J. (2006). Making authentic practices accessible to learners: Design challenges and strategies. *Cambridge handbook of the learning sciences*, 335–354.
6. Fegraus, E. H. , Lin, K., Ahumada, J.A., Baru, C., Chandra, S., Youn, C. Data acquisition and management software for camera trap data: A case study from the TEAM Network, Ecological Informatics, Volume 6, Issue 6, November 2011, Pages 345-353
7. Gallagher, J. (2002). *The learning theory of Piaget and Inhelder*. iUniverse.
8. Gentner, D., & Toupin, C. (1988). Systematicity and surface similarity in the development of analogy. *Cognitive Science*, 10, 277-300.
9. Hammerman, J. K., & Rubin, A. (2004). Strategies for managing statistical complexity with new software tools. *Statistics Education Research Journal*, 3(2), 17-41
10. Hancock, C., Kaput, J. J., & Goldsmith, L. T. (1992). Authentic enquiry with data: Critical barriers to classroom implementation. *Educational Psychologist, 27(3),* 337–364.
11. Heer, J., & Shneiderman, B. (2012). Interactive dynamics for visual analysis. *Communications of the ACM, 55*(4), 45 -55.
12. Konold, C., & Higgins, T. L. (2002). Highlights of related research. In S. J. Russell, D. Schifter & V. Bastable (Eds.), *Developing mathematical ideas (DMI): Working with data casebook,* (pp. 165–201). Parsippany, NY: Dale Seymour Publications.
13. Konold, C., Higgins, T. L., Russell, S. J., & Khalil, K. (2003). Data seen through different lenses. Unpublished manuscript, Amherst, MA.
14. Konold, C., & Miller, C. (2004). TinkerPlots^{TM} Dynamic Data Exploration (Version Beta 1.0). Emeryville, CA: Key Curriculum Press.

15. Krajcik, J., Blumenfeld, P., Marx, R. and Soloway, E. (2000). Instructional, curricular, and technological supports for inquiry in science classrooms. In J. Minstrell and E. H. van Zee (eds), Inquiring into Inquiry Learning and Teaching in Science (Washington, DC: American Association for the Advancement of Science), 283–315.
16. Lee, H. and Songer, N. (2003). Making authentic science accessible to students, International Journal of Science Education, 25(8), 923-948.
17. Linn, M.C., Clark, D., & Slotta, J.D. (2003). WISE design for knowledge integration. Science Education, 87, 517–538.
18. Marx, R. W., Blumenfeld, P. C., Krajcik, J. S., Fishman, B., Soloway, E., Geier, R., & Tal, R. T. (2004). Inquiry-based science in the middle grades: Assessment of learning in urban systemic reform. Journal of Research in Science Teaching, 41(10), 1063-1080
19. Metz, K. E. (2004). Children's Understanding of Scientific Inquiry: Their Conceptualization of Uncertainty in Investigations of Their Own Design. Cog. and Instruction, 22(2), 219-290.
20. Miller, J., Friedman, B., & Jancke, G. (2007). Value tensions in design: the value sensitive design, development, and appropriation of a corporation's groupware system. *GROUP '07 Proceedings of the 2007 international ACM conference on Supporting group work*, 281–290.
21. Moher, T., Brown, J., Reiser, B.J., Silva, A., Shelley, T., Lyons, L. (2013). The Urban Game Park: A Pilot Study of Student Investigations of Animal Behavior Using Motion-Detecting Cameras. *American Educational Research Association Annual Meeting 2013.*
22. Piaget, J. (1977). Problems of equilibration. In *Topics in cognitive development* (pp. 3-13). Springer US.
23. Reiser, B. J., Tabak, I., Sandoval, W. A., Smith, B. K., Steinmuller, F., & Leone, A. J. (2001). BGuILE: Strategic and conceptual scaffolds for scientific inquiry in biology classrooms. In S. M. Carver & D. Klahr (Eds.), *Cognition and instruction: Twenty-five years of progress* (pp. 263-305). Mahwah, NJ: Erlbaum.
24. Resnick, M., Berg, R., & Eisenberg, M. (2000). Beyond black boxes: Bringing transparency and aesthetics back to scientific investigation. *The Journal of the Learning Sciences, 9*(1), 7-30.
25. Silva , A., Dasgupta, C., Shelley, T., Lopez Silva, B.A., Lyons, L., Moher, T. (2014) .Shaping the Construction of Learner Questions. In review: *American Educational Research Association Annual Meeting 2014*
26. Simons, D. J., & Keil, F. C. (1995). An abstract to concrete shift in the development of biological thought: the insides story. *Cognition*, *56*(2), 129-163.
27. Songer, N. (2006). BioKIDS: An Animated Conversation on the Development of Curricular Activity Structures for Inquiry Science. In R. K. Sawyer (Ed.), *The Cambridge Handbook of the Learning Sciences*. New York, NY: Cambridge University Press.
28. Tobler, M. (2013). Camera Base. http://www.atrium-biodiversity.org/tools/camerabase/.
29. Wellman, H.M., & Gelman, S.A. (1992). Cognitive development: foundational theories of core domains. *Annual Review of Psychology*, 43, 337-375.
30. Yoo, D., Huldtgren, A., & Woelfer, J. (2013). A value sensitive action-reflection model: evolving a co-design space with stakeholder and designer prompts. *Proceedings of the SIGCHI Conference on Human Factors in Computing Systems*, 419–428.

CHI 2014 Author Index

CHI 2014 Author Index

CHI 2014 Author Index

CHI 2014 Author Index

CHI 2014 Author Index

CHI 2014 Author Index

www.ingramcontent.com/pod-product-compliance
Ingram Content Group UK Ltd.
Pitfield, Milton Keynes, MK11 3LW, UK
UKHW051419290926
15471UKWH00009B/1687

9 781450 332880